FAR

FEDERAL AVIATION REGULATIONS

FOR AVIATION MECHANICS

PUBLISHED BY

ASA PUBLICATIONS, INC.
600 SIXTH AVENUE, SOUTH
SEATTLE, WASHINGTON 98108-33007

ISBN 0-940732-85-8

TABLE OF CONTENTS

Part 1 — DEFINITIONS AND ABBREVIATIONS ....

Part 13 — INVESTIGATION AND ENFORCEMENT PROCEDURE ....

Part 21 — CERTIFICATION PROCEDURES FOR PRODUCTS AND PARTS..............

Part 23 — AIRWORTHINESS STANDARDS: Normal, Utility, and
Acrobatic Category Airplanes..............................

Part 33 — AIRWORTHINESS STANDARDS: Aircraft Engines........................

Part 35 — AIRWORTHINESS STANDARDS: Propellers ....

Part 39 — AIRWORTHINESS DIRECTIVES ....

Part 43 — MAINTENANCE, PREVENTIVE MAINTENANCE,
REBUILDING, AND ALTERATION ....

Part 45 — IDENTIFICATION AND REGISTRATION MARKING ....

Part 47 — AIRCRAFT REGISTRATION ....

Part 65 — CERTIFICATION: Airmen Other Than Flight Crewmembers...............

Part 91 — GENERAL OPERATING AND FLIGHT RULES ....

Part 125 — CERTIFICATION AND OPERATIONS: Airplanes Having a
Seating Capacity of 20 or More Passengers or a
Maximum Payload Capacity of 6,000 Pounds or More ....

Part 135 — AIR TAXI OPERATORS AND COMMERCIAL OPERATORS....................

Part 145 — REPAIR STATIONS ....

FEDERAL AVIATION REGULATIONS

PART 1
DEFINITIONS AND ABBREVIATIONS

1989 EDITION

SUBCHAPTER A—DEFINITIONS

PART 1—DEFINITIONS AND ABBREVIATIONS

Sec.
1.1 General definitions.
1.2 Abbreviations and symbols.
1.3 Rules of construction.

AUTHORITY: 49 U.S.C. 1347, 1348, 1354(a), 1357(d)(2), 1372, 1421 through 1430, 1432, 1442, 1443, 1472, 1510, 1522, 1652(e), 1655(c), 1657(f), 49 U.S.C. 106(g) (Revised Pub. L. 97–449, Jan. 12, 1983).

§ 1.1 General definitions.

As used in Subchapters A through K of this chapter, unless the context requires otherwise:

"Administrator" means the Federal Aviation Administrator or any person to whom he has delegated his authority in the matter concerned.

"Aerodynamic coefficients" means non-dimensional coefficients for aerodynamic forces and moments.

"Air carrier" means a person who undertakes directly by lease, or other arrangement, to engage in air transportation.

"Air commerce" means interstate, overseas, or foreign air commerce or the transportation of mail by aircraft or any operation or navigation of aircraft within the limits of any Federal airway or any operation or navigation of aircraft which directly affects, or which may endanger safety in, interstate, overseas, or foreign air commerce.

"Aircraft" means a device that is used or intended to be used for flight in the air.

"Aircraft engine" means an engine that is used or intended to be used for propelling aircraft. It includes turbosuperchargers, appurtenances, and accessories necessary for its functioning, but does not include propellers.

"Airframe" means the fuselage, booms, nacelles, cowlings, fairings, airfoil surfaces (including rotors but excluding propellers and rotating airfoils of engines), and landing gear of an aircraft and their accessories and controls.

"Airplane" means an engine-driven fixed-wing aircraft heavier than air, that is supported in flight by the dynamic reaction of the air against its wings.

"Airport" means an area of land or water that is used or intended to be used for the landing and takeoff of aircraft, and includes its buildings and facilities, if any.

"Airport traffic area" means, unless otherwise specifically designated in Part 93, that airspace within a horizontal radius of 5 statute miles from the geographical center of any airport at which a control tower is operating, extending from the surface up to, but not including, an altitude of 3,000 feet above the elevation of the airport.

"Airship" means an engine-driven lighter-than-air aircraft that can be steered.

"Air traffic" means aircraft operating in the air or on an airport surface, exclusive of loading ramps and parking areas.

"Air traffic clearance" means an authorization by air traffic control, for the purpose of preventing collision between known aircraft, for an aircraft to proceed under specified traffic conditions within controlled airspace.

"Air traffic control" means a service operated by appropriate authority to promote the safe, orderly, and expeditious flow of air traffic.

"Air transportation" means interstate, overseas, or foreign air transportation or the transportation of mail by aircraft.

"Alternate airport" means an airport at which an aircraft may land if a landing at the intended airport becomes inadvisable.

"Altitude engine" means a reciprocating aircraft engine having a rated takeoff power that is producible from sea level to an established higher altitude.

"Appliance" means any instrument, mechanism, equipment, part, apparatus, appurtenance, or accessory, including communications equipment, that is used or intended to be used in operating or controlling an aircraft in flight, is installed in or attached to the aircraft, and is not part of an airframe, engine, or propeller.

"Approved", unless used with reference to another person, means approved by the Administrator.

"Area navigation (RNAV)" means a method of navigation that permits aircraft operations on any desired course within the coverage of station-referenced navigation signals or within the limits of self-contained system capability.

"Area navigation low route" means an area navigation route within the airspace extending upward from 1,200 feet above the surface of the earth to, but not including, 18,000 feet MSL.

"Area navigation high route" means an area navigation route within the airspace extending upward from, and including, 18,000 feet MSL to flight level 450.

"Armed Forces" means the Army, Navy, Air Force, Marine Corps, and Coast Guard, including their regular and reserve components and members serving without component status.

"Autorotation" means a rotorcraft flight condition in which the lifting rotor is driven entirely by action of the air when the rotorcraft is in motion.

"Auxiliary rotor" means a rotor that serves either to counteract the effect of the main rotor torque on a rotorcraft or to maneuver the rotorcraft about one or more of its three principal axes.

"Balloon" means a lighter-than-air aircraft that is not engine driven.

"Brake horsepower" means the power delivered at the propeller shaft (main drive or main output) of an aircraft engine.

"Calibrated airspeed" means the indicated airspeed of an aircraft, corrected for position and instrument error. Calibrated airspeed is equal to true airspeed in standard atmosphere at sea level.

"Category":

(1) As used with respect to the certification, ratings, privileges, and limitations of airmen, means a broad classification of aircraft. Examples include: airplane; rotorcraft; glider; and lighter-than-air; and

(2) As used with respect to the certification of aircraft, means a grouping of aircraft based upon intended use or operating limitations. Examples include: transport, normal, utility, acrobatic, limited, restricted, and provisional.

"Category A," with respect to transport category rotorcraft, means multiengine rotorcraft designed with engine and system isolation features specified in Part 29 and utilizing scheduled takeoff and landing operations under a critical engine failure concept which assures adequate designated surface area and adequate performance capability for continued safe flight in the event of engine failure.

"Category B," with respect to transport category rotorcraft, means single-engine or multiengine rotorcraft which do not fully meet all Category A standards. Category B rotorcraft have no guaranteed stay-up ability in the event of engine failure and unscheduled landing is assumed.

"Category II operations", with respect to the operation of aircraft, means a straight-in ILS approach to the runway of an airport under a Category II ILS instrument approach procedure issued by the Administrator or other appropriate authority.

"Category III operations," with respect to the operation of aircraft, means an ILS approach to, and landing on, the runway of an airport using a Category III ILS instrument approach procedure issued by the Administrator or other appropriate authority.

"Ceiling" means the height above the earth's surface of the lowest layer of clouds or obscuring phenomena that is reported as "broken", "overcast", or "obscuration", and not classified as "thin" or "partial".

"Civil aircraft" means aircraft other than public aircraft.

"Class":

(1) As used with respect to the certification, ratings, privileges, and limitations of airmen, means a classification of aircraft within a category having similar operating characteristics. Examples include: single engine; multiengine; land; water; gyroplane; helicopter; airship; and free balloon; and

(2) As used with respect to the certification of aircraft, means a broad grouping of aircraft having similar characteristics of propulsion, flight, or landing. Examples include: airplane;

rotorcraft; glider; balloon; landplane; and seaplane.

"Clearway" means:

(1) For turbine engine powered airplanes certificated after August 29, 1959, an area beyond the runway, not less than 500 feet wide, centrally located about the extended centerline of the runway, and under the control of the airport authorities. The clearway is expressed in terms of a clearway plane, extending from the end of the runway with an upward slope not exceeding 1.25 percent, above which no object nor any terrain protrudes. However, threshold lights may protrude above the plane if their height above the end of the runway is 26 inches or less and if they are located to each side of the runway.

(2) For turbine engine powered airplanes certificated after September 30, 1958, but before August 30, 1959, an area beyond the takeoff runway extending no less than 300 feet on either side of the extended centerline of the runway, at an elevation no higher than the elevation of the end of the runway, clear of all fixed obstacles, and under the control of the airport authorities.

"Climbout speed," with respect to rotorcraft, means a referenced airspeed which results in a flight path clear of the height-velocity envelope during initial climbout.

"Commercial operator" means a person who, for compensation or hire, engages in the carriage by aircraft in air commerce of persons or property, other than as an air carrier or foreign air carrier or under the authority of Part 375 of this title. Where it is doubtful that an operation is for "compensation or hire", the test applied is whether the carriage by air is merely incidental to the person's other business or is, in itself, a major enterprise for profit.

"Controlled airspace" means airspace designated as a continental control area, control area, control zone, terminal control area, or transition area, within which some or all aircraft may be subject to air traffic control.

"Crewmember" means a person assigned to perform duty in an aircraft during flight time.

"Critical altitude" means the maximum altitude at which, in standard atmosphere, it is possible to maintain, at a specified rotational speed, a specified power or a specified manifold pressure. Unless otherwise stated, the critical altitude is the maximum altitude at which it is possible to maintain, at the maximum continuous rotational speed, one of the following:

(1) The maximum continuous power, in the case of engines for which this power rating is the same at sea level and at the rated altitude.

(2) The maximum continuous rated manifold pressure, in the case of engines, the maximum continuous power of which is governed by a constant manifold pressure.

"Critical engine" means the engine whose failure would most adversely affect the performance or handling qualities of an aircraft.

"Decision height," with respect to the operation of aircraft, means the height at which a decision must be made, during an ILS or PAR instrument approach, to either continue the approach or to execute a missed approach.

"Equivalent airspeed" means the calibrated airspeed of an aircraft corrected for adiabatic compressible flow for the particular altitude. Equivalent airspeed is equal to calibrated airspeed in standard atmosphere at sea level.

"Extended over-water operation" means—

(1) With respect to aircraft other than helicopters, an operation over water at a horizontal distance of more than 50 nautical miles from the nearest shoreline; and

(2) With respect to helicopters, an operation over water at a horizontal distance of more than 50 nautical miles from the nearest shoreline and more than 50 nautical miles from an off-shore heliport structure.

"External load" means a load that is carried, or extends, outside of the aircraft fuselage.

"External-load attaching means" means the structural components used to attach an external load to an aircraft, including external-load containers, the backup structure at the attachment points, and any quick-release device used to jettison the external load.

"Fireproof"—

(1) With respect to materials and parts used to confine fire in a designated fire zone, means the capacity to withstand at least as well as steel in dimensions appropriate for the purpose for which they are used, the heat produced when there is a severe fire of extended duration in that zone; and

(2) With respect to other materials and parts, means the capacity to withstand the heat associated with fire at least as well as steel in dimensions appropriate for the purpose for which they are used.

"Fire resistant"—

(1) With respect to sheet or structural members means the capacity to withstand the heat associated with fire at least as well as aluminum alloy in dimensions appropriate for the purpose for which they are used; and

(2) With respect to fluid-carrying lines, fluid system parts, wiring, air ducts, fittings, and powerplant controls, means the capacity to perform the intended functions under the heat and other conditions likely to occur when there is a fire at the place concerned.

"Flame resistant" means not susceptible to combustion to the point of propagating a flame, beyond safe limits, after the ignition source is removed.

"Flammable", with respect to a fluid or gas, means susceptible to igniting readily or to exploding.

"Flap extended speed" means the highest speed permissible with wing flaps in a prescribed extended position.

"Flash resistant" means not susceptible to burning violently when ignited.

"Flightcrew member" means a pilot, flight engineer, or flight navigator assigned to duty in an aircraft during flight time.

"Flight level" means a level of constant atmospheric pressure related to a reference datum of 29.92 inches of mercury. Each is stated in three digits that represent hundreds of feet. For example, flight level 250 represents a barometric altimeter indication of 25,000 feet; flight level 255, an indication of 25,500 feet.

"Flight plan" means specified information, relating to the intended flight of an aircraft, that is filed orally or in writing with air traffic control.

"Flight time" means the time from the moment the aircraft first moves under its own power for the purpose of flight until the moment it comes to rest at the next point of landing. ("Block-to-block" time.) Hobb / TACH

"Flight visibility" means the average forward horizontal distance, from the cockpit of an aircraft in flight, at which prominent unlighted objects may be seen and identified by day and prominent lighted objects may be seen and identified by night.

"Foreign air carrier" means any person other than a citizen of the United States, who undertakes directly, by lease or other arrangement, to engage in air transportation.

"Foreign air commerce" means the carriage by aircraft of persons or property for compensation or hire, or the carriage of mail by aircraft, or the operation or navigation of aircraft in the conduct or furtherance of a business or vocation, in commerce between a place in the United States and any place outside thereof; whether such commerce moves wholly by aircraft or partly by aircraft and partly by other forms of transportation.

"Foreign air transportation" means the carriage by aircraft of persons or property as a common carrier for compensation or hire, or the carriage of mail by aircraft, in commerce between a place in the United States and any place outside of the United States, whether that commerce moves wholly by aircraft or partly by aircraft and partly by other forms of transportation.

"Glider" means a heavier-than-air aircraft, that is supported in flight by the dynamic reaction of the air against its lifting surfaces and whose free flight does not depend principally on an engine.

"Ground visibility" means prevailing horizontal visibility near the earth's surface as reported by the United States National Weather Service or an accredited observer.

"Load factor" means the ratio of a specified load to the total weight of the aircraft. The specified load is expressed in terms of any of the following: aerodynamic forces, inertia forces, or ground or water reactions.

"Mach number" means the ratio of true airspeed to the speed of sound.

"Main rotor" means the rotor that supplies the principal lift to a rotorcraft.

"Maintenance" means inspection, overhaul, repair, preservation, and the replacement of parts, but excludes preventive maintenance.

"Major alteration" means an alteration not listed in the aircraft, aircraft engine, or propeller specifications—

(1) That might appreciably affect weight, balance, structural strength, performance, powerplant operation, flight characteristics, or other qualities affecting airworthiness; or

(2) That is not done according to accepted practices or cannot be done by elementary operations.

"Major repair" means a repair:

(1) That, if improperly done, might appreciably affect weight, balance, structural strength, performance, powerplant operation, flight characteristics, or other qualities affecting airworthiness; or

(2) That is not done according to accepted practices or cannot be done by elementary operations.

"Manifold pressure" means absolute pressure as measured at the appropriate point in the induction system and usually expressed in inches of mercury.

"Medical certificate" means acceptable evidence of physical fitness on a form prescribed by the Administrator.

"Minimum descent altitude" means the lowest altitude, expressed in feet above mean sea level, to which descent is authorized on final approach or during circle-to-land maneuvering in execution of a standard instrument approach procedure, where no electronic glide slope is provided.

"Minor alteration" means an alteration other than a major alteration.

"Minor repair" means a repair other than a major repair.

"Navigable airspace" means airspace at and above the minimum flight altitudes prescribed by or under this chapter, including airspace needed for safe takeoff and landing.

"Night" means the time between the end of evening civil twilight and the beginning of morning civil twilight, as published in the American Air Almanac, converted to local time.

"Nonprecision approach procedure" means a standard instrument approach procedure in which no electronic glide slope is provided.

"Operate," with respect to aircraft, means use, cause to use or authorize to use aircraft, for the purpose (except as provided in § 91.10 of this chapter) of air navigation including the piloting of aircraft, with or without the right of legal control (as owner, lessee, or otherwise).

"Operational control", with respect to a flight, means the exercise of authority over initiating, conducting or terminating a flight.

"Overseas air commerce" means the carriage by aircraft of persons or property for compensation or hire, or the carriage of mail by aircraft, or the operation or navigation of aircraft in the conduct or furtherance of a business or vocation, in commerce between a place in any State of the United States, or the District of Columbia, and any place in a territory or possession of the United States; or between a place in a territory or possession of the United States, and a place in any other territory or possession of the United States.

"Overseas air transportation" means the carriage by aircraft of persons or property as a common carrier for compensation or hire, or the carriage of mail by aircraft, in commerce:

(1) Between a place in a State or the District of Columbia and a place in a possession of the United States; or

(2) Between a place in a possession of the United States and a place in another possession of the United States; whether that commerce moves wholly by aircraft or partly by aircraft and partly by other forms of transportation.

"Over-the-top" means above the layer of clouds or other obscuring phenomena forming the ceiling.

"Parachute" means a device used or intended to be used to retard the fall of a body or object through the air.

"Gyrodyne" means a rotorcraft whose rotors are normally engine-driven for takeoff, hovering, and landing, and for forward flight through part of its speed range, and whose means of propulsion, consisting usually of conventional propellers, is independent of the rotor system.

"Gyroplane" means a rotorcraft whose rotors are not engine-driven, except for initial starting, but are made to rotate by action of the air when the rotorcraft is moving; and whose means of propulsion, consisting usually of conventional propellers, is independent of the rotor system.

"Helicopter" means a rotorcraft that, for its horizontal motion, depends principally on its engine-driven rotors.

"Heliport" means an area of land, water, or structure used or intended to be used for the landing and takeoff of helicopters.

"Idle thrust" means the jet thrust obtained with the engine power control level set at the stop for the least thrust position at which it can be placed.

"IFR conditions" means weather conditions below the minimum for flight under visual flight rules.

"IFR over-the-top", with respect to the operation of aircraft, means the operation of an aircraft over-the-top on an IFR flight plan when cleared by air traffic control to maintain "VFR conditions" or "VFR conditions on top".

"Indicated airspeed" means the speed of an aircraft as shown on its pitot static airspeed indicator calibrated to reflect standard atmosphere adiabatic compressible flow at sea level uncorrected for airspeed system errors.

"Instrument" means a device using an internal mechanism to show visually or aurally the attitude, altitude, or operation of an aircraft or aircraft part. It includes electronic devices for automatically controlling an aircraft in flight.

"Interstate air commerce" means the carriage by aircraft of persons or property for compensation or hire, or the carriage of mail by aircraft, or the operation or navigation of aircraft in the conduct or furtherance of a busi-ness or vocation, in commerce between a place in any State of the United States, or the District of Columbia, and a place in any other State of the United States, or the District of Columbia; or between places in the same State of the United States through the airspace over any place outside thereof; or between places in the same territory or possession of the United States, or the District of Columbia.

"Interstate air transportation" means the carriage by aircraft of persons or property as a common carrier for compensation or hire, or the carriage of mail by aircraft in commerce:

(1) Between a place in a State or the District of Columbia and another place in another State or the District of Columbia;

(2) Between places in the same State through the airspace over any place outside that State; or

(3) Between places in the same possession of the United States;

Whether that commerce moves wholly by aircraft of partly by aircraft and partly by other forms of transportation.

"Intrastate air transportation" means the carriage of persons or property as a common carrier for compensation or hire, by turbojet-powered aircraft capable of carrying thirty or more persons, wholly within the same State of the United States.

"Kite" means a framework, covered with paper, cloth, metal, or other material, intended to be flown at the end of a rope or cable, and having as its only support the force of the wind moving past its surfaces.

"Landing gear extended speed" means the maximum speed at which an aircraft can be safely flown with the landing gear extended.

"Landing gear operating speed" means the maximum speed at which the landing gear can be safely extended or retracted.

"Large aircraft" means aircraft of more than 12,500 pounds, maximum certificated takeoff weight.

"Lighter-than-air aircraft" means aircraft that can rise and remain suspended by using contained gas weighing less than the air that is displaced by the gas.

"Person" means an individual, firm, partnership, corporation, company, association, joint-stock association, or governmental entity. It includes a trustee, receiver, assignee, or similar representative of any of them.

"Pilotage"means navigation by visual reference to landmarks.

"Pilot in command" means the pilot responsible for the operation and safety of an aircraft during flight time.

"Pitch setting" means the propeller blade setting as determined by the blade angle measured in a manner, and at a radius, specified by the instructional manual for the propeller.

"Positive control" means control of all air traffic, within designated airspace, by air traffic control.

"Precision approach procedure" means a standard instrument approach procedure in which an electronic glide slope is provided, such as ILS and PAR.

"Preventive maintenance" means simple or minor preservation operations and the replacement of small standard parts not involving complex assembly operations.

"Prohibited area" means designated airspace within which the flight of the aircraft is prohibited.

"Propeller" means a device for propelling an aircraft that has blades on an engine-driven shaft and that, when rotated, produces by its action on the air, a thrust approximately perpendicular to its plane of rotation. It includes control components normally supplied by its manufacturer, but does not include main and auxilliary rotors or rotating airfoils of engines.

"Public aircraft" means aircraft used only in the service of a government or a political subdivision. It does not include any government-owned aircraft engaged in carrying persons or property for commercial purposes.

"Rated continuous OEI power," with respect to rotorcraft turbine engines, means the approved brake horsepower developed under static conditions at specified altitudes and temperatures within the operating limitations established for the engine under Part 33 of this chapter, and limited in use to the time required to complete the flight after the failure of one engine of a multiengine rotorcraft.

"Rated maximum continuous augmented thrust", with respect to turbojet engine type certification, means the approved jet thrust that is developed statically or in flight, in standard atmosphere at a specified altitude, with fluid injection or with the burning of fuel in a separate combustion chamber, within the engine operating limitations established under Part 33 of this chapter, and approved for unrestricted periods of use.

of this chapter, and approved for unrestricted periods of use.

"Rated maximum continuous power," with respect to reciprocating, turbopropeller, and turboshaft engines, means the approved brake horsepower that is developed statically or in flight, in standard atmosphere at a specified altitude, within the engine operating limitations established under Part 33, and approved for unrestricted periods of use.

"Rated maximum continuous thrust", with respect to turbojet engine type certification, means the approved jet thrust that is developed statically or in flight, in standard atmosphere at a specified altitude, without fluid injection and without the burning of fuel in a separate combustion chamber, within the engine operating limitations established under Part 33 of this chapter, and approved for unrestricted periods of use.

"Rated takeoff augmented thrust", with respect to turbojet engine type certification, means the approved jet thrust that is developed statically under standard sea level conditions, with fluid injection or with the burning of fuel in a separate combustion chamber, within the engine operating limitations established under Part 33 of this chapter, and limited in use to periods of not over 5 minutes for takeoff operation.

"Rated takeoff power", with respect to reciprocating, turbopropeller, and turboshaft engine type certification, means the approved brake horsepower that is developed statically under standard sea level conditions, within the engine operating limitations established under Part 33, and limited in use to periods of not over 5 minutes for takeoff operation.

"Rated takeoff thrust", with respect to turbojet engine type certification, means the approved jet thrust that is developed statically under standard sea level conditions, without fluid injection and without the burning of fuel in a separate combustion chamber, within the engine operating limitations established under Part 33 of this chapter, and limited in use to periods of not over 5 minutes for takeoff operation.

"Rated 30 minute OEI power," with respect to rotorcraft turbine engines, means the approved brake horsepower develped under static conditions at specified altitudes and temperatures within the operating limitations established for the engine under Part 33 of this chapter, and limited in use to a period of not more than 30 minutes after the failure of one engine of a multiengine rotorcraft.

"Rated 2½-minute OEI power," with respect to rotorcraft turbine engines, means the approved brake horsepower developed under static conditons at specified altitudes and temperatures within the operating limitations established for the engine under part 33 of this chapter, and limited in use to a period of not more than 2½ minutes after the failure of one engine of a multiengine rotorcraft.

"Rating" means a statement that, as a part of a certitificate, sets forth special conditons, privileges, or limitations.

"Reporting point" means a geographical location in relation to which the position of an aircaft is reported.

"Restricted area" means airspace designated under Part 73 of this chapter within which the flight of aircraft while not wholly prohibited, is subject to restriction.

"RNAV way point (W/P)" means a predetermined geographical position used for route or instrument approach definition or progress reporting purposes that is defined relative to a VORTAC station position.

"Rocket" means an aircraft propelled by ejected expanding gases generated in the engine from self-contained propellants and not dependent on the intake of outside substances. It includes any part which becomes separated during the operation.

"Rotorcraft" means a heavier-than-air aircraft that depends principally for its support in flight on the lift generated by one or more rotors.

"Rotorcraft-load combination means the combination of a rotorcraft and an external load, including the external-load attaching means. Rotorcraft-load combinations are designated as Class A, Class B, Class C, and Class D, as follows:

(1) "Class A rotorcraft-load combination" means one in which the external load cannot move freely, cannot be jettisoned, and does not extend below the landing gear.

(2) "Class B rotorcraft-load combination" means one in which the external load is jettisonable and is lifted free of land or water during the rotorcraft operation.

(3) "Class C rotorcraft-load combination" means one in which the external load is jettisonable and remains in contact with land or water during the rotorcraft operation.

(4) "Class D rotorcraft-load combination" means one in which the external-load is other than a Class A, B, or C and has been specifically approved by the Administrator for that operation.

"Route segment" means a part of a route. Each end of that part is identified by:

(1) A continental or insular geographical location; or

(2) A point at which a definite radio fix can be established.

"Sea level engine" means a reciprocating aircraft engine having a rated takeoff power that is producible only at sea level.

"Second in command" means a pilot who is designated to be second in command of an aircraft during flight time.

"Show", unless the context otherwise requires, means to show to the satisfaction of the Administrator.

"Small aircraft" means aircraft of 12,500 pounds or less, maximum certificated takeoff weight.

"Standard atmosphere" means the atmosphere defined in U.S. Standard Atmosphere, 1962 (Geopotential altitude tables).

"Stopway" means an area beyond the takeoff runway, no less wide than the runway and centered upon the extended centerline of the runway, able to support the airplane during an aborted takeoff, without causing structural damage to the airplane, and designated by the airport authorities for use in decelerating the airplane during an aborted takeoff.

"Takeoff power":

(1) With respect to reciprocating engines, means the brake horsepower that is developed under standard sea level conditions, and under the maximum conditions of crankshaft rota-

tional speed and engine manifold pressure approved for the normal takeoff, and limited in continuous use to the period of time shown in the approved engine specification; and

(2) With respect to turbine engines, means the brake horsepower that is developed under static conditions at a specified altitude and atmospheric temperature, and under the maximum conditions of rotor shaft rotational speed and gas temperature approved for the normal takeoff, and limited in continuous use to the period of time shown in the approved engine specification.

"Takeoff safety speed" means a referenced airspeed obtained after lift-off at which the required one-engine-inoperative climb performance can be achieved.

"Takeoff thrust", with respect to turbine engines, means the jet thrust that is developed under static conditions at a specific altitude and atmospheric temperature under the maximum conditions of rotorshaft rotational speed and gas temperature approved for the normal takeoff, and limited in continuous use to the period of time shown in the approved engine specification.

"Time in service", with respect to maintenance time records, means the time from the moment an aircraft leaves the surface of the earth until it touches it at the next point of landing.

"True airspeed" means the airspeed of an aircraft relative to undisturbed air. True airspeed is equal to equivalent airspeed multiplied by $(\rho0/\rho)^{1/2}$.

"Traffic pattern" means the traffic flow that is prescribed for aircraft landing at, taxiing on, or taking off from, an airport.

"Type":

(1) As used with respect to the certification, ratings, privileges, and limitations of airmen, means a specific make and basic model of aircraft, including modifications thereto that do not change its handling or flight characteristics. Examples include: DC-7, 1049, and F-27; and

(2) As used with respect to the certification of aircraft, means those aircraft which are similar in design. Examples include: DC-7 and DC-7C;

1049G and 1049H; and F-27 and F-27F.

(3) As used with respect to the certification of aircraft engines means those engines which are similar in design. For example, JT8D and JT8D-7 are engines of the same type, and JT9D-3A and JT9D-7 are engines of the same type.

"United States", in a geographical sense, means (1) the States, the District of Columbia, Puerto Rico, and the possessions, including the territorial waters, and (2) the airspace of those areas.

"United States air carrier" means a citizen of the United States who undertakes directly by lease, or other arrangement, to engage in air transportation.

"VFR over-the-top", with respect to the operation of aircraft, means the operation of an aircraft over-the-top under VFR when it is not being operated on an IFR flight plan.

[Doc. No. 1150, 27 FR 4588, May 15, 1962]

EDITORIAL NOTE: For Federal Register citations affecting §1.1, see the List of CFR Sections Affected appearing in the Finding Aids section of this volume.

§1.2 Abbreviations and symbols.

In Subchapters A through K of this chapter:

"AGL" means above ground level.

"ALS" means approach light system.

"ASR" means airport surveillance radar.

"ATC" means air traffic control.

"CAS" means calibrated airspeed.

"CAT II" means Category II.

"CONSOL or CONSOLAN" means a kind of low or medium frequency long range navigational aid.

"DH" means decision height.

"DME" means distance measuring equipment compatible with TACAN.

"EAS" means equivalent airspeed.

"FAA" means Federal Aviation Administration.

"FM" means fan marker.

"GS" means glide slope.

"HIRL" means high-intensity runway light system.

"IAS" means indicated airspeed.

"ICAO" means International Civil Aviation Organization.

"IFR" means instrument flight rules.

"ILS" means instrument landing system.

"IM" means ILS inner marker.

"INT" means intersection.

"LDA" means localizer-type directional aid.

"LFR" means low-frequency radio range.

"LMM" means compass locator at middle marker.

"LOC" means ILS localizer.

"LOM" means compass locator at outer marker.

"*M*" means mach number.

"MAA" means maximum authorized IFR altitude.

"MALS" means medium intensity approach light system.

"MALSR" means medium intensity approach light system with runway alignment indicator lights.

"MCA" means minimum crossing altitude.

"MDA" means minimum descent altitude.

"MEA" means minimum en route IFR altitude.

"MM" means ILS middle marker.

"MOCA" means minimum obstruction clearance altitude.

"MRA" means minimum reception altitude.

"MSL" means mean sea level.

"NDB(ADF)" means nondirectional beacon (automatic direction finder).

"NOPT" means no procedure turn required.

"OEI" means one engine inoperative.

"OM" means ILS outer marker.

"PAR" means precision approach radar.

"RAIL" means runway alignment indicator light system.

"RBN" means radio beacon.

"RCLM" means runway centerline marking.

"RCLS" means runway centerline light system.

"REIL" means runway end identification lights.

"RR" means low or medium frequency radio range station.

"RVR" means runway visual range as measured in the touchdown zone area.

"SALS" means short approach light system.

"SSALS" means simplified short approach light system.

"SSALSR" means simplified short approach light system with runway alignment indicator lights.

"TACAN" means ultra-high frequency tactical air navigational aid.

"TAS" means true airspeed.

"TDZL" means touchdown zone lights.

"TVOR" means very high frequency terminal omnirange station.

V_A means design maneuvering speed.

V_B means design speed for maximum gust intensity.

V_C means design cruising speed.

V_D means design diving speed.

V_{DF}/M_{DF} means demonstrated flight diving speed.

V_F means design flap speed.

V_{FC}/M_{FC} means maximum speed for stability characteristics.

V_{FE} means maximum flap extended speed.

V_H means maximum speed in level flight with maximum continuous power.

V_{LE} means maximum landing gear extended speed.

V_{LO} means maximum landing gear operating speed.

V_{LOF} means lift-off speed.

V_{MC} means minimum control speed with the critical engine inoperative.

V_{MO}/M_{MO} means maximum operating limit speed.

V_{MU} means minimum unstick speed.

V_{NE} means never-exceed speed.

V_{NO} means maximum structural cruising speed.

V_R means rotation speed.

V_S means the stalling speed or the minimum steady flight speed at which the airplane is controllable.

V_{SO} means the stalling speed or the minimum steady flight speed in the landing configuration.

V_{S1} means the stalling speed or the minimum steady flight speed obtained in a specific configuration.

V_{TOSS} means takeoff safety speed for Category A rotorcraft.

V_X means speed for best angle of climb.

V_Y means speed for best rate of climb.

V_1 means takeoff decision speed (formerly denoted as critical engine failure speed).

V_2 means takeoff safety speed.

V_2 min means minimum takeoff safety speed.

"VFR" means visual flight rules.

"VHF" means very high frequency.

"VOR" means very high frequency omnirange station.

"VORTAC" means collocated VOR and TACAN.

[Doc. No. 1150, 27 FR 4590, May 15, 1962]

EDITORIAL NOTE: For FEDERAL REGISTER citations affecting § 1.2, see the List of CFR Sections Affected appearing in the Finding Aids, section of this volume.

§ 1.3 Rules of construction.

(a) In Subchapters A through K of this chapter, unless the context requires otherwise:

(1) Words importing the singular include the plural;

(2) Words importing the plural include the singular; and

(3) Words importing the masculine gender include the feminine.

(b) In Subchapters A through K of this chapter, the word:

(1) "Shall" is used in an imperative sense;

(2) "May" is used in a permissive sense to state authority or permission to do the act prescribed, and the words "no person may * * *" or "a person may not * * *" mean that no person is required, authorized, or permitted to do the act prescribed; and

(3) "Includes" means "includes but is not limited to".

[Doc. No. 1150, 27 FR 4590, May 15, 1962, as amended by Amdt. 1-10, 31 FR 5055, Mar. 29, 1966]

FEDERAL AVIATION REGULATIONS

PART 13
INVESTIGATION AND ENFORCEMENT PROCEDURE

1989 EDITION

Federal Aviation Administration, DOT — Part 13

PART 13 — INVESTIGATIVE AND ENFORCEMENT PROCEDURES

Subpart A — Investigative Procedures

Sec.
13.1   Reports of violations.
13.3   Investigations (general).
13.5   Formal complaints.
13.7   Records, documents and reports.

Subpart B — Administrative Actions

13.11 Administrative disposition of certain violations.

Subpart C — Legal Enforcement Actions

13.13 Consent orders.
13.15 Civil penalties: Federal Aviaiton Act of 1958.
13.16 Civil penalties: Hazardous Materials Transportation Act.
13.17 Seizure of aircraft.
13.19 Certificate action.
13.20 Orders of compliance, cease and desist orders, orders of denial and other orders.
13.21 Military personnel.
13.23 Criminal penalties.
13.25 Injunctons.
13.27 Final order of Hearing Officer in certificate of aircraft registration proceedings.

Subpart D — Rules of Practice for FAA Hearings

13.31 Applicability.
13.33 Appearances.
13.35 Request for hearing.
13.37 Hearing Officer's powers.
13.39 Disqualificaitons of Hearing Officer.
13.41 [Reserved]
13.43 Service and filing of pleadings, motions, and documents.
13.44 Computation of time and extension of time.
13.45 Amendment of notice and answer.
13.47 Withdrawal of notice or request for hearing.
13.49 Motions.
13.51 Intervention.
13.53 Depositions.
13.55 Notice of hearing.
13.57 Subpoenas and witness fees.
13.59 Evidence.
13.61 Argument and submittals.
13.63 Record.

Subpart E — Orders of Compliance Under the Hazardous Materials Transportation Act

13.71 Applicability
13.73 Notice of proposed order of compliance.
13.75 Reply or request for hearing.
13.77 Consent order of compliance.
13.79 Hearing.
13.81 Order of immediate compliance.
13.83 Appeal.

13.85 Filing, service, and computation of time.
13.87 Extension of time.

Subpart F — Formal Fact-Finding Investigation Under an Order of Investigation

13.101 Applicability.
13.103 Order of investigation.
13.105 Notification.
13.107 Designation of additional parties.
13.109 Convening of the investigation.
13.111 Subpoenas.
13.113 Noncompliance with the investigative process.
13.115 Public proceedings.
13.117 Conduct of investigative proceeding or deposition.
13.119 Rights of persons against self-incrimination.
13.121 Witness fees.
13.123 Submission by party to the investigation.
13.125 Depositions.
13.127 Reports, decisions and orders.
13.129 Post-investigation action.
13.131 Other procedures.

Subpart G — Rules of Practice in FAA Civil Penalty Actions

13.201 Applicability.
13.202 Definitions.
13.203 Separation of functions.
13.204 Appearances and rights of parties.
13.205 Administrative law judges.
13.206 Intervention.
13.207 Certification of documents.
13.208 Complaint.
13.209 Answer.
13.210 Filing of documents.
13.211 Service of documents.
13.212 Computation of time.
13.213 Extension of time.
13.214 Amendment of pleadings.
13.215 Withdrawal of a complaint or request for a hearing.
13.216 Waivers.
13.217 Joint procedural or discovery schedule.
13.218 Motions.
13.219 Interlocutory appeals.
13.220 Discovery.
13.221 Notice of hearing.
13.222 Evidence.
13.223 Standard of proof.
13.224 Burden of proof.
13.225 Offer of proof.
13.226 Public disclosure of evidence.
13.227 Testimony by agency employees.
13.228 Subpoenas.
13.229 Witness fees.

1989   [FAR 34]   ASA-13

13.230 Record.
13.231 Argument before the administrative law judge.
13.232 Initial decision.
13.233 Appeals from initial decisions.
13.234 Petitions to reconsider or modify a final decision and order of the FAA decisionmaker on appeal.
13.235 Judicial review of final decision and order.

Subpart A — Investigative Procedures

§ 13.1 Reports of violations.

(a) Any person who knows of a violation of the Federal Aviation Act of 1958, as amended, the Hazardous Materials Transportation Act relating to the transportation or shipment by air of hazardous materials, the Airport and Airway Development Act of 1970, the Airport and Airway Improvement Act of 1982, the Air-

port and Airway Improvement Act of 1982 as amended by the Airport and Airway Safety and Capacity Expansion Act of 1987, or any rule, regulation, or order issued thereunder, should report it to appropriate personnel of any FAA regional or district office.

(b) Each report made under this section, together with any other information the FAA may have that is relevant to the matter reported, will be reviewed by FAA personnel to determine the nature and type of any additional investigation or enforcement action the FAA will take.

§ 13.3 Investigations (general).

(a) Under the Federal Aviation Act of 1958, as amended, (49 U.S.C. 1301 *et seq.*), the Hazardous Materials Transportation Act (49, U.S.C. 1801 *et seq.*), the Airport and Airway Development Act of 1970 (49 U.S.C. 1701 *et seq.*), the Airport and Airway Improvement Act of 1982 (49 U.S.C. 2201 *et seq.*), the Airport and Airway Improvement Act of 1982 (as amended, 49 U.S.C. App. 2201 *et. seq.*, Airport and Airway Safety and Capacity Expansion Act of 1987), and the Regulations of the Office of the Secretary of Transportation (49 CFR 1 *et seq.*), the Administrator may conduct investigations, hold hearings, issue subpoenas, require the production of relevant documents, records, and property, and take evidence and depositions.

(b) For the purpose of investigating alleged violations of the Federal Aviation Act of 1958, as amended (except Title V of that Act), the Hazardous Materials Transportation Act, the Airport and Airway Development Act of 1970, the Airport and Airway Development Act of 1982, the Airport and Airway Development Act of 1982 as amended by the Airport and Airway Safety and Capacity Expansion Act of 1987, or any rule, regulation, or order issued thereunder, the Administrator's authority has been delegated to the various services and or offices for matters within their respective areas for all routine investigations. When the compulsory processes of sections 313 and 1004 (49 U.S.C. 1354 and 1484) of the Federal Aviation Act, or section 109 of the Hazardous Materials Transportation Act (49 U.S.C. 1808) are invoked, the Administrator's authority has been delegated to the Chief Counsel, the Deputy Chief Counsel, each Assistant Chief Counsel, and each Regional Counsel. For the purpose of investigating alleged violations of Title V of the Federal Aviation Act, or any regulation or order issued under it, the Administrator's authority has been delegated to the Chief Counsel, the Deputy Chief

Counsel, and the Aeronautical Center Counsel.

(c) In conducting formal investigations, the Chief Counsel, the Deputy Chief Counsel, each Assistant Chief Counsel, each Regional Counsel, and the Aeronautical Center Counsel may issue an order of investigation in accordance with Subpart F of this part.

§13.5 Formal complaints.

(a) Any person may file a complaint with the Administrator with respect to anything done or omitted to be done by any person in contravention of any provision of any Act or of any regulation or order issued under it, as to matters within the jurisdiction of the Administrator. This section does not apply to complaints against the Administrator or employees of the FAA acting within the scope of their employment.

(b) Complaints filed under this section must—

(1) Be submitted in writing and identified as a complaint filed for the purpose of seeking an appropriate order or other enforcement action;

(2) Be submitted to the Federal Aviation Administration, Office of the Chief Counsel, Attention: Enforcement Docket (AGC-209), 800 Independence Avenue, S.W., Washington, D.C. 20591;

(3) Set forth the name and address, if known, of each person who is the subject of the complaint and, with respect to each person, the specific provisions of the Act or regulation or order that the complainant believes were violated;

(4) Contain a concise but complete statement of the facts relied upon to substantiate each allegation;

(5) State the name, address and telephone number of the person filing the complaint; and

(6) Be signed by the person filing the complaint or a duly authorized representative.

(c) Complaints which do not meet the requirements of paragraph (b) of this section will be considered reports under §13.1.

(d) Complaints which meet the requirements of paragraph (b) of this section will be docketed and a copy mailed to each person named in the complaint.

(e) Any complaint filed against a member of the Armed Forces of the United States acting in the performance of official duties shall be referred to the Secretary of the Department concerned for action in accordance with the procedures set forth in §13.21 of this part.

(f) The person named in the complaint shall file an answer within 20 days after service of a copy of the complaint.

(g) After the complaint has been answered or after the allotted time in which to file an answer has expired, the Administrator shall determine if there are reasonable grounds for investigating the complaint.

(h) If the Administrator determines that a complaint does not state facts which warrant an investigation or action, the complaint may be dismissed without a hearing and the reason for the dismissal shall be given, in writing, to the person who filed the complaint and the person named in the complaint.

(i) If the Administrator determines that reasonable grounds exist, an informal investigation may be initiated or an order of investigation may be issued in accordance with Subpart F of this part, or both. Each person named in the complaint shall be advised which official has been delegated the responsibility under §13.3(b) or (c) for conducting the investigation.

(j) If the investigation substantiates the allegations set forth in the complaint, a notice of proposed order may be issued or other enforcement action taken in accordance with this part.

(k) The complaint and other pleadings and official FAA records relating to the disposition of the complaint are maintained in current docket form in the Enforcement Docket (AGC-209), Office of the Chief Counsel, Federal Aviation Administration, 800 Independence Avenue, S.W., Washington, D. C. 20591. Any interested person may examine any docketed material at that office, at any time after the docket is established, except material that is ordered withheld from the public under applicable law or regulations, and may obtain a photostatic or duplicate copy upon paying the cost of the copy.

§ 13.7 Records, document and reports.

Each record, document and report that the Federal Aviation Regulations require to be maintained, exhibited or submitted to the Administrator may be used in any investigation conducted by the Administrator; and, except to the extent the use may be specifically limited or prohibited by the section which imposes the requirement, the records, documents and reports may be used in any civil penalty action, certificate action, or other legal proceeding.

Subpart B — Administrative Actions

§ 13.11 Administrative disposition of certain violations.

(a) If it is determined that a violation or an alleged violation of the Federal Aviation Act of 1958, or an order or regulation issued under it, or of the Hazardous Materials Transportation Act, or an order or regulation issued under it, does not require legal enforcement action, an appropriate official of the FAA field office responsible for processing the enforcement case or other appropriate FAA official take administrative action in disposition of the case.

(b) An administrative action under this section does not constitute a formal adjudication of the matter, and may be taken by issuing the alleged violator—

(1) A "Warning Notice" which recites available facts and information about the incident or condition and indicates that it may have been a violation; or

(2) A "Letter of Correction" which confirms the FAA decision in the matter and states the necessary corrective action the alleged violator has taken or agrees to take. If the agreed corrective action is not fully completed, legal enforcement action a may be taken.

Subpart C — Legal Enforcement Actions

§ 13.13 Consent orders.

(a) At any time before the issuance of an order under this subpart, the official who issued the notice may agree to dispose of the case by the issuance of a consent order by the official.

(b) A proposal for a consent order, submitted to the official who issued the notice, under this section must include—

(1) A proposed order;

(2) An admission of all jurisdictional facts;

(3) An express waiver of the right to further procedural steps and of all rights to judicial review; and

(4) An incorporation by reference of the notice and an acknowledgment that the notice may be used to construe the terms of the order.

(c) If the issuance of a consent order has been agreed upon after the filing of a request for hearing in accordance with Subpart D of this part, the proposal for a consent order shall include a request to be filed with the Hearing Officer withdrawing the request for a hearing and requesting that the case be dismissed.

§ 13.15 Civil penalties: Federal Aviation Act of 1958   involving an amount in controversy in excess   of $50,000; an in rem action; seizure of aircraft;   or injunctive relief.

(a) The following penalties apply to persons who violate the Federal Aviation Act of 1958, as amended:

(1) Any person who violates any provision of Title III, V, VI, or XII of the Federal Aviation Act of 1958, as amended, or any rule, regulation, or order issued thereunder, is subject to a civil penalty of not more than $1000 for each violation, in accordance with section 901 of the Federal Aviation Act of 1958, as amended (49 U.S.C. 1471, *et seq.*).

(2) Any person who violates section 404(d) of the Federal Aviation Act of 1958, as amended, or any rule, regulation, or order issued thereunder, is subject to a civil penalty of not more than $2,000 for each violation, in accordance with section 901 of the Federal Aviation Act of 1958, as amended (49 U.S.C. 1471, *et seq.*)

(3) Any person who operates aircraft for the carriage of persons or property for compensation or hire (other than an airman serving in the capacity of an airman) is subject to a civil penalty of not more than $10,000 for each violation of Title III, VI, or XII of the Federal Aviation Act of 1958, as amended, or any rule, regulation, or order issued thereunder, occuring after December 30, 1987, in accordance with section 901 of the Federal Aviation Act of 1958, as amended (49 U.S.C. 1471, *et seq.*).

(b) The authority of the Administrator, under section 901 of of the Federal Aviation Act of 1958, as amended, to propose a civil penalty for a violation of that Act, or a rule, regulation, or order issued thereunder, and the ability to refer cases to the United States Attorney General, or the delegate of the Attorney General, for prosecution of civil penalty actions proposed by the Administrator, involving an amount in controversy in excess of $50,000, an *in rem* action, seizure of aircraft subject to lien, or suit for injunctive relief, or for collection of an assessed civil penalty, is delegated to the Chief Counsel, the Assistant Chief Counsel for Regulations and Enforcement, and the Assistant Chief Counsel for a region or center.

(c) The Administrator may compromise any civil penalty, proposed in accordance with section 901 of the Federal Aviation Act of 1958, as amended, involving an amount in controversy in excess of $50,000, an *in rem* action, seizure of aircraft subject to lien, or suit for injunctive relief, prior to referral of the civil penalty action to the United States Attorney General, or the delegate of the Attorney General, for prosecution.

(1) The Administrator, through the Chief Counsel, the Assistant Chief Counsel for Regulations and Enforcement, and the Assistant Chief Counsel for a region or center, sends a civil penalty letter to the person charged with a violation of the Federal Aviation Act of 1958, as amended, or a rule, regulation, or order issued thereunder. The civil penalty letter contains a statement of the charges, the applicable law, rule, regulation, or order, the amount of civil penalty that the Administrator will accept in full settlement of the action or an offer to compromise the civil penalty.

(2) Not later than 30 days after receipt of the civil penalty letter, the person charged with a violation may present any material or information in answer to the charges to the agency attorney, either orally or in writing, that may explain, mitigate, or deny the violation or that may show extenuating circumstances. The Administrator will consider any material or information submitted in accordance with this paragraph to determine whether the person is

subject to a civil penalty or to determine the amount for which the Administrator will compromise the action.

(3) If the person charged with the violation offers to compromise for a specific amount, that person shall send a certified check or money order for that amount, payable to the Federal Aviation Administration, to the agency attorney. The Chief Counsel, the Assistant Chief Counsel for Regulations and Enforcement, or the Assistant Chief Counsel for a region or center, may accept the certified check or money order or may refuse and return the certified check or money order.

(4) If the offer to compromise is accepted by the Administrator, the agency attorney will send a letter to the person charged with the violation stating that the certified check or money order is accepted in full settlement of the civil penalty action.

(5) If the parties cannot agree to compromise the civil penalty action or the offer to compromise is rejected and the certified check or money order submitted in compromise is returned, the Administrator may refer the civil penalty action to the United States Attorney General, or the delegate of the Attorney General, to begin proceedings in a United States District Court, pursuant to the authority in section 903 of the Federal Aviation Act, as amended (49 U.S.C. 1473), to prosecute and collect the civil penalty.

§ 13.16 Civil Penalties: Federal Aviation Act of 1958, involving an amount in controversy not exceeding $50,000; Hazardous Materials Transportation Act.

(a) The following penalties apply to persons who violate the Federal Aviation Act of 1958, as amended, and the Hazardous Materials Transportation Act:

(1) Any person who violates any provision of Title III, V, VI, or XII of the Federal Aviation Act of 1958, as amended, or any rule, regulation, or order issued thereunder, is subject to a civil penalty of not more than $1,000 for each violation, in accordance with section 901 of the Federal Aviation Act of 1958, as amended (49 U.S.C. 1471, et seq.).

(2) Any person who violates section 404(d) of the Federal Aviation Act of 1958, as amended, or any rule, regulation, or order issued thereunder, is subject to a civil penalty of not more than $2,000, for each violation, in accordance with section 901 of the Federal Aviation Act of 1958, as amended, (49 U.S.C. 1471 et seq.).

(3) Any person who operates aircraft for the carriage of persons or property for compen-

sation or hire (other than an airman serving in the capacity of an airman) is subject to a civil penalty of not more than $10,000 for each violation of Title III, VI, or XII of the Federal Aviation Act of 1958, as amended, or any rule, regulation, or order issued thereunder, occurring after December 30, 1987, in accordance with section 901 of the Federal Aviation Act of 1958, as amended, (49 U.S.C. 1471, et seq.).

(4) Any person who knowingly commits an act in violation of the Hazardous Materials Transportation Act, or any rule, regulation, or order issued thereunder is subject to a civil penalty of not more than $10,000 for each violation, in accordance with section 901 of the Federal Aviation Act of 1958, as amended, and section 110 of the Hazardous Materials Transportation Act (49 U.S.C. 1471 and 1809 et seq.). An order assessing civil penalty for a violation under the Hazardous Materials Transportation Act, or a rule, regulation, or order issued thereunder, will be issued only after consideration of—

(i) The nature and circumstances of the violation;

(ii) The extent and gravity of the violation;

(iii) The person's degree of culpability;

(iv) The person's history of prior violations;

(v) The person's ability to pay the civil penalty;

(vi) The effect on the person's ability to continue in business; and

(vii) Such other matters as justice may require.

(b) An order assessing civil penalty may be issued for a violation described in paragraphs (a)(1), (a)(2), (a)(3), and (a)(4) of this section after notice and opportunity for a hearing.

(c) The authority of the Administrator, under sections 901 and § 905 of the Federal Aviation Act of 1958, as amended, and section 110 of the Hazardous Materials Transportation Act, to initiate and assess civil penalties for a violation of those Acts, or a rule, regulation, or order issued thereunder and the authority under section 901 of the Federal Aviation Act of 1958, as amended, and the ability to refer cases to the United States Attorney General, or the delegate of the Attorney General, for collection of assessed civil penalties, is delegated to the Chief Counsel, the Assistant Chief Counsel for Regulations and Enforcement, and the Assistant Chief Counsel for a region or center.

(d) *Notice of proposed civil penalty.* A civil penalty action is initiated by sending a notice of proposed civil penalty to the person charged with a violation of the Federal Aviation Act of 1958 as amended, the Hazardous Materials Transportation Act, or a rule, regulation, or order issued thereunder. The notice of proposed civil penalty contains a statement of the charges and the amount of the proposed civil penalty.

(e) *Procedures following receipt of notice of proposed civil penalty.* Not later than 30 days after receipt of the notice of proposed civil penalty, the person charged with a violation shall do one of the following:

(1) The person shall submit the amount of the proposed civil penalty in which case an order assessing civil penalty shall be issued in that amount.

(2) The person shall participate in the informal procedures provided in paragraph (f) of this section.

(3) The person shall request a hearing, pursuant to paragraph (i) of this section, in which case an order of civil penalty shall be issued and shall be filed with the hearing docket clerk as the complaint in the proceedings.

(f) *Informal procedures.* Not later than 30 days after receipt of the notice of proposed civil penalty, the person charged with a violation, who wants to participate in informal procedures, shall do one of the following:

(1) The person shall submit any information, including documents and witness statements, in writing, to the agency attorney, demonstrating that a violation of the regulations did not occur or that the penalty or the amount of the penalty is not warranted by the circumstances.

(2) the person shall submit a written request to the agency attorney to reduce the proposed civil penalty and shall submit, in writing, the reasons and documents supporting the reduction of the proposed civil penalty, including records indicating a financial inability to pay or records showing that payment of the proposed civil penalty would prevent the person from continuing in business, or

(3) The person shall submit a written request to the agency attorney for an informal conference to discuss the matter with the agency attorney and to submit relevant information or documents to the agency attorney.

(g) *Procedures following interim reply or informal conference.* Not later than 10 days after the person charged with a violation receives an interim reply to any submission made in accordance with paragraphs (f)(1) or (f)(2) or not later than 10 days after an informal conference, the person charged with the violation shall do one of the following:

(1) The person shall submit the amount of the proposed civil penalty in which case an order assessing civil penalty shall be issued in that amount.

(2) The person shall submit additional written information to the agency attorney for consideration.

(3) The person shall request a hearing, pursuant to paragraph (i) of this section, in which case an order of civil penalty shall be issued and shall be filed with the hearing docket clerk as the the complaint in the proceedings.

(h) *Order of civil penalty.* An order of civil penalty shall be issued if the person charged with a violation requests a hearing in accordance with paragraph (e)(3) or paragraph (g)(3) of this section.

(i) *Request for a hearing.* Any person who recieves a notice of proposed civil penalty may request a hearing, pursuant to paragraph (e)(3) or paragraph (g)(3) of this section, to be conducted in accordance with the procedures in Subpart G of this part. A person requesting a hearing shall file a written request for a hearing with the agency attorney. The request for a hearing may be in the form of a letter but must be dated and signed by the person requesting a hearing. The request for a hearing may be typewritten or may be legibly handwritten. A person requesting a hearing shall include a suggested location for the hearing in the request of a hearing.

(j) *Order assessing civil penalty.* An order assessing civil penalty shall be issued if the person charged with a violation—

(1) Submits the amount of the proposed civil penalty in which case the order assessing civil penalty shall reflect receipt of the civil penalty:

(2) Does not respond in a timely manner to the notice of proposed civil penalty:

(3) Does not respond in a timely manner to interim replies from the agency attorney under paragraph (g) of this section; or

(4) Does not comply with any agreement reached between the parties during an informal conference.

(k) *Payment.* A person charged with a violation may pay the amount of the civil penalty proposed in the notice or stated in the order, or an amount agreed upon, by sending a certified check or money order, payable to the Federal Aviation Administration, to the agency attorney.

(l) *Hearing.* If the person charged with the violation requests a hearing pursuant to paragraph (e)(3) or paragraph (g)(3) of this section, the order of civil penalty shall be issued and shall be filed with the hearing docket clerk as the complaint in the proceedings. The procedural rules in Subpart G of this part apply to the hearing and any appeal. At the close of the hearing, the administrative law judge shall issue, either orally on the record or in writing, an initial decision, including the reasons for the decision, that affirms, modifies, or reverses the order of civil penalty. An order of civil penalty as affirmed or modified by the administrative law judge, shall become an order assessing civil penalty if a party does not appeal the administrative law judge's initial decision to the FAA decisionmaker.

(m) *Appeal.* Either party may appeal the administrative law judge's initial decision to the FAA decisionmaker pursuant to the procedures in Subpart G of this part. If a party files a notice of appeal pursuant to § 13.233 of Subpart G, the effectiveness of any order assessing civil penalty is stayed until a final decision and order of the Administrator has been entered on the record. The FAA decisionmaker shall review the record of the hearing and issue a final decision and order of the Administrator that affirms, modifies, or reverses the order assessing civil penalty. The FAA decisionmaker shall not assess a civil penalty in an amount greater than the amount stated in the order of civil penalty.

(n) *Exhaustion of administrative remedies.* A party may only appeal a final decision and order of the Administrator to the courts of appeals of the United States or the United States Court of Appeals for the District of Columbia pursuant to section 1006 of the

Federal Aviation Act of 1958, as amended. An order or an initial decision of an administrative law judge, that has not been appealed to the FAA decisionmaker, does not constitute a final order of the Administrator for the purposes of judicial appellate review under section 1006 of the Federal Aviation Act of 1958, as amended.

(o) If a person subject to an order assessing civil penalty does not pay the assessed civil penalty within 60 days after service of the order assessing civil penalty, the Administrator may refer the order to the United States Attorney General, or the delegate of the Attorney General, to begin proceedings in a United States District Court, pursuant to the authority in section 903 of the Federal Aviation Act of 1958, as amended (49 U.S.C. 1473), or section 110 of the Hazardous Materials Transportation Act (49 U.S.C. 1809), to collect the civil penalty.

(p) *Compromise.* The Administrator may compromise any civil penalty, assessed in accordance with sections 901 and 905 of the Federal Aviation Act of 1958, as amended, involving an amount in controversy not exceeding $50,000, or any civil penalty assessed in accordance with section 901 of the Federal Aviation Act of 1958, as amended, and section 110 of the Hazardous Materials Transportation Act, at any time prior to referring the order assessing civil penalty to the United States attorney for collection.

§ 13.17 Seizure of aircraft

(a) Under section 903 of the Federal Aviation act of 1958 (49 U.S.C. 1473), a State or Federal law enforcement officer, or a Federal Aviation Administration safety inspector, authorized in an order of seizure issued by the Regional Director of the region, or by the Chief Counsel, may summarily seize an aircraft that is involved in a violation for which a civil penalty may be imposed on its owner or operator

(b) Each person seizing an aircraft under this section shall place it in the nearest available and adequate public storage facility in the judicial district in which it was seized

(c) The Regional Director or Chief Counsel, without delay, sends a written notice and copy of this section, to the registered owner of the seized aircraft, and to each other persons shown by FAA records to have an interest in it, stating the —

(1) Time, date, and place of seizure;

(2) Name and address of the custodian of the aircraft;

(3) Reasons for the seizure, including the violations believed, or judicially determined, to have been committed; and

(4) Amount that may be tendered as —

(i) A compromise of a civil penalty for the alleged violation; or

(ii) Payment for a civil penalty imposed by a Federal court for a proven violation

(d) The Chief Counsel or Regional Counsel of the region, in which an aircraft is seized under this section immediately sends a report to the United States District Attorney for the judicial district in which it was seized, requesting the District Attorney to institute proceedings to enforce a lien against the aircraft

(e) The Regional Director or Chief Counsel directs the release or a seized aircraft whenever—

(1) The alleged violator pays a civil penalty or an amount agreed upon in compromise, and the costs of seizing, storing, and maintaining the aircraft;

(2) The aircraft is seized under an order of a Federal Court in proceedings in rem to enforce a lien against the aircraft, or the United States District Attorney for the judicial district concerned notifies the FAA that the District Attorney refuses to institute those proceedings; or

(3) A bond in the amount and with the sureties prescribed by the Chief Counsel or the Regional Counsel is deposited, conditioned on payment of the penalty, or the compromise amount, and the costs of seizing, storing, and maintaining the aircraft.

§ 13.19 Certificate action.

(a) Under section 609 of the Federal Aviation Act of 1958 (49 U.S.C. 1429), the Administrator may reinspect any civil aircraft, aircraft engine, propeller, appliance, air navigation facility, or air agency, and may re-examine any civil airman. Under section 501(e) of the FA Act, any Certificate of Aircraft Registration may be suspended or revoked by the Administrator for any cause that renders the aircraft ineligible for registration.

(b) If, as a result of such a reinspection re-examination, or other investigation made by the Administrator under section 609 of the FA Act, the Administrator determines that the public interest and safety in air commerce requires it, the Administrator may issue an order amending, suspending, or revoking, all or part of any type certificate, production certificate, airworthiness certificate, airman certificate, air carrier operating certificate, air navigation facility certificate, or air agency certificate. This authority may be exercised for remedial purposes in cases involving the Hazardous Materials Transportation Act (49 U.S.C. 1801 et seq.) or regulations issued under that Act. This authority is also exercised by the Chief Counsel, the Assistant Chief Counsel for Regulations and Enforcement, and the Regional Counsel concerned. If the Administrator finds that any aircraft registered under Part 47 of this chapter is ineligible for registration or if the holder of a Certificate of Aircraft Registration has refused or failed to submit AC Form 8050-73, as required by § 47.51 of this chapter, the Administrator issues an order suspending or revoking that certificate. This authority as to aircraft found ineligible for registration is also exercised by the Aeronautical Center Counsel.

(c) Before issuing an order under paragraph (b) of this section, the Chief Counsel, the Assistant Chief Counsel for Regulations and Enforcement, the Regional Counsel concerned, or the Aeronautical Center Counsel (as to matters under Title V of the FA Act) advises the certificate holder of the charges or other reasons upon which the Administrator bases the proposed action and, except in an emergency, allows the holder to answer any charges and to be heard as to why the certificate should not be amended, suspended, or revoked. The holder may, by checking the appropriate box on the form that is sent to the holder with the notice of proposed certificate action, elect to—

(1) Admit the charges and surrender his or her certificate;

(2) Answer the charges in writing;

(3) Request that an order be issued in accordance with the notice of proposed certificate action so that the certificate holder may appeal to the National Transportation Safety Board, if the charges concerning a matter under Title VI of the FA Act;

(4) Request an opportunity to be heard in an informal conference with the FAA counsel; or

(5) Request a hearing in accordance with Subpart D of this part if the charges concern a matter under Title V of the FA Act.

Except as provided in § 13.35(b), unless the certificate holder returns the form and, where required, an answer or motion, with a postmark of not later than 15 days after the date of receipt of the notice, the order of the Administrator is issued as proposed. If the certificate holder has requested an informal conference with the FAA counsel and the charges concern a matter under Title V of the FAAct, the holder may after that conference also request a formal hearing in writing with a postmark of not later than 10 days after the close of the conference. After considering any information submitted by the certificate holder, the Chief Counsel, the Assistant Chief Counsel for Regulations and Enforcement, the Regional Counsel concerned, or the Aeronautical Center Counsel (as to matters under Title V of the FA Act) issues the order of the Administrator, except that if the holder has made a valid request for a formal hearing on a matter under Title V of the FA Act initially or after an informal conference, Subpart D of this part governs further proceedings.

(d) Any person whose certificate is affected by an order issued under this section may appeal to the National Transportation Safety Board. If the certificate holder files an appeal with the Board, the Administrator's order is stayed unless the Administrator advises the Board that an emergency exists and safety in air commerce requires that the order become effective immediately. If the Board is so advised, the order remains effective and the Board shall finally dispose of the appeal within 60 days after the date of the advice. This paragraph does not apply to any person whose Certificate of Aircraft Registration is affected by an order issued under this section.

[Doc. No. 13-14, 44 FR 63723, Nov. 5, 1979, as amended by Amdt. 13-15, 45 FR 20773, Mar. 31, 1980]

§ 13.20 Orders of compliance, cease and desist orders, orders of denial and other orders.

(a) This section applies to orders of compliance, cease and desist orders, orders of denial, and other orders issued by the Administrator to carry out the provisions of the Federal Aviation Act of 1958, as amended, the Hazardous Materials Transportation Act, of 1970, and the Airport and Airway Improvement Act of 1982, or the Airport and Airway Improvement Act of 1982 as amended by the Airport and Airway Safety and Capacity Expansion Act of 1987. This section does not apply to orders issued pursuant to section 602 or section 609 of the Federal Aviation Act of 1958, as amended.

order shall be provided with notice prior to issuance.

(c) Within 30 days after service of the notice, the person subject to the order may reply in writing or request a hearing in accordance with Subpart D of this part.

(d) If a reply is filed, as to any charges not dismissed or not subject to a consent order, the person subject to the order may, within 10 days after receipt of notice that the remaining charges are not dismissed, request a hearing in accordance with Subpart D of this part.

(e) Failure to request a hearing within the period provided in paragraphs (c) or (d) of this section—

(1) Constitutes a waiver of the right to appeal and the right to a hearing, and

(2) Authorizes the official who issued the notice to find the facts to be as alleged in the notice, or as modified as the official may determine necessary based on any written response, and to issue an appropriate order, without further notice or proceedings.

(f) If a hearing is requested in accordance with paragraph (c) or (d) of this section, the procedure of Subpart D of this part applies. At the close of the hearing, the Hearing Officer, on the record or subsequently in writing, shall set forth findings and conclusions and the reasons therefor, and either—

(1) Dismiss the notice; or

(2) Issue an order.

(g) Any party to the hearing may appeal from the order of the Hearing Officer by filing a notice of appeal with the Administrator within 20 days after the date of issuance of the order.

(h) If a notice of appeal is not filed from the order issued by a Hearing Officer, such order is the final agency order.

(i) Any person filing an appeal authorized by paragraph (g) of this section shall file an appeal brief with the Administrator within 40 days after the date of issuance of the order, and serve a copy on the other party. A reply brief must be filed within 20 days after service of the appeal brief and a copy served on the appellant.

(j) On appeal the Administrator reviews the available record of the proceeding, and issues an order dismissing, reversing, modifying or affirming the order. The Administrator's order includes the reasons for the Administrator's action.

(k) For good cause shown, requests for extensions of time to file any document under this section may be granted by—

(1) The official who issued the order, if the request is filed prior to the designation of a Hearing Officer; or

(2) The Hearing Officer, if the request is filed prior to the filing of a notice of appeal; or

(3) The Administrator, if the request is filed after the filing of a notice of appeal.

(l) Except in the case of an appeal from the decision of a Hearing Officer, the authority of the Administrator under this section is also exercised by the Chief Counsel, Deputy Chief Counsel, each Assistant Chief Counsel and each Regional Counsel and the Aeronautical Center Counsel (as to matters under Title V of the Federal Aviation Act of 1958).

(m) Filing and service of documents under this section shall be accomplished in accordance with § 13.43; and the periods of time specified in this section shall be computed in accordance with § 13.44.

§ 13.21   Military personnel.

If a report made under this part indicates that, while performing official duties, a member of the Armed Forces, or a civilian employee of the Department of Defense who is subject to the Uniform Code of Military Justice (10 U.S.C. Ch. 47), has violated the Federal Aviation Act of 1958, or a regulation or order issued under it, the Chief Counsel, the Assistant Chief Counsel for Regulations and Enforcement, or the Regional Counsel concerned sends a copy of the report to the appropriate military authority for such disciplinary action as that authority considers appropriate and a report to the Administrator thereon.

§ 13.23   Criminal penalties.

(a) Sections 902 and 1203 of the Federal Aviation Act of 1958 (49 U.S.C. 1472 and 1523), provide criminal penalties for any person who knowingly and willfully violates specified provisions of that Act, or any regulation or order issued under those provisions. Section 110(b) of the Hazardous Materials Transportation Act (49 U.S.C. 1809(b)) provides for a criminal penalty of a fine of not more than $25,000, imprisonment for not more than five years, or both, for any person who willfully violates a provision of that Act or a regulation or order issued under it.

(b) If an inspector or other employee of the FAA becomes aware of a possible violation of any criminal provision of the Federal Aviation Act of 1958 (except a violation of section 902 (i) through (m) which is reported directly to the Federal Bureau of Investigation), or of the Hazardous Materials Transportation Act, relating to the transportation or shipment by air of hazardous materials, he or she shall report it to the Office of the Chief Counsel or the Regional Counsel concerned. If appropriate, that office refers the report to the Department of Justice for criminal prosecution of the offender. If such an inspector or other employee becomes aware of a possible violation of a Federal statute that is within the investigatory jurisdiction of another Federal agency, he or she shall immediately report it to that agency according to standard FAA practices.

§ 13.25 Injunctions.

(a) Whenever it is determined that a person has engaged, or is about to engage, in any act or practice constituting a violation of the Federal Aviation Act of 1958, or any regulation or order issued under it for which the FAA exercises enforcement responsibility, or, with respect to the transportation or shipment by air of any hazardous materials, in any act or practice constituting a violation of the Hazardous Materials Transportation Act, or any regulation or order issued under it for which the FAA exercises enforcement responsibility, the Chief Counsel, the Assistant Chief Counsel for Regulations and Enforcement the Regional Counsel concerned, or the Aeronautical Center Counsel may request the United States Attorney General, or the delegate of the Attorney

General, to bring an action in the appropriate United States District Court for such relief as is necessary or appropriate, including mandatory or prohibitive injunctive relief, interim equitable relief, and punitive damages, as provided by section 1007 of the Federal Aviation Act of 1958 (49 U.S.C. 1487) and section 111(a) of the Hazardous Materials Transportation Act (49 U.S.C. 1810).

(b) Whenever it is determined that there is substantial likelihood that death, serious illness, or severe personal injury, will result from the transportation by air of a particular hazardous material before an order of compliance proceeding, or other administrative hearing or formal proceeding to abate the risk of the harm can be completed, the Chief Counsel, the Assistant Chief Counsel for Regulations and Enforcement, or the Regional Counsel concerned may bring, or request the United States Attorney General to bring, an action in the appropriate United States District Court for an order suspending or restricting the transportation by air of the hazardous material or for such other order as is necessary to eliminate or ameliorate the imminent hazard, as provided by section 111(b) of the Hazardous Materials Transportation Act (49 U.S.C. 1810).

§ 13.27 Final order of Hearing Officer in certificate of aircraft registration proceedings.

(a) If, in proceedings under section 501(b) of the Federal Aviation Act of 1958 (49 USC 1401), the Hearing Officer determines that the holder of the Certificate of Aircraft Registration has refused or failed to submit AC Form 8050-73, as required by § 47.51 of this chapter, or that the aircraft is ineligible for a Certificate of Aircraft Registration, the Hearing Officer shall suspend or revoke the respondent's certificate, as proposed in the notice of proposed certificate action.

(b) If the final order of the Hearing Officer makes a decision on the merits, it shall contain a statement of the findings and conclusions of law on all material issues of fact and law. If the Hearing Officer finds that the allegations of the notice have been proven, but that no sanction is required, the Hearing Officer shall make appropriate findings and issue an order terminating the notice. If the Hearing Officer finds that the allegations of the notice have not been proven, the Hearing Officer shall issue an order dismissing the notice. If the Hearing Officer finds it to be equitable and in the public interest, the Hearing Officer shall issue an order terminating the proceeding upon payment by the respondent of a civil penalty in an amount agreed upon by the parties.

(c) If the order is issued in writing, it shall be served upon the parties.

[Doc. No. 13–14, 44 FR 63723, Nov. 5, 1979; as amended by Amdt. 13–15, 45 FR 20773, Mar. 31, 1980]

Subpart D—Rules of Practice for FAA Hearings

§ 13.31 Applicability.

This subpart applies to proceedings in which a hearing has been requested in accordance with §§ 13.19(c)(5), 13.20(c), 13.20(d), 13.75(a)(2), 13.75(b), or 13.81(e).

§ 13.33 Appearances.

Any party to a proceeding under this subpart may appear and be heard in person or by attorney.

§ 13.35 Request for hearing.

(a) A request for hearing must be made in writing to the Hearing Docket, Room 914E, Federal Aviation Administration, 800 Independence Avenue, S.W., Washington, D.C. 20591. It must describe briefly the action proposed by the FAA, and must contain a statement that a hearing is requested. A copy of the request for hearing and a copy of the answer required by paragraph (b) of this section must be served on the official who issued the notice of proposed action.

(b) An answer to the notice of proposed action must be filed with the request for hearing. All allegations in the notice not specifically denied in the answer are deemed admitted.

(c) Within 15 days after service of the copy of the request for hearing,

the official who issued the notice of proposed action forwards a copy of that notice, which serves as the complaint, to the Hearing Docket.

§ 13.37 Hearing Officer's powers.

Any Hearing Officer may—

(a) Give notice concerning, and hold, prehearing conferences and hearings;

(b) Administrator oaths and affirmations;

(c) Examine witnesses;

(d) Adopt procedures for the submission of evidence in written form;

(e) Issue subpoenas and take depositions or cause them to be taken;

(f) Rule on offers of proof;

(g) Receive evidence;

(h) Regulate the course of the hearing;

(i) Hold conferences, before and during the hearing, to settle and simplify issues by consent of the parties;

(j) Dispose of procedural requests and similar matters; and

(k) Issue decisions, make findings of fact, make assessments, and issue orders, as appropriate.

§ 13.39 Disqualification of Hearing Officer.

If disqualified for any reason, the Hearing Officer shall withdraw from the case.

§ 13.41 [Reserved]

§ 13.43 Service and filing of pleadings, motions, and documents.

(a) Copies of all pleadings, motions, and documents filed with the Hearing Docket must be served upon all parties to the proceedings by the person filing them.

(b) Service may be made by personal delivery or by mail.

(c) A certificate of service shall accompany all documents when they are tendered for filing and shall consist of a certificate of personal delivery or a certificate of mailing, executed by the person making the personal delivery or mailing the document.

(d) Whenever proof of service by mail is made, the date of mailing or the date as shown on the postmark shall be the date of service, and where personal service is made, the date of personal delivery shall be the date of service.

(e) The date of filing is the date the document is actually received.

§ 13.44 Computation of time and extension of time.

(a) In computing any period of time prescribed or allowed by this subpart, the date of the act, event, default, notice or order after which the designated period of time begins to run is not to be included in the computation. The last day of the period so computed is to be included unless it is a Saturday, Sunday, or legal holiday for the FAA, in which event the period runs until the end of the next day which is neither a Saturday, Sunday nor a legal holiday.

(b) Upon written request filed with the Hearing Docket and served upon all parties, and for good cause shown, a Hearing Officer may grant an extension of time to file any documents specified in this subpart.

§ 13.45 Amendment of notice and answer.

At any time more than 10 days before the date of hearing, any party may amend his or her notice, answer, or other pleading, by filing the amendment with the Hearing Officer and serving a copy of it on each other party. After that time, amendments may be allowed only in the discretion of the Hearing Officer. If an amendment to an initial pleading has been allowed, the Hearing Officer shall allow the other parties a reasonable opportunity to answer.

§ 13.47 Withdrawal of notice or request for hearing.

At any time before the hearing, the FAA counsel may withdraw the notice of proposed action, and the party requesting the hearing may withdraw the request for hearing.

§ 13.49 Motions.

(a) *Motion to dismiss for insufficiency.* A respondent who requests a formal hearing may, in place of an answer, file a motion to dismiss for failure of the allegations in the notice of proposed action to state a violation of the FA Act or of this chapter or to show lack of qualification of the re-

spondent. If the Hearing Officer denies the motion, the respondent shall file an answer within 10 days.

(b) [Reserved]

(c) *Motion for more definite statement.* The certificate holder may, in place of an answer, file a motion that the allegations in the notice be made more definite and certain. If the Hearing Officer grants the motion, the FAA counsel shall comply within 10 days after the date it is granted. If the Hearing Officer denies the motion the certificate holder shall file an answer within 10 days after the date it is denied.

(d) *Motion for judgment on the pleadings.* After the pleadings are closed, either party may move for a judgment on the pleadings.

(e) *Motion to strike.* Upon motion of either party, the Hearing Officer may order stricken, from any pleadings, any insufficient allegation or defense, or any immaterial, impertinent, or scandalous matter.

(f) *Motion for production of documents.* Upon motion of any party showing good cause, the Hearing Officer may, in the manner provided by Rule 34, Federal Rules of Civil Procedure, order any party to produce any designated document, paper, book, account, letter, photograph, object, or other tangible thing, that is not privileged, that constitutes or contains evidence relevant to the subject matter of the hearings, and that is in the party's possession, custody, or control.

(g) *Consolidation of motions.* A party who makes a motion under this section shall join with it all other motions that are then available to the party. Any objection that is not so raised is considered to be waived.

(h) *Answers to motions.* Any party may file an answer to any motion under this section within 5 days after service of the motion.

§ 13.51 Intervention.

Any person may move for leave to intervene in a proceeding and may become a party thereto, if the Hearing Officer, after the case is sent to the Hearing Officer for hearing, finds that the person may be bound by the order to be issued in the proceedings or has a property or financial interest that may not be adequately represented by existing parties, and that the intervention will not unduly broaden the issues or delay the proceedings. Except for good cause shown, a motion for leave to intervene may not be considered if it is filed less than 10 days before the hearing.

§13.53 Depositions.

After the respondent has filed a request for hearing and an answer, either party may take testimony by deposition in accordance with section 1004 of the Federal Aviation Act of 1958 (49 U.S.C. 1484) or Rule 26, Federal Rules of Civil Procedure.

§13.55 Notice of hearing.

The Hearing Officer shall set a reasonable date, time, and place for the hearing, and shall give the parties adequate notice thereof and of the nature of the hearing. Due regard shall be given to the convenience of the parties with respect to the place of the hearing.

§13.57 Subpoenas and witness fees.

(a) The Hearing Officer to whom a case is assigned may, upon application by any party to the proceeding, issue subpoenas requiring the attendance of witnesses or the production of documentary or tangible evidence at a hearing or for the purpose of taking depositions. However, the application for producing evidence must show its general relevance and reasonable scope. This paragraph does not apply to the attendance of FAA employees or to the production of documentary evidence in the custody of such an employee at a hearing.

(b) A person who applies for the production of a document in the custody of an FAA employee must follow the procedure in §13.49(f). A person who applies for the attendance of an FAA employee must send the application, in writing, to the Hearing Officer setting forth the need for that employee's attendance.

(c) A witness in a proceeding under this subpart is entitled to the same fees and mileage as is paid to a witness in a court of the United States under comparable circumstances. The party at whose instance the witness is subpoenaed or appears shall pay the witness fees.

(d) Notwithstanding the provisions of paragraph (c) of this section, the FAA pays the witness fees and mileage if the Hearing Officer who issued the subpoena determines, on the basis of a written request and good cause shown, that—

(1) The presence of the witness will materially advance the proceeding; and

(2) The party at whose instance the witness is subpoenaed would suffer a serious hardship if required to pay the witness fees and mileage.

§13.59 Evidence.

(a) Each party to a hearing may present the party's case or defense by oral or documentary evidence, submit evidence in rebuttal, and conduct such cross-examination as may be needed for a full disclosure of the facts.

(b) Except with respect to affirmative defenses and orders of denial, the burden of proof is upon the FAA counsel.

(c) The Hearing Officer may order information contained in any report or document filed or in any testimony given pursuant to this subpart withheld from public disclosure when, in the judgment of the Hearing Officer, disclosure would adversely affect the interests of any person and is not required in the public interest or is not otherwise required by statute to be made available to the public. Any person may make written objection to the public disclosure of such information, stating the ground for such objection.

§13.61 Argument and submittals.

The Hearing Officer shall give the parties adequate opportunity to present arguments in support of motions, objections, and the final order. The Hearing Officer may determine whether arguments are to be oral or written. At the end of the hearing the Hearing Officer may, in the discretion of the Hearing Officer, allow each party to submit written proposed findings and conclusions and supporting reasons for them.

§ 13.63   Record.

The testimony and exhibits presented at a hearing, together with all papers, requests, and rulings filed in the proceedings are the exclusive basis for the issuance of an order. Either party may obtain a transcript from the official reporter upon payment of the fees fixed therefor.

Subpart E—Orders of Compliance Under the Hazardous Materials Transportation Act

§ 13.71   Applicability.

Whenever the Chief Counsel, the Assistant Chief Counsel for Regulations and Enforcement, or the Regional Counsel concerned has reason to believe that a person is engaging in the transportation or shipment by air of hazardous materials in violation of the Hazardous Materials Transportation Act, or any regulation or order issued under it for which the FAA exercises enforcement responsibility, and the circumstances do not require the issuance of an order of immediate compliance, he may conduct proceedings pursuant to section 109 of that Act (49 U.S.C. 1808) to determine the nature and extent of the violation, and may thereafter issue an order directing compliance.

§ 13.73   Notice of proposed order of compliance.

A compliance order proceeding commences when the Chief Counsel, the Assistant Chief Counsel for Regulations and Enforcement, or the Regional Counsel concerned sends the alleged violator a notice of proposed order of compliance advising the alleged violator of the charges and setting forth the remedial action sought in the form of a proposed order of compliance.

§ 13.75   Reply or request for hearing.

(a) Within 30 days after service upon the alleged violator of a notice of proposed order of compliance, the alleged violator may—

(1) File a reply in writing with the official who issued the notice; or

(2) Request a hearing in accordance with Subpart D of this part.

(b) If a reply is filed, as to any charges not dismissed or not subject to a consent order of compliance, the alleged violator may, within 10 days after receipt of notice that the remaining charges are not dismissed, request a hearing in accordance with Subpart D of this part.

(c) Failure of the alleged violator to file a reply or request a hearing within the period provided in paragraph (a) or (b) of this section—

(1) Constitutes a waiver of the right to a hearing and the right to an appeal, and

(2) Authorizes the official who issued the notice to find the facts to be as alleged in the notice and to issue an appropriate order directing compliance, without further notice or proceedings.

§ 13.77   Consent order of compliance.

(a) At any time before the issuance of an order of compliance, the official who issued the notice and the alleged violator may agree to dispose of the case by the issuance of a consent order of compliance by the official.

(b) A proposal for a consent order submitted to the official who issued the notice under this section must include—

(1) A proposed order of compliance;

(2) An admission of all jurisdictional facts;

(3) An express waiver of right to further procedural steps and of all rights to judicial review;

(4) An incorporation by reference of the notice and an acknowledgement that the notice may be used to construe the terms of the order of compliance; and

(5) If the issuance of a consent order has been agreed upon after the filing of a request for hearing in accordance with Subpart D of this part, the proposal for a consent order shall include a request to be filed with the Hearing Officer withdrawing the request for a hearing and requesting that the case be dismissed.

§ 13.79   Hearing.

If an alleged violator requests a hearing in accordance with § 13.75, the procedure of Subpart D of this part applies. At the close of the hearing, the Hearing Officer, on the record or subsequently in writing, sets forth the Hearing Officer's findings and conclusion and the reasons therefor, and either—

(a) Dismisses the notice of proposed order of compliance; or

(b) Issues an order of compliance.

§ 13.81 **Order of immediate compliance.**

(a) Notwithstanding §§ 13.73 through 13.79, the Chief Counsel, the Assistant Chief Counsel for Regulations and Enforcement, or the Regional Counsel concerned may issue an order of immediate compliance, which is effective upon issuance, if the person who issues the order finds that—

(1) There is strong probability that a violation is occurring or is about to occur;

(2) The violation poses a substantial risk to health or to safety of life or property; and

(3) The public interest requires the avoidance or amelioration of that risk through immediate compliance and waiver of the procedures afforded under §§ 13.73 through 13.79.

(b) An order of immediate compliance is served promptly upon the person against whom the order is issued by telephone or telegram, and a written statement of the relevant facts and the legal basis for the order, including the findings required by paragraph (a) of this section, is served promptly by personal service or by mail.

(c) The official who issued the order of immediate compliance may rescind or suspend the order if it appears that the criteria set forth in paragraph (a) of this section are no longer satisfied, and, when appropriate, may issue a notice of proposed order of compliance under § 13.73 in lieu thereof.

(d) If at any time in the course of a proceeding commenced in accordance with § 13.73 the criteria set forth in paragraph (a) of this section are satisfied, the offical who issued the notice may issue an order of immediate compliance, even if the period for filing a reply or requesting a hearing specified in § 13.75 has not expired.

(e) Within three days after receipt of service of an order of immediate compliance, the alleged violator may request a hearing in accordance with Subpart D of this part and the procedure in that subpart will apply except that—

(1) The case will be heard within fifteen days after the date of the order of immediate compliance unless the alleged violator requests a later date;

(2) The order will serve as the complaint; and

(3) The Hearing Officer shall issue his decision and order dismissing, reversing, modifying, or affirming the order of immediate compliance on the record at the close of the hearing.

(f) The filing of a request for hearing in accordance with paragraph (e) of this section does not stay the effectiveness of an order of immediate compliance.

(g) At any time after an order of immediate compliance has become effective, the official who issued the order may request the United States Attorney General, or the delegate of the Attorney General, to bring an action for appropriate relief in accordance with § 13.25.

§ 13.83 **Appeal.**

(a) Any party to the hearing may appeal from the order of the Hearing Officer by filing a notice of appeal with the Administrator within 20 days after the date of issuance of the order.

(b) Any person against whom an order of immediate compliance has been issued in accordance with § 13.81 or the official who issued the order of immediate compliance may appeal from the order of the Hearing Officer by filing a notice of appeal with the Administrator within three days after the date of issuance of the order by the Hearing Officer.

(c) Unless the Administrator expressly so provides, the filing of a notice of appeal does not stay the effectiveness of an order of immediate compliance.

(d) If a notice of appeal is not filed from the order of compliance issued by a Hearing Officer, such order is the final agency order of compliance.

(e) Any person filing an appeal authorized by paragraph (a) of this section shall file an appeal brief with the Administrator within 40 days after the date of the issuance of the order, and serve a copy on the other party. Any reply brief must be filed within 20 days after service of the appeal brief. A copy of the reply brief must be served on the appellant.

(f) Any person filing an appeal authorized by paragraph (b) of this section shall file an appeal brief with the Administrator with the notice of appeal and serve a copy on the other party. Any reply brief must be filed within 3 days after receipt of the appeal brief. A copy of the reply brief must be served on the appellant.

(g) On appeal the Administrator reviews the available record of the proceeding, and issues an order dismissing, reversing, modifying or affirming the order of compliance or the order of immediate compliance. The Administrator's order includes the reasons for the action.

(h) In cases involving an order of immediate compliance, the Administrator's order on appeal is issued within ten days after the filing of the notice of appeal.

§ 13.85 Filing, service and computation of time.

Filing and service of documents under this subpart shall be accomplished in accordance with § 13.43 except service of orders of immediate compliance under § 13.81(b); and the periods of time specified in this subpart shall be computed in accordance with § 13.44.

§ 13.87 Extension of time.

(a) The official who issued the notice of proposed order of compliance, for good cause shown, may grant an extension of time to file any document specified in this subpart, except documents to be filed with the Administrator.

(b) Extensions of time to file documents with the Administrator may be granted by the Administrator upon written request, served upon all parties, and for good cause shown.

Subpart F—Formal Fact-Finding Investigation Under an Order of Investigation

§ 13.101 Applicability.

(a) This subpart applies to fact-finding investigations in which an order of investigation has been issued under § 13.3(c) or § 13.5(i) of this part.

(b) This subpart does not limit the authority of duly designated persons to issue subpoenas, administer oaths, examine witnesses and receive evidence in any informal investigation as provided for in sections 313 and 1004(a) of the Federal Aviation Act (49 U.S.C. 1354 and 1484(a)) and section 109(a) of the Hazardous Materials Transportation Act (49 U.S.C. 1808(a)).

§ 13.103 Order of investigation.

The order of investigation—

(a) Defines the scope of the investigation by describing the information sought in terms of its subject matter or its relevancy to specified FAA functions;

(b) Sets forth the form of the investigation which may be either by individual deposition or investigative proceeding or both; and

(c) Names the official who is authorized to conduct the investigation and serve as the Presiding Officer.

§ 13.105 Notification.

Any person under investigation and any person required to testify and produce documentary or physical evidence during the investigation will be advised of the purpose of the investigation, and of the place where the investigative proceeding or deposition will be convened. This may be accomplished by a notice of investigation or by a subpoena. A copy of the order of investigation may be sent to such persons, when appropriate.

§ 13.107 Designation of additional parties.

(a) The Presiding Officer may designate additional persons as parties to the investigation, if in the discretion of the Presiding Officer, it will aid in the conduct of the investigation.

(b) The Presiding Officer may designate any person as a party to the investigation if that person—

(1) Petitions the Presiding Officer to participate as a party; and

(2) Is so situated that the disposition of the investigation may as a practical matter impair the ability to protect that person's interest unless allowed to participate as a party, and

(3) Is not adequately represented by existing parties.

§ 13.109 Convening the investigation.

The investigation shall be conducted at such place or places designated by the Presiding Officer, and as convenient to the parties involved as expeditious and efficient handling of the investigation permits.

§ 13.111 Subpoenas.

(a) Upon motion of the Presiding Officer, or upon the request of a party to the investigation, the Presiding Officer may issue a subpoena directing any person to appear at a designated time and place to testify or to produce documentary or physical evidence relating to any matter under investigation.

(b) Subpoenas shall be served by personal service, or upon an agent designated in writing for the purpose, or by registered or certified mail addressed to such person or agent. Whenever service is made by registered or certified mail, the date of mailing shall be considered as the time when service is made.

(c) Subpoenas shall extend in jurisdiction throughout the United States or any territory or possession thereof.

§ 13.113 Noncompliance with the investigative process.

If any person fails to comply with the provisions of this subpart or with any subpoena or order issued by the Presiding Officer or the designee of the Presiding Officer, judicial enforcement may be initiated against that person under applicable statutes.

§ 13.115 Public proceedings.

(a) All investigative proceedings and depositions shall be public unless the Presiding Officer determines that the public interest requires otherwise.

(b) The Presiding Officer may order information contained in any report or document filed or in any testimony given pursuant to this subpart withheld from public disclosure when, in the judgment of the Presiding Officer, disclosure would adversely affect the interests of any person and is not required in the public interest or is not otherwise required by statute to be made available to the public. Any person may make written objection to the public disclosure of such information, stating the grounds for such objection.

§ 13.117 Conduct of investigative proceeding or deposition.

(a) The Presiding Officer or the designee of the Presiding Officer may question witnesses.

(b) Any witness may be accompanied by counsel.

(c) Any party may be accompanied by counsel and either the party or counsel may—

(1) Question witnesses, provided the questions are relevant and material to the matters under investigation and would not unduly impede the progress of the investigation; and

(2) Make objections on the record and argue the basis for such objections.

(d) Copies of all notices or written communications sent to a party or witness shall upon request be sent to that person's attorney of record.

§ 13.119 Rights of persons against self-incrimination.

(a) Whenever a person refuses, on the basis of a privilege against self-incrimination, to testify or provide other information during the course of any investigation conducted under this subpart, the Presiding Officer may, with the approval of the Attorney General of the United States, issue an order requiring the person to give testimony or provide other information. However, no testimony or other information so compelled (or any information directly or indirectly derived from such testimony or other information) may be used against the person in any criminal case, except in a prosecution for perjury, giving a false statement, or otherwise failing to comply with the order.

(b) The Presiding Officer may issue an order under this section if—

(1) The testimony or other information from the witness may be necessary to the public interest; and

(2) The witness has refused or is likely to refuse to testify or provide other information on the basis of a privilege against self-incrimination.

(c) Immunity provided by this section will not become effective until the person has refused to testify or provide other information on the basis of a privilege against self-incrimination, and an order under this section has been issued. An order, however, may be issued prospectively to become effective in the event of a claim of the privilege.

§ 13.121   Witness fees.

All witnesses appearing shall be compensated at the same rate as a witness appearing before a United States District Court.

§ 13.123   Submission by party to the investigation.

(a) During an investigation conducted under this subpart, a party may submit to the Presiding Officer—

(1) A list of witnesses to be called, specifying the subject matter of the expected testimony of each witness, and

(2) A list of exhibits to be considered for inclusion in the record.

(b) If the Presiding Officer determines that the testimony of a witness or the receipt of an exhibit in accordance with paragraph (a) of this section will be relevant, competent and material to the investigation, the Presiding Officer may subpoena the witness or use the exhibit during the investigation.

§ 13.125   Depositions.

Depositions for investigative purposes may be taken at the discretion of the Presiding Officer with reasonable notice to the party under investigation. Such depositions shall be taken before the Presiding Officer or other person authorized to administer oaths and designated by the Presiding Officer. The testimony shall be reduced to writing by the person taking the deposition, or under the direction of that person, and where possible shall then be subscribed by the deponent. Any person may be compelled to appear and testify and to produce physical and documentary evidence.

§ 13.127   Reports, decisions and orders.

The Presiding Officer shall issue a written report based on the record developed during the formal investigation, including a summary of principal conclusions. A summary of principal conclusions shall be prepared by the official who issued the order of investigation in every case which results in no action, or no action as to a particular party to the investigation. All such reports shall be furnished to the parties to the investigation and filed in the public docket. Insertion of the report in the Public Docket shall constitute "entering of record" and publication as prescribed by section 313(b) of the Federal Aviation Act.

§ 13.129   Post-investigation action.

A decision on whether to initiate subsequent action shall be made on the basis of the record developed during the formal investigation and any other information in the possession of the Administrator.

§ 13.131   Other procedures.

Any question concerning the scope or conduct of a formal investigation not covered in this subpart may be ruled on by the Presiding Officer on motion of the Presiding Officer, or on the motion of a party or a person testifying or producing evidence.

Subpart G — Rules of Practice in FAA Civil Penalty Actions

§ 13.201 Applicability.

(a) This subpart applies to the following actions:

(1) A civil penalty action, initiated after September 7, 1988, in which an order of civil penalty has been issued not exceeding $50,000 for a violation arising under the Federal Aviation Act of 1958, as amended, (49 U.S.C. 1301 et seq.), or a rule, regulation, or order issued thereunder.

(2) A civil penalty action inititated after September 7, 1988, in which an order of civil penalty has been issued for a violation arising under the Federal Aviation Act of 1958, as amended (49 U.S.C. 1471 *et seq.*) and the Hazardous Materials Transportation Act (49 U.S.C. 1801 *et seq.*), or a rule, regulation, or order issued thereunder.

(b) This subpart applies only to proceedings initiated after September 7, 1988. All other cases, hearings, or other proceedings pending or in progress at the time this subpart is effective are not affected by the rules in this subpart.

(c) Notwithstanding the provisions of paragraph (a) of this section, the United States district courts shall have exclusive jurisdiction of any civil penalty action initiated by the Administrator—

(1) Which involves an amount in controversy in excess of $50,000;

(2) Which is an *in rem* action or in which an *in rem* action based on the same violation has been brought;

(3) Regarding which an aircraft subject to lien has been seized by the United States; and

(4) In which a suit for injunctive relief based on the violation giving rise to the civil penalty has also been brought.

§ 13.202 Definitions.

"Administrative law judge" means an administrative law judge appointed pursuant to the provisions of 5 U.S.C. 3105.

"Agency attorney" means the Assistant Chief Counsel for Regulations and Enforcement, the Assistant Chief Counsel for a region or center, or an attorney designated to prosecute a case. An agency attorney shall not include any attorney who advises the FAA decisionmaker regarding an initial decision or any appeal to the FAA decisionmaker or who is supervised by a person who provides advice to the FAA decisionmaker in a case.

"Attorney" means a person licensed by a state, the District of Columbia, or a territory of the United States to practice law or appear before the courts of that state or territory.

"Complaint" means an order of civil penalty issued pursuant to the Federal Aviation Act of 1958, as amended, or a rule, regulation, or order issued thereunder, or the Hazardous Materials Transportation Act, or a rule, regulation, or order issued thereunder, which has been filed with the Hearing Docket after a hearing has been requested.

"FAA decisionmaker" means the Administrator of the Federal Aviation Administration, acting in the capacity of the decision maker on appeal, or any person to whom the Administrator has delegated the Administrator's decisionmaking authority in a civil penalty action. As used in this subpart, the FAA decisionmaker is the official authorized to issue a final decision and order of the Administrator in a civil penalty action.

"Mail" includes U.S. certified mail, U.S. registered mail, or use of an overnight express courier service.

"Order assessing civil penalty" means an order that contains a finding or determination of violation arising under the Federal Aviation Act, as amended, or a rule, regulation, or order issued thereunder, or a violation of the Hazardous Materials Transportation Act, or a rule, regulation, or order issued thereunder, and directs a person to pay a civil penalty for the violation.

"Order of civil penalty" means an order issued after a person requests a hearing pursuant to § 13.16(e)(3) or 13.16(g)(3) of this part and which is filed with the docket clerk as the complaint in the proceedings.

"Party" means the agency attorney or the respondent named in an order of civil penalty.

"Personal delivery" includes hand-delivery or use of a contract or express messenger service. "Personal delivery" does not include use of government interoffice mail service.

"Pleading" means a complaint, an answer, and any amendment of these documents permitted under this subpart.

"Properly addressed" means a document that shows an address contained in FAA records, a residential, business, or other address submitted by a person on any other document provided by this subpart, or any other address shown by other reasonable and available means.

"Respondent" means a person to whom a civil penalty is directed and who has received an order of civil penalty.

§ 13.203 Separation of functions.

(a) Civil penalty proceedings, including hearings, shall be prosecuted by an agency attorney.

(b) Any agency attorney engaged in the performance of prosecutorial functions in a case shall not, in that case or a factually related case, participate in, or advise the FAA decisionmaker regarding, an initial decision or any appeal to the FAA decisionmaker under this subpart, except as a witness or counsel in public proceedings. The prohibition described in this paragraph shall begin at the time that notice of proposed civil penalty is issued.

(c) The Chief Counsel shall not perform prosecutorial functions in a case and shall not supervise the agency attorney in the performance of prosecutorial functions in a case. The prohibitions described in this paragraph shall begin at the time that the notice of proposed civil penalty is issued.

(d) The Chief Counsel or the delegate of the Chief Counsel, other than individuals described in paragraph (a) of this section, shall advise the FAA decisionmaker regarding an initial decision or any appeal to the FAA decisionmaker under this subpart.

§ 13.204 Appearances and rights of parties.

(a) Any party may appear and be heard in person.

(b) Any party may be accompanied, represented or advised by an attorney or representative designated by the party and may be examined by that attorney or representative in any proceeding governed by this subpart. An attorney or representative who represents a party may file a notice of appearance in the action, in the manner provided in § 13.210 of this subpart, and shall serve a copy of the notice of appearance on each party, in the manner provided in § 13.211 of this subpart, before participating in any proceeding governed by this subpart. The attorney or representative shall include the name, address, and telephone number of the attorney or representative in the notice of appearance.

(c) Any person may request a copy of a document upon payment of reasonable costs. A person may keep an original document, data, or evidence, with the consent of the administrative law judge, by substituting a legible copy of the document for the record.

§ 13.205 Administrative law judges.

(a) *Powers of an administrative law judge.* In accordance wtih the rules of this subpart, an administrative law judge may—

(1) Give notice of, and hold, prehearing conferences and hearings:

(2) Administer oaths and affirmations;

(3) Issue subpoenas authorized by law and issue notices of deposition requested by the parties;

(4) Rule on offers of proof;

(5) Receive relevant and material evidence;

(6) Regulate the course of the hearing in accordance with the rules of this subpart;

(7) Hold conferences to settle or to simplify the issues by consent of the consent parties;

(8) Dispose of procedural motions and requests; and

(9) Make findings of fact and conclusions of law, and issue an initial decision.

(b) *Limitations on the power of the administrative law judge.* The administrative law judge shall not issue an order of contempt, award costs to any party, or impose any sanction not specified in this subpart. If the administrative law judge imposes any sanction not specified in this subpart, a party may file an interlocutory appeal of right with the FAA decisionmaker pursuant to § 13.219(c)(4) of this subpart. This section does not preclude an administrative law judge from issuing an order that bars a person from a specific proceeding based on a finding of obstreperous or disruptive behavior in that specific proceeding.

(c) *Disqualification.* The administrative law judge may disqualify himself or herself at any time. A party may file a motion, pursuant to § 13.218(f)(6), requesting that an administrative law judge be disqualified from the proceedings.

§ 13.206 Intervention.

(a) Any person who has a statutory right to participate in the proceedings shall be allowed to intervene in the proceedings by the administrative law judge.

(b) In all other cases, the administrative judge shall not allow any person to intervene in any proceeding governed by this subpart.

§ 13.207 Certification of documents.

(a) *Signature required.* The attorney of record, the party, or the party's representative shall sign each document tendered for filing with the hearing docket clerk, the administrative law judge, the FAA decisionmaker on appeal, or served on each party.

(b) *Effect of signing a document.* By signing a document, the attorney of record, the party, or the party's representative certifies that the attorney or party has read the document and, based on reasonable inquiry and to the best of the attorney or party's knowledge, information, and belief, the document is—

(1) Consistent with these rules:

(2) Warranted by existing law or that a good faith argument exists for extension, mod-

ification, or reversal of existing law; and

(3) Not unreasonable or unduly burdensome or expensive, not made to harass any person, not made to cause unnecessary delay, not made to cause needless increase in the cost of the proceedings, or for any other improper purpose.

(c) *Sanctions.* If the attorney of record, the party, or the party's representative signs a document in violation of this section, the administrative law judge or the FAA decisionmaker shall—

(1) Strike the pleading signed in violation of this section;

(2) Strike the request for discovery or the discovery response signed in violation of this section and preclude further discovery by the party;

(3) Deny the motion or request signed in violation of this section;

(4) Exclude the document signed in violation of this section from the record;

(5) Dismiss the interlocutory appeal and preclude further appeal on that issue by the party who filed the appeal until an initial decision has been entered on the record; or

(6) Dismiss the appeal of the administrative law judge's initial decision to the FAA decisionmaker.

§ 13.208 Complaint.

(a) In accordance with § § 13.16(e)(3) and 13.16(g)(3), an order of civil penalty shall serve as the complaint. The agency attorney shall serve the original order of civil penalty on the person requesting the hearing.

(b) The agency attorney shall file the complaint, attaching a copy of the request for a hearing, and shall suggest a location for the hearing, with the hearing docket clerk not later than 20 days after receipt of a person's request for hearing.

(c) If the agency attorney and the person requesting the hearing do not agree on the location for the hearing, the hearing docket clerk shall assign a hearing location near the place where the incident occured.

§ 13.209 Answer.

(a) *Writing required.* A person who receives an order of civil penalty shall file a written answer to the order, or a motion pursuant to § 13.218(f)(1-4) of this subpart, not later than 30 days after service of the order of civil penalty. The answer may be in the form of a letter but must be dated and signed by the person responding to the order of civil penalty. An answer may be typewritten or may be legibly handwritten.

(b) *Filing and address.* a person filing an answer shall personally deliver or mail the answer for filing with the hearing docket clerk to the Hearing Docket, Federal Aviation Administration, 800 Independence Avenue SW., Room 914E, Washington, DC 20591. Attn: Hearing Docket Clerk.

(c) *Contents.* A person filing an answer shall include a brief statement of the relief requested by the person in the answer. The person shall include specifically any affirmative defense in the answer that the person intends to assert at the hearing.

(d) *Specific denial of allegations required.* A person filing an answer shall admit, deny, or state that the person is without sufficient knowledge of information to admit or deny each allegation in each numbered paragraph of the order of civil penalty. A general denial of the order of civil penalty is deemed a failure to file an answer. Any statement or allegation contained in the order of civil penalty that is not specifically denied in the answer is deemed an admission of the truth of that allegation.

(e) *Service.* A person filing an answer shall comply with the service requirements of § 13.211 of this subpart.

(f) *Failure to file answer.* A person's failure to file an answer without good cause is deemed an admission of the truth of each allegation contained in the order of civil penalty and an order assessing civil penalty shall be issued.

§ 13.210 Filing of documents.

(a) *Address and method of filing.* A person tendering a document for filing shall personally deliver or mail the signed original and one copy of each document to the Hearing Docket, Federal Aviation Administration, 800 Independence Avenue SW., Room 914E, Washington, DC 20591, Attn: Hearing Docket Clerk. After an administrative law judge has been assigned to the proceedings, a person shall personally deliver or mail the signed original of each document to the hearing docket clerk and shall serve a copy of each document on each party and the administrative law judge.

(b) *Date of filing* A document shall be considered to be filed on the date of persoanl delivery; or if mailed, the mailing date shown on the certificate of service, the date shown on the postmark if there is no certificate of service, or other mailing date shown by other evidence if there is no certificate of service or postmark.

(c) *Form.* Each document shall be typewritten or legibly handwritten.

(d) *Contents.* Unless otherwise specified in this subpart, each document must contain a short, plain statement of the facts on which the person's case rests and a brief statement of the action requested in the document.

§ 13.211 Service of documents.

(a) *General.* A person shall serve a copy of any document filed with the Hearing Docket on the administrative law judge and on each party at the time of filing.

(b) *Type of service.* A person may serve documents by personal delivery or by mail.

(c) *Certificate of service.* A person may attach a certificate of service to a document tendered for filing with the hearing docket clerk. A certificate of service shall consist of a statement, dated and signed by the person filing the document, that the document was personally delivered or mailed to each party on a specific date.

(d) *Date of service.* The date of service shall be the date of personal delivery; or if mailed, the mailing date shown on the certificate of service, the date shown on the postmark if there is no certificate of service, or other mailing date shown by other evidence if there is no certificate of service or postmark.

(e) *Additional time after service by mail.* Whenever a party has a right or duty to act or to make any response within a prescribed period after service by mail, or on a date certain after service by mail, 5 days shall be added to the prescribed period.

(f) *Service by the administrative law judge.* The administrative law judge shall serve a copy of each document including, but not limited to, notices of prehearing conferences and hearings, rulings on motions, decisions, and orders, upon each party to the proceedings by personal delivery or by mail.

(g) *Valid service.* A document that was properly addressed, was sent in accordance with this subpart, and that was returned, that was not claimed, or that was refused, is deemed to have been served in accordance with this subpart. The service shall be considered valid as of the date and the time that the document was deposited with a contract or express messenger, the document was mailed, or personal delivery of the document was refused.

(h) *Presumption of service.* There shall be a presumption of service where a party or a person, who customarily receives mail, or receives it in the ordinary course of business, at either the person's residence or the person's principal place of business, acknowledges receipt of the document.

§ 13.212 Computation of time.

(a) This section applies to any period of time prescribed or allowed by this subpart, by notice or order of administrative law judge,

or by any applicable statute.

(b) The date of an act, event, or default, after which a designated time period begins to run, is not included in a computation of time under this subpart.

(c) The last day of a time period is included in a computation of time unless it is a Saturday, Sunday, or a legal holiday. If the last day of the time period is a Saturday, Sunday, or legal holiday, the time period runs until the end of the next day that is not a Saturday, Sunday, or legal holiday.

§ 13.213 Extension of time.

(a) *Oral requests.* The parties may reasonably agree to extend the time for filing a document under this subpart. If the parties agree, the administrative law judge shall grant one extension of time to each party. The party seeking the extension of time shall submit a draft order to the administrative law judge to be signed by the and filed with the hearing docket clerk. The administrative law judge may grant additional oral requests for an extension of time where the parties agree to the extension.

(b) *Written motion.* A party shall file a written motion for an extension of time with the administrative law judge not later than 7 days before the document is due unless good cause for the late filing is shown. A party filing a written motion for an extension of time shall serve a copy of the motion on each party. The administrative law judge may grant the extension of time if good cause for the extension is shown.

(c) *Failure to rule.* If the administrative law judge fails to rule on a written motion for an extension of time by the date the document was due, the motion for an extension of time is deemed granted for no more than 20 days after the original date the document was to be filed.

§ 13.214 Amendment of pleadings.

(a) *Filing and service.* A party shall file the admendment with the administrative law judge and shall serve a copy of the amendment on all parties to the proceeding.

(b) *Time.* A party shall file an amendment to a complaint or an answer within the following:

(1) Not later than 15 days before the scheduled date of a hearing, a party may amend a complaint or an answer without the consent of the administrative law judge.

(2) Less than 15 days before the scheduled date of a hearing, the administrative law judge may allow amendment of a complaint or an answer only for good cause shown in a motion to amend.

(c) *Responses.* The administrative law judge shall allow a reasonable time, but not more than 20 days from the date of filing, for other parties to respond if an amendment to a complaint, answer, or other pleading has been filed with the administrative law judge.

§ 13.215 Withdrawal of a complaint or request for a hearing.

At any time before or during a hearing, the agency attorney may withdraw a complaint or a party may withdraw a request for a hearing without the consent of the administrative law judge. If the agency attorney withdraws the complaint or a party withdraws the request for a hearing and the answer, the administrative law judge shall dismiss the proceedings in this subpart with prejudice.

§ 13.216. Waivers.

Waivers of any rights provided by statute or regulation shall be in writing or by stipulation made at a hearing and entered into the record. The parties shall set forth the precise terms of the waiver and any conditions.

§ 13.217 Joint procedural or discovery schedule.

(a) *General.* The parties may agree to submit a schedule for fitting all prehearing motions, a schedule for conducting discovery in the proceedings, or a schedule that will govern all prehearing motions and discovery in the proceedings.

(b) *Form and content of schedule.* If the parties agree to a joint procedural or discovery schedule, one of the parties shall file the joint schedule with the administrative law judge, setting forth the dates to which the parties have agreed, and shall serve a copy of the joint schedule on each party.

(1) The joint schedule may include, but need not be limited to, requests for discovery, any objections to discovery requests, responses to discovery requests to which there are no objections, submission of prehearing motions, responses to prehearing motions, exchange of exhibits to be introduced at the hearing, and a list of witnesses that may be called at the hearing.

(2) Each party shall sign the original joint schedule to be filed with the administrative law judge.

(c) *Time.* The parties may agree to submit all prehearing motions and responses and may agree to close discovery in the proceedings under the joint schedule within a reasonable time before the date of the hearing, but not later than 15 days before the hearing.

(d) *Order establishing joint schedule.* The administrative law judge shall approve the joint schedule filed by the parties. One party shall submit a draft order establishing a joint schedule to the administrative law judge to be signed by the administrative law judge and filed with the hearing docket clerk.

(e) *Disputes.* The administrative law judge shall resolve disputes regarding discovery or disputes regarding compliance with the joint schedule as soon as possible so that the parties may continue to comply with the joint schedule.

(f) *Sanctions for failure to comply with joint schedule.* If a party fails to comply with the administrative law judge's order establishing a joint schedule, the administrative law judge may direct that party to comply with a motion or discovery request or, limited to the extent of the party's failure to comply with a motion or discovery request, the administrative law judge may—

(1) Strike that portion of a party's pleadings;

(2) Preclude prehearing or discovery motions by that party;

(3) Preclude admission of that portion of a party's evidence at the hearing; or

(4) Preclude that portion of the testimony of that party's witnesses at the hearing.

§ 13.218 Motions.

(a) *General.* A party applying for an order or ruling not specifically provided in this subpart shall do so by motion. A party shall comply with the requirements of this section when filing a motion with the administrative law judge. A party shall serve a copy of each motion on each party.

(b) *Form and contents.* A party shall state the relief sought by the motion and the particular grounds supporting that relief. If a party has evidence in support of a motion, the party shall attach any supporting evidence, including affidavits, to the motion.

(c) *Filing of motions.* A motion made prior to the hearing must be in writing. Unless otherwise agreed by the parties or for good cause shown, a party shall file any prehearing motion, and shall serve a copy on each party, not later than 30 days before the hearing. Motions introduced during a hearing may be made orally on the record unless the administrative law judge directs otherwise.

(d) *Answers to motions.* Any party may file an answer, with affadivits or other evidence in support of the answer, not later than 10 days after service of a written motion on that party. When a motion is made during a hearing, the answer may be made at the hearing on the record, orally or in writing, within a reasonable time determined by the administrative law judge.

(e) *Rulings on motions.* The administrative law judge shall rule on all motions as follows:

(1) *Discovery motions.* The administrative law judge shall resolve all pending discovery motions not later than 10 days before the hearing.

(2) *Prehearing motions.* The administrative law judge shall resolve all pending prehearing motions not later than 7 days before the hearing. If the administrative law judge issues a ruling or order orally, the administrative law judge shall serve a written copy of the ruling or order, within 3 days, on each party. In all other cases, the administrative law judge shall issue rulings and orders in writing and shall serve a copy of the ruling or order on each party.

(3) *Motions made during the hearing.* The administrative law judge may issue rulings and orders on motions made during the hearing orally. Oral rulings or orders on motions must be made on the record.

(f) *Specific motions.* A party may file the following motions with the administrative law judge:

(1) *Motion to dismiss for insufficiency.* A party may file a motion to dismiss the order of civil penalty for insufficiency instead of an answer. If the administrative law judge denies the motion to dismiss the order of civil penalty for insufficiency, the party who received the order of civil penalty shall file an answer not later than 10 days of service of the administrative law judge's denial of motion. A motion to dismiss the order of civil penalty for insufficiency must show that the order of civil penalty fails to state a violation of the Federal Aviation Act of 1958, as amended, or a rule, regulation, or order issued thereunder, or a violation of the Hazardous Materials Transportation Act, or a rule, regulation, or order issued thereunder.

(2) *Motion to dismiss.* A party may file a motion to dismiss an order of civil penalty instead of an answer, specifying the grounds for dismissal.

(i) If the motion to dismiss is not granted, the respondent shall file an answwer with the administrative law judge and shall serve a copy of the answer on each party not later than 10 days after service of the administrative law judge's ruling or order on the motion to dismiss.

(ii) If the administrative law judge grants a motion to dismiss and terminates the proceedings without a hearing, the agency at-torney may file an appeal pursuant to § 13.233 of this subpart. If the administrative law judge grants a motion to dismiss in part, the agency attorney may appeal the administrative law judge's decision to dismiss part of the order of civil penalty under the provisions of § 13.219(c) of this subpart. If required by the decision on appeal, the respondent shall file an answer with the administrative law judge, and shall serve a copy of the answer on each party, not later than 10 days after service of the decision on appeal.

(3) *Motion for more definite statement.* A party may file a motion for more definite statement of any pleading which requires a response under this subpart. A party shall set forth, in detail, the indefinite or uncertain allegations contained in an order of civil penalty or response to any pleading and shall submit the details that the party believes would would make the allegation or response definite and certain.

(i) *Order of civil penalty.* A party may file a motion requesting a more definite statement of the allegations contained in the order of civil penalty instead of an answer. If the administrative law judge grants the motion, and the agency attorney does not supply a more definite statement not later than 15 days after service of the order granting the motion, the administrative law judge shall strike the allegations in the order of civil penalty to which the motion is directed. If the administrative law judge denies the motion, the respondent shall file an answer with the administrative law judge and shall serve a copy of the answer on each party not later than 10 days after service of the order of denial.

(ii) *Answer.* A party may file a motion requesting a more definite statement if an answer fails to clearly respond to the allegations in the order of civil penalty. If the administrative law judge grants the motion, the respondent shall supply a more definite statement not later than 15 days after service of the ruling on the motion. If the respondent fails to supply a more definite statement, the administrative law judge shall strike those statements in the answer to which the motion is directed. A party's failure to supply a more definite statement is deemed a failure to anwser and the unanswered allegations in the order of civil penalty are deemed admitted.

(4) *Motion to strike.* Any party may make a motion to strike any insufficient allegation or defense, or any redundant, immaterial, or irrelevant matter in a pleading. A party shall file a motion to strike with the administrative law judge and shall serve a copy on each party before a response is required under this subpart or, if a response is not required, not later than 10 days after service of the pleading.

(5) *Motion for decision.* A party may make a motion for decision, regarding all or any part of the proceedings, at any time before the administrative law judge has issued an initial decision in the proceedings. The administrative law judge shall grant a party's motion for decision if the pleadings, depositions, answers to interrogatories, admissions, matters that the administrative law judge has officially noticed, or evidence introduced during the hearing show that there is no genuine issue of material fact and that the party making the motion is entitled to a decision as a matter of law. The party making the motion for decision has the burden of showing that there is no genuine issue of material fact disputed by the parties.

(6) *Motion for disqualification.* A party may file a motion for disqualification with the administrative law judge and shall serve a copy on each party. A party may file the motion at any time after the administrative law judge has been assigned to the proceedings but shall make the motion before the administrative law judge files an initial decision in the proceedings.

(i) *Motion and supporting affidavit.* A party shall state the grounds for disqualification, including, but not limited to, personal bias, pecuniary interest, or other factors showing disqualification, in the motion for disqualification. A party shall submit an affidavit with the motion for disqualification that sets forth, in detail, the matters alleged to constitute grounds for disqualification.

(ii) *Answer.* A party shall respond to the motion for disqualification not later than 5 days after service of the motion for disqualification.

(iii) *Decision on motion for disqualification.* The administrative law judge shall render a decision on the motion for disqualification not later than 15 days after the motion has been filed. If the administrative law judge finds that the motion for and supporting affidavit show a basis for disqualification, the administrative law judge shall withdraw from the proceedings immediately. If the administrative law judge finds that disqualification is not warranted, the adminis-

trative law judge shall deny the motion and state the grounds for the denial on the record. If the administrative law judge fails to rule on a party's motion for disqualification within 15 days after the motion has been filed, the motion is deemed granted.

(iv) *Appeal.* A party may appeal the administrative law judge's denial of the motion for disqualification in accordance with §13.219 of this subpart.

§ 13.219 Interlocutory appeals.

(a) *General.* Unless otherwise provided in this subpart, a party may not appeal a ruling or decision of the FAA decisionmaker until the initial decision has been entered on the record. A decision or order of the FAA decisionmaker on the interlocutory appeal does not constitute a final order of the Administrator for the purposes of judicial appellate review under section 1006 of the Federal Aviation Act of 1958, as amended.

(b) *Interlocutory appeal for cause.* If a party files a written request for an interlocutory appeal for cause with the administrative law judge, or orally requests an interlocutory appeal for cause, the proceedings are stayed until the administrative law judge issues a decision on the request. If the administrative law judge grants the request, the proceedings are stayed until the FAA decisionmaker issues a decision on the interlocutory appeal. The administrative law judge shall grant an interlocutory appeal for cause if a party shows that delay of the appeal would be detrimental to the public interest or would result in undue prejudice to any party.

(c) *Interlocutory appeals of right.* If a party notifies the administrative law judge of an interlocutory appeal of right, the proceedings are stayed until the FAA decisionmaker issues a decision on the interlocutory appeal. A party may file an interlocutory appeal with the FAA decisionmaker, without the consent of the administrative law judge, before an initial decision has been entered in the case of—

(1) A rule or order by the administrative law judge barring a person from the proceedings;

(2) Failure of the administrative law judge to dismiss the proceedings in accordance with §13.215 of this subpart;

(3) A ruling or order by the administrative law judge in violation of §13.205(b) of this subpart; and

(4) A ruling by the the administrative law judge granting, in part, a respondent's motion to dismiss an order of civil penalty pursuant to §13.218(f)(2)(B).

(d) *Procedure.* A party shall file a notice of

interlocutory appeal, with supporting documents, with the FAA decisionmaker and the hearing docket clerk, and shall serve a copy of the notice and sup porting documents on each party and the administrative law judge, not later than 3 days after the the administrative law judge's decision forming the basis of the appeal. A party shall file a reply brief, if any, with the FAA decisionmaker and serve a copy of the reply brief on each party, not later than 10 days after the service of the appeal brief. If the FAA decisionmaker does not issue a decision on the interlocutory appeal or does not seek additional information within 10 days of the filing of the appeal, the stay of the proceeding is dissolved. The FAA decisionmaker shall render a decision on the interlocutory appeal, on the record and as a part of the decision in the proceedings, within a reasonable time after receipt of the interlocutory appeal.

(e) The FAA decisionmaker may reject frivolous, repetitive, or dilatory appeals, and may issue an order precluding one or more parties from making further interlocutory appeals in a proceeding in which there have been frivolous, repetitive, or dilatory interlocutory appeals.

§ 13.220   Discovery

(a) *Initiation of discovery.* Any party may initiate discovery described in this section without the consent or approval of the administrative law judge, at any time after a complaint has been filed in the proceedings.

(b) *Methods of discovery.* The following methods of discovery are permitted under this section: Depositions on oral examination or written questions of any person; written interrogatories directed to a party; requests for production of documents or tangible items to any person; and requests for admission by a party. A party is not required to file written interrogatories and responses, requests for production of documents or tangible items and responses, and requests for admission and responses with the administrative law judge or the hearing docket clerk. In the event of a discovery dispute, a party shall attach a copy of these documents in support of a motion made under this section.

(c) *Service on the agency.* A party shall serve each discovery request directed to the agency or an agency employee on the agency attorney of record.

(d) *Time for responses to discovery requests.* Unless otherwise directed by the parties, a party shall respond to a request for discovery, including filing objections to a reqeust for discovery, not later than 30 days of service of the request.

(e) *Scope of discovery.* Subject to the limits on discovery set forth paragraph (f) of this section, a party may discover any matter that is not privileged and that is relevant to the subject matter of the proceedings. A party may discovery information that relates to the claim or defense of any party including the existence, description, nature, custody, condition, and location of any document or other tangible item and the identity and location of any person having knowledge of discoverable matter. A party may discover facts known, or opinions held, by an expert who any other party expects to call to testify at the hearing. A party has no ground to object to a discovery request on the basis that the information sought would not be admissible at the hearing if the information sought during discovery is reasonably calculated to lead to the discovery of admissible evidence.

(f) *Limiting discovery.* The administrative law judge shall limit the frequency and extent of discovery permitted by this section if a party shows that—

(1) The information request is cumulative or repetitious;

(2) The information requested can be obtained from another less burdensome and more convenient source;

(3) The party requesting the information has had ample opportunity to obtain the information through other discovery methods permitted under this seciton;

(4) The method or scope of discovery requested by the party is unduly burdensome or expensive.

(g) *Confidential orders.* A party or person who has received a discovery request for information that is related to a trade secret, confidential or sensitive material, competitive or commercial information, proprietary data, or information on research and development, may file a motion for a confidential order with the the administrative law judge and shall serve a copy of the motion for a confidential order on each party.

(1) The party or person making the motion must show that the confidential order is necessary to protect the information from disclosure to the public.

(2) If the administrative law judge determines that the requested material is not necessary to decide the case, the administrative law judge shall preclude any inquiry into the matter by any party.

(3) If the administrative law judge determines that the requested material may be disclosed during discovery, the administrative

law judge may order that the material may be discovered and disclosed under limited conditions or may be used only under certain terms and conditions.

(4) If the administrative law judge determines that the requested material is necessary to decide the case and that a confidential order is warranted. the administrative law judge shall provide—

(i) An opportunity for review of the document by the parties off the record:

(ii) Procedures for excluding the information from the record; and

(iii) Order that the parties shall not disclose the information in any manner and the parties shall not use the information in any other proceeding.

(h) *Protective orders.* A party or a person who has received a request for discovery may file a motion for protective order with the administrative law judge and shall serve a copy of the motion for protective order on each party. The party or person making the motion must show that the protective order is necessary to protect the party or the person from annoyance, embarassment, oppression, or undue burden or expense. As part of the protective order, the administrative law judge may—

(1) Deny the discovery request;

(2) Order that discovery be conducted only on specified terms and conditions, including a designation of the time or place for discovery or a determination of the method of discovery; or

(3) Limit the scope of discovery or preclude any inquiry into certain matters during discovery.

(i) *Duty to supplement or amend responses.* A party who has responded to a discovery request has a duty to supplement or amend the response, as soon as the information is known, as follows:

(1) A party shall supplement or amend any response to a question requesting the identity and location of any person having knowledge of discoverable matters.

(2) A party shall supplement or amend any response to a question requesting the identity of each person who will be called to testify at the hearing as an expert witness' the subject matter and substance of that witness, testimony.

(3) A party shall supplement or amend any response that was incorrect when made or any response that was correct when made but is no longer correct, accurate, or complete.

(i) *Depositions.* The following rules apply to depositions taken pursuant to this section:

(1) *Form.* A deposition shall be taken on the record and reduced to writing. The person being deposed shall sign the deposition unless the parties agree to waive the requirement of a signature.

(2) *Administration of oaths.* Within the United States, or a territory or possession subject to the jurisdiction of the United States, a party shall take a deposition before a person authorized to administer oaths by the laws of the United States or authorized by the law of the place where the examination is held. In foreign countries, a party shall take a deposition in any manner allowed by the *Federal Rules of Civil Procedure.*

(3) *Notice of deposition.* A party shall serve a notice of deposition, stating the time and place of the deposition and the name and address of each person to be examined, on the person to be deposed, on the administrative law judge, on the hearing docket clerk, and on each party not later than 7 days before the deposition. A party may serve a notice of deposition less than 7 days before the deposition only with the consent of the administrative law judge. If a subpoena *duces tecum* is to be served on the person to be examined, the party shall attach a copy of the subpoena *duces tecum*, that describes the materials to be produced at the deposition, to the notice of deposition.

(4) *Use of depositions.* A party may use any part or all of a deposition at a hearing authorized under this subpart only upon a showing of good cause. The deposition may be used against any party who was present or represented at the deposition or who had reasonable notice of the deposition.

(k) *Interrogatories.* A party shall not serve more than 30 interrogatories to each other party. Each subpart of an interrogatory shall be counted as a separate interrogatory.

(1) A party shall answer each interrogatory separately and completely in writing and under oath. A party's attorney may sign the response to the interrogatories if the attorney has verification of authority to sign from the party. If a party objects to an interrogatory, the party shall state the objection and the reasons for the objection.

(2) A party shall file a motion for leave to serve additional interrogatories on a party with the administrative law judge before serving additional interrogatories on a party. The administrative law judge shall grant the motion only if the party shows good cause for the party's failure to inquire about the information previously and that the information can not reasonably be obtained from other sources.

(1) *Requests for admission.* A party may serve a written request for admission of the truth of any matter within the scope of discovery under this section or the authenticity of any document described in the request. A party shall set forth each request for admission separately. A party shall serve copies of documents referenced in the request for admission unless the documents have been provided or are reasonably available for inspection and copying.

(1) *Time.* A party's failure to respond to a request for admision, in writing and signed by the attorney or the party, not later than 30 days after service of the request, is deemed an admission of the truth of the statement or statements contained in the request for admission. The admission judge may determine that a failure to respond to a request for admission is not deemed an admission of the truth if a party shows that the failure was due to circumstances beyond the control of the party or the party's attorney.

(2) *Response.* A party may object to a request for admission and shall state the reasons for objection. A party may specifically deny the truth of the matter or describe the reasons why the party is unable to truthfully deny or admit the matter. If a party is unable to deny or admit the truth of the matter, the party shall show that the party has made reasonable inquiry into the matter or that the information known to, or readily-obtainable by, the party is insufficient to enable the party to admit or deny the matter. A party may admit or deny any part of the request for admission. If the administrative law judge determines that a response does not comply with the requirements of this rule or that the response is insufficient, the matter is deemed admitted.

(3) *Effect of admission.* Any matter admitted or deemed admitted under this section is conclusively established for the purpose of the hearing and appeal. Any matter admitted or deemed admitted under this section that results in a finding of violation may be used by the Administrator in a subsequent enforcement proceeding.

(m) *Motion to compel discovery.* A party may make a motion to compel discovery if a person refuses to answer a question during a deposition, a party fails or refuses to answer an interrogatory, if a person gives an evasive or incomplete answer during a depostion or when responding to an interrogatory, or a party fails or refuses to produce documents or tangible items. During a deposition, the proponent of a question may complete the deposition or may adjourn the examination before making a motion to compel if a person refuses to answer.

(n) *Failure to comply with a discovery order or order to compel.* If a party fails to comply with a discovery order or an order to compel, the administrative law judge, limited to the extent of the party's failure to comply with the discovery order or motion to compel, may—

(1) Strike that portion of a party's pleadings;

(2) Preclude prehearing or discovery motions by that party;

(3) Preclude admission of that portion of a party's evidence at the hearing; or

(4) Preclude that portion of the testimony of that party's witnesses at the hearing.

§ 13.221 Notice of hearing.

(a) *Notice.* The administrative law judge shall give each party at least 60 days notice of the date and time of the hearing.

(b) *Date and time of hearing.* The administrative law judge to whom the proceedings have been assigned shall set a reasonable date and a time for the hearing. The administrative law judge shall consider the need for discovery and any joint procedural or discovery schedule submitted by the parties when determining the hearing date.

(c) *Location of the hearing.* After assignment of an administrative law judge to the proceedings. a party may file a motion to change the location of the hearing or the administrative law judge on his own motion may change the location of the hearing. The administrative law judge shall give due regard to where the majority of the witnesses reside or work, the convenience of the parties, and whether the location is served by scheduled air carrier.

(d) *Earlier hearing.* With the consent of the administrative law judge, the parties may agree to hold the hearing on an earlier date than the date specified in the notice of hearing.

§ 13.222 Evidence.

(a) *General.* A party is entitled to present the party's case or defense by oral, documentary, or demonstrative evidence, to submit rebuttal evidence, and to conduct any cross-examination that may be required for a full and true disclosure of the facts.

(b) *Admissibility.* A party may introduce any oral, documentary, or demonstrative evidence in support of the party's case or defense. The administrative law judge shall admit any oral, documentary, or demonstrative evidence introduced by a party but shall exclude irrelevant, immaterial, or unduly repetitious evidence.

(c) *Hearsay evidence.* Hearsay evidence is admissible in proceedings governed by this subpart. The fact that evidence submitted by a party is hearsay goes only to the weight of the evidence and does not affect its admissibility.

§ 13.223 Standard of proof.

The administrative law judge shall issue an initial decision or shall rule in a party's favor only if the decision or ruling is supported by, and in accordance with, the reliable, probative, and substantial evidence contained in the record. In order to prevail, the party with the burden of proof shall prove the party's case or defense by a preponderance of reliable, probative, and substantial evidence.

§ 13.224 Burden of proof.

(a) Except in the case of an affirmative defense, the burden of proof is on the agency.

(b) Except as otherwise provided by statute or rule, the proponent of a motion, request, or order has the burden of proof.

(c) A party who has asserted an affirmative defense has the burden of proving the affirmative defense.

§ 13.225 Offer of proof.

A party whose evidence has been exluded by a ruling of the administrative law judge may offer the evidece for the record on appeal.

§ 13.226 Public disclosure of evidence.

(a) The administrative law judge may order that any information contained in the record be withheld from public disclosure. Any person may object to disclosure of information in the record by filing a written motion to withhold specific information with the administrative law judge and serving a copy of the motion on each party. The party shall state the specific grounds for nondisclosure in the motion.

(b) The administrative law judge shall grant the motion to withhold information in the record if, based on the motion and any response to the motion, the administrative law judge determines that disclosure would be detrimental to aviation safety, disclosure would not be in the public interest, or that the information is not otherwise required to be made available to the public.

§ 13.227 Testimony by agency employees.

An employee of the agency may not testify as an expert or opinion witness, for any party other than the agency, in any proceeding governed by this subpart. An employee of the agency may testify in a proceeding governed by this subpart only as to facts, within the employee's personal knowledge, giving rise to the incident or violation.

§ 13.228 Subpoenas.

(a) *Request for subpoena.* A party may obtain a subpoena to compel the attendance of a witness at a deposition or hearing or to require the production of documents or tangible items from the hearing docket clerk. The hearing docket clerk shall deliver the subpoena, signed by the hearing docket clerk or an administrative law judge but otherwise in blank, to the party. The party shall complete the subpoena, stating the title of the action and the date and time for the witness' attendance or production of documents or items. The party who obtained the subpoena shall serve the subpoena on the witness.

(b) *Motion to quash or modify the subpoena.* Any person upon whom a subpoena has been served may file a motion to quash or modify the subpoena with the administrative law judge at or before the time specified in the subpoena for compliance. The applicant shall describe, in detail, the basis for the application to quash or modify the subpoena including, but not limited to, a statement that the testimony or the documents or tangible evidence is not relevant to the proceeding, that that subpoena is not reasonable tailored to the scope of the proceeding, or that the subpoena is unreasonable and oppressive. A motion to quash or modify the subpoena will stay the effect of the subpoena pending a decision by the administrative law judge on the motion.

(c) *Enforcement of subpoena.* Upon a showing that a person has failed or refused to comply with a subpoena, a party may apply to the local Federal district court to seek judicial enforcement of the subpoena in accordance with section 1004 of the Federal Aviation Act of 1958, as amended.

§ 13.229 Witness fees.

(a) *General.* Unless otherwise authorized by the administrative law judge, the party who applies for a subpoena to compel the attendance of a witness at a deposition or hearing, or the party at whose request a witness appears at a deposition or hearing, shall pay the witness fees descibed in this section.

(b) *Amount.* Except for an FAA employee who appears at the direction of the agency, a witness who appears at a disposition or hearing is entitled to the same fees and mileage expenses as are paid to a witness in a court of the United States in comparable circumstances.

§ 13.230 Record.

(a) *Exclusive record.* The transcript of all testimony in the hearing, all exhibits received into evidence, and all motions, applications, requests, and rulings shall constitute the exclusive record for decision of the proceedings and the basis for the issuance of any orders in the proceeding. Any proceedings regarding the disqualification of an administrative law judge shall be included in the record.

(b) *Examiniation and copying of record.* Any person may examine the record at the Hearing Docket, Federal Aviation Administration, 800 Independence Avenue, SW., Room 914E, Washington, DC 20591. Any person may have a copy of the record after payment of reasonable costs to copy the record.

§ 13.231 Argument before the administrative law judge.

(a) *Arguments during the hearing.* During the hearing, the administrative law judge shall give the parties a reasonable opportunity to present oral arguments on the record, supporting or opposing motions, objections, and rulings if the parties request an opportunity for argument. Only in a clearly complex or unusual case, the administrative law judge may request or the parties may agree to file written arguments with the administrative law judge.

(b) *Final oral argument.* At the conclusion of the hearing and before the administrative law judge issues an initial decision in the proceedings, the parties are entitled to submit oral proposed findings of fact and conclusions of law, exceptions to rulings of the administrative law judge, and supporting arguments for the findings, conclusions, or exceptions. At the conclusion of the hearing, a party may waive final oral argument.

(c) *Posthearing briefs.* Only in a clearly complex or unusual case, the administrative law judge may request or the parties may agree to file written posthearing briefs, instead of final oral argument, before the administrative law judge issues an initial

decision in the proceedings. If a party files a written posthearing brief, the party shall include proposed findings of fact and conclusions of law, exceptions to rulings of the administrative law judge, and supporting arguments for the findings, conclusions, or exceptions. The administrative law judge shall give the parties a reasonable opportunity, not more than 30 days after receipt of the transcript, to prepare and submit the briefs.

§ 13.232 Initial decision.

(a) *Contents.* The administrative law judge shall issue an initial decision at the conclusion of the hearing and may affirm, modify, or reverse the order of civil penalty. In each oral or written decision, the administrative law judge shall include findings of fact and conclulsions of law, and the grounds supporting those findings and conclusions, upon all material issues of fact, the credibility of witnesses, the applicable law, any excercise of the administrative law judge's discretion, the reasonableness of any sanction contained in the order of civil penalty, and a discussion of the basis for any order issued in the proceedings. The administrative law judge is not required to provide a written explanation for rulings on objections, procedural motions, and other matters not directly relevant to the substance of the initial decision. If the administrative law judge reduces the civil penalty contained in the order of civil penalty, the administrative law judge shall provide a basis supporting the reduction in civil penalty. If the administrative law judge refers to any previous unreported or unpublished initial decision, the administrative law judge shall make copies of that initial decision available to the parties and the FAA decisionmaker.

(b) *Oral decision.* Except as provided in paragraph (c) of this section, at the conclusion of the hearing, the administrative law judge shall issue the intial decision and order orally on the record.

(c) *Written decision.* Only in a clearly complex or unusual case, the administrative law judge may issue a written initial decision not later than 30 days after the conclusion of the hearing or submission of the last posthearing brief. The administrative law judge shall serve a copy of the written initial decision on each party.

(d) *Order assessing civil penalty.* If the administrative law judge affirms or modifies the order of civil penalty, the order shall become an order assessing civil penalty.

§ 13.233 Appeals from initial decisions.

(a) *Notice of appeal.* A party may appeal the initial decision, and any decision not previously appealed pursuant to § 13.219, by filing a notice of appeal with the FAA decisionmaker. A party shall file the notice of appeal with the Federal Aviation Administration, 800 Independence Avenue SW., Room 914E, Washington, DC 20591. Attn: Appellate Docket Clerk. A party shall file the notice of appeal not later than 10 days after entry of the oral initial decision on the record or service of the written initial decision on the parties and shall serve a copy of the notice of appeal on each party.

(b) *Issues on appeal.* A party may appeal only the following issues:

(1) Whether each filing of fact is supported by a preponderance of reliable, probative, and substantial evidence;

(2) Whether each conclusion of law is made in accordance with applicable law, precedent, and public policy; and

(3) Whether the administrative law judge committed any prejudicial errors during the hearing that support the appeal.

(c) *Perfecting an appeal.* Unless otherwise agreed by the parties, a party shall perfect an appeal, not later than 50 days after entry of the oral initial decision on the record or service of the written initial decision on the party, by filing an appeal brief with the FAA decisionmaker.

(1) *Extension of time by agreement of the parties.* The parties may agree to extend the time for perfecting the appeal with the consent of the FAA decisionmaker. If the FAA decisionmaker grants an extension of time to perfect the appeal, the appellate docket clerk shall serve a letter confirming the extension of time on each party.

(2) *Written motion for extension.* If the parties do not agree to an extension of time for perfecting an appeal, a party desiring an extension of time may file a written motion for an extension with the FAA decisionmaker and shall serve a copy of the motion on each party. The FAA decisionmaker may grant an extension if good cause for extension is shown in the motion.

(d) Appeal briefs. A party shall file the appeal brief with the FAA decisionmaker and shall serve a copy of the appeal brief on each party.

(1) A party shall set forth, in detail, the party's specific objections to the initial decision or rulings in the appeal brief. A party also shall set forth, in detail, the basis for the appeal, the reasons supporting the appeal, and the relief requested in the appeal. If the party relies on evidence contained in the record for the appeal, the party shall specifically refer to the pertinent evidence contained in the transcript in the appeal brief.

(2) The FAA decisionmaker may dismiss an appeal, on the FAA decisionmaker's own initiative or upon motion of any other party, where a party has filed a notice of appeal but fails to perfect the appeal by timely filing of an appeal brief with the FAA decisionmaker.

(e) *Reply brief.* Unless otherwise agreed by the parties, any party may file a reply brief with the FAA decisionmaker not later than 35 days after the appeal brief has been served on that party. The party filing the reply brief shall serve a copy of the reply brief on each party. If the party relies on evidence contained in the record for the reply, the party shall specifically refer to the pertinent evidence contained in the transcript in the reply brief.

(1) *Extensions of time by agreement of the parties.* The parties may agree to extend the time for filing a reply brief with the consent of the FAA decisionmaker. If the FAA decisionmaker grants an extension of time to file the reply brief, the appellate docket clerk shall serve a letter confirming the extension of time on each party.

(2) *Written motion for extension.* If the parties do not agree to an extension of time for filing a reply brief, a party desiring an extension of time may file a written motion for an extension with the FAA decisionmaker and shall serve a copy of the motion on each party. The FAA decisionmaker may grant an extension if good cause for the extension is shown in the motion.

(f) *Other briefs.* The FAA decisionmaker may allow any person to submit an *amicus curiae* brief in an appeal of an initial decision. A party may not file more than one appeal brief or reply brief. A party may petition the The FAA decisionmaker, in writing, for leave to file an additional brief and shall serve a copy of the petition on each party. The party may not file the additional brief with the petition. The FAA decisionmaker may grant leave to file an additional brief if the party demonstrates good cause for allowing additional argument on the appeal. The FAA decisionmaker will allow a reasonable time for each party to file the additional brief.

(g) *Number of copies.* A party shall file the original appeal brief or the original reply brief, and 2 copies of the brief, with the FAA decisionmaker.

(h) *Oral argument.* The FAA decisionmaker has sole discretion to permit oral argument on the appeal. On the FAA decisionmaker's own initiative or upon written motion by any party, the FAA decisionmaker may find that oral argument will contribute substantially to the development of the issues on appeal and may grant the parties an opportunity for oral argument.

(i) *Waiver of objections on appeal.* If a party fails to object to any alleged error regarding the proceedings in an appeal or a reply brief, the party waives any objection to the alleged error. The FAA decisionmaker is not required to consider any objection in an appeal brief or any argument in the reply brief if a party's objection is based on evidence contained on the record and the party does not specifically refer to the pertinent evidence from the record in the brief.

(j) *FAA decisionmaker's decision on appeal.* The FAA decisionmaker will review the briefs on appeal and the oral argument, if any, to determine if the administrative law judge committed prejudicial error in the proceedings or that the order should be affirmed, modified, or reversed. The FAA decisionmaker may affirm, modify, or reverse the initial decision, make any necessary findings, or may remand the case for any proceedings that the FAA decisionmaker determines may be necessary.

(1) The FAA decisionmaker may raise any issue, on the FAA decisionmaker's own initiative, that is required for proper dispostion of the proceedings. The FAA decisionmaker will give the parties a reasonable opportunity to submit arguments on the new issues before making a decision on appeal.

(2) The FAA decisionmaker will issue the final decision and order of the Administrator on appeal in writing and will serve a copy of the decision and order on each party.

(3) A final decision and order of the Administrator after appeal is precedent in any other civil penalty action. Any issue, finding or conclusion, order, ruling, or initial decision of an administrative law judge that has not been appealed to the FAA decisionmaker is not precedent in any other civil penalty action.

§ 13.234 Petitions to reconsider or modify a final decision and order of the FAA decisionmaker on appeal.

(a) *General.* Any party may petition the FAA decisionmaker to reconsider or modify a final decision and order issued by the FAA decisionmaker on appeal from an initial decision. A party shall file a petition to reconsider or modify with the FAA decisionmaker not later than 30 days after service of the FAA decisionmaker's final decision and order on appeal and shall serve a copy of the petition on each party. The FAA decisionmaker will not reconsider or modify an initial decision and order issued by an administrative law judge that has not been appealed by any party to the FAA decisionmaker.

(b) *Form and number of copies.* A party shall file a petition to reconsider or modify in writing with the FAA decisionmaker. The party shall file the original petition with the FAA decisionmaker and shall serve a copy of the petition on each party.

(c) *Contents.* A party shall state briefly and specifically the alleged errors in the final decision and order on appeal, the relief sought by the party, and the grounds that support the petition to reconsider or modify.

(1) If the petition is based, in whole or in part, on allegations regarding the consequences of the FAA decisionmaker's decision, the party shall describe these allegations and shall describe, and support, the basis for the allegations.

(2) If the petition is based, in whole or in part, on new material not previously raised in the proceedings, the party shall set forth the new material and include affidavits of prospective witnesses and authenticated documents that would be introduced in support of the new material. The party shall explain, in detail, why the new material was not discovered through due diligence prior to the hearing.

(d) *Repetitious and frivolous petitions.* The FAA decisionmaker will not consider repetitious or frivolous petitions. The FAA decisionmaker may summarily dismiss repetitious or frivolous petitions to reconsider or modify.

(e) *Reply petitions.* Any other party may reply to a petition to reconsider or modify, not later than 10 days after service of the petition on that party, by filing a reply with the FAA decisionmaker. A party shall serve a copy of the reply on each party.

(f) *Effect of filing petition.* Unless otherwise ordered by the FAA decisionmaker, filing of a petition pursuant to this section will not stay or delay the effective date of the FAA decisionmaker's final decision and order on appeal and shall not toll the time allowed for judicial review.

(g) *FAA decisionmaker's decision on petition.* The FAA decisionmaker has sole discretion to grant or deny a petition to reconsider or modify. The FAA decisionmaker will grant or deny a petition to reconsider or modify within a reasonable time after receipt of the petition or receipt of the reply petition, if any. The FAA decisionmaker may affirm, modify, or reverse the final decision and order on appeal, or may remand the case for any proceedings that the FAA decisionmaker determines may be necessary.

§ 13.235 Judicial review of final decision and order.

A person may seek judicial review of a final decision and order of the Administrator as provided in § 1006 of the Federal Aviation Act of 1958, as amended. A party seeking judicial review of a final decision and order shall file a petition for review not later than 60 days after the final decision and order has been served on the party.

FEDERAL AVIATION REGULATIONS

PART 21
CERTIFICATION PROCEDURES FOR PRODUCTS AND PARTS

1989 EDITION

SUBCHAPTER C—AIRCRAFT

PART 21—CERTIFICATION PROCEDURES FOR PRODUCTS AND PARTS

Subpart A—General

Sec.
21.1 Applicability.
21.3 Reporting of failures, malfunctions, and defects.
21.5 Airplane or Rotorcraft Flight Manual.

Subpart B—Type Certificates

21.11 Applicability.
21.13 Eligibility.
21.15 Application for type certificate.
21.16 Special conditions.
21.17 Designation of applicable regulations.
21.19 Changes requiring a new type certificate.
21.21 Issue of type certificate: normal, utility, acrobatic, commuter, and transport category aircraft; manned free balloons; special classes of aircraft; aircraft engines; propellers.
21.23 [Reserved]
21.25 Issue of type certificate: Restricted category aircraft.
21.27 Issue of type certificate: surplus aircraft of the Armed Forces.
21.29 Issue of type certificate: import products.
21.31 Type design.
21.33 Inspection and tests.
21.35 Flight tests.
21.37 Flight test pilot.
21.39 Flight test instrument calibration and correction report.
21.41 Type certificate.
21.43 Location of manufacturing facilities.
21.45 Privileges.
21.47 Transferability.
21.49 Availability.
21.50 Instructions for continued airworthiness and manufacturer's maintenance manuals having airworthiness limitations sections.
21.51 Duration.
21.53 Statement of conformity.

Subpart C—Provisional Type Certificates

21.71 Applicability.
21.73 Eligibility.
21.75 Application.
21.77 Duration.
21.79 Transferability.
21.81 Requirements for issue and amendment of Class I provisional type certificates.
21.83 Requirements for issue and amendment of Class II provisional type certificates.
21.85 Provisional amendments to type certificates.

Subpart D—Changes to Type Certificates

21.91 Applicability.
21.93 Classification of changes in type design.
21.95 Approval of minor changes in type design.
21.97 Approval of major changes in type design.
21.99 Required design changes.
21.101 Designation of applicable regulations.

Subpart E—Supplemental Type Certificates

21.111 Applicability.
21.113 Requirement of supplemental type certificate.
21.115 Applicable requirements.
21.117 Issue of supplemental type certificates.
21.119 Privileges.

Subpart F—Production Under Type Certificate Only

21.121 Applicability.
21.123 Production under type certificate.
21.125 Production inspection system: Materials Review Board.
21.127 Tests: aircraft.
21.128 Tests: aircraft engines.
21.129 Tests: propellers.
21.130 Statement of conformity.

Subpart G—Production Certificates

21.131 Applicability.
21.133 Eligibility.
21.135 Requirements for issuance.
21.137 Location of manufacturing facilities.
21.139 Quality control.
21.143 Quality control data requirements; prime manufacturer.
21.147 Changes in quality control system.
21.149 Multiple products.
21.151 Production limitation record.
21.153 Amendment of the production certificates.
21.155 Transferability.
21.157 Inspections and tests.

21.159   Duration.
21.161   Display.
21.163   Privileges.
21.165   Responsibility of holder.

Subpart H—Airworthiness Certificates

21.171   Applicability.
21.173   Eligibility.
21.175   Airworthiness certificates: classification.
21.177   Amendment or modification.
21.179   Transferability.
21.181   Duration.
21.182   Aircraft identification.
21.183   Issue of standard airworthiness certificates for normal, utility, acrobatic, commuter, and transport category aircraft; manned free balloons; and special classes of aircraft.
21.185   Issue of airworthiness certificates for restricted category aircraft.
21.187   Issue of multiple airworthiness certification.
21.189   Issue of airworthiness certificate for limited category aircraft.
21.191   Experimental certificates.
21.193   Experimental certificates: general.
21.195   Experimental certificates: Aircraft to be used for market surveys, sales demonstrations, and customer crew training.
21.197   Special flight permits.
21.199   Issue of special flight permits.

Subpart I—Provisional Airworthiness Certificates

21.211   Applicability.
21.213   Eligibility.
21.215   Application.
21.217   Duration.
21.219   Transferability.
21.221   Class I provisional airworthiness certificates.
21.223   Class II provisional airworthiness certificates.
21.225   Provisional airworthiness certificates corresponding with provisional amendments to type certificates.

Subpart J—Delegation Option Authorization Procedures

21.231   Applicability
21.235   Application.
21.239   Eligibility.
21.243   Duration.
21.245   Maintenance of eligibility.
21.247   Transferability.
21.249   Inspections.
21.251   Limits of applicability.
21.253   Type certificates: application.
21.257   Type certificates: issue.
21.261   Equivalent safety provisions.
21.267   Production certificates.
21.269   Export airworthiness approvals.

21.271   Airworthiness approval tags.
21.273   Airworthiness certificates other than experimental.
21.275   Experimental certificates.
21.277   Data review and service experience.
21.289   Major repairs, rebuilding and alteration.
21.293   Current records.

Subpart K—Approval of Materials, Parts, Processes, and Appliances

21.301   Applicability.
21.303   Replacement and modification parts.
21.305   Approval of materials, parts, processes, and appliances.

Subpart L—Export Airworthiness Approvals

21.321   Applicability.
21.323   Eligibility.
21.325   Export airworthiness approvals.
21.327   Application.
21.329   Issue of export certificates of airworthiness for Class I products.
21.331   Issue of airworthiness approval tags for Class II products.
21.333   Issue of export airworthiness approval tags for Class III products.
21.335   Responsibilities of exporters.
21.337   Performance of inspections and overhauls.
21.339   Special export airworthiness approval for aircraft.

Subpart M—Designated Alteration Station Authorization Procedures

21.431   Applicability.
21.435   Application.
21.439   Eligibility.
21.441   Procedure manual.
21.443   Duration.
21.445   Maintenance of eligibility.
21.447   Transferability.
21.449   Inspections.
21.451   Limits of applicability.
21.461   Equivalent safety provisions.
21.463   Supplemental type certificates.
21.473   Airworthiness certificates other than experimental.
21.475   Experimental certificates.
21.477   Data review and service experience.
21.493   Current records.

Subpart N—Approval of Engines, Propellers, Materials, Parts, and Appliances: Import

21.500   Approval of engines and propellers.
21.502   Approval of materials, parts, and appliances.

Subpart O—Technical Standard Order Authorizations

21.601   Applicability.

21.603 TSO marking and privileges.
21.605 Application and issue.
21.607 General rules governing holders of TSO authorizations.
21.609 Approval for deviation.
21.611 Design changes.
21.613 Recordkeeping requirements.
21.615 FAA inspection.
21.617 Issue of letters of TSO design approval: import appliances.
21.619 Noncompliance.
21.621 Transferability and duration.

AUTHORITY: 49 U.S.C. 1344, 1348(c), 1352, 1354(a), 1355, 1421 through 1431, 1502, 1651(b)(2), 42 U.S.C. 1857f-10, 4321 et. seq.; E.O. 11514; 49 U.S.C. 106(g) (Revised Pub. L. 97-449, Jan. 12, 1983).

Subpart A—General

§ 21.1 Applicability.

(a) This part prescribes—

(1) Procedural requirements for the issue of type certificates and changes to those certificates; the issue of production certificates; the issue of airworthiness certificates; and the issue of export airworthiness approvals.

(2) Rules governing the holders of any certificate specified in paragraph (a)(1) of this section; and

(3) Procedural requirements for the approval of certain materials, parts, processes, and appliances.

(b) For the purposes of this part, the word "product" means an aircraft, aircraft engine, or propeller. In addition, for the purposes of Subpart L only, it includes components and parts of aircraft, of aircraft engines, and of propellers; also parts, materials, and appliances, approved under the Technical Standard Order system.

[Doc. No. 5085, 29 FR 14563, Oct. 24, 1964, as amended by Amdt. 21-2, 30 FR 8465, July 2, 1965; Amdt. 21-6, 30 FR 11379, Sept. 8, 1965]

§ 21.3 Reporting of failures, malfunctions, and defects.

(a) Except as provided in paragraph (d) of this section, the holder of a Type Certificate (including a Supplemental Type Certificate), a Parts Manufacturer Approval (PMA), or a TSO authorization, or the licensee of a Type Certificate shall report any failure, malfunction, or defect in any product, part, process, or article manufactured by it that it determines has resulted in any of the occurrences listed in paragraph (c) of this section.

(b) The holder of a Type Certificate (including a Supplemental Type Certificate), a Parts Manufacturer Approval (PMA), or a TSO authorization, or the licensee of a Type of Certificate shall report any defect in any product, part, or article manufactured by it that has left its quality control system and that it determines could result in any of the occurrences listed in paragraph (c) of this section.

(c) The following occurrences must be reported as provided in paragraphs (a) and (b) of this section:

(1) Fires caused by a system or equipment failure, malfunction, or defect.

(2) An engine exhaust system failure, malfunction, or defect which causes damage to the engine, adjacent aircraft structure, equipment, or components.

(3) The accumulation or circulation of toxic or noxious gases in the crew compartment or passenger cabin.

(4) A malfunction, failure, or defect of a propeller control system.

(5) A propeller or rotorcraft hub or blade structural failure.

(6) Flammable fluid leakage in areas where an ignition source normally exists.

(7) A brake system failure caused by structural or material failure during operation.

(8) A significant aircraft primary structural defect or failure caused by any autogenous condition (fatigue, understrength, corrosion, etc.).

(9) Any abnormal vibration or buffeting caused by a structural or system malfunction, defect, or failure.

(10) An engine failure.

(11) Any structural or flight control system malfunction, defect, or failure which causes an interference with normal control of the aircraft for which derogates the flying qualities.

(12) A complete loss of more than one electrical power generating system or hydraulic power system during a given operation of the aircraft.

(13) A failure or malfunction of more than one attitude, airspeed, or altitude instrument during a given operation of the aircraft.

(d) The requirements of paragraph (a) of this section do not apply to—

(1) Failures, malfunctions, or defects that the holder of a Type Certificate (including a Supplemental Type Certificate), Parts Manufacturer Approval (PMA), or TSO authorization, or the licensee of a Type Certificate—

(i) Determines were caused by improper maintenance, or improper usage;

(ii) Knows were reported to the FAA by another person under the Federal Aviation Regulations; or

(iii) Has already reported under the accident reporting provisions of Part 430 of the regulations of the National Transportation Safety Board.

(2) Failures, malfunctions, or defects in products, parts, or articles manufactured by a foreign manufacturer under a U.S. Type Certificate issued under §21.29 or §21.617, or exported to the United States under §21.502.

(e) Each report required by this section—

(1) Shall be made to the FAA Regional Office in the region in which the person required to make the report is located within 24 hours after it has determined that the failure, malfunction, or defect required to be reported has occurred. However, a report that is due on a Saturday or a Sunday may be delivered on the following Monday and one that is due on a holiday may be delivered on the next workday;

(2) Shall be transmitted in a manner and form acceptable to the Administrator and by the most expeditious method available; and

(3) Shall include as much of the following information as is available and applicable:

(i) Aircraft serial number.

(ii) When the failure, malfunction, or defect is associated with an article approved under a TSO authorization, the article serial number and model designation, as appropriate.

(iii) When the failure, malfunction, or defect is associated with an engine or propeller, the engine or propeller serial number, as appropriate.

(iv) Product model.

(v) Identification of the part, component, or system involved. The identification must include the part number.

(vi) Nature of the failure, malfunction, or defect.

(f) Whenever the investigation of an accident or service difficulty report shows that an article manufactured under a TSO authorization is unsafe because of a manufacturing or design defect, the manufacturer shall, upon request of the Administrator, report to the Administrator the results of its investigation and any action taken or proposed by the manufacturer to correct that defect. If action is required to correct the defect in existing articles, the manufacturer shall submit the data necessary for the issuance of an appropriate airworthiness directive to the Chief, Engineering and Manufacturing Branch (or in the case of the Western Region, the Chief, Aircraft Engineering Division), of the FAA regional office in the region in which it is located.

[Amdt. 21–36, 35 FR 18187, Nov. 28, 1970, as amended by Amdt. 21–37, 35 FR 18450, Dec. 4, 1970; Amdt. 21–50, 45 FR 38346, June 9, 1980]

§21.5 Airplane or Rotorcraft Flight Manual.

(a) With each airplane or rotorcraft that was not type certificated with an Airplane or Rotorcraft Flight Manual and that has had no flight time prior to March 1, 1979, the holder of a Type Certificate (including a Supplemental Type Certificate) or the licensee of a Type Certificate shall make available to the owner at the time of delivery of the aircraft a current approved Airplane or Rotorcraft Flight Manual.

(b) The Airplane or Rotorcraft Flight Manual required by paragraph (a) of this section must contain the following information:

(1) The operating limitations and information required to be furnished in an Airplane or Rotorcraft Flight Manual or in manual material, markings, and placards, by the applicable regulations under which the airplane or rotorcraft was type certificated.

(2) The maximum ambient atmospheric temperature for which engine

cooling was demonstrated must be stated in the performance information section of the Flight Manual, if the applicable regulations under which the aircraft was type certificated do not require ambient temperature on engine cooling operating limitations in the Flight Manual.

[Amdt. 21-46, 43 FR 2316, Jan. 16, 1978]

Subpart B—Type Certificates

SOURCE: Docket No. 5085, 29 FR 14564, Oct. 24, 1964, unless otherwise noted.

§ 21.11 Applicability.

This subpart prescribes—
(a) Procedural requirements for the issue of type certificates for aircraft, aircraft engines, and propellers; and
(b) Rules governing the holders of those certificates.

§ 21.13 Eligibility.

Any interested person may apply for a type certificate.

[Amdt. 21-25, 34 FR 14068, Sept. 5, 1969]

§ 21.15 Application for type certificate.

(a) An application for a type certificate is made on a form and in a manner prescribed by the Administrator and is submitted to the appropriate FAA regional office.
(b) An application for an aircraft type certificate must be accompanied by a three-view drawing of that aircraft and available preliminary basic data.
(c) An application for an aircraft engine type certificate must be accompanied by a description of the engine design features, the engine operating characteristics, and the proposed engine operating limitations.

[Doc. No. 5085, 29 FR 14564, Oct. 24, 1964, as amended by Amdt. 21-40, 39 FR 35459, Oct. 1, 1974]

§ 21.16 Special conditions.

If the Administrator finds that the airworthiness regulations of this subchapter do not contain adequate or appropriate safety standards for an aircraft, aircraft engine, or propeller because of a novel or unusual design feature of the aircraft, aircraft engine or propeller, he prescribes special conditions and amendments thereto for the product. The special conditions are issued in accordance with Part 11 of this chapter and contain such safety standards for the aircraft, aircraft engine or propeller as the Administrator finds necessary to establish a level of safety equivalent to that established in the regulations.

[Amdt. 21-19, 32 FR 17851, Dec. 13, 1967; as amended by Amdt. 21-51, 45 FR 60170, Sept. 11, 1980]

§ 21.17 Designation of applicable regulations.

(a) Except as provided in § 23.2, § 25.2 and in Part 36 of this chapter, an applicant for a type certificate must show that the aircraft, aircraft engine, or propeller concerned meets—
(1) The applicable requirements of this subchapter that are effective on the date of application for that certificate unless—
(i) Otherwise specified by the Administrator; or
(ii) Compliance with later effective amendments is elected or required under this section; and
(2) Any special conditions prescribed by the Administrator.
(b) For special classes of aircraft, including the engines and propellers installed thereon (e.g., gliders, airships, and other nonconventional aircraft), for which airworthiness standards have not been issued under this subchapter, the applicable requirements will be the portions of those other airworthiness requirements contained in Parts 23, 25, 27, 29, 31, 33, and 35 found by the Administrator to be appropriate for the aircraft and applicable to a specific type design, or such airworthiness criteria as the Administrator may find provide an equivalent level of safety to those parts.
(c) An application for type certification of a transport category aircraft is effective for 5 years and an application for any other type certificate is effective for 3 years, unless an applicant shows at the time of application that his product requires a longer period of time for design, development, and testing, and the Administrator approves a longer period.

(d) In a case where a type certificate has not been issued, or it is clear that a type certificate will not be issued, within the time limit established under paragraph (c) of this section, the applicant may—

(1) File a new application for a type certificate and comply with all the provisions of paragraph (a) of this section applicable to an original application; or

(2) File for an extension of the original application and comply with the applicable airworthiness requirements of this subchapter that were effective on a date, to be selected by the applicant, not earlier than the date which precedes the date of issue of the type certificate by the time limit established under paragraph (c) of this section for the original application.

(e) If an applicant elects to comply with an amendment to this subchapter that is effective after the filing of the application for a type certificate, he must also comply with any other amendment that the Administrator finds is directly related.

[Doc. No. 5085, 29 FR 14564, Oct. 24, 1964, as amended by Amdt. 21-19, 32 FR 17851, Dec. 13, 1967; Amdt. 21-24, 34 FR 364, Jan. 10, 1969; Amdt. 21-42, 40 FR 1033, Jan. 6, 1975; Amdt. 21-58, 50 FR 46877, Nov. 13, 1985; Amdt. 21-60, 52 FR 8042, Mar. 13, 1987]

§ 21.19 Changes requiring a new type certificate.

Any person who proposes to change a product must make a new application for a type certificate if—

(a) The Administrator finds that the proposed change in design, configuration, power, power limitations (engines), speed limitations (engines), or weight is so extensive that a substantially complete investigation of compliance with the applicable regulations is required;

(b) In the case of a normal, utility, acrobatic, commuter or transport category aircraft, the proposed change is—

(1) In the number of engines or rotors; or

(2) To engines or rotors using different principles of propulsion or to rotors using different principles of operation;

(c) In the case of an aircraft engine, the proposed change is in the principle of operation; or

(d) In the case of propellers, the proposed change is in the number of blades or principle of pitch change operation.

[Doc. No. 5085, 29 FR 14564, Oct. 24, 1964, as amended by Amdt. 23-34, 52 FR 1835, Jan. 15, 1987]

§ 21.21 Issue of type certificate: normal, utility, acrobatic, commuter, and transport category aircraft; manned free balloons; special classes of aircraft; aircraft engines; propellers.

An applicant is entitled to a type certificate for an aircraft in the normal, utility, acrobatic, commuter, or transport category, or for a manned free balloon, special class of aircraft, or an aircraft engine or propeller, if—

(a) The product qualifies under § 21.27; or

(b) The applicant submits the type design, test reports, and computations necessary to show that the product to be certificated meets the applicable airworthiness and aircraft noise requirements of the Federal Aviation Regulations and any special conditions prescribed by the Administrator, and the Administrator finds—

(1) Upon examination of the type design, and after completing all tests and inspections, that the type design and the product meet the applicable aircraft noise requirements of the Federal Aviation Regulations, and further finds that they meet the applicable airworthiness requirements of the Federal Aviation Regulations or that any airworthiness provisions not complied with are compensated for by factors that provide an equivalent level of safety; and

(2) For an aircraft, that no feature or characteristic makes it unsafe for the category in which certification is requested.

[Doc. No. 5085, 29 FR 14564, Oct. 24, 1964, as amended by Amdt. 21-15, 32 FR 3735, Mar. 4, 1967; Amdt. 21-27, 34 FR 18368, Nov. 18, 1969; Amdt. 21-60, 52 FR 8042, Mar. 13, 1987]

§ 21.23 [Reserved]

§ 21.25 Issue of type certificate: Restricted category aircraft.

(a) An applicant is entitled to a type certificate for an aircraft in the restricted category for special purpose operations if he shows compliance with the applicable noise requirements of Part 36 of this chapter, and if he shows that no feature or characteristic of the aircraft makes it unsafe when it is operated under the limitations prescribed for its intended use, and that the aircraft—

(1) Meets the airworthiness requirements of an aircraft category except those requirments that the Administrator finds inappropriate for the special purpose for which the aircraft is to be used; or

(2) Is of a type that has been manufactured in accordance with the requirements of and accepted for use by, an Armed Force of the United States and has been later modified for a special purpose.

(b) For the purposes of this section, "special purpose operations" includes—

(1) Agricultural (spraying, dusting, and seeding, and livestock and predatory animal control);

(2) Forest and wildlife conservation;

(3) Aerial surveying (photography, mapping, and oil and mineral exploration);

(4) Patrolling (pipelines, power lines, and canals);

(5) Weather control (cloud seeding);

(6) Aerial advertising (skywriting, banner towing, airborne signs and public address systems); and

(7) Any other operation specified by the Administrator.

[Doc. No. 5085, 29 FR 14564, Oct. 24, 1964, as amended by Amdt. 21-42, 40 FR 1033, Jan. 6, 1975]

§ 21.27 Issue of type certificate: surplus aircraft of the Armed Forces.

(a) Except as provided in paragraph (b) of this section an applicant is entitled to a type certificate for an aircraft in the normal, utility, acrobatic, commuter, or transport category that was designed and constructed in the United States, accepted for operational use, and declared surplus by, an Armed Force of the United States, and that is shown to comply with the applicable certification requirements in paragraph (f) of this section.

(b) An applicant is entitled to a type certificate for a surplus aircraft of the Armed Forces of the United States that is a counterpart of a previously type certificated civil aircraft, if he shows compliance with the regulations governing the original civil aircraft type certificate.

(c) Aircraft engines, propellers, and their related accessories installed in surplus Armed Forces aircraft, for which a type certificate is sought under this section, will be approved for use on those aircraft if the applicant shows that on the basis of the previous military qualifications, acceptance, and service record, the product provides substantially the same level of airworthiness as would be provided if the engines or propellers were type certificated under Part 33 or 35 of the Federal Aviation Regulations.

(d) The Administrator may relieve an applicant from strict compliance with a specific provision of the applicable requirements in paragraph (f) of this section, if the Administrator finds that the method of compliance proposed by the applicant provides substantially the same level of airworthiness and that strict compliance with those regulations would impose a severe burden on the applicant. The Administrator may use experience that was satisfactory to an Armed Force of the United States in making such a determination.

(e) The Administrator may require an applicant to comply with special conditions and later requirements than those in paragraphs (c) and (f) of this section, if the Administrator finds that compliance with the listed regulations would not ensure an adequate level of airworthiness for the aircraft.

(f) Except as provided in paragraphs (b) through (e) of this section, an applicant for a type certificate under this section must comply with the appropriate regulations listed in the following table:

Type of aircraft	Date accepted for operational use by the Armed Forces of the United States	Regulations that apply [1]
Small reciprocating-engine powered airplanes...........	Before May 16, 1956.................	CAR Part 3, as effective May 15, 1956.
	After May 15, 1956...................	CAR Part 3, or FAR Part 23.
Small turbine engine-powered airplanes...................	Before Oct. 2, 1959.................	CAR Part 3, as effective Oct. 1, 1959.
	After Oct. 1, 1959.....................	CAR Part 3 or FAR Part 23.
Commuter category airplanes................................	After (Feb. 17, 1987)..................	
	FAR Part 23 as of (Feb. 17, 1987)..	
Large reciprocating-engine powered airplanes..........	Before Aug. 26, 1955.................	CAR Part 4b, as effective Aug. 25, 1955.
	After Aug. 25, 1959	CAR Part 4b or FAR Part 25.
Large turbine engine-powered airplanes.................	Before Oct. 2, 1959.................	CAR Part 4b, as effective Oct. 1, 1959.
	After Oct. 1, 1959	CAR Part 4b or FAR Part 25.
Rotorcraft with maximum certificated takeoff weight of:		
6,000 pounds or less..	Before Oct. 2, 1959.................	CAR Part 6, as effective Oct. 1, 1959.
	After Oct. 1, 1959.....................	CAR Part 6, or FAR Part 27.
Over 6,000 pounds...	Before Oct. 2, 1959.................	CAR Part 7, as effective Oct. 1, 1959.
	After Oct. 1, 1959.....................	CAR Part 7, or FAR Part 29.

[1] Where no specific date is listed, the applicable regulations are those in effect on the date that the first aircraft of the particular model was accepted for operational use by the Armed Forces.

[Doc. No. 5085, 29 FR 14564, Oct. 24, 1964, as amended by Amdt. 21-59, 52 FR 1835, Jan. 15, 1987; 52 FR 7261, Mar. 9, 1987]

§ 21.29 Issue of type certificate: import products.

(a) A type certificate may be issued for a product that is manufactured in a foreign country with which the United States has an agreement for the acceptance of these products for export and import and that is to be imported into the United States if—

(1) The country in which the product was manufactured certifies that the product has been examined, tested, and found to meet—

(i) The applicable aircraft noise requirements of this subchapter as designated in § 21.17 or the applicable aircraft noise requirements of the country in which the product was manufactured and any other requirements the Administrator may prescribe to provide noise levels no greater than those provided by the applicable aircraft noise requirements of this subchapter as designated in § 21.17; and

(ii) The applicable airworthiness requirements of this subchapter as designated in § 21.17, or the applicable airworthiness requirements of the country in which the product was manufactured and any other requirements the Administrator may prescribe to provide a level of safety equivalent to that provided by the applicable airworthiness requirements of this subchapter as designated in § 21.17;

(2) The applicant has submitted the technical data, concerning aircraft noise and airworthiness, respecting the product required by the Administrator; and

(3) The manuals, placards, listings, and instrument markings required by the applicable airworthiness (and noise, where applicable) requirements are presented in the English language.

(b) A product type certificated under this section is considered to be type certificated under the noise standards of Part 36 of the Federal Aviation Regulations where compliance therewith is certified under paragraph (a)(1)(i) of this section, and under the airworthiness standards of that part of the Federal Aviation Regulations with which compliance is certified under paragraph (a)(1)(ii) of this section or to which an equivalent level of safety is certified under paragraph (a)(1)(ii) of this section.

[Amdt. 21-27, 34 FR 18363, Nov. 18, 1969]

§ 21.31 Type design.

The type design consists of—

(a) The drawings and specifications, and a listing of those drawings and specifications, necessary to define the configuration and the design features of the product shown to comply with the requirements of that part of this subchapter applicable to the product;

(b) Information on dimensions, materials, and processes necessary to define the structural strength of the product;

(c) The Airworthiness Limitations section of the Instructions for Continued Airworthiness as required by Parts 23, 25, 27, 29, 31, 33, and 35 of this chapter; and as specified in the applicable airworthiness criteria for special classes of aircraft defined in § 21.17(b); and

(d) Any other data necessary to allow, by comparison, the determination of the airworthiness and noise characteristics (where applicable) of later products of the same type.

[Doc. No. 5085, 29 FR 14564, Oct. 24, 1964, as amended by Amdt. 21-27, 34 FR 18363, Nov. 18, 1969; Amdt. 21-51, 45 FR 60170, Sept. 11, 1980; Amdt. 21-60, 52 FR 8042, Mar. 13, 1987]

§ 21.33   Inspection and tests.

(a) Each applicant must allow the Administrator to make any inspection and any flight and ground test necessary to determine compliance with the applicable requirements of the Federal Aviation Regulations. However, unless otherwise authorized by the Administrator—

(1) No aircraft, aircraft engine, propeller, or part thereof may be presented to the Administrator for test unless compliance with paragraphs (b)(2) through (b)(4) of this section has been shown for that aircraft, aircraft engine, propeller, or part thereof; and

(2) No change may be made to an aircraft, aircraft engine, propeller, or part thereof between the time that compliance with paragraphs (b)(2) through (b)(4) of this section is shown for that aircraft, aircraft engine, propeller, or part thereof and the time that it is presented to the Administrator for test.

(b) Each applicant must make all inspections and tests necessary to determine—

(1) Compliance with the applicable airworthiness and aircraft noise requirements;

(2) That materials and products conform to the specifications in the type design;

(3) That parts of the products conform to the drawings in the type design; and

(4) That the manufacturing processes, construction and assembly conform to those specified in the type design.

[Doc. No. 5085, 29 FR 14564, Oct. 24, 1964, as amended by Amdt. 21-17, 32 FR 14926, Oct. 28, 1967; Amdt. 21-27, 34 FR 18363, Nov. 18, 1969; Amdt. 21-44, 41 FR 55463, Dec. 20, 1976]

§ 21.35   Flight tests.

(a) Each applicant for an aircraft type certificate (other than under §§ 21.25 through 21.29) must make the tests listed in paragraph (b) of this section. Before making the tests the applicant must show—

(1) Compliance with the applicable structural requirements of this subchapter;

(2) Completion of necessary ground inspections and tests;

(3) That the aircraft conforms with the type design; and

(4) That the Administrator received a flight test report from the applicant (signed, in the case of aircraft to be certificated under Part 25 [New] of this chapter, by the applicant's test pilot) containing the results of his tests.

(b) Upon showing compliance with paragraph (a) of this section, the applicant must make all flight tests that the Administrator finds necessary—

(1) To determine compliance with the applicable requirements of this subchapter; and

(2) For aircraft to be certificated under this subchapter, except gliders and except airplanes of 6,000 lbs. or less maximum certificated weight that are to be certificated under Part 23 of this chapter, to determine whether there is reasonable assurance that the aircraft, its components, and its equipment are reliable and function properly.

(c) Each applicant must, if practicable, make the tests prescribed in paragraph (b)(2) of this section upon the aircraft that was used to show compliance with—

(1) Paragraph (b)(1) of this section; and

(2) For rotorcraft, the rotor drive endurance tests prescribed in § 27.923 or § 29.923 of this chapter, as applicable.

(d) Each applicant must show for each flight test (except in a glider or a manned free balloon) that adequate provision is made for the flight test crew for emergency egress and the use of parachutes.

(e) Except in gliders and manned free balloons, an applicant must discontinue flight tests under this section until he shows that corrective action has been taken, whenever—

(1) The applicant's test pilot is unable or unwilling to make any of the required flight tests; or

(2) Items of noncompliance with requirements are found that may make additional test data meaningless or that would make further testing unduly hazardous.

(f) The flight tests prescribed in paragraph (b)(2) of this section must include—

(1) For aircraft incorporating turbine engines of a type not previously used in a type certificated aircraft, at least 300 hours of operation with a full complement of engines that conform to a type certificate; and

(2) For all other aircraft, at least 150 hours of operation.

[Doc. No. 5085, 29 FR 14564, Oct. 24, 1964, as amended by Amdt. No. 21-40, 39 FR 35459, Oct. 1, 1974; Amdt. 21-51, 45 FR 60170, Sept. 11, 1980]

§ 21.37 Flight test pilot.

Each applicant for a normal, utility, acrobatic, commuter, or transport category aircraft type certificate must provide a person holding an appropriate pilot certificate to make the flight tests required by this part.

[Doc. No. 5085, 29 FR 14564, Oct. 24, 1964, as amended by Amdt. 21-59, 52 FR 1835, Jan. 15, 1987]

§ 21.39 Flight test instrument calibration and correction report.

(a) Each applicant for a normal, utility, acrobatic, commuter, or transport category aircraft type certificate must submit a report to the Administrator showing the computations and tests required in connection with the calibration of instruments used for test purposes and in the correction of test results to standard atmospheric conditions.

(b) Each applicant must allow the Administrator to conduct any flight tests that he finds necessary to check the accuracy of the report submitted under paragraph (a) of this section.

[Doc. No. 5085, 29 FR 14564, Oct. 24, 1964, as amended by Amdt. 21-59, 52 FR 1835, Jan. 15, 1987]

§ 21.41 Type certificate.

Each type certificate is considered to include the type design, the operating limitations, the certificate data sheet, the applicable regulations of this subchapter with which the Administrator records compliance, and any other conditions or limitations prescribed for the product in this subchapter.

§ 21.43 Location of manufacturing facilities.

Except as provided in § 21.29, the Administrator does not issue a type certificate if the manufacturing facilities for the product are located outside of the United States, unless the Administrator finds that the location of the manufacturer's facilities places no undue burden on the FAA in administering applicable airworthiness requirements.

§ 21.45 Privileges.

The holder or licensee of a type certificate for a product may—

(a) In the case of aircraft, upon compliance with §§ 21.173 through 21.189, obtain airworthiness certificates;

(b) In the case of aircraft engines or propellers, obtain approval for installation or certified aircraft;

(c) In the case of any product, upon compliance with §§ 21.133 through 21.163, obtain a production certificate for the type certificated product;

(d) Obtain approval of replacement parts for that product.

§ 21.47 Transferability.

A type certificate may be transferred to or made available to third persons by licensing agreements. Each grantor shall, within 30 days after the transfer of a certificate or execution or termination of a licensing agreement, notify in writing the appropriate FAA Regional Office. The notification must state the name and address of the transferee or licensee, date of the transaction, and in the case of a licensing agreement, the extent of authority granted the licensee.

§ 21.49 Availability.

The holder of a type certificate shall make the certificate available for examination upon the request of the Administrator or the National Transportation Safety Board.

[Doc. No. 5085, 29 FR 14564, Oct. 24, 1964, as amended by Doc. No. 8084, 32 FR 5769, Apr. 11, 1967]

§ 21.50 Instructions for continued airworthiness and manufacturer's maintenance manuals having airworthiness limitations sections.

(a) The holder of a type certificate for a rotorcraft for which a Rotorcraft Maintenance Manual containing an "Airworthiness Limitations" section has been issued under § 27.1529 (a)(2) or § 29.1529 (a)(2) of this chapter, and who obtains approval of changes to any replacement time, inspection interval, or related procedure in that section of the manual, shall make those changes available upon request to any operator of the same type of rotorcraft.

(b) The holder of a design approval, including either the type certificate or supplemental type certificate for an aircraft, aircraft engine, or propeller for which application was made after January 28, 1981, shall furnish at least one set of complete Instructions for Continued Airworthiness, prepared in accordance with §§ 23.1529, 25.1529, 27.1529, 29.1529, 31.82, 33.4, or 35.4 of this chapter, or as specified in the applicable airworthiness criteria for special classes of aircraft defined in § 21.17(b), as applicable, to the owner of each type of aircraft, aircraft engine, or propeller upon its delivery, or upon issuance of the first standard airworthiness certificate for the affected aircraft, whichever occurs later, and thereafter make those instructions available to any other person required by this chapter to comply with any of the terms of these instructions. In addition, changes to the Instructions for Continued Airworthiness

shall be made available to any person required by this chapter to comply with any of those instructions.

[Amdt. No. 21-23, 33 FR 14105, Sept. 18, 1968, as amended by Amdt. No 21-51, 45 FR 60170, Sept. 11, 1980; Amdt. 21-60, 52 FR 8042, Mar. 13, 1987]

§ 21.51 Duration.

A type certificate is effective until surrendered, suspended, revoked, or a termination date is otherwise established by the Administrator.

§ 21.53 Statement of conformity.

(a) Each applicant must submit a statement of conformity (FAA Form 317) to the Administrator for each aircraft engine and propeller presented to the Administrator for type certification. This statement of conformity must include a statement that the aircraft engine or propeller conforms to the type design therefor.

(b) Each applicant must submit a statement of conformity to the Administrator for each aircraft or part thereof presented to the Administrator for tests. This statement of conformity must include a statement that the applicant has complied with § 21.33(a) (unless otherwise authorized under that paragraph).

[Amdt. 21-17, 32 FR 14926, Oct. 28, 1967]

Subpart C—Provisional Type Certificates

Source: Docket No. 5085, 29 FR 14566, Oct. 24, 1964, unless otherwise noted.

§ 21.71 Applicability.

This subpart prescribes—

(a) Procedural requirements for the issue of provisional type certificates, amendments to provisional type certificates, and provisional amendments to type certificates; and

(b) Rules government the holders of those certificates.

§ 21.73 Eligibility.

(a) Any manufacturer of aircraft manufactured within the United States who is a United States citizen may apply for Class I or Class II provisional type certificates, for amendments to provisional type certificates held by him, and for provisional amendments to type certificates held by him.

(b) Any manufacturer of aircraft manufactured in a foreign country with which the United States has an agreement for the acceptance of those aircraft for export and import may apply for a Class II provisional type certificate, for amendments to provisional type certificates held by him, and for provisional amendments to type certificates held by him.

(c) An aircraft engine manufacturer who is a United States citizen and who has altered a type certificated aircraft by installing different type certificated aircraft engines manufactured by him within the United States may apply for a Class I provisional type certificate for the aircraft, and for amendments to Class I provisional type certificates held by him, if the basic aircraft, before alteration, was type certificated in the normal, utility, acrobatic, commuter, or transport category.

[Doc. No. 5085, 29 FR 14566, Oct. 24, 1964, as amended by Amdt. 21-12, 31 FR 13380, Oct. 15, 1966; Amdt. 21-59, 52 FR 1836, Jan. 15, 1987]

§ 21.75 Application.

Applications for provisional type certificates, for amendments thereto, and for provisional amendments to type certificates must be submitted to the Chief, Engineering and Manufacturing Branch, Flight Standards Division, of the region in which the applicant is located (or, in the case of the Western Region, the Chief, Aircraft Engineering Division, and in the case of the European, African, and Middle East Region, the Chief Aircraft Engineering Division), and must be accompanied by the pertinent information specified in this subpart.

[Doc. No. 5085, 29 FR 14566, Oct. 24, 1964, as amended by Amdt. 21-12, 31 FR 13388, Oct. 15, 1966]

§ 21.77 Duration.

(a) Unless sooner surrendered, superseded, revoked, or otherwise terminated, provisional type certificates and amendments thereto are effective for the periods specified in this section.

(b) A Class I provisional type certificate is effective for 24 months after the date of issue.

(c) A Class II provisional type certificate is effective for twelve months after the date of issue.

(d) An amendment to a Class I or Class II provisional type certificate is effective for the duration of the amended certificate.

(e) A provisional amendment to a type certificate is effective for six months after its approval or until the amendment of the type certificate is approved, whichever is first.

[Doc. No. 5085, 29 FR 14566, Oct. 24, 1964 as amended by Amdt. 21-7, 30 FR 14311, Nov. 16, 1965]

§ 21.79 Transferability.

Provisional type certificates are not transferable.

§ 21.81 Requirements for issue and amendment of Class I provisional type certificates.

(a) An applicant is entitled to the issue or amendment of a Class I provisional type certificate if he shows compliance with this section and the Administrator finds that there is no feature, characteristic, or condition that would make the aircraft unsafe when operated in accordance with the limitations established in paragraph (e) of this section and in § 91.41 of this chapter.

(b) The applicant must apply for the issue of a type or supplemental type certificate for the aircraft.

(c) The applicant must certify that—

(1) The aircraft has been designed and constructed in accordance with the airworthiness requirements applicable to the issue of the type or supplemental type certificate applied for;

(2) The aircraft substantially meets the applicable flight characteristic requirements for the type or supplemental type certificate applied for; and

(3) The aircraft can be operated safely under the appropriate operating limitations specified in paragraph (a) of this section.

(d) The applicant must submit a report showing that the aircraft had been flown in all maneuvers necessary to show compliance with the flight requirements for the issue of the type or supplemental type certificate applied for, and to establish that the aircraft can be operated safely in accordance with the limitations contained in this subchapter.

(e) The applicant must establish all limitations required for the issue of the type or supplemental type certificate applied for, including limitations on weights, speeds, flight maneuvers, loading, and operation of controls and equipment unless, for each limitation not so established, appropriate operating restrictions are established for the aircraft.

(f) The applicant must establish an inspection and maintenance program for the continued airworthiness of the aircraft.

(g) The applicant must show that a prototype aircraft has been flown for at least 50 hours under an experimental certificate issued under §§ 21.191 through 21.195, or under the auspices of an Armed Force of the United States. However, in the case of an amendment to a provisional type certificate, the Administrator may reduce the number of required flight hours.

§ 21.83 Requirements for issue and amendment of Class II provisional type certificates.

(a) An applicant who manufactures aircraft within the United States is entitled to the issue or amendment of a Class II provisional type certificate if he shows compliance with this section and the Administrator finds that there is no feature, characteristic, or condition that would make the aircraft unsafe when operated in accordance with the limitations in paragraph (h) of this section, and §§ 91.41 and 121.207 of this chapter.

(b) An applicant who manufactures aircraft in a country with which the United States has an agreement for the acceptance of those aircraft for export and import is entitled to the issue or amendment of a Class II provisional type certificate if the country in which the aircraft was manufactured certifies that the applicant has shown compliance with this section, that the aircraft meets the requirements of paragraph (f) of this section and that there is no feature, charac-

teristic, or condition that would make the aircraft unsafe when operated in accordance with the limitations in paragraph (h) of this section and §§ 91.41 and 121.207 of this chapter.

(c) The applicant must apply for a type certificate, in the transport category, for the aircraft.

(d) The applicant must hold a U.S. type certificate for at least one other aircraft in the same transport category as the subject aircraft.

(e) The FAA's official flight test program or the flight test program conducted by the authorities of the country in which the aircraft was manufactured, with respect to the issue of a type certificate for that aircraft, must be in progress.

(f) The applicant or, in the case of a foreign manufactured aircraft, the country in which the aircraft was manufactured, must certify that—

(1) The aircraft has been designed and constructed in accordance with the airworthiness requirements applicable to the issue of the type certificate applied for;

(2) The aircraft substantially complies with the applicable flight characteristic requirements for the type certificate applied for; and

(3) The aircraft can be operated safely under the appropriate operating limitations in this subchapter.

(g) The applicant must submit a report showing that the aircraft has been flown in all maneuvers necessary to show compliance with the flight requirements for the issue of the type certificate and to establish that the aircraft can be operated safely in accordance with the limitations in this subchapter.

(h) The applicant must prepare a provisional aircraft flight manual containing all limitations required for the issue of the type certificate applied for, including limitations on weights, speeds, flight maneuvers, loading, and operation of controls and equipment unless, for each limitation not so established, appropriate operating restrictions are established for the aircraft.

(i) The applicant must establish an inspection and maintenance program for the continued airworthiness of the aircraft.

(j) The applicant must show that a prototype aircraft has been flown for at least 100 hours. In the case of an amendment to a provisional type certificate, the Administrator may reduce the number of required flight hours.

[Amdt. 21-12, 31 FR 13386, Oct. 15, 1966]

§ 21.85 Provisional amendments to type certificates.

(a) An applicant who manufactures aircraft within the United States is entitled to a provisional amendment to a type certificate if he shows compliance with this section and the Administrator finds that there is no feature, characteristic, or condition that would make the aircraft unsafe when operated under the appropriate limitations contained in this subchapter.

(b) An applicant who manufactures aircraft in a foreign country with which the United States has an agreement for the acceptance of those aircraft for export and import is entitled to a provisional amendment to a type certificate if the country in which the aircraft was manufactured certifies that the applicant has shown compliance with this section, that the aircraft meets the requirements of paragraph (e) of this section and that there is no feature, characteristic, or condition that would make the aircraft unsafe when operated under the appropriate limitations contained in this subchapter.

(c) The applicant must apply for an amendment to the type certificate.

(d) The FAA's official flight test program or the flight test program conducted by the authorities of the country in which the aircraft was manufactured, with respect to the amendment of the type certificate, must be in progress.

(e) The applicant or, in the case of foreign manufactured aircraft, the country in which the aircraft was manufactured, must certify that—

(1) The modification involved in the amendment to the type certificate has been designed and constructed in accordance with the airworthiness requirements applicable to the issue of the type certificate for the aircraft;

(2) The aircraft substantially complies with the applicable flight charac-teristic requirements for the type certificate; and

(3) The aircraft can be operated safely under the appropriate operating limitations in this subchapter.

(f) The applicant must submit a report showing that the aircraft incorporating the modifications involved has been flown in all maneuvers necessary to show compliance with the flight requirements applicable to those modifications and to establish that the aircraft can be operated safely in accordance with the limitations specified in §§ 91.41 and 121.207 of this chapter.

(g) The applicant must establish and publish, in a provisional aircraft flight manual or other document and on appropriate placards, all limitations required for the issue of the type certificate applied for, including weight, speed, flight maneuvers, loading, and operation of controls and equipment, unless, for each limitation not so established, appropriate operating restrictions are established for the aircraft.

(h) The applicant must establish an inspection and maintenance program for the continued airworthiness of the aircraft.

(i) The applicant must operate a prototype aircraft modified in accordance with the corresponding amendment to the type certificate for the number of hours found necessary by the Administrator.

[Amdt. 21-12, 31 FR 13388, Oct. 15, 1966]

Subpart D—Changes to Type Certificates

SOURCE: Docket No. 5085, 29 FR 14567, Oct. 24, 1964, unless otherwise noted.

§ 21.91 Applicability.

This subpart prescribes procedural requirements for the approval of changes to type certificates.

§ 21.93 Classification of changes in type design.

(a) In addition to changes in type design specified in paragraph (b) of this section, changes in type design are classified as minor and major. A "minor change" is one that has no appreciable effect on the weight, balance, structural strength, reliability, operational characteristics, or other characteristics affecting the airworthiness of the product. All other changes are "major changes" (except as provided in paragraph (b) of this section).

(b) For the purpose of complying with Part 36 of this chapter, and except as provided in paragraphs (b)(2), (b)(3), and (b)(4) of this section, any voluntary change in the type design of an aircraft that may increase the noise levels of that aircraft is an "acoustical change" (in addition to being a minor or major change as classified in paragraph (a) of this section) for the following aircraft.

(1) Transport category large airplanes.

(2) Turbojet powered airplanes (regardless of category). For airplanes to which this paragraph applies, "acoustical changes" do not include changes in type design that are limited to one of the following—

(i) Gear down flight with one or more retractable landing gear down during the entire flight, or

(ii) Spare engine and nacelle carriage external to the skin of the airplane (and return of the pylon or other external mount), or

(iii) Time-limited engine and/or nacelle changes, where the change in type design specifies that the airplane may not be operated for a period of more than 90 days unless compliance with the applicable acoustical change provisions of Part 36 of this chapter is shown for that change in type design.

(3) Propeller driven commuter category and small airplanes in the normal, utility, acrobatic, transport, and restricted categories (except for those airplanes that are designated for 'agricultural aircraft operations' (as defined in § 137.3 of this chapter, as effective on January 1, 1966) or for dispensing fire fighting materials to which § 36.1583 of this chapter does not apply). For airplanes to which this paragraph applies, "acoustical changes" are limited to the following type design changes:

(i) Any change to, or removal of, a muffler or other component designed for noise control.

(ii) Any change to, or installation of, a powerplant or propeller that increases maximum continuous power or thrust at sea level, or increases the propeller tip speed at that power or thrust, over that previously approved for the airplane.

(4) Helicopters, (except for those helicopters that are designated exclusively for "agri-cultural aircraft operations", as defined in § 137.3 of this chapter, as effective on January 1, 1966, for dispensing fire fighting materials, or for carrying external loads, as defined in § 133.1(b) of this chapter, as effective on December 20, 1976). For helicopters to which this paragraph applies, "acoustical changes" include the following type design changes:

(i) Any changes to, or removal of, a muffler or other component designed for noise control.

(ii) Any other design or configuration change (including a change in the operating limitations of the aircraft) that, based on FAA-approved analytical or test data, the Administrator determines may result in an increase in noise level.

§ 21.95 Approval of minor changes in type design.

Minor changes in a type design may be approved under a method acceptable to the Administrator before submitting to the Administrator any substantiating or descriptive data.

§ 21.97 Approval of major changes in type design.

(a) In the case of a major change in type design, the applicant must submit substantiating data and necessary descriptive data for inclusion in the type design.

(b) Approval of a major change in the type design of an aircraft engine is limited to the specific engine configuration upon which the change is made unless the applicant identifies in the necessary descriptive data for inclusion in the type design the other configurations of the same engine type for which approval is requested and shows that the change is compatible with the other configurations.

§ 21.99 Required design changes.

(a) When an Airworthiness Directive is issued under Part 39 the holder of the type certificate for the product concerned must—

(1) If the Administrator finds that design changes are necessary to correct the unsafe condition of the product, and upon his request, submit appropriate design changes for approval; and

(2) Upon approval of the design changes, make available the descriptive data covering the changes to all operators of products previously certificated under the type certificate.

(b) In a case where there are no current unsafe conditions, but the Administrator or the holder of the type certificate finds through service experience that changes in type design will contribute to the safety of the product, the holder of the type certificate may submit appropriate design changes for approval. Upon approval of the changes, the manufacturer shall make information on the design changes available to all operators of the same type of product.

[Doc. No. 5085, 29 FR 14567, Oct. 24, 1964, as amended by Amdt. 21–3, 30 FR 8826, July 24, 1965]

§ 21.101 Designation of applicable regulations.

(a) Except as provided in § 23.2, § 25.2 and in Part 36 of this chapter, an applicant for a change to a type certificate must comply with either—

(1) The regulations incorporated by reference in the type certificate; or

(2) The applicable regulations in effect on the date of the application, plus any other amendments the Administrator finds to be directly related.

(b) If the Administrator finds that a proposed change consists of a new design or a substantially complete redesign of a component, equipment installation, or system installation, and that the regulations incorporated by reference in the type certificate for the product do not provide adequate standards with respect to the proposed change, the applicant must comply with—

(1) The applicable provisions of this subchapter, in effect on the date of the application for the change, that the Administrator finds necessary to provide a level of safety equal to that established by the regulations incorporated by reference in the type certificate for the product; and

(2) Any special conditions, and amendments to those special conditions, prescribed by the Administrator to provide a level of safety equal to that established by the regulations incorporated by reference in the type certificate for the product.

(c) Unless otherwise required by § 21.19(a), an applicant for a change to a type certificate for a transport category airplane involving the replacement of reciprocating engines with the same number of turbopropeller powerplants must comply with the requirements of Part 25 of this chapter applicable to the airplane as type certificat-

ed with reciprocating engines, and with the following:

(1) The certification performance requirements prescribed in §§ 25.101 through 25.125 and 25.149, 25.1533, 25.1583, and 25.1587.

(2) The powerplant requirements of Part 25 of this chapter applicable to turbopropeller engine-powered airplanes.

(3) The requirements of Part 25 of this chapter for the standardization of cockpit controls and instruments, unless the Administrator finds that compliance with a particular detailed requirement would be impractical and would not contribute materially to standardization.

(4) Any other requirement of Part 25 of this chapter applicable to turbopropeller engine-powered airplanes that the Administrator finds to be related to the changes in engines and that are necessary to ensure a level of safety equal to that of the airplane certificated with reciprocating engines.

For each new limitation established with respect to weight, speed, or altitude that is significantly altered from those approved for the airplane with reciprocating engines, the applicant must show compliance with the requirements of Part 25 of this chapter applicable to the limitations being changed.

[Doc. No. 5085, 29 FR 14567, Oct. 24, 1964, as amended by Amdt. 21–16, 32 FR 13262, Sept. 20, 1967; Amdt. 21–19, 32 FR 17851, Dec. 13, 1967; Amdt. 21–27, 34 FR 18363, Nov. 18, 1969; Amdt. 21–42, 40 FR 1033, Jan. 6, 1975; Amdt. 21–58, 50 FR 46877, Nov. 13, 1985]

Subpart E—Supplemental Type Certificates

STC

Source: Docket No. 5085, 29 FR 14568, Oct. 24, 1964, unless otherwise noted.

§ 21.111 Applicability.

This subpart prescribes procedural requirements for the issue of supplemental type certificates.

§ 21.113 Requirement of supplemental type certificate.

Any person who alters a product by introducing a major change in type design, not great enough to require a new application for a type certificate under § 21.19, shall apply to the Administrator for a supplemental type certificate, except that the holder of a type certificate for the product may apply for amendment of the original type certificate. The application must be made in a form and manner prescribed by the Administrator.

§ 21.115 Applicable requirements.

(a) Each applicant for a supplemental type certificate must show that the altered product meets applicable airworthiness requirements as specified in paragraphs (a) and (b) of § 21.101 and in the case of an acoustical change described in § 21.93(b), show compliance with the applicable noise requirements of §§ 36.7, 36.9, or 36.11 of this chapter.

(b) Each applicant for a supplemental type certificate must meet §§ 21.33 and 21.53 with respect to each change in the type design.

[Amdt. 21-17, 32 FR 14927, Oct. 28, 1967, as amended by Amdt. 21-42, 40 FR 1033, Jan. 6, 1975; Amdt. 21-52A, 45 FR 79009, Nov. 28, 1980]

§ 21.117 Issue of supplemental type certificates.

(a) An applicant is entitled to a supplemental type certificate if he meets the requirements of §§ 21.113 and 21.115.

(b) A supplemental type certificate consists of—

(1) The approval by the Administrator of a change in the type design of the product; and

(2) The type certificate previously issued for the product.

§ 21.119 Privileges.

The holder of a supplemental type certificate may—

(a) In the case of aircraft, obtain airworthiness certificates;

(b) In the case of other products, obtain approval for installation on certificated aircraft; and

(c) Obtain a production certificate for the change in the type design that was approved by that supplemental type certificate.

Subpart F—Production Under Type Certificate Only

SOURCE: Docket No. 5085, 29 FR 14568, Oct. 24, 1964, unless otherwise noted.

§ 21.121 Applicability.

This subpart prescribes rules for production under a type certificate only.

§ 21.123 Production under type certificate.

Each manufacturer of a product being manufactured under a type certificate only shall—

(a) Make each product available for inspection by the Administrator;

(b) Maintain at the place of manufacture the technical data and drawings necessary for the Administrator to determine whether the product and its parts conform to the type design;

(c) Except as otherwise authorized by the Regional Director in the region in which the manufacturer is located, for products manufactured more than 6 months after the date of issue of the type certificate, establish and maintain an approved production inspection system that insures that each product conforms to the type design and is in condition for safe operation; and

(d) Upon the establishment of the approved production inspection system (as required by paragraph (c) of this section) submit to the Administrator a manual that describes that system and the means for making the determinations required by § 21.125(b).

[Doc. No. 5085, 29 FR 14568, Oct. 24, 1964, as amended by Amdt. 21-34, 35 FR 13008, Aug. 15, 1970; Amdt. 21-51, 45 FR 60170, Sept. 11, 1980]

§ 21.125 Production inspection system: Materials Review Board.

(a) Each manufacturer required to establish a production inspection system by § 21.123(c) shall—

(1) Establish a Materials Review Board (to include representatives from the inspection and engineering departments) and materials review procedures; and

(2) Maintain complete records of Materials Review Board action for at least two years.

(b) The production inspection system required in §21.123(c) must provide a means for determining at least the following:

(1) Incoming materials, and bought or subcontracted parts, used in the finished product must be as specified in the type design data, or must be suitable equivalents.

(2) Incoming materials, and bought or subcontracted parts, must be properly identified if their physical or chemical properties cannot be readily and accurately determined.

(3) Materials subject to damage and deterioration must be suitably stored and adequately protected.

(4) Processes affecting the quality and safety of the finished product must be accomplished in accordance with acceptable industry or United States specifications.

(5) Parts and components in process must be inspected for conformity with the type design data at points in production where accurate determinations can be made.

(6) Current design drawings must be readily available to manufacturing and inspection personnel, and used when necessary.

(7) Design changes, including material substitutions, must be controlled and approved before being incorporated in the finished product.

(8) Rejected materials and parts must be segregated and identified in a manner that precludes installation in the finished product.

(9) Materials and parts that are withheld because of departures from design data or specifications, and that are to be considered for installation in the finished product, must be processed through the Materials Review Board. Those materials and parts determined by the Board to be serviceable must be properly identified and reinspected if rework or repair is necessary. Materials and parts rejected by the Board must be marked and disposed of to ensure that they are not incorporated in the final product.

(10) Inspection records must be maintained, identified with the completed product where practicable, and retained by the manufacturer for at least two years.

§21.127 Tests: aircraft.

(a) Each person manufacturing aircraft under a type certificate only shall establish an approved production flight test procedure and flight check-off form, and in accordance with that form, flight test each aircraft produced.

(b) Each production flight test procedure must include the following:

(1) An operational check of the trim, controllability, or other flight characteristics to establish that the production aircraft has the same range and degree of control as the prototype aircraft.

(2) An operational check of each part or system operated by the crew while in flight to establish that, during flight, instrument readings are within normal range.

(3) A determination that all instruments are properly marked, and that all placards and required flight manuals are installed after flight test.

(4) A check of the operational characteristics of the aircraft on the ground.

(5) A check on any other items peculiar to the aircraft being tested that can best be done during the ground or flight operation of the aircraft.

§21.128 Tests: aircraft engines.

(a) Each person manufacturing aircraft engines under a type certificate only shall subject each engine (except rocket engines for which the manufacturer must establish a sampling technique) to an acceptable test run that includes the following:

(1) Break-in runs that include a determination of fuel and oil consumption and a determination of power characteristics at rated maximum continuous power or thrust and, if applicable, at rated takeoff power or thrust.

(2) At least five hours of operation at rated maximum continuous power or thrust. For engines having a rated takeoff power or thrust higher than rated maximum continuous power or thrust, the five-hour run must include 30 minutes at rated takeoff power or thrust.

(b) The test runs required by paragraph (a) of this section may be made with the engine appropriately mounted and using current types of power and thrust measuring equipment.

[Doc. No. 5085, 29 FR 14568, Oct. 24, 1964, as amended by Amdt. 21-5, 32 FR 3735, Mar. 4, 1967]

§ 21.129 Tests: propellers.

Each person manufacturing propellers under a type certificate only shall give each variable pitch propeller an acceptable functional test to determine if it operates properly throughout the normal range of operation.

§ 21.130 Statement of conformity.

Each holder or licensee of a type certificate only, for a product manufactured in the United States, shall, upon the initial transfer by him of the ownership of such product manufactured under that type certificate, or upon application for the original issue of an aircraft airworthiness certificate or an aircraft engine or propeller airworthiness approval tag (FAA Form 8130-3), give the Administrator a statement of conformity (FAA Form 317). This statement must be signed by an authorized person who holds a responsible position in the manufacturing organization, and must include—

(a) For each product, a statement that the product conforms to its type certificate and is in condition for safe operation;

(b) For each aircraft, a statement that the aircraft has been flight checked; and

(c) For each aircraft engine or variable pitch propeller, a statement that the engine or propeller has been subjected by the manufacturer to a final operational check.

However, in the case of a product manufactured for an Armed Force of the United States, a statement of conformity is not required if the product has been accepted by that Armed Force.

[Amdt. 21-25, 34 FR 14068, Sept. 5, 1969]

Subpart G—Production Certificates

SOURCE: Docket No. 5085, 29 FR 14569, Oct. 24, 1964, unless otherwise noted.

§ 21.131 Applicability.

This subpart prescribes procedural requirements for the issue of production certificates and rules governing the holders of those certificates.

§ 21.133 Eligibility.

(a) Any person may apply for a production certificate if he holds, for the product concerned, a—

(1) Current type certificate;

(2) Right to the benefits of that type certificate under a licensing agreement; or

(3) Supplemental type certificate.

(b) Each application for a production certificate must be made in a form and manner prescribed by the Administrator.

§ 21.135 Requirements for issuance.

An applicant is entitled to a production certificate if the Administrator finds, after examination of the supporting data and after inspection of the organization and production facilities, that the applicant has complied with §§ 21.139 and 21.143.

§ 21.137 Location of manufacturing facilities.

The Administrator does not issue a production certificate if the manufacturing facilities concerned are located outside the United States, unless the Administrator finds no undue burden on the United States in administering the applicable requirements of the Federal Aviation Act of 1958 or of the Federal Aviation Regulations.

§ 21.139 Quality control.

The applicant must show that he has established and can maintain a quality control system for any product, for which he requests a production certificate, so that each article will meet the design provisions of the pertinent type certificate.

§ 21.143 Quality control data requirements; prime manufacturer.

(a) Each applicant must submit, for approval, data describing the inspection and test procedures necessary to ensure that each article produced conforms to the type design and is in a condition for safe operation, including as applicable—

(1) A statement describing assigned responsibilities and delegated authority of the quality control organization, together with a chart indicating the functional relationship of the quality control organization to management and to other organizational components, and indicating the chain of authority and responsibility within the quality control organization;

(2) A description of inspection procedures for raw materials, purchased items, and parts and assemblies produced by manufacturers' suppliers including methods used to ensure acceptable quality of parts and assemblies that cannot be completely inspected for conformity and quality when delivered to the prime manufacturer's plant;

(3) A description of the methods used for production inspection of individual parts and complete assemblies, including the identification of any special manufacturing processes involved, the means used to control the processes, the final test procedure for the complete product, and, in the case of aircraft, a copy of the manufacturer's production flight test procedures and checkoff list;

(4) An outline of the materials review system, including the procedure for recording review board decisions and disposing of rejected parts;

(5) An outline of a system for informing company inspectors of current changes in engineering drawings, specifications, and quality control procedures; and

(6) A list or chart showing the location and type of inspection stations.

(b) Each prime manufacturer shall make available to the Administrator information regarding all delegation of authority to suppliers to make major inspections of parts or assemblies for which the prime manufacturer is responsible.

[Doc. No. 5085, 29 FR 14569, Oct. 24, 1964, as amended by Amdt. 21-51, 45 FR 60170, Sept. 11, 1980]

§21.147 Changes in quality control system.

After the issue of a production certificate, each change to the quality control system is subject to review by the Administrator. The holder of a production certificate shall immediately notify the Administrator, in writing of any change that may affect the inspection, conformity, or airworthiness of the product.

§21.149 Multiple products.

The Administrator may authorize more than one type certificated product to be manufactured under the terms of one production certificate, if the products have similar production characteristics.

§21.151 Production limitation record.

A production limitation record is issued as part of a production certificate. The record lists the type certificate of every product that the applicant is authorized to manufacture under the terms of the production certificate.

§21.153 Amendment of the production certificates.

The holder of a production certificate desiring to amend it to add a type certificate or model, or both, must apply therefor in a form and manner prescribed by the Administrator. The applicant must comply with the applicable requirements of §§ 21.139, 21.143, and 21.147.

§21.155 Transferability.

A production certificate is not transferable.

§21.157 Inspections and tests.

Each holder of a production certificate shall allow the Administrator to make any inspections and tests necessary to determine compliance with the applicable regulations in this subchapter.

§21.159 Duration.

A production certificate is effective until surrendered, suspended, revoked, or a termination date is otherwise established by the Administrator, or the location of the manufacturing facility is changed.

§ 21.161 Display.

The holder of a production certificate shall display it prominently in the main office of the factory in which the product concerned is manufactured.

§ 21.163 Privileges.

The holder of a production certificate may—

(a) Obtain an aircraft airworthiness certificate without further showing, except that the Administrator may inspect the aircraft for conformity with the type design; or

(b) In the case of other products, obtain approval for installation on certificated aircraft.

§ 21.165 Responsibility of holder.

The holder of a production certificate shall—

(a) Maintain the quality control system in conformity with the data and procedures approved for the production certificate; and

(b) Determine that each completed product submitted for airworthiness certification or approval conforms to the type design and is in a condition for safe operation.

Subpart H—Airworthiness Certificates

SOURCE: Docket No. 5085, 29 FR 14570, Oct. 24, 1964, unless otherwise noted.

§ 21.171 Applicability.

This subpart prescribes procedural requirements for the issue of airworthiness certificates.

§ 21.173 Eligibility.

Any registered owner of a U.S.-registered aircraft (or the agent of the owner) may apply for an airworthiness certificate for that aircraft. An application for an airworthiness certificate must be made in a form and manner acceptable to the Administrator, and may be submitted to any FAA office.

[Amdt. 21-26, 34 FR 15244, Sept. 30, 1969]

§ 21.175 Airworthiness certificates: classification.

(a) Standard airworthiness certificates are airworthiness certificates issued for aircraft type certificated in the normal, utility, acrobatic, commuter, or transport category, and for manned free balloons, and for aircraft designated by the Administrator as special classes of aircraft.

(b) Special airworthiness certificates are restricted, limited, and provisional airworthiness certificates, special flight permits, and experimental certificates.

[Amdt. 21-21, 33 FR 6858, May 7, 1968, as amended by Amdt. 21-60, 52 FR 8043, Mar. 13, 1987]

§ 21.177 Amendment or modification.

An airworthiness certificate may be amended or modified only upon application to the Administrator.

§ 21.179 Transferability.

An airworthiness certificate is transferred with the aircraft.

§ 21.181 Duration.

(a) Unless sooner surrendered, suspended, revoked, or a termination date is otherwise established by the Administrator, airworthiness certificates are effective as follows:

(1) Standard airworthiness certificates and airworthiness certificates issued for restricted or limited category aircraft are effective as long as the maintenance, preventive maintenance, and alterations are performed in accordance with Parts 43 and 91 of this chapter and the aircraft are registered in the United States.

(2) A special flight permit is effective for the period of time specified in the permit.

(3) An experimental certificate for research and development, showing compliance with regulations, crew training, or market surveys is effective for one year after the date of issue or renewal unless a shorter period is prescribed by the Administrator. The duration of amateur-built, exhibition, and air-racing experimental certificates will be unlimited unless the Administrator finds for good cause that a specific period should be established.

(b) The owner, operator, or bailee of the aircraft shall, upon request, make it available for inspection by the Administrator.

(c) Upon suspension, revocation, or termination by order of the Administrator of an airworthiness certificate, the owner, operator, or bailee of an aircraft shall, upon request, surrender the certificate to the Administrator.

[Amdt. 21-21, 33 FR 6858, May 7, 1968, as amended by Amdt. 21-49, 44 FR 46781, Aug. 9, 1979]

§ 21.182   Aircraft identification.

(a) Except as provided in paragraph (b) of this section, each applicant for an airworthiness certificate under this subpart must show that his aircraft is identified as prescribed in § 45.11.

(b) Paragraph (a) of this section does not apply to applicants for the following:

(1) A special flight permit.

(2) An experimental certificate for an aircraft that is not amateur built.

(3) A change from one airworthiness classification to another, for an aircraft already identified as prescribed in § 45.11.

[Amdt. 21-13, 32 FR 188, Jan. 10, 1967, as amended by Amdt. 21-51, 45 FR 60170, Sept. 11, 1980]

§ 21.183   Issue of standard airworthiness certificates for normal, utility, acrobatic, commuter, and transport category aircraft; manned free balloons; and special classes of aircraft.

(a) *New aircraft manufactured under a production certificate.* An applicant for a standard airworthiness certificate for a new aircraft manufactured under a production certificate is entitled to a standard airworthiness certificate without further showing, except that the Administrator may inspect the aircraft to determine conformity to the type design and condition for safe operation.

(b) *New aircraft manufactured under type certificate only.* An applicant for a standard airworthiness certificate for a new aircraft manufactured under a type certificate only is entitled to a standard airworthiness certificate upon presentation, by the holder or licensee of the type certificate, of the statement of conformity prescribed in § 21.130 if the Administrator finds after inspection that the aircraft conforms to the type design and is in condition for safe operation.

(c) *Import aircraft.* An applicant for a standard airworthiness certificate for an import aircraft type certificated in accordance with § 21.29 is entitled to an airworthiness certificate if the country in which the aircraft was manufactured certifies, and the Administrator finds, that the aircraft conforms to the type design and is in condition for safe operation.

(d) *Other aircraft.* An applicant for a standard airworthiness certificate for aircraft not covered by paragraphs (a) through (c) of this section is entitled to a standard airworthiness certificate if—

(1) He presents evidence to the Administrator that the aircraft conforms to a type design approved under a type certificate or a supplemental type certificate and to applicable Airworthiness Directives;

(2) The aircraft (except an experimentally certificated aircraft that previously had been issued a different airworthiness certificate under this section) has been inspected in accordance with the performance rules for 100-hour inspections set forth in § 43.15 of this chapter and found airworthy by—

(i) The manufacturer;

(ii) The holder of a repair station certificate as provided in Part 145 of this chapter;

(iii) The holder of a mechanic certificate as authorized in Part 65 of this chapter; or

(iv) The holder of a certificate issued under Part 121 or 127 of this chapter, and having a maintenance and inspection organization appropriate to the aircraft type; and

(3) The Administrator finds after inspection, that the aircraft conforms to the type design, and is in condition for safe operation.

(e) *Noise requirements.* Notwithstanding all other provisions of this section, the following must be complied with for the original issuance of a standard airworthiness certificate:

(1) For transport category large airplanes and turbojet powered airplanes that have not had any flight time before the dates specified in § 36.1(d), no standard airworthiness certificate is originally issued under this section unless the Administrator finds that the type design complies with the

noise requirements in § 36.1(d) in addition to the applicable airworthiness requirements in this section. For import airplanes, compliance with this paragraph is shown if the country in which the airplane was manufactured certifies, and the Administrator finds, that § 36.1(d) (or the applicable airplane noise requirements of the country in which the airplane was manufactured and any other requirements the Administrator may prescribe to provide noise levels no greater than those provided by compliance with § 36.1(d)) and paragraph (c) of this section are complied with.

(2) For normal, utility, acrobatic, commuter, or transport category propeller driven small airplanes (except for those airplanes that are designed for "agricultural aircraft operations" (as defined in § 137.3 of this chapter, as effective on January 1, 1966) or for dispensing fire fighting materials to which § 36.1583 of this chapter does not apply) that have not had any flight time before the applicable date specified in Part 36 of this chapter, no standard airworthiness certificate is originally issued under this section unless the applicant shows that the type design complies with the applicable noise requirements of Part 36 of this chapter in addition to the applicable airworthiness requirements in this section. For import airplanes, compliance with this paragraph is shown if the country in which the airplane was manufactured certifies, and the Administrator finds, that the applicable requirements of Part 36 of this chapter (or the applicable airplane noise requirements of the country in which the airplane was manufactured and any other requirements the Administrator may prescribe to provide noise levels no greater than those provided by compliance with the applicable requirements of Part 36 of this chapter) and paragraph (c) of this section are complied with.

[Amdt. 21-17, 32 FR 14927, Oct. 28, 1967, as amended by Amdt. 21-20, 33 FR 3055, Feb. 16, 1968; Amdt. 21-25, 34 FR 14068, Sept. 5, 1969; Amdt. 21-42, 40 FR 1033, Jan. 6, 1975; Amdt. 21-47, 43 FR 28419, June 29, 1978; Amdt. 21-52, 45 FR 67066, Oct. 9, 1980; Amdt. 21-59, 52 FR 1836, Jan. 15, 1987; Amdt. 21-60, 52 FR 8043, Mar. 13, 1987]

§ 21.185   Issue of airworthiness certificates for restricted category aircraft.

(a) *Aircraft manufactured under a production certificate or type certificate only.* An applicant for the original issue of a restricted category airworthiness certificate for an aircraft type certificated in the restricted category, that was not previously type certificated in any other category, must comply with the appropriate provisions of § 21.183.

(b) *Other aircraft.* An applicant for a restricted category airworthiness certificate for an aircraft type certificated in the restricted category, that was either a surplus aircraft of the Armed Forces or previously type certificated in another category, is entitled to an airworthiness certificate if the aircraft has been inspected by the Administrator and found by him to be in a good state of preservation and repair and in a condition for safe operation.

(c) *Import aircraft.* An applicant for the original issue of a restricted category airworthiness certificate for an import aircraft type certificated in the restricted category only in accordance with § 21.29 is entitled to an airworthiness certificate if the country in which the aircraft was manufactured certifies, and the Administrator finds, that the aircraft conforms to the type design and is in a condition for safe operation.

(d) *Noise requirements.* For propeller-driven small airplanes (except airplanes designed for "agricultural aircraft operations," as defined in § 137.3 of this chapter, as effective on January 1, 1966, or for dispensing fire fighting materials) that have not had any flight time before the applicable date specified in Part 36 of this chapter, and notwithstanding the other provisions of this section, no original restricted category airworthiness certificate is issued under this section unless the Administrator finds that the type design complies with the applicable noise requirements of Part 36 of this chapter in addition to the applicable airworthiness requirements of this section. For import airplanes, compliance with this paragraph is shown if the country in which the airplane was manufactured certifies, and the Administrator finds, that the applicable requirements of Part 36 of this chapter (or the applicable airplane noise requirements of the country in which the airplane was manufactured and any other requirements the Administrator may prescribe to provide noise levels no greater than those provided by compliance with the applicable requirements of Part 36 of this chapter) and paragraph (c) of this section are complied with.

[Amdt. 21-10, 31 FR 9211, July 6, 1966; as amended by Amdt. 21-32, 35 FR 10202, June 23, 1970; Amdt. 21-42, 40 FR 1034, Jan. 6, 1975]

§ 21.187 Issue of multiple airworthiness certification.

(a) An applicant for an airworthiness certificate in the restricted category, and in one or more other categories, is entitled to the certificate, if—

(1) He shows compliance with the requirements for each category, when the aircraft is in the configuration for that category; and

(2) He shows that the aircraft can be converted from one category to another by removing or adding equipment by simple mechanical means.

(b) The operator of an aircraft certificated under this section shall have the aircraft inspected by the Administrator, or by a certificated mechanic with an appropriate airframe rating, to determine airworthiness each time the aircraft is converted from the restricted category to another category for the carriage of passengers for compensation or hire, unless the Administrator finds this unnecessary for safety in a particular case.

§ 21.189 Issue of airworthiness certificate for limited category aircraft.

(a) An applicant for an airworthiness certificate for an aircraft in the limited category is entitled to the certificate when—

(1) He shows that the aircraft has been previously issued a limited category type certificate and that the aircraft conforms to that type certificate; and

(2) The Administrator finds, after inspection (including a flight check by the applicant), that the aircraft is in a good state of preservation and repair and is in a condition for safe operation.

(b) The Administrator prescribes limitations and conditions necessary for safe operation.

[Doc. No. 5085, 29 FR 14570, Oct. 24, 1964, as amended by Amdt. 21-4, 30 FR 9437, July 29, 1965]

§ 21.191 Experimental certificates.

Experimental certificates are issued for the following purposes:

(a) *Research and development.* Testing new aircraft design concepts, new aircraft equipment, new aircraft installations, new aircraft operating techniques, or new uses for aircraft.

(b) *Showing compliance with regulations.* Conducting flight tests and other operations to show compliance with the airworthiness regulations including flights to show compliance for issuance of type and supplemental type certificates, flights to substantiate major design changes, and flights to show compliance with the function and reliability requirements of the regulations.

(c) *Crew training.* Training of the applicant's flight crews.

(d) *Exhibition.* Exhibiting the aircraft's flight capabilities, performance, or unusual characteristics at air shows, motion picture, television, and similar productions, and the maintenance of exhibition flight proficiency, including (for persons exhibiting aircraft) flying to and from such air shows and productions.

(e) *Air racing.* Participating in air races, including (for such participants) practicing for such air races and flying to and from racing events.

(f) *Market surveys.* Use of aircraft for purposes of conducting market surveys, sales demonstrations, and customer crew training only as provided in § 21.195.

(g) *Operating amateur-built aircraft.* Operating an aircraft the major portion of which has been fabricated and assembled by persons who undertook the construction project solely for their own education or recreation.

[Amdt. 21-21, 38 FR 6858, May 7, 1968, as amended by Amdt. 21-57, 49 FR 39651, Oct. 9, 1984]

§ 21.193 Experimental certificates: general.

An applicant for an experimental certificate must submit the following information:

(a) A statement, in a form and manner prescribed by the Administrator setting forth the purpose for which the aircraft is to be used.

(b) Enough data (such as photographs) to identify the aircraft.

(c) Upon inspection of the aircraft, any pertinent information found necessary by the Administrator to safeguard the general public.

(d) In the case of an aircraft to be used for experimental purposes—

(1) The purpose of the experiment;

(2) The estimated time or number of flights required for the experiment;

(3) The areas over which the experiment will be conducted; and

(4) Except for aircraft converted from a previously certificated type without appreciable change in the external configuration, three-view drawings or three-view dimensioned photographs of the aircraft.

§ 21.195 Experimental certificates: Aircraft to be used for market surveys, sales demonstrations, and customer crew training.

(a) A manufacturer of aircraft manufactured within the United States may apply for an experimental certificate for an aircraft that is to be used for market surveys, sales demonstrations, or customer crew training.

(b) A manufacturer of aircraft engines who has altered a type certificated aircraft by installing different engines, manufactured by him within the United States, may apply for an experimental certificate for that aircraft to be used for market surveys, sales demonstrations, or customer crew training, if the basic aircraft, before alteration, was type certificated in the normal, acrobatic, commuter, or transport category.

(c) A person who has altered the design of a type certificated aircraft may apply for an experimental certificate for the altered aircraft to be used for market surveys, sales demonstrations, or customer crew training if the basic aircraft, before alteration, was type certificated in the normal, utility, acrobatic, or transport category.

(d) An applicant for an experimental certificate under this section is entitled to that certificate if, in addition to meeting the requirements of § 21.193—

(1) He has established an inspection and maintenance program for the continued airworthiness of the aircraft; and

(2) He shows that the aircraft has been flown for at least 50 hours, or for at least 5 hours if it is a type certificated aircraft which has been modified.

[Amdt. 21-21, 33 FR 6858, May 7, 1968, as amended by Amdt. 21-28, 35 FR 2818, Feb. 11, 1970; Amdt. 21-57, 49 FR 39651, Oct. 9, 1984; Amdt. 21-59, 52 FR 1836, Jan. 15, 1987]

§ 21.197 Special flight permits.

(a) A special flight permit may be issued for an aircraft that may not currently meet applicable airworthiness requirements but is capable of safe flight, for the following purposes:

(1) Flying the aircraft to a base where repairs, alterations, or maintenance are to be performed, or to a point of storage.

(2) Delivering or exporting the aircraft.

(3) Production flight testing new production aircraft.

(4) Evacuating aircraft from areas of impending danger.

(5) Conducting customer demonstration flights in new production aircraft that have satisfactorily completed production flight tests.

(b) A special flight permit may also be issued to authorize the operation of an aircraft at a weight in excess of its maximum certificated takeoff weight for flight beyond the normal range over water, or over land areas where adequate landing facilities or appropriate fuel is not available. The excess weight that may be authorized under this paragraph is limited to the additional fuel, fuel-carrying facilities, and navigation equipment necessary for the flight.

(c) Upon application, as prescribed in §§ 121.79, 127.27, and 135.17 of this chapter, a special flight permit with a continuing authorization may be issued for aircraft that may not meet applicable airworthiness requirements but are capable of safe flight for the purpose of flying aircraft to a base where maintenance or alterations are to be performed. The permit issued under this paragraph is an authorization, including conditions and limitations for flight, which is set forth in the certificate holder's operations specifications. The permit issued under this paragraph may be issued to—

(1) Certificate holders authorized to conduct operations under Part 121 or Part 127 of this chapter; or

(2) Certificate holders authorized to conduct operations under Part 135 for those aircraft they operate and maintain under a continuous airworthiness maintenance program prescribed by § 135.411 (a)(2) or (b) of that part.

The permit issued under this paragraph is an authorization, including any conditions and limitations for flight, which is set forth in the certificate holder's operations specifications.

[Doc. No. 5085, 29 FR 14570, Oct. 24, 1964, as amended by Amdt. 21-21, 33 FR 6859, May 7, 1968; Amdt. 21—51, 45 FR 60170, Sept. 11, 1980; Amdt. 21-54, 46 FR 37878, July 23, 1981]

§ 21.199 Issue of special flight permits.

(a) Except as provided in § 21.197(c), an applicant for a special flight permit must submit a statement in a form and manner prescribed by the Administrator, indicating—

(1) The purpose of the flight.

(2) The proposed itinerary.

(3) The crew required to operate the aircraft and its equipment, e.g., pilot, co-pilot, navigator, etc.

(4) The ways, if any, in which the aircraft does not comply with the applicable airworthiness requirements.

(5) Any restriction the applicant considers necessary for safe operation of the aircraft.

(6) Any other information considered necessary by the Administrator for the purpose of prescribing operating limitations.

(b) The Administrator may make, or require the applicant to make appropriate inspections or tests necessary for safety.

[Doc. No. 5085, 29 FR 14570, Oct. 24, 1964, as amended by Amdt. 21-21, 33 FR 6859, May 7, 1968; Amdt. 21-22, 33 FR 11901, Aug. 22, 1968]

Subpart I—Provisional Airworthiness Certificates

SOURCE: Docket No. 5085, 29 FR 14571, Oct. 24, 1964, unless otherwise noted.

§ 21.211 Applicability.

This subpart prescribes procedural requirements for the issue of provisional airworthiness certificates.

§ 21.213 Eligibility.

(a) A manufacturer who is a United States citizen may apply for a Class I or Class II provisional airworthiness certificate for aircraft manufactured by him within the U.S.

(b) Any holder of an air carrier operating certificate under Part 121 or Part 127 of this chapter who is a United States citizen may apply for a Class II provisional airworthiness certificate for transport category aircraft that meet either of the following:

(1) The aircraft has a current Class II provisional type certificate or an amendment thereto.

(2) The aircraft has a current provisional amendment to a type certificate that was preceded by a corresponding Class II provisional type certificate.

(c) An aircraft engine manufacturer who is a United States citizen and who has altered a type certificated aircraft by installing different type certificated engines, manufactured by him within the United States, may apply for a Class I provisional airworthiness certificate for that aircraft, if the basic aircraft, before alteration, was type certificated in the normal, utility, acrobatic, commuter, or transport category.

[Doc. No. 5085, 29 FR 14571, Oct. 24, 1964, as amended by Amdt. 21-59, 52 FR 1836, Jan. 15, 1987]

§ 21.215 Application.

Applications for provisional airworthiness certificates must be submitted to the Chief, Engineering and Manufacturing Branch, Flight Standards Division, of the region in which the

FAA Regional Office for the area in which the manufacturer or air carrier is located (or, in the case of the Western Region, the Chief, Aircraft Engineering Division). The application must be accompanied by the pertinent information specified in this subpart.

§ 21.217 Duration.

Unless sooner surrendered, superseded, revoked, or otherwise terminated, provisional airworthiness certificates are effective for the duration of the corresponding provisional type certificate, amendment to a provisional type certificate, or provisional amendment to the type certificate.

§ 21.219 Transferability.

Class I provisional airworthiness certificates are not transferable. Class II provisional airworthiness certificates may be transferred to an air carrier eligible to apply for a certificate under § 21.213(b).

§ 21.221 Class I provisional airworthiness certificates.

(a) Except as provided in § 21.225, an applicant is entitled to a Class I provisional airworthiness certificate for an aircraft for which a Class I provisional type certificate has been issued if—

(1) He meets the eligibility requirements of § 21.213 and he complies with this section; and

(2) The Administrator finds that there is no feature, characteristic or condition of the aircraft that would make the aircraft unsafe when operated in accordance with the limitations established in §§ 21.81(e) and 91.41 of this subchapter.

(b) The manufacturer must hold a provisional type certificate for the aircraft.

(c) The manufacturer must submit a statement that the aircraft conforms to the type design corresponding to the provisional type certificate and has been found by him to be in safe operating condition under all applicable limitations.

(d) The aircraft must be flown at least five hours by the manufacturer.

(e) The aircraft must be supplied with a provisional aircraft flight manual or other document and appropriate placards containing the limitations established by §§ 21.81(e) and 91.41.

§ 21.223 Class II provisional airworthiness certificates.

(a) Except as provided in § 21.225, an applicant is entitled to a Class II provisional airworthiness certificate for an aircraft for which a Class II provisional type certificate has been issued if—

(1) He meets the eligibility requirements of § 21.213 and he complies with this section; and

(2) The Administrator finds that there is no feature, characteristic, or condition of the aircraft that would make the aircraft unsafe when operated in accordance with the limitations established in §§ 21.83(h), 91.41, and 121.207 of this chapter.

(b) The applicant must show that a Class II provisional type certificate for the aircraft has been issued to the manufacturer.

(c) The applicant must submit a statement by the manufacturer that the aircraft has been manufactured under a quality control system adequate to ensure that the aircraft conforms to the type design corresponding with the provisional type certificate.

(d) The applicant must submit a statement that the aircraft has been found by him to be in a safe operating condition under the applicable limitations.

(e) The aircraft must be flown at least five hours by the manufacturer.

(f) The aircraft must be supplied with a provisional aircraft flight manual containing the limitations established by §§ 21.83(h), 91.41, and 121.207 of this chapter.

[Doc. No. 5085, 29 FR 14571, Oct. 24, 1964, as amended by Amdt. 21-12, 31 FR 13389, Oct. 15, 1966]

§ 21.225 Provisional airworthiness certificates corresponding with provisional amendments to type certificates.

(a) An applicant is entitled to a Class I or a Class II provisional airworthiness certificate, for an aircraft, for which a provisional amendment to the type certificate has been issued, if—

(1) He meets the eligibility requirements of § 21.213 and he complies with this section; and

(2) The Administrator finds that there is no feature, characteristic, or condition of the aircraft, as modified in accordance with the provisionally amended type certificate, that would make the aircraft unsafe when operated in accordance with the applicable limitations established in §§ 21.85(g), 91.41, and 121.207 of this chapter.

(b) The applicant must show that the modification was made under a quality control system adequate to ensure that the modification conforms to the provisionally amended type certificate.

(c) The applicant must submit a statement that the aircraft has been found by him to be in a safe operating condition under the applicable limitations.

(d) The aircraft must be flown at least five hours by the manufacturer.

(e) The aircraft must be supplied with a provisional aircraft flight manual or other document and appropriate placards containing the limitations required by §§ 21.85(g), 91.41, and 121.207 of this chapter.

[Doc. No. 5085, 29 FR 14571, Oct. 24, 1964, as amended by Amdt. 21-12, 31 FR 13389, Oct. 15, 1966]

Subpart J—Delegation Option Authorization Procedures

SOURCE: Amdt. 21-5, 30 FR 11375, Sept. 8, 1965, unless otherwise noted.

§ 21.231 Applicability.

This subpart prescribes procedures for—

(a) Obtaining and using a delegation option authorization for type, production, and airworthiness certification (as applicable) of—

(1) Small airplanes and small gliders;

(2) Commuter category airplanes;

(3) Normal category rotorcraft;

(4) Turbojet engines of not more than 1,000 pounds thrust;

(5) Turbopropeller and reciprocating engines of not more than 500 brake horsepower; and

(6) Propellers manufactured for use on engines covered by paragraph (a)(4) of this section; and

(b) Issuing airworthiness approval tags for engines, propellers, and parts of products covered by paragraph (a) of this section.

[Amdt. 21-5, 30 FR 11375, Sept. 8, 1965, as amended by Amdt. 21-59, 52 FR 1836, Jan. 15, 1987]

§ 21.235 Application.

(a) An application for a delegation option authorization must be submitted, in a form and manner prescribed by the Administrator, to the FAA Regional Office for the area in which the manufacturer is located.

(b) The application must include the names, signatures, and titles of the persons for whom authorization to sign airworthiness certificates, repair and alteration forms, and inspection forms is requested.

§ 21.239 Eligibility.

To be eligible for a delegation option authorization, the applicant must—

(a) Hold a current type certificate, issued to him under the standard procedures, for a product type certificated under the same part as the products for which the delegation option authorization is sought;

(b) Hold a current production certificate issued under the standard procedures;

(c) Employ a staff of engineering, flight test, production and inspection personnel who can determine compliance with the applicable airworthiness requirements of this chapter; and

(d) Meet the requirements of this subpart.

§ 21.243 Duration.

A delegation option authorization is effective until it is surrendered or the Administrator suspends, revokes, or otherwise terminates it.

§ 21.245 Maintenance of eligibility.

The holder of a delegation option authorization shall continue to meet the requirements for issue of the authorization or shall notify the Administrator within 48 hours of any change (including a change of personnel) that could affect the ability of the holder to meet those requirements.

§ 21.247   Transferability.

A delegation option authorization is not transferable.

§ 21.249   Inspections.

Upon request, each holder of a delegation option authorization and each applicant shall let the Administrator inspect his organization, facilities, product, and records.

§ 21.251   Limits of applicability.

(a) Delegation option authorizations apply only to products that are manufactured by the holder of the authorization.

(b) Delegation option authorizations may be used for—

(1) Type certification;

(2) Changes in the type design of products for which the manufacturer holds, or obtains, a type certificate;

(3) The amendment of a production certificate held by the manufacturer to include additional models or additional types for which he holds or obtains a type certificate; and

(4) The issue of—

(i) Experimental certificates for aircraft for which the manufacturer has applied for a type certificate or amended type certificate under § 21.253, to permit the operation of those aircraft for the purpose of research and development, crew training, market surveys, or the showing of compliance with the applicable airworthiness requirements;

(ii) Airworthiness certificates (other than experimental certificates) for aircraft for which the manufacturer holds a type certificate and holds or is in the process of obtaining a production certificate;

(iii) Airworthiness approval tags (FAA Form 8130-3) for engines and propellers for which the manufacturer holds a type certificate and holds or is in the process of obtaining a production certificate; and

(iv) Airworthiness approval tags (FAA Form 8130-3) for parts of products covered by this section.

(c) Delegation option procedures may be applied to one or more types selected by the manufacturer, who must notify the FAA of each model, and of the first serial number of each model manufactured by him under the delegation option procedures. Other types or models may remain under the standard procedures.

(d) Delegation option authorizations are subject to any additional limitations prescribed by the Administrator after inspection of the applicant's facilities or review of the staff qualifications.

[Amdt. 21-5, 30 FR 11375, Sept. 8, 1965, as amended by Amdt. 21-31, 35 FR 7292, May 9, 1970; Amdt. 21-43, 40 FR 2576, Jan. 14, 1975]

§ 21.253   Type certificates: application.

(a) To obtain, under the delegation option authorization, a type certificate for a new product or an amended type certificate, the manufacturer must submit to the Administrator—

(1) An application for a type certificate (FAA Form 312);

(2) A statement listing the airworthiness requirements of this chapter (by part number and effective date) that the manufacturer considers applicable;

(3) After determining that the type design meets the applicable requirements, a statement certifying that this determination has been made;

(4) After placing the required technical data and type inspection report in the technical data file required by § 21.293(a)(1)(i), a statement certifying that this has been done;

(5) A proposed type certificate data sheet; and

(6) An Aircraft Flight Manual (if required) or a summary of required operating limitations and other information necessary for safe operation of the product.

§ 21.257   Type certificates: issue.

An applicant is entitled to a type certificate for a product manufactured under a delegation option authorization if the Administrator finds that the product meets the applicable airworthiness and noise requirements (including applicable acoustical change requirements in the case of changes in type design).

[Doc. No. 13243, 40 FR 1034, Jan. 6, 1975]

§ 21.261   Equivalent safety provisions.

The manufacturer shall obtain the Administrator's concurrence on the application of all equivalent safety provisions applied under § 21.21.

§ 21.267 Production certificates.

To have a new model or new type certificate listed on his production certificate (issued under Subpart G of this part), the manufacturer must submit to the Administrator—

(a) An application for an amendment to the production certificate;

(b) After determining that the production certification requirements of Subpart G, with respect to the new model or type, are met, a statement certifying that this determination has been made;

(c) A statement identifying the type certificate number under which the product is being manufactured; and

(d) After placing the manufacturing and quality control data required by § 21.143 with the data required by § 21.293(a)(1)(ii), a statement certifying that this has been done.

§ 21.269 Export airworthiness approvals.

The manufacturer may issue export airworthiness approvals.

§ 21.271 Airworthiness approval tags.

(a) A manufacturer may issue an airworthiness approval tag (FAA Form 8130–3) for each engine and propeller covered by § 21.251(b)(4), and may issue an airworthiness approval tag for parts of each product covered by that section, if he finds, on the basis of inspection and operation tests, that those products conform to a type design for which he holds a type certificate and are in condition for safe operation.

(b) When a new model has been included on the Production Limitation Record, the production certification number shall be stamped on the engine or propeller identification data place instead of issuing an airworthiness approval tag.

[Amdt. 21–5, 30 FR 11375, Sept. 8, 1965, as amended by Amdt. 21–43, 40 FR 2577, Jan. 14, 1975]

§ 21.273 Airworthiness certificates other than experimental.

(a) The manufacturer may issue an airworthiness certificate for aircraft manufactured under a delegation option authorization if he finds, on the basis of the inspection and production flight check, that each aircraft conforms to a type design for which he holds a type certificate and is in a condition for safe operation.

(b) The manufacturer may authorize any employee to sign airworthiness certificates if that employee—

(1) Performs, or is in direct charge of, the inspection specified in paragraph (a) of this section; and

(2) Is listed on the manufacturer's application for the delegation option authorization, or on amendments thereof.

[Amdt. 21–5, 30 FR 11375, Sept. 8, 1965, as amended by Amdt. 21–18, 32 FR 15472, Nov. 7, 1967]

§ 21.275 Experimental certificates.

(a) The manufacturer shall, before issuing an experimental certificate, obtain from the Administration any limitations and conditions that the Administrator considers necessary for safety.

(b) For experimental certificates issued by the manufacturer, under this subpart, for aircraft for which the manufacturer holds the type certificate and which have undergone changes to the type design requiring flight test, the manufacturer may prescribe any operating limitations that he considers necessary.

§ 21.277 Data review and service experience.

(a) If the Administrator finds that a product for which a type certificate was issued under this subpart does not meet the applicable airworthiness requirements, or that an unsafe feature or characteristic caused by a defect in design or manufacture exists, the manufacturer, upon notification by the Administrator, shall investigate the matter and report to the Administrator the results of the investigation and the action, if any, taken or proposed.

(b) If corrective action by the user of the product is necessary for safety because of any noncompliance or defect specified in paragraph (a) of this section, the manufacturer shall submit the information necessary for the issue of an Airworthiness Directive under Part 39.

§ 21.289 Major repairs, rebuilding and alteration.

For types covered by a delegation option authorization, a manufacturer may—

(a) After finding that a major repair or major alteration meets the applicable airworthiness requirements of this chapter, approve that repair or alteration; and

(b) Authorize any employee to execute and sign FAA Form 337 and make required log book entries if that employee—

(1) Inspects, or is in direct charge of inspecting, the repair, rebuilding, or alteration; and

(2) Is listed on the application for the delegation option authorization, or on amendments thereof.

§ 21.293 Current records.

(a) The manufacturer shall maintain at his factory, for each product type certificated under a delegation option authorization, current records containing the following:

(1) For the duration of the manufacturing operating under the delegation option authorization—

(i) A technical data file that includes the type design drawings, specifications, reports on tests prescribed by this part, and the original type inspection report and amendments to that report;

(ii) The data (including amendments) required to be submitted with the original application for each production certificate; and

(iii) A record of any rebuilding and alteration performed by the manufacturer on products manufactured under the delegation option authorization.

(2) For 2 years—

(i) A complete inspection record for each product manufactured, by serial number, and data covering the processes and tests to which materials and parts are subjected; and

(ii) A record of reported service difficulties.

(b) The records and data specified in paragraph (a) of this section shall be—

(1) Made available, upon the Administrator's request, for examination by the Administrator at any time; and

(2) Identified and sent to the Administrator as soon as the manufacturer no longer operates under the delegation option procedures.

Subpart K—Approval of Materials, Parts, Processes, and Appliances

SOURCE: Docket No. 5085, 29 FR 14574, Oct. 24, 1964, unless otherwise noted.

§ 21.301 Applicability.

This subpart prescribes procedural requirements for the approval of certain materials, parts, processes, and appliances.

§ 21.303 Replacement and modification parts.

(a) Except as provided in paragraph (b) of this section, no person may produce a modification or replacement part for sale for installation on a type certificated product unless it is produced pursuant to a Parts Manufacturer Approval issued under this subpart.

(b) This section does not apply to the following:

(1) Parts produced under a type or production certificate.

(2) Parts produced by an owner or operator for maintaining or altering his own product.

(3) Parts produced under an FAA Technical Standard Order.

(4) Standard parts (such as bolts and nuts) conforming to established industry or U.S. specifications.

(c) An application for a Parts Manufacturer Approval is made to the Regional Office of the region in which the manufacturing facility is located and must include the following:

(1) The identity of the product on which the part is to be installed.

(2) The name and address of the manufacturing facilities at which these parts are to be manufactured.

(3) The design of the part, which consists of—

(i) Drawings and specifications necessary to show the configuration of the part; and

(ii) Information on dimensions, materials, and processes necessary to define the structural strength of the part.

(4) Test reports and computations necessary to show that the design of the part meets the airworthiness requirements of the Federal Aviation Regulations applicable to the product on which the part is to be installed, unless the applicant shows that the design of the part is identical to the design of a part that is covered under a type certificate. If the design of the part was obtained by a licensing agreement, evidence of that agreement must be furnished.

(d) An applicant is entitled to a Parts Manufacturer Approval for a replacement or modification part if—

(1) The Administrator finds, upon examination of the design and after completing all tests and inspections, that the design meets the airworthiness requirements of the Federal Aviation Regulations applicable to the product on which the part is to be installed; and

(2) He submits a statement certifying that he has established the fabrication inspection system required by paragraph (h) of this section.

(e) Each applicant for a Parts Manufacturer Approval must allow the Administrator to make any inspection or test necessary to determine compliance with the applicable Federal Aviation Regulations. However, unless otherwise authorized by the Administrator—

(1) No part may be presented to the Administrator for an inspection or test unless compliance with paragraphs (f) (2) through (4) of this section has been shown for that part; and

(2) No change may be made to a part between the time that compliance with paragraphs (f) (2) through (4) of this section is shown for that part and the time that the part is presented to the Administrator for the inspection or test.

(f) Each applicant for a Parts Manufacturer Approval must make all inspections and tests necessary to determine—

(1) Compliance with the applicable airworthiness requirements;

(2) That materials conform to the specifications in the design;

(3) That the part conforms to the drawings in the design; and

(4) That the fabrication processes, construction, and assembly conform to those specified in the design.

(g) The Administrator does not issue a Parts Manufacturer Approval if the manufacturing facilities for the part are located outside of the United States, unless the Administrator finds that the location of the manufacturing facilities places no burden on the FAA in administering applicable airworthiness requirements.

(h) Each holder of a Parts Manufacturer Approval shall establish and maintain a fabrication inspection system that ensures that each completed part conforms to its design data and is safe for installation on applicable type certificated products. The system shall include the following:

(1) Incoming materials used in the finished part must be as specified in the design data.

(2) Incoming materials must be properly identified if their physical and chemical properties cannot otherwise be readily and accurately determined.

(3) Materials subject to damage and deterioration must be suitably stored and adequately protected.

(4) Processes affecting the quality and safety of the finished product must be accomplished in accordance with acceptable specifications.

(5) Parts in process must be inspected for conformity with the design data at points in production where accurate determination can be made. Statistical quality control procedures may be employed where it is shown that a satisfactory level of quality will be maintained for the particular part involved.

(6) Current design drawings must be readily available to manufacturing and inspection personnel, and used when necessary.

(7) Major changes to the basic design must be adequately controlled and approved before being incorporated in the finished part.

(8) Rejected materials and components must be segregated and identified in such a manner as to preclude their use in the finished part.

(9) Inspection records must be maintained, identified with the completed part, where practicable, and retained in the manufacturer's file for a period of at least 2 years after the part has been completed.

(i) A Parts Manufacturer Approval issued under this section is not transferable and is effective until surrendered or withdrawn or otherwise terminated by the Administrator.

(j) The holder of a Parts Manufacturer Approval shall notify the FAA in writing within 10 days from the date the manufacturing facility at which the parts are manufactured is relocated or expanded to include additional facilities at other locations.

(k) Each holder of a Parts Manufacturer Approval shall determine that each completed part conforms to the design data and is safe for installation on type certificated products.

[Amdt. 21-38, 37 FR 10659, May 26, 1972, as amended by Amdt. 21-41, 39 FR 41965, Dec. 4, 1974]

§ 21.305 Approval of materials, parts, processes, and appliances.

Whenever a material, part, process, or appliance is required to be approved under this chapter, it may be approved—

(a) Under a Parts Manufacturer Approval issued under § 21.303;

(b) Under a Technical Standard Order issued by the Administrator. Advisory Circular 20-110 contains a list of Technical Standard Orders that may be used to obtain approval. Copies of the Advisory Circular may be obtained from the U.S. Department of Transportation, Publication Section (M-443.1), Washington, D.C. 20590;

(c) In conjunction with type certification procedures for a product; or

(d) In any other manner approved by the Administrator.

[Amdt. 21-38, 37 FR 10659, May 26, 1972, as amended by Amdt. 21-50, 45 FR 38346, June 9, 1980]

Subpart L—Export Airworthiness Approvals

Source: Amdt. 21-2, 30 FR 8465, July 2, 1965, unless otherwise noted.

§ 21.321 Applicability.

(a) This subpart prescribes—

(1) Procedural requirements for the issue of export airworthiness approvals; and

(2) Rules governing the holders of those approvals.

(b) For the purposes of this subpart—

(1) A Class I product is a complete aircraft, aircraft engine, or propeller, which—

(i) Has been type certificated in accordance with the applicable Federal Aviation Regulations and for which Federal Aviation Specifications or type certificate data sheets have been issued; or

(ii) Is identical to a type certificated product specified in paragraph (b)(1)(i) of this section in all respects except as is otherwise acceptable to the civil aviation authority of the importing state.

(2) A Class II product is a major component of a Class I product (e.g., wings, fuselages, empennage assemblies, landing gears, power transmissions, control surfaces, etc), the failure of which would jeopardize the safety of a Class I product; or any part, material, or appliance, approved and manufactured under the Technical Standard Order (TSO) system in the "C" series.

(3) A Class III product is any part or component which is not a Class I or Class II product and includes standard parts, i.e., those designated as AN, NAS, SAE, etc.

(4) The words "newly overhauled" when used to describe a product means that the product has not been operated or placed in service, except for functional testing, since having been overhauled, inspected and approved for return to service in accordance with the applicable Federal Aviation Regulations.

[Amdt. 21-2, 30 FR 11375, July 2, 1965, as amended by Amdt. 21-48, 44 FR 15649, Mar. 15, 1979]

§ 21.323 Eligibility.

(a) Any exporter or his authorized representative may obtain an export airworthiness approval for a Class I or Class II product.

(b) Any manufacturer may obtain an export airworthiness approval for a Class III product if the manufacturer—

(1) Has in his employ a designated representative of the Administrator who has been authorized to issue that approval; and

(2) Holds for that product—

(i) A production certificate;

(ii) An approved production inspection system;

(iii) An FAA Parts Manufacturer Approval (PMA); or

(iv) A Technical Standard Order authorization.

§ 21.325   Export airworthiness approvals.

(a) *Kinds of approvals.* (1) Export airworthiness approval of Class I products is issued in the form of Export Certificates of Airworthiness, FAA Form 8130–4. Such a certificate does not authorize the operation of aircraft.

(2) Export airworthiness approval of Class II and III products is issued in the form of Airworthiness Approval Tags, FAA Form 8130–3.

(b) *Products which may be approved.* Export airworthiness approvals are issued for—

(1) New aircraft that are assembled and that have been flight-tested, and other Class I products located in the United States, except that export airworthiness approval may be issued for any of the following without assembly or flight-test:

(i) A small airplane type certificated under Part 3 or 4a of the Civil Air Regulations, or Part 23 of the Federal Aviation Regulations, and manufactured under a production certificate;

(ii) A glider type certificated under § 21.23 of this part and manufactured under a production certificate; or

(iii) A normal category rotorcraft type certificated under Part 6 of the Civil Air Regulations or Part 27 of the Federal Aviation Regulations and manufactured under a production certificate.

(2) Used aircraft possessing a valid U.S. airworthiness certificate, or other used Class I products that have been maintained in accordance with the applicable CAR's or FAR's and are located in a foreign country, if the Administrator finds that the location places no undue burden upon the FAA in administering the provisions of this regulation.

(3) Class II and III products that are manufactured and located in the United States.

(c) *Export airworthiness approval exceptions.* If the export airworthiness approval is issued on the basis of a written statement by the importing state as provided for in § 21.327(e)(4), the requirements that are not met and the differences in configuration, if any, between the product to be exported and the related type certificated product, are listed on the export airworthiness approval as exceptions.

[Amdt. 21–2, 30 FR 8465, July 2, 1965, as amended by Amdt. 21–14, 32 FR 2999, Feb. 17, 1967; Amdt. 21–43, 40 FR 2577, Jan. 14, 1975; Amdt. 21–48, 44 FR 15649, Mar. 15, 1979]

§ 21.327   Application.

(a) Except as provided in paragraph (b) of this section, an application for export airworthiness approval for a Class I or Class II product is made on a form and in a manner prescribed by the Administrator and is submitted to the appropriate Flight Standards District Office or to the nearest international field office.

(b) A manufacturer holding a production certificate may apply orally to the appropriate Flight Standards District Office or the nearest international field office for export airworthiness approval of a Class II product approved under his production certificate.

(c) Application for export airworthiness approval of Class III products is made to the designated representative of the Administrator authorized to issue those approvals.

(d) A separate application must be made for—

(1) Each aircraft;

(2) Each engine and propeller, except that one application may be made for more than one engine or propeller, if all are of the same type and model and are exported to the same purchaser and country; and

(3) Each type of Class II product, except that one application may be

used for more than one type of Class II product when—

(i) They are separated and identified in the application as to the type and model of the related Class I product; and

(ii) They are to be exported to the same purchaser and country.

(e) Each application must be accompanied by a written statement from the importing country that will validate the export airworthiness approval if the product being exported is—

(1) An aircraft manufactured outside the United States and being exported to a country with which the United States has a reciprocal agreement concerning the validation of export certificates;

(2) An unassembled aircraft which has not been flight-tested;

(3) A product that does not meet the special requirement of the importing country; or

(4) A product that does not meet a requirement specified in §§ 21.329, 21.331, or 21.333, as applicable, for the issuance of an export airworthiness approval. The written statement must list the requirements not met.

(f) Each application for export airworthiness approval of a Class I product must include, as applicable:

(1) A Statement of Conformity, FAA Form 8130-9, for each new product that has not been manufactured under a production certificate.

(2) A weight and balance report, with a loading schedule when applicable, for each aircraft in accordance with Part 43 of this chapter. For transport aircraft and commuter category airplanes this report must be based on an actual weighing of the aircraft within the preceding twelve months, but after any major repairs or alterations to the aircraft. Changes in equipment not classed as major changes that are made after the actual weighing may be accounted for on a "computed" basis and the report revised accordingly. Manufacturers of new nontransport category airplanes, normal category rotorcraft, and gliders may submit reports having computed weight and balance data, in place of an actual weighing of the aircraft, if fleet weight control procedures approved by the FAA have been

established for such aircraft. In such a case, the following statement must be entered in each report: "The weight and balance data shown in this report are computed on the basis of Federal Aviation Administration approved procedures for establishing fleet weight averages." The weight and balance report must include an equipment list showing weights and moment arms of all required and optional items of equipment that are included in the certificated empty weight.

(3) A maintenance manual for each new product when such a manual is required by the applicable airworthiness rules.

(4) Evidence of compliance with the applicable airworthiness directives. A suitable notation must be made when such directives are not complied with.

(5) When temporary installations are incorporated in an aircraft for the purpose of export delivery, the application form must include a general description of the installations together with a statement that the installation will be removed and the aircraft restored to the approved configuration upon completion of the delivery flight.

(6) Historical records such as aircraft and engine log books, repair and alteration forms, etc., for used aircraft and newly overhauled products.

(7) For products intended for overseas shipment, the application form must describe the methods used, if any, for the preservation and packaging of such products to protect them against corrosion and damage while in transit or storage. The description must also indicate the duration of the effectiveness of such methods.

(8) The Airplane or Rotorcraft Flight Manual when such material is required by the applicable airworthiness regulations for the particular aircraft.

(9) A statement as to the date when title passed or is expected to pass to a foreign purchaser.

(10) The data required by the special requirements of the importing country.

[Amdt. 21-2, 30 FR 8465, July 2, 1965, as amended by Doc. No. 8084, 32 FR 5769, Apr. 11, 1967; Amdt. 21-48, 44 FR 15650, Mar. 15, 1979; Amdt. 21-59, 52 FR 1836, Jan. 15, 1987]

§21.329 Issue of export certificates of airworthiness for Class I products.

An applicant is entitled to an export certificate of airworthiness for a Class I product if that applicant shows at the time the product is submitted to the Administrator for export airworthiness approval that it meets the requirements of paragraphs (a) through (f) of this section, as applicable, except as provided in paragraph (g) of this section:

(a) New or used aircraft manufactured in the United States must meet the airworthiness requirement for a standard U.S. airworthiness certificate under §21.183, or meet the airworthiness certification requirements for a "restricted" airworthiness certificate under §21.185.

(b) New or used aircraft manufactured outside the United States must have a valid U.S. standard airworthiness certificate.

(c) Used aircraft must have undergone an annual type inspection and be approved for return to service in accordance with Part 43 of this chapter. The inspection must have been performed and properly documented within 30 days before the date the application is made for an export certificate of airworthiness. In complying with this paragraph, consideration may be given to the inspections performed on an aircraft maintained in accordance with a continuous airworthiness maintenance program under Part 121 or 127 of this chapter or a progressive inspection program under Part 91 of this chapter, within the 30 days prior to the date the application is made for an export certificate of airworthiness.

(d) New engines and propellers must conform to the type design and must be in a condition for safe operation.

(e) Used engines and propellers which are not being exported as part of a certificated aircraft must have been newly overhauled.

(f) The special requirements of the importing country must have been met.

(g) A product need not meet a requirement specified in paragraphs (a) through (f) of this section, as applicable, if acceptable to the importing country and the importing country in-

dicates that acceptability in accordance with §21.327(e)(4) of this part.

[Amdt. 21-2, 30 FR 8465, July 2, 1965, as amended by Amdt. 21-8, 31 FR 2421, Feb. 5, 1966; Amdt. 21-9, 31 FR 3336, Mar. 3, 1966; Amdt. 21-48, 44 FR 15650, Mar. 15, 1979]

§21.331 Issue of airworthiness approval tags for Class II products.

(a) An applicant is entitled to an export airworthiness approval tag for Class II products if that applicant shows, except as provided in paragraph (b) of this section, that—

(1) The products are new or have been newly overhauled and conform to the approved design data;

(2) The products are in a condition for safe operation;

(3) The products are identified with at least the manufacturer's name, part number, model designation (when applicable), and serial number or equivalent; and

(4) The products meet the special requirements of the importing country.

(b) A product need not meet a requirement specified in paragraph (a) of this section if acceptable to the importing country and the importing country indicates that acceptability in accordance with §21.327(e)(4) of this part.

[Amdt. 21-2, 30 FR 8465, July 2, 1965, as amended by Amdt. 21-48, 44 FR 15650, Mar. 15, 1979]

§21.333 Issue of export airworthiness approval tags for Class III products.

(a) An applicant is entitled to an export airworthiness approval tag for Class III products if that applicant shows, except as provided in paragraph (b) of this section, that—

(1) The products conform to the approved design data applicable to the Class I or Class II product of which they are a part;

(2) The products are in a condition for safe operation; and

(3) The products comply with the special requirements of the importing country.

(b) A product need not meet a requirement specified in paragraph (a) of this section if acceptable to the importing country and the importing country indicates that acceptability in accordance with § 21.327(e)(4) of this part.

[Amdt. 21-2, 30 FR 8465, July 2, 1965, as amended by Amdt. 21-48, 44 FR 15650, Mar. 15, 1979]

§ 21.335 Responsibilities of exporters.

Each exporter receiving an export airworthiness approval for a product shall—

(a) Forward to the air authority of the importing country all documents and information necessary for the proper operation of the products being exported, e.g., Flight Manuals, Maintenance Manuals, Service Bulletins, and assembly instructions, and such other material as is stipulated in the special requirements of the importing country. The documents, information, and material may be forwarded by any means consistent with the special requirements of the importing country;

(b) Forward the manufacturer's assembly instructions and an FAA-approved flight test checkoff form to the air authority of the importing country when unassembled aircraft are being exported. These instructions must be in sufficient detail to permit whatever rigging, alignment, and ground testing is necessary to ensure that the aircraft will conform to the approved configuration when assembled;

(c) Remove or cause to be removed any temporary installation incorporated on an aircraft for the purpose of export delivery and restore the aircraft to the approved configuration upon completion of the delivery flight;

(d) Secure all proper foreign entry clearances from all the countries involved when conducting sales demonstrations or delivery flights; and

(e) When title to an aircraft passes or has passed to a foreign purchaser—

(1) Request cancellation of the U.S. registration and airworthiness certificates, giving the date of transfer of title, and the name and address of the foreign owner;

(2) Return the Registration and Airworthiness Certificates, AC Form 8050.3 and FAA Form 8100-2, to the FAA; and

(3) Submit a statement certifying that the United States' identification and registration numbers have been removed from the aircraft in compliance with § 45.33.

[Amdt. 21-2, 30 FR 8465, July 2, 1965, as amended by Amdt. 21-48, 44 FR 15650, Mar. 15, 1979]

§ 21.337 Performance of inspections and overhauls.

Unless otherwise provided for in this subpart, each inspection and overhaul required for export airworthiness approval of Class I and Class II products must be performed and approved by one of the following:

(a) The manufacturer of the product.

(b) An appropriately certificated domestic repair station.

(c) An appropriately certificated foreign repair station having adequate overhaul facilities, and maintenance organization appropriate to the product involved, when the product is a Class I product located in a foreign country and an international office of Flight Standards Service has approved the use of such foreign repair station.

(d) The holder of an inspection authorization as provided in Part 65 of this chapter.

(e) An air carrier, when the product is one that the carrier has maintained under its own or another air carrier's continuous airworthiness maintenance program and maintenance manuals as provided in Part 121 or 127 of this chapter.

(f) A commercial operator, when the product is one that the operator has maintained under its continuous airworthiness maintenance program and maintenance manual as provided in Part 121 of this chapter.

[Amdt. 21-2, 30 FR 8465, July 2, 1965, as amended by Amdt. 21-8, 31 FR 2421, Feb. 5, 1966]

§ 21.339 Special export airworthiness approval for aircraft.

A special export certificate of airworthiness may be issued for an aircraft located in the United States that is to be flown to several foreign countries for the purpose of sale, without returning the aircraft to the United States for the certificate if—

(a) The aircraft possesses either—

(1) A standard U.S. certificate of airworthiness; or

(2) A special U.S. certificate of airworthiness in the restricted category issued under § 21.185;

(b) The owner files an application as required by § 21.327 except that items 3 and 4 of the application (FAA Form 8130-1) need not be completed;

(c) The aircraft is inspected by the Administrator before leaving the United States and is found to comply with all the applicable requirements;

(d) A list of foreign countries in which it is intended to conduct sales demonstrations, together with the expected dates and duration of such demonstration, is included in the application;

(e) For each prospective importing country, the applicant shows that—

(1) He has met that country's special requirements, other than those requiring that documents, information, and materials be furnished; and

(2) He has the documents, information, and materials necessary to meet the special requirements of that country; and

(f) All other requirements for the issuance of a Class I export certificate of airworthiness are met.

[Amdt. 21-12, 31 FR 12565, Sept. 23, 1966, as amended by Amdt. 21-43, 40 FR 2577, Jan. 14, 1975; Amdt. 21-55, 46 FR 44737, Sept. 8, 1981]

Subpart M—Designated Alteration Station Authorization Procedures

SOURCE: Amdt. 21-6, 30 FR 11379, Sept. 8, 1965; 30 FR 11849, Sept. 16, 1965, unless otherwise noted.

§ 21.431 Applicability.

(a) This subpart prescribes Designated Alteration Station (DAS) authorization procedures for—

(1) Issuing supplemental type certificates;

(2) Issuing experimental certificates; and

(3) Amending standard airworthiness certificates.

(b) This subpart applies to domestic repair stations, air carriers (except air taxi operators), commercial operators of large aircraft, and manufacturers of products.

§ 21.435 Application.

The applicant for a DAS authorization must submit an application, in writing and signed by an official of the applicant, to the FAA Regional Office for the region in which the applicant is located. The application must contain—

(a) The repair station certificate number held by the repair station applicant, and the current ratings covered by the certificate;

(b) The air carrier or commercial operator operating certificate number held by the air carrier or commercial operator applicant, and the products that it may operate and maintain under the certificate;

(c) A statement by the manufacturer applicant of the products for which he holds the type certificate;

(d) The names, signatures, and titles of the persons for whom authorization to issue supplemental type certificates or experimental certificates, or amend airworthiness certificates, is requested; and

(e) A description of the applicant's facilities, and of the staff with which compliance with § 21.439(a)(4) is to be shown.

§ 21.439 Eligibility.

(a) To be eligible for a DAS authorization, the applicant must—

(1) Hold a current domestic repair station certificate under Part 145, or air carrier or commercial operator operating certificate under Part 121;

(2) Be a manufacturer of a product for which it has alteration authority under § 43.3(i) of this subchapter;

(3) Have adequate maintenance facilities and personnel, in the United States, appropriate to the products that it may operate and maintain under its certificate; and

(4) Employ, or have available, a staff of engineering, flight test, and inspection personnel who can determine compliance with the applicable airworthiness requirements of this chapter.

(b) At least one member of the staff required by paragraph (a)(4) of this section must have all of the following qualifications:

(1) A thorough working knowledge of the applicable requirements of this chapter.

(2) A position, on the applicant's staff, with authority to establish alteration programs that ensure that altered products meet the applicable requirements of this chapter.

(3) At least one year of satisfactory experience in direct contact with the FAA (or its predecessor agency (CAA)) while processing engineering work for type certification or alteration projects.

(4) At least eight years of aeronautical engineering experience (which may include the one year required by paragraph (b)(3) of this section).

(5) The general technical knowledge and experience necessary to determine that altered products, of the types for which a DAS authorization is requested, are in condition for safe operation.

§ 21.441 Procedure manual.

(a) No DAS may exercise any authority under this subpart unless it submits, and obtains approval of, a procedure manual containing—

(1) The procedures for issuing STCs; and

(2) The names, signatures, and responsibilities of officials and of each staff member required by § 21.439(a)(4), identifying those persons who—

(i) Have authority to make changes in procedures that require a revision to the procedure manual; and

(ii) Are to conduct inspections (including conformity and compliance inspections) or approve inspection reports, prepare or approve data, plan or conduct tests, approve the results of tests, amend airworthiness certificates, issue experimental certificates, approve changes to operating limitations or Aircraft Flight Manuals, and sign supplemental type certificates.

(b) No DAS may continue to perform any DAS function affected by any change in facilities or staff necessary to continue to meet the requirements of § 21.439, or affected by any change in procedures from those approved under paragraph (a) of this section, unless that change is approved and entered in the manual. For this purpose, the manual shall contain a log-of-revisions page with space for the identification of each revised item, page, or date, and the signature of the person approving the change for the Administrator.

§ 21.443 Duration.

(a) A DAS authorization is effective until it is surrendered or the Administrator suspends, revokes, or otherwise terminates it.

(b) The DAS shall return the authorization certificate to the Administrator when it is no longer effective.

§ 21.445 Maintenance of eligibility.

The DAS shall continue to meet the requirements for issue of the authorization or shall notify the Administrator within 48 hours of any change (including a change of personnel) that could affect the ability of the DAS to meet those requirements.

§ 21.447 Transferability.

A DAS authorization is not transferable.

§ 21.449 Inspections.

Upon request, each DAS and each applicant shall let the Administrator inspect his facilities, products, and records.

§ 21.451 Limits of applicability.

(a) DAS authorizations apply only to products—

(1) Covered by the ratings of the repair station applicant;

(2) Covered by the operating certificate and maintenance manual of the air carrier or commercial operator applicant; and

(3) For which the manufacturer applicant has alteration authority under § 43.3(i) of this subchapter.

(b) DAS authorizations may be used for—

(1) The issue of supplemental type certificates;

(2) The issue of experimental certificates for aircraft that—

(i) Are altered by the DAS under a supplemental type certificate issued by the DAS; and

(ii) Require flight tests in order to show compliance with the applicable airworthiness requirements of this chapter; and

(3) The amendment of standard airworthiness certificates for aircraft altered under this subpart.

(c) DAS authorizations are subject to any additional limitations prescribed by the Administrator after inspection of the applicant's facilities or review of the staff qualifications.

(d) Notwithstanding any other provision of this subpart, a DAS may not issue a supplemental type certificate involving the acoustical change requirements of Part 36 of this chapter until the Administrator finds that those requirements are met.

[Amdt. 21-6, 30 FR 11379, Sept. 8, 1965; 30 FR 11849, Sept. 16, 1965, as amended by Amdt. 21-42, 40 FR 1034, Jan. 6, 1975]

§ 21.461 Equivalent safety provisions.

The DAS shall obtain the Administrator's concurrence on the application of all equivalent safety provisions applied under § 21.21.

§ 21.463 Supplemental type certificates.

(a) For each supplemental type certificate issued under this subpart, the DAS shall follow the procedure manual prescribed in § 21.441 and shall, before issuing the certificate—

(1) Submit to the Administrator a statement describing—

(i) The type design change;

(ii) The airworthiness requirements of this chapter (by part and effective date) that the DAS considers applicable; and

(iii) The proposed program for meeting the applicable airworthiness requirements;

(2) Find that each applicable airworthiness requirement is met; and

(3) Find that the type of product for which the STC is to be issued, as modified by the supplemental type design data upon which the STC is based, is of proper design for safe operation.

(b) Within 30 days after the date of issue of the STC, the DAS shall submit to the Administrator—

(1) Two copies of the STC;

(2) One copy of the design data approved by the DAS and referred to in the STC;

(3) One copy of each inspection and test report; and

(4) Two copies of each revision to the Aircraft Flight Manual or to the operating limitations, and any other information necessary for safe operation of the product.

§ 21.473 Airworthiness certificates other than experimental.

For each amendment made to a standard airworthiness certificate under this subpart, the DAS shall follow the procedure manual prescribed in § 21.441 and shall, before making that amendment—

(a) Complete each flight test necessary to meet the applicable airworthiness requirements of this chapter;

(b) Find that each applicable airworthiness requirement of this chapter is met; and

(c) Find that the aircraft is in condition for safe operation.

§ 21.475 Experimental certificates.

The DAS shall, before issuing an experimental certificate, obtain from the Administrator any limitations and conditions that the Administrator considers necessary for safety.

§ 21.477 Data review and service experience.

(a) If the Administrator finds that a product for which an STC was issued under this subpart does not meet the applicable airworthiness requirements, or that an unsafe feature or characteristic caused by a defect in design or manufacture exists, the DAS, upon notification by the Administrator, shall investigate the matter and report to the Administrator the results of the investigation and the action, if any, taken or proposed.

(b) If corrective action by the user of the product is necessary for safety because of any noncompliance or defect specified in paragraph (a) of this section, the DAS shall submit the information necessary for the issue of an Airworthiness Directive under Part 39.

§ 21.493 Current records.

(a) The DAS shall maintain, at its facility, current records containing—

(1) For each product for which it has issued an STC under this subpart, a technical data file that includes any

data and amendments thereto (including drawings, photographs, specifications, instructions, and reports) necessary for the STC;

(2) A list of products by make, model, manufacturer's serial number and, if applicable, any FAA identification, that have been altered under the DAS authorization; and

(3) A file of information from all available sources on alteration difficulties of products altered under the DAS authorization.

(b) The records prescribed in paragraph (a) of this section shall be—

(1) Made available by the DAS, upon the Administrator's request, for examination by the Administrator at any time; and

(2) In the case of the data file prescribed in paragraph (a)(1) of this section, identified by the DAS and sent to the Administrator as soon as the DAS no longer operates under this subpart.

Subpart N—Approval of Engines, Propellers, Materials, Parts, and Appliances: Import

§ 21.500 Approval of engines and propellers.

Each holder or licensee of a U.S. type certificate for an aircraft engine or propeller manufactured in a foreign country with which the United States has an agreement for the acceptance of those products for export and import, shall furnish with each such aircraft engine or propeller imported into this country, a certificate of airworthiness for export issued by the country of manufacture certifying that the individual aircraft engine or propeller—

(a) Conforms to its U.S. type certificate and is in condition for safe operation; and

(b) Has been subjected by the manufacturer to a final operational check.

[Amdt. 21–25, 34 FR 14068, Sept. 5, 1969]

§ 21.502 Approval of materials, parts, and appliances.

(a) A material, part, or appliance, manufactured in a foreign country with which the United States has an agreement for the acceptance of those materials, parts, or appliances for export and import, is considered to meet the requirements for approval in the Federal Aviation Regulations when the country of manufacture issues a certificate of airworthiness for export certifying that the individual material, part, or appliance meets those requirements, unless the Administrator finds, based on the technical data submitted under paragraph (b) of this section, that the material, part, or appliance is otherwise not consistent with the intent of the Federal Aviation Regulations.

(b) An applicant for approval of a material, part, or appliance must, upon request, submit to the Administrator any technical data respecting that material, part, or appliance.

[Amdt. 21–25, 34 FR 14068, Sept. 5, 1969]

Subpart O—Technical Standard Order Authorizations

SOURCE: Docket No. 19589, 45 FR 38346, June 9, 1980, unless otherwise noted.

§ 21.601 Applicability.

(a) This subpart prescribes—

(1) Procedural requirements for the issue of Technical Standard Order authorizations;

(2) Rules governing the holders of Technical Standard Order authorizations; and

(3) Procedural requirements for the issuance of a letter of Technical Standard Order design approval.

(b) For the purpose of this subpart—

(1) A Technical Standard Order (referred to in this subpart as "TSO") is issued by the Administrator and is a minimum performance standard for specified articles (for the purpose of this subpart, articles means materials, parts, processes, or appliances) used on civil aircraft.

(2) A TSO authorization is an FAA design and production approval issued to the manufacturer of an article which has been found to meet a specific TSO.

(3) A letter of TSO design approval is an FAA design approval for a foreign-manufactured article which has been found to meet a specific TSO in accordance with the procedures of § 21.617.

(4) An article manufactured under a TSO authorization, an FAA letter of acceptance as described in § 21.603(b), or an appliance manufactured under a letter of TSO design approval described in § 21.617 is an approved article or appliance for the purpose of meeting the regulations of this chapter that require the article to be approved.

(5) An article manufacturer is the person who controls the design and quality of the article produced (or to be produced, in the case of an application), including the parts of them and any processes or services related to them that are procured from an outside source.

(c) The Administrator does not issue a TSO authorization if the manufacturing facilities for the product are located outside of the United States, unless the Administrator finds that the location of the manufacturer's facilities places no undue burden on the FAA in administering applicable airworthiness requirements.

§ 21.603 TSO marking and privileges.

(a) Except as provided in paragraph (b) of this section and § 21.617(c), no person may identify an article with a TSO marking unless that person holds a TSO authorization and the article meets applicable TSO performance standards.

(b) The holder of an FAA letter of acceptance of a statement of conformance issued for an article before July 1, 1962, or any TSO authorization issued after July 1, 1962, may continue to manufacture that article without obtaining a new TSO authorization but shall comply with the requirements of §§ 21.3, 21.607 through 21.615, 21.619, and 21.621.

(c) Notwithstanding paragraphs (a) and (b) of this section, after August 6, 1976, no person may identify or mark an article with any of the following TSO numbers:

(1) TSO–C18, –C18a, –C18b, –C18c.

(2) TSO–C24.

(3) TSO–C33.

(4) TSO–C61 or C61a.

§ 21.605 Application and issue.

(a) The manufacturer (or an authorized agent) shall submit an application for a TSO authorization, together with the following documents, to the Chief, Engineering and Manufacturing Branch, Flight Standards Division, of the region in which the applicant is located (or in the case of the Western Region, the Chief, Aircraft Engineering Division):

(1) A statement of conformance certifying that the applicant has met the requirements of this subpart and that the article concerned meets the applicable TSO that is effective on the date of application for that article.

(2) One copy of the technical data required in the applicable TSO.

(3) A description of its quality control system in the detail specified in § 21.143. In complying with this section, the applicant may refer to current quality control data filed with the FAA as part of a previous TSO authorization application.

(b) When a series of minor changes in accordance with § 21.611 is anticipated, the applicant may set forth in its application the basic model number of the article and the part number of the components with open brackets after it to denote that suffix change letters or numbers (or combinations of them) will be added from time to time.

(c) After receiving the application and other documents required by paragraph (a) of this section to substantiate compliance with this part, and after a determination has been made of its ability to produce duplicate articles under this part, the Administrator issues a TSO authorization (including all TSO deviations granted to the applicant) to the applicant to identify the article with the applicable TSO marking.

(d) If the application is deficient, the applicant must, when requested by the Administrator, submit any additional information necessary to show compliance with this part. If the applicant fails to submit the additional information within 30 days after the Administrator's request, the application is denied and the applicant is so notified.

(e) The Administrator issues or denies the application within 30 days after its receipt or, if additional information has been requested, within 30 days after receiving that information.

§ 21.607 General rules governing holders of TSO authorizations.

Each manufacturer of an article for which a TSO authorization has been issued under this part shall—

(a) Manufacture the article in accordance with this part and the applicable TSO;

(b) Conduct all required tests and inspections and establish and maintain a quality control system adequate to ensure that the article meets the requirements of paragraph (a) of this section and is in condition for safe operation;

(c) Prepare and maintain, for each model of each article for which a TSO authorization has been issued, a current file of complete technical data and records in accordance with § 21.613; and

(d) Permanently and legibly mark each article to which this section applies with the following information:

(1) The name and address of the manufacturer.

(2) The name, type, part number, or model designation of the article.

(3) The serial number or the date of manufacture of the article or both.

(4) The applicable TSO number.

§ 21.609 Approval for deviation.

(a) Each manufacturer who requests approval to deviate from any performance standard of a TSO shall show that the standards from which a deviation is requested are compensated for by factors or design features providing an equivalent level of safety.

(b) The request for approval to deviate, together with all pertinent data, must be submitted to the Chief, Engineering and Manufacturing Branch, Flight Standards Division, of the region in which the manufacturer is located (or in the case of the Western Region, the Chief, Aircraft Engineering Division). If the article is manufactured in a foreign country, the request for approval to deviate, together with all pertinent data, must be submitted through the civil aviation authority in that country to the FAA.

§ 21.611 Design changes.

(a) *Minor changes by the manufacturer holding a TSO authorization.* The manufacturer of an article under an authorization issued under this part may make minor design changes (any change other than a major change) without further approval by the Administrator. In this case, the changed article keeps the original model number (part numbers may be used to identify minor changes) and the manufacturer shall forward to the appropriate Chief, Engineering and Manufacturing Branch (or in the case of the Western Region, the Chief, Aircraft Engineering Division), any revised data that are necessary for compliance with § 21.605(b).

(b) *Major changes by manufacturer holding a TSO authorization.* Any design change by the manufacturer that is extensive enough to require a substantially complete investigation to determine compliance with a TSO is a major change. Before making such a change, the manufacturer shall assign a new type or model designation to the article and apply for an authorization under § 21.605.

(c) *Changes by person other than manufacturer.* No design change by any person (other than the manufacturer who submitted the statement of conformance for the article) is eligible for approval under this part unless the person seeking the approval is a manufacturer and applies under § 21.605(a) for a separate TSO authorization. Persons other than a manufacturer may obtain approval for design changes under Part 43 or under the applicable airworthiness regulations.

§ 21.613 Recordkeeping requirements.

(a) *Keeping the records.* Each manufacturer holding a TSO authorization under this part shall, for each article manufactured under that authorization, keep the following records at its factory:

(1) A complete and current technical data file for each type or model article, including design drawings and specifications.

(2) Complete and current inspection records showing that all inspections and tests required to ensure compliance with this part have been properly completed and documented.

(b) *Retention of records.* The manufacturer shall retain the records described in paragraph (a)(1) of this section until it no longer manufactures the article. At that time, copies of these records shall be sent to the Administrator. The manufacturer shall retain the records described in paragraph (a)(2) of this section for a period of at least 2 years.

§ 21.615   FAA inspection.

Upon the request of the Administrator, each manufacturer of an article under a TSO authorization shall allow the Administrator to—

(a) Inspect any article manufactured under that authorization;

(b) Inspect the manufacturer's quality control system;

(c) Witness any tests;

(d) Inspect the manufacturing facilities; and

(e) Inspect the technical data files on that article.

§ 21.617   Issue of letters of TSO design approval: import appliances.

(a) A letter of TSO design approval may be issued for an appliance that is manufactured in a foreign country with which the United States has an agreement for the acceptance of these appliances for export and import and that is to be imported into the United States if—

(1) The country in which the appliance was manufactured certifies that the appliance has been examined, tested, and found to meet the applicable TSO designated in § 21.305(b) or the applicable performance standards of the country in which the appliance was manufactured and any other performance standards the Administrator may prescribe to provide a level of safety equivalent to that provided by the TSO designated in § 21.305(b); and

(2) The manufacturer has submitted one copy of the technical data required in the applicable performance standard through its civil aviation authority.

(b) The letter of TSO design approval will be issued by the Administrator and must list any deviation granted to the manufacturer under § 21.609.

(c) After the Administrator has issued a letter of TSO design approval and the country of manufacture issues a Certificate of Airworthiness for

Export as specified in § 21.502(a), the manufacturer shall be authorized to identify the appliance with the TSO marking requirements described in § 21.607(d) and in the applicable TSO. Each appliance must be accompanied by a Certificate of Airworthiness for Export as specified in § 21.502(a) issued by the country of manufacture.

§ 21.619   Noncompliance.

The Administrator may, upon notice, withdraw the TSO authorization or letter of TSO design approval of any manufacturer who identifies with a TSO marking an article not meeting the performance standards of the applicable TSO.

§ 21.621   Transferability and duration.

A TSO authorization or letter of TSO design approval issued under this part is not transferable and is effective until surrendered, withdrawn, or otherwise terminated by the Administrator.

FEDERAL AVIATION REGULATIONS

PART 23
AIRWORTHINESS STANDARDS:
Normal, Utility, and Acrobatic Category Airplanes

1989 EDITION

PART 23—AIRWORTHINESS STAND-ARDS: NORMAL, UTILITY, ACRO-BATIC, AND COMMUTER CATEGO-RY AIRPLANES

Subpart A—General

Sec.
23.1 Applicability.
23.2 Special retroactive requirements.
23.3 Airplane categories.

Subpart B—Flight

GENERAL

23.21 Proof of compliance.
23.23 Load distribution limits.
23.25 Weight limits.

23.29 Empty weight and corresponding center of gravity.
23.31 Removable ballast.
23.33 Propeller speed and pitch limits.

PERFORMANCE

23.45 General.
23.49 Stalling speed.
23.51 Takeoff.
23.53 Takeoff speeds.

23.55   Accelerate–stop distance.
23.57   Takeoff path.
23.59   Takeoff distance and takeoff run.
23.61   Takeoff flight path.
23.65   Climb: All engines operating.
23.67   Climb: one engine inoperative.
23.75   Landing.
23.77   Balked landing.

FLIGHT CHARACTERISTICS

23.141 General.

CONTROLLABILITY AND MANEUVERABILITY

23.143 General.
23.145 Longitudinal control.
23.147 Directional and lateral control.
23.149 Minimum control speed.
23.151 Acrobatic maneuvers.
23.153 Control during landings.
23.155 Elevator control force in maneuvers.
23.157 Rate of roll.

TRIM

23.161 Trim.

STABILITY

23.171 General.
23.173 Static longitudinal stability.
23.175 Demonstration of static longitudinal stability.
23.177 Static directional and lateral stability.
23.179 Instrumented stick force measurements.
23.181 Dynamic stability.

STALLS

23.201 Wings level stall.
23.203 Turning flight and accelerated stalls.
23.205 Critical engine inoperative stalls.
23.207 Stall warning.

SPINNING

23.221 Spinning.

GROUND AND WATER HANDLING CHARACTERISTICS

23.231 Longitudinal stability and control.
23.233 Directional stability and control.
23.235 Taxiing condition.
23.239 Spray characteristics.

MISCELLANEOUS FLIGHT REQUIREMENTS

23.251 Vibration and buffeting.
23.253 High speed characteristics.

Subpart C—Structure

GENERAL

23.301 Loads.
23.303 Factor of safety.
23.305 Strength and deformation.
23.307 Proof of structure.

FLIGHT LOADS

23.321 General.
23.331 Symmetrical flight conditions.
23.333 Flight envelope.
23.335 Design airspeeds.
23.337 Limit maneuvering load factors.
23.341 Gust loads factors.
23.345 High lift devices.
23.347 Unsymmetrical flight conditions.
23.349 Rolling conditions.
23.351 Yawing conditions.
23.361 Engine torque.
23.363 Side load on engine mount.
23.365 Pressurized cabin loads.
23.367 Unsymmetrical loads due to engine failure.
23.369 Special conditions for rear lift truss.
23.371 Gyroscopic loads.
23.373 Speed control devices.

CONTROL SURFACE AND SYSTEM LOADS

23.391 Control surface loads.
23.395 Control system loads.
23.397 Limit control forces and torques.
23.399 Dual control system.
23.405 Secondary control system.
23.407 Trim tab effects.
23.409 Tabs.
23.415 Ground gust conditions.

HORIZONTAL TAIL SURFACES

23.421 Balancing loads.
23.423 Maneuvering loads.
23.425 Gust loads.
23.427 Unsymmetrical loads.

VERTICAL TAIL SURFACES

23.441 Maneuvering loads.
23.443 Gust loads.
23.445 Outboard fins.

AILERONS, WING FLAPS, AND SPECIAL DEVICES

23.455 Ailerons.
23.457 Wing flaps.
23.459 Special devices.

GROUND LOADS

23.471 General.
23.473 Ground load conditions and assumptions.
23.477 Landing gear arrangement.
23.479 Level landing conditions.
23.481 Tail down landing conditions.
23.483 One-wheel landing conditions.
23.485 Side load conditions.
23.493 Braked roll conditions.
23.497 Supplementary conditions for tail wheels.
23.499 Supplementary conditions for nose wheels.
23.505 Supplementary conditions for skiplanes.
23.507 Jacking loads.
23.509 Towing loads.

23.511 Ground load; unsymmetrical loads on multiple-wheel units.

WATER LOADS

23.521 Water load conditions.

EMERGENCY LANDING CONDITIONS

23.561 General.

FATIGUE EVALUATION

23.571 Pressurized cabin.
23.572 Flight structure.

Subpart D—Design and Construction

23.601 General.
23.603 Materials and workmanship.
23.605 Fabrication methods.
23.607 Self-locking nuts.
23.609 Protection of structure.
23.611 Accessibility.
23.613 Material strength properties and design values.
23.615 Design properties.
23.619 Special factors.
23.621 Casting factors.
23.623 Bearing factors.
23.625 Fitting factors.
23.627 Fatigue strength.
23.629 Flutter.

WINGS

23.641 Proof of strength.

CONTROL SURFACES

23.651 Proof of strength.
23.655 Installation.
23.657 Hinges.
23.659 Mass balance.

CONTROL SYSTEMS

23.671 General.
23.673 Primary flight controls.
23.675 Stops.
23.677 Trim systems.
23.679 Control system locks.
23.681 Limit load static tests.
23.683 Operation tests.
23.685 Control system details.
23.687 Spring devices.
23.689 Cable systems.
23.693 Joints.
23.697 Wing flap controls.
23.699 Wing flap position indicator.
23.701 Flap interconnection.

LANDING GEAR

23.721 General.
23.723 Shock absorption tests.
23.725 Limit drop tests.
23.726 Ground load dynamic tests.
23.727 Reserve energy absorption drop test.
23.729 Landing gear extension and retraction system.

23.731 Wheels.
23.733 Tires.
23.735 Brakes.
23.737 Skis.

FLOATS AND HULLS

23.751 Main float buoyancy.
23.753 Main float design.
23.755 Hulls.
23.757 Auxiliary floats.

PERSONNEL AND CARGO ACCOMMODATIONS

23.771 Pilot compartment.
23.773 Pilot compartment view.
23.775 Windshields and windows.
23.777 Cockpit controls.
23.779 Motion and effect of cockpit controls.
23.781 Cockpit control knob shape.
23.783 Doors.
23.785 Seats, berths, safety belts, and harnesses.
23.787 Cargo compartments.
23.803 Emergency evacuation.
23.807 Emergency exits.
23.815 Width of aisle.
23.831 Ventilation.

PRESSURIZATION

23.841 Pressurized cabins.
23.843 Pressurization tests.

FIRE PROTECTION

23.851 Fire extinguishers.
23.853 Compartment interiors.
23.859 Combustion heater fire protection.
23.863 Flammable fluid fire protection.
23.865 Fire protection of flight controls and other flight structure.

LIGHTNING EVALUATION

23.867 Lightning protection of structure.

MISCELLANEOUS

23.871 Leveling means.

Subpart E—Powerplant

GENERAL

23.901 Installation.
23.903 Engines.
23.905 Propellers.
23.907 Propeller vibration.
23.909 Turbosuperchargers.
23.925 Propeller clearance.
23.929 Engine installation ice protection.
23.933 Reversing systems.
23.937 Turbopropeller-drag limiting systems.
23.939 Powerplant operating characteristics.
23.943 Negative acceleration.

FUEL SYSTEM

23.951 General.
23.953 Fuel system independence.
23.954 Fuel system lightning protection.
23.955 Fuel flow.
23.957 Flow between interconnected tanks.
23.959 Unusable fuel suppy.
23.961 Fuel system hot weather operation.
23.963 Fuel tanks: General.
23.965 Fuel tank tests.
23.967 Fuel tank installation.
23.969 Fuel tank expansion space.
23.971 Fuel tank sump.
23.973 Fuel tank filler connection.
23.975 Fuel tank vents and carburetor vapor vents.
23.977 Fuel tank outlet.
23.979 Pressure fueling systems.

FUEL SYSTEM COMPONENTS

23.991 Fuel pumps.
23.993 Fuel system lines and fittings.
23.994 Fuel system components.
23.995 Fuel valves and controls.
23.997 Fuel strainer or filter.
23.999 Fuel system drains.
23.1001 Fuel jettisoning system.

OIL SYSTEM

23.1011 General.
23.1013 Oil tanks.
23.1015 Oil tank tests.
23.1017 Oil lines and fittings.
23.1019 Oil strainer or filter.
23.1021 Oil system drains.
23.1023 Oil radiators.
23.1027 Propeller feathering system.

COOLING

23.1041 General.
23.1043 Cooling tests.
23.1045 Cooling test procedures for turbine engine powered airplanes.
23.1047 Cooling test procedures for reciprocating engine-powered airplanes.

LIQUID COOLING

23.1061 Installation.
23.1063 Coolant tank tests.

INDUCTION SYSTEM

23.1091 Air induction.
23.1093 Induction system icing protection.
23.1095 Carburetor deicing fluid flow rate.
23.1097 Carburetor deicing fluid system capacity.
23.1099 Carburetor deicing fluid system detail design.
23.1101 Carburetor air preheater design.
23.1103 Induction system ducts.
23.1105 Induction system screens.
23.1111 Turbine engine bleed air system.

EXHAUST SYSTEM

23.1121 General.

23.1123 Exhaust manifold.
23.1125 Exhaust heat exchangers.

POWERPLANT CONTROLS AND ACCESSORIES

23.1141 Powerplant controls: General.
23.1143 Engine controls.
23.1145 Ignition switches.
23.1147 Mixture controls.
23.1149 Propeller speed and pitch controls.
23.1153 Propeller feathering controls.
23.1155 Turbine engine reverse thrust and propeller pitch settings below the flight regime.
23.1157 Carburetor air temperature controls.
23.1163 Powerplant accessories.
23.1165 Engine ignition systems.

POWERPLANT FIRE PROTECTION

23.1182 Nacelle areas behind firewalls.
23.1183 Lines, fittings, and components.
23.1189 Shutoff means.
23.1191 Firewalls.
23.1192 Engine accessory compartment diaphragm.
23.1193 Cowling and nacelle.
23.1195 Fire extinguishing systems.
23.1197 Fire extinguishing agents.
23.1199 Extinguishing agent containers.
23.1201 Fire extinguishing systems materials.
23.1203 Fire detector system.

Subpart F—Equipment

GENERAL

23.1301 Function and installation.
23.1303 Flight and navigation instruments.
23.1305 Powerplant instruments.
23.1307 Miscellaneous equipment.
23.1309 Equipment, systems, and installations.

INSTRUMENTS: INSTALLATION

23.1321 Arrangement and visibility.
23.1322 Warning, caution, and advisory lights.
23.1323 Airspeed indicating system.
23.1325 Static pressure system.
23.1327 Magnetic direction indicator.
23.1329 Automatic pilot system.
23.1331 Instruments using a power supply.
23.1335 Flight director systems.
23.1337 Powerplant instruments.

ELECTRICAL SYSTEMS AND EQUIPMENT

23.1351 General.
23.1353 Storage battery design and installation.
23.1357 Circuit protective devices.
23.1361 Master switch arrangement.
23.1365 Electric cables and equipment.
23.1367 Switches.

LIGHTS

23.1381 Instrument lights.
23.1383 Landing lights.
23.1385 Position light system installation.
23.1387 Position light system dihedral angles.
23.1389 Position light distribution and intensities.
23.1391 Minimum intensities in the horizontal plane of forward and rear position lights.
23.1393 Minimum intensities in any vertical plane of forward and rear position lights.
23.1395 Maximum intensities in overlapping beams of forward and rear position lights.
23.1397 Color specifications.
23.1399 Riding light.
23.1401 Anticollision light system.

SAFETY EQUIPMENT

23.1411 General.
23.1413 Safety belts and harnesses.
23.1415 Ditching equipment.
23.1416 Pneumatic de-icer boot system.
23.1419 Ice protection.

MISCELLANEOUS EQUIPMENT

23.1431 Electronic equipment.
23.1435 Hydraulic systems.
23.1437 Accessories for multiengine airplanes.
23.1438 Pressurization and pneumatic systems.
23.1441 Oxygen equipment and supply.
23.1443 Minimum mass flow of supplemental oxygen.
23.1447 Equipment standards for oxygen dispensing units.
23.1449 Means for determining use of oxygen.
23.1450 Chemical oxygen generators.
23.1461 Equipment containing high energy rotors.

Subpart G—Operating Limitations and Information

23.1501 General.
23.1505 Airspeed limitations.
23.1507 Maneuvering speed.
23.1511 Flap extended speed.
23.1513 Minimum control speed.
23.1519 Weight and center of gravity.
23.1521 Powerplant limitations.
23.1523 Minimum flight crew.
23.1524 Maximum passenger seating configuration.
23.1525 Kinds of operation.
23.1527 Maximum operating altitude.
23.1529 Instructions for Continued Airworthiness.

MARKINGS AND PLACARDS

23.1541 General.

23.1543 Instrument markings: General.
23.1545 Airspeed indicator.
23.1547 Magnetic direction indicator.
23.1549 Powerplant instruments.
23.1551 Oil quantity indicator.
23.1553 Fuel quantity indicator.
23.1555 Control markings.
23.1557 Miscellaneous markings and placards.
23.1559 Operating limitations placard.
23.1561 Safety equipment.
23.1563 Airspeed placards.
23.1567 Flight maneuver placard.

AIRPLANE FLIGHT MANUAL AND APPROVED MANUAL MATERIAL

23.1581 General.
23.1583 Operating limitations.
23.1585 Operating procedures.
23.1587 Performance information.
23.1589 Loading information.

APPENDIX A—SIMPLIFIED DESIGN LOAD CRITERIA FOR CONVENTIONAL, SINGLE-ENGINE AIRPLANES OF 6,000 POUNDS OR LESS MAXIMUM WEIGHT
APPENDIX B—CONTROL SURFACE LOADINGS
APPENDIX C—BASIC LANDING CONDITIONS
APPENDIX D—WHEEL SPIN-UP LOADS
APPENDIX E—LIMITED WEIGHT CREDIT FOR AIRPLANES EQUIPPED WITH STANDBY POWER
APPENDIX F—TEST PROCEDURE
APPENDIX G—INSTRUCTIONS FOR CONTINUED AIRWORTHINESS

AUTHORITY: 49 U.S.C. 1344, 1354(a), 1355, 1421, 1423, 1425, 1428, 1429, 1430; (49 U.S.C. 106(g)) (Revised Pub. L. 97–449, January 12, 1983).

SOURCE: Docket No. 4080, 29 FR 17955, Dec. 18. 1964; 30 FR 258, Jan. 9, 1965, unless otherwise noted.

**INTENTIONALLY
LEFT
BLANK**

Subpart A — General

§ 23.1 Applicabilty.

(a) This part prescribes airworthiness standards for the issue of type certificates, and changes to those certificates, for airplanes in the normal, utility, acrobatic, and commuter categories.

(b) Each person who applies under Part 21 for such a certificate or change must show compliance with the applicable requirements of this part.

§ 23.2 Special retroactive requirements.

(a) Notwithstanding §§ 21.17 and 21.101 of this chapter and irrespective of the type certification basis, each normal, utility, and acrobatic category airplane having a passenger seating configuration, excluding pilot seats, of nine or less, manufactured after December 12, 1986, or any such foreign airplane for entry into the United States must provide a safety belt and shoulder harness for each forward- or aft-facing seat which will protect the occupant from serious head injury when subjected to the inertia loads resulting from the ultimate static load factors prescribed in § 23.561(b)(2) of this part, or which will provide the occupant protection specified in §23.562 of this part when that section is applicable to the airplane. For other seat orientations, the seat/restraint system must be designed to provide a level of occupant protection equivalent to that provided for forward- or aft-facing seats with a safety belt and shoulder harness installed.

(b) Each shoulder harness installed at a flight crewmember station, as required by this section, must allow the crewmember, when seated with the safety belt and shoulder harness fastened, to perform all functions necessary for flight operations.

(c) For the purpose of this section, the date of manufacture is:

(1) The date the inspection acceptance records, or equivalent, reflect that the airplane is complete and meets the FAA approved type design data; or

(2) In the case of a foreign manufactured airplane, the date the foreign civil airworthiness authority certifies the airplane is complete and issues an original standard airworthiness certificate, or the equivalent in that country.

§ 23.3 Airplane categories.

(a) The normal category is limited to airplanes that have a seating configuration, excluding pilot seats, of nine or less, a maximum certificated takeoff weight of 12,500 pounds or less, and intended for nonacrobatic operation. Nonacrobatic operation includes:

(1) Any maneuver incident to normal flying;

(2) Stalls (except whip stalls); and

(3) Lazy eights, chandelles, and steep turns, in which the angle of bank is not more than 60 degrees.

(b) The utility category is limited to airplanes that have a seating configuration, excluding pilot seats, of nine or less, a maximum certificated takeoff weight of 12,500 pounds or less, and intended for limited acrobatic operation. Airplanes certificated in the utility category may be used in any of the operations covered under paragraph (a) of this section and in limited acrobatic operations. Limited acrobatic operation includes:

(1) Spins (if approved for the particular type of airplane); and

(2) Lazy eights, chandelles, and steep turns, in which the angle of bank is more than 60 degrees.

(c) The acrobatic category is limited to airplanes that have a seating configuration, excluding pilot seats, of nine or less, a maximum certificated takeoff weight of 12,500 pounds or less, and intended for use without restrictions, other than those shown to be necessary as a result of required flight tests.

(d) The commuter category is limited to propeller-driven, multiengine airplanes that have a seating configuration excluding pilot seats, of 19 or less, and a maximum certificated takeoff weight of 19,000 pounds or less, intended for nonacrobatic operation as described in paragraph (a) of this section.

(e) Airplanes may be type certificated in more than one category of this part if the requirements of each requested category are met.

[Doc. No. 4080, 29 FR 17955, Dec. 18, 1964, as amended by Amdt. 23-4, 32 FR 5934, Apr. 14, 1967; Amdt. 23-34, 52 FR 1825, Jan. 15, 1987; 52 FR 34745, Sept. 14, 1987]

Subpart B—Flight

GENERAL

§ 23.21 Proof of compliance.

(a) Each requirement of this subpart must be met at each appropriate combination of weight and center of gravity within the range of loading conditions for which certification is requested. This must be shown—

(1) By tests upon an airplane of the type for which certification is requested, or by calculations based on, and equal in accuracy to, the results of testing; and

(2) By systematic investigation of each probable combination of weight and center of gravity, if compliance cannot be reasonably inferred from combinations investigated.

(b) The following general tolerances are allowed during flight testing. However, greater tolerances may be allowed in particular tests:

Item	Tolerance
Weight	+5%, −10%.
Critical items affected by weight	+5%, −1%.
C.G	±7% total travel.

§ 23.23 Load distribution limits.

Ranges of weight and centers of gravity within which the airplane may be safely operated must be established and must include the range for lateral centers of gravity if possible loading conditions can result in significant variation of their positions. If low fuel adversely affects balance or stability, the airplane must be tested under conditions simulating those that would exist when the amount of usable fuel does not exceed one gallon for each 12 maximum continuous horsepower of the engine or engines.

[Doc. No. 4080, 29 FR 17955, Dec. 18, 1964, as amended by Amdt. 23-17, 41 FR 55463, Dec. 20, 1976]

§ 23.25 Weight limits.

(a) *Maximum weight.* The maximum weight is the highest weight at which compliance with each applicable requirement of this Part (other than those complied with at the design landing weight) is shown. In addition, for commuter category airplanes, the applicant must establish a maximum zero fuel weight. The maximum weight must be established so that it is—

(1) Not more than—

(i) The highest weight selected by the applicant;

(ii) The design maximum weight, which is the highest weight at which compliance with each applicable structural loading condition of this part (other than those complied with at the design landing weight) is shown; or

(iii) The highest weight at which compliance with each applicable flight requirement is shown, except for airplanes equipped with standby power rocket engines, in which case it is the highest weight established in accordance with Appendix E of this part; or

(2) Assuming a weight of 170 pounds for each occupant of each seat for normal and commuter category airplanes and 190 pounds (unless otherwise placarded) for utility and acrobatic category airplanes, not less than the weight with—

(i) Each seat occupied, oil at full tank capacity, and at least enough fuel for one-half hour of operation at rated maximum continuous power; or

(ii) The required minimum crew, and fuel and oil to full tank capacity.

(b) *Minimum weight.* The minimum weight (the lowest weight at which compliance with each applicable requirement of this part is shown) must be established so that it is not more than the sum of—

(1) The empty weight determined under § 23.29;

(2) The weight of the required minimum crew (assuming a weight of 170 pounds for each crewmember); and

(3) The weight of—

(i) For turbojet powered airplanes, 5 percent of the total fuel capacity of that particular fuel tank arrangement under investigation, and

(ii) For other airplanes, the fuel necessary for one-half hour of operation at maximum continuous power.

[Doc. No. 4080, 29 FR 17955, Dec. 18, 1964, as amended by Amdt. 23-7, 34 FR 13086, Aug. 13, 1969; Amdt. 23-21, 43 FR 2317, Jan.

16, 1978; Amdt. 23-34, 52 FR 1825, Jan. 15, 1987]

§ 23.29 Empty weight and corresponding center of gravity.

(a) The empty weight and corresponding center of gravity must be determined by weighing the airplane with—

(1) Fixed ballast;

(2) Unusable fuel determined under § 23.959; and

(3) Full operating fluids, including—

(i) Oil;

(ii) Hydraulic fluid; and

(iii) Other fluids required for normal operation of airplane systems, except potable water, lavatory precharge water, and water intended for injection in the engines.

(b) The condition of the airplane at the time of determining empty weight must be one that is well defined and can be easily repeated.

[Doc. No. 4080, 29 FR 17955, Dec. 18, 1964; 30 FR 258, Jan. 9, 1965, as amended by Amdt. 23-21, 43 FR 2317, Jan. 16, 1978]

§ 23.31 Removable ballast.

Removable ballast may be used in showing compliance with the flight requirements of this subpart, if—

(a) The place for carrying ballast is properly designed and installed, and is marked under § 23.1557; and

(b) Instructions are included in the airplane flight manual, approved manual material, or markings and placards, for the proper placement of the removable ballast under each loading condition for which removable ballast is necessary.

[Doc. No. 4080, 29 FR 17955, Dec. 18, 1964; 30 FR 258, Jan. 9, 1965, as amended by Amdt. 23-13, 37 FR 20023, Sept. 23, 1972]

§ 23.33 Propeller speed and pitch limits.

(a) *General.* The propeller speed and pitch must be limited to values that will assure safe operation under normal operating conditions.

(b) *Propellers not controllable in flight.* For each propeller whose pitch cannot be controlled in flight—

(1) During takeoff and initial climb at V^y, the propeller must limit the engine r.p.m., at full throttle or at maximum allowable takeoff manifold pressure, to a speed not greater than the maximum allowable takeoff r.p.m.; and

(2) During a closed throttle glide at the placarded "never-exceed speed", the propeller may not cause an engine speed above 110 percent of maximum continuous speed.

(c) *Controllable pitch propellers without constant speed controls.* Each propeller that can be controlled in flight, but that does not have constant speed controls, must have a means to limit the pitch range so that—

(1) The lowest possible pitch allows compliance with paragraph (b)(1) of this section; and

(2) The highest possible pitch allows compliance with paragraph (b)(2) of this section.

(d) *Controllable pitch propellers with constant speed controls.* Each controllable pitch propeller with constant speed controls must have—

(1) With the governor in operation, a means at the governor to limit the maximum engine speed to the maximum allowable takeoff r.p.m.; and

(2) With the governor inoperative, a means to limit the maximum engine speed to 103 percent of the maximum allowable takeoff r.p.m. with the propeller blades at the lowest possible pitch and with takeoff manifold pressure, the airplane stationary, and no wind.

PERFORMANCE

§ 23.45 General.

(a) Unless otherwise prescribed, the performance requirements of this subpart must be met for still air; and

(1) Standard atmospheric conditions for normal, utility, and acrobatic category airplanes; or

(2) Ambient atmospheric conditions for commuter category airplanes.

(b) The performance must correspond to the propulsive thrust available under the particular ambient atmospheric conditions, the particular flight condition, and the relative humidity specified in paragraph (d) or (e) of this section, as appropriate.

(c) The available propulsive thrust must correspond to engine power or thrust, not exceeding the approved power or thrust, less—

(1) Installation losses; and

(2) The power or equivalent thrust absorbed by the accessories and services appropriate to the particular ambient atmospheric conditions and the particular flight condition.

(d) For reciprocating engine-powered airplanes, the performance, as affected by engine power, must be based on a relative humidity of 80 percent in a standard atmosphere.

(e) For turbine engine-powered airplanes, the performance, as affected by engine power or thrust, must be based on a relative humidity of—

(1) 80 percent, at and below standard temperature; and

(2) 34 percent, at and above standard temperature plus 50 degrees F.

Between these two temperatures, the relative humidity must vary linearly.

(f) For commuter category airplanes, the following also apply:

(1) Unless otherwise prescribed, the applicant must select the takeoff, en route, approach, and landing configurations for the airplane;

(2) The airplane configuration may vary with weight, altitude, and temperature, to the extent they are compatible with the operating procedures required by paragraph (f)(3) of this section;

(3) Unless otherwise prescribed, in determining the critical-engine-inoperative takeoff performance, takeoff flight path, the accelerate-stop distance, takeoff distance, and landing distance, changes in the airplane's configuration, speed, power, and thrust must be made in accordance with procedures established by the applicant for operation in service;

(4) Procedures for the execution of missed approaches and balked landings associated with the conditions prescribed in §§ 23.67(e)(3) and 23.77(c) must be established; and

(5) The procedures established under paragraphs (f)(3) and (f)(4) of this section must—

(i) Be able to be consistently executed by a crew of average skill;

(ii) Use methods or devices that are safe and reliable; and

(iii) Include allowance for any reasonably expected time delays in the execution of the procedures.

[Amdt. 23-21, 43 FR 2317, Jan. 16, 1978, as amended by Amdt. 23-34, 52 FR 1826, Jan. 15, 1987]

§ 23.49　Stalling speed.

(a) V_{so} is the stalling speed, if obtainable, or the minimum steady speed, in knots (CAS), at which the airplane is controllable, with the—

(1) Applicable power or thrust condition set forth in paragraph (e) of this section;

(2) Propellers in the takeoff position;

(3) Landing gear extended;

(4) Wing flaps in the landing position;

(5) Cowl flaps closed;

(6) Center of gravity in the most unfavorable position within the allowable landing range; and

(7) Weight used when V_{so} is being used as a factor to determine compliance with a required performance standard.

(b) V_{so} at maximum weight may not exceed 61 knots for—

(1) Single-engine airplanes; and

(2) Multiengine airplanes of 6,000 pounds or less maximum weight that cannot meet the minimum rate of climb specified in § 23.67(b) with the critical engine inoperative.

(c) V_{s1} is the calibrated stalling speed, if obtainable, or the minimum steady speed, in knots, at which the airplane is controllable, with the—

(1) Applicable power or thrust condition set forth in paragraph (e) of this section;

(2) Propellers in the takeoff position;

(3) Airplane in the condition existing in the test in which V_{s1} is being used; and

(4) Weight used when V_{s1} is being used as a factor to determine compliance with a required performance standard.

(d) V_{so} and V_{s1} must be determined by flight tests, using the procedure specified in § 23.201.

(e) The following power or thrust conditions must be used to meet the requirements of this section:

(1) For reciprocating engine-powered airplanes, engines idling, throttles closed or at not more than the power necessary for zero thrust at a speed

not more than 110 percent of the stalling speed.

(2) For turbine engine-powered airplanes, the propulsive thrust may not be greater than zero at the stalling speed, or, if the resultant thrust has no appreciable effect on the stalling speed, with engines idling and throttles closed.

[Doc. No. 4080, 29 FR 17955, Dec. 18, 1964, as amended by Amdt. 23-7, 34 FR 13086, Aug. 13, 1969; Amdt. 23-21, 43 FR 2317, Jan. 16, 1978]

§ 23.51 Takeoff.

(a) For each airplane (except a skiplane for which landplane takeoff data has been determined under this paragraph and furnished in the Airplane Flight Manual) the distance required to takeoff and climb over a 50-foot obstacle must be determined with—

(1) The engines operating within approved operating limitations; and

(2) The cowl flaps in the normal takeoff position.

(b) The starting point for measuring seaplane and amphibian takeoff distance may be the point at which a speed of not more than three knots is reached.

(c) Takeoffs made to determine the data required by this section may not require exceptional piloting skill or exceptionally favorable conditions.

(d) For commuter category airplanes, takeoff performance and data as required by §§ 23.53 through 23.59 must be determined and included in the Airplane Flight Manual—

(1) For each weight, altitude, and ambient temperature within the operational limits selected by the applicant;

(2) For the selected configuration for takeoff;

(3) For the most unfavorable center of gravity position;

(4) With the operating engine within approved operating limitations;

(5) On a smooth, dry, hard surface runway; and

(6) Corrected for the following operational correction factors:

(i) Not more than 50 percent of nominal wind components along the takeoff path opposite to the direction of takeoff and not less than 150 percent of nominal wind components along the takeoff path in the direction of takeoff; and

(ii) Effective runway gradients.

[Amdt. 23-21, 43 FR 2317, Jan. 16, 1978, as amended by Amdt. 23-34, 52 FR 1826, Jan. 15, 1987]

§ 23.53 Takeoff speeds.

(a) For multiengine airplanes, the lift-off speed, V_{LOF}, may not be less than V_{MC} determined in accordance with § 23.149.

(b) Each normal, utility, and acrobatic category airplane, upon reaching a height of 50 feet above the takeoff surface level, must have reached a speed of not less than the following:

(1) For multiengine airplanes, the higher of—

(i) 1.1 V_{MC}; or

(ii) 1.3 V_{S1}, or any lesser speed, not less than V_X plus 4 knots, that is shown to be safe under all conditions, including turbulence and complete engine failure.

(2) For single engine airplanes—

(i) 1.3 V_{S1}; or

(ii) Any lesser speed, not less than V_X plus 4 knots, that is shown to be safe under all conditions, including turbulence and complete engine failure.

(c) For commuter category airplanes, the following apply:

(1) The takeoff decision speed, V_1, is the calibrated airspeed on the ground at which, as a result of engine failure or other reasons, the pilot is assumed to have made a decision to continue or discontinue the takeoff. The takeoff decision speed, V_1, must be selected by the applicant but may not be less than the greater of the following:

(i) 1.10 V_{S1};

(ii) 1.10 V_{MC} established in accordance with § 23.149;

(iii) A speed at which the airplane can be rotated for takeoff and shown to be adequate to safely continue the takeoff, using normal piloting skill, when the critical engine is suddenly made inoperative; or

(iv) V_{EF} plus the speed gained with the critcial engine inoperative during the time interval between the instant that the critical engine is failed and the instant at which the pilot recognizes and reacts to the engine failure as indicated by the pilot's application of the first retarding means during the accelerate-stop determination of § 23.55.

(2) The takeoff safety speed, V_2, in terms of calibrated airspeed, must be selected by the applicant so as to allow the gradient of climb required in § 23.67 but must not be less than V_1 or less than $1.2V_{S1}$.

(3) The critical engine failure speed, V_{EF}, is the calibrated airspeed at which the critical engine is assumed to fail. V_{EF} must be selected by the applicant but not less than V_{MC} determined in accordance with § 23.149.

(4) The rotation speed, V_R in terms of calibrated airspeed, must be selected by the applicant and may not be less than the greater of the following:

(i) V_1; or

(ii) The speed determined in accordance with § 23.57(c) that allows attaining the initial climb out speed, V_2, before reaching a height of 35 feet above the takeoff surface.

(5) For any given set of conditions, such as weight, altitude, configuration, and temperature, a single value of V_R must be used to show compliance with both the one-engine-inoperative takeoff and all-engines-operating takeoff requirements:

(i) One-engine-inoperative takeoff determined in accordance with § 23.57; and

(ii) All-engines-operating takeoff determined in accordance with § 23.59.

(6) The one-engine-inoperative takeoff distance, using a normal rotation rate at a speed of 5 knots less than V_R established in accordance with paragraphs (c)(4) and (5) of this section, must be shown not to exceed the corresponding one-engine-inoperative takeoff distance determined in accordance with §§ 23.57 and 23.59 using the established V_R. The take off distance determined in accordance with § 23.59 and the takeoff must be safely continued from the point at which the airplane is 35 feet above the takeoff surface at a speed not less than 5 knots less than the established V_2 speed.

(7) The applicant must show, with all engines operating, that marked increases in the scheduled takeoff distances determined in accordance with

§ 23.59 do not result from over-rotation of the airplane and out-of-trim conditions.

[Amdt. 23-34, 52 FR 1826, Jan. 15, 1987; 52 FR 34745, Sept. 14, 1987]

§ 23.55 Accelerate-stop distance.

For each commuter category airplane, the accelerate-stop distance must be determined as follows:

(a) The accelerate-stop distance is the sum of the distances necessary to—

(1) Accelerate the airplane from a standing start to V_1; and

(2) Come to a full stop from the point at which V_1 is reached assuming that in the case of engine failure, the pilot has decided to stop as indicated by application of the first retarding means at the speed V_1.

(b) Means other than wheel brakes may be used to determine the accelerate-stop distance if that means is available with the critical engine inoperative and if that means—

(1) Is safe and reliable;

(2) Is used so that consistent results can be expected under normal operating conditions; and

(3) Is such that exceptional skill is not required to control the airplane.

[Amdt. 23-34, 52 FR 1826, Jan. 15, 1987]

§ 23.57 Takeoff path.

For each commuter category airplane, the takeoff path is as follows:

(a) The takeoff path extends from a standing start to a point in the takeoff at which the airplane is 1,500 feet above the takeoff surface or at which the transition from the takeoff to the en route configuration is completed, whichever point is higher; and

(1) The takeoff path must be based on the procedures prescribed in § 23.45;

(2) The airplane must be accelerated on the ground to V_{EF} at which point the critical engine must be made inoperative and remain inoperative for the rest of the takeoff; and

(3) After reaching V_{EF}, the airplane must be accelerated to V_2.

(b) During the acceleration to speed V_2, the nose gear may be raised off the ground at a speed not less than V_R. However, landing gear retraction may not be initiated until the airplane is airborne.

(c) During the takeoff path determination, in accordance with paragraphs (a) and (b) of this section—

(1) The slope of the airborne part of the takeoff path must be positive at each point;

(2) The airplane must reach V_2 before it is 35 feet above the takeoff surface, and must continue at a speed as close as practical to, but not less than V_2, until it is 400 feet above the takeoff surface;

(3) At each point along the takeoff path, starting at the point at which the airplane reaches 400 feet above the takeoff surface, the available gradient of climb may not be less than—

(i) 1.2 percent for two-engine airplanes;

(ii) 1.5 percent for three-engine airplanes;

(iii) 1.7 percent for four-engine airplanes; and

(4) Except for gear retraction and automatic propeller feathering, the airplane configuration may not be changed, and no change in power or thrust that requires action by the pilot may be made, until the airplane is 400 feet above the takeoff surface.

(d) The takeoff path must be determined by a continuous demonstrated takeoff or by synthesis from segments. If the takeoff path is determined by the segmental method—

(1) The segments must be clearly defined and must be related to the distinct changes in the configuration, power or thrust, and speed;

(2) The weight of the airplane, the configuration, and the power or thrust must be constant throughout each segment and must correspond to the most critical condition prevailing in the segment;

(3) The flight path must be based on the airplane's performance without ground effect;

(4) The takeoff path data must be checked by continuous demonstrated takeoffs up to the point at which the airplane is out of ground effect and its speed is stabilized to ensure that the path is conservative relative to the continuous path; and

(5) The airplane is considered to be out of the ground effect when it reaches a height equal to its wing span.

[Amdt. 23–34, 52 FR 1827, Jan. 15, 1987]

§ 23.59 Takeoff distance and takeoff run.

For each commuter category airplane—

(a) Takeoff distance is the greater of—

(1) The horizontal distance along the takeoff path from the start of the takeoff to the point at which the airplane is 35 feet above the takeoff surface as determined under § 23.57; or

(2) With all engines operating, 115 percent of the horizontal distance along the takeoff path, with all engines operating, from the start of the takeoff to the point at which the airplane is 35 feet above the takeoff surface, as determined by a procedure consistent with § 23.57.

(b) If the takeoff distance includes a clearway, the takeoff run is the greater of—

(1) The horizontal distance along the takeoff path from the start of the takeoff to a point equidistant between the point at which V_{LOF} is reached and the point at which the airplane is 35 feet above the takeoff surface as determined under § 23.57; or

(2) With all engines operating, 115 percent of the horizontal distance along the takeoff path, with all engines operating, from the start of the takeoff to a point equidistant between the point at which V_{LOF} is reached and the point at which the airplane is 35 feet above the takeoff surface determined by a procedure consistent with § 23.57.

[Amdt. 23–34, 52 FR 1827, Jan. 15, 1987]

§ 23.61 Takeoff flight path.

For each commuter category airplane, the takeoff flight path must be determined as follows:

(a) The takeoff flight path begins 35 feet above the takeoff surface at the end of the takeoff distance determined in accordance with § 23.59.

(b) The net takeoff flight path data must be determined so that they represent the actual takeoff flight paths, as determined in accordance with § 23.57 and with paragraph (a) of this section, reduced at each point by a gradient of climb equal to—

(1) 0.8 percent for two-engine airplanes;

(2) 0.9 percent for three-engine airplanes; and

(3) 1.0 percent for four-engine airplanes.

(c) The prescribed reduction in climb gradient may be applied as an equivalent reduction in acceleration along that part of the takeoff flight path at which the airplane is accelerated in level flight.

[Amdt. 23-34, 52 FR 1827, Jan. 15, 1987]

§ 23.65   Climb: All engines operating.

(a) Each airplane must have a steady rate of climb at sea level of at least 300 feet per minute and a steady angle of climb of at least 1:12 for landplanes or 1:15 for seaplanes and amphibians with—

(1) Not more than maximum continuous power on each engine;

(2) The landing gear retracted;

(3) The wing flaps in the takeoff position; and

(4) The cowl flaps or other means for controlling the engine cooling air supply in the position used in the cooling tests required by §§ 23.1041 through 23.1047.

(b) Each airplane with engines for which the takeoff and maximum continuous power ratings are identical and that has fixed-pitch, two-position, or similar propellers, may use a lower propeller pitch setting than that allowed by § 23.33 to obtain rated engine r.p.m. at Vx, if—

(1) The airplane shows marginal performance (such as when it can meet the rate of climb requirements of paragraph (a) of this section but has difficulty in meeting the angle of climb requirements of paragraph (a) of this section or of § 23.77); and

(2) Acceptable engine cooling is shown at the lower speed associated with the best angle of climb.

(c) Each turbine engine-powered airplane must be able to maintain a steady gradient of climb of at least 4 percent at a pressure altitude of 5,000 feet and a temperature of 81 degrees F (standard temperature plus 40 degree F) with the airplane in the configura-

tion prescribed in paragraph (a) of this section.

(d) In addition for commuter category airplanes, performance data must be determined for variations in weight, altitude, and temperature at the most critical center of gravity for which approval is requested.

[Doc. No. 4080, 29 FR 17955, Dec. 18, 1964, as amended by Amdt. 23-7, 34 FR 13086, Aug. 13, 1969; Amdt. 23-21, 43 FR 2317, Jan. 16, 1978; Amdt. 23-34, 52 FR 1827, Jan. 15, 1987; Amdt. 23-24, 52 FR 34745, Sept. 14, 1987]

§ 23.67   Climb: one engine inoperative.

(a) Each normal, utility, and acrobatic category reciprocating engine-powered multiengine airplane of more than 6,000 pounds maximum weight must be able to maintain a steady rate of climb of at least $0.027\ V_{so}^2$ (that is, the number of feet per minute is obtained by multiplying the square of the number of knots by 0.027 at an altitude of 5,000 feet with the—

(1) Critical engine inoperative, and its propeller in the minimum drag position;

(2) Remaining engines at not more than maximum continuous power;

(3) Landing gear retracted;

(4) Wing flaps in the most favorable position; and

(5) Cowl flaps in the position used in the cooling tests required by §§ 23.1041 through 23.1047.

(b) For normal, utility, and acrobatic category reciprocating engine-powered multiengine airplanes of 6,000 pounds or less maximum weight, the following apply:

(1) Each airplane with a V_{so} of more than 61 knots must be able to maintain a steady rate of climb of at least $0.027\ V_{so}^2$ (that is, the number of feet per minute is obtained by multiplying the square of the number of knots by 0.027), at an altitude of 5,000 feet with the—

(i) Critical engine inoperative and its propeller in the minimum drag position;

(ii) Remaining engines at not more than maximum continuous power;

(iii) Landing gear retracted;

(iv) Wing flaps in the most favorable position; and

(v) Cowl flaps in the position used in the cooling tests required by §§ 23.1041 through 23.1047.

(2) For each airplane with a stalling speed of 61 knots or less, the steady rate of climb at 5,000 feet must be determined with the—

(i) Critical engine inoperative and its propeller in the minimum drag position;

(ii) Remaining engines at not more than maximum continuous power;

(iii) Landing gear retracted;

(iv) Wing flaps in the most favorable position; and

(v) Cowl flaps in the position used in the cooling tests required by §§ 23.1041 through 23.1047.

(c) For normal, utility, and acrobatic category turbine-powered multiengine airplanes the following apply:

(1) The steady gradient of climb must be determined at each weight, altitude, and ambient temperature within the operational limits established by the applicant, with the—

(i) Critical engine inoperative, and its propeller in the minimum drag position;

(ii) Remaining engines at not more than maximum continuous power or thrust;

(iii) Landing gear retracted;

(iv) Wing flaps in the most favorable position; and

(v) The means for controlling the engine cooling air supply in the position used in the engine cooling tests required by §§ 23.1041 through 23.1047.

(2) Each airplane must be able to maintain the following climb gradients with the airplane in the configuration prescribed in paragraph (c)(1) of this section:

(i) 1.2 percent (or, if greater, a gradient equivalent to a rate of climb of 0.027 $Vs_0{}^2$) at a pressure altitude of 5,000 feet and standard temperature (41 degrees F).

(ii) 0.6 percent (or, if greater, a gradient equivalent to a rate of climb of 0.014 $Vs_0{}^2$) at a pressure altitude of 5,000 feet and 81 degrees F (standard temperature plus 40 degrees F).

(3) The minimum climb gradient specified in paragraphs (c)(2) (i) and (ii) of this section must vary linearly between 41 degrees F and 81 degrees F

and must change at the same rate up to the maximum operating termperature approved for the airplane.

(4) In paragraphs (c)(2) (i) and (ii) of this section, rate of climb is expressed in feet per minute and Vs_0 is expressed in knots.

(d) For all multiengine airplanes, the speed for best rate of climb with one engine inoperative must be determined.

(e) For commuter category airplanes, the following apply:

(1) *Takeoff climb:* The maximum weight at which the airplane meets the minimum climb performance specified in paragraphs (e)(1) (i) and (ii) of this section must be determined for each altitude and ambient temperature within the operating limitations established for the airplane, out of ground effect in free air, with the airplane in the takeoff configuration, with the most critical center of gravity, the critical engine inoperative, the remaining engines at the maximum takeoff power or thrust, and the propeller of the inoperative engine windmilling with the propeller controls in the normal position, except that, if an approved automatic propeller feathering system is installed, the propeller may be in the feathered position:

(i) *Takeoff, landing gear extended.* The minimum steady gradient of climb between the lift-off speed, V_{LOF}, and until the landing gear is retracted must be measurably positive for two-engine airplanes, not less than 0.3 percent for three-engine airplanes, or 0.5 percent for four-engine airplanes at all points along the flight path; and

(ii) *Takeoff, landing gear retracted.* The minimum steady gradient of climb must not be less than 2 percent for two-engine airplanes, 2.3 percent for three-engine airplanes, and 2.6 percent for four-engine airplanes at the speed V_2, until the airplane is 400 feet above the takeoff surface. For airplanes with fixed landing gear, this requirement must be met with the landing gear extended.

(2) *En route climb:* The maximum weight must be determined for each altitude and ambient temperature within the operational limits established for the airplane, at which the steady gradient of climb is not less

than 1.2 percent for two-engine airplanes, 1.5 percent for three-engine airplanes, and 1.7 percent for four-engine airplanes at an altitude of 1,500 feet above the takeoff surface, with the airplane in the en route configuration, the critical engine inoperative, the remaining engine at the maximum continuous power or thrust, and the most unfavorable center of gravity.

(3) *Approach:* In the approach configuration corresponding to the normal all-engines-operating procedure in which V_{s1} for this configuration does not exceed 110 percent of the V_{s1} for the related landing configuration, the steady gradient of climb may not be less than 2.1 percent for two-engine airplanes, 2.4 percent for three-engine airplanes, and 2.7 percent for four-engine airplanes, with—

(i) The critical engine inoperative and the remaining engines at the available takeoff power or thrust;

(ii) The maximum landing weight; and

(iii) A climb speed established in connection with the normal landing procedures but not exceeding 1.5 V_{s1}.

[Amdt. 23-21, 43 FR 2317, Jan. 16, 1978, as amended by Amdt. 23-34, 52 FR 1827, Jan. 15, 1987; Amdt. 23-24, 52 FR 34745, Sept. 14, 1987]

§ 23.75 Landing.

For airplanes (except skiplanes for which landplane landing data have been determined under this section and furnished in the Airplane Flight Manual), the horizontal distance necessary to land and come to a complete stop (or to a speed of approximately 3 knots for water landings of seaplanes and amphibians) from a point 50 feet above the landing surface must be determined as follows:

(a) A steady gliding approach with a calibrated airspeed of at least 1.3 V_{s1} must be maintained down to the 50-foot height.

(b) The landing may not require exceptional piloting skill or exceptionally favorable conditions.

(c) The landing must be made without excessive vertical acceleration or tendency to bounce, nose over, ground loop, porpoise, or water loop.

(d) It must be shown that a safe transition to the balked landing condi-

tions of § 23.77 can be made from the conditions that exist at the 50-foot height.

(e) The pressures on the wheel braking system may not exceed those specified by the brake manufacturer.

(f) Means other than wheel brakes may be used if that means—

(1) Is safe and reliable;

(2) Is used so that consistent results can be expected in service; and

(3) Is such that exceptional skill is not required to control the airplane.

(g) In addition, for commuter category airplanes, the following apply:

(1) The landing distance must be determined for standard temperatures at each weight, altitude, and wind condition within the operational limits established by the applicant;

(2) A steady gliding approach, or a steady approach at a gradient of descent not greater than 5.2 percent (3°), at a calibrated airspeed not less than 1.3V_{s1} must be maintained down to the 50-foot height; and

(3) The landing distance data must include correction factors for not more than 50 percent of the nominal wind components along the landing path opposite to the direction of landing and not less than 150 percent of the nominal wind components along the landing path in the direction of landing.

[Amdt. 23-21, 43 FR 2318, Jan. 16, 1978, as amended by Amdt. 23-34, 52 FR 1828, Jan. 15, 1987]

§ 23.77 Balked landing.

(a) For balked landings, each normal, utility, and acrobatic category airplane must be able to maintain a steady angle of climb at sea level of at least 1:30 with—

(1) Takeoff power on each engine;

(2) The landing gear extended; and

(3) The wing flaps in the landing position, except that if the flaps may safely be retracted in two seconds or less without loss of altitude and without sudden changes of angle of attack or exceptional piloting skill, they may be retracted.

(b) Each normal, utility, and acrobatic category turbine engine-powered airplane must be able to maintain a steady rate of climb of at least zero at a pressure altitude of 5,000 feet at 81 degrees F (standard temperature plus 40 degrees F), with the airplanes in the configuration prescribed in paragraph (a) of this section.

(c) For each commuter category airplane, with all engines operating, the maximum weight must be determined with the airplane in the landing configuration for each altitude and ambient temperature within the operational limits established for the airplane, with the most unfavorable center of gravity and out-of-ground effect in free air, at which the steady gradient of climb will not be less than 3.3 percent with—

(1) The engines at the power or thrust that is available 8 seconds after initiation of movement of the power or thrust controls from the minimum flight-idle position to the takeoff position.

(2) A climb speed not greater than the approach speed established under § 23.75 and not less than the greater of $1.05 V_{MC}$ or $1.10 V_{S1}$.

[Amdt. 23-21, 43 FR 2318, Jan. 16, 1978, as amended by Amdt. 23-34, 52 FR 1828, Jan. 15, 1987; Amdt. 23-24, 52 FR 34745, Sept. 14, 1987]

FLIGHT CHARACTERISTICS

§ 23.141 General.

The airplane must meet the requirements of §§ 23.143 through 23.253 at the normally expected operating altitudes without exceptional piloting skill, alertness, or strength.

[Amdt. 23-17, 41 FR 55464, Dec. 20, 1976]

CONTROLLABILITY AND MANEUVERABILITY

§ 23.143 General.

(a) The airplane must be safely controllable and maneuverable during—

(1) Takeoff;

(2) Climb;

(3) Level flight;

(4) Dive; and

(5) Landing (power on and power off with the wing flaps extended and retracted).

(b) It must be possible to make a smooth transition from one flight condition to another (including turns and slips) without danger of exceeding the limit load factor, under any probable operating condition (including, for multiengine airplanes, those conditions normally encountered in the sudden failure of any engine).

(c) If marginal conditions exist with regard to required pilot strength, the "strength of pilots" limits must be shown by quantitative tests. In no case may the limits exceed those prescribed in the following table:

Values in pounds of force as applied to the control wheel or rudder pedals	Pitch	Roll	Yaw
(a) For temporary application:			
Stick	60	30	
Wheel (applied to rim)	75	60	
Rudder pedal			150
(b) For prolonged application	10	5	20

[Doc. No. 4080, 29 FR 17955, Dec. 18, 1964, as amended by Amdt. 23-14, 38 FR 31819, Nov. 19, 1973; Amdt. 23-17, 41 FR 55464, Dec. 20, 1976]

§ 23.145 Longitudinal control.

(a) It must be possible, at speeds below the trim speed, to pitch the nose downward so that the rate of increase in airspeed allows prompt acceleration to the trim speed with—

(1) Maximum continuous power on each engine and the airplane trimmed at V_X;

(2) Power off and the airplane trimmed at a speed determined in accordance with § 23.161(c)(3) or (4) as appropriate or at the minimum trim speed, whichever is higher; and

(3) Wing flaps and landing gear (i) retracted, and (ii) extended.

(b) With the landing gear extended no change in trim or exertion of more control force than can be readily applied with one hand for a short period of time may be required for the following maneuvers:

(1) With power off, flaps retracted, and the airplane trimmed at $1.4V_{S1}$ or the minimum trim speed, whichever is higher, extend the flaps as rapidly as possible and allow the airspeed to transition from $1.4V_{S1}$ to $1.4V_{S0}$, or if appropriate from the minimum trim speed to a speed equal to V_{S0} increased by the same percentage that the minimum trim speed at the initial condition was greater than V_{S1}.

(2) With power off, flaps extended, and the airplane trimmed at $1.4V_{So}$ or the minimum trim speed, whichever is higher, retract the flaps as rapidly as possible and allow the airspeed to transition from $1.4V_{So}$ to $1.4V_{S1}$, or if appropriate, from the minimum trim speed to a speed equal to $1.4V_{S1}$ increased by the same percentage that the minimum trim speed at the initial condition was greater than V_{So}.

(3) Repeat paragraph (b)(2) of this section except with maximum continuous power.

(4) With power off, flaps retracted, and the airplane trimmed at a speed determined in accordance with § 23.161 (c)(3) or (4), as appropriate or at the minimum trim speed, whichever is higher, apply takeoff power rapidly while maintaining the same airspeed.

(5) Repeat subparagraph (4) of this paragraph, except with the flaps extended.

(6) With power off, flaps extended, and the airplane trimmed at a speed determined in accordance with § 23.161 (c)(3) or (4), as appropriate or at the minimum trim speed, whichever is higher, obtain and maintain airspeeds between $1.1\ V_{S1}$ and either $1.7\ V_{S1}$ or V_F, whichever is lower.

(c) It must be possible to maintain approximately level flight when flap retraction from any position is made during steady horizontal flight at $1.1\ V_{S1}$ with simultaneous application of not more than maximum continuous power.

(d) It must be possible, with a pilot control force of not more than 10 pounds, to maintain a speed of not more than the speed determined in accordance with § 23.161(c)(4), during a power-off glide with landing gear and wing flaps extended.

(e) By using normal flight and power controls, except as otherwise noted in paragraphs (e)(1) and (e)(2), it must be possible in the following airplanes to establish a zero rate of descent at an attitude suitable for a controlled landing without exceeding the operational and structural limitations of the airplane:

(1) For single engine and multiengine airplanes, without the use of the primary longitudinal control system.

(2) For multiengine airplanes—

(i) Without the use of the primary directional control; and

(ii) If a single failure of any one connecting or transmitting link would affect both the longitudinal and directional primary control system, without the primary longitudinal and directional control system.

[Doc. No. 4080, 29 FR 17955, Dec. 18, 1964, as amended by Amdt. 23-7, 34 FR 13086, Aug. 13, 1969; Amdt. 23-14, 38 FR 31819, Nov. 19, 1973; Amdt. 23-17, 41 FR 55464, Dec. 20, 1976]

§ 23.147   Directional and lateral control.

(a) For each multiengine airplane, it must be possible to make turns with 15 degrees of bank both towards and away from an inoperative engine, from a steady climb at $1.4\ V_{S1}$ or V_Y with—

(1) One engine inoperative and its propeller in the minimum drag position;

(2) The remaining engines at not more than maximum continuous power;

(3) The rearmost allowable center of gravity;

(4) The landing gear (i) retracted, and (ii) extended;

(5) The flaps in the most favorable climb position; and

(6) Maximum weight.

(b) For each multiengine airplane, it must be possible, while holding the wings level within five degrees, to make sudden changes in heading safely in both directions. This must be shown at $1.4\ V_{S1}$ or V_Y with heading changes up to 15 degrees (except that the heading change at which the rudder force corresponds to the limits specified in § 23.143 need not be exceeded), with the—

(1) Critical engine inoperative and its propeller in the minimum drag position;

(2) Remaining engines at maximum continuous power;

(3) Landing gear (i) retracted, and (ii) extended;

(4) Flaps in the most favorable climb position; and

(5) Center of gravity at its rearmost allowable position.

§ 23.149 Minimum control speed.

(a) V_{MC} is the calibrated airspeed, at which, when the critical engine is suddenly made inoperative, it is possible to recover control of the airplane with that engine still inoperative and maintain straight flight either with zero yaw or, at the option of the applicant, with an angle of bank of not more than five degrees. The method used to simulate critical engine failure must represent the most critical mode of powerplant failure with respect to controllability expected in service.

(b) For reciprocating engine-powered airplanes, V_{MC} may not exceed 1.2 V_{S_1} (where V_{S_1} is determined at the maximum takeoff weight with—

(1) Takeoff or maximum available power on the engines;

(2) The most unfavorable center of gravity;

(3) The airplane trimmed for takeoff;

(4) The maximum sea level takeoff weight (or any lesser weight necessary to show V_{MC});

(5) Flaps in the takeoff position;

(6) Landing gear retracted;

(7) Cowl flaps in the normal takeoff position;

(8) The propeller of the inoperative engine—

(i) Windmilling;

(ii) In the most probable position for the specific design of the propeller control; or

(iii) Feathered, if the airplane has an automatic feathering device; and

(9) The airplane airborne and the ground effect negligible.

(c) For turbine engine-powered airplanes, V_{MC} may not exceed 1.2 V_{S_1} (where V_{S_1} is determined at the maximum takeoff weight) with—

(1) Maximum available takeoff power or thrust on the engines;

(2) The most unfavorable center of gravity;

(3) The airplane trimmed for takeoff;

(4) The maximum sea level takeoff weight for any lesser weight necessary to show V_{MC});

(5) The airplane in the most critical takeoff configuration except with the landing gear retracted; and

(6) The airplane airborne and the ground effect negligible.

(d) At V_{MC}, the rudder pedal force required to maintain control may not exceed 150 pounds, and it may not be necessary to reduce power or thrust of the operative engines. During recovery, the airplane may not assume any dangerous attitude and it must be possible to prevent a heading change of more than 20 degrees.

[Amdt. 23–21, 43 FR 2318, Jan. 16, 1978]

§ 23.151 Acrobatic maneuvers.

Each acrobatic and utility category airplane must be able to perform safely the acrobatic maneuvers for which certification is requested. Safe entry speeds for these maneuvers must be determined.

§ 23.153 Control during landings.

For an airplane that has a maximum weight of more than 6,000 pounds, it must be possible, while in the landing configuration, to safely complete a landing without encountering forces in excess of those prescribed in § 23.143(c) following an approach to land:

(a) At a speed 5 knots less than the speed used in complying with § 23.75 and with the airplane in trim or as nearly as possible in trim;

(b) With neither the trimming control being moved throughout the maneuver nor the power being increased during the landing flare; and

(c) With the thrust settings used in demonstrating compliance with § 23.75.

[Amdt. 23–14, 38 FR 31819, Nov. 19, 1973]

§ 23.155 Elevator control force in maneuvers.

(a) The elevator control force needed to achieve the positive limit maneuvering load factor may not be less than:

(1) For wheel controls, $W/100$ (where W is the maximum weight) or 20 pounds, whichever is greater, except that it need not be greater than 50 pounds; or

(2) For stick controls, $W/140$ (where W is the maximum weight) or 15 pounds, whichever is greater, except that it need not be greater than 35 pounds.

(b) The requirement of paragraph (a) of this section must be met with wing flaps and landing gear retracted under each of the following conditions:

(1) At 75 percent of maximum continuous power for reciprocating engines, or the maximum power or thrust selected by the applicant as an operating limitation for use during cruise for reciprocating or turbine engines.

(2) In a turn, after the airplane is trimmed with wings level at the minimum speed at which the required normal acceleration can be achieved without stalling, and at the maximum level flight trim speed except that the speed may not exceed V_{NE} or V_{MO}/M_{MO}, whichever is appropriate.

(c) Compliance with the requirements of this section may be demonstrated by measuring the normal acceleration that is achieved with the limiting stick force or by establishing the stick force per g gradient and extrapolating to the appropriate limit.

[Amdt. 23-14, 38 FR 31819, Nov. 19, 1973; 38 FR 32784, Nov. 28, 1973]

§ 23.157   Rate of roll.

(a) *Takeoff.* It must be possible, using a favorable combination of controls, to roll the airplane from a steady 30-degree banked turn through an angle of 60 degrees, so as to reverse the direction of the turn within:

(1) For an airplane of 6,000 pounds or less maximum weight, 5 seconds from initiation of roll; and

(2) For an airplane of over 6,000 pounds maximum weight,

$$(W+500)/1,300$$

seconds, where W is the weight in pounds.

(b) The requirement of paragraph (a) must be met when rolling the airplane in either direction in the following condition:

(1) Flaps in the takeoff position;

(2) Landing gear retracted;

(3) For a single engine airplane, at maximum takeoff power or thrust; and for a multiengine airplane, with the critical engine inoperative, the propeller in the minimum drag position, and the other engines at maximum continuous power or thrust; and

(4) The airplane trimmed at $1.2V_{S1}$, or as nearly as possible in trim for straight flight.

(c) *Approach.* It must be possible, using a favorable combination of controls, to roll the airplane from a steady 30-degree banked turn through an angle of 60 degrees, so as to reverse the direction of the turn within:

(1) For an airplane of 6,000 pounds or less maximum weight, 4 seconds from initiation of roll; and

(2) For an airplane of over 6,000 pounds maximum weight,

$$(W+2,800)/2,200$$

seconds, where W is the weight in pounds.

(d) The requirement of paragraph (c) must be met when rolling the airplane in either direction in the following conditions:

(1) Flaps extended;

(2) Landing gear extended;

(3) All engines operating at idle power or thrust and with all engines operating at the power or thrust for level flight; and

(4) The airplane trimmed at the speed that is used in determining compliance with § 23.75.

[Amdt. 23-14, 38 FR 31819, Nov. 19, 1973]

TRIM

§ 23.161   Trim.

(a) *General.* Each airplane must meet the trim requirements of this section after being trimmed, and without further pressure upon, or movement of, the primary controls or their corresponding trim controls by the pilot or the automatic pilot.

(b) *Lateral and directional trim.* The airplane must maintain lateral and directional trim in level flight with the landing gear and wing flaps retracted as follows:

(1) For normal, utility, and acrobatic category airplanes, at a speed of $0.9V_H$ or V_C, whichever is lower; and

(2) For commuter category airplanes, at a speed of V_H or V_{MO}/M_{MO}, whichever is lower.

(c) *Longitudinal trim.* The airplane must maintain longitudinal trim under each of the following conditions, except that it need not maintain trim at a speed greater than V_{MO}/M_{MO}:

(1) A climb with maximum continuous power at a speed between V_X and 1.4 V_{S_1}, with—

(i) The landing gear and wing flaps retracted; and

(ii) The landing gear retracted and the wing flaps in the takeoff position.

(2) A power approach with a 3 degree angle of descent, the landing gear extended, and with—

(i) The wing flaps retracted and at a speed of 1.4 V_{S_1}; and

(ii) The applicable airspeed and flap position used in showing compliance with § 23.75.

(3) Level flight at any speed with the landing gear and wing flaps retracted as follows:

(i) For normal, utility, and acrobatic category airplanes, at any speed from $0.9V_H$ to either V_X or $1.4V_{S1}$; and

(ii) For commuter category airplanes, at a speed of V_H or V_{MO}/M_{MO}, whichever is lower, to either V_X or $1.4V_{S1}$.

(d) In addition, each multiengine airplane must maintain longitudinal and directional trim at a speed between V_Y and 1.4 V_{S1}, with—

(1) The critical engine inoperative;

(2) The remaining engines at maximum continuous power;

(3) The landing gear retracted;

(4) The wing flaps retracted; and

(5) An angle of bank of not more than five degrees.

[Doc. No. 4080, 29 FR 17955, Dec. 18, 1964, as amended by Amdt. 23–21, 43 FR 2318, Jan. 16, 1978, Amdt. 23–34, 52 FR 1828, Jan. 15, 1987]

STABILITY

§ 23.171 General.

The airplane must be longitudinally, directionally, and laterally stable under §§ 23.173 through 23.181. In addition, the airplane must show suitable stability and control "feel" (static stability) in any condition normally encountered in service, if flight tests show it is necessary for safe operation.

§ 23.173 Static longitudinal stability.

Under the conditions specified in § 23.175 and with the airplane trimmed as indicated, the characteristics of the elevator control forces and the friction within the control system must be as follows:

(a) A pull must be required to obtain and maintain speeds below the specified trim speed and a push required to obtain and maintain speeds above the specified trim speed. This must be shown at any speed that can be obtained, except that speeds requiring a control force in excess of 40 pounds or speeds above the maximum allowable speed or below the minimum speed for steady unstalled flight, need not be considered.

(b) The airspeed must return to within the tolerances specified for applicable categories of airplanes when the control force is slowly released at any speed within the speed range specified in paragraph (a) of this section. The applicable tolerances are—

(1) The airspeed must return to within plus or minus 10 percent of the original trim airspeed; and

(2) For commuter category airplanes, the airspeed must return to within plus or minus 7.5 percent of the original trim airspeed for the cruising condition specified in § 23.175(b).

(c) The stick force must vary with speed so that any substantial speed change results in a stick force clearly perceptible to the pilot.

[Doc. No. 4080, 29 FR 17955, Dec. 18, 1964, as amended by Amdt. 23–14, 38 FR 31820 Nov. 19, 1973, Amdt. 23–34, 52 FR 1828, Jan. 15, 1987]

§ 23.175 Demonstration of static longitudinal stability.

Static longitudinal stability must be shown as follows:

(a) *Climb.* The stick force curve must have a stable slope, at speeds between 85 and 115 percent of the trim speed, with—

(1) Flaps in the climb position;

(2) Landing gear retracted;

(3) 75 percent of maximum continuous power for reciprocating engines or the maximum power or thrust selected by the applicant as an operating limitation for use during a climb for turbine engines; and

(4) The airplane trimmed for V_Y, except that the speed need not be less than 1.4 V_{S1}.

(b) *Cruise—Landing gear retracted (or fixed gear).* (1) For the cruise conditions specified in paragraphs (b) (2) and (3) of this section, the following apply:

(i) The speed need not be less than 1.3 V_{S1}.

(ii) For airplanes with V_{NE} established under § 23.1505(a), the speed need not be greater than V_{NE}.

(iii) For airplanes with V_{MO}/M_{MO} established under § 23.1505(c), the speed need not be greater than a speed midway between V_{MO}/M_{MO} and the lesser of V_D/M_D or the speed demonstrated under § 23.251, except that for altitudes where Mach number in the limiting factor, the speed need not exceed that corresponding to the Mach number at which effective speed warning occurs.

(2) *High speed cruise.* The stick force curve must have a stable slope at all speeds within a range that is the greater of 15 percent of the trim speed plus the resulting free return speed range or 40 knots plus the resulting free return speed range for normal, utility, and acrobatic category airplanes, above and below the trim speed. For commuter category airplanes, the stick force curve must have a stable slope for a speed range of 50 knots from the trim speed, except that the speeds need not exceed V_{FC}/M_{FC} or be less than 1.4 V_{S1} and this speed range is considered to begin at the outer extremes of the friction band with a stick force not to exceed 50 pounds. In addition, for commuter category airplanes, V_{FC}/M_{FC} may not be less than a speed midway between V_{MO}/M_{MO} and V_{DF}/M_{DF}, except that, for altitudes where Mach number is the limiting factor, M_{FC} need not exceed the Mach number at which effective speed warning occurs. These requirements for all categories of airplane must be met with—

(i) Flaps retracted.

(ii) Seventy-five percent of maximum continuous power for reciprocating engines or, for turbine engines, the maximum cruising power or thrust selected by the applicant as an operating limitation, except that the power need not exceed that required at V_{NE} for airplanes with V_{NE} established under § 23.1505(a), or that required at $V_{MO}/$

M_{MO} for airplanes with V_{MO}/M_{MO} established under § 23.1505(c).

(iii) The airplane trimmed for level flight.

(3) *Low speed cruise.* The stick force curve must have a stable slope under all the conditions prescribed in paragraph (b)(2) of this section, except that the power is that required for level flight at a speed midway between 1.3 V_{S1} and the trim speed obtained in the high speed cruise condition under paragraph (b)(2) of this section.

(c) *Landing gear extended (airplanes with retractable gear).* The stick force curve must have a stable slope at all speeds within a range from 15 percent of the trim speed plus the resulting free return speed range below the trim speed, to the trim speed (except that the speed range need not include speeds less than 1.4 V_{S1} nor speeds greater than V_{LE}, with—

(1) Landing gear extended;

(2) Flaps retracted;

(3) 75 percent of maximum continuous power for reciprocating engines, or for turbine engines, the maximum cruising power or thrust selected by the applicant as an operating limitation, except that the power need not exceed that required for level flight at V_{LE}; and

(4) The airplane trimmed for level flight.

(d) *Approach and landing.* The stick force curve must have a stable slope at speeds between 1.1 V_{S1} and 1.8 V_{S1} with—

(1) Wing flaps in the landing position;

(2) Landing gear extended;

(3) The airplane trimmed at a speed in compliance with § 23.161(c)(4).

(4) Both power off and enough power to maintain a 3° angle of descent.

[Amdt. 23-7, 34 FR 13087, Aug. 13, 1969, as amended by Amdt. 23-14, 38 FR 31820, Nov. 19, 1973; Amdt. 23-17, 41 FR 55464, Dec. 20, 1976; Amdt. 23-34, 52 FR 1828, Jan. 15, 1987]

§ 23.177 Static directional and lateral stability.

(a) *Three-control airplanes.* The stability requirements for three-control airplanes are as follows:

(1) The static directional stability, as shown by the tendency to recover from a skid with the rudder free, must be positive for any landing gear and flap position appropriate to the takeoff, climb, cruise, and approach configurations. This must be shown with symmetrical power up to maximum continuous power, and at speeds from 1.2 V_{S1} up to the maximum allowable speed for the condition being investigated. The angle of skid for these tests must be appropriate to the type of airplane. At larger angles of skid up to that at which full rudder is used or a control force limit in § 23.143 is reached, whichever occurs first, and at speeds from 1.2 V_{S1} to V_A, the rudder pedal force must not reverse.

(2) The static lateral stability, as shown by the tendency to raise the low wing in a slip, must be positive for any landing gear and flap positions. This must be shown with symmetrical power up to 75 percent of maximum continuous power at speeds above 1.2 V_{S1}, up to the maximum allowable speed for the configuration being investigated. The static lateral stability may not be negative at 1.2 V_{S1}. The angle of slip for these tests must be appropriate to the type of airplane, but in no case may the slip angle be less than that obtainable with 10 degrees of bank.

(3) In straight, steady slips at 1.2 V_{S1} for any landing gear and flap positions, and for any symmetrical power conditions up to 50 percent of maximum continuous power, the aileron and rudder control movements and forces must increase steadily (but not necessarily in constant proportion) as the angle of slip is increased up to the maximum appropriate to the type of airplane. At larger slip angles up to the angle at which the full rudder or aileron control is used or a control force limit contained in § 23.143 is obtained, the rudder pedal force may not reverse. Enough bank must accompany slipping to hold a constant heading. Rapid entry into, or recovery from, a maximum slip may not result in uncontrollable flight characteristics.

(b) *Two-control (or simplified control) airplanes.* The stability requirements for two-control airplanes are as follows:

(1) The directional stability of the airplane must be shown by showing that, in each configuration, it can be rapidly rolled from a 45 degree bank in one direction to a 45 degree bank in the opposite direction without showing dangerous skid characteristics.

(2) The lateral stability of the airplane must be shown by showing that it will not assume a dangerous attitude or speed when the controls are abandoned for two minutes. This must be done in moderately smooth air with the airplane trimmed for straight level flight at 0.9 V_H or V_C, whichever is lower, with flaps and landing gear retracted, and with a rearward center of gravity.

[Doc. No. 4080, 29 FR 17955, Dec. 18, 1964; 30 FR 258, Jan, 9, 1965, as amended by Amdt. 23–21, 43 FR 2318, Jan. 16, 1978]

§ 23.179 Instrumented stick force measurements.

Instrumented stick force measurements must be made unless—

(a) Changes in speed are clearly reflected by changes in stick forces; and

(b) The maximum forces obtained under §§ 23.173 and 23.175 are not excessive.

§ 23.181 Dynamic stability.

(a) Any short period oscillation not including combined lateral-directional oscillations occurring between the stalling speed and the maximum allowable speed appropriate to the configuration of the airplane must be heavily damped with the primary controls—

(1) Free; and

(2) In a fixed position.

(b) Any combined lateral-directional oscillations ("Dutch roll") occurring between the stalling speed and the maximum allowable speed appropriate to the configuration of the airplane must be damped to 1/10 amplitude in 7 cycles with the primary controls—

(1) Free; and

(2) In a fixed position.

[Amdt. 23–21, 43 FR 2318, Jan. 16, 1978]

STALLS

§ 23.201 Wings level stall.

(a) For an airplane with independently controlled roll and directional controls, it must be possible to produce and to correct roll by unreversed use of the rolling control and to produce and to correct yaw by unreversed use of the directional control, up to the time the airplane pitches.

(b) For an airplane with interconnected lateral and directional controls (2 controls) and for an airplane with only one of these controls, it must be possible to produce and correct roll by unreversed use of the rolling control without producing excessive yaw, up to the time the airplane pitches.

(c) The wing level stall characteristics of the airplane must be demonstrated in flight as follows: The airplane speed must be reduced with the elevator control until the speed is slightly above the stalling speed, then the elevator control must be pulled back so that the rate of speed reduction will not exceed one knot per second until a stall is produced, as shown by an uncontrollable downward pitching motion of the airplane, or until the control reaches the stop. Normal use of the elevator control for recovery is allowed after the pitching motion has unmistakably developed.

(d) Except where made inapplicable by the special features of a particular type of airplane, the following apply to the measurement of loss of altitude during a stall:

(1) The loss of altitude encountered in the stall (power on or power off) is the change in altitude (as observed on the sensitive altimeter testing installation) between the altitude at which the airplane pitches and the altitude at which horizontal flight is regained.

(2) If power or thrust is required during stall recovery the power or thrust used must be that which would be used under the normal operating procedures selected by the applicant for this maneuver. However, the power used to regain level flight may not be applied until flying control is regained.

(e) During the recovery part of the maneuver, it must be possible to pre-

vent more than 15 degrees of roll or yaw by the normal use of controls.

(f) Compliance with the requirements of this section must be shown under the following conditions:

(1) *Wing flaps:* Full up, full down, and intermediate, if appropriate.

(2) *Landing gear:* Retracted and extended.

(3) *Cowl flaps:* Appropriate to configuration.

(4) *Power:* Power or thrust off, and 75 percent maximum continuous power or thrust.

(5) *Trim:* 1.5 V_{S1} or at the minimum trim speed, whichever is higher.

(6) *Propeller:* Full increase rpm position for the power off condition.

[Amdt. 23-14, 38 FR 31820, Nov. 19, 1973]

§ 23.203 Turning flight and accelerated stalls.

Turning flight and accelerated stalls must be demonstrated in flight tests as follows:

(a) Establish and maintain a coordinated turn in a 30 degree bank. Reduce speed by steadily and progressively tightening the turn with the elevator until the airplane is stalled or until the elevator has reached its stop. The rate of speed reduction must be constant, and:

(1) For a turning flight stall, may not exceed one knot per second; and

(2) For an accelerated stall, be 3 to 5 knots per second with steadily increasing normal acceleration.

(b) When the stall has fully developed or the elevator has reached its stop, it must be possible to regain level flight without:

(1) Excessive loss of altitude;

(2) Undue pitchup;

(3) Uncontrollable tendency to spin;

(4) Exceeding 60 degree of roll in either direction from the established 30 degree bank; and

(5) For accelerated entry stalls, without exceeding the maximum permissible speed or the allowable limit load factor.

(c) Compliance with the requirements of this section must be shown with:

(1) *Wing flaps:* Retracted and fully extended for turning flight and accelerated entry stalls, and intermediate,

if appropriate, for accelerated entry stalls;

(2) *Landing gear:* Retracted and extended;

(3) *Cowl flaps:* Appropriate to configuration;

(4) *Power:* 75 percent maximum continuous power; and

(5) *Trim:* 1.5 V_{S1} or minimum trim speed, whichever is higher.

[Amdt. 23-14, 38 FR 31820, Nov. 19, 1973]

§ 23.205 Critical engine inoperative stalls.

(a) A multiengine airplane may not display any undue spinning tendency and must be safely recoverable without applying power to the inoperative engine when stalled. The operating engines may be throttled back during the recovery from stall.

(b) Compliance with paragraph (a) of the section must be shown with:

(1) *Wing flaps:* Retracted.

(2) *Landing gear:* Retracted.

(3) *Cowl flaps:* Appropriate to level flight critical engine inoperative.

(4) *Power:* Critical engine inoperative and the remaining engine(s) at 75 percent maximum continuous power or thrust or the power or thrust at which the use of maximum control travel just holds the wings laterally level in the approach to stall, whichever is lesser.

(5) *Propeller:* Normal inoperative position for the inoperative engine.

(6) *Trim:* Level flight, critical engine inoperative, except that for an airplane of 6,000 pounds or less maximum weight that has a stalling speed of 61 knots or less and cannot maintain level flight with the critical engine inoperative, the airplane must be trimmed for straight flight, critical engine inoperative, at a speed not greater than 1.5V_{S1}.

[Amdt. 23-14, 38 FR 31820, Nov. 19, 1973]

§ 23.207 Stall warning.

(a) There must be a clear and distinctive stall warning, with the flaps and landing gear in any normal position, in straight and turning flight.

(b) The stall warning may be furnished either through the inherent aerodynamic qualities of the airplane or by a device that will give clearly distinguishable indications under expected conditions of flight. However, a visual stall warning device that requires the attention of the crew within the cockpit is not acceptable by itself.

(c) The stall warning must begin at a speed exceeding the stalling speed by a margin of not less than 5 knots, but not more than the greater of 10 knots or 15 percent of the stalling speed, and must continue until the stall occurs.

[Amdt. 23-7, 34 FR 13087, Aug. 13, 1969]

SPINNING

§ 23.221 Spinning.

(a) *Normal category.* A single-engine, normal category airplane must be able to recover from a one-turn spin or a 3-second spin, whichever takes longer, in not more than one additional turn, with the controls used in the manner normally used for recovery. In addition—

(1) For both the flaps-retracted and flaps-extended conditions, the applicable airspeed limit and positive limit maneuvering load factor may not be exceeded;

(2) There may be no excessive back pressure during the spin or recovery; and

(3) It must be impossible to obtain uncontrollable spins with any use of the controls.

For the flaps-extended condition, the flaps may be retracted during recovery.

(b) *Utility category.* A utility category airplane must meet the requirements of paragraph (a) of this section or the requirements of paragraph (c) of this section.

(c) *Acrobatic category.* An acrobatic category airplane must meet the following requirements:

(1) The airplane must recover from any point in a spin, in not more than one and one-half additional turns after normal recovery application of the controls. Prior to normal recovery application of the controls, the spin test must proceed for six turns or 3 seconds, whichever takes longer, with flaps retracted, and one turn or 3 seconds, whichever takes longer, with flaps extended. However, beyond 3 seconds, the spin may be discontinued

when spiral characteristics appear with flaps retracted.

(2) For both the flaps-retracted and flaps-extended conditions, the applicable airspeed limit and positive limit maneuvering load factor may not be exceeded. For the flaps-extended condition, the flaps may be retracted during recovery, if a placard is installed prohibiting intentional spins with flaps extended.

(3) It must be impossible to obtain uncontrollable spins with any use of the controls.

(d) *Airplanes "characteristically incapable of spinning".* If it is desired to designate an airplane as "characteristically incapable of spinning", this characteristic must be shown with—

(1) A weight five percent more than the highest weight for which approval is requested;

(2) A center of gravity at least three percent aft of the rearmost position for which approval is requested;

(3) An available elevator up-travel four degrees in excess of that to which the elevator travel is to be limited for approval; and

(4) An available rudder travel seven degrees, in both directions, in excess of that to which the rudder travel is to be limited for approval.

[Doc. No. 4080, 29 FR 17955, Dec. 18, 1964, as amended by Amdt. 23-7, 34 FR 13087, Aug. 13, 1969]

GROUND AND WATER HANDLING CHARACTERISTICS

§ 23.231 Longitudinal stability and control.

(a) A landplane may have no uncontrollable tendency to nose over in any reasonably expected operating condition, including rebound during landing or takeoff. Wheel brakes must operate smoothly and may not induce any undue tendency to nose over.

(b) A seaplane or amphibian may not have dangerous or uncontrollable porpoising characteristics at any normal operating speed on the water.

§ 23.233 Directional stability and control.

(a) There may be no uncontrollable ground or water looping tendency in 90 degree cross winds, up to a wind velocity of 0.2 V_{SO}, at any speed at which the airplane may be expected to be operated on the ground or water.

(b) A landplane must be satisfactorily controllable, without exceptional piloting skill or alertness, in power-off landings at normal landing speed, without using brakes or engine power to maintain a straight path.

(c) The airplane must have adequate directional control during taxiing.

§ 23.235 Taxiing condition.

The shock-absorbing mechanism may not damage the structure of the airplane when the airplane is taxied on the roughest ground that may reasonably be expected in normal operation.

§ 23.239 Spray characteristics.

Spray may not dangerously obscure the vision of the pilots or damage the propellers or other parts of a seaplane or amphibian at any time during taxiing, takeoff, and landing.

MISCELLANEOUS FLIGHT REQUIREMENTS

§ 23.251 Vibration and buffeting.

Each part of the airplane must be free from excessive vibration under any appropriate speed and power conditions up to at least the minimum value of V_D allowed in § 23.335. In addition, there may be no buffeting, in any normal flight condition, severe enough to interfere with the satisfactory control of the airplane, cause excessive fatigue to the crew, or result in structural damage. Stall warning buffeting within these limits is allowable.

§ 23.253 High speed characteristics.

If a maximum operating speed V_{MO}/M_{MO} is established under § 23.1505(c), the following speed increase and recovery characteristics must be met:

(a) Operating conditions and characteristics likely to cause inadvertent speed increases (including upsets in pitch and roll) must be simulated with the airplane trimmed at any likely cruise speed up to V_{MO}/M_{MO}. These conditions and characteristics include gust upsets, inadvertent control movements, low stick force gradient in relation to control friction, passenger movement, leveling off from climb, and descent from Mach to airspeed limit altitude.

(b) Allowing for pilot reaction time after effective inherent or artificial speed warning occurs, it must be shown that the airplane can be recovered to a normal attitude and its speed reduced to V_{MO}/M_{MO}, without—

(1) Exceptional piloting strength or skill;

(2) Exceeding V_D/M_D, the maximum speed shown under § 23.251, or the structural limitations; or

(3) Buffeting that would impair the pilot's ability to read the instruments or to control the airplane for recovery.

(c) There may be no control reversal about any axis at any speed up to the maximum speed shown under § 23.251. Any reversal of elevator control force or tendency of the airplane to pitch, roll, or yaw must be mild and readily controllable, using normal piloting techniques.

[Amdt. 23-7, 34 FR 13087, Aug. 13, 1969; as amended by Amdt. 23-26, 45 FR 60170, Sept. 11, 1980]

Subpart C—Structure

GENERAL

§ 23.301 Loads.

(a) Strength requirements are specified in terms of limit loads (the maximum loads to be expected in service) and ultimate loads (limit loads multiplied by prescribed factors of safety). Unless otherwise provided, prescribed loads are limit loads.

(b) Unless otherwise provided, the air, ground, and water loads must be placed in equilibrium with inertia forces, considering each item of mass in the airplane. These loads must be distributed to conservatively approximate or closely represent actual conditions.

(c) If deflections under load would significantly change the distribution of external or internal loads, this redistribution must be taken into account.

(d) Simplified structural design criteria may be used if they result in design loads not less than those prescribed in §§ 23.331 through 23.521. For conventional, single-engine airplanes with design weights of 6,000

pounds or less, the design criteria of Appendix A of this part are an approved equivalent of §§ 23.321 through 23.459. If Appendix A is used, the entire Appendix must be substituted for the corresponding sections of this part.

[Doc. No. 4080, 29 FR 17955, Dec. 18, 1964; 30 FR 258, Jan. 9, 1965, as amended by Amdt. 23-28, 47 FR 13315, Mar. 29, 1982]

§ 23.303 Factor of safety.

Unless otherwise provided, a factor of safety of 1.5 must be used.

§ 23.305 Strength and deformation.

(a) The structure must be able to support limit loads without detrimental, permanent deformation. At any load up to limit loads, the deformation may not interfere with safe operation.

(b) The structure must be able to support ultimate loads without failure for at least three seconds. However, when proof of strength is shown by dynamic tests simulating actual load conditions, the three second limit does not apply.

§ 23.307 Proof of structure.

(a) Compliance with the strength and deformation requirements of § 23.305 must be shown for each critical load condition. Structural analysis may be used only if the structure conforms to those for which experience has shown this method to be reliable. In other cases, substantiating load tests must be made. Dynamic tests, including structural flight tests, are acceptable if the design load conditions have been simulated.

(b) Certain parts of the structure must be tested as specified in Subpart D of this part.

FLIGHT LOADS

§ 23.321 General.

(a) Flight load factors represent the ratio of the aerodynamic force component (acting normal to the assumed longitudinal axis of the airplane) to the weight of the airplane. A positive flight load factor is one in which the aerodynamic force acts upward, with respect to the airplane.

(b) Compliance with the flight load requirements of this subpart must be shown—

(1) At each critical altitude within the range in which the airplane may be expected to operate;

(2) At each weight from the design minimum weight to the design maximum weight; and

(3) For each required altitude and weight, for any practicable distribution of disposable load within the operating limitations specified in §§ 23.1583 through 23.1589.

§ 23.331 Symmetrical flight conditions.

(a) The appropriate balancing horizontal tail load must be accounted for in a rational or conservative manner when determining the wing loads and linear inertia loads corresponding to any of the symmetrical flight conditions specified in §§ 23.331 through 23.341.

(b) The incremental horizontal tail loads due to maneuvering and gusts must be reacted by the angular inertia of the airplane in a rational or conservative manner.

§ 23.333 Flight envelope.

(a) *General.* Compliance with the strength requirements of this subpart must be shown at any combination of airspeed and load factor on and within the boundaries of a flight envelope (similar to the one in paragraph (d) of this section) that represents the envelope of the flight loading conditions specified by the maneuvering and gust criteria of paragraphs (b) and (c) of this section respectively.

(b) *Maneuvering envelope.* Except where limited by maximum (static) lift coefficients, the airplane is assumed to be subjected to symmetrical maneuvers resulting in the following limit load factors:

(1) The positive maneuvering load factor specified in § 23.337 at speeds up to V_D;

(2) The negative maneuvering load factor specified in § 23.337 at V_C; and

(3) Factors varying linearly with speed from the specified value at V_C to 0.0 at V_D for the normal and commuter category, and —1.0 at V_D for the acrobatic and utility categories.

(c) *Gust envelope.* (1) The airplane is assumed to be subjected to symmetrical vertical gusts in level flight. The resulting limit load factors must correspond to the conditions determined as follows:

(i) Positive (up) and negative (down) gusts of 50 f.p.s. at V_C must be considered at altitudes between sea level and 20,000 feet. The gust velocity may be reduced linearly from 50 f.p.s. at 20,000 feet to 25 f.p.s. at 50,000 feet.

(ii) Positive and negative gusts of 25 f.p.s. at V_D must be considered at altitudes between sea level and 20,000 feet. The gust velocity may be reduced linearly from 25 f.p.s. at 20,000 feet to 12.5 f.p.s. at 50,000 feet.

(iii) In addition, for commuter category airplanes, positive (up) and negative (down) rough air gusts of 66 f.p.s. at V_B must be considered at altitudes between sea level and 20,000 feet. The gust velocity may be reduced linearly from 66 f.p.s. at 20,000 feet to 38 f.p.s. at 50,000 feet.

(2) The following assumptions must be made:

(i) The shape of the gust is—

$$U = \frac{U_{de}}{2} \left(1 - \cos \frac{2\pi s}{25C} \right)$$

Where—

s =Distance penetrated into gust (ft.);
C =Mean geometric chord of wing (ft.); and
U_{de} =Derived gust velocity referred to in subparagraph (1) of this section.

(ii) Gust load factors vary linearly with speed between V_C and V_D .

(d) *Flight envelope.*

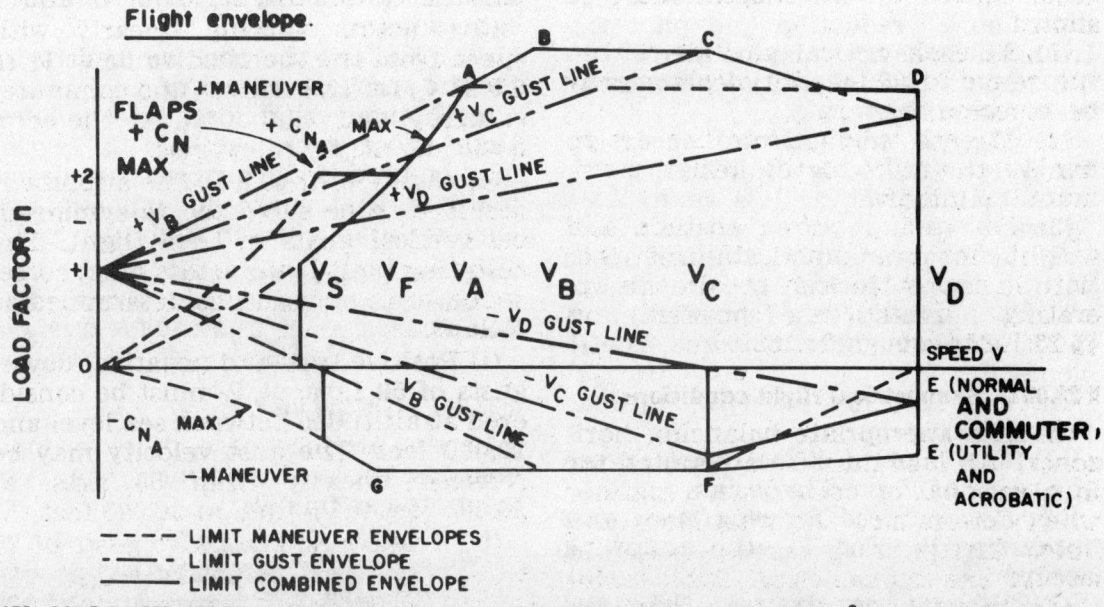

Flight envelope.

NOTE: POINT G NEED NOT BE INVESTIGATED WHEN THE SUPPLEMENTARY CONDITION SPECIFIED IN §23.369 IS INVESTIGATED

[Doc. No. 4080, 29 FR 17955, Dec. 18, 1964, as amended by Amdt. 23-7, 34 FR 13087, Aug. 13, 1969; Amdt. 23-34, 52 FR 1829, Jan. 15, 1987]

§ 23.335 **Design airspeeds.**

Except as provided in paragraph (a) (4) of this section, the selected design airspeeds are equivalent airspeeds (EAS).

(a) *Design cruising speed, V_C.* For V_C the following apply:

(1) V_C (in knots) may not be less than—

(i) 33 W/S (for normal, utility, and commuter category airplanes); and

(ii) $36\sqrt{W/S}$ (for acrobatic category airplanes).

(2) For values of W/S more than 20, the multiplying factors may be decreased linearly with W/S to a value of 28.6 where W/S =100.

(3) V_C need not be more than 0.9 V_H at sea level.

(4) At altitudes where an M_D is established, a cruising speed M_C limited by compressibility may be selected.

(b) *Design dive speed V_D.* For V_D, the following apply:

(1) V_D/M_D may not be less than 1.25 V_C/M_C; and

(2) With $V_{C\ min}$, the required minimum design cruising speed, V_C (in knots) may not be less than—

(i) 1.40 $V_{C\ min}$ (for normal and commuter category airplanes);

(ii) 1.50 $V_{C\ min}$ (for utility category airplanes); and

(iii) 1.55 $V_{C\ min}$ (for acrobatic category airplanes).

(3) For values of W/S more than 20, the multiplying factors in paragraph (b)(2) of this section may be decreased linearly with W/S to a value of 1.35 where W/S = 100.

(4) Compliance with paragraphs (b) (1) and (2) of this section need not be shown if V_D/M_D is selected so that the minimum speed margin between V_C/M_C and V_D/M_D is the greater of the following:

(i) The speed increase resulting when, from the initial condition of stabilized flight at V_C/M_C, the airplane is assumed to be upset, flown for 20 seconds along a flight path 7.5° below the initial path, and then pulled up with a load factor of 1.5 (0.5 *g.* acceleration increment). At least 75 percent maximum continuous power for reciprocating engines, and maximum cruising power for turbines, or, if less, the power required for V_C/M_C for both kinds of engines, must be assumed until the pullup is initiated, at which point power reduction and pilot-controlled drag devices may be used.

(ii) Mach 0.05 (at altitudes where an M_D is established).

(c) *Design maneuvering speed V_A*. For V_A, the following applies:

(1) V_A may not be less than $V_S\sqrt{n}$ where—

(i) V_S is a computed stalling speed with flaps retracted at the design weight, normally based on the maximum airplane normal force coefficients, C_{NA}; and

(ii) n is the limit maneuvering load factor used in design

(2) The value of V_A need not exceed the value of V_C used in design.

(d) *Design speed for maximum gust intensity, V_B.* For V_B, the following apply:

(1) V_B may not be less than the speed determined by the intersection of the line representing the maximum positive lift $C_{n\ max}$ and the line representing the rough air gust velocity on the gust V-n diagram, or $\sqrt{(n_g)}\ V_{S1}$, whichever is less, where:

(i) n_g the positive airplane gust load factor due to gust, at speed V_C (in accordance with § 23.341), and at the particular weight under consideration; and

(ii) V_{S1} is the stalling speed with the flaps retracted at the particular weight under consideration.

(2) V_B need not be greater than V_C.

[Doc. No. 4080, 29 FR 17955, Dec. 18, 1964, as amended by Amdt. 23-7, 34 FR 13088, Aug. 13, 1969; Amdt. 23-16, 40 FR 2577, Jan. 14, 1975; Amdt. 23-34, 52 FR 1829, Jan. 15, 1987; Amdt. 23-24, 52 FR 34745, Sept. 14, 1987]

§ 23.337   Limit maneuvering load factors.

(a) The positive limit maneuvering load factor n may not be less than—

(1)

$$2.1 + [24{,}000/(W+10{,}000)]$$

for normal and commuter category airplanes, except that n need not be more than 3.8

(2) 4.4 for utility category airplanes; or

(3) 6.0 for acrobatic category airplanes.

(b) The negative limit maneuvering load factor may not be less than—

(1) 0.4 times the positive load factor for the normal utility and commuter categories; or

(2) 0.5 times the positive load factor for the acrobatic category.

(c) Maneuvering load factors lower than those specified in this section may be used if the airplane has design features that make it impossible to exceed these values in flight.

[Doc. No. 4080, 29 FR 17955, Dec. 18, 1964, as amended by Amdt. 23-7, 34 FR 13088, Aug. 13, 1969; Amdt. 23-34, 52 FR 1829, Jan. 15, 1987]

§ 23.341   Gust loads factors.

In the absence of a more rational analysis, the gust load factors must be computed as follows:

$$n = 1 + \frac{K_g U_{de} V a}{498(W/S)}$$

Where—

$K_g = 0.88\mu_g/5.3 + \mu_g =$ gust alleviation factor;

$\mu_g = 2(W/S)/\rho Cag =$ airplane mass ratio;

$U_{de} =$ Derived gust velocities referred to in § 23.333(c) (f.p.s.);

$\rho =$ Density of air (slugs/cu.ft.);

$W/S =$ Wing loading (p.s.f.);

$C =$ Mean geometric chord (ft.);

$g =$ Acceleration due to gravity (ft./sec.^{2})

$V =$ Airplane equivalent speed (knots); and

$a =$ Slope of the airplane normal force coefficient curve C_{NA} per radian if the gust loads are applied to the wings and horizontal tail surfaces simultaneously by a rational method. The wing lift curve slope C_L per radian may be used when the gust load is applied to the wings only and the horizontal tail gust loads are treated as a separate condition.

[Amdt. 23-7, 34 FR 13088, Aug. 13, 1969]

§ 23.345   High lift devices.

(a) If flaps or similar high lift devices to be used for takeoff, approach, or landing are installed, the airplane, with the flaps fully deflected at V_F, is assumed to be subjected to symmetrical maneuvers and gusts resulting in limit load factors within the range determined by—

(1) Maneuvering, to a positive limit load factor of 2.0; and

(2) Positive and negative gust of 25 feet per second acting normal to the flight path in level flight.

(b) V_F must be assumed to be not less than 1.4 V_S or 1.8 V_{SF}, whichever is greater, where—

V_S is the computed stalling speed with flaps retracted at the design weight; and
V_{SF} is the computed stalling speed with flaps fully extended at the design weight.

However, if an automatic flap load limiting device is used, the airplane may be designed for the critical combinations of airspeed and flap position allowed by that device.

(c) In designing the flaps and supporting structures, the following must be accounted for:

(1) A head-on gust having a velocity of 25 feet per second (EAS).

(2) The slipstream effects specified in §23.457(b).

(d) In determining external loads on the airplane as a whole, thrust, slipstream, and pitching acceleration may be assumed to be zero.

(e) The requirements of §23.457, and this section may be complied with separately or in combination.

[Doc. No. 4080, 29 FR 17955, Dec. 18, 1964, as amended by Amdt. 23-7, 34 FR 13088, Aug. 13, 1969; Amdt. 23-23, 43 FR 50592, Oct. 30, 1978]

§23.347 Unsymmetrical flight conditions.

The airplane is assumed to be subjected to the unsymmetrical flight conditions of §§23.349 and 23.351. Unbalanced aerodynamic moments about the center of gravity must be reacted in a rational or conservative manner, considering the principal masses furnishing the reacting inertia forces.

§23.349 Rolling conditions.

The wing and wing bracing must be designed for the following loading conditions:

(a) Unsymmetrical wing loads appropriate to the category. Unless the following values result in unrealistic loads, the rolling accelerations may be obtained by modifying the symmetrical flight conditions in §23.333(d) as follows:

(1) For the acrobatic category, in conditions A and F, assume that 100 percent of the semispan wing airload acts on one side of the plane of symmetry and 60 percent of this load acts on the other side.

(2) For normal, utility, and commuter categories, in Condition A, assume that 100 percent of the semispan wing airload acts on one side of the airplane, and 70 percent of this load acts on the other side. For airplanes of more than 1,000 pounds design weight, the latter percentage may be increased linearly with weight up through 75 percent at 12,500 pounds to the maximum gross weight of the airplane.

(b) The loads resulting from the aileron deflections and speeds specified in §23.455, in combination with an airplane load factor of at least two thirds of the positive maneuvering load factor used for design. Unless the following values result in unrealistic loads, the effect of aileron displacement on wing torsion may be accounted for by adding the following increment to the basic airfoil moment coefficient over the aileron portion of the span in the critical condition determined in §23.333(d):

$$\Delta c_m = -0.01\delta$$

where—

Δc_m is the moment coefficient increment; and
δ is the down aileron deflection in degrees in the critical condition.

[Doc. No. 4080, 29 FR 17955, Dec. 18, 1964, as amended by Amdt. 23-7, 34 FR 13088, Aug. 13, 1969; Amdt. 23-34, 52 FR 1829, Jan. 15, 1987]

§23.351 Yawing conditions.

The airplane must be designed for yawing loads on the vertical tail surfaces resulting from the loads specified in §§23.441 through 23.445.

§23.361 Engine torque.

(a) Each engine mount and its supporting structure must be designed for the effects of—

(1) A limit engine torque corresponding to takeoff power and propeller speed acting simultaneously with 75 percent of the limit loads from flight condition A of §23.333(d);

(2) The limit engine torque as specified in §23.361(c) acting simultaneously with the time loads from flight condition A of §23.333(d); and

(3) For turbopropeller installations, in addition to the conditions specified in paragraphs (a)(1) and (a)(2) of this

section, a limit engine torque corresponding to takeoff power and propeller speed, multiplied by a factor accounting for propeller control system malfunction, including quick feathering, acting simultaneously with lg level flight loads. In the absence of a rational analysis, a factor of 1.6 must be used.

(b) For turbine engine installations, the engine mounts and supporting structure must be designed to withstand each of the following:

(1) A limit engine torque load imposed by sudden engine stoppage due to malfunction or structural failure (such as compressor jamming).

(2) A limit engine torque load imposed by the maximum acceleration of the engine.

(c) The limit engine torque to be considered under paragraph (a)(2) of this section must be obtained by multiplying the mean torque for maximum continuous power by a factor of—

(1) 1.25 for turbopropeller installations;

(2) 1.33 for engines with five or more cylinders; and

(3) Two, three, or four, for engines with four, three, or two cylinders, respectively.

[Amdt. 23-26, 45 FR 60171, Sept. 11, 1980]

§ 23.363   Side load on engine mount.

(a) Each engine mount and its supporting structure must be designed for a limit load factor in a lateral direction, for the side load on the engine mount, of not less than—

(1) 1.33, or

(2) One-third of the limit load factor for flight condition A.

(b) The side load prescribed in paragraph (a) of this section may be assumed to be independent of other flight conditions.

§ 23.365   Pressurized cabin loads.

For each pressurized compartment, the following apply:

(a) The airplane structure must be strong enough to withstand the flight loads combined with pressure differential loads from zero up to the maximum relief valve setting.

(b) The external pressure distribution in flight, and any stress concentrations, must be accounted for.

(c) If landings may be made with the cabin pressurized, landing loads must be combined with pressure differential loads from zero up to the maximum allowed during landing.

(d) The airplane structure must be strong enough to withstand the pressure differential loads corresponding to the maximum relief valve setting multiplied by a factor of 1.33, omitting other loads.

(e) If a pressurized cabin has two or more compartments separated by bulkheads or a floor, the primary structure must be designed for the effects of sudden release of pressure in any compartment with external doors or windows. This condition must be investigated for the effects of failure of the largest opening in the compartment. The effects of intercompartmental venting may be considered.

§ 23.367   Unsymmetrical loads due to engine failure.

(a) Turbopropeller airplanes must be designed for the unsymmetrical loads resulting from the failure of the critical engine including the following conditions in combination with a single malfunction of the propeller drag limiting system, considering the probable pilot corrective action on the flight controls:

(1) At speeds between V_{MC} and V_D, the loads resulting from power failure because of fuel flow interruption are considered to be limit loads.

(2) At speeds between V_{MC} and V_C, the loads resulting from the disconnection of the engine compressor from the turbine or from loss of the turbine blades are considered to be ultimate loads.

(3) The time history of the thrust decay and drag buildup occurring as a result of the prescribed engine failures must be substantiated by test or other data applicable to the particular engine-propeller combination.

(4) The timing and magnitude of the probable pilot corrective action must be conservatively estimated, considering the characteristics of the particular engine-propeller-airplane combination.

(b) Pilot corrective action may be assumed to be initiated at the time maximum yawing velocity is reached, but not earlier than 2 seconds after the engine failure. The magnitude of the corrective action may be based on the limit pilot forces specified in § 23.397 except that lower forces may be assumed where it is shown by analysis or test that these forces can control the yaw and roll resulting from the prescribed engine failure conditions.

[Amdt. 23–7, 34 FR 13089, Aug. 13, 1969]

§ 23.369 Special conditions for rear lift truss.

(a) If a rear lift truss is used, it must be designed for conditions of reversed airflow at a design speed of—

$$V = 8.7 \sqrt{W/S} + 8.7 \text{ (knots)}$$

(b) Either aerodynamic data for the particular wing section used, or a value of C_L equalling -0.8 with a chordwise distribution that is triangular between a peak at the trailing edge and zero at the leading edge, must be used.

[Doc. No. 4080, 29 FR 17955, Dec. 18, 1964, as amended by Amdt. 23–7, 34 FR 13089, Aug. 13, 1969; 34 FR 17509, Oct. 30, 1969]

§ 23.371 Gyroscopic loads.

For turbine powered airplanes, each engine mount and its supporting structure must be designed for the gyroscopic loads that result, with the engines at maximum continuous r.p.m., under either of the following conditions:

(a) The conditions prescribed in §§ 23.351 and 23.423.

(b) All possible combinations of the following:

(1) A yaw velocity of 2.5 radians per second.

(2) A pitch velocity of 1 radian per second.

(3) A normal load factor of 2.5.

(4) Maximum continuous thrust.

[Amdt. 23–7, 34 FR 13089, Aug. 13, 1969, as amended by Amdt. 23–26, 45 FR 60171, Sept. 11, 1980]

§ 23.373 Speed control devices.

If speed control devices (such as spoilers and drag flaps) are incorporated for use in enroute conditions—

(a) The airplane must be designed for the symmetrical maneuvers and gusts prescribed in §§ 23.333, 23.337, and 23.341, and the yawing maneuvers and lateral gusts in §§ 23.441 and 23.443, with the device extended at speeds up to the placard device extended speed; and

(b) If the device has automatic operating or load limiting features, the airplane must be designed for the maneuver and gust conditions prescribed in paragraph (a) of this section at the speeds and corresponding device positions that the mechanism allows.

[Amdt. 23–7, 34 FR 13089, Aug. 13, 1969]

CONTROL SURFACE AND SYSTEM LOADS

§ 23.391 Control surface loads.

(a) The control surface loads specified in §§ 23.397 through 23.459 are assumed to occur in the conditions described in §§ 23.331 through 23.351.

(b) If allowed by the following sections, the values of control surface loading in Appendix B of this part may be used, instead of particular control surface data, to determine the detailed rational requirements of §§ 23.397 through 23.459, unless these values result in unrealistic loads.

§ 23.395 Control system loads.

(a) Each flight control system and its supporting structure must be designed for loads corresponding to at least 125 percent of the computed hinge moments of the movable control surface in the conditions prescribed in §§ 23.391 through 23.459. In addition, the following apply:

(1) The system limit loads need not exceed the higher of the loads that can be produced by the pilot and automatic devices operating the controls. However, autopilot forces need not be added to pilot forces. The system must be designed for the maximum effort of the pilot or autopilot, whichever is higher. In addition, if the pilot and the autopilot act in opposition, the part of the system between them may be designed for the maximum effort of the one that imposes the lesser load. Pilot forces used for design need not exceed the maximum forces prescribed in § 23.397(b).

(2) The design must, in any case, provide a rugged system for service

use, considering jamming, ground gusts, taxiing downwind, control inertia, and friction. Compliance with this subparagraph may be shown by designing for loads resulting from application of the minimum forces prescribed in § 23.397(b).

(b) A 125 percent factor on computed hinge moments must be used to design elevator, aileron, and rudder systems. However, a factor as low as 1.0 may be used if hinge moments are based on accurate flight test data, the exact reduction depending upon the accuracy and reliability of the data.

(c) Pilot forces used for design are assumed to act at the appropriate control grips or pads as they would in flight, and to react at the attachments of the control system to the control surface horns.

[Doc. No. 4080, 29 FR 17955, Dec. 18, 1964, as amended by Amdt. 23-7, 34 FR 13089, Aug. 13, 1969]

§ 23.397   Limit control forces and torques.

(a) In the control surface flight loading condition, the airloads on movable surfaces and the corresponding deflections need not exceed those that would result in flight from the application of any pilot force within the ranges specified in paragraph (b) of this section. In applying this criterion, the effects of control system boost and servo-mechanisms, and the effects of tabs must be considered. The automatic pilot effort must be used for design if it alone can produce higher control surface loads than the human pilot.

(b) The limit pilot forces and torques are as follows:

Control	Maximum forces or torques for design weight, weight equal to or less than 5,000 pounds [1]	Minimum forces or torques [2]
Aileron:		
Stick	67 lbs	40 lbs.
Wheel [3]	50 D in.-lbs [4]	40 D in.-lbs. [4]
Elevator:		
Stick	167 lbs	100 lbs.
Wheel (symmetrical)	200 lbs	100 lbs.
Wheel (unsymmetrical) [5].		100 lbs.
Rudder	200 lbs	130 lbs.

[1] For design weight (W) more than 5,000 pounds, the specified maximum values must be increased linearly with weight to 1.18 times the specified values at a design weight of 12,500 pounds and for commuter category airplanes, the specified values must be increased linearly with weight to 1.35 times the specified values at a design weight of 19,000 pounds.

[2] If the design of any individual set of control systems or surfaces makes these specified minimum forces or torques inapplicable, values corresponding to the present hinge moments obtained under § 23.415, but not less than 0.6 of the specified minimum forces or torques, may be used.

[3] The critical parts of the aileron control system must also be designed for a single tangential force with a limit value of 1.25 times the couple force determined from the above criteria.

[4] D=wheel diameter (inches).

[5] The unsymmetrical force must be applied at one of the normal handgrip points on the control wheel.

[Doc. No. 4080, 29 FR 17955, Dec. 18, 1964, as amended by Amdt. 23-7, 34 FR 13089, Aug. 13, 1969; Amdt. 23-17, 41 FR 55464, Dec. 20, 1976; Amdt. 23-34, 52 FR 1829, Jan. 15, 1987]

§ 23.399   Dual control system.

Each dual control system must be designed for the pilots operating in opposition, using individual pilot forces not less than—

(a) 0.75 times those obtained under § 23.395; or

(b) The minimum forces specified in § 23.397(b).

§ 23.405   Secondary control system.

Secondary controls, such as wheel brakes, spoilers, and tab controls, must be designed for the maximum forces that a pilot is likely to apply to those controls.

§ 23.407   Trim tab effects.

The effects of trim tabs on the control surface design conditions must be accounted for only where the surface loads are limited by maximum pilot effort. In these cases, the tabs are considered to be deflected in the direction that would assist the pilot. These deflections must correspond to the maximum degree of "out of trim" expected at the speed for the condition under consideration.

§ 23.409   Tabs.

Control surface tabs must be designed for the most severe combination of airspeed and tab deflection likely to be obtained within the flight envelope for any usable loading condition.

§ 23.415   Ground gust conditions.

(a) The control system must be investigated as follows for control surface loads due to ground gusts and taxiing downwind:

(1) If an investigation of the control system for ground gust loads is not required by paragraph (a)(2) of this section, but the applicant elects to design a part of the control system of these loads, these loads need only be carried from control surface horns through the nearest stops or gust locks and their supporting structures.

(2) If pilot forces less than the minimums specified in § 23.397(b) are used for design, the effects of surface loads due to ground gusts and taxiing downwind must be investigated for the entire control system according to the formula:

$$H = KcSq$$

where—

H = limit hinge moment (ft.-lbs.);
c = means chord of the control surface aft of the hinge line (ft.);
S = area of control surface aft of the hinge line (sq. ft.);
q = Dynamic pressure (p.s.f.) based on a design speed not less than $14.6\sqrt{W/S}$-%14.6 (f.p.s.) except that the design speed need not exceed 88 (f.p.s.); and
K = limit hinge moment factor for ground gusts derived in paragraph (b) of this section. (For ailerons and elevators, a positive value of K indicates a moment tending to depress the surface and a negative value of K indicates a moment tending to raise the surface).

(b) The limit hinge moment factor K for ground gusts must be derived as follows:

Surface	K	Position of controls
(a) Aileron	0.75	Control column locked lashed in mid-position.
(b) Aileron	±0.50	Ailerons at full throw; + moment on one aileron, − moment on the other.
(c) Elevator	±0.75	(c) Elevator full up (−).
(d) Elevator		(d) Elevator full down (+).
(e) Rudder	±0.75	(e) Rudder in neutral.
(f) Rudder		(f) Rudder at full throw.

[Doc. No. 4080, 29 FR 17955, Dec. 18, 1964, as amended by Amdt. 23–7, 34 FR 13089, Aug. 13, 1969]

HORIZONTAL TAIL SURFACES

§ 23.421 **Balancing loads.**

(a) A horizontal tail balancing load is a load necessary to maintain equilibrium in any specified flight condition with no pitching acceleration.

(b) Horizontal tail surfaces must be designed for the balancing loads occurring at any point on the limit maneuvering envelope and in the flap conditions specified in § 23.345. The distribution in figure B6 of Appendix B may be used.

[Doc. No. 4080, 29 FR 17955, Dec. 18, 1964, as amended by Amdt. 23–7, 34 FR 13089, Aug. 13, 1969]

§ 23.423 **Maneuvering loads.**

Each horizontal tail surface must be designed for maneuvering loads imposed by the following conditions:

(a) A sudden deflection of the elevator control, at V_A, to (1) the maximum upward deflection, and (2) the maximum downward deflection, as limited by the control stops, or pilot effort, whichever is critical. The average loading of B23.11 of Appendix B and the distribution in figure B7 of Appendix B may be used.

(b) A sudden upward deflection of the elevator, at speeds above V_A followed by a downward deflection of the elevator, resulting in the following combinations of normal and angular acceleration:

Condition	Normal acceleration (n)	Angular acceleration (radian/sec.²)
Down load	1.0	$+\dfrac{39}{V} n_m (n_m - 1.5)$
Up load	n_m	$-\dfrac{39}{V} n_m (n_m - 1.5)$

where—

(1) n_m = positive limit maneuvering load factor used in the design of the airplane; and

(2) V = initial speed in knots.

The conditions in this paragraph involve loads corresponding to the loads that may occur in a "checked maneuver" (a maneuver in which the pitching control is suddenly displaced in one direction and then suddenly moved in the opposite direction), the deflections and timing avoiding exceeding the limit maneuvering load factor. The total tail load for both down and up load conditions is the sum of the balancing tail loads at V

and the specified value of the normal load factor n, plus the maneuvering load increment due to the specified value of the angular acceleration. The maneuvering load increment in figure B2 of Appendix B and the distributions in figure B7 (for down loads) and in figure B8 (for up loads) of Appendix B may be used.

[Doc. No. 4080, 29 FR 17955, Dec. 18, 1964, as amended by Amdt. 23-7, 34 FR 13089, Aug. 13, 1969]

§ 23.425 Gust loads.

(a) Each horizontal tail surface must be designed for loads resulting from—

(1) Gust velocities specified in § 23.333(c) with flaps retracted; and

(2) Positive and negative gusts of 25 f.p.s. nominal intensity at V_F corresponding to the flight conditions specified in § 23.345(a)(2).

(b) The average loadings in figures B3 and B4 of Appendix B and the distribution in figure B8 of Appendix B may be used instead of the requirements of paragraph (a)(1) of this section.

(c) When determining the total load on the horizontal tail for the conditions specified in paragraph (a) of this section, the initial balancing tail loads for steady unaccelerated flight at the pertinent design speeds V_F, V_C, and V_D must first be determined. The incremental tail load resulting from the gusts must be added to the initial balancing tail load to obtain the total tail load.

(d) In the absence of a more rational analysis, the incremental tail load due to the gust must be computed as follows:

$$\Delta L_{ht} = \frac{K_g\, U_{de}\, V a_{ht}\, S_{ht}}{498} \left(1 - \frac{d\epsilon}{d\alpha}\right)$$

where—

ΔL_{ht} = Incremental horizontal tailload (lbs.);
K_g = Gust alleviation factor defined in § 23.341;
U_{de} = Derived gust velocity (f.p.s.);
V = Airplane equivalent speed (knots);
a_{ht} = Slope of horizontal tail lift curve (per radian);
S_{ht} = Area of horizontal tail (ft.²); and

$$\left(1 - \frac{d\epsilon}{d\alpha}\right) = \text{Downwash factor}$$

[Doc. No. 4080, 20 FR 17955, Dec. 18, 1964, as amended by Amdt. 23-7, 34 FR 13089 Aug. 13, 1969]

§ 23.427 Unsymmetrical loads.

(a) Horizontal tail surfaces and their supporting structure must be designed for unsymmetrical loads arising from yawing and slipstream effects, in combination with the loads prescribed for the flight conditions set forth in §§ 23.421 through 23.425.

(b) In the absence of more rational data for airplanes that are conventional in regard to location of engines, wings, tail surfaces, and fuselage shape:

(1) 100 percent of the maximum loading from the symmetrical flight conditions may be assumed on the surface on one side of the plane of symmetry; and

(2) The following percentage of that loading must be applied to the opposite side:

Percent = $100 - 10\ (n-1)$, where n is the specified positive maneuvering load factor, but this value may not be more than 80 percent.

(c) For airplanes that are not conventional (such as airplanes with horizontal tail surfaces having appreciable dihedral or supported by the vertical tail surfaces) the surfaces and supporting structures must be designed for combined vertical and horizontal surface loads resulting from each prescribed flight condition taken separately.

[Amdt. 23-14, 38 FR 31820, Nov. 19, 1973]

VERTICAL TAIL SURFACES

§ 23.441 Maneuvering loads.

(a) At speeds up to V_A, the vertical tail surfaces must be designed to withstand the following conditions. In computing the tail loads, the yawing velocity may be assumed to be zero:

(1) With the airplane in unaccelerated flight at zero yaw, it is assumed that the rudder control is suddenly displaced to the maximum deflection,

as limited by the control stops or by limit pilot forces.

(2) With the rudder deflected as specified in paragraph (a)(1) of this section, it is assumed that the airplane yaws to the resulting sideslip angle. In lieu of a rational analysis, an over-swing angle equal to 1.3 times the static sideslip angle of paragraph (a)(3) of this section may be assumed.

(3) A yaw angle of 15 degrees with the rudder control maintained in the neutral position (except as limited by pilot strength).

(b) The average loading of B23.11 and figure B1 of Appendix B and the distribution in figures B6, B7, and B8 of Appendix B may be used instead of the requirements of paragraphs (a)(2), (a)(1), and (a)(3), respectively, of this section.

(c) The yaw angles specified in paragraph (a)(3) of this section may be reduced if the yaw angle chosen for a particular speed cannot be exceeded in—

(1) Steady slip conditions;

(2) Uncoordinated rolls from steep banks; or

(3) Sudden failure of the critical engine with delayed corrective action.

[Doc. No. 4080, 29 FR 17955, Dec. 18, 1964, as amended by Amdt. 23-7, 34 FR 13090, Aug. 13, 1969; Amdt. 23-14, 38 FR 31821, Nov. 19, 1973; Amdt. 23-28, 47 FR 13315, Mar. 29, 1982]

§23.443 Gust loads.

(a) Vertical tail surfaces must be designed to withstand, in unaccelerated flight at speed V_C, lateral gusts of the values prescribed for V_C in §23.333(c).

(b) In addition, for commuter category airplanes, the airplane is assumed to encounter derived gusts normal to the plane of symmetry while in unaccelerated flight at V_B, V_C, V_D, and V_F. The derived gusts and airplane speeds corresponding to these conditions, as determined by §§23.341 and 23.345, must be investigated. The shape of the gust must be as specified in §23.333(c)(2)(i).

(c) In the absence of a more rational analysis, the gust load must be computed as follows:

$$L_{vt} = K_{gt} U_{de} V a_{vt} S_{vt} \div 498$$

where—

L_{vt} = Vertical tail load (lbs.);
$K_{gt} = 0.88\mu_{gt} \div 5.3 + \mu_{gt}$ = gust alleviation factor;
$\mu_{gt} = 2W \div PC_t g a_{vt} S_{vt}(K \div 1_t)^2$ = lateral mass ratio;
U_{de} = Derived gust velocity (f.p.s.);
P = Air density (slugs/cu.ft.);
W = Airplane weight (lbs.);
S_{vt} = Area of vertical tail (ft.²);
C_t = Mean geometric chord of vertical surface (ft.);
a_{vt} = Lift curve slope of vertical tail (per radian);
K = Radius of gyration in yaw (ft.);
1_t = Distance from airplane c.g. to lift center of vertical surface (ft.);
g = Acceleration due to gravity (ft./sec.²); and
V = Airplane equivalent speed (knots).

(d) The average loading in figure B5 and the distribution in figure B8 of Appendix B may be used.

[Amdt. 23-7, 34 FR 13090, Aug. 13, 1969, as amended by Amdt. 23-34, 52 FR 1830, Jan. 15, 1987; 52 FR 7262, Mar. 9, 1987; Amdt. 23-24, 52 FR 34745, Sept. 14, 1987]

§23.445 Outboard fins.

(a) If outboard fins are on the horizontal tail surface, the tail surfaces must be designed for the maximum horizontal surface load in combination with the corresponding loads induced on the vertical surfaces by endplate effects. These induced effects need not be combined with other vertical surface loads.

(b) If outboard fins extend above and below the horizontal surface, the critical vertical surface loading (the load per unit area as determined under §§23.441 and 23.443) must be applied to—

(1) The part of the vertical surfaces above the horizontal surface with 80 percent of that loading applied to the part below the horizontal surface; and

(2) The part of the vertical surfaces below the horizontal surface with 80 percent of that loading applied to the part above the horizontal surface.

(c) The end plate effects of outboard fins must be taken into account in applying the yawing conditions of §§23.441 and 23.443 to the vertical surfaces in paragraph (b) of this section.

[Doc. No. 4080, 29 FR 17955, Dec. 18, 1964, as amended by Amdt. 23-14, 38 FR 31821, Nov. 19, 1973]

AILERONS, WING FLAPS, AND SPECIAL
DEVICES

§ 23.455   Ailerons.

(a) The ailerons must be designed for the loads to which they are subjected—

(1) In the neutral position during symmetrical flight conditions; and

(2) By the following deflections (except as limited by pilot effort), during unsymmetrical flight conditions:

(i) Sudden maximum displacement of the aileron control at V_A. Suitable allowance may be made for control system deflections.

(ii) Sufficient deflection at V_C, where V_C is more than V_A, to produce a rate of roll not less than obtained in paragraph (a)(2)(i) of this section.

(iii) Sufficient deflection at V_D to produce a rate of roll not less than one-third of that obtained in paragraph (a)(2)(i) of this section.

(b) The average loading in § B23.11 and figure B1 of Appendix B and the distribution in figure B9 of Appendix B may be used.

[Doc. No. 4080, 29 FR 17955, Dec. 18, 1964, as amended by Amdt. 23-7, 34 FR 13090, Aug. 13, 1969]

§ 23.457   Wing flaps.

(a) The wing flaps, their operating mechanisms, and their supporting structures must be designed for critical loads occurring in the flaps-extended flight conditions with the flaps in any position. However, if an automatic flap load limiting device is used, these components may be designed for the critical combinations of airspeed and flap position allowed by that device.

(b) The effects of propeller slipstream, corresponding to takeoff power, must be taken into account at not less than 1.4 V_S, where V_S is the computed stalling speed with flaps fully retracted at the design weight. For the investigation of slipstream effects, the load factor may be assumed to be 1.0.

§ 23.459   Special devices.

The loading for special devices using aerodynamic surfaces (such as slots and spoilers) must be determined from test data.

GROUND LOADS

§ 23.471   General.

The limit ground loads specified in this subpart are considered to be external loads and inertia forces that act upon an airplane structure. In each specified ground load condition, the external reactions must be placed in equilibrium with the linear and angular inertia forces in a rational or conservative manner.

§ 23.473   Ground load conditions and assumptions.

(a) The ground load requirements of this subpart must be complied with at the design maximum weight except that §§ 23.479, 23.481, and 23.483 may be complied with at a design landing weight (the highest weight for landing conditions at the maximum descent velocity) allowed under paragraphs (b) and (c) of this section.

(b) The design landing weight may be as low as—

(1) 95 percent of the maximum weight if the minimum fuel capacity is enough for at least one-half hour of operation at maximum continuous power plus a capacity equal to a fuel weight which is the difference between the design maximum weight and the design landing weight; or

(2) The design maximum weight less the weight of 25 percent of the total fuel capacity.

(c) The design landing weight of a multiengine airplane may be less than that allowed under paragraph (b) of this section if—

(1) The airplane meets the one-engine-inoperative climb requirements of § 23.67 (a) or (b)(1); and

(2) Compliance is shown with the fuel jettisoning system requirements of § 23.1001.

(d) The selected limit vertical inertia load factor at the center of gravity of the airplane for the ground load conditions prescribed in this subpart may not be less than that which would be obtained when landing with a descent velocity (V), in feet per second, equal to 4.4 (W/S)¼, except that this velocity need not be more than 10 feet per second and may not be less than seven feet per second.

(e) Wing lift not exceeding two-thirds of the weight of the airplane may be assumed to exist throughout the landing impact and to act through the center of gravity. The ground reaction load factor may be equal to the inertia load factor minus the ratio of the above assumed wing lift to the airplane weight.

(f) Energy absorption tests (to determine the limit load factor corresponding to the required limit descent velocities) must be made under § 23.723(a).

(g) No inertia load factor used for design purposes may be less than 2.67, nor may the limit ground reaction load factor be less than 2.0 at design maximum weight, unless these lower values will not be exceeded in taxiing at speeds up to takeoff speed over terrain as rough as that expected in service.

[Doc. No. 4080, 29 FR 17955, Dec. 18, 1964, as amended by Amdt. 23–7, 34 FR 13090, Aug. 13, 1969; Amdt. 23–28, 47 FR 13315, Mar. 29, 1982]

§ 23.477 Landing gear arrangement.

Sections 23.479 through 23.483, or the conditions in Appendix C, apply to airplanes with conventional arrangements of main and nose gear, or main and tail gear.

§ 23.479 Level landing conditions.

(a) For a level landing, the airplane is assumed to be in the following attitudes:

(1) For airplanes with tail wheels, a normal level flight attitude.

(2) For airplanes with nose wheels, attitudes in which—

(i) The nose and main wheels contact the ground simultaneously; and

(ii) The main wheels contact the ground and the nose wheel is just clear of the ground.

The attitude used in paragraph (a)(2)(i) of this section may be used in the analysis required under paragraph (a)(2)(ii) of this section.

(b) When investigating landing conditions, the drag components simulating the forces required to accelerate the tires and wheels up to the landing speed must be properly combined with the corresponding instantaneous vertical ground reactions, assuming wing lift and a tire-sliding coefficient of friction of 0.8. However, the drag loads may not be less than 25 percent of the maximum vertical ground reactions (neglecting wing lift).

(c) In determining the wheel spin-up loads for landing conditions, the method set forth in Appendix D or the arbitrary drag components in Appendix C must be used. However, if Appendix D is used, the 25 percent value for the minimum drag component must be used.

(d) For airplanes with tip tanks or large overhung masses (such as turbopropeller or jet engines) supported by the wing, the tip tanks and the structure supporting the tanks or overhung masses must be designed for the effects of dynamic responses under the level landing conditions of either paragraph (a)(1) or (a)(2)(ii) of this section. In evaluating the effects of dynamic response, an airplane lift equal to the weight of the airplane may be assumed.

[Doc. No. 4080, 29 FR 17955, Dec. 18, 1964, as amended by Amdt. 23–17, 41 FR 55464, Dec. 20, 1976]

§ 23.481 Tail down landing conditions.

(a) For a tail down landing, the airplane is assumed to be in the following attitudes:

(1) For airplanes with tail wheels, an attitude in which the main and tail wheels contact the ground simultaneously.

(2) For airplanes with nose wheels, a stalling attitude, or the maximum angle allowing ground clearance by each part of the airplane, whichever is less.

(b) For airplanes with either tail or nose wheels, ground reactions are assumed to be vertical, with the wheels up to speed before the maximum vertical load is attained.

§ 23.483 One-wheel landing conditions.

For the one-wheel landing condition, the airplane is assumed to be in the level attitude and to contact the ground on one side of the main landing gear. In this attitude, the ground reactions must be the same as those obtained on that side under § 23.479.

§ 23.485 Side load conditions.

(a) For the side load condition, the airplane is assumed to be in a level attitude with only the main wheels contacting the ground and with the shock absorbers and tires in their static positions.

(b) The limit vertical load factor must be 1.33, with the vertical ground reaction divided equally between the main wheels.

(c) The limit side inertia factor must be 0.83, with the side ground reaction divided between the main wheels so that—

(1) 0.5 (W) is acting inboard on one side; and

(2) 0.33 (W) is acting outboard on the other side.

§ 23.493 Braked roll conditions.

Under braked roll conditions, with the shock absorbers and tires in their static positions, the following apply:

(a) The limit vertical load factor must be 1.33.

(b) The attitudes and ground contacts must be those described in § 23.479 for level landings.

(c) A drag reaction equal to the vertical reaction at the wheel multiplied by a coefficient of friction of 0.8 must be applied at the ground contact point of each wheel with brakes, except that the drag reaction need not exceed the maximum value based on limiting brake torque.

§ 23.497 Supplementary conditions for tail wheels.

In determining the ground loads on the tail wheel and affected supporting structures, the following apply:

(a) For the obstruction load, the limit ground reaction obtained in the tail down landing condition is assumed to act up and aft through the axle at 45 degrees. The shock absorber and tire may be assumed to be in their static positions.

(b) For the side load, a limit vertical ground reaction equal to the static load on the tail wheel, in combination with a side component of equal magnitude, is assumed. In addition—

(1) If a swivel is used, the tail wheel is assumed to be swiveled 90 degrees to the airplane longitudinal axis with the resultant ground load passing through the axle;

(2) If a lock, steering device, or shimmy damper is used, the tail wheel is also assumed to be in the trailing position with the side load acting at the ground contact point; and

(3) The shock absorber and tire are assumed to be in their static positions.

§ 23.499 Supplementary conditions for nose wheels.

In determining the ground loads on nose wheels and affected supporting structures, and assuming that the shock absorbers and tires are in their static positions, the following conditions must be met:

(a) For aft loads, the limit force components at the axle must be—

(1) A vertical component of 2.25 times the static load on the wheel; and

(2) A drag component of 0.8 times the vertical load.

(b) For forward loads, the limit force components at the axle must be—

(1) A vertical component of 2.25 times the static load on the wheel; and

(2) A forward component of 0.4 times the vertical load.

(c) For side loads, the limit force components at ground contact must be—

(1) A vertical component of 2.25 times the static load on the wheel; and

(2) A side component of 0.7 times the vertical load.

§ 23.505 Supplementary conditions for skiplanes.

In determining ground loads for skiplanes, and assuming that the airplane is resting on the ground with one main ski frozen at rest and the other skis free to slide, a limit side force equal to 0.036 times the design maximum weight must be applied near the tail assembly, with a factor of safety of 1.

[Amdt. 23-7, 34 FR 13090, Aug. 13, 1969]

§ 23.507 Jacking loads.

(a) The airplane must be designed for the loads developed when the aircraft is supported on jacks at the design maximum weight assuming the following load factors for landing gear jacking points at a three-point attitude and for primary flight structure jacking points in the level attitude:

(1) Vertical-load factor of 1.35 times the static reactions.

(2) Fore, aft, and lateral load factors of 0.4 times the vertical static reactions.

(b) The horizontal loads at the jack points must be reacted by inertia forces so as to result in no change in the direction of the resultant loads at the jack points.

(c) The horizontal loads must be considered in all combinations with the vertical load.

[Amdt. 23-14, 38 FR 31821, Nov. 19, 1973]

§ 23.509   Towing loads.

The towing loads of this section must be applied to the design of tow fittings and their immediate attaching structure.

(a) The towing loads specified in paragraph (d) of this section must be considered separately. These loads must be applied at the towing fittings and must act parallel to the ground. In addition:

(1) A vertical load factor equal to 1.0 must be considered acting at the center of gravity; and

(2) The shock struts and tires must be in there static positions.

(b) For towing points not on the landing gear but near the plane of symmetry of the airplane, the drag and side tow load components specified for the auxiliary gear apply. For towing points located outboard of the main gear, the drag and side tow load components specified for the main gear apply. Where the specified angle of swivel cannot be reached, the maximum obtainable angle must be used.

(c) The towing loads specified in paragraph (d) of this section must be reacted as follows:

(1) The side component of the towing load at the main gear must be reacted by a side force at the static ground line of the wheel to which the load is applied.

(2) The towing loads at the auxiliary gear and the drag components of the towing loads at the main gear must be reacted as follows:

(i) A reaction with a maximum value equal to the vertical reaction must be applied at the axle of the wheel to which the load is applied. Enough airplane inertia to achieve equilibrium must be applied.

(ii) The loads must be reacted by airplane inertia.

(d) The prescribed towing loads are as follows, where W is the design maximum weight:

Tow point	Position	Load		
		Magnitude	No.	Direction
Main gear	....	0.225W	1	Forward, parallel to drag axis.
			2	Forward, at 30° to drag axis.
			3	Aft, parallel to drag axis.
			4	Aft, at 30° to drag axis.
Auxiliary gear............................	Swiveled forward..................................	0.3W	5	Forward.
			6	Aft.
	Swiveled aft	0.3W	7	Forward.
			8	Aft.
	Swiveled 45° from forward	0.15W	9	Forward, in plane of wheel.
			10	Aft, in plane of wheel.
	Swiveled 45° from aft........................	0.15W	11	Forward, in plane of wheel.
			12	Aft, in plane of wheel.

[Amdt. 23-14, 38 FR 31821, Nov. 19, 1973]

§ 23.511   Ground   load;   unsymmetrical loads on multiple-wheel units.

(a) *Pivoting loads.* The airplane is assumed to pivot about on side of the main gear with—

(1) The brakes on the pivoting unit locked; and

(2) Loads corresponding to a limit vertical load factor of 1, and coefficient of friction of 0.8 applied to the main gear and its supporting structure.

(b) *Unequal tire loads.* The loads established under §§ 23.471 through 23.483 must be applied in turn, in a 60/40 percent distribution, to the dual wheels and tires in each dual wheel landing gear unit.

(c) *Deflated tire loads.* For the deflated tire condition—

(1) 60 percent of the loads established under §§ 23.471 through 23.483 must be applied in turn to each wheel in a landing gear unit; and

(2) 60 percent of the limit drag and side loads, and 100 percent of the limit vertical load established under §§ 23.485 and 23.493 or lesser vertical load obtained under paragraph (c)(1) of this section, must be applied in turn to each wheel in the dual wheel landing gear unit.

WATER LOADS

§ 23.521 Water load conditions.

(a) The structure of seaplanes and amphibians must be designed for water loads developed during takeoff and landing with the seaplane in any attitude likely to occur in normal operation at appropriate forward and sinking velocities under the most severe sea conditions likely to be encountered.

(b) Unless the applicant makes a rational analysis of the water loads, or uses the standards in ANC-3, §§ 25.523 through 25.537 of this chapter apply.

(c) Floats certificated under Part 4a of this chapter before November 9, 1945, may be installed on airplanes that are designed under this part.

EMERGENCY LANDING CONDITIONS

§ 23.561 General.

(a) The airplane, although it may be damaged in emergency landing conditions, must be designed as prescribed in this section to protect each occupant under those conditions.

(b) The structure must be designed to protect each occupant during emergency landing conditions when—

(1) Proper use is made of the seats, safety belts, and shoulder harnesses provided for in the design;

(2) The occupant experiences the static inertia loads corresponding to the following ultimate load factors—

(i) Upward, 3.0g for normal, utility, and commuter category airplanes, or 4.5g for acrobatic category airplanes;

(ii) Forward, 9.0g;

(iii) Sideward, 1.5g; and

(3) The items of mass within the cabin, that could injure an occupant, experience the static inertia loads corresponding to the following ultimate load factors—

(i) Upward, 3.0g;

(ii) Forward, 18.0g; and

(iii) Sideward, 4.5g.

(c) Each airplane with retractable landing gear must be designed to protect each occupant in a landing—

(1) With the wheels retracted;

(2) With moderate descent velocity; and

(3) Assuming, in the absence of a more rational analysis—

(i) A downward ultimate inertia force of 3 g; and

(ii) A coefficient of friction of 0.5 at the ground.

(d) If it is not established that a turnover is unlikely during an emergency landing, the structure must be designed to protect the occupants in a complete turnover as follows:

(1) The likelihood of a turnover may be shown by an analysis assuming the following conditions—

(i) Maximum weight;

(ii) Most forward center of gravity position;

(iii) Longitudinal load factor of 9.0g;

(iv) Vertical load factor of 1.0g; and

(v) For airplanes with tricycle landing gear, the nose wheel strut failed with the nose contacting the ground.

(2) For determining the loads to be applied to the inverted airplane after a turnover, an upward ultimate inertia load factor of 3.0g and a coefficient of friction with the ground of 0.5 must be used.

(e) Except as provided in § 23.787 the supporting structure must be designed to restrain, under loads up to those specified in paragraph (b)(2) of this section, each item of mass that could injure an occupant if it came loose in a minor crash landing.

§ 23.562 Emergency landing dynamic conditions.

(a) Each seat/restraint system for use in a normal, utility, or acrobatic category airplane must be designed to protect each occupant during an emergency landing when—

(1) Proper use is made of seats, safety belts, and shoulder harnesses provided for in the design; and

(2) The occupant is exposed to the loads resulting from the conditions prescribed in this section.

(b) Each seat/restraint system, for crew or passenger occupancy in a normal, utility, or acrobatic category airplane, must successfully complete dynamic tests or be demonstrated by rational analysis supported by dynamic tests, in accordance with each of the following conditions. These tests must be conducted with an occupant simulated by an anthropomorphic test dummy (ATD) defined by 49 CFR Part 572, Subpart B, or an FAA-approved equivalent, with a nominal weight of 170 pounds and seated in the normal upright position.

(1) For the first test, the change in velocity may not be less than 31 feet per second. The

seat/restraint system must be oriented in its nominal position with respect to the airplane and with the horizontal plane of the airplane pitched up 60 degrees, with no yaw, relative to the impact vector. For seat/restraint systems to be installed in the first row of the airplane, peak deceleration must occur in not more than 0.05 seconds after impact and must reach a minimum of 19g. For all other seat/restraint systems, peak deceleration must occur in not more than 0.06 seconds after impact and must reach a minimum of 15g.

(2) For the second test, the change in velocity may not be less than 42 feet per second. The seat/restraint system must be oriented in its nominal position with respect to the airplane and with the vertical plane of the airplane yawed 10 degrees, with no pitch, relative to the impact vector in a direction that results in the greatest load on the shoulder harness. For seat/restraint systems to be installed in the first row of the airplane, peak deceleration must occur in not more than 0.05 seconds after impact and must reach a minimum of 26g. For all other seat/restraint systems, peak deceleration must occur in not more than 0.06 seconds after impact and must reach a minimum of 21g.

(3) To account for floor warpage, the floor rails or attachment devices used to attach the seat/restraint system to the airframe structure must be preloaded to misalign with respect to each other by at least 10 degrees vertically (i.e., pitch out of parallel) and one of the rails or attachment devices must be preloaded to misalign by 10 degrees in roll prior to conducting the test defined by paragraph (b)(2) of this section.

(c) Compliance with the following requirements must be shown during the dynamic tests conducted in accordance with paragraph (b) of this section:

(1) The seat/restraint system must restrain the ATD although seat/restraint system components may experience deformation, elongation, displacement, or crushing intended as part of the design.

(2) The attachment between the seat/restraint system and the test fixture must remain intact, although the seat structure may have deformed.

(3) Each shoulder harness strap must remain on the ATD's shoulder during the impact.

(4) The safety belt must remain on the ATD's pelvis during the impact.

(5) The results of the dynamic tests must show that the occupant is protected from serious head injury.

(i) When contact with adjacent seats, structure, or other items in the cabin can occur, protection must be provided so that the head impact does not exceed a head injury criteria (HIC) of 1,000.

(ii) the value of HIC is defined as—

$$HIC = \left\{ (t_2 - t_1) \left[\frac{1}{(t_2 - t_1)} \int_{t_1}^{t_2} a(t)dt \right]^{2.5} \right\}_{Max}$$

Where t_1 is the initial integration time, expressed in seconds, t_2 is the final integration time, expressed in seconds ($t_2 - t_1$) is the time duration of the major head impact, expressed in seconds, and a(t) is the resultant deceleration at the center of gravity of the head form expressed as a multiple of g (units of gravity).

(iii) Compliance with the HIC limit must be demonstrated by measuring the head impact during dynamic testing as prescribed in paragraphs (b)(1) and (b)(2) of this section or by a separate showing of compliance with the head injury criteria using test or analysis procedures.

(6) Loads in individual shoulder harness straps may not exceed 1,750 pounds. If dual straps are used for retaining the upper torso, the total strap loads may not exceed 2,000 pounds.

(7) The compression load measured between the pelvis and the lumbar spine of the ATD may not exceed 1,500 pounds.

(d) An alternate approach that achieves an equivalent, or greater, level of occupant protection to that required by this section may be used if substantiated on a rational basis.

FATIGUE EVALUATION

§ 23.571 Pressurized cabin.

The strength, detail design, and fabrication of the pressure cabin structure must be evaluated under either of the following:

(a) A fatigue strength investigation, in which the structure is shown by analysis, tests, or both to be able to withstand the repeated loads of variable magnitude expected in service. Analysis alone is considered acceptable only when it is conservative and applied to simple structures.

(b) A fail safe strength investigation, in which it is shown by analysis, tests, or both that catastrophic failure of the structure is not probable after fatigue failure, or obvious partial failure, of a principal structural element, and that the remaining structures are able to withstand a static ultimate load factor of 75 percent of the limit load factor at V_c, considering the combined effects of normal operating pressures, expected external aerodynamic pressures, and flight loads. These loads must be multiplied by a factor of 1.15 unless the dynamic effects of failure under static load are otherwise considered.

[Doc. No. 4080, 29 FR 17955, Dec. 18, 1964, as amended by Amdt. 23-14, 38 FR 31821, Nov. 19, 1973]

§ 23.572   Flight structure.

(a) For normal, utility, and acrobatic catgory airplanes, the strength, detail design, and fabrication of those parts of the wing, wing carrythrough, and attaching structure whose failure would be catastrophic must be evaluated under either of the following unless it is shown that the structure, operating stress level, materials, and expected use are comparable, from a fatigue standpoint, to a similar design that has had extensive satisfactory service experience:

(1) A fatigue strength investigation, in which the structure is shown by analysis, tests, or both, to be able to withstand the repeated loads of variable magnitude expected in service. Analysis alone is acceptable only when it is conservative and applied to simple structures.

(2) A fail-safe strength investigation in which it is shown by analysis, tests, or both, that catastrophic failure of the structure is not probably after fatigue failure, or obvious partial failure, of a principal structural element, and that the remaining structure is able to withstand a static ultimate load factor of 75 percent of the critical limit load factor at V_o. These loads must be multiplied by a factor of 1.15 unless the

dynamic effects of failure under static load are otherwise considered.

(b) For commuter category airplanes, unless it is shown that the structure, operating stress levels, materials, and expected use are comparable from a fatigue standpoint to similar design which has had a substantial satisfactory service experience, the strength, detail design, and the fabrication of those parts of the wing, wing carrythrough, vertical fin, horizontal stabilizer, and attaching structure whose failure would be catastrophic must be evaluated under either—

(1) A fatigue strength investigation, in which the structure is shown by analysis, tests, or both, to be able to withstand the repeated loads of variable magnitude expected in service. Analysis alone is acceptable only when it is conservative and applied to simple structures; or

(2) A fail-safe strength investigation in which analysis, tests, or both, show that catastrophic failure of the structure is not probable after fatigue failure, or obvious partial failure, of a principal structural element and that the remaining structure is able to withstand a static ultimate load factor of 75 percent of the critical limit load at V_c. These loads must be multiplied by a factor of 1.15 unless the dynamic effects of failure under static load are otherwise considered.

[Amdt. 23-7, 34 FR 13090, Aug. 13, 1969, as amended by Amdt. 23-14, 38 FR 31821, Nov. 19, 1973; Amdt. 23-34, 52 FR 1830, Jan. 15, 1987]

Subpart D—Design and Construction

§ 23.601   General.

The suitability of each questionable design detail and part having an important bearing on safety in operations, must be established by tests.

§ 23.603   Materials and workmanship.

(a) The suitability and durability of materials used for parts, the failure of which could adversely affect safety, must—

(1) Be established by experience or tests;

(2) Meet approved specifications that ensure their having the strength

and other properties assumed in the design data; and

(3) Take into account the effects of environmental conditions, such as temperature and humidity, expected in service.

(b) Workmanship must be of a high standard.

[Doc. No. 4080, 29 FR 17955, Dec. 18, 1964, as amended by Amdt. 23-17, 41 FR 55464, Dec. 20, 1976; Amdt. 23-23, 43 FR 50592, Oct. 10, 1978]

§ 23.605 Fabrication methods.

(a) The methods of fabrication used must produce consistently sound structures. If a fabrication process (such as gluing, spot welding, or heat-treating) requires close control to reach this objective, the process must be performed under an approved process specification.

(b) Each new aircraft fabrication method must be substantiated by a test program.

[Doc. No. 4080, 29 FR 17955, Dec. 18, 1964; 30 FR 258, Jan. 9, 1965, as amended by Amdt. 23-23, 43 FR 50592, Oct. 10, 1978]

§ 23.607 Self-locking nuts.

No self-locking nut may be used on any bolt subject to rotation in operation unless a nonfriction locking device is used in addition to the self-locking device.

[Amdt. 23-17, 41 FR 55464, Dec. 20, 1976]

§ 23.609 Protection of structure.

Each part of the structure must—

(a) Be suitably protected against deterioration or loss of strength in service due to any cause, including—

(1) Weathering;

(2) Corrosion; and

(3) Abrasion; and

(b) Have adequate provisions for ventilation and drainage.

§ 23.611 Accessibility.

Means must be provided to allow inspection (including inspection of principal structural elements and control systems), close examination, repair, and replacement of each part requiring maintenance, adjustments for proper alignment and function, lubrication or servicing.

[Amdt. 23-7, 34 FR 13090, Aug. 13, 1969]

§ 23.613 Material strength properties and design values.

(a) Material strength properties must be based on enough tests of material meeting specifications to establish design values on a statistical basis.

(b) The design values must be chosen so that the probability of any structure being understrength because of material variations is extremely remote.

(c) Design values must be those contained in the following publications (obtainable from the Superintendent of Documents, Government Printing Office, Washington, D.C. 20402) or other values approved by the Administrator:

MIL-HDBK-5, "Metallic Materials and Elements for Flight Vehicle Structure";

MIL-HDBK-17, "Plastics for Flight Vehicles";

ANC-18, "Design of Wood Aircraft Structures"; and

MIL-HDBK-23, "Composite Construction for Flight Vehicles".

[Doc. No. 4080, 29 FR 17955, Dec. 18, 1964; 30 FR 258, Jan. 9, 1965, as amended by Amdt. 23-23, 43 FR 50592, Oct. 30, 1978]

§ 23.615 Design properties.

(a) Design properties outlined in MIL-HDBK-5 may be used subject to the following conditions:

(1) Where applied loads are eventually distributed through a single member within an assembly, the failure of which would result in the loss of the structural integrity of the component involved, the guaranteed minimum design mechanical properties ("A" values) when listed in MIL-HDBK-5 must be met.

(2) Redundant structures in which the partial failure of individual elements would result in applied loads being safely distributed to other load carrying members may be designed on the basis of the "90 percent probability" ("B" values) when listed in MIL-HDBK-5. Examples of these items are sheet-stiffener combinations and multirivet or multiple-bolt connections.

(b) Design values greater than the guaranteed minimums required by paragraph (a) of this section may be used if a "premium selection" of the material is made in which a specimen of each individual item is tested before use to determine that the actual strength properties of that particular item will equal or exceed those used in design.

(c) Material correction factors for structural items such as sheets, sheet-stringer combinations, and riveted joints, may be omitted if sufficient test data are obtained to allow a probability analysis showing that 90 percent or more of the elements will equal or exceed allowable selected design values.

[Doc. No. 4080, 29 FR 17955, Dec. 18, 1964, as amended by Amdt. 23-7, 34 FR 13090, Aug. 13, 1969]

§ 23.619 Special factors.

The factor of safety prescribed in § 23.303 must be multiplied by the highest pertinent special factors of safety prescribed in §§ 23.621 through 23.625 for each part of the structure whose strength is—

(a) Uncertain;

(b) Likely to deteriorate in service before normal replacement; or

(c) Subject to appreciable variability because of uncertainties in manufacturing processes or inspection methods.

[Amdt. 23-7, 34 FR 13091, Aug. 13, 1969]

§ 23.621 Casting factors.

(a) *General.* The factors, tests, and inspections specified in paragraphs (b) through (d) of this section must be applied in addition to those necessary to establish foundry quality control. The inspections must meet approved specifications. Paragraphs (c) and (d) of this section apply to any structural castings except castings that are pressure tested as parts of hydraulic or other fluid systems and do not support structural loads.

(b) *Bearing stresses and surfaces.* The casting factors specified in paragraphs (c) and (d) of this section—

(1) Need not exceed 1.25 with respect to bearing stresses regardless of the method of inspection used; and

(2) Need not be used with respect to the bearing surfaces of a part whose bearing factor is larger than the applicable casting factor.

(c) *Critical castings.* For each casting whose failure would preclude continued safe flight and landing of the airplane or result in serious injury to occupants, the following apply:

(1) Each critical casting must—

(i) Have a casting factor of not less than 1.25; and

(ii) Receive 100 percent inspection by visual, radiographic, and magnetic particle or penetrant inspection methods or approved equivalent nondestructive inspection methods.

(2) For each critical casting with a casting factor less than 1.50, three sample castings must be static tested and shown to meet—

(i) The strength requirements of § 23.305 at an ultimate load corresponding to a casting factor of 1.25; and

(ii) The deformation requirements of § 23.305 at a load of 1.15 times the limit load.

(3) Examples of these castings are structural attachment fittings, parts of flight control systems, control surface hinges and balance weight attachments, seat, berth, safety belt, and fuel and oil tank supports and attachments, and cabin pressure valves.

(d) *Noncritical castings.* For each casting other than those specified in paragraph (c) of this section, the following apply:

(1) Except as provided in paragraphs (d) (2) and (3) of this section, the casting factors and corresponding inspections must meet the following table:

Casting factor	Inspection
2.0 or more........................	100 percent visual.
Less than 2.0 but more than 1.5.	100 percent visual, and magnetic particle or penetrant or equivalent nondestructive inspection methods.
1.25 through 1.50..............	100 percent visual, magnetic particle or penetrant, and radiographic, or approved equivalent nondestructive inspection methods.

(2) The percentage of castings inspected by nonvisual methods may be reduced below that specified in subparagraph (d)(1) of this section when an approved quality control procedure is established.

(3) For castings procured to a specification that guarantees the mechanical properties of the material in the casting and provides for demonstration of these properties by test of coupons cut from the castings on a sampling basis—

(i) A casting factor of 1.0 may be used; and

(ii) The castings must be inspected as provided in paragraph (d)(1) of this section for casting factors of "1.25 through 1.50" and tested under paragraph (c)(2) of this section.

§ 23.623 Bearing factors.

(a) Each part that has clearance (free fit), and that is subject to pounding or vibration, must have a bearing factor large enough to provide for the effects of normal relative motion.

(b) For control surface hinges and control system joints, compliance with the factors prescribed in §§ 23.657 and 23.693, respectively, meets paragraph (a) of this section.

[Amdt. 23-7, 34 FR 13091, Aug. 13, 1969]

§ 23.625 Fitting factors.

For each fitting (a part or terminal used to join one structural member to another), the following apply:

(a) For each fitting whose strength is not proven by limit and ultimate load tests in which actual stress conditions are simulated in the fitting and surrounding structures, a fitting factor of at least 1.15 must be applied to each part of—

(1) The fitting;

(2) The means of attachment; and

(3) The bearing on the joined members.

(b) No fitting factor need be used for joint designs based on comprehensive test data (such as continuous joints in metal plating, welded joints, and scarf joints in wood).

(c) For each integral fitting, the part must be treated as a fitting up to the point at which the section properties become typical of the member.

(d) For each seat, berth, safety belt, and harness, its attachment to the structure must be shown, by analysis, tests, or both, to be able to withstand the inertia forces prescribed in § 23.561 multiplied by a fitting factor of 1.33.

[Doc. No. 4080, 29 FR 17955, Dec. 18, 1964, as amended by Amdt. 23-7, 34 FR 13091, Aug. 13, 1969]

§ 23.627 Fatigue strength.

The structure must be designed, as far as practicable, to avoid points of stress concentration where variable stresses above the fatigue limit are likely to occur in normal service.

§ 23.629 Flutter.

(a) It must be shown by one of the methods specified in paragraph (b), (c), or (d) of this section, or a combination of these methods, that the airplane is free from flutter, control reversal, and divergence for any condition of operation within the limit V-n envelope, and at all speeds up to the speed specified for the selected method. In addition—

(1) Adequate tolerances must be established for quantities which affect flutter, including speed, damping, mass balance, and control system stiffness; and

(2) The natural frequencies of main structural components must be determined by vibration tests or other approved methods.

(b) A rational analysis may be used to show that the airplane is free from flutter, control reversal, and divergence if the analysis shows freedom from flutter for all speeds up to $1.2V_D$.

(c) Flight flutter tests may be used to show that the airplane is free from flutter, control reversal, and divergence if it is shown by these tests that—

(1) Proper and adequate attempts to induce flutter have been made within the speed range up to V_D;

(2) The vibratory response of the structure during the test indicates freedom from flutter;

(3) A proper margin of damping exists at V_D; and

(4) There is no large and rapid reduction in damping as V_D is approached.

(d) Compliance with the rigidity and mass balance criteria (pages 4-12), in Airframe and Equipment Engineering Report No. 45 (as corrected) "Simplified Flutter Prevention Criteria" (published by the Federal Aviation Administration) may be accomplished to show that the airplane is free from flutter, control reversal, or divergence if—

(1) V for the airplane is less than 260 knots (EAS) at altitudes below 14,000 feet and less than Mach 0.6 at altitudes at and above 14,000 feet,

(2) The wing and aileron flutter prevention criteria, as represented by the wing torsional stiffness and aileron balance criteria, are limited in use to airplanes without large mass concentrations (such as engines, floats, or fuel tanks in outer wing panels) along the wing span, and

(3) The airplane—

(i) Does not have a T-tail or boom tail,

(ii) Does not have unusual mass distributions or other unconventional design features that affect the applicability of the criteria, and

(iii) Has fixed-fin and fixed-stabilizer surfaces.

(e) For turbopropeller-powered airplanes, the dynamic evaluation must include—

(1) Whirl mode degree of freedom which takes into account the stability of the plane of rotation of the propeller and significant elastic, inertial, and aerodynamic forces, and

(2) Propeller, engine, engine mount, and airplane structure stiffness and damping variations appropriate to the particular configuration.

(f) Freedom from flutter, control reversal, and divergence up to V_D/M_D must be shown as follows:

(1) For airplanes that meet the criteria of paragraphs (d)(1) through (d)(3) of this section, after the failure, malfunction, or disconnection of any single element in any tab control system.

(2) For airplanes other than those described in paragraph (f)(1) of this section, after the failure, malfunction, or disconnection of any single element in the primary flight control system, any tab control system, or any flutter damper.

[Amdt. 23-23, 43 FR 50592, Oct. 30, 1978, as amended by Amdt. 23-31, 49 FR 46867, Nov. 28, 1984]

WINGS

§ 23.641   Proof of strength.

The strength of stressed-skin wings must be proven by load tests or by combined structural analysis and load tests.

CONTROL SURFACES

§ 23.651   Proof of strength.

(a) Limit load tests of control surfaces are required. These tests must include the horn or fitting to which the control system is attached.

(b) In structural analyses, rigging loads due to wire bracing must be accounted for in a rational or conservative manner.

§ 23.655   Installation.

(a) Movable tail surfaces must be installed so that there is no interference between any surfaces or their bracing when one surface is held in its extreme position and the others are operated through their full angular movement.

(b) If an adjustable stabilizer is used, it must have stops that will limit its range of travel to that allowing safe flight and landing.

§ 23.657   Hinges.

(a) Control surface hinges, except ball and roller bearing hinges, must have a factor of safety of not less than 6.67 with respect to the ultimate bearing strength of the softest material used as a bearing.

(b) For ball or roller bearing hinges, the approved rating of the bearing may not be exceeded.

(c) Hinges must have enough strength and rigidity for loads parallel to the hinge line.

§ 23.659   Mass balance.

The supporting structure and the attachment of concentrated mass balance weights used on control surfaces must be designed for—

(a) 24 g normal to the plane of control surface;

(b) 12 g fore and aft; and

(c) 12 g parallel to the hinge line.

CONTROL SYSTEMS

§ 23.671 General.

(a) Each control must operate easily, smoothly, and positively enough to allow proper performance of its functions.

(b) Controls must be arranged and identified to provide for convenience in operation and to prevent the possibility of confusion and subsequent inadvertent operation.

§ 23.673 Primary flight controls.

(a) Primary flight controls are those used by the pilot for the immediate control of pitch, roll, and yaw.

(b) The design of two-control airplanes must minimize the likelihood of complete loss of lateral or directional control in the event of failure of any connecting or transmitting element in the control system.

§ 23.675 Stops.

(a) Each control system must have stops that positively limit the range of motion of each movable aerodynamic surface controlled by the system.

(b) Each stop must be located so that wear, slackness, or takeup adjustments will not adversely affect the control characteristics of the airplane because of a change in the range of surface travel.

(c) Each stop must be able to withstand any loads corresponding to the design conditions for the control system.

[Amdt. 23-17, 41 FR 55464, Dec. 20, 1976]

§ 23.677 Trim systems.

(a) Proper precautions must be taken to prevent inadvertent, improper, or abrupt trim tab operation. There must be means near the trim control to indicate to the pilot the direction of trim control movement relative to airplane motion. In addition, there must be means to indicate to the pilot the position of the trim device with respect to the range of adjustment. This means must be visible to the pilot and must be located and designed to prevent confusion.

(b) Trimming devices must be designed so that, when any one connecting or transmitting element in the pri-

mary flight control system fails, adequate control for safe flight and landing is available with—

(1) For single-engine airplanes, the longitudinal trimming devices; or

(2) For multiengine airplanes, the longitudinal and directional trimming devices.

(c) Tab controls must be irreversible unless the tab is properly balanced and has no unsafe flutter characteristics. Irreversible tab systems must have adequate rigidity and reliability in the portion of the system from the tab to the attachment of the irreversible unit to the airplane structure.

(d) In addition, for commuter category airplanes, a demonstration must show that the airplane is safely controllable and that a pilot can perform all the maneuvers and operations necessary to effect a safe landing following any probable electric trim tab runaway which might be reasonably expected in service allowing for appropriate time delay after pilot recognition of the runaway. This demonstration must be conducted at the critical airplane weights and center of gravity positions.

[Doc. No. 4080, 29 FR 17955, Dec. 18, 1964, as amended by Amdt. 23-7, 34 FR 13091, Aug. 13, 1969; Amdt. 23-34, 52 FR 1830, Jan. 15, 1987]

§ 23.679 Control system locks.

If there is a device to lock the control system on the ground or water, there must be means to—

(a) Give unmistakable warning to the pilot when the lock is engaged; and

(b) Prevent the lock from engaging in flight.

§ 23.681 Limit load static tests.

(a) Compliance with the limit load requirements of this part must be shown by tests in which—

(1) The direction of the test loads produces the most severe loading in the control system; and

(2) Each fitting, pulley, and bracket used in attaching the system to the main structure is included.

(b) Compliance must be shown (by analyses or individual load tests) with the special factor requirements for control system joints subject to angular motion.

§ 23.683 Operation tests.

(a) It must be shown by operation tests that, when the controls are operated from the pilot compartment with the system loaded as prescribed in paragraph (b) of this section, the system is free from—

(1) Jamming;

(2) Excessive friction; and

(3) Excessive deflection.

(b) The prescribed test loads are—

(1) For the entire system, loads corresponding to the limit airloads on the appropriate surface, or the limit pilot forces in § 23.397(b), whichever are less; and

(2) For secondary controls, loads not less than those corresponding to the maximum pilot effort established under § 23.405.

[Doc. No. 4080, 29 FR 17955, Dec. 18, 1964, as amended by Amdt. 23-7, 34 FR 13091, Aug. 13, 1969]

§ 23.685 Control system details.

(a) Each detail of each control system must be designed and installed to prevent jamming, chafing, and interference from cargo, passengers, loose objects, or the freezing of moisture.

(b) There must be means in the cockpit to prevent the entry of foreign objects into places where they would jam the system.

(c) There must be means to prevent the slapping of cables or tubes against other parts.

(d) Each element of the flight control system must have design features, or must be distinctively and permanently marked, to minimize the possibility of incorrect assembly that could result in malfunctioning of the control system.

[Doc. No. 4080, 29 FR 17955, Dec. 18, 1964, as amended by Amdt. 23-17, 41 FR 55464, Dec. 20, 1976]

§ 23.687 Spring devices.

The reliability of any spring device used in the control system must be established by tests simulating service conditions unless failure of the spring will not cause flutter or unsafe flight characteristics.

§ 23.689 Cable systems.

(a) Each cable, cable fitting, turnbuckle, splice, and pulley used must meet approved specifications. In addition—

(1) No cable smaller than ⅛ inch diameter may be used in primary control systems;

(2) Each cable system must be designed so that there will be no hazardous change in cable tension throughout the range of travel under operating conditions and temperature variations; and

(3) There must be means for visual inspection at each fairlead, pulley, terminal, and turnbuckle.

(b) Each kind and size of pulley must correspond to the cable with which it is used. Each pulley must have closely fitted guards to prevent the cables from being misplaced or fouled, even when slack. Each pulley must lie in the plane passing through the cable so that the cable does not rub against the pulley flange.

(c) Fairleads must be installed so that they do not cause a change in cable direction of more than three degrees.

(d) Clevis pins subject to load or motion and retained only by cotter pins may not be used in the control system.

(e) Turnbuckles must be attached to parts having angular motion in a manner that will positively prevent binding throughout the range of travel.

(f) Tab control cables are not part of the primary control system and may be less than ⅛ inch diameter in airplanes that are safely controllable with the tabs in the most adverse positions.

[Doc. No. 4080, 29 FR 17955, Dec. 18, 1964, as amended by Amdt. 23-7, 34 FR 13091, Aug. 13, 1969]

§ 23.693 Joints.

Control system joints (in push-pull systems) that are subject to angular motion, except those in ball and roller bearing systems, must have a special factor of safety of not less than 3.33 with respect to the ultimate bearing strength of the softest material used as a bearing. This factor may be reduced to 2.0 for joints in cable control systems. For ball or roller bearings, the approved ratings may not be exceeded.

§ 23.697 Wing flap controls.

(a) Each wing flap control must be designed so that, when the flap has been placed in any position upon which compliance with the performance requirements of this part is based, the flap will not move from that position unless the control is adjusted or is moved by the automatic operation of a flap load limiting device.

(b) The rate of movement of the flaps in response to the operation of the pilot's control or automatic device must give satisfactory flight and performance characteristics under steady or changing conditions of airspeed, engine power, and attitude.

§ 23.699 Wing flap position indicator.

There must be a wing flap position indicator for—

(a) Flap installations with only the retracted and fully extended position, unless—

(1) A direct operating mechanism provides a sense of "feel" and position (such as when a mechanical linkage is employed); or

(2) The flap position is readily determined without seriously detracting from other piloting duties under any flight condition, day or night; and

(b) Flap installation with intermediate flap positions if—

(1) Any flap position other than retracted or fully extended is used to show compliance with the performance requirements of this part; and

(2) The flap installation does not meet the requirements of paragraph (a)(1) of this section.

§ 23.701 Flap interconnection.

(a) The motion of flaps on opposite sides of the plane of symmetry must be synchronized by a mechanical interconnection unless the airplane has safe flight characteristics with the flaps retracted on one side and extended on the other.

(b) If an interconnection is used in multiengine airplanes, it must be designed to account for the unsummetri-

cal loads resulting from flight with the engines on one side of the plane of symmetry inoperative and the remaining engines at takeoff power. For single-engine airplanes, and multiengine airplanes with no slipstream effects on the flaps, it may be assumed that 100 percent of the critical air load acts on one side and 70 percent on the other.

[Doc. No. 4080, 29 FR 17955, Dec. 18, 1964, as amended by Amdt. 23-14, 38 FR 31821, Nov. 19, 1973]

LANDING GEAR

§ 23.721 General.

For commuter category airplanes that have a passenger seating configuration, excluding pilot seats, of 10 or more, the following general requirements for the landing gear apply:

(a) The main landing-gear system must be designed so that if it fails due to overloads during takeoff and landing (assuming the overloads to act in the upward and aft directions), the failure mode is not likely to cause the spillage of enough fuel from any part of the fuel system to consitute a fire hazard.

(b) Each airplane must be designed so that, with the airplane under control, it can be landed on a paved runway with any one or more landing-gear legs not extended without sustaining a structural component failure that is likely to cause the spillage of enough fuel to consitute a fire hazard.

(c) Compliance with the provisions of this section may be shown by analysis or tests, or both.

[Amdt. 23-34, 52 FR 1830, Jan. 15, 1987]

§ 23.723 Shock absorption tests.

(a) It must be shown that the limit load factors selected for design in accordance with § 23.473 for takeoff and landing weights, respectively, will not be exceeded. This must be shown by energy absorption tests except that analysis based on tests conducted on a landing gear system with identical energy absorption characteristics may be used for increases in previously approved takeoff and landing weights.

(b) The landing gear may not fail, but may yield, in a test showing its reserved energy absorption capacity, simulating a descent velocity of 1.2 times the limit descent velocity, assuming wing lift equal to the weight of the airplane.

[Doc. No. 4080, 29 FR 17955, Dec. 18, 1964; 30 FR 258, Jan. 9, 1965, as amended by Amdt. 23-23, 43 FR 50593, Oct. 30, 1978]

§ 23.725   Limit drop tests.

(a) If compliance with § 23.723(a) is shown by free drop tests, these tests must be made on the complete airplane, or on units consisting of wheel, tire, and shock absorber, in their proper relation, from free drop heights not less than those determined by the following formula:

$$h \text{ (inches)} = 3.6 \, (W/S)^{1/2}$$

However, the free drop height may not be less than 9.2 inches and need not be more than 18.7 inches.

(b) If the effect of wing lift is provided for in free drop tests, the landing gear must be dropped with an effective weight equal to

$$W_e = W \times \frac{h+(1-L)d}{h+d}$$

where—

W_e = the effective weight to be used in the drop test (lbs.);

h = specified free drop height (inches);

d = deflection under impact of the tire (at the approved inflation pressure) plus the vertical component of the axle travel relative to the drop mass (inches);

$W = W_M$ for main gear units (lbs), equal to the static weight on that unit with the airplane in the level attitude (with the nose wheel clear in the case of nose wheel type airplanes);

$W = W_T$ for tail gear units (lbs.), equal to the static weight on the tail unit with the airplane in the tail-down attitude;

$W = W_N$ for nose wheel units lbs.), equal to the vertical component of the static reaction that would exist at the nose wheel, assuming that the mass of the airplane acts at the center of gravity and exerts a force of 1.0 g downward and 0.33 g forward; and

L = the ratio of the assumed wing lift to the airplane weight, but not more than 0.667.

(c) The limit inertia load factor must be determined in a rational or conservative manner, during the drop test,

using a landing gear unit attitude, and applied drag loads, that represent the landing conditions.

(d) The value of d used in the computation of W_e in paragraph (b) of this section may not exceed the value actually obtained in the drop test.

(e) The limit inertia load factor must be determined from the drop test in paragraph (b) of this section according to the following formula:

$$n = n_j \, \frac{W_e}{W} + L$$

where—

n_j = the load factor developed in the drop test (that is, the acceleration (dv/dt) in g's recorded in the drop test) plus 1.0; and

W_e, W, and L are the same as in the drop test computation.

(f) The value of n determined in accordance with paragraph (e) may not be more than the limit inertia load factor used in the landing conditions in § 23.473.

[Doc. No. 4080, 29 FR 17955, Dec. 18, 1964, as amended by Amdt. 23-7, 34 FR 13091, Aug. 13, 1969]

§ 23.726   Ground load dynamic tests.

(a) If compliance with the ground load requirements of §§ 23.479 through 23.483 is shown dynamically by drop test, one drop test must be conducted that meets § 23.725 except that the drop height must be—

(1) 2.25 times the drop height prescribed in § 23.725(a); or

(2) Sufficient to develop 1.5 times the limit load factor.

(b) The critical landing condition for each of the design conditions specified in §§ 23.479 through 23.483 must be used for proof of strength.

[Amdt. 23-7, 34 FR 13091, Aug. 13, 1969]

§ 23.727   Reserve energy absorption drop test.

(a) If compliance with the reserve energy absorption requirement in § 23.723(b) is shown by free drop tests, the drop height may not be less than 1.44 times that specified in § 23.725.

(b) If the effect of wing lift is provided for, the units must be dropped with an effective mass equal to $W_e = Wh/(h+d)$, when the symbols and other details are the same as in § 23.725.

[Doc. No. 4080, 29 FR 17955, Dec. 18, 1964, as amended by Amdt. 23-7, 34 FR 13091, Aug. 13, 1969]

§ 23.729 Landing gear extension and retraction system.

(a) *General.* For airplanes with retractable landing gear, the following apply:

(1) Each landing gear retracting mechanism and its supporting structure must be designed for maximum flight load factors with the gear retracted and must be designed for the combination of friction, inertia, brake torque, and air loads, occurring during retraction at any airspeed up to 1.6 V_{S1} with flaps retracted, and for any load factor up to those specified in § 23.345 for the flaps-extended condition.

(2) The landing gear and retracting mechanism, including the wheel well doors, must withstand flight loads, including loads resulting from all yawing conditions specified in § 23.351, with the landing gear extended at any speed up to at least 1.6 V_{S1} with the flaps retracted.

(b) *Landing gear lock.* There must be positive means (other than the use of hydraulic pressure) to keep the landing gear extended.

(c) *Emergency operation.* For a landplane having retractable landing gear that cannot be extended manually, there must be means to extend the landing gear in the event of either—

(1) Any reasonably probable failure in the normal landing gear operation system; or

(2) Any reasonably probable failure in a power source that would prevent the operation of the normal landing gear operation system.

(d) *Operation test.* The proper functioning of the retracting mechanism must be shown by operation tests.

(e) *Position indicator.* If a retractable landing gear is used, there must be a landing gear position indicator (as well as necessary switches to actuate the indicator) or other means to inform the pilot that the gear is secured in the extended (or retracted) position. If switches are used, they must be located and coupled to the landing gear mechanical system in a manner that prevents an erroneous indication of either "down and locked" if the landing gear is not in a fully extended position, or of "up and locked" if the landing gear is not in the fully retracted position. The switches may be located where they are operated by the actual landing gear locking latch or device.

(f) *Landing gear warning.* For landplanes, the following aural or equally effective landing gear warning devices must be provided:

(1) A device that functions continuously when one or more throttles are closed if the landing gear is not fully extended and locked. A throttle stop may not be used in place of an aural device. If there is a manual shutoff for the warning device prescribed in this paragraph, the warning system must be designed so that, when the warning has been suspended after one or more throttles are closed, subsequent retardation of any throttle to or beyond the position for normal landing approach will activate the warning device.

(2) A device that functions continuously when the wing flaps are extended to or beyond the approach flap position, using a normal landing procedure, if the landing gear is not fully extended and locked. There may not be a manual shutoff for this warning device. The flap position sensing unit may be installed at any suitable location. The system for this device may use any part of the system (including the aural warning device) for the device required in paragraph (f)(1) of this section.

[Doc. No. 4080, 29 FR 17955, Dec. 18, 1964, as amended by Amdt. 23-7, 34 FR 13091, Aug. 13, 1969; Amdt. 23-21, 43 FR 2318, Jan. 1978; Amdt. 23-26, 45 FR 60171, Sept. 11, 1980]

§ 23.731 Wheels.

(a) Each main and nose wheel must be approved.

(b) The maximum static load rating of each wheel may not be less than the corresponding static ground reaction with—

(1) Design maximum weight; and

(2) Critical center of gravity.

(c) The maximum limit load rating of each wheel must equal or exceed the maximum radial limit load determined under the applicable ground load requirements of this part.

§ 23.733 Tires.

(a) Each landing gear wheel must have a tire whose tire rating (assigned by the Tire and Rim Association or the Administrator) is not exceeded—

(1) By a load on each main wheel tire equal to the corresponding static ground reaction under the design maximum weight and critical center of gravity; and

(2) By a load on nose wheel tires (to be compared with the dynamic rating established for such tires) equal to the reaction obtained at the nose wheel, assuming the mass of the airplane to be concentrated at the most critical center of gravity and exerting a force of 1.0 *W* downward and 0.31 *W* forward (where *W* is the design maximum weight), with the reactions distributed to the nose and main wheels by the principles of statics, and with the drag reaction at the ground applied only at wheels with brakes.

(b) If specially constructed tires are used, the wheels must be plainly and conspicuously marked to that effect. The markings must include the make, size, number of plies, and identification marking of the proper tire.

(c) Each tire installed on a retractable landing gear system must, at the maximum size of the tire type expected in service, have a clearance to surrounding structure and systems that is adequate to prevent contact between the tire and any part of the structure of systems.

[Doc. No. 4080, 29 FR 17955, Dec. 18, 1964, as amended by Amdt. 23-7, 34 FR 13092, Aug. 13, 1969; Amdt. 23-17, 41 FR 55464, Dec. 20, 1976]

§ 23.735 Brakes.

(a) Brakes must be provided so that the brake kinetic energy capacity rating of each main wheel brake assembly is not less than the kinetic energy absorption requirements determined under either of the following methods:

(1) The brake kinetic energy absorption requirements must be based on a conservative rational analysis of the sequence of events expected during landing at the design landing weight.

(2) Instead of a rational analysis, the kinetic energy absorption requirements for each main wheel brake assembly may be derived from the following formula:

$$KE = 0.0443\ WV^2/N$$

where—

KE = Kinetic energy per wheel (ft.-lb.);

W = Design landing weight (lb.);

V = Airplane speed in knots. V must be not less than $V_s\sqrt{\ }$, the poweroff stalling speed of the airplane at sea level, at the design landing weight, and in the landing configuration; and

N = Number of main wheels with brakes.

(b) Brakes must be able to prevent the wheels from rolling on a paved runway with takeoff power on the critical engine, but need not prevent movement of the airplane with wheels locked.

[Amdt. 23-7, 34 FR 13092, Aug. 13, 1969, as amended by Amdt. 23-24, 44 FR 68742, Nov. 29, 1979]

§ 23.737 Skis.

Each ski must be approved. The maximum limit load rating of each ski must equal or exceed the maximum limit load determined under the applicable ground load requirements of this part.

FLOATS AND HULLS

§ 23.751 Main float buoyancy.

(a) Each main float must have—

(1) A buoyancy of 80 percent in excess of that required to support the maximum weight of the seaplane or amphibian in fresh water; and

(2) Enough watertight compartments to provide reasonable assurance that the seaplane or amphibian will stay afloat if any two compartments of the main floats are flooded.

(b) Each main float must contain at least four watertight compartments approximately equal in volume.

§ 23.753 Main float design.

Each seaplane main float must be approved and must meet the requirements of § 23.521.

§ 23.755 Hulls.

(a) The hull of a hull seaplane or amphibian of 1,500 pounds or more maximum weight must have watertight compartments designed and arranged so that the hull auxiliary floats, and tires (if used), will keep the airplane afloat in fresh water when—

(1) For airplanes of 5,000 pounds or more maximum weight, any two adjacent compartments are flooded; and

(2) For airplanes of 1,500 pounds up to, but not including, 5,000 pounds maximum weight, any single compartment is flooded.

(b) The hulls of hull seaplanes or amphibians of less than 1,500 pounds maximum weight need not be compartmented.

(c) Bulkheads with watertight doors may be used for communication between compartments.

§ 23.757 Auxiliary floats.

Auxiliary floats must be arranged so that, when completely submerged in fresh water, they provide a righting moment of at least 1.5 times the upsetting moment caused by the seaplane or amphibian being tilted.

PERSONNEL AND CARGO
ACCOMMODATIONS

§ 23.771 Pilot compartment.

For each pilot compartment—

(a) The compartment and its equipment must allow each pilot to perform his duties without unreasonable concentration or fatigue;

(b) Where the flight crew are separated from the passengers by a partition, an opening or openable window or door must be provided to facilitate communication between flight crew and the passengers; and

(c) The aerodynamic controls listed in § 23.779, excluding cables and control rods, must be located with respect to the propellers so that no part of the pilot or the controls lies in the region between the plane of rotation of any inboard propeller and the surface generated by a line passing through the center of the propeller hub making an angle of 5 degrees forward or aft of the plane of rotation of the propeller.

[Doc. No. 4080, 29 FR 17955, Dec. 18, 1964, as amended by Amdt. 23–14, 38 FR 31821, Nov. 19, 1973]

§ 23.773 Pilot compartment view.

(a) Each pilot compartment must be free from glare and reflections that could interfere with the pilot's vision, and designed so that—

(1) The pilot's view is sufficiently extensive, clear, and undistorted, for safe operation;

(2) Each pilot is protected from the elements so that moderate rain conditions do not unduly impair his view of the flight path in normal flight and while landing; and

(3) Internal fogging of the windows covered under paragraph (a)(1) of this section can be easily cleared by each pilot unless means are provided to prevent fogging.

(b) If certification for night operation is requested, compliance with paragraph (a) of this section must be shown in night flight tests.

[Doc. No. 4080, 29 FR 17955, Dec. 18, 1964, as amended by Amdt. 23–14, 38 FR 31822, Nov. 19, 1973]

§ 23.775 Windshields and windows.

(a) Nonsplintering safety glass must be used in internal glass panes.

(b) The design of windshields, windows, and canopies in pressurized airplanes must be based on factors peculiar to high altitude operation, including—

(1) The effects of continuous and cyclic pressurization loadings;

(2) The inherent characteristics of the material used; and

(3) The effects of temperatures and temperature gradients.

(c) On pressurized airplanes that do not comply with the fail-safe requirements of paragraph (e) of this section, an enclosure canopy including a representative part of the installation must be subjected to special tests to account for the combined effects of continuous and cyclic pressurization loadings and flight loads.

(d) The windshield and side windows forward of the pilot's back when he is seated in the normal flight position must have a luminous transmittance value of not less than 70 percent.

(e) If certification for operation above 25,000 feet is requested the windshields, window panels, and canopies must be strong enough to withstand the maximum cabin pressure differential loads combined with critical aerodynamic pressure and temperature effects, after failure of any load-carrying element of the windshield, window panel, or canopy.

[Doc. No. 4080, 29 FR 17955, Dec. 18, 1964, as amended by Amdt. 23-7, 34 FR 13092, Aug. 13, 1969]

§ 23.777 Cockpit controls.

(a) Each cockpit control must be located and (except where its function is obvious) identified to provide convenient operation and to prevent confusion and inadvertent operation.

(b) The controls must be located and arranged so that the pilot, when seated, has full and unrestricted movement of each control without interference from either his clothing or the cockpit structure.

(c) Powerplant controls must be located—

(1) For multiengine airplanes, on the pedestal or overhead at or near the center of the cockpit;

(2) For tandem seated single-engine airplanes, on the left side console or instrument panel;

(3) For other single-engine airplanes at or near the center of the cockpit, on the pedestal, instrument panel, or overhead; and

(4) For airplanes, with side-by-side pilot seats and with two sets of powerplant controls, on left and right consoles.

(d) The control location order from left to right must be power (thrust) lever, propeller (rpm control), and mixture control (condition lever and fuel cutoff for turbine-powered airplanes). Power (thrust) levers must be at least one inch higher or longer to make them more prominent than propeller (rpm control) or mixture controls. Carburetor heat or alternate air control must be to the left of the throttle or at least eight inches from the mixture control when located other than on a pedestal. Carburetor heat or alternate air control, when located on a pedestal must be aft or below the power (thrust) lever. Super-

charger controls must be located below or aft of the propeller controls. Airplanes with tandem seating or single-place airplanes may utilize control locations on the left side of the cabin compartment; however, location order from left to right must be power (thrust) lever, propeller (rpm control) and mixture control.

(e) Identical powerplant controls for each engine must be located to prevent confusion as to the engines they control.

(1) Conventional multiengine powerplant controls must be located so that the left control(s) operates the left engines(s) and the right control(s) operates the right engine(s).

(2) On twin-engine airplanes with front and rear engine locations (tandem), the left powerplant controls must operate the front engine and the right powerplant controls must operate the rear engine.

(f) Wing flap and auxiliary lift device controls must be located—

(1) Centrally, or to the right of the pedestal or powerplant throttle control centerline; and

(2) Far enough away from the landing gear control to avoid confusion.

(g) The landing gear control must be located to the left of the throttle centerline or pedestal centerline.

(h) Each fuel feed selector control must comply with § 23.995 and be located and arranged so that the pilot can see and reach it without moving any seat or primary flight control when his seat is at any position in which it can be placed.

(1) For a mechanical fuel selector:

(i) The indication of the selected fuel valve position must be by means of a pointer and must provide positive identification and feel (detent, etc.) of the selected position.

(ii) The position indicator pointer must be located at the part of the handle that is the maximum dimension of the handle measured from the center of rotation.

(2) For electrical or electronic fuel selector:

(i) Digital controls or electrical switches must be properly labelled.

(ii) Means must be provided to indicate to the flight crew the tank or function selected. Selector switch position is not acceptable as a means of indication. The "off" or "closed" position must be indicated in red.

(3) If the fuel valve selector handle or electrical or digital selection is also a fuel shut-off selector, the off position marking must be colored red. If a separate emergency shut-off means is provided, it also must be colored red.

[Doc. No. 4080, 29 FR 17955, Dec. 18, 1964, as amended by Amdt. 23–7, 34 FR 13092, Aug. 13, 1969; Amdt. 23–33, 51 FR 26656, July 24, 1986]

§ 23.779 Motion and effect of cockpit controls.

Cockpit controls must be designed so that they operate in accordance with the following movement and actuation:

(a) Aerodynamic controls:

Motion and effect

(1) *Primary controls:*

Aileron	Right (clockwise) for right wing down.
Elevator	Rearward for nose up.
Rudder	Right pedal forward for nose right.

(2) *Secondary controls:*

Flaps (or auxiliary lift devices).	Forward or up for flaps up or auxiliary device stowed; rearward or down for flaps down or auxiliary device deployed.
Trim tabs (or equivalent).	Switch motion or mechanical rotation of control to produce similar rotation of the airplane about an axis parallel to the axis control. Axis of roll trim control may be displaced to accommodate comfortable actuation by the pilot. For single-engine airplanes, direction of pilot's hand movement must be in the same sense as airplane response for rudder trim if only a portion of a rotational element is accessible.

(b) Powerplant and auxiliary controls:

Motion and effect

(1) *Powerplant controls:*

Power (thrust) lever.	Forward to increase forward thrust and rearward to increase rearward thrust.
Propellers	Forward to increase rpm.
Mixture	Forward or upward for rich.
Carburetor, air heat or alternate air.	Forward or upward for cold.
Supercharger.	Forward or upward for low blower.
Turbosuperchargers.	Forward, upward, or clockwise to increase pressure.
Rotary controls.	Clockwise from off to full on.

(2) *Auxiliary controls:*

Fuel tank selector.	Right for right tanks, left for left tanks.
Landing gear.	Down to extend.
Speed brakes.	Aft to extend.

[Amdt. 23–33, 51 FR 26656, July 24, 1986]

§ 23.781 Cockpit control knob shape.

(a) Flap and landing gear control knobs must conform to the general shapes (but not necessarily the exact sizes or specific proportions) in the following figure:

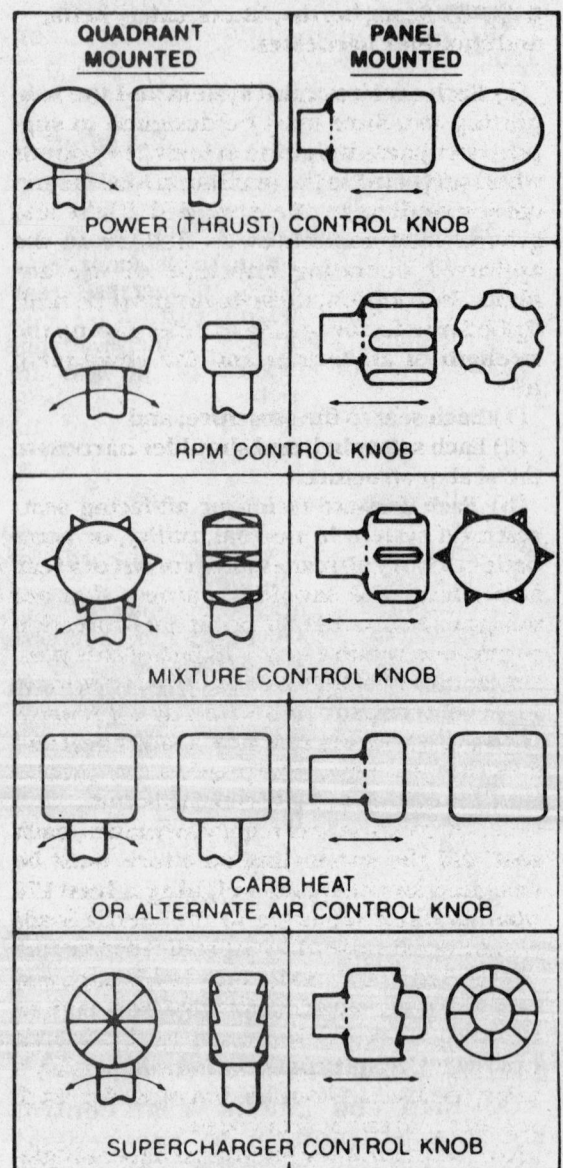

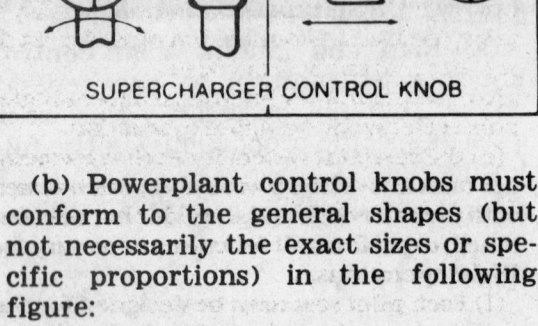

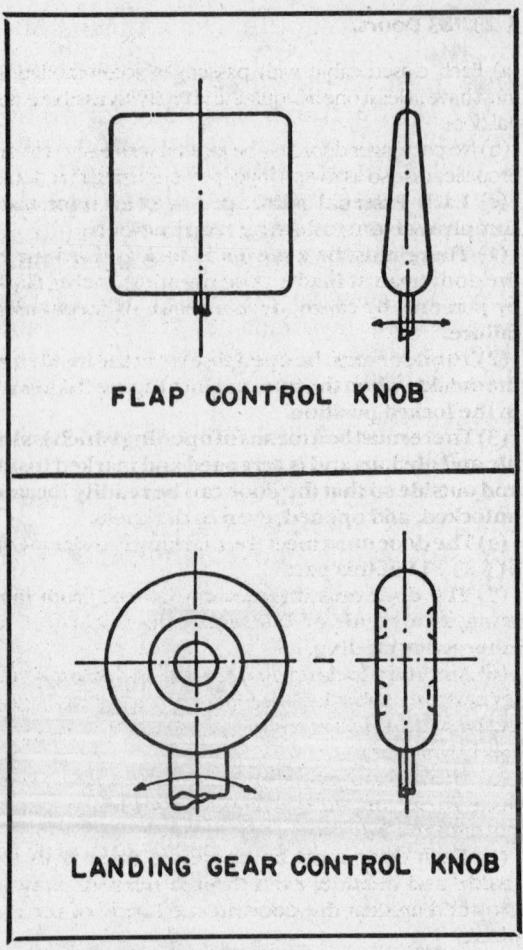

(b) Powerplant control knobs must conform to the general shapes (but not necessarily the exact sizes or specific proportions) in the following figure:

[Doc. No. 4080, 29 FR 17955, Dec. 18, 1964; 30 FR 258, Jan. 9, 1965, as amended by Amdt. 23-33, 51 FR 26657, July 24, 1986]

§ 23.783 **Doors.**

(a) Each closed cabin with passenger accommodations must have at least one adequate and easily accessible external door.

(b) No passenger door may be located with respect to any propeller disc so as to endanger persons using that door.

(c) **Each external passenger or crew door must comply with the following requirements:**

(1) **There must be a means to lock and safeguard the door against inadvertent opening during flight by persons, by cargo, or as a result of mechanical failure.**

(2) **The door must be openable from the inside and the outside when the internal locking mechanism is in the locked position.**

(3) **There must be a means of opening which is simple and obvious and is arranged and marked inside and outside so that the door can be readily located, unlocked, and opened, even in darkness.**

(4) **The door must meet the marking requirements of § 23.811 of this part.**

(5) **The door must be reasonably free from jamming as a result of fuselage deformation in an emergency landing.**

(6) **Auxiliary locking devices that are actuated externally to the airplane may be used but such devices must be overriden by the normal internal opening means.**

(d) **In addition, each external passenger or crew door, for a commuter category airplane, must comply with the following requirements:**

(1) **Each door must be openable from both the inside and outside, even though persons may be crowded against the door on the inside of the airplane.**

(2) **If inward opening doors are used, there must be a means to prevent occupants from crowding against the door to the extent that would interfere with opening the door.**

(3) **Auxiliary locking devices may be used.**

(e) **Each external door on a commuter category airplane, each external door forward of any engine or propeller on a normal, utility, or acrobatic category airplane, and each door of the pressure vessel on a pressurized airplane must comply with the following requirements:**

(1) **There must be a means to lock and safeguard each external door, including cargo and service type doors, against inadvertent opening in flight, by persons, by cargo, or as a result of mechanical failure or failure of a single structural element, either during or after closure.**

(2) **There must be a provision for direct visual inspection of the locking mechanism to determine if the external door, for which the initial opening movement is not inward, is fully closed and locked. The provisions must be discernible, by a crewmember using a flashlight or an equivalent lighting source.**

(3) **There must be a visual warning means to signal a flight crewmember if the external door is not fully closed and locked. The means must be designed so that any failure, or combination of failures, that would result in an erroneous closed and locked indication is improbable for doors for which the initial opening movement is not inward.**

§ 23.785 **Seats, berths, litters, safety belts, and shoulder harnesses.**

(a) **Each seat/restraint system and the supporting structure must be designed to support occupants weighing at least 215 pounds when subjected to the maximum load factors corresponding to the specified flight and ground load conditions, as defined in the approved operating envelope of the airplane. In addition, these loads must be multiplied by a factor of 1.33 in determining the strength of all fittings and the attachment of—**

(1) **Each seat to the structure; and**

(2) **Each safety belt and shoulder harness to the seat or structure.**

(b) **Each forward-facing or aft-facing seat/restraint system in normal, utility, or acrobatic category airplanes must consist of a seat, safety belt, and shoulder harness that are designed to provide the occupant protection provisions required in § 23.562 of this part. Other seat orientations must provide the same level of occupant protection as a forward-facing or aft-facing seat with a safety belt and shoulder harness, and provide the protection provisions of § 23.562 of this part.**

(c) **For commuter category airplanes, each seat and the supporting structure must be designed for occupants weighing at least 170 pounds when subjected to the inertia loads resulting from the ultimate static load factors prescribed in § 23.561(b)(2) of this part, and each occupant must be protected from serious head injury when subjected to the inertia loads resulting from these load factors by a safety belt and shoulder harness, for each seat other than the front seats.**

(d) **Each restraint system must have a single-point release for occupant evacuation.**

(e) **the restraint system for each crewmember must allow the crewmember, when seated with the safety belt and shoulder harness fastened, to perform all functions necessary for flight operations.**

(f) **Each pilot seat must be designed for the reactions resulting from the application of pilot forces to the primary flight controls as prescribed in § 23.395 of this part.**

(g) **There must be a means to secure each safety belt and shoulder harness, when not in use, to prevent interference with the operation of the airplane and with rapid occupant egress in an emergency.**

(h) **Unless otherwise placarded, each seat in a utility or acrobatic category airplane must be designed to accommodate an occupant wearing a parachute.**

(i) **The cabin area surrounding each seat, including the structure, interior walls, in-**

strument panel, control wheel, pedals, and seats within striking distance of the occupant's head or torso (with the restraint system fastened) must be free of potentially injurious objects, sharp edges, protuberances, and hard surfaces. If energy absorbing designs or devices are used to meet this requirement, they must protect the occupant from serious injury when the occupant is subjected to the inertia loads resulting from the ultimate static load factors prescribed in § 23.561(b)(2) of this part, or they must comply with the occupant protection provisions of § 23.562 of this part, as required in paragraphs (b) and (c) of this section.

(j) Each seat track must be fitted with stops to prevent the seat from sliding off the track.

(k) Each seat/restraint system may use design features, such as crushing or separation of certain components, to reduce occupant loads when showing compliance with the requirements of § 23.562 of this part; otherwise, the system must remain intact.

(l) For the purposes of this section, a front seat is a seat located at a flight crewmember station or any seat located alongside such a seat.

(m) Each berth, or provisions for a litter, installed parallel to the longitudinal axis of the airplane, must be designed so that the forward part has a padded endboard, canvas diaphragm, or equivalent means that can withstand the load reactions from a 215-pound occupant when subjected to the inertia loads resulting from the ultimate static load factors of § 23.561(b)(3) of this part. In addition—

(1) Each berth or litter must have an occupant restraint system and may not have corners or other parts likely to cause serious injury to a person occupying it during emergency landing conditions; and

(2) Occupant restraint system attachments for the berth or litter must withstand the inertia loads resulting from the ultimate static load factors of § 23.561 (b)(3) of this part.

(n) Proof of compliance with the static strength requirements of this section for seats and berths approved as part of the type design and for seat and berth installations may be shown by—

(1) Structural analysis, if the structure conforms to conventional airplane types for which existing methods of analysis are known to be reliable;

(2) A combination of structural analysis and static load tests to limit load; or

(3) Static load tests to ultimate loads.

§ 23.787 Baggage and cargo compartments.

(a) Each cargo compartment must be designed for its placarded maximum weight of contents and for the critical load distributions at the appropriate maximum load factors corresponding to the flight and ground load conditions of this part.

(b) There must be means to prevent the contents of any cargo compartment from becoming a hazard by shifting, and to protect any controls, wiring, lines, equipment or accessories whose damage or failure would affect safe operations.

(c) There must be a means to protect occupants from injury by the contents of any baggage or cargo compartment located aft of the occupants and separated by structure, when the ultimate forward inertia load factor is 9g and assuming the maximun allowed baggage or cargo weight for the compartment.

(d) Cargo compartments must be constructed of materials which are at least flame resistant.

(e) Designs which provide for baggage or cargo to be carried in the same compartment as passengers must have a means to protect the occupants from injury when the cargo is subjected to the inertia loads resulting from the ultimate static load factors of § 23.561(b)(3) of this part, assuming the maximum allowed baggage or cargo weight for the compartment.

(f) If cargo compartment lamps are installed, each lamp must be installed so as to prevent contact between lamp bulb and cargo.

(g) Baggage compartments used in commuter category airplanes must also meet the requirements of paragraphs (a), (b), (d) and (f) of this section.

§ 23.803 Emergency evacuation.

For commuter category airplanes, an evacuation demonstration must be conducted utilizing the maximum number of occupants for which certification is desired. The demonstration must be conducted under simulated night conditions using only the emergency exits on the most critical side of the airplane. The participants must be representative of average airline passengers with no prior practice or rehearsal for the demonstration. Evacuation must be completed within 90 seconds.

[Amdt. 23–34, 52 FR 1831, Jan. 15, 1987]

§ 23.807 Emergency exits.

(a) *Number and location.* Emergency exits must be located to allow escape without crowding in any probable crash attitude. The airplane must have at least the following emergency exits:

(1) For all airplanes with a seating capacity of two or more, excluding airplanes with canopies, at least one emergency exit on the opposite side of the cabin from the main door specified in § 23.783 of this part.

(2) [Reserved]

(3) If the pilot compartment is separated from the cabin by a door that is likely to block the pilot's escape in a minor crash, there must be an exit in the pilot's compartment. The number of exits required by paragraph (a)(1) of this section must then be separately determined for the passenger compartment, using the seating capacity of that compartment.

(b) *Type and operation.* Emergency exits must be movable windows, panels, canopies, or external doors, openable from both inside and outside the airplane that provide a clear and unobstructed opening large enough to admit a 19-by-26-inch ellipse. Auxiliary locking devices used to secure the airplane must be designed to be overridden by the normal internal opening means. In addition, each emergency exit must—

(1) Be readily accessible, requiring no exceptional agility to be used in emergencies;

(2) Have a method of opening that is simple and obvious;

(3) Be arranged and marked for easy location and operation, even in darkness;

(4) Have reasonable provisions against jamming by fuselage deformation; and

(5) In the case of acrobatic category airplanes, allow each occupant to bail out quickly with parachutes at any speed between V_{SO} and V_D.

(c) *Tests.* The proper functioning of each emergency exit must be shown by tests.

(d) *Doors and exits.* In addition, for commuter category airplanes the following requirements apply:

(1) The passenger entrance door must qualify as a floor level emergency exit. If an integral stair is installed at such a passenger entry door, the stair must be designed so that when subjected to the inertia forces specified in § 23.561, and following the collapse of one or more legs of the landing gear, it will not interfere to an extent that will reduce the effectiveness of emergency egress through the passenger entry door. Each additional required emergency exit, except floor level exits, must be located over the wing or must be provided with acceptable means to assist the occupants in descending to the ground. In addition to the passenger entrance door—

(i) For a total passenger seating capacity of 15 or less, an emergency exit as defined in paragraph (b) of this section is required on each side of the cabin; and

(ii) For a total passenger seating capacity of 16 through 19, three emergency exits, as defined in paragraph (b) of this section, are required with one on the same side as the door and two on the side opposite the door.

(2) A means must be provided to lock each emergency exit and to safeguard against its opening in flight, either inadvertently by persons or as a result of mechanical failure. In addition, a means for direct visual inspection of the locking mechanism must be provided to determine that each emergen-

cy exit for which the initial opening movement is outward is fully locked.

§ 23.811 Emergency exit marking.

(a) Each emergency exit and external door in the passenger compartment must be externally marked and readily identifiable from outside the airplane by—

(1) A conspicuous visual identification scheme; and

(2) A permanent decal or placard on or adjacent to the emergency exit which shows the means of opening the emergency exit, including any special instructions, if applicable.

(b) In addition, for commuter category airplanes, these exits and doors must be internally marked with the word "exit" by a sign which has white letters 1 inch high on a red background 2 inches high, be self-illuminated or independently, internally electrically illuminated, and have a minimum brightness of at least 160 microlamberts. The color may be reversed if the passenger compartment illumination is essentially the same.

§ 23.813 Emergency exit access.

For commuter category airplanes, access to window-type emergency exits may not be obstructed by seats or seat backs.

§ 23.815 Width of aisle.

For commuter category airplanes, the width of the main passenger aisle at any point between seats must equal or exceed the values in the following table:

Number of passenger seats	Minimum main passenger aisle width	
	Less than 25 inches from floor	25 inches and more from floor
10 through 19..........	9 inches..................	15 inches.

§ 23.831 Ventilation.

(a) Each passenger and crew compartment must be suitably ventilated. Carbon monoxide concentration may not exceed one part in 20,000 parts of air.

(b) In addition, for pressurized commuter category airplanes, the ventilating air in the flightcrew and passenger compartments must be free of harmful or hazardous concentrations of gases and vapors in normal operations and in the event of reasonably probable failures or malfunctioning of the ventilating, heating, pressurization, or other systems and equipment. If accumulation of hazardous quantities of smoke in the cockpit area is reasonably probable, smoke evacuation must be readily accomplished starting with full pressurization and without depressurizing beyond safe limits.

[Docket No. 4080, 29 FR 17955, Dec. 18, 1964; 30 FR 258, Jan. 9, 1965, as amended by Amdt. 23-34, 52 FR 1831, Jan. 15, 1987]

PRESSURIZATION

§ 23.841 Pressurized cabins.

(a) If certification for operation over 31,000 feet is requested, the airplane must be able to maintain a cabin pressure altitude of not more than 15,000 feet in event of any probable failure or malfunction in the pressurization system.

(b) Pressurized cabins must have at least the following valves, controls, and indicators, for controlling cabin pressure:

(1) Two pressure relief valves to automatically limit the positive pressure differential to a predetermined value at the maximum rate of flow delivered by the pressure source. The combined capacity of the relief valves must be large enough so that the failure of any one valve would not cause an appreciable rise in the pressure differential. The pressure differential is positive when the internal pressure is greater than the external.

(2) Two reverse pressure differential relief valves (or their equivalent) to automatically prevent a negative pressure differential that would damage the structure. However, one valve is enough if it is of a design that reasonably precludes its malfunctioning.

(3) A means by which the pressure differential can be rapidly equalized.

(4) An automatic or manual regulator for controlling the intake or exhaust airflow, or both, for maintaining the required internal pressures and airflow rates.

(5) Instruments to indicate to the pilot the pressure differential, the cabin pressure altitude, and the rate of change of cabin pressure altitude.

(6) Warning indication at the pilot station to indicate when the safe or preset pressure differential is exceeded and when a cabin pressure altitude of 10,000 feet is exceeded.

(7) A warning placard for the pilot if the structure is not designed for pressure differentials up to the maximum relief valve setting in combination with landing loads.

(8) A means to stop rotation of the compressor or to divert airflow from the cabin if continued rotation of an engine-driven cabin compressor or continued flow of any compressor bleed air will create a hazard if a malfunction occurs.

[Amdt. 23–14, 38 FR 31822, Nov. 19, 1973, as amended by Amdt. 23–17, 41 FR 55464, Dec. 20, 1976]

§ 23.843 Pressurization tests.

(a) *Strength test.* The complete pressurized cabin, including doors, windows, canopy, and valves, must be tested as a pressure vessel for the pressure differential specified in § 23.365(d).

(b) *Functional tests.* The following functional tests must be performed:

(1) Tests of the functioning and capacity of the positive and negative pressure differential valves, and of the emergency release valve, to simulate the effects of closed regulator valves.

(2) Tests of the pressurization system to show proper functioning under each possible condition of pressure, temperature, and moisture, up to the maximum altitude for which certification is requested.

(3) Flight tests, to show the performance of the pressure supply, pressure and flow regulators, indicators, and warning signals, in steady and stepped climbs and descents at rates corresponding to the maximum attainable within the operating limitations of the airplane, up to the maximum altitude for which certification is requested.

(4) Tests of each door and emergency exit, to show that they operate properly after being subjected to the flight tests prescribed in paragraph (b)(3) of this section.

FIRE PROTECTION

§ 23.851 Fire extinguishers.

For the commuter category airplanes, the following apply:

(a) At least one hand fire extinguisher must be located conveniently in the pilot compartment; and

(b) At least one hand fire extinguisher must be located conveniently in the passenger compartment.

[Amdt. 23–34, 52 FR 1831, Jan. 15, 1987]

§ 23.853 Compartment interiors.

For each compartment to be used by the crew or passengers:

(a) The materials must be at least flame-resistant;

(b) [Reserved]

(c) If smoking is to be prohibited, there must be a placard so stating, and if smoking is to be allowed—

(1) There must be an adequate number of self-contained, removable ashtrays; and

(2) Where the crew compartment is separated from the passenger compartment, there must be at least one illuminated sign (using either letters or symbols) notifying all passengers when smoking is prohibited. Signs which notify when smoking is prohibited must—

(i) When illuminated, be legible to each passenger seated in the passenger cabin under all probable lighting conditions; and

(ii) Be so constructed that the crew can turn the illumination on and off; and

(d) In addition, for commuter category airplanes the following requirements apply:

(1) Each disposal receptacle for towels, paper, or waste must be fully enclosed and constructed of at least fire resistant materials and must contain fires likely to occur in it under normal use. The ability of the disposal receptacle to contain those fires under all probable conditions of wear, misalignment, and ventilation expected in service must be demonstrated by test. A placard containing the legible words "No Cigarette Disposal" must be located on or near each disposal receptacle door.

(2) Lavatories must have "No Smoking" or "No Smoking in Lavatory" placards located conspicuously on each side of the entry door and self-contained, removable ashtrays located conspicuously on or near the entry side of each lavatory door, except that one ashtray may serve more than one lavatory door if it can be seen from the cabin side of each lavatory door served. The placards must have red letters at least ½ inch high on a white background at least 1 inch high (a "No

Smoking" symbol may be included on the placard).

(3) Materials (including finishes or decorative surfaces applied to the materials) used in each compartment occupied by the crew or passengers must meet the following test criteria as applicable:

(i) Interior ceiling panels, interior wall panels, partitions, galley structure, large cabinet walls, structural flooring, and materials used in the construction of stowage compartments (other than underseat stowage compartments and compartments for stowing small items such as magazines and maps) must be self-extinguishing when tested vertically in accordance with the applicable portions of Appendix F of this part or by other equivalent methods. The average burn length may not exceed 6 inches and the average flame time after removal of the flame source may not exceed 15 seconds. Drippings from the test specimen may not continue to flame for more than an average of 3 seconds after falling.

(ii) Floor covering, textiles (including draperies and upholstery), seat cushions, padding, decorative and non-decorative coated fabrics, leather, trays and galley furnishings, electrical conduit, thermal and acoustical insulation and insulation covering, air ducting, joint and edge covering, cargo compartment liners, insulation blankets, cargo covers and transparencies, molded and thermoformed parts, air ducting joints, and trim strips (decorative and chafing), that are constructed of materials not covered in paragraph (d)(3)(iv) of this section must be self extinguishing when tested vertically in accordance with the applicable portions of Appendix F of this part or other approved equivalent methods. The average burn length may not exceed 8 inches and the average flame time after removal of the flame source may not exceed 15 seconds. Drippings from the test specimen may not continue to flame for more than an average of 5 seconds after falling.

(iii) Motion picture film must be safety film meeting the Standard Specifications for Safety Photographic Film PH1.25 (available from the American National Standards Institute,

1430 Broadway, New York, N.Y. 10018) or an FAA approved equivalent. If the film travels through ducts, the ducts must meet the requirements of paragraph (d)(3)(ii) of this section.

(iv) Acrylic windows and signs, parts constructed in whole or in part of elastomeric materials, edge-lighted instrument assemblies consisting of two or more instruments in a common housing, seatbelts, shoulder harnesses, and cargo and baggage tiedown equipment, including containers, bins, pallets, etc., used in passenger or crew compartments, may not have an average burn rate greater than 2.5 inches per minute when tested horizontally in accordance with the applicable portions of Appendix F of this part or by other approved equivalent methods.

(v) Except for electrical wire cable insulation, and for small parts (such as knobs, handles, rollers, fasteners, clips, grommets, rub strips, pulleys, and small electrical parts) that the Administrator finds would not contribute significantly to the propagation of a fire, materials in items not specified in paragraphs (d)(3) (i), (ii), (iii), or (iv) of this section may not have a burn rate greater than 4.0 inches per minute when tested horizontally in accordance with the applicable portions of Appendix F of this part or by other approved equivalent methods.

(e) Lines, tanks, or equipment containing fuel, oil, or other flammable fluids may not be installed in such compartments unless adequately shielded, isolated, or otherwise protected so that any breakage or failure of such an item would not create a hazard.

(f) Airplane materials located on the cabin side of the firewall must be self-extinguishing or be located at such a distance from the firewall, or otherwise protected, so that ignition will not occur if the firewall is subjected to a flame temperature of not less than 2,000 degrees F for 15 minutes. For self-extinguishing materials (except electrical wire and cable insulation and small parts that the Administrator finds would not contribute significantly to the propagation of a fire), a vertifical self-extinguishing test must be conducted in accordance with Appendix F of this part or an equivalent method approved by the Administrator. The average burn length of the material may not exceed 6 inches and the average flame time after removal of the flame source may not exceed 15 seconds. Drippings from the material test specimen may not continue to flame for more than an average of 3 seconds after falling.

[Amdt. 23-14, 23 FR 31822, Nov. 19, 1973, as amended by Amdt. 23-23, 43 FR 50593, Oct. 30, 1978; Amdt. 23-25, 45 FR 7755, Feb. 4, 1980; Amdt. 23-34, 52 FR 1831, Jan. 15, 1987]

§23.859 Combustion heater fire protection.

(a) *Combustion heater fire regions.* The following combustion heater fire regions must be protected from fire in accordance with the applicable provisions of §§23.1182 through 23.1191 and 23.1203:

(1) The region surrounding the heater, if this region contains any flammable fluid system components (excluding the heater fuel system) that could—

(i) Be damaged by heater malfunctioning; or

(ii) Allow flammable fluids or vapors to reach the heater in case of leakage.

(2) The region surrounding the heater, if the heater fuel system has fittings that, if they leaked, would allow fuel vapor to enter this region.

(3) The part of the ventilating air passage that surrounds the combustion chamber.

(b) *Ventilating air ducts.* Each ventilating air duct passing through any fire region must be fireproof. In addition—

(1) Unless isolation is provided by fireproof valves or by equally effective means, the ventilating air duct downstream of each heater must be fireproof for a distance great enough to ensure that any fire originating in the heater can be contained in the duct; and

(2) Each part of any ventilating duct passing through any region having a flammable fluid system must be constructed or isolated from that system so that the malfunctioning of any component of that system cannot introduce flammable fluids or vapors into the ventilating airstream.

(c) *Combustion air ducts.* Each combustion air duct must be fireproof for a distance great enough to prevent damage from backfiring or reverse flame propagation. In addition—

(1) No combustion air duct may have a common opening with the ventilating airstream unless flames from backfires or reverse burning cannot enter the ventilating airstream under any operating condition, including reverse flow or malfunctioning of the heater or its associated components; and

(2) No combustion air duct may restrict the prompt relief of any backfire that, if so restricted, could cause heater failure.

(d) *Heater controls: general.* Provision must be made to prevent the hazardous accumulation of water or ice on or in any heater control component, control system tubing, or safety control.

(e) *Heater safety controls.* (1) Each combustion heater must have the following safety controls:

(i) Means independent of the components for the normal continuous control of air temperature, airflow, and fuel flow must be provided to automatically shut off the ignition and fuel supply to that heater at a point remote from that heater when any of the following occurs:

(A) The heater exchanger temperature exceeds safe limits.

(B) The ventilating air temperature exceeds safe limits.

(C) The combustion airflow becomes inadequate for safe operation.

(D) The ventilating airflow becomes inadequate for safe operation.

(ii) Means to warn the crew when any heater whose heat output is essential for safe operation has been shut off by the automatic means prescribed in paragraph (e)(1)(i) of this section.

(2) The means for complying with paragraph (e)(1)(i) of this section for any individual heater must—

(i) Be independent of components serving any other heater whose heat output is essential for safe operations; and

(ii) Keep the heater off until restarted by the crew.

(f) *Air intakes.* Each combustion and ventilating air intake must be located so that no flammable fluids or vapors can enter the heater system under any operating condition—

(1) During normal operation; or

(2) As a result of the malfunctioning of any other component.

(g) *Heater exhaust.* Heater exhaust systems must meet the provisions of §§ 23.1121 and 23.1123. In addition, there must be provisions in the design of the heater exhaust system to safely expel the products of combustion to prevent the occurrence of—

(1) Fuel leakage from the exhaust to surrounding compartments;

(2) Exhaust gas impingement on surrounding equipment or structure;

(3) Ignition of flammable fluids by the exhaust, if the exhaust is in a compartment containing flammable fluid lines; and

(4) Restrictions in the exhaust system to relieve backfires that, if so restricted, could cause heater failure.

(h) *Heater fuel systems.* Each heater fuel system must meet each powerplant fuel system requirement affecting safe heater operation. Each heater fuel system component within the ventilating airstream must be protected by shrouds so that no leakage from those components can enter the ventilating airstream.

(i) *Drains.* There must be means to safely drain fuel that might accumulate within the combustion chamber or the heater exchanger. In addition—

(1) Each part of any drain that operates at high temperatures must be protected in the same manner as heater exhausts; and

(2) Each drain must be protected from hazardous ice accumulation under any operating condition.

[Amdt. 23—27, 45 FR 70387, Oct. 23, 1980]

§ 23.863 Flammable fluid fire protection.

(a) In each area where flammable fluids or vapors might escape by leakage of a fluid system, there must be means to minimize the probability of ignition of the fluids and vapors, and the resultant hazard if ignition does occur.

(b) Compliance with paragraph (a) of this section must be shown by analysis or tests, and the following factors must be considered:

(1) Possible sources and paths of fluid leakage, and means of detecting leakage.

(2) Flammability characteristics of fluids, including effects of any combustible or absorbing materials.

(3) Possible ignition sources, including electrical faults, overheating of equipment, and malfunctioning of protective devices.

(4) Means available for controlling or extinguishing a fire, such as stopping flow of fluids, shutting down equipment, fireproof containment, or use of extinguishing agents.

(5) Ability of airplane components that are critical to safety of flight to withstand fire and heat.

(c) If action by the flight crew is required to prevent or counteract a fluid fire (e.g. equipment shutdown or actuation of a fire extinguisher), quick acting means must be provided to alert the crew.

(d) Each area where flammable fluids or vapors might escape by leakage of a fluid system must be identified and defined.

[Amdt. 23-23, 43 FR 50593, Oct. 30, 1978]

§ 23.865 Fire protection of flight controls and other flight structure.

Flight controls, engine mounts, and other flight structure located in the engine compartment must be constructed of fireproof material or shielded so that they will withstand the effect of a fire.

[Amdt. 23-14, 38 FR 31822, Nov. 19, 1973]

LIGHTNING EVALUATION

§ 23.867 Lightning protection of structure.

(a) The airplane must be protected against catastrophic effects from lightning.

(b) For metallic components, compliance with paragraph (a) of this section may be shown by—

(1) Bonding the components properly to the airframe; or

(2) Designing the components so that a strike will not endanger the airplane.

(c) For nonmetallic components, compliance with paragraph (a) of this section may be shown by—

(1) Designing the components to minimize the effect of a strike; or

(2) Incorporating acceptable means of diverting the resulting electrical current so as not to endanger the airplane.

[Amdt. 23–7, 34 FR 13092, Aug. 13, 1969]

MISCELLANEOUS

§ 23.871 Leveling means.

There must be means for determining when the airplane is in a level position on the ground.

[Amdt. 23–7, 34 FR 13092, Aug. 13, 1969]

Subpart E—Powerplant

GENERAL

§ 23.901 Installation.

(a) For the purpose of this part, the airplane powerplant installation includes each component that—

(1) Is necessary for propulsion; and

(2) Affects the safety of the major propulsive units.

(b) Each powerplant must be constructed, arranged, and installed to—

(1) Insure safe operation to the maximum altitude for which approval is requested.

(2) Be accessible for necessary inspections and maintenance.

(3) For turbopropeller-powered commuter category airplanes, not result in vibration characteristics exceeding those established during the type certification of the engine.

(c) Engine cowls and nacelles must be easily removable or openable by the pilot to provide adequate access to and exposure of the engine compartment for preflight checks.

(d) Each turbine engine powerplant must be constructed, arranged, and installed to provide continued safe operation without a hazardous loss of power or thrust for a period of 3 minutes each at rated takeoff power or thrust and flight idle in rainfall with an ambient liquid water content of not less than 4 percent of engine airflow by weight.

(e) The installation must comply with—

(1) The installation instructions provided under § 33.5 of this chapter; and

(2) The applicable provisions of this subpart.

[Doc. No. 4080, 29 FR 17955, Dec. 18, 1964, as amended by Amdt. 23–7, 34 FR 13092, Aug. 13, 1969; Amdt. 23–18, 42 FR 15041, Mar. 17, 1977; Amdt. 23–29, 49 FR 6846, Feb. 23, 1984; Amdt. 23–34, 52 FR 1832, Jan. 15, 1987; Amdt. 23–24, 52 FR 34745, Sept. 14, 1987]

§ 23.903 Engines.

(a) *Engine type certificate.* (1) Each engine must have a type certificate.

(2) Each turbine engine must either—

(i) Comply with § 33.77 of this chapter in effect on October 31, 1974, or as later amended; or

(ii) Be shown to have a foreign object ingestion service history in similar installation locations which has not resulted in any unsafe condition.

(b) *Turbine engine installations.* For turbine engine installations—

(1) Design precautions must be taken to minimize the hazards to the airplane in the event of an engine rotor failure or of a fire originating inside the engine which burns through the engine case.

(2) The powerplant systems associated with engine control devices, systems, and instrumentation must be designed to give reasonable assurance that those operating limitations that adversely affect turbine rotor structural integrity will not be exceeded in service.

(c) The powerplants must be arranged and isolated from each other to allow operation, in at least one configuration, so that the failure or malfunction of any engine, or the failure or malfunction (including destruction by fire in the engine compartment) of any system that can affect an engine (other than a fuel tank if only one fuel tank is installed), will not:

(1) Prevent the continued safe operation of the remaining engines; or

(2) Require immediate action by any crewmember for continued safe operation of the remaining engines.

(d) *Starting and stopping (piston engine).* (1) The design of the installation must be such that risk of fire or mechanical damage to the engine or airplane, as a result of starting the engine in any conditions in which starting is to be permitted, is reduced to a minimum. Any techniques and associated limitations for engine starting must be established and included in the Airplane Flight Manual, approved manual material, or applicable operating placards. For multiengine airplanes, means must be provided for stopping and restarting each engine in flight. For single-engine airplanes, means must be provided for stopping the engine in flight after engine failure if overspeeding might be caused by windmilling of the propeller.

(2) In addition, for commuter category airplanes, the following apply:

(i) Each component of the stopping system on the engine side of the firewall that might be exposed to fire must be at least fire resistant.

(ii) If hydraulic propeller feathering systems are used for this purpose, the feathering lines must be at least fire resistant under the operating conditions that may be expected to exist during feathering.

(e) *Starting and stopping (turbine engine).* Turbine engine installations must comply with the following:

(1) The design of the installation must be such that risk of fire or mechanical damage to the engine or the airplane, as a result of starting the engine in any conditions in which starting is to be permitted, is reduced to a minimum. Any techniques and associated limitations must be established and included in the Airplane Flight Manual, approved manual material, or applicable operating placards.

(2) A means must be provided for stopping combustion and rotation of any engine. All those components provided for compliance with this requirement, which are within any engine compartment on the engine side of the firewall, must be fire resistant. In addition, for commuter category airplanes, each component of the restarting system on the engine side of the firewall and those components that might be exposed to fire must be at least fire resistant. If hydraulic propeller feathering systems are used for this purpose, the feathering lines must be at least fire resistant under the operating conditions that may be expected to exist during feathering.

(3) It must be possible to restart an engine in flight. Any techniques and associated limitations must be established and included in the Airplane Flight Manual, approved manual material, or applicable operating placards.

(4) It must be demonstrated in flight that when restarting engines following a false start, all fuel or vapor is discharged in such a way that it does not constitute a fire hazard.

(f) *Restart capability.* An altitude and airspeed envelope must be established for the airplane for in-flight engine restarting and each installed engine must have a restart capability within that envelope.

(g) For turbine engine powered airplanes, if the minimum windmilling speed of the engines, following the in-flight shutdown of all engines, is insufficient to provide the necessary electrical power for engine ignition, a power source independent of the engine-driven electrical power generating system must be provided to permit in-flight engine ignition for restarting.

[Amdt. 23-14, 38 FR 31822, Nov. 19, 1973, as amended by Amdt. 23-17, 41 FR 55464, Dec. 20, 1976; Amdt. 23-26, 45 FR 60171, Sept. 11, 1980; Amdt. 23-29, 49 FR 6847, Feb. 23, 1984; Amdt. 23-34, 52 FR 1832, Jan. 15, 1987]

§ 23.905 Propellers.

(a) Each propeller must have a type certificate.

(b) Engine power and propeller shaft rotational speed may not exceed the limits for which the propeller is certificated.

(c) Each featherable propeller must have a means to unfeather it in flight.

(d) Each component of the propeller blade pitch control system must meet the requirements of § 35.42 of this chapter.

[Doc. No. 4080, 29 FR 17955, Dec. 18, 1964, as amended by Amdt. 23-26, 45 FR 60171, Sept. 11, 1980; Amdt. 23-29, 49 FR 6847, Feb. 23, 1984]

§ 23.907 Propeller vibration.

(a) Each propeller with metal blades or highly stressed metal components must be shown to have vibration stresses, in normal operating conditions, that do not exceed values that have been shown by the propeller manufacturer to be safe for continuous operation. This must be shown by—

(1) Measurement of stresses through direct testing of the propeller;

(2) Comparison with similar installations for which these measurements have been made; or

(3) Any other acceptable test method or service experience that proves the safety of the installation.

(b) Proof of safe vibration characteristics for any type of propeller, except for conventional, fixed-pitch, wood propellers must be shown where necessary.

§23.909 Turbosuperchargers.

(a) Each turbosupercharger must be approved under the engine type certificate or it must be shown that the turbosupercharger system—

(1) Can withstand, without defect, an endurance test of 150 hours that meets the applicable requirements of §33.49 of this subchapter; and

(2) Will have no adverse effect upon the engine.

(b) Control system malfunctions, vibrations, and abnormal speeds and temperatures expected in service may not damage the turbosupercharger compressor or turbine.

(c) Each turbosupercharger case must be able to contain fragments of a compressor or turbine that fails at the highest speed that is obtainable with normal speed control devices inoperative.

[Amdt. 23-7, 34 FR 13092, Aug. 13, 1969]

§23.925 Propeller clearance.

Unless smaller clearances are substantiated, propeller clearances with the airplane at maximum weight, with the most adverse center of gravity, and with the propeller in the most adverse pitch position, may not be less than the following:

(a) *Ground clearance.* There must be a clearance of at least seven inches (for each airplane with nose wheel landing gear) or nine inches (for each airplane with tail wheel landing gear) between each propeller and the ground with the landing gear statically deflected and in the level, normal takeoff, or taxing attitude, whichever

is most critical. In addition, for each airplane with conventional landing gear struts using fluid or mechanical means for absorbing landing shocks, there must be positive clearance between the propeller and the ground in the level takeoff attitude with the critical tire completely deflated and the corresponding landing gear strut bottomed. Positive clearance for airplanes using leaf spring struts is shown with a deflection corresponding to 1.5*g*.

(b) *Water clearance.* There must be a clearance of at least 18 inches between each propeller and the water, unless compliance with §23.239 can be shown with a lesser clearance.

(c) *Structural clearance.* There must be—

(1) At least one inch radial clearance between the blade tips and the airplane structural, plus any additional radial clearance necessary to prevent harmful vibration;

(2) At least one-half inch longitudinal clearance between the propeller blades or cuffs and stationary parts of the airplane; and

(3) Positive clearance between other rotating parts of the propeller or spinner and stationary parts of the airplane.

§23.929 Engine installation ice protection.

Propellers (except wooden propellers) and other components of complete engine installations must be protected against the accumulation of ice as necessary to enable satisfactory functioning without appreciable loss of power when operated in the icing conditions for which certification is requested.

[Amdt. 23-14, 33 FR 31822, Nov. 19, 1973]

§23.933 Reversing systems.

(a) Reversing systems intended for ground operation only must be designed so that no single failure or malfunction of the system will result in unwanted reverse thrust under any expected operating condition. Failure of structural elements need not be considered if the probability of this kind of failure is extremely remote.

(b) Turbojet reversing systems intended for inflight use must be designed so that no unsafe condition will result during normal operation of the system, or from any failure (or reasonably likely combination of failures) of the reversing system, under any anticipated condition of operation of the airplane including ground operation. Failure of structural elements need not be considered if the probability of this kind of failure is extremely remote.

(c) Each turbojet reversing system must have means to prevent the engine from producing more than idle forward thrust when the reversing system malfunctions, except that it may produce any greater forward thrust that is shown to allow directional control to be maintained, with aerodynamic means alone, under the most critical reversing condition expected in operation.

(d) For turbopropeller-powered, commuter category airplanes, the requirements of paragraphs (b) and (c) of this section apply. Compliance with this section must be shown by failure analysis, testing, or both, for propeller systems that allow the propeller blades to move from the flight low-pitch position to a position that is substantially less than that at the normal flight, low-pitch stop position. The analysis may include, or be supported by, the analysis made to show compliance for the type certification of the propeller and associated installation components. Credit will be given for pertinent analysis and testing completed by the engine and propeller manufacturers.

[Amdt. 23-7, 34 FR 13092, Aug. 13, 1969, as amended by Amdt. 23-17, 41 FR 55465, Dec. 20, 1976; Amdt. 23-34, 52 FR 1832, Jan. 15, 1987]

§ 23.937 Turbopropeller-drag limiting systems.

Turbopropeller-powered airplane propeller-drag limiting systems must be designed so that no single failure or malfunction of any of the systems during normal or emergency operation results in propeller drag in excess of that for which the airplane was designed under the structural requirements of this part. Failure of structural elements of the drag limiting systems need not be considered if the

probability of this kind of failure is extremely remote.

[Amdt. 23-7, 34 FR 13093, Aug. 13, 1969]

§ 23.939 Powerplant operating characteristics.

(a) Turbine engine powerplant operating characteristics must be investigated in flight to determine that no adverse characteristics (such as stall, surge, or flameout) are present, to a hazardous degree, during normal and emergency operation within the range of operating limitations of the airplane and of the engine.

(b) [Reserved]

(c) The vibration characteristics of turbine engine components whose failure could be catastrophic may not be adversely affected during normal operation.

[Amdt. 23-7, 34 FR 13093 Aug. 13, 1969, as amended by Amdt. 23-14, 38 FR 31823, Nov. 19, 1973; Amdt. 23-18, 42 FR 15041, Mar. 17, 1977]

§ 23.943 Negative acceleration.

No hazardous malfunction of an engine, an auxiliary power unit approved for use in flight, or any component or system associated with the powerplant or auxiliary power unit may occur when the airplane is operated at the negative accelerations within the flight envelopes prescribed in § 23.333. This must be shown for the greatest duration expected for the acceleration.

[Amdt. 23-18, 42 FR 15041, Mar. 17, 1977]

FUEL SYSTEM

§ 23.951 General.

(a) Each fuel system must be constructed and arranged to insure a flow of fuel at a rate and pressure established for proper engine functioning under each likely operating condition, including any maneuver for which certification is requested.

(b) Each fuel system must be arranged so that—

(1) No fuel pump can draw fuel from more than one tank at a time; or

(2) There are means to prevent introducing air into the system.

(c) Each fuel system for a turbine engine must be capable of sustained operation throughout its flow and pressure range with fuel initially saturated with water at 80° F and having 0.75cc of free water per gallon added and cooled to the most critical condition for icing likely to be encountered in operation.

[Amdt. 23-15, 39 FR 35459, Oct. 1, 1974]

§ 23.953   Fuel system independence.

(a) Each fuel system for a multiengine airplane must be arranged so that, in at least one system configuration, the failure of any one component (other than a fuel tank) will not result in the loss of power of more than one engine or require immediate action by the pilot to prevent the loss of power of more than one engine.

(b) If a single fuel tank (or series of fuel tanks interconnected to function as a single fuel tank) is used on a multiengine airplane, the following must be provided:

(1) Independent tank outlets for each engine, each incorporating a shut-off valve at the tank. This shut-off valve may also serve as the fire wall shutoff valve required if the line between the valve and the engine compartment does not contain more than one quart of fuel (or any greater amount shown to be safe) that can drain into the engine compartment.

(2) At least two vents arranged to minimize the probability of both vents becoming obstructed simultaneously.

(3) Filler caps designed to minimize the probability of incorrect installation or inflight loss.

(4) A fuel system in which those parts of the system from each tank outlet to any engine are independent of each part of the system supplying fuel to any other engine.

[Doc. No. 4080, 29 FR 17955, Dec. 18, 1964, as amended by Amdt. 23-7, 34 FR 13093 Aug. 13, 1969]

§ 23.954   Fuel system lightning protection.

The fuel system must be designed and arranged to prevent the ignition of fuel vapor within the system by—

(a) Direct lightning strikes to areas having a high probability of stroke attachment;

(b) Swept lightning strokes on areas where swept strokes are highly probable; and

(c) Corona or streamering at fuel vent outlets.

[Amdt. 23-7, 34 FR 13093, Aug. 13, 1969]

§ 23.955   Fuel flow.

(a) *General.* The ability of the fuel system to provide fuel at the rates specified in this section and at a pressure sufficient for proper carburetor operation must be shown in the attitude that is most critical with respect to fuel feed and quantity of unusable fuel. These conditions may be simulated in a suitable mockup. In addition—

(1) The quantity of fuel in the tank may not exceed the amount established as the unusable fuel supply for that tank under § 23.959 plus that necessary to show compliance with this section; and

(2) If there is a fuel flowmeter, it must be blocked during the flow test and the fuel must flow through the meter bypass.

(b) *Gravity systems.* The fuel flow rate for gravity systems (main and reserve supply) must be 150 percent of the takeoff fuel consumption of the engine.

(c) *Pump systems.* The fuel flow rate for each pump system (main and reserve supply) for each reciprocating engine must be 125 percent of the take-off fuel flow of the engine at the maximum power approved for takeoff under Part 33 of this chapter or lesser power selected and approved for takeoff under this part.

(1) This flow rate is required for each primary engine-driven pump and each emergency pump, and must be available when the pump is running as it would during takeoff; and

(2) For each hand-operated pump, this rate must occur at not more than 60 complete cycles (120 single strokes) per minute.

(d) *Auxiliary fuel systems and fuel transfer systems.* Paragraphs (b), (c), and (f) of this section apply to each auxiliary and transfer system, except that—

(1) The required fuel flow rate must be established upon the basis of maximum continuous power and engine ro-

tational speed, instead of takeoff power and fuel consumption; and

(2) A lesser flow rate may be used for a small auxiliary tank feeding into a large main tank, if there is a suitable placard stating that the auxiliary tank is not to be opened to the main tank unless a predetermined amount of fuel remains in the main tank.

(e) *Multiple fuel tanks.* If a reciprocating engine can be supplied with fuel from more than one tank, it must be possible, in level flight, to regain full power and fuel pressure to that engine in not more than 10 seconds (for single-engine airplanes) or 20 seconds (for multiengine airplanes) after switching to any full tank after engine malfunctioning due to fuel depletion becomes apparent while the engine is being supplied from any other tank.

(f) *Turbine engine fuel systems.* Each turbine engine fuel system must provide at least 100 percent of the fuel flow required by the engine under each intended operation condition and maneuver. The conditions may be simulated in a suitable mockup. This flow must—

(1) Be shown with the airplane in the most adverse fuel feed condition (with respect to altitudes, attitudes, and other conditions) that is expected in operation; and

(2) Be automatically uninterrupted with respect to any engine until all fuel scheduled for use by the engine has been consumed.

[Doc. No. 4080, 29 FR 17955, Dec. 18, 1964, as amended by Amdt. 23-7, 34 FR 13093, Aug. 13, 1969]

§ 23.957 Flow between interconnected tanks.

It must be impossible, in a gravity feed system with interconnected tank outlets, for enough fuel to flow between the tanks to cause an overflow of fuel from any tank vent under the conditions in § 23.959, except that full tanks must be used.

§ 23.959 Unusable fuel supply.

The unusable fuel supply for each tank must be established as not less than that quantity at which the first evidence of malfunctioning occurs under the most adverse fuel feed condition occurring under each intended

operation and flight maneuver involving that tank. Fuel system component failures need not be considered.

[Amdt. 23-7, 34 FR 13093, Aug. 13, 1969, as amended by Amdt. 23-18, 42 FR 15041, Mar. 17, 1977]

§ 23.961 Fuel system hot weather operation.

Each fuel system conducive to vapor formation must be free from vapor lock when using fuel at a temperature of 110° F. under critical operating conditions.

§ 23.963 Fuel tanks: general.

(a) Each fuel tank must be able to withstand, without failure, the vibration, inertia, fluid, and structural loads that it may be subjected to in operation.

(b) Each flexible fuel tank liner must be of an acceptable kind.

(c) Each integral fuel tank must have adequate facilities for interior inspection and repair.

(d) The total usable capacity of the fuel tanks must be enough for at least one-half hour of operation at maximum continuous power.

(e) Each fuel quantity indicator must be adjusted, as specified in § 23.1337(b), to account for the unusable fuel supply determined under § 23.959.

(f) For commuter category airplanes, fuel tanks within the fuselage contour must be able to resist rupture and to retain fuel under the inertia forces prescribed for the emergency landing conditions in § 23.561. In addition, these tanks must be in a protected position so that exposure of the tanks to scraping action with the ground is unlikely.

[Doc. No. 4080, 29 FR 17955, Dec. 18, 1964; 30 FR 258, Jan. 9, 1965, as amended by Amdt 23-34, 52 FR 1832, Jan. 15, 1987]

§ 23.965 Fuel tank tests.

(a) Each fuel tank must be able to withstand the following pressures without failure or leakage:

(1) For each conventional metal tank and nonmetallic tank with walls not supported by the airplane structure, a pressure of 3.5 p.s.i., or that pressure developed during maximum ultimate

acceleration with a full tank, whichever is greater.

(2) For each integral tank, the pressure developed during the maximum limit acceleration of the airplane with a full tank, with simultaneous application of the critical limit structural loads.

(3) For each nonmetallic tank with walls supported by the airplane structure and constructed in an acceptable manner using acceptable basic tank material, and with actual or simulated support conditions, a pressure of 2 p.s.i. for the first tank of a specific design. The supporting structure must be designed for the critical loads occurring in the flight or landing strength conditions combined with the fuel pressure loads resulting from the corresponding accelerations.

(b) Each fuel tank with large, unsupported, or unstiffened flat areas must be able to withstand the following test without leakage or failure:

(1) Each complete tank assembly and its supports must be vibration tested while mounted to simulate the actual installation.

(2) Except as specified in paragraph (b)(4) of this section, the tank assembly must be vibrated for 25 hours at an amplitude of not less than $\frac{1}{32}$ of an inch (unless another amplitude is substantiated) while $\frac{2}{3}$ filled with water or other suitable test fluid.

(3) The test frequency of vibration must be as follows:

(i) If no frequency of vibration resulting from any r.p.m. within the normal operating range of engine speeds is critical, the test frequency of vibration, in number of cycles per minute, must be the number obtained by multiplying the maximum continuous engine speed (r.p.m.) by 0.9.

(ii) If only one frequency of vibration resulting from any r.p.m. within the normal operating range of engine speeds is critical, that frequency of vibration must be the test frequency.

(iii) If more than one frequency of vibration resulting from any r.p.m. within the normal operating range of engine speeds is critical, the most critical of these frequencies must be the test frequency.

(4) Under paragraphs (b)(3) (ii) and (iii) of this section, the time of test must be adjusted to accomplish the same number of vibration cycles that would be accomplished in 25 hours at the frequency specified in paragraph (b)(3)(i) of this section.

(5) During the test, the tank assembly must be rocked at a rate of 16 to 20 complete cycles per minute, through an angle of 15 degrees on either side of the horizontal (30 degrees total), about an axis parallel to the axis of the fuselage, for 25 hours.

(c) Each integral tank using methods of construction and sealing not previously proven to be adequate by test data or service experience must be able to withstand the vibration test specified in paragraphs (b) (1) through (4) of this section.

(d) Each tank with a nonmetallic liner must be subjected to the sloshing test outlined in paragraph (b)(5) of this section, with the fuel at room temperature. In addition, a specimen liner of the same basic construction as that to be used in the airplane must, when installed in a suitable test tank, withstand the sloshing test with fuel at a temperature of 110° F.

§ 23.967 Fuel tank installation.

(a) Each fuel tank must be supported so that tank loads are not concentrated. In addition—

(1) There must be pads, if necessary, to prevent chafing between each tank and its supports;

(2) Padding must be nonabsorbent or treated to prevent the absorption of fuel;

(3) If a flexible tank liner is used, it must be supported so that it is not required to withstand fluid loads;

(4) Interior surfaces adjacent to the liner must be smooth and free from projections that could cause wear, unless—

(i) Provisions are made for protection of the liner at those points; or

(ii) The construction of the liner itself provides such protection; and

(5) A positive pressure must be maintained within the vapor space of each bladder cell under any condition of operation, except for a particular condition for which it is shown that a zero or negative pressure will not cause the bladder cell to collapse; and

(6) Syphoning of fuel (other than minor spillage) or collapse of bladder fuel cells may not result from improper securing or loss of the fuel filler cap.

(b) Each tank compartment must be ventilated and drained to prevent the accumulation of flammable fluids or vapors. Each compartment adjacent to a tank that is an integral part of the airplane structure must also be ventilated and drained.

(c) No fuel tank may be on the engine side of the firewall. There must be at least one-half inch of clearance between the fuel tank and the firewall. No part of the engine nacelle skin that lies immediately behind a major air opening from the engine compartment may act as the wall of an integral tank.

(d) No fuel tank may be installed in the personnel compartment of a multi-engine airplane. If a fuel tank is installed in the personnel compartment of a single-engine airplane, it must be isolated by fume and fuel-proof enclosures that are drained and vented to the exterior of the airplane. A bladder type fuel cell, if used, must have a retaining shell at least equivalent to a metal fuel tank in structural integrity.

(e) Fuel tanks must be designed, located, and installed so as to retain fuel:

(1) When subjected to the inertia loads resulting from the ultimate static load factors prescribed in § 23.561(b)(2) of this part; and

(2) Under conditions likely to occur when the airplane lands on a paved runway at a normal landing speed under each of the following conditions:

(i) The airplane in a normal landing attitude and its landing gear retracted.

(ii) the most critical landing gear leg collapsed and the other landing gear legs extended.

In showing compliance with the paragraph (e)(2) of this section, the tearing away of an engine mount must be considered unless all the engines are installed above the wing or on the tail or fuselage of the airplane.

Mar. 17, 1977; Amdt. 23-26, 45 FR 60171, Sept. 11, 1980]

§ 23.969   Fuel tank expansion space

Each fuel tank must have an expansion space of not less than two percent of the tank capacity, unless the tank vent discharges clear of the airplane (in which case no expansion space is required). It must be impossible to fill the expansion space inadvertently with the airplane in the normal ground attitude.

§ 23.971   Fuel tank sump.

(a) Each fuel tank must have a drainable sump with an effective capacity, in the normal ground and flight attitudes, of 0.25 percent of the tank capacity, or $\frac{1}{16}$ gallon, whichever is greater, unless—

(1) The fuel system has a sediment bowl or chamber that is accessible for drainage and has a capacity of 1 ounce for every 20 gallons of fuel tank capacity; and

(2) Each fuel tank outlet is located so that, in the normal ground attitude, water will drain from all parts of the tank to the sediment bowl or chamber.

(b) Each sump, sediment bowl, and sediment chamber drain required by paragraph (a) of this section must comply with the drain provisions of § 23.999(b) (1), (2), and (3).

[Doc. No. 4080, 29 FR 17955, Dec. 18, 1964, as amended by Amdt. 23-17, 41 FR 55465, Dec. 20, 1976]

§ 23.973   Fuel tank filler connection.

(a) Each fuel tank filler connection must be marked as prescribed in § 23.1557(c).

(b) Spilled fuel must be prevented from entering the fuel tank compartment or any part of the airplane other than the tank itself.

(c) Each filler cap must provide a fuel-tight seal for the main filler opening. However, there may be small openings in the fuel tank cap for venting purposes or for the purpose of allowing passage of a fuel gauge through the cap.

(d) Each fuel filling point, except pressure fueling connection points, must have a provision for electrically bonding the airplane to ground fueling equipment.

[Doc. No. 4080, 29 FR 17955, Dec. 18, 1964; 30 FR 258, Jan. 9, 1965, as amended by Amdt. 23-18, 42 FR 15041, Mar. 17, 1977]

§ 23.975 Fuel tank vents and carburetor vapor vents.

(a) Each fuel tank must be vented from the top part of the expansion space. In addition—

(1) Each vent outlet must be located and constructed in a manner that minimizes the possibility of its being obstructed by ice or other foreign matter;

(2) Each vent must be constructed to prevent siphoning of fuel during normal operation;

(3) The venting capacity must allow the rapid relief of excessive differences of pressure between the interior and exterior of the tank;

(4) Airspaces of tanks with interconnected outlets must be interconnected;

(5) There may be no undrainable points in any vent line where moisture can accumulate with the airplane in either the ground or level flight attitudes;

(6) No vent may terminate at a point where the discharge of fuel from the vent outlet will constitute a fire hazard or from which fumes may enter personnel compartments; and

(7) Vents must be arranged to prevent the loss of fuel, except fuel discharged because of thermal expansion, when the airplane is parked in any direction on a ramp having a one-percent slope.

(b) Each carburetor with vapor elimination connections and each fuel injection engine employing vapor return provisions must have a separate vent line to lead vapors back to the top of one of the fuel tanks. If there is more than one tank and it is necessary to use these tanks in a definite sequence for any reason, the vapor vent line must lead back to the fuel tank to be used first, unless the relative capacities of the tanks are such that return to another tank is preferable.

(c) For acrobatic category airplanes, excessive loss of fuel during acrobatic maneuvers, including short periods of inverted flight, must be prevented. It must be impossible for fuel to siphon from the vent when normal flight has been resumed after any acrobatic maneuver for which certification is requested.

[Doc. No. 4080, 29 FR 17955, Dec. 18, 1964; 30 FR 258, Jan. 9, 1965, as amended by Amdt. 23-18, 42 FR 15041, Mar. 17, 1977; Amdt. 23-29, 49 FR 6847, Feb. 23, 1984]

§ 23.977 Fuel tank outlet.

(a) There must be a fuel strainer for the fuel tank outlet or for the booster pump. This strainer must—

(1) For reciprocating engine powered airplanes, have 8 to 16 meshes per inch; and

(2) For turbine engine powered airplanes, prevent the passage of any object that could restrict fuel flow or damage any fuel system component.

(b) The clear area of each fuel tank outlet strainer must be at least five times the area of the outlet line.

(c) The diameter of each strainer must be at least that of the fuel tank outlet.

(d) Each finger strainer must be accessible for inspection and cleaning.

[Amdt. 23-17, 41 FR 55465, Dec. 20, 1976]

§ 23.979 Pressure fueling systems.

For pressure fueling systems, the following apply:

(a) Each pressure fueling system fuel manifold connection must have means to prevent the escape of hazardous quantities of fuel from the system if the fuel entry valve fails.

(b) An automatic shutoff means must be provided to prevent the quantity of fuel in each tank from exceeding the maximum quantity approved for that tank. This means must allow checking for proper shutoff operation before each fueling of the tank.

(c) A means must be provided to prevent damage to the fuel system in the event of failure of the automatic shutoff means prescribed in paragraph (b) of this section.

(d) All parts of the fuel system up to the tank which are subjected to fueling pressures must have a proof pressure of 1.33 times, and an ultimate pressure of at least 2.0 times, the surge pressure likely to occur during fueling.

[Amdt. 23-14, 38 FR 31823, Nov. 19, 1973]

Read for 131

FUEL SYSTEM COMPONENTS

§ 23.991 Fuel pumps.

(a) *Main pumps.* For main pumps, the following apply:

(1) For reciprocating engine installations having fuel pumps to supply fuel to the engine, at least one pump for each engine must be directly driven by the engine and must meet § 23.955. This pump is a main pump.

(2) For turbine engine installations, each fuel pump required for proper engine operation, or required to meet the fuel system requirements of this subpart (other than those in paragraph (b) of this section), is a main pump. In addition—

(i) There must be at least one main pump for each turbine engine;

(ii) The power supply for the main pump for each engine must be independent of the power supply for each main pump for any other engine; and

(iii) For each main pump, provision must be made to allow the bypass of each positive displacement fuel pump other than a fuel injection pump approved as part of the engine.

(b) *Emergency pumps.* There must be an emergency pump immediately available to supply fuel to the engine if any main pump (other than a fuel injection pump approved as part of an engine) fails. The power supply for each emergency pump must be independent of the power supply for each corresponding main pump.

(c) *Warning means.* If both the normal pump and emergency pump operate continuously, there must be a means to indicate to the appropriate flight crewmembers a malfunction of either pump.

(d) Operation of any fuel pump may not affect engine operation so as to create a hazard, regardless of the engine power or thrust setting or the functional status of any other fuel pump.

[Doc. No. 4080, 29 FR 17955, Dec. 18, 1964, as amended by Amdt. 23-7, 34 FR 13093, Aug. 13, 1969; Amdt. 23-26, 45 FR 60171, Sept. 11, 1980]

§ 23.993 Fuel system lines and fittings.

(a) Each fuel line must be installed and supported to prevent excessive vibration and to withstand loads due to fuel pressure and accelerated flight conditions.

(b) Each fuel line connected to components of the airplane between which relative motion could exist must have provisions for flexibility.

(c) Each flexible connection in fuel lines that may be under pressure and subjected to axial loading must use flexible hose assemblies.

(d) Each flexible hose must be approved or must be shown to be suitable for the particular application.

(e) No flexible hose that might be adversely affected by exposure to high temperatures may be used where excessive temperatures will exist during operation or after engine shutdown.

§ 23.994 Fuel system components.

Fuel system components in an engine nacelle or in the fuselage must be protected from damage which could result in spillage of enough fuel to constitute a fire hazard as a result of a wheels-up landing on a paved runway.

[Amdt. 23-29, 49 FR 6847, Feb. 23, 1984]

§ 23.995 Fuel valves and controls.

(a) There must be a means to allow appropriate flight crew members to rapidly shut off, in flight, the fuel to each engine individually.

(b) No shutoff valve may be on the engine side of any firewall. In addition, there must be means to—

(1) Guard against inadvertent operation of each shutoff valve; and

(2) Allow appropriate flight crew members to reopen each valve rapidly after it has been closed.

(c) Each valve and fuel system control must be supported so that loads resulting from its operation or from accelerated flight conditions are not transmitted to the lines connected to the valve.

(d) Each valve and fuel system control must be installed so that gravity and vibration will not affect the selected position.

(e) Each fuel valve handle and its connections to the valve mechanism must have design features that minimize the possibility of incorrect installation.

(f) Each check valve must be constructed, or otherwise incorporate provisions, to preclude incorrect assembly or connection of the valve.

(g) Fuel tank selector valves must—

(1) Require a separate and distinct action to place the selector in the "OFF" position; and

(2) Have the tank selector positions located in such a manner that it is impossible for the selector to pass through the "OFF" position when changing from one tank to another.

[Doc. No. 4080, 29 FR 17955, Dec. 18, 1964, as amended by Amdt. 23-14, 38 FR 31823, Nov. 19, 1973; Amdt. 23-17, 41 FR 55465, Dec. 20, 1976; Amdt. 23-18, 42 FR 15041, Mar. 17, 1977; Amdt. 23-29, 49 FR 6847, Feb. 23, 1984]

§23.997 Fuel strainer or filter.

There must be a fuel strainer or filter between the fuel tank outlet and the inlet of either the fuel metering device or an engine driven positive displacement pump, whichever is nearer the fuel tank outlet. This fuel strainer or filter must—

(a) Be accessible for draining and cleaning and must incorporate a screen or element which is easily removable;

(b) Have a sediment trap and drain except that it need not have a drain if the strainer or filter is easily removable for drain purposes;

(c) Be mounted so that its weight is not supported by the connecting lines or by the inlet or outlet connections of the strainer or filter itself, unless adequate strength margins under all loading conditions are provided in the lines and connections; and

(d) Have the capacity (with respect to operating limitations established for the engine) to ensure that engine fuel system functioning is not impaired, with the fuel contaminated to a degree (with respect to particle size and density) that is greater than that established for the engine in Part 33 of this chapter.

(e) In addition, for commuter category airplanes, unless means are provided in the fuel system to prevent the accumulation of ice on the filter, a means must be provided to automatically maintain the fuel flow if ice clogging of the filter occurs.

[Amdt. 23-15, 39 FR 35459, Oct. 1, 1974, as amended by Amdt. 23-29, 49 FR 6847, Feb.

23, 1984; Amdt. 23-34, 52 FR 1832, Jan. 15, 1987]

§23.999 Fuel system drains.

(a) There must be at least one drain to allow safe drainage of the entire fuel system with the airplane in its normal ground attitude.

(b) Each drain required by paragraph (a) of this section and §23.971 must—

(1) Discharge clear of all parts of the airplane;

(2) Have manual or automatic means for positive locking in the closed position; and

(3) Have a drain valve—

(i) That is readily accessible and which can be easily opened and closed; and

(ii) That is either located or protected to prevent fuel spillage in the event of a landing with landing gear retracted.

[Doc. No. 4080, 29 FR 17955, Dec. 18, 1964, as amended by Amdt. 23-17, 41 FR 55465, Dec. 20, 1976]

§23.1001 Fuel jettisoning system.

(a) If the design landing weight is less than that permitted under the requirements of §23.473(b), the airplane must have a fuel jettisoning system installed that is able to jettison enough fuel to bring the maximum weight down to the design landing weight. The average rate of fuel jettisoning must be at least 1 percent of the maximum weight per minute, except that the time required to jettison the fuel need not be less than 10 minutes.

(b) Fuel jettisoning must be demonstrated at maximum weight with flaps and landing gear up and in—

(1) A power-off glide at $1.4 V_{S1}$;

(2) A climb at the one-engine-inoperative best rate-of-climb speed, with the critical engine inoperative and the remaining engines at maximum continuous power; and

(3) Level flight at $1.4 V_{S1}$, if the results of the tests in the conditions specified in paragraphs (b)(1) and (2) of this section show that this condition could be critical.

(c) During the flight tests prescribed in paragraph (b) of this section, it must be shown that—

(1) The fuel jettisoning system and its operation are free from fire hazard;

(2) The fuel discharges clear of any part of the airplane;

(3) Fuel or fumes do not enter any parts of the airplane; and

(4) The jettisoning operation does not adversely affect the controllability of the airplane.

(d) For reciprocating engine powered airplanes, the jettisoning system must be designed so that it is not possible to jettison the fuel in the tanks used for takeoff and landing below the level allowing 45 minutes flight at 75 percent maximum continuous power. However, if there is an auxiliary control independent of the main jettisoning control, the system may be designed to jettison all the fuel.

(e) For turbine engine powered airplanes, the jettisoning system must be designed so that it is not possible to jettison fuel in the tanks used for takeoff and landing below the level allowing climb from sea level to 10,000 feet and thereafter allowing 45 minutes cruise at a speed for maximum range.

(f) The fuel jettisoning valve must be designed to allow flight personnel to close the valve during any part of the jettisoning operation.

(g) Unless it is shown that using any means (including flaps, slots, and slats) for changing the airflow across or around the wings does not adversely affect fuel jettisoning, there must be a placard, adjacent to the jettisoning control, to warn flight crewmembers against jettisoning fuel while the means that change the airflow are being used.

(h) The fuel jettisoning system must be designed so that any reasonably probable single malfunction in the system will not result in a hazardous condition due to unsymmetrical jettisoning of, or inability to jettison, fuel.

[Amdt. 23–7, 34 FR 13094, Aug. 13, 1969]

OIL SYSTEM

§ 23.1011   General.

(a) Each engine must have an independent oil system that can supply it with an appropriate quantity of oil at a temperature not above that safe for continuous operation.

(b) The usable oil tank capacity may not be less than the product of the endurance of the airplane under critical operating conditions and the maximum oil consumption of the engine under the same conditions, plus a suitable margin to ensure adequate circulation and cooling.

(c) For an oil system without an oil transfer system, only the usable oil tank capacity may be considered. The amount of oil in the engine oil lines, the oil radiator, and the feathering reserve, may not be considered.

(d) If an oil transfer system is used, and the transfer pump can pump some of the oil in the transfer lines into the main engine oil tanks, the amount of oil in these lines that can be pumped by the transfer pump may be included in the oil capacity.

§ 23.1013   Oil tanks.

(a) *Installation.* Each oil tank must be installed to—

(1) Meet the requirements of § 23.967 (a) and (b); and

(2) Withstand any vibration, inertia, and fluid loads expected in operation.

(b) *Expansion space.* Oil tank expansion space must be provided so that—

(1) Each oil tank used with a reciprocating engine has an expansion space of not less than the greater of 10 percent of the tank capacity or 0.5 gallon, and each oil tank used with a turbine engine has an expansion space of not less than 10 percent of the tank capacity; and

(2) It is impossible to fill the expansion space inadvertently with the airplane in the normal ground attitude.

(c) *Filler connection.* Each oil tank filler connection must be marked as specified in § 23.1557(c). Each recessed oil tank filler connection of an oil tank used with a turbine engine, that can retain any appreciable quantity of oil, must have provisions for fitting a drain.

(d) *Vent.* Oil tanks must be vented as follows:

(1) Each oil tank must be vented to the engine crankcase from the top part of the expansion space so that the vent connection is not covered by oil under any normal flight condition.

(2) Oil tank vents must be arranged so that condensed water vapor that might freeze and obstruct the line cannot accumulate at any point.

(3) For acrobatic category airplanes, there must be means to prevent hazardous loss of oil during acrobatic maneuvers, including short periods of inverted flight.

(e) *Outlet.* No oil tank outlet may be enclosed by any screen or guard that would reduce the flow of oil below a safe value at any operating temperature. No oil tank outlet diameter may be less than the diameter of the engine oil pump inlet. Each oil tank used with a turbine engine must have means to prevent entrance into the tank itself, or into the tank outlet, of any object that might obstruct the flow of oil through the system. There must be a shutoff valve at the outlet of each oil tank used with a turbine engine, unless the external portion of the oil system (including oil tank supports) is fireproof.

(f) *Flexible liners.* Each flexible oil tank liner must be of an acceptable kind.

(g) Each oil tank filler cap of an oil tank that is used with a turbine engine must provide an oiltight seal.

[Doc. No. 4080, 29 FR 17955, Dec. 18, 1964, as amended by Amdt. 23-15, 39 FR 35459 Oct. 1, 1974]

§ 23.1015 Oil tank tests.

Each oil tank must be tested under § 23.965, except that—

(a) The applied pressure must be five p.s.i. for the tank construction instead of the pressures specified in § 23.965(a);

(b) For a tank with a nonmetallic liner the test fluid must be oil rather than fuel as specified in § 23.965(d), and the slosh test on a specimen liner must be conducted with the oil at 250° F.; and

(c) For pressurized tanks used with a turbine engine, the test pressure may not be less than 5 p.s.i. plus the maximum operating pressure of the tank.

[Doc. No. 4080, 29 FR 17955, Dec. 18, 1964, as amended by Amdt. 23-15, 39 FR 35460, Oct. 1, 1974]

§ 23.1017 Oil lines and fittings.

(a) *Oil lines.* Oil lines must meet § 23.993 and must accommodate a flow of oil at a rate and pressure adequate for proper engine functioning under any normal operating condition.

(b) *Breather lines.* Breather lines must be arranged so that—

(1) Condensed water vapor or oil that might freeze and obstruct the line cannot accumulate at any point;

(2) The breather discharge will not constitute a fire hazard if foaming occurs, or cause emitted oil to strike the pilot's windshield;

(3) The breather does not discharge into the engine air induction system; and

(4) For acrobatic category airplanes, there is no excessive loss of oil from the breather during acrobatic maneuvers, including short periods of inverted flight.

(5) The breather outlet is protected against blockage by ice or foreign matter.

[Doc. No. 4080, 29 FR 17955, Dec. 18, 1964, as amended by Amdt. 23-7, 34 FR 13094, Aug. 13, 1969; Amdt. 23-14, 38 FR 31823, Nov. 19, 1973]

§ 23.1019 Oil strainer or filter.

(a) Each turbine engine installation must incorporate an oil strainer or filter through which all of the engine oil flows and which meets the following requirements:

(1) Each oil strainer or filter that has a bypass, must be constructed and installed so that oil will flow at the normal rate through the rest of the system with the strainer or filter completely blocked.

(2) The oil strainer or filter must have the capacity (with respect to operating limitations established for the engine) to ensure that engine oil system functioning is not impaired when the oil is contaminated to a degree (with respect to particle size and density) that is greater than that established for the engine under Part 33 of this chapter.

(3) The oil strainer or filter, unless it is installed at an oil tank outlet, must incorporate an indicator that will indicate contamination before it reaches

the capacity established in accordance with paragraph (a)(2) of this section.

(4) The bypass of a strainer or filter must be constructed and installed so that the release of collected contaminants is minimized by appropriate location of the bypass to ensure that collected contaminants are not in the bypass flow path.

(5) An oil strainer or filter that has no bypass, except one that is installed at an oil tank outlet, must have a means to connect it to the warning system required in § 23.1305(u).

(b) Each oil strainer or filter in a powerplant installation using reciprocating engines must be constructed and installed so that oil will flow at the normal rate through the rest of the system with the strainer or filter element completely blocked.

[Amdt. 23-15, 39 FR 35460, Oct. 1, 1974, as amended by Amdt. 23-29, 49 FR 6847, Feb. 23, 1984]

§ 23.1021   Oil system drains.

A drain (or drains) must be provided to allow safe drainage of the oil system. Each drain must—

(a) Be accessible; and

(b) Have manual or automatic means for positive locking in the closed position.

[Amdt. 23-29, 49 FR 6847, Feb. 23, 1984]

§ 23.1023   Oil radiators.

Each oil radiator and its supporting structures must be able to withstand the vibration, inertia, and oil pressure loads to which it would be subjected in operation.

§ 23.1027   Propeller feathering system.

(a) If the propeller feathering system depends on engine oil, there must be means to trap an amount of oil in the tank if the supply becomes depleted due to failure of any part of the lubricating system, other than the tank itself.

(b) The amount of trapped oil must be enough to accomplish feathering and must be available only to the feathering pump.

(c) The ability of the system to accomplish feathering with the trapped oil must be shown.

(d) Provision must be made to prevent sludge or other foreign matter from affecting the safe operation of the propeller feathering system.

[Doc. No. 4080, 29 FR 17955, Dec. 18, 1964, as amended by Amdt. 23-14, 38 FR 31823, Nov. 19, 1973]

COOLING

§ 23.1041   General.

The powerplant cooling provisions must be able to maintain the temperatures of powerplant components and engine fluids, within the temperature limit established during ground and flight operation to the maximum altitude for which approval is requested.

[Amdt. 23-7, 34 FR 13094, Aug. 13, 1969]

§ 23.1043   Cooling tests.

(a) *General.* Compliance with § 23.1041 must be shown under critical ground, water, and flight operating conditions to the maximum altitude for which approval is requested. For turbosupercharged engines, each turbosupercharger must be operated through that part of the climb profile for which operation with the turbosupercharger is requested and in a manner consistent with its intended operation. For these tests, the following apply:

(1) If the tests are conducted under conditions deviating from the maximum ambient atmospheric temperatures specified in paragraph (b) of this section, the recorded powerplant temperatures must be corrected under paragraphs (c) and (d) of this section, unless a more rational correction method is applicable.

(2) No corrected temperature determined under paragraph (a)(1) of this section may exceed established limits.

(3) The fuel uses during the cooling tests must be of the minimum grade approved for the engines, and the mixture settings must be those used in normal operation.

(4) [Reserved]

(5) Water taxing tests must be conducted on each hull seaplane that may reasonably be expected to be taxied for extended periods.

(b) *Maximum ambient atmospheric temperature.* A maximum ambient atmospheric temperature corresponding to sea level conditions of at least 100 degrees F must be established. The assumed temperature lapse rate is 3.6 degrees F per thousand feet of altitude above sea level until a temperature of −69.7 degrees F is reached, above which altitude the temperature is considered constant at −69.7 degrees F. However, for winterization installations, the applicant may select a maximum ambient atmospheric temperature corresponding to sea level conditions of less than 100 degrees F.

(c) *Correction factor (except cylinder barrels)*. Unless a more rational correction applies, temperatures of engine fluids and powerplant components (except cylinder barrels) for which temperature limits are established, must be corrected by adding to them the difference between the maximum ambient atmospheric temperature and the temperature of the ambient air at the time of the first occurrence of the maximum component or fluid temperature recorded during the cooling test.

(d) *Correction factor for cylinder barrel temperatures*. Cylinder barrel temperatures must be corrected by adding to them 0.7 times the difference between the maximum ambient atmospheric temperature and the temperature of the ambient air at the time of the first occurrence of the maximum cylinder barrel temperature recorded during the cooling test.

[Doc. No. 4080, 29 FR 17955, Dec. 18, 1964, as amended by Amdt. 23–7, 34 FR 13094, Aug. 13, 1969; Amdt. 23–21, 43 FR 2319, Jan. 16, 1978]

§ 23.1045 Cooling test procedures for turbine engine powered airplanes.

(a) Compliance with § 23.1041 must be shown for the takeoff, climb, en route, and landing stages of flight that correspond to the applicable performance requirements. The cooling tests must be conducted with the airplane in the configuration, and operating under the conditions, that are critical relative to cooling during each stage of flight. For the cooling tests, a temperature is "stabilized" when its rate of change is less than 2° F. per minute.

(b) Temperatures must be stabilized under the conditions from which entry is made into each stage of flight being investigated, unless the entry condition normally is not one during which component and engine fluid temperatures would stabilize (in which case, operation through the full entry condition must be conducted before entry into the stage of flight being investigated in order to allow temperatures to reach their natural levels at the time of entry). The takeoff cooling test must be preceded by a period during which the powerplant component and engine fluid temperatures are stabilized with the engines at ground idle.

(c) Cooling tests for each stage of flight must be continued until—

(1) The component and engine fluid temperatures stabilize;

(2) The stage of flight is completed; or

(3) An operating limitation is reached.

[Amdt. 23–7, 34 FR 13094, Aug. 13, 1969]

§ 23.1047 Cooling test procedures for reciprocating engine-powered airplanes.

(a) For each single-engine airplane powered with a reciprocating engine, engine cooling tests must be conducted as follows:

(1) Engine temperatures must be stabilized in flight with the engines at not less than 75 percent of maximum continuous power.

(2) After temperatures have stabilized, a climb must be begun at the lowest practicable altitude and continued for 1 minute with the engine at takeoff power.

(3) At the end of 1 minute, the climb must be continued at maximum continuous power for at least 5 minutes after the occurrence of the highest temperature recorded.

(b) The climb required in paragraph (a) of this section must be conducted at a speed not more than the best rate-of-climb speed with maximum continuous power unless—

(1) The slope of the flight path at the speed chosen for the cooling test is equal to or greater than the minimum required angle of climb determined under § 23.65; and

(2) The airplane has a cylinder head temperature indicator as specified in § 23.1337(e).

(c) The stabilizing and climb parts of the test must be conducted with cowl flap settings selected by the applicant.

(d) For each multiengine airplane powered with reciprocating engines, that meets the minimum one-engine-inoperative climb performance specified in § 23.67(a) or § 23.67(b)(1), engine cooling tests must be conducted as follows:

(1) The airplane must be in the configuration specified in § 23.67(a) or § 23.67(b)(1), except that, when above the critical altitude, the operating engines must be at maximum continuous power or at full throttle.

(2) The stabilizing and climb parts of the tests must be conducted with cowl flap settings selected by the applicant.

(3) The temperatures of the operating engines must be stabilized in flight, with the engines at not less than 75 percent of the maximum continuous power.

(4) After engine temperatures have stabilized, a climb must be—

(i) Begun from 1,000 feet below the critical altitude (or, if this is impracticable, at the lowest altitude that the terrain will allow) or 1,000 feet below the altitude at which the single-engine-inoperative rate of climb is 0.02 V_{so}^2 whichever is lower; and

(ii) Continued for at least 5 minutes after the highest temperature has been recorded.

(5) The climb must be conducted at a speed not more than the highest speed at which compliance with the climb requirement of § 23.67(a) or § 23.67(b)(1) can be shown. If the speed used exceeds the speed for best rate of climb with one engine inoperative, the airplane must have a cylinder head temperature indicator as specified in § 23.1337(e).

(e) For each multiengine airplane powered with reciprocating engines that cannot meet the minimum one-engine-inoperative climb performance specified in § 23.67(a) or § 23.67(b)(1), engine cooling tests must be conducted as prescribed in paragraph (d) of this section, except that, after stabilizing temperatures in flight, the climb (or descent, for airplanes with zero or negative one-engine-inoperative rates of climb) must be—

(1) Begun as close to sea level as is practicable; and

(2) Conducted at the best rate-of-climb speed (or the speed of minimum rate of descent, for airplanes with zero or negative one-engine-inoperative rates of climb).

[Amdt. 23-7, 34 FR 13094, Aug. 13, 1969, as amended by Amdt. 23-21, 43 FR 2319, Jan. 16, 1978]

LIQUID COOLING

§ 23.1061 Installation.

(a) *General.* Each liquid-cooled engine must have an independent cooling system (including coolant tank) installed so that—

(1) Each coolant tank is supported so that tank loads are distributed over a large part of the tank surface;

(2) There are pads between the tank and its supports to prevent chafing; and

(3) No air or vapor can be trapped in any part of the system, except the expansion tank, during filling or during operation.

Padding must be nonabsorbent or must be treated to prevent the absorption of flammable fluids.

(b) *Coolant tank.* The tank capacity must be at least one gallon, plus 10 percent of the cooling system capacity. In addition—

(1) Each coolant tank must be able to withstand the vibration, inertia, and fluid loads to which it may be subjected in operation;

(2) Each coolant tank must have an expansion space of at least 10 percent of the total cooling system capacity; and

(3) It must be impossible to fill the expansion space inadvertently with the airplane in the normal ground attitude.

(c) *Filler connection.* Each coolant tank filler connection must be marked as specified in § 23.1557(c). In addition—

(1) Spilled coolant must be prevented from entering the coolant tank compartment or any part of the airplane other than the tank itself; and

(2) Each recessed coolant filler connection must have a drain that discharges clear of the entire airplane.

(d) *Lines and fittings.* Each coolant system line and fitting must meet the requirements of § 23.993, except that the inside diameter of the engine coolant inlet and outlet lines may not be less than the diameter of the corresponding engine inlet and outlet connections.

(e) *Radiators.* Each coolant radiator must be able to withstand any vibration, inertia, and coolant pressure load to which it may normally be subjected. In addition—

(1) Each radiator must be supported to allow expansion due to operating temperatures and prevent the transmittal of harmful vibration to the radiator; and

(2) If flammable coolant is used, the air intake duct to the coolant radiator must be located so that (in case of fire) flames from the nacelle cannot strike the radiator.

(f) *Drains.* There must be an accessible drain that—

(1) Drains the entire cooling system (including the coolant tank, radiator, and the engine) when the airplane is in the normal ground altitude;

(2) Discharges clear of the entire airplane; and

(3) Has means to positively lock it closed.

§ 23.1063 Coolant tank tests.

Each coolant tank must be tested under § 23.965, except that—

(a) The test required by § 23.965(a)(1) must be replaced with a similar test using the sum of the pressure developed during the maximum ultimate acceleration with a full tank or a pressure of 3.5 pounds per square inch, whichever is greater, plus the maximum working pressure of the system; and

(b) For a tank with a nonmetallic liner the test fluid must be coolant rather than fuel as specified in § 23.965(d), and the slosh test on a specimen liner must be conducted with the coolant at operating temperature.

INDUCTION SYSTEM N

§ 23.1091 Air induction.

(a) The air induction system for each engine must supply the air required by that engine under the operating conditions for which certification is requested.

(b) Each reciprocating engine installation must have at least two separate air intake sources and must meet the following:

(1) Primary air intakes may open within the cowling if that part of the cowling is isolated from the engine accessory section by a fire-resistant diaphragm or if there are means to prevent the emergence of backfire flames.

(2) Each alternate air intake must be located in a sheltered position and may not open within the cowling if the emergence of backfire flames will result in a hazard.

(3) The supplying of air to the engine through the alternate air intake system may not result in a loss of excessive power in addition to the power loss due to the rise in air temperature.

(c) For turbine engine powered airplanes—

(1) There must be means to prevent hazardous quantities of fuel leakage or overflow from drains, vents, or other components of flammable fluid systems from entering the engine intake system; and

(2) The air inlet ducts must be located or protected so as to minimize the ingestion of foreign matter during takeoff, landing, and taxiing.

[Doc. No. 4080, 29 FR 17955, Dec. 18, 1964, as amended by Amdt. 23–7, 34 FR 13095, Aug. 13, 1969]

§ 23.1093 Induction system icing protection.

(a) Each reciprocating engine air induction system must have means to prevent and eliminate icing. Unless this is done by other means, it must be shown that, in air free of visible moisture at a temperature of 30° F.—

(1) Each airplane with sea level engines using conventional venturi carburetors has a preheater that can provide a heat rise of 90° F. with the engines at 75 percent of maximum continuous power;

(2) Each airplane with altitude engines using conventional venturi carburetors has a preheater that can provide a heat rise of 120° F. with the en-

gines at 75 percent of maximum continuous power;

(3) Each airplane with altitude engines using carburetors tending to prevent icing has a preheater that, with the engines at 60 percent of maximum continuous power, can provide a heat rise of—

(i) 100° F.; or

(ii) 40° F., if a fluid deicing system meeting the requirements of §§ 23.1095 through 23.1099 is installed;

(4) Each single-engine airplane with a sea level engine using a carburetor tending to prevent icing has a sheltered alternate source of air with a preheat of not less than that provided by the engine cooling air down-stream of the cylinders; and

(5) Each multiengine airplane with sea level engines using a carburetor tending to prevent icing has a preheater that can provide a heat rise of 90° F. with the engines at 75 percent of maximum continuous power.

(b) *Turbine engines.*

(1) Each turbine engine and its air inlet system must operate throughout the flight power range of the engine (including idling), within the limitations established for the airplane, without the accumulation of ice on engine or inlet system components that would adversely affect engine operation or cause a serious loss of power or thrust—

(i) Under the icing conditions specified in Appendix C of Part 25 of this chapter; and

(ii) In snow, both falling and blowing.

(2) Each turbine engine must idle for 30 minutes on the ground, with the air bleed available for engine icing protection at its critical condition, without adverse effect, in an atmosphere that is at a temperature between 15° and 30°F (between −9° and −1°C) and has a liquid water content not less than 0.3 grams per cubic meter in the form of drops having a mean effective diameter not less than 20 microns, followed by momentary operation at takeoff power or thrust. During the 30 minutes of idle operation, the engine may be run up periodically to a moderate power or thrust setting in a manner acceptable to the Administrator.

(c) For airplanes with reciprocating engines having superchargers to pressurize the air before it enters the carburetor, the heat rise in the air caused by that supercharging at any altitude may be utilized in determining compliance with paragraph (a) of this section if the heat rise utilized is that which will be available, automatically, for the applicable altitudes and operating condition because of supercharging.

[Amdt. 23-7, 34 FR 13095, Aug. 13, 1969, as amended by Amdt. 23-15, 39 FR 35460, Oct. 1, 1974; Amdt. 23-17, 41 FR 55465, Dec. 20, 1976; Amdt. 23-18, 42 FR 15041, Mar. 17, 1977; Amdt. 23-29, 49 FR 6847, Feb. 23, 1984]

§ 23.1095 Carburetor deicing fluid flow rate.

(a) If a carburetor deicing fluid system is used, it must be able to simultaneously supply each engine with a rate of fluid flow, expressed in pounds per hour, of not less than 2.5 times the square root of the maximum continuous power of the engine.

(b) The fluid must be introduced into the air induction system—

(1) Close to, and upstream of, the carburetor; and

(2) So that it is equally distributed over the entire cross section of the induction system air passages.

§ 23.1097 Carburetor deicing fluid system capacity.

(a) The capacity of each carburetor deicing fluid system—

(1) May not be less than the greater of—

(i) That required to provide fluid at the rate specified in § 23.1095 for a time equal to three percent of the maximum endurance of the airplane; or

(ii) 20 minutes at that flow rate; and

(2) Need not exceed that required for two hours of operation.

(b) If the available preheat exceeds 50° F. but is less than 100° F., the capacity of the system may be decreased in proportion to the heat rise available in excess of 50° F.

§ 23.1099 Carburetor deicing fluid system detail design.

Each carburetor deicing fluid system must meet the applicable requirements for the design of a fuel system, except as specified in §§ 23.1095 and 23.1097.

§ 23.1101 Carburetor air preheater design.

Each carburetor air preheater must be designed and constructed to—

(a) Ensure ventilation of the preheater when the engine is operated in cold air;

(b) Allow inspection of the exhaust manifold parts that it surrounds; and

(c) Allow inspection of critical parts of the preheater itself.

§ 23.1103 Induction system ducts.

(a) Each induction system duct must have a drain to prevent the accumulation of fuel or moisture in the normal ground and flight attitudes. No drain may discharge where it will cause a fire hazard.

(b) Each duct connected to components between which relative motion could exist must have means for flexibility.

[Doc. No. 4080, 29 FR 17955, Dec. 18, 1964, as amended by Amdt. 23-7, 34 FR 13095, Aug. 13, 1969]

§ 23.1105 Induction system screens.

If induction system screens are used—

(a) Each screen must be upstream of the carburetor;

(b) No screen may be in any part of the induction system that is the only passage through which air can reach the engine, unless—

(1) The available preheat is at least 100° F.; and

(2) The screen can be deiced by heated air;

(c) No screen may be deiced by alcohol alone; and

(d) It must be impossible for fuel to strike any screen.

§ 23.1111 Turbine engine bleed air system.

For turbine engine bleed air systems, the following apply:

(a) No hazard may result if duct rupture or failure occurs anywhere between the engine port and the airplane unit served by the bleed air.

(b) The effect on airplane and engine performance of using maximum bleed air must be established.

(c) Hazardous contamination of cabin air systems may not result from failures of the engine lubricating system.

[Amdt. 23-7, 34 FR 13095, Aug. 13, 1969, as amended by Amdt. 23-17, 41 FR 55465, Dec. 20, 1976]

EXHAUST SYSTEM

§ 23.1121 General.

(a) Each exhaust system must ensure safe disposal of exhaust gases without fire hazard or carbon monoxide contamination in any personnel compartment.

(b) Each exhaust system part with a surface hot enough to ignite flammable fluids or vapors must be located or shielded so that leakage from any system carrying flammable fluids or vapors will not result in a fire caused by impingement of the fluids or vapors on any part of the exhaust system including shields for the exhaust system.

(c) Each exhaust system component must be separated by fireproof shields from adjacent flammable parts of the airplane that are outside the engine compartment.

(d) No exhaust gases may discharge dangerously near any fuel or oil system drain.

(e) No exhaust gases may be discharged where they will cause a glare seriously affecting pilot vision at night.

(f) Each exhaust system component must be ventilated to prevent points of excessively high temperature.

(g) If significant traps exists, each turbine engine exhaust system must have drains discharging clear of the airplane, in any normal ground and flight attitude, to prevent fuel accumulation after the failure of an attempted engine start.

(h) Each exhaust heat exchanger must incorporate means to prevent blockage of the exhaust port after any internal heat exchanger failure.

[Doc. No. 4080, 29 FR 17955, Dec. 18, 1964, as amended by Amdt. 23-7, 34 FR 13095, Aug. 13, 1969; Amdt. 23-18, 42 FR 15042, Mar. 17, 1977]

§ 23.1123 Exhaust manifold.

(a) Each exhaust manifold must be fireproof and corrosion-resistant, and must have means to prevent failure due to expansion by operating temperatures.

(b) Each exhaust manifold must be supported to withstand the vibration and inertia loads to which it may be subjected in operation.

(c) Parts of the manifold connected to components between which relative motion could exist must have means for flexibility.

§ 23.1125 Exhaust heat exchangers.

For reciprocating engine powered airplanes the following apply:

(a) Each exhaust heat exchanger must be constructed and installed to withstand the vibration, inertia, and other loads that it may be subjected to in normal operation. In addition—

(1) Each exchanger must be suitable for continued operation at high temperatures and resistant to corrosion from exhaust gases;

(2) There must be means for inspection of critical parts of each exchanger; and

(3) Each exchanger must have cooling provisions wherever it is subject to contact with exhaust gases.

(b) Each heat exchanger used for heating ventilating air must be constructed so that exhaust gases may not enter the ventilating air.

[Doc. No. 4080, 29 FR 17955, Dec. 18, 1964, as amended by Amdt. 23-17, 41 FR 55465, Dec. 20, 1976]

POWERPLANT CONTROLS AND ACCESSORIES

§ 23.1141 Powerplant controls: general.

(a) Powerplant controls must be located and arranged under § 23.777 and marked under § 23.1555(a).

(b) Each flexible control must be of an acceptable kind.

(c) Each control must be able to maintain any necessary position without—

(1) Constant attention by flight crew members; or

(2) Tendency to creep due to control loads or vibration.

(d) Each control must be able to withstand operating loads without failure or excessive deflection.

(e) For turbine engine powered airplanes, no single failure or malfunction, or probable combination thereof, in any powerplant control system may cause the failure of any powerplant function necessary for safety.

(f) The portion of each powerplant control located in the engine compartment that is required to be operated in the event of fire must be at least fire resistant.

(g) Powerplant valve controls located in the cockpit must have—

(1) For manual valves, positive stops or in the case of fuel valves suitable index provisions, in the open and closed position; and

(2) For power-assisted valves, a means to indicate to the flight crew when the valve—

(i) Is in the fully open or fully closed position; or

(ii) Is moving between the fully open and fully closed position.

[Doc. No. 4080, 29 FR 17955, Dec. 18, 1964, as amended by Amdt. 23-7, 34 FR 13095, Aug. 13, 1969; Amdt. 23-14, 38 FR 31823, Nov. 19, 1973; Amdt. 23-18, 42 FR 15042, Mar. 17, 1977]

§ 23.1143 Engine controls.

(a) There must be a separate power or thrust control for each engine and a separate control for each supercharger that requires a control.

(b) Power, thrust, and supercharger controls must be arranged to allow—

(1) Separate control of each engine and each supercharger; and

(2) Simultaneous control of all engines and all superchargers.

(c) Each power, thrust, or supercharger control must give a positive and immediate responsive means of controlling its engine or supercharger.

(d) The power, thrust, or supercharger controls for each engine or supercharger must be independent of those for every other engine or supercharger.

(e) For each fluid injection (other than fuel) system and its controls not provided and approved as part of the engine, the applicant must show that the flow of the injection fluid is adequately controlled.

(f) If a power or thrust control incorporates a fuel shutoff feature, the control must have a means to prevent the inadvertent movement of the control into the shutoff position. The means must—

(1) Have a positive lock or stop at the idle position; and

(2) Require a separate and distinct operation to place the control in the shutoff position.

[Amdt. 23-7, 34 FR 13095, Aug. 13, 1969, as amended by Amdt. 23-17, 41 FR 55465, Dec. 20, 1976; Amdt. 23-29, 49 FR 6847, Feb. 23, 1984]

§ 23.1145 Ignition switches.

(a) Ignition switches must control each ignition circuit on each engine.

(b) There must be means to quickly shut off all ignition on multiengine airplanes by the grouping of switches or by a master ignition control.

(c) Each group of ignition switches, except ignition switches for turbine engines for which continuous ignition is not required, and each master ignition control must have a means to prevent its inadvertent operation.

[Doc. No. 4080, 29 FR 17955, Dec. 18, 1964; 30 FR 258, Jan. 9, 1965, as amended by Amdt. 23-18, 42 FR 15042, Mar. 17, 1977]

§ 23.1147 Mixture controls.

If there are mixture controls, each engine must have a separate control, and each mixture control must have guards or must be shaped or arranged to prevent confusion by feel with other controls.

(a) The controls must be grouped and arranged to allow—

(1) Separate control of each engine; and

(2) Simultaneous control of all engines.

(b) The controls must require a separate and distinct operation to move the control toward lean or shut-off position.

[Doc. No. 4080, 29 FR 17955, Dec. 18, 1964, as amended by Amdt. 23-7, 34 FR 13096,

Aug. 13, 1969; Amdt. 23-33, 51 FR 26657, July 24, 1986]

§ 23.1149 Propeller speed and pitch controls.

(a) If there are propeller speed or pitch controls, they must be grouped and arranged to allow—

(1) Separate control of each propeller; and

(2) Simultaneous control of all propellers.

(b) The controls must allow ready synchronization of all propellers on multiengine airplanes.

§ 23.1153 Propeller feathering controls.

If there are propeller feathering controls, each propeller must have a separate control. Each control must have means to prevent inadvertent operation.

§ 23.1155 Turbine engine reverse thrust and propeller pitch settings below the flight regime.

For turbine engine installations, each control for reverse thrust and for propeller pitch settings below the flight regime must have means to prevent its inadvertent operation. The means must have a positive lock or stop at the flight idle position and must require a separate and distinct operation by the crew to displace the control from the flight regime (forward thrust regime for turbojet powered airplanes).

[Amdt. 23-7, 34 FR 13096, Aug. 13, 1969]

§ 23.1157 Carburetor air temperature controls.

There must be a separate carburetor air temperature control for each engine.

§ 23.1163 Powerplant accessories.

(a) Each engine mounted accessory must—

(1) Be approved for mounting on the engine involved;

(2) Use the provisions on the engine for mounting; and

(3) Be sealed to prevent contamination of the engine oil system and the accessory system.

(b) Electrical equipment subject to arcing or sparking must be installed to minimize the probability of contact with any flammable fluids or vapors that might be present in a free state.

(c) Each generator rated at or more than 6 kilowatts must be designed and installed to minimize the probability of a fire hazard in the event it malfunctions.

(d) In addition, for commuter category airplanes, if the continued rotation of any accessory remotely driven by the engine is hazardous when malfunctioning occurs, a means to prevent rotation without interfering with the continued operation of the engine must be provided.

[Doc. No. 4080, 29 FR 17955, Dec. 18, 1964, as amended by Amdt. 23-14, 38 FR 31823, Nov. 19, 1973; Amdt. 23-29, 49 FR 6847, Feb. 23, 1984; Amdt. 23-34, 52 FR 1832, Jan. 15, 1987]

§ 23.1165   Engine ignition systems.

(a) Each battery ignition system must be supplemented by a generator that is automatically available as an alternate source of electrical energy to allow continued engine operation if any battery becomes depleted.

(b) The capacity of batteries and generators must be large enough to meet the simultaneous demands of the engine ignition system and the greatest demands of any electrical system components that draw from the same source.

(c) The design of the engine ignition system must account for—

(1) The condition of an inoperative generator;

(2) The condition of a completely depleted battery with the generator running at its normal operating speed; and

(3) The condition of a completely depleted battery with the generator operating at idling speed, if there is only one battery.

(d) There must be means to warn appropriate crewmembers if malfunctioning of any part of the electrical system is causing the continuous discharge of any battery used for engine ignition.

(e) Each turbine engine ignition system must be independent of any electrical circuit that is not used for assisting, controlling, or analyzing the operation of that system.

(f) In addition, for commuter category airplanes, each turbopropeller ignition system must be an essential electrical load.

[Doc. No. 4080, 29 FR 17955, Dec. 18, 1964, as amended by Amdt. 23-17, 41 FR 55465 Dec. 20, 1976; Amdt. 23-34, 52 FR 1832, Jan. 15, 1987]

POWERPLANT FIRE PROTECTION

§ 23.1182   Nacelle areas behind firewalls.

Components, lines, and fittings, except those subject to the provisions of § 23.1351(e), located behind the engine-compartment firewall must be constructed of such materials and located at such distances from the firewall that they will not suffer damage sufficient to endanger the airplane if a portion of the engine side of the firewall is subjected to a flame temperature of not less than 2000° F for 15 minutes.

[Amdt. 23-16, 38 FR 31823, Nov. 19, 1973]

§ 23.1183   Lines, fittings, and components.

(a) Except as provided in paragraph (b) of this section, each component, line, and fitting carrying flammable fluids, gas, or air in any area subject to engine fire conditions must be at least fire resistant, except that flammable fluid tanks and supports which are part of and attached to the engine must be fireproof or be enclosed by a fireproof shield unless damage by fire to any non-fireproof part will not cause leakage or spillage of flammable fluid. Components must be shielded or located so as to safeguard against the ignition of leaking flammable fluid. Flexible hose assemblies (hose and end fittings) must be approved. An integral oil sump of less than 25-quart capacity on a reciprocating engine need not be fireproof nor be enclosed by a fireproof shield.

(b) Paragraph (a) of this section does not apply to—

(1) Lines, fittings, and components which are already approved as part of a type certificated engine; and

(2) Vent and drain lines, and their fittings, whose failure will not result in, or add to, a fire hazard.

[Doc. No. 4080, 29 FR 17955, Dec. 18, 1964, as amended by Amdt. 23-5, 32 FR 6912, May

5, 1967; Amdt. 23–15, 39 FR 35460, Oct. 1, 1974; Amdt. 23–29, 49 FR 6847, Feb. 23, 1984]

§ 23.1189 Shutoff means.

(a) For each multiengine airplane subject to § 23.67(a) or § 23.67(b)(1), the following apply:

(1) Each engine installation must have means to shut off or otherwise prevent hazardous quantities of fuel, oil, deicing fluid, and other flammable liquids from flowing into, within, or through any engine compartment, except in lines, fittings, and components forming an integral part of an engine.

(2) The closing of the fuel shutoff valve for any engine may not make any fuel unavailable to the remaining engines that would be available to those engines with that valve open.

(3) Operation of any shutoff means may not interfere with the later emergency operation of other equipment such as propeller feathering devices.

(4) Each shutoff must be outside of the engine compartment unless an equal degree of safety is provided with the shutoff inside the compartment.

(5) No hazardous amount of flammable fluid may drain into the engine compartment after shutoff.

(6) There must be means to guard against inadvertent operation of each shutoff means, and to make it possible for the crew to reopen the shutoff means in flight after it has been closed.

(b) Turbine engine installations need not have an engine oil system shutoff if—

(1) The oil tank is integral with, or mounted on, the engine; and

(2) All oil system components external to the engine are fireproof or located in areas not subject to engine fire conditions.

(c) Power operated valves must have means to indicate to the flight crew when the valve has reached the selected position and must be designed so that the valve will not move from the selected position under vibration conditions likely to exist at the valve location.

[Doc. No. 4080, 29 FR 17955, Dec. 18, 1964, as amended by Amdt. 23–7, 34 FR 13096, Aug. 13, 1969; Amdt. 23–14, 38 FR 31823,

Nov. 19, 1973; Amdt. 23–29, 49 FR 6847, Feb. 23, 1984]

§ 23.1191 Firewalls.

(a) Each engine, auxiliary power unit, fuel burning heater, and other combustion equipment intended for operation in flight, must be isolated from the rest of the airplane by firewalls, shrouds, or equivalent means.

(b) Each firewall or shroud must be constructed so that no hazardous quantity of liquid, gas, or flame can pass from the engine compartment to other parts of the airplane.

(c) Each opening in the firewall or shroud must be sealed with close fitting, fireproof grommets, bushings, or firewall fittings.

(d) Fire-resistant seals may be used on single-engine airplanes and multiengine airplanes not subject to § 23.67(a) or (b)(1), if—

(1) Each engine has a volumetric displacement of 1,000 cubic inches or less; and

(2) No opening in the firewall or shroud will allow the passage of a hazardous amount of flame without seals.

(e) Each firewall and shroud must be fireproof and protected against corrosion.

(f) Compliance with the criteria for fireproof materials or components must be shown as follows:

(1) The flame to which the materials or components are subjected must be $2,000\pm50°F$.

(2) Sheet materials approximately 10 inches square must be subjected to the flame from a suitable burner.

(3) The flame must be large enough to maintain the required test temperature over an area approximately five inches square.

(g) Firewall materials and fittings must resist flame penetration for at least 15 minutes.

(h) The following materials may be used in firewalls or shrouds without being tested as required by this section:

(1) Stainless steel sheet, 0.015 inch thick.

(2) Mild steel sheet (coated with aluminum or otherwise protected against corrosion) 0.018 inch thick.

(3) Terne plate, 0.018 inch thick.

(4) Monel metal, 0.018 inch thick.

(5) Steel or copper base alloy firewall fittings.

§ 23.1192 Engine accessory compartment diaphragm.

For aircooled radial engines, the engine power section and all portions of the exhaust sytem must be isolated from the engine accessory compartment by a diaphragm that meets the firewall requirements of § 23.1191.

[Amdt. 23-14, 38 FR 31823, Nov. 19, 1973]

§ 23.1193 Cowling and nacelle.

(a) Each cowling must be constructed and supported so that it can resist any vibration, inertia, and air loads to which it may be subjected in operation.

(b) There must be means for rapid and complete drainage of each part of the cowling in the normal ground and flight attitudes. No drain may discharge where it will cause a fire hazard.

(c) Cowling must be at least fire resistant.

(d) Each part behind an opening in at least fire resistant for a distance of at least 24 inches aft of the opening.

(e) Each part of the cowling subjected to high temperatures due to its nearness to exhaust sytem ports or exhaust gas impingement, must be fire proof.

(f) Each nacelle of a multiengine airplane with supercharged engines must be designed and constructed so that with the landing gear retracted, a fire in the engine compartment will not burn through a cowling or nacelle and enter a nacelle area other than the engine compartment.

(g) In addition, for commuter category airplanes, the airplane must be designed so that no fire originating in any engine compartment can enter, either through openings or by burnthrough, any other region where it would create additional hazards.

[Doc. No. 4080, 29 FR 17955, Dec. 18, 1964; 30 FR 258, Jan. 9, 1965, as amended by Amdt. 23-18, 42 FR 15042, Mar. 17, 1977; Amdt. 23-34, 52 FR 1833, Jan. 15, 1987]

§ 23.1195 Fire extinguishing systems.

For commuter category airplanes, fire extinguishing systems must be installed and compliance shown with the following:

(a) Except for combustor, turbine, and tailpipe sections of turbine-engine installations that contain lines or components carrying flammable fluids or gases for which a fire originating in these sections is shown to be controllable, a fire extinguisher system must serve each engine compartment;

(b) The fire extinguishing system, the quantity of the extinguishing agent, the rate of discharge, and the discharge distribution must be adequate to extinguish fires. An individual "one shot" system may be used.

(c) The fire extinguishing system for a nacelle must be able to simultaneously protect each compartment of the nacelle for which protection is provided.

[Amdt. 23-34, 52 FR 1833, Jan. 15, 1987]

§ 23.1197 Fire extinguishing agents.

For commuter category airplanes, the following applies:

(a) Fire extinguishing agents must—

(1) Be capable of extinguishing flames emanating from any burning of fluids or other combustible materials in the area protected by the fire extinguishing system; and

(2) Have thermal stability over the temperature range likely to be experienced in the compartment in which they are stored.

(b) If any toxic extinguishing agent is used, provisions must be made to prevent harmful concentrations of fluid or fluid vapors (from leakage during normal operation of the airplane or as a result of discharging the fire extinguisher on the ground or in flight) from entering any personnel compartment, even though a defect may exist in the extinguishing system. This must be shown by test except for built-in carbon dioxide fuselage compartment fire extinguishing systems for which—

(1) Five pounds or less of carbon dioxide will be discharged, under established fire control procedures, into any fuselage compartment; or

(2) Protective breathing equipment is available for each flight crewmember on flight deck duty.

[Amdt. 23-34, 52 FR 1833, Jan. 15, 1987]

§ 23.1199 Extinguishing agent containers.

For commuter category airplanes, the following applies:

(a) Each extinguishing agent container must have a pressure relief to prevent bursting of the container by excessive internal pressures.

(b) The discharge end of each discharge line from a pressure relief connection must be located so that discharge of the fire extinguishing agent would not damage the airplane. The line must also be located or protected to prevent clogging caused by ice or other foreign matter.

(c) A means must be provided for each fire extinguishing agent container to indicate that the container has discharged or that the charging pressure is below the established minimum necessary for proper functioning.

(d) The temperature of each container must be maintained, under intended operating conditions, to prevent the pressure in the container from—

(1) Falling below that necessary to provide an adequate rate of discharge; or

(2) Rising high enough to cause premature discharge.

(e) If a pyrotechnic capsule is used to discharge the extinguishing agent, each container must be installed so that temperature conditions will not cause hazardous deterioration of the pyrotechnic capsule.

[Amdt. 23-34, 52 FR 1833, Jan. 15, 1987; 52 FR 34745, Sept. 14, 1987]

§ 23.1201 Fire extinguishing system materials.

For commuter category airplanes, the following apply:

(a) No material in any fire extinguishing system may react chemically with any extinguishing agent so as to create a hazard.

(b) Each system component in an engine compartment must be fireproof.

[Amdt. 23-34, 52 FR 1833, Jan. 15, 1987; 52 FR 7262, Mar. 9, 1987]

§ 23.1203 Fire detector system.

For multiengine turbine powered airplanes, multiengine reciprocating engine powered airplanes incorporating turbo-superchargers, and all commuter category airplanes the following apply:

(a) There must be a means which ensures the prompt detection of a fire in an engine compartment.

(b) Each fire detector must be constructed and installed to withstand the vibration, inertia, and other loads to which it may be subjected in operation.

(c) No fire detector may be affected by any oil, water, other fluids, or fumes that might be present.

(d) There must be means to allow the crew to check, in flight, the functioning of each fire detector electric circuit.

(e) Wiring and other components of each fire detector system in an engine compartment must be at least fire resistant.

[Amdt. 23-18, 42 FR 15042, Mar. 17, 1977, as amended by Amdt. 23-34, 52 FR 1833, Jan. 15, 1987]

Subpart F—Equipment

GENERAL

§ 23.1301 Function and installation.

Each item of installed equipment must—

(a) Be of a kind and design appropriate to its intended function.

(b) Be labeled as to its identification, function, or operating limitations, or any applicable combination of these factors;

(c) Be installed according to limitations specified for that equipment; and

(d) Function properly when installed.

[Amdt. 23-20, 42 FR 36968, July 18, 1977]

§ 23.1303 Flight and navigation instruments.

The following are required flight and navigational instruments:

(a) An airspeed indicator.

(b) An altimeter.

(c) A magnetic direction indicator.

(d) For turbine engine powered airplanes, a free air temperature indicator or an air-temperature indicator which provides indications that are convertible to free-air.

(e) A speed warning device for—

(1) Turbine engine powered airplanes; and

(2) Other airplanes for which VMO/MMO and VD/MD are established under §§ 23.335(b)(4) and 23.1505(c) if VMO/MMO is greater than 0.8 VD/MD.

The speed warning device must give effective aural warning (differing distinctively from aural warnings used for other purposes) to the pilots whenever the speed exceeds VMO plus 6 knots or MMO+0.01. The upper limit of the production tolerance for the warning device may not exceed the prescribed warning speed.

[Doc. No. 4080, 29 FR 17955, Dec. 18, 1964, as amended by Amdt. 23-17, 41 FR 55465, Dec. 20, 1976]

§ 23.1305 Powerplant instruments.

The following are required powerplant instruments:

(a) A fuel quantity indicator for each fuel tank.

(b) An oil pressure indicator for each engine and for each turbosupercharger oil system that is separate from other oil systems.

(c) An oil temperature indicator for each engine and for each turbosupercharger oil system that is separate from other oil systems.

(d) A tachometer for each reciprocating engine.

(e) A tachometer (to indicate the speed of the rotors with established limiting speeds) for each turbine engine.

(f) A cylinder head temperature indicator for—

(1) Each air-cooled engine with cowl flaps and for each airplane for which compliance with § 23.1041 is shown at a speed higher than Vy; and

(2) Each reciprocating engine-powered commuter category airplane.

(g) A fuel pressure indicator for pump-fed engines.

(h) A manifold pressure indicator for—

(1) Each altitude engine; and

(2) Each reciprocating engine-powered commuter category airplane.

(i) An oil quantity indicator for each oil tank.

(j) A gas temperature indicator for each turbine engine.

(k) A fuel flowmeter for—

(1) Each turbine engine or fuel tank if pilot action is required to maintain fuel flow within limits; and

(2) Each turbine engine of turbine-powered commuter category airplane.

(l) An indicator to indicate engine thrust or to indicate a gas stream pressure that can be related to thrust, for each turbojet engine, including a free air temperature indicator if needed for this purpose.

(m) A torque indicator for each turbopropeller engine.

(n) A blade position indicating means for each turbopropeller engine propeller to provide an indication to the flight crew when the propeller blade angle is below the flight low pitch position. The required indicator must begin indicating before the blade moves more than 8° below the flight low pitch stop. The source of indication must directly sense the blade position.

(o) A position indicating means to indicate to the flight crew when the thrust reverser is in the reverse thrust position for each turbojet engine.

(p) For turbosupercharger installations, if limitations are established for either carburetor air inlet temperature or exhaust gas temperature, indicators must be furnished for each temperature for which the limitation is established unless it is shown that the limitation will not be exceeded in all intended operations.

(q) A low oil pressure warning means for each turbine engine.

(r) An induction system air temperature indicator for each engine equipped with a preheater and having induction air temperature limitations which can be exceeded with preheat.

(s) For each turbine engine, an indicator to indicate the functioning of the powerplant ice protection system.

(t) For each turbine engine, an indicator for the fuel strainer or filter required by § 23.997 to indicate the occurrence of contamination of the strainer or filter before it reaches the capacity established in accordance with § 23.997 (d).

(u) For each turbine engine, a warning means for the oil strainer or filter required by § 23.1019, if it has no bypass, to warn the pilot of the occurrence of contamination of the strainer or filter screen before it reaches the capacity established in accordance with § 23.1019 (a)(2).

(v) An indicator to indicate the functioning of any heater used to prevent ice clogging of fuel system components.

(w) A fire warning indicator for those airplanes required to comply with § 23.1203.

[Amdt. 23-7, 34 FR 13096, Aug. 13, 1969, as amended by Amdt. 23-14, 38 FR 31823, Nov. 19, 1973; Amdt. 23-15, 39 FR 35460, Oct. 1, 1974; Amdt. 23-18, 42 FR 15042, Mar. 17, 1977; Amdt. 23-26, 45 FR 60171, Sept. 11, 1980; Amdt. 23-34, 52 FR 1833, Jan. 15, 1987; 52 FR 34745, Sept. 14, 1987]

§ 23.1307 Miscellaneous equipment.

(a) There must be an approved seat or berth for each occupant.

(b) The following miscellaneous equipment is required as prescribed in this subpart:

(1) A master switch arrangement.

(2) An adequate source of electrical energy.

(3) Electrical protective devices.

[Doc. No. 4080, 29 FR 17955, Dec. 18, 1964; 30 FR 258, Jan. 9, 1965, as amended by Amdt. 23-23, 43 FR 50593, Oct. 30, 1978]

§ 23.1309 Equipment, systems, and installations.

(a) Each item of equipment, when performing its intended function, may not adversely affect:

(1) The response, operation, or accuracy of any equipment essential to safe operation; or

(2) The response, operation, or accuracy of any other equipment unless there is a means to inform the pilot of the effect.

(b) The equipment, system and installations of a multiengine airplane must be designed to prevent hazards to the airplane in the event of a probable malfunction or failure.

(c) The equipment, systems, and installations of a single-engine airplane must be designed to minimize hazards to the airplane in the event of a probable malfunction or failure.

(d) In addition, for commuter category airplanes, systems and installations must be designed to safeguard against hazards to the airplane in the event of their malfunction or failure.

When an installation requires a power supply and the function of that installation is necessary to show compliance with the applicable requirements, the installation must be considered an essential load on the power supply. The power sources and the distribution system must be capable of supplying the following power loads in probable operation combinations and for probable durations;

(1) All essential loads after failure of any prime mover, power converter, or energy storage device;

(2) All essential loads after failure of any one engine on two-engine airplanes; and

(3) In determining the probable operating combinations and durations of essential loads for the power failure conditions described in paragraphs (d) (1) and (2) of this section, the assumption may be that the power loads are reduced in accordance with a monitoring procedure which is consistent with safety for the types of operations for which approval is requested.

[Amdt. 23-14, 38 FR 31823, Nov. 19, 1973, as amended by Amdt. 23-17, 41 FR 55465, Dec. 20, 1976; Amdt. 23-34, 52 FR 1833, Jan. 15, 1987]

INSTRUMENTS: INSTALLATION

§ 23.1321 Arrangement and visibility.

(a) Each flight, navigation, and powerplant instrument for use by any pilot must be plainly visible to him from his station with the minimum practicable deviation from his normal position and line of vision when he is looking forward along the flight path.

(b) For each multiengine airplane, identical powerplant instruments must be located so as to prevent confusion as to which engine each instrument relates.

(c) Instrument panel vibration may not damage, or impair the accuracy of, any instrument.

(d) For each airplane of more than 6,000 pounds maximum weight, the flight instruments required by § 23.1303, and as applicable, by Part 91 of this chapter must be grouped on the instrument panel and centered as nearly as practicable about the vertical plane of the pilot's forward vision. In addition:

(1) The instrument that most effectively indicates the attitude must be on the panel in the top center position;

(2) The instrument that most effectively indicates airspeed must be adjacent to and directly to the left of the instrument in the top center position;

(3) The instrument that most effectively indicates altitude must be adjacent to and directly to the right of the instrument in the top center position; and

(4) The instrument that most effectively indicates direction of flight, other than the magnetic direction indicator required by § 23.1303(c), must be adjacent to and directly below the instrument in the top center position.

(e) If a visual indicator is provided to indicate malfunction of an instrument, it must be effective under all probable cockpit lighting conditions.

[Doc. No. 4080, 29 FR 17955, Dec. 18, 1964, as amended by Amdt. 23-14, 38 FR 31824, Nov. 19, 1973; Amdt. 23-20, 42 FR 36968, July 18, 1977]

§ 23.1322   Warning, caution, and advisory lights.

If warning, caution, or advisory lights are installed in the cockpit, they must, unless otherwise approved by the Administrator, be—

(a) Red, for warning lights (lights indicating a hazard which may require immediate corrective action);

(b) Amber, for caution lights (lights indicating the possible need for future corrective action);

(c) Green, for safe operation lights; and

(d) Any other color, including white, for lights not described in paragraphs (a) through (c) of this section, provided the color differs sufficiently from the colors prescribed in paragraphs (a) through (c) of this section to avoid possible confusion.

[Amdt. 23-17, 41 FR 55465, Dec. 20, 1976]

§ 23.1323   Airspeed indicating system.

(a) Each airspeed indicating instrument must be calibrated to indicate true airspeed (at sea level with a standard atmosphere) with a minimum practicable instrument calibration error when the corresponding pitot and static pressures are applied.

(b) Each airspeed system must be calibrated in flight to determine the system error. The system error, including position error, but excluding the airspeed indicator instrument calibration error, may not exceed three percent of the calibrated airspeed or five knots, whichever is greater, throughout the following speed ranges:

(1) 1.3 V_{S1} to V_{MO}/M_{MO} or V_{NE}, whichever is appropriate with flaps retracted. sd

(2) 1.3 V_{S1} to V_{FE} with flaps extended.

(c) In addition, for commuter category airplanes, the airspeed indicating system must be calibrated to determine the system error in flight and during the accelerate-takeoff ground run. The ground run calibration must be obtained between 0.8 of the minimum value of V_I, and 1.2 times the maximum value of V_I considering the approved ranges of altitude and weight. The ground run calibration must be determined assuming an engine failure at the minimum value of V_I.

(d) For commuter category airplanes, the information showing the relationship between IAS and CAS determined in accordance with paragraph (c) of this section must be shown in the Airplane Flight Manual.

[Amdt. 23-20, 42 FR 36968, July 18, 1977, as amended by Amdt. 23-34, 52 FR 1834, Jan. 15, 1987; 52 FR 34745, Sept. 14, 1987]

§ 23.1325   Static pressure system.

(a) Each instrument provided with static pressure case connections must be so vented that the influence of airplane speed, the opening and closing of windows, airflow variations, moisture, or other foreign matter will least affect the accuracy of the instruments except as noted in paragraph (b)(3) of this section.

(b) If a static pressure system is necessary for the functioning of instruments, systems, or devices, it must comply with the provisions of paragraphs (b)(1) through (3) of this section.

(1) The design and installation of a static pressure system must be such that—

(i) Positive drainage of moisture is provided;

(ii) Chafing of the tubing, and excessive distortion or restriction at bends in the tubing, is avoided; and

(iii) The materials used are durable, suitable for the purpose intended, and protected against corrosion.

(2) A proof test must be conducted to demonstrate the integrity of the static pressure system in the following manner:

(i) *Unpressurized airplanes.* Evacuate the static pressure system to a pressure differential of approximately 1 inch of mercury or to a reading on the altimeter, 1,000 feet above the aircraft elevation at the time of the test. Without additional pumping for a period of 1 minute, the loss of indicated altitude must not exceed 100 feet on the altimeter.

(ii) *Pressurized airplanes.* Evacuate the static pressure system until a pressure differential equivalent to the maximum cabin pressure differential for which the airplane is type certificated is achieved. Without additional pumping for a period of 1 minute, the loss of indicated altitude must not exceed 2 percent of the equivalent altitude of the maximum cabin differential pressure or 100 feet, whichever is greater.

(3) If a static pressure system is provided for any instrument, device, or system required by the operating rules of this chapter, each static pressure port must be designed or located in such a manner that the correlation between air pressure in the static pressure system and true ambient atmospheric static pressure is not altered when the airplane encounters icing conditions. An antiicing means or an alternate source of static pressure may be used in showing compliance with this requirement. If the reading of the altimeter, when on the alternate static pressure system differs from the reading of the altimeter when on the primary static system by more than 50 feet, a correction card must be provided for the alternate static system.

(c) Except as provided in paragraph (d) of this section, if the static pressure system incorporates both a primary and an alternate static pressure source, the means for selecting one or the other source must be designed so that—

(1) When either source is selected, the other is blocked off; and

(2) Both sources cannot be blocked off simultaneously.

(d) For unpressurized airplanes, paragraph (c)(1) of this section does not apply if it can be demonstrated that the static pressure system calibration, when either static pressure source is selected, is not changed by the other static pressure source being open or blocked.

(e) Each system must be designed and installed so that the error in indicated pressure altitude, at sea level, with a standard atmosphere, excluding instrument calibration error, does not result in an error of more than ±30 feet per 100 knots speed for the appropriate configuration in the speed range between 1.3 V_{s0} with flaps extended and 1.8 V_{s1} with flaps retracted. However, the error need not be less than ±30 feet.

(f) For commuter category airplanes, the altimeter system calibration, required by paragraph (e) of this section, must be shown in the Airplane Flight Manual.

[Amdt. 23-1, 30 FR 8261, June 29, 1965, as amended by Amdt. 23-6, 32 FR 7586, May 24, 1967; 32 FR 13505, Sept. 27, 1967; 32 FR 13714, Sept. 30, 1967; Amdt. 23-20, 42 FR 36968, July 18, 1977; Amdt. 23-34, 52 FR 1834, Jan. 15, 1987]

§23.1327 Magnetic direction indicator.

(a) Except as provided in paragraph (b) of this section—

(1) Each magnetic direction indicator must be installed so that its accuracy is not excessively affected by the airplane's vibration or magnetic fields; and

(2) The compensated installation may not have a deviation in level flight, greater than ten degrees on any heading.

(b) A magnetic nonstabilized direction indicator may deviate more than ten degrees due to the operation of electrically powered systems such as electrically heated windshields if either a magnetic stabilized direction indicator, which does not have a deviation in level flight greater than ten degrees on any heading, or a gyroscopic direction indicator, is installed. Deviations of a magnetic nonstabilized direction indicator of more than 10 degrees must be placarded in accordance with § 23.1547(e).

[Amdt. 23-20, 42 FR 36969, July 18, 1977]

§ 23.1329 Automatic pilot system.

If an automatic pilot system is installed, it must meet the following:

(a) Each system must be designed so that the automatic pilot can—

(1) Be quickly and positively disengaged by the pilots to prevent it from interfering with their control of the airplane; or

(2) Be sufficiently overpowered by one pilot to let him control the airplane.

(b) Unless there is automatic synchronization, each system must have a means to readily indicate to the pilot the alignment of the actuating device in relation to the control system it operates.

(c) Each manually operated control for the system operation must be readily accessible to the pilot. Each control must operate in the same plane and sense of motion as specified in § 23.779 for cockpit controls. The direction of motion must be plainly indicated on or near each control.

(d) Each system must be designed and adjusted so that, within the range of adjustment available to the pilot, it cannot produce hazardous loads on the airplane or create hazardous deviations in the flight path, under any flight condition appropriate to its use, either during normal operation or in the event of a malfunction, assuming that corrective action begins within a reasonable period of time.

(e) Each system must be designed so that a single malfunction will not produce a hardover signal in more than one control axis. If the automatic pilot integrates signals from auxiliary controls or furnishes signals for operation of other equipment, positive interlocks and sequencing of engagement to prevent improper operation are required.

(f) There must be protection against adverse interaction of integrated components, resulting from a malfunction.

(g) If the automatic pilot system can be coupled to airborne navigation equipment, means must be provided to indicate to the flight crew the current mode of operation. Selector switch position is not acceptable as a means of indication.

[Doc. No. 4080, 29 FR 17955, Dec. 18, 1964; 30 FR 258, Jan. 9, 1965, as amended by Amdt. 23-23, 43 FR 50593, Oct. 30, 1978]

§ 23.1331 Instruments using a power supply.

(a) For each airplane—

(1) Each gyroscopic instrument must derive its energy from power sources adequate to maintain its required accuracy at any speed above the best rate-of-climb speed;

(2) Each gyroscopic instrument must be installed so as to prevent malfunction due to rain, oil, and other detrimental elements; and

(3) There must be a means to indicate the adequacy of the power being supplied to the instruments.

(b) For each multiengine airplane—

(1) There must be at least two independent sources of power (not driven by the same engine), a manual or an automatic means to select each power source, and a means to indicate the adequacy of the power being supplied by each source; and

(2) The installation and power supply systems must be designed so that—

(i) The failure of one instrument will not interfere with the proper supply of energy to the remaining instruments; and

(ii) The failure of the energy supply from one source will not interfere with the proper supply of energy from any other source.

§ 23.1335 Flight director systems.

If a flight director system is installed, means must be provided to indicate to the flight crew its current mode of operation. Selector switch position is not acceptable as a means of indication.

[Amdt. 23-20, 42 FR 36969, July 18, 1977]

§ 23.1337 Powerplant instruments.

(a) *Instruments and instrument lines.*

(1) Each powerplant instrument line must meet the requirements of § 23.993.

(2) Each line carrying flammable fluids under pressure must—

(i) Have restricting orifices or other safety devices at the source of pressure to prevent the escape of excessive fluid if the line fails; and

(ii) Be installed and located so that the escape of fluids would not create a hazard.

(3) Each powerplant instrument that utilizes flammable fluids must be installed and located so that the escape of fluid would not create a hazard.

(b) *Fuel quantity indicator.* There must be a means to indicate to the flight crewmembers the quantity of fuel in each tank during flight. An indicator, calibrated in either gallons or pounds, and clearly marked to indicate which scale is being used, may be used. In addition—

(1) Each fuel quantity indicator must be calibrated to read "zero" during level flight when the quantity of fuel remaining in the tank is equal to the unusable fuel supply determined under § 23.959;

(2) Each exposed sight gauge used as a fuel quantity indicator must be protected against damage;

(3) Each sight gauge that forms a trap in which water can collect and freeze must have means to allow drainage on the ground;

(4) Tanks with interconnected outlets and airspaces may be considered as one tank and need not have separate indicators; and

(5) No fuel quantity indicator is required for a small auxiliary tank that is used only to transfer fuel to other tanks if the relative size of the tank, the rate of fuel transfer, and operating instructions are adequate to—

(i) Guard against overflow; and

(ii) Give the flight crewmembers prompt warning if transfer is not proceeding as planned.

(c) *Fuel flowmeter system.* If a fuel flowmeter system is installed, each metering component must have a means to by-pass the fuel supply if malfunctioning of that component severely restricts fuel flow.

(d) *Oil quantity indicator.* There must be a means to indicate the quantity of oil in each tank—

(1) On the ground (such as by a stick gauge); and

(2) In flight, to the flight crew members, if there is an oil transfer system or a reserve oil supply system.

[Doc. No. 4080, 29 FR 17955, Dec. 18, 1964, as amended by Amdt. 23-7, 34 FR 13096, Aug. 13, 1969; Amdt. 23-18, 42 FR 15042, Mar. 17, 1977]

ELECTRICAL SYSTEMS AND EQUIPMENT

§ 23.1351 General.

(a) *Electrical system capacity.* Each electrical system must be adequate for the intended use. In addition—

(1) Electric power sources, their transmission cables, and their associated control and protective devices, must be able to furnish the required power at the proper voltage to each load circuit essential for safe operation; and

(2) Compliance with paragraph (a)(1) of this section must be shown as follows—

(i) For normal, utility, and acrobatic category airplanes, by an electrical load analysis or by electrical measurements that account for the electrical loads applied to the electrical system in probable combinations and for probable durations; and

(ii) For commuter category airplanes, by an electrical load analysis that accounts for the electrical loads applied to the electrical system in probable combinations and for probable durations.

(b) *Function.* For each electrical system, the following apply:

(1) Each system, when installed, must be—

(i) Free from hazards in itself, in its method of operation, and in its effects on other parts of the airplane;

(ii) Protected from fuel, oil, water, other detrimental substances, and mechanical damage; and

(iii) So designed that the risk of electrical shock to crew, passengers, and ground personnel is reduced to a minimum.

(2) Electric power sources must function properly when connected in combination or independently, except alternators installed in normal, utility,

and acrobatic category airplanes, may depend on a battery for initial excitation or for stabilization.

(3) No failure or malfunction of any electric power source may impair the ability of any remaining source to supply load circuits essential for safe operation, except the operation of an alternator that depends on a battery for initial excitation or for stabilization may be stopped by failure of that battery in normal, utility, and acrobatic category airplanes.

(4) Each electric power source control must allow the independent operation of each source, except in normal, utility and acrobatic category airplanes, controls associated with alternators which depend on a battery for initial excitation or for stabilization need not break the connection between the alternator and its battery.

(5) In addition, for commuter category airplanes, the following apply:

(i) Each system must be designed so that essential load circuits can be supplied in the event of reasonably probable faults or open circuits including faults in heavy current carrying cables;

(ii) A means must be accessible in flight to the flight crewmembers for the individual and collective disconnection of the electrical power sources from the system;

(iii) The system must be designed so that voltage and frequency, if applicable, at the terminals of all essential load equipment can be maintained within the limits for which the equipment is designed during any probable operating conditions;

(iv) If two independent sources of electrical power for particular equipment or systems are required, their electrical energy supply must be ensured by means such as duplicate electrical equipment, throwover switching, or multichannel or loop circuits separately routed; and

(v) For the purpose of complying with paragraph (b)(5) of this section, the distribution system includes the distribution busses, their associated feeders, and each control and protective device.

(c) *Generating system.* There must be at least one generator if the electrical system supplies power to load cir-

cuits essential for safe operation. In addition—

(1) Each generator must be able to deliver its continuous rated power;

(2) Generator voltage control equipment must be able to dependably regulate the generator output within rated limits;

(3) Each generator must have a reverse current cutout designed to· disconnect the generator from the battery and from the other generators when enough reverse current exists to damage that generator;

(4) There must be a means to give immediate warning to the flight crew of a failure of any generator; and

(5) Each generator must have an overvoltage control designed and installed to prevent damage to the electrical system, or to equipment supplied by the electrical system, that could result if that generator were to develop an overvoltage condition.

(d) *Instruments.* A means must exist to indicate to appropriate flight crewmembers the electric power system quantities essential for safe operation.

(1) For normal, utility, and acrobatic category airplanes with direct current systems, an ammeter that can be switched into each generator feeder may be used and, if only one generator exists, the ammeter may be in the battery feeder.

(2) For commuter category airplanes, the essential electric power system quantities include the voltage and current supplied by each generator.

(e) *Fire resistance.* Electrical equipment must be so designed and installed that in the event of a fire in the engine compartment, during which the surface of the firewall adjacent to the fire is heated to 2,000° F for 5 minutes or to a lesser temperature substantiated by the applicant, the equipment essential to continued safe operation and located behind the firewall will function satisfactorily and will not create an additional fire hazard.

(f) *External power.* If provisions are made for connecting external power to the airplane, and that external power can be electrically connected to equipment other than that used for engine starting, means must be provided to ensure that no external power supply having a reverse polarity, or a reverse phase sequence, can supply power to the airplane's electrical system.

[Doc. No. 4080, 29 FR 17955, Dec. 18, 1964, as amended by Amdt. 23-7, 34 FR 13096, Aug. 13, 1969; Amdt. 23-14, 38 FR 31824, Nov. 19, 1973; Amdt. 23-17, 41 FR 55465, Dec. 20, 1976; Amdt. 23-20, 42 FR 36969, July 18, 1977; Amdt. 23-34, 52 FR 1834, Jan. 15, 1987; 52 FR 34745, Sept. 14, 1987]

§ 23.1353 Storage battery design and installation.

(a) Each storage battery must be designed and installed as prescribed in this section.

(b) Safe cell temperatures and pressures must be maintained during any probable charging and discharging condition. No uncontrolled increase in cell temperature may result when the battery is recharged (after previous complete discharge)—

(1) At maximum regulated voltage or power;

(2) During a flight of maximum duration; and

(3) Under the most adverse cooling condition likely to occur in service.

(c) Compliance with paragraph (b) of this section must be shown by tests unless experience with similar batteries and installations has shown that maintaining safe cell temperatures and pressures presents no problem.

(d) No explosive or toxic gases emitted by any battery in normal operation, or as the result of any probable malfunction in the charging system or battery installation, may accumulate in hazardous quantities within the airplane.

(e) No corrosive fluids or gases that may escape from the battery may damage surrounding structures or adjacent essential equipment.

(f) Each nickel cadmium battery installation capable of being used to start an engine or auxiliary power unit must have provisions to prevent any hazardous effect on structure or essential systems that may be caused by the maximum amount of heat the battery can generate during a short circuit of the battery or of its individual cells.

(g) Nickel cadmium battery installations capable of being used to start an engine or auxiliary power unit must have—

(1) A system to control the charging rate of the battery automatically so as to prevent battery overheating;

(2) A battery temperature sensing and over-temperature warning system with a means for disconnecting the battery from its charging source in the event of an over-temperature condition; or

(3) A battery failure sensing and warning system with a means for disconnecting the battery from its charging source in the event of battery failure.

[Doc. No. 4080, 29 FR 17955, Dec. 18, 1964; 30 FR 258, Jan. 9, 1965, as amended by Amdt. 23-20, 42 FR 36969, July 18, 1977; Amdt. 23-21, 43 FR 2319, Jan. 16, 1978]

§ 23.1357 Circuit protective devices.

(a) Protective devices, such as fuses or circuit breakers, must be installed in all electrical circuits other than—

(1) The main circuits of starter motors; and

(2) Circuits in which no hazard is presented by their omission.

(b) A protective device for a circuit essential to flight safety may not be used to protect any other circuit.

(c) Each resettable circuit protective device ("trip free" device in which the tripping mechanism cannot be overridden by the operating control) must be designed so that—

(1) A manual operation is required to restore service after tripping; and

(2) If an overload or circuit fault exists, the device will open the circuit regardless of the position of the operating control.

(d) If the ability to reset a circuit breaker or replace a fuse is essential to safety in flight, that circuit breaker or fuse must be so located and identified that it can be readily reset or replaced in flight.

(e) If fuses are used, there must be one spare of each rating, or 50 percent spare fuses of each rating, whichever is greater.

[Doc. No. 4080, 29 FR 17955, Dec. 18, 1964; 30 FR 258, Jan. 9, 1965, as amended by Amdt. 23-20, 42 FR 36969, July 18, 1977]

§ 23.1361 Master switch arrangement.

(a) There must be a master switch arrangement to allow ready disconnection of electric power sources from the main bus. The point of disconnection must be adjacent to the sources controlled by the switch.

(b) Load circuits may be connected so that they remain energized after the switch is opened, if they are protected by circuit protective devices, rated at five amperes or less, adjacent to the electric power source. These circuits must be isolated, or phsyically shielded, to prevent their igniting flammable fluids or vapors that might be liberated by the leakage or rupture of flammable fluid systems.

(c) The master switch or its controls must be so installed that the switch is easily discernible and accessible to a crewmember in flight.

[Doc. No. 4080, 29 FR 17955, Dec. 18, 1964; 30 FR 258, Jan. 9, 1965, as amended by Amdt. 23-20, 42 FR 36969, July 18, 1977]

§ 23.1365 Electric cables and equipment.

(a) Each electric connecting cable must be of adequate capacity.

(b) Each cable and associated equipment that would overheat in the event of circuit overload or fault must be at least flame resistant and may not emit dangerous quantities of toxic fumes.

[Doc. No. 4080, 29 FR 17955, Dec. 18, 1964, as amended by Amdt. 23-14, 38 FR 31824, Nov. 19, 1973]

§ 23.1367 Switches.

Each switch must be—

(a) Able to carry its rated current;

(b) Constructed with enough distance or insulating material between current carrying parts and the housing so that vibration in flight will not cause shorting;

(c) Accessible to appropriate flight crewmembers; and

(d) Labeled as to operation and the circuit controlled.

LIGHTS

§ 23.1381 Instrument lights.

The instrument lights must—

(a) Make each instrument and control easily readable and discernible;

(b) Be installed so that their direct rays, and rays reflected from the windshield or other surface, are shielded from the pilot's eyes; and

(c) Have enough distance or insulating material between current carrying parts and the housing so that vibration in flight will not cause shorting.

A cabin dome light is not an instrument light.

§ 23.1383 Landing lights.

(a) Each installed landing light must be acceptable.

(b) Each landing light must be installed so that—

(1) No dangerous glare is visible to the pilot;

(2) The pilot is not seriously affected by halation; and

(3) It provides enough light for night landing.

§ 23.1385 Position light system installation.

(a) *General.* Each part of each position light system must meet the applicable requirements of this section and each system as a whole must meet the requirements of §§ 23.1387 through 23.1397.

(b) *Forward position lights.* Forward position lights must consist of a red and a green light spaced laterally as far apart as practicable and installed forward on the airplane so that, with the airplane in the normal flying position, the red light is on the left side and the green light is on the right side. Each light must be approved.

(c) *Rear position light.* The rear position light must be a white light mounted as far aft as practicable on the tail or on each wing tip, and must be approved.

(d) *Circuit.* The two forward position lights and the rear position light must make a single circuit.

(e) *Light covers and color filters.* Each light cover or color filter must be at least flame resistant and may not change color or shape or lose any appreciable light transmission during normal use.

[Doc. No. 4080, 29 FR 17955, Dec. 18, 1964, as amended by Amdt. 23-17, 41 FR 55465, Dec. 20, 1976]

§ 23.1387 Position light system dihedral angles.

(a) Except as provided in paragraph (e) of this section, each forward and rear position light must, as installed, show unbroken light within the dihedral angles described in this section.

(b) Dihedral angle *L* (left) is formed by two intersecting vertical planes, the first parallel to the longitudinal axis of the airplane, and the other at 110 degrees to the left of the first, as viewed when looking forward along the longitudinal axis.

(c) Dihedral angle *R* (right) is formed by two intersecting vertical planes, the first parallel to the longitudinal axis of the airplane, and the other at 110 degrees to the right of the first, as viewed when looking forward along the longitudinal axis.

(d) Dihedral angle *A* (aft) is formed by two intersecting vertical planes making angles of 70 degrees to the right and to the left, respectively, to a vertical plane passing through the longitudinal axis, as viewed when looking aft along the longitudinal axis.

(e) If the rear position light, when mounted as far aft as practicable in accordance with § 23.1385(c), cannot show unbroken light within dihedral angle A (as defined in paragraph (d) of this section), a solid angle or angles of obstructed visibility totaling not more than 0.04 steradians is allowable within that dihedral angle, if such solid angle is within a cone whose apex is at the rear position light and whose elements make an angle of 30° with a vertical line passing through the rear position light.

[Doc. No. 4080, 29 FR 17955, Dec. 18, 1964; 30 FR 258, Jan. 9, 1965, as amended by Amdt. 23–12, 36 FR 21278, Nov. 5, 1971]

§ 23.1389 Position light distribution and intensities.

(a) *General.* The intensities prescribed in this section must be provided by new equipment with each light cover and color filter in place. Intensities must be determined with the light source operating at a steady value equal to the average luminous output of the source at the normal operating voltage of the airplane. The light distribution and intensity of each position light must meet the requirements of paragraph (b) of this section.

(b) *Forward and rear position lights.* The light distribution and intensities of forward and rear position lights must be expressed in terms of minimum intensities in the horizontal plane, minimum intensities in any vertical plane, and maximum intensities in overlapping beams, within dihedral angles *L*, *R*, and *A*, and must meet the following requirements:

(1) *Intensities in the horizontal plane.* Each intensity in the horizontal plane (the plane containing the longitudinal axis of the airplane and perpendicular to the plane of symmetry of the airplane) must equal or exceed the values in § 23.1391.

(2) *Intensities in any vertical plane.* Each intensity in any vertical plane (the plane perpendicular to the horizontal plane) must equal or exceed the appropriate value in § 23.1393, where *I* is the minimum intensity prescribed in § 23.1391 for the corresponding angles in the horizontal plane.

(3) *Intensities in overlaps between adjacent signals.* No intensity in any overlap between adjacent signals may exceed the values in § 23.1395, except that higher intensities in overlaps may be used with main beam intensities substantially greater than the minima specified in §§ 23.1391 and 23.1393, if the overlap intensities in relation to the main beam intensities do not adversely affect signal clarity. When the peak intensity of the forward position lights is more than 100 candles, the maximum overlap intensities between them may exceed the values in § 23.1395 if the overlap intensity in Area A is not more than 10 percent of peak position light intensity and the overlap intensity in Area B is not more than 2.5 percent of peak position light intensity.

(c) *Rear position light installation.* A single rear position light may be installed in a position displaced laterally from the plane of symmetry of an airplane if—

(1) The axis of the maximum cone of illumination is parallel to the flight path in level flight; and

(2) There is no obstruction aft of the light and between planes 70 degrees to

the right and left of the axis of maximum illumination.

§ 23.1391   Minimum intensities in the horizontal plane of forward and rear position lights.

Each position light intensity must equal or exceed the applicable values in the following table:

Dihedral angle (light included)	Angle from right or left of longitudinal axis, measured from dead ahead	Intensity (candles)
L and R (forward red and green).	0° to 10°	40
	10° to 20°	30
	20° to 110°	5
A (rear white)	110° to 180°	20

§ 23.1393   Minimum intensities in any vertical plane of forward and rear position lights.

Each position light intensity must equal or exceed the applicable values in the following table:

Angle above or below the horizontal plane	Intensity, I
0°	1.00
0° to 5°	0.90
5° to 10°	0.80
10° to 15°	0.70
15° to 20°	0.50
20° to 30°	0.30
30° to 40°	0.10
40° to 90°	0.05

§ 23.1395   Maximum intensities in overlapping beams of forward and rear position lights.

No position light intensity may exceed the applicable values in the following equal or exceed the applicable values in § 23.1389(b)(3):

Overlaps	Maximum intensity	
	Area A (candles)	Area B (candles)
Green in dihedral angle L	10	1
Red in dihedral angle R	10	1
Green in dihedral angle A	5	1
Red in dihedral angle A	5	1
Rear white in dihedral angle L	5	1
Rear white in dihedral angle R	5	1

Where—

(a) Area A includes all directions in the adjacent dihedral angle that pass through the light source and intersect the common boundary plane at more than 10 degrees but less than 20 degrees; and

(b) Area B includes all directions in the adjacent dihedral angle that pass through the light source and intersect the common boundary plane at more than 20 degrees.

§ 23.1397   Color specifications.

Each position light color must have the applicable International Commission on Illumination chromaticity coordinates as follows:

(a) *Aviation red*—

"y" is not greater than 0.335; and
"z" is not greater than 0.002.

(b) *Aviation green*—

"x" is not greater than $0.440-0.320\,y$;
"x" is not greater than $y-0.170$; and
"y" is not less than $0.390-0.170\,x$.

(c) *Aviation white*—

"x" is not less than 0.300 and not greater than 0.540;
"y" is not less than "$x-0.040$" or "$y_0-0.010$," whichever is the smaller; and
"y" is not greater than "$x+0.020$" nor "$0.636-0.400\,x$";

Where "y_0" is the "y" coordinate of the Planckian radiator for the value of "x" considered.

[Doc. No. 4080, 29 FR 17955, Dec. 18, 1964, amended by Amdt. 23-11, 36 FR 12971, July 10, 1971]

§ 23.1399   Riding light.

(a) Each riding (anchor) light required for a seaplane or amphibian, must be installed so that it can—

(1) Show a white light for at least two miles at night under clear atmospheric conditions; and

(2) Show the maximum unbroken light practicable when the airplane is moored or drifting on the water.

(b) Externally hung lights may be used.

§ 23.1401   Anticollision light system.

(a) *General.* If certification for night operation is requested, the airplane must have an anticollision light system that—

(1) Consists of one or more approved anticollision lights located so that their light will not impair the flight

crewmembers' vision or detract from the conspicuity of the position lights; and

(2) Meets the requirements of paragraphs (b) through (f) of this section.

(b) *Field of coverage.* The system must consist of enough lights to illuminate the vital areas around the airplane, considering the physical configuration and flight characteristics of the airplane. The field of coverage must extend in each direction within at least 75 degrees above and 75 degrees below the horizontal plane of the airplane, except that there may be solid angles of obstructed visibility totaling not more than 0.5 steradians.

(c) *Flashing characteristics.* The arrangement of the system, that is, the number of light sources, beam width, speed of rotation, and other characteristics, must give an effective flash frequency of not less than 40, nor more than 100, cycles per minute. The effective flash frequency is the frequency at which the airplane's complete anticollision light system is observed from a distance, and applies to each sector of light including any overlaps that exist when the system consists of more than one light source. In overlaps, flash frequencies may exceed 100, but not 180, cycles per minute.

(d) *Color.* Each anticollision light must be either aviation red or aviation white and must meet the applicable requirements of §23.1397.

(e) *Light intensity.* The minimum light intensities in any vertical plane, measured with the red filter (if used) and expressed in terms of "effective" intensities, must meet the requirements of paragraph (f) of this section. The following relation must be assumed:

$$I_e = \frac{\int_{t_1}^{t_2} I(t)dt}{0.2 + (t_2 - t_1)}$$

where:

I_e = effective intensity (candles).
$I(t)$ = instantaneous intensity as a function of time.
$t_2 - t_1$ = flash time interval (seconds).

Normally, the maximum value of effective intensity is obtained when t_2 and t_1 are chosen so that the effective intensity is equal to the instantaneous intensity at t_2 and t_1.

(f) *Minimum effective intensities for anticollision lights.* Each anticollision light effective intensity must equal or exceed the applicable values in the following table.

Angle above or below the horizontal plane	Effective intensity (candles)
0° to 5°	400
5° to 10°	240
10° to 20°	80
20° to 30°	40
30° to 75°	20

[Doc. No. 4080, 29 FR 17955, Dec. 18, 1964, as amended by Amdt. 23-11, 36 FR 12972, July 10, 1971; Amdt. 23-20, 42 FR 36969, July 18, 1977]

SAFETY EQUIPMENT

§23.1411 General.

(a) Required safety equipment to be used by the flight crew in an emergency, such as automatic liferaft releases, must be readily accessible.

(b) Stowage provisions for required safety equipment must be furnished and must—

(1) Be arranged so that the equipment is directly accessible and its location is obvious; and

(2) Protect the safety equipment from damage caused by being subjected to the inertia loads resulting from the ultimate static load factors specified in §23.561(b)(3) of this part.

§23.1413 Safety belts and harnessess.

Each safety belt and shoulder harness must be equipped with a metal-to-metal latching device.

[Doc. No. 4080, 29 FR 17955, Dec. 18, 1964, as amended by Amdt. 23-7, 34 FR 13096, Aug. 13, 1969; Amdt. 23-22, 43 FR 46233, Oct. 5, 1978]

§ 23.1415 Ditching equipment.

(a) Emergency flotation and signaling equipment required by any operating rule in this chapter must be installed so that it is readily available to the crew and passengers.

(b) Each raft and each life preserver must be approved.

(c) Each raft released automatically or by the pilot must be attached to the airplane by a line to keep it alongside the airplane. This line must be weak enough to break before submerging the empty raft to which it is attached.

(d) Each signaling device required by any operating rule in this chapter, must be accessible, function satisfactorily, and must be free of any hazard in its operation.

§ 23.1416 Pneumatic de-icer boot system.

If certification with ice protection provisions is desired and a pneumatic de-icer boot system is installed—

(a) The system must meet the requirements specified in § 23.1419.

(b) The system and its components must be designed to perform their intended function under any normal system operating temperature or pressure, and

(c) Means to indicate to the flight crew that the pneumatic de-icer boot system is receiving adequate pressure and is functioning normally must be provided.

[Amdt. 23-23, 43 FR 50593, Oct. 30, 1978]

§ 23.1419 Ice protection.

If certification with ice protection provisions is desired, compliance with the following requirements must be shown:

(a) The recommended procedures for the use of the ice protection equipment must be set forth in the Airplane Flight Manual or in approved manual material.

(b) An analysis must be performed to establish, on the basis of the airplane's operational needs, the adequacy of the ice protection system for the various components of the airplane. In addition, tests of the ice protection system must be conducted to demonstrate that the airplane is capable of operating safely in continuous maximum and intermittent maximum icing conditions as described in Appendix C of Part 25 of this chapter.

(c) Compliance with all or portions of this section may be accomplished by reference, where applicable because of similarity of the designs, to analysis and tests performed for the type certification of a type certificated aircraft.

(d) When monitoring of the external surfaces of the airplane by the flight crew is required for proper operation of the ice protection equipment, external lighting must be provided which is adequate to enable the monitoring to be done at night.

[Amdt. No. 23-14, 38 FR 31824, Nov. 19, 1973]

MISCELLANEOUS EQUIPMENT

§ 23.1431 Electronic equipment.

Radio equipment and installations must be free from hazards in themselves, in their method of operation, and in their effects on other components.

§ 23.1435 Hydraulic systems.

(a) *Design.* Each hydraulic system must be designed as follows:

(1) Each hydraulic system and its elements must withstand, without yielding, the structural loads expected in addition to hydraulic loads.

(2) A means to indicate the pressure in each hydraulic system which supplies two or more primary functions must be provided to the flight crew.

(3) There must be means to ensure that the pressure, including transient (surge) pressure, in any part of the system will not exceed the safe limit above design operating pressure and to prevent excessive pressure resulting from fluid volumetric changes in all lines which are likely to remain closed long enough for such changes to occur.

(4) The minimum design burst pressure must be 2.5 times the operating pressure.

(b) *Tests.* Each system must be substantiated by proof pressure tests. When proof tested, no part of any system may fail, malfunction, or experience a permanent set. The proof load of each system must be at least 1.5 times the maximum operating pressure of that system.

(c) *Accumulators.* No hydraulic accumulator or pressurized reservoir may be installed on the engine side of any firewall, unless it is an integral part of an engine or propeller.

[Doc. No. 4080, 29 FR 17955, Dec. 18, 1964, as amended by Amdt. 23-7, 34 FR 13096, Aug. 13, 1969; Amdt. 23-14, 38 FR 31824, Nov. 19, 1973]

§ 23.1437 Accessories for multiengine airplanes.

For multiengine airplanes, engine-driven accessories essential to safe operation must be distributed among two or more engines so that the failure of any one engine will not impair safe operation through the malfunctioning of these accessories.

§ 23.1438 Pressurization and pneumatic systems.

(a) Pressurization system elements must be burst pressure tested to 2.0 times, and proof pressure tested to 1.5 times, the maximum normal operating pressure.

(b) Pneumatic system elements must be burst pressure tested to 3.0 times, and proof pressure tested to 1.5 times, the maximum normal operating pressure.

(c) An analysis, or a combination of analysis and test, may be substituted for any test required by paragraph (a) or (b) of this section if the Administrator finds it equivalent to the required test.

[Amdt. 23-20, 42 FR 36969, July 18, 1977]

§ 23.1441 Oxygen equipment and supply.

(a) If certification with supplemental oxygen equipment is requested, the equipment must meet the requirements of this section and §§ 23.1443 through 23.1449. Portable oxygen equipment may be used to meet the requirements.

(b) The oxygen system must be free from hazards in itself, in its method of operation, and its effect upon other components.

(c) There must be a means to allow the crew to readily determine, during the flight, the quantity of oxygen available in each source of supply.

(d) Demand flow oxygen equipment, and oxygen equipment for use above 40,000 feet (MSL), must be approved.

[Amdt. 23-9, 35 FR 6386, Apr. 21, 1970]

§ 23.1443 Minimum mass flow of supplemental oxygen.

If continuous flow oxygen equipment is installed for use by occupants of the airplane, the mass flow of supplemental oxygen supplied for each user must be at a rate not less than that shown in the following figure for each altitude up to and including the maximum operating altitude of the airplane:

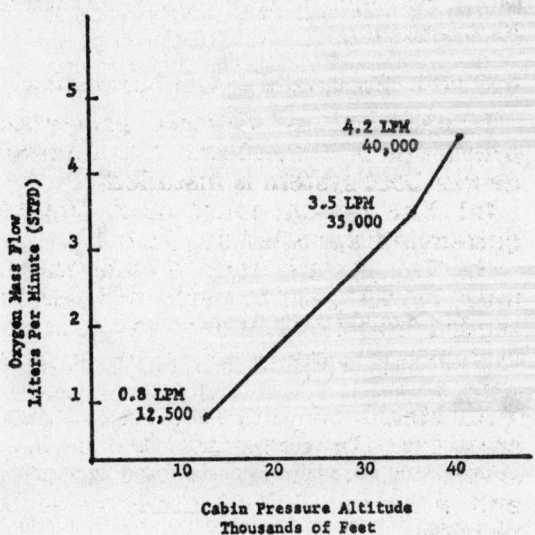

[Amdt. 23-9, 35 FR 6386, Apr. 21, 1970]

§ 23.1447 Equipment standards for oxygen dispensing units.

If oxygen dispensing units are installed, the following apply:

(a) There must be an individual dispensing unit for each occupant for whom supplemental oxygen is to be supplied. Each dispensing unit must:

(1) Provide for effective utilization of the oxygen being delivered to the unit.

(2) Be capable of being readily placed into position on the face of the user.

(3) Be equipped with a suitable means to retain the unit in position on the face.

(b) If certification for operation up to and including 18,000 feet (MSL) is requested, each oxygen dispensing unit must:

(1) Cover the nose and mouth of the user; or

(2) Be a nasal cannula, in which case one oxygen dispensing unit covering both the nose and mouth of the user must be available. In addition, each nasal cannula or its connecting tubing must have permanently affixed—

(i) A visible warning against smoking while in use;

(ii) An illustration of the correct method of donning; and

(iii) A visible warning against use with nasal obstructions or head colds with resultant nasal congestion.

(c) If certification for operation above 18,000 feet (MSL) is requested, each oxygen dispensing unit must cover the nose and mouth of the user.

(d) For a pressurized airplane designed to operate at flight altitudes above 25,000 feet (MSL), an oxygen dispensing unit connected to an oxygen supply terminal must be immediately available to each occupant, wherever seated.

(e) If certification for operation above 30,000 feet is requested, the dispensing units providing the required oxygen flow rate must be automatically presented to each occupant before the cabin pressue altitude exceeds 15,000 feet.

(f) If an automatic dispensing unit (hose and mask, or other unit) system is installed, the crew must be provided with a manual means to make the dispensing units immediately available in the event or failure of the automatic system.

§ 23.1449 Means for determining use of oxygen.

There must be a means to allow the crew to determine whether oxygen is being delivered to the dispensing equipment.

§23.1450 Chemical oxygen generators.

(a) For the purpose of this section, a chemical oxygen generator is defined as a device which produces oxygen by chemical reaction.

(b) Each chemical oxygen generator must be designed and installed in accordance with the following requirements:

(1) Surface temperature developed by the generator during operation may not create a hazard to the airplane or to its occupants.

(2) Means must be provided to relieve any internal pressure that may be hazardous.

(c) In addition to meeting the requirements in paragraph (b) of this section, each portable chemical oxygen generator that is capable of sustained operation by successive replacement of a generator element must be placarded to show—

(1) The rate of oxygen flow, in liters per minute;

(2) The duration of oxygen flow, in minutes, for the replaceable generator element; and

(3) A warning that the replaceable generator may be hot, unless the element construction is such that the surface temperature cannot exceed 100°F.

§ 23.1457 Cockpit voice recorders.

(a) Each cockpit voice recorder required by the operating rules of this chapter must be approved and must be installed so that it will record the following:

(1) Voice communications transmitted from or received in the airplane by radio.

(2) Voice communications of flight crewmembers on the flight deck.

(3) Voice communications of flight crewmembers on the flight deck, using the airplane's interphone system.

(4) Voice or audio signals identifying navigation or approach aids introduced into a headset or speaker.

(5) Voice communications of flight crewmembers using the passenger loudspeaker system, if there is such a system and if the fourth channel is available in accordance with the requirements of paragraph (c)(4)(ii) of this section.

(b) The recording requirements of paragraph (a)(2) of this section must be met by installing a cockpit-mounted area microphone, located in the best position for recording voice communications originating at the first and second pilot stations and voice communications of other crewmembers on the flight deck when directed to those stations. The microphone must be so located and, if necessary, the preamplifiers and filters of the recorder must be so adjusted or supplemented, so that the intelligibility of the recorded communications is as high as practicable when recorded under flight cockpit noise conditions and played back. Repeated aural or visual playback of the record may be used in evaluating intelligibility.

(c) Each cockpit voice recorder must be installed so that the part of the communication or audio signals specified in paragraph (a) of this section obtained from each of the following sources is recorded on a separate channel:

(1) For the first channel, from each boom, mask, or handheld microphone, headset, or speaker used at the first pilot station.

(2) For the second channel from each boom, mask, or handheld microphone, headset, or speaker used at the second pilot station.

(3) For the third channel — from the cockpit-mounted area microphone.

(4) For the fourth channel from:

(i) Each boom, mask, or handheld microphone, headset, or speaker used at the station for the third and fourth crewmembers.

(ii) If the stations specified in paragraph (c)(4)(i) of this section are not required or if the signal at such a station is picked up by another channel, each microphone on the flight deck that is used with the passenger loudspeaker system, if its signals are not picked up by another channel.

(5) And that as far as is practicable all sounds received by the microphone listed in paragraphs (c) (1), (2), and (4) of this section must be recorded without interruption irrespective of the position of the interphone-transmitter key switch. The design shall ensure that sidetone for the flight crew is produced only when the interphone, public address system, or radio transmitters are in use.

(d) Each cockpit voice recorder must be installed so that:

(1) It receives its electric power from the bus that provides the maximum reliability for operation of the cockpit voice recorder without jeopardizing service to essential or emergency loads.

(2) There is an automatic means to simultaneously stop the recorder and prevent each erasure feature from functioning, within 10 minutes after crash impact; and

(3) There is an aural or visual means for preflight checking of the recorder for proper operation.

(e) The record container must be located and mounted to minimize the probability of rupture of the container as a result of crash impact and consequent heat damage to the record from fire. In meeting this requirement, the record container must be as far aft as practicable, but may not be where aft mounted engines may crush the container during impact. However, it need not be outside of the pressurized compartment.

(f) If the cockpit voice recorder has a bulk erasure device, the installation must be designed to minimize the probability of inadvertent operation and actuation of the device during crash impact.

(g) Each recorder container must:

(1) Be either bright orange or bright yellow;

(2) Have reflective tape affixed to its external surface to facilitate its location under water; and

(3) Have an underwater locating device, when required by the operating rules of this chapter, on or adjacent to the container which is secured in such manner that they are not likely to be separated during crash impact.

§ 23.1459 Flight Recorders

(a) Each flight recorder required by the operating rules of this chapter must be installed so that:

(1) It is supplied with airspeed, altitude, and directional data obtained from sources that meet the accuracy requirements of §§ 23.1323, 23.1325, and 23.1327, as appropriate;

(2) The vertical acceleration sensor is rigidly attached, and located longitudinally either within the approved center of gravity limits of the airplane, or at a distance forward or aft of these limits that does not exceed 25 percent of the airplane's mean aerodynamic chord;

(3) It receives its electrical power power from the bus that provides the maximum reliability for operation of the flight recorder without jeopardizing service to essential or emergency loads;

(4) There is an aural or visual means for preflight checking of the recorder for proper recording of data in the storage medium

(5) Except for recorders powered solely by the engine-driven electrical generator system, there is an automatic means to simultaneously stop a recorder that has a data erasure feature and prevent each erasure feature from functioning, within 10 minutes after crash impact; and

(b) Each nonejectable record container must be located and mounted so as to minimize the probability of container rupture resulting from crash impact and subsequent damage to the record from fire. In meeting this requirement the record container must be located as far aft as practicable, but need not be aft of the pressurized compartment, and may not be where aft-mounted engines may crush the container upon impact

(c) A correlation must be established between the flight recorder readings of airspeed, altitude, and heading and the corresponding readings (taking into account correction factors) of the first pilot's instruments. The correlation must cover the airspeed range over which the airplane is to be operated, the range of altitude to which the airplane is limited, and 360 degrees of heading. Correlation may be established on the ground as appropriate

(d) Each recorder container must:

(1) Be either bright orange or bright yellow;

(2) Have reflective tape affixed to its external surface to facilitate its location under water; and

(3) Have an underwater locating device, when required by the operating rules of this chapter, on or adjacent to the container which is secured in such a manner that they are not likely to be separated during crash impact

(e) Any novel or unique design or operational characteristics of the aircraft shall be evaluated to determine if any dedicated parameters must be recorded on flight recorders in addition to or in place of existing requirements.

§ 23.1461 Equipment containing high energy rotors.

(a) Equipment containing high energy rotors must meet paragraph (b), (c), or (d) of this section

(b) High energy rotors contained in equipment must be able to withstand damage caused by malfunctions, vibration, abnormal speeds, and abnormal temperatures. In addition—

(1) Auxiliary rotor cases must be able to contain damage caused by the failure of high energy rotor blades; and

(2) Equipment control devices, systems, and instrumentation must reasonably ensure that no operating limitations affecting the integrity of high energy rotors will be exceeded in service

(c) It must be shown by test that equipment containing high energy rotors can contain any failure of a high energy rotor that occurs at the highest speed obtainable with the normal speed control devices inoperative.

(d) Equipment containing high energy rotors must be located where rotor failure will neither endanger the occupants nor adversely affect continued safe flight.

[Amdt. 23-20, 42 FR 36969, July 18, 1977]

Subpart G—Operating Limitations and Information

§ 23.1501 General.

(a) Each operating limitation specified in §§ 23.1505 through 23.1527 and other limitations and information necessary for safe operation must be established.

(b) The operating limitations and other information necessary for safe operation must be made available to the crewmembers as prescribed in §§ 23.1541 through 23.1589.

[Amdt. 23-21, 43 FR 2319, Jan. 16, 1978]

§ 23.1505 Airspeed limitations.

(a) The never-exceed speed V_{NE} must be established so that it is—

(1) Not less than 0.9 times the minimum value of V_D allowed under § 23.335; and

(2) Not more than the lesser of—

(i) 0.9 V_D established under § 23.335; or

(ii) 0.9 times the maximum speed shown under § 23.251.

(b) The maximum structural cruising speed V_{NO} must be established so that it is—

(1) Not less than the minimum value of V_C allowed under § 23.335; and

(2) Not more than the lesser of—

(i) V_C established under § 23.335; or

(ii) 0.89 V_{NE} established under paragraph (a) of this section.

(c) Paragraphs (a) and (b) of this section do not apply to turbine airplanes or to airplanes for which a design diving speed V_D/M_D is established under § 23.335(b)(4). For those airplanes, a maximum operating limit speed (V_{MO}/M_{MO}-airspeed or Mach number, whichever is critical at a particular altitude) must be established as a speed that may not be deliberately exceeded in any regime of flight (climb, cruise, or descent) unless a higher speed is authorized for flight test or pilot training operations. V_{MO}/M_{MO} must be established so that it is not greater than the design cruising speed V_C/M_C and so that it is sufficiently below V_D/M_D and the maximum speed shown under § 23.251 to make it highly improbable that the latter speeds will be inadvertently exceeded in operations. The speed margin between V_{MO}/M_{MO} and V_D/M_D or the maximum speed shown under § 23.251 may not be less than the speed margin established between V_C/M_C and V_D/M_D under § 23.335(b), or the speed margin found necessary in the flight test conducted under § 23.253.

[Doc. No. 4080, 29 FR 17955, Dec. 18, 1964, as amended by Amdt. 23-7, 34 FR 13096, Aug. 13, 1969]

§ 23.1507 Maneuvering speed.

The maneuvering speed V_A, determined under § 23.335, must be established as an operating limitation.

§ 23.1511 Flap extended speed.

(a) The flap extended speed V_{FE} must be established so that it is—

(1) Not less than the minimum value of V_F allowed in §§ 23.345 and 23.457; and

(2) Not more than the lesser of—

(i) V_F established under § 23.345; or

(ii) V_F established under § 23.457.

(b) Additional combinations of flap setting, airspeed, and engine power may be established if the structure has been proven for the corresponding design conditions.

§ 23.1513 Minimum control speed.

The minimum control speed V_{MC}, determined under § 23.149, must be established as an operating limitation.

§ 23.1519 Weight and center of gravity.

The weight and center of gravity limitations determined under § 23.23 must be established as operating limitations.

§ 23.1521 Powerplant limitations.

(a) *General.* The powerplant limitations prescribed in this section must be established so that they do not exceed the corresponding limits for which the engines or propellers are type certificated.

(b) *Takeoff operation.* The power-plant takeoff operation must be limited by—

(1) The maximum rotational speed (rpm);

(2) The maximum allowable manifold pressure (for reciprocating engines);

(3) The maximum allowable gas temperature (for turbine engines);

(4) The time limit for the use of the power or thrust corresponding to the limitations established in paragraphs (b)(1) through (3) of this section; and

(5) If the time limit in paragraph (b)(4) of this section exceeds two minutes, the maximum allowable cylinder head (as applicable), liquid coolant, and oil temperatures.

(c) *Continuous operation.* The continuous operation must be limited by—

(1) The maximum rotational speed;

(2) The maximum allowable manifold pressure (for reciprocating engines);

(3) The maximum allowable gas temperature (for turbine engines); and

(4) The maximum allowable cylinder head, oil, and liquid coolant temperatures.

(d) *Fuel grade or designation.* The minimum fuel grade (for reciprocating engines), or fuel designation (for turbine engines), must be established so that it is not less than that required for the operation of the engines within the limitations in paragraphs (b) and (c) of this section.

(e) *Ambient temperature.* For turbine engines, ambient temperature limitations (including limitations for winterization installations if applicable) must be established as the maximum ambient atmospheric temperature at which compliance with the cooling provisions of §§ 23.1041 through 23.1047 is shown.

[Doc. No. 4080, 29 FR 17955, Dec. 18, 1964; 30 FR 258, Jan. 9, 1965, as amended by Amdt. 23-21, 43 FR 2319, Jan. 16, 1978]

§ 23.1523 Minimum flight crew.

The minimum flight crew must be established so that it is sufficient for safe operation considering—

(a) The workload on individual crewmembers and, in addition for commuter category airplanes, each crewmember workload determination must consider the following:

(1) Flight path control,

(2) Collision avoidance,

(3) Navigation,

(4) Communications,

(5) Operation and monitoring of all essential airplane systems,

(6) Command decisions, and

(7) The accessibility and ease of operation of necessary controls by the appropriate crewmember during all normal and emergency operations when at the crewmember flight station;

(b) The accessibility and ease of operation of necessary controls by the appropriate crewmember; and

(c) The kinds of operation authorized under § 23.1525.

[Amdt. 23-21, 43 FR 2319, Jan. 16, 1978, as amended by Amdt. 23-34, 52 FR 1834, Jan. 15, 1987]

§ 23.1524 Maximum passenger seating configuration.

The maximum passenger seating configuration must be established.

[Amdt. 23-10, 36 FR 2864, Feb. 11, 1971]

§ 23.1525 Kinds of operation.

The kinds of operation to which the airplane is limited are established by the category in which it is eligible for certification and by the installed equipment.

§ 23.1527 Maximum operating altitude.

(a) A maximum operating altitude limitation of not more than 25,000 feet must be established for pressurized airplanes, unless compliance with § 23.775(e) is shown.

(b) For turbine engine powered airplanes and turbosupercharged airplanes, the maximum altitude up to which operation is allowed, as limited by flight, structural, powerplant, functional, or equipment characteristics must be established.

[Amdt. 23-7, 34 FR 13096, Aug. 13, 1969]

§ 23.1529 Instructions for Continued Airworthiness.

The applicant must prepare Instructions for Continued Airworthiness in accordance with Appendix G to this part that are acceptable to the Administrator. The instructions may be incomplete at type certification if a program exists to ensure their completion prior to delivery of the first airplane or issuance of a standard certificate of airworthiness, whichever occurs later.

[Amdt. 23-26, 45 FR 60171, Sept. 11, 1980]

MARKINGS AND PLACARDS

§ 23.1541 General.

(a) The airplane must contain—

(1) The markings and placards specified in §§ 23.1545 through 23.1567; and

(2) Any additional information, instrument markings, and placards required for the safe operation if it has unusual design, operating, or handling characteristics.

(b) Each marking and placard prescribed in paragraph (a) of this section—

(1) Must be displayed in a conspicuous place; and

(2) May not be easily erased, disfigured, or obscured.

(c) For airplanes which are to be certificated in more than one category—

(1) The applicant must select one category upon which the placards and markings are to be based; and

(2) The placards and marking information for all categories in which the airplane is to be certificated must be furnished in the Airplane Flight Manual.

[Doc. No. 4080, 29 FR 17955, Dec. 18, 1964; 30 FR 258, Jan. 9, 1965, as amended by Amdt. 23-21, 43 FR 2319, Jan. 16, 1978]

§ 23.1543 Instrument markings: general.

For each instrument—

(a) When markings are on the cover glass of the instrument, there must be means to maintain the correct alignment of the glass cover with the face of the dial; and

(b) Each arc and line must be wide enough and located to be clearly visible to the pilot.

§ 23.1545 Airspeed indicator.

(a) Each airspeed indicator must be marked as specified in paragraph (b) of this section, with the marks located at the corresponding indicated airspeeds.

(b) The following markings must be made:

(1) For the never-exceed speed V_{NE}, a radial red line.

(2) For the caution range, a yellow arc extending from the red line specified in paragraph (b)(1) of this section to the upper limit of the green arc specified in paragraph (b)(3) of this section.

(3) For the normal operating range, a green arc with the lower limit at V_{S1} with maximum weight and with landing gear and wing flaps retracted, and the upper limit at the maximum structural cruising speed V_{NO} established under § 23.1505(b).

(4) For the flap operating range, a white arc with the lower limit at V_{S0} at the maximum weight, and the upper limit at the flaps-extended speed V_{FE} established under § 23.1511.

(5) For the one-engine-inoperative best rate of climb speed, V_y, a blue sector extending from the V_y speed at sea level to the V_y speed at—

(i) An altitude of 5,000 feet, if the one-engine-inoperative best rate of climb at that altitude is less than 100 feet per minute, or

(ii) The highest 1,000-foot altitude (at or above 5,000 feet) at which the one-engine-inoperative best rate of climb is 100 feet per minute or more.

Each side of the sector must be labeled to show the altitude for the corresponding V_y.

(6) For the minimum control speed (one-engine-inoperative), V_{mc}', a red radial line.

(c) If V_{NE} or V_{NO} vary with altitude, there must be means to indicate to the pilot the appropriate limitations throughout the operating altitude range.

(d) Paragraphs (b)(1) through (b)(3) and paragraph (c) of this section do not apply to aircraft for which a maximum operating speed V_{MO}/M_{MO} is established under § 23.1505(c). For those aircraft there must either be a maximum allowable airspeed indication showing the variation of V_{MO}/M_{MO} with altitude or compressibility limitations (as appropriate), or a radial red line marking for V_{MO}/M_{MO} must be made at lowest value of V_{MO}/M_{MO} established for any altitude up to the maximum operating altitude for the airplane.

[Doc. No. 4080, 29 FR 17955, Dec. 18, 1964, as amended by Amdt. 23-3, 30 FR 14240, Nov. 13, 1965; Amdt. 23-7, 34 FR 13097, Aug. 13, 1969; Amdt. 23-23, 43 FR 50593, Oct. 30, 1978]

§23.1547 Magnetic direction indicator.

(a) A placard meeting the requirements of this section must be installed on or near the magnetic direction indicator.

(b) The placard must show the calibration of the instrument in level flight with the engines operating.

(c) The placard must state whether the calibration was made with radio receivers on or off.

(d) Each calibration reading must be in terms of magnetic headings in not more than 30 degree increments.

(e) If a magnetic nonstabilized direction indicator can have a deviation of more than 10 degrees caused by the operation of electrical equipment, the placard must state which electrical loads, or combination of loads, would cause a deviation of more than 10 degrees when turned on.

[Doc. No. 4080, 29 FR 17955, Dec. 18, 1964; 30 FR 258, Jan. 9, 1965, as amended by Amdt. 23-20, 42 FR 36969, July 18, 1977]

§23.1549 Powerplant instruments.

For each required powerplant instrument, as appropriate to the type of instruments—

(a) Each maximum and, if applicable, minimum safe operating limit must be marked with a red radial or a red line;

(b) Each normal operating range must be marked with a green arc or green line, not extending beyond the maximum and minimum safe limits;

(c) Each takeoff and precautionary range must be marked with a yellow arc or a yellow line; and

(d) Each engine or propeller range that is restricted because of excessive vibration stresses must be marked with red arcs or red lines.

[Amdt. 23-12, 41 FR 55466, Dec. 20, 1976, as amended by Amdt. 23-28, 47 FR 13315, Mar. 29, 1982]

§23.1551 Oil quantity indicator.

Each oil quantity indicator must be marked in sufficient increments to indicate readily and accurately the quantity of oil.

§23.1553 Fuel quantity indicator.

If the unusable fuel supply for any tank exceeds one gallon, or five percent of the tank capacity, whichever is greater, a red arc must be marked on its indicator extending from the calibrated zero reading to the lowest reading obtainable in level flight.

§23.1555 Control markings.

(a) Each cockpit control, other than primary flight controls and simple push button type starter switches, must be plainly marked as to its function and method of operation.

(b) Each secondary control must be suitably marked.

(c) For powerplant fuel controls—

(1) Each fuel tank selector control must be marked to indicate the position corresponding to each tank and to each existing cross feed position;

(2) If safe operation requires the use of any tanks in a specific sequence, that sequence must be marked on or near the selector for those tanks;

(3) The conditions under which the full amount of usable fuel in any restricted usage fuel tank can safely be used must be stated on a placard adjacent to the selector valve for that tank; and

(4) Each valve control for any engine of a multiengine airplane must be marked to indicate the position corresponding to each engine controlled.

(d) Usable fuel capacity must be marked as follows:

(1) For fuel systems having no selector controls, the usable fuel capacity of the system must be indicated at the fuel quantity indicator.

(2) For fuel systems having selector controls, the usable fuel capacity available at each selector control position must be indicated near the selector control.

(e) For accessory, auxiliary, and emergency controls—

(1) If retractable landing gear is used, the indicator required by § 23.729 must be marked so that the pilot can, at any time, ascertain that the wheels are secured in the extreme positions; and

(2) Each emergency control must be red and must be marked as to method of operation.

[Doc. No. 4080, 29 FR 17955, Dec. 18, 1964; 30 FR 258, Jan. 9, 1965, as amended by Amdt. 23-21, 43 FR 2319, Jan. 16, 1978]

§ 23.1557 Miscellaneous markings and placards.

(a) *Baggage and cargo compartments, and ballast location.* Each baggage and cargo compartment, and each ballast location, must have a placard stating any limitations on contents, including weight, that are necessary under the loading requirements.

(b) *Seats.* If the maximum allowable weight to be carried in a seat is less than 170 pounds, a placard stating the lesser weight must be permanently attached to the seat structure.

(c) *Fuel and oil filler openings.* The following apply:

(1) Fuel filler openings must be marked at or near the filler cover with—

(i) The word "fuel";

(ii) For reciprocating engine powered airplanes, the minimum fuel grade;

(iii) For turbine engine powered airplanes, the permissible fuel designations; and

(iv) For pressure fueling systems, the maximum permissible fueling supply pressure and the maximum permissible defueling pressure.

(2) Oil filler openings must be marked at or near the filler cover with the word "oil."

(d) *Emergency exit placards.* Each placard and operating control for each emergency exit must be red. A placard must be near each emergency exit control and must clearly indicate the location of that exit and its method of operation.

(e) The system voltage of each direct current installation must be clearly marked adjacent to its exernal power connection.

(f) *Unusable fuel.* If the unusable fuel supply in any tank exceeds five percent of the tank capacity, or one

gallon, whichever is greater, a placard must be installed next to the fuel quantity indicator for that tank, stating that the fuel remaining when the quantity indicator reads "zero" in level flight cannot be used safely in flight.

[Doc. No. 4080, 29 FR 17955, Dec. 18, 1964; as amended by Amdt. 23-21, 42 FR 15042, Mar. 17, 1977; Amdt. 23-23, 43 FR 50594, Oct. 30, 1978]

§ 23.1559 Operating limitations placard.

(a) There must be a placard in clear view of the pilot stating—

(1) For airplanes certificated in one category:

The markings and placards installed in this airplane contain operating limitations which must be complied with when operating this airplane in the ——————— category. (Insert category.) Other operating limitations which must be complied with when operating this airplane in this category are contained in the Airplane Flight Manual.

(2) For airplanes certificated in more than one category:

The markings and placards installed in this airplane contain operating limitations which must be complied with when operating this airplane in the ———— category. (Insert category.) Other operating limitations which must be complied with when operating this airplane in this category or in the ———— category are contained in the Airplane Flight Manual. (Insert category or categories.)

(b) There must be a placard in clear view of the pilot that specifies the kind of operations (such as VFR, IFR, day, or night) and the meteorological conditions (such as icing conditions) to which the operation of the airplane is limited, or from which it is prohibited, by the equipment installed.

[Doc. No. 4080, 29 FR 17955, Dec. 18, 1964; 30 FR 258, Jan. 9, 1965, as amended by Amdt. 23-13, 37 FR 20023, Sept. 23, 1972; 37 FR 21320, Oct. 7, 1972; Amdt. 23-21, 43 FR 2319, Jan. 16, 1978]

§ 23.1561 Safety equipment.

(a) Safety equipment must be plainly marked as to method of operation.

(b) Stowage provisions for required safety equipment must be marked for the benefit of occupants.

§ 23.1563 Airspeed placards.

There must be an airspeed placard in clear view of the pilot and as close as practicable to the airspeed indicator. This placard must list—

(a) The design maneuvering speed V_A; and

(b) The maximum landing gear operating speed V_{LO}.

[Amdt. 23–7, 34 FR 13097, Aug. 13, 1969]

§ 23.1567 Flight maneuver placard.

(a) For normal category airplanes, there must be a placard in front of and in clear view of the pilot stating: "No acrobatic maneuvers, including spins, approved."

(b) For utility category airplanes, there must be—

(1) A placard in clear view of the pilot stating: "Acrobatic maneuvers are limited to the following ——" (list approved maneuvers and the recommended entry speed for each); and

(2) For those airplanes that do not meet the spin requirements for acrobatic category airplanes, an additional placard in clear view of the pilot stating: "Spins Prohibited."

(c) For acrobatic category airplanes, there must be a placard in clear view of the pilot listing the approved acrobatic maneuvers and the recommended entry airspeed for each. If inverted flight maneuvers are not approved, the placard must bear a notation to this effect.

[Doc. No. 4080, 29 FR 17955, Dec. 18, 1964; 30 FR 258, Jan. 9, 1965, as amended by Amdt. 23–13, 37 FR 20023, Sept. 23, 1972; Amdt. 23–21, 43 FR 2319, Jan. 16, 1978]

AIRPLANE FLIGHT MANUAL AND
APPROVED MANUAL MATERIAL

§ 23.1581 General.

(a) *Furnishing information.* An Airplane Flight Manual must be furnished with each airplane, and it must contain the following:

(1) Information required by §§ 23.1583 through 23.1589.

(2) Other information that is necessary for safe operation because of design, operating, or handling characteristics.

(b) *Approved information.* (1) Except as provided in paragraph (b)(2) of this section, each part of the Airplane Flight Manual containing information prescribed in §§ 23.1583 through 23.1589 must be approved, segregated, identified and clearly distinguished from each unapproved part of that Airplane Flight Manual.

(2) The requirements of paragraph (b)(1) of this section do not apply if the following is met:

(i) Each part of the Airplane Flight Manual containing information prescribed in § 23.1583 must be limited to such information, and must be approved, identified, and clearly distinguished from each other part of the Airplane Flight Manual.

(ii) The information prescribed in §§ 23.1585 through 23.1589 must be determined in accordance with the applicable requirements of this part and presented in its entirety in a manner acceptable to the Administrator.

(3) Each page of the Airplane Flight Manual containing information prescribed in this section must be of a type that is not easily erased, disfigured, or misplaced, and is capable of being inserted in a manual provided by the applicant, or in a folder, or in any other permanent binder.

(c) [Reserved]

(d) *Table of contents.* Each Airplane Flight Manual must include a table of contents if the complexity of the manual indicates a need for it.

(e) Provision must be made for stowing the Airplane Flight Manual in a suitable fixed container which is readily accessible to the pilot.

[Amdt. 23–21, 43 FR 2319, Jan. 16, 1978, as amended by Amdt. 23–34, 52 FR 1834, Jan. 15, 1987]

§ 23.1583 Operating limitations.

(a) *Airspeed limitations.* The following information must be furnished:

(1) Information necessary for the marking of the airspeed limits on the indicator as required in § 23.1545, and the significance of each of those limits and of the color coding used on the indicator.

(2) The speeds V_A, V_{LE}, and V_{LO} and their significance.

(3) In addition, for commuter category airplanes—

(i) The maximum operating limit speed, V_{MO}/M_{MO} and a statement that this speed may not be deliberately exceeded in any regime of flight (climb, cruise, or descent) unless a higher speed is authorized for flight test or pilot training;

(ii) If an airspeed limitation is based upon compressibility effects, a statement to this effect and information as to any symptoms, the probable behavior of the airplane, and the recommended recovery procedures; and

(iii) The airspeed limits must be shown in terms of V_{MO}/M_{MO} instead of V_{NO} and V_{NE}.

(b) *Powerplant limitations.* The following information must be furnished:

(1) Limitations required by § 23.1521.

(2) Explanation of the limitations, when appropriate.

(3) Information necessary for marking the instruments required by § 23.1549 through § 23.1553.

(c) *Weight.* The airplane flight manual must include—

(1) The maximum weight; and

(2) The maximum landing weight, if the design landing weight selected by the applicant is less than the maximum weight.

(3) In addition, for commuter category airplanes, the maximum takeoff weight for each altitude, ambient temperature, and required takeoff runway length within the range selected by the applicant may not exceed the weight at which—

(i) The all-engine-operating distance determined under § 23.59 or the accelerate-stop distance determined under § 23.55, whichever is greater, is equal to the available runway length;

(ii) The airplane complies with the one-engine-inoperative takeoff distance requirements of § 23.59; and

(iii) The airplane complies with the one-engine-inoperative takeoff and en route climb requirements of §§ 23.57 and 23.67.

(4) In addition, for commuter category airplanes, the maximum landing weight for each altitude, ambient temperature, and required landing runway length, within the range selected by the applicant. The maximum landing weights may not exceed:

(i) The weight at which the landing distance is determined under § 23.75; or

(ii) The weight at which compliance with § 23.77 is shown.

(d) *Center of gravity.* The established center of gravity limits must be furnished.

(e) *Maneuvers.* The following authorized maneuvers, appropriate airspeed limitations, and unauthorized maneuvers must be furnished as prescribed in this section.

(1) *Normal category airplanes.* For normal category airplanes, acrobatic maneuvers, including spins, are unauthorized. If the airplane has been shown to be "characteristically incapable of spinning" under § 23.221(d), a statement to this effect must be entered. Other normal category airplanes must be placarded against spins.

(2) *Utility category airplanes.* For utility category airplanes, authorized maneuvers shown in the type flight tests must be furnished, together with recommended entry speeds. No other maneuver is authorized. If the airplane has been shown to be "characteristically incapable of spinning" under § 23.221(d), a statement to this effect must be entered.

(3) *Acrobatic category airplanes.* For acrobatic category airplanes, the approved flight maneuvers shown in the type flight tests must be included, together with recommended entry speeds. A placard listing the use of the controls required to recover from spinning maneuvers must be in the cockpit.

(4) *Commuter category airplanes.* For commuter category airplanes, acrobatic maneuvers, including spins, are unauthorized.

(f) *Flight load factor.* The positive limit load factors, in *g*'s, must be furnished.

(g) *Flight crew.* If a flight crew of more than one is required for safety, the number and functions of the minimum flight crew must be furnished.

(h) *Kinds of operation.* The kinds of operation (such as VFR, IFR, day, or night) in which the airplane may or may not be used, and the meteorological conditions under which it may or may not be used, must be furnished.

Any installed equipment that affects any operating limitation must be listed and identified as to operational function.

(i)—(j) [Reserved]

(k) *Maximum operating altitude.* The maximum altitude established under § 23.1527 must be furnished.

(l) *Maximum passenger seating configuration.* The maximum passenger seating configuration must be furnished.

[Doc. No. 4080, 29 FR 17955, Dec. 18, 1964, as amended by Amdt. 23-7, 34 FR 13097, Aug. 13, 1969; Amdt. 23-10, 36 FR 2864, Feb. 11, 1971; Amdt. 23-21, 43 FR 2320, Jan. 16, 1978; Amdt. 23-23, 43 FR 50594, Oct. 30, 1978; Amdt. 23-34, 52 FR 1834, Jan. 15, 1987]

§ 23.1585   **Operating procedures.**

(a) For each airplane, information concerning normal and emergency procedures and other pertinent information necessary to safe operation must be furnished, including—

(1) The demonstrated crosswind velocity and procedures and information pertinent to operation of the airplane in crosswinds; and

(2) The airspeeds, procedures, and information pertinent to the use of the following airspeeds:

(i) The recommended climb speed and any variation with altitude.

(ii) V_x and any variation with altitude.

(iii) The approach speeds, including speeds for transition to the balked landing condition.

(b) [Reserved]

(c) For multiengine airplanes, the information must include:

(1) Procedures for maintaining or recovering control of the airplane with one engine inoperative at speeds above and below V_{MC}.

(2) Procedures for making a landing with one engine inoperative and procedures for making a go-around with one engine inoperative, if this latter maneuver can be performed safely; otherwise, a warning against attempting the maneuver.

(3) Procedures for obtaining the best performance with one engine inoperative, including the effects of the airplane configuration.

(4) Procedures for takeoff determined in accordance with § 23.51.

(d) For multiengine airplanes, information identifying each operating condition in which the fuel system independence prescribed in § 23.953 is necessary for safety must be furnished, together with instructions for placing the fuel system in a configuration used to show compliance with that section.

(e) For each airplane showing compliance with § 23.1353 (g)(2) or (g)(3), the operating procedures for disconnecting the battery from its charging source must be furnished.

(f) If the unusable fuel supply in any tank exceeds 5 percent of the tank capacity, or 1 gallon, whichever is greater, information must be furnished which indicates that when the fuel quantity indicator reads "zero" in level flight, any fuel remaining in the fuel tank cannot be used safely in flight.

(g) Information on the total quantity of usable fuel for each fuel tank must be furnished.

(h) In addition, for commuter category airplanes, the procedures for restarting turbine engines in flight, including the effects of altitude, must be set forth in the Airplane Flight Manual.

[Doc. No. 4080, 29 FR 17955, Dec. 18, 1964, as amended by Amdt. 23-3, 30 FR 14240, Nov. 13, 1965; Amdt. 23-5, 32 FR 6912, May 5, 1967; Amdt. 23-7, 34 FR 13097, Aug. 13, 1969; Amdt. 23-21, 43 FR 2320, Jan. 16, 1978; Amdt. 23-23, 43 FR 50594, Oct. 30, 1978; Amdt. 23-34, 52 FR 1835, Jan. 15, 1987]

§ 23.1587   **Performance information.**

(a) *General.* For each airplane, the following information must be furnished:

(1) Any loss of altitude more than 100 feet, or any pitch more than 30 degrees below flight level, occurring during the recovery part of the maneuver prescribed in § 23.201(c).

(2) The conditions under which the full amount of usable fuel in each tank can safely be used.

(3) The stalling speed, V_{s_0}, at maximum weight.

(4) The stalling speed, V_{s_t}, at maximum weight and with landing gear and wing flaps retracted and the effect

upon this stalling speed of angles of bank up to 60 degrees.

(5) The takeoff distance determined under § 23.51, the airspeed at the 50-foot height, the airplane configuration (if pertinent), the kind of surface in the tests, and the pertinent information with respect to cowl flap position, use of flight path control devices, and use of the landing gear retraction system.

(6) The landing distance determined under § 23.75, the airplane configuration (if pertinent), the kind of surface used in the tests, and the pertinent information with respect to flap position and the use of flight path control devices.

(7) The steady rate or gradient of climb determined under §§ 23.65 and 23.77, the airspeed, power, and the airplane configuration.

(8) The calculated approximate effect on takeoff distance (paragraph (a)(5) of this section), landing distance (paragraph (a)(6) of this section), and steady rates of climb (paragraph (a)(7) of this section), of variations in—

(i) Altitude from sea level to 8,000 feet; and

(ii) Temperature at these altitudes from 60 degrees F below standard to 40 degrees F above standard.

(9) For reciprocating engine-powered airplanes, the maximum atmospheric temperature at which compliance with the cooling provisions of §§ 23.1041 through 23.1047 is shown.

(b) *Skiplanes.* For skiplanes, a statement of the approximate reduction in climb performance may be used instead of complete new data for skiplane configuration, if—

(1) The landing gear is fixed in both landplane and skiplane configurations;

(2) The climb requirements are not critical; and

(3) The climb reduction in the skiplane configurations is small (30 to 50 feet per minute).

(c) *Multiengine airplanes.* For multiengine airplanes, the following information must be furnished:

(1) The loss of altitude during the one-engine-inoperative stall shown under § 23.205 (as measured from the altitude at which the airplane starts to pitch uncontrollably to the altitude at which level flight is regained) and the pitch angle during that maneuver.

(2) The best rate of climb speed or the minimum rate of descent speed with one engine inoperative.

(3) The speed used in showing compliance with the cooling and climb requirements of § 23.1047(d)(5), if this speed is greater than the best rate of climb speed with one engine inoperative.

(4) The steady rate or gradient of climb determined under § 23.67 and the airspeed, power, and airplane configuration.

(5) The calculated approximate effect on the climb performance determined under § 23.67 of variations in—

(i) Altitude from sea level to 8,000 feet in a standard atmosphere and cruise configuration; and

(ii) Temperature at those altitudes from 60 degrees F below standard to 40 degrees F above standard.

(d) *Commuter category airplanes.* In addition, for commuter category airplanes, the Airplane Flight Manual must contain at least the following performance information:

(1) Sufficient information so that the takeoff weight limits specified in § 23.1583 can be determined for all temperatures and altitudes within the operational limitations selected by the applicant;

(2) The conditions under which the performance information was obtained including the airspeed at the 50-foot height used to determine the landing distance as required by § 23.75;

(3) The performance information (determined by extrapolation and computed for the range of weights between the maximum landing and maximum takeoff weights) for—

(i) Climb in the landing configuration as determined by § 23.77; and

(ii) Landing distance as determined by § 23.75;

(4) Procedures information established in accordance with the limitations and other information for safe operation of the airplane in the form of recommended procedures;

(5) An explanation of significant or unusual flight and ground handling characteristics of the airplane; and

(6) Airspeed, as calibrated airspeed, corresponding to those established

while showing compliance to §23.53, Takeoff speeds.

[Amdt. 23-21, 43 FR 2320, Jan. 16, 1978, as amended by Amdt. 23-28, 47 FR 13315, Mar. 29, 1982; Amdt. 23-34, 52 FR 1835, Jan. 15, 1987]

§23.1589 Loading information.

The following loading information must be furnished:

(a) The weight and location of each item of equipment installed when the airplane was weighed under §23.25.

(b) Appropriate loading instructions for each possible loading condition between the maximum and minimum weights determined under §23.25 that can result in a center of gravity beyond—

(1) The extremes selected by the applicant;

(2) The extremes within which the structure is proven; or

(3) The extremes within which compliance with each functional requirement is shown.

APPENDIX A TO PART 23—SIMPLIFIED DESIGN LOAD CRITERIA FOR CONVENTIONAL, SINGLE-ENGINE AIRPLANES OF 6,000 POUNDS OR LESS MAXIMUM WEIGHT

A23.1 *General.*

(a) The design load criteria in this appendix are an approved equivalent of those in §§23.321 through 23.459 of this subchapter for the certification of conventional, single-engine airplanes of 6,000 pounds or less maximum weight.

(b) Unless otherwise stated, the nomenclature and symbols in this Appendix are the same as the corresponding nomenclature and symbols in Part 23.

A23.3 *Special symbols.*

n_1 = Airplane Positive Maneuvering Limit Load Factor.
n_2 = Airplane Negative Maneuvering Limit Load Factor.
n_3 = Airplane Positive Gust Limit Load Factor at V_C.
n_4 = Airplane Negative Gust Limit Load Factor at V_C.
n_{flap} = Airplane Positive Limit Load Factor With Flaps Fully Extended at V_F.

* $V_{F min}$ = Minimum Design Flap Speed = $11.0\sqrt{n_1 W/S}$ [kts]

* $V_{A min}$ = Minimum Design Maneuvering Speed = $15.0\sqrt{n_1 W/S}$ [kts]

* $V_{C min}$ = Minimum Design Cruising Speed = $17.0\sqrt{n_1 W/S}$ [kts]

* $V_{D min}$ = Minimum Design Dive Speed = $24.0\sqrt{n_1 W/S}$ [kts]

A23.5 *Certification in more than one category.*

The criteria in this appendix may be used for certification in the normal, utility, and acrobatic categories, or in any combination of these categories. If certification in more than one category is desired, the design category weights must be selected to make the term "$n_1 W$" constant for all categories or greater for one desired category than for others. The wings and control surfaces (including wing flaps and tabs) need only be investigated for the maximum value of "$n_1 W$", or for the category corresponding to the maximum design weight, where "$n_1 W$" is constant. If the acrobatic category is selected, a special unsymmetrical flight load investigation in accordance with paragraphs A23.9(c)(2) and A23.11(c)(2) of this appendix must be completed. The wing, wing carrythrough, and the horizontal tail structures must be checked for this condition. The basic fuselage structure need only be investigated for the highest load factor design category selected. The local supporting structure for dead weight items need only be designed for the highest load factor imposed when the particular items are installed in the airplane. The engine mount, however, must be designed for a higher side load factor, if certification in the acrobatic category is desired, than that required for certification in the normal and utility categories. When designing for landing loads, the landing gear and the airplane as a whole need only be investigated for the category corresponding to the maximum design weight. These simplifications apply to single-engine aircraft of conventional types for which experience is available, and the Administrator may require additional investigations for aircraft with unusual design features.

A23.7 *Flight loads.*

(a) Each flight load may be considered independent of altitude and, except for the local supporting structure for dead weight items, only the maximum design weight conditions must be investigated.

(b) Table 1 and figures 3 and 4 of this Appendix must be used to determine values of n_1, n_2, n_3, and n_4, corresponding to the maximum design weights in the desired categories.

(c) Figures 1 and 2 of this Appendix must be used to determine values of n_3 and n_4 corresponding to the minimum flying weights in the desired categories, and, if these load factors are greater than the load factors at the design weight, the supporting structure for dead weight items must be substantiated for the resulting higher load factors.

(d) Each specified wing and tail loading is independent of the center of gravity range. The applicant, however, must select a c.g. range, and the basic fuselage structure must be investigated for the most adverse dead weight loading conditions for the c.g. range selected.

(e) The following loads and loading conditions are the minimums for which strength must be provided in the structure:

(1) *Airplane equilibrium.* The aerodynamic wing loads may be considered to act normal to the relative wind, and to have a magnitude of 1.05 times the airplane normal loads (as determined from paragraphs A23.9 (b) and (c) of this appendix) for the positive flight conditions and a magnitude equal to the airplane normal loads for the negative conditions. Each chordwise and normal component of this wing load must be considered.

(2) *Minimum design airspeeds.* The minimum design airspeeds may be chosen by the applicant except that they may not be less than the minimum speeds found by using figure 3 of this Appendix. In addition, V_{Cmin} need not exceed values of 0.9 V_H actually obtained at sea level for the lowest design weight category for which certification is desired. In computing these minimum design airspeeds, n_1 may not be less than 3.8.

(3) *Flight load factor.* The limit flight load factors specified in Table 1 of this Appendix represent the ratio of the aerodynamic force component (acting normal to the assumed longitudinal axis of the airplane) to the weight of the airplane. A positive flight load factor is an aerodynamic force acting upward, with respect to the airplane.

A23.9   *Flight conditions.*

(a) *General.* Each design condition in paragraphs (b) and (c) of this section must be used to assure sufficient strength for each condition of speed and load factor on or within the boundary of a $V-n$ diagram for the airplane similar to the diagram in figure 4 of this Appendix. This diagram must also be used to determine the airplane structural operating limitations as specified

in §§ 23.1501(c) through 23.1513 and § 23.1519.

(b) *Symmetrical flight conditions.* The airplane must be designed for symmetrical flight conditions as follows:

(1) The airplane must be designed for at least the four basic flight conditions, "A", "D", "E", and "G" as noted on the flight envelope of figure 4 of this Appendix. In addition, the following requirements apply:

(i) The design limit flight load factors corresponding to conditions "D" and "E" of figure 4 must be at least as great as those specified in Table 1 and figure 4 of this Appendix, and the design speed for these conditions must be at least equal to the value of V_D found from figure 3 of this Appendix.

(ii) For conditions "A" and "G" of figure 4, the load factors must correspond to those specified in Table 1 of this Appendix, and the design speeds must be computed using these load factors with the maximum static lift coefficient C_{NA} determined by the applicant. However, in the absence of more precise computations, these latter conditions may be based on a value of $C_{NA} = \pm 1.35$ and the design speed for condition "A" may be less than V_{Amin}.

(iii) Conditions "C" and "F" of figure 4 need only be investigated when n_3W/S or n_4W/S are greater than n_1W/S or n_2W/S of this Appendix, respectively.

(2) If flaps or other high lift devices intended for use at the relatively low airspeed of approach, landing, and takeoff, are installed, the airplane must be designed for the two flight conditions corresponding to the values of limit flap-down factors specified in Table 1 of this Appendix with the flaps fully extended at not less than the design flap speed V_{Fmin} from figure 3 of this Appendix.

(c) *Unsymmetrical flight conditions.* Each affected structure must be designed for unsymmetrical loadings as follows:

(1) The aft fuselage-to-wing attachment must be designed for the critical vertical surface load determined in accordance with paragraph SA23.11(c) (1) and (2) of this Appendix.

(2) The wing and wing carry-through structures must be designed for 100 percent of condition "A" loading on one side of the plane of symmetry and 70 percent on the opposite side for certification in the normal and utility categories, or 60 percent on the opposite side for certification in the acrobatic category.

(3) The wing and wing carry-through structures must be designed for the loads resulting from a combination of 75 percent of the positive maneuvering wing loading on both sides of the plane of symmetry and the maximum wing torsion resulting from aileron displacement. The effect of aileron displacement on wing torsion at V_C or V_A using

the basic airfoil moment coefficient modified over the aileron portion of the span, must be computed as follows:

(i) $Cm = Cm + 0.01\delta\mu$ (up aileron side) wing basic airfoil.

(ii) $Cm = Cm - 0.01\delta\mu$ (down aileron side) wing basic airfoil, where $\delta\mu$ is the up aileron deflection and δd is the down aileron deflection.

(4) Δ critical, which is the sum of $\delta\mu + \delta d$ must be computed as follows:

(i) Compute Δ_a and Δ_b from the formulas:

$$\Delta_a = \frac{V_A}{V_C} \times \Delta_p \quad \text{and}$$

$$\Delta_b = 0.5 \frac{V_A}{V_D} \times \Delta_p$$

Where Δ_p = the maximum total deflection (sum of both aileron deflections) at V_A with V_A, V_C, and V_D described in subparagraph (2) of § 23.7(e) of this Appendix.

(ii) Compute K from the formula:

$$K = \frac{(C_m - 0.01\delta_b) \, V_D{}^2}{(C_m - 0.01\delta_a) \, V_C{}^2}$$

where δ_a is the down aileron deflection corresponding to Δ_a, and δ_b is the down aileron deflection corresponding to Δb as computed in step (i).

(iii) If K is less than 1.0, Δ_a is Δ critical and must be used to determine δ_u and δd. In this case, V_C is the critical speed which must be used in computing the wing torsion loads over the aileron span.

(iv) If K is equal to or greater than 1.0, Δ_b is Δ critical and must be used to determine δ_u and δ_d. In this case, V_d is the critical speed which must be used in computing the wing torsion loads over the aileron span.

(d) *Supplementary conditions; rear lift truss; engine torque; side load on engine mount.* Each of the following supplementary conditions must be investigated:

(1) In designing the rear lift truss, the special condition specified in § 23.369 may be investigated instead of condition "G" of figure 4 of this Appendix. If this is done, and if certification in more than one category is desired, the value of W/S used in the formula appearing in § 23.369 must be that for the category corresponding to the maximum gross weight.

(2) Each engine mount and its supporting structures must be designed for the maximum limit torque corresponding to METO power and propeller speed acting simultaneously with the limit loads resulting from

the maximum positive maneuvering flight load factor n_1. The limit torque must be obtained by multiplying the mean torque by a factor of 1.33 for engines with five or more cylinders. For 4, 3, and 2 cylinder engines, the factor must be 2, 3, and 4, respectively.

(3) Each engine mount and its supporting structure must be designed for the loads resulting from a lateral limit load factor of not less than 1.47 for the normal and utility categories, or 2.0 for the acrobatic category.

A23.11 *Control surface loads.*

(a) *General.* Each control surface load must be determined using the criteria of paragraph (b) of this section and must lie within the simplified loadings of paragraph (c) of this section.

(b) *Limit pilot forces.* In each control surface loading condition described in paragraphs (c) through (e) of this section, the airloads on the movable surfaces and the corresponding deflections need not exceed those which could be obtained in flight by employing the maximum limit pilot forces specified in the table in § 23.397(b). If the surface loads are limited by these maximum limit pilot forces, the tabs must either be considered to be deflected to their maximum travel in the direction which would assist the pilot or the deflection must correspond to the maximum degree of "out of trim" expected at the speed for the condition under consideration. The tab load, however, need not exceed the value specified in Table 2 of this Appendix.

(c) *Surface loading conditions.* Each surface loading condition must be investigated as follows:

(1) Simplified limit surface loadings and distributions for the horizontal tail, vertical tail, aileron, wing flaps, and trim tabs are specified in Table 2 and figures 5 and 6 of this Appendix. If more than one distribution is given, each distribution must be investigated.

(2) If certification in the acrobatic category is desired, the horizontal tail must be investigated for an unsymmetrical load of 100 percent *w* on one side of the airplane centerline and 50 percent on the other side of the airplane centerline.

(d) *Outboard fins.* Outboard fins must meet the requirements of § 23.455.

(e) *Special devices.* Special devices must meet the requirements of § 23.459.

A23.13 *Control system loads.*

(a) *Primary flight controls and systems.* Each primary flight control and system must be designed as follows:

(1) The flight control system and its supporting structure must be designed for loads corresponding to 125 percent of the computed hinge moments of the movable control

surface in the conditions prescribed in A23.11 of this Appendix. In addition—

(i) The system limit loads need not exceed those that could be produced by the pilot and automatic devices operating the controls; and

(ii) The design must provide a rugged system for service use, including jamming, ground gusts, taxiing downwind, control inertia, and friction.

(2) Acceptable maximum and minimum limit pilot forces for elevator, aileron, and rudder controls are shown in the table in § 23.397(b). These pilots loads must be assumed to act at the appropriate control grips or pads as they would under flight conditions, and to be reacted at the attachments of the control system to the control surface horn.

(b) *Dual controls.* If there are dual controls, the systems must be designed for pilots operating in opposition, using individual pilot loads equal to 75 percent of those obtained in accordance with paragraph (a) of this section, except that individual pilot loads may not be less than the minimum limit pilot forces shown in the table in § 23.397(b).

(c) *Ground gust conditions.* Ground gust conditions must meet the requirements of § 23.415.

(d) *Secondary controls and systems.* Secondary controls and systems must meet the requirements of § 23.405.

TABLE 1—LIMIT FLIGHT LOAD FACTORS

[Limit flight load factors]

Flight load factors	Normal category	Utility category	Acrobatic category
Flaps up:			
n_1	3.8	4.4	6.0
n_2	$-0.5\,n_1$		
n_3	(1)		
n_4	(2)		
Flaps down:			
n flap	$0.5\,n_1$		
n flap	3 Zero		

[1] Find n_3 from Fig. 1
[2] Find n_4 from Fig. 2
[3] Vertical wing load may be assumed equal to zero and only the flap part of the wing need be checked for this condition.

TABLE 2—AVERAGE LIMIT CONTROL SURFACE LOADING

AVERAGE LIMIT CONTROL SURFACE LOADING

SURFACE	DIRECTION OF LOADING	MAGNITUDE OF LOADING	CHORDWISE DISTRIBUTION
HORIZONTAL TAIL I	a) Up and Down	Figure 5 Curve (2)	(A)
	b) Unsymmetrical loading (Up and Down)	100% w̄ on one side airplane ℄ 65% w̄ on other side of airplane ℄ for the normal and utility categories. For the acrobatic category see A23.11(c).	(B)
VERTICAL TAIL II	a) Right and Left	Figure 5 Curve (1)	Same as (A) above
	b) Right and Left	Figure 5 Curve (1)	Same as (B) above
AILERON III	a) Up and Down	Figure 6 Curve (5)	(C)
WING FLAP IV	a) Up	Figure 6 Curve (4)	(D)
	b) Down	.25 x Up Load (a)	Same as (D) above
TRIM TAB V	a) Up and Down	Figure 6 Curve (3)	Same as (D) above

NOTE: The surface loadings I, II, III, and V above, are based on speeds $V_{A\,min}$ and $V_{D\,min}$. The loading of IV is based on $V_{F\,min}$. If values of speeds greater than these minimums are selected for design, the appropriate surface loadings must be multiplied by the ratio $\left[\frac{V_{selected}}{V_{minimum}}\right]^2$. For conditions I, II, III and V the multiplying factor used must be the higher of $\left[\frac{V_{A\,sel.}}{V_{A\,min}}\right]^2$ or $\left[\frac{V_{D\,sel.}}{V_{D\,min}}\right]^2$.

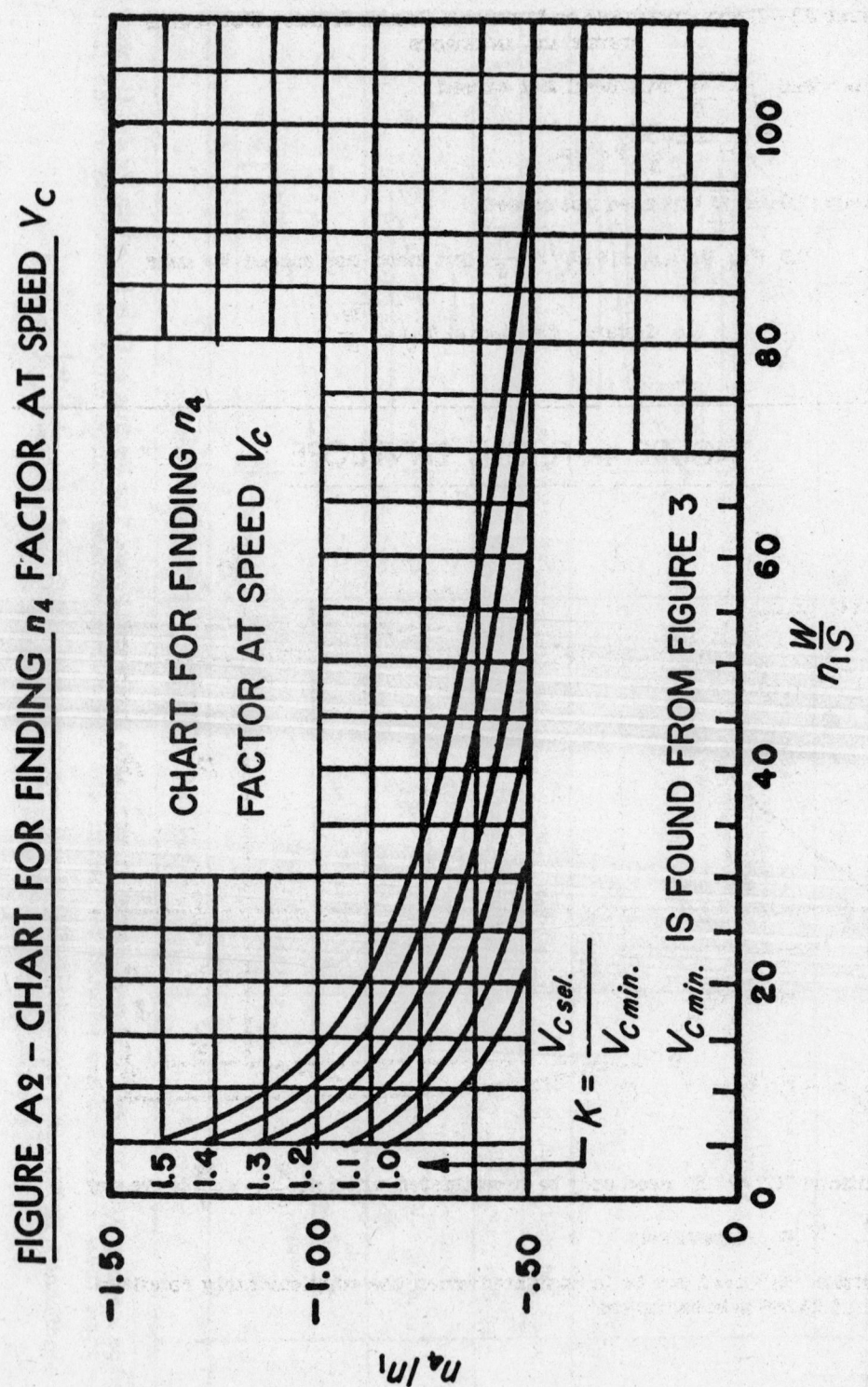

FIGURE A2 – CHART FOR FINDING n_4 FACTOR AT SPEED V_C

FIGURE A3—DETERMINATIONS OF MINIMUM DESIGN SPEEDS—EQUATIONS
SPEEDS ARE IN KNOTS

$$V_{D \ min} = 24.0 \sqrt{n_1 \frac{W}{S}} \text{ but need not exceed}$$

$$1.4 \sqrt{\frac{n_1}{3.8}} V_{C \ min};$$

$$V_{C \ min} = 17.0 \sqrt{n_1 \frac{W}{S}} \text{ but need not exceed}$$

$$0.9 \ V_H; \quad V_{A \ min} = 15.0 \sqrt{n_1 \frac{W}{S}} \text{ but need not exceed } V_C \text{ used}$$

$$\text{in design.} \quad V_{F \ min} = 11.0 \sqrt{n_1 \frac{W}{S}}$$

FIGURE 4—FLIGHT ENVELOPE

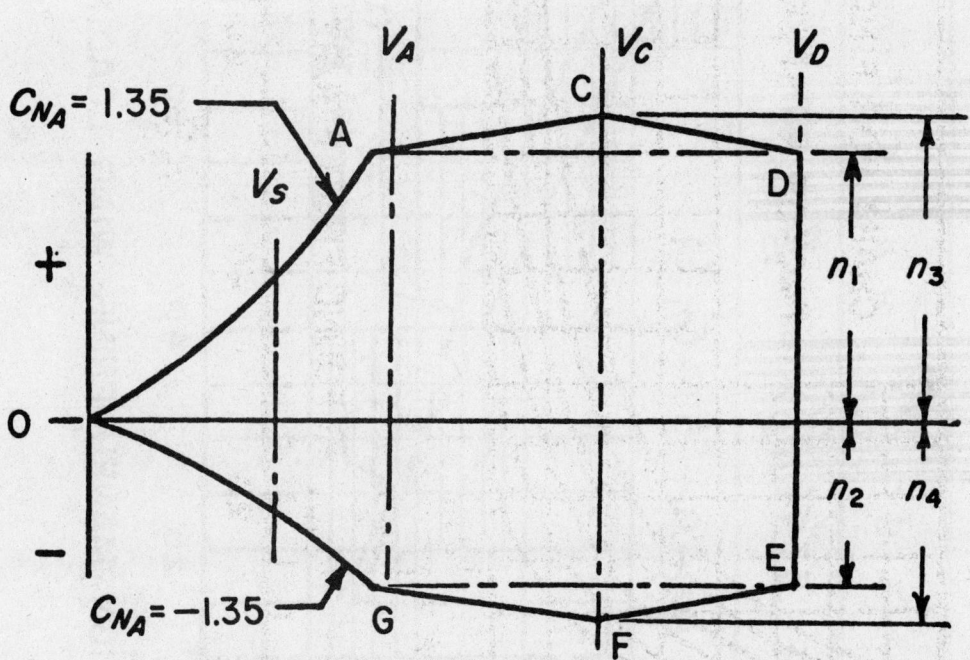

1. Conditions "C" or "F" need only be investigated when $n_3 \frac{W}{S}$ or $n_4 \frac{W}{S}$ is greater than $n_1 \frac{W}{S}$ W |ϖ, respectively.

2. Condition "G" need not be investigated when the supplementary condition specified in § 23.369 is investigated.

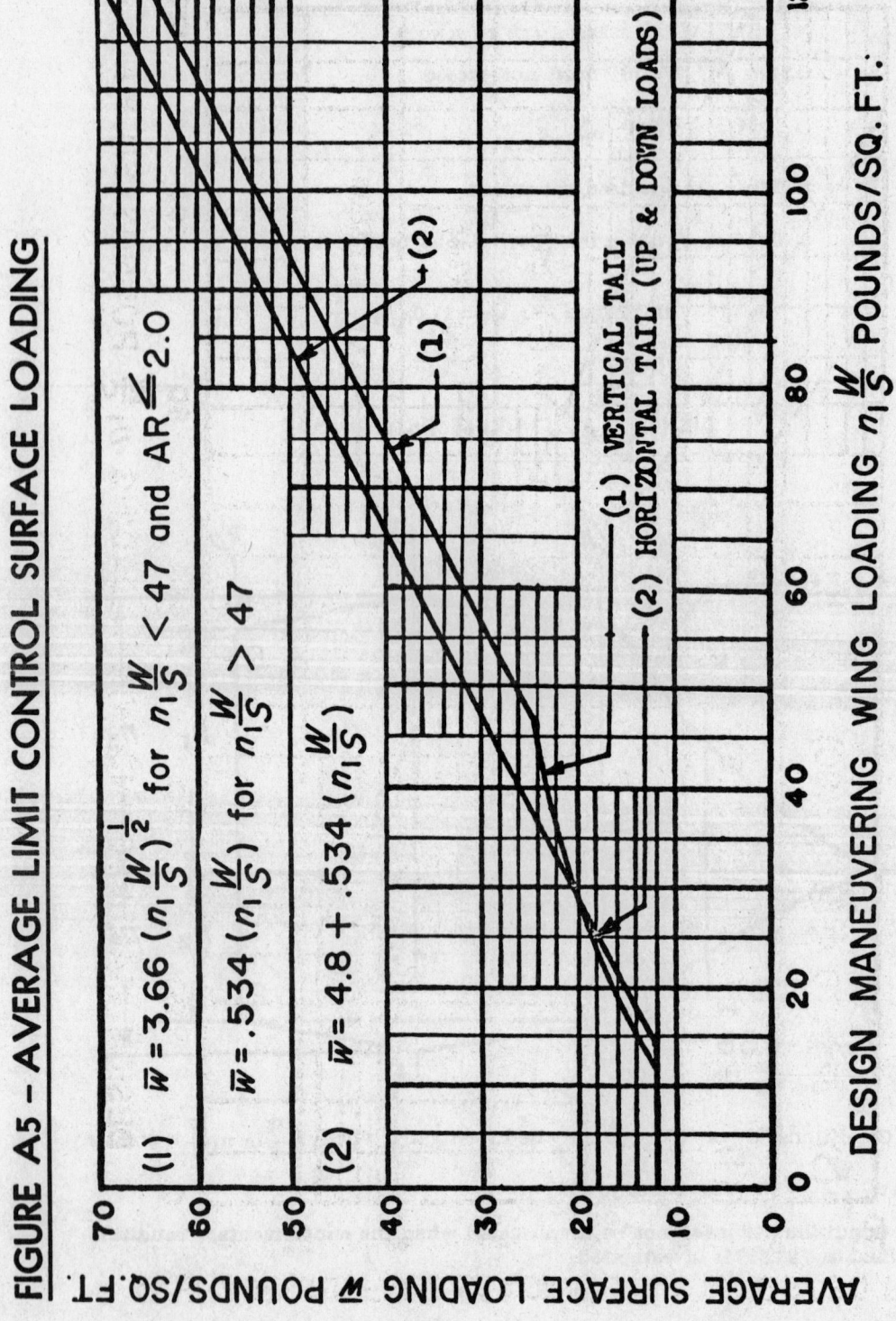

FIGURE A5 – AVERAGE LIMIT CONTROL SURFACE LOADING

$$\bar{w} = 3.66 \left(n_1 \frac{W}{S}\right)^{\frac{1}{2}} \text{ for } n_1 \frac{W}{S} < 47 \text{ and } AR \leq 2.0$$

$$\bar{w} = .534 \left(n_1 \frac{W}{S}\right) \text{ for } n_1 \frac{W}{S} > 47$$

$$\bar{w} = 4.8 + .534 \left(n_1 \frac{W}{S}\right)$$

(1) VERTICAL TAIL

(2) HORIZONTAL TAIL (UP & DOWN LOADS)

DESIGN MANEUVERING WING LOADING $n_1 \frac{W}{S}$ POUNDS/SQ. FT.

AVERAGE SURFACE LOADING $\bar{w}$ POUNDS/SQ.FT.

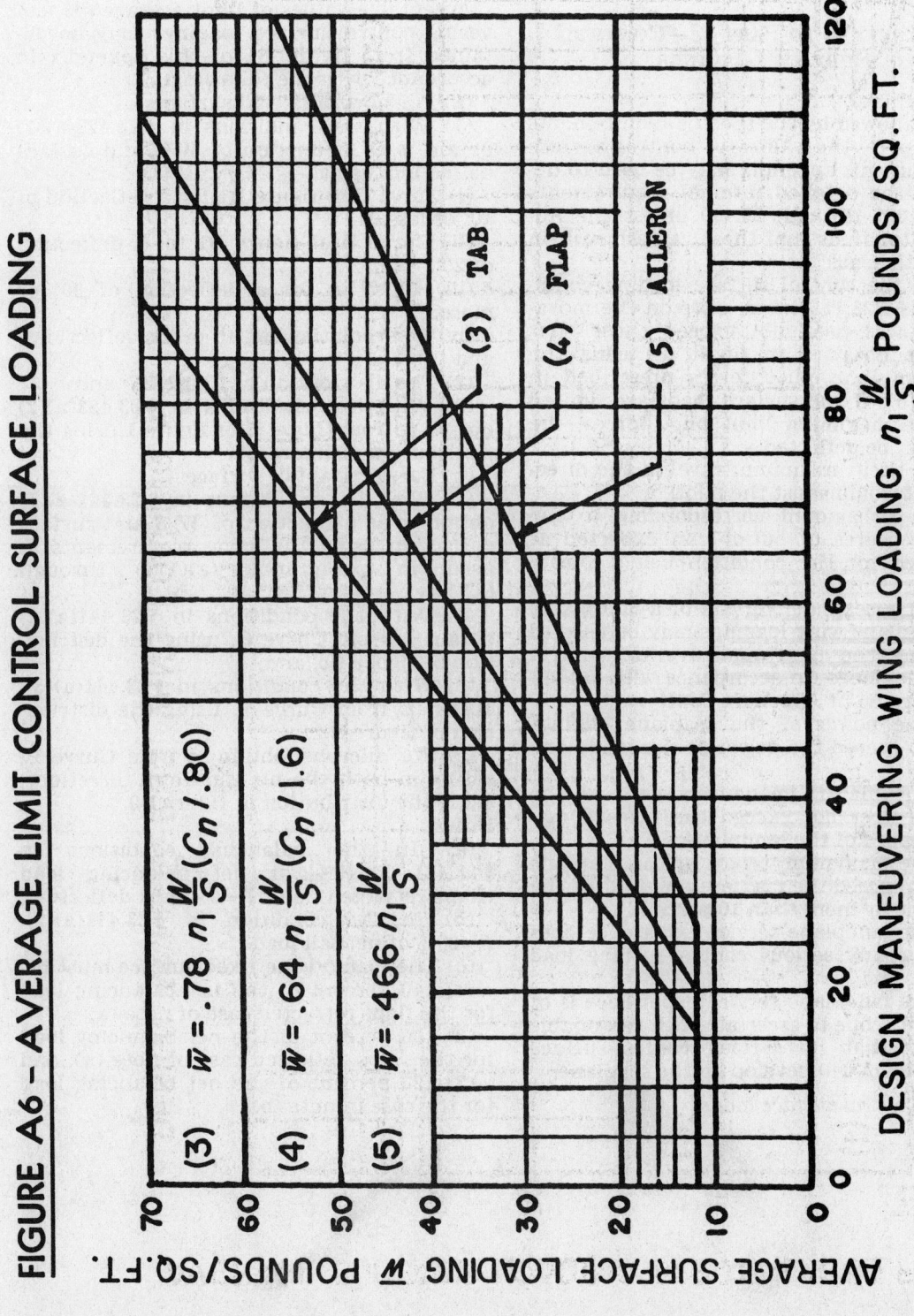

FIGURE A6 – AVERAGE LIMIT CONTROL SURFACE LOADING

$$\bar{w} = .78\, n_1 \frac{W}{S}\left(C_n / .80\right) \quad (3)$$

$$\bar{w} = .64\, n_1 \frac{W}{S}\left(C_n / 1.6\right) \quad (4)$$

$$\bar{w} = .466\, n_1 \frac{W}{S} \quad (5)$$

AVERAGE SURFACE LOADING $\bar{w}$ POUNDS/SQ.FT.

DESIGN MANEUVERING WING LOADING $n_1 \frac{W}{S}$ POUNDS/SQ. FT.

(3) TAB
(4) FLAP
(5) AILERON

[Doc. No. 4080, 29 FR 17955, Dec. 18, 1964, as amended by Amdt. 23–7, 34 FR 13097, Aug. 13, 1969; 34 FR 14727, Sept. 24, 1969; Amdt. 23–16, 40 FR 2577, Jan. 14, 1975; Amdt. 23–28, 47 FR 13315, Mar. 29, 1982]

APPENDIX B TO PART 23—CONTROL SURFACE LOADINGS

B23.1 *General.*

(a) If allowed by the specific requirements in this part, the values of control surface loading in this appendix may be used to determine the detailed rational requirements of §§ 23.397 through 23.459 unless the Administrator finds that these values result in unrealistic loads.

(b) In the control surface loading conditions of § B23.11, the airloads on the movable surfaces need not exceed those that could be obtained in flight by using the maximum limit pilot forces prescribed in § 23.397(b). If the surface loads are limited by these maximum limit pilot forces. the tabs must be deflected—

(1) To their maximum travel in the direction that would assist the pilot; or

(2) In an amount corresponding to the greatest degree of out-of-trim expected at the speed for the condition being considered.

(c) For a seaplane version of a landplane, the landplane wing loadings may be used to determine the limit maneuvering control surface loadings (in accordance with B23.11 and figure B1 of Appendix B) if—

(1) The power of the seaplane engines does not exceed the power of the landplane engines:

(2) The placard maneuver speed of the seaplane does not exceed the placard maneuver speed of the landplane;

(3) The maximum weight of the seaplane does not exceed the maximum weight of the landplane by more than 10 percent;

(4) The landplane service experience does not show any serious control-surface load problem; and

(5) The landplane service experience is of sufficient scope to ascertain with reasonable accuracy that no serious control-surface load problem will develop on the seaplane.

B23.11 *Control surface loads.*

Acceptable values of limit average maneuvering control-surface loadings may be obtained from figure B1 of this appendix in accordance with the following:

(a) For horizontal tail surfaces—

(1) With the conditions in § 23.423(a)(1) obtain w as a function of W/S and surface deflection, using—

(i) Curve C of figure B1 for a deflection of 10° or less;

(ii) Curve B of figure B1 for a deflection of 20°;

(iii) Curve A for a deflection of 30° or more;

(iv) Interpolation for all other deflections; and

(v) The distribution of figure B7; and

(2) With the conditions in § 23.423(a)(2) obtain w from Curve B of figure 1 using the distribution of figure B7.

(b) For vertical tail surfaces—

(1) With the conditions in § 23.441(a)(1) obtain w as a function of W/S and surface deflection using the same requirements as used in paragraphs (a)(1)(i) through (a)(1)(v):

(2) With the conditions in § 23.441(a)(2) obtain w from Curve C, using the distribution of figure B6; and

(3) With the conditions in § 23.441(a)(3), obtain w from Curve A, using the distribution of figure B8.

(c) For ailerons, obtain w from Curve B, acting in both the up and down directions, using the distribution of figure B9.

Notes:

(a) In the balancing conditions in § 23.421—$P=40\%$ of net balancing load (flaps retracted); and $P=0$ (flaps deflected).

(b) In the condition in § 23.441(a)(2), $P=20\%$ of net tail load.

(c) The load on the fixed surface must be:

(1) 140 percent of the net balancing load for the flaps retracted case of note (a);

(2) 100 percent of the net balancing load for the flaps deflected case of note (a); and

(3) 120 percent of the net balancing load for the case in note (b).

FIGURE B1—LIMIT AVERAGE MANUFACTURING CONTROL SURFACE LOADING

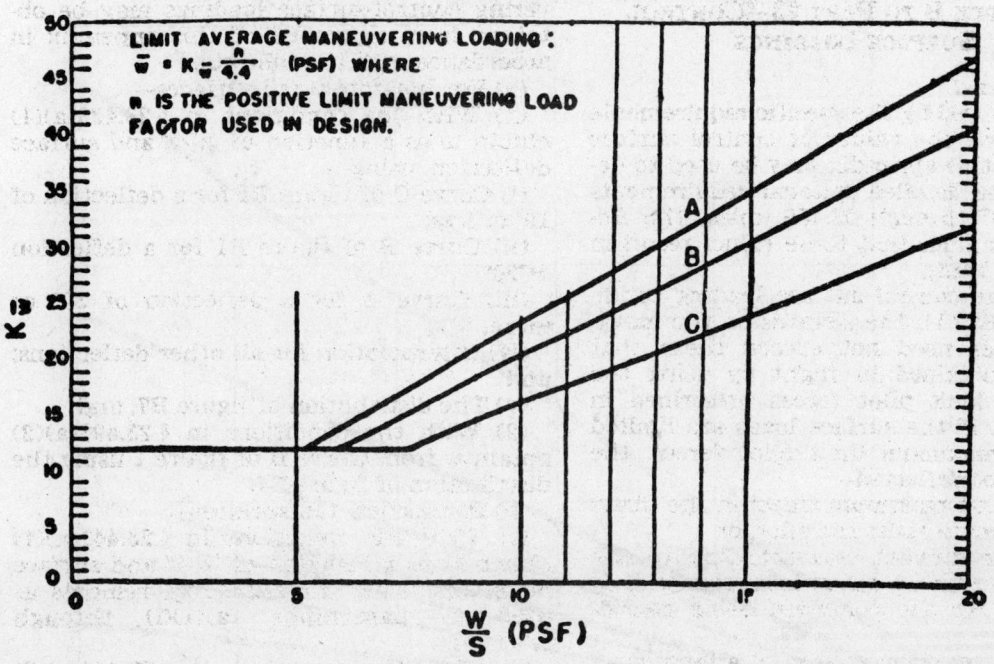

Note: In no case may $\bar{w}$ be less than 12 psf.

FIGURE B2—MANEUVERING TAIL LOAD INCREMENT (UP OR DOWN)

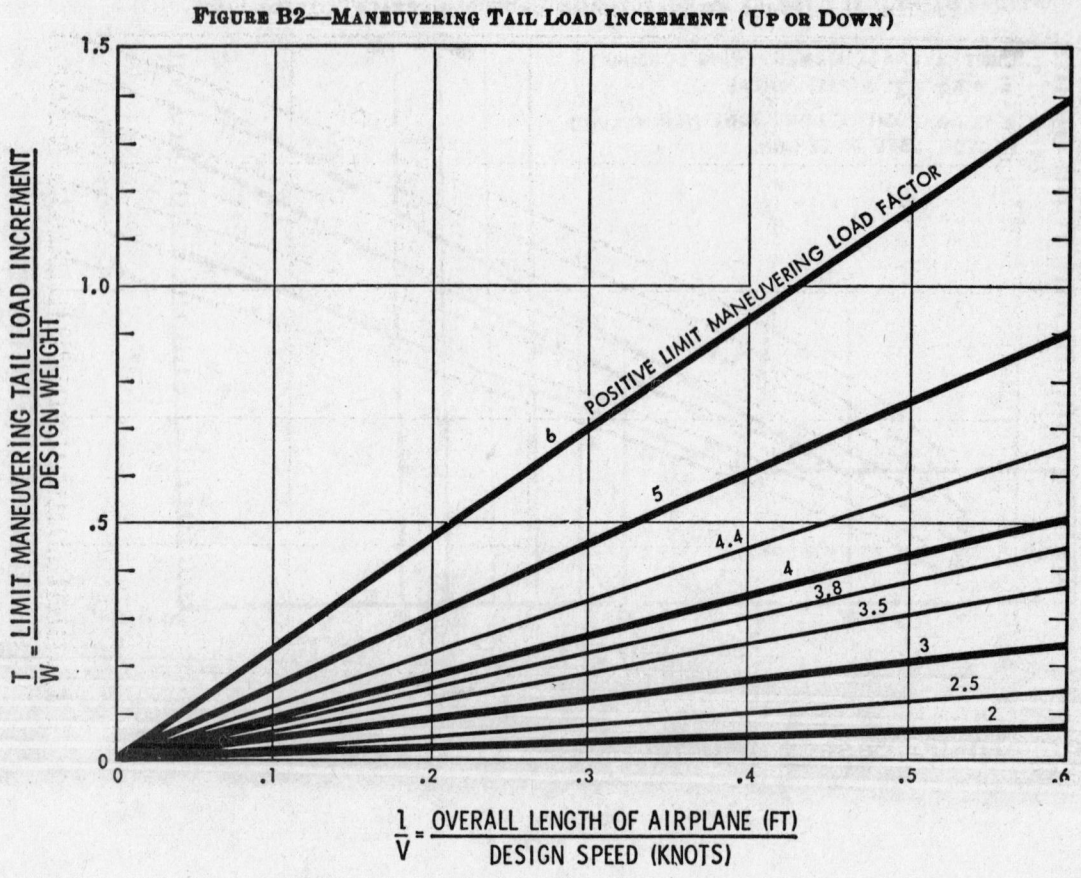

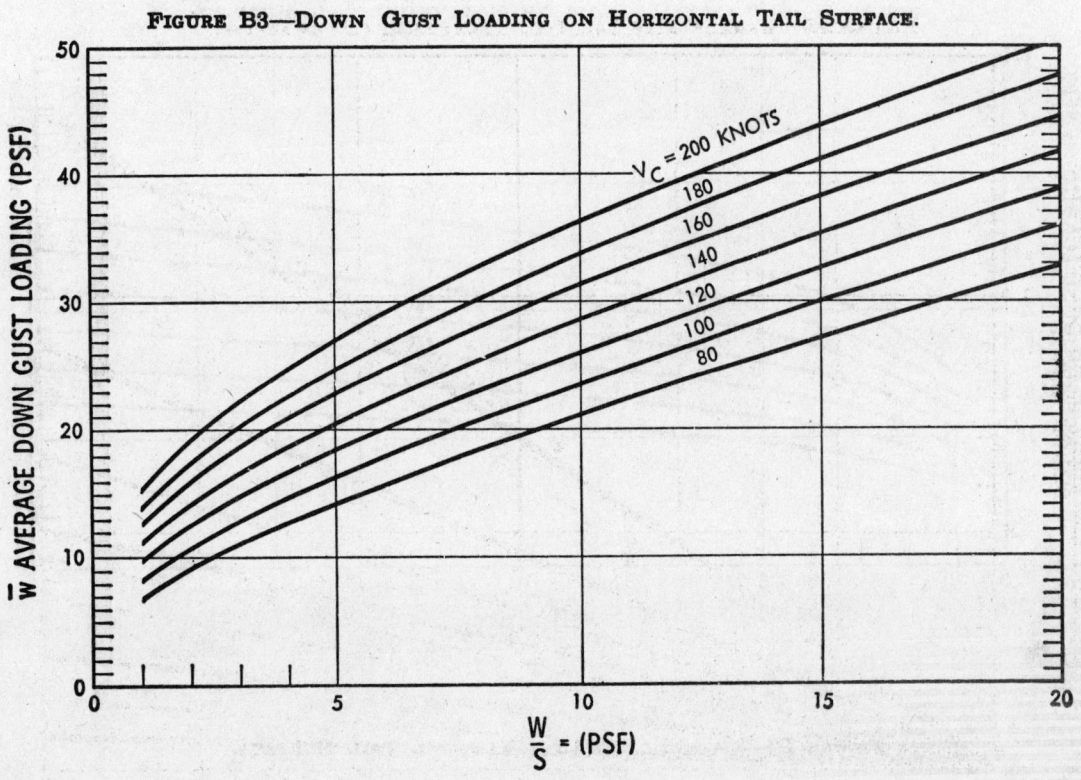

FIGURE B3—DOWN GUST LOADING ON HORIZONTAL TAIL SURFACE.

FIGURE B4—UP GUST LOADING ON HORIZONTAL TAIL SURFACE.

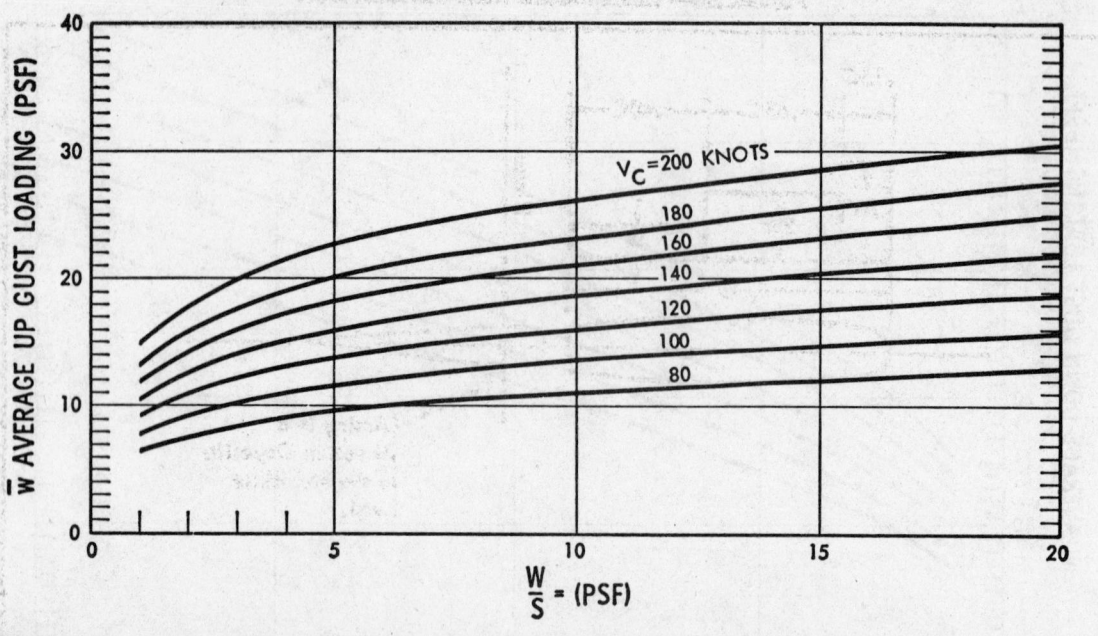

FIGURE B5—GUST LOADING ON VERTICAL TAIL SURFACE.

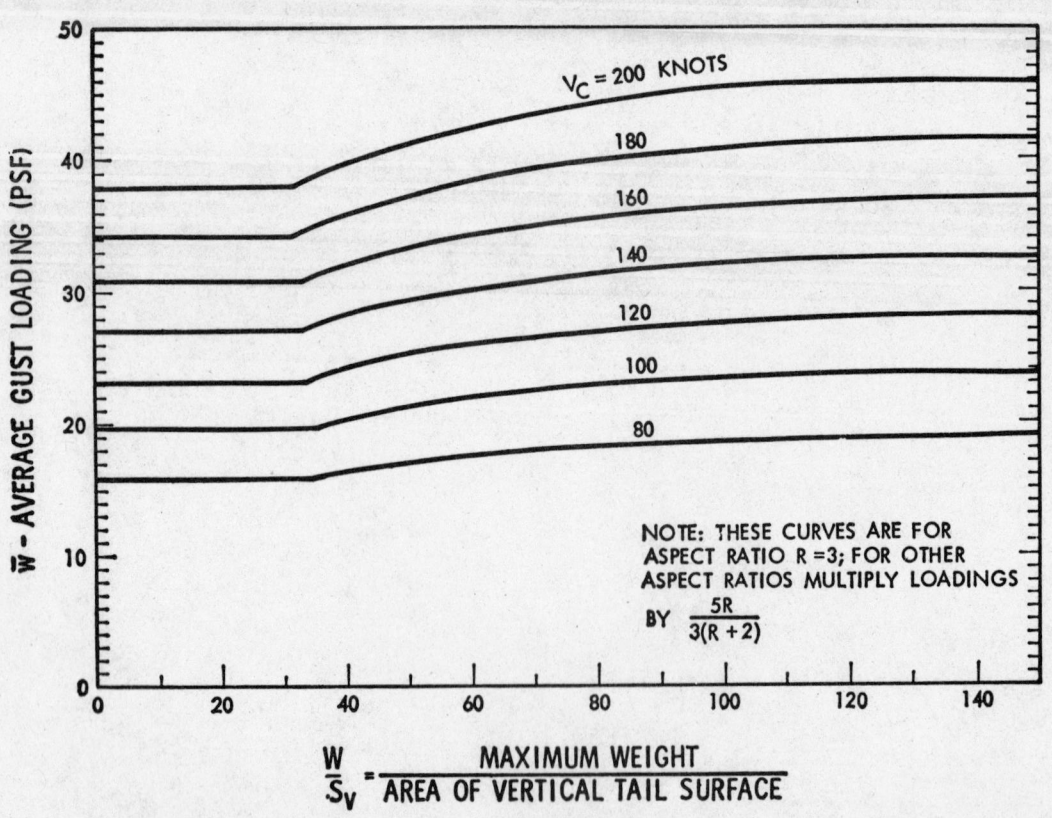

NOTE: THESE CURVES ARE FOR ASPECT RATIO R =3; FOR OTHER ASPECT RATIOS MULTIPLY LOADINGS BY $\dfrac{5R}{3(R+2)}$

$$\frac{W}{S_V} = \frac{\text{MAXIMUM WEIGHT}}{\text{AREA OF VERTICAL TAIL SURFACE}}$$

FIGURE B6—TAIL SURFACE LOAD DISTRIBUTION

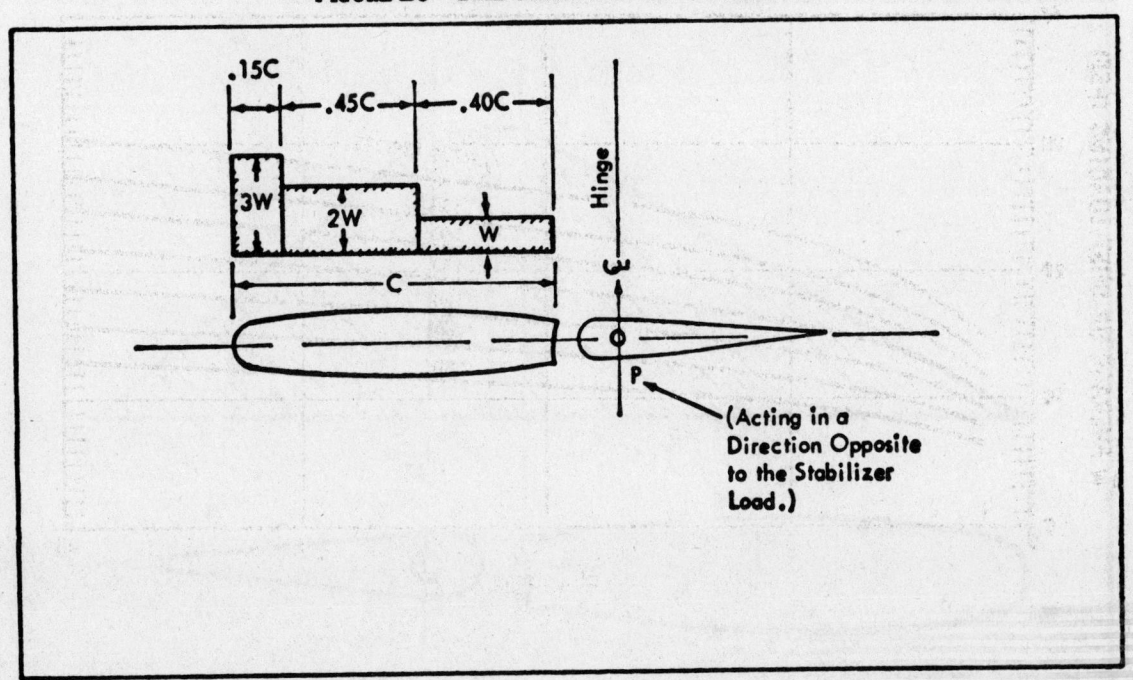

FIGURE B7—TAIL SURFACE LOAD DISTRIBUTION

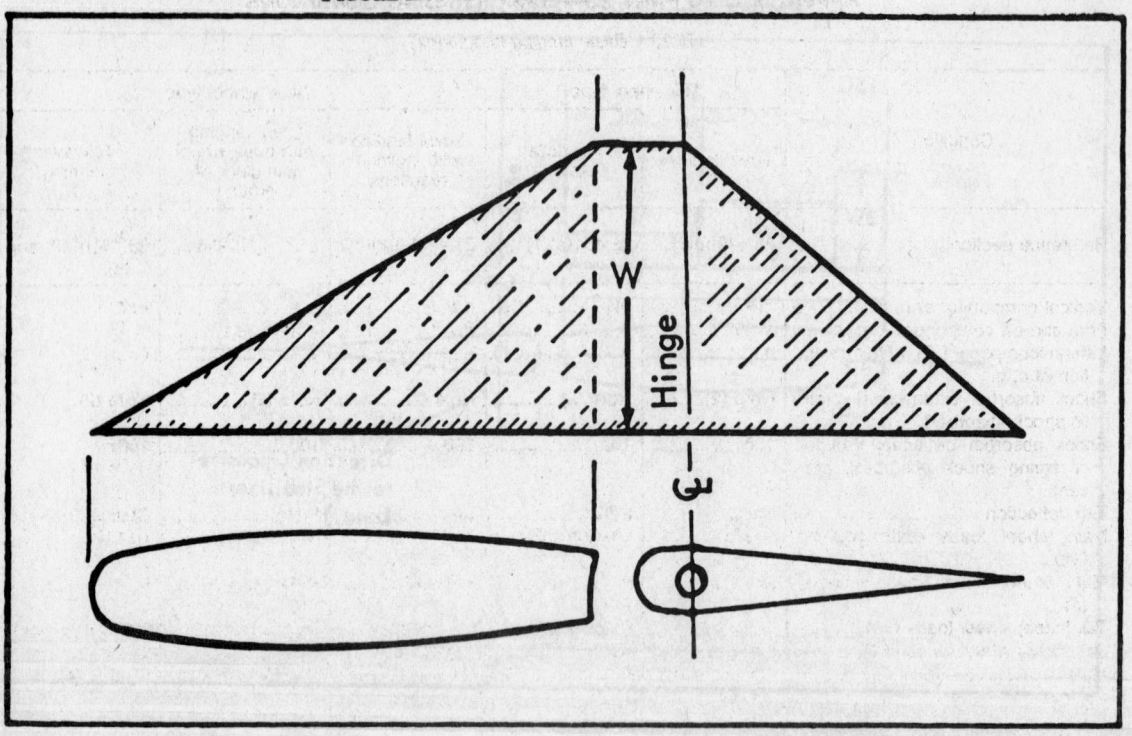

FIGURE B8—TAIL SURFACE LOAD DISTRIBUTION

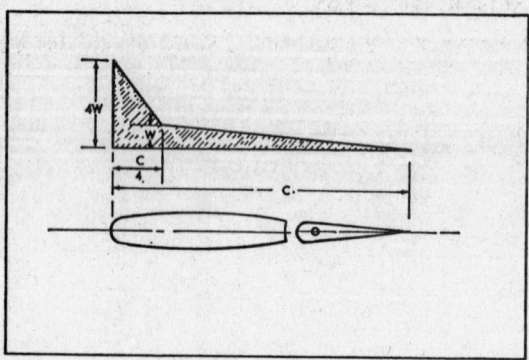

FIGURE B9—AILERON LOAD DISTRIBUTION

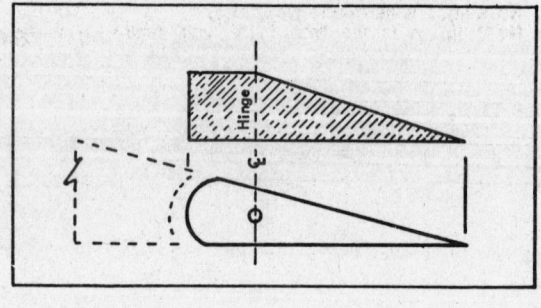

APPENDIX C TO PART 23—BASIC LANDING CONDITIONS

[C23.1 *Basic landing conditions*]

Condition	Tail wheel type		Nose wheel type		
	Level landing	Tail-down landing	Level landing with inclined reactions	Level landing with nose wheel just clear of ground	Tail-down landing
Reference section	23.479(a)(1)	23.481(a)(1)	23.479(a)(2)(i)	23.479(a)(2)(ii)	23.481(a)(2) and (b).
Vertical component at c. g	nW	nW	nW	nW	nW.
Fore and aft component at c. g	KnW	0	KnW	KnW	0.
Lateral component in either direction at c. g.	0	0	0	0	0.
Shock absorber extension (hydraulic shock absorber).	Note (2)	Note (2)	Note (2)	Note (2)	Note (2).
Shock absorber deflection (rubber or spring shock absorber), percent.	100	100	100	100	100.
Tire deflection	Static	Static	Static	Static	Static.
Main wheel loads (both wheels) (Vr).	$(n-L)W$	$(n-L)W$ b/d	$(n-L)W$ a′/d′	$(n-L)W$	$(n-L)W$.
Main wheel loads (both wheels) (Dr).	KnW	0	KnW a′/d′	KnW	0.
Tail (nose) wheel loads (Vf)	0	$(n-L)W$ a/d	$(n-L)W$ b′/d′	0	0.
Tail (nose) wheel loads (Df)	0	0	KnW b′/d′	0	0.
Notes	(1), (3), and (4).	(4)	(1)	(1), (3), and (4)	(3) and (4).

NOTE (1). K may be determined as follows: $K=0.25$ for $W=3,000$ pounds or less; $K=0.33$ for $W=6,000$ pounds or greater, with linear variation of K between these weights.

NOTE (2). For the purpose of design, the maximum load factor is assumed to occur throughout the shock absorber stroke from 25 percent deflection to 100 percent deflection unless otherwise shown and the load factor must be used with whatever shock absorber extension is most critical for each element of the landing gear.

NOTE (3). Unbalanced moments must be balanced by a rational or conservative method.

NOTE (4). L is defined in § 23.735(b).

NOTE (5). n is the limit inertia load factor, at the c.g. of the airplane, selected under § 23.473 (d), (f), and (g).

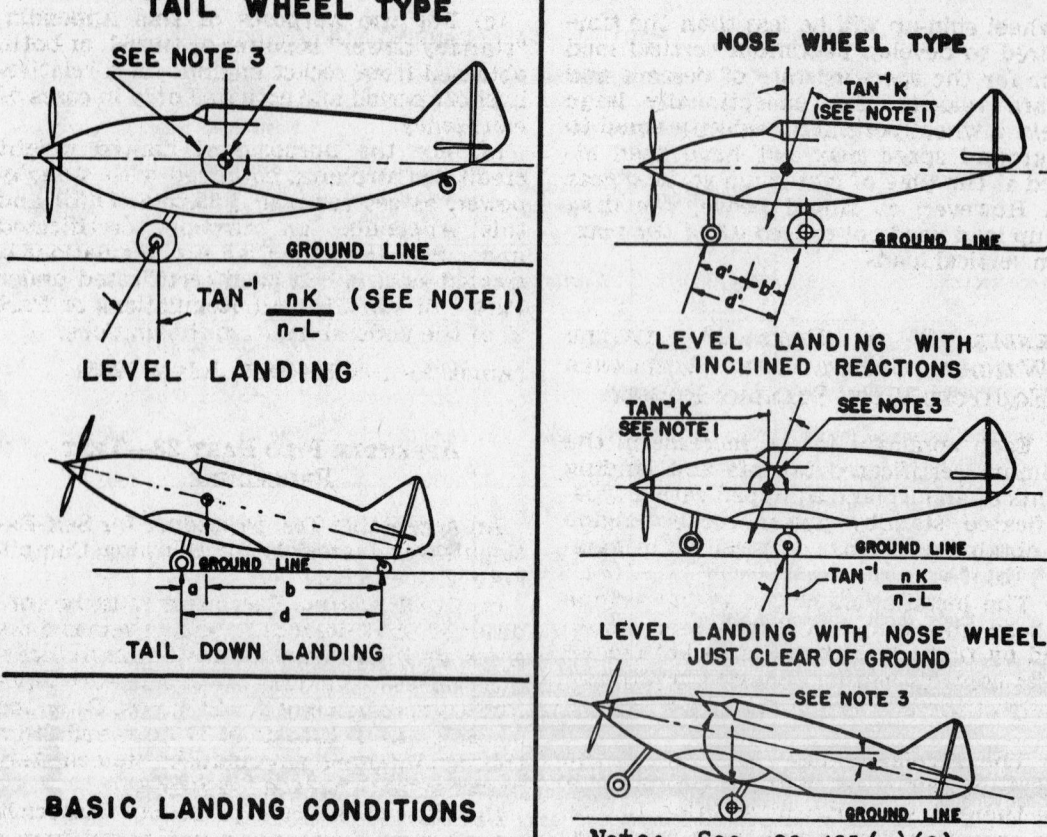

TAIL WHEEL TYPE

SEE NOTE 3

GROUND LINE

$\mathrm{TAN}^{-1} \dfrac{nK}{n-L}$ (SEE NOTE I)

LEVEL LANDING

GROUND LINE

TAIL DOWN LANDING

BASIC LANDING CONDITIONS

NOSE WHEEL TYPE

TAN^{-1} K (SEE NOTE I)

GROUND LINE

LEVEL LANDING WITH INCLINED REACTIONS

TAN^{-1} K SEE NOTE I

SEE NOTE 3

GROUND LINE

$\mathrm{TAN}^{-1} \dfrac{nK}{n-L}$

LEVEL LANDING WITH NOSE WHEEL JUST CLEAR OF GROUND

SEE NOTE 3

GROUND LINE

Note: See s23.481(a)(2)

TAIL DOWN LANDING

[Doc. No. 4080, 29 FR 17955, Dec. 18, 1964, as amended by Amdt. 23-7, 34 FR 13099, Aug. 13, 1969]

APPENDIX D TO PART 23—WHEEL SPIN-UP LOADS

D23.1 *Wheel spin-up loads.*

(a) The following method for determining wheel spin-up loads for landing conditions is based on NACA T.N. 863. However, the drag component used for design may not be less than the drag load prescribed in § 23.479(b).

$$F_{Hmax} = 1/r_e \sqrt{2I_w(V_H - V_c)nF_{Vmax}/t_S}$$

where—

F_{Hmax} = maximum rearward horizontal force acting on the wheel (in pounds);

r_e = effective rolling radius of wheel under impact based on recommended operating tire pressure (which may be assumed to be equal to the rolling radius under a static load of $n_j W_e$) in feet;

I_w = rotational mass moment of inertia of rolling assembly (in slug feet);

V_H = linear velocity of airplane parallel to ground at instant of contact (assumed to be 1.2 V_{So}, in feet per second);

V_c = peripheral speed of tire, if prerotation is used (in feet per second) (there must be a positive means of pre-rotation before pre-rotation may be considered);

n = equals effective coefficient of friction (0.80 may be used);

F_{Vmax} = maximum vertical force on wheel (pounds) = $n_j W_e$, where W_e and n_j are defined in § 23.725;

t_s = time interval between ground contact and attainment of maximum vertical force on wheel (seconds). (However, if the value of F_{Vmax}, from the above equation exceeds 0.8 F_{Vmax}, the latter value must be used for F_{Hmax}.)

(b) The equation assumes a linear variation of load factor with time until the peak load is reached and under this assumption, the equation determines the drag force at the time that the wheel peripheral velocity at radius r_e equals the airplane velocity. Most shock absorbers do not exactly follow a linear variation of load factor with time. Therefore, rational or conservative allowances must be made to compensate for these variations. On most landing gears, the time for wheel spin-up will be less than the time required to develop maximum vertical load factor for the specified rate of descent and forward velocity. For exceptionally large wheels, a wheel peripheral velocity equal to the ground speed may not have been attained at the time of maximum vertical gear load. However, as stated above, the drag spin-up load need not exceed 0.8 of the maximum vertical loads.

APPENDIX E TO PART 23—LIMITED WEIGHT CREDIT FOR AIRPLANES EQUIPPED WITH STANDBY POWER

(a) Each applicant for an increase in the maximum certificated takeoff and landing weights of an airplane equipped with a type-certificated standby power rocket engine may obtain an increase as specified in paragraph (b) if—

(1) The installation of the rocket engine has been approved and it has been established by flight test that the rocket engine and its controls can be operated safely and reliably at the increase in maximum weight; and

(2) The Airplane Flight Manual, or the placard, markings or manuals required in place thereof, set forth in addition to any other operating limitations the Administrator may require, the increased weight approved under this regulation and a prohibition against the operation of the airplane at the approved increased weight when—

(i) The installed standby power rocket engines have been stored or installed in excess of the time limit established by the manufacturer of the rocket engine (usually stenciled on the engine casing); or

(ii) The rocket engine fuel has been expended or discharged.

(b) The currently approved maximum takeoff and landing weights at which an airplane is certificated without a standby power rocket engine installation may be increased by an amount which does not exceed any of the following:

(1) An amount equal in pounds to 0.014 IN, where I is the maximum usable impulse in pounds-seconds available from each standby power rocket engine and N is the number of rocket engines installed.

(2) An amount equal to 5 percent of the maximum certificated weight approved in accordance with the applicable airworthiness regulations without standby power rocket engines installed.

(3) An amount equal to the weight of the rocket engine installation.

(4) An amount that, together with the currently approved maximum weight, would equal the maximum structural weight established for the airplane without standby rocket engines installed.

(c) For the purposes of this Appendix, "standby power" is power or thrust, or both, obtained from rocket engines for a relatively short period and actuated only in cases of emergency.

(d) For the purposes of limited weight credit for airplanes equipped with standby power, as set forth in § 23.25(a)(1)(iii) and this Appendix, an airplane certificated under Part 4a of the Civil Air Regulations is treated as if it had been certificated under Part 3 of the Civil Air Regulations or Part 23 of the Federal Aviation Regulations.

[Amdt. 23-2, 30 FR 8468, July 2, 1965]

APPENDIX F TO PART 23—TEST PROCEDURE

An Acceptable Test Procedure for Self-Extinguishing Materials for Showing Compliance with § 23.853.

(a) *Conditioning.* Specimens must be conditioned to 70 degrees F, plus or minus 5 degrees, and at 50 percent plus or minus 5 percent relative humidity until moisture equilibrium is reached or for 24 hours. Only one specimen at a time may be removed from the conditioning environment immediately before subjecting it to the flame.

(b) *Specimen configuration.* Materials must be tested either as a section cut from a fabricated part as installed in the airplane or as a specimen simulating a cut section, such as a specimen cut from a flat sheet of the material or a model of the fabricated part. The specimen may be cut from any location in a fabricated part; however, fabricated units, such as sandwich panels, may not be separated for test. The specimen thickness must be no thicker than the minimum thickness to be qualified for use in the airplane, except that thick foam parts must be tested in ½-inch thickness. In the case of fabrics, both the warp and fill direction of the weave must be tested to determine the most critical flammability conditions. When performing the test prescribed in paragraphs (d) and (e) of this Appendix, the specimen must be mounted in a metal frame so that: (1) The two long edges and the upper edge are held securely; (2) the exposed area of the specimen is at least 2 inches wide and 12 inches long, unless the actual size used in the airplane is smaller; and (3) the edge to which the burner flame is applied must not consist of the finished or protected edge of the specimen but must be representative of the actual cross section of the material or part installed in the airplane.

(c) *Apparatus.* Except as provided in paragraph (e) of this Appendix, tests must be conducted in a draft-free cabinet in accordance with Federal Test Method Standard 191 Method 5903 (revised Method 5902) which is available from the General Services Administration, Business Service Center, Region 3, Seventh and D Streets SW., Washington, D.C. 20407, or with some other approved equivalent method. Specimens which are too large for the cabinet must be tested in similar draft-free conditions.

(d) *Vertical test.* A minimum of three specimens must be tested and the results averaged. For fabrics, the direction of weave corresponding to the most critical flammability conditions must be parallel to the longest dimension. Each specimen must be supported vertically. The specimen must be exposed to a Bunsen or Tirrill burner with a nominal ⅜-inch I.D. tube adjusted to give a flame of 1½ inches in height. The minimum flame temperature measured by a calibrated thermocouple pryometer in the center of the flame must be 1550° F. The lower edge of the specimen must be three-fourths inch above the top edge of the burner. The flame must be applied to the center line of the lower edge of the specimen. For materials covered by §§ 23.853(d)(3)(i) and 23.853(f), the flame must be applied for 60 seconds and then removed. For materials covered by § 23.853(d)(3)(ii), the flame must be applied for 12 seconds and then removed. Flame time, burn length, and flaming time of drippings, if any, must be recorded. The burn length determined in accordance with paragraph (f) of this Appendix must be measured to the nearest one-tenth inch.

(e) *Horizontal test.* A minimum of three specimens must be tested and the results averaged. Each specimen must be supported horizontally. The exposed surface when installed in the airplane must be face down for the test. The specimen must be exposed to a Bunsen burner or Tirrill burner with a nominal ⅜-inch I.D. tube adjusted to give a flame of 1½ inches in height. The minimum flame temperature measured by a calibrated thermocouple pyrometer in the center of the flame must be 1550° F. The specimen must be positioned so that the edge being tested is three-fourths of an inch above the top of, and on the center line of, the burner. The flame must be applied for 15 seconds and then removed. A minimum of 10 inches of the specimen must be used for timing purposes, approximately 1½ inches must burn before the burning front reaches the timing zone, and the average burn rate must be recorded.

(f) *Burn length.* Burn length is the distance from the original edge to the farthest evidence of damage to the test specimen due to flame impingement, including areas of partial or complete consumption, charring, or embrittlement, but not including areas sooted, stained, warped, or discolored, nor areas where material has shrunk or melted away from the heat source.

[Amdt. 23-23, 43 FR 50594, Oct. 30, 1978, as amended by Amdt. 23-34, 52 FR 1835, Jan. 15, 1987; 52 FR 34745, Sept. 14, 1987]

APPENDIX G TO PART 23—INSTRUCTIONS FOR CONTINUED AIRWORTHINESS

G23.1 *General.* (a) This appendix specifies requirements for the preparation of Instructions for Continued Airworthiness as required by § 23.1529.

(b) The Instructions for Continued Airworthiness for each airplane must include the Instructions for Continued Airworthiness for each engine and propeller (hereinafter designated 'products'), for each appliance required by this chapter, and any required information relating to the interface of those appliances and products with the airplane. If Instructions for Continued Airworthiness are not supplied by the manufacturer of an appliance or product installed in the airplane, the Instructions for Continued Airworthiness for the airplane must include the information essential to the continued airworthiness of the airplane.

(c) The applicant must submit to the FAA a program to show how changes to the Instructions for Continued Airworthiness made by the applicant or by the manufacturers of products and appliances installed in the airplane will be distributed.

G23.2 *Format.* (a) The Instructions for Continued Airworthiness must be in the form of a manual or manuals as appropriate for the quantity of data to be provided.

(b) The format of the manual or manuals must provide for a practical arrangement.

G23.3 *Content.* The contents of the manual or manuals must be prepared in the English language. The Instructions for Continued Airworthiness must contain the following manuals or sections, as appropriate, and information:

(a) *Airplane maintenance manual or section.* (1) Introduction information that includes an explanation of the airplane's features and data to the extent necessary for maintenance or preventive maintenance.

(2) A description of the airplane and its systems and installations including its engines, propellers, and appliances.

(3) Basic control and operation information describing how the airplane components and systems are controlled and how they operate, including any special procedures and limitations that apply.

(4) Servicing information that covers details regarding servicing points, capacities of tanks, reservoirs, types of fluids to be used, pressures applicable to the various systems, location of access panels for inspection and servicing, locations of lubrication points, lubricants to be used, equipment required for

servicing, tow instructions and limitations, mooring, jacking, and leveling information.

(b) *Maintenance instructions.* (1) Scheduling information for each part of the airplane and its engines, auxiliary power units, propellers, accessories, instruments, and equipment that provides the recommended periods at which they should be cleaned, inspected, adjusted, tested, and lubricated, and the degree of inspection, the applicable wear tolerances, and work recommended at these periods. However, the applicant may refer to an accessory, instrument, or equipment manufacturer as the source of this information if the applicant shows that the item has an exceptionally high degree of complexity requiring specialized maintenance techniques, test equipment, or expertise. The recommended overhaul periods and necessary cross reference to the Airworthiness Limitations section of the manual must also be included. In addition, the applicant must include an inspection program that includes the frequency and extent of the inspections necessary to provide for the continued airworthiness of the airplane.

(2) Troubleshooting information describing probable malfunctions, how to recognize those malfunctions, and the remedial action for those malfunctions.

(3) Information describing the order and method of removing and replacing products and parts with any necessary precautions to be taken.

(4) Other general procedural instructions including procedures for system testing during ground running, symmetry checks, weighing and determining the center of gravity, lifting and shoring, and storage limitations.

(c) Diagrams of structural access plates and information needed to gain access for inspections when access plates are not provided.

(d) Details for the application of special inspection techniques including radiographic and ultrasonic testing where such processes are specified.

(e) Information needed to apply protective treatments to the structure after inspection.

(f) All data relative to structural fasteners such as identification, discard recommendations, and torque values.

(g) A list of special tools needed.

(h) In addition, for commuter category airplanes, the following information must be furnished:

(1) Electrical loads applicable to the various systems;

(2) Methods of balancing control surfaces;

(3) Identification of primary and secondary structures; and

(4) Special repair methods applicable to the airplane.

G23.4 *Airworthiness Limitations section.* The Instructions for Continued Airworthiness must contain a section titled Airworthiness Limitations that is segregated and clearly distinguishable from the rest of the document. This section must set forth each mandatory replacement time, structural inspection interval, and related structural inspection procedure required for type certification. If the Instructions for Continued Airworthiness consist of multiple documents, the section required by this paragraph must be included in the principal manual. This section must contain a legible statement in a prominent location that reads: "The Airworthiness Limitations section is FAA approved and specifies maintenance required under §§ 43.16 and 91.163 of the Federal Aviation Regulations unless an alternative program has been FAA approved."

[Amdt. 23–26, 45 FR 60171, Sept. 11, 1980, as amended by Amdt. 23–34, 52 FR 1835, Jan. 15, 1987; 52 FR 34745, Sept. 14, 1987]

FEDERAL AVIATION REGULATIONS

PART 33
AIRWORTHINESS STANDARDS:
Aircraft Engines

1989 EDITION

PART 33—AIRWORTHINESS
STANDARDS: AIRCRAFT ENGINES

Subpart A—General

Sec.
33.1　Applicability.
33.3　General.
33.4　Instructions for Continued Airworthiness.
33.5　Instruction manual for installing and operating the engine.
33.7　Engine ratings and operating limitations.
33.8　Selection of engine power and thrust ratings.

Subpart B—Design and Construction; General

33.11　Applicability.
33.13　[Reserved]
33.14　Start-stop cyclic stress (low-cycle fatigue).
33.15　Materials.
33.17　Fire prevention.
33.19　Durability.
33.21　Engine cooling.
33.23　Engine mounting attachments and structure.
33.25　Accessory attachments.
33.27　Turbine, compressor, fan, and turbo-supercharger rotors.
33.29　Instrument connection.

Subpart C—Design and Construction; Reciprocating Aircraft Engines

33.31　Applicability.
33.33　Vibration.
33.35　Fuel and induction system.
33.37　Ignition system.
33.39　Lubrication system.

Subpart D—Block Tests; Reciprocating Aircraft Engines

33.41　Applicability.
33.42　General.
33.43　Vibration test.
33.45　Calibration tests.
33.47　Detonation test.
33.49　Endurance test.
33.51　Operation test.
33.53　Engine component tests.
33.55　Teardown inspection.
33.57　General conduct of block tests.

Subpart E—Design and Construction; Turbine Aircraft Engines

33.61　Applicability.
33.62　Stress analysis.
33.63　Vibration.
33.65　Surge and stall characteristics.
33.66　Bleed air system.
33.67　Fuel system.

33.68   Induction system icing.
33.69   Ignitions system.
33.71   Lubrication system.
33.72   Hydraulic actuating systems.
33.73   Power or thrust response.
33.75   Safety analysis.
33.77   Foreign object ingestion.
33.79   Fuel burning thrust augmentor.

Subpart F—Block Tests; Turbine Aircraft Engines

33.81   Applicability.
33.82   General.
33.83   Vibration test.
33.85   Calibration tests.
33.87   Endurance test.
33.88   Engine overtemperature test.
33.89   Operation test.
33.90   Initial maintenance inspection.
33.91   Engine component tests.
33.92   Windmilling tests.
33.93   Teardown inspection.
33.94   Blade containment and rotor unbalance tests.
33.95   Engine-propeller systems tests.
33.96   Engine tests in auxiliary power unit (APU) mode.
33.97   Thrust reversers.
33.99   General conduct of block tests.

APPENDIX A—INSTRUCTIONS FOR CONTINUED AIRWORTHINESS

AUTHORITY: Secs. 313, 601, 608, 72 Stat. 752, 775; 49 U.S.C. 1354, 1421, 1423.

SOURCE: Docket No. 3025, 29 FR 7453, June 10, 1964, unless otherwise noted.

NOTE: For miscellaneous amendments to cross references in this Part 33, see Amdt. 33-2, 31 FR 9211, July 6, 1966.

Subpart A—General

§ 33.1 Applicability.

(a) This part prescribes airworthiness standards for the issue of type certificates and changes to those certificates, for aircraft engines.

(b) Each person who applies under Part 21 for such a certificate or change must show compliance with the applicable requirements of this part.

[Amdt. 33-7, 41 FR 55474, Dec. 20, 1976]

§ 33.3 General.

Each applicant must show that the aircraft engine concerned meets the applicable requirements of this part.

§ 33.4 Instructions for Continued Airworthiness.

The applicant must prepare Instructions for Continued Airworthiness in accordance with Appendix A to this part that are acceptable to the Administrator. The instructions may be incomplete at type certification if a program exists to ensure their completion prior to delivery of the first aircraft with the engine installed, or upon issuance of a standard certificate of airworthiness for the aircraft with the engine installed, whichever occurs later.

[Amdt. 33-9, 45 FR 60181, Sept. 11, 1980]

§ 33.5 Instruction manual for installing and operating the engine.

Each applicant must prepare and make available to the Administrator prior to the issuance of the type certificate, and to the owner at the time of delivery of the engine, approved instructions for installing and operating the engine. The instructions must include at least the following:

(a) *Installation instructions.* (1) The location of engine mounting attachments, the method of attaching the engine to the aircraft, and the maximum allowable load for the mounting attachments and related structure.

(2) The location and description of engine connections to be attached to accessories, pipes, wires, cables, ducts, and cowling.

(3) An outline drawing of the engine including overall dimensions.

(b) *Operation instructions.* (1) The operating limitations established by the Administrator.

(2) The power or thrust ratings and procedures for correcting for nonstandard atmosphere.

(3) The recommended procedures, under normal and extreme ambient conditions for—

(i) Starting;
(ii) Operating on the ground; and
(iii) Operating during flight.

[Amdt. 33-6, 39 FR 35463, Oct. 1, 1974, as amended by Amdt. 33-9, 45 FR 60181, Sept. 11, 1980]

§ 33.7 Engine ratings and operating limitations.

(a) Engine ratings and operating limitations are established by the Administrator and included in the engine certificate data sheet specified in § 21.41 of this chapter, including ratings and limitations based on the operating conditions and information specified in this section, as applicable, and any other information found necessary for safe operation of the engine.

(b) For reciprocating engines, ratings and operating limitations are established relating to the following:

(1) Horsepower or torque, r.p.m., manifold pressure, and time at critical pressure altitude and sea level pressure altitude for—

(i) Rated maximum continuous power (relating to unsupercharged operation or to operation in each supercharger mode as applicable); and

(ii) Rated takeoff power (relating to unsupercharged operation or to operation in each supercharger mode as applicable).

(2) Fuel grade or specification.

(3) Oil grade or specification.

(4) Temperature of the—

(i) Cylinder;

(ii) Oil at the oil inlet; and

(iii) Turbosupercharger turbine wheel inlet gas.

(5) Pressure of—

(i) Fuel at the fuel inlet; and

(ii) Oil at the main oil gallery.

(6) Accessory drive torque and overhang moment.

(7) Component life.

(8) Turbosupercharger turbine wheel r.p.m.

(c) For turbine engines, ratings and operating limitations are established relating to the following:

(1) Horsepower, torque, or thrust, r.p.m., gas temperature, and time for—

(i) Rated maximum continuous power or thrust (augmented);

(ii) Rated maximum continuous power or thrust (unaugmented);

(iii) Rated takeoff power or thrust (augmented);

(iv) Rated takeoff power or thrust (unaugmented);

(v) Rated 30-minute OEI power;

(vi) Rated 2½-minute OEI power;

(vii) Rated continuous OEI power; and

(viii) Auxiliary power unit (APU) mode of operation.

(2) Fuel designation or specification.

(3) Oil grade or specification.

(4) Hydraulic fluid specification.

(5) Temperature of—

(i) Oil at a location specified by the applicant;

(ii) Induction air at the inlet face of a supersonic engine, including steady state operation and transient overtemperature and time allowed;

(iii) Hydraulic fluid of a supersonic engine;

(iv) Fuel at a location specified by the applicant; and

(v) External surfaces of the engine, if specified by the applicant.

(6) Pressure of—

(i) Fuel at the fuel inlet;

(ii) Oil at a location specified by the applicant;

(iii) Induction air at the inlet face of a supersonic engine, including steady state operation and transient overpressure and time allowed; and

(iv) Hydraulic fluid.

(7) Accessory drive torque and overhang moment.

(8) Component life.

(9) Fuel filtration.

(10) Oil filtration.

(11) Bleed air.

(12) The number of start-stop stress cycles approved for each rotor disc and spacer.

(13) Inlet air distortion at the engine inlet.

(14) Transient rotor shaft overspeed r.p.m., and number of overspeed occurrences.

(15) Transient gas overtemperature, and number of overtemperature occurrences.

(16) For engines to be used in supersonic aircraft, engine rotor windmilling rotational r.p.m.

[Amdt. 33–6, 39 FR 35463, Oct. 1, 1974, as amended by Amdt. 33–10, 49 FR 6850, Feb. 23, 1984; Amdt. 33–11, 51 FR 10346, Mar. 25, 1986]

§ 33.8 Selection of engine power and thrust ratings.

(a) Requested engine power and thrust ratings must be selected by the applicant.

(b) Each selected rating must be for the lowest power or thrust that all engines of the same type may be expect-

§ 33.11

14 CFR Ch. 1 (1-1-89 Edition)

ed to produce under the conditions used to determine that rating.

[Amdt. 33-3, 32 FR 3736, Mar. 4, 1967]

Subpart B—Design and Construction; General

§ 33.11 Applicability.

This subpart prescribes the general design and construction requirements for reciprocating and turbine aircraft engines.

§ 33.13 [Reserved]

§ 33.14 Start-stop cyclic stress (low-cycle fatigue).

By a procedure approved by the FAA, operating limitations must be established which specify the maximum allowable number of start-stop stress cycles for each rotor structural part (such as discs, spacers, hubs, and shafts of the compressors and turbines), the failure of which could produce a hazard to the aircraft. A start-stop stress cycle consists of a flight cycle profile or an equivalent representation of engine usage. It includes starting the engine, accelerating to maximum rated power or thrust, decelerating, and stopping. For each cycle, the rotor structural parts must reach stabilized temperature during engine operation at a maximum rate power or thrust and after engine shutdown, unless it is shown that the parts undergo the same stress range without temperature stabilization.

[Amdt. 33-10, 49 FR 6850, Feb. 23, 1984]

§ 33.15 Materials.

The suitability and durability of materials used in the engine must—

(a) Be established on the basis of experience or tests; and

(b) Conform to approved specifications (such as industry or military specifications) that ensure their having the strength and other properties assumed in the design data.

(Secs. 313(a), 601, and 603, 72 Stat. 759, 775, 49 U.S.C. 1354(a), 1421, and 1423; sec. 6(c), 49 U.S.C. 1655(c))

[Amdt. 33-8, 42 FR 15047, Mar. 17, 1977, as amended by Amdt. 33-10, 49 FR 6850, Feb. 23, 1984]

§ 33.17 Fire prevention.

(a) The design and construction of the engine and the materials used must minimize the probability of the occurrence and spread of fire. In addition, the design and construction of turbine engines must minimize the probability of the occurrence of an internal fire that could result in structural failure, overheating, or other hazardous conditions.

(b) Except as provided in paragraphs (c), (d), and (e) of this section, each external line, fitting, and other component, which contains or conveys flammable fluid must be fire resistant. Components must be shielded or located to safeguard against the ignition of leaking flammable fluid.

(c) Flammable fluid tanks and supports which are part of and attached to the engine must be fireproof or be enclosed by a fireproof shield unless damage by fire to any non-fireproof part will not cause leakage or spillage of flammable fluid. For a reciprocating engine having an integral oil sump of less than 25-quart capacity, the oil sump need not be fireproof nor be enclosed by fireproof shield.

(d) For turbine engines type certificated for use in supersonic aircraft, each external component which conveys or contains flammable fluid must be fireproof.

(e) Unwanted accumulation of flammable fluid and vapor must be prevented by draining and venting.

(Secs. 313(a), 601, and 603, 72 Stat. 759, 775, 49 U.S.C. 1354(a), 1421, and 1423; sec. 6(c), 49 U.S.C. 1655(c))

[Amdt. 33-6, 39 FR 35464, Oct. 1, 1974, as amended by Amdt. 33-8, 42 FR 15047, Mar. 17, 1977; Amdt. 33-10, 49 FR 6850, Feb. 23, 1984]

§ 33.19 Durability.

(a) Engine design and construction must minimize the development of an unsafe condition of the engine between overhaul periods. The design of the compressor and turbine rotor cases must provide for the containment of damage from rotor blade failure. Energy levels and trajectories of fragments resulting from rotor blade failure that lie outside the compressor

off

ASA-216   [FAR 616]   1989

and turbine rotor cases must be defined.

(b) Each component of the propeller blade pitch control system which is a part of the engine type design must meet the requirements of § 35.42 of this chapter.

[Doc. No. 3025, 29 FR 7453, June 10, 1964, as amended by Amdt. 33-9, 45 FR 60181, Sept. 11, 1980; Amdt. 33-10, 49 FR 6851, Feb. 23, 1984]

§ 33.21 Engine cooling.

Engine design and construction must provide the necessary cooling under conditions in which the airplane is expected to operate.

§ 33.23 Engine mounting attachments and structure.

(a) The maximum allowable limit and ultimate loads for engine mounting attachments and related engine structure must be specified.

(b) The engine mounting attachments and related engine structure must be able to withstand—

(1) The specified limit loads without permanent deformation; and

(2) The specified ultimate loads without failure, but may exhibit permanent deformation.

[Amdt. 33-10, 49 FR 6851, Feb. 23, 1984]

§ 33.25 Accessory attachments.

The engine must operate properly with the accessory drive and mounting attachments loaded. Each engine accessory drive and mounting attachment must include provisions for sealing to prevent contamination of, or unacceptable leakage from, the engine interior. A drive and mounting attachment requiring lubrication for external drive splines, or coupling by engine oil, must include provisions for sealing to prevent unacceptable loss of oil and to prevent contamination from sources outside the chamber enclosing the drive connection. The design of the engine must allow for the examination, adjustment, or removal of each accessory required for engine operation.

[Amdt. 33-10, 49 FR 6851, Feb. 23, 1984]

§ 33.27 Turbine, compressor, fan, and turbosupercharger rotors.

(a) Turbine, compressor, fan, and turbosupercharger rotors must have sufficient strength to withstand the test conditions specified in paragraph (c) of this section.

(b) The design and functioning of engine control devices, systems, and instruments must give reasonable assurance that those engine operating limitations that affect turbine, compressor, fan, and turbosupercharger rotor structural integrity will not be exceeded in service.

(c) The most critically stressed rotor component (except blades) of each turbine, compressor, and fan, including integral drum rotors and centrifugal compressors in an engine or turbosupercharger, as determined by analysis or other acceptable means, must be tested for a period of 5 minutes—

(1) At its maximum operating temperature, except as provided in paragraph (c)(2)(iv) of this section; and

(2) At the highest speed of the following, as applicable:

(i) 120 percent of its maximum permissible r.p.m. if tested on a rig and equipped with blades or blade weights.

(ii) 115 percent of its maximum permissible r.p.m. if tested on an engine.

(iii) 115 percent of its maximum permissible r.p.m. if tested on turbosupercharger driven by a hot gas supply from a special burner rig.

(iv) 120 percent of the r.p.m. at which, while cold spinning, it is subject to operating stresses that are equivalent to those induced at the maximum operating temperature and maximum permissible r.p.m.

(v) 105 percent of the highest speed that would result from failure of the most critical component or system in a representative installation of the engine.

(vi) The highest speed that would result from the failure of any component or system in a representative installation of the engine, in combination with any failure of a component or system that would not normally be detected during a routine preflight check or during normal flight operation.

Following the test, each rotor must be within approved dimensional limits for an overspeed condition and may not be cracked.

[Amdt. 33-10, 49 FR 6851, Feb. 23, 1984]

§ 33.29 Instrument connection.

(a) Unless it is constructed to prevent its connection to an incorrect instrument, each connection provided for powerplant instruments required by aircraft airworthiness regulations or necessary to insure operation of the engine in compliance with any engine limitation must be marked to identify it with its corresponding instrument.

(b) A connection must be provided on each turbojet engine for an indicator system to indicate rotor system unbalance.

[Amdt. 33-5, 39 FR 1831, Jan. 15, 1974, as amended by Amdt. 33-6, 39 FR 35465, Oct. 1, 1974]

Subpart C—Design and Construction; Reciprocating Aircraft Engines

§ 33.31 Applicability.

This subpart prescribes additional design and construction requirements for reciprocating aircraft engines.

§ 33.33 Vibration.

The engine must be designed and constructed to function throughout its normal operating range of crankshaft rotational speeds and engine powers without inducing excessive stress in any of the engine parts because of vibration and without imparting excessive vibration forces to the aircraft structure.

§ 33.35 Fuel and induction system.

(a) The fuel system of the engine must be designed and constructed to supply an appropriate mixture of fuel to the cylinders throughout the complete operating range of the engine under all flight and atmospheric conditions.

(b) The intake passages of the engine through which air or fuel in combination with air passes for combustion purposes must be designed and constructed to minimize the danger of ice accretion in those passages. The engine must be designed and con-

structed to permit the use of a means for ice prevention.

(c) The type and degree of fuel filtering necessary for protection of the engine fuel system against foreign particles in the fuel must be specified. The applicant must show that foreign particles passing through the prescribed filtering means will not critically impair engine fuel system functioning.

(d) Each passage in the induction system that conducts a mixture of fuel and air must be self-draining, to prevent a liquid lock in the cylinders, in all attitudes that the applicant establishes as those the engine can have when the aircraft in which it is installed is in the static ground attitude.

(e) If provided as part of the engine, the applicant must show for each fluid injection (other than fuel) system and its controls that the flow of the injected fluid is adequately controlled.

[Doc. No. 3025, 29 FR 7453, June 10, 1964, as amended by Amdt. 33-10, 49 FR 6851, Feb. 23, 1984]

§ 33.37 Ignition system.

Each spark ignition engine must have a dual ignition system with at least two spark plugs for each cylinder and two separate electric circuits with separate sources of electrical energy, or have an ignition system of equivalent in-flight reliability.

§ 33.39 Lubrication system.

(a) The lubrication system of the engine must be designed and constructed so that it will function properly in all flight attitudes and atmospheric conditions in which the airplane is expected to operate. In wet sump engines, this requirement must be met when only one-half of the maximum lubricant supply is in the engine.

(b) The lubrication system of the engine must be designed and constructed to allow installing a means of cooling the lubricant.

(c) The crankcase must be vented to the atmosphere to preclude leakage of oil from excessive pressure in the crankcase.

Subpart D—Block Tests; Reciprocating Aircraft Engines

§ 33.41 Applicability.

This subpart prescribes the block tests and inspections for reciprocating aircraft engines.

§ 33.42 General.

Before each endurance test required by this subpart, the adjustment setting and functioning characteristic of each component having an adjustment setting and a functioning characteristic that can be established independent of installation on the engine must be established and recorded.

[Amdt. 33–6, 39 FR 35465, Oct. 1, 1974]

§ 33.43 Vibration test.

(a) Each engine must undergo a vibration survey to establish the torsional and bending vibration characteristics of the crankshaft and the propeller shaft or other output shaft, over the range of crankshaft speed and engine power, under steady state and transient conditions, from idling speed to either 110 percent of the desired maximum continuous speed rating or 103 percent of the maximum desired takeoff speed rating, whichever is higher. The survey must be conducted using, for airplane engines, the same configuration of the propeller type which is used for the endurance test, and using, for other engines, the same configuration of the loading device type which is used for the endurance test.

(b) The torsional and bending vibration stresses of the crankshaft and the propeller shaft or other output shaft may not exceed the endurance limit stress of the material from which the shaft is made. If the maximum stress in the shaft cannot be shown to be below the endurance limit by measurement, the vibration frequency and amplitude must be measured. The peak amplitude must be shown to produce a stress below the endurance limit; if not, the engine must be run at the condition producing the peak amplitude until, for steel shafts, 10 million stress reversals have been sustained without fatigue failure and, for other shafts, until it is shown that fatigue will not occur within the endurance limit stress of the material.

(c) Each accessory drive and mounting attachment must be loaded, with the loads imposed by each accessory used only for an aircraft service being the limit load specified by the applicant for the drive or attachment point.

(d) The vibration survey described in paragraph (a) of this section must be repeated with that cylinder not firing which has the most adverse vibration effect, in order to establish the conditions under which the engine can be operated safely in that abnormal state. However, for this vibration survey, the engine speed range need only extend from idle to the maximum desired takeoff speed, and compliance with paragraph (b) of this section need not be shown.

[Amdt. 33–6, 39 FR 35465, Oct. 1, 1974, as amended by Amdt. 33–10, 49 FR 6851, Feb. 23, 1984]

§ 33.45 Calibration tests.

(a) Each engine must be subjected to the calibration tests necessary to establish its power characteristics and the conditions for the endurance test specified in § 33.49. The results of the power characteristics calibration tests form the basis for establishing the characteristics of the engine over its entire operating range of crankshaft rotational speeds, manifold pressures, fuel/air mixture settings, and altitudes. Power ratings are based upon standard atmospheric conditions with only those accessories installed which are essential for engine functioning.

(b) A power check at sea level conditions must be accomplished on the endurance test engine after the endurance test. Any change in power characteristics which occurs during the endurance test must be determined. Measurements taken during the final portion of the endurance test may be used in showing compliance with the requirements of this paragraph.

[Doc. No. 3025, 29 FR 7453, June 10, 1964, as amended by Amdt. 33–6, 39 FR 35465, Oct. 1, 1974]

§ 33.47 Detonation test.

Each engine must be tested to establish that the engine can function without detonation throughout its range of intended conditions of operation.

§ 33.49 Endurance test.

(a) *General.* Each engine must be subjected to an endurance test that includes a total of 150 hours of operation (except as provided in paragraph (e)(1)(iii) of this section) and, depending upon the type and contemplated use of the engine, consists of one of the series of runs specified in paragraphs (b) through (e) of this section, as applicable. The runs must be made in the order found appropriate by the Administrator for the particular engine being tested. During the endurance test the engine power and the crankshaft rotational speed must be kept within ±3 percent of the rated values. During the runs at rated takeoff power and for at least 35 hours at rated maximum continuous power, one cylinder must be operated at not less than the limiting temperature, the other cylinders must be operated at a temperature not lower than 50 degrees F. below the limiting temperature, and the oil inlet temperature must be maintained within ±10 degrees F. of the limiting temperature. An engine that is equipped with a propeller shaft must be fitted for the endurance test with a propeller that thrust-loads the engine to the maximum thrust which the engine is designed to resist at each applicable operating condition specified in this section. Each accessory drive and mounting attachment must be loaded. During operation at rated takeoff power and rated maximum continuous power, the load imposed by each accessory used only for an aircraft service must be the limit load specified by the applicant for the engine drive or attachment point.

(b) *Unsupercharged engines and engines incorporating a gear-driven single-speed supercharger.* For engines not incorporating a supercharger and for engines incorporating a gear-driven single-speed supercharger the applicant must conduct the following runs:

(1) A 30-hour run consisting of alternate periods of 5 minutes at rated takeoff power with takeoff speed, and 5 minutes at maximum best economy cruising power or maximum recommended cruising power.

(2) A 20-hour run consisting of alternate periods of 1½ hours at rated maximum continuous power with maximum continuous speed, and ½ hour at 75 percent rated maximum continuous power and 91 percent maximum continuous speed.

(3) A 20-hour run consisting of alternate periods of 1½ hours at rated maximum continuous power with maximum continuous speed, and ½ hour at 70 percent rated maximum continuous power and 89 percent maximum continuous speed.

(4) A 20-hour run consisting of alternate periods of 1½ hours at rated maximum continuous power with maximum continuous speed, and ½ hour at 65 percent rated maximum continuous power and 87 percent maximum continuous speed.

(5) A 20-hour run consisting of alternate periods of 1½ hours at rated maximum continuous power with maximum continuous speed, and ½ hour at 60 percent rated maximum continuous power and 84.5 percent maximum continuous speed.

(6) A 20-hour run consisting of alternate periods of 1½ hours at rated maximum continuous power with maximum continuous speed, and ½ hour at 50 percent rated maximum continuous power and 79.5 percent maximum continuous speed.

(7) A 20-hour run consisting of alternate periods of 2½ hours at rated maximum continuous power with maximum continuous speed, and 2½ hours at maximum best economy cruising power or at maximum recommended cruising power.

(c) *Engines incorporating a gear-driven two-speed supercharger.* For engines incorporating a gear-driven two-speed supercharger the applicant must conduct the following runs:

(1) A 30-hour run consisting of alternate periods in the lower gear ratio of 5 minutes at rated takeoff power with takeoff speed, and 5 minutes at maximum best economy cruising power or at maximum recommended cruising power. If a takeoff power rating is desired in the higher gear ratio, 15 hours of the 30-hour run must be made in the higher gear ratio in alternate peri-

ods of 5 minutes at the observed horsepower obtainable with the takeoff critical altitude manifold pressure and takeoff speed, and 5 minutes at 70 percent high ratio rated maximum continuous power and 89 percent high ratio maximum continuous speed.

(2) A 15-hour run consisting of alternate periods in the lower gear ratio of 1 hour at rated maximum continuous power with maximum continuous speed, and ½ hour at 75 percent rated maximum continuous power and 91 percent maximum continuous speed.

(3) A 15-hour run consisting of alternate periods in the lower gear ratio of 1 hour at rated maximum continuous power with maximum continuous speed, and ½ hour at 70 percent rated maximum continuous power and 89 percent maximum continuous speed.

(4) A 30-hour run in the higher gear ratio at rated maximum continuous power with maximum continuous speed.

(5) A 5-hour run consisting of alternate periods of 5 minutes in each of the supercharger gear ratios. The first 5 minutes of the test must be made at maximum continuous speed in the higher gear ratio and the observed horsepower obtainable with 90 percent of maximum continuous manifold pressure in the higher gear ratio under sea level conditions. The condition for operation for the alternate 5 minutes in the lower gear ratio must be that obtained by shifting to the lower gear ratio at constant speed.

(6) A 10-hour run consisting of alternate periods in the lower gear ratio of 1 hour at rated maximum continuous power with maximum continuous speed, and 1 hour at 65 percent rated maximum continuous power and 87 percent maximum continuous speed.

(7) A 10-hour run consisting of alternate periods in the lower gear ratio of 1 hour at rated maximum continuous power with maximum continuous speed, and 1 hour at 60 percent rated maximum continuous power and 84.5 percent maximum continuous speed.

(8) A 10-hour run consisting of alternate periods in the lower gear ratio of 1 hour at rated maximum continuous power with maximum continuous speed, and 1 hour at 50 percent rated

maximum continuous power and 79.5 percent maximum continuous speed.

(9) A 20-hour run consisting of alternate periods in the lower gear ratio of 2 hours at rated maximum continuous power with maximum continuous speed, and 2 hours at maximum best economy cruising power and speed or at maximum recommended cruising power.

(10) A 5-hour run in the lower gear ratio at maximum best economy cruising power and speed or at maximum recommended cruising power and speed.

Where simulated altitude test equipment is not available when operating in the higher gear ratio, the runs may be made at the observed horsepower obtained with the critical altitude manifold pressure or specified percentages thereof, and the fuel-air mixtures may be adjusted to be rich enough to suppress detonation.

(d) *Helicopter engines.* To be eligible for use on a helicopter each engine must either comply with paragraphs (a) through (j) of § 29.923 of this chapter, or must undergo the following series of runs:

(1) A 35-hour run consisting of alternate periods of 30 minutes each at rated takeoff power with takeoff speed, and at rated maximum continuous power with maximum continuous speed.

(2) A 25-hour run consisting of alternate periods of 2½ hours each at rated maximum continuous power with maximum continuous speed, and at 70 percent rated maximum continuous power with maximum continuous speed.

(3) A 25-hour run consisting of alternate periods of 2½ hours each at rated maximum continuous power with maximum continuous speed, and at 70 percent rated maximum continuous power with 80 to 90 percent maximum continuous speed.

(4) A 25-hour run consisting of alternate periods of 2½ hours each at 30 percent rated maximum continuous power with takeoff speed, and at 30 percent rated maximum continuous power with 80 to 90 percent maximum continuous speed.

(5) A 25-hour run consisting of alternate periods of 2½ hours each at 80 percent rated maximum continuous power with takeoff speed, and at either rated maximum continuous power with 110 percent maximum continuous speed or at rated takeoff power with 103 percent takeoff speed, whichever results in the greater speed.

(6) A 15-hour run at 105 percent rated maximum continuous power with 105 percent maximum continuous speed or at full throttle and corresponding speed at standard sea level carburetor entrance pressure, if 105 percent of the rated maximum continuous power is not exceeded.

(e) *Turbosupercharged engines.* For engines incorporating a turbosupercharger the following apply except that altitude testing may be simulated provided the applicant shows that the engine and supercharger are being subjected to mechanical loads and operating temperatures no less severe than if run at actual altitude conditions:

(1) For engines used in airplanes the applicant must conduct the runs specified in paragraph (b) of this section, except—

(i) The entire run specified in paragraph (b)(1) of this section must be made at sea level altitude pressure;

(ii) The portions of the runs specified in paragraphs (b) (2) through (7) of this section at rated maximum continuous power must be made at critical altitude pressure, and the portions of the runs at other power must be made at 8,000 feet altitude pressure; and

(iii) The turbosupercharger used during the 150-hour endurance test must be run on the bench for an additional 50 hours at the limiting turbine wheel inlet gas temperature and rotational speed for rated maximum continuous power operation unless the limiting temperature and speed are maintained during 50 hours of the rated maximum continuous power operation.

(2) For engines used in helicopters the applicant must conduct the runs specified in paragraph (d) of this section, except—

(i) The entire run specified in paragraph (d)(1) of this section must be made at critical altitude pressure;

(ii) The portions of the runs specified in paragraphs (d) (2) and (3) of this section at rated maximum continuous power must be made at critical altitude pressure and the portions of the runs at other power must be made at 8,000 feet altitude pressure;

(iii) The entire run specified in paragraph (d)(4) of this section must be made at 8,000 feet altitude pressure;

(iv) The portion of the runs specified in paragraph (d)(5) of this section at 80 percent of rated maximum continuous power must be made at 8,000 feet altitude pressure and the portions of the runs at other power must be made at critical altitude pressure;

(v) The entire run specified in paragraph (d)(6) of this section must be made at critical altitude pressure; and

(vi) The turbosupercharger used during the endurance test must be run on the bench for 50 hours at the limiting turbine wheel inlet gas temperature and rotational speed for rated maximum continuous power operation unless the limiting temperature and speed are maintained during 50 hours of the rated maximum continuous power operation.

[Amdt. 33-3, 32 FR 3736, Mar. 4, 1967, as amended by Amdt. 33-6, 39 FR 35465, Oct. 1, 1974; Amdt. 33-10, 49 FR 6851, Feb. 23, 1984]

§ 33.51   Operation test.

The operation test must include the testing found necessary by the Administrator to demonstrate backfire characteristics, starting, idling, acceleration, overspeeding, functioning of propeller and ignition, and any other operational characteristic of the engine. If the engine incorporates a multispeed supercharger drive, the design and construction must allow the supercharger to be shifted from operation at the lower speed ratio to the higher and the power appropriate to the manifold pressure and speed settings for rated maximum continuous power at the higher supercharger speed ratio must be obtainable within five seconds.

[Doc. No. 3025, 29 FR 7453, June 10, 1964, as amended by Amdt. 33-3, 32 FR 3737, Mar. 4, 1967]

§33.53 Engine component tests.

(a) For each engine that cannot be adequately substantiated by endurance testing in accordance with §33.49, the applicant must conduct additional tests to establish that components are able to function reliably in all normally anticipated flight and atmospheric conditions.

(b) Temperature limits must be established for each component that requires temperature controlling provisions in the aircraft installation to assure satisfactory functioning, reliability, and durability.

§33.55 Teardown inspection.

After completing the endurance test—

(a) Each engine must be completely disassembled;

(b) Each component having an adjustment setting and a functioning characteristic that can be established independent of installation on the engine must retain each setting and functioning characteristic within the limits that were established and recorded at the beginning of the test; and

(c) Each engine component must conform to the type design and be eligible for incorporation into an engine for continued operation, in accordance with information submitted in compliance with §33.4.

[Amdt. 33-6, 39 FR 35466, Oct. 1, 1974, as amended by Amdt. 33-9, 45 FR 60181, Sept. 11, 1980]

§33.57 General conduct of block tests.

(a) The applicant may, in conducting the block tests, use separate engines of identical design and construction in the vibration, calibration, detonation, endurance, and operation tests, except that, if a separate engine is used for the endurance test it must be subjected to a calibration check before starting the endurance test.

(b) The applicant may service and make minor repairs to the engine during the block tests in accordance with the service and maintenance instructions submitted in compliance with §33.4. If the frequency of the service is excessive, or the number of stops due to engine malfunction is ex-

cessive, or a major repair, or replacement of a part is found necessary during the block tests or as the result of findings from the teardown inspection, the engine or its parts may be subjected to any additional test the Administrator finds necessary.

(c) Each applicant must furnish all testing facilities, including equipment and competent personnel, to conduct the block tests.

[Doc. No. 3025, 29 FR 7453, June 10, 1964, as amended by Amdt. 33-6, 39 FR 35466, Oct. 1, 1974; Amdt. 33-9, 45 FR 60181, Sept. 11, 1980]

Subpart E—Design and Construction; Turbine Aircraft Engines

§33.61 Applicability.

This subpart prescribes additional design and construction requirements for turbine aircraft engines.

§33.62 Stress analysis.

A stress analysis must be performed on each turbine engine showing the design safety margin of each turbine engine rotor, spacer, and rotor shaft.

[Amdt. 33-6, 39 FR 35466, Oct. 1, 1974]

§33.63 Vibration.

Each engine must be designed and constructed to function throughout its operating range of rotational speeds and engine power without inducing excessive stress in any engine part because of vibration and without imparting excessive vibration forces to the aircraft structure.

[Doc. No. 3025, 29 FR 7453, June 10, 1964, as amended by Amdt. 33-10, 49 FR 6851, Feb. 23, 1984]

§33.65 Surge and stall characteristics.

When the engine is operated in accordance with operating instructions required by §33.5(b), starting, a change of power or thrust, power or thrust augmentation, limiting inlet air distortion, or inlet air temperature may not cause surge or stall to the extent that flameout, structural failure, overtemperature, or failure of the engine to recover power or thrust will occur at any point in the operating envelope.

[Amdt. 33-6, 39 FR 35466, Oct. 1, 1974]

§ 33.66   Bleed air system.

The engine must supply bleed air without adverse effect on the engine, excluding reduced thrust or power output, at all conditions up to the discharge flow conditions established as a limitation under § 33.7(c)(11). If bleed air used for engine anti-icing can be controlled, provision must be made for a means to indicate the functioning of the engine ice protection system.

[Amdt. 33-10, 49 FR 6851, Feb. 23, 1984]

§ 33.67   Fuel system.

(a) With fuel supplied to the engine at the flow and pressure specified by the applicant, the engine must function properly under each operating condition required by this part. Each fuel control adjusting means that may not be manipulated while the fuel control device is mounted on the engine must be secured by a locking device and sealed, or otherwise be inaccessible. All other fuel control adjusting means must be accessible and marked to indicate the function of the adjustment unless the function is obvious.

(b) There must be a fuel strainer or filter between the engine fuel inlet opening and the inlet of either the fuel metering device or the engine-driven positive displacement pump whichever is nearer the engine fuel inlet. In addition, the following provisions apply to each strainer or filter required by this paragraph (b):

(1) It must be accessible for draining and cleaning and must incorporate a screen or element that is easily removable.

(2) It must have a sediment trap and drain except that it need not have a drain if the strainer or filter is easily removable for drain purposes.

(3) It must be mounted so that its weight is not supported by the connecting lines or by the inlet or outlet connections of the strainer or filter, unless adequate strength margins under all loading conditions are provided in the lines and connections.

(4) It must have the type and degree of fuel filtering specified as necessary for protection of the engine fuel system against foreign particles in the fuel. The applicant must show:

(i) That foreign particles passing through the specified filtering means do not impair the engine fuel system functioning; and

(ii) That the fuel system is capable of sustained operation throughout its flow and pressure range with the fuel initially saturated with water at 80° F (27° C) and having 0.025 fluid ounces per gallon (0.20 milliliters per liter) of free water added and cooled to the most critical condition for icing likely to be encountered in operation. However, this requirement may be met by demonstrating the effectiveness of specified approved fuel anti-icing additives, or that the fuel system incorporates a fuel heater which maintains the fuel temperature at the fuel strainer or fuel inlet above 32° F (0° C) under the most critical conditions.

(5) The applicant must demonstrate that the filtering means has the capacity (with respect to engine operating limitations) to ensure that the engine will continue to operate within approved limits, with fuel contaminated to the maximum degree of particle size and density likely to be encountered in service. Operation under these conditions must be demonstrated for a period acceptable to the Administrator, beginning when indication of impending filter blockage is first given by either:

(i) Existing engine instrumentation; or

(ii) Additional means incorporated into the engine fuel system.

(6) Any strainer or filter bypass must be designed and constructed so that the release of collected contaminants is minimized by appropriate location of the bypass to ensure that collected contaminants are not in the bypass flow path.

(c) If provided as part of the engine, the applicant must show for each fluid injection (other than fuel) system and its controls that the flow of the injected fluid is adequately controlled.

[Amdt. 33-6, 39 FR 35466, Oct. 1, 1974, as amended by Amdt. 33-10, 49 FR 6851, Feb. 23, 1984]

§ 33.68   Induction system icing.

Each engine, with all icing protection systems operating, must—

(a) Operate throughout its flight power range (including idling) without the accumulation of ice on the engine components that adversely affects engine operation or that causes a serious loss of power or thrust in continuous maximum and intermittent maximum icing conditions as defined in Appendix C of Part 25 of this chapter; and

(b) Idle for 30 minutes on the ground, with the available air bleed for icing protection at its critical condition, without adverse effect, in an atmosphere that is at a temperature between 15° and 30° F (between −9° and −1° C) and has a liquid water content not less than 0.3 grams per cubic meter in the form of drops having a mean effective diameter not less than 20 microns, followed by a momentary operation at takeoff power or thrust. During the 30 minutes of idle operation the engine may be run up periodically to a moderate power or thrust setting in a manner acceptable to the Administrator.

[Amdt. 33–6, 39 FR 35466, Oct. 1, 1974, as amended by Amdt. 33–10, 49 FR 6852, Feb. 23, 1984]

§ 33.69 Ignitions system.

Each engine must be equipped with an ignition system for starting the engine on the ground and in flight. An electric ignition system must have at least two igniters and two separate secondary electric circuits, except that only one igniter is required for fuel burning augmentation systems.

[Amdt. 33–6, 39 FR 35466, Oct. 1, 1974]

§ 33.71 Lubrication system.

(a) *General.* Each lubrication system must function properly in the flight attitudes and atmospheric conditions in which an aircraft is expected to operate.

(b) *Oil strainer or filter.* There must be an oil strainer or filter through which all of the engine oil flows. In addition:

(1) Each strainer or filter required by this paragraph that has a bypass must be constructed and installed so that oil will flow at the normal rate through the rest of the system with the strainer or filter element completely blocked.

(2) The type and degree of filtering necessary for protection of the engine oil system against foreign particles in the oil must be specified. The applicant must demonstrate that foreign particles passing through the specified filtering means do not impair engine oil system functioning.

(3) Each strainer or filter required by this paragraph must have the capacity (with respect to operating limitations established for the engine) to ensure that engine oil system functioning is not impaired with the oil contaminated to a degree (with respect to particle size and density) that is greater than that established for the engine in paragraph (b)(2) of this section.

(4) For each strainer or filter required by this paragraph, except the strainer or filter at the oil tank outlet, there must be means to indicate contamination before it reaches the capacity established in accordance with paragraph (b)(3) of this section.

(5) Any filter bypass must be designed and constructed so that the release of collected contaminants is minimized by appropriate location of the bypass to ensure that the collected contaminants are not in the bypass flow path.

(6) Each strainer or filter required by this paragraph that has no bypass, except the strainer or filter at an oil tank outlet or for a scavenge pump, must have provisions for connection with a warning means to warn the pilot of the occurence of contamination of the screen before it reaches the capacity established in accordance with paragraph (b)(3) of this section.

(7) Each strainer or filter required by this paragraph must be accessible for draining and cleaning.

(c) *Oil tanks.* (1) Each oil tank must have an expansion space of not less than 10 percent of the tank capacity.

(2) It must be impossible to inadvertently fill the oil tank expansion space.

(3) Each recessed oil tank filler connection that can retain any appreciable quantity of oil must have provision for fitting a drain.

(4) Each oil tank cap must provide an oil-tight seal.

(5) Each oil tank filler must be marked with the word "oil."

(6) Each oil tank must be vented from the top part of the expansion space, with the vent so arranged that condensed water vapor that might freeze and obstruct the line cannot accumulate at any point.

(7) There must be means to prevent entrance into the oil tank or into any oil tank outlet, of any object that might obstruct the flow of oil through the system.

(8) There must be a shutoff valve at the outlet of each oil tank, unless the external portion of the oil system (including oil tank supports) is fireproof.

(9) Each unpressurized oil tank may not leak when subjected to a maximum operating temperature and an internal pressure of 5 p.s.i., and each pressurized oil tank may not leak when subjected to maximum operating temperature and an internal pressure that is not less than 5 p.s.i. plus the maximum operating pressure of the tank.

(10) Leaked or spilled oil may not accumulate between the tank and the remainder of the engine.

(11) Each oil tank must have an oil quantity indicator or provisions for one.

(12) If the propeller feathering system depends on engine oil—

(i) There must be means to trap an amount of oil in the tank if the supply becomes depleted due to failure of any part of the lubricating system other than the tank itself;

(ii) The amount of trapped oil must be enough to accomplish the feathering opeation and must be available only to the feathering pump; and

(iii) Provision must be made to prevent sludge or other foreign matter from affecting the safe operation of the propeller feathering system.

(d) *Oil drains.* A drain (or drains) must be provided to allow safe drainage of the oil system. Each drain must—

(1) Be accessible; and

(2) Have manual or automatic means for positive locking in the closed position.

(e) *Oil radiators.* Each oil radiator must withstand, without failure, any vibration, inertia, and oil pressure load to which it is subjected during the block tests.

[Amdt. 33-6, 39 FR 35466, Oct. 1, 1974, as amended by Amdt. 33-10, 49 FR 6852, Feb. 23, 1984]

§ 33.72   Hydraulic actuating systems.

Each hydraulic actuating system must function properly under all conditions in which the engine is expected to operate. Each filter or screen must be accessible for servicing and each tank must meet the design criteria of § 33.71.

[Amdt. 33-6, 39 FR 35467, Oct. 1, 1974]

§ 33.73   Power or thrust response.

The design and construction of the engine must enable an increase—

(a) From minimum to rated takeoff power or thrust with the maximum bleed air and power extraction to be permitted in an aircraft, without overtemperature, surge, stall, or other detrimental factors occurring to the engine whenever the power control lever is moved from the minimum to the maximum position in not more than 1 second, except that the Administrator may allow additional time increments for different regimes of control operation requiring control scheduling; and

(b) From the fixed minimum flight idle power lever position when provided, or if not provided, from not more than 15 percent of the rated takeoff power or thrust available to 95 percent rated takeoff power or thrust in not over 5 seconds. The 5-second power or thrust response must occur from a stabilized static condition using only the bleed air and accessories loads necessary to run the engine. This takeoff rating is specified by the applicant and need not include thrust augmentation.

[Amdt. 33-1, 36 FR 5493, Mar. 24, 1971]

§ 33.75   Safety analysis.

It must be shown by analysis that any probable malfunction or any probable single or multiple failure, or any probable improper operation of the engine will not cause the engine to—

(a) Catch fire;

(b) Burst (release hazardous fragments through the engine case);

(c) Generate loads greater than those ultimate loads specified in §33.23(a); or

(d) Lose the capability of being shut down.

[Amdt. 33-6, 39 FR 35467, Oct. 1, 1974, as amended by Amdt. 33-10, 49 FR 6852, Feb. 23, 1984]

§33.77 Foreign object ingestion.

(a) Ingestion of a 4-pound bird, under the conditions prescribed in paragraph (e) of this section, may not cause the engine to—

(1) Catch fire;

(2) Burst (release hazardous fragments through the engine case);

(3) Generate loads greater than those ultimate loads specified in §33.23(a); or

(4) Lose the capability of being shut down.

(b) Ingestion of 3-ounce birds or 1½-pound birds, under the conditions prescribed in paragraph (e) of this section, may not—

(1) Cause more than a sustained 25 percent power or thrust loss;

(2) Require the engine to be shut down within 5 minutes from the time of ingestion; or

(3) Result in a potentially hazardous condition.

(c) Ingestion of water, ice, or hail, under the conditions prescribed in paragraph (e) of this section, may not cause a sustained power or thrust loss or require the engine to be shut down. It must be demonstrated that the engine can accelerate and decelerate safely while inducting a mixture of at least 4 percent water by weight of engine airflow following stabilized operation at both flight idle and takeoff power settings with at least a 4 percent water-to-air ratio.

(d) For an engine that incorporates a protection device, compliance with this section need not be demonstrated with respect to foreign objects to be ingested under the conditions prescribed in paragraph (e) of this section if it is shown that—

(1) Such foreign objects are of a size that will not pass through the protective device;

(2) The protective device will withstand the impact of the foreign objects; and

(3) The foreign object, or objects, stopped by the protective device will not obstruct the flow of induction air into the engine with a resultant sustained reduction in power or thrust greater than those values required by paragraphs (b) and (c) of this section.

(e) Compliance with paragraphs (a), (b), and (c) of this section must be shown by engine test under the following ingestion conditions:

Foreign object	Test quantity	Speed of foreign object	Engine operation	Ingestion
Birds:				
3-ounce size..........	One for each 50 square inches of inlet area or fraction thereof up to a maximum of 16 birds. Three-ounce bird ingestion not required if a 1½-pound bird will pass the inlet guide vanes into the rotor blades.	Liftoff speed of typical aircraft.	Takeoff........................	In rapid sequence to simulate a flock encounter and aimed at selected critical areas.
1½-pound size......	One for the first 300 square inches of inlet area, if it can enter the inlet, plus one for each additional 600 square inches of inlet area or fraction thereof up to a maximum of 8 birds.	Initial climb speed of typical aircraft.	Takeoff........................	In rapid sequence to simulate a flock encounter and aimed at selected critical areas.
4-pound size..........	One, if it can enter the inlet...........	Maximum climb speed of typical aircraft if the engine has inlet guide vanes.	Maximum cruise........	Aimed at critical area.
		Liftoff speed of typical aircraft, if the engine does not have inlet guide vanes.	Takeoff........................	Aimed at critical area.

Foreign object	Test quantity	Speed of foreign object	Engine operation	Ingestion
Ice..............................	Maximum accumulation on a typical inlet cowl and engine face resulting from a 2-minute delay in actuating anti-icing system, or a slab of ice which is comparable in weight or thickness for that size engine.	Sucked in	Maximum cruise........	To simulate a continuous maximum icing encounter at 25°F.
Hail (0.8 to 0.9 specific gravity).	For all engines: With inlet area of not more than 100 square inches: one 1-inch hailstone. With inlet area of more than 100 square inches: one 1-inch and one 2-inch hailstone for each 150 square inches of inlet area or fraction thereof.	Rough air flight speed of typical aircraft.	Maximum cruise at 15,000 feet altitude.	In a volley to simulate a hailstone encounter. One-half the number of hailstones aimed at random area over the face of the inlet and the other half aimed at the critical face area.
	For supersonic engines (in addition): 3 hailstones each having a diameter equal to that in a straight line variation from 1 inch at 35,000 feet to ¼ inch at 60,000 feet using diameter corresponding to the lowest supersonic cruise altitude expected.	Supersonic cruise velocity. Alternatively, use subsonic velocities with larger hailstones to give equivalent kinetic energy.	Maximum cruise........	Aimed at critical engine face area.
Water..................	At least 4 percent of engine airflow by weight.	Sucked in	Flight idle, acceleration, takeoff, deceleration.	For 3 minutes each at idle and takeoff, and during acceleration and deceleration in spray to simulate rain.

NOTE.—The term "inlet area" as used in this section means the engine inlet projected area at the front face of the engine. It includes the projected area of any spinner or bullet nose that is provided.

[Amdt. 33-10, 49 FR 6852, Feb. 23, 1984]

§ 33.79 Fuel burning thrust augmentor.

Each fuel burning thrust augmentor, including the nozzle, must—

(a) Provide cutoff of the fuel burning thrust augmentor;

(b) Permit on-off cycling;

(c) Be controllable within the intended range of operation;

(d) Upon a failure or malfunction of augmentor combustion, not cause the engine to lose thrust other than that provided by the augmentor; and

(e) Have controls that function compatibly with the other engine controls and automatically shut off augmentor fuel flow if the engine rotor speed drops below the minimum rotational speed at which the augmentor is intended to function.

[Amdt. 33-6, 39 FR 35468, Oct. 1, 1974]

Subpart F—Block Tests; Turbine Aircraft Engines

§ 33.81 Applicability.

This subpart prescribes the block tests and inspections for turbine engines.

[Doc. 3025, 29 FR 7453, June 10, 1964, as amended by Amdt. 33-6, 39 FR 35468, Oct. 1, 1974]

§ 33.82 General.

Before each endurance test required by this subpart, the adjustment setting and functioning characteristic of each component having an adjustment setting and a functioning characteristic that can be established independent of installation on the engine must be established and recorded.

[Amdt. 36-6, 39 FR 35468. Oct. 1, 1974]

§ 33.83 Vibration test.

(a) Each engine must undergo a vibration survey to establish the vibration characteristics of the rotor discs, rotor blades, rotor shafts, stator blades, and any other components that are subject to vibratory exciting forces which could induce failure at the maximum inlet distortion limit. The survey is to cover the range of rotor speeds and engine power or thrust, under steady state and transient conditions, from idling speed to 103 percent of the maximum permissible speed. The survey must be conducted using the same configuration of the loading device which is used for the endurance test, except that the Administrator may allow the use of a modified configuration if that loading device type is incompatible with the necessary vibration instrumentation.

(b) The vibration stresses (or strains) of rotor and stator components determined under paragraph (a) of this section must be less, by a margin acceptable to the Administrator, than the endurance limit of the material from which these parts are made, adjusted for the most severe operating conditions.

(c) Each accessory drive and mounting attachment must be loaded, with the load imposed by each accessory used only for an aircraft service being the limit load specified by the applicant for the engine drive or attachment point.

[Amdt. 33-6, 39 FR 35468, Oct. 1, 1974, as amended by Amdt. 33-10, 49 FR 6853, Feb. 23, 1984]

§ 33.85 Calibration tests.

(a) Each engine must be subjected to those calibration tests necessary to establish its power characteristics and the conditions for the endurance test specified § 33.87. The results of the power characteristics calibration tests form the basis for establishing the characteristics of the engine over its entire operating range of speeds, pressures, temperatures, and altitudes. Power ratings are based upon standard atmospheric conditions with no airbleed for aircraft services and with only those accessories installed which are essential for engine functioning.

(b) A power check at sea level conditions must be accomplished on the endurance test engine after the endurance test and any change in power

characteristics which occurs during the endurance test must be determined. Measurements taken during the final portion of the endurance test may be used in showing compliance with the requirements of this paragraph.

[Doc. No. 3025, 29 FR 7453, June 10, 1964, as amended by Amdt. 33-6, 39 FR 35468, Oct. 1, 1974]

§ 33.87 Endurance test.

(a) *General.* Each engine must be subjected to an endurance test that includes a total of 150 hours of operation and, depending upon the type and contemplated use of the engine, consists of one of the series of runs specified in paragraphs (b) through (f) of this section, as applicable. For engines tested under paragraph (b), (c), (d), or (e) of this section, the prescribed 6-hour test sequence must be conducted 25 times to complete the required 150 hours of operation. The following test requirements apply:

(1) The runs must be made in the order found appropriate by the Administrator for the particular engine being tested.

(2) Any automatic engine control that is part of the engine must control the engine during the endurance test except for operations where automatic control is normally overridden by manual control or where manual control is otherwise specified for a particular test run.

(3) Except as provided in paragraph (a)(5) of this section, power or thrust, gas temperature, rotor shaft rotational speed, and, if limited, temperature of external surfaces of the engine must be at least 100 percent of the value associated with the particular engine operation being tested. More than one test may be run if all parameters cannot be held at the 100 percent level simultaneously.

(4) The runs must be made using fuel, lubricants and hydraulic fluid which conform to the specifications specified in complying with § 33.7(c).

(5) Maximum air bleed for engine and aircraft services must be used during at least one-fifth of the runs. However, for these runs, the power or thrust or the rotor shaft rotational

speed may be less than 100 percent of the value associated with the particular operation being tested if the Administrator finds that the validity of the endurance test is not compromised.

(6) Each accessory drive and mounting attachment must be loaded. The load imposed by each accessory used only for aircraft service must be the limit load specified by the applicant for the engine drive and attachment point during rated maximum continuous power or thrust and higher output. The endurance test of any accessory drive and mounting attachment under load may be accomplished on a separate rig if the validity of the test is confirmed by an approved analysis.

(7) During the runs at any rated power or thrust the gas temperature and the oil inlet temperature must be maintained at the limiting temperature except where the test periods are not longer than 5 minutes and do not allow stabilization. At least one run must be made with fuel, oil, and hydraulic fluid at the minimum pressure limit and at least one run must be made with fuel, oil, and hydraulic fluid at the maximum pressure limit with fluid temperature reduced as necessary to allow maximum pressure to be attained.

(8) If the number of occurrences of either transient rotor shaft overspeed or transient gas overtemperature is limited, that number of the accelerations required by paragraphs (b), (c), (d), and (e) of this section must be made at the limiting overspeed or overtemperature. If the number of occurrences is not limited, half the required accelerations must be made at the limiting overspeed or overtemperature.

(9) For each engine type certificated for use on supersonic aircraft the following additional test requirements apply:

(i) To change the thrust setting, the power control lever must be moved from the initial position to the final position in not more than one second except for movements into the fuel burning thrust augmentor augmentation position if additional time to confirm ignition is necessary.

(ii) During the runs at any rated augmented thrust the hydraulic fluid temperature must be maintained at the limiting temperature except where the test periods are not long enough to allow stabilization.

(iii) During the simulated supersonic runs the fuel temperature and induction air temperature may not be less than the limiting temperature.

(iv) The endurance test must be conducted with the fuel burning thrust augmentor installed, with the primary and secondary exhaust nozzles installed, and with the variable area exhaust nozzles operated during each run according to the methods specified in complying with § 33.5(b).

(v) During the runs at thrust settings, for maximum continuous thrust and percentages thereof, the engine must be operated with the inlet air distortion at the limit for those thrust settings.

(b) *Engines other than certain rotorcraft engines.* For each engine, except a rotorcraft engine for which a rating is desired under paragraph (c), (d), or (e) of this section, the applicant must conduct the following runs:

(1) *Takeoff and idling.* One hour of alternate five-minute periods at rated takeoff power and thrust and at idling power and thrust. The developed powers and thrusts at takeoff and idling conditions and their corresponding rotor speed and gas temperature conditions must be as established by the power control in accordance with the schedule established by the manufacturer. The applicant may, during any one period, manually control the rotor speed, power, and thrust while taking data to check performance. For engines with augmented takeoff power ratings that involve increases in turbine inlet temperature, rotor speed, or shaft power, this period of running at takeoff must be at the augmented rating. For engines with augmented takeoff power ratings that do not materially increase operating severity, the amount of running conducted at the augmented rating is determined by the Administrator. In changing the power setting after each period, the power-control lever must be moved in the manner prescribed in paragraph (b)(5) of this section.

(2) *Rated maximum continuous and takeoff power and thrust.* **Thirty minutes at—**

(i) Rated maximum continuous power and thrust during fifteen of the twenty-five 6-hour endurance test cycles; and

(ii) Rated takeoff power and thrust during ten of the twenty-five 6-hour endurance test cycles.

(3) *Rated maximum continuous power and thrust.* One hour and 30 minutes at rated maximum continuous power and thrust.

(4) *Incremental cruise power and thrust.* Two hours and 30 minutes at the successive power lever positions corresponding to at least 15 approximately equal speed and time increments between maximum continuous engine rotational speed and ground or minimum idle rotational speed. For engines operating at constant speed, the thrust and power may be varied in place of speed. If there is significant peak vibration anywhere between ground idle and maximum continuous conditions, the number of increments chosen may be changed to increase the amount of running made while subject to the peak vibrations up to not more than 50 percent of the total time spent in incremental running.

(5) *Acceleration and deceleration runs.* 30 minutes of accelerations and decelerations, consisting of six cycles from idling power and thrust to rated takeoff power and thrust and maintained at the takeoff power lever position for 30 seconds and at the idling power lever position for approximately four and one-half minutes. In complying with this paragraph, the power-control lever must be moved from one extreme poition to the other in not more than one second, except that, if different regimes of control operations are incorporated necessitating scheduling of the power-control lever motion in going from one extreme position to the other, a longer period of time is acceptable, but not more than two seconds.

(6) *Starts.* One hundred starts must be made, of which 25 starts must be preceded by at least a two-hour engine shutdown. There must be at least 10 false engine starts, pausing for the applicant's specified minimum fuel drainage time, before attempting a normal start. There must be at least 10 normal restarts with not longer

than 15 minutes since engine shutdown. The remaining starts may be made after completing the 150 hours of endurance testing.

(c) *Rotorcraft engines for which a 30-minute OEI power rating is desired.* **For each rotorcraft engine for which a 30-minute OEI power rating is desired, the applicant must conduct the following series of tests:**

(1) *Takeoff and idling.* **One hour of alternate 5-minute periods at rated takeoff power and at idling power. The developed powers at takeoff and idling conditions and their corresponding rotor speed and gas temperature conditions must be as established by the power control in accordance with the schedule established by the manufacturer. During any one period, the rotor speed and power may be controlled manually while taking data to check performance. For engines with augmented takeoff power ratings that involve increases in turbine inlet temperature, rotor speed, or shaft power, this period of running at rated takeoff power must be at the augmented power rating. In changing the power setting after each period, the power control lever must be moved in the manner prescribed in paragraph (c)(5) of this section.**

(2) *Rated 30-minute OEI power.* **Thirty minutes at rated 30-minute OEI power.**

(3) *Rated maximum continuous power.* **Two hours at rated maximum continuous power.**

(4) *Incremental cruise power.* **Two hours at the successive power lever positions corresponding with not less than 12 approximately equal speed and time increments between maximum continuous engine rotational speed and ground or minimum idle rotational speed. For engines operating at constant speed, power may be varied in place of speed. If there are significant peak vibrations anywhere between ground idle and maximum continuous conditions, the number of increments chosen must be changed**

to increase the amount of running conducted while being subjected to the peak vibrations up to not more than 50 percent of the total time spent in incremental running.

(5) *Acceleration and deceleration runs.* Thirty minutes of accelerations and decelerations, consisting of six cycles from idling power to rated takeoff power and maintained at the takeoff power lever position for 30 seconds and at the idling power lever position for approximately 4½ minutes. In complying with this paragraph, the power control lever must be moved from one extreme position to the other in not more than 1 second, except that if different regimes of control operations are incorporated necessitating scheduling of the power control lever motion in going from one extreme position to the other, a longer period of time is acceptable, but not more than 2 seconds.

(6) *Starts.* One hundred starts must be made, of which 25 starts must be preceded by at least a two-hour engine shutdown. There must be at least 10 false engine starts, pausing for the applicant's specified minimum fuel drainage time, before attempting a normal start. There must be at least 10 normal restarts with not longer than 15 minutes since engine shutdown. The remaining starts may be made after completing the 150 hours of endurance testing.

(d) *Rotorcraft engines for which a continuous OEI rating is desired.* For each rotorcraft engine for which a continuous OEI power rating is desired, the applicant must conduct the following series of tests:

(1) *Takeoff and idling.* One hour of alternate 5-minute periods at rated takeoff power and at idling power. The developed powers at takeoff and idling conditions and their corresponding rotor speed and gas temperature conditions must be as established by the power control in accordance with the schedule established by the manufacturer. During any one period the rotor speed and power may be controlled manually while taking data to check performance. For engines with augmented takeoff power ratings that involve increases in turbine inlet temperature, rotor speed, or shaft power, this period of running at rated takeoff power must be at the augmented power rating. In changing the power setting after each period, the power contol lever must be moved in the manner prescribed in paragraph (c)(5) of this section.

(2) *Rated maximum continuous and takeoff power.* Thirty minutes at—

(i) Rated maximum continuous power during fifteen of the twenty-five 6-hour endurance test cycles; and

(ii) Rated takeoff power during ten of the twenty-five 6-hour endurance test cycles.

(3) *Rated continuous OEI power.* One hour at rated continuous OEI power.

(4) *Rated maximum continuous power.* One hour at rated maximum continuous power.

(5) *Incremental cruise power.* Two hours at the successive power lever positions corresponding with not less than 12 approximately equal speed and time increments between maximum continuous engine rotational speed and ground or minimum idle rotational speed. For engines operating at constant speed, power may be varied in place of speed. If there are significant peak vibrations any where between ground idle and maximum con-

tinuous conditions, the number of increments chosen must be changed to increase the amount of running conducted while being subjected to the peak vibrations up to not more than 50 percent of the total time spent in incremental running.

(6) *Acceleration and deceleration runs.* Thirty minutes of accelerations and decelerations, consisting of six cycles from idling power to rated takeoff power and maintained at the takeoff power lever position for 30 seconds and at the idling power lever position for approximately 4½ minutes. In complying with this paragraph, the power control lever must be moved from one extreme position to the other in not more than 1 second, except that if different regimes of control operations are incorporated necessitating scheduling of the power control lever motion in going from one extreme position to the other, a longer period of time is acceptable, but not more than 2 seconds.

(7) *Starts.* One hundred starts, of which 25 starts must be preceded by at least a 2-hour engine shutdown. There must be at least 10 false engine starts, pausing for the applicant's specified minimum fuel drainage time, before attempting a normal start. There must be at least 10 normal restarts with not longer than 15 minutes since engine shutdown. The remaining starts may be made after completing the 150 hours of endurance testing.

(e) *Rotorcraft engines for which a 2½-minute OEI power rating is desired.* For each rotorcraft engine for which a 2½ minute OEI power rating is desired, the applicant must conduct the following series of tests:

(1) *Takeoff, 2½-minute OEI, and idling.* One hour of alternate 5-minute periods at rated takeoff power and at idling power except that, during the third and sixth takeoff power periods, only 2½ minutes need be conducted at rated takeoff power, and the remaining 2½ minutes must be conducted at rated 2½-minute OEI power. The developed powers at takeoff, 2½-minute OEI, and idling conditions and their corresponding rotor speed and gas temperature conditions must be as established by the power control in accordance with the schedule established by the manufacturer. The applicant may, during any one period, control manually the rotor speed and power while taking data to check performance. For engines with augmented takeoff power ratings that involve increases in turbine inlet temperature, rotor speed, or shaft power, this period of running at rated takeoff power must be at the augmented rating. In changing the power setting after or during each period, the power control lever must be moved in the manner prescribed in paragraph (d)(6) of this section.

(2) The tests required in paragraphs (b)(2) through (b)(6), or (c)(2) through (c)(6), or (d)(2) through (d)(7) of this section, as applicable, except that in one of the 6-hour test sequences, the last 5 minutes of the 30 minutes at takeoff power test period of paragraph (b)(2) of this section, or of the 30 minutes at 30-minute OEI power test period of paragraph (c)(2) of this section, or of the 1 hour at continuous OEI power test period of paragraph (d)(3) of this section, must be run at 2½-minute OEI power.

(f) *Supersonic aircraft engines.* For each engine type certificated for use on supersonic aircraft the applicant must conduct the following:

(1) *Subsonic test under sea level ambient atmospheric conditions.* Thirty runs of one hour each must be made, consisting of—

(i) Two periods of 5 minutes at rated takeoff augmented thrust each followed by 5 minutes at idle thrust;

(ii) One period of 5 minutes at rated takeoff thrust followed by 5 minutes at not more than 15 percent of rated takeoff thrust;

(iii) One period of 10 minutes at rated takeoff augmented thrust followed by 2 minutes at idle thrust, except that if rated maximum continuous augmented thrust is lower than rated takeoff augmented thrust, 5 of the 10-minute periods must be at rated maximum continuous augmented thrust; and

(iv) Six periods of 1 minute at rated takeoff augmented thrust each followed by 2 minutes, including acceleration and deceleration time, at idle thrust.

(2) *Simulated supersonic test.* Each run of the simulated supersonic test must be preceded by changing the inlet air temperature and pressure from that attained at subsonic condition to the temperature and pressure attained at supersonic velocity, and must be followed by a return to the temperature attained at subsonic condition. Thirty runs of 4 hours each must be made, consisting of—

(i) One period of 30 minutes at the thrust obtained with the power control lever set at the position for rated maximum continuous augmented thrust followed by 10 minutes at the thrust obtained with the power control lever set at the position for 90 percent of rated maximum continuous augmented thrust. The end of this period in the first five runs must be made with the induction air temperature at the limiting condition of transient overtemperature, but need not be repeated during the periods specified in paragraphs (e)(2) (ii) through (iv) of this section;

(ii) One period repeating the run specified in paragraph (e)(2)(i) of this section, except that it must be followed by 10 minutes at the thrust obtained with the power control lever set at the position for 80 percent of rated maximum continuous augmented thrust;

(iii) One period repeating the run specified in paragraph (e)(2)(i) of this section, except that it must be followed by 10 minutes at the thrust obtained with the power control lever set at the position for 60 percent of rated maximum continuous augmented thrust and then 10 minutes at not more than 15 percent of rated takeoff thrust;

(iv) One period repeating the runs specified in paragraphs (e)(2) (i) and (ii) of this section; and

(v) One period of 30 minutes with 25 of the runs made at the thrust obtained with the power control lever set at the position for rated maximum continuous augmented thrust, each followed by idle thrust and with the remaining 5 runs at the thrust obtained with the power control lever set at the position for rated maximum continuous augmented thrust for 25 minutes each, followed by subsonic operation at not more than 15 percent or rated takeoff thrust and accelerated to rated takeoff thrust for 5 minutes using hot fuel.

(3) *Starts.* One hundred starts must be made, of which 25 starts must be preceded by an engine shutdown of least 2 hours. There must be at least 10 false engine starts, pausing for the applicant's specified minimum fuel drainage time before attempting a normal start. At least 10 starts must be normal restarts, each made no later than 15 minutes after engine shutdown. The starts may be made at any time, including the period of endurance testing.

§ 33.88 Engine overtemperature test.

Each engine must be run for 5 minutes at maximum permissible r.p.m with the gas temperature at least 75°F (42°C) higher than the maximum operating limit. Following this run, the turbine assembly must be within serviceable limits.

§ 33.89 Operation test.

(a) The operation test must include testing found necessary by the Administrator to demonstrate—

(1) Starting, idling, acceleration, overspeeding, ignition, functioning of the propeller (if the engine is designated to operate with a propeller);

(2) Compliance with the engine response requirements of § 33.73; and

(3) The minimum power or thrust response time to 95 percent rated takeoff power or thrust, from power lever postions representative of minimum idle and of minimum flight idle, starting from stabilized idle operation, under the following engine load conditions:

(i) No bleed air and power extraction for aircraft use.

(ii) Maximum allowable bleed air and power extraction for aircraft use.

(iii) An intermediate value for bleed air and power extraction representative of that which might be used as a maximum for aircraft during approach to a landing.

(4) If testing facilities are not available, the determination of power extraction required in paragraph (a)(3)(ii) and (iii) of this section may be accomplished through appropriate analytical means.

(b) The operation test must include all testing found necessary by the Administrator to demonstrate that the engine has safe operating characteristics throughout its specified operating envelope.

[Amdt. 33–4, 36 FR 5493, Mar. 24, 1971, as amended by Amdt. 33–6, 39 FR 35469, Oct. 1, 1974; Amdt. 33–10, 49 FR 6853, Feb. 23, 1984]

§ 33.90 Initial maintenance inspection.

Each engine, except engines being type certificated through amendment of an existing type certificate or through supplemental type certification procedures, must undergo an approved test run that simulates the conditions in which the engine is expected to operate in service, including typical start-stop cycles, to establish when the initial maintenance inspection is required. The test run must be accomplished on an engine which substantially conforms to the final type design.

[Amdt. 33–10, 49 FR 6854, Feb. 23, 1984]

§ 33.91 Engine component tests.

(a) For those systems that cannot be adequately substantiated by endurance testing in accordance with the provisions of § 33.87, additional tests must be made to establish that components are able to function reliably in all normally anticipated flight and atmospheric conditions.

(b) Temperature limits must be established for those components that require temperature controlling provisions in the aircraft installation to assure satisfactory functioning, reliability, and durability.

(c) Each unpressurized hydraulic fluid tank may not fail or leak when subjected to maximum operating temperature and an internal pressure of 5 p.s.i., and each pressurized hydraulic fluid tank may not fail or leak when subjected to maximum operating temperature and an internal pressure not less than 5 p.s.i. plus the maximum operating pressure of the tank.

(d) For an engine type certificated for use in supersonic aircraft, the systems, safety devices, and external components that may fail because of operation at maximum and minimum operating temperatures must be identified and tested at maximum and minimum

operating temperatures 'and while temperature and other operating conditions are cycled between maximum and minimum operating values.

[Doc. No. 3025, 29 FR 7453, June 10, 1964, as amended by Amdt. 33–6, 39 FR 35469, Oct. 1, 1974]

§ 33.92 Windmilling tests.

(a) For engines to be used in supersonic aircraft, unless means are incorporated in the engine to stop rotation of the engine rotors when the engine is shut down in flight, each engine rotor must either seize or be capable of rotation for 3 hours at the limiting windmilling rotational r.p.m. with no oil in the engine system, without the engine—

(1) Catching fire;

(2) Bursting (releasing hazardous uncontained fragments); or

(3) Generating loads greater than those ultimate loads specified in § 33.23(a).

(b) A turbojet or turbofan engine incorporating means to stop rotation of the engine rotors when the engine is shut down in flight must be subjected to 25 operations under the following conditions:

(1) Each engine must be shut down while operating at rated maximum continuous thrust.

(2) For engines certificated for use on supersonic aircraft, the temperature of the induction air and the external surfaces of the engine must be held at the maximum limit during the tests required by this paragraph.

[Amdt. 33–6, 39 FR 35470, Oct. 1, 1974, as amended by Amdt. 33–10, 49 FR 6854, Feb. 23, 1984]

§ 33.93 Teardown inspection.

After completing the endurance test each engine must be completely disassembled, and—

(a) Each component having an adjustment setting and a functioning characteristic that can be established independent of installation on the engine must retain each setting and functioning characteristic within the limits that were established and recorded at the beginning of the test; and

(b) Each engine part must conform to the type design and be eligible for incorporation into an engine for continued operation, in accordance with information submitted in compliance with §33.4.

[Amdt. 33-6, 39 FR 35470, Oct. 1, 1974, as amended by Amdt. 33-9, 45 FR 60181, Sept. 11, 1980; Amdt. 33-10, 49 FR 6854, Feb. 23, 1984]

§33.94 Blade containment and rotor unbalance tests.

(a) Except as provided in paragraph (b) of this section, it must be demonstrated by engine tests that the engine is capable of containing damage without catching fire and without failure of its mounting attachments when operated for at least 15 seconds, unless the resulting engine damage induces a self shutdown, after each of the following events:

(1) Failure of the most critical compressor or fan blade while operating at maximum permissible r.p.m. The blade failure must occur at the outermost retention groove or, for integrally-bladed rotor discs, at least 80 percent of the blade must fail.

(2) Failure of the most critical turbine blade while operating at maximum permissible r.p.m. The blade failure must occur at the outermost retention groove or, for integrally-bladed rotor discs, at least 80 percent of the blade must fail. The most critical turbine blade must be determined by considering turbine blade weight and the strength of the adjacent turbine case at case temperatures and pressures associated with operation at maximum permissible r.p.m.

(b) Analysis based on rig testing, component testing, or service experience may be substitute for one of the engine tests prescribed in paragraphs (a)(1) and (a)(2) of this section if—

(1) That test, of the two prescribed, produces the least rotor unbalance; and

(2) The analysis is shown to be equivalent to the test.

(Secs. 313(a), 601, and 603, Federal Aviation Act of 1958 (49 U.S.C. 1354(a), 1421, and 1423); and 49 U.S.C. 106(g) Revised, Pub. L. 97-449, Jan. 12, 1983)

[Amdt. 33-10, 49 FR 6854, Feb. 23, 1984]

§33.95 Engine-propeller systems tests.

If the engine is designed to operate with a propeller, the following tests must be made with a representative propeller installed by either including the tests in the endurance run or otherwise performing them in a manner acceptable to the Administrator:

(a) Feathering operation: 25 cycles.

(b) Negative torque and thrust system operation: 25 cycles from rated maximum continuous power.

(c) Automatic decoupler operation: 25 cycles from rated maximum continuous power (if repeated decoupling and recoupling in service is the intended function of the device).

(d) Reverse thrust operation: 175 cycles from the flight-idle position to full reverse and 25 cycles at rated maximum continuous power from full forward to full reverse thrust. At the end of each cycle the propeller must be operated in reverse pitch for a period of 30 seconds at the maximum rotational speed and power specified by the applicant for reverse pitch operation.

[Doc. No. 3025, 29 FR 7453, June 10, 1964, as amended by Amdt. 33-3, 32 FR 3737, Mar. 4, 1967]

§33.96 Engine tests in auxiliary power unit (APU) mode.

If the engine is designed with a propeller brake which will allow the propeller to be brought to a stop while the gas generator portion of the engine remains in operation, and remain stopped during operation of the engine as an auxiliary power unit ("APU mode"), in addition to the requirements of §33.87, the applicant must conduct the following tests:

(a) Ground locking: A total of 45 hours with the propeller brake engaged in a manner which clearly demonstrates its ability to function without adverse effects on the complete engine while the engine is operating in the APU mode under the maximum conditions of engine speed, torque, temperature, air bleed, and power extraction as specified by the applicant.

(b) Dynamic braking: A total of 400 application-release cycles of brake engagements must be made in a manner which clearly demonstrates its ability to function without adverse effects on the complete engine under the maximum conditions of engine acceleration/deceleration rate, speed, torque, and temperature as specified by the applicant. The propeller must be stopped prior to brake release.

(c) One hundred engine starts and stops with the propeller brake engaged.

(d) The tests required by paragraphs (a), (b), and (c) of this section must be performed on the same engine, but this engine need not be the same engine used for the tests required by § 33.87.

(e) The tests required by paragraphs (a), (b), and (c) of this section must be followed by engine disassembly to the extent necessary to show compliance with the requirements of § 33.93(a) and § 33.93(b).

[Amdt. 33-11, 51 FR 10346, Mar. 25, 1986]

§ 33.97   Thrust reversers.

(a) If the engine incorporates a reverser, the endurance calibration, operation, and vibration tests prescribed in this subpart must be run with the reverser installed. In complying with this section, the power control lever must be moved from one extreme position to the other in not more than one second except, if regimes of control operations are incorporated necessitating scheduling of the power-control lever motion in going from one extreme position to the other, a longer period of time is acceptable but not more than three seconds. In addition, the test prescribed in paragraph (b) of this section must be made. This test may be scheduled as part of the endurance run.

(b) 175 reversals must be made from flight-idle forward thrust to maximum reverse thrust and 25 reversals must be made from rated takeoff thrust to maximum reverse thrust. After each reversal the reverser must be operated at full reverse thrust for a period of one minute, except that, in the case of a reverser intended for use only as a braking means on the ground, the reverser need only be operated at full reverse thrust for 30 seconds.

[Doc. No. 3025, 29 FR 7453, June 10, 1964, as amended by Amdt. 33-3, 32 FR 3737, Mar. 4, 1967]

§ 33.99   General conduct of block tests.

(a) Each applicant may, in making a block test, use separate engines of identical design and construction in the vibration, calibration, endurance, and operation tests, except that, if a separate engine is used for the endurance test it must be subjected to a calibration check before starting the endurance test.

(b) Each applicant may service and make minor repairs to the engine during the block tests in accordance with the service and maintenance instructions submitted in compliance with § 33.4. If the frequency of the service is excessive, or the number of stops due to engine malfunction is excessive, or a major repair, or replacement of a part is found necessary during the block tests or as the result of findings from the teardown inspection, the engine or its parts must be subjected to any additional tests the Administrator finds necessary.

(c) Each applicant must furnish all testing facilities, including equipment and competent personnel, to conduct the block tests.

[Doc. No. 3025, 29 FR 7453, June 10, 1964, as amended by Amdt. 33-6, 39 FR 35470, Oct. 1, 1974; Amdt. 33-9, 45 FR 60181, Sept. 11, 1980]

APPENDIX A—INSTRUCTIONS FOR CONTINUED AIRWORTHINESS

A33.1   GENERAL

(a) This appendix specifies requirements for the preparation of Instructions for Continued Airworthiness as required by § 33.4.

(b) The Instructions for Continued Airworthiness for each engine must include the Instructions for Continued Airworthiness for all engine parts. If Instructions for Continued Airworthiness are not supplied by the engine part manufacturer for an engine part, the Instructions for Continued Airworthiness for the engine must include the information essential to the continued airworthiness of the engine.

(c) The applicant must submit to the FAA a program to show how changes to the Instructions for Continued Airworthiness made by the applicant or by the manufacturers of engine parts will be distributed.

A33.2 FORMAT

(a) The Instructions for Continued Airworthiness must be in the form of a manual or manuals as appropriate for the quantity of data to be provided.

(b) The format of the manual or manuals must provide for a practical arrangement.

A33.3 CONTENT

The contents of the manual or manuals must be prepared in the English language. The Instructions for Continued Airworthiness must contain the following manuals or sections, as appropriate, and information:

(a) *Engine Maintenance Manual or Section.* (1) Introduction information that includes an explanation of the engine's features and data to the extent necessary for maintenance or preventive maintenance.

(2) A detailed description of the engine and its components, systems, and installations.

(3) Installation instructions, including proper procedures for uncrating, deinhibiting, acceptance checking, lifting, and attaching accessories, with any necessary checks.

(4) Basic control and operating information describing how the engine components, systems, and installations operate, and information describing the methods of starting, running, testing, and stopping the engine and its parts including any special procedures and limitations that apply.

(5) Servicing information that covers details regarding servicing points, capacities of tanks, reservoirs, types of fluids to be used, pressures applicable to the various systems, locations of lubrication points, lubricants to be used, and equipment required for servicing.

(6) Scheduling information for each part of the engine that provides the recommended periods at which it should be cleaned, inspected, adjusted, tested, and lubricated, and the degree of inspection the applicable wear tolerances, and work recommended at these periods. However, the applicant may refer to an accessory, instrument, or equipment manufacturer as the source of this information if the applicant shows that the item has an exceptionally high degree of complexity requiring specialized maintenance techniques, test equipment, or expertise. The recommended overhaul periods and necessary cross references to the Airworthiness Limitations section of the manual must also be included. In addition, the applicant must include an inspection program that includes the frequency and extent of the inspections necessary to provide for the continued airworthiness of the engine.

(7) Troubleshooting information describing probable malfunctions, how to recognize those malfunctions, and the remedial action for those malfunctions.

(8) Information describing the order and method of removing the engine and its parts and replacing parts, with any necessary precautions to be taken. Instructions for proper ground handling, crating, and shipping must also be included.

(9) A list of the tools and equipment necessary for maintenance and directions as to their method of use.

(b) *Engine Overhaul Manual or Section.* (1) Disassembly information including the order and method of disassembly for overhaul.

(2) Cleaning and inspection instructions that cover the materials and apparatus to be used and methods and precautions to be taken during overhaul. Methods of overhaul inspection must also be included.

(3) Details of all fits and clearances relevant to overhaul.

(4) Details of repair methods for worn or otherwise substandard parts and components along with the information necessary to determine when replacement is necessary.

(5) The order and method of assembly at overhaul.

(6) Instructions for testing after overhaul.

(7) Instructions for storage preparation, including any storage limits.

(8) A list of tools needed for overhaul.

A33.4 AIRWORTHINESS LIMITATIONS SECTION

The Instructions for Continued Airworthiness must contain a section titled Airworthiness Limitations that is segregated and clearly distinguishable from the rest of the document. This section must set forth each mandatory replacement time, inspection interval, and related procedure required for type certification. If the Instructions for Continued Airworthiness consist of multiple documents, the section required by this paragraph must be included in the principal manual. This section must contain a legible statement in a prominent location that reads: "The Airworthiness Limitations section is FAA approved and specifies maintenance required under §§ 43.16 and 91.163 of the Federal Aviation Regulations unless an alternative program has been FAA approved."

[Amdt. 33-9, 45 FR 60181, Sept. 11, 1980]

FEDERAL AVIATION REGULATIONS

PART 35
AIRWORTHINESS STANDARDS:
Propellers

1989 EDITION

PART 35—AIRWORTHINESS STANDARDS: PROPELLERS

Subpart A—General

Sec.
35.1 Applicability.
35.3 Instruction manual for installing and operating the propeller.
35.4 Instructions for continued airworthiness.
35.5 Propeller operating limitations.

Subpart B—Design and Construction

35.11 Applicability.
35.13 General.
35.15 Design features.
35.17 Materials.
35.19 Durability.
35.21 Reversible propellers.
35.23 Pitch control and indication.

Subpart C—Tests and Inspections

35.31 Applicability.
35.33 General.
35.35 Blade retention test.
35.37 Fatigue limit tests.
35.39 Endurance test.
35.41 Functional test.
35.42 Blade pitch control system component test.
35.43 Special tests.
35.45 Teardown inspection.
35.47 Propeller adjustments and parts replacements.
APPENDIX A—INSTRUCTIONS FOR CONTINUED AIRWORTHINESS

AUTHORITY: Secs. 313, 601, 603, 72 Stat. 752, 775; 49 U.S.C. 1354, 1421, 1423.

SOURCE: Docket No. 2095, 29 FR 7458, June 10, 1964, unless otherwise noted.

Subpart A—General

§ 35.1 Applicability.

(a) This part prescribes airworthiness standards for the issue of type certificates and changes to those certificates, for propellers.

(b) Each person who applies under Part 21 for such a certificate or change must show compliance with the applicable requirements of this part.

[Amdt. 35-3, 41 FR 55475, Dec. 20, 1976]

§ 35.3 Instruction manual for installing and operating the propeller.

Each applicant must prepare and make available an approved manual or manuals containing instructions for installing and operating the propeller.

[Amdt. 35-5, 45 FR 60181, Sept. 11, 1980]

§ 35.4 Instructions for continued airworthiness.

The applicant must prepare Instructions for Continued Airworthiness in accordance with Appendix A to this part that are acceptable to the Administrator. The instructions may be incomplete at type certification if a program exists to ensure their completion prior to delivery of the first aircraft with the propeller installed, or upon issuance of a standard certificate of airworthiness for an aircraft with the propeller installed, whichever occurs later.

[Amdt. 35-5, 45 FR 60181, Sept. 11, 1980]

§ 35.5 Propeller operating limitations.

Propeller operating limitations are established by the Administrator, are included in the propeller type certificate data sheet specified in § 21.41 of this chapter, and include limitations based on the operating conditions demonstrated during the tests required by this part and any other information found necessary for the safe operation of the propeller.

[Amdt. 35-5, 45 FR 60182, Sept. 11, 1980]

Subpart B—Design and Construction

§ 35.11 Applicability.

This subpart prescribes the design and construction requirements for propellers.

§ 35.13 General.

Each applicant must show that the propeller concerned meets the design and construction requirements of this subpart.

§ 35.15 Design features.

The propeller may not have design features that experience has shown to be hazardous or unreliable. The suitability of each questionable design detail or part must be established by tests.

§ 35.17 Materials.

The suitability and durability of materials used in the propeller must—

(a) Be established on the basis of experience or tests; and

(b) Conform to approved specifications (such as industry or military specifications, or Technical Standard Orders) that ensure their having the strength and other properties assumed in the design data.

(Secs. 313(a), 601, and 603, 72 Stat. 752, 775, 49 U.S.C. 1354(a), 1421, and 1423; sec. 6(c), 49 U.S.C. 1655(c))

[Amdt. 35-4, 42 FR 15047, Mar. 17, 1977]

§ 35.19 Durability.

Each part of the propeller must be designed and constructed to minimize the development of any unsafe condition of the propeller between overhaul periods.

§ 35.21 Reversible propellers.

A reversible propeller must be adaptable for use with a reversing system in an airplane so that no single failure or malfunction in that system during normal or emergency operation will result in unwanted travel of the propeller blades to a position substantially below the normal flight low-pitch stop. Failure of structural elements need not be considered if the occurrence of such a failure is expected to be extremely remote. For the purposes of this section the term "reversing system" means that part of the complete reversing system that is in the propeller itself and those other parts that are supplied by the applicant for installation in the aircraft.

§ 35.23 Pitch control and indication.

(a) No loss of normal propeller pitch control may cause hazardous overspeeding of the propeller under intended operating conditions.

(b) Each pitch control system that is within the propeller, or supplied with the propeller, and that uses engine oil for feathering, must incorporate means to override or bypass the normally operative hydraulic system com-

ponents so as to allow feathering if those components fail or malfunction.

(c) Each propeller approved for installation on a turbopropeller engine must incorporate a provision for an indicator to indicate when the propeller blade angle is below the flight low pitch position. The provision must directly sense the blade position and be arranged to cause an indicator to indicate that the blade angle is below the flight low pitch position before the blade moves more than 8° below the flight low pitch stop.

[Amdt. 35-2, 32 FR 3737, Mar. 4, 1967, as amended by Amdt. 35—5, 45 FR 60182, Sept. 11, 1980]

Subpart C—Tests and Inspections

§ 35.31 Applicability.

This subpart prescribes the tests and inspections for propellers and their essential accessories.

§ 35.33 General.

(a) Each applicant must show that the propeller concerned and its essential accessories complete the tests and inspections of this subpart without evidence of failure or malfunction.

(b) Each applicant must furnish testing facilities, including equipment, and competent personnel, to conduct the required tests.

§ 35.35 Blade retention test.

The hub and blade retention arrangement of propellers with detachable blades must be subjected to a centrifugal load of twice the maximum centrifugal force to which the propeller would be subjected during operations within the limitations established for the propeller. This may be done by either a whirl test or a static pull test.

(Secs. 313(a), 601, and 603, 72 Stat. 752, 775, 49 U.S.C. 1354(a), 1421, and 1423; sec. 6(c), 49 U.S.C. 1655(c))

[Amdt. 35-4, 42 FR 15047, Mar. 17, 1977]

§ 35.37 Fatigue limit tests.

A fatigue evalution must be made and the fatigue limits determined for each metallic hub and blade, and each primary load carrying metal component of nonmetallic blades. The fatigue evaluation must include consideration of all reasonably foreseeable vibration load patterns. The fatigue limits must account for the permissible service deteriortion (such as nicks, grooves, galling, bearing wear, and variations in material properties).

[Amdt. 35–5, 45 FR 60182, Sept. 11, 1980]

§ 35.39 Endurance test.

(a) *Fixed-pitch wood propellers.* Fixed-pitch wood propellers must be subjected to one of the following tests:

(1) A 10-hour endurance block test on an engine with a propeller of the greatest pitch and diameter for which certification is sought at the rated rotational speed.

(2) A 50-hour flight test in level flight or in climb. At least five hours of this flight test must be with the propeller operated at the rated rotational speed, and the remainder of the 50 hours must be with the propeller operated at not less than 90 percent of the rated rotational speed. This test must be conducted on a propeller of the greatest diameter for which certification is requested.

(3) A 50-hour endurance block test on an engine at the power and propeller rotational speed for which certification is sought. This test must be conducted on a propeller of the greatest diameter for which certification is requested.

(b) *Fixed-pitch metal propellers and ground adjustable-pitch propellers.* Each fixed-pitch metal propeller or ground adjustable-pitch propeller must be subjected to the test prescribed in either paragraph (a)(2) or (a)(3) of this section.

(c) *Variable-pitch propellers.* Compliance with this paragraph must be shown for a propeller of the greatest diameter for which certification is requested. Each variable-pitch propeller (a propeller the pitch setting of which can be changed by the flight crew or by automatic means while the propeller is rotating) must be subjected to one of the following tests:

(1) A 100-hour test on a representative engine with the same or higher power and rotational speed and the same or more severe vibration characteristics as the engine with which the propeller is to be used. Each test must be made at the maximum continuous rotational speed and power rating of the propeller. If a takeoff rating greater than the maximum continuous rating is to be established, and additional 10-hour block test must be made at the maximum power and rotational speed for the takeoff rating.

(2) Operation of the propeller throughout the engine endurance tests prescribed in Part 33 of this subchapter.

[Doc. No. 2095, 29 FR 7458, June 10, 1964, as amended by Amdt. 35–2, 32 FR 3737, Mar. 4, 1967; Amdt. 35–3, 41 FR 55475, Dec. 20, 1976]

§ 35.41 Functional test.

(a) Each variable-pitch propeller must be subjected to the applicable functional tests of this section. The same propeller used in the endurance test must be used in the functional tests and must be driven by an engine on a test stand or on an aircraft.

(b) *Manually controllable propellers.* 500 complete cycles of control must be made throughout the pitch and rotational speed ranges.

(c) *Automatically controllable propellers.* 1,500 complete cycles of control must be made throughout the pitch and rotational speed ranges.

(d) *Feathering propellers.* 50 cycles of feathering operation must be made.

(e) *Reversible-pitch propellers.* Two hundred complete cycles of control must be made from lowest normal pitch to maximum reverse pitch, and, while in maximum reverse pitch, during each cycle, the propeller must be run for 30 seconds at the maximum power and rotational speed selected by the applicant for maximum reverse pitch.

[Doc. No. 2095, 29 FR 7458, June 10, 1964, as amended by Amdt. 35–3, 41 FR 55475, Dec. 20, 1976]

§ 35.42 Blade pitch control system component test.

The following durability requirements apply to propeller blade pitch control system components:

(a) Except as provided in paragraph (b) of this section, each propeller blade pitch control system component, including governors, pitch change assemblies, pitch locks, mechanical stops, and feathering system components, must be subjected in tests to cyclic loadings that simulate the frequency and amplitude those to which the component would be subjected during 1,000 hours of propeller operation.

(b) Compliance with paragraph (a) of this section may be shown by a rational analysis based on the results of tests on similar components.

[Amdt. 35-5, 45 FR 60182, Sept. 11, 1980]

§ 35.43   Special tests.

The Administrator may require any additional tests he finds necessary to substantiate the use of any unconventional features of design, material, or construction.

§ 35.45   Teardown inspection.

(a) After completion of the tests prescribed in this subpart, the propeller must be completely disassembled and a detailed inspection must be made of the propeller parts for cracks, wear, distortion, and any other unusual conditions.

(b) After the inspection the applicant must make any changes to the design or any additional tests that the Administrator finds necessary to establish the airworthiness of the propeller.

[Doc. No. 3095, 29 FR 7458, June 10, 1964, as amended by Amdt. 35-3, 41 FR 55475, Dec. 20, 1976]

§ 35.47   Propeller adjustments and parts replacements.

The applicant may service and make minor repairs to the propeller during the tests. If major repairs or replacement of parts are found necessary during the tests or in the teardown inspection, the parts in question must be subjected to any additional tests the Administrator finds necessary.

APPENDIX A—INSTRUCTIONS FOR CONTINUED AIRWORTHINESS

A35.1   GENERAL

(a) This appendix specifies requirements for the preparation of Instructions for Continued Airworthiness as required by § 35.4.

(b) The Instructions for Continued Airworthiness for each propeller must include the Instructions for Continued Airworthiness for all propeller parts. If Instructions for Continued Airworthiness are not supplied by the propeller part manufacturer for a propeller part, the Instructions for Continued Airworthiness for the propeller must include the information essential to the continued airworthiness of the propeller.

(c) The applicant must submit to the FAA a program to show how changes to the Instructions for Continued Airworthiness made by the applicant or by the manufacturers of propeller parts will be distributed.

A35.2   FORMAT

(a) The Instructions for Continued Airworthiness must be in the form of a manual or manuals as appropriate for the quantity of data to be provided.

(b) The format of the manual or manuals must provide for a practical arrangement.

A35.3   CONTENT

The contents of the manual must be prepared in the English language. The Instructions for Continued Airworthiness must contain the following sections and information:

(a) *Propeller Maintenance Section.* (1) Introduction information that includes an explanation of the propeller's features and data to the extent necessary for maintenance or preventive maintenance.

(2) A detailed description of the propeller and its systems and installations.

(3) Basic control and operation information describing how the propeller components and systems are controlled and how they operate, including any special procedures that apply.

(4) Instructions for uncrating, acceptance checking, lifting, and installing the propeller.

(5) Instructions for propeller operational checks.

(6) Scheduling information for each part of the propeller that provides the recommended periods at which it should be cleaned, adjusted, and tested, the applicable wear tolerances, and the degree of work recommended at these periods. However, the applicant may refer to an accessory, instrument, or equipment manufacturer as the source of this information if it shows that the item has an exceptionally high degree of complexity requiring specialized maintenance techniques, test equipment, or expertise. The recommended overhaul periods and necessary cross-references to the Airworthiness Limitations section of the manual must also be included. In addition, the applicant must include an inspection program that includes the frequency and

extent of the inspections necessary to provide for the continued airworthiness of the propeller.

(7) Troubleshooting information describing probable malfunctions, how to recognize those malfunctions, and the remedial action for those malfunctions.

(8) Information describing the order and method of removing and replacing propeller parts with any necessary precautions to be taken.

(9) A list of the special tools needed for maintenance other than for overhauls.

(b) *Propeller Overhaul Section.* (1) Disassembly information including the order and method of disassembly for overhaul.

(2) Cleaning and inspection instructions that cover the materials and apparatus to be used and methods and precautions to be taken during overhaul. Methods of overhaul inspection must also be included.

(3) Details of all fits and clearances relevant to overhaul.

(4) Details of repair methods for worn or otherwise substandard parts and components along with information necessary to determine when replacement is necessary.

(5) The order and method of assembly at overhaul.

(6) Instructions for testing after overhaul.

(7) Instructions for storage preparation including any storage limits.

(8) A list of tools needed for overhaul.

A35.4 AIRWORTHINESS LIMITATIONS SECTION

The Instructions for Continued Airworthiness must contain a section titled Airworthiness Limitations that is segregated and clearly distinguishable from the rest of the document. This section must set forth each mandatory replacement time, inspection interval, and related procedure required for type certification. This section must contain a legible statement in a prominent location that reads: "The Airworthiness Limitations section is FAA approved and specifies maintenance required under §§ 43.16 and 91.163 of the Federal Aviation Regulations unless an alternative program has been FAA approved."

[Amdt. 35-5, 45 FR 60182, Sept. 11, 1980]

FEDERAL AVIATION REGULATIONS

PART 39
AIRWORTHINESS DIRECTIVES

1989 EDITION

PART 39—AIRWORTHINESS DIRECTIVES

Subpart A—General

Sec.
39.1 Applicability.
39.3 General.

Subpart B—Airworthiness Directives

39.11 Applicability.
39.13 Airworthiness directives.

AUTHORITY: Secs. 601 and 603, 72 Stat. 775, 776; 49 U.S.C. 1421, 1423.

SOURCE: Docket No. 5061, 29 FR 14403, Oct. 20, 1964, unless otherwise noted.

Subpart A—General

§ 39.1 **Applicability.**

This part prescribes airworthiness directives that apply to aircraft, aircraft engines, propellers, or appliances (hereinafter referred to in this part as "products") when—

(a) An unsafe condition exists in a product; and

(b) That condition is likely to exist or develop in other products of the same type design.

[Doc. No. 5061, 29 FR 14403, Oct. 20, 1964, as amended by Amdt. 39 106, 30 FR 8826, July 14, 1965]

§ 39.3 **General.**

No person may operate a product to which an airworthiness directive applies except in accordance with the requirements of that airworthiness directive.

§ 39.11 **Applicability.**

This subpart identifies those products in which the Administrator has found an unsafe condition as described in § 39.1 and, as appropriate, prescribes inspections and the conditions and limitations, if any, under which those products may continue to be operated.

§ 39.13 **Airworthiness directives.**

All airworthiness directives contained in § 507.10 of the regulations of the Administrator are hereby transferred to this section of the Federal Aviation Regulations.

EDITORIAL NOTE: Airworthiness directives prescribed under this subpart were published in full in the FEDERAL REGISTER at 21 FR 9449, Dec. 4, 1956. For Federal Register citations to amendments in 1957 and subsequent years, see former § 507.10 of this title, in a separate volume entitled "List of Sections Affected 1949-1963." See also § 39.13 in a separate volume entitled "List of CFR Sections Affected, 1964-1972," and the List of CFR Sections Affected at the end of this volume.

FEDERAL AVIATION REGULATIONS

PART 43
MAINTENANCE, PREVENTIVE MAINTENANCE, REBUILDING, AND ALTERATION

1989 EDITION

PART 43—MAINTENANCE, PREVENTIVE MAINTENANCE, REBUILDING, AND ALTERATION

Sec.
43.1　Applicability.
43.2　Records of overhaul and rebuilding.
43.3　Persons authorized to perform maintenance, preventive maintenance, rebuilding, and alterations.
43.5　Approval for return to service after maintenance, preventive maintenance, rebuilding, or alteration.
43.7　Persons authorized to approve aircraft, airframes, aircraft engines, propellers, appliances, or component parts for return to service after maintenance, preventive maintenance, rebuilding, or alteration.
43.9　Content, form, and disposition of maintenance, preventive maintenance, rebuilding, and alteration records (except inspections performed in accordance with Part 91, Part 123, Part 125, § 135.411(a)(1), and § 135.419 of this chapter).

Sec.

43.11 Content, form, and disposition of the records for inspections conducted under Parts 91, 123, 125, § 135.411(a)(1), and § 135.419 of this chapter.

43.12 Maintenance records: Falsification, reproduction, or alteration.

43.13 Performance rules (general).

43.15 Additional performance rules for inspections.

43.16 Airworthiness Limitations.

43.17 Mechanical work performed on U.S. registered aircraft by certain Canadian persons.

APPENDIX A—MAJOR ALTERATIONS, MAJOR REPAIRS, AND PREVENTIVE MAINTENANCE

APPENDIX B—RECORDING OF MAJOR REPAIRS AND MAJOR ALTERATIONS

APPENDIX C—[RESERVED]

APPENDIX D—SCOPE AND DETAIL OF ITEMS (AS APPLICABLE TO THE PARTICULAR AIRCRAFT) TO BE INCLUDED IN ANNUAL AND 100-HOUR INSPECTIONS

APPENDIX E—ALTIMETER SYSTEM TEST AND INSPECTION

APPENDIX F—ATC TRANSPONDER TESTS AND INSPECTIONS

AUTHORITY: 49 U.S.C. 1354, 1421 through 1430; 49 U.S.C. 106(g) (Revised Pub. L. 97-449, Jan. 12, 1983).

SOURCE: Docket No. 1993, 29 FR 5451, Apr. 23, 1964, unless otherwise noted.

EDITORIAL NOTE: For miscellaneous technical amendments to this Part 43, see Amdt. 43-3, 31 FR 3336, Mar. 3, 1966, and Amdt. 43-6, 31 FR 9211, July 6, 1966.

SPECIAL FEDERAL AVIATION REGULATION No. 27—FUEL VENTING AND EXHAUST EMISSION REQUIREMENTS FOR TURBINE ENGINE POWERED AIRPLANES

EDITORIAL NOTE: For the text of SFAR No. 27, see Part 11 of this chapter.

§ 43.1 Applicability.

(a) Except as provided in paragraph (b) of this section, this part prescribes rules governing the maintenance, preventive maintenance, rebuilding, and alteration of any—

(1) Aircraft having a U.S. airworthiness certificate;

(2) Foreign-registered civil aircraft used in common carriage or carriage of mail under the provisions of Part 121, 127, or 135 of this chapter; and

(3) Airframe, aircraft engines, propellers, appliances, and component parts of such aircraft.

(b) This part does not apply to any aircraft for which an experimental airworthiness certificate has been issued, unless a different kind of airworthiness certificate had previously been issued for that aircraft.

[Doc. No. 1993, 29 FR 5451, Apr. 23, 1964, as amended by Amdt. 43-23, 47 FR 41084, Sept. 16, 1982]

§ 43.2 Records of overhaul and rebuilding.

(a) No person may describe in any required maintenance entry or form an aircraft, airframe, aircraft engine, propeller, appliance, or component part as being overhauled unless—

(1) Using methods, techniques, and practices acceptable to the Administrator, it has been disassembled, cleaned, inspected, repaired as necessary, and reassembled; and

(2) It has been tested in accordance with approved standards and technical data, or in accordance with current standards and technical data acceptable to the Administrator, which have been developed and documented by the holder of the type certificate, supplemental type certificate, or a material, part, process, or applicance approval under § 21.305 of this chapter.

(b) No person may describe in any required maintenace entry or form an aircraft, airframe, aircraft engine, propeller, appliance, or component part as being rebuilt unless it has been disassembled, cleaned, inspected, repaired as necessary, reassembled, and tested to the same tolerances and limits as a new item, using either new parts or used parts that either conform to new part tolerances and limits or to approved oversized or undersized dimensions.

[Amdt. 43-23, 47 FR 41084, Sept. 16, 1982]

§ 43.3 Persons authorized to perform maintenance, preventive maintenance, rebuilding, and alterations.

(a) Except as provided in this section and § 43.17, no person may maintain, rebuild, alter, or perform preventive maintenance on an aircraft, airframe, aircraft engine, propeller, appliance, or component part to which this part applies. Those items, the performance of which is a major alteration, a major repair, or preventive maintenance, are listed in Appendix A.

(b) The holder of a mechanic certificate may perform maintenance, preventive maintenance, and alterations as provided in Part 65 of this chapter.

(c) The holder of a repairman certificate may perform maintenance and preventive maintenance as provided in Part 65 of this chapter.

(d) A person working under the supervision of a holder of a mechanic or repairman certificate may perform the maintenance, preventive maintenance, and alterations that his supervisor is authorized to perform, if the supervisor personally observes the work being done to the extent necessary to ensure that it is being done properly and if the supervisor is readily available, in person, for consultation. However, this paragraph does not authorize the performance of any inspection required by Part 91 or Part 125 of this chapter or any inspection performed after a major repair or alteration.

(e) The holder of a repair station certificate may perform maintenance, preventive maintenance, and alterations as provided in Part 145 of this chapter.

(f) The holder of an air carrier operating certificate or an operating certificate issued under Part 121, 127, or 135, may perform maintenance, preventive maintenance, and alterations as provided in Part 121, 127, or 135.

(g) The holder of a pilot certificate issued under Part 61 may perform preventive maintenance on any aircraft owned or operated by that pilot which is not used under Part 121, 127, 129, or 135.

(h) Notwithstanding the provisions of paragraph (g) of this section, the Administrator may approve a certificate holder under Part 135 of this chapter, operating rotorcraft in a remote area, to allow a pilot to perform specific preventive maintenance items provided—

(1) The items of preventive maintenance are a result of a known or suspected mechanical difficulty or malfunction that occurred en route to or in a remote area;

(2) The pilot has satisfactorily completed an approved training program and is authorized in writing by the certificate holder for each item of preventive maintenance that the pilot is authorized to perform;

(3) There is no certificated mechanic available to perform preventive maintenance;

(4) The certificate holder has procedures to evaluate the accomplishment of a preventive maintenance item that requires a decision concerning the airworthiness of the rotorcraft; and

(5) The items of preventive maintenance authorized by this section are those listed in paragraph (c) of Appendix A of this part.

(i) A manufacturer may—

(1) Rebuild or alter any aircraft, aircraft engine, propeller, or appliance manufactured by him under a type or production certificate;

(2) Rebuild or alter any appliance or part of aircraft, aircraft engines, propellers, or appliances manufactured by him under a Technical Standard Order Authorization, an FAA-Parts Manufacturer Approval, or Product and Process Specification issued by the Administrator; and

(3) Perform any inspection required by Part 91 or Part 125 of this chapter on aircraft it manufacturers, while currently operating under a production certificate or under a currently approved production inspection system for such aircraft.

[Doc. No. 1993, 29 FR 5451, Apr. 23, 1964, as amended by Amdt. 43-4, 31 FR 5249, Apr. 1, 1966; Amdt. 43-23, 47 FR 41084, Sept. 16, 1982; Amdt. 43-25, 51 FR 40702, Nov. 7, 1986]

§ 43.5 Approval for return to service after maintenance, preventive maintenance, rebuilding, or alteration.

No person may approve for return to service any aircraft, airframe, aircraft engine, propeller, or appliance, that has undergone maintenance, preventive maintenance, rebuilding, or alteration unless—

(a) The maintenance record entry required by § 43.9 or § 43.11, as appropriate, has been made;

(b) The repair or alteration form authorized by or furnished by the Administrator has been executed in a manner prescribed by the Administrator; and

(c) If a repair or an alteration results in any change in the aircraft operating limitations or flight data contained in the approved aircraft flight manual, those operating limitations or flight data are appropriately revised and set forth as prescribed in § 91.31 of this chapter.

[Docket No. 1993, 29 FR 5451, Apr. 23, 1964, as amended by Amdt. 43-23, 47 FR 41084, Sept. 16, 1982]

§ 43.7 Persons authorized to approve aircraft, airframes, aircraft engines, propellers, appliances, or component parts for return to service after maintenance, preventive maintenance, rebuilding, or alteration.

(a) Except as provided in this section and § 43.17, no person, other than the Administrator, may approve an aircraft, airframe, aircraft engine, propeller, appliance, or component part for return to service after it has undergone maintenance, preventive maintenance, rebuilding, or alteration.

(b) The holder of a mechanic certificate or an inspection authorization may approve an aircraft, airframe, aircraft engine, propeller, appliance, or component part for return to service as provided in Part 65 of this chapter.

(c) The holder of a repair station certificate may approve an aircraft, airframe, aircraft engine, propeller, appliance, or component part for return to service as provided in Part 145 of this chapter.

(d) A manufacturer may approve for return to service any aircraft, airframe, aircraft engine, propeller, appliance, or component part which that manufacturer has worked on under § 43.3(h). However, except for minor alterations, the work must have been done in accordance with technical data approved by the Administrator.

(e) The holder of an air carrier operating certificate or an operating certificate issued under Part 121, 127, or 135, may approve an aircraft, airframe, aircraft engine, propeller, appliance, or component part for return to service as provided in Part 121, 127, or 135 of this chapter, as applicable.

(f) A person holding at least a private pilot certificate may approve an aircraft for return to service after performing preventive maintenance under the provisions of § 43.3(g).

[Amdt. 43-23, 47 FR 41084, Sept. 16, 1982]

§ 43.9 Content, form, and disposition of maintenance, preventive maintenance, rebuilding, and alteration records (except inspections performed in accordance with Part 91, Part 123, Part 125, § 135.411(a)(1), and § 135.419 of this chapter).

(a) *Maintenance record entries.* Except as provided in paragraphs (b) and (c) of this section, each person who maintains, performs preventive maintenance, rebuilds, or alters an aircraft, airframe, aircraft engine, propeller, appliance, or component part shall make an entry in the maintenance record of that equipment containing the following information:

(1) A description (or reference to data acceptable to the Administrator) of work performed.

(2) The date of completion of the work performed.

(3) The name of the person performing the work if other than the person specified in paragraph (a)(4) of this section.

(4) If the work performed on the aircraft, airframe, aircraft engine, propeller, appliance, or component part has been performed satisfactorily, the signature, certificate number, and kind of certificate held by the person approving the work. The signature constitutes the approval for return to service only for the work performed.

In addition to the entry required by this paragraph, major repairs and major alterations shall be entered on a form, and the form disposed of, in the manner prescribed in Appendix B, by the person performing the work.

(b) Each holder of an air carrier operating certificate or an operating certificate issued under Part 121, 127, or 135, that is required by its approved operations specifications to provide for a continuous airworthiness maintenance program, shall make a record of the maintenance, preventive maintenance, rebuilding, and alteration, on aircraft, airframes, aircraft engines, propellers, appliances, or component parts which it operates in accordance with the applicable provisions of Part

121, 127, or 135 of this chapter, as appropriate.

(c) This section does not apply to persons performing inspections in accordance with Part 91, 123, 125, § 135.411(a)(1), or § 135.419 of this chapter.

[Amdt. 43-23, 47 FR 41085, Sept. 16, 1982]

§ 43.11 Content, form, and disposition of the records for inspections conducted under Parts 91, 123, 125, § 135.411(a)(1), and § 135.419 of this chapter.

(a) *Maintenance record entries.* The person approving or disapproving for return to service an aircraft, airframe, aircraft engine, propeller, appliance, or component part after any inspection performed in accordance with Part 91, 123, 125, § 135.411(a)(1), or § 135.419 shall make an entry in the maintenance record of that equipment containing the following information:

(1) The type of inspection and a brief description of the extent of the inspection.

(2) The date of the inspection and aircraft total time in service.

(3) The signature, the certificate number, and kind of certificate held by the person approving or disapproving for return to service the aircraft, airframe, aircraft engine, propeller, appliance, component part, or portions thereof.

(4) Except for progressive inspections, if the aircraft is found to be airworthy and approved for return to service, the following or a similarly worded statement—"I certify that this aircraft has been inspected in accordance with (insert type) inspection and was determined to be in airworthy condition."

(5) Except for progressive inspections, if the aircraft is not approved for return to service because of needed maintenance, noncompliance with applicable specifications, airworthiness directives, or other approved data, the following or a similarly worded statement—"I certify that this aircraft has been inspected in accordance with (insert type) inspection and a list of discrepancies and unairworthy items dated (date) has been provided for the aircraft owner or operator."

(6) For progressive inspections, the following or a similarly worded statement—"I certify that in accordance with a progressive inspection program, a routine inspection of (identify whether aircraft or components) and a detailed inspection of (identify components) were performed and the (aircraft or components) are (approved or disapproved) for return to service." If disapproved, the entry will further state "and a list of discrepancies and unairworthy items dated (date) has been provided to the aircraft owner or operator."

(7) If an inspection is conducted under an inspection program provided for in Part 91, 123, 125, or § 135.411(a)(1), the entry must identify the inspection program, that part of the inspection program accomplished, and contain a statement that the inspection was performed in accordance with the inspections and procedures for that particular program.

(b) *Listing of discrepancies.* If the person performing any inspection required by Part 91, 123, 125, or § 135.411(a)(1) of this chapter finds that the aircraft is unairworthy or does not meet the applicable type certificate data, airworthiness directives, or other approved data upon which its airworthiness depends, that person must give the owner or lessee a signed and dated list of those discrepancies.

[Amdt. 43-23, 47 FR 41085, Sept. 16, 1982]

§ 43.12 Maintenance records: Falsification, reproduction, or alteration.

(a) No person may make or cause to be made:

(1) Any fraudulent or intentionally false entry in any record or report that is required to be made, kept, or used to show compliance with any requirement under this part;

(2) Any reproduction, for fraudulent purpose, of any record or report under this part; or

(3) Any alteration, for fraudulent purpose, of any record or report under this part.

(b) The commission by any person of an act prohibited under paragraph (a) of this section is a basis for suspending or revoking the applicable airman, operator, or production certificate, Technical Standard Order Authorization, FAA-Parts Manufacturer Approval, or

Product and Process Specification issued by the Administrator and held by that person.

[Amdt. 43-19, 43 FR 22639, May 25, 1978, as amended by Amdt. 43-23, 47 FR 41085, Sept. 16, 1982]

§ 43.13 Performance rules (general).

(a) Each person performing maintenance, alteration, or preventive maintenance on an aircraft, engine, propeller, or appliance shall use the methods, techniques, and practices prescribed in the current manufacturer's maintenance manual or Instructions for Continued Airworthiness prepared by its manufacturer, or other methods, techniques, and practices acceptable to the Administrator, except as noted in § 43.16. He shall use the tools, equipment, and test apparatus necessary to assure completion of the work in accordance with accepted industry practices. If special equipment or test apparatus is recommended by the manufacturer involved, he must use that equipment or apparatus or its equivalent acceptable to the Administrator.

(b) Each person maintaining or altering, or performing preventive maintenance, shall do that work in such a manner and use materials of such a quality, that the condition of the aircraft, airframe, aircraft engine, propeller, or appliance worked on will be at least equal to its original or properly altered condition (with regard to aerodynamic function, structural strength, resistance to vibration and deterioration, and other qualities affecting airworthiness).

(c) *Special provisions for holders of air carrier operating certificates and operating certificates issued under the provisions of Part 121, 127, or 135 and Part 129 operators holding operations specifications.* Unless otherwise notified by the administrator, the methods, techniques, and practices contained in the maintenance manual or the maintenance part of the manual of the holder of an air carrier operating certificate or an operating certificate under Part 121, 127, or 135 and Part 129 operators holding operations specifications (that is required by its operating specifications to provide a continuous airworthiness maintenance

and inspection program) constitute acceptable means of compliance with this section.

[Doc. No. 1993, 29 FR 5451, Apr. 23, 1964, as amended by Amdt. 43-20, 45 FR 60182, Sept. 11, 1980; Amdt. 43-23, 47 FR 41085, Sept. 16, 1982; Amdt. 43-28, 52 FR 20028, June 16, 1987]

§ 43.15 Additional performance rules for inspections.

(a) *General.* Each person performing an inspection required by Part 91, 123, 125, or 135 of this chapter, shall—

(1) Perform the inspection so as to determine whether the aircraft, or portion(s) thereof under inspection, meets all applicable airworthiness requirements; and

(2) If the inspection is one provided for in Part 123, 125, 135, or § 91.169(e) of this chapter, perform the inspection in accordance with the instructions and procedures set forth in the inspection program for the aircraft being inspected.

(b) *Rotorcraft.* Each person performing an inspection required by Part 91 on a rotorcraft shall inspect the following systems in accordance with the maintenance manual or Instructions for Continued Airworthiness of the manufacturer concerned:

(1) The drive shafts or similar systems.

(2) The main rotor transmission gear box for obvious defects.

(3) The main rotor and center section (or the equivalent area).

(4) The auxiliary rotor on helicopters.

(c) *Annual and 100-hour inspections.* (1) Each person performing an annual or 100-hour inspection shall use a checklist while performing the inspection. The checklist may be of the person's own design, one provided by the manufacturer of the equipment being inspected or one obtained from another source. This checklist must include the scope and detail of the items contained in Appendix D to this part and paragraph (b) of this section.

(2) Each person approving a reciprocating-engine-powered aircraft for return to service after an annual or 100-hour inspection shall, before that approval, run the aircraft engine or

engines to determine satisfactory performance in accordance with the manufacturer's recommendations of—

(i) Power output (static and idle r.p.m.);

(ii) Magnetos;

(iii) Fuel and oil pressure; and

(iv) Cylinder and oil temperature.

(3) Each person approving a turbine-engine-powered aircraft for return to service after an annual, 100-hour, or progressive inspection shall, before that approval, run the aircraft engine or engines to determine satisfactory performance in accordance with the manufacturer's recommendations.

(d) *Progressive inspection.* (1) Each person performing a progressive inspection shall, at the start of a progressive inspection system, inspect the aircraft completely. After this initial inspection, routine and detailed inspections must be conducted as prescribed in the progressive inspection schedule. Routine inspections consist of visual examination or check of the appliances, the aircraft, and its components and systems, insofar as practicable without disassembly. Detailed inspections consist of a thorough examination of the appliances, the aircraft, and its components and systems, with such disassembly as is necessary. For the purposes of this subparagraph, the overhaul of a component or system is considered to be a detailed inspection.

(2) If the aircraft is away from the station where inspections are normally conducted, an appropriately rated mechanic, a certificated repair station, or the manufacturer of the aircraft may perform inspections in accordance with the procedures and using the forms of the person who would otherwise perform the inspection.

[Doc. No. 1993, 29 FR 5451, Apr. 23, 1964, as amended by Amdt. 43-23, 47 FR 41086, Sept. 16, 1982; Amdt. 43-25, 51 FR 40702, Nov. 7, 1986]

§ 43.16 Airworthiness Limitations.

Each person performing an inspection or other maintenance specified in an Airworthiness Limitations section of a manufacturer's maintenance manual or Instructions for Continued Airworthiness shall perform the inspection or other maintenance in accordance with that section, or in ac-

cordance with operations specifications approved by the Administrator under Parts 121, 123, 127, or 135, or an inspection program approved under § 91.169(e).

[Amdt. 43-20, 45 FR 60183, Sept. 11, 1980, as amended by Amdt. 43-23, 47 FR 41086, Sept. 16, 1982]

§ 43.17 Mechanical work performed on U.S. registered aircraft by certain Canadian persons.

(a) A person holding a valid mechanic certificate of competence (Aircraft Maintenance Engineer license) and appropriate ratings issued by the Canadian Government, or a person who is an authorized employee (Approved Inspector) performing work for a company whose system of quality control for the inspection and maintenance of aircraft has been approved by the Canadian Department of Transport may, in connection with aircraft of U.S. registry in Canada:

(1) Perform maintenance, preventive maintenance and alterations if those operations are done in accordance with § 43.13 and the maintenance record entries are made in accordance with § 43.9.

(2) Except for an annual inspection, perform any inspection required by § 91.169 of this chapter, if the inspection is done in accordance with § 43.15 and the maintenance record entries are made in accordance with § 43.11.

(3) Approve (certify) maintenance, preventive maintenance, and alterations performed under this section except that a Canadian Aircraft Maintenance Engineer may not approve a major repair or major alteration.

(b) A Canadian Department of Transport Airworthiness Inspector, or an authorized employee (Approved Inspector) performing work for a company approved by the Canadian Department of Transport, may approve (certify) a major repair or major alteration performed under this section if the work was done in accordance with technical data approved by the Administrator.

(c) No person may operate in air commerce an aircraft, airframe, aircraft engine, propeller, or appliance on which maintenance, preventive maintenance, or alteration has been performed under this section unless it has been approved by a person authorized in this section.

[Amdt. 43–10, 33 FR 15988, Oct. 31, 1968; 33 FR 16273, Nov. 6, 1968, as amended by Amdt. 43–23, 47 FR 41086, Sept. 16, 1982]

APPENDIX A—MAJOR ALTERATIONS, MAJOR REPAIRS, AND PREVENTIVE MAINTENANCE

(a) *Major alterations—*(1) *Airframe major alterations.* Alterations of the following parts and alterations of the following types, when not listed in the aircraft specifications issued by the FAA, are airframe major alterations:

(i) Wings.
(ii) Tail surfaces.
(iii) Fuselage.
(iv) Engine mounts.
(v) Control system.
(vi) Landing gear.
(vii) Hull or floats.
(viii) Elements of an airframe including spars, ribs, fittings, shock absorbers, bracing, cowling, fairings, and balance weights.
(ix) Hydraulic and electrical actuating system of components.
(x) Rotor blades.
(xi) Changes to the empty weight or empty balance which result in an increase in the maximum certificated weight or center of gravity limits of the aircraft.
(xii) Changes to the basic design of the fuel, oil, cooling, heating, cabin pressurization, electrical, hydraulic, de-icing, or exhaust systems.
(xiii) Changes to the wing or to fixed or movable control surfaces which affect flutter and vibration characteristics.

(2) *Powerplant major alterations.* The following alterations of a powerplant when not listed in the engine specifications issued by the FAA, are powerplant major alterations.

(i) Conversion of an aircraft engine from one approved model to another, involving any changes in compression ratio, propeller reduction gear, impeller gear ratios or the substitution of major engine parts which requires extensive rework and testing of the engine.
(ii) Changes to the engine by replacing aircraft engine structural parts with parts not supplied by the original manufacturer or parts not specifically approved by the Administrator.
(iii) Installation of an accessory which is not approved for the engine.
(iv) Removal of accessories that are listed as required equipment on the aircraft or engine specification.

(v) Installation of structural parts other than the type of parts approved for the installation.
(vi) Conversions of any sort for the purpose of using fuel of a rating or grade other than that listed in the engine specifications.

(3) *Propeller major alterations.* The following alterations of a propeller when not authorized in the propeller specifications issued by the FAA are propeller major alterations:

(i) Changes in blade design.
(ii) Changes in hub design.
(iii) Changes in the governor or control design.
(iv) Installation of a propeller governor or feathering system.
(v) Installation of propeller de-icing system.
(vi) Installation of parts not approved for the propeller.

(4) *Appliance major alterations.* Alterations of the basic design not made in accordance with recommendations of the appliance manufacturer or in accordance with an FAA Airworthiness Directive are appliance major alterations. In addition, changes in the basic design of radio communication and navigation equipment approved under type certification or a Technical Standard Order that have an effect on frequency stability, noise level, sensitivity, selectivity, distortion, spurious radiation, AVC characteristics, or ability to meet environmental test conditions and other changes that have an effect on the performance of the equipment are also major alterations.

(b) *Major repairs—*(1) *Airframe major repairs.* Repairs to the following parts of an airframe and repairs of the following types, involving the strengthening, reinforcing, splicing, and manufacturing of primary structural members or their replacement, when replacement is by fabrication such as riveting or welding, are airframe major repairs.

(i) Box beams.
(ii) Monocoque or semimonocoque wings or control surfaces.
(iii) Wing stringers or chord members.
(iv) Spars.
(v) Spar flanges.
(vi) Members of truss-type beams.
(vii) Thin sheet webs of beams.
(viii) Keel and chine members of boat hulls or floats.
(ix) Corrugated sheet compression members which act as flange material of wings or tail surfaces.
(x) Wing main ribs and compression members.
(xi) Wing or tail surface brace struts.
(xii) Engine mounts.
(xiii) Fuselage longerons.
(xiv) Members of the side truss, horizontal truss, or bulkheads.

(xv) Main seat support braces and brackets.

(xvi) Landing gear brace struts.

(xvii) Axles.

(xviii) Wheels.

(xix) Skis, and ski pedestals.

(xx) Parts of the control system such as control columns, pedals, shafts, brackets, or horns.

(xxi) Repairs involving the substitution of material.

(xxii) The repair of damaged areas in metal or plywood stressed covering exceeding six inches in any direction.

(xxiii) The repair of portions of skin sheets by making additional seams.

(xxiv) The splicing of skin sheets.

(xxv) The repair of three or more adjacent wing or control surface ribs or the leading edge of wings and control surfaces, between such adjacent ribs.

(xxvi) Repair of fabric covering involving an area greater than that required to repair two adjacent ribs.

(xxvii) Replacement of fabric on fabric covered parts such as wings, fuselages, stabilizers, and control surfaces.

(xxviii) Repairing, including rebottoming, of removable or integral fuel tanks and oil tanks.

(2) *Powerplant major repairs.* Repairs of the following parts of an engine and repairs of the following types, are powerplant major repairs:

(i) Separation or disassembly of a crankcase or crankshaft of a reciprocating engine equipped with an integral supercharger.

(ii) Separation or disassembly of a crankcase or crankshaft of a reciprocating engine equipped with other than spur-type propeller reduction gearing.

(iii) Special repairs to structural engine parts by welding, plating, metalizing, or other methods.

(3) *Propeller major repairs.* Repairs of the following types to a propeller are propeller major repairs:

(i) Any repairs to, or straightening of steel blades.

(ii) Repairing or machining of steel hubs.

(iii) Shortening of blades.

(iv) Retipping of wood propellers.

(v) Replacement of outer laminations on fixed pitch wood propellers.

(vi) Repairing elongated bolt holes in the hub of fixed pitch wood propellers.

(vii) Inlay work on wood blades.

(viii) Repairs to composition blades.

(ix) Replacement of tip fabric.

(x) Replacement of plastic covering.

(xi) Repair of propeller governors.

(xii) Overhaul of controllable pitch propellers.

(xiii) Repairs to deep dents, cuts, scars, nicks, etc., and straightening of aluminum blades.

(xiv) The repair or replacement of internal elements of blades.

(4) *Appliance major repairs.* Repairs of the following types to appliances are appliance major repairs:

(i) Calibration and repair of instruments.

(ii) Calibration of radio equipment.

(iii) Rewinding the field coil of an electrical accessory.

(iv) Complete disassembly of complex hydraulic power valves.

(v) Overhaul of pressure type carburetors, and pressure type fuel, oil and hydraulic pumps.

(c) *Preventive maintenance.* Preventive maintenance is limited to the following work, provided it does not involve complex assembly operations:

(1) Removal, installation, and repair of landing gear tires.

(2) Replacing elastic shock absorber cords on landing gear.

(3) Servicing landing gear shock struts by adding oil, air, or both.

(4) Servicing landing gear wheel bearings, such as cleaning and greasing.

(5) Replacing defective safety wiring or cotter keys.

(6) Lubrication not requiring disassembly other than removal of nonstructural items such as cover plates, cowlings, and fairings.

(7) Making simple fabric patches not requiring rib stitching or the removal of structural parts or control surfaces. In the case of balloons, the making of small fabric repairs to envelopes (as defined in, and in accordance with, the balloon manufacturers' instructions) not requiring load tape repair or replacement.

(8) Replenishing hydraulic fluid in the hydraulic reservoir.

(9) Refinishing decorative coating of fuselage, balloon baskets, wings tail group surfaces (excluding balanced control surfaces), fairings, cowlings, landing gear, cabin, or cockpit interior when removal or disassembly of any primary structure or operating system is not required.

(10) Applying preservative or protective material to components where no disassembly of any primary structure or operating system is involved and where such coating is not prohibited or is not contrary to good practices.

(11) Repairing upholstery and decorative furnishings of the cabin, cockpit, or balloon basket interior when the repairing does not require disassembly of any primary structure or operating system or interfere with an operating system or affect the primary structure of the aircraft.

(12) Making small simple repairs to fairings, nonstructural cover plates, cowlings, and small patches and reinforcements not changing the contour so as to interfere with proper air flow.

(13) Replacing side windows where that work does not interfere with the structure or any operating system such as controls, electrical equipment, etc.

(14) Replacing safety belts.

(15) Replacing seats or seat parts with replacement parts approved for the aircraft, not involving disassembly of any primary structure or operating system.

(16) Trouble shooting and repairing broken circuits in landing light wiring circuits.

(17) Replacing bulbs, reflectors, and lenses of position and landing lights.

(18) Replacing wheels and skis where no weight and balance computation is involved.

(19) Replacing any cowling not requiring removal of the propeller or disconnection of flight controls.

(20) Replacing or cleaning spark plugs and setting of spark plug gap clearance.

(21) Replacing any hose connection except hydraulic connections.

(22) Replacing prefabricated fuel lines.

(23) Cleaning or replacing fuel and oil strainers or filter elements.

(24) Replacing and servicing batteries.

(25) Cleaning of balloon burner pilot and main nozzles in accordance with the balloon manufacturer's instructions.

(26) Replacement or adjustment of non-structural standard fasteners incidental to operations.

(27) The interchange of balloon baskets and burners on envelopes when the basket or burner is designated as interchangeable in the balloon type certificate data and the baskets and burners are specifically designed for quick removal and installation.

(28) The installations of anti-misfueling devices to reduce the diameter of fuel tank filler openings provided the specific device has been made a part of the aircraft type certificiate data by the aircraft manufacturer, the aircraft manufacturer has provided FAA-approved instructions for installation of the specific device, and installation does not involve the disassembly of the existing tank filler opening.

(29) Removing, checking, and replacing magnetic chip detectors.

(Secs. 313, 601 through 610, and 1102, Federal Aviation Act of 1958 as amended (49 U.S.C. 1354, 1421 through 1430 and 1502); (49 U.S.C. 106(g) (Revised Pub. L. 97-449, Jan. 21, 1983); and 14 CFR 11.45)

[Doc. No. 1993, 29 FR 5451, Apr. 23, 1964, as amended by Amdt. 43-14, 37 FR 14291, June 19, 1972; Amdt. 43-23, 47 FR 41086, Sept. 16, 1982; Amdt. 43-24, 49 FR 44602, Nov. 7, 1984; Amdt. 43-25, 51 FR 40703, Nov. 7, 1986; Amdt. 43-27, 52 FR 17277, May 6, 1987]

Appendix B—Recording of Major Repairs and Major Alterations

(a) Except as provided in paragraphs (b), (c), and (d) of this appendix, each person performing a major repair or major alteration shall—

(1) Execute FAA Form 337 at least in duplicate;

(2) Give a signed copy of that form to the aircraft owner; and

(3) Forward a copy of that form to the local Flight Standards District Office within 48 hours after the aircraft, airframe, aircraft engine, propeller, or appliance is approved for return to service.

(b) For major repairs made in accordance with a manual or specifications acceptable to the Administrator, a certificated repair station may, in place of the requirements of paragraph (a)—

(1) Use the customer's work order upon which the repair is recorded;

(2) Give the aircraft owner a signed copy of the work order and retain a duplicate copy for at least two years from the date of approval for return to service of the aircraft, airframe, aircraft engine, propeller, or appliance;

(3) Give the aircraft owner a maintenance release signed by an authorized representative of the repair station and incorporating the following information:

(i) Identity of the aircraft, airframe, aircraft engine, propeller or appliance.

(ii) If an aircraft, the make, model, serial number, nationality and registration marks, and location of the repaired area.

(iii) If an airframe, aircraft engine, propeller, or appliance, give the manufacturer's name, name of the part, model, and serial numbers (if any); and

(4) Include the following or a similarly worded statement—

"The aircraft, airframe, aircraft engine, propeller, or appliance identified above was repaired and inspected in accordance with current Regulations of the Federal Aviation Agency and is approved for return to service.

Pertinent details of the repair are on file at this repair station under Order No. ———, Date ———————————————— Signed ———————————————— (For signature of authorized representative)

————————————————————
(Repair station name)   (Certificate No.)
————————————."
(Address)

(c) For a major repair or major alteration made by a person authorized in § 43.17, the person who performs the major repair or major alteration and the person authorized by § 43.17 to approve that work shall execute a FAA Form 337 at least in duplicate. A completed copy of that form shall be—

(1) Given to the aircraft owner; and

(2) Forwarded to the Federal Aviation Administration, Aircraft Registration Branch, Post Office Box 25082, Oklahoma City, Okla. 73125, within 48 hours after the work is inspected.

(d) For extended-range fuel tanks installed within the passenger compartment or a baggage compartment, the person who performs the work and the person authorized to approve the work by § 43.7 of this part shall execute an FAA Form 337 in at least triplicate. One (1) copy of the FAA Form 337 shall be placed on board the aircraft as specified in § 91.173 of this chapter. The remaining forms shall be distributed as required by paragraph (a) (2) and (3) or (c) (1) and (2) of this paragraph as appropriate.

(Secs. 101, 610, 72 Stat. 737, 780, 49 U.S.C. 1301, 1430)

[Doc. No. 1993, 29 FR 5451, Apr. 23, 1964, as amended by Amdt. 43-10, 33 FR 15989, Oct. 31, 1968; Amdt. 43-29, 52 FR 34101, Sept. 9, 1987]

APPENDIX C—[RESERVED]

APPENDIX D—SCOPE AND DETAIL OF ITEMS (AS APPLICABLE TO THE PARTICULAR AIRCRAFT) TO BE INCLUDED IN ANNUAL AND 100-HOUR INSPECTIONS

(a) Each person performing an annual or 100-hour inspection shall, before that inspection, remove or open all necessary inspection plates, access doors, fairing, and cowling. He shall thoroughly clean the aircraft and aircraft engine.

(b) Each person performing an annual or 100-hour inspection shall inspect (where applicable) the following components of the fuselage and hull group:

(1) Fabric and skin—for deterioration, distortion, other evidence of failure, and defective or insecure attachment of fittings.

(2) Systems and components—for improper installation, apparent defects, and unsatisfactory operation.

(3) Envelope, gas bags, ballast tanks, and related parts—for poor condition.

(c) Each person performing an annual or 100-hour inspection shall inspect (where applicable) the following components of the cabin and cockpit group:

(1) Generally—for uncleanliness and loose equipment that might foul the controls.

(2) Seats and safety belts—for poor condition and apparent defects.

(3) Windows and windshields—for deterioration and breakage.

(4) Instruments—for poor condition, mounting, marking, and (where practicable) improper operation.

(5) Flight and engine controls—for improper installation and improper operation.

(6) Batteries—for improper installation and improper charge.

(7) All systems—for improper installation, poor general condition, apparent and obvious defects, and insecurity of attachment.

(d) Each person performing an annual or 100-hour inspection shall inspect (where applicable) components of the engine and nacelle group as follows:

(1) Engine section—for visual evidence of excessive oil, fuel, or hydraulic leaks, and sources of such leaks.

(2) Studs and nuts—for improper torquing and obvious defects.

(3) Internal engine—for cylinder compression and for metal particles or foreign matter on screens and sump drain plugs. If there is weak cylinder compression, for improper internal condition and improper internal tolerances.

(4) Engine mount—for cracks, looseness of mounting, and looseness of engine to mount.

(5) Flexible vibration dampeners—for poor condition and deterioration.

(6) Engine controls—for defects, improper travel, and improper safetying.

(7) Lines, hoses, and clamps—for leaks, improper condition and looseness.

(8) Exhaust stacks—for cracks, defects, and improper attachment.

(9) Accessories—for apparent defects in security of mounting.

(10) All systems—for improper installation, poor general condition, defects, and insecure attachment.

(11) Cowling—for cracks, and defects.

(e) Each person performing an annual or 100-hour inspection shall inspect (where applicable) the following components of the landing gear group:

(1) All units—for poor condition and insecurity of attachment.

(2) Shock absorbing devices—for improper oleo fluid level.

(3) Linkages, trusses, and members—for undue or excessive wear fatigue, and distortion.

(4) Retracting and locking mechanism—for improper operation.

(5) Hydraulic lines—for leakage.

(6) Electrical system—for chafing and improper operation of switches.

(7) Wheels—for cracks, defects, and condition of bearings.

(8) Tires—for wear and cuts.

(9) Brakes—for improper adjustment.

(10) Floats and skis—for insecure attachment and obvious or apparent defects.

(f) Each person performing an annual or 100-hour inspection shall inspect (where applicable) all components of the wing and center section assembly for poor general condition, fabric or skin deterioration, distortion, evidence of failure, and insecurity of attachment.

(g) Each person performing an annual or 100-hour inspection shall inspect (where applicable) all components and systems that make up the complete empennage assembly for poor general condition, fabric or skin deterioration, distortion, evidence of failure, insecure attachment, improper component installation, and improper component operation.

(h) Each person performing an annual or 100-hour inspection shall inspect (where applicable) the following components of the propeller group:

(1) Propeller assembly—for cracks, nicks, binds, and oil leakage.

(2) Bolts—for improper torquing and lack of safetying.

(3) Anti-icing devices—for improper operations and obvious defects.

(4) Control mechanisms—for improper operation, insecure mounting, and restricted travel.

(i) Each person performing an annual or 100-hour inspection shall inspect (where applicable) the following components of the radio group:

(1) Radio and electronic equipment—for improper installation and insecure mounting.

(2) Wiring and conduits—for improper routing, insecure mounting, and obvious defects.

(3) Bonding and shielding—for improper installation and poor condition.

(4) Antenna including trailing antenna—for poor condition, insecure mounting, and improper operation.

(j) Each person performing an annual or 100-hour inspection shall inspect (where applicable) each installed miscellaneous item that is not otherwise covered by this listing for improper installation and improper operation.

APPENDIX E—ALTIMETER SYSTEM TEST AND INSPECTION

Each person performing the altimeter system tests and inspections required by § 91.171 shall comply with the following:

(a) Static pressure system:

(1) Ensure freedom from entrapped moisture and restrictions.

(2) Determine that leakage is within the tolerances established in § 23.1325 or § 25.1325, whichever is applicable.

(3) Determine that the static port heater, if installed, is operative.

(4) Ensure that no alterations or deformations of the airframe surface have been made that would affect the relationship between air pressure in the static pressure system and true ambient static air pressure for any flight condition.

(b) Altimeter:

(1) Test by an appropriately rated repair facility in accordance with the following subparagraphs. Unless otherwise specified, each test for performance may be conducted with the instrument subjected to vibration. When tests are conducted with the temperature substantially different from ambient temperature of approximately 25 degrees C., allowance shall be made for the variation from the specified condition.

(i) *Scale error.* With the barometric pressure scale at 29.92 inches of mercury, the altimeter shall be subjected successively to pressures corresponding to the altitude specified in Table I up to the maximum normally expected operating altitude of the airplane in which the altimeter is to be installed. The reduction in pressure shall be made at a rate not in excess of 20,000 feet per minute to within approximately 2,000 feet of the test point. The test point shall be approached at a rate compatible with the test equipment. The altimeter shall be kept at the pressure corresponding to each test point for at least 1 minute, but not more than 10 minutes, before a reading is taken. The error at all test points must not exceed the tolerances specified in Table I.

(ii) *Hysteresis.* The hysteresis test shall begin not more than 15 minutes after the altimeter's initial exposure to the pressure corresponding to the upper limit of the scale error test prescribed in subparagraph (i); and while the altimeter is at this pressure, the hysteresis test shall commence. Pressure shall be increased at a rate simulating a descent in altitude at the rate of 5,000 to 20,000 feet per minute until within 3,000 feet of the first test point (50 percent of maximum altitude). The test point shall then be approached at a rate of approximately 3,000 feet per minute. The altimeter shall be kept at this pressure for at least 5 minutes, but not more than 15 minutes, before the test reading is taken. After the reading has been taken, the pressure shall be increased further, in the same manner as before, until the pressure corresponding to the second test point (40 percent of maximum altitude) is reached. The altimeter shall be kept at this pressure for at least 1 minute, but not more than 10 minutes, before the test reading is taken. After the reading has been taken, the pressure shall be increased further, in the same manner as before, until atmospheric pressure is reached. The reading of the altimeter at either of the two test points shall not differ by more than the tolerance specified in Table II from the reading of the altimeter for the corresponding altitude recorded during the scale error test prescribed in paragraph (b)(i).

(iii) *After effect.* Not more than 5 minutes after the completion of the hysteresis test prescribed in paragraph (b)(ii), the reading of the altimeter (corrected for any change in atmospheric pressure) shall not differ from the original atmospheric pressure reading by more than the tolerance specified in Table II.

(iv) *Friction.* The altimeter shall be subjected to a steady rate of decrease of pressure approximating 750 feet per minute. At each altitude listed in Table III, the change in reading of the pointers after vibration shall not exceed the corresponding tolerance listed in Table III.

(v) *Case leak.* The leakage of the altimeter case, when the pressure within it corresponds to an altitude of 18,000 feet, shall not change the altimeter reading by more than the tolerance shown in Table II during an interval of 1 minute.

(vi) *Barometric scale error.* At constant atmospheric pressure, the barometric pressure scale shall be set at each of the pressures (falling within its range of adjustment) that are listed in Table IV, and shall cause the pointer to indicate the equivalent altitude difference shown in Table IV with a tolerance of 25 feet.

(2) Altimeters which are the air data computer type with associated computing systems, or which incorporate air data correction internally, may be tested in a manner and to specifications developed by the manufacturer which are acceptable to the Administrator.

(c) Automatic Pressure Altitude Reporting Equipment and ATC Transponder System Integration Test. The test must be conducted by an appropriately rated person under the conditions specified in paragraph (a). Measure the automatic pressure altitude at the output of the installed ATC transponder when interrogated on Mode C at a sufficient number of test points to ensure that the altitude reporting equipment, altimeters, and ATC transponders perform their intended functions as installed in the aircraft. The difference between the automatic reporting output and the altitude displayed at the altimeter shall not exceed 125 feet.

(d) Records: Comply with the provisions of § 43.9 of this chapter as to content, form, and disposition of the records. The person performing the altimeter tests shall record on the altimeter the date and maximum altitude to which the altimeter has been tested and the persons approving the airplane for return to service shall enter that data in the airplane log or other permanent record.

TABLE I

Altitude	Equivalent pressure (inches of mercury)	Tolerance ±(feet)
−1,000	31.018	20
0	29.921	20
500	29.385	20
1,000	28.856	20
1,500	28.335	25
2,000	27.821	30
3,000	26.817	30
4,000	25.842	35
6,000	23.978	40
8,000	22.225	60
10,000	20.577	80
12,000	19.029	90
14,000	17.577	100
16,000	16.216	110
18,000	14.942	120
20,000	13.750	130
22,000	12.636	140
25,000	11.104	155
30,000	8.885	180
35,000	7.041	205
40,000	5.538	230
45,000	4.355	255
50,000	3.425	280

TABLE II—TEST TOLERANCES

Test	Tolerance (feet)
Case Leak Test	±100
Hysteresis Test:	
First Test Point (50 percent of maximum altitude)	75
Second Test Point (40 percent of maximum altitude)	75
After Effect Test	30

TABLE III—FRICTION

Altitude (feet)	Tolerance (feet)
1,000	±70
2,000	70
3,000	70
5,000	70
10,000	80
15,000	90
20,000	100
25,000	120
30,000	140
35,000	160
40,000	180
50,000	250

TABLE IV—PRESSURE-ALTITUDE DIFFERENCE

Pressure (inches of Hg)	Altitude difference (feet)
28.10	−1,727
28.50	−1,340
29.00	−863
29.50	−392
29.92	0
30.50	+531
30.90	+893
30.99	+974

(Secs. 313, 314, and 601 through 610 of the Federal Aviation Act of 1958 (49 U.S.C. 1354, 1355, and 1421 through 1430) and sec. 6(c), Dept. of Transportation Act (49 U.S.C. 1655(c)))

[Amdt. 43-2, 30 FR 8262, June 29, 1965, as amended by Amdt. 43-7, 32 FR 7587, May 24, 1967; Amdt. 43-19, 43 FR 22639, May 25, 1978; Amdt. 43-23, 47 FR 41086, Sept. 16, 1982]

Appendix F—ATC Transponder Tests and Inspections

The ATC transponder tests required by § 91.172 of this chapter may be conducted using a bench check or portable test equipment and must meet the requirements prescribed in paragraphs (a) through (j) of this appendix. If portable test equipment with appropriate coupling to the aircraft antenna system is used, operate the test equipment for ATCRBS transponders at a nominal rate of 235 interrogations per second to avoid possible ATCRBS interference. Operate the test equipment at a nominal rate of 50 Mode S interrogations per second for Mode S. An additional 3 dB loss is allowed to compensate for antenna coupling errors during receiver sensitivity measurements conducted in accordance with paragraph (c)(1) when using portable test equipment.

(a) Radio Reply Frequency:

(1) For all classes of ATCRBS transponders, interrogate the transponder and verify that the reply frequency is 1090±3 Megahertz (MHz).

(2) For classes 1B, 2B, and 3B Mode S transponders, interrogate the transponder and verify that the reply frequency is 1090±3 MHz.

(3) For classes 1B, 2B, and 3B Mode S transponders that incorporate the optional 1090±1 MHz reply frequency, interrogate the transponder and verify that the reply frequency is correct.

(4) For classes 1A, 2A, 3A, and 4 Mode S transponders, interrogate the transponder and verify that the reply frequency is 1090±1 MHz.

(b) Suppression: When Classes 1B and 2B ATCRBS Transponders, or Classes 1B, 2B, and 3B Mode S transponders are interrogated Mode 3/A at an interrogation rate between 230 and 1,000 interrogations per second; or when Classes 1A and 2A ATCRBS Transponders, or Classes 1B, 2A, 3A, and 4 Mode S transponders are interrogated at a rate between 230 and 1,200 Mode 3/A interrogations per second:

(1) Verify that the transponder does not respond to more than 1 percent of ATCRBS interrogations when the amplitude of P_2 pulse is equal to the P_1 pulse.

(2) Verify that the transponder replies to at least 90 percent of ATCRBS interrogations when the amplitude of the P_2 pulse is 9 dB less than the P_1 pulse. If the test is conducted with a radiated test signal, the interrogation rate shall be 235±5 interrogations per second unless a higher rate has been approved for the test equipment used at that location.

(c) Receiver Sensitivity:

(1) Verify that for any class of ATCRBS Transponder, the receiver minimum triggering level (MTL) of the system is −73±4 dbm, or that for any class of Mode S transponder the receiver MTL for Mode S format (P6 type) interrogations is −74±3 dbm by use of a test set either:

(i) Connected to the antenna end of the transmission line;

(ii) Connected to the antenna terminal of the transponder with a correction for transmission line loss; or

(iii) Utilized radiated signal.

(2) Verify that the difference in Mode 3/A and Mode C receiver sensitivity does not exceed 1 db for either any class of ATCRBS transponder or any class of Mode S transponder.

(d) Radio Frequency (RF) Peak Output Power:

(1) Verify that the transponder RF output power is within specifications for the class of transponder. Use the same conditions as described in (c)(1) (i), (ii), and (iii) above.

(i) For Class 1A and 2A ATCRBS transponders, verify that the minimum RF peak output power is at least 21.0 dbw (125 watts).

(ii) For Class 1B and 2B ATCRBS Transponders, verify that the minimum RF peak output power is at least 18.5 dbw (70 watts).

(iii) For Class 1A, 2A, 3A, and 4 and those Class 1B, 2B, and 3B Mode S transponders that include the optional high RF peak output power, verify that the minimum RF peak output power is at least 21.0 dbw (125 watts).

(iv) For Classes 1B, 2B, and 3B Mode S transponders, verify that the minimum RF peak output power is at least 18.5 dbw (70 watts).

(v) For any class of ATCRBS or any class of Mode S transponders, verify that the maximum RF peak output power does not exceed 27.0 dbw (500 watts).

Note: The tests in (e) through (j) apply only to Mode S transponders.

(e) Mode S Diversity Transmission Channel Isolation: For any class of Mode S transponder that incorporates diversity operation, verify that the RF peak output power transmitted from the selected antenna exceeds the power transmitted from the nonselected antenna by at least 20 db.

(f) Mode S Address: Interrogate the Mode S transponder and verify that it replies only to its assigned address. Use the correct address and at least two incorrect addresses. The interrogations should be made at a nominal rate of 50 interrogations per second.

(g) Mode S Formats: Interrogate the Mode S transponder with uplink formats (UF') for which it is equipped and verify that the replies are made in the correct format. Use the surveillance formats UF=4 and 5. Verify that the altitude reported in the replies to UF=4 are the same as that reported in a valid ATCRBS Mode C reply. Verify that the identity reported in the replies to UF=5 are the same as that reported in a valid ATCRBS Mode 3/A reply. If the transponder is so equipped, use the communication formats UF=20, 21, and 24.

(h) Mode S All-Call Interrogations: Interrogate the Mode S transponder with the Mode S-only all-call format UF=11, and the ATCRBS/Mode S all-call formats (1.6 microsecond P_4 pulse) and verify that the correct address and capability are reported in the replies (downlink format DF=11).

(i) ATCRBS-Only All-Call Interrogation: Interrogate the Mode S transponder with the ATCRBS-only all-call interrogation (0.8 microsecond P_4 pulse) and verify that no reply is generated.

(j) Squitter: Verify that the Mode S transponder generates a correct squitter approximately once per second.

(k) Records: Comply with the provisions of § 43.9 of this chapter as to content, form, and disposition of the records.

[Amdt. 43-26, 52 FR 3390, Feb. 3, 1987; 52 FR 6651, Mar. 4, 1987]

FEDERAL AVIATION REGULATIONS

PART 45
IDENTIFICATION AND REGISTRATION MARKING

1989 EDITION

PART 45—IDENTIFICATION AND REGISTRATION MARKING

Subpart A—General

Sec.
45.1 Applicability.

Subpart B—Identification of Aircraft and Related Products

45.11 General.
45.13 Identification data.
45.14 Identification of critical components.
45.15 Replacement and modification parts.

Subpart C—Nationality and Registration Marks

45.21 General.
45.22 Exhibition, antique, and other aircraft: Special rules.
45.23 Display of marks; general.
45 25 Location of marks on fixed-wing aircraft.
45.27 Location of marks; nonfixed-wing aircraft.
45.29 Size of marks.
45.31 Marking of export aircraft.
45.33 Sale of aircraft: removal of marks.

AUTHORITY: 49 U.S.C. 1348, 1354, 1401, 1402, 1421, 1423, 1522, 1655(c); (Revised Pub. L. 97-449, Jan. 12, 1983).

SOURCE: Docket No. 2047, 29 FR 3223, Mar. 11, 1964, unless otherwise noted.

Subpart A—General

§ 45.1 Applicability.

This part prescribes the requirements for—

(a) Identification of aircraft, and identification of aircraft engines and propellers that are manufactured under the terms of a type or production certificate;

(b) Identification of certain replacement and modified parts produced for installation on type certificated products; and

(c) Nationality and registration marking of U.S. registered aircraft.

[Doc. No. 2047, 29 FR 3223, Mar. 11, 1964, as amended by Amdt. 45-3, 32 FR 188, Jan. 10, 1967]

Subpart B—Identification of Aircraft and Related Products

§ 45.11 General.

(a) *Aircraft and aircraft engines.* Aircraft covered under § 21.182 of this chapter must be identified, and each person who manufacturers an aircraft engine under a type or production certificate shall identify that engine, by means of a fireproof plate that has the information specified in § 45.13 of this part marked on it by etching, stamping, engraving, or other approved method of fireproof marking. The identification plate for aircraft must be secured in such a manner that it will not likely be defaced or removed during normal service, or lost or destroyed in an accident. Except as provided in paragraphs (c) and (d) of this section, the aircraft identification plate must be secured to the aircraft fuselage exterior so that it is legible to a person on the ground, and must be either adjacent to and aft of the rear-most entrance door or on the fuselage surface near the tail surfaces. For aircraft engines, the identification plate must be affixed to the engine at an accessible location in such a manner that it will not likely be defaced or removed during normal service, or lost or destroyed in an accident.

(b) *Propellers and propeller blades and hubs.* Each person who manufactures a propeller, propeller blade, or propeller hub under the terms of a type or production certificate shall identify his product by means of a plate, stamping, engraving, etching, or other approved method of fireproof identification that is placed on it on a noncritical surface, contains the information specified in § 45.13, and will not be likely to be defaced or removed during normal service or lost or destroyed in an accident.

(c) For manned free balloons, the identification plate prescribed in paragraph (a) of this section must be secured to the balloon envelope and must be located, if practicable, where it is legible to the operator when the balloon is inflated. In addition, the basket and heater assembly must be permanently and legibly marked with the manufacturer's name, part number (or equivalent) and serial number (or equivalent).

(d) On aircraft manufactured before March 7, 1988, the identification plate required by paragraph (a) of this section may be secured at an accessible exterior or interior location near an entrance, if the model designation and builder's serial number are also displayed on the aircraft fuselage exterior. The model designation and builder's serial number must be legible to a person on the ground and must be located either adjacent to and aft of the rear-most entrance door or on the fuselage near the tail surfaces. The model designation and builder's serial number must be displayed in such a manner that they are not likely to be defaced or removed during normal service.

[Amdt. 45-3, 32 FR 188, Jan. 10, 1967 as amended by Amdt. 45-7, 33 FR 14402, Sept. 25, 1968; Amdt. 45-12, 45 FR 60183, Sept. 11, 1980; 45 FR 85597, Dec. 29, 1980; Amdt. 45-17, 52 FR 34101, Sept. 9, 1987; 52 FR 36566, Sept. 30, 1987]

§ 45.13 Identification data.

(a) The identification required by § 45.11 (a) and (b) shall include the following information:

(1) Builder's name.
(2) Model designation.
(3) Builder's serial number.
(4) Type certificate number, if any.
(5) Production certificate number, if any.
(6) For aircraft engines, the established rating.
(7) Any other information the Administrator finds appropriate.

(b) Except as provided in paragraph (d)(1) of this section, no person may remove, change, or place identification information required by paragraph (a) of this section, on any aircraft, aircraft engine, propeller, propeller blade, or propeller hub, without the approval of the Administrator.

(c) Except as provided in paragraph (d)(2) of this section, no person may remove or install any identification plate required by § 45.11 of this part, without the approval of the Administrator.

(d) Persons performing work under the provisions of Part 43 of this chapter may, in accordance with methods, techniques, and practices acceptable to the Administrator—

(1) Remove, change, or place the identification information required by paragraph (a) of this section on any aircraft, aircraft engine, propeller, propeller blade, or propeller hub; or

(2) Remove an identification plate required by § 45.11 when necessary during maintenance operations.

(e) No person may install an identification plate removed in accordance with paragraph (d)(2) of this section on any aircraft, aircraft engine, propeller, propeller blade, or propeller hub other than the one from which it was removed.

[Amdt. 45-3, 32 FR 188, Jan. 10, 1967, as amended by Amdt. 45-10, 44 FR 45379, Aug. 2, 1979; Amdt. 45-12, 45 FR 60183, Sept. 11, 1980]

§ 45.14 Identification of critical components.

Each person who produces a part for which a replacement time, inspection interval, or related procedure is specified in the Airworthiness Limitations section of a manufacturer's maintenance manual or Instructions for Continued Airworthiness shall permanently and legibly mark that component with a part number (or equivalent) and a serial number (or equivalent).

[Amdt. 45-16, 51 FR 40703, Nov. 7, 1986]

§ 45.15 Replacement and modification parts.

(a) Except as provided in paragraph (b) of this section, each person who produces a replacement or modification part under a Parts Manufacturer Approval issued under § 21.303 of this chapter shall permanently and legibly mark the part with—

(1) The letters "FAA-PMA";

(2) The name, trademark, or symbol of the holder of the Parts Manufacturer Approval;

(3) The part number; and

(4) The name and model designation of each type certificated product on which the part is eligible for installation.

(b) If the Administrator finds that a part is too small or that it is otherwise impractical to mark a part with any of the information required by paragraph (a) of this section, a tag attached to the part or its container must include the information that could not be marked on the part. If the marking required by paragraph (a)(4) of this section is so extensive that to mark it on a tag is impractical, the tag attached to the part or the container may refer to a specific readily available manual or catalog for part eligibility information.

[Amdt. 45-8, 37 FR 10660, May 26, 1972, as amended by Amdt. 45-14, 47 FR 13315, Mar. 29, 1982]

Subpart C—Nationality and Registration Marks

§ 45.21 General.

(a) Except as provided in § 45.22, no person may operate a U.S.-registered aircraft unless that aircraft displays nationality and registration marks in accordance with the requirements of this section and §§ 45.23 through 45.33.

(b) Unless otherwise authorized by the Administrator, no person may place on any aircraft a design, mark, or symbol that modifies or confuses the nationality and registration marks.

(c) Aircraft nationality and registration marks must—

(1) Except as provided in paragraph (d) of this section, be painted on the aircraft or affixed by any other means insuring a similar degree of permanence;

(2) Have no ornamentation;

(3) Contrast in color with the background; and

(4) Be legible.

(d) The aircraft nationality and registration marks may be affixed to an aircraft with readily removable material if—

(1) It is intended for immediate delivery to a foreign purchaser;

(2) It is bearing a temporary registration number; or

(3) It is marked temporarily to meet the requirements of § 45.22(c)(1) or § 45.29(h) of this part, or both.

[Doc. No. 8093, Amdt. 45-5, 33 FR 450, Jan 12, 1968, as amended by Amdt. 45-17, 52 FR 34102, Sept. 9, 1987]

§ 45.22 Exhibition, antique, and other aircraft: Special rules.

(a) When display of aircraft nationality and registration marks in accordance with §§ 45.21 and 45.23 through 45.33 would be inconsistent with exhibition of that aircraft, a U.S.-registered aircraft may be operated without displaying those marks anywhere on the aircraft if:

(1) It is operated for the purpose of exhibition, including a motion picture or television production, or an airshow;

(2) Except for practice and test fights necessary for exhibition purposes, it is operated only at the location of the exhibition, between the exhibition locations, and between those locations and the base of operations of the aircraft; and

(3) For each flight in the United States:

(i) It is operated with the prior approval of the General Aviation District Office, in the case of a flight within the designated airport control zone of the takeoff airport, or within 5 miles of that airport if it has no designated control zone; or

(ii) It is operated under a flight plan filed under § 91.83 of this chapter describing the marks it displays, in the case of any other flight.

(b) A small U.S.-registered aircraft built at least 30 years ago or a U.S.-registered aircraft for which an experimental certificate has been issued under § 21.191(d) or 21.191(g) for operation as an exhibition aircraft or as an amateur-built aircraft and which has the same external configuration as an aircraft built at least 30 years ago may be operated without displaying marks in accordance with §§ 45.21 and 45.23 through 45.33 if:

(1) It displays in accordance with § 45.21(c) marks at least 2 inches high on each side of the fuselage or vertical tail surface consisting of the Roman capital letter "N" followed by:

(i) The U.S. registration number of the aircraft; or

(ii) The symbol appropriate to the airworthiness certificate of the aircraft ("C", standard; "R", restricted; "L", limited; or "X", experimental) followed by the U.S. registration number of the aircraft; and

(2) It displays no other mark that begins with the letter "N" anywhere on the aircraft, unless it is the same mark that is displayed under paragraph (b)(1) of this section.

(c) No person may operate an aircraft under paragraph (a) or (b) of this section—

(1) In an ADIZ or DEWIZ described in Part 99 of this chapter unless it temporarily bears marks in accordance with §§ 45.21 and 45.23 through 45.33;

(2) In a foreign country unless that country consents to that operation; or

(3) In any operation conducted under Part 121, 127, 133, 135, or 137 of this chapter.

(d) If, due to the configuration of an aircraft, it is impossible for a person to mark it in accordance with §§ 45.21 and 45.23 through 45.33, he may apply to the Administrator for a different marking procedure.

[Doc. No. 8093, Amdt. 45-5, 33 FR 450, Jan. 12, 1968, as amended by Amdt. 45-13, 46 FR 48603, Oct. 1, 1981]

§ 45.23 Display of marks; general.

(a) Each operator of an aircraft shall display on that aircraft marks consisting of the Roman capital letter "N" (denoting United States registration) followed by the registration number of the aircraft. Each suffix letter used in the marks displayed must also be a Roman capital letter.

(b) When marks that include only the Roman capital letter "N" and the registration number are displayed on limited or restricted category aircraft or experimental or provisionally certificated aircraft, the operator shall also display on that aircraft near each entrance to the cabin or cockpit, in letters not less than 2 inches nor more than 6 inches in height, the words "limited," "restricted," "experimental," or "provisional airworthiness," as the case may be.

[Doc. No. 8093, Amdt. 45-5, 33 FR 450, Jan. 12, 1968, as amended by Amdt. 45-9, 42 FR 41102, Aug. 15, 1977]

§ 45.25 **Location of marks on fixed-wing aircraft.**

(a) The operator of a fixed-wing aircraft shall display the required marks on either the vertical tail surfaces or the sides of the fuselage, except as provided in § 45.29(f).

(b) The marks required by paragraph (a) of this section shall be displayed as follows:

(1) If displayed on the vertical tail surfaces, horizontally on both surfaces, horizontally on both surfaces of a single vertical tail or on the outer surfaces of a multivertical tail. However, on aircraft on which marks at least 3 inches high may be displayed in accordance with § 45.29(b)(1), the marks may be displayed vertically on the vertical tail surfaces.

(2) If displayed on the fuselage surfaces, horizontally on both sides of the fuselage between the trailing edge of the wing and the leading edge of the horizontal stabilizer. However, if engine pods or other appurtenances are located in this area and are an integral part of the fuselage side surfaces, the operator may place the marks on those pods or appurtenances.

[Amdt. 45-9, 42 FR 41102, Aug. 15, 1977]

§ 45.27 **Location of marks; nonfixed-wing aircraft.**

(a) *Rotorcraft.* Each operator of a rotorcraft shall display on that rotorcraft horizontally on both surfaces of the cabin, fuselage, boom, or tail the marks required by § 45.23.

(b) *Airships.* Each operator of an airship shall display on that airship the marks required by § 45.23, horizontally on—

(1) The upper surface of the right horizontal stabilizer and on the under surface of the left horizontal stabilizer with the top of the marks toward the leading edge of each stabilizer; and

(2) Each side of the bottom half of the vertical stabilizer.

(c) *Spherical balloons.* Each operator of a spherical balloon shall display the marks required by § 45.23 in two places diametrically opposite and near the maximum horizontal circumference of that balloon.

(d) *Nonspherical balloons.* Each operator of a nonspherical balloon shall display the marks required by § 45.23 on each side of the balloon near its maximum cross section and immediately above either the rigging band or the points of attachment of the basket or cabin suspension cables.

[Doc. No. 2047, 29 FR 3223, Mar. 11, 1964, as amended by Amdt. 45-15, 48 FR 11392, Mar. 17, 1983]

§ 45.29 **Size of marks.**

(a) Except as provided in paragraph (f) of this section, each operator of an aircraft shall display marks on the aircraft meeting the size requirements of this section.

(b) *Height.* Except as provided in paragraph (h) of this part, the nationality and registration marks must be of equal height and on—

(1) Fixed-wing aircraft, must be at least 12 inches high, except that:

(i) An aircraft displaying marks at least 2 inches high before November 1, 1981 and an aircraft manufactured after November 2, 1981, but before January 1, 1983, may display those marks until the aircraft is repainted or the marks are repainted, restored, or changed;

(ii) Marks at least 3 inches high may be displayed on a glider;

(iii) Marks at least 3 inches high may be displayed on an aircraft for which an experimental certificate has been issued under § 21.191(d) or 21.191(g) for operating as an exhibition aircraft or as an amateur-built aircraft when the maximum cruising speed of the aircraft does not exceed 180 knots CAS; and

(iv) Marks may be displayed on an exhibition, antique, or other aircraft in accordance with § 45.22.

(2) Airships, spherical balloons, and nonspherical balloons, must be at least 3 inches high; and

(3) Rotorcraft, must be at least 12 inches high, except that rotorcraft displaying before April 18, 1983, marks required by § 45.29(b)(3) in effect on April 17, 1983, and rotorcraft manufactured on or after April 18, 1983, but before December 31, 1983, may display those marks until the aircraft is re-

painted or the marks are repainted, restored, or changed.

(c) *Width.* Characters must be two-thirds as wide as they are high, except the number "1", which must be one-sixth as wide as it is high, and the letters "M" and "W" which may be as wide as they are high.

(d) *Thickness.* Characters must be formed by solid lines one-sixth as thick as the character is high.

(e) *Spacing.* The space between each character may not be less than one-fourth of the character width.

(f) If either one of the surfaces authorized for displaying required marks under § 45.25 is large enough for display of marks meeting the size requirements of this section and the other is not, full-size marks shall be placed on the larger surface. If neither surface is large enough for full-size marks, marks as large as practicable shall be displayed on the larger of the two surfaces. If any surface authorized to be marked by § 45.27 is not large enough for full-size marks, marks as large as practicable shall be placed on the largest of the authorized surfaces.

(g) *Uniformity.* The marks required by this part for fixed-wing aircraft must have the same height, width, thickness, and spacing on both sides of the aircraft.

(h) After March 7, 1988, each operator of an aircraft penetrating an ADIZ or DEWIZ shall display on that aircraft temporary or permanent nationality and registration marks at least 12 inches high.

[Doc. No. 2047, 29 FR 3223, Mar. 11, 1964, as amended by Amdt. 45-2, 31 FR 9863, July 21, 1966; Amdt. 45-9, 42 FR 41102, Aug. 15, 1977; Amdt. 45-13, 46 FR 48604, Oct. 1, 1981; Amdt. 45-15, 48 FR 11392, Mar. 17, 1983; Amdt. 45-17, 52 FR 34102, Sept. 9, 1987; 52 FR 36566, Sept. 30, 1987]

§ 45.31   Marking of export aircraft.

A person who manufactures an aircraft in the United States for delivery outside thereof may display on that aircraft any marks required by the State of registry of the aircraft. However, no person may operate an aircraft so marked within the United States, except for test and demonstration flights for a limited period of time, or while in necessary transit to the purchaser.

§ 45.33   Sale of aircraft; removal of marks.

When an aircraft that is registered in the United States is sold, the holder of the Certificate of Aircraft Registration shall remove, before its delivery to the purchaser, all United States marks from the aircraft, unless the purchaser is—

(a) A citizen of the United States;

(b) An individual citizen of a foreign country who is lawfully admitted for permanent residence in the United States; or

(c) When the aircraft is to be based and primarily used in the United States, a corporation (other than a corporation which is a citizen of the United States) lawfully organized and doing business under the laws of the United States or any State thereof.

[Amdt. 45-11, 44 FR 61938, Oct. 29, 1979]

FEDERAL AVIATION REGULATIONS

PART 47
AIRCRAFT REGISTRATION

1989 EDITION

PART 47—AIRCRAFT REGISTRATION

Subpart A—General

Sec.
47.1 Applicability.
47.3 Definition.
47.5 Registration required.
47.7 Applicant.
47.7 United States citizens and resident aliens.
47.8 Voting trusts.
47.9 Corporations not U.S. citizens.
47.11 Evidence of ownership.
47.13 Signature and statements made by representatives.
47.15 Identification number.
47.16 Temporary registration numbers.
47.17 Fees.
47.19 T.A. airworthiness certificate.

Subpart B—Certificate of Aircraft Registration

47.31 Application.
47.33 Aircraft not previously registered anywhere.
47.35 Aircraft last previously registered in a foreign country.
47.37 Aircraft last previously registered in the United States.
47.39 Duration and return of Certificate.
47.40 Renewal of registration.
47.41 Duration of Certificate.
47.43 Invalid registration.
47.45 Change of address.
47.47 Cancellation of Certificate for export purposes.
47.49 Replacement of Certificate.

PART 47—AIRCRAFT REGISTRATION

Subpart A—General

Sec.
47.1   Applicability.
47.2   Definitions.
47.3   Registration required.
47.5   Applicants.
47.7   United States citizens and resident aliens.
47.8   Voting trusts.
47.9   Corporations not U.S. citizens.
47.11   Evidence of ownership.
47.13   Signatures and instruments made by representatives.
47.15   Identification number.
47.16   Temporary registration numbers.
47.17   Fees.
47.19   FAA Aircraft Registry.

Subpart B—Certificates of Aircraft Registration

47.31   Application.
47.33   Aircraft not previously registered anywhere.
47.35   Aircraft last previously registered in the United States.
47.37   Aircraft last previously registered in a foreign country.
47.39   Effective date of registration.
47.41   Duration and return of Certificate.
47.43   Invalid registration.
47.45   Change of address.
47.47   Cancellation of Certificate for export purpose.
47.49   Replacement of Certificate.

47.51   Triennial aircraft registration report.

Subpart C—Dealer's Aircraft Registration Certificate

47.61   Dealers' Aircraft Registration Certificate.
47.63   Application.
47.65   Eligibility.
47.67   Evidence of ownership.
47.69   Limitations.
47.71   Duration of Certificate; change of status.

AUTHORITY: Secs. 307, 313, 501, 503, 505, 506, and 1102, 72 Stat. 749, 752, 771, 772, 774, 797; 49 U.S.C. 1348, 1354, 1401, 1403, 1405, 1406, and 1502, and the Convention of the International Recognition of Rights in Aircraft; 4 U.S.C. 1830.

SOURCE: Docket No. 7190, 31 FR 4495, Mar. 17, 1966, unless otherwise noted.

Subpart A—General

§ 47.1   Applicability.

This part prescribes the requirements for registering aircraft under section 501 of the Federal Aviation Act of 1958 (49 U.S.C. 1401). Subpart B applies to each applicant for, and holder of, a Certificate of Aircraft Registration. Subpart C applies to each applicant for, and holder of, a Dealers' Aircraft Registration Certificate.

§ 47.2   Definitions.

The following are definitions of terms used in this part:

"Act" means the Federal Aviation Act of 1958 (49 U.S.C. section 1301 *et seq.*).

"Resident alien" means an individual citizen of a foreign country lawfully admitted for permanent residence in the United States as an immigrant in conformity with the regulations of the Immigration and Naturalization Service of the Department of Justice (8 CFR Chapter 1).

"U.S. citizen" means one of the following:

(1) An individual who is a citizen of the United States or one of its possessions.

(2) A partnership of which each member is such an individual.

(3) A corporation or association created or organized under the laws of the United States or of any State, Territory, or possession of the United States, of which the president and two-thirds or more of the board of directors and other managing officers thereof are such individuals and in which at least 75 percent of the voting interest is owned or controlled by persons who are citizens of the United States or of one of its possessions.

[Amdt. 47-20, 44 FR 61939, Oct. 29, 1979]

§ 47.3   Registration required.

(a) Section 501(b) of the Federal Aviation Act of 1958 (49 U.S.C. 1401 (b)) defines eligibility for registration as follows:

(b) An aircraft shall be eligible for registration if, but only if—

(1)(A) it is—

(i) owned by a citizen of the United States or by an individual citizen of a foreign country who has lawfully been admitted for permanent residence in the United States; or

(ii) owned by a corporation (other than a corporation which is a citizen of the United States) lawfully organized and doing business under the laws of the United States or any State thereof so long as such aircraft is based and primarily used in the United States; and

(B) it is not registered under the laws of any foreign country; or

(2) it is an aircraft of the Federal Government, or of a State, territory, or possession of the United States or the District of Columbia or a political subdivision thereof.

(b) No person may operate on aircraft that is eligible for registration under section 501 of the Federal Aviation Act of 1958 unless the aircraft—

(1) Has been registered by its owner;

(2) Is carrying aboard the temporary authorization required by § 47.31(b); or

(3) Is an aircraft of the Armed Forces.

(c) Governmental units are those named in paragraph (a) of this section and Puerto Rico.

[Doc. No. 7190, 31 FR 4495, Mar. 17, 1966, as amended by Amdt. 47-20, 44 FR 61939, Oct. 29, 1979]

§ 47.5   Applicants.

(a) A person who wishes to register an aircraft in the United States must submit an Application for Aircraft Registration under this part.

(b) An aircraft may be registered only by and in the legal name of its owner.

(c) Section 501(f) of the Act (49 U.S.C. 1401(f)), provides that registration is not evidence of ownership of aircraft in any proceeding in which ownership by a particular person is in issue. The FAA does not issue any certificate of ownership or endorse any information with respect to ownership on a Certificate of Aircraft Registration. The FAA issues a Certificate of Aircraft Registration to the person who appears to be the owner on the basis of the evidence of ownership submitted pursuant to § 47.11 with the Application for Aircraft Registration, or recorded at the FAA Aircraft Registry.

(d) In this part, "owner" includes a buyer in possession, a bailee, or a lessee of an aircraft under a contract of conditional sale, and the assignee of that person.

[Amdt. 47-20, 44 FR 61939, Oct. 29, 1979]

§ 47.7 United States citizens and resident aliens.

(a) *United States Citizens.* An applicant for aircraft registration under this part who is a U.S. citizen must certify to this in the application.

(b) *Resident aliens.* An applicant for aircraft registration under section 501(b)(1)(A)(i) of the Act who is a resident alien must furnish a representation of permanent residence and the applicant's alien registration number issued by the Immigration and Naturalization Service.

(c) *Trustees.* An applicant for aircraft registration under section 501(b)(1)(A)(i) of the Act that holds legal title to an aircraft in trust must comply with the following requirements:

(1) Each trustee must be either a U.S. citizen or a resident alien.

(2) The applicant must submit with the application—

(i) A copy of each document legally affecting a relationship under the trust;

(ii) If each beneficiary under the trust, including each person whose security interest in the aircraft is incorporated in the trust, is either a U.S.

citizen or a resident alien, an affidavit by the applicant to that effect; and

(iii) If any beneficiary under the trust, including any person whose security interest in the aircraft is incorporated in the trust, is not a U.S. citizen or resident alien, an affidavit from each trustee stating that the trustee is not aware of any reason, situation, or relationship (involving beneficiaries or other persons who are not U.S. citizens or resident aliens) as a result of which those persons together would have more than 25 percent of the aggregate power to influence or limit the exercise of the trustee's authority.

(3) If persons who are neither U.S. citizens nor resident aliens have the power to direct or remove a trustee, either directly or indirectly through the control of another person, the trust instrument must provide that those persons together may not have more than 25 percent of the aggregate power to direct or remove a trustee. Nothing in this paragraph prevents those persons from having more than 25 percent of the beneficial interest in the trust.

(d) *Partnerships.* A partnership may apply for a Certificate of Aircraft Registration under section 501(b)(1)(A)(i) of the Act only if each partner, whether a general or limited partner, is a citizen of the United States. Nothing in this section makes ineligible for registration an aircraft which is not owned as a partnership asset but is co-owned by—

(1) Resident aliens; or

(2) One or more resident aliens and one or more U.S. citizens.

[Amdt. 47-20, 44 FR 61939, Oct. 29, 1979]

§ 47.8 Voting trusts.

(a) If a voting trust is used to qualify a domestic corporation as a U.S. citizen, the corporate applicant must submit to the FAA Aircraft Registry—

(1) A true copy of the fully executed voting trust agreement, which must identify each voting interest of the applicant, and which must be binding upon each voting trustee, the applicant corporation, all foreign stockholders, and each other party to the transaction; and

(2) An affidavit executed by each person designated as voting trustee in the voting trust agreement, in which each affiant represents—

(i) That each voting trustee is a citizen of the United States within the meaning of section 101(16) of the Act;

(ii) That each voting trustee is not a past, present, or prospective director, officer, employee, attorney, or agent of any other party to the trust agreement;

(iii) That each voting trustee is not a present or prospective beneficiary, creditor, debtor, supplier or contractor of any other party to the trust agreement;

(iv) That each voting trustee is not aware of any reason, situation, or relationship under which any other party to the agreement might influence the exercise of the voting trustee's totally independent judgment under the voting trust agreement.

(b) Each voting trust agreement submitted under paragraph (a)(1) of this section must provide for the succession of a voting trustee in the event of death, disability, resignation, termination of citizenship, or any other event leading to the replacement of any voting trustee. Upon succession, the replacement voting trustee shall immediately submit to the FAA Aircraft Registry the affidavit required by paragraph (a)(2) of this section.

(c) If the voting trust terminates or is modified, and the result is less than 75 percent control of the voting interest in the corporation by citizens of the United States, a loss of citizenship of the holder of the registration certificate occurs, and § 47.41(a)(5) of this part applies.

(d) A voting trust agreement may not empower a trustee to act through a proxy.

[Amdt. 47-20, 44 FR 61939, Oct. 29, 1979]

§ 47.9   Corporations not U.S. citizens.

(a) Each corporation applying for registration of an aircraft under section 501(b)(1)(A)(ii) of the Act must submit to the FAA Registry with the application—

(1) A certified copy of its certificate of incorporation;

(2) A certification that it is lawfully qualified to do business in one or more States;

(3) A certification that the aircraft will be based and primarily used in the United States; and

(4) The location where the records required by paragraph (e) of this section will be maintained.

(b) For the purposes of registration, an aircraft is based and primarily used in the United States if the flight hours accumulated within the United States amount to at least 60 percent of the total flight hours of the aircraft during—

(1) For aircraft registered on or before January 1, 1980, the 6-calendar month period beginning on January 1, 1980, and each 6-calendar month period thereafter; and

(2) For aircraft registered after January 1, 1980, the period consisting in the remainder of the registration month and the succeeding 6 calendar months and each 6-calendar month period thereafter.

(c) For the purpose of this section, only those flight hours accumulated during non-stop (except for stops in emergencies or for purposes of refueling) flight between two points in the United States, even if the aircraft is outside of the United States during part of the flight, are considered flight hours accumulated within the United States.

(d) In determining compliance with this section, any periods during which the aircraft is not validly registered in the United States are disregarded.

(e) The corporation that registers an aircraft pursuant to section 501(b)(1)(A)(ii) of the Act shall maintain, and make available for inspection by the Administrator upon request, records containing the total flight hours in the United States of the aircraft for three calendar years after the year in which the flight hours were accumulated.

(f) The corporation that registers an aircraft pursuant to section 501(b)(1)(A)(ii) of the Act shall send to the FAA Aircraft Registry, at the end of each period of time described in paragraphs (b) (1) and (2) of this section, either—

(1) A signed report containing—

(i) The total time in service of the airframe as provided in §91.173(a)(2)(i), accumulated during that period; and

(ii) The total flight hours in the United States of the aircraft accumulated during that period; or

(2) A signed statement that the total flight hours of the aircraft, while registered in the United States during that period, have been exclusively within the United States.

[Amdt. No. 47-20, 44 FR 61940, Oct. 29, 1979]

EDITORIAL NOTE: For documents relating to the effective date of reporting requirements in §47.9 and the correction of certain reporting periods, see 46 FR 35491, July 9, 1981 and 47 FR 8158, February 25, 1982.

§47.11 Evidence of ownership.

Except as provided in §§47.33 and 47.35, each person that submits an Application for Aircraft Registration under this part must also submit the required evidence of ownership, recordable under §§49.13 and 49.17 of this chapter, as follows:

(a) The buyer in possession, the bailee, or the lessee of an aircraft under a contract of conditional sale must submit the contract. The assignee under a contract of conditional sale must submit both the contract (unless it is already recorded at the FAA Aircraft Registry), and his assignment from the original buyer, bailee, lessee, or prior assignee.

(b) The repossessor of an aircraft must submit—

(1) A certificate of repossession on FAA Form 8050-4, or its equivalent, signed by the applicant and stating that the aircraft was repossessed or otherwise seized under the security agreement involved and applicable local law;

(2) The security agreement (unless it is already recorded at the FAA Aircraft Registry), or a copy thereof certified as true under §49.21 of this chapter; and

(3) When repossession was through foreclosure proceedings resulting in sale, a bill of sale signed by the sheriff, auctioneer, or other authorized person who conducted the sale, and stating that the sale was made under applicable local law.

(c) The buyer of an aircraft at a judicial sale, or at a sale to satisfy a lien or charge, must submit a bill of sale signed by the sheriff, auctioneer, or other authorized person who conducted the sale, and stating that the sale was made under applicable local law.

(d) The owner of an aircraft, the title to which has been in controversy and has been determined by a court, must submit a certified copy of the decision of the court.

(e) The executor or administrator of the estate of the deceased former owner of an aircraft must submit a certified copy of the letters testamentary or letters of administration appointing him executor or administrator. The Certificate of Aircraft Registration is issued to the applicant as executor or administrator.

(f) The buyer of an aircraft from the estate of a deceased former owner must submit both a bill of sale, signed for the estate by the executor or administrator, and a certified copy of the letters testamentary or letters of administration. When no executor or administrator has been or is to be appointed, the applicant must submit both a bill of sale, signed by the heir-at-law of the deceased former owner, and an affidavit of the heir-at-law stating that no application for appointment of an executor or administrator has been made, that so far as he can determine none will be made, and that he is the person entitled to, or having the right to dispose of, the aircraft under applicable local law.

(g) The guardian of another person's property that includes an aircraft must submit a certified copy of the order of the court appointing him guardian. The Certificate of Aircraft Registration is issued to the applicant as guardian.

(h) The trustee of property that includes an aircraft, as described in §47.7(c), must submit either a certified copy of the order of the court appointing the trustee, or a complete and true copy of the instrument creating the trust. If there is more than one trustee, each trustee must sign the application. The Certificate of Aircraft

Registration is issued to a single applicant as trustee, or to several trustees jointly as co-trustees.

[Doc. No. 7190, 31 FR 4495, Mar. 17, 1966, as amended by Amdt. 47-20, 44 FR 61940, Oct. 29, 1979]

§ 47.13 Signatures and instruments made by representatives.

(a) Each signature on an Application for Aircraft Registration, on a request for cancellation of a Certificate of Aircraft Registration or on a document submitted as supporting evidence under this part, must be in ink.

(b) When one or more persons doing business under a trade name submits an Application for Aircraft Registration or a request for cancellation of a Certificate of Aircraft Registration, the application or request must be signed by, or in behalf of, each person who shares title to the aircraft.

(c) When an agent submits an Application for Aircraft Registration or a request for cancellation of a Certificate of Aircraft Registration in behalf of the owner, he must—

(1) State the name of the owner on the application or request;

(2) Sign as agent or attorney-in-fact on the application or request; and

(3) Submit a signed power of attorney, or a true copy thereof certified under § 49.21 of this chapter, with the application or request.

(d) When a corporation submits an Application for Aircraft Registration or a request for cancellation of a Certificate of Aircraft Registration, it must—

(1) Have an authorized person sign the application or request;

(2) Show the title of the signer's office on the application or request; and

(3) Submit a copy of the authorization from the board of directors to sign for the corporation, certified as true under § 49.21 of this chapter by a corporate officer or other person in a managerial position therein, with the application or request, unless—

(i) The signer of the application or request is a corporate officer or other person in a managerial position in the corporation and the title of his office is stated in connection with his signature; or

(ii) A valid authorization to sign is on file at the FAA Aircraft Registry.

(e) When a partnership submits an Application for Aircraft Registration or a request for cancellation of a Certificate of Aircraft Registration, it must—

(1) State the full name of the partnership on the application or request;

(2) State the name of each general partner on the application or request; and

(3) Have a general partner sign the application or request.

(f) When co-owners, who are not engaged in business as partners, submit an Application for Aircraft Registration or a request for cancellation of a Certificate of Aircraft Registration, each person who shares title to the aircraft under the arrangement must sign the application or request.

(g) A power of attorney or other evidence of a person's authority to sign for another, submitted under this part, is valid for the purposes of this section, unless sooner revoked, until—

(1) Its expiration date stated therein; or

(2) If an expiration date is not stated therein, for not more than 3 years after the date—

(i) It is signed; or

(ii) The grantor (a corporate officer or other person in a managerial position therein, where the grantor is a corporation) certifies in writing that the authority to sign shown by the power of attorney or other evidence is still in effect.

[Doc. No. 7190, 31 FR 4495, Mar. 17, 1966, as amended by Amdt. 47-2, 31 FR 15349, Dec. 8, 1966; Amdt. 47-3, 32 FR 6554, Apr. 28, 1967; Amdt. 47-12, 36 FR 8661, May 11, 1971]

§ 47.15 Identification number.

(a) *Number required.* An applicant for Aircraft Registration must place a U.S. identification number (registration mark) on his Aircraft Registration Application, AC Form 8050-1, and on any evidence submitted with the application. There is no charge for the assignment of numbers provided in this paragraph. This paragraph does not apply to an aircraft manufacturer who applies for a group of U.S. identification numbers under paragraph (c) of this section; a person who applies for a special identification number under paragraphs (d) through (g) of this section; or a holder of a Dealer's Aircraft Registration Certificate who applies for a temporary registration number under § 47.16.

(1) *Aircraft not previously registered anywhere.* The applicant must obtain the U.S. identification number from the FAA Aircraft Registry by request in writing describing the aircraft by make, type, model, and serial number (or, if it is amateur-built, as provided in § 47.33(b)) and stating that the aircraft has not previously been registered anywhere. If the aircraft was brought into the United States from a foreign country, the applicant must submit evidence that the aircraft has never been registered in a foreign country.

(2) *Aircraft last previously registered in the United States.* Unless he applies for a different number under paragraphs (d) through (g) of this section, the applicant must place the U.S. identification number that is already assigned to the aircraft on his application and the supporting evidence.

(3) *Aircraft last previously registered in a foreign country.* Whether or not the foreign registration has ended, the applicant must obtain a U.S. identification number from the FAA Aircraft Registry for an aircraft last previously registered in a foreign country, by request in writing describing the aircraft by make, model, and serial number, accompanied by—

(i) Evidence of termination of foreign registration in accordance with § 47.37(b) or the applicant's affidavit showing that foreign registration has ended; or

(ii) If foreign registration has not ended, the applicant's affidavit stating that the number will not be placed on the aircraft until foreign registration has ended.

Authority to use the identification number obtained under paragraph (a)(1) or (3) of this section expires 90 days after the date it is issued unless the applicant submits an Aircraft Registration Application, AC Form 8050-1, and complies with § 47.33 or § 47.37, as applicable, within that period of time.

However, the applicant may obtain an extension of this 90-day period from the FAA Aircraft Registry if he shows that his delay in complying with that section is due to circumstances beyond his control.

(b) A U.S. identification number may not exceed five symbols in addition to the prefix letter "N". These symbols may be all numbers (N10000), one to four numbers and one suffix letter (N 1000A), or one to three numbers and two suffix letters (N 100AB). The letters "I" and "O" may not be used. The first zero in a number must always be preceded by at least one of the numbers 1 through 9.

(c) An aircraft manufacturer may apply to the FAA Aircraft Registry for enough U.S. identification numbers to supply his estimated production for the next 18 months. There is no charge for this assignment of numbers.

(d) Any unassigned U.S. identification number may be assigned as a special identification number. An applicant who wants a special identification number or wants to change the identification number of his aircraft may apply for it to the FAA Aircraft Registry. The fee required by § 47.17 must accompany the application.

(e) [Reserved]

(f) The FAA Aircraft Registry assigns a special identification number on AC Form 8050-64. Within 5 days after he affixes the special identification number to his aircraft, the owner must complete and sign the receipt contained in AC Form 8050-64, state the date he affixed the number to his aircraft, and return the original form to the FAA Aircraft Registry. The owner shall carry the duplicate of AC Form 8050-64 and the present Certificate of Aircraft Registration in the aircraft as temporary authority to operate it. This temporary authority is valid until the date the owner receives the revised Certificate of Aircraft Registration issued by the FAA Aircraft Registry.

(g) [Reserved]

(h) A special identification number may be reserved for no more than 1 year. If a person wishes to renew his reservation from year to year, he must apply to the FAA aircraft Registry for renewal and submit the fee required by § 47.17 for a special identification number.

(Sec. 3(e), 80 Stat. 931, 49 U.S.C. 1652; secs. 307(c), 313(a), 501, 503, 1102, Federal Aviation Act of 1958, as amended (49 U.S.C. 1348(c), 1354(a), 1401, 1403, 1502), and sec. 6(c), Dept. of Transportation Act (49 U.S.C. 1655(c))

[Doc. No. 7190, 31 FR 4495, Mar. 17, 1966, as amended by Amdt. 47-1, 31 FR 13314, Oct. 14, 1966; Amdt. 47-5, 32 FR 13505, Sept. 27, 1967; Amdt. 47-7, 34 FR 2480, Feb. 21, 1969; Amdt. 47-13, 36 FR 16187, Aug. 20, 1971; Amdt. 47-15, 37 FR 21528, Oct. 12, 1972; Amdt. 47-16, 37 FR 25487, Dec. 1, 1972; Amdt. 47-17, 39 FR 1353, Jan. 8, 1974; Amdt. 47-22, 47 FR 12153, Mar. 22, 1982]

§ 47.16 Temporary registration numbers.

(a) Temporary registration numbers are issued by the FAA to manufacturers, distributors, and dealers who are holders of Dealer's Aircraft Registration Certificates for temporary display on aircraft during flight allowed under Subpart C of this part.

(b) The holder of a Dealer's Aircraft Registration Certificate may apply to the FAA Aircraft Registry for as many temporary registration numbers as are necessary for his business. The application must be in writing and include—

(1) Sufficient information to justify the need for the temporary registration numbers requested; and

(2) The number of each Dealer's Aircraft Registration Certificate held by the applicant.

There is no charge for these numbers.

(c) The use of temporary registration numbers is subject to the following conditions:

(1) The numbers may be used and reused—

(i) Only in connection with the holder's Dealer's Aircraft Registration Certificate;

(ii) Within the limitations of § 47.69 where applicable, including the requirements of § 47.67; and

(iii) On aircraft not registered under Subpart B of this part or in a foreign country, and not displaying any other identification markings.

(2) A temporary registration number may not be used on more than one aircraft in flight at the same time.

(3) Temporary registration numbers may not be used to fly aircraft into the United States for the purpose of importation.

(d) The assignment of any temporary registration number to any person lapses upon the expiration of all of his Dealer's Aircraft Registration Certificates. When a temporary registration number is used on a flight outside the United States for delivery purposes, the holder shall record the assignment of that number to the aircraft and shall keep that record for at least 1 year after the removal of the number from that aircraft. Whenever the owner of an aircraft bearing a temporary registration number applies for an airworthiness certificate under Part 21 of this chapter he shall furnish that number in the application. The temporary registration number must be removed from the aircraft not later than the date on which either title or possession passes to another person.

[Amdt. 47-4, 32 FR 12556, Aug. 30, 1967]

§ 47.17 Fees.

(a) The fees for applications under this part are as follows:

(1) Certificate of Aircraft Registration (each aircraft)	$5.00
(2) Dealer's Aircraft Registration Certificate	10.00
(3) Additional Dealer's Aircraft Registration Certificate (issued to same dealer)	2.00
(4) Special identification number (each number)	10.00
(5) Changed, reassigned, or reserved identification number	10.00
(6) Duplicate Certificate of Registration	2.00

(b) Each application must be accompanied by the proper fee, that may be paid by check or money order to the Federal Aviation Administration.

[Doc. No. 7190, 31 FR 4495, Mar. 17, 1966; 31 FR 5483, Apr. 7, 1966, as amended by Doc. No. 8084, 32 FR 5769, Apr. 11, 1967]

§ 47.19 FAA Aircraft Registry.

Each application, request, notification, or other communication sent to the FAA under this part must be mailed to the FAA Aircraft Registry, Department of Transportation, Post Office Box 25504, Oklahoma City, Oklahoma 73125, or delivered to the

Registry at 6400 South MacArthur Boulevard, Oklahoma City, Oklahoma.

[Doc. No. 13890, 41 FR 34009, Aug. 12, 1976]

Subpart B—Certificates of Aircraft Registration

§47.31 Application.

(a) Each applicant for a Certificate of Aircraft Registration must submit the following to the FAA Aircraft Registry—

(1) The original (white) and one copy (green) of the Aircraft Registration Application, AC Form 8050-1;

(2) The original Aircraft Bill of Sale, ACC Form 8050-2, or other evidence of ownership authorized by §§47.33, 47.35, or 47.37 (unless already recorded at the FAA Aircraft Registry); and

(3) The fee required by §47.17.

The FAA rejects an application when any form is not completed, or when the name and signature of the applicant are not the same throughout.

(b) After he complies with paragraph (a) of this section, the applicant shall carry the second duplicate copy (pink) of the Aircraft Registration Application, AC Form 8050-1, in the aircraft as temporary authority to operate it without registration. This temporary authority is valid until the date the applicant receives the certificate of the Aircraft Registration, AC Form 8050-3, or until the date the FAA denies the application, but in no case for more than 90 days after the date the applicant signs the application. If by 90 days after the date the applicant signs the application, the FAA has neither issued the Certificate of Aircraft Registration nor denied the application, the FAA aircraft Registry issues a letter of extension that serves as authority to continue to operate the aircraft without registration while it is carried in the aircraft.

(c) Paragraph (b) of this section applies to each application submitted under paragraph (a) of this section, and signed after October 5, 1967. If, after that date, an applicant signs an application and the second duplicate copy (pink) of the Aircraft Registration Application, AC Form 8050-1, bears an obsolete statement limiting its validity to 30 days, the applicant

may strike out the number "30" on that form, and insert the number "90" in place thereof.

(Sec. 1001, 72 Stat. 788, 49 U.S.C. 1481)

[Doc. No. 7190, 31 FR 4495, Mar. 17, 1966; 31 FR 5483, Apr. 7, 1966, as amended by Amdt. 47-6, 33 FR 11, Jan. 3, 1968; Amdt. 47-15, 37 FR 21528, Oct. 12, 1972; Amdt. 47-16, 37 FR 25487, Dec. 1, 1972]

§47.33 Aircraft not previously registered anywhere.

(a) A person who is the owner of an aircraft that has not been registered under the Federal Aviation Act of 1958, under other law of the United States, or under foreign law, may register it under this part if he—

(1) Complies with §§47.3, 47.7, 47.8, 47.9, 47.11, 47.13, 47.15, and 47.17, as applicable; and

(2) Submits with his application an aircraft Bill of Sale, AC Form 8050-2, signed by the seller, an equivalent bill of sale, or other evidence of ownership authorized by §47.11.

(b) If, for good reason, the applicant cannot produce the evidence of ownership required by paragraph (a) of this section, he must submit other evidence that is satisfactory to the Administrator. This other evidence may be an affidavit stating why he cannot produce the required evidence, accompanied by whatever further evidence is available to prove the transaction.

(c) The owner of an amateur-built aircraft who applies for registration under paragraphs (a) and (b) of this section must describe the aircraft by class (airplane, rotorcraft, glider, or balloon), serial number, number of seats, type of engine installed, (reciprocating, turbopropeller, turbojet, or other), number of engines installed, and make, model, and serial number of each engine installed; and must state whether the aircraft is built for land or water operation. Also, he must submit as evidence of ownership an affidavit giving the U.S. identification number, and stating that the aircraft was built from parts and that he is the owner. If he built the aircraft from a kit, the applicant must also submit a bill of sale from the manufacturer of the kit.

(d) The owner, other than the holder of the type certificate, of an aircraft that he assembles from parts to conform to the approved type design, must describe the aircraft and engine in the manner required by paragraph (c) of this section, and also submit evidence of ownership satisfactory to the Administrator, such as bills of sale, for all major components of the aircraft.

[Doc. No. 7190, 31 FR 4495, Mar. 17, 1966; 31 FR 5483, Apr. 7, 1966, as amended by Amdt. 47-16, 37 FR 25487, Dec. 1, 1972; Amdt. 47-20, 44 FR 61940, Oct. 29, 1979]

§ 47.35 Aircraft last previously registered in the United States.

(a) A person who is the owner of an aircraft last previously registered under the Federal Aviation Act of 1958, or under other law of the United States, may register it under this part if he complies with §§ 47.3, 47.7, 47.8, 47.9, 47.11, 47.13, 47.15, and 47.17, as applicable and submits with his application an Aircraft Bill of Sale, AC Form 8050-2, signed by the seller or an equivalent conveyance, or other evidence of ownership authorized by § 47.11:

(1) If the applicant bought the aircraft from the last registered owner, the conveyance must be from that owner to the applicant.

(2) If the applicant did not buy the aircraft from the last registered owner, he must submit conveyances or other instruments showing consecutive transactions from the last registered owner through each intervening owner to the applicant.

(b) If, for good reason, the applicant cannot produce the evidence of ownership required by paragraph (a) of this section, he must submit other evidence that is satisfactory to the Administrator. This other evidence may be an affidavit stating why he cannot produce the required evidence, accompanied by whatever further evidence is available to prove the transaction.

[Doc. No. 7190, 31 FR 4495, Mar. 17, 1966, as amended by Amdt. 47-16, 37 FR 25487, Dec. 1, 1972; Amdt. 47-20, 44 FR 61940, Oct. 29, 1979]

§ 47.37 Aircraft last previously registered in a foreign country.

(a) A person who is the owner of an aircraft last previously registered under the law of a foreign country may register it under this part if he—

(1) Complies with §§ 47.3, 47.7, 47.8, 47.9, 47.11, 47.13, 47.15, and 47.17, as applicable;

(2) Submits with his application a bill of sale from the foreign seller or other evidence satisfactory to the Administrator that he owns the aircraft; and

(3) Submits evidence satisfactory to the Administrator that—

(i) If the country in which the aircraft was registered has not ratified the Convention on the International Recognition of Rights in Aircraft (4 U.S.T. 1830), the foreign registration has ended or is invalid; or

(ii) If that country has ratified the convention, the foreign registration has ended or is invalid, and each holder of a recorded right against the aircraft has been satisfied or has consented to the transfer, or ownership in the country of export has been ended by a sale in execution under the terms of the convention.

(b) For the purposes of paragraph (a)(3) of this section, satisfactory evidence of termination of the foreign registration may be—

(1) A statement, by the official having jurisdiction over the national aircraft registry of the foreign country, that the registration has ended or is invalid, and showing the official's name and title and describing the aircraft by make, model, and serial number; or

(2) A final judgment or decree of a court of competent jurisdiction that determines, under the law of the country concerned, that the registration has in fact become invalid.

[Doc. No. 7190, 31 FR 4495, Mar. 17, 1966, as amended by Amdt. 47-20, 44 FR 61940, Oct. 29, 1979]

§ 47.39 Effective date of registration.

(a) Except for an aircraft last previously registered in a foreign country, an aircraft is registered under this subpart on the date and at the time the FAA Aircraft Registry receives the documents required by §47.33 or §47.35.

(b) An aircraft last previously registered in a foreign country is registered under this subpart on the date and at the time the FAA Aircraft Registry issues the Certificate of Aircraft Registration, AC Form 8050-3, after the documents required by §47.37 have been received and examined.

[Doc. No. 7190, 31 FR 4495, Mar. 17, 1966, as amended by Amdt. 47-16, 37 FR 25487, Dec. 1, 1972]

§47.41 Duration and return of Certificate.

(a) Each Certificate of Aircraft Registration issued by the FAA under this subpart is effective, unless suspended or revoked, until the date upon which—

(1) Subject to the Convention on the International Recognition of Rights in Aircraft when applicable, the aircraft is registered under the laws of a foreign country;

(2) The registration is canceled at the written request of the holder of the certificate;

(3) The aircraft is totally destroyed or scrapped;

(4) Ownership of the aircraft is transferred;

(5) The holder of the certificate loses his U.S. citizenship;

(6) 30 days have elapsed since the death of the holder of the certificate;

(7) The owner, if an individual who is not a citizen of the United States, loses status as a resident alien, unless that person becomes a citizen of the United States at the same time; or

(8) If the owner is a corporation other than a corporation which is a citizen of the United States—

(i) The corporation ceases to be lawfully organized and doing business under the laws of the United States or any State thereof; or

(ii) A period described in §47.9(b) ends and the aircraft was not based and primarily used in the United States during that period.

(9) If the trustee in whose name the aircraft is registered—

(i) Loses U.S. citizenship;

(ii) Loses status as a resident alien and does not become a citizen of the United States at the same time; or

(iii) In any manner ceases to act as trustee and is not immediately replaced by another who meets the requirements of §47.7(c).

(b) The Certificate of Aircraft Registration, with the reverse side completed, must be returned to the FAA Aircraft Registry—

(1) In case of registration under the laws of a foreign country, by the person who was the owner of the aircraft before foreign registration;

(2) Within 60 days after the death of the holder of the certificate, by the administrator or executor of his estate, or by his heir-at-law if no administrator or executor has been or is to be appointed; or

(3) Upon the termination of the registration, by the holder of the Certificate of Aircraft Registration in all other cases mentioned in paragraph (a) of this section.

[Doc. No. 7190, 31 FR 4495, Mar. 17, 1966; 31 FR 5483, Apr. 7, 1966, as amended by Amdt. 47-20, 44 FR 61940, Oct. 29, 1979]

§47.43 Invalid registration.

(a) The registration of an aircraft is invalid if, at the time it is made—

(1) The aircraft is registered in a foreign country;

(2) The applicant is not the owner;

(3) The applicant is not qualified to submit an application under this part; or

(4) The interest of the applicant in the aircraft was created by a transaction that was not entered into in good faith, but rather was made to avoid (with or without the owner's knowledge) compliance with section 501 of the Federal Aviation Act of 1958 (49 U.S.C. 1401).

(b) If the registration of an aircraft is invalid under paragraph (a) of this section, the holder of the invalid Certificate of Aircraft Registration shall return it as soon as possible to the FAA Aircraft Registry.

[Doc. No. 7190, 31 FR 4495, Mar. 17, 1966; 31 FR 5483, Apr. 7, 1966, as amended by Amdt. 47-20, 44 FR 61940, Oct. 29, 1979]

§47.45 Change of address.

Within 30 days after any change in his permanent mailing address, the holder of a Certificate of Aircraft Registration for an aircraft shall notify the FAA Aircraft Registry of his new address. A revised Certificate of Aircraft Registration is then issued, without charge.

§ 47.47 Cancellation of certificate for export purpose.

(a) The holder of a Certificate of Aircraft Registration who wishes to cancel the Certificate for the purpose of export must submit the FAA Aircraft Registry—

(1) A written request for cancellation of the Certificate describing the aircraft by make, model, and serial number, stating the U.S. identification number and the country to which the aircraft will be exported; and

(2) Evidence satisfactory to the Administrator that each holder of a recorded right has been satisfied or has consented to the transfer.

(i) When the aircraft is under a contract of conditional sale, the written consent of the seller, bailor, or lessor under the contract.

(ii) When the aircraft is subject to a recorded right other than a contract of conditional sale, evidence satisfactory to the Administrator that the holder of the recorded tight has been satisfied, or has consented to the transfer.

(b) The FAA notifies the country to which the aircraft is to be exported of the cancellation by ordinary mail, or by airmail at the owner's request. The owner must arrange and pay for the transmission of this notice by means other than ordinary mail or airmail.

§ 47.49 Replacement of Certificate.

(a) If a Certificate of Aircraft Registration is lost, stolen, or mutilated, the holder of the Certificate of Aircraft Registration may apply to the FAA Aircraft Registry for a duplicate certificate, accompanying his application with the fee required by § 47.17.

(b) If the holder has applied and has paid the fee for a duplicate Certificate of Aircraft Registration and needs to operate his aircraft before receiving it, he may request a temporary certificate. The FAA Aircraft Registry issues a temporary certificate, by a collect telegram, to be carried in the aircraft. This temporary certificate is valid

until he receives the duplicate Certificate of Aircraft Registration.

§ 47.51 Triennial aircraft registration report.

(a) Unless one of the registration activities listed in paragraph (b) of this section has occurred within the preceding 36 calendar months, the holder of each Certificate of Aircraft Registration issued under this subpart shall submit, on the form provided by the FAA Aircraft Registry and in the manner described in paragraph (c) of this section, a Triennial Aircraft Registration Report, certifying—

(1) The current identification number (registration mark) assigned to the aircraft;

(2) The name and permanent mailing address of the certificate holder;

(3) The name of the manufacturer of the aircraft and its model and serial number;

(4) Whether the certificate holder is—

(i) A citizen of the United States;

(ii) An individual citizen of a foreign country who has lawfully been admitted for permanent residence in the United States; or

(iii) A corporation (other than a corporation which is a citizen of the United States) lawfully organized and doing business under the laws of the United States or any State thereof; and

(5) Whether the aircraft is currently registered under the laws of any foreign country.

(b) The FAA Aircraft Registry will forward a Triennial Aircraft Registration Report to each holder of a Certificate of Aircraft Registration whenever 36 months has expired since the latest of the following registration activities occurred with respect to the certificate holder's aircraft:

(1) The submission of an Application for Aircraft Registration.

(2) The submission of a report or statement required by § 47.9(f).

(3) The filing of a notice of change of permanent mailing address.

(4) The filing of an application for a duplicate Certificate of Aircraft Registration.

(5) The filing of an application for a change of aircraft identification number.

(6) The submission of an Aircraft Registration Eligibility, Identification, and Activity Report, Part 1, AC Form 8050-73, under former § 47.44.

(7) The submission of a Triennial Aircraft Registration Report under this section.

(c) The holder of the Certificate of Aircraft Registration shall return the Triennial Aircraft Registration Report to the FAA Aircraft Registry within 60 days after issuance by the FAA Aircraft Registry. The report must be dated, legibly executed, and signed by the certificate holder in the manner prescribed by § 47.13, except that any co-owner may sign for all co-owners.

(d) Refusal or failure to submit the Triennial Aircraft Registration Report with the information required by this section may be cause for suspension or revocation of the Certificate of Aircraft Registration in accordance with Part 13 of this chapter.

(Secs. 313(a), 501, 601(a), Federal Aviation Act of 1958, as amended (49 U.S.C. 1354(a), 1401, and 1421(a)); sec. 6(c), Dept. of Transportation Act (49 U.S.C. 1655(c)))

[Amdt. 47-21, 45 FR 20773, Mar. 31, 1980]

Subpart C—Dealers' Aircraft Registration Certificate

§ 47.61 Dealers' Aircraft Registration Certificates.

(a) The FAA issues a Dealers' Aircraft Registration Certificate, AC Form 8050-6, to manufacturers and dealers so as to—

(1) Allow manufacturers to make any required flight tests of aircraft.

(2) Facilitate operating, demonstrating, and merchandising aircraft by the manufacturer or dealer without the burden of obtaining a Certificate of Aircraft Registration for each aircraft with each transfer of ownership, under Subpart B of this part.

(b) A Dealers' Aircraft Registration Certificate is an alternative for the Certificate of Aircraft Registration issued under Subpart B of this part. A dealer may, under this subpart, obtain one or more Dealers' Aircraft Registration Certificates in addition to his original certificate, and he may use a Dealer's Aircraft Registration Certificate for any aircraft he owns.

[Doc. No. 7190, 31 FR 4495, Mar. 17, 1966; as amended by Amdt. 47-9, 35 FR 802, Jan. 21, 1970; Amdt. 47-16, 37 FR 25487, Dec. 1, 1972]

§ 47.63 Application.

A manufacturer or dealer that wishes to obtain a Dealer's Aircraft Registration Certificate, AC Form 8050-6, must submit—

(a) An Application for Dealers' Aircraft Registration Certificates, AC Form 8050-5; and

(b) The fee required by § 47.17.

[Doc. No. 7190, 31 FR 4495, Mar. 17, 1966, as amended by Amdt. 47-16, 37 FR 25487, Dec. 1, 1972]

§ 47.65 Eligibility.

To be eligible for a Dealer's Aircraft Registration Certificate, a person must have an established place of business in the United States, must be substantially engaged in manufacturing or selling aircraft, and must be a citizen of the United States, as defined by section 101(13) of the Federal Aviation Act of 1958 (49 U.S.C. 1301).

[Amdt. 47-9, 35 FR 802, Jan. 21, 1970]

§ 47.67 Evidence of ownership.

Before using his Dealer's Aircraft Registration Certificate for operating an aircraft, the holder of the certificate (other than a manufacturer) must send to the FAA Aircraft Registry evidence satisfactory to the Administrator that he is the owner of that aircraft. An Aircraft Bill of Sale, or its equivalent, may be used as evidence of ownership. There is no recording fee.

§ 47.69 Limitations.

A Dealer's Aircraft Registration Certificate is valid only in connection with use of aircraft—

(a) By the owner of the aircraft to whom it was issued, his agent or employee, or a prospective buyer, and in the case of a dealer other than a manufacturer, only after he has complied with § 47.67;

(b) Within the United States, except when used to deliver to a foreign pur-

chaser an aircraft displaying a temporary registration number and carrying
an airworthiness certificate on which
that number is written;

(c) While a certificate is carried
within the aircraft; and

(d) On a flight that is—

(1) For required flight testing of aircraft; or

(2) Necessary for, or incident to, sale
of the aircraft.

However, a prospective buyer may operate an aircraft for demonstration
purposes only while he is under the
direct supervision of the holder of the
Dealer's Aircraft Registration Certificate or his agent.

[Doc. No. 7190 31 FR 4495, Mar. 17, 1966; 31
FR 5483, Apr. 7, 1966, as amended by Amdt.
47-4, 32 FR 12556, Aug. 30, 1967]

§ 47.71 Duration of Certificate; change of
status.

(a) A Dealer's Aircraft Registration
Certificate expires 1 year after the
date it is issued. Each additional certificate expires on the date the original
certificate expires.

(b) The holder of a Dealer's Aircraft
Registration Certificate shall immediately notify the FAA Aircraft Registry
of any of the following—

(1) A change of his name;

(2) A change of his address;

(3) A change that affects his status
as a citizen of the United States; or

(4) The discontinuance of his business.

FEDERAL AVIATION REGULATIONS

PART 65

CERTIFICATION:
Airmen Other Than Flight Crewmembers

1989 EDITION

PART 65—CERTIFICATION: AIRMEN OTHER THAN FLIGHT CREWMEMBERS

Subpart A—General

Sec.
65.1 Applicability.
65.3 Certification of foreign airmen other than flight crewmembers.
65.11 Application and issue.
65.12 Offenses involving alcohol or drugs.
65.13 Temporary certificate.
65.15 Duration of certificates.
65.16 Change of name: Replacement of lost or destroyed certificate.
65.17 Tests: General procedure.
65.18 Written tests: Cheating or other unauthorized conduct.
65.19 Retesting after failure.
65.20 Applications, certificates, logbooks reports, and records: Falsification reproduction, or alteration.
65.21 Change of address.

Subpart B—Air-Traffic Control Tower Operators

65.31 Required certificates, and rating or qualification.
65.33 Eligibility requirements: General.
65.35 Knowledge requirements.
65.37 Skill requirements: Operating positions.
65.39 Practical experience requirements: Facility rating.
65.41 Skill requirements: Facility ratings.
65.43 Rating privileges and exchange.
65.45 Performance of duties.
65.47 Maximum hours.
65.49 General operating rules.
65.50 Currency requirements.

Subpart C—Aircraft Dispatchers

65.51 Certificate required.
65.53 Eligibility requirements: General.
65.55 Knowledge requirements.
65.57 Experience requirements.
65.59 Skill requirements.
65.61 Aircraft dispatcher courses.

Subpart D—Mechanics

65.71 Eligibility requirements: General.
65.73 Ratings.
65.75 Knowledge requirements.
65.77 Experience requirements.
65.79 Skill requirements.

65.80 Certificated aviation maintenance technician school students.
65.81 General privileges and limitations.
65.83 Recent experience requirements.
65.85 Airframe rating; additional privileges.
65.87 Powerplant rating; additional privileges.
65.89 Display of certificate.
65.91 Inspection authorization.
65.92 Inspection authorization: Duration.
65.93 Inspection authorization: Renewal.
65.95 Inspection authorization: Privileges and limitations.

Subpart E—Repairmen

65.101 Eligibility requirements: General.
65.103 Repairman certificate: Privileges and limitations.
65.104 Repairman certificate—experimental aircraft builder—Eligibility, privileges and limitations.
65.105 Display of certificate.

Subpart F—Parachute Riggers

65.111 Certificate required.
65.113 Eligibility requirements: General.
65.115 Senior parachute rigger certificate: Experience, knowledge, and skill requirements.
65.117 Military riggers or former military riggers: Special certification rule.
65.119 Master parachute rigger certificate: Experience, knowledge, and skill requirements.
65.121 Type ratings.
65.123 Additional type ratings: Requirements.
65.125 Certificates: Privileges.
65.127 Facilities and equipment.
65.129 Performance standards.
65.131 Records.
65.133 Seal.

APPENDIX A—AIRCRAFT DISPATCHER COURSES

AUTHORITY: 49 U.S.C. 1354(a), 1355, 1421, 1422, and 1427; 49 U.S.C. 106(g) (revised), Pub. L. 97-449, January 12, 1983).

SOURCE: Docket No. 1179, 27 FR 7973, Aug. 10, 1962, unless otherwise noted.

Subpart A—General

§ 65.1 Applicability.

This part prescribes the requirements for issuing the following certificates and associated ratings and the general operating rules for the holders of those certificates and ratings:

(a) Air-traffic control-tower operators.

(b) Aircraft dispatchers.

(c) Mechanics.
(d) Repairmen.
(e) Parachute riggers.

§ 65.3 Certification of foreign airmen other than flight crewmembers.

A person who is neither a U.S. citizen nor a resident alien is issued a certificate under Subpart D of this part, outside the United States, only when the Administrator finds that the certificate is needed for the operation or continued airworthiness of a U.S.-registered civil aircraft.

[Doc. 65-28, FR 35693, Aug. 16, 1982]

§ 65.11 Application and issue.

(a) Application for a certificate and appropriate class rating, or for an additional rating, under this part must be made on a form and in a manner prescribed by the Administrator. Each person who is neither a U.S. citizen nor a resident alien and who applies for a written or practical test to be administered outside the United States or for any certificate or rating issued under this part must show evidence that the fee prescribed in Appendix A of Part 187 of this chapter has been paid.

(b) An applicant who meets the requirements of this part is entitled to an appropriate certificate and rating.

(c) Unless authorized by the Administrator, a person whose air traffic control tower operator, mechanic, or parachute rigger certificate is suspended may not apply for any rating to be added to that certificate during the period of suspension.

(d) Unless the order of revocation provides otherwise—

(1) A person whose air traffic control tower operator, aircraft dispatcher, or parachute rigger certificate is revoked may not apply for the same kind of certificate for 1 year after the date of revocation; and

(2) A person whose mechanic or repairman certificate is revoked may not apply for either of those kinds of certificates for 1 year after the date of revocation.

[Doc. No. 1179, 27 FR 7973, Aug. 10, 1962, as amended by Amdt. 65-9, 31 FR 13524, Oct. 20, 1966; Amdt. 65-28, 47 FR 35693, Aug. 16, 1982]

§ 65.12 Offenses involving alcohol or drugs.

(a) A conviction for the violation of any Federal or state statute relating to the growing, processing, manufacture, sale, disposition, possession, transportation, or importation of narcotic drugs, marihuana, or depressant or stimulant drugs or substances is grounds for—

(1) Denial of an application for any certificate or rating issued under this part for a period of up to 1 year after the date of final conviction; or

(2) Suspension or revocation of any certificate or rating issued under this part.

(b) The commission of an act prohibited by § 91.12(a) of this chapter is grounds for—

(1) Denial of an application for a certificate or rating issued under this part for a period of up to 1 year after the date of that act; or

(2) Suspension or revocation of any certificate or rating issued under this part.

[Doc. No. 21956, Amdt. 65-29, 50 FR 15379, Apr. 17, 1985]

§ 65.13 Temporary certificate.

A certificate and ratings effective for a period of not more than 120 days may be issued to a qualified applicant, pending review of his application and supplementary documents and the issue of the certificate and ratings for which he applied.

[Doc. No. 1179, 27 FR 7973, Aug. 10, 1962, as amended by Amdt. 65-23, 43 FR 22640, May 25, 1978]

§ 65.15 Duration of certificates.

(a) Except for repairman certificates, a certificate or rating issued under this part is effective until it is surrendered, suspended, or revoked.

(b) Unless it is sooner surrendered, suspended, or revoked, a repairman certificate is effective until the holder is relieved from the duties for which the holder was employed and certificated.

(c) The holder of a certificate issued under this part that is suspended, revoked, or no longer effective shall return it to the Administrator.

[Amdt. 65-28, 47 FR 35693, Aug. 16, 1982]

§ 65.16 Change of name: Replacement of lost or destroyed certificate.

(a) An application for a change of name on a certificate issued under this part must be accompanied by the applicant's current certificate and the marriage license, court order, or other document verifying the change. The documents are returned to the applicant after inspection.

(b) An application for a replacement of a lost or destroyed certificate is made by letter to the Department of Transportation, Federal Aviation Administration, Airman Certification Branch, Post Office Box 25082, Oklahoma City, Okla. 73125. The letter must—

(1) Contain the name in which the certificate was issued, the permanent mailing address (including zip code), social security number (if any), and date and place of birth of the certificate holder, and any available information regarding the grade, number, and date of issue of the certificate, and the ratings on it; and

(2) Be accompanied by a check or money order for $2, payable to the Federal Aviation Administration.

(c) An application for a replacement of a lost or destroyed medical certificate is made by letter to the Department of Transportation, Federal Aviation Administration, Civil Aeromedical Institute, Aeromedical Certification Branch, Post Office Box 25082, Oklahoma City, Okla. 73125, accompanied by a check or money order for $2.00.

(d) A person whose certificate issued under this part or medical certificate, or both, has been lost may obtain a telegram from the FAA confirming that it was issued. The telegram may be carried as a certificate for a period not to exceed 60 days pending his receiving a duplicate certificate under paragraph (b) or (c) of this section, unless he has been notified that the certificate has been suspended or revoked. The request for such a telegram may be made by prepaid telegram, stating the date upon which a duplicate certificate was requested, or including the request for a duplicate and a money order for the necessary amount. The request for a telegraphic certificate should be sent to the office prescribed in paragraph (b) or (c) of this section, as appropriate. However, a request for both at the same time should be sent to the office prescribed in paragraph (b) of this section.

[Amdt. 65-9, 31 FR 13524, Oct. 20, 1966, as amended by Doc. No. 8084, 32 FR 5769, Apr. 11, 1967; Amdt. 65-16, 35 FR 14075, Sept. 4, 1970; Amdt. 65-17, 36 FR 2865, Feb. 11, 1971]

§ 65.17 Tests: General procedure.

(a) Tests prescribed by or under this part are given at times and places, and by persons, designated by the Administrator.

(b) The minimum passing grade for each test is 70 percent.

§ 65.18 Written tests: Cheating or other unauthorized conduct.

(a) Except as authorized by the Administrator, no person may—

(1) Copy, or intentionally remove, a written test under this part;

(2) Give to another, or receive from another, any part or copy of that test;

(3) Give help on that test to, or receive help on that test from, any person during the period that test is being given;

(4) Take any part of that test in behalf of another person;

(5) Use any material or aid during the period that test is being given; or

(6) Intentionally cause, assist, or participate in any act prohibited by this paragraph.

(b) No person who commits an act prohibited by paragraph (a) of this section is eligible for any airman or ground instructor certificate or rating under this chapter for a period of 1 year after the date of that act. In addition, the commission of that act is a basis for suspending or revoking any airman or ground instructor certificate or rating held by that person.

[Amdt. 65-3, 30 FR 2196, Feb. 18, 1965]

§ 65.19 Retesting after failure.

An applicant for a written, oral, or practical test for a certificate and rating, or for an additional rating under this part, may apply for retesting—

(a) After 30 days after the date the applicant failed the test; or

(b) Before the 30 days have expired if the applicant presents a signed statement from an airman holding the certificate and rating sought by the applicant, certifying that the airman has given the applicant additional instruction in each of the subjects failed and that the airman considers the applicant ready for retesting.

[Amdt. 65-23, 43 FR 22640, May 25, 1978]

§ 65.20 Applications, certificates, logbooks, reports, and records: Falsification, reproduction, or alteration.

(a) No person may make or cause to be made—

(1) Any fraudulent or intentionally false statement on any application for a certificate or rating under this part;

(2) Any fraudulent or intentionally false entry in any logbook, record, or report that is required to be kept, made, or used, to show compliance with any requirement for any certificate or rating under this part;

(3) Any reproduction, for fraudulent purpose, of any certificate or rating under this part; or

(4) Any alteration of any certificate or rating under this part.

(b) The commission by any person of an act prohibited under paragraph (a) of this section is a basis for suspending or revoking any airman or ground instructor certificate or rating held by that person.

[Amdt. 65-3, 30 FR 2196, Feb. 18, 1965]

§ 65.21 Change of address.

Within 30 days after any change in his permanent mailing address, the holder of a certificate issued under this part shall notify the Department of Transportation, Federal Aviation Administration, Airman Certification Branch, Post Office Box 25082, Oklahoma City, Okla. 73125, in writing, of his new address.

[Amdt. 65-16, 35 FR 14075, Sept. 4, 1970]

Subpart B—Air Traffic Control Tower Operators

SOURCE: Amdt. 65-15, 35 FR 12326, Aug. 1, 1970, unless otherwise noted.

§ 65.31 Required certificates, and rating or qualification.

No person may act as an air traffic control tower operator at an air traffic control tower in connection with civil aircraft unless he—

(a) Holds an air traffic control tower operator certificate issued to him under this subpart;

(b) Holds a facility rating for that control tower issued to him under this subpart, or has qualified for the operating position at which he acts and is under the supervision of the holder of a facility rating for that control tower; and

For the purpose of this subpart, "operating position" means an air traffic control function performed within or directly associated with the control tower;

(c) Except for a person employed by the FAA or employed by, or on active duty with, the Department of the Air Force, Army, or Navy or the Coast Guard, holds at least a second-class medical certificate issued under Part 67 of this chapter.

[Amdt. 65-15, 35 FR 12326, Aug. 1, 1970, as amended by Amdt. 65-25, 45 FR 18911, Mar. 24, 1980; Amdt. 65-31, 52 FR 17518, May 8, 1987]

§ 65.33 Eligibility requirements: General.

To be eligible for an air traffic control tower operator certificate a person must—

(a) Be at least 18 years of age;

(b) Be of good moral character;

(c) Be able to read, write, and understand the English language and speak it without accent or impediment of speech that would interfere with two-way radio conversation;

(d) Except for a person employed by the FAA or employed by, or on active duty with, the Department of the Air Force, Army, or Navy or the Coast Guard, holds at least a second-class medical certificate issued under Part 67 of this chapter within the 12 months before the date application is made; and

(e) Comply with § 65.35.

[Amdt. 65-15, 35 FR 12326, Aug. 1, 1970, as amended by Amdt. 65-25, 45 FR 18911, Mar.

24, 1980; Amdt. 65-31, 52 FR 17518, May 8, 1987]

§ 65.35   Knowledge requirements.

Each applicant for an air traffic control tower operator certificate must pass a written test on—

(a) The flight rules in Part 91 of this chapter:

(b) Airport traffic control procedures, and this subpart:

(c) En route traffic control procedures;

(d) Communications operating procedures;

(e) Flight assistance service;

(f) Air navigation, and aids to air navigation; and

(g) Aviation weather.

§ 65.37   Skill requirements: Operating positions.

No person may act as an air traffic control tower operator at any operating position unless he has passed a practical test on—

(a) Control tower equipment and its use;

(b) Weather reporting procedures and use of reports;

(c) Notices to Airmen, and use of the Airman's Information Manual;

(d) Use of operational forms;

(e) Performance of noncontrol operational duties; and

(f) Each of the following procedures that is applicable to that operating position and is required by the person examining him:

(1) The airport, including rules, equipment, runways, taxiways, and obstructions.

(2) The control zone, including terrain features, visual checkpoints, and obstructions.

(3) Traffic patterns and associated procedures for use of preferential runways and noise abatement.

(4) Operational agreements.

(5) The center, alternate airports, and those airways, routes, reporting points, and air navigation aids used for terminal air traffic control.

(6) Search and rescue procedures.

(7) Terminal air traffic control procedures and phraseology.

(8) Holding procedures, prescribed instrument approach, and departure procedures.

(9) Radar alignment and technical operation.

(10) The application of the prescribed radar and nonradar separation standard, as appropriate.

§ 65.39   Practical experience requirements: Facility rating.

Each applicant for a facility rating at any air traffic control tower must have satisfactorily served—

(a) As an air traffic control tower operator at that control tower without a facility rating for at least 6 months; or

(b) As an air traffic control tower operator with a facility rating at a different control tower for at least 6 months before the date he applies for the rating.

However, an applicant who is a member of an Armed Force of the United States meets the requirements of this section if he has satisfactorily served as an air traffic control tower operator for at least 6 months.

[Doc. No. 1179, 27 FR 7973, Aug. 10, 1962, as amended by Amdt. 65-19, 36 FR 21280, Nov. 5, 1971]

§ 65.41   Skill requirements: Facility ratings.

Each applicant for a facility rating at an air traffic control tower must have passed a practical test on each item listed in § 65.37 of this part that is applicable to each operating position at the control tower at which the rating is sought.

§ 65.43   Rating privileges and exchange.

(a) The holder of a senior rating on August 31, 1970, may at any time after that date exchange his rating for a facility rating at the same air traffic control tower. However, if he does not do so before August 31, 1971, he may not thereafter exercise the privileges of his senior rating at the control tower concerned until he makes the exchange.

(b) The holder of a junior rating on August 31, 1970, may not control air traffic, at any operating position at the control tower concerned, until he has met the applicable requirements of § 65.37 of this part. However, before meeting those requirements he may control air traffic under the supervision, where required, of an operator with a senior rating (or facility rating) in accordance with § 65.41 of this part in effect before August 31, 1970.

§ 65.45 Performance of duties.

(a) An air traffic control tower operator shall perform his duties in accordance with the limitations on his certificate and the procedures and practices prescribed in air traffic control manuals of the FAA, to provide for the safe, orderly, and expeditious flow of air traffic.

(b) An operator with a facility rating may control traffic at any operating position at the control tower at which he holds a facility rating. However, he may not issue an air traffic clearance for IFR flight without authorization from the appropriate facility exercising IFR control at that location.

(c) An operator who does not hold a facility rating for a particular control tower may act at each operating position for which he has qualified, under the supervision of an operator holding a facility rating for that control tower.

[Amdt. 65-15, 35 FR 12326, Aug. 1, 1970, as amended by Amdt. 65-16, 35 FR 14075, Sept. 4, 1970]

§ 65.47 Maximum hours.

Except in an emergency, a certificated air traffic control tower operator must be relieved of all duties for at least 24 consecutive hours at least once during each 7 consecutive days. Such an operator may not serve or be required to serve—

(a) For more than 10 consecutive hours; or

(b) For more than 10 hours during a period of 24 consecutive hours, unless he has had a rest period of at least 8 hours at or before the end of the 10 hours of duty.

§ 65.49 General operating rules.

(a) Except for a person employed by the FAA or employed by, or on active duty with, the Department of the Air Force, Army, or Navy, or the Coast Guard, no person may act as an air traffic control tower operator under a certificate issued to him or her under this part unless he or she has in his or her personal possession an appropriate current medical certificate issued under Part 67 of this chapter.

(b) Each person holding an air traffic control tower operator certificate shall keep it readily available when performing duties in an air traffic control tower, and shall present that certificate or his medical certificate or both for inspection upon the request of the Administrator or an authorized representative of the National Transportation Safety Board, or of any Federal, State, or local law enforcement officer.

(c) A certificated air traffic control tower operator who does not hold a facility rating for a particular control tower may not act at any operating position at the control tower concerned unless there is maintained at that control tower, readily available to persons named in paragraph (b) of this section, a current record of the operating positions at which he has qualified.

(d) An air traffic control tower operator may not perform duties under his certificate during any period of known physical deficiency that would make him unable to meet the physical requirements for his current medical certificate. However, if the deficiency is temporary, he may perform duties that are not affected by it whenever another certificated and qualified operator is present and on duty.

(e) A certificated air traffic control tower operator may not control air traffic with equipment that the Administrator has found to be inadequate.

(f) The holder of an air traffic control tower operator certificate, or an applicant for one, shall, upon the reasonable request of the Administrator, cooperate fully in any test that is made of him.

[Doc. No. 1179, 27 FR 7973, Aug. 10, 1962, as amended by Amdt. 65-31, 52 FR 17519, May 8, 1987]

§ 65.50 Currency requirements.

The holder of an air traffic control tower operator certificate may not perform any duties under that certificate unless—

(a) He has served for at least three of the preceding 6 months as an air traffic control tower operator at the control tower to which his facility rating applies, or at the operating positions for which he has qualified; or

(b) He has shown that he meets the requirements for his certificate and facility rating at the control tower concerned, or for operating at positions for which he has previously qualified.

Subpart C—Aircraft Dispatchers

§ 65.51   Certificate required.

(a) No person may serve as an aircraft dispatcher (exercising responsibility with the pilot in command in the operational control of a flight) in connection with any civil aircraft in air commerce unless he has in his personal possession a current aircraft dispatcher certificate issued under this subpart.

(b) Each person who holds an aircraft dispatcher certificate shall present it for inspection upon the request of the Administrator or an authorized representative of the National Transportation Safety Board, or of any Federal, State, or local law enforcement officer.

[Doc. No. 1179, 27 FR 7973, Aug. 10, 1962, as amended by Amdt. 65-9, 31 FR 13524, Oct. 20, 1966; 32 FR 5769, Apr. 11, 1967]

§ 65.53   Eligibility requirements: General.

To be eligible for an aircraft dispatcher certificate, a person must—

(a) Be at least 23 years of age;

(b) Be able to read, speak, and understand the English language, or have an appropriate limitation placed on his certificate;

(c) Comply with §§ 65.55, 65.57, and 65.59.

§ 65.55   Knowledge requirements.

(a) An applicant for an aircraft dispatcher certificate must pass a written test on—

(1) The regulations of this chapter that apply to the duties of an aircraft dispatcher;

(2) The general system of collecting and disseminating weather information;

(3) Interpreting aviation weather reports, including abbreviations and symbols, as prescribed in "National Weather Service Federal Meteorological Handbook No. 1," as amended;

(4) The fundamentals of meteorology as applied to aircraft operations, particularly as to—

(i) Surface and upper air weather maps and general characteristics of air masses, pressure systems, and frontal systems, including their symbols and nomenclature;

(ii) Cloud forms and their significance; and

(iii) Icing, turbulence, thunderstorms, fog and low ceilings, winds aloft, pressure pattern flying, the influence of terrain on meteorological conditions, and general principles of forecasting and analysis;

(5) Principles of aircraft navigation with particular respect to instrument operation and procedures;

(6) Communications facilities and procedures;

(7) Air navigation facilities and procedures; and

(8) Air traffic control procedures.

(b) A report of the test is sent to the applicant. A passing grade is evidence, for a period of 24 months after the date the test is given, that the applicant has complied with this section.

[Doc. No. 1179, 27 FR 7973, Aug. 10, 1962, as amended by Amdt. 65-18, 36 FR 13911, July 28, 1971]

§ 65.57   Experience requirements.

An applicant for an aircraft dispatcher certificate must present documentary evidence satisfactory to the Administrator that he has the experience prescribed in any one of the following paragraphs:

(a) A total of at least 2 of the 3 years before the date he applies, in scheduled air carrier operations, scheduled military aviation operations, or any other aircraft operations that the Administrator finds provides equivalent experience—

(1) As a pilot member of a flight crew;

(2) As a flight radio operator or ground radio operator;

(3) As a flight navigator;

(4) As a meteorologist;

(5) Performing the duties of an aircraft dispatcher or his assistant; or

(6) Performing other duties that the Administrator finds provide equivalent experience.

(b) A total of at least 2 of the 3 years before the date he applies, as an air route traffic controller or a certificated air-traffic control-tower operator.

(c) A total of at least 1 of the 2 years before the date he applies, as an assistant in dispatching scheduled air carrier aircraft performing the duties of an aircraft dispatcher under the direct supervision of a certificated dispatcher.

(d) Within 90 days before the date he applies, successful completion of a course of instruction approved by the Administrator as adequate for the training of an aircraft dispatcher.

An applicant is entitled to credit any combination of experience in paragraph (a), or paragraphs (a) and (b), of this section, if the aggregate of that experience is at least 2 years.

§ 65.59 Skill requirements.

An applicant for an aircraft dispatcher certificate must pass a practical test—

(a) With respect to any one type of large aircraft used in air carrier operations, on—

(1) Weight and balance limitations;

(2) Performance operating limitations;

(3) Using cruise control charts;

(4) Fuel and oil capacities and rates of consumption; and

(5) Using the operations manual;

(b) On the characteristics of air routes and airports with particular reference to—

(1) Landing areas;

(2) Lighting facilities; and

(3) Approach and landing facilities and procedures;

(c) On the use and limitations of sensitive-type altimeters;

(d) On applying available weather forecasts and reports to determine whether a flight can be made safely;

(e) On using the Airman's Guide and the Flight Information Manual;

(f) On dispatching and assisting a flight under adverse weather conditions; and

(g) On emergency procedures.

§ 65.61 Aircraft dispatcher courses.

An applicant for approval of an aircraft dispatcher course shall submit a letter to the Administrator requesting approval, and shall also submit three copies of the course outline, a description of his equipment and facilities and a list of the instructors and their qualifications. Requirements for the course and the outline are set forth in Appendix A to this part.

Subpart D—Mechanics

§ 65.71 Eligibility requirements: General.

(a) To be eligible for a mechanic certificate and associated ratings, a person must—

(1) Be at least 18 years of age;

(2) Be able to read, write, speak, and understand the English language, or in the case of an applicant who does not meet this requirement and who is employed outside of the United States by a U.S. air carrier, have his certificate endorsed "Valid only outside the United States";

(3) Have passed all of the prescribed tests within a period of 24 months; and

(4) Comply with the sections of this subpart that apply to the rating he seeks.

(b) A certificated mechanic who applies for an additional rating must meet the requirements of § 65.77 and, within a period of 24 months, pass the tests prescribed by §§ 65.75 and 65.79 for the additional rating sought.

[Doc. No. 1179, 27 FR 7973, Aug. 10, 1962, as amended by Amdt. 65-6, 31 FR 5950, Apr. 19, 1966]

§ 65.73 Ratings.

(a) The following ratings are issued under this subpart:

(1) Airframe.

(2) Powerplant.

(b) A mechanic certificate with an aircraft or aircraft engine rating, or both, that was issued before, and was valid on, June 15, 1952, is equal to a mechanic certificate with an airframe or powerplant rating, or both, as the case may be, and may be exchanged for such a corresponding certificate and rating or ratings.

§ 65.75 Knowledge requirements.

(a) Each applicant for a mechanic certificate or rating must, after meeting the applicable experience requirements of § 65.77, pass a written test covering the construction and maintenance of aircraft appropriate to the rating he seeks, the regulations in this subpart, and the applicable provisions of Parts 43 and 91 of this chapter. The basic principles covering the installation and maintenance of propellers are included in the powerplant test.

(b) The applicant must pass each section of the test before applying for the oral and practical tests prescribed by § 65.79. A report of the written test is sent to the applicant.

[Doc. No. 1179, 27 FR 7973, Aug. 10, 1962, as amended by Amdt. 65–1, 27 FR 10410, Oct. 25, 1962; Amdt. 65–6, 31 FR 5950, Apr. 19, 1966]

§ 65.77 Experience requirements.

Each applicant for a mechanic certificate or rating must present either an appropriate graduation certificate or certificate of completion from a certificated cated aviation maintenance technician school or documentary evidence, satisfactory to the Administrator, of—

(a) At least 18 months of practical experience with the procedures, practices, materials, tools, machine tools, and equipment generally used in constructing, maintaining, or altering airframes, or powerplants appropriate to the rating sought; or

(b) At least 30 months of practical experience concurrently performing the duties appropriate to both the airframe and powerplant ratings.

[Doc. No. 1179, 27 FR, 7973, Aug. 10, 1962, as amended by Amdt. 65–14, 35 FR, 5533, Apr. 3, 1970]

§ 65.79 Skill requirements.

Each applicant for a mechanic certificate or rating must pass an oral and a practical test on the rating he seeks. The tests cover the applicant's basic skill in performing practical projects on the subjects covered by the written test for that rating. An applicant for a powerplant rating must show his ability to make satisfactory minor repairs to, and minor alterations of, propellers.

§ 65.80 Certificated aviation maintenance technician school students.

Whenever an aviation maintenance technician school certificated under Part 147 of this chapter shows to an FAA inspector that any of its students has made satisfactory progress at the school and is prepared to take the oral and practical tests prescribed by § 65.79, that student may take those tests during the final subjects of his training in the approved curriculum, before he meets the applicable experience requirements of § 65.77 and before he passes each section of the written test prescribed by § 65.75.

[Amdt. 65–14, 35 FR, 5533, Apr. 3, 1970]

§ 65.81 General privileges and limitations.

(a) A certificated mechanic may perform or supervise the maintenance, preventive maintenance or alteration of an aircraft or appliance, or a part thereof, for which he is rated (but excluding major repairs to, and major alterations of, propellers, and any repair to, or alteration of, instruments), and may perform additional duties in accordance with §§ 65.85, 65.87, and 65.95. However, he may not supervise the maintenance, preventive maintenance, or alteration of, or approve and return to service, any aircraft or appliance, or part thereof, for which he is rated unless he has satisfactorily performed the work concerned at an earlier date. If he has not so performed that work at an earlier date, he may show his ability to do it by performing it to the satisfaction of the Administrator or under the direct supervision of a certificated and appropriately rated mechanic, or a certificated repairman, who has had previous experience in the specific operation concerned.

(b) A certificated mechanic may not exercise the privileges of his certificate and rating unless he understands the current instructions of the manufacturer, and the maintenance manuals, for the specific operation concerned.

[Doc. No. 1179, 27 FR 7973, Aug. 10, 1962, as amended by Amdt. 65–2, 29 FR 5451, Apr. 23, 1964; Amdt. 65–26, 45 FR 46737, July 10, 1980]

§ 65.83   Recent experience requirements.

A certificated mechanic may not exercise the privileges of his certificate and rating unless, within the preceding 24 months—

(a) The Administrator has found that he is able to do that work; or

(b) He has, for at least 6 months—

(1) Served as a mechanic under his certificate and rating;

(2) Technically supervised other mechanics;

(3) Supervised, in an executive capacity, the maintenance or alteration of aircraft; or

(4) Been engaged in any combination of paragraph (b) (1), (2), or (3) of this section.

§ 65.85   Airframe rating; additional privileges.

A certificated mechanic with an airframe rating may approve and return to service an airframe, or any related part or appliance, after he has performed, supervised, or inspected its maintenance or alteration (excluding major repairs and major alterations). In addition, he may perform the 100-hour inspection required by Part 91 of this chapter on an airframe, or any related part or appliance, and approve and return it to service.

[Doc. No. 1179, 27 FR 7973, Aug. 10, 1962, as amended by Amdt. 65–10, 32 FR 5770, Apr. 11, 1967]

§ 65.87   Powerplant   rating;   additional privileges.

A certificated mechanic with a powerplant rating may approve and return to service a powerplant or propeller or any related part or appliance, after he has performed, supervised, or inspected its maintenance or alteration (excluding major repairs and major alterations). In addition, he may perform the 100-hour inspection required by Part 91 of this chapter on a powerplant or propeller, or any part thereof, and approve and return it to service.

[Doc. No. 1179, 27 FR 7973, Aug. 10, 1962, as amended by Amdt. 65–10, 32 FR 5770, Apr. 11, 1967]

§ 65.89   Display of certificate.

Each person who holds a mechanic certificate shall keep it within the immediate area where he normally exercises the privileges of the certificate and shall present it for inspection upon the request of the Administrator or an authorized representative of the National Transportation Safety Board, or of any Federal, State, or local law enforcement officer.

[Amdt. 65–9, 31 FR 13524, Oct. 20, 1966, as amended by Doc. No. 8084, 32 FR 5769, Apr. 11, 1967]

§ 65.91   Inspection authorization.

(a) An application for an inspection authorization is made on a form and in a manner prescribed by the Administrator.

(b) An applicant who meets the requirements of this section is entitled to an inspection authorization.

(c) To be eligible for an inspection authorization, an applicant must—

(1) Hold a currently effective mechanic certificate with both an airframe rating and a powerplant rating, each of which is currently effective and has been in effect for a total of at least 3 years;

(2) Have been actively engaged, for at least the 2-year period before the date he applies, in maintaining aircraft certificated and maintained in accordance with this chapter;

(3) Have a fixed base of operations at which he may be located in person or by telephone during a normal working week but it need not be the place where he will exercise his inspection authority;

(4) Have available to him the equipment, facilities, and inspection data necessary to properly inspect airframes, powerplants, propellers, or any related part or appliance; and

(5) Pass a written test on his ability to inspect according to safety standards for returning aircraft to service after major repairs and major alterations and annual and progressive inspections performed under Part 43 of this chapter.

An applicant who fails the test prescribed in paragraph (c)(5) of this section may not apply for retesting until at least 90 days after the date he failed the test.

[Doc. No. 1179, 27 FR 7973, Aug. 10, 1962, as amended by Amdt. 65–5, 31 FR 3337, Mar. 3,

1966; Amdt. 65-22, 42 FR 46279, Sept. 15, 1977; Amdt. 65-30, 50 FR 15700, Apr. 19, 1985]

§ 65.92 Inspection authorization: Duration.

(a) Each inspection authorization expires on March 31 of each year. However, the holder may exercise the privileges of that authorization only while he holds a currently effective mechanic certificate with both a currently effective airframe rating and a currently effective powerplant rating.

(b) An inspection authorization ceases to be effective whenever any of the following occurs:

(1) The authorization is surrendered, suspended, or revoked.

(2) The holder no longer has a fixed base of operation.

(3) The holder no longer has the equipment, facilities, and inspection data required by § 65.91(c) (3) and (4) for issuance of his authorization.

(c) The holder of an inspection authorization that is suspended or revoked shall, upon the Administrator's request, return it to the Administrator.

[Doc. No. 12537, Amdt. 65-22, 42 FR 46279, Sept. 15, 1977]

§ 65.93 Inspection authorization: Renewal.

(a) To be eligible for renewal of an inspection authorization for a 1-year period an applicant must present evidence annually, during the month of March, at an FAA General Aviation District Office, a Flight Standards District Office, or an International Field Office that the applicant still meets the requirements of § 65.91(c) (1) through (4) and must show that, during the current period that the applicant held the inspection authorization, the applicant—

(1) Has performed at least one annual inspection for each 90 days that the applicant held the current authority; or

(2) Has performed inspections of at least two major repairs or major alterations for each 90 days that the applicant held the current authority; or

(3) Has performed or supervised and approved at least one progressive inspection in accordance with standards prescribed by the Administrator; or

(4) Has attended and successfully completed a refresher course, acceptable to the Administrator, of not less than 8 hours of instruction during the 12-month period preceding the application for renewal; or

(5) Has passed on oral test by an FAA inspector to determine that the applicant's knowledge of applicable regulations and standards is current.

(b) The holder of an inspection authorization that has been in effect for less than 90 days before the expiration date need not comply with paragraphs (a) (1) through (5) of this section.

[Doc. No. 18241, Amdt. 65-26, 45 FR 46738, July 10, 1980]

§ 65.95 Inspection authorization: Privileges and limitations.

(a) The holder of an inspection authorization may—

(1) Inspect and approve for return to service any aircraft or related part or appliance (except any aircraft maintained in accordance with a continuous airworthiness program under Part 121 or 127 of this chapter) after a major repair or major alteration to it in accordance with Part 43 [New] of this chapter, if the work was done in accordance with technical data approved by the Administrator; and

(2) Perform an annual, or perform or supervise a progressive inspection according to §§ 43.13 and 43.15 of this chapter.

(b) When he exercises the privileges of an inspection authorization the holder shall keep it available for inspection by the aircraft owner, the mechanic submitting the aircraft, repair, or alteration for approval (if any), and shall present it upon the request of the Administrator or an authorized representative of the National Transportation Safety Board, or of any Federal, State, or local law enforcement officer.

(c) If the holder of an inspection authorization changes his fixed base of operation, he may not exercise the privileges of the authorization until he has notified the FAA General Aviation District Office or International Field Office for the area in which the new base is located, in writing, of the change.

[Doc. No. 1179, 27 FR 7973, Aug. 10, 1962, as amended by Amdt. 65-2, 29 FR 5451, Apr. 23, 1964; Amdt. 65-4, 30 FR 3638, Mar. 14, 1965; Amdt. 65-5, 31 FR 3337, Mar. 3, 1966; Amdt. 65-9, 31 FR 13524, Oct. 20, 1966; 32 FR 5769, Apr. 11, 1967]

Subpart E—Repairmen

§ 65.101 Eligibility requirements: General.

(a) To be eligible for a repairman certificate a person must—

(1) Be at least 18 years of age;

(2) Be specially qualified to perform maintenance on aircraft or components thereof, appropriate to the job for which he is employed;

(3) Be employed for a specific job requiring those special qualifications by a certificated repair station, or by a certificated commercial operator or certificated air carrier, that is required by its operating certificate or approved operations specifications to provide a continuous airworthiness maintenance program according to its maintenance manuals;

(4) Be recommended for certification by his employer, to the satisfaction of the Administrator, as able to satisfactorily maintain aircraft or components, appropriate to the job for which he is employed;

(5) Have either—

(i) At least 18 months of practical experience in the procedures, practices, inspection methods, materials, tools, machine tools, and equipment generally used in the maintenance duties of the specific job for which the person is to be employed and certificated; or

(ii) Completed formal training that is acceptable to the Administrator and is specifically designed to qualify the applicant for the job on which the applicant is to be employed; and

(6) Be able to read, write, speak, and understand the English language, or, in the case of an applicant who does not meet this requirement and who is employed outside the United States by a certificated repair station, a certificated U.S. commercial operator, or a certificated U.S. air carrier, described in paragraph (c) of this section, have his certificate endorsed "Valid only outside the United States."

(b) This section does not apply to the issuance of repairman certificates (experimental aircraft builder) under § 65.104.

[Doc. No. 1179, 27 FR 7973, Aug. 10, 1962, as amended by Amdt. 65-11, 32 FR 13506, Sept. 27, 1967; Amdt. 65-24, 44 FR 46781, Aug. 9, 1979; Amdt. 65-27, 47 FR 13316, Mar. 29, 1982]

§ 65.103 Repairman certificate: Privileges and limitations.

(a) A certificated repairman may perform or supervise the maintenance, preventive maintenance, or alteration of aircraft or aircraft components appropriate to the job for which the repairman was employed and certificated, but only in connection with duties for the certificate holder by whom the repairman was employed and recommended.

(b) A certificated repairman may not perform or supervise duties under the repairman certificate unless the repairman understands the current instructions of the certificate holder by whom the repairman is employed and the manufacturer's instructions for continued airworthiness relating to the specific operations concerned.

[Doc. No. 18241, Amdt. 65-26, 45 FR 46738, July 10, 1980]

§ 65.104 Repairman certificate—experimental aircraft builder—Eligibility, privileges and limitations.

(a) To be eligible for a repairman certificate (experimental aircraft builder), an individual must—

(1) Be at least 18 years of age;

(2) Be the primary builder of the aircraft to which the privileges of the certificate are applicable;

(3) Show to the satisfaction of the Administrator that the individual has the requisite skill to determine whether the aircraft is in a condition for safe operations; and

(4) Be a citizen of the United States or an individual citizen of a foreign country who has lawfully been admitted for permanent residence in the United States.

(b) The holder of a repairman certificate (experimental aircraft builder) may perform condition inspections on the aircraft constructed by the holder in accordace with the operating limitations of that aircraft.

(c) Section 65.103 does not apply to the holder of a repairman certificate (experimental aircraft builder) while performing under that certificate.

[Amdt. 65-24, 44 FR 46781, Aug. 9, 1979]

§ 65.105 Display of certificate.

Each person who holds a repairman certificate shall keep it within the immediate area where he normally exercises the privileges of the certificate and shall present it for inspection upon the request of the Administrator or an authorized representative of the National Transportation Safety Board, or of any Federal, State, or local law enforcement officer.

[Amdt. 65-9, 31 FR 13524, Oct. 20, 1966, as amended by Doc. No. 8084, 32 FR 5769, Apr. 11, 1967]

Subpart F—Parachute Riggers

§ 65.111 Certificate required.

(a) No person may pack, maintain, or alter any personnel-carrying parachute intended for emergency use in connection with civil aircraft of the United States (including the auxiliary parachute of a dual parachute pack to be used for intentional jumping) unless he holds an appropriate current certificate and type rating issued under this subpart and complies with §§ 65.127 through 65.133.

(b) No person may pack, maintain, or alter any main parachute of a dual parachute pack to be used for intentional jumping in connection with civil aircraft of the United States unless he has an appropriate current certificate issued under this subpart. However, a person who does not hold such a certificate may pack the main parachute of a dual parachute pack that is to be used by him for intentional jumping.

(c) Each person who holds a parachute rigger certificate shall present it for inspection upon the request of the Administrator or an authorized representative of the National Transportation Safety Board, or of any Federal, State, or local law enforcement officer.

(d) The following parachute rigger certificates are issued under this part:

(1) Senior parachute rigger.

(2) Master parachute rigger.

(e) Sections 65.127 through 65.133 do not apply to parachutes packed, maintained, or altered for the use of the armed forces.

[Doc. No. 1179, 27 FR 7973, Aug. 10, 1962, as amended by Amdt. 65-9, 31 FR 13524, Oct. 20, 1966; 32 FR 5769, Apr. 11, 1967]

§ 65.113 Eligibility requirements: General.

(a) To be eligible for a parachute rigger certificate, a person must—

(1) Be at least 18 years of age;

(2) Be able to read, write, speak, and understand the English language, or, in the case of a citizen of Puerto Rico, or a person who is employed outside of the United States by a U.S. air carrier, and who does not meet this requirement, be issued a certificate that is valid only in Puerto Rico or while he is employed outside of the United States by that air carrier, as the case may be; and

(3) Comply with the sections of this subpart that apply to the certificate and type rating he seeks.

(b) Except for a master parachute rigger certificate, a parachute rigger certificate that was issued before, and was valid on, October 31, 1962, is equal to a senior parachute rigger certificate, and may be exchanged for such a corresponding certificate.

§ 65.115 Senior parachute rigger certificate: Experience, knowledge, and skill requirements.

Except as provided in § 65.117, an applicant for a senior parachute rigger certificate must—

(a) Present evidence satisfactory to the Administrator that he has packed at least 20 parachutes of each type for which he seeks a rating, in accordance with the manufacturer's instructions and under the supervision of a certificated parachute rigger holding a rating for that type or a person holding an appropriate military rating;

(b) Pass a written test, with respect to parachutes in common use, on—

(1) Their construction, packing, and maintenance;

(2) The manufacturer's instructions;

(3) The regulations of this subpart; and

(c) Pass an oral and practical test showing his ability to pack and maintain at least one type of parachute in common use, appropriate to the type rating he seeks.

[Doc. No. 10468, Amdt. 65-20, 37 FR 13251, July 6, 1972]

§ 65.117 Military riggers or former military riggers: Special certification rule.

In place of the procedure in § 65.115, an applicant for a senior parachute rigger certificate is entitled to it if he passes a written test on the regulations of this subpart and presents satisfactory documentary evidence that he—

(a) Is a member or civilian employee of an Armed Force of the United States, is a civilian employee of a regular armed force of a foreign country, or has, within the 12 months before he applies, been honorably discharged or released from any status covered by this paragraph;

(b) Is serving, or has served within the 12 months before he applies, as a parachute rigger for such an Armed Force; and

(c) Has the experience required by § 65.115(a).

§ 65.119 Master parachute rigger certificate: Experience, knowledge, and skill requirements.

An applicant for a master parachute rigger certificate must meet the following requirements:

(a) Present evidence satisfactory to the Administrator that he has had at least 3 years of experience as a parachute rigger and has satisfactorily packed at least 100 parachutes of each of two types in common use, in accordance with the manufacturer's instructions—

(1) While a certificated and appropriately rated senior parachute rigger; or

(2) While under the supervision of a certificated and appropriately rated parachute rigger or a person holding appropriate military ratings.

An applicant may combine experience specified in paragraphs (a) (1) and (2) of this section to meet the requirements of this paragraph.

(b) If the applicant is not the holder of a senior parachute rigger certifi-

cate, pass a written test, with respect to parachutes in common use, on—

(1) Their construction, packing, and maintenance;

(2) The manufacturer's instructions; and

(3) The regulations of this subpart.

(c) Pass an oral and practical test showing his ability to pack and maintain two types of parachutes in common use, appropriate to the type ratings he seeks.

[Doc. No. 10468, Amdt. 65-20, 37 FR 13252, July 6, 1972]

§ 65.121 Type ratings.

(a) The following type ratings are issued under this subpart:

(1) Seat.

(2) Back.

(3) Chest.

(4) Lap.

(b) The holder of a senior parachute rigger certificate who qualifies for a master parachute rigger certificate is entitled to have placed on his master parachute rigger certificate the ratings that were on his senior parachute rigger certificate.

§ 65.123 Additional type ratings: Requirements.

A certificated parachute rigger who applies for an additional type rating must—

(a) Present evidence satisfactory to the Administrator that he has packed at least 20 parachutes of the type for which he seeks a rating, in accordance with the manufacturer's instructions and under the supervision of a certificated parachute rigger holding a rating for that type or a person holding an appropriate military rating; and

(b) Pass a practical test, to the satisfaction of the Administrator, showing his ability to pack and maintain the type of parachute for which he seeks a rating.

[Doc. No. 1179, 27 FR 7973, Aug. 10, 1962, as amended by Amdt. 65-20, 37 FR 13251, July 6, 1972]

§ 65.125 Certificates: Privileges.

(a) A certificated senior parachute rigger may—

(1) Pack or maintain (except for major repair) any type of parachute for which he is rated; and

(2) Supervise other persons in packing any type of parachute for which he is rated.

(b) A certificated master parachute rigger may—

(1) Pack, maintain, or alter any type of parachute for which he is rated; and

(2) Supervise other persons in packing, maintaining, or altering any type of parachute for which he is rated.

(c) A certificated parachute rigger need not comply with §§ 65.127 through 65.133 (relating to facilities, equipment, performance standards, records, recent experience, and seal) in packing, maintaining, or altering (if authorized) the main parachute of a dual parachute pack to be used for intentional jumping.

[Doc. No. 1179, 27 FR 7973, Aug. 10, 1962, as amended by Amdt. 65-20, 37 FR 13252, July 6, 1972]

§ 65.127 Facilities and equipment.

No certificated parachute rigger may exercise the privileges of his certificate unless he has at least the following facilities and equipment available to him:

(a) A smooth top table at least three feet wide by 40 feet long.

(b) Suitable housing that is adequately heated, lighted, and ventilated for drying and airing parachutes.

(c) Enough packing tools and other equipment to pack and maintain the types of parachutes that he services.

(d) Adequate housing facilities to perform his duties and to protect his tools and equipment.

[Doc. No. 1179, 27 FR 7973, Aug. 10, 1962, as amended by Amdt. 65-27, 47 FR 13316, Mar. 29, 1982]

§ 65.129 Performance standards.

No certificated parachute rigger may—

(a) Pack, maintain, or alter any parachute unless he is rated for that type;

(b) Pack a parachute that is not safe for emergency use;

(c) Pack a parachute that has not been thoroughly dried and aired;

(d) Alter a parachute in a manner that is not specifically authorized by the Administrator or the manufacturer;

(e) Pack, maintain, or alter a parachute in any manner that deviates from procedures approved by the Administrator or the manufacturer of the parachute; or

(f) Exercise the privileges of his certificate and type rating unless he understands the current manufacturer's instructions for the operation involved and has—

(1) Performed duties under his certificate for at least 90 days within the preceding 12 months; or

(2) Shown the Administrator that he is able to perform those duties.

§ 65.131 Records.

(a) Each certificated parachute rigger shall keep a record of the packing, maintenance, and alteration of parachutes performed or supervised by him. He shall keep in that record, with respect to each parachute worked on, a statement of—

(1) Its type and make;

(2) Its serial number;

(3) The name and address of its owner;

(4) The kind and extent of the work performed;

(5) The date when and place where the work was performed; and

(6) The results of any drop tests made with it.

(b) Each person who makes a record under paragraph (a) of this section shall keep it for at least 2 years after the date it is made.

(c) Each certificated parachute rigger who packs a parachute shall write, on the parachute packing record attached to the parachute, the date and place of the packing and a notation of any defects he finds on inspection. He shall sign that record with his name and the number of his certificate.

§ 65.133 Seal.

Each certificated parachute rigger must have a seal with an identifying mark prescribed by the Administrator, and a seal press. After packing a parachute he shall seal the pack with his seal in accordance with the manufacturer's recommendation for that type of parachute.

APPENDIX A—AIRCRAFT DISPATCHER COURSES

(a) *Training course outline.* It is not mandatory that the training course outline have the subject headings arranged exactly as listed in the following example. Any arrangement of headings and subheadings will be satisfactory provided all the subjects listed in this section are included. Each general subject of the outline shall be broken down, in detail, showing the items to be covered. Additional subjects, especially those which are not closely associated with the training of aircraft dispatchers, may be listed so long as the hourly requirements devoted to the subjects are not included as a part of the basic minimum hours.

(b) *Format of the training outline and course requirements.* The course outline submitted for approval must be in looseleaf form, must include a table of contents and minimum coverage of the course material, and must include the following:

Subject	Classroom hours
Federal Aviation Regulations	15
Subpart C of part 65 of this chapter.	
Parts 25, 91, 103, and 121 of this chapter.	
Part 430 of the Regulations of the National Transportation Safety Board, "Rules Pertaining to Aircraft Accidents, Incidents, Overdue Aircraft, and Safety Investigation", on sale at the Government Printing Office	
Meteorology	75
Basic properties of the atmosphere:	
Composition.	
Density.	
Measurement.	
General circulation.	
Solar heating.	

Subject	Classroom hours
Clouds:	
Formation.	
Condensation.	
Precipitation.	
Use of cloud knowledge in forecasting.	
Stability and instability.	
Air mass analysis:	
Classification.	
Flying conditions to be encountered.	
Use of air mass knowledge in forecasting.	
Analysis of fronts:	
Structure and characteristics.	
Cloud sequences in fronts.	
Establishing position of front by cloud types.	
Fronts in North America and seasonal variations	
Flying weather in fronts.	
Cyclones and anticyclones.	
Fog:	
Types.	
Cause and formation.	
Ice:	
Type.	
Cause and formation.	
Thunderstorms, hurricanes, tornados:	
Causes.	
Methods of forecasting.	
Structure and complexity of internal winds.	
Hail, its cause and formation.	
Turbulence:	
Determining the smooth level of flights.	
Cause.	
Interpreting weather data:	
Weather sequences and symbols.	
Weather map symbols.	
Drawing a weather map.	
Reading a weather map.	
Upper-level charts.	
Adiabatic charts.	
Winds-aloft charts.	
Instruments used to gather and record the weather	
Weather forecasting:	
Extrapolation.	
Movement of fronts and air masses.	
Isobars.	
Barometric tendency.	
Application of weather knowledge:	
Planning a flight.	
Navigation	30

Subject	Classroom hours	Subject	Classroom hours
Study of the earth as a planet (charts, maps, and projections):		Instrument familiarization.	
Mercator projections.		Bracketing.	
Gnomonic projections.		Orientation.	
Lambert projections.		Holding procedure.	
Polyconic projections.		Let-down procedure.	
Chart reading:		Missed-approach procedure.	
Symbols, landmarks, etc.		Air Traffic Control...	30
Dead reckoning:		Air route traffic control procedures and equipment.	
Magnetic variation, compass deviation terms, winds and vectors		Airport traffic control procedures and equipment.	
Correction angle.		Practical Dispatching	15
Findings wind drift-off course.		Preflight:	
Off course problems.		Safety.	
Wind velocity by single and double drift.		Economic advantage.	
Interception problems.		Crew.	
Radius of action—problems.		Notams.	
Search problems.		The course and distance.	
Computer use—problems.		Horizontal and vertical extent of the weather.	
Radio navigation:		Winds.	
Principles of the radio range, radio compass direction finder, marker beacons, ILS, CCA, radio altimeter, LORAN, and any other		Forecast.	
		Minimum safe altitude.	
		The cruising altitude.	
Navigation instruments:		Flight plan.	
Altimeter, air-speed indicator, compass, drift and rate of climb indicator		The alternate plan.	
		Clearances, company air traffic control.	
Aircraft..	15	The fuel.	
Weight and balance:		The load.	
Center of gravity.		The departure time.	
How determined.			
Center of gravity limits.		In-flight:	
Problem in loading.		Position report.	
Engine specifications—Powerplant:		Altimeter settings.	
Operating limits.		Weather reports.	
Fuel consumption.		Changes in forecast.	
Accessories.		Changing instrument altitude.	
Operating manual.		Changing from VFR to IFR.	
Airplane specifications:		Additional clearances.	
Operational equipment.		Emergency procedures.	
Flight controls, landing gear hydraulic system, electrical system, loading characteristics, fuel capacity heating and ventilating system, and deicing equipment		Post-flight:	
		Arrival report.	
		Differences between the forecasted and actual weather encountered for subsequent flights	
Performance:			
Effect of weight, wind, air density, and runway surfaces on take-off performance of aircraft			
Power setting and cockpit procedure.			
Types of cruise control.			
Communications...	8		
Radio-telephone rules and regulations.			
FCC rules and regulations.			
Company communications:			
Air to ground radio communications and procedures			
Point to point communications and procedures.			
Equipment air to ground and point to point.			
FAA communications:			
Air to ground radio communications and procedures			
Point to point communications and procedures.			
Equipment air to ground and point to point.			
Simulated instrument flight	10		

(c) *Facilities, equipment, and material.* An applicant for authority to operate an approved aircraft dispatcher course of study must have the following facilities, equipment, and materials:

(1) *Facilities.* Suitable classrooms, adequate to accommodate the largest number of students scheduled for attendance at any one time. Such classrooms shall be properly heated, lighted, and ventilated.

(2) *Equipment and materials.* Suitable devices for the teaching of simulated instrument flight, navigation, and meteorology, acceptable textbooks, operations manuals, wall maps, charts, blackboards, and visual aids of a quantity which will provide for each student the theoretical and practical aspects of aircraft dispatching.

(d) *Instructors.* (1) The number of instructors available for conducting the course of study shall be determined according to the needs and facilities of the applicant. However, the ratio of students per instructor may not exceed 25 students for one instructor.

(2) At least one instructor who possesses a currently effective aircraft dispatcher certificate must be available for coordination of the training course instruction.

(e) *Revision of training course.* Requests for revision of course outlines, facilities, and equipment shall be accomplished in the same manner established for securing approval of the original course of study. Revisions must be submitted in such form that an entire page or pages of the approved outline can be removed and replaced by the revision.

The list of instructors may be revised at any time without request for approval, provided the minimum requirements are maintained and the local inspector is notified.

(f) *Credit for previous experience or training.* A course operator may evaluate an entrant's previous experience or training and where the training or experience is provable and comparable to portions of the approved course curriculum, may, as each individual case warrants, allow credit for such, commensurate with accepted training practices. Where credit is allowed, the basis for allowance and the total hours credited must be incorporated as a part of the student's records, provided for in paragraph (g) of this Appendix.

(g) *Student records and reports.* Approval of a course may not be continued in effect unless the course operator keeps an accurate record of each student, including a chronological log of all instructions, subjects covered, and course examinations and grades, and unless he prepares and transmits to the FAA not later than January 31 of each year, a report containing the following information:

(1) The names of all students graduated, together with school grades for aircraft dispatcher courses.

(2) The names of all students failed or dropped, together with school grades and reasons for dropping.

(h) *Quality of instruction.* Approval of a course may not be continued in effect unless at least 80 percent of the students who apply within 90 days after graduation are able to qualify on the first attempt for certification as aircraft dispatchers.

(i) *Statement of graduation.* Each student who successfully completes the approved aircraft dispatcher course shall be given a statement of graduation.

(j) *Change of ownership, name, or location*—(1) *Change of ownership.* Approval of an aircraft dispatcher course may not be continued in effect after the course has changed ownership. The new owner must obtain a new approval by following the procedures prescribed for original approval.

(2) *Change in name.* An approved course changed in name but not changed in owner-

ship remains valid if the change is reported by the approved course operator to the local inspector who will issue a letter of approval under the new name.

(3) *Change in location.* An approved course remains in effect even though the approved course operator changes location if the change is reported without delay by the operator to the local inspector who will inspect the facilities to be used in the new location and, if they are found to be adequate, issue a letter of approval showing the new location.

(k) *Cancellation of approval.* (1) Failure to meet or maintain any of the standards set forth herein for the approval or operation of an approved aircraft dispatcher course is considered to be a sufficient reason for discontinuing approval of the course.

(2) If an operator desires voluntary cancellation of his approved course, he shall send a letter requesting cancellation to the Administrator of the Federal Aviation Administration through the local inspector.

(1) *Duration.* The authority to operate an approved aircraft dispatcher course of study expires 24 months after the last day of the month of issuance.

(m) *Renewal.* Application for renewal of an approved aircraft dispatcher course shall be made by letter addressed to the Administrator of the Federal Aviation Administration through the local inspector at any time within 60 days of the expiration date. Renewal of approval will depend on the course operator's meeting the current conditions of course approval and having a satisfactory record as a course operator.

[Doc. No. 1179, 27 FR 7973, Aug. 10, 1962, as amended by Amdt. 65-10, 32 FR 5770, Apr. 11, 1967; Amdt. 65-16, 35 FR 14075, Sept. 4, 1970]

FEDERAL AVIATION REGULATIONS

PART 91
GENERAL OPERATING AND FLIGHT RULES

1989 EDITION

Subpart A—General

§ 91.1 Applicability.

(a) Except as provided in paragraph (b) of this section, this part describes rules governing the operation of aircraft (other than moored balloons, kites, unmanned rockets, and unmanned free balloons) within the United States.

(b) Each person operating a civil aircraft of U.S. registry outside of the United States shall—

(1) When over the high seas, comply with Annex 2 (Rules of the Air) to the Convention on International Civil Aviation and with §§ 91.70(c), 91.88, and 91.90 of Subpart B;

(2) When within a foreign country, comply with the regulations relating to the flight and maneuver of aircraft there in force;

(3) Except for §§ 91.15(b), 91.17, 91.38 and 91.43, comply with Subparts A, C, and D of this part so far as they are not inconsistent with applicable regulations of the foreign country where the aircraft is operated or Annex 2 to the Convention on International Civil Aviation; and

(4) When over the North Atlantic within airspace designated as Minimum Navigation Performance Specifications airspace, comply with § 91.20.

(c) Annex 2 to the Convention on International Civil Aviation, Sixth Edition—September 1970, with amendments through Amendment 20 effective August 1976, to which reference is made in this part is incorporated into this part and made a part hereof as provided in 5 U.S.C. 552 and pursuant to 1 CFR Part 51, Annex 2 (including a complete historic file of changes thereto) is available for public inspection at the Rules Docket, AGC-24, Federal Aviation Administration, 800 Independence Avenue, SW., Washington, D.C. 20591. In addition, Annex 2 may be purchased from the International Civil Aviation Organization (Attention: Distribution Officer), P.O. Box 400, Succursale; Place de L'Aviation Internationale, 1000 Sherbrooke Street West, Montreal, Quebec, Canada H3A 2R2.

[Amdt. 61-22, 31 FR 8355, June 15, 1966, as amended by Amdt. 91-78, 35 FR 7784, May 21, 1970; Amdt. 91-112, 38 FR 8054, Mar. 28, 1973; Amdt. 91-137, 42 FR 22139, May 2, 1977; Amdt. 91-144, 42 FR 64881, Dec. 29, 1977; Amdt. 91-153, 43 FR 28420, June 29, 1978; Amdt. 91-187, 50 FR 9258, Mar. 6, 1985]

§ 91.2   Certificate of authorization for certain Category II operations.

The Admistrator may issue a certificate of authorization authorizing deviations from the requirements of §§ 91.6, 91.33(f), and 91.34 for the operation of small aircrafts identified as Category A aircraft in § 97.3 of this chapter in Category II operations, if he finds that the proposed operation can be safely conducted under the terms of the certificate. Such authorization does not permit operation of the aircraft carrying persons or property for compensation or hire.

[Amdt. 91-88, 36 FR 4592, Mar. 10, 1971, as amended by Amdt. 91-196, 51 FR 40707, Nov. 7, 1986]

§ 91.3   Responsibility and authority of the pilot in command.

(a) The pilot in command of an aircraft is directly responsible for, and is the final authority as to, the operation of that aircraft.

(b) In an emergency requiring immediate action, the pilot in command may deviate from any rule of this subpart or of Subpart B to the extent required to meet that emergency.

(c) Each pilot in command who deviates from a rule under paragraph (b) of this section shall, upon the request of the Administrator, send a written report of that deviation to the Administrator.

§ 91.4   Pilot in command of aircraft requiring more than one required pilot.

No person may operate an aircraft that is type certificated for more than one required pilot flight crewmember unless the pilot flight crew consists of a pilot in command who meets the requirements of § 61.58 of this chapter.

[Doc. No. 10916, Amdt. 91-111, 38 FR 3179, Feb. 1, 1973, as amended by Amdt. 91-133, 41 FR 47228, Oct. 28, 1976]

§ 91.5   Preflight action.

Each pilot in command shall, before beginning a flight, familiarize himself with all available information concerning that flight. This information must include:

(a) For a flight under IFR or a flight not in the vicinity of an airport, weather reports and forecasts, fuel requirements, alternatives available if the planned flight cannot be completed, and any known traffic delays of which he has been advised by ATC.

(b) For any flight, runway lengths at airports of intended use, and the following takeoff and landing distance information:

(1) For civil aircraft for which an approved airplane or rotorcraft flight manual containing takeoff and landing distance data is required, the takeoff and landing distance data contained therein; and

(2) For civil aircraft other than those specified in paragraph (b)(1) of this section, other reliable information appropriate to the aircraft, relating to aircraft performance under expected values of airport elevation and runway slope, aircraft gross weight, and wind and temperature.

[Amdt. 91-87, 36 FR 2482, Feb. 5, 1971]

§ 91.6   Category II and III operations: General operating rules.

(a) No person may operate a civil aircraft in a Category II or Category III operation unless:

(1) The flightcrew of the aircraft consists of a pilot in command and a second in command who hold the appropriate authorizations and ratings prescribed in § 61.3 of this chapter;

(2) Each flight crewmember has adequate knowledge of, and familiarity

with, the aircraft and the procedures to be used; and

(3) The instrument panel in front of the pilot who is controlling the aircraft has appropriate instrumentation for the type of flight control guidance system that is being used.

(b) Unless otherwise authorized by the Administrator, no person may operate a civil aircraft in a Category II or Category III operation unless each ground component required for that operation and the related airborne equipment is installed and operating.

(c) For the purpose of this section, when the approach procedure being used provides for and requires use of a DH, the authorized decision height is the DH prescribed by the approach procedure, the DH prescribed for the pilot in command, or the DH for which the aircraft is equipped, whichever is higher.

(d) Unless otherwise authorized by the Administrator, no pilot operating an aircraft in a Category II or Category III approach that provides and requires use of a DH may continue the approach below the authorized decision height unless the following conditions are met:

(1) The aircraft is in a position from which a descent to a landing on the intended runway can be made at a normal rate of descent using normal maneuvers, and where that descent rate will allow touchdown to occur within the touchdown zone of the runway of intended landing.

(2) At least one of the following visual references for the intended runway is distinctly visible and identifiable to the pilot:

(i) The approach light system, except that the pilot may not descend below 100 feet above the touchdown zone elevation using the approach lights as a reference unless the red terminating bars or the red side row bars are also distinctly visible and identifiable.

(ii) The threshold.

(iii) The threshold markings.

(iv) The threshold lights.

(v) The touchdown zone or touchdown zone markings.

(vi) The touchdown zone lights.

(e) Unless otherwise authorized by the Administrator, each pilot operating an aircraft shall immediately execute an appropriate missed approach whenever prior to touchdown the requirements of paragraph (d) of this section are not met.

(f) No person operating an aircraft using a Category III approach without decision height may land that aircraft except in accordance with the provisions of the letter of authorization issued by the Administrator.

(g) Paragraphs (a) through (f) of this section do not apply to operations conducted by the holders of certificates issued under Part 121, 123, 125, 129, or 135 of this chapter. No person may operate a civil aircraft in a Category II or Category III operation conducted by the holder of a certificate issued under Part 121, 123, 125, 129, or 135 of this chapter unless the operation is conducted in accordance with that certificate holder's operations specifications.

[Amdt. 91-173, 46 FR 2289, Jan. 8, 1981]

§ 91.7 Flight crewmembers at stations.

(a) During takeoff and landing, and while en route, each required flight crewmember shall—

(1) Be at his station unless his absence is necessary in the performance of his duties in connection with the operation of the aircraft or in connection with his physiological needs; and

(2) Keep his seat belt fastened while at his station.

(b) After July 18, 1978, each required flight crewmember of a U.S. registered civil airplane shall, during takeoff and landing, keep the shoulder harness fastened while at his station. This paragraph does not apply if—

(1) The seat at the crewmember's station is not equipped with a shoulder harness; or

(2) The crewmember would be unable to perform his required duties with the shoulder harness fastened.

[Doc. No. 1580, Amdt. 1-1, 28 FR 6704, June 29, 1963, as amended by Amdt. 91-24, 30 FR 13120, Oct. 15, 1965; Amdt. 91-139, 42 FR 30603, June 16, 1977]

§ 91.8 Prohibition against interference with crewmembers.

(a) No person may assault, threaten, intimidate, or interfere with a crewmember in the performance of the crewmember's duties aboard an aircraft being operated.

[Amdt. 91-152, 43 FR 22640, May 25, 1978]

§ 91.9   Careless or reckless operation.

No person may operate an aircraft in a careless or reckless manner so as to endanger the life or property of another.

§ 91.10   Careless or reckless operation other than for the purpose of air navigation.

No person may operate an aircraft other than for the purpose of air navigation, on any part of the surface of an airport used by aircraft for air commerce (including areas used by those aircraft for receiving or discharging persons or cargo), in a careless or reckless manner so as to endanger the life or property of another.

[Amdt. 91-43, 32 FR 9641, July 4, 1967]

§ 91.11   Alcohol or drugs.

(a) No person may act or attempt to act as a crewmember of a civil aircraft—

(1) Within 8 hours after the consumption of any alcoholic beverage;

(2) While under the influence of alcohol;

(3) While using any drug that affects the person's faculties in any way contrary to safety; or

(4) While having .04 percent by weight or more alcohol in the blood.

(b) Except in an emergency, no pilot of a civil aircraft may allow a person who appears to be intoxicated or who demonstrates by manner or physical indications that the individual is under the influence of drugs (except a medical patient under proper care) to be carried in that aircraft.

(c) A crewmember shall do the following:

(1) On request of a law enforcement officer, submit to a test to indicate the percentage by weight of alcohol in the blood, when—

(i) The law enforcement officer is authorized under State or local law to conduct the test or to have the test conducted; and

(ii) The law enforcement officer is requesting submission to the test to investigate a suspected violation of State or local law governing the same or substantially similar conduct prohibited by paragraph (a)(1), (a)(2), or (a)(4) of this section.

(2) Whenever the Administrator has a reasonable basis to believe that a person may have violated paragraph (a)(1), (a)(2), or (a)(4) of this section, that person shall, upon request by the Administrator, furnish the Administrator, or authorize any clinic, hospital, doctor, or other person to release to the Administrator, the results of each test taken within 4 hours after acting or attempting to act as a crewmember that indicates percentage by weight of alcohol in the blood.

(d) Whenever the Administrator has a reasonable basis to believe that a person may have violated paragraph (a)(3) of this section, that person shall, upon request by the Administrator, furnish the Administrator, or authorize any clinic, hospital, doctor, or other person to release to the Administrator, the results of each test taken within 4 hours after acting or attempting to act as a crewmember that indicates the presence of any drugs in the body.

(e) Any test information obtained by the Administrator under paragraph (c) or (d) of this section may be evaluated in determining a person's qualifications for any airman certificate or possible violations of this chapter and may be used as evidence in any legal proceeding under section 602, 609, or 901 of the Federal Aviation Act of 1958.

[Doc. No. 21956, Amdt. 91-188, 50 FR 15380, Apr. 17 1985, as amended by Amdt. 91-194, 51 FR 1229, Jan. 9, 1986]

§ 91.12   Carriage of narcotic drugs, marihuana, and depressant or stimulant drugs or substances.

(a) Except as provided in paragraph (b) of this section, no person may operate a civil aircraft within the United States with knowledge that narcotic drugs, marihuana, and depressant or stimulant drugs or substances as defined in Federal or State statutes are carried in the aircraft.

(b) Paragraph (a) of this section does not apply to any carriage of narcotic drugs, marihuana, and depressant or stimulant drugs or substances authorized by or under any Federal or State statute or by any Federal or State agency.

[Doc. No. 12035, Amdt. 91-117, 38 FR 17493, July 2, 1973]

§ 91.13   Dropping objects.

No pilot in command of a civil aircraft may allow any object to be dropped from that aircraft in flight that creates a hazard to persons or property. However, this section does not prohibit the dropping of any object if reasonable precautions are taken to avoid injury or damage to persons or property.

§ 91.14   Use of safety belts and shoulder harnesses.

(a) Unless otherwise authorized by the Administrator—

(1) No pilot may take off a U.S. registered civil aircraft (except a free balloon that incorporates a basket or gondola and an airship) unless the pilot in command of that aircraft ensures that each person on board is briefed on how to fasten and unfasten that person's safety belt and shoulder harness, if installed.

(2) No pilot may take off or land a U.S. registered civil aircraft (except free ballons that incorporate baskets or gondolas and airships) unless the pilot in command of that aircraft ensures that each person on board has been notified to fasten his safety belt and shoulder harness, if installed.

(3) During the takeoff and landing of U.S. registered civil aircraft (except free balloons that incorporate baskets or gondolas and airships), each person on board that aircraft must occupy a seat or berth with a safety belt and shoulder harness, if installed, properly secured about him. However, a person who has not reached his second birthday may be held by an adult who is occupying a seat or berth, and a person on board for the purpose of engaging in sport parachuting may use the floor of the aircraft as a seat.

(b) This section does not apply to operations conducted under Part 121, 123, or 127 of this chapter. Paragraph (a)(3) of this section does not apply to persons subject to § 91.7.

[Amdt. 91-89, 36 FR 12571, July 1, 1971; 36 FR 14128, July 30, 1971, as amended by Amdt. 91-135, 41 FR 55475, Dec. 20, 1976; Amdt. 91-154, 43 FR 46233, Oct. 5, 1978; Amdt. 91-191, 50 FR 46877, Nov. 13, 1985]

§ 91.15   Parachutes and parachuting.

(a) No pilot of a civil aircraft may allow a parachute that is available for emergency use to be carried in that aircraft unless it is an approved type and—

(1) If a chair type (canopy in back), it has been packed by a certificated and appropriately rated parachute rigger within the preceding 120 days; or

(2) If any other type, it has been packed by a certificated and appropriately rated parachute rigger—

(i) Within the preceding 120 days, if its canopy, shrouds, and harness are composed exclusively of nylon, rayon, or other similar synthetic fiber or materials that are substantial resistant to damage from mold, mildew, or other fungi and other rotting agents propagated in a moist environment; or

(ii) Within the preceding 60 days, if any part of the parachute is composed of silk, pongee, or other natural fiber, or materials not specified in paragraph (a)(2)(i) of this section.

(b) Except in an emergency, no pilot in command may allow, and no person may make, a parachute jump from an aircraft within the United States except in accordance with Part 105 of this chapter.

(c) Unless each occupant of the aircraft is wearing an approved parachute, no pilot of a civil aircraft, carrying any person (other than a crewmember) may execute any intentional maneuver that exceeds—

(1) A bank of 60° relative to the horizon; or

(2) A nose-up or nose-down attitude of 30° relative to the horizon.

(d) Paragraph (c) of this section does not apply to—

(1) Flight tests for pilot certification or rating; or

(2) Spins and other flight maneuvers required by the regulations for any certificate or rating when given by—

(i) A certificated flight instructor; or

(ii) An airline transport pilot instructing in accordance with § 61.169 of this chapter.

(e) For the purposes of this section, "approved parachute" means—

(1) A parachute manufactured under a type certificate or a technical standard order (C-23 series); or

(2) A personnel-carrying military parachute identified by an NAF, AAF, or AN drawing number, an AAF order number, or any other military designation or specification number.

[Doc. No. 1580, Amdt. 1-1, 28 FR 6704, June 29, 1963, as amended by Amdt. 91-29, 31 FR 8355, June 15, 1966; Amdt. 91-65, 34 FR 12883, Aug. 8, 1969; Amdt. 91-100, 37 FR 13252, July 6, 1972; Amdt. 91-114, 38 FR 12203, May 10, 1973; Amdt. 91-152, 43 FR 22640, May 25, 1978]

§ 91.17 Towing: Gliders.

(a) No person may operate a civil aircraft towing a glider unless:

(1) The pilot in command of the towing aircraft is qualified under § 61.69 of this chapter.

(2) The towing aircraft is equipped with a towhitch of a kind, and installed in a manner, approved by the Administrator.

(3) The towline used has a breaking strength not less than 80 percent of the maximum certificated operating weight of the glider, and not more than twice this operating weight. However, the towline used may have a breaking strength more than twice the maximum certificated operating weight of the glider if—

(i) A safety link is installed at the point of attachment of the towline to the glider, with a breaking strength not less than 80 percent of the maximum certificated operating weight of the glider, and not greater than twice this operating weight; and

(ii) A safety link is installed at the point of attachment of the towline to the towing aircraft with a breaking strength greater, but not more than 25 percent greater, than that of the safety link at the towed glider end of the towline, and not greater than twice the maximum certificated operating weight of the glider.

(4) Before conducting any towing operations within a control zone, or before making each towing flight within a control zone if required by ATC, the pilot in command notifies the control tower if one is in operation in that control zone. If such a control tower is not in operation, he must notify the FAA flight service station serving the control zone before conducting any towing operations in that control zone.

(5) The pilots of the towing aircraft and the glider have agreed upon a general course of action including takeoff and release signals, airspeeds, and emergency procedures for each pilot.

(b) No pilot of a civil aircraft may intentionally release a towline, after release of a glider, in a manner so as to endanger the life or property of another.

[Amdt. 91-38, 32 FR 3000, Feb. 17, 1967, as amended by Amdt. 91-133, 41 FR 47228, Oct. 28, 1976; Amdt. 91-152, 43 FR 22640, May 25, 1978]

§ 91.18 Towing: Other than under § 91.17.

(a) No pilot of a civil aircraft may tow anything with that aircraft (other than under § 91.17) except in accordance with the terms of a certificate of waiver issued by the Administrator.

(b) An application for a certificate of waiver under this section is made on a form and in a manner prescribed by the Administrator and must be submitted to the nearest Flight Standards District Office.

[Amdt. 91-38, 32 FR 3001, Feb. 17, 1967, as amended by Amdt. 91-114, 38 FR 12203, May 10, 1973; Amdt. 91-152, 43 FR 22640, May 25, 1978]

§ 91.19 Portable electronic devices.

(a) Except as provided in paragraph (b) of this section, no person may operate, nor may any operator or pilot in command of an aircraft allow the operation of, any portable electronic device on any of the following U.S. registered civil aircraft:

(1) Aircraft operated by an air carrier or commercial operator; or

(2) Any other aircraft while it is operated under IFR.

(b) Paragraph (a) of this section does not apply to:

(1) Portable voice recorders;

(2) Hearing aids;

(3) Heart pacemakers;

(4) Electric shavers; or

(5) Any other portable electronic device that the operator of the aircraft has determined will not cause interference with the navigation or communication system of the aircraft on which it is to be used.

(c) In the case of an aircraft operated by an air carrier or commercial operator, the determination required by paragraph (b)(5) of this section shall be made by the air carrier or commercial operator of the aircraft on which the particular device is to be used. In the case of other aircraft, the determination may be made by the pilot in command or other operator of the aircraft.

[Amdt. 91-35, 31 FR 15318, Dec. 7, 1966]

§ 91.20 Operations Within the North Atlantic Minimum Navigation Performance Specifications Airspace.

Unless otherwise authorized by the Administrator, no person may operate a civil aircraft of U.S. registry in North Atlantic (NAT) airspace designated as Minimum Navigation Performance Specifications (MNPS) airspace unless that aircraft has approved navigation performance capability which complies with the requirements of Appendix C to this part. The Administrator authorizes deviations from the requirements of this section in accordance with section 3 of Appendix C to this part.

[Amdt. 91-144, 42 FR 64881, Dec. 29, 1977]

§ 91.21 Flight instruction; simulated instrument flight and certain flight tests.

(a) No person may operate a civil aircraft (except a manned free balloon) that is being used for flight instruction unless that aircraft has fully functioning dual controls. However, instrument flight instruction may be given in a single-engine airplane equipped with a single, functioning, throwover control wheel, in place of fixed, dual controls of the elevator and ailerons, when:

(1) The instructor has determined that the flight can be conducted safely; and

(2) The person manipulating the controls has at least a private pilot

certificate with appropriate category and class ratings.

(b) No person may operate a civil aircraft in simulated instrument flight unless—

(1) An appropriately rated pilot occupies the other control seat as safety pilot;

(2) The safety pilot has adequate vision forward and to each side of the aircraft, or a competent observer in the aircraft adequately supplements the vision of the safety pilot; and

(3) Except in the case of lighter-than-air aircraft, that aircraft is equipped with fully functioning dual controls. However, simulated instrument flight may be conducted in a single-engine airplane, equipped with a single, functioning, throwover control wheel, in place of fixed, dual controls of the elevator and ailerons, when—

(i) The safety pilot has determined that the flight can be conducted safely; and

(ii) The person manipulating the control has at least a private pilot certificate with appropriate category and class ratings.

(c) No person may operate a civil aircraft that is being used for a flight test for an airline transport pilot certificate or a class or type rating on that certificate, or for a Federal Aviation Regulation Part 121 proficiency flight test, unless the pilot seated at the controls, other than the pilot being checked, is fully qualified to act as pilot in command of the aircraft.

[Doc. No. 1580, Amdt. 1-1, 28 FR 6704, June 29, 1963, as amended by Amdt. 91-36, 32 FR 262, Jan. 11, 1967; Amdt. 91-135, 41 FR 54475, Dec. 20, 1976; Amdt 91-154, 43 FR 46233, Oct. 5, 1978]

§ 91.22 Fuel requirements for flight under VFR.

(a) No person may begin a flight in an airplane under VFR unless (considering wind and forecast weather conditions) there is enough fuel to fly to the first point of intended landing and, assuming normal cruising speed—

(1) During the day, to fly after that for at least 30 minutes; or

(2) At night, to fly after that for at least 45 minutes.

(b) No person may begin a flight in a rotorcraft under VFR unless (considering wind and forecast weather conditions) there is enough fuel to fly to the first point of intended landing and, assuming normal cruising speed, to fly after that for at least 20 minutes.

§ 91.23 Fuel requirements for flight in IFR conditions.

(a) Except as provided in paragraph (b) of this section, no person may operate a civil aircraft in IFR conditions unless it carries enough fuel (considering weather reports and forecasts, and weather conditions) to—

(1) Complete the flight to the first airport of intended landing;

(2) Fly from that airport to the alternate airport; and

(3) Fly after that for 45 minutes at normal crusing speed or, for helicopters, fly after that for 30 minutes at normal crusing speed.

(b) Paragraph (a)(2) of this section does not apply if—

(1) Part 97 of this subchapter prescribes a standard instrument approach procedure for the first airport of intended landing; and

(2) For at least 1 hour before and 1 hour after the estimated time of arrival at the airport, the weather reports or forecasts or any combination of them, indicate—

(i) The ceiling will be at least 2,000 feet above airport elevation; and

(ii) Visibility will be at least 3 miles.

§ 91.24 ATC transponder and altitude reporting equipment and use.

(a) *All airspace: U.S.-registered civil aircraft.* For operations not conducted under parts 121, 127, or 135 of this chapter, ATC transponder equipment installed within the time periods indicated below must meet the performance and environmental requirements of the following TSO's:.

(1) *Through January 1, 1992:* (i) Any class of TSO-C74b or any class of TSO-C74c as appropriate, provided that the equiment was manufactured before January 1, 1990; or

(ii) The appropriate class of TSO-C112 (Mode S).

(2) *After January 1, 1992:* The appropriate class of TSO-C112 (Mode S). For purposes of paragraph (a)(2) of this section "installation" does not include—

(i) Temporary installation of TSO-C74b or TSO-C74c substitute equipment, as appropriate, during maintenance of the permanent equipment;

(ii) Reinstallation of equipment after temporary removal for maintenance; or

(iii) For fleet operations, installation of equipment in a fleet aircraft after removal of the equipment for maintenance from another aircraft in the same operator's fleet.

(b) *All airspace.* No person may operate an aircraft in the airspace described in paragraphs (b)(1) through (b)(5) of this section, unless that aircraft is equipped with an operable coded radar beacon transponder having either Mode 3/A 4096 code capability, replying to Mode 3/A interrogations with the code specified by ATC or a Mode S capability, replying to Mode 3/A interrogations with the code specified by ATC and intermode and Mode S interrogations in accordance with the applicable provisions specified in TSO C-112, and that aircraft is equipped with automatic pressure altitude reporting equipment having a Mode C capability that automatically replies to Mode C interrogations by transmitting pressure altitude information in 100-foot increments. This requirement applies—

(1) *All aircraft.* In terminal control areas and positive control areas;

(2) *Effective July 1 1989. All aircraft.* In all airspace within 30 nautical miles of a terminal control area primary airport, from the surface upward to 10,000 feet MSL;

(3) *Effective July 1,1989.* Notwithstanding paragraph (b)(2) of this section, any aircraft which was not originally certificated with an engine-driven electrical system or which has not subsequently been certified with such a system installed, balloon, or glider may conduct operations in the airspace within 30 nautical miles of a terminal control area primary airport provided such operations are conducted—

(i) Outside any terminal control area and positive control area; and

(ii) Below the altitude of the terminal control area ceiling or 10,000 feet MSL, whichever is lower; and

(4) *Effective December 30, 1990— All aircraft.*

(i) In the airspace of an airport radar service area, and

(ii) In all airspace above the ceiling and within the lateral boundaries of an airport radar service area upward to 10,000 feet MSL; and

(5) *All aircraft except any aircraft which was not originally certificated with an engine-driven electrical system or which has not subsequently been certified with such a system installed, balloon, or glider.*

(i) In all airspace of the 48 contiguous states and the District of Columbia:

(A) *Through June 30, 1989.* Above 12,500 feet MSL and below the floor of a positive control area, excluding the airspace at and below 2,500 feet AGL.

(B) *Effective July 1, 1989.* At and above 10,000 feet MSL and below the floor of a positive control area, excluding the airspace at and below 2,500 feet AGL; and

(ii) *Effective December 30, 1990.* In the airspace from the surface to 10,000 feet MSL within a 10-nautical-mile radius of any airport listed in Appendix D of this part excluding the airspace below 1,200 feet AGL outside of the airport traffic area for that airport.

(c) *Transponder-on operation.* While in the airspace as specified in (b) of this section or in all controlled airspace, each person operating an aircraft equipped with an operable ATC transponder maintained in accordance with §91.172 of this part shall operate the transponder, including Mode C equipment if installed, and shall reply on the appropriate code or as assigned by ATC.

(c) *Controlled Airspace, all aircraft, transponder-on operation.* While in controlled airspace, each person operating an aircraft equipped with an operable ATC transponder maintained in accordance with § 91.172 of this Part shall operate the transponder, including Mode C equipment if installed, and shall reply on the appropriate code or as assigned by ATC.

(d) *ATC authorized deviations.* ATC may authorize deviations from paragraph (b) of this section—

(1) Immediately, to allow an aircraft with an inoperative transponder to continue to the airport of ultimate destination, including any intermediate stops, or to proceed to a place where suitable repairs can be made, or both;

(2) Immediately, for operations of aircraft with an operating transponder but without operating automatic pressure altitude reporting equipment having a Model C capability; and

(3) On a continuing basis, or for individual flights, for operations of aircraft without a transponder, in which case the request for a deviation must be submitted to the ATC facility having jurisdiction over the airspace concerned at least one hour before the proposed operation.

§ 91.25 VOR equipment check for IFR operations.

(a) No person may operate a civil aircraft under IFR using the VOR system of radio navigation unless the VOR equipment of that aircraft—

(1) Is maintained, checked, and inspected under an approved procedure; or

(2) Has been operationally checked within the preceding 30 days and was found to be within the limits of the permissible indicated bearing error set forth in paragraph (b) or (c) of this section.

(b) Except as provided in paragraph (c) of this section, each person conducting a VOR check under paragraph (a)(2) of this section shall—

(1) Use, at the airport of intended departure, an FAA operated or approved test signal or a test signal radiated by a certificated and appropriately rated radio repair station or, outside the United States, a test signal operated or approved by appropriate authority, to check the VOR equipment (the maximum permissible indicated bearing error is plus or minus 4 degrees).

(2) If a test signal is not available at the airport of intended departure, use a point on an airport surface designated as a VOR system checkpoint by the Administrator or, outside the United States, by appropriate authority (the maximum permissible bearing error is plus or minus 4 degrees);

(3) If neither a test signal nor a designated checkpoint on the surface is available, use an airborne checkpoint designated by the Administrator or, outside the United States, by appropriate authority (the maximum permissible bearing error is plus or minus 6 degrees) or

(4) If no check signal or point is available, while in flight—

(i) Select a VOR radial that lies along the centerline of an established VOR airway;

(ii) Select a prominent ground point along the selected radial preferably more than 20 miles from the VOR ground facility and maneuver the aircraft directly over the point at a reasonably low altitude; and

(iii) Note the VOR bearing indicated by the receiver when over the ground point (the maximum permissible variation between the published radial and the indicated bearing is 6 degrees).

(c) If dual system VOR (units independent of each other except for the antenna) is installed in the aircraft, the person checking the equipment may check one system against the other in place of the check procedures specified in paragraph (b) of this section. He shall tune both systems to the same VOR ground facility and note the indicated bearings to that station. The maximum permissible variation between the two indicated bearings is 4 degrees.

(d) Each person making the VOR operational check as specified in paragraph (b) or (c) of this section shall enter the date, place, bearing error, and sign the aircraft log or other record. In addition, if a test signal radiated by a repair station, as specified in paragraph (b)(1) of this section, is used, an entry must be made in the aircraft log or other record by the repair station certificate holder or the certificate holder's representative certifying to the bearing transmitted by the repair station for the check and the date of transmission.

[Doc. No. 1580, Amdt. 1-1, 28 FR 6704, June 29, 1963, as amended by Doc. No. 8254, 32 FR 16483, Dec. 1, 1967; Amdt. 91-122, 39 FR 19204, May 31, 1974; Amdt. 91-154, 43 FR 46234, Oct. 5, 1978]

§ 91.27 Civil aircraft: Certifications required.

(a) Except as provided in § 91.28, no person may operate a civil aircraft unless it has within it the following:

(1) An appropriate and current airworthiness certificate. Each U.S. airworthiness certificate used to comply with this paragraph (except a special flight permit, a copy of the applicable operations specifications issued under § 21.197(c) of this chapter, appropriate sections of the air carrier manual required by Parts 121 and 127 of this chapter containing that portion of the operations specifications issued under § 21.197(c), or an authorization under § 91.45), must have on it the registration number assigned to the aircraft under Part 47 of this chapter. However, the airworthiness certificate need not have on it an assigned special identification number before 10 days after that number is first affixed to the aircraft. A revised airworthiness certificate having on it an assigned special identification number, that has been affixed to an aircraft, may only be obtained upon application to an FAA Flight Standards District Office.

(2) A registration certificate issued to its owner.

(b) No person may operate a civil aircraft unless the airworthiness certificate required by paragraph (a) of this section or a special flight authorization issued under § 91.28 is displayed at the cabin or cockpit entrance so that it is legible to passengers or crew.

(c) No person may operate an aircraft with a fuel tank installed within the passenger compartment or a baggage compartment unless the installation was accomplished pursuant to Part 43 of this chapter, and a copy of FAA Form 337 authorizing that installation is on board the aircraft.

[Amdt. 91-9, 29 FR 14563, Oct. 24, 1964, as amended by Amdt. 91-15, 30 FR 3638, Mar. 19, 1965; Amdt. 91-54, 33 FR 7623, May 23, 1968; Amdt. 91-56, 33 FR 11901, Aug. 22, 1968; Amdt. 91-20, 39 FR 1353, Jan. 8, 1974; Amdt. 91-206, 52 FR 34102, Sept. 9, 1987]

§ 91.28 Special flight authorizations for foreign civil aircraft.

(a) Foreign civil aircraft may be operated without airworthiness certificates required under § 91.27 if a special flight authorization for that operation is issued under this section. Application for a special flight authorization must be made to the Regional Director of the FAA region in which the applicant is located, or to the region within which the U.S. point of entry is located. However, in the case of an aircraft to be operated in the U.S. for the purpose of demonstration at an air show, the application may be made to the Regional Director of the FAA region in which the air show is located.

(b) The Administrator may issue a special flight authorization for a foreign civil aircraft subject to any conditions and limitations that the Administrator considers necessary for safe operation in the U.S. airspace.

(c) No person may operate a foreign civil aircraft under a special flight authorization unless that operation also complies with Part 375 of the Special Regulations of the Civil Aeronautics Board (14 CFR Part 375).

[Amdt. 91-178, 47 FR 13316, Mar. 29, 1982]

§ 91.29 Civil aircraft airworthiness.

(a) No person may operate a civil aircraft unless it is in an airworthy condition.

(b) The pilot in command of a civil aircraft is responsible for determining whether that aircraft is in condition for safe flight. He shall discontinue the flight when unairworthy mechanical or structural conditions occur.

§91.30 Inoperable instruments and equipment for multiengine aircraft.

(a) No person may take off a multiengine civil aircraft with inoperable instruments or equipment installed unless the following conditions are met:

(1) An approved Minimum Equipment List exists for that aircraft.

(2) The aircraft has within it a letter of authorization, issued by the FAA Flight Standards Office having jurisdiction over the area in which the operator is located, authorizing operation of the aircraft under the Minimum Equipment List. The letter of authorization may be obtained by written request of the airworthiness certificate holder. The Minimum Equipment List and the letter of authorization constitute a supplemental type certificate for the aircraft.

(3) The approved Minimum Equipment List must:

(i) Be prepared in accordance with the limitations specified in paragraph (b) of this section.

(ii) Provide for the operation of the aircraft with the instruments and equipment in an inoperable condition.

(4) The aircraft records available to the pilot must include an entry describing the inoperable instruments and equipment.

(5) The aircraft is operated under all applicable conditions and limitations contained in the Minimum Equipment List and the letter authorizing the use of the list.

(b) The following instruments and equipment may not be included in a Minimum Equipment List:

(1) Instruments and equipment that are either specifically or otherwise required by the airworthiness requirements under which the aircraft is type certificated and which are essential for safe operations under all operating conditions.

(2) Instruments and equipment required by an airworthiness directive to be in operable condition unless the airworthiness directive provides otherwise.

(3) Instruments and equipment required for specific operations by this part.

(c) A person authorized to use an approved Minimum Equipment List issued under Part 121 or 135 for a specific aircraft may use that Minimum Equipment List in connection with operations conducted with that aircraft under this part.

(d) Notwithstanding any other provision of this section, an aircraft with inoperable instruments or equipment may be operated under a special flight permit issued in accordance with §§ 21.197 and 21.199 of this chapter.

[Amdt. 91-157, 44 FR 43716, July 26, 1979]

§91.31 Civil aircraft flight manual, marking, and placard requirements.

(a) Except as provided in paragraph (d) of this section, no person may operate a civil aircraft without complying with the operating limitations specified in the approved Airplane or Rotorcraft Flight Manual, markings, and placards, or as otherwise prescribed by the certificating authority of the country of registry.

(b) No person may operate a U.S. registered civil aircraft—

(1) For which an Airplane or Rotorcraft Flight Manual is required by § 21.5 unless there is available in the aircraft a current approved Airplane of Rotorcraft Flight Manual or the manual provided for in § 121.141(b); and

(2) For which an Airplane or Rotorcraft Flight Manual is not required by § 21.5, unless there is available in the aircraft a current approved Airplane or Rotorcraft Flight Manual, approved manual material, markings, and placards, or any combination thereof.

(c) No person may operate a U.S. registered civil aircraft unless that aircraft is identified in accordance with Part 45.

(d) Any person taking off or landing a helicopter certificated under Part 29 of this chapter at a heliport constructed over water may make such momentary flight as is necessary for takeoff or landing through the prohibited range of the limiting height-speed envelope established for that helicopter if that flight through the prohibited range takes place over water on which a safe ditching can be accomplished, and if the helicopter is amphibious or is equipped with floats or other emergency flotation gear adequate to accomplish a safe emergency ditching on open water.

[Doc. No. 1580, Amdt. 1-1, 28 FR 6704, June 29, 1963, as amended by Amdt. 91-30, 31 FR 9211, July 6, 1966, as amended by Amdt. 91-103, 37 FR 20024, Sept. 23, 1972; Amdt. 91-115, 38 FR 12905, May 17, 1973; Amdt. 91-145, 43 FR 2328, Jan. 16, 1978; Amdt. 91-185, 49 FR 44440, Nov. 6, 1984]

§ 91.32 Supplemental oxygen.

(a) *General.* No person may operate a civil aircraft of U.S. registry—

(1) At cabin pressure altitudes above 12,500 feet (MSL) up to and including 14,000 feet (MSL), unless the required minimum flight crew is provided with and uses supplemental oxygen for that part of the flight at those altitudes that is of more than 30 minutes duration;

(2) At cabin pressure altitudes above 14,000 feet (MSL), unless the required minimum flight crew is provided with and uses supplemental oxygen during the entire flight time at those altitudes; and

(3) At cabin pressure altitudes above 15,000 feet (MSL), unless each occupant of the aircraft is provided with supplemental oxygen.

(b) *Pressurized cabin aircraft.* (1) No person may operate a civil aircraft of U.S. registry with a pressurized cabin—

(i) At flight altitudes above flight level 250, unless at least a 10-minute supply of supplemental oxygen in addition to any oxygen required to satisfy paragraph (a) of this section, is available for each occupant of the aircraft for use in the event that a descent is necessitated by loss of cabin pressurization; and

(ii) At flight altitudes above flight level 350, unless one pilot at the controls of the airplane is wearing and using an oxygen mask that is secured and sealed, and that either supplies oxygen at all times or automatically supplies oxygen whenever the cabin pressure altitude of the airplane exceeds 14,000 feet (MSL), except that the one pilot need not wear and use an

oxygen mask while at or below flight level 410 if there are two pilots at the controls and each pilot has a quick-donning type of oxygen mask that can be placed on the face with one hand from the ready position within five seconds, supplying oxygen and properly secured and sealed.

(2) Notwithstanding paragraph (b)(1)(ii) of this section, if for any reason at any time it is necessary for one pilot to leave his station at the controls of the aircraft when operating at flight altitudes above flight level 350, the remaining pilot at the controls shall put on and use his oxygen mask until the other pilot has returned to his station.

[Amdt. 91-75, 35 FR 6387, Apr. 21, 1970]

§ 91.33 Powered civil aircraft with standard category U.S. airworthiness certificates; instrument and equipment requirements.

(a) *General.* Except as provided in paragraphs (c)(3) and (e) of this section, no person may operate a powered civil aircraft with a standard category U.S. airworthiness certificate in any operation described in paragraphs (b) through (f) of this section unless that aircraft contains the instruments and equipment specified in those paragraphs for FAA-approved equivalents for that type of operation, and those instruments and items of equipment are in operable condition.

(b) *Visual flight rules (day).* For VFR flight during the day the following instruments and equipment are required.

(1) Airspeed indicator.
(2) Altimeter.
(3) Magnetic direction indicator.
(4) Tachometer for each engine.
(5) Oil pressure gauge for each engine using pressure system.
(6) Temperature gauge for each liquid-cooled engine.
(7) Oil temperature gauge for each air-cooled engine.
(8) Manifold pressure gauge for each altitude engine.
(9) Fuel gauge indicating the quantity of fuel in each tank.
(10) Landing gear position indicator, if the aircraft has a retractable landing gear.

(11) If the aircraft is operated for hire over water and beyond power-off gliding distance from shore, approved flotation gear readily available to each occupant, and at least one pyrotechnic signaling device.

(12) Except as to airships, an approved safety belt for all occupants who have reached their second birthday. After December 4, 1981, each safety belt must be equipped with an approved metal to metal latching device. The rated strength of each safety belt shall not be less than that corresponding with the ultimate load factors specified in the current applicable aircraft airworthiness requirements considering the dimensional characteristics of the safety belt installation for the specific seat or berth arrangement. The webbing of each safety belt shall be replaced as required by the Administrator.

(13) For small civil airplanes manufactured after July 18, 1978, an approved shoulder harness for each front seat. The shoulder harness must be designed to protect the occupant from serious head injury when the occupant experiences the ultimate intertia forces specified in § 23.561(b)(2) of this chapter. Each shoulder harness installed at a flight crewmember station must permit the crewmember, when seated and with his safety belt and shoulder harness fastened, to perform all functions necessary for flight operations. For purposes of this paragraph—

(i) The date of manufacture of an airplane is the date the inspection acceptance records reflect that the airplane is complete and meets the FAA Approved Type Design Data; and

(ii) A front seat is a seat located at a flight crewmember station or any seat located alongside such a seat.

(14) For normal, utility, and acrobatic category airplanes with a seating configuration, excluding pilot seats, of nine or less, manufactured after December 12, 1986, a shoulder harness for—

(i) Each front seat that meets the requirements of § 23.785 (g) and (h) of this chapter in effect on December 12, 1985;

(ii) Each additional seat that meets the requirements of § 23.785(g) of this

chapter in effect on December 12, 1985.

(c) *Visual flight rules (night)*. For VFR flight at night the following instruments and equipment are required:

(1) Instruments and equipment specified in paragraph (b) of this section.

(2) Approved position lights.

(3) An approved aviation red or aviation white anticollision light system on all U.S. registered civil aircraft. Anticollision light systems initially installed after August 11, 1971, on aircraft for which a type certificate was issued or applied for before August 11, 1971, must at least meet the anticollision light standards of Part 23, 25, 27, or 29, as applicable, that were in effect on August 10, 1971, except that the color may be either aviation red or aviation white. In the event of failure of any light of the anticollision light system, operations with the aircraft may be continued to a stop where repairs or replacement can be made.

(4) If the aircraft is operated for hire, one electric landing light.

(5) An adequate source of electrical energy for all installed electrical and radio equipment.

(6) One spare set of fuses, or three spare fuses of each kind required.

(d) *Instrument flight rules*. For IFR flight the following instruments and equipment are required:

(1) Instruments and equipment specified in paragraph (b) of this section and for night flight, instruments and equipment specified in paragraph (c) of this section.

(2) Two-way radio communications system and navigational equipment appropriate to the ground facilities to be used.

(3) Gyroscopic rate-of-turn indicator, except on the following aircraft:

(i) Large airplanes with a third attitude instrument system useable through flight attitudes of 360 degrees of pitch and roll and installed in accordance with § 121.305(j) of this chapter; and

(ii) Rotorcraft, type certificated under Part 29 of this chapter, with a third attitude instrument system useable through flight attitudes of ±80 degrees of pitch and ±120 degrees of roll and installed in accordance with § 29.1303(g) of this chapter.

(4) Slip-skid indicator.

(5) Sensitive altimeter adjustable for barometric presure.

(6) A clock displaying hours, minutes, and seconds with a sweep-second pointer or digital presentation.

(7) Generator of adequate capacity.

(8) Gyroscopic bank and pitch indicator (artificial horizon).

(9) Gyroscopic direction indicator (directional gyro or equivalent).

(e) *Flight at and above 24,000 feet MSL.* If VOR naviagtional equipment is required under paragraph (d)(2) of this section, no person may operate a U.S. registered civil aircraft within the 50 states, and the District of Columbia, at or above 24,000 feet MSL unless that aircraft is equipped with approved distance measuring equipment (DME). When DME required by this paragraph fails at and above 24,000 feet MSL, the pilot in command of the aircraft shall notify ATC immediatley, and may then continue operations at and above 24,000 feet MSL to the next airport of intended landing at which repairs or replacement of the equipment can be made.

(f) *Category II operations.* For Category II operations the instruments and equipment specified in paragraph (d) of this section and Appendix A to this part are required. This pargraph does not apply to operations conducted by the holder of a certificate issued under Part 121 of this chapter.

§ 91.34 Category II manual.

(a) No person may operate a civil aircraft of U.S. registry in a Category II operation unless—

(1) There is available in the aircraft a current approved Category II manual for that aircraft;

(2) The operation is conducted in accordance with the procedures, instructions, and limitations in that manual; and

(3) The instruments and equipment listed in the manual that are required for a particular Category II operation have been inspected and maintained in accordance with the maintenance program contained in that manual.

(b) Each operator shall keep a current copy of the approved manual at its principal base of operations and shall make it available for inspection upon request of the Administrator.

(c) This section does not apply to operations conducted by the holder of a certificate issued under Part 121 of this chapter.

§ 91.35 Flight recorders and cockpit voice recorders.

(a) No holder of an air carrier or commercial operator certificate may conduct any operation under this part with an aircraft listed in his operations specifications or current list of aircraft used in air transportation unless that aircraft complies with any applicable flight recorder and cockpit voice recorder requirements of the part under which its certificate is issued; except that it may—

(1) Ferry an aircraft with an inoperative flight recorder or cockpit voice recorder from a place where repair or replacement cannot be made to a place where they can be made;

(2) Continue a flight as originally planned, if the flight recorder or cockpit voice recorder becomes inoperative after the aircraft has taken off;

(3) Conduct an airworthiness flight test , during whiich the flight recorder or cockpit voice recorder is turned off to test it or to test any communications or electrical equipment installed in the aircraft; or

(4) Ferry a newly acquired aircraft from the place where possession of it was taken to a place where the flight recorder or cockpitvoice recorder is to be installed.

(b) No person may operate a U.S. civil registered, multiengine, turbine-powered airplane or rotorcraft having a passenger seating configuration, excluding any pilot seats of 10 or more that has been manufactured after October 11, 1991, unless it is equipped with one or more approved flight recorders that utilize a digital method of recording and storing data and a method of readily retrieving that data from the storage medium, that are capable of recording the data specified in Appendix E, for an airplane, or Appendix F, for a rotorcraft, of this part within the range, accuracy, and recording interval specified, and that are capable of retaining no less than 8 hours of aircraft operation.

(c) Whenever a flight recorder, required by this section, is installed, it must be operated continuously from the instant the airplane begins the takeoff roll or the rotorcraft begins lift-off until the airplane has completed the landing roll or the rotorcraft has landed at its destination.

(d) Unless otherwise authorized by the Administrator, after October 11, 1991, no person may operate a U.S. civil registered, multiengine, turbine-powered airplane or rotorcraft having a passenger seating configuration of six passengers or more and for which two pilots are required by type certification or operating rule unless it is equipped with an approved cockpit voice recorder that:

(1) Is installed in compliance with § 23.1457 (a)(1) and (2), (b), (c), (d), (e), (f), and (g); §25.1457 (a) (1) and (2), (b), (c), (d), (e), (f), and (g); §27.1457(a) (1) and (2), (b), (c), (d), (e), (f), and (g): or § 29.1457(a) (1) and (2), (b), (c), (d), (e), (f), and (g) of this chapter as applicable; and

(2) Is operated continuously from the use of the check list before the flight to completion of the final check list at the end of the flight.

(e) In complying with this section, an approved cockpit voice recorder having an erasure feature may be used, so that at any time during the operation of the recorder, information recorded more than 15 minutes earlier may be erased or otherwise obliterated.

(f) In the event of an accident or occurrence requiring immediate notification to the National Transportation Safety Board under Part 830 of its regulations that results in the termination of the flight, any operator who has installed approved flight recorders and approved cockpit voice recorders shall keep the recorded information for at least 60 days, or if requested by the Administrator or the Board, for a longer period. Information obtained from the record is used to assist in determining the cause of accidents or occurrences in connection with investigation under Part 830. The Administrator does not use the cockpit voice recorder record in any civil penalty or certificate action.

§ 91.36 Data correspondence between automatically reported pressure altitude data and the pilot's altitude reference.

No person may operate any automatic pressure altitude reporting equipment associated with a radar beacon transponder—

(a) When deactivation of that equipment is directed by ATC;

(b) Unless, as installed, that equipment was tested and calibrated to transmit altitude data corresponding within 125 feet (on a 95-percent probability basis) of the indicated or calibrated datum of the altimeter normally used to maintain flight altitude, with that altimeter referenced to 29.92 inches of mercury for altitudes from sea level to the maximum operating altitude of the aircraft; or

(c) After September 1, 1979, unless the altimeters and digitizers in that equipment meet the standards in TSO-C10b and TSO-C88, respectively.

§ 91.37 Transport category civil airplane weight limitations

(a) No person may take off any transport category airplane (other than a turbine engine powered airplane certificated after September 30, 1958) unless—

(1) The takeoff weight does not exceed the authorized maximum takeoff weight for the elevation of the airport of takeoff;

(2) The elevation of the airport of takeoff is within the altitude range for which maximum takeoff weights have been determined;

(3) Normal consumption of fuel and oil in flight to the airport of intended landing will leave a weight on arrival not in excess of the authorized maximum landing weight for the elevation of that airport; and

(4) The elevations of the airport of intended landing and of all specified alternate airports are within the altitude range for which maximum landing weights have been determined.

(b) No person may operate a turbine engine powered transport category airplane certificated after September 30, 1958 contrary to the Airplane Flight Manual, nor take off that airplane unless—

(1) The takeoff weight does not exceed the takeoff weight specified in the Airplane Flight Manual for the elevation of the airport and for the ambient temperature existing at the time of takeoff;

(2) Normal consumption of fuel and oil in flight to the airport of intended landing and to the alternate airports will leave a weight on arrival not in excess of the landing weight specified in the Airplane Flight Manual for the elevation of each of the airports involved and for the ambient temperatures expected at the time of landing;

(3) The takeoff weight does not exceed the weight shown in the Airplane Flight Manual to correspond with the minimum distances required for takeoff considering the elevation of the airport, the runway to be used, the effective runway gradient, and the ambient temperature and wind component existing at the time of takeoff; and

(4) Where the takeoff distance includes a clearway, the clearway distance is not greater than one-half of—

(i) The takeoff run, in the case of airplanes certificated after September 30, 1958 and before August 30, 1959; or

(ii) The runway length, in the case of airplanes certificated after August 29, 1959.

(c) No person may take off a turbine engine powered transport category airplane certificated after August 29, 1959 unless, in addition to the requirements of paragraph (b) of this section—

(1) The accelerate-stop distance is no greater than the length of the runway plus the length of the stopway (if present);

(2) The takeoff distance is no greater than the length of the runway plus the length of the clearway (if present); and

(3) The takeoff run is no greater than the length of the runway.

[Amdt. 91-10, 29 FR 18290, Dec. 24, 1964]

§ 91.38 Increased maximum certificated weights for certain airplanes operated in Alaska.

(a) Notwithstanding any other provision of the Federal Aviation Regulations, the Administrator will, as provided in this section, approve an increase in the maximum certificated weight of any airplane type certificated under Aeronautics Bulletin No. 7-A of the U.S. Department of Commerce dated January 1, 1931, as amended, or under the normal category of Part 4a of the former Civil Air Regulations (Part 4a of this chapter, 1964 ed.), if that airplane is operated in the State of Alaska by—

(1) An air taxi operator or other air carrier; or

(2) The U.S. Department of Interior in conducting its game and fish law enforcement activities or its management, fire detection, and fire suppression activities concerning public lands.

(b) The maximum certificated weight approved under this section may not exceed—

(1) 12,500 pounds;

(2) 115 percent of the maximum weight listed in the FAA Aircraft Specifications;

(3) The weight at which the airplane meets the positive maneuvering load factor requirement for the normal category specified in § 23.337 of this chapter; or

(4) The weight at which the airplane meets the climb performance requirements under which it was type certificated.

(c) In determining the maximum certificated weight the Administrator considers the structural soundness of the airplane and the terrain to be traversed.

(d) The maximum certificated weight determined under this section is added to the airplane's operation limitations and is identified as the maximum weight authorized for operations within the State of Alaska.

[Amdt. 91-27, 31 FR 5250, Apr. 1, 1966, as amended by Amdt. 91-41, 32 FR 8406, June 13, 1967]

§ 91.39 Restricted category civil aircraft; operating limitations.

(a) No person may operate a restricted category civil aircraft:

(1) For other than the special purpose for which it is certificated; or

(2) In an operation other than one necessary for the accomplishment of the work activity directly associated with that special purpose.

For the purposes of this paragraph, the operation of a restricted category civil aircraft to provide flight crewmember training in a special purpose operation for which the aircraft is certificated is considered to be an operation for that special purpose.

(b) No person may operate a restricted category civil aircraft carrying persons or property for compensation or hire. For the purposes of this paragraph, a special purpose operation involving the carriage of persons or materials necessary for the accomplishment of that operation such as crop dusting, seeding, spraying, and banner towing (including the carrying of required persons or materials to the location of that operation), and an operation for the purpose of providing flight crew-member training in a special purpose operation, are not considered to be the carrying of persons or property for compensation or hire.

(c) No person may be carried on a restricted category civil aircraft unless:

(1) He is a flight crewmember;

(2) He is a flight crewmember trainee;

(3) He performs an essential function in connection with a special purpose operation for which the aircraft is certificated; or

(4) He is necessary for the accomplishment of the work activity directly associated with that special purpose.

(d) Except when operating in accordance with the terms and conditions of a certificate of waiver or special operating limitations issued by the Administrator, no person may operate a restricted category civil aircraft within the United States—

(1) Over a densely populated area;

(2) In a congested airway; or

(3) Near a busy airport where passenger transport operations are conducted.

(e) An application for a certificate of waiver under paragraph (d) of this section is made on a form and in a manner prescribed by the Administrator and must be submitted to the Flight Standards District Office having jurisdiction over the area in which the applicant is located.

(f) After December 9, 1977, this section does not apply to nonpassenger-carrying civil rotorcraft external-load operations conducted under Part 133 of this chapter.

(g) No person may operate a small restricted category civil airplane, manufactured after July 18, 1978, unless an approved shoulder harness is installed for each front seat. The shoulder harness must be designed to protect each occupant from serious head injury when the occupant experiences the ultimate inertia forces specified in §23.561(b)(2) of this chapter. The shoulder harness installation at each flight crewmember station must permit the crewmember, when seated and with his safety belt and shoulder harness fastened, to perform all functions necessary for flight operations. For purposes of this paragraph—

(1) The date of manufacture of an airplane is the date the inspection acceptance records reflect that the airplane is complete and meets the FAA Approved Type Design Data; and

(2) A front seat is a seat located at a flight crewmember station or any seat located alongside such a seat.

[Doc. No. 1580, Amdt. 1-1, 28 FR 6704, June 29, 1963, as amended by Amdt. 91-12, 30 FR 2532, Feb. 26, 1965; Amdt. 91-29, 21 FR 8355, June 15, 1966; Amdt. 91-58, 33 FR 12826, Sept. 11, 1968; Amdt. 91-138, 42 FR 24197, May 12, 1977; Amdt. 91-139, 42 FR 30603, June 16, 1977]

§91.40 Limited category civil aircraft; operating limitations.

No person may operate a limited category civil aircraft carrying persons or property for compensation or hire.

[Amdt. 91-9, 29 FR 14563, Oct. 24, 1964]

§91.41 Provisionally certificated civil aircraft; operating limitations.

(a) No person may operate a provisionally certificated civil aircraft unless he is eligible for a provisional airworthiness certificate under §21.213 of this chapter.

(b) No person may operate a provisionally certificated civil aircraft outside the United States unless he has specific authority to do so from the Administrator and each foreign country involved.

(c) Unless otherwise authorized by the Director of Airworthiness, no person may operate a provisionally certificated civil aircraft in air transportation.

(d) Unless otherwise authorized by the Administrator, no person may operate a provisionally certificated civil aircraft except—

(1) In direct conjunction with the type or supplemental type certification of that aircraft;

(2) For training flight crews, including simulated air carrier operations;

(3) Demonstration flights by the manufacturer for prospective purchasers;

(4) Market surveys by the manufacturer;

(5) Flight checking of instruments, accessories, and equipment, that do not affect the basic airworthiness of the aircraft; or

(6) Service testing of the aircraft.

(e) Each person operating a provisionally certificated civil aircraft shall operate within the prescribed limitations displayed in the aircraft or set forth in the provisional aircraft flight manual or other appropriate document. However, when operating in direct conjunction with the type or supplemental type certification of the aircraft, he shall operate under the experimental aircraft limitations of §21.191 of this chapter and when flight testing, shall operate under the requirements of §91.93 of this chapter.

(f) Each person operating a provisionally certificated civil aircraft shall establish approved procedures for—

(1) The use and guidance of flight and ground personnel in operating under this section; and

(2) Operating in and out of airports where takeoffs or approaches over populated areas are necessary.

No person may operate that aircraft except in compliance with the approved procedures.

(g) Each person operating a provisionally certificated civil aircraft shall ensure that each flight crewmember is properly certificated and has adequate knowledge of, and familiarity with, the aircraft and procedures to be used by that crewmember.

(h) Each person operating a provisionally certificated civil aircraft shall maintain it as required by applicable regulations and as may be specially prescribed by the Administrator.

(i) Whenever the manufacturer, or the Administrator, determines that a change in design, construction or operation is necessary to ensure safe operation, no person may operate a provisionally certificated civil aircraft until that change has been made and approved. Section 21.99 of this chapter applies to operations under this section.

(j) Each person operating a provisionally certificated civil aircraft—

(1) May carry in that aircraft only persons who have a proper interest in the operations allowed by this section or who are specifically authorized by both the manufacturer and the Administrator; and

(2) Shall advise each person carried that the aircraft is provisionally certificated.

(k) The Administrator may prescribe additional limitations or procedures that he considers necessary, including limitations on the number of persons who may be carried in the aircraft.

[Doc. No. 1580, Amdt. 1–1, 28 FR 6704, June 29, 1963, as amended by Amdt. 91–30, 31 FR 9211, July 6, 1966; Amdt. 91–166, 45 FR 47838, July 17, 1980]

§ 91.42 Aircraft having experimental certificates; operating limitations.

(a) No person may operate an aircraft that has an experimental certificate:

(1) For other than the purpose for which the certificate was issued; or

(2) Carrying persons or property for compensation or hire.

(b) No person may operate an aircraft that has an experimental certificate outside of an area assigned by the Administrator until it is shown that:

(1) The aircraft is controllable throughout its normal range of speeds and throughout all the maneuvers to be executed; and

(2) The aircraft has no hazardous operating characteristics or design features.

(c) Unless otherwise authorized by the Administrator in special operating limitations, no person may operate an aircraft that has an experimental certificate over a densely populated area or in a congested airway. The Administrator may issue special operating limitations for particular aircraft to permit takeoffs and landings to be conducted over a densely populated area or in a congested airway, in accordance with terms and conditions specified in the authorization in the interest of safety in air commerce.

(d) Each person operating an aircraft that has an experimental certificate shall:

(1) Advise each person carried of the experimental nature of the aircraft;

(2) Operate under VFR, day only, unless otherwise specifically authorized by the Administrator; and

(3) Notify the control tower of the experimental nature of the aircraft when operating the aircraft into or out of airports with operating control towers.

(e) The Administrator may prescribe additional limitations that he considers necessary, including limitations on the persons that may be carried in the aircraft.

[Amdt. 91–53, 33 FR 6859, May 7, 1968, as amended by Amdt. 91–109, 38 FR 1176, Jan. 10, 1973]

§ 91.43 Special rules for foreign civil aircraft.

(a) *General.* In addition to the other applicable regulations of this part, each person operating a foreign civil aircraft within the United States shall comply with this section.

(b) *VFR.* No person may conduct VFR operations which require two-way radio communications under this part, unless at least one crewmember of that aircraft is able to conduct two-way radio communications in the English language and is on duty during that operation.

(c) *IFR.* No person may operate a foreign civil aircraft under IFR unless—

(1) That aircraft is equipped with—

(i) Radio equipment allowing two-way radio communication with ATC when it is operated in a control zone or control area; and

(ii) Radio navigational equipment appropriate to the navigational facilities to be used.

(2) Each person piloting the aircraft—

(i) Holds a current United States instrument rating or is authorized by his foreign airman certificate to pilot under IFR; and

(ii) Is thoroughly familiar with the United States en route, holding, and letdown procedures; and

(3) At least one crewmember of that aircraft is able to conduct two-way radiotelephone communications in the English language and that crewmember is on duty while the aircraft is approaching, operating within, or leaving the United States.

(d) *Overwater.* Each person operating a foreign civil aircraft overwater off the shores of the United States shall give flight notification or file a flight plan, in accordance with the Supplementary Procedures for the ICAO region concerned.

(e) *Flight at and above 24,000 feet MSL.* If VOR navigation equipment is required under paragraph (c)(1)(ii) of this section, no person may operate a foreign civil aircraft within the 50 states and the District of Columbia at or above 24,000 feet MSL, unless the aircraft is equipped with distance measuring equipment (DME) capable of receiving and indicating distance information from the VORTAC facilities to be used. When DME required by this paragraph fails at and above 24,000 feet MSL the pilot in command of the aircraft shall notify ATC immediately, and may then continue operations at and above 24,000 feet MSL to the next airport of intended landing at

which repairs or replacement of the equipment can be made.

However, paragraph (e) of this section does not apply to foreign civil aircraft that are not equipped with DME when operated for the following purposes, and if ATC is notified prior to each takeoff:

(1) Ferry flights to and from a place in the United States where repairs or alterations are to be made.

(2) Ferry flights to a new country of registry.

(3) Flight of a new aircraft of U.S. manufacture for the purpose of—

(i) Flight testing the aircraft;

(ii) Training foreign flight crews in the operation of the aircraft; or

(iii) Ferrying the aircraft for export delivery outside the United States.

(4) Ferry, demonstration, and test flights of an aircraft brought to the United States for the purpose of demonstration or testing the whole or any part thereof.

[Doc. No. 1580, Amdt. 1–1, 28 FR 6704, June 29, 1963, as amended by Amdt. 91–23, 30 FR 10288, Aug. 19, 1965; Amdt. 91–28, 31 FR 6265, Apr. 23, 1966; Amdt. 91–48, 32 FR 16392, Nov. 30, 1967; Amdt. 91–59, 33 FR 12825, Sept. 11, 1968; Amdt. 91–133, 41 FR 47228, Oct. 28, 1976; Amdt. 91–152, 43 FR 22640, May 25, 1978]

§ 91.45 Authorization for ferry flights with one engine inoperative.

(a) *General.* The holder of an air carrier operating certificate, an operating certificate issued under Part 125, or until January 1, 1983, an operating certificate issued under Part 121, may conduct a ferry flight of a four-engine airplane or a turbine-engine-powered airplane equipped with three engines, with one engine inoperative, to a base for the purpose of repairing that engine subject to the following:

(1) The airplane model has been test flown and found satisfactory for safe flight in accordance with paragraph (b) or (c) of this section, as appropriate. However, each operator who before November 19, 1966, has shown that a model of airplane with an engine inoperative is satisfactory for safe flight by a test flight conducted in accordance with performance data contained in the applicable Airplane

Flight Manual under paragraph (a)(2) of this section need not repeat the test flight for that model.

(2) The approved Airplane Flight Manual contains the following performance data and the flight is conducted in accordance with that data:

(i) Maximum weight.

(ii) Center of gravity limits.

(iii) Configuration of the inoperative propeller (if applicable).

(iv) Runway length for takeoff (including temperature accountability).

(v) Altitude range.

(vi) Certificate limitations.

(vii) Ranges of operational limits.

(viii) Performance information.

(ix) Operating procedures.

(3) The operator's manual contains operating procedures for the safe operation of the airplane, including specific requirements for—

(i) A limitation that the operating weight on any ferry flight must be the minimum necessary therefor with the necessary reserve fuel load;

(ii) A limitation that takeoffs must be made from dry runways unless, based on a showing of actual operating takeoff techniques on wet runways with one engine inoperative, takeoffs with full controllability from wet runways have been approved for the specific model aircraft and included in the Airplane Flight Manual;

(iii) Operations from airports where the runways may require a takeoff or approach over populated areas; and

(iv) Inspection procedures for determining the operating condition of the operative engines.

(4) No person may take off an airplane under this section if—

(i) The initial climb is over thickly populated areas; or

(ii) Weather conditions at the takeoff or destination airport are less than those required for VFR flight.

(5) Persons other than required flight crewmembers shall not be carried during the flight.

(6) No person may use a flight crewmember for flight under this section unless that crewmember is thoroughly familiar with the operating procedures for one-engine inoperative ferry flight contained in the certificate holder's manual, and the limitations and performance information in the Airplane Flight Manual.

(b) *Flight tests: Reciprocating engine powered airplanes.* The airplane performance of a reciprocating engine powered airplane with one engine inoperative must be determined by flight test as follows:

(1) A speed not less than $1.3V_{s1}$ must be chosen at which the airplane may be controlled satisfactorily in a climb with the critical engine inoperative (with its propeller removed or in a configuration desired by the operator) and with all other engines operating at the maximum power determined in paragraph (b)(3) of this section.

(2) The distance required to accelerate to the speed listed in paragraph (b)(1) of this section and to climb to 50 feet must be determined with—

(i) The landing gear extended;

(ii) The critical engine inoperative and its propeller removed or in a configuration desired by the operator; and

(iii) The other engines operating at not more than the maximum power established under paragraph (b)(3) of this section.

(3) The takeoff, flight, and landing procedures such as the approximate trim settings, method of power application, maximum power, and speed, must be established.

(4) The performance must be determined at a maximum weight not greater than the weight that allows a rate of climb of at least 400 feet a minute in the en route configuration set forth in § 25.67(d) of this chapter at an altitude of 5,000 feet.

(5) The performance must be determined using temperature accountability for the takeoff field length, computed in accordance with § 25.61 of this chapter.

(c) *Flight tests: Turbine engine powered airplanes.* The airplane performance of a turbine engine powered airplane with one engine inoperative must be determined in accordance with the following, by flight tests including at least three takeoff tests:

(1) Takeoff speeds V_R and V_2, not less than the corresponding speeds under which the airplane was type certificated under § 25.107 of this chapter, must be chosen at which the airplane may be controlled satisfactorily

with the critical engine inoperative (with its propeller removed or in a configuration desired by the operator, if applicable) and with all other engines operating at not more than the power selected for type certification, as set forth in § 25.101 of this chapter.

(2) The minimum takeoff field length must be the horizontal distance required to accelerate, and climb to the 35-foot height at V_2 speed (including any additional speed increment obtained in the tests), multiplied by 115 percent, and determined with—

(i) The landing gear extended;

(ii) The critical engine inoperative and its propeller removed or in a configuration desired by the operator (if applicable); and

(iii) The other engines operating at not more than the power selected for type certification, as set forth in § 25.101 of this chapter.

(3) The takeoff, flight, and landing procedures such as the approximate trim settings, method of power application, maximum power, and speed, must be established. The airplane must be satisfactorily controllable during the entire takeoff run when operated according to these procedures.

(4) The performance must be determined at a maximum weight not greater than the weight determined under § 25.121(c) of this chapter, but with—

(i) The actual steady gradient of the final takeoff climb requirement not less than 1.2 percent at the end of the takeoff path with two critical engines inoperative; and

(ii) The climb speed not less than the two-engine inoperative trim speed for the actual steady gradient of the final takeoff climb prescribed by paragraph (c)(4)(i) of this section.

(5) The airplane must be satisfactorily controllable in a climb with two critical engines inoperative. Climb performance may be shown by calculations based on, and equal in accuracy to, the results of testing.

(6) The performance must be determined using temperature accountability for takeoff distance and final takeoff climb, computed in accordance with § 25.101 of this chapter.

For the purposes of paragraphs (c) (4) and (5) of this section, "two critical engines" means two adjacent engines on one side of an airplane with four engines, and the center engine and one outboard engine on an airplane with three engines.

[Amdt. 91-33, 31 FR 13526, Oct. 20, 1966, as amended by Amdt. 91-34, 31 FR 14929, Nov. 26, 1966; Amdt. 91-133, 41 FR 47228, Oct. 28, 1976; Amdt. 91-179, 47 FR 25117, June 10, 1982]

§ 91.47 Emergency exits for airplanes carrying passengers for hire.

(a) Notwithstanding any other provision of this chapter, no person may operate a large airplane (type certificated under the Civil Air Regulations effective before April 9, 1957) in passenger-carrying operations for hire, with more than the number of occupants:

(1) Allowed under Civil Air Regulation § 4b.362 (a), (b), and (c) of this chapter, as in effect on December 20 1951; or

(2) Approved under Special Civil Air Regulations SR-387, SR-389, SR-389A or SR-389B, or under this section as in effect.

However, an airplane type listed in the following table may be operated with up to the listed number of occupants (including crewmembers) and the corresponding number of exits (including emergency exits and doors) approved for the emergency exit of passengers or with an occupant-exit configuration approved under paragraph (b) or (c) of this section:

Airplane type	Maximum number of occupants including all crewmembers	Corresponding number of exits authorized for passenger use
B-307	61	4
B-377	96	9
C-46	67	4
CV-240	53	6
CV-340 and CV-440	53	6
DC-3	35	4
DC-3(Super)	39	5
DC-4	86	5
DC-6	87	7
DC-6B	112	11
L-18	17	3
L-049, L-649, L-749	87	7
L-1049 series	96	9
M-202	53	6
M-404	53	7

Airplane type	Maximum number of occupants including all crewmembers	Corresponding number of exits authorized for passenger use
Viscount 700 series	53	7

(b) Occupants in addition to those authorized under paragraph (a) of this section may be carried as follows:

(1) For each additional floor-level exit at least 24 inches wide by 48 inches high, with an unobstructed 20-inch wide access aisleway between the exit and the main passenger aisle: 12 additional occupants.

(2) For each additional window exit located over a wing that meets the requirements of the airworthiness standards under which the airplane was type certificated or that is large enough to inscribe an ellipse 19 x 26 inches: Eight additional occupants.

(3) For each additional window exit that is not located over a wing but that otherwise complies with paragraph (b)(2) of this section: Five additional occupants.

(4) For each airplane having a ratio (as computed from the table in paragraph (a) of this section) of maximum number of occupants to number of exits greater than 14:1, and for each airplane that does not have at least one full-size door-type exit in the side of the fuselage in the rear part of the cabin, the first additional exit must be a floor-level exit that complies with paragraph (b)(1) of this section and must be located in the rear part of the cabin on the opposite side of the fuselage from the main entrance door. However, no person may operate an airplane under this section carrying more than 115 occupants unless there is such an exit on each side of the fuselage in the rear part of the cabin.

(c) No person may eliminate any approved exit except in accordance with the following:

(1) The previously authorized maximum number of occupants must be reduced by the same number of additional occupants authorized for that exit under this section.

(2) Exits must be eliminated in accordance with the following priority schedule: First, non-over-wing window exits; second, over-wing-window exits; third, floor-level exits located in the forward part of the cabin; fourth, floor-level exits located in the rear of the cabin.

(3) At least one exit must be retained on each side of the fuselage regardless of the number of occupants.

(4) No person may remove any exit that would result in a ratio of maximum number of occupants to approved exits greater than 14:1.

(d) This section does not relieve any person operating under Part 121 of this chapter from complying with § 121.291 of this chapter.

[Amdt. 91-22, 30 FR 8516, July 3, 1965]

§ 91.49   Aural speed warning device.

No person may operate a transport category airplane in air commerce unless that airplane is equipped with an aural speed warning device that complies with § 25.1303(c)(1).

[Amdt. 91-15, 30, FR 3638, Mar. 19, 1965, as amended by Amdt. 91-97, 37 FR 4327, Mar. 2, 1972]

§ 91.50   [Reserved]

§ 91.51   Altitude alerting system or device; turbojet powered civil airplanes.

(a) Except as provided in paragraph (d) of this section, no person may operate a turbojet powered U.S. registered civil airplane unless that airplane is equipped with an approved altitude alerting system or device that is in operable condition and meets the requirements of paragraph (b) of this section.

(b) Each altitude alerting system or device required by paragraph (a) of this section must be able to—

(1) Alert the pilot: (i) Upon approaching a preselected altitude in either ascent or descent, by a sequence of both aural and visual signals in sufficient time to establish level flight at that preselected altitude; or

(ii) Upon approaching a preselected altitude in either ascent or descent, by a sequence of visual signals in sufficient time to establish level flight at that preselected altitude, and when deviating above and below that preselected altitude, by an aural signal;

(2) Provide the required signals from sea level to the highest operating altitude approved for the airplane in which it is installed;

(3) Preselect altitudes in increments that are commensurate with the altitudes at which the aircraft is operated;

(4) Be tested without special equipment to determine proper operation of the alerting signals; and

(5) Accept necessary barometric pressure settings if the system or device operates on barometric pressure.

However, for operations below 3,000 feet AGL, the system or device need only provide one signal, either visual or aural, to comply with this paragraph. A radio altimeter may be included to provide the signal, if the operator has an approved procedure for its use to determine DH or MDA, as appropriate.

(c) Each operator to which this section applies must establish and assign procedures for the use of the altitude alerting system or device and each flight crewmember must comply with those procedures assigned to him.

(d) Paragraph (a) of this section does not apply to any operation of an airplane that has an experimental certificate or to the operation of an airplane for the following purposes:

(1) Ferrying a newly acquired airplane from the place where possession of it was taken to a place where the altitude alerting system or device is to be installed.

(2) Continuing a flight as originally planned, if the altitude alerting system or device becomes inoperative after the airplane has taken off; however, the flight may not depart from a place where repair or replacement can be made.

(3) Ferrying an airplane with an inoperative altitude alerting system or device from a place where repair or replacement cannot be made to a place where they can be made.

(4) Conducting an airworthiness flight test of the airplane.

(5) Ferrying an airplane to a place outside the United States for the purpose of registering it in a foreign country.

(6) Conducting a sales demonstration of the operation of the airplane.

(7) Training foreign flight crews in the operation of the airplane prior to ferrying it to a place outside the United States for the purpose of registering it in a foreign country.

[Amdt. 91-57, 33 FR 12180, Aug. 29, 1968, as amended by Amdt. 91-97, 37 FR 4327, Mar. 2, 1972; Amdt. 91-133, 41 FR 47228, Oct. 28, 1976; Amdt. No. 91-142, 42 FR 42187, Aug. 22, 1977]

§91.52 **Emergency locator transmitters.**

(a) Except as provided in paragraphs (e) and (f) of this section, no person may operate a U.S. registered civil airplane unless it meets the applicable requirements of paragraphs (b), (c), and (d) of this section.

(b) To comply with paragraph (a) of this section, each U.S. registered civil airplane must be equipped as follows:

(1) For operations governed by the supplemental air carrier and commercial operator rules of Part 121 of this chapter, or the air travel club rules of Part 123 of this chapter, there must be attached to the airplane an automatic type emergency locator transmitter that is in operable condition and meets the applicable requirements of TSO-C91;

(2) For charter flights governed by the domestic and flag air carrier rules of Part 121 of this chapter, there must be attached to the airplane an automatic type emergency locator transmitter that is in operable condition and meets the applicable requirements of TSO-C91;

(3) For operations governed by Part 135 of this chapter, there must be attached to the airplane an automatic type emergency locator transmitter that is in operable condition and meets the applicable requirements of TSO-C91; and

(4) For operations other than those specified in paragraphs (b) (1), (2), and (3) of this section, there must be attached to the airplane a personal type or an automatic type emergency locator transmitter that is in operable condition and meets the applicable requirements of TSO-C91.

(c) Each emergency locator transmitter required by paragraphs (a) and

(b) of this section must be attached to the airplane in such a manner that the probability of damage to the transmitter, in the event of crash impact, is minimized. Fixed and deployable automatic type transmitters must be attached to the airplane as far aft as practicable.

(d) Batteries used in the emergency locator transmitters required by paragraphs (a) and (b) of this section must be replaced (or recharged, if the battery is rechargeable)—

(1) When the transmitter has been in use for more than one cumulative hour; or

(2) When 50 percent of their useful life (or, for rechargeable batteries, 50 percent of their useful life of charge), as established by the transmitter manufacturer under TSO-C91, paragraph (g)(2) has expired.

The new expiration date for the replacement (or recharge) of the battery must be legibly marked on the outside of the transmitter and entered in the aircraft maintenance record. Paragraph (d)(2) of this section does not apply to batteries (such as water-activated batteries) that are essentially unaffected during probable storage intervals.

(e) Notwithstanding paragraphs (a) and (b) of this section, a person may—

(1) Ferry a newly acquired airplane from the place where possession of it was taken to a place where the emergency locator transmitter is to be installed; and

(2) Ferry an airplane with an inoperative emergency locator transmitter from a place where repairs or replacement cannot be made to a place where they can be made.

No persons other than required crewmembers may be carried aboard an airplane being ferried pursuant to this paragraph (e).

(f) Paragraphs (a) and (b) of this section do not apply to—

(1) Turbojet-powered aircraft;

(2) Aircraft while engaged in scheduled flights by scheduled air carriers certificated by the Civil Aeronautics Board;

(3) Aircraft while engaged in training operations conducted entirely within a 50-mile radius of the airport from which such local flight operations began;

(4) Aircraft while engaged in flight operations incident to design and testing;

(5) New aircraft while engaged in flight operations incident to their manufacture, preparation, and delivery;

(6) Aircraft while engaged in flight operations incident to the aerial application of chemicals and other substances for agricultural purposes;

(7) Aircraft certificated by the Administrator for research and development purposes;

(8) Aircraft while used for showing compliance with regulations, crew training, exhibition, air racing, or market surveys;

(9) Aircraft equipped to carry not more than one person; and

(10) An aircraft during any period for which the transmitter has been temporarily removed for inspection, repair, modification or replacement, subject to the following:

(i) No person may operate the aircraft unless the aircraft records contain an entry which includes the date of initial removal, the make, model, serial number and reason for removal of the transmitter, and a placard is located in view of the pilot to show "ELT not installed."

(ii) No person may operate the aircraft more than 90 days after the ELT is initially removed from the aircraft.

[Doc. No. 10915, Amdt. 91-95, 36 FR 18723, Sept. 21, 1971, as amended by Amdt. 91-121, 39 FR 6516, Feb. 20, 1974; Amdt. 91-123, 39 FR 25315, July 10, 1974; Amdt. 91-133, 41 FR 47228, Oct. 28, 1976; Amdt. 91-151, 43 FR 10905, Mar. 16, 1978; Amdt. 91-152, 43 FR 22640, May 25, 1978; Amdt. 91-163, 45 FR 38348, June 9, 1980]

§ 91.53 [Reserved]

§ 91.54 Truth in leasing clause requirement in leases and conditional sales contracts.

(a) Except as provided in paragraph (b) of this section, the parties to a lease or contract of conditional sale involving a United States registered large civil aircraft and entered into after January 2, 1973, shall execute a written lease or contract and include therein a written truth in leasing clause as a concluding paragraph in large print, immediately preceding the space for the signature of the parties, which contains the following with respect to each such aircraft:

(1) Identification of the Federal Aviation Regulations under which the aircraft has been maintained and inspected during the 12 months preceding the execution of the lease or contract of conditional sale; and certification by the parties thereto regarding the aircraft's status of compliance with applicable maintenance and inspection requirements in this part for the operation to be conducted under the lease or contract of conditional sale.

(2) The name and address (printed or typed) and the signature of the person responsible for operational control of the aircraft under the lease or contract of conditional sale, and certification that each person understands that person's responsibilities for compliance with applicable Federal Aviation Regulations.

(3) A statement that an explanation of factors bearing on operational control and pertinent Federal Aviation Regulations can be obtained from the nearest FAA Flight Standards District Office, General Aviation District Office, or Air Carrier District Office.

(b) The requirements of paragraph (a) of this section do not apply—

(1) To a lease or contract of conditional sale when:

(i) The party to whom the aircraft is furnished is a foreign air carrier or certificate holder under Part 121, 123, 125, 127, 135, or 141 of this chapter; or

(ii) The party furnishing the aircraft is a foreign air carrier, certificate holder under Part 121, 123, 125, 127, or 141 of this chapter, or a certificate holder under Part 135 of this chapter having appropriate authority to engage in air taxi operations with large aircraft.

(2) To a contract of conditional sale, when the aircraft involved has not been registered anywhere prior to the execution of the contract, except as a new aircraft under a dealer's aircraft registration certificate issued in accordance with § 47.61 of this chapter.

(c) No person may operate a large civil aircraft of U.S. registry that is subject to a lease or contract of conditional sale to which paragraph (a) of this section applies, unless—

(1) The lessee or conditional buyer, or the registered owner if the lessee is not a citizen of the United States, has mailed a copy of the lease or contract that complies with the requirements of paragraph (a) of this section, within 24 hours of its execution, to the Flight Standards Technical Division, Post Office Box 25724, Oklahoma City, OK 73125;

(2) A copy of the lease or contract that complies with the requirements of paragraph (a) of this section is carried in the aircraft. The copy of the lease or contract shall be made available for review upon request by the Administrator; and

(3) The lessee or conditional buyer, or the registered owner if the lessee is not a citizen of the United States, has notified by telephone or in person, the FAA Flight Standards District Office, General Aviation District Office, Air Carrier District Office, or International Field Office nearest the airport where the flight will originate. Unless otherwise authorized by that office, the notification shall be given at least 48 hours prior to takeoff in the case of the first flight of that aircraft under that lease or contract and inform the FAA of—

(i) The location of the airport of departure;

(ii) The departure time; and

(iii) The registration number of the aircraft involved.

(d) The copy of the lease or contract furnished to the FAA under paragraph (c) of this section is commercial or financial information obtained from a person. It is, therefore, privileged and confidential, and will not be made available by the FAA for public inspection or copying under 5 U.S.C. 552(b)(4), unless recorded with the FAA under Part 49 of this chapter.

(e) For the purpose of this section, a lease means any agreement by a person to furnish an aircraft to another person for compensation or hire, whether with or without flight crewmembers, other than an agreement for the sale of an aircraft and a contract of conditional sale under section 101 of the Federal Aviation Act of 1958. The person furnishing the aircraft is referred to as the lessor and the person to whom it is furnished the lessee.

[Amdt. 91-104, 37 FR 20935, Oct. 5, 1972, as amended by Amdt. 91-108, 38 FR 852, Jan. 5, 1973; Amdt. 91-143, 42 FR 57448, Nov. 3, 1977; Amdt. 91-154, 43 FR 46234, Oct. 5, 1978; Amdt. 91-169, 45 FR 67234, Oct. 9, 1980]

§ 91.55 Civil aircraft sonic boom.

(a) No person may operate a civil aircraft in the United States at a true flight Mach number greater than 1 except in compliance with conditions and limitations in an authorization to exceed Mach 1 issued to the operator under Appendix B of this part.

(b) In addition, no person may operate a civil aircraft, for which the maximum operating limit speed M_{mo} exceeds a Mach number of 1, to or from an airport in the United States unless—

(1) Information available to the flight crew includes flight limitations that insure that flights entering or leaving the United States will not cause a sonic boom to reach the surface within the United States; and

(2) The operator complies with the flight limitations prescribed in paragraph (b)(1) of this section or complies with conditions and limitations in an authorization to exceed Mach 1 issued under Appendix B of this part.

[Doc. No. 10261, Amdt. 91-112, 38 FR 8054, Mar. 28, 1973; Amdt. 91-153, 43 FR 28421, June 29, 1978]

§ 91.56 Agricultural and fire fighting airplanes; noise operating limitations.

(a) This section applies to propeller-driven, small airplanes having standard airworthiness certificates, that are designed for "agricultural aircraft operations" (as defined in § 137.3 of this chapter, as efective on January 1, 1966) or for dispensing fire fighting materials.

(b) If the Airplane Flight Manual, or other approved manual material, information, markings, or placards for the airplane indicate that the airplane has not been shown to comply with the noise limits under Part 36 of this chapter, no person may operate that airplane, except—

(1) To the extent necessary to accomplish the work activity directly associated with the purpose for which it is designed;

(2) To provide flight crewmember training in the special purpose operation for which the airplane is designed; and

(3) To conduct "nondispensing aerial work operations" in accordance with the requirements under § 137.29(c) of this chapter.

[Doc. No. 16382, Amdt. 91-168, 45 FR 67066, Oct. 9, 1980]

§ 91.57 Aviation Safety Reporting Program; prohibition against use of reports for enforcement purposes.

The Administrator of the FAA will not use reports submitted to the National Aeronautics and Space Administration under the Aviation Safety Reporting Program (or information derived therefrom) in any enforcement action, except information concerning criminal offenses or accidents which are wholly excluded from the Program.

[Doc. No. 19301, Amdt. 91-156, 44 FR 37625, June 28, 1979]

§ 91.58 Materials for compartment interiors.

No person may operate an airplane that conforms to an amended or supplemental type certificate issued in accordance with SFAR No. 41 for a maximum certificated takeoff weight in excess of 12,500 pounds, unless within one year after issuance of the initial airworthiness certificate under that SFAR, the airplane meets the compartment interior requirements set forth in § 25.853 (a), (b), (b-1), (b-2), and (b-3) of this chapter in effect on September 26, 1978.

[Doc. No. 18315, Amdt. 91-159, 44 FR 53731, Sept. 17, 1979]

§ 91.59 Carriage of candidates in Federal elections.

(a) An aircraft operator, other than one operating an aircraft under the rules of Part 121, 127, or 135 of this chapter, may receive payment for the carriage of a candidate in a Federal election, an agent of the candidate, or a person traveling on behalf of the candidate, if—

(1) That operator's primary business is not as an air carrier or commercial operator;

(2) The carriage is conducted under the rules of Part 91; and

(3) The payment for the carriage is required, and does not exceed the amount required to be paid, by regulations of the Federal Election Commission (11 CFR et seq.).

(b) For the purposes of this section, the terms "candidate" and "election" have the same meaning as that set forth in the regulations of the Federal Election Commission.

[Doc. No. 18313, Amdt. 91-164, 45 FR 43162, June 26, 1980]

Subpart B—Flight Rules

GENERAL

§91.61 Applicability.

This subpart prescribes flight rules governing the operation of aircraft within the United States.

§91.63 Waivers.

(a) The Administrator may issue a certificate of waiver authorizing the operation of aircraft in deviation of any rule of this subpart if he finds that the proposed operation can be safely conducted under the terms of that certificate of waiver.

(b) An application for a certificate of waiver under this section is made on a form and in a manner prescribed by the Administrator and may be submitted to any FAA office.

(c) A certificate of waiver is effective as specified in that certificate.

§91.65 Operating near other aircraft.

(a) No person may operate an aircraft so close to another aircraft as to create a collision hazard.

(b) No person may operate an aircraft in formation flight except by arrangement with the pilot in command of each aircraft in the formation.

(c) No person may operate an aircraft, carrying passengers for hire, in formation flight.

(d) Unless otherwise authorized by ATC, no person operating an aircraft may operate his aircraft in accordance with any clearance or instruction that has been issued to the pilot of another aircraft for radar Air Traffic Control purposes.

[Doc. No. 1580, Amdt. 1-1, 28 FR 6704, June 29, 1963, as amended by Amdt. 91-8, 29 FR 14404, Oct. 20, 1964]

§91.67 Right-of-way rules; except water operations.

(a) *General.* When weather conditions permit, regardless of whether an operation is conducted under Instrument Flight Rules or Visual Flight Rules, vigilance shall be maintained by each person operating an aircraft so as to see and avoid other aircraft in compliance with this section. When a rule of this section gives another aircraft the right of way, he shall give way to that aircraft and may not pass over, under, or ahead of it, unless well clear.

(b) *In distress.* An aircraft in distress has the right of way over all other air traffic.

(c) *Converging.* When aircraft of the same category are converging at approximately the same altitude (except head-on, or nearly so) the aircraft to the other's right has the right of way. If the aircraft are of different categories—

(1) A balloon has the right of way over any other category of aircraft;

(2) A glider has the right of way over an airship, airplane or rotorcraft; and

(3) An airship has the right of way over an airplane or rotorcraft.

However, an aircraft towing or refueling other aircraft has the right of way over all other engine-driven aircraft.

(d) *Approaching head-on.* When aircraft are approaching each other head-on, or nearly so, each pilot of each aircraft shall alter course to the right.

(e) *Overtaking.* Each aircraft that is being overtaken has the right of way and each pilot of an overtaking aircraft shall alter course to the right to pass well clear.

(f) *Landing.* Aircraft, while on final approach to land, or while landing, have the right of way over other aircraft in flight or operating on the surface. When two or more aircraft are approaching an airport for the purpose of landing, the aircraft at the lower altitude has the right of way, but it shall not take advantage of this rule to cut in front of another which is on final approach to land, or to overtake that aircraft.

(g) *Inapplicability.* This section does not apply to the operation of an aircraft on water.

[Doc. No. 1580, Amdt. 1-1, 28 FR 6704, June 29, 1963, as amended by Amdt. 91-55, 33 FR 10505, July 24, 1968]

§ 91.69 Right-of-way rules; water operations.

(a) *General.* Each person operating an aircraft on the water shall, insofar as possible, keep clear of all vessels and avoid impeding their navigation, and shall give way to any vessel or other aircraft that is given the right of way by any rule of this section.

(b) *Crossing.* When aircraft, or an aircraft and a vessel are on crossing courses, the aircraft or vessel to the others right has the right of way.

(c) *Approaching head-on.* When aircraft, or an aircraft and a vessel, are approaching head-on or nearly so, each shall alter its course to the right to keep well clear.

(d) *Overtaking.* Each aircraft or vessel that is being overtaken has the right of way, and the one overtaking shall alter course to keep well clear.

(e) *Special circumstances.* When aircraft, or an aircraft and a vessel, approach so as to involve risk of collision, each aircraft or vessel shall proceed with careful regard to existing circumstances, including the limitations of the respective craft.

§ 91.70 Aircraft speed.

(a) Unless otherwise authorized by the Administrator, no person may operate an aircraft below 10,000 feet MSL at an indicated airspeed of more than 250 knots (288 m.p.h.).

(b) Unless otherwise authorized or required by ATC, no person may operate an aircraft within an airport traffic area at an indicated airspeed of more than—

(1) In the case of a reciprocating engine aircraft, 156 knots (180 m.p.h.); or

(2) In the case of a turbine-powered aircraft, 200 knots (230 m.p.h.).

Paragraph (b) of this section does not apply to any operations within a Terminal Control Area. Such operations shall comply with paragraph (a) of this section.

(c) No person may operate an aircraft in the airspace underlying a terminal control area, or in a VFR corridor designated through a terminal control area, at an indicated airspeed of more than 200 knots (230 m.p.h.).

However, if the minimum safe airspeed for any particular operation is greater than the maximum speed prescribed in this section, the aircraft may be operated at that minimum speed.

[Doc. No. 13543, Amdt. 91-47, 32 FR 15709, Nov. 15, 1967, as amended by Amdt. 91-78, 35 FR 7784, May 21, 1970; Amdt. 91-113, 38 FR 8135, Mar. 29, 1973; Amdt. 91-125, 39 FR 26888, July 24, 1974]

§ 91.71 Acrobatic flight.

No person may operate an aircraft in acrobatic flight—

(a) Over any congested area of a city, town, or settlement;

(b) Over an open air assembly of persons;

(c) Within a control zone or Federal Airway;

(d) Below an altitude of 1,500 feet above the surface; or

(e) When flight visibility is less than three miles.

For the purposes of this section, acrobatic flight means an intentional maneuver involving an abrupt change in an aircraft's attitude, an abnormal attitude, or abnormal acceleration, not necessary for normal flight.

[Doc. No. 1580, Amdt. 1-1, 28 FR 6704, June 29, 1963, as amended by Amdt. 91-6, 29 FR 9823, July 22, 1964, Amdt. 91-65, 34 FR 12883, Aug. 8, 1969; Amdt. 91-65, 34 FR 13467, Aug. 21, 1969]

§ 91.73 Aircraft lights.

No person may, during the period from sunset to sunrise (or, in Alaska, during the period a prominent unlighted object cannot be seen from a distance of three statute miles or the sun is more than six degrees below the horizon)—

(a) Operate an aircraft unless it has lighted position lights;

(b) Park or move an aircraft in, or in dangerous proximity to, a night flight operations area of an airport unless the aircraft—

(1) Is clearly illuminated;

(2) Has lighted position lights; or

(3) Is in an area which is marked by obstruction lights.

(c) Anchor an aircraft unless the aircraft—

(1) Has lighted anchor lights; or

(2) Is in an area where anchor lights are not required on vessels; or

(d) Operate an aircraft, required by § 91.33(c)(3) to be equipped with an anticollision light system, unless it has approved and lighted aviation red or aviation white anticollision lights. However, the anticollision lights need not be lighted when the pilot in command determines that, because of operating conditions, it would be in the interest of safety to turn the lights off.

[Doc. No. 1580, Amdt. 1-1, 28 FR 6704, June 29, 1963, as amended by Amdt. 91-152, 43 FR 22640, May 25, 1978]

§ 91.75 Compliance with ATC clearances and instructions.

(a) When an ATC clearance has been obtained, no pilot in command may deviate from that clearance, except in an emergency, unless he obtains an amended clearance. However, except in positive controlled airspace, this paragraph does not prohibit him from cancelling an IFR flight plan if he is operating in VFR weather conditions. If a pilot is uncertain of the meaning of an ATC clearance, he shall immediately request clarification from ATC.

(b) Except in an emergency, no person may, in an area in which air traffic control is exercised, operate an aircraft contrary to an ATC instruction.

(c) Each pilot in command who deviates, in an emergency, from an ATC clearance or instruction shall notify ATC of that deviation as soon as possible.

(d) Each pilot in command who (though not deviating from a rule of this subpart) is given priority by ATC in an emergency, shall, if requested by ATC, submit a detailed report of that emergency within 48 hours to the chief of that ATC facility.

[Doc. No. 1580, Amdt. 1-1, 28 FR 6704, June 29, 1963, as amended by Amdt. 91-50, 33 FR 452, Jan. 12, 1968; Amdt. 91-126, 40 FR 10451, Mar. 6, 1975]

§ 91.77 ATC light signals.

ATC light signals have the meaning shown in the following table:

Color and type of signal	Meaning with respect to aircraft on the surface	Meaning with respect to aircraft in flight
Steady green	Cleared for take-off	Cleared to land.
Flashing green	Cleared to taxi	Return for landing (to be followed by steady green at proper time).
Steady red	Stop	Give way to other aircraft and continue circling.
Flashing red	Taxi clear of runway in use.	Airport unsafe—do not land.
Flashing white	Return to starting point on airport.	Not applicable.
Alternating red and green.	Exercise extreme caution.	Exercise extreme caution.

§ 91.79 Minimum safe altitudes; general.

Except when necessary for takeoff or landing, no person may operate an aircraft below the following altitudes:

(a) *Anywhere.* An altitude allowing, if a power unit fails, an emergency landing without undue hazard to persons or property on the surface.

(b) *Over congested areas.* Over any congested area of a city, town, or settlement, or over any open air assembly of persons, an altitude of 1,000 feet above the highest obstacle within a horizontal radius of 2,000 feet of the aircraft.

(c) *Over other than congested areas.* An altitude of 500 feet above the surface except over open water or sparsely populated areas. In that case, the aircraft may not be operated closer than 500 feet to any person, vessel, vehicle, or structure.

(d) *Helicopters.* Helicopters may be operated at less than the minimums prescribed in paragraph (b) or (c) of this section if the operation is conducted without hazard to persons or property on the surface. In addition, each person operating a helicopter shall comply with routes or altitudes specifically prescribed for helicopters by the Administrator.

§ 91.81   Altimeter settings.

(a) Each person operating an aircraft shall maintain the cruising altitude or flight level of that aircraft, as the case may be, by reference to an altimeter that is set, when operating—

(1) Below 18,000 feet MSL, to—

(i) The current reported altimeter setting of a station along the route and within 100 nautical miles of the aircraft;

(ii) If there is no station within the area prescribed in paragraph (a)(1)(i) of this section, the current reported altimeter setting of an appropriate available station; or

(iii) In the case of an aircraft not equipped with a radio, the elevation of the departure airport or an appropriate altimeter setting available before departure; or

(2) At or above 18,000 feet MSL, to 29.92″ Hg.

(b) The lowest usable flight level is determined by the atmospheric pressure in the area of operation, as shown in the following table:

Current altimeter setting	Lowest usable flight level
29.92 or higher	180
29.91 through 29.42	185
29.41 through 28.92	190
28.91 through 28.42	195
28.41 through 27.92	200
27.91 through 27.42	205
27.41 through 26.92	210

(c) To convert minimum altitude prescribed under §§ 91.79 and 91.119 to the minimum flight level, the pilot shall take the flight-level equivalent of the minimum altitude in feet and add the appropriate number of feet specified below, according to the current reported altimeter setting:

Current altimeter setting	Adjustment factor
29.92 or higher	None.
29.91 through 29.42	500 feet.
29.41 through 28.92	1,000 feet.
28.91 through 28.42	1,500 feet.
28.41 through 27.92	2,000 feet.
27.91 through 27.42	2,500 feet.
27.41 through 26.92	3,000 feet.

[Amdt. 91-7, 29 FR 9894, July 23, 1964]

§ 91.83   Flight plan; information required.

(a) Unless otherwise authorized by ATC, each person filing an IFR or VFR flight plan shall include in it the following information:

(1) The aircraft identification number and, if necessary, its radio call sign.

(2) The type of the aircraft or, in the case of a formation flight, the type of each aircraft and the number of aircraft in the formation.

(3) The full name and address of the pilot in command or, in the case of a formation flight, the formation commander.

(4) The point and proposed time of departure.

(5) The proposed route, cruising altitude (or flight level), and true air speed at that altitude.

(6) The point of first intended landing and the estimated elapsed time until over that point.

(7) The radio frequencies to be used.

(8) The amount of fuel on board (in hours).

(9) In the case of an IFR flight plan, an alternate airport, except as provided in paragraph (b) of this section.

(10) The number of persons in the aircraft, except where that information is otherwise readily available to the FAA.

(11) Any other information the pilot in command or ATC believes is necessary for ATC purposes.

(b) *Exceptions to applicability of paragraph (a)(9) of this section.* Paragraph (a)(9) of this section does not apply if Part 97 of this subchapter prescribes a standard instrument approach procedure for the first airport of intended landing and, for at least one hour before and one hour after the estimated time of arrival, the weather reports or forecasts or any combination of them, indicate—

(1) The ceiling will be at least 2,000 feet above the airport elevation; and

(2) Visibility will be at least 3 miles.

(c) *IFR alternate airport weather minimums.* Unless otherwise authorized by the Administrator, no person may include an alternate airport in an IFR flight plan unless current weather forecasts indicate that, at the estimated time of arrival at the alternate airport, the ceiling and visibility at that airport will be at or above the following alternate airport weather minimums:

(1) If an instrument approach procedure has been published in Part 97 of this chapter for that airport, the alternate airport minimums specified in that procedure or, if none are so specified, the following minimums:

(i) Precision approach procedure: Ceiling 600 feet and visibility 2 statute miles.

(ii) Nonprecision approach procedure: Ceiling 800 feet and visibility 2 statute miles.

(2) If no instrument approach procedure has been published in Part 97 of this chapter for that airport, the ceiling and visibility minimums are those allowing descent from the MEA, approach, and landing, under basic VFR.

(d) *Cancellation.* When a flight plan has been activated, the pilot in command, upon cancelling or completing the flight under the flight plan, shall notify an FAA Flight Service Station or ATC facility.

[Doc. No. 1580, Amdt. 1-1, 28 FR 6704, June 29, 1963, as amended by Amdt. 91-18, 30 FR 6070, Apr. 29, 1965; Amdt. 91-44, 32 FR 13910, Oct. 6, 1967; Amdt. 91-152, 43 FR 22640, May 25, 1978; Amdt. 91-154, 43 FR 46234, Oct. 5, 1978; Amdt. 91-155, 44 FR 15656, Mar. 15, 1979]

§91.84 Flights between Mexico or Canada and the United States.

Unless otherwise authorized by ATC, no person may operate a civil aircraft between Mexico or Canada and the United States without filing an IFR or VFR flight plan, as appropriate.

[Doc. No. 12035, Amdt. 91-117, 38 FR 17493, July 2, 1973]

§91.85 Operating on or in the vicinity of an airport; general rules.

(a) Unless otherwise required by Part 93 of this chapter, each person operating an aircraft on or in the vicinity of an airport shall comply with the requirements of this section and of §§ 91.87 and 91.89.

(b) Unless otherwise authorized or required by ATC, no person may operate an aircraft within an airport traffic area except for the purpose of landing at, or taking off from, an airport within that area. ATC authorizations may be given as individual approval of specific operations or may be contained in written agreements between airport users and the tower concerned.

(c) After March 28, 1977, except when necessary for training or certification, the pilot in command of a civil turbojet-powered airplane shall use, as a final landing flap setting, the minimum certificated landing flap setting set forth in the approved performance information in the Airplane Flight Manual for the applicable conditions. However, each pilot in command has the final authority and responsibility for the safe operation of his airplane, and he may use a different flap setting approved for that airplane if he determines that it is necessary in the interest of safety.

[Doc. No. 1580, Amdt. 1-1, 28 FR 6704, June 29, 1963, as amended by Amdt. 91-47, 32 FR 15709, Nov. 15, 1967; Amdt. 91-134, 41 FR 52392, Nov. 29, 1976]

§91.87 Operation at airports with operating control towers.

(a) *General.* Unless otherwise authorized or required by ATC, each person operating an aircraft to, from, or on an airport with an operating control tower shall comply with the applicable provisions of this section.

(b) *Communications with control towers operated by the United States.* No person may, within an airport traffic area, operate an aircraft to, from, or on an airport having a control tower operated by the United States unless two-way radio communications are maintained between that aircraft and the control tower. However, if the aircraft radio fails in flight, he may operate that aircraft and land if weather conditions are at or above basic VFR weather minimums, he maintains visual contact with the tower, and he receives a clearance to land. If the aircraft radio fails while in flight under IFR, he must comply with § 91.127.

(c) *Communications with other control towers.* No person may, within an airport traffic area, operate an aircraft to, from, or on an airport having a control tower that is operated by any person other than the United States unless—

(1) If that aircraft's radio equipment so allows, two-way radio communications are maintained between the aircraft and the tower; or

(2) If that aircraft's radio equipment allows only reception from the tower, the pilot has the tower's frequency monitored.

(d) *Minimum altitudes.* When operating to an airport with an operating control tower, each pilot of—

(1) A turbine-powered airplane or a large airplane shall, unless otherwise required by the applicable distance from cloud criteria, enter the airport traffic area at an altitude of at least 1,500 feet above the surface of the airport and maintain at least 1,500 feet within the airport traffic area, including the traffic pattern, until further descent is required for a safe landing;

(2) A turbine-powered airplane or a large airplane approaching to land on a runway being served by an ILS, shall, if the airplane is ILS equipped, fly that airplane at an altitude at or above the glide slope between the outer marker (or the point of interception with the glide slope, if compliance with the applicable distance from clouds criteria requires interception closer in) and the middle marker; and

(3) An airplane approaching to land on a runway served by a visual approach slope indicator, shall maintain an altitude at or above the glide slope until a lower altitude is necessary for a safe landing.

However, paragraphs (d) (2) and (3) of this section do not prohibit normal bracketing maneuvers above or below the glide slope that are conducted for the purpose of remaining on the glide slope.

(e) *Approaches.* When approaching to land at an airport with an operating control tower, each pilot of—

(1) An airplane, shall circle the airport to the left; and

(2) A helicopter, shall avoid the flow of fixed-wing aircraft.

(f) *Departures.* No person may operate an aircraft taking off from an airport with an operating control tower except in compliance with the following:

(1) Each pilot shall comply with any departure procedures established for that airport by the FAA.

(2) Unless otherwise required by the departure procedure or the applicable distance from clouds criteria, each pilot of a turbine-powered airplane and each pilot of a large airplane shall climb to an altitude of 1,500 feet above the surface as rapidly as practicable.

(g) *Noise abatement runway system.* When landing or taking off from an airport with an operating control tower, and for which a formal runway use program has been established by the FAA, each pilot of a turbine-powered airplane and each pilot of a large airplane assigned a noise abatement runway by ATC, shall use that runway. However, consistent with the final authority of the pilot in command concerning the safe operation of the aircraft as prescribed in § 91.3(a), ATC may assign a different runway if requested by the pilot in the interest of safety.

(h) *Clearances required.* No person may, at any airport with an operating control tower, operate an aircraft on a runway or taxiway, or takeoff or land an aircraft, unless an appropriate clearance is received from ATC. A clearance to "taxi to" the takeoff runway assigned to the aircraft is not a clearance to cross that assigned takeoff runway, or to taxi on that runway at any point, but is a clearance to cross other runways that intersect the taxi route to that assigned takeoff runway. A clearance to "taxi to" any point other than an assigned takeoff runway is a clearance to cross all runways that intersect the taxi route to that point.

[Doc. No. 1580, Amdt. 1-1, 28 FR 6704, June 29, 1963, as amended by Amdt. 91-46. 32 FR 15422, Nov. 4, 1967; Amdt. 91-129, 40 FR

§91.88 Airport radar service areas.

(a) *General.* For the purposes of this section, the primary airport is the airport designated in Part 71, Subpart L, for which the airport radar service area is designated. A satellite airport is any other airport within the airport radar service area.

(b) *Deviations.* An operator may deviate from any provision of this section under the provisions of an ATC authorization issued by the ATC facility having jurisdiction of the airport radar service area. ATC may authorize a deviation on a continuing basis or for an individual flight, as appropriate.

(c) *Arrivals and Overflights.* No person may operate an aircraft in an airport radar service area unless two-way radio communication is established with ATC prior to entering that area and is thereafter maintained with ATC while within that area.

(d) *Departures.* No person may operate an aircraft within an airport radar service area unless two-way radio communication is maintained with ATC while within that area, except that for aircraft departing a satellite airport, two-way radio communication is established as soon as practicable and thereafter maintained with ATC while within that area.

(e) *Traffic Patterns.* No person may take off or land an aircraft at a satellite airport within an airport radar service area except in compliance with FAA arrival and departure traffic patterns.

(f) *Equipment requirement.* Unless otherwise authorized by ATC, no person may operate an aircraft within an airport radar service area unless that aircraft is equipped with the applicable equipment specified in § 91.24

§91.89 Operation at airports without control towers.

(a) Each person operating an aircraft to or from an airport without an operating control tower shall—

(1) In the case of an airplane approaching to land, make all turns of that airplane to the left unless the airport displays approved light signals or visual markings indicating that turns should be made to the right, in which case the pilot shall make all turns to the right;

(2) In the case of a helicopter approaching to land, avoid the flow of fixed-wing aircraft; and

(3) In the case of an aircraft departing the airport, comply with any FAA traffic pattern for that airport.

[Amdt. 91-17, 30 FR 5507, Apr. 17, 1965]

§ 91.90 Terminal control areas.

(a) *Operating rules.* No person may operate an aircraft within a terminal control area designated in Part 71 of this chapter except in compliance with the following rules:.

(1) No person may operate an aircraft within a terminal control area unless that person has received an appropriate authorization from ATC prior to operation of that aircraft in that area.

(2) Unless otherwise authorized by ATC, each person operating a large turbine engine-powered airplane to or from a primary airport shall operate at or above the designated floors while within the lateral limits of the terminal control area.

(3) Any person conducting pilot training operations at an airport within a terminal control area shall comply with any procedures established by ATC for such operations in terminal control area.

(b) *Pilot requirements.* (1) No person may takeoff or land a civil aircraft at an airport within a terminal control area or operate a civil aircraft within a terminal control area unless:

(i) The pilot-in-command holds at least a private pilot certificate; or

(ii) The aircraft is operated by a student pilot who has met the requirements of § 61.95.

(2) Notwithstanding the provisions of (b)(1)(ii) of this section, at the following TCA primary airports, no person may takeoff or land a civil aircraft unless the pilot-in-command holds at least a private pilot certificate:

(i)   Atlanta Hartsfield Airport, GA.

(ii)   Boston Logan Airport, MA.

(iii) Chicago O'Hare International Airport, IL.

(iv)   Dallas/Forth Worth International Airport, TX.

(v)   Los Angeles International Airport, CA.

(vi)   Miami International Airport, FL.

(vii) Newark International Airport, NJ.

(viii) New York Kennedy Airport, NY.

(ix)   New York LaGuardia Airport, NY.

(x)   San Francisco International Airport, CA.

(xi)   Washington National Airport, DC.

(xii) Andrews Air Force Base, MD.

(c) *Communications and navigation equipment requirements.* Unless otherwise authorized by ATC, no person may operate an aircraft within a terminal control area unless that aircraft is equipped with—

(1) An operable VOR or TACAN receiver (except for helicopter operations prior to July 1, 1989); and

(2) An operable two-way radio capable of communications with ATC on appropriate frequencies for that terminal control area.

(d) *Transponder requirement.* No person may operate an aircraft in a terminal control area unless the aircraft is equipped with the applicable operating transponder and automatic altitude reporting equipment specified in paragraph (a) of § 91.24 except as provided in paragraph (d) of that section.

§ 91.91   Temporary flight restrictions.

(a) The Administrator will issue a Notice to Airmen (NOTAM) designating an area within which temporary flight restrictions apply and specifying the hazard or condition requiring their imposition, whenever he determines it is necessary in order to—

(1) protect persons and property on the surface or in the air from a hazard associated with an incident on the surface;

(2) provide a safe environment for the operation of disaster relief aircraft; or

(3) prevent an unsafe congestion of sightseeing and other aircraft above an incident or event which may generate a high degree of public interest.

The Notice to Airmen will specify the hazard or condition that requires the imposition of temporary flight restrictions.

(b) When a NOTAM has been issued under paragraph (a)(1) of this section, no person may operate an aircraft within the designated area unless that aircraft is participating in the hazard relief activities and is being operated under the direction of the official in charge of on scene emergency response activities.

(c) When a NOTAM has been issued under paragraph (a)(2) of this section, no person may operate an aircraft within the designated area unless at least one of the following conditions are met:

(1) The aircraft is participating in hazard relief activities and is being operated under the direction of the official in charge of on scene emergency response activities.

(2) The aircraft is carrying law enforcement officials.

(3) The aircraft is operating under an ATC approved IFR flight plan.

(4) The operation is conducted directly to or from an airport within the area, or is necessitated by the impracticability of VFR flight above or around the area due to weather, or terrain; notification is given to the Flight Service Station (FSS) or ATC facility specified in the NOTAM to receive advisories concerning disaster relief aircraft operations; and the operation does not hamper or endanger relief activities and is not conducted for the purpose of observing the disaster.

(5) The aircraft is carrying properly accredited news representatives, and, prior to entering the area, a flight plan is filed with the appropriate FAA or ATC facility specified in the Notice to Airmen and the operation is conducted above the altitude used by the disaster relief aircraft, unless otherwise authorized by the official in charge of on scene emergency response activities.

(d) When a NOTAM has been issued under paragraph (a)(3) of this section, no person may operate an aircraft within the designated area unless at least one of the following conditions is met:

(1) The operation is conducted directly to or from an airport within the area, or is necessitated by the impracticability of VFR flight above or around the area due to weather or terrain, and the operation is not conducted for the purpose of observing the incident or event.

(2) The aircraft is operating under an ATC approved IFR flight plan.

(3) The aircraft is carrying incident or event personnel, or law enforcement officials.

(4) The aircraft is carrying properly accredited news representatives and, prior to entering that area, a flight plan is filed with the appropriate FSS or ATC facility specified in the NOTAM.

(e) Flight plans filed and notifications made with an FSS or ATC facility under this section shall include the following information:

(1) Aircraft identification, type and color.

(2) Radio communications frequencies to be used.

(3) Proposed times of entry of, and exit from, the designated area.

(4) Name of news media or organization and purpose of flight.

(5) Any other information requested by ATC.

[Doc. No. 22961, Amdt. 91-186, 49 FR 48032, Dec. 10, 1984]

§91.93 Flight test areas.

No person may flight test an aircraft except over open water, or sparsely populated areas, having light air traffic.

[Amdt. 91-21, 30 FR 8473, July 2, 1965]

§91.95 Restricted and prohibited areas.

(a) No person may operate an aircraft within a restricted area (designated in Part 73 contrary to the restrictions imposed, or within a prohibited area, unless he has the permission of the using or controlling agency, as appropriate.

(b) Each person conducting, within a restricted area, an aircraft operation (approved by the using agency) that creates the same hazards as the operations for which the restricted area was designated, may deviate from the rules of this subpart that are not compatible with his operation of the aircraft.

§91.97 Positive control areas and route segments.

(a) Except as provided in paragraph (b) of this section, no person may operate an aircraft within a positive control area, or positive control route segment designated in Part 71 of this chapter, unless that aircraft is—

(1) Operated under IFR at a specific flight level assigned by ATC;

(2) Equipped with instruments and equipment required for IFR operations;

(3) Flown by a pilot rated for instrument flight; and

(4) Equipped, when in a positive control area, with—

(i) The applicable equipment specified in §91.24; and

(ii) A radio providing direct pilot/controller communication on the frequency specified by ATC for the area concerned.

(b) ATC may authorize deviations from the requirements of paragraph (a) of this section. In the case of an inoperative transponder, ATC may immediately approve an operation within a positive control area allowing flight to continue, if desired, to the airport of ultimate destination, including any intermediate stops, or to proceed to a place where suitable repairs can be made, or both. A request for authorization to deviate from a requirement of paragraph (a) of this section, other than for operation with an inoperative transponder as outlined above, must be submitted at least 4 days before the proposed operation, in writing, to the ATC center having jurisdiction over the positive control area concerned. ATC may authorize a deviation on a continuing basis or for an individual flight, as appropriate.

[Amdt. No. 91-32, 31 FR 10517, Aug. 5, 1966, as amended at 31 FR 11641, Sept. 3, 1966; Amdt. 91-116, 38 FR 14677, June 4, 1973; Amdt. 91-147, 43 FR 7205, Feb. 21, 1978]

§ 91.100   Emergency air traffic rules.

(a) This section prescribes a process for utilizing Notices to Airmen (NOTAM) to advise of the issuance and operations under emergency air traffic rules and regulations and designates the official who is authorized to issue NOTAMs on behalf of the Administrator in certain matters under this section.

(b) Whenever the Administrator determines that an emergency condition exists, or will exist, relating to the FAA's ability to operate the Air Traffic Control System and during which normal flight operations under this chapter cannot be conducted consistent with the required levels of safety and efficiency—

(1) The Administrator issues an immediately effective Air Traffic rule or regulation in response to that emergency condition, and

(2) The Administrator, or the Director, Air Traffic Service, may utilize the Notice to Airmen (NOTAMs) system to provide notification of the issuance of the rule or regulation.

Those NOTAMs communicate information concerning the rules and regulations that govern flight operations, the use of navigation facilities, and designation of that airspace in which the rules and regulations apply.

(c) When a NOTAM has been issued under this section, no person may operate an aircraft, or other device governed by the regulation concerned, within the designated airspace, except in accordance with the authorizations, terms, and conditions prescribed in the regulation covered by the NOTAM.

[Amdt. 91-175, 46 FR 16891, Mar. 16, 1981]

§ 91.101   Operations to Cuba.

No person may operate a civil aircraft from the United States to Cuba unless—

(a) Departure is from an international airport of entry designated in § 6.13 of the Air Commerce Regulations of the Bureau of Customs (19 CFR 6.13); and

(b) In the case of departure from any of the 48 contiguous States or the District of Columbia, the pilot in command of the aircraft has filed—

(1) A DVFR or IFR flight plan as prescribed in § 99.11 or § 99.13 of this chapter; and

(2) A written statement, within one hour before departure, with the office of Immigration and Naturalization Service at the airport of departure, containing—

(i) All information in the flight plan;

(ii) The name of each occupant of the aircraft;

(iii) The number of occupants of the aircraft; and

(iv) A description of the cargo, if any.

This section does not apply to the operation of aircraft by a scheduled air carrier over routes authorized in operations specifications issued by the Administrator.

[Doc. No. 1580, Amdt. 1-1, 28 FR 6704, June 29, 1966, as amended by Amdt. 91-30, 31 FR 9211, July 6, 1966; Amdt. 91-105, 37 FR 21990, Oct. 18, 1972]

§ 91.102   Flight limitation in the proximity of space flight operations.

No person may operate any aircraft of U.S. registry, or pilot any aircraft under the authority of an airman certificate issued by the Federal Aviation Administration within areas designated in a NOTAM for space flight operations except when authorized by ATC, or operated under the control of the Department of Defense Manager for Space Transportation System Contingency Support Operations.

[Doc. No. 25069, Amdt. 91-195, 51 FR 31098, Sept. 2, 1986]

§ 91.103 Operation of civil aircraft of Cuban registry.

No person may operate a civil aircraft of Cuban registry except in controlled airspace and in accordance with air traffic clearances or air traffic control instructions that may require use of specific airways or routes and landings at specific airports.

[Amdt. 91-15, 30 FR 3638, Mar. 19, 1965]

§ 91.104 Flight restrictions in the proximity of the Presidential and other parties.

No person may operate an aircraft over or in the vicinity of any area to be visited or traveled by the President, the Vice President, or other public figures contrary to the restrictions established by the Administrator and published in a Notice to Airmen (NOTAM).

[Amdt. 91-64, 34 FR 2551, Feb. 25, 1969]

VISUAL FLIGHT RULES

§ 91.105 Basic VFR weather minimums.

(a) Except as provided in § 91.107, no person may operate an aircraft under VFR when the flight visibility is less, or at a distance from clouds that is less, than that prescribed for the corresponding altitude in the following table:

Altitude	Flight visibility	Distance from clouds
1,200 feet or less above the surface (regardless of MSL altitude)—		
Within controlled airspace	3 statute miles	500 feet below. 1,000 feet above. 2,000 feet horizontal.
Outside controlled airspace	1 statute mile except as provided in § 91.105(b).	Clear of clouds.
More than 1,200 feet above the surface but less than 10,000 feet MSL—		
Within controlled airspace	3 statute miles	500 feet below. 1,000 feet above. 2,000 feet horizontal.
Outside controlled airspace	1 statute mile	500 feet below. 1,000 feet above. 2,000 feet horizontal.
More than 1,200 feet above the surface and at or above 10,000 feet MSL..	5 statute miles	1,000 feet below. 1,000 feet above. 1 mile horizontal.

(b) When the visibility is less than one mile, a helicopter may be operated outside controlled airspace at 1,200 feet or less above the surface if operated at a speed that allows the pilot adequate opportunity to see any air traffic or other obstruction in time to avoid a collision.

(c) Except as provided in § 91.107, no person may operate an aircraft, under VFR, within a control zone beneath the ceiling when the ceiling is less than 1,000 feet.

(d) Except as provided in § 91.107, no person may take off or land an aircraft, or enter the traffic pattern of an airport, under VFR, within a control zone—

(1) Unless ground visibility at that airport is at least 3 statute miles; or

(2) If ground visibility is not reported at that airport, unless flight visibility during landing or takeoff, or while operating in the traffic pattern, is at least 3 statute miles.

(e) For the purposes of this section, an aircraft operating at the base altitude of a transition area or control area is considered to be within the airspace directly below that area.

[Amdt. 91-51, 33 FR 2992, Feb. 15, 1968]

§ 91.107 Special VFR weather minimums.

(a) Except as provided in § 93.113 of this chapter, when a person has received an appropriate ATC clearance, the special weather minimums of this section instead of those contained in § 91.105 apply to the operation of an aircraft by that person in a control zone under VFR.

(b) No person may operate an aircraft in a control zone under VFR except clear of clouds.

(c) No person may operate an aircraft (other than a helicopter) in a control zone under VFR unless flight visibility is at least one statute mile.

(d) No person may takeoff or land an aircraft (other than a helicopter) at any airport in a control zone under VFR—

(1) Unless ground visibility at that airport is at least 1 statute mile; or

(2) If ground visibility is not reported at that airport, unless flight visibility during landing or takeoff is at least 1 statute mile.

(e) No person may operate an aircraft (other than a helicopter) in a control zone under the special weather minimums of this section, between sunset and sunrise (or in Alaska, when the sun is more than 6 degrees below the horizon) unless:

(1) That person meets the applicable requirements for instrument flight under Part 61 of this chapter; and

(2) The aircraft is equipped as required in § 91.33(d).

[Doc No. 1580, Amdt. 1-1, 28 FR 6704, June 29, 1963, as amended by Amdt. 91-37, 32 FR 2940, Feb. 16, 1967; Amdt. 91-52, 33 FR 4096, Mar. 2, 1968; Amdt. 91-99, 37 FR 10435, May 23, 1972]

§ 91.109 VFR cruising altitude or flight level.

Except while holding in a holding pattern of 2 minutes or less, or while turning, each person operating an aircraft under VFR in level cruising flight more than 3,000 feet above the surface shall maintain the appropriate altitude or flight level prescribed below, unless otherwise authorized by ATC:

(a) When operating below 18,000 feet MSL and—

(1) On a magnetic course of zero degrees through 179 degrees, any odd thousand foot MSL altitude plus 500 feet (such as 3,500, 5,500, or 7,500); or

(2) On a magnetic course of 180 degrees through 359 degrees, any even thousand foot MSL altitude plus 500 feet (such as 4,500, 6,500, or 8,500).

(b) When operating above 18,000 feet MSL to flight level 290 (inclusive), and—

(1) On a magnetic course of zero degrees through 179 degrees, any odd flight level plus 500 feet (such as 195, 215, or 235); or

(2) On a magnetic course of 180 degrees through 359 degrees, any even flight level plus 500 feet (such as 185, 205, or 225).

(c) When operating above flight level 290 and—

(1) On a magnetic course of zero degrees through 179 degrees, any flight level, at 4,000 foot intervals, beginning at and including flight level 300 (such as flight level 300, 340, or 380); or

(2) On a magnetic course of 180 degrees through 359 degrees, any flight level, at 4,000 foot intervals, beginning at and including flight level 320 (such as flight level 320, 360, or 400).

[Amdt. 91-7, 29 FR 9894, July 23, 1964, as amended by Amdt. 91-84, 36 FR 43, Jan. 5, 1971; Amdt. 91-149, 43 FR 10904, Mar. 16, 1978]

INSTRUMENT FLIGHT RULES

§ 91.115 ATC clearance and flight plan required.

No person may operate an aircraft in controlled airspace under IFR unless—

(a) He has filed an IFR flight plan; and

(b) He has received an appropriate ATC clearance.

§ 91.116 Takeoff and landing under IFR: General.

(a) *Instrument approaches to civil airports.* Unless otherwise authorized by the Administrator for paragraphs (a) through (k) of this section, when an instrument letdown to a civil airport is necessary, each person operating an aircraft, except a military aircraft of the United States, shall use a standard instrument approach procedure prescribed for the airport in Part 97 of this chapter.

(b) *Authorized DH or MDA.* For the purpose of this section, when the approach procedure being used provides for and requires use of a DH or MDA, the authorized decision height or authorized minimum descent altitude is the DH or MDA prescribed by the approach procedure, the DH or MDA prescribed for the pilot in command, or the DH or MDA for which the aircraft is equipped, whichever is higher.

(c) *Operation below DH or MDA.* Where a DH or MDA is applicable, no pilot may operate an aircraft, except a military aircraft of the United States, at any airport below the authorized MDA or continue an approach below the authorized DH unless—

(1) The aircraft is continuously in a position from which a descent to a landing on the intended runway can be made at a normal rate of descent using normal maneuvers, and for operations conducted under Part 121 or Part 135 unless that descent rate will allow touchdown to occur within the touchdown zone of the runway of intended landing;

(2) The flight visibility is not less than the visibility prescribed in the standard instrument approach procedure being used;

(3) Except for a Category II or Category III approach where any necessary visual reference requirements are specified by the Administrator, at least one of the following visual references for the intended runway is distinctly visible and identifiable to the pilot:

(i) The approach light system, except that the pilot may not descend below 100 feet above the touchdown zone elevation using the approach lights as a reference unless the red terminating bars or the red side row bars are also distinctly visible and identifiable.

(ii) The threshold.

(iii) The threshold markings.

(iv) The threshold lights.

(v) The runway end identifier lights.

(vi) The visual approach slope indicator.

(vii) The touchdown zone or touchdown zone markings.

(viii) The touchdown zone lights.

(ix) The runway or runway markings.

(x) The runway lights; and

(4) When the aircraft is on a straight-in nonprecision approach procedure which incorporates a visual descent point, the aircraft has reached the visual descent point, except where the aircraft is not equipped for or capable of establishing that point or a descent to the runway cannot be made using normal procedures or rates of descent if descent is delayed until reaching that point.

(d) *Landing.* No pilot operating an aircraft, except a military aircraft of the United States, may land that aircraft when the flight visibility is less than the visibility prescribed in the standard instrument approach procedure being used.

(e) *Missed approach procedures.* Each pilot operating an aircraft, except a military aircraft of the United States, shall immediately execute an appropriate missed approach procedure when either of the following conditions exist:

(1) Whenever the requirements of paragraph (c) of this section are not met at either of the following times:

(i) When the aircraft is being operated below MDA; or

(ii) Upon arrival at the missed approach point, including a DH where a DH is specified and its use is required, and at any time after that until touchdown.

(2) Whenever an identifiable part of the airport is not distinctly visible to the pilot during a circling maneuver at or above MDA, unless the inability to see an identifiable part of the airport results only from a normal bank of the aircraft during the circling approach.

(f) *Civil airport takeoff minimums.* Unless otherwise authorized by the Administrator, no person operating an aircraft under Part 121, 125, 127, 129, or 135 of this chapter may take off from a civil airport under IFR unless weather conditions are at or above the weather minimums for IFR takeoff prescribed for that airport under Part 97 of this chapter. If takeoff minimums are not prescribed under Part 97 of this chapter for a particular airport, the following minimums apply to takeoffs under IFR for aircraft operating under those parts:

(1) For aircraft, other than helicopters, having two engines or less—1 statute mile visibility.

(2) For aircraft having more than two engines—½ statute mile visibility.

(3) For helicopters—1/2 statute mile visibility.

(g) *Military airports.* Unless otherwise prescribed by the Administrator, each person operating a civil aircraft under IFR into or out of a military airport shall comply with the instrument approach procedures and the takeoff and landing minimums prescribed by the military authority having jurisdiction of that airport.

(h) *Comparable values of RVR and ground visibility.* (1) Except for Category II or Category III minimums, if RVR minimums for takeoff or landing are prescribed in an instrument approach procedure, but RVR is not reported for the runway of intended operation, the RVR minimum shall be converted to ground visibility in accordance with the table in paragraph (h)(2) of this section and shall be the visibility minimum for takeoff or landing on that runway.

(2)

RVR (feet)	Visibility (statute miles)
1,600	¼
2,400	½
3,200	⅝
4,000	¾
4,500	⅞
5,000	1
6,000	1¼

(i) *Operations on unpublished routes and use of radar in instrument approach procedures.* When radar is approved at certain locations for ATC purposes, it may be used not only for surveillance and precision radar approaches, as applicable, but also may be used in conjunction with instrument approach procedures predicated on other types of radio navigational aids. Radar vectors may be authorized to provide course guidance through the segments of an approach procedure to the final approach course or fix. When operating on an unpublished route or while being radar vectored, the pilot, when an approach clearance is received, shall, in addition to complying with § 91.119, maintain the last altitude assigned to that pilot until the aircraft is established on a segment of a published route or instrument approach procedure unless a different altitude is assigned by ATC. After the aircraft is so established, published altitudes apply to descent within each succeeding route or approach segment unless a different altitude is assigned by ATC. Upon reaching the final approach course or fix, the pilot may either complete the instrument approach in accordance with a procedure approved for the facility or continue a surveillance or precision radar approach to a landing.

(j) *Limitation on procedure turns.* In the case of a radar vector to a final approach course or fix, a timed approach from a holding fix, or an approach for which the procedure specifies "No PT", no pilot may make a procedure turn unless cleared to do so by ATC.

(k) *ILS components.* The basic ground components of an ILS are the localizer, glide slope, outer marker, middle marker, and, when installed for use with Category II or Category III instrument approach procedures, an inner marker. A compass locator or precision radar may be substituted for the outer or middle marker. DME, VOR, or nondirectional beacon fixes authorized in the standard instrument approach procedure or surveillance radar may be substituted for the outer marker. Applicability of, and substitution for, the inner marker for Category II or III approaches is determined by the appropriate Part 97 approach procedure, letter of authorization, or operations specification pertinent to the operation.

[Amdt. 91-173, 46 FR 2290, Jan. 8, 1981, as amended by Amdt. 91-196, 51 FR 40707, Nov. 7, 1986]

§ 91.117　[Reserved]

§ 91.119　Minimum altitudes for IFR operations.

(a) Except when necessary for takeoff or landing, or unless otherwise authorized by the Administrator, no person may operate an aircraft under IFR below—

(1) The applicable minimum altitudes prescribed in Parts 95 and 97 of this chapter; or

(2) If no applicable minimum altitude is prescribed in those parts—

(i) In the case of operations over an area designated as a mountainous area in Part 95 an altitude of 2,000 feet above the highest obstacle within a horizontal distance of five statute miles from the course to be flown; or

(ii) In any other case, an altitude of 1,000 feet above the highest obstacle within a horizontal distance of five statute miles from the course to be flown.

However, if both a MEA and a MOCA are prescribed for a particular route or route segment, a person may operate an aircraft below the MEA down to, but not below, the MOCA, when within 25 statute miles of the VOR concerned (based on the pilot's reasonable estimate of that distance).

(b) *Climb.* Climb to a higher minimum IFR altitude shall begin immediately after passing the point beyond which that minimum altitude applies, except that, when ground obstructions intervene, the point beyond which the higher minimum altitude applies shall be crossed at or above the applicable MCA.

§ 91.121 IFR cruising altitude or flight level.

(a) *In controlled airspace.* Each person operating an aircraft under IFR in level cruising flight in controlled airspace shall maintain the altitude or flight level assigned that aircraft by ATC. However, if the ATC clearance assigns "VFR conditions on-top," he shall maintain an altitude or flight level as prescribed by § 91.109.

(b) *In uncontrolled airspace.* Except while holding in a holding pattern of two minutes or less, or while turning, each person operating an aircraft under IFR in level cruising flight, in uncontrolled airspace, shall maintain an appropriate altitude as follows:

(1) When operating below 18,000 feet MSL and—

(i) On a magnetic course of zero degrees through 179 degrees, any odd thousand foot MSL altitude (such as 3,000, 5,000, or 7,000); or

(ii) On a magnetic course of 180 degrees through 359 degrees, any even thousand foot MSL altitude (such as 2,000, 4,000, or 6,000).

(2) When operating at or above 18,000 feet MSL but below flight level 290, and—

(i) On a magnetic course of zero degrees through 179 degrees, any odd flight level (such as 190, 210, or 230); or

(ii) On a magnetic course of 180 degrees through 359 degrees, any even flight level (such as 180, 200, or 220).

(3) When operating at flight level 290 and above, and—

(i) On a magnetic course of zero degrees through 179 degrees, any flight level, at 4,000 foot intervals, beginning at and including flight level 290 (such as flight level 290, 330, or 370); or

(ii) On a magnetic course of 180 degrees through 359 degrees, any flight level, at 4,000 foot intervals, beginning at and including flight level 310 (such as flight level 310, 350, or 390).

[Amdt. 91-7, 29 FR 9894, July 23, 1964]

§ 91.123 Course to be flown.

Unless otherwise authorized by ATC, no person may operate an aircraft within controlled airspace, under IFR, except as follows:

(a) On a Federal airway, along the centerline of that airway.

(b) On any other route, along the direct course between the navigational aids or fixes defining that route.

However, this section does not prohibit maneuvering the aircraft to pass well clear of other air traffic or the maneuvering of the aircraft, in VFR conditions to clear the intended flight path both before and during climb or descent.

§ 91.125 IFR radio communications.

The pilot in command of each aircraft operated under IFR in controlled airspace shall have a continuous watch maintained on the appropriate frequency and shall report by radio as soon as possible—

(a) The time and altitude of passing each designated reporting point, or the reporting points specified by ATC, except that while the aircraft is under radar control, only the passing of those reporting points specifically requested by ATC need be reported;

(b) Any unforecast weather conditions encountered; and

(c) Any other information relating to the safety of flight.

[Doc. No. 1580, Amdt. 1-1, 28 FR 6704, June 29, 1963, as amended by Amdt. 91-5, 30 FR 15322, Dec. 11, 1965]

§ 91.127 IFR operations; two-way radio communications failure.

(a) *General.* Unless otherwise authorized by ATC, each pilot who has two-way radio communications failure when operating under IFR shall comply with the rules of this section.

(b) *VFR conditions.* If the failure occurs in VFR conditions, or if VFR conditions are encountered after the failure, each pilot shall continue the flight under VFR and land as soon as practicable.

(c) *IFR conditions.* If the failure occurs in IFR conditions, or if paragraph (b) of this section cannot be complied with, each pilot shall continue the flight according to the following:

(1) *Route.* (i) By the route assigned in the last ATC clearance received;

(ii) If being radar vectored, by the direct route from the point of radio failure to the fix, route, or airway specified in the vector clearance;

(iii) In the absence of an assigned route, by the route that ATC has advised may be expected in a further clearance; or

(iv) In the absence of an assigned route or a route that ATC has advised may be expected in a further clearance, by the route filed in the flight plan.

(2) *Altitude.* At the highest of the following altitudes or flight levels for the route segment being flown:

(i) The altitude or flight level assigned in the last ATC clearance received;

(ii) The minimum altitude (converted, if appropriate, to minimum flight level as prescribed in § 91.81(c)) for IFR operations; or

(iii) The altitude or flight level ATC has advised may be expected in a further clearance.

(3) *Leave clearance limit.* (i) When the clearance limit is a fix from which an approach begins, commence descent or descent and approach as close as possible to the expect further clearance time if one has been received, or if one has not been received, as close as possible to the estimated time of arrival as calculated from the filed or amended (with ATC) estimated time en route.

(ii) If the clearance limit is not a fix from which an approach begins, leave the clearance limit at the expect further clearance time if one has been received, or if none has been received, upon arrival over the clearance limit, and proceed to a fix from which an approach begins and commence descent or descent and approach as close as possible to the estimated time of arrival as calculated from the filed or amended (with ATC) estimated time en route.

[Doc. No. 1580, Amdt. 1-1, 28 FR 6704, June 29, 1963, as amended by Amdt. 91-14, 30 FR 3706, Mar. 20, 1965; Amdt. 91-86, 36 FR 2481, Feb. 5, 1971; Amdt. 91-189, 50 FR 31588, Aug. 5, 1985]

§ 91.129 Operation under IFR in controlled airspace; malfunction reports.

(a) The pilot in command of each aircraft operated in controlled airspace under IFR, shall report immediately to ATC any of the following malfunctions of equipment occurring in flight:

(1) Loss of VOR, TACAN, ADF, or low frequency navigation receiver capability.

(2) Complete or partial loss of ILS receiver capability.

(3) Impairment of air/ground communications capability.

(b) In each report required by paragraph (a) of this section, the pilot in command shall include the—

(1) Aircraft identification;

(2) Equipment affected;

(3) Degree to which the capability of the pilot to operate under IFR in the ATC system is impaired; and

(4) Nature and extent of assistance he desires from ATC.

Subpart C—Maintenance, Preventive Maintenance, and Alterations

§ 91.161 Applicability.

(a) This subpart prescribes rules governing the maintenance, preventative maintenance, and alteration of U.S. registered civil aircraft operating within or without the United States.

(b) Sections 91.165, 91.169, 91.171, 91.173, and 91.174 of this subpart do not apply to an aircraft maintained in accordance with a continuous airworthiness maintenance program as provided in Part 121, 127, 129, or § 135.411(a)(2) of this chapter.

(c) Sections 91.165, 91.169, 91.171, and Subpart D of this part do not apply to an airplane inspected in accordance with Part 125 of this chapter.

[Amdt. 91-29, 31 FR 8355, June 15, 1966; as amended by Amdt. 91-169, 45 FR 67234, Oct. 9, 1980; Amdt. 91-181, 47 FR 41086, Sept. 16, 1982; Amdt. 91-201, 52 FR 20028, May 28, 1987]

§ 91.163 General.

(a) The owner or operator of an aircraft is primarily responsible for maintaining that aircraft in an airworthy condition, including compliance with Part 39 of this chapter.

(b) No person may perform maintenance, preventive maintenance, or alterations on an aircraft other than as prescribed in this subpart and other applicable regulations, including Part 43 of this chapter.

(c) No person may operate an aircraft for which a manufacturer's maintenance manual or Instructions for Continued Airworthiness has been issued that contains an Airworthiness Limitations section unless the mandatory replacement times, inspection intervals, and related procedures specified in that section or alternative inspection intervals and related procedures set forth in an operations specification approved by the Administrator under Parts 121, 123, 127, or 135, or in accordance with an inspection program approved under § 91.217(e), have been complied with.

[Amdt. 91-19, 30 FR 8033, June 23, 1965, as amended by Amdt. 91-29, 31 FR 8355, June 15, 1966; Amdt. 91-167, 45 FR 60183, Sept. 11, 1980]

§ 91.165 Maintenance required.

Each owner or operator of an aircraft shall have that aircraft inspected as prescribed in §§ 91.169, 91.171, and 91.172 and shall, between required inspections, have discrepancies repaired as prescribed in Part 43 of this chapter. In addition, each owner or operator shall ensure that maintenance personnel make appropriate entries in the aircraft maintenance records indicating that the aircraft has been approved for return to service.

[Doc. No. 21071, Amdt. 91-181, 47 FR 41086, Sept. 16, 1982]

§ 91.167 Operation after maintenance, preventive maintenance, rebuilding, or alteration.

(a) No person may operate any aircraft that has undergone maintenance, preventive maintenance, rebuilding, or alteration unless—

(1) It has been approved for return to service by a person authorized under § 43.7 of this chapter; and

(2) The maintenance record entry required by §43.9 or §43.11, as applicable, of this chapter has been made.

(b) No person may carry any person (other than crewmembers) in an aircraft that has been maintained, rebuilt, or altered in a manner that may have appreciably changed its flight characteristics or substantially affected its operation in flight until an appropriately rated pilot with at least a private pilot certificate flies the aircraft, makes an operational check of the maintenance performed or alteration made, and logs the flight in the aircraft records.

(c) The aircraft does not have to be flown as required by paragraph (b) of this section if, prior to flight, ground tests, inspections, or both show conclusively that the maintenance, preventive maintenance, rebuilding, or alteration has not appreciably changed the flight characteristics or substantially affected the flight operation of the aircraft.

(Approved by the Office of Management and Budget under OMB control number 2120-0005)

[Doc. No. 21071, Amdt. 91-181, 47 FR 41086, Sept. 16, 1982]

§ 91.169 Inspections.

(a) Except as provided in paragraph (c) of this section, no person may operate an aircraft unless, within the preceding 12 calendar months, it has had—

(1) An annual inspection in accordance with Part 43 of this chapter and has been approved for return to service by a person authorized by § 43.7 of this chapter; or

(2) An inspection for the issue of an airworthiness certificate.

No inspection performed under paragraph (b) of this section may be substituted for any inspection required by this paragraph unless it is performed by a person authorized to perform annual inspections, and is entered as an "annual" inspection in the required maintenance records.

(b) Except as provided in paragraph (c) of this section, no person may operate an aircraft carrying any person (other than a crewmember) for hire, and no person may give flight instruction for hire in an aircraft which that person provides, unless within the preceding 100 hours of time in service it has received an annual or 100-hour inspection and been approved for return to service in accordance with Part 43 of this chapter, or received an inspection for the issuance of an airworthiness certificate in accordance with Part 21 of this chapter. The 100-hour limitation may be exceeded by not more than 10 hours if necessary to reach a place at which the inspection can be done. The excess time, however, is included in computing the next 100 hours of time in service.

(c) Paragraphs (a) and (b) of this section do not apply to—

(1) An aircraft that carries a special flight permit, a current experimental certificate, or a provisional airworthiness certificate;

(2) An aircraft inspected in accordance with an approved aircraft inspection program under Part 123, 125, or 135 of this chapter and so identified by the registration number in the operations specifications of the certificate holder having the approved inspection program; or

(3) An aircraft subject to the requirements of paragraph (d) or (e) of this section.

(d) *Progressive inspection.* Each registered owner or operator of an aircraft desiring to use a progressive inspection program must submit a written request to the FAA Flight Standards district office having jurisdiction over the area in which the applicant is located, and shall provide—

(1) A certificated mechanic holding an inspection authorization, a certificated airframe repair station, or the manufacturer of the aircraft to supervise or conduct the progressive inspection;

(2) A current inspection procedures manual available and readily understandable to pilot and maintenance personnel containing, in detail—

(i) An explanation of the progressive inspection, including the continuity of inspection responsibility, the making of reports, and the keeping of records and technical reference material;

(ii) An inspection schedule, specifying the intervals in hours or days when routine and detailed inspections will be performed and including instructions for exceeding an inspection interval by not more than 10 hours while en route and for changing an inspection interval because of service experience;

(iii) Sample routine and detailed inspection forms and instructions for their use; and

(iv) Sample reports and records and instructions for their use;

(3) Enough housing and equipment for necessary disassembly and proper inspection of the aircraft; and

(4) Appropriate current technical information for the aircraft.

The frequency and detail of the progressive inspection shall provide for the complete inspection of the aircraft within each 12-calendar months and be consistent with the manufacturer's recommendations, field service experience, and the kind of operation in which the aircraft is engaged. The progressive inspection schedule must ensure that the aircraft, at all times, will be airworthy and will conform to all applicable FAA aircraft specifications, type certificate data sheets, airworthiness directives, and other approved data. If the progressive inspection is discontinued, the owner or operator shall immediately notify the local FAA Flight Standards district office, in writing, of the discontinuance. After the discontinuance, the first annual inspection under §91.169(a) is due within 12-calendar months after the last complete inspection of the aircraft under the progressive inspection. The 100-hour inspection under §91.169(b) is due within 100 hours after that complete inspection. A complete inspection of the aircraft, for the purpose of determining when the annual and 100-hour inspections are due, requires a detailed inspection of the aircraft and all its components in accordance with the progressive inspection. A routine inspection of the aircraft and a detailed inspection of several components is not considered to be a complete inspection.

(e) *Large airplanes (to which Part 125 is not applicable), turbojet multiengine airplanes, and turbopropeller-powered multiengine airplanes.* No person may operate a large airplane, turbojet multiengine airplane, or turbopropeller-powered multiengine airplane unless the replacement times for life-limited parts specified in the aircraft specifications, type data sheets, or other documents approved by the Administrator are complied with and the airplane, including the airframe, engines, propellers, appliances, survival equipment, and emergency equipment, is inspected in accordance with an inspection program selected under the provisions of paragraph (f) of this section.

(f) *Selection of inspection programs under paragraph (e) of this section.* The registered owner or operator of each airplane described in paragraph (e) of this section must select, identify in the aircraft maintenance records, and use one of the following programs for the inspection of that airplane:

(1) A continuous airworthiness inspection program that is part of a continuous airworthiness maintenance program currently in use by a person holding an air carrier operating certificate or an operating certificate issued under Part 121, 127, or 135 of this

chapter and operating that make and model airplane under Part 121 or 127 or operating that make and model under Part 135 and maintaining it under §135.411(a)(2).

(2) An approved aircraft inspection program approved under §135.419 of this chapter and currently in use by a person holding an operating certificate issued under Part 135.

(3) An approved continuous inspection program currently in use by a person certificated under Part 123 of this chapter.

(4) A current inspection program recommended by the manufacturer.

(5) Any other inspection program established by the registered owner or operator of that airplane and approved by the Administrator under paragraph (g) of this section. However, the Administrator may require revision to this inspection program in accordance with the provisions of §91.170.

Each operator shall include in the selected program the name and address of the person responsible for scheduling the inspections required by the program and make a copy of that program available to the person performing inspections on the airplane and, upon request, to the Administrator.

(g) *Inspection program approval under paragraph (e) of this section.* Each operator of an airplane desiring to establish or change an approved inspection program under paragraph (f)(5) of this section must submit the program for approval to the local FAA Flight Standards district office having jurisdiction over the area in which the airplane is based. The program must be in writing and include at least the following information:

(1) Instruction and procedures for the conduct of inspections for the particular make and model airplane, including necessary tests and checks. The instructions and procedures must set forth in detail the parts and areas of the airframe, engines, propellers, and appliances, including survival and emergency equipment required to be inspected.

(2) A schedule for performing the inspections that must be performed under the program expressed in terms

of the time in service, calendar time, number of system operations, or any combination of these.

(h) *Changes from one inspection program to another.* When an operator changes from one inspection program under paragraph (f) of this section to another, the time in service, calendar times, or cycles of operation accumulated under the previous program must be applied in determining inspection due times under the new program.

(Approved by the Office of Management and Budget under OMB control number 2120–0005)

[Doc. No. 1580, Amdt. 1-1, 28 FR 6704, June 29, 1963, as amended by Amdt. 91-26, 31 FR 3337, Mar. 3, 1966; Amdt. 91-30, 31 FR 9211, July 6, 1966; Amdt. 91-74, 35 FR 4116, Mar. 5, 1970; Amdt. 91-181, 47 FR 41086, Sept. 16, 1982]

§ 91.170 Changes to aircraft inspection programs.

(a) Whenever the Administrator finds that revisions to an approved aircraft inspection program under § 91.169(f)(5) are necessary for the continued adequacy of the program, the owner or operator shall, after notification by the Administrator, make any changes in the program found to be necessary by the Administrator.

(b) The owner or operator may petition the Administrator to reconsider the notice to make any changes in a program in accordance with paragraph (a) of this section.

(c) The petition must be filed with the FAA Flight Standards district office which requested the change to the program within 30 days after the certificate holder receives the notice.

(d) Except in the case of an emergency requiring immediate action in the interest of safety, the filing of the petition stays the notice pending a decision by the Administrator.

[Doc. No. 21071, Amdt. 91-181, 47 FR 41087, Sept. 16, 1982]

§ 91.171 Altimeter system and altitude reporting equipment tests and inspections.

(a) No person may operate an airplane or helicopter in controlled airspace under IFR unless—

(1) Within the preceding 24 calendar months, each static pressure system, each altimeter instrument, and each automatic pressure altitude reporting system has been tested and inspected and found to comply with Appendices E and F of Part 43 of this chapter;

(2) Except for the use of system drain and alternate static pressure valves, following any opening and closing of the static pressure system, that system has been tested and inspected and found to comply with paragraph (a), Appendix E, of Part 43 of this chapter; and

(3) Following installation or maintenance on the automatic pressure altitude reporting system or the ATC transponder where data correspondence error could be introduced, the integrated system has been tested, inspected, and found to comply with paragraph (c), Appendix E, of Part 43 of this chapter.

(b) The tests required by paragraph (a) of this section must be conducted by—

(1) The manufacturer of the airplane or helicopter on which the tests and inspections are to be performed;

(2) A certificated repair station properly equipped to perform those functions and holding—

(i) An instrument rating, Class I;

(ii) A limited instrument rating appropriate to the make and model of appliance to be tested;

(iii) A limited rating appropriate to the test to be performed;

(iv) An airframe rating appropriate to the airplane or helicopter to be tested; or

(v) A limited rating for a manufacturer issued for the appliance in accordance with § 145.101(b)(4) of this chapter; or

(3) A certificated mechanic with an airframe rating (static pressure system tests and inspections only).

(c) Altimeter and altitude reporting equipment approved under Technical Standard Orders are considered to be tested and inspected as of the date of their manufacture.

(d) No person may operate an airplane or helicopter in controlled airspace under IFR at an altitude above the maximum altitude at which all altimeters and the automatic altitude reporting system of that airplane have been tested.

[Doc. No. 21071, Amdt. 91–181, 47 FR 41088, Sept. 16, 1982, as amended by Amdt. 91–196, 51 FR 40707, Nov. 7, 1986]

§ 91.172 ATC transponder tests and inspections.

(a) No person may use an ATC transponder that is specified in Part 125, § 91.24(a), § 121.345(c), § 127.123(b) or § 135.143(c) of this chapter unless, within the preceding 24 calendar months, that ATC transponder has been tested and inspected and found to comply with Appendix F of Part 43 of this chapter; and

(b) Following any installation or maintenance on an ATC transponder where data correspondence error could be introduced, the integrated system has been tested, inspected, and found to comply with paragraph (c), Appendix E, of Part 43 of this chapter.

(c) The tests and inspections specified in this section must be conducted by—

(1) A certificated repair station properly equipped to perform those functions and holding—

(i) A radio rating, Class III;

(ii) A limited radio rating appropriate to the make and model transponder to be tested;

(iii) A limited rating appropriate to the test to be performed;

(iv) A limited rating for a manufacturer issued for the transponder in accordance with § 145.101(b)(4) of this chapter; or

(2) A holder of a continuous airworthiness maintenance program as provided in Part 121, 127, or § 135.411(a)(2) of this chapter; or

(3) The manufacturer of the aircraft on which the transponder to be tested is installed, if the transponder was installed by that manufacturer.

[Doc. No. 21071, Amdt. 91–181, 47 FR 41088, Sept. 16, 1982; 47 FR 44246, Oct. 7, 1982]

§ 91.173 Maintenance records.

(a) Except for work performed in accordance with § 91.171, each registered owner or operator shall keep the following records for the periods specified in paragraph (b) of this section:

(1) Records of the maintenance, preventive maintenance, and alteration, and records of the 100-hour, annual, progressive, and other required or approved inspections, as appropriate, for each aircraft (including the airframe) and each engine, propeller, rotor, and appliance of an aircraft. The records must include—

(i) A description (or reference to data acceptable to the Administrator) of the work performed;

(ii) The date of completion of the work performed; and

(iii) The signature and certificate number of the person approving the aircraft for return to service.

(2) Records containing the following information:

(i) The total time in service of the airframe, each engine and each propeller.

(ii) The current status of life-limited parts of each airframe, engine, propeller, rotor, and appliance.

(iii) The time since last overhaul of all items installed on the aircraft which are required to be overhauled on a specified time basis.

(iv) The identification of the current inspection status of the aircraft, including the times since the last inspections required by the inspection program under which the aircraft and its appliances are maintained.

(v) The current status of applicable airworthiness directives (AD) including, for each, the method of compliance, the AD number, and revision date. If the AD involves recurring action, the time and date when the next action is required.

(vi) Copies of the forms prescribed by § 43.9(a) of this chapter for each major alteration to the airframe and currently installed engines, rotors, propellers, and appliances.

(b) The owner or operator shall retain the following records for the periods prescribed:

(1) The records specified in paragraph (a)(1) of this section shall be retained until the work is repeated or superseded by other work or for 1 year after the work is performed.

(2) The records specified in paragraph (a)(2) of this section shall be retained and transferred with the aircraft at the time the aircraft is sold.

(3) A list of defects furnished to a registered owner or operator under § 43.11 of this chapter, shall be retained until the defects are repaired

and the aircraft is approved for return to service.

(c) The owner or operator shall make all maintenance records required to be kept by this section available for inspection by the Administrator or any authorized representative of the National Transportation Safety Board (NTSB). In addition, the owner or operator shall present the Form 337 described in paragraph (d) of this section for inspection upon request of any law enforcement officer.

(d) When a fuel tank is installed within the passenger compartment or a baggage compartment pursuant to Part 43, a copy of the FAA Form 337 shall be kept on board the modified aircraft by the owner or operator.

(Approved by the Office of Management and Budget under OMB control number 2120-0005)

[Doc. No. 10658, Amdt. 91-102, 37 FR 15983, Aug. 9, 1972, as amended by Amdt. 91-152, 43 FR 22640, May 25, 1978; Amdt. 91-167, 45 FR 60183, Sept. 11, 1980; Amdt. 91-181, 47 FR 41088, Sept. 16, 1982; Amdt. 91-200, 52 FR 17277, May 6, 1987; Amdt. 91-206, 52 FR 34102, Sept. 9, 1987]

§ 91.174 Transfer of maintenance records.

Any owner or operator who sells a U.S. registered aircraft shall transfer to the purchaser, at the time of sale, the following records of that aircraft, in plain language form or in coded form at the election of the purchaser, if the coded form provides for the preservation and retrieval of information in a manner acceptable to the Administrator:

(a) The records specified in § 91.173(a)(2).

(b) The records specified in § 91.173(a)(1) which are not included in the records covered by paragraph (a) of this section, except that the purchaser may permit the seller to keep physical custody of such records. However, custody of records in the seller does not relieve the purchaser of his responsibility under § 91.173(c), to make the records available for inspection by the Administrator or any authorized representative of the National Transportation Safety Board (NTSB).

[Doc. No. 10658, Amdt. 91-102, 37 FR 15983, Aug. 9, 1972]

§ 91.175 Rebuilt engine maintenance records.

(a) The owner or operator may use a new maintenance record, without previous operating history, for an aircraft engine rebuilt by the manufacturer or by an agency approved by the manufacturer.

(b) Each manufacturer or agency that grants zero time to an engine rebuilt by it shall enter, in the new record—

(1) A signed statement of the date the engine was rebuilt;

(2) Each change made as required by Airworthiness Directives; and

(3) Each change made in compliance with manufacturer's service bulletins, if the entry is specifically requested in that bulletin.

(c) For the purposes of this section, a rebuilt engine is a used engine that has been completely disassembled, inspected, repaired as necessary, reassembled, tested, and approved in the same manner and to the same tolerances and limits as a new engine with either new or used parts. However, all parts used in it must conform to the production drawing tolerances and limits for new parts or be of approved oversize or undersize dimensions for a new engine.

Subpart D—Large and Turbine-Powered Multiengine Airplanes

SOURCE: Docket No. 11437, Amdt. 91-101, 37 FR 14763, July 25, 1972, unless otherwise noted.

§ 91.181 Applicability.

(a) Sections 91.181 through 91.215 prescribe operating rules, in addition to those prescribed in other subparts of this part, governing the operation of large and of turbojet-powered multiengine civil airplanes of U.S. registry. The operating rules in this subpart do not apply to those airplanes when they are required to be operated under Parts 121, 123, 125, 129, 135, and 137 of this chapter. Section 91.169 prescribes an inspection program for large and for turbine-powered (turbojet and turboprop) multiengine airplanes of U.S. registry when they are operated under this part or Part 129 or 137.

(b) Operations that may be conducted under the rules in this subpart instead of those in Parts 121, 123, 129, 135, and 137 of this chapter, when common carriage is not involved, include—

(1) Ferry or training flights;

(2) Aerial work operations such as aerial photography or survey, or pipeline patrol, but not including firefighting operations;

(3) Flights for the demonstration of an airplane to prospective customers when no charge is made except for those specified in paragraph (d) of this section;

(4) Flights conducted by the operator of an airplane for his personal transportation, or the transportation of his guests when no charge, assessment, or fee is made for the transportation;

(5) The carriage of officials, employees, guests, and property of a company on an airplane operated by that company, or the parent or a subsidiary of that company or a subsidiary of the parent, when the carriage is within the scope of, and incidental to, the business of the company (other than transportation by air) and no charge, assessment or fee is made for the carriage in excess of the cost of owning, operating, and maintaining the airplane, except that no charge of any kind may be made for the carriage of a guest of a company, when the carriage is not within the scope of, and incidental to, the business of that company;

(6) The carriage of company officials, employees, and guests of the company on an airplane operated under a time sharing, interchange, or joint ownership agreement as defined in paragraph (c) of this section;

(7) The carriage of property (other than mail) on an airplane operated by a person in the furtherance of a business or employment (other than transportation by air) when the carriage is within the scope of, and incidental to, that business or employment and no charge, assessment, or fee is made for the carriage other than those specified in paragraph (d) of this section;

(8) The carriage on an airplane of an athletic team, sports group, choral group, or similar group having a common purpose or objective when there is no charge, assessment, or fee of any kind made by any person for that carriage; and

(9) The carriage of persons on an airplane operated by a person in the furtherance of a business (other than transportation by air) for the purpose of selling to them land, goods, or property, including franchises or distributorships, when the carriage is within the scope of, and incidental to, that business and no charge, assessment, or fee is made for that carriage.

(c) As used in this section:

(1) A "time sharing agreement" means an arrangement whereby a person leases his airplane with flight crew to another person, and no charge is made for the flights conducted under that arrangement other than those specified in paragraph (d) of this section;

(2) An "interchange agreement" means an arrangement whereby a person leases his airplane to another person in exchange for equal time, when needed, on the other person's airplane, and no charge, assessment, or fee is made, except that a charge may be made not to exceed the difference between the cost of owning, operating, and maintaining the two airplanes;

(3) A "joint ownership agreement" means an arrangement whereby one of the registered joint owners of an airplane employs and furnishes the flight crew for that airplane and each of the registered joint owners pays a share of the charges specified in the agreement.

(d) The following may be charged, as expenses of a specific flight, for transportation as authorized by paragraphs (b)(3) and (7) and (c)(1) of this section:

(1) Fuel, oil, lubricants, and other additives.

(2) Travel expenses of the crew, including food, lodging, and ground transportation.

(3) Hangar and tie-down costs away from the aircraft's base of operations.

(4) Insurance obtained for the specific flight.

(5) Landing fees, airport taxes, and similar assessments.

(6) Customs, foreign permit, and similar fees directly related to the flight.

(7) In flight food and beverages.

(8) Passenger ground transportation.

(9) Flight planning and weather contract services.

(10) An additional charge equal to 100 percent of the expenses listed in paragraph (d)(1) of this section.

[Doc. No. 11437, Amdt. 91-101, 37 FR 14763, July 25, 1972, as amended by Amdt. 91-118, 38 FR 19025, July 17, 1973; Amdt. 91-133, 41 FR 47229, Oct. 28, 1976; Amdt. 91-164, 45 FR 67234, Oct. 9, 1980; Amdt. 91-181, 47 FR 41088, Sept. 16, 1982]

§ 91.183 Flying equipment and operating information.

(a) The pilot in command of an airplane shall insure that the following flying equipment and aeronautical charts and data, in current and appropriate form, are accessible for each flight at the pilot station of the airplane:

(1) A flashlight having at least two size D cells, or the equivalent, that is in good working order.

(2) A cockpit checklist containing the procedures required by paragraph (b) of this section.

(3) Pertinent aeronautical charts.

(4) For IFR, VFR over-the-top, or night operations, each pertinent navigational en route, terminal area, and approach and letdown chart.

(5) In the case of multiengine airplanes, one-engine inoperative climb performance data.

(b) Each cockpit checklist must contain the following procedures and shall be used by the flight crewmembers when operating the airplane:

(1) Before starting engines.

(2) Before takeoff.

(3) Cruise.

(4) Before landing.

(5) After landing.

(6) Stopping engines.

(7) Emergencies.

(c) Each emergency cockpit checklist procedure required by paragraph (b)(7) of this section must contain the following procedures, as appropriate:

(1) Emergency operation of fuel, hydraulic, electrical, and mechanical systems.

(2) Emergency operation of instruments and controls.

(3) Engine inoperative procedures.

(4) Any other procedures necessary for safety.

(d) The equipment, charts, and data prescribed in this section shall be used by the pilot in command and other members of the flight crew, when pertinent.

§ 91.185 Familiarity with operating limitations and emergency equipment.

(a) Each pilot in command of an airplane shall, before beginning a flight, familiarize himself with the airplane flight manual for that airplane, if one is required, and with any placards, listings, instrument markings, or any combination thereof, containing each operating limitation prescribed for that airplane by the Administrator, including those specified in § 91.31(b).

(b) Each required member of the crew shall, before beginning a flight, familiarize himself with the emergency equipment installed on the airplane to which he is assigned and with the procedures to be followed for the use of that equipment in an emergency situation.

§ 91.187 Equipment requirements: Over-the-top, or night VFR operations.

No person may operate an airplane over-the-top, or at night under VFR unless that airplane is equipped with the instruments and equipment required for IFR operations under § 91.33(d) and one electric landing light for night operations. Each required instrument and item of equipment must be in operable condition.

§ 91.189 Survival equipment for overwater operations.

(a) No person may take off an airplane for a flight over water more than 50 nautical miles from the nearest shoreline, unless that airplane is equipped with a life preserver or an approved flotation means for each occupant of the airplane.

(b) No person may take off an airplane for a flight over water more than 30 minutes flying time or 100 nautical miles from the nearest shoreline, unless it has on board the following survival equipment:

(1) A life preserver equipped with an approved survivor locator light, for each occupant of the airplane.

(2) Enough liferafts (each equipped with an approved survivor locator light) of a rated capacity and buoyancy to accommodate the occupants of the airplane.

(3) At least one pyrotechnic signaling device for each raft.

(4) One self-buoyant, water-resistant, portable emergency radio signaling device, that is capable of transmission on the appropriate emergency frequency or frequencies, and not dependent upon the airplane power supply.

(5) After June 26, 1979, a lifeline stored in accordance with § 25.1411(g) of this chapter.

(c) The required liferafts, life preservers, and signaling devices must be installed in conspicuously marked locations and easily accessible in the event of a ditching without appreciable time for preparatory procedures.

(d) A survival kit, appropriately equipped for the route to be flown, must be attached to each required liferaft.

[Doc. No. 1580, Amdt. 1-1, 28 FR 6704, June 29, 1963, as amended by Amdt. 91-152, 43 FR 22641, May 25, 1978]

§ 91.191 Radio equipment for overwater operations.

(a) Except as provided in paragraphs (c) and (d) of this section, no person may takeoff an airplane for a flight over water more than 30 minutes flying time or 100 nautical miles from the nearest shoreline, unless it has at least the following operable radio communication and navigational equipment appropriate to the facilities to be used and able to transmit to, and receive from, at any place on the route, at least one surface facility:

(1) Two transmitters.

(2) Two microphones.

(3) Two headsets or one headset and one speaker.

(4) Two independent receivers for navigation.

(5) Two independent receivers for communications.

However, a receiver that can receive both communications and navigational signals may be used in place of a separate communications receiver and a separate navigational signal receiver.

(b) For the purposes of paragraphs (a)(4) and (5) of this section, a receiver is independent if the function of any part of it does not depend on the functioning of any part of another receiver.

(c) Notwithstanding the provisions of paragraph (a) of this section, a person may operate an airplane on which no passengers are carried from a place where repairs or replacement cannot be made to a place where they can be made, if not more than one of each of the dual items of radio communication and navigation equipment specified in paragraphs (a)(1) through (5) of this section malfunctions or becomes inoperative.

(d) Notwithstanding the provisions of paragraph (a) of this section, when both VHF and HF communications equipment are required for the route and the airplane has two VHF transmitters and two VHF receivers for communications, only one HF transmitter and one HF receiver is required for communications.

[Doc. No. 11437, Amdt. 91-101, 37 FR 14763, July 25, 1972, as amended by Amdt. 91-132, 41 FR 16795, Apr. 22, 1976]

§ 91.193 Emergency equipment.

(a) No person may operate an airplane unless it is equipped with the emergency equipment listed in this section:

(b) Each item of equipment—

(1) Must be inspected in accordance with § 91.217 to insure its continued serviceability and immediate readiness for its intended purposes;

(2) Must be readily accessible to the crew;

(3) Must clearly indicate its method of operation; and

(4) When carried in a compartment or container, must have that compartment or container marked as to contents and date of last inspection.

(c) Hand fire extinguishers must be provided for use in crew, passenger, and cargo compartments in accordance with the following:

(1) The type and quantity of extinguishing agent must be suitable for the kinds of fires likely to occur in the

compartment where the extinguisher is intended to be used.

(2) At least one hand fire extinguisher must be provided and located on or near the flight deck in a place that is readily accessible to the flight crew.

(3) At least one hand fire extinguisher must be conveniently located in the passenger compartment of each airplane accommodating more than six but less than 31 passengers, and at least two hand fire extinguishers must be conveniently located in the passenger compartment of each airplane accommodating more than 30 passengers.

(4) Hand fire extinguishers must be installed and secured in such a manner that they will not interfere with the safe operation of the airplane or adversely affect the safety of the crew and passengers. They must be readily accessible, and unless the locations of the fire extinguishers are obvious, their stowage provisions must be properly identified.

(d) First aid kits for treatment of injuries likely to occur in flight or in minor accidents must be provided.

(e) Each airplane accommodating more than 19 passengers must be equipped with a crash ax.

(f) Each passenger-carrying airplane must have a portable battery-powered megaphone or megaphones readily accessible to the crewmembers assigned to direct emergency evacuation, installed as follows:

(1) One megaphone on each airplane with a seating capacity of more than 60 but less than 100 passengers, at the most rearward location in the passenger cabin where it would be readily accessible to a normal flight attendant seat. However, the Administrator may grant a deviation from the requirements of this paragraph if he finds that a different location would be more useful for evacuation of persons during an emergency.

(2) Two megaphones in the passenger cabin on each airplane with a seating capacity of more than 99 passengers, one installed at the forward end and the other at the most rearward location where it would be readily accessible to a normal flight attendant seat.

[Doc. No. 11437, Amdt. 91-101, 37 FR 14763, July 25, 1972, as amended by Amdt. 91-167, 45 FR 60183, Sept. 11, 1980]

§ 91.195 Flight altitude rules.

(a) Notwithstanding § 91.79, and except as provided in paragraph (b) of this section, no person may operate an airplane under VFR at less than—

(1) One thousand feet above the surface, or 1,000 feet from any mountain, hill, or other obstruction to flight, for day operations; and

(2) The altitudes prescribed in § 91.119, for night operations.

(b) This section does not apply—

(1) During takeoff or landing;

(2) When a different altitude is authorized by a waiver to this section under § 91.63; or

(3) When a flight is conducted under the special VFR weather minimums of § 91.107 with an appropriate clearance from ATC.

§ 91.197 Smoking and safety belt signs.

(a) Except as provided in paragraph (b) of this section, no person may operate an airplane carrying passengers unless it is equipped with signs that are visible to passengers and cabin attendants to notify them when smoking is prohibited and when safety belts should be fastened. The signs must be so constructed that the crew can turn them on and off. They must be turned on for each takeoff and each landing and when otherwise considered to be necessary by the pilot in command.

(b) The pilot in command of an airplane that is not equipped as provided in paragraph (a) of this section shall insure that the passengers are orally notified each time that it is necessary to fasten their safety belts and when smoking is prohibited.

§ 91.199 Passenger briefing.

(a) Before each takeoff the pilot in command of an airplane carrying passengers shall ensure that all passengers have been orally briefed on:

(1) Smoking;

(2) Use of safety belts;

(3) Location and means for opening the passenger entry door and emergency exits;

(4) Location of survival equipment;

(5) Ditching procedures and the use of flotation equipment required under § 91.189 for a flight over water; and

(6) The normal and emergency use of oxygen equipment installed on the airplane.

(b) The oral briefing required by paragraph (a) of this section shall be given by the pilot in command or a member of the crew, but need not be given when the pilot in command determines that the passengers are familiar with the contents of the briefing. It may be supplemented by printed cards for the use of each passenger containing—

(1) A diagram of, and methods of operating, the emergency exits; and

(2) Other instructions necessary for use of emergency equipment.

Each card used under this paragraph must be carried in convenient locations on the airplane for use of each passenger and must contain information that is pertinent only to the type and model airplane on which it is used.

§ 91.200 Shoulder harness.

(a) No person may operate a transport category airplane that was type certificated after January 1, 1958, unless it is equipped at each seat at a flight-deck station with a combined safety belt and shoulder harness that meets the applicable requirements specified in § 25.785 of this chapter, except that—

(1) Shoulder harnesses and combined safety belt and shoulder harnesses that were approved and installed before March 6, 1980, may continue to be used; and

(2) Safety belt and shoulder harness restraint systems may be designed to the inertia load factors established under the certification basis of the airplane.

(b) No person may operate a transport category airplane unless it is equipped at each required flight attendant seat in the passenger compartment with a combined safety belt and shoulder harness that meets the applicable requirements specified in § 25.785 of this chapter, except that—

(1) Shoulder harnesses and combined safety belt and shoulder harnesses that were approved and in-

stalled before March 6, 1980, may continue to be used; and

(2) Safety belt and shoulder harness restraint systems may be designed to the inertia load factors established under the certification basis of the airplane.

[Doc. No. 23584, Amdt. 91-183, 48 FR 13663, Mar. 31, 1983]

§ 91.201 Carry-on-baggage.

No pilot in command of an airplane having a seating capacity of more than 19 passengers may permit a passenger to stow his baggage aboard that airplane except—

(a) In a suitable baggage or cargo storage compartment, or as provided in § 91.203; or

(b) Under a passenger seat in such a way that it will not slide forward under crash impacts severe enough to induce the ultimate inertia forces specified in § 25.561(b)(3) of this chapter, or the requirements of the regulations under which the airplane was type certificated. After December 4, 1979, restraining devices must also limit sideward motion of under-seat baggage and be designed to withstand crash impacts severe enough to induce sideward forces specified in § 25.561(b)(3) of this chapter.

[Doc. No. 1580, Amdt. 91-1, 28 FR 6704, June 29, 1963, as amended by Amdt. 91-154, 43 FR 46234, Oct. 5, 1978]

§ 91.203 Carriage of cargo.

(a) No pilot in command may permit cargo to be carried in any airplane unless—

(1) It is carried in an approved cargo rack, bin, or compartment installed in the airplane;

(2) It is secured by means approved by the Administrator; or

(3) It is carried in accordance with each of the following:

(i) It is properly secured by a safety belt or other tiedown having enough strength to eliminate the possibility of shifting under all normally anticipated flight and ground conditions.

(ii) It is packaged or covered to avoid possible injury to passengers.

(iii) It does not impose any load on seats or on the floor structure that exceeds the load limitation for those components.

(iv) It is not located in a position that restricts the access to or use of any required emergency or regular exit, or the use of the aisle between the crew and the passenger compartment.

(v) It is not carried directly above seated passengers.

(b) When cargo is carried in cargo compartments that are designed to require the physical entry of a crewmember to extinguish any fire that may occur during flight, the cargo must be loaded so as to allow a crewmember to effectively reach all parts of the compartment with the contents of a hand fire extinguisher.

§ 91.205 Transport category airplane weight limitations.

No person may take off a transport category airplane, except in accordance with the weight limitations prescribed for that airplane in § 91.37.

§ 91.209 Operating in icing conditions.

(a) No pilot may take off an airplane that has—

(1) Frost, snow, or ice adhering to any propeller, windshield, or powerplant installation, or to an airspeed, altimeter, rate of climb, or flight attitude instrument system;

(2) Snow or ice adhering to the wings, or stabilizing or control surfaces; or

(3) Any frost adhering to the wings, or stabilizing or control surfaces, unless that frost has been polished to make it smooth.

(b) Except for an airplane that has ice protection provisions that meet the requirements in section 34 of Special Federal Aviation Regulation No. 23, or those for transport category airplane type certification, no pilot may fly—

(1) Under IFR into known or forecast moderate icing conditions; or

(2) Under VFR into known light or moderate icing conditions; unless the aircraft has functioning de-icing or anti-icing equipment protecting each propeller, windshield, wing, stabilizing or control surface, and each airspeed, altimeter, rate of climb, or flight attitude instrument system.

(c) Except for an airplane that has ice protection provisions that meet the requirements in section 34 of Special Federal Aviation Regulation No. 23, or those for transport category airplane type certification, no pilot may fly an airplane into known or forecast severe icing conditions.

(d) If current weather reports and briefing information relied upon by the pilot in command indicate that the forecast icing conditions that would otherwise prohibit the flight will not be encountered during the flight because of changed weather conditions since the forecast, the restrictions in paragraphs (b) and (c) of this section based on forecast conditions do not apply.

§ 91.211 Flight engineer requirements.

(a) No person may operate the following airplanes without a flight crewmember holding a current flight engineer certificate:

(1) An airplane for which a type certificate was issued before January 2, 1964, having a maximum certificated takeoff weight of more than 80,000 pounds.

(2) An airplane type certificated after January 1, 1964, for which a flight engineer is required by the type certification requirements.

(b) No person may serve as a required flight engineer on an airplane unless, within the preceding 6 calendar months, he has had at least 50 hours of flight time as a flight engineer on that type airplane, or the Administrator has checked him on that type airplane and determined that he is familiar and competent with all essential current information and operating procedures.

§ 91.213 Second in command requirements.

(a) Except as provided in paragraph (b) of this section, no person may operate the following airplanes without a pilot who is designated as second in command of that airplane:

(1) A large airplane, except that a person may operate an airplane certificated under SFAR 41 without a pilot who is designated as second in com-

marid if that airplane is certificated for operation with one pilot.

(2) A turbojet-powered multiengine airplane for which two pilots are required under the type certification requirements for that airplane.

(3) A commuter category airplane, except that a person may operate a commuter category airplane notwithstanding paragraph (a)(1) of this section, that has a passenger seating configuration, excluding pilot seats, of nine or less without a pilot who is designated as second in command if that airplane is type certificated for operations with one pilot.

(b) The Administrator may issue a letter of authorization for the operation of an airplane without compliance with the requirements of paragraph (a) of this section if that airplane is designed for and type certificated with only one pilot station. The authorization contains any conditions that the Administrator finds necessary for safe operation.

(c) No person may designate a pilot to serve as second in command nor may any pilot serve as second in command of an airplane required under this section to have two pilots, unless that pilot meets the qualifications for second in command prescribed in § 61.55 of this chapter.

[Doc. No. 11437, Amdt. 91-101, 37 FR 14763, July 25, 1972, as amended by Amdt. 91-133, 41 FR 47229, Oct. 28, 1976; Amdt. 91-154, 43 FR 46234, Oct. 5, 1978; Amdt. 91-180, 47 FR 30947, July 15, 1982; Amdt. 91-197, 52 FR 1836, Jan. 15, 1987]

§ 91.215 Flight-attendant requirements.

(a) No person may operate an airplane unless at least the following number of flight attendants are on board the airplane:

(1) For airplanes having more than 19 but less than 51 passengers on board—one flight attendant.

(2) For airplanes having more than 50 but less than 101 passengers on board—two flight attendants.

(3) For airplanes having more than 100 passengers on board—two flight attendants plus one additional flight attendant for each unit (or part of a unit) of 50 passengers above 100.

(b) No person may serve as a flight attendant on an airplane when re-

quired by paragraph (a) of this section, unless that person has demonstrated to the pilot in command that he is familiar with the necessary functions to be performed in an emergency or a situation requiring emergency evacuation and is capable of using the emergency equipment installed on that airplane for the performance of those functions.

Subpart E—Operating Noise Limits

AUTHORITY: Secs. 307, 313(a), 601, 603, 604, and 611, Federal Aviation Act of 1958 (49 U.S.C. 1348, 1354(a), 1421, 1423, 1424 and 1431 as amended by the Noise Control Act of 1972 (Pub. L. 92-574)); sec. 6(c), Dept. of Transportation Act.

§ 91.301 Applicability; relation to Part 36.

(a) This subpart prescribes operating noise limits and related requirements that apply, as follows, to the operation of civil aircraft in the United States:

(1) Sections 91.303, 91.305, 91.306, and 91.307 apply to civil subsonic turbojet airplanes with maximum weights of more than 75,000 pounds and—

(i) If U.S. registered, that have standard airworthiness certificates; or

(ii) If foreign registered, that would be required by this chapter to have a U.S. standard airworthiness certificate in order to conduct the operations intended for the airplane were it registered in the United States.

Those sections apply to operations to or from airports in the United States under this part and Parts 121, 123, 129, and 135 of this chapter.

(2) Section 91.308 applies to U.S. operators of civil subsonic turbojet airplanes covered by this subpart. That section applies to operators operating to or from airports in the United States under this part and Parts 121, 123, 125, and 135 but not to those operating under Part 129 of this chapter.

(3) Sections 91.302, 91.309 and 91.311 apply to U.S. registered civil supersonic airplanes having standard airworthiness certificates, and to foreign registered civil supersonic airplanes that, if registered in the United States, would be required by this chapter to have a U.S. standard airworthiness certificate in order to conduct the operations intended for the airplane. Those sec-

tions apply to operations under this part and under Parts 121, 123, 125, 129, and 135 of this chapter.

(b) Unless otherwise specified, as used in this subpart "Part 36" refers to 14 CFR Part 36, including the noise levels under Appendix C of that part, notwithstanding the provisions of that part excepting certain airplanes from the specified noise requirements. For purposes of this subpart, the various stages of noise levels, the terms used to describe airplanes with respect to those levels, and the terms "subsonic airplane" and "supersonic airplane" have the meanings specified under Part 36 of this chapter. For purposes of this subpart, for subsonic airplanes operated in foreign air commerce in the United States, the Administrator may accept compliance with the noise requirements under Annex 16 of the International Civil Aviation Organization when those requirements have been shown to be substantially compatible with, and achieve results equivalent to those achievable under, Part 36 for that airplane. Determinations made under these provisions are subject to the limitations of § 36.5 of this chapter as if those noise levels were Part 36 noise levels.

[Docs. 13582 and 14317, Amdt. 91-136, 41 FR 56055, Dec. 23, 1976, as amended by Amdt. 91-153, 43 FR 28421, June 29, 1978; Amdt. 91-161, 44 FR 75562, Dec. 20, 1979; Amdt. 91-170, 45 FR 67259, Oct. 9, 1980; Amdt. 91-171, 45 FR 79315, Nov. 28, 1980]

§ 91.302 Part 125 operators: Designation of applicable regulations.

For airplanes covered by this subpart and operated under Part 125, the following regulations apply as specified:

(a) For each airplane operation to which requirements prescribed under this subpart applied before November 29, 1980, those requirements of this subpart continue to apply.

(b) For each subsonic airplane operation to which requirements prescribed under this subpart did not apply before November 29, 1980, because the airplane was not operated in the United States under this part or Part 121, 123, 129 or 135, the requirements prescribed under §§ 91.303,

91.306, 91.307, and 91.308 of this subpart apply.

(c) For each supersonic airplane operation to which requirements prescribed under this subpart did not apply before November 29, 1980, because the airplane was not operated in the United States under this part or Part 121, 123, 129, or 135, the requirements of §§ 91.309 and 91.311 of this subpart apply.

(d) For each airplane required to operate under Part 125 for which a deviation under that part is approved to operate, in whole or in part, under this part or Part 121, 123, 129, or 135, notwithstanding the approval, the requirements prescribed under paragraphs (a), (b), and (c) of this section continue to apply.

[Doc. No. 20813, Amdt. 91-170, 45 FR 67259, Oct. 9, 1980, as amended by Amdt. 91-170A, 45 FR 79302, Nov. 28, 1980]

§ 91.303 Final compliance: Subsonic airplanes.

Except as provided in §§ 91.306 and 91.307, on and after January 1, 1985, no person may operate to or from an airport in the United States any subsonic airplane covered by this subpart, unless that airplane has been shown to comply with Stage 2 or Stage 3 noise levels under Part 36 of this chapter.

[Doc. No. 20251, Amdt. 91-171, 45 FR 79315, Nov. 28, 1980]

§ 91.305 Phased compliance under Parts 121, and 135: Subsonic airplanes.

(a) General. Each person operating airplanes under Parts 121 or 135 of this chapter, regardless of the State of registry of the airplane, shall comply with this section with respect to subsonic airplanes covered by this subpart.

(b) Compliance schedule. Except for airplanes shown to be operated in foreign air commerce under paragraph (c) of this section or covered by an exemption (including those issued under § 91.307), airplanes operated by U.S. operators in air commerce in the United States must be shown to comply with Stage 2 or Stage 3 noise levels under Part 36, in accordance with the following schedule, or they may not be operated to or from airports in the United States:

(1) By January 1, 1981:

(i) At least one quarter of the airplanes that have four engines with no bypass ratio or with a bypass ratio less that two.

(ii) At least half of the airplanes powered by engines with any other bypass ratio or by another number of engines.

(2) By January 1, 1983:

(i) At least one half of the airplanes that have four engines with no bypass ratio or with a bypass ratio less than two.

(ii) All airplanes powered by engines with any other bypass ratio or by another number of engines.

(c) *Apportionment of airplanes.* For purposes of paragraph (b) of this section, a person operating airplanes engaged in domestic and foreign air commerce in the United States may elect not to comply with the phased schedule with respect to that portion of the airplanes operated by that person shown, under an approved method of apportionment, to be engaged in foreign air commerce in the United States.

[Doc. No. 20251, Amdt. 91-171, 45 FR 79315, Nov. 28, 1980]

§ 91.306 Replacement airplanes.

A Stage 1 airplane may be operated after the otherwise applicable compliance dates prescribed under §§ 91.303 and 91.305 if, under an approved plan, a replacement airplane has been ordered by the operator under a binding contract as follows:

(a) For replacement of an airplane powered by two engines, until January 1, 1986, but not after the date specified in the plan, if the contract is entered into by January 1, 1983, and specifies delivery before January 1, 1986, of a replacement airplane which has been shown to comply with Stage 3 noise levels under Part 36 of this chapter.

(b) For replacement of an airplane powered by three engines, until January 1, 1985, but not after the date specified in the plan, if the contract is entered into by January 1, 1983, and specifies delivery before January 1, 1985, of a replacement airplane which

has been shown to comply with Stage 3 noise levels under Part 36 of this chapter.

(c) For replacement of any other airplane, until January 1, 1985, but not after the date specified in the plan, if the contract specifies delivery before January 1, 1985, of a replacement airplane which—

(1) Has been shown to comply with Stage 2 or Stage 3 noise levels under Part 36 of this chapter prior to issuance of an original standard airworthiness certificate; or

(2) Has been shown to comply with Stage 3 noise levels under Part 36 of this chapter prior to issuance of a standard airworthiness certificate other than original issue.

(d) Each operator of a Stage 1 airplane for which approval of a replacement plan is requested under this section shall submit to the FAA Director of the Office of Environment and Energy an application constituting the proposed replacement plan (or revised Plan) that contains the information specified under this paragraph and which is certified (under penalty of 18 U.S.C. 1001) as true and correct. Each application for approval must provide information corresponding to that specified in the contract, upon which the FAA may rely in considering its approval, as follows:

(1) Name and address of the applicant.

(2) Aircraft type and model and registration number for each airplane to be replaced under the plan.

(3) Aircraft type and model of each replacement airplane.

(4) Scheduled dates of delivery and introduction into service of each replacement airplane.

(5) Name and addresses of the parties to the contract and any other persons who may effectively cancel the contract or otherwise control the performance of any party.

(6) Information specifying the anticipated disposition of the airplanes to be replaced.

(7) A statement that the contract represents a legally enforceable, mutual agreement for delivery of an eligible replacement airplane.

(8) Any other information or documentation requested by the Director,

Office of Environment and Energy reasonably necessary to determine whether the plan should be approved.

[Doc. No. 20251, Amdt. 91-171, 45 FR 79315, Nov. 28, 1980]

§ 91.307 Service to small communities exemption: Two-engine, subsonic airplanes.

(a) A Stage 1 airplane powered by two engines may be operated after the compliance dates prescribed under §§ 91.303, 92.305, and 91.306, when, with respect to that airplane, the Administrator issues an exemption to the operator from the noise level requirements under this subpart. Each exemption issued under this section terminates on the earlier of the following dates—

(1) For an exempted airplane sold, or otherwise disposed of, to another person on or after January 1, 1983—on the date of delivery to that person;

(2) For an exempted airplane with a seating configuration of 100 passenger seats or less—on January 1, 1988; or

(3) For an exempted airplane with a seating configuration of more than 100 passenger seats—on January 1, 1985.

(b) For purposes of this section, the seating configuration of an airplane is governed by that shown to exist on December 1, 1979, or an earlier date established for that airplane by the Administrator.

[Doc. No. 20251, Amdt. 91-171, 45 FR 79316, Nov. 28, 1980]

§ 91.308 Compliance plans and status: U.S. operators of subsonic airplanes.

(a) Each U.S. operator of a civil subsonic airplane covered by this subpart (regardless of the State of registry) shall submit to the FAA, Director of the Office of Environment and Energy, in accordance with this section, the operator's current compliance status and plan for achieving and maintaining compliance with the applicable noise level requirements of this subpart. If appropriate, an operator may substitute for the required plan a notice, certified as true (under penalty of 18 U.S.C. 1001) by that operator, that no change in the plan or status of any airplane affected by the plan has occurred since the date of the

plan most recently submitted under this section.

(b) Each compliance plan, including any revised plans, must contain the information specified under paragraph (c) of this section for each airplane covered by this section that is operated by the operator. Unless otherwise approved by the Administrator, compliance plans must provide the required plan and status information as it exists on the date 30 days before the date specified for submission of the plan. Plans must be certified by the operator as true and complete (under penalty of 18 U.S.C. 1001) and be submitted for each airplane covered by this section on or before the following dates—

(1) May 1, 1980 or 90 days after initially commencing operation of airplanes covered by this section, whichever is later, and thereafter;

(2) Thirty days after any change in the operator's fleet or compliance planning decisions that has a separate or cumulative effect on 10 percent or more of the airplanes in either class of airplanes covered by § 91.305(b); and

(3) Thirty days after each compliance date applicable to that airplane under this subpart and annually thereafter through 1985 or until any later compliance date for that airplane prescribed under this subpart, on the anniversary of that submission date, to show continuous compliance with this subpart.

(c) Each compliance plan submitted under this section must identify the operator and include information regarding the compliance plan and status for each airplane covered by the plan as follows:

(1) Name and address of the airplane operator.

(2) Name and telephone number of the person designated by the operator to be responsible for the preparation of the compliance plan and its submission.

(3) The total number of airplanes covered by this section and in each of the following classes and subclasses:

(i) Airplanes engaged in domestic air commerce.

(A) Airplanes powered by four turbojet engines with no bypass ratio or with a bypass ratio less than two.

(B) Airplanes powered by engines with any other bypass ratio or by another number of engines.

(C) Airplanes covered by an exemption issued under § 91.307 of this subpart.

(ii) Airplanes engaged in foreign air commerce under an approved apportionment plan.

(A) Airplanes powered by four turbojet engines with no bypass ratio or with a bypass ratio less than two.

(B) Airplanes powered by engines with any other bypass ratio or by another number of engines.

(C) Airplanes covered by an exemption issued under § 91.307 of this subpart.

(4) For each airplane covered by this section—

(i) Aircraft type and model;

(ii) Aircraft registration number;

(iii) Aircraft manufacturer serial number;

(iv) Aircraft power plant make and model;

(v) Aircraft year of manufacture;

(vi) Whether Part 36 noise level compliance has been shown: Yes/No;

(vii) [Reserved]

(viii) The appropriate code prescribed under paragraph (c)(5) of this section which indicates the acoustical technology installed, or to be installed, on the airplane;

(ix) For airplanes on which acoustical technology has been or will be applied, following the appropriate code entry, the actual or scheduled month and year of installation on the airplane;

(x) For DC–8 and B–707 airplanes operated in domestic U.S. air commerce which have been or will be retired from service in the United States without replacement between January 24, 1977, and January 1, 1985, the appropriate code prescribed under paragraph (c)(5) of this section followed by the actual or scheduled month and year of retirement of the airplane from service;

(xi) For DC–8 and B–707 airplanes operated in foreign air commerce in the United States, which have been or will be retired from service in the United States without replacement between April 14, 1980, and January 1, 1985, the appropriate code prescribed

under paragraph (c)(5) of this section followed by the actual or scheduled month and year of retirement of the airplane from service;

(xii) For airplanes covered by an approved replacement plan under § 91.305(c) of this subpart, the appropriate code prescribed under paragraph (c)(5) of this section followed by the scheduled month and year for replacement of the airplane;

(xiii) For airplanes designated as "engaged in foreign commerce" in accordance with an approved method of apportionment under § 91.305(c) of this subpart, the appropriate code prescribed under paragraph (c)(5) of this section;

(xiv) For airplanes covered by an exemption issued to the operator granting relief from noise level requirements of this subpart, the appropriate code prescribed under paragraph (c)(5) of this section followed by the actual or scheduled month and year of expiration of the exemption and the appropriate code and applicable dates which indicate the compliance strategy planned or implemented for the airplane;

(xv) For all airplanes covered by this section, the number of spare shipsets of acoustical components needed for continuous compliance and the number available on demand to the operator in support of those airplanes; and

(xvi) For airplanes for which none of the other codes prescribed under paragraph (c)(5) of this section describes either the technology applied, or to be applied to the airplane in accordance with the certification requirements under Parts 21 and 36 of this chapter, or the compliance strategy or methodology, following the code "OTH" enter the date of any certificate action and attach an addendum to the plan explaining the nature and extent of the certificated technology, strategy, or methodology employed, together with reference to the type certificate documentation.

(5) TABLE OF ACOUSTICAL TECHNOLOGY/ STRATEGY CODES

Code	Airplane type/ model	Certificated technology
A	B-707-120B B-707-320B/C B-720B	Quiet nacelles + 1-ring.
B	B-727-100	Double wall fan duct treatment.
C	B-727-200	Double wall fan duct treatment (pre-January 1977 installations and amended type certificate).
D	B-727-200 B-737-100 B-737-200	Quiet nacelles + double wall fan duct treatement.
E	B-747-100 [1] B-747-200 [1]	Fixed lip inlets + sound absorbing material treatment.
F	DC-8	New extended inlet and bullet with treatment + fan duct treatment areas.
G	DC-9	P-36 sound absorbing material treatment kit.
H	BAC-111-200	Silencer kit (BAC acoustic report 522).
I	BAC-111-400	(To be identified later if certificated.)
J	B-707 DC-8	Reengined with high bypass ratio turbojet engines + quiet nacelles (if certificated under stage 3 noise level requirements).

[1] Pre-December 1971.

REP—For airplanes covered by an approved replacement plan under § 91.305(c) of this subpart.

EFC—For airplanes designated as "engated in foreign commerce" in accordance with an approved method of apportionment under § 91.307 of this subpart.

RET—For DC-8 and B-707 airplanes operated in domestic U.S. air commerce and retired from service in the United States without replacement between January 24, 1977, and January 1, 1985.

RFC—For DC-8 and B-707 airplanes operated by U.S. operators in foreign air commerce in the United States and retired from service in the United States without replacement between April 14, 1980, and January 1, 1985.

EXD—For airplanes exempted from showing compliance with the noise level requirements of this subpart.

OTH—For airplanes for which no other prescribed code describes either the certificated technology applied, or to be applied to the airplane, or the compliance strategy or methodology. (An addendum must explain the nature and extent of technology, strategy or methodology and reference the type certificate documentation.

[Doc. Nos. 18955 and 18924, Amdt. 91-161, 44 FR 75563, Dec. 20, 1979; Amdt. 91-161A,

45 FR 6923, Jan. 31, 1980; Amdt. 91-171, 45 FR 79316, Nov. 28, 1980]

§ 91.309 Civil supersonic airplanes that do not comply with Part 36.

(a) *Applicability.* This section applies to civil supersonic airplanes that have not been shown to comply with the stage 2 noise limits of Part 36 in effect on October 13, 1977, using applicable tradeoff provisions, and that are operated in the United States after July 31, 1978.

(b) *Airport use.* Except in an emergency, the following apply to each person who operates a civil supersonic airplane to or from an airport in the United States:

(1) Regardless of whether a type design change approval is applied for under Part 21 of this chapter, no person may land or take off an airplane, covered by this section, for which the type design is changed, after July 31, 1978, in a manner constituting an "acoustical change" under § 21.93, unless the acoustical change requirements of Part 36 are complied with.

(2) No flight may be scheduled, or otherwise planned, for takeoff or landing after 10 p.m. and before 7 a.m. local time.

[Amdt. 91-153, 43 FR 28421, June 29, 1978]

§ 91.311 Civil supersonic airplanes: Noise limits.

Except for Concorde airplanes having flight time before January 1, 1980, no person may, after July 31, 1978, operate, in the United States, a civil supersonic airplane that does not comply with the stage 2 noise limits of Part 36 in effect on October 13, 1977, using applicable trade-off provisions.

[Amdt. 91-153, 43 FR 28421, June 29, 1978]

APPENDIX A—CATEGORY II OPERATIONS: MANUAL, INSTRUMENTS, EQUIPMENT AND MAINTENANCE

1. *Category II Manual*—(a) *Application for approval.* An applicant for approval of a Category II manual or an amendment to an approved Category II manual must submit the proposed manual or amendment to the Flight Standards District Office having jurisdiction of the area in which the applicant

is located. If the application requests an evaluation program, it must include the following:

(1) The location of the aircraft and the place where the demonstrations are to be conducted; and

(2) The date the demonstrations are to commence (at least 10 days after filing the application).

(b) *Contents.* Each Category II manual must contain—

(1) the registration number, make, and model of the aircraft to which it applies;

(2) A maintenance program as specified in section 4 of this appendix; and

(3) The procedures and instructions related to recognition of decision height, use of runway visual range information, approach monitoring, the decision region (the region between the middle marker and the decision height), the maximum permissible deviations of the basic ILS indicator within the decision region, a missed approach, use of airborne low approach equipment, minimum altitude for the use of the autopilot, instrument and equipment failure warning systems, instrument failure, and other procedures, instructions, and limitations that may be found necessary by the Administrator.

2. *Required instruments and equipment.* The instruments and equipment listed in this section must be installed in each aircraft operated in a Category II operation. This section does not require duplication of instruments and equipment required by § 91.33 or any other provisions of this chapter.

(a) *Group I.* (1) Two localizer and glide slope receiving systems. Each system must provide a basic ILS display and each side of the instrument panel must have a basic ILS display. However, a single localizer antenna and a single glide slope antenna may be used.

(2) A communications system that does not affect the operation of at least one of the ILS systems.

(3) A marker beacon receiver that provides distinctive aural and visual indications of the outer and the middle marker.

(4) Two gyroscopic pitch and bank indicating systems.

(5) Two gyroscopic direction indicating systems.

(6) Two airspeed indicators.

(7) Two sensitive altimeters adjustable for barometric pressure, each having a placarded correction for altimeter scale error and for the wheel height of the aircraft. After June 26, 1979, two sensitive altimeters adjustable for barometric pressure, having markings at 20-foot intervals and each having a placarded correction for altimeter scale error and for the wheel height of the aircraft.

(8) Two vertical speed indicators.

(9) A flight control guidance system that consists of either an automatic approach coupler or a flight director system. A flight director system must display computed information as steering command in relation to an ILS localizer and, on the same instrument, either computed information as pitch command in relation to an ILS glide slope or basic ILS glide slope information. An automatic approach coupler must provide at least automatic steering in relation to an ILS localizer. The flight control guidance system may be operated from one of the receiving systems required by paragraph (1) of this paragraph (a).

(10) For Category II operations with decision heights below 150 feet, either a marker beacon receiver providing aural and visual indications of the inner marker or a radio altimeter.

(b) *Group II.* (1) Warning systems for immediate detection by the pilot of system faults in items (1), (4), (5), and (9) of Group I and, if installed, for use in Category II operations, the radio altimeter and auto throttle system.

(2) Dual controls.

(3) An externally vented static pressure system with an alternate static pressure source.

(4) A windshield wiper or equivalent means of providing adequate cockpit visibility for a safe visual transition by either pilot to touch down and roll out.

(5) A heat source for each airspeed system pitot tube installed or an equivalent means of preventing malfunctioning due to icing of the pitot system.

3. *Instruments and equipment approval—* (a) *General.* The instruments and equipment required by section 2 of this appendix must be approved as provided in this section before being used in Category II operations. Before presenting an aircraft for approval of the instruments and equipment, it must be shown that, since the beginning of the 12th calendar month before the date of submission—

(1) The ILS localizer and glide slope equipment were bench checked according to the manufacturer's instructions and found to meet those standards specified in RTCA Paper 23-63/DO-117, dated March 14, 1963. "Standard Adjustment Criteria for Airborne Localizer and Glide Slope Receivers," which may be obtained from the RTCA Secretariat, 2000 K Street NW., Washington, D.C. 20006, at cost of 50 cents per copy, payment in cash or by check or money order payable to the Radio Technical Commission for Aeronautics;

(2) The altimeters and the static pressure systems were tested and inspected in accordance with Appendix E to Part 43 of this chapter; and

(3) All other instruments and items of equipment specified in section 2(a) of this appendix that are listed in the proposed maintenance program were bench checked and found to meet the manufacturer's specifications.

(b) *Flight control guidance system.* All components of the flight control guidance system must be approved as installed by the evaluation program specified in paragraph (e) of this section if they have not been approved for Category II operations under applicable type or supplemental type certification procedures. In addition, subsequent changes to make, model or design of these components must be approved under this paragraph. Related systems or devices such as the auto throttle and computed missed approach guidance system must be approved in the same manner if they are to be used for Category II operations.

(c) *Radio altimeter.* A radio altimeter must meet the performance criteria of this paragraph for original approval and after each subsequent alteration.

(1) It must display to the flight crew clearly and positively the wheel height of the main landing gear above the terrain.

(2) It must display wheel height above the terrain to an accuracy of plus or minus 5 feet or 5 percent, whichever is greater, under the following conditions:

(i) Pitch angles of zero to plus or minus 5 degrees about the mean approach altitude.

(ii) Roll angles of zero to 20 degrees in either direction.

(iii) Forward velocities from minimum approach speed up to 200 knots.

(iv) Sink rates from zero to 15 feet per second at altitudes from 100 to 200 feet.

(3) Over level ground, it must track the actual altitude of the aircraft without significant lag or oscillation.

(4) With the aircraft at an altitude of 200 feet or less, any abrupt change in terrain representing no more than 10 percent of the aircraft's altitude must not cause the altimeter to unlock, and indicator response to such changes must not exceed 0.1 second and in addition, if the system unlocks for greater changes, it must reacquire the signal in less than 1 second.

(5) Systems that contain a push-to-test feature must test the entire system (with or without an antenna) at a simulated altitude of less than 500 feet.

(6) The system must provide to the flight crew a positive failure warning display any time there is a loss of power or an absence of ground return signals within the designed range of operating altitudes.

(d) *Other instruments and equipment.* All other instruments and items of equipment required by section 2 of this appendix must be capable of performing as necessary for Category II operations. Approval is also required after each subsequent alteration to these instruments and items of equipment.

(e) *Evaluation program*—(1) *Application.* Approval by evaluation is requested as a part of the application for approval of the Category II manual.

(2) *Demonstrations.* Unless otherwise authorized by the Administrator, the evaluation program for each aircraft requires the demonstrations specified in this paragraph. At least 50 ILS approaches must be flown with at least five approaches on each of three different ILS facilities and no more than one-half of the total approaches on any one ILS facility. All approaches shall be flown under simulated instrument conditions to a 100-foot decision height and 90 percent of the total approaches made must be successful. A successful approach is one in which—

(i) At the 100-foot decision height, the indicated airspeed and heading are satisfactory for a normal flare and landing (speed must be plus or minus 5 knots of programed airspeed but may not be less than computed threshold speed, if auto throttles are used);

(ii) The aircraft, at the 100-foot decision height, is positioned so that the cockpit is within, and tracking so as to remain within, the lateral confines of the runway extended;

(iii) Deviation from glide slope after leaving the outer marker does not exceed 50 percent of full scale deflection as displayed on the ILS indicator;

(iv) No unusual roughness or excessive attitude changes occur after leaving the middle marker; and

(v) In the case of an aircraft equipped with an approach coupler, the aircraft is sufficiently in trim when the approach coupler is disconnected at the decision height to allow for the continuation of a normal approach and landing.

(3) *Records.* During the evaluation program the following information must be maintained by the applicant for the aircraft with respect to each approach and made available to the Administrator upon request:

(i) Each deficiency in airborne instruments and equipment that prevented the initiation of an approach.

(ii) The reasons for discontinuing an approach including the altitude above the runway at which it was discontinued.

(iii) Speed control at the 100-foot decision height if auto throttles are used.

(iv) Trim condition of the aircraft upon disconnecting the auto coupler with respect to continuation to flare and landing.

(v) Position of the aircraft at the middle marker and at the decision height indicated both on a diagram of the basic ILS display and a diagram of the runway extended to the middle marker. Estimated touch down point must be indicated on the runway diagram.

(vi) Compatibility of flight director with the auto coupler, if applicable.

(vii) Quality of overall system performance.

(4) *Evaluation.* A final evaluation of the flight control guidance system is made upon successful completion of the demonstrations. If no hazardous tendencies have been displayed or are otherwise known to exist, the system is approved as installed.

4. *Maintenance program.* (a) Each maintenance program must contain the following:

(1) A list of each instrument and item of equipment specified in section 2 of this ppendix that is installed in the aircraft and approved for Category II operations, including the make and model of those specified in section 2(a).

(2) A schedule that provides for the performance of inspections under subparagraph (5) of this paragraph within 3 calendar months after the date of the previous inspection. The inspection must be performed by a person authorized by Part 43 of this chapter, except that each alternate inspection may be replaced by a functional flight check. This functional flight check must be performed by a pilot holding a Category II pilot authorization for the type aircraft checked.

(3) A schedule that provides for the performance of bench checks for each listed instrument and item of equipment that is specified in section 2(a) within 12 calendar months after the date of the previous bench check.

(4) A schedule that provides for the performance of a test and inspection of each static pressure system in accordance with Appendix E to Part 43 of this chapter within 12 calendar months after the date of the previous test and inspection.

(5) The procedures for the performance of the periodic inspections and functional flight checks to determine the ability of each listed instrument and item of equipment specified in section 2(a) of this Appendix to perform as approved for Category II operations including a procedure for recording functional flight checks.

(6) A procedure for assuring that the pilot is informed of all defects in listed instruments and items of equipment.

(7) A procedure for assuring that the condition of each listed instrument and item of equipment upon which maintenance is performed is at least equal to its Category II approval condition before it is returned to service for Category II operations.

(8) A procedure for an entry in the maintenance records required by § 43.9 of this chapter that shows the date, airport, and reasons for each discontinued Category II operation because of a malfunction of a listed instrument or item of equipment.

(b) *Bench check.* A bench check required by this section must comply with this paragraph.

(1) It must be performed by a certificated repair station holding one of the following ratings as appropriate to the equipment checked:

(i) An instrument rating.

(ii) A radio rating.

(iii) A rating issued under Subpart D of Part 145.

(2) It must consist of removal of an instrument or item of equipment and performance of the following:

(i) A visual inspection for cleanliness, impending failure, and the need for lubrication, repair, or replacement of parts;

(ii) Correction of items found by that visual inspection; and

(iii) Calibration to at least the manufacturer's specifications unless otherwise specified in the approved Category II manual for the aircraft in which the instrument or item of equipment is installed.

(c) *Extensions.* After the completion of one maintenance cycle of 12 calendar months a request to extend the period for checks, tests, and inspections is approved if it is shown that the performance of particular equipment justifies the requested extension.

[Amdt. 91–39, 32 FR 6906, May 5, 1967; 32 FR 8127, June 7, 1967; Amdt. 91–63, 33 FR 17291, Nov. 22, 1968; Amdt. 91–152, 43 FR 22641, May 25, 1978; Amdt. 91–196, 51 FR 40707, Nov. 7, 1986]

APPENDIX B—AUTHORIZATIONS TO EXCEED MACH 1 (§ 91.55)

SECTION 1. *Application.* (*a*) An applicant for an authorization to exceed mach 1 must apply in a form and manner prescribed by the Administrator and must comply with this appendix.

(b) In addition, each application for an authorization to exceed mach 1 covered by section 2(a) of this appendix must contain all information, requested by the Administrator, that he deems necessary to assist him in determining whether the designation of a particular test area, or issuance of a particular authorization, is a "major Federal action significantly affecting the quality of the human environment" within the meaning of the National Environmental Policy Act of 1969 (42 U.S.C. 4321 et seq.), and to assist him in complying with that Act, and with related Executive orders, guidelines, and orders, prior to such action.

(c) In addition, each application for an authorization to exceed mach 1 covered by section 2(a) of this appendix must contain—

(1) Information showing that operation at a speed greater than mach 1 is necessary to

accomplish one or more of the purposes specified in section 2(a) of this appendix, including a showing that the purpose of the test cannot be safely or properly accomplished by overocean testing;

(2) A description of the test area proposed by the applicant, including an environmental analysis of that area meeting the requirements of paragraph (b) of this section; and

(3) Conditions and limitations that will insure that no measurable sonic boom overpressure will reach the surface outside of the designated test area.

(d) An application is denied if the Administrator finds that such action is necessary to protect or enhance the environment.

SEC. 2. *Issuance.* (a) For a flight in a designated test area, an authorization to exceed mach 1 may be issued when the Administrator has taken the environmental protective actions specified in section 1(b) of this appendix, and the applicant shows one or more of the following:

(1) The flight is necessary to show compliance with airworthiness requirements.

(2) The flight is necessary to determine the sonic boom characteristics of the airplane, or is necessary to establish means of reducing or eliminating the effects of sonic boom.

(3) The flight is necessary to demonstrate the conditions and limitations under which speeds greater than a true flight mach number of 1 will not cause a measurable sonic boom overpressure to reach the surface.

(b) For a flight outside of a designated test area, an authorization to exceed mach 1 may be issued if the applicant shows conservatively under paragraph (a)(3) of this section that—

(1) The flight will not cause a measurable sonic boom overpressure to reach the surface when the aircraft is operated under conditions and limitations demonstrated under paragraph (a)(3) of this section; and

(2) Those conditions and limitations represent all foreseeable operating conditions.

SEC. 3. *Duration.* (a) An authorization to exceed mach 1 is effective until it expires or is surrendered, or until it is suspended or terminated by the Administrator. Such an authorization may be amended or suspended by the Administrator at any time if he finds that such action is necessary to protect the environment. Within 30 days of notification of amendment, the holder of the authorization must request reconsideration or the amendment becomes final. Within 30 days of notification of suspension, the holder of the authorization must request reconsideration or the authorization is automatically terminated. If reconsideration is requested within the 30-day period, the amendment or suspension continues until the holder shows why, in his opinion, the

authorization should not be amended or terminated. Upon such showing, the Administrator may terminate or amend the authorization if he finds that such action is necessary to protect the environment, or he may reinstate the authorization without amendment if he finds that termination or amendment is not necessary to protect the environment.

(b) Findings and actions by the Administrator under this section do not affect any certificate issued under title VI of the Federal Aviation Act of 1958.

(Sec. 307(c), 313(a), 611, Federal Aviation Act of 1958, 49 U.S.C. 1348(c), 1354(a), 1431; sec. 2(b)(2), 6(c), Department of Transportation Act, 49 U.S.C. 1651(b)(2), 1655(c), Title I of the National Environmental Policy Act of 1969, 42 U.S.C. 4321 et seq., E. O. 11514, Protection and Enhancement of Environmental Quality, Mar. 5, 1970)

[Doc. No. 10261, Amdt. 91-112, 38 FR 8055, Mar. 28, 1973]

APPENDIX C—OPERATIONS IN THE NORTH ATLANTIC (NAT) MINIMUM NAVIGATION PERFORMANCE SPECIFICATIONS (MNPS) AIRSPACE

Section 1. NAT MNPS airspace is that volume of airspace between FL 275 and FL 400 extending between latitude 27 degrees north and the North Pole, bounded in the east by the eastern boundaries of control areas Santa Maria Oceanic, Shanwick Oceanic, and Reykjavik Oceanic and in the west by the western boundary of Reykjavik Oceanic Control Area, the western boundary of Gander Oceanic Control Area, and the western boundary of New York Oceanic Control Area, excluding the areas west of 60 degrees west and south of 38 degrees 30 minutes north.

Section 2. The navigation performance capability required for aircraft to be operated in the airspace defined in Sec. 1 of this appendix is as follows:

(a) The standard deviation of lateral track errors shall be less than 6.3 NM (11.7 Km). Standard deviation is a statistical measure of data about a mean value. The mean is zero nautical miles. The overall form of data is such that the plus and minus one standard deviation about the mean encompasses approximately 68 percent of the data and plus or minus two deviations encompasses approximately 95 percent.

(b) The proportion of the total flight time spent by aircraft 30 NM (55.6 Km) or more off the cleared track shall be less than 5.3×10^{-4} (less than one hour in 1,887 flight hours).

(c) The proportion of the total flight time spent by aircraft between 50 NM and 70 NM

(92.6 Km and 129.6 Km) off the cleared track shall be less than 13 x 10⁻⁵ (less than one hour in 7,693 hours).

Section 3. Air traffic control (ATC) may authorize an aircraft operator to deviate from the requirements of § 91.20 for a speicific flight if, at the time of flight plan filing for that flight, ATC determines that the aircraft may be provided appropriate separation and that the flight will not interfere with, or impose a burden upon, the operations of other aircraft which meet the requirements of § 91.20.

APPENDIX D — AIRPORTS/LOCATIONS WHERE THE TRANSPONDER REQUIRE- MENTS OF SECTION 91.24(b)(5)(ii) APPLY

Section 1. The requirements of §91.24(b) (5)(ii) apply to operation in the vicinity of each of the following airports.

Logan International Airport, Billings, MT

Hector International Airport, Fargo ND

APPENDIX E—AIRPLANE FLIGHT RECORDER SPECIFICATIONS

Parameters	Range	Installed system [1] minimum accuracy (to recovered data)	Sampling interval (per second)	Resolution [4] read out
Relative Time (From Recorded on Prior to Takeoff).	8 hr minimum	±0.125% per hour	1	1 sec.
Indicated Airspeed	V_{so} to V_D (KIAS)	±5% or ±10 kts., whichever is greater. Resolution 2 kts. below 175 KIAS.	1	1% [3]
Altitude	−1,000 ft. to max cert. alt. of A/C	±100 to ±700 ft. (see Table 1, TSO C51–a).	1	25 to 150 ft.
Magnetic Heading	360°	±5°	1	1°
Vertical Acceleration	−3g to +6g	±0.2g in addition to ±0.3g maximum datum.	4 (or 1 per second where peaks, ref. to 1g are recorded).	0.03g.
Longitudinal Acceleration	±1.0g	±1.5% max. range excluding datum error of ±5%.	2	0.01g.
Pitch Altitude	100% of useable	±2°	1	0.8°.
Roll Altitude	±60° or 100% of usale range, whichever is greater.	±2°	1	0.8°
Stabilizer Trim Position, or	Full Range	±3% unless higher uniquely required	1	1% [3]
Pitch Control Position.	Full Range	±3% unless higher uniquely required	1	1% [3]
Engine Power, Each Engine: Fan or N_1 Speed or EPR or Cockpit indications Used for Aircraft Certification OR.	Maximum Range	±5%	1	1% [3]
Prop. speed and Torque (Sample Once/Sec as Close together as Practicable).			1 (prop Speed) / 1 (torque)	1% [3] / 1% [3]
Altitude Rate [2] (need depends on altitude resolution).	±8,000 fpm	±10%. Resolution 250 fpm below 12,000 ft. indicated.	1	250 fpm. below 12,000.
Angle of Attack [2] (need depends on altitude resolution).	−20° to 40° or of usable range	±2°	1	0.8°% [3]
Radio Transmitter Keying (Discrete)	On/Off.		1	
TE Flaps (Discrete or Analog)	Each discrete position (U, D, T/O, AAP) OR		1	
	Analog 0–100% range	±3°	1	1% [3]
LE Flaps (Discrete or Analog)	Each discrete position (U, D, T/O, AAP) OR		1	
	Analog 0–100% range	±3°	1	1% [3]
Thrust Reverser, Each Engine (Discrete)	Stowed or full reverse		1	
Spoiler/Speedbrake (Discrete)	Stowed or out.		1	
Autopilot Engaged (Discrete)	Engaged or Disengaged		1	

[1] When data sources are aircraft instruments (except altimeters) of acceptable quality to fly the aircraft the recording system excluding these sensors (but including all other characteristics of the recording system) shall contribute no more than half of the values in this column.
[2] If data from the altitude encoding altimeter (100 ft. resolution) is used, then either one of these parameters should also be recorded. If however, altitude is recorded at a minimum resolution of 25 feet, then these two parameters can be omitted.
[3] Per cent of full range.
[4] This column applies to aircraft manufactured after October 11, 1991

APPENDIX F—HELICOPTER FLIGHT RECORDER SPECIFICATION

Parameters	Range	Installed system [1] minimum accuracy (to recovered data)	Sampling interval (per second)	Resolution [3] read out
Relative Time (From Recorded on Prior to Takeoff).	4 hr minimum	±0.125% per hour	1	1 sec
Indicated Airspeed	V_m in to V_D (KIAS) (minimum airspeed signal attainable with installed pilot-static system).	±5% or ±10 kts., whichever is greater.	1	1 kt
Altitude	−1,000 ft. to 20,000 ft. pressure altitude	±100 to ±700 ft. (see Table 1, TSO C51–a).	1	25 to 150 ft.
Magnetic Heading	360°	±5°	1	1°
Vertical Acceleration	−3g to +6g	±0.2g in addition to ±0.3g maximum datum.	4 (or 1 per second where peaks, ref. to 1g are recorded).	0.05g.
Longitudinal Acceleration	±1.0g	±1.5% max. range excluding datum error of ±5%.	2	0.03g.
Pitch Attitude	100% of usable range	±2°	1	0.8°
Roll Attitude	±60° or 100% of usable range, whichever is greater.	±2°	1	0.8°
Altitude Rate	±8,000 fpm	±10% Resolution 250 fpm below 12,000 ft. indicated.	1	250 fpm below 12,000.
Engine Power, Each Engine				
Main Rotor Speed	Maximum Range	±5%	1	1% [2]
Free or Power Turbine	Maximum Range	+5%	1	1% [2]
Engine Torque	Maximum Range	±5%	1	1% [2]

FEDERAL AVIATION REGULATIONS

PART 125

CERTIFICATION AND OPERATIONS:
Airplanes Having a Seating Capacity of 20 or More Passengers or a Maximum Payload Capacity of 6,000 Pounds or More

1989 EDITION

PART 125—CERTIFICATION AND OPERATIONS: AIRPLANES HAVING A SEATING CAPACITY OF 20 OR MORE PASSENGERS OR A MAXIMUM PAYLOAD CAPACITY OF 6,000 POUNDS OR MORE

Subpart A—General

Sec.
125.1 Applicability.
125.3 Deviation authority.
125.5 Operating certificate and operations specifications required.
125.7 Display of certificate.
125.9 Definitions.
125.11 Certificate eligibility and prohibited operations.

Subpart B—Certification Rules and Miscellaneous Requirements

125.21 Application for operating certificate.
125.23 Rules applicable to operations subject to this part.
125.25 Management personnel required.
125.27 Issue of certificate.
125.29 Duration of certificate.
125.31 Contents of certificate and operations specifications.
125.33 Operations specifications not a part of certificate.
125.35 Amendment of operations specifications.

125.37 Duty time limitations.
125.39 Carriage of narcotic drugs, marihuana, and depressant or stimulant drugs or substances.
125.41 Availability of certificate and operations specifications.
125.43 Use of operations specifications.
125.45 Inspection authority.
125.47 Change of address.
125.49 Airport requirements.
125.51 En route navigational facilities.
125.53 Flight locating requirements.

Subpart C—Manual Requirements

125.71 Preparation.
125.73 Contents.
125.75 Airplane flight manual.

Subpart D—Airplane Requirements

125.91 Airplane requirements: General.
125.93 Airplane limitations.

Subpart E—Special Airworthiness Requirements

125.111 General.
125.113 Cabin interiors.
125.115 Internal doors.
125.117 Ventilation.
125.119 Fire precautions.
125.121 Proof of compliance with § 125.119.
125.123 Propeller deicing fluid.
125.125 Pressure cross-feed arrangements.
125.127 Location of fuel tanks.
125.129 Fuel system lines and fittings.
125.131 Fuel lines and fittings in designated fire zones.
125.133 Fuel valves.
125.135 Oil lines and fittings in designated fire zones.
125.137 Oil valves.
125.139 Oil system drains.
125.141 Engine breather lines.
125.143 Firewalls.
125.145 Firewall construction.
125.147 Cowling.
125.149 Engine accessory section diaphragm.
125.151 Powerplant fire protection.
125.153 Flammable fluids.
125.155 Shutoff means.
125.157 Lines and fittings.
125.159 Vent and drain lines.
125.161 Fire-extinguishing systems.
125.163 Fire-extinguishing agents.
125.165 Extinguishing agent container pressure relief.
125.167 Extinguishing agent container compartment temperature.
125.169 Fire-extinguishing system materials.
125.171 Fire-detector systems.
125.173 Fire detectors.
125.175 Protection of other airplane components against fire.
125.177 Control of engine rotation.
125.179 Fuel system independence.
125.181 Induction system ice prevention.
125.183 Carriage of cargo in passenger compartments.
125.185 Carriage of cargo in cargo compartments.
125.187 Landing gear: Aural warning device.
125.189 Demonstration of emergency evacuation procedures.

Subpart F—Instrument and Equipment Requirements

125.201 Inoperable instruments and equipment.
125.202 Flight recorders and cockpit voice recorders.
125.203 Radio and navigational equipment.
125.205 Equipment requirements: Airplanes under IFR.
125.206 Pitot heat indication systems.
125.207 Emergency equipment requirements.

125.209 Emergency equipment: Extended overwater operations.
125.211 Seat and safety belts.
125.213 Miscellaneous equipment.
125.215 Operating information required.
125.217 Passenger information.
125.219 Oxygen for medical use by passengers.
125.221 Icing conditions: Operating limitations.
125.223 Airborne weather radar equipment requirements.

Subpart G—Maintenance

125.241 Applicability.
125.243 Certificate holder's responsibilities.
125.245 Organization required to perform maintenance, preventive maintenance, and alteration.
125.247 Inspection programs and maintenance.
125.249 Maintenance manual requirements.
125.251 Required inspection personnel.

Subpart H—Airman and Crewmember Requirements

125.261 Airman: Limitations on use of services.
125.263 Composition of flightcrew.
125.265 Flight engineer requirements.
125.267 Flight navigator and long-range navigation equipment.
125.269 Flight attendants.
125.271 Emergency and emergency evacuation duties.

Subpart I—Flight Crewmember Requirements

125.281 Pilot-in-command qualifications.
125.283 Second-in-command qualifications.
125.285 Pilot qualifications: Recent experience.
125.287 Initial and recurrent pilot testing requirements.
125.289 Initial and recurrent flight attendant crewmember testing requirements.
125.291 Pilot in command: Instrument proficiency check requirements.
125.293 Crewmember: Tests and checks, grace provisions, accepted standards.
125.295 Check airman authorization: Application and issue.
125.297 Approval of airplane simulators and other training devices.

Subpart J—Flight Operations

125.311 Flight crewmembers at controls.
125.313 Manipulation of controls when carrying passengers.
125.315 Admission to flight deck.
125.317 Inspector's credentials: Admission to pilots' compartment: Forward observer's seat.

125.319 Emergencies.
125.321 Reporting potentially hazardous meteorological conditions and irregularities of ground and navigation facilities.
125.323 Reporting mechanical irregularities.
125.325 Instrument approach procedures and IFR landing minimums.
125.327 Briefing of passengers before flight.
125.329 Minimum altitudes for use of autopilot.
125.331 Carriage of persons without compliance with the passenger-carrying requirements of this part.

Subpart K—Flight Release Rules

125.351 Flight release authority.
125.353 Facilities and services.
125.355 Airplane equipment.
125.357 Communication and navigation facilities.
125.359 Flight release under VFR.
125.361 Flight release under IFR or over-the-top.
125.363 Flight release over water.
125.365 Alternate airport for departure.
125.367 Alternate airport for destination: IFR or over-the-top.
125.369 Alternate airport weather minimums.
125.371 Continuing flight in unsafe conditions.
125.373 Original flight release or amendment of flight release.
125.375 Fuel supply: Nonturbine and turbopropeller-powered airplanes.
125.377 Fuel supply: Turbine-engine-powered airplanes other than turbopropeller.
125.379 Landing weather minimums: IFR.
125.381 Takeoff and landing weather minimums: IFR.
125.383 Load manifest.

Subpart L—Records and Reports

125.401 Crewmember record.
125.403 Flight release form.
125.405 Disposition of load manifest, flight release, and flight plans.
125.407 Maintenance log: Airplanes.
125.409 Reports of defects or unairworthy conditions.
125.411 Airworthiness release or maintenance record entry.

APPENDIX A—ADDITIONAL EMERGENCY EQUIPMENT
APPENDIX B—CRITERIA FOR DEMONSTRATION OF EMERGENCY EVACUATION PROCEDURES UNDER § 125.189
APPENDIX C—ICE PROTECTION
APPENDIX D — AIRPLANE FLIGHT RECORDER SPECIFICATION

SOURCE: Docket No. 19779, 45 FR 67235, Oct. 9, 1980, unless otherwise noted.

SPECIAL FEDERAL AVIATION REGULATION No. 38-2

EDITORIAL NOTE: For the text of SFAR No. 38-2, see Part 121 of this chapter.

Subpart A—General

§ 125.1 Applicability.

(a) Except as provided in paragraphs (b) and (c) of this section, this part prescribes rules governing the operations of U.S.-registered civil airplanes which have a seating configuration of 20 or more passengers, or a maximum payload capacity of 6,000 pounds or more when common carriage is not involved.

(b) The rules of this part do not apply to the operations of airplanes specified in paragraph (a) of this section, when—

(1) They are required to be operated under Part 121, 129, 135, or 137 of this chapter;

(2) They have been issued restricted, limited, or provisional airworthiness certificates, special flight permits, or experimental certificates;

(3) They are being operated by a Part 125 certificate holder without carrying passengers or cargo under Part 91 for training, ferrying, positioning, or maintenance purposes;

(4) They are being operated under Part 91 by an operator certificated to operate those airplanes under Part 121, 135, or 137 of this chapter or are being operated by a foreign air carrier or a foreign person in common carriage solely outside the United States under Part 91 of this chapter; or

(5) They are being operated under a deviation authority issued under § 125.3 of this chapter.

(c) The rules of this part, except § 125.247, do not apply to the operation of airplanes specified in paragraph (a) when they are operated outside the United States by a person who is not a citizen of the United States.

[Doc. No. 19779, 45 FR 67235, Oct. 9, 1980, as amended by Amdt. 125-4, 47 FR 44719, Oct. 12, 1982; Amdt. 125-5, 49 FR 34816, Sept. 4, 1984; Amdt. 125-6, 51 FR 873, Jan.

8, 1986; Amdt. 125-9, 52 FR 20028, May 28, 1987]

§ 125.3 Deviation authority.

(a) The Associate Administrator for Aviation Standards may, upon consideration of the circumstances of a particular operation, issue deviation authority providing relief from specified sections of Part 125. This deviation authority will be issued as a Letter of Deviation Authority.

(b) A Letter of Deviation Authority may be terminated or amended at any time by the Associate Administrator for Aviation Standards.

(c) A request for deviation authority must be submitted to the Department of Transportation, Federal Aviation Administration, Associate Administrator for Aviation Standards, 800 Independence Ave., S.W., Washington, D.C. 20591, not less than 60 days prior to the date of intended operations. A request for deviation authority must contain a complete statement of the circumstances and justification for the deviation requested.

§ 125.5 Operating certificate and operations specifications required.

(a) After February 3, 1981, no person may engage in operations governed by this part unless that person holds a certificate and operations specification or appropriate deviation authority.

(b) Applicants who file an application before June 1, 1981 shall continue to operate under the rules applicable to their operations on February 2, 1981 until the application for an operating certificate required by this part has been denied or the operating certificate and operations specifications required by this part have been issued.

(c) The rules of this part which apply to a certificate holder also apply to any person who engages in any operation governed by this part without an appropriate certificate and operations specifications required by this part or a Letter of Deviation Authority issued under § 125.3.

[Doc. No. 19779, 45 FR 67235, Oct. 9, 1980, as amended by Amdt. 125-1A, 46 FR 10903, Feb. 5, 1981]

§ 125.7 Display of certificate.

(a) The certificate holder must display a true copy of the certificate in each of its aircraft.

(b) Each operator holding a Letter of Deviation Authority issued under this part must carry a true copy in each of its airplanes.

§ 125.9 Definitions.

(a) For the purposes of this part, "maximum payload capacity" means:

(1) For an airplane for which a maximum zero fuel weight is prescribed in FAA technical specifications, the maximum zero fuel weight, less empty weight, less all justifiable airplane equipment, and less the operating load (consisting of minimum flightcrew, foods and beverages and supplies and equipment related to foods and beverages, but not including disposable fuel or oil):

(2) For all other airplanes, the maximum certificated takeoff weight of an airplane, less the empty weight, less all justifiable airplane equipment, and less the operating load (consisting of minimum fuel load, oil, and flightcrew). The allowance for the weight of the crew, oil, and fuel is as follows:

(i) Crew—200 pounds for each crewmember required under this chapter

(ii) Oil—350 pounds.

(iii) Fuel—the minimum weight of fuel required under this chapter for a flight between domestic points 174 nautical miles apart under VFR weather conditions that does not involve extended overwater operations.

(b) For the purposes of this part, "empty weight" means the weight of the airframe, engines, propellers, and fixed equipment. Empty weight excludes the weight of the crew and payload, but includes the weight of all fixed ballast, unusable fuel supply, undrainable oil, total quantity of engine coolant, and total quantity of hydraulic fluid.

(c) For the purposes of this part, "maximum zero fuel weight" means the maximum permissible weight of an airplane with no disposable fuel or oil. The zero fuel weight figure may be found in either the airplane type certificate data sheet or the approved Airplane Flight Manual, or both.

(d) For the purposes of this section, "justifiable airplane equipment" means any equipment necessary for the operation of the airplane. It does not include equipment or ballast specifically installed, permanently or otherwise, for the purpose of altering the empty weight of an airplane to meet the maximum payload capacity.

§125.11 **Certificate eligibility and prohibited operations.**

(a) No person is eligible for a certificate or operations specifications under this part if the person holds the appropriate operating certificate and/or operations specifications necessary to conduct operations under Part 121, 129 or 135 of this chapter.

(b) No certificate holder may conduct any operation which results directly or indirectly from any person's holding out to the public to furnish transportation.

(c) No person holding operations specifications under this part may operate or list on its operations specifications any aircraft listed on any operations specifications or other required aircraft listing under Part 121, 129, or 135 of this chapter.

[Doc. No. 19779, 45 FR 67235, Oct. 9, 1980 as amended by Amdt. 125-9, 52 FR 20028, May 28, 1987]

Subpart B—Certification Rules and Miscellaneous Requirements

§125.21 **Application for operating certificate.**

(a) Each applicant for the issuance of an operating certificate must submit an application in a form and manner prescribed by the Administrator to the FAA Flight Standards district office in whose area the applicant proposes to establish or has established its principal operations base. The application must be submitted at least 60 days before the date of intended operations.

(b) Each application submitted under paragraph (a) of this section must contain a signed statement showing the following:

(1) The name and address of each director and each officer or person employed or who will be employed in a management position described in §125.25.

(2) A list of flight crewmembers with the type of airman certificate held, including ratings and certificate numbers.

§125.23 **Rules applicable to operations subject to this part.**

Each person operating an airplane in operations under this part shall—

(a) While operating inside the United States, comply with the applicable rules in Part 91 of this chapter; and

(b) While operating outside the United States, comply with Annex 2, Rules of the Air, to the Convention on International Civil Aviation or the regulations of any foreign country, whichever applies, and with any rules of Parts 61 and 91 of this chapter and this part that are more restrictive than that Annex or those regulations and that can be complied with without violating that Annex or those regulations. Annex 2 is incorporated by reference in §91.1(c) of this chapter.

§125.25 **Management personnel required.**

(a) Each applicant for a certificate under this part must show that it has enough management personnel, including at least a director of operations, to assure that its operations are conducted in accordance with the requirements of this part.

(b) Each applicant shall—

(1) Set forth the duties, responsibilities, and authority of each of its management personnel in the general policy section of its manual;

(2) List in the manual the names and addresses of each of its management personnel;

(3) Designate a person as responsible for the scheduling of inspections required by the manual and for the updating of the approved weight and balance system on all airplanes.

(c) Each certificate holder shall notify the FAA Flight Standards district office charged with the overall inspection of the certificate holder of any change made in the assignment of persons to the listed positions within 10 days, excluding Saturdays, Sundays, and Federal holidays, of such change.

§ 125.27 Issue of certificate.

(a) An applicant for a certificate under this subpart is entitled to a certificate if the Administrator finds that the applicant is properly and adequately equipped and able to conduct a safe operation in accordance with the requirements of this part and the operations specifications provided for in this part.

(b) The Administrator may deny an application for a certificate under this subpart if the Administrator finds—

(1) That an operating certificate required under this part or Part 121, 123, or 135 of this chapter previously issued to the applicant was revoked; or

(2) That a person who was employed in a management position under § 125.25 of this part with (or has exercised control with respect to) any certificate holder under Part 121, 123, 125, or 135 of this chapter whose operating certificate has been revoked, will be employed in any of those positions or a similar position with the applicant and that the person's employment or control contributed materially to the reasons for revoking that certificate.

§ 125.29 Duration of certificate.

(a) A certificate issued under this part is effective until surrendered, suspended, or revoked.

(b) The Administrator may suspend or revoke a certificate under section 609 of the Federal Aviation Act of 1958 and the applicable procedures of Part 13 of this chapter for any cause that, at the time of suspension or revocation, would have been grounds for denying an application for a certificate.

(c) If the Administrator suspends or revokes a certificate or it is otherwise terminated, the holder of that certificate shall return it to the Administrator.

§ 125.31 Contents of certificate and operations specifications.

(a) Each certificate issued under this part contains the following:

(1) The holder's name.

(2) A description of the operations authorized.

(3) The date it is issued.

(b) The operations specifications issued under this part contain the following:

(1) The kinds of operations authorized.

(2) The types and registration numbers of airplanes authorized for use.

(3) Approval of the provisions of the operator's manual relating to airplane inspections, together with necessary conditions and limitations.

(4) Registration numbers of airplanes that are to be inspected under an approved airplane inspection program under § 125.247.

(5) Procedures for control of weight and balance of airplanes.

(6) Any other item that the Administrator determines is necessary to cover a particular situation.

§ 125.33 Operations specifications not a part of certificate.

Operations specifications are not a part of an operating certificate.

§ 125.35 Amendment of operations specifications.

(a) The FAA Flight Standards district office charged with the overall inspection of the certificate holder may amend any operations specifications issued under this part if—

(1) It determines that safety in air commerce requires that amendment; or

(2) Upon application by the holder, that district office determines that safety in air commerce allows that amendment.

(b) The certificate holder must file an application to amend operations specifications at least 15 days before the date proposed by the applicant for the amendment to become effective, unless a shorter filing period is approved. The application must be on a form and in a manner prescribed by the Administrator and be submitted to the FAA Flight Standards district office charged with the overall inspection of the certificate holder.

(c) Within 30 days after a notice of refusal to approve a holder's application for amendment is received, the holder may petition the Director of Airworthiness or the Director of Flight Operations, as appropriate, to reconsider the refusal to amend.

(d) When the FAA Flight Standards district office charged with the overall inspection of the certificate holder amends operations specifications, that district office gives notice in writing to the holder of a proposed amendment to the operations specifications, fixing a period of not less than 7 days within which the holder may submit written information, views, and arguments concerning the proposed amendment. After consideration of all relevant matter presented, that district office notifies the holder of any amendment adopted, or a rescission of the notice. That amendment becomes effective not less than 30 days after the holder receives notice of the adoption of the amendment, unless the holder petitions the Director of Airworthiness or the Director of Flight Operations, as appropriate, for reconsideration of the amendment. In that case, the effective date of the amendment is stayed pending a decision by the Director. If the Director finds there is an emergency requiring immediate action as to safety in air commerce that makes the provisions of this paragraph impracticable or contrary to the public interest, the Director notifies the certificate holder that the amendment is effective on the date of receipt, without previous notice.

§ 125.37 Duty time limitations.

(a) Each flight crewmember must be relieved from all duty for at least 8 consecutive hours during any 24-hour period.

(b) The Administrator may specify rest, flight time, and duty time limitations in the operations specifications that are other than those specified in paragraph (a) of this section.

§ 125.39 Carriage of narcotic drugs, marihuana, and depressant or stimulant drugs or substances.

If the holder of a certificate issued under this part permits any airplane owned or leased by that holder to be engaged in any operation that the certificate holder knows to be in violation of § 91.12(a) of this chapter, that oper-

ation is a basis for suspending or revoking the certificate.

§ 125.41 Availability of certificate and operations specifications.

Each certificate holder shall make its operating certificate and operations specifications available for inspection by the Administrator at its principal operations base.

§ 125.43 Use of operations specifications.

(a) Each certificate holder shall keep each of its employees informed of the provisions of its operations specifications that apply to the employee's duties and responsibilities.

(b) Each certificate holder shall maintain a complete and separate set of its operations specifications. In addition, each certificate holder shall insert pertinent excerpts of its operations specifications, or reference thereto, in its manual in such a manner that they retain their identity as operations specifications.

§ 125.45 Inspection authority.

Each certificate holder shall allow the Administrator, at any time or place, to make any inspections or tests to determine its compliance with the Federal Aviation Act of 1958, the Federal Aviation Regulations, its operating certificate and operations specifications, its letter of deviation authority, or its eligibililty to continue to hold its certificate or its letter of deviation authority.

§ 125.47 Change of address.

Each certificate holder shall notify the FAA Flight Standards district office charged with the overall inspection of its operations, in writing, at least 30 days in advance, of any change in the address of its principal business office, its principal operations base, or its principal maintenance base.

§ 125.49 Airport requirements.

(a) No certificate holder may use any airport unless it is adequate for the proposed operation, considering such items as size, surface, obstructions, and lighting.

(b) No pilot of an airplane carrying passengers at night may take off from, or land on, an airport unless—

(1) That pilot has determined the wind direction from an illuminated wind direction indicator or local ground communications, or, in the case of takeoff, that pilot's personal observations; and

(2) The limits of the area to be used for landing or takeoff are clearly shown by boundary or runway marker lights.

(c) For the purposes of paragraph (b) of this section, if the area to be used for takeoff or landing is marked by flare pots or lanterns, their use must be approved by the Administrator.

§ 125.51 En route navigational facilities.

(a) Except as provided in paragraph (b) of this section, no certificate holder may conduct any operation over a route unless nonvisual ground aids are—

(1) Available over the route for navigating airplanes within the degree of accuracy required for ATC; and

(2) Located to allow navigation to any airport of destination, or alternate airport, within the degree of accuracy necessary for the operation involved.

(b) Nonvisual ground aids are not required for—

(1) Day VFR operations that can be conducted safely by pilotage because of the characteristics of the terrain;

(2) Night VFR operations on routes that the Administrator determines have reliable landmarks adequate for safe operation; or

(3) Operations where the use of celestial or other specialized means of navigation, such as an inertial navigation system, is approved.

§ 125.53 Flight locating requirements.

(a) Each certificate holder must have procedures established for locating each flight for which an FAA flight plan is not filed that—

(1) Provide the certificate holder with at least the information required to be included in a VFR flight plan;

(2) Provide for timely notification of an FAA facility or search and rescue facility, if an airplane is overdue or missing; and

(3) Provide the certificate holder with the location, date, and estimated time for reestablishing radio or telephone communications, if the flight will operate in an area where communications cannot be maintained.

(b) Flight locating information shall be retained at the certificate holder's principal operations base, or at other places designated by the certificate holder in the flight locating procedures, until the completion of the flight.

(c) Each certificate holder shall furnish the representative of the Administrator assigned to it with a copy of its flight locating procedures and any changes or additions, unless those procedures are included in a manual required under this part.

Subpart C—Manual Requirements

§ 125.71 Preparation.

(a) Each certificate holder shall prepare and keep current a manual setting forth the certificate holder's procedures and policies acceptable to the Administrator. This manual must be used by the certificate holder's flight, ground, and maintenance personnel in conducting its operations. However, the Administrator may authorize a deviation from this paragraph if the Administrator finds that, because of the limited size of the operation, all or part of the manual is not necessary for guidance of flight, ground, or maintenance personnel.

(b) Each certificate holder shall maintain at least one copy of the manual at its principal operations base.

(c) The manual must not be contrary to any applicable Federal regulations, foreign regulation applicable to the certificate holder's operations in foreign countries, or the certificate holder's operating certificate or operations specifications.

(d) A copy of the manual, or appropriate portions of the manual (and changes and additions) shall be made available to maintenance and ground operations personnel by the certificate holder and furnished to—

(1) Its flight crewmembers; and

(2) The FAA Flight Standards district office charged with the overall inspection of its operations.

(e) Each employee of the certificate holder to whom a manual or appropriate portions of it are furnished under paragraph (d)(1) of this section shall keep it up to. date with the changes and additions furnished to them.

(f) Except as provided in paragraph (g) of this section, each certificate holder shall carry appropriate parts of the manual in each airplane when away from the principal operations base. The appropriate parts must be available for use by ground or flight personnel. If a certificate holder carries aboard an airplane all or any portion of the maintenance part of its manual in microfilm, it must also carry a reading device that provides a legible facsimile image of the microfilmed maintenance information and instructions.

(g) If a certificate holder conducts airplane inspections or maintenance at specified stations where it keeps the approved inspection program manual, it is not required to carry the manual aboard the airplane en route to those stations.

§ 125.73 Contents.

Each manual shall have the date of the last revision and revision number on each revised page. The manual must include—

(a) The name of each management person who is authorized to act for the certificate holder, the person's assigned area of responsibility, and the person's duties, responsibilities, and authority;

(b) Procedures for ensuring compliance with airplane weight and balance limitations;

(c) Copies of the certificate holder's operations specifications or appropriate extracted information, including area of operations authorized, category and class of airplane authorized, crew complements, and types of operations authorized;

(d) Procedures for complying with accident notification requirements;

(e) Procedures for ensuring that the pilot in command knows that required airworthiness inspections have been made and that the airplane has been approved for return to service in compliance with applicable maintenance requirements;

(f) Procedures for reporting and recording mechanical irregularities that come to the attention of the pilot in command before, during, and after completion of a flight;

(g) Procedures to be followed by the pilot in command for determining that mechanical irregularities or defects reported for previous flights have been corrected or that correction has been deferred;

(h) Procedures to be followed by the pilot in command to obtain maintenance, preventive maintenance, and servicing of the airplane at a place where previous arrangements have not been made by the operator, when the pilot is authorized to so act for the operator;

(i) Procedures for the release for, or continuation of, flight if any item of equipment required for the particular type of operation becomes inoperative or unserviceable en route;

(j) Procedures for refueling airplanes, eliminating fuel contamination, protecting from fire (including electrostatic protection), and supervising and protecting passengers during refueling;

(k) Procedures to be followed by the pilot in command in the briefing under § 125.327;

(l) Flight locating procedures, when applicable;

(m) Procedures for ensuring compliance with emergency procedures, including a list of the functions assigned each category of required crewmembers in connection with an emergency and emergency evacuation;

(n) The approved airplane inspection program;

(o) Procedures and instructions to enable personnel to recognize hazardous materials, as defined in Title 49 CFR, and if these materials are to be carried, stored, or handled, procedures and instructions for—

(1) Accepting shipment of hazardous material required by Title 49 CFR, to assure proper packaging, marking, labeling, shipping documents, compatibility of articles, and instructions on their loading, storage, and handling;

(2) Notification and reporting hazardous material incidents as required by Title 49 CFR; and

(3) Notification of the pilot in command when there are hazardous materials aboard, as required by Title 49 CFR;

(p) Procedures for the evacuation of persons who may need the assistance of another person to move expeditiously to an exit if an emergency occurs;

(q) The identity of each person who will administer tests required by this part, including the designation of the tests authorized to be given by the person; and

(r) Other procedures and policy instructions regarding the certificate holder's operations that are issued by the certificate holder.

§ 125.75 Airplane flight manual.

(a) Each certificate holder shall keep a current approved Airplane Flight Manual or approved equivalent for each type airplane that it operates.

(b) Each certificate holder shall carry the approved Airplane Flight Manual or the approved equivalent aboard each airplane it operates. A certificate holder may elect to carry a combination of the manuals required by this section and § 125.71. If it so elects, the certificate holder may revise the operating procedures sections and modify the presentation of performance from the applicable Airplane Flight Manual if the revised operating procedures and modified performance data presentation are approved by the Administrator.

Subpart D—Airplane Requirements

§ 125.91 Airplane requirements: General.

(a) No certificate holder may operate an airplane governed by this part unless it—

(1) Carries an appropriate current airworthiness certificate issued under this chapter; and

(2) Is in an airworthy condition and meets the applicable airworthiness requirements of this chapter, including those relating to identification and equipment.

(b) No person may operate an airplane unless the current empty weight and center of gravity are calculated from the values established by actual weighing of the airplane within the preceding 36 calendar months.

(c) Paragraph (b) of this section does not apply to airplanes issued an original airworthiness certificate within the preceding 36 calendar months.

§ 125.93 Airplane limitations.

No certificate holder may operate a land airplane (other than a DC-3, C-46, CV-240, CV-340, CV-440, CV-580, CV-600, CV-640, or Martin 404) in an extended overwater operation unless it is certificated or approved as adequate for ditching under the ditching provisions of Part 25 of this chapter.

Subpart E—Special Airworthiness Requirements

§ 125.111 General.

(a) Except as provided in paragraph (b) of this section, no certificate holder may use an airplane powered by airplane engines rated at more than 600 horsepower each for maximum continuous operation unless that airplane meets the requirements of §§ 125.113 through 125.181.

(b) If the Administrator determines that, for a particular model of airplane used in cargo service, literal compliance with any requirement under paragraph (a) of this section would be extremely difficult and that compliance would not contribute materially to the objective sought, the Administrator may require compliance with only those requirements that are necessary to accomplish the basic objectives of this part.

(c) This section does not apply to any airplane certificated under—

(1) Part 4b of the Civil Air Regulations in effect after October 31, 1946;

(2) Part 25 of this chapter; or

(3) Special Civil Air Regulation 422, 422A, or 422B.

§ 125.113 Cabin interiors.

(a) Upon the first major overhaul of an airplane cabin or refurbishing of the cabin interior, all materials in each compartment used by the crew or passengers that do not meet the following requirements must be replaced with materials that meet these requirements:

(1) For an airplane for which the application for the type certificate was filed prior to May 1, 1972, § 25.853 in effect on April 30, 1972.

(2) For an airplane for which the application for the type certificate was filed on or after May 1, 1972, the materials requirement under which the airplane was type certificated.

(b) Except as provided in paragraph (a) of this section, each compartment used by the crew or passengers must meet the following requirements:

(1) Materials must be at least flash resistant.

(2) The wall and ceiling linings and the covering of upholstering, floors, and furnishings must be flame resistant.

(3) Each compartment where smoking is to be allowed must be equipped with self-contained ash trays that are completely removable and other compartments must be placarded against smoking.

(4) Each receptacle for used towels, papers, and wastes must be of fire-resistant material and must have a cover or other means of containing possible fires started in the receptacles.

§ 125.115 Internal doors.

In any case where internal doors are equipped with louvres or other ventilating means, there must be a means convenient to the crew for closing the flow of air through the door when necessary.

§ 125.117 Ventilation.

Each passenger or crew compartment must be suitably ventilated. Carbon monoxide concentration may not be more than one part in 20,000 parts of air, and fuel fumes may not be present. In any case where partitions between compartments have louvres or other means allowing air to flow between compartments, there must be a means convenient to the crew for closing the flow of air through the partitions when necessary.

§ 125.119 Fire precautions.

(a) Each compartment must be designed so that, when used for storing cargo or baggage, it meets the following requirements:

(1) No compartment may include controls, wiring, lines, equipment, or accessories that would upon damage or failure, affect the safe operation of the airplane unless the item is adequately shielded, isolated, or otherwise protected so that it cannot be damaged by movement of cargo in the compartment and so that damage to or failure of the item would not create a fire hazard in the compartment.

(2) Cargo or baggage may not interfere with the functioning of the fire-protective features of the compartment.

(3) Materials used in the construction of the compartments, including tie-down equipment, must be at least flame resistant.

(4) Each compartment must include provisions for safeguarding against fires according to the classifications set forth in paragraphs (b) through (f) of this section.

(b) *Class A.* Cargo and baggage compartments are classified in the "A" category if a fire therein would be readily discernible to a member of the crew while at that crewmember's station, and all parts of the compartment are easily accessible in flight. There must be a hand fire extinguisher available for each Class A compartment.

(c) *Class B.* Cargo and baggage compartments are classified in the "B" category if enough access is provided while in flight to enable a member of the crew to effectively reach all of the compartment and its contents with a hand fire extinguisher and the compartment is so designed that, when the access provisions are being used, no hazardous amount of smoke, flames, or extinguishing agent enters any compartment occupied by the crew or passengers. Each Class B compartment must comply with the following:

(1) It must have a separate approved smoke or fire detector system to give warning at the pilot or flight engineer station.

(2) There must be a hand-held fire extinguisher available for the compartment.

(3) It must be lined with fire-resistant material, except that additional

service lining of flame-resistant material may be used.

(d) *Class C.* Cargo and baggage compartments are classified in the "C" category if they do not conform with the requirements for the "A", "B", "D", or "E" categories. Each Class C compartment must comply with the following:

(1) It must have a separate approved smoke or fire detector system to give warning at the pilot or flight engineer station.

(2) It must have an approved built-in fire-extinguishing system controlled from the pilot or flight engineer station.

(3) It must be designed to exclude hazardous quantities of smoke, flames, or extinguishing agents from entering into any compartment occupied by the crew or passengers.

(4) It must have ventilation and draft control so that the extinguishing agent provided can control any fire that may start in the compartment.

(5) It must be lined with fire-resistant material, except that additional service lining of flame-resistant material may be used.

(e) *Class D.* Cargo and baggage compartments are classified in the "D" category if they are so designed and constructed that a fire occurring therein will be completely confined without endangering the safety of the airplane or the occupants. Each Class D compartment must comply with the following:

(1) It must have a means to exclude hazardous quantities of smoke, flames, or noxious gases from entering any compartment occupied by the crew or passengers.

(2) Ventilation and drafts must be controlled within each compartment so that any fire likely to occur in the compartment will not progress beyond safe limits.

(3) It must be completely lined with fire-resistant material.

(4) Consideration must be given to the effect of heat within the compartment on adjacent critical parts of the airplane.

(f) *Class E.* On airplanes used for the carriage of cargo only, the cabin area may be classified as a Class "E"

compartment. Each Class E compartment must comply with the following:

(1) It must be completely lined with fire-resistant material.

(2) It must have a separate system of an approved type smoke or fire detector to give warning at the pilot or flight engineer station.

(3) It must have a means to shut off the ventilating air flow to or within the compartment and the controls for that means must be accessible to the flightcrew in the crew compartment.

(4) It must have a means to exclude hazardous quantities of smoke, flames, or noxious gases from entering the flightcrew compartment.

(5) Required crew emergency exits must be accessible under all cargo loading conditions.

§ 125.121 Proof of compliance with § 125.119.

Compliance with those provisions of § 125.119 that refer to compartment accessibility, the entry of hazardous quantities of smoke or extinguishing agent into compartment occupied by the crew or passengers, and the dissipation of the extinguishing agent in Class "C" compartments must be shown by tests in flight. During these tests it must be shown that no inadvertent operation of smoke or fire detectors in other compartments within the airplane would occur as a result of fire contained in any one compartment, either during the time it is being extinguished, or thereafter, unless the extinguishing system floods those compartments simultaneously.

§ 125.123 Propeller deicing fluid.

If combustible fluid is used for propeller deicing, the certificate holder must comply with § 125.153.

§ 125.125 Pressure cross-feed arrangements.

(a) Pressure cross-feed lines may not pass through parts of the airplane used for carrying persons or cargo unless there is a means to allow crewmembers to shut off the supply of fuel to these lines or the lines are enclosed in a fuel and fume-proof enclosure that is ventilated and drained to the exterior of the airplane. However, such an enclosure need not be used if those lines incorporate no fittings on or within the personnel or cargo areas and are suitably routed or protected to prevent accidental damage.

(b) Lines that can be isolated from the rest of the fuel system by valves at each end must incorporate provisions for relieving excessive pressures that may result from exposure of the isolated line to high temperatures.

§ 125.127 Location of fuel tanks.

(a) Fuel tanks must be located in accordance with § 125.153.

(b) No part of the engine nacelle skin that lies immediately behind a major air outlet from the engine compartment may be used as the wall of an integral tank.

(c) Fuel tanks must be isolated from personnel compartments by means of fume- and fuel-proof enclosures.

§ 125.129 Fuel system lines and fittings.

(a) Fuel lines must be installed and supported so as to prevent excessive vibration and so as to be adequate to withstand loads due to fuel pressure and accelerated flight conditions.

(b) Lines connected to components of the airplane between which there may be relative motion must incorporate provisions for flexibility.

(c) Flexible connections in lines that may be under pressure and subject to axial loading must use flexible hose assemblies rather than hose clamp connections.

(d) Flexible hoses must be of an acceptable type or proven suitable for the particular application.

§ 125.131 Fuel lines and fittings in designated fire zones.

Fuel lines and fittings in each designated fire zone must comply with § 125.157.

§ 125.133 Fuel valves.

Each fuel valve must—

(a) Comply with § 125.155;

(b) Have positive stops or suitable index provisions in the "on" and "off" positions; and

(c) Be supported so that loads resulting from its operation or from accelerated flight conditions are not trans-

mitted to the lines connected to the valve.

§ 125.135 Oil lines and fittings in designated fire zones.

Oil lines and fittings in each designated fire zone must comply with § 125.157.

§ 125.137 Oil valves.

(a) Each oil valve must—

(1) Comply with § 125.155;

(2) Have positive stops or suitable index provisions in the "on" and "off" positions; and

(3) Be supported so that loads resulting from its operation or from accelerated flight conditions are not transmitted to the lines attached to the valve.

(b) The closing of an oil shutoff means must not prevent feathering the propeller, unless equivalent safety provisions are incorporated.

§ 125.139 Oil system drains.

Accessible drains incorporating either a manual or automatic means for positive locking in the closed position must be provided to allow safe drainage of the entire oil system.

§ 125.141 Engine breather lines.

(a) Engine breather lines must be so arranged that condensed water vapor that may freeze and obstruct the line cannot accumulate at any point.

(b) Engine breathers must discharge in a location that does not constitute a fire hazard in case foaming occurs and so that oil emitted from the line does not impinge upon the pilots' windshield.

(c) Engine breathers may not discharge into the engine air induction system.

§ 125.143 Firewalls.

Each engine, auxiliary power unit, fuel-burning heater, or other item of combusting equipment that is intended for operation in flight must be isolated from the rest of the airplane by means of firewalls or shrouds, or by other equivalent means.

§ 125.145 Firewall construction.

Each firewall and shroud must—

(a) Be so made that no hazardous quantity of air, fluids, or flame can pass from the engine compartment to other parts of the airplane;

(b) Have all openings in the firewall or shroud sealed with close-fitting fireproof grommets, bushings, or firewall fittings;

(c) Be made of fireproof material; and

(d) Be protected against corrosion.

§ 125.147 Cowling.

(a) Cowling must be made and supported so as to resist the vibration, inertia, and air loads to which it may be normally subjected.

(b) Provisions must be made to allow rapid and complete drainage of the cowling in normal ground and flight attitudes. Drains must not discharge in locations constituting a fire hazard. Parts of the cowling that are subjected to high temperatures because they are near exhaust system parts or because of exhaust gas impingement must be made of fireproof material. Unless otherwise specified in these regulations, all other parts of the cowling must be made of material that is at least fire resistant.

§ 125.149 Engine accessory section diaphragm.

Unless equivalent protection can be shown by other means, a diaphragm that complies with § 125.145 must be provided on air-cooled engines to isolate the engine power section and all parts of the exhaust system from the engine accessory compartment.

§ 125.151 Powerplant fire protection.

(a) Designated fire zones must be protected from fire by compliance with §§ 125.153 through 125.159.

(b) Designated fire zones are—

(1) Engine accessory sections;

(2) Installations where no isolation is provided between the engine and accessory compartment; and

(3) Areas that contain auxiliary power units, fuel-burning heaters, and other combustion equipment.

§ 125.153 Flammable fluids.

(a) No tanks or reservoirs that are a part of a system containing flammable fluids or gases may be located in designated fire zones, except where the fluid contained, the design of the system, the materials used in the tank, the shutoff means, and the connections, lines, and controls provide equivalent safety.

(b) At least one-half inch of clear airspace must be provided between any tank or reservoir and a firewall or shroud isolating a designated fire zone.

§ 125.155 Shutoff means.

(a) Each engine must have a means for shutting off or otherwise preventing hazardous amounts of fuel, oil, deicer, and other flammable fluids from flowing into, within, or through any designated fire zone. However, means need not be provided to shut off flow in lines that are an integral part of an engine.

(b) The shutoff means must allow an emergency operating sequence that is compatible with the emergency operation of other equipment, such as feathering the propeller, to facilitate rapid and effective control of fires.

(c) Shutoff means must be located outside of designated fire zones, unless equivalent safety is provided, and it must be shown that no hazardous amount of flammable fluid will drain into any designated fire zone after a shutoff.

(d) Adequate provisions must be made to guard against inadvertent operation of the shutoff means and to make it possible for the crew to reopen the shutoff means after it has been closed.

§ 125.157 Lines and fittings.

(a) Each line, and its fittings, that is located in a designated fire zone, if it carries flammable fluids or gases under pressure, or is attached directly to the engine, or is subject to relative motion between components (except lines and fittings forming an integral part of the engine), must be flexible and fire-resistant with fire-resistant, factory-fixed, detachable, or other approved fire-resistant ends.

(b) Lines and fittings that are not subject to pressure or to relative motion between components must be of fire-resistant materials.

§ 125.159 Vent and drain lines.

All vent and drain lines, and their fittings, that are located in a designated fire zone must, if they carry flammable fluids or gases, comply with § 125.157, if the Administrator finds that the rupture or breakage of any vent or drain line may result in a fire hazard.

§ 125.161 Fire-extinguishing systems.

(a) Unless the certificate holder shows that equivalent protection against destruction of the airplane in case of fire is provided by the use of fireproof materials in the nacelle and other components that would be subjected to flame, fire-extinguishing systems must be provided to serve all designated fire zones.

(b) Materials in the fire-extinguishing system must not react chemically with the extinguishing agent so as to be a hazard.

§ 125.163 Fire-extinguishing agents.

Only methyl bromide, carbon dioxide, or another agent that has been shown to provide equivalent extinguishing action may be used as a fire-extinguishing agent. If methyl bromide or any other toxic extinguishing agent is used, provisions must be made to prevent harmful concentrations of fluid or fluid vapors from entering any personnel compartment either because of leakage during normal operation of the airplane or because of discharging the fire extinguisher on the ground or in flight when there is a defect in the extinguishing system. If a methyl bromide system is used, the containers must be charged with dry agent and sealed by the fire-extinguisher manufacturer or some other person using satisfactory recharging equipment. If carbon dioxide is used, it must not be possible to discharge enough gas into the personnel compartments to create a danger of suffocating the occupants.

§ 125.165 Extinguishing agent container pressure relief.

Extinguishing agent containers must be provided with a pressure relief to prevent bursting of the container because of excessive internal pressures. The discharge line from the relief connection must terminate outside the airplane in a place convenient for inspection on the ground. An indicator must be provided at the discharge end of the line to provide a visual indication when the container has discharged.

§ 125.167 Extinguishing agent container compartment temperature.

Precautions must be taken to ensure that the extinguishing agent containers are installed in places where reasonable temperatures can be maintained for effective use of the extinguishing system.

§ 125.169 Fire-extinguishing system materials.

(a) Except as provided in paragraph (b) of this section, each component of a fire-extinguishing system that is in a designated fire zone must be made of fireproof materials.

(b) Connections that are subject to relative motion between components of the airplane must be made of flexible materials that are at least fire-resistant and be located so as to minimize the probability of failure.

§ 125.171 Fire-detector systems.

Enough quick-acting fire detectors must be provided in each designated fire zone to assure the detection of any fire that may occur in that zone.

§ 125.173 Fire detectors.

Fire detectors must be made and installed in a manner that assures their ability to resist, without failure, all vibration, inertia, and other loads to which they may be normally subjected. Fire detectors must be unaffected by exposure to fumes, oil, water, or other fluids that may be present.

§ 125.175 Protection of other airplane components against fire.

(a) Except as provided in paragraph (b) of this section, all airplane surfaces aft of the nacelles in the area of one nacelle diameter on both sides of the nacelle centerline must be made of material that is at least fire resistant.

(b) Paragraph (a) of this section does not apply to tail surfaces lying behind nacelles unless the dimensional configuration of the airplane is such that the tail surfaces could be affected readily by heat, flames, or sparks emanating from a designated fire zone or from the engine from a designated fire zone or from the engine compartment of any nacelle.

§ 125.177   Control of engine rotation.

(a) Except as provided in paragraph (b) of this section, each airplane must have a means of individually stopping and restarting the rotation of any engine in flight.

(b) In the case of turbine engine installations, a means of stopping rotation need be provided only if the Administrator finds that rotation could jeopardize the safety of the airplane.

§ 125.179   Fuel system independence.

(a) Each airplane fuel system must be arranged so that the failure of any one component does not result in the irrecoverable loss of power of more than one engine.

(b) A separate fuel tank need not be provided for each engine if the certificate holder shows that the fuel system incorporates features that provide equivalent safety.

§ 125.181   Induction system ice prevention.

A means for preventing the malfunctioning of each engine due to ice accumulation in the engine air induction system must be provided for each airplane.

§ 125.183   Carriage of cargo in passenger compartments.

(a) Except as provided in paragraph (b) or (c) of this section, no certificate holder may carry cargo in the passenger compartment of an airplane.

(b) Cargo may be carried aft of the foremost seated passengers if it is carried in an approved cargo bin that meets the following requirements:

(1) The bin must withstand the load factors and emergency landing conditions applicable to the passenger seats of the airplane in which the bin is installed, multiplied by a factor of 1.15, using the combined weight of the bin and the maximum weight of cargo that may be carried in the bin.

(2) The maximum weight of cargo that the bin is approved to carry and any instructions necessary to ensure

proper weight distribution within the bin must be conspicuously marked on the bin.

(3) The bin may not impose any load on the floor or other structure of the airplane that exceeds the load limitations of that structure.

(4) The bin must be attached to the seat tracks or to the floor structure of the airplane, and its attachment must withstand the load factors and emergency landing conditions applicable to the passenger seats of the airplane in which the bin is installed, multiplied by either the factor 1.15 or the seat attachment factor specified for the airplane, whichever is greater, using the combined weight of the bin and the maximum weight of cargo that may be carried in the bin.

(5) The bin may not be installed in a position that restricts access to or use of any required emergency exit, or of the aisle in the passenger compartment.

(6) The bin must be fully enclosed and made of material that is at least flame-resistant.

(7) Suitable safeguards must be provided within the bin to prevent the cargo from shifting under emergency landing conditions.

(8) The bin may not be installed in a position that obscures any passenger's view of the "seat belt" sign, "no smoking" sign, or any required exit sign, unless an auxiliary sign or other approved means for proper notification of the passenger is provided.

(c) All cargo may be carried forward of the foremost seated passengers and carry-on baggage may be carried alongside the foremost seated passengers if the cargo (including carry-on baggage) is carried either in approved bins as specified in paragraph (b) of this section or in accordance with the following:

(1) It is properly secured by a safety belt or other tie down having enough strength to eliminate the possibility of shifting under all normally anticipated flight and ground conditions.

(2) It is packaged or covered in a manner to avoid possible injury to passengers.

(3) It does not impose any load on seats or the floor structure that ex-

ceeds the load limitation for those components.

(4) Its location does not restrict access to or use of any required emergency or regular exit, or of the aisle in the passenger compartment.

(5) Its location does not obscure any passenger's view of the "seat belt" sign, "no smoking" sign, or required exit sign, unless an auxiliary sign or other approved means for proper notification of the passenger is provided.

§ 125.185 Carriage of cargo in cargo compartments.

When cargo is carried in cargo compartments that are designed to require the physical entry of a crewmember to extinguish any fire that may occur during flight, the cargo must be loaded so as to allow a crewmember to effectively reach all parts of the compartment with the contents of a hand-held fire extinguisher.

§ 125.187 Landing gear: Aural warning device.

(a) Each airplane must have a landing gear aural warning device that functions continuously under the following conditions:

(1) For airplanes with an established approach wing-flap position, whenever the wing flaps are extended beyond the maximum certificated approach climb configuration position in the Airplane Flight Manual and the landing gear is not fully extended and locked.

(2) For airplanes without an established approach climb wing-flap position, whenever the wing flaps are extended beyond the position at which landing gear extension is normally performed and the landing gear is not fully extended and locked.

(b) The warning system required by paragraph (a) of this section—

(1) May not have a manual shutoff;

(2) Must be in addition to the throttle-actuated device installed under the type certification airworthiness requirements; and

(3) May utilize any part of the throttle-actuated system including the aural warning device.

(c) The flap position sensing unit may be installed at any suitable place in the airplane.

§ 125.189 Demonstration of emergency evacuation procedures.

(a) Each certificate holder must show, by actual demonstration conducted in accordance with paragraph (a) of Appendix B of this part, that the emergency evacuation procedures for each type and model of airplane with a seating of more than 44 passengers, that is used in its passenger-carrying operations, allow the evacuation of the full seating capacity, including crewmembers, in 90 seconds or less, in each of the following circumstances:

(1) A demonstration must be conducted by the certificate holder upon the initial introduction of a type and model of airplane into passenger-carrying operations. However, the demonstration need not be repeated for any airplane type or model that has the same number and type of exits, the same cabin configuration, and the same emergency equipment as any other airplane used by the certificate holder in successfully demonstrating emergency evacuation in compliance with this paragraph.

(2) A demonstration must be conducted—

(i) Upon increasing by more than 5 percent the passenger seating capacity for which successful demonstration has been conducted; or

(ii) Upon a major change in the passenger cabin interior configuration that will affect the emergency evacuation of passengers.

(b) If a certificate holder has conducted a successful demonstration required by § 121.291(a) in the same type airplane as a Part 121 or Part 123 certificate holder, it need not conduct a demonstration under this paragraph in that type airplane to achieve certification under Part 125.

(c) Each certificate holder operating or proposing to operate one or more landplanes in extended overwater operations, or otherwise required to have certain equipment under § 125.209, must show, by a simulated ditching conducted in accordance with paragraph (b) of Appendix B of this part, that it has the ability to efficiently carry out its ditching procedures.

(d) If a certificate holder has conducted a successful demonstration required by § 121. 291(b) in the same type airplane as Part 121 or Part 123 certificate holder, it need not conduct a demonstration under this paragraph in that type airplane to achieve certification under Part 125.

Subpart F - Instrument and Equipment Requirements

§ 125.201 Inoperable instruments and equipment.

(a) No person may take off an airplane unless the following instruments and equipment are in an operable condition:

(1) Instruments and equipment that are either specifically or otherwise required by the airworthiness requirements under which the airplane is type certificated and which are essential for safe operations under all operating conditions.

(2) Instruments and equipment required by an airworthiness directive to be in operable condition unless the airworthiness directive provides otherwise.

(b) No person may take off any airplane with inoperable instruments or equipment installed, other than those described in paragraph (a) of this section, unless the following conditions are met:

(1) An approved Minimum Equipment List exists for the airplane type.

(2) The airplane has within it a letter of authorization, issued by the FAA Flight Standards district office having certification responsibility for the certificate holder, authorizing operation of the airplane under the Minimum Equipment List. The letter of authorization may be obtained by written request of the certificate holder. The Minimum Equipment

List and the letter of authorization constitute a supplemental type certificate for the airplane.

(3) The approved Minimum Equipment List must provide for the operation of the airplane with the instruments and equipment in an inoperable condition.

(4) The airplane records available to the pilot must include an entry describing the inoperable instruments and equipment.

(5) The airplane is operated under all applicable conditions and limitations contained in the Minimum Equipment List and the letter authorizing the use of the list.

(c) Without regard to the requirements of paragraph (a)(1) of this section, an airplane with inoperable instruments or equipment may be operated under a special flight permit under § § 21.197 and 21.199 of this chapter.

§ 125.203 Radio and naviagational equipment.

(a) No person may operate an airplane unless it has two-way radio communications equipment able, at least in flight, to transmit to, and receive from, ground facilities 25 miles away.

(b) No person may operate an airplane over-the-top unless it has radio navigational equipment able to receive radio signals from the ground facilities to be used.

(c) No person may operate an airplane carrying passengers under IFR or in extended overwater operations unless it has at least the following radio communication and navigational equipment appropriate to the facilities to be used which are capable of transmitting to, and receiving from, at any place on the route to be flown, at least one ground facility:

(1) Two transmitters, (2) two microphones, (3) two headsets or one headset and one speaker (4) a marker beacon receiver, (5) two independent receivers for navigation, and (6) two independent receivers for communications.

(d) For the purposes of paragraphs (c)(5) and (c)(6) of this section, a receiver is independent if the function of any part of it does not depend on the functioning of any part of another receiver. However, a receiver that can receive both communications and navigational signals may be used in place of a separate communications receiver and a separate navigational signal receiver.

§125.205 Equipment requirements: Airplanes under IFR.

No person may operate an airplane under IFR unless it has—

(a) A vertical speed indicator;

(b) A free-air temperature indicator;

(c) A heated pitot tube for each airspeed indicator;

(d) A power failure warning device or vacuum indicator to show the power available for gyroscopic instruments from each power source;

(e) An alternate source of static pressure for the altimeter and the airspeed and vertical speed indicators;

(f) At least two generators each of which is on a separate engine, or which any combination of one-half of the total number are rated sufficiently to supply the electrical loads of all required instruments and equipment necessary for safe emergency operation of the airplane; and

(g) Two independent sources of energy (with means of selecting either), of which at least one is an engine-driven pump or generator, each of which is able to drive all gyroscopic instruments and installed so that failure of one instrument or source does not interfere with the energy supply to the remaining instruments or the other energy source. For the purposes of this paragraph, each engine-driven source of energy must be on a different engine.

(h) For the purposes of paragraph (f) of this section, a continuous inflight electrical load includes one that draws current continuously during flight, such as radio equipment, electrically driven instruments, and lights, but does not include occasional intermittent loads.

(i) An airspeed indicating system with heated pitot tube or equivalent means for preventing malfunctioning due to icing.

(j) A sensitive altimeter.

(k) Instrument lights providing enough light to make each required instrument, switch, or similar instrument easily readable and installed so that the direct rays are shielded from the flight crewmembers' eyes and that no objectionable reflections are visible to them. There must be a means of controlling the intensity of illumination unless it is shown that nondimming instrument lights are satisfactory.

§125.206 Pitot heat indication systems.

(a) Except as provided in paragraph (b) of this section, after April 12, 1981, no person may operate a transport category airplane equipped with a flight instrument pitot heating system unless the airplane is equipped with an operable pitot heat indication system that complies with §25.1326 of this chapter in effect on April 12, 1978.

(b) A certificate holder may obtain an extension of the April 12, 1981, compliance date specified in paragraph (a) of this section, but not beyond April 12, 1983, from the Director of Flight Operations if the certificate holder—

(1) Shows that due to circumstances beyond its control it cannot comply by the specified compliance date; and

(2) Submits by the specified compliance date a schedule for compliance acceptable to the Director, indicating that compliance will be achieved at the earliest practicable date.

[Amdt. 125-3, 46 FR 43806, Aug. 31, 1981]

§125.207 Emergency equipment requirements.

(a) No person may operate an airplane having a seating capacity of 20 or more passengers unless it is equipped with the following emergency equipment:

(1) One approved first aid kit for treatment of injuries likely to occur in flight or in a minor accident, which meets the following specifications and requirements:

(i) Each first aid kit must be dust and moisture proof and contain only materials that either meet Federal Specifications GGK–391a, as revised, or as approved by the Administrator.

(ii) Required first aid kits must be readily accessible to the cabin flight attendants.

(iii) At time of takeoff, each first aid kit must contain at least the following or other contents approved by the Administrator:

Contents:	Quantity
Adhesive bandage compressors, 1 in	16
Antiseptic swabs	20
Ammonia inhalents	10
Bandage compressors, 4 in	8
Triangular bandage compressors, 40 in	5
Burn compound, ⅛ oz or an equivalent of other burn remedy	6
Arm splint, noninflatable	1
Leg splint, noninflatable	1
Roller bandage, 4 in	4
Adhesive tape, 1-in standard roll	2
Bandage scissors	1

(2) A crash axe carried so as to be accessible to the crew but inaccessible to passengers during normal operations.

(3) Signs that are visible to all occupants to notify them when smoking is prohibited and when safety belts should be fastened. The signs must be so constructed that they can be turned on and off by a crewmember. They must be turned on for each takeoff and each landing and when otherwise considered to be necessary by the pilot in command.

(4) The additional emergency equipment specified in Appendix A of this part.

(b) *Megaphones.* Each passenger-carrying airplane must have a portable battery-powered megaphone or megaphones readily accessible to the crewmembers assigned to direct emergency evacuation, installed as follows:

(1) One megaphone on each airplane with a seating capacity of more than 60 and less than 100 passengers, at the most rearward location in the passenger cabin where it would be readily ac-cessible to a normal flight attendant seat. However, the Administrator may grant a deviation from the requirements of this paragraph if the Administrator finds that a different location would be more useful for evacuation of persons during an emergency.

(2) Two megaphones in the passenger cabin on each airplane with a seating capacity of more than 99 and less than 200 passengers, one installed at the forward end and the other at the most rearward location where it would be readily accessible to a normal flight attendant seat.

(3) Three megaphones in the passenger cabin on each airplane with a seating capacity of more than 199 passengers, one installed at the forward end, one installed at the most rearward location where it would be readily accessible to a normal flight attendant seat, and one installed in a readily accessible location in the mid-section of the airplane.

§ 125.209 Emergency equipment: Extended overwater operations.

(a) No person may operate an airplane in extended overwater operations unless it carries, installed in conspicuously marked locations easily accessible to the occupants if a ditching occurs, the following equipment:

(1) An approved life preserver equipped with an approved survivor locator light, or an approved flotation means, for each occupant of the aircraft. The life preserver or other flotation means must be easily accessible to each seated occupant. If a flotation means other than a life preserver is used, it must be readily removable from the airplane.

(2) Enough approved life rafts (with proper buoyancy) to carry all occupants of the airplane, and at least the following equipment for each raft clearly marked for easy identification—

(i) One canopy (for sail, sunshade, or rain catcher);

(ii) One radar reflector (or similar device);

(iii) One life raft repair kit;

(iv) One bailing bucket;

(v) One signaling mirror;

(vi) One police whistle;

(vii) One raft knife;

(viii) One CO_2 bottle for emergency inflation;

(ix) One inflation pump;

(x) Two oars;

(xi) One 75-foot retaining line;

(xii) One magnetic compass;

(xiii) One dye marker;

(xiv) One flashlight having at least two size "D" cells or equivalent;

(xv) At least one approved pyrotechnic signaling device;

(xvi) A 2-day supply of emergency food rations supplying at least 1,000 calories a day for each person;

(xvii) One sea water desalting kit for each two persons that raft is rated to carry, or two pints of water for each person the raft is rated to carry;

(xviii) One fishing kit; and

(xix) One book on survival appropriate for the area in which the airplane is operated.

(b) No person may operate an airplane in extended overwater operations unless there is attached to one of the life rafts required by paragraph (a) of this section, a survival type emergency locator transmitter that meets TSO-C91. Batteries used in this transmitter must be replaced (or recharged, if the batteries are rechargeable) when the transmitter has been in use for more than 1 cumulative hour, and also when 50 percent of their useful life (or for rechargeable batteries, 50 percent of their useful life of charge), as established by the transmitter manufacturer under TSO-C91 has expired. The new expiration date for the replacement or recharged batteries must be legibly marked on the outside of the transmitter. The battery useful life or useful life of charge requirements of this paragraph do not apply to batteries (such as water-activated batteries) that are essentially unaffected during probably storage intervals.

§ 125.211 **Seat and safety belts.**

(a) No person may operate an airplane unless there are available during the takeoff, en route flight, and landing—

(1) An approved seat or berth for each person on board the airplane who is at least 2 years old; and

(2) An approved safety belt for separate use by each person on board the airplane who is at least 2 years old, except that two persons occupying a berth may share one approved safety belt and two persons occupying a multiple lounge or divan seat may share one approved safety belt during en route flight only.

(b) During the takeoff and landing of an airplane, each person on board shall occupy an approved seat or berth with a separate safety belt properly secured about that person. However, a person who is not at least 2 years old may be held by an adult who is occupying a seat or berth. A safety belt provided for the occupant of a seat may not be used during takeoff and landing by more than one person who is at least 2 years old.

(c) Each sideward facing seat must comply with the applicable requirements of § 25.785(c) of this chapter.

(d) No certificate holder may take off or land an airplane unless each passenger seat back is in the upright position. Each passenger shall comply with instructions given by a crewmember in compliance with this paragraph. This paragraph does not apply to seats on which cargo or persons who are unable to sit erect for a medical reason are carried in accordance with procedures in the certificate holder's manual if the seat back does not obstruct any passenger's access to the aisle or to any emergency exit.

(e) Each occupant of a seat equipped with a shoulder harness must fasten the shoulder harness during takeoff and landing, except that, in the case of crewmembers, the shoulder harness need not be fastened if the crewmember cannot perform his required duties with the shoulder harness fastened.

§ 125.213 **Miscellaneous equipment.**

No person may conduct any operation unless the following equipment is installed in the airplane:

(a) If protective fuses are installed on an airplane, the number of spare fuses approved for the airplane and appropriately described in the certificate holder's manual.

(b) A windshield wiper or equivalent for each pilot station.

(c) A power supply and distribution system that meets the requirements of §§ 25.1309, 25.1331, 25.1351 (a) and (b) (1) through (4), 25.1353, 25.1355, and 25.1431(b) or that is able to produce and distribute the load for the required instruments and equipment, with use of an external power supply if any one power source or component of the power distribution system fails. The use of common elements in the system may be approved if the Administrator finds that they are designed to be reasonably protected against malfunctioning. Engine-driven sources of energy, when used, must be on separate engines.

(d) A means for indicating the adequacy of the power being supplied to required flight instruments.

(e) Two independent static pressure systems, vented to the outside atmospheric pressure so that they will be least affected by air flow variation or moisture or other foreign matter, and installed so as to be airtight except for the vent. When a means is provided for transferring an instrument from its primary operating system to an alternative system, the means must include a positive positioning control and must be marked to indicate clearly which system is being used.

(f) A placard on each door that is the means of access to a required passenger emergency exit to indicate that it must be open during takeoff and landing.

(g) A means for the crew, in an emergency, to unlock each door that leads to a compartment that is normally accessible to passengers and that can be locked by passengers.

§ 125.215   Operating information required.

(a) The operator of an airplane must provide the following materials, in current and appropriate form, accessible to the pilot at the pilot station, and the pilot shall use them:

(1) A cockpit checklist.

(2) An emergency cockpit checklist containing the procedures required by paragraph (c) of this section, as appropriate.

(3) Pertinent aeronautical charts.

(4) For IFR operations, each pertinent navigational en route, terminal area, and approach and letdown chart;

(5) One-engine-inoperative climb performance data and, if the airplane is approved for use in IFR or over-the-top operations, that data must be sufficient to enable the pilot to determine that the airplane is capable of carrying passengers over-the-top or in IFR conditions at a weight that will allow it to climb, with the critical engine inoperative, at least 50 feet a minute when operating at the MEA's of the route to be flown or 5,000 feet MSL, whichever is higher.

(b) Each cockpit checklist required by paragraph (a)(1) of this section must contain the following procedures:

(1) Before starting engines;

(2) Before take-off;

(3) Cruise;

(4) Before landing;

(5) After landing;

(6) Stopping engines.

(c) Each emergency cockpit checklist required by paragraph (a)(2) of this section must contain the following procedures, as appropriate:

(1) Emergency operation of fuel, hydraulic, electrical, and mechanical systems.

(2) Emergency operation of instruments and controls.

(3) Engine inoperative procedures.

(4) Any other emergency procedures necessary for safety.

§ 125.217   Passenger information.

(a) No person may operate an airplane carrying passengers unless it is equipped with passenger information signs that meet the requirements of § 25.791 of this chapter. The signs must be constructed so that the crewmembers can turn them on and off. They must be turned on for each takeoff and each landing and when otherwise considered to be necessary by the pilot in command.

(b) No passenger or crewmember may smoke while the no smoking sign is lighted and each passenger shall fasten that passenger's seat belt and keep it fastened while the seat belt sign is lighted.

§ 125.219 Oxygen for medical use by passengers.

(a) Except as provided in paragraphs (d) and (e) of this section, no certificate holder may allow the carriage or operation of equipment for the storage, generation or dispensing of medical oxygen unless the unit to be carried is constructed so that all valves, fittings, and gauges are protected from damage during that carriage or operation and unless the following conditions are met:

(1) The equipment must be—

(i) Of an approved type or in conformity with the manufacturing, packaging, marking, labeling, and maintenance requirements of Title 49 CFR Parts 171, 172, and 173, except § 173.24(a)(1);

(ii) When owned by the certificate holder, maintained under the certificate holder's approved maintenance program;

(iii) Free of flammable contaminants on all exterior surfaces; and

(iv) Appropriately secured.

(2) When the oxygen is stored in the form of a liquid, the equipment must have been under the certificate holder's approved maintenance program since its purchase new or since the storage container was last purged.

(3) When the oxygen is stored in the form of a compressed gas as defined in Title 49 CFR 173.300(a)—

(i) When owned by the certificate holder, it must be maintained under its approved maintenance program; and

(ii) The pressure in any oxygen cylinder must not exceed the rated cylinder pressure.

(4) The pilot in command must be advised when the equipment is on board and when it is intended to be used.

(5) The equipment must be stowed, and each person using the equipment must be seated so as not to restrict access to or use of any required emergency or regular exit or of the aisle in the passenger compartment.

(b) When oxygen is being used, no person may smoke and no certificate holder may allow any person to smoke within 10 feet of oxygen storage and dispensing equipment carried under paragraph (a) of this section.

(c) No certificate holder may allow any person other than a person trained in the use of medical oxygen equipment to connect or disconnect oxygen bottles or any other ancillary component while any passenger is aboard the airplane.

(d) Paragraph (a)(1)(i) of this section does not apply when that equipment is furnished by a professional or medical emergency service for use on board an airplane in a medical emergency when no other practical means of transportation (including any other properly equipped certificate holder) is reasonably available and the person carried under the medical emergency is accompanied by a person trained in the use of medical oxygen.

(e) Each certificate holder who, under the authority of paragraph (d) of this section, deviates from paragraph (a)(1)(i) of this section under a medical emergency shall, within 10 days, excluding Saturdays, Sundays, and Federal holidays, after the deviation, send to the FAA Flight Standards district office charged with the overall inspection of the certificate holder a complete report of the operation involved, including a description of the deviation and the reasons for it.

§ 125.221 Icing conditions: Operating limitations.

(a) No pilot may take off an airplane that has—

(1) Frost, snow, or ice adhering to any propeller, windshield, or powerplant installation, or to an airspeed, altimeter, rate of climb, or flight attitude instrument system;

(2) Snow or ice adhering to the wings or stabilizing or control surfaces; or

(3) Any frost adhering to the wings, or stabilizing or control surfaces, unless that frost has been polished to make it smooth.

(b) Except for an airplane that has ice protection provisions that meet Appendix C of this part or those for transport category airplane type certification, no pilot may fly—

(1) Under IFR into known or forecast light or moderate icing conditions; or

(2) Under VFR into known light or moderate icing conditions, unless the airplane has functioning de-icing or anti-icing equipment protecting each propeller, windshield, wing, stabilizing or control surface, and each airspeed, altimeter, rate of climb, or flight attitude instrument system.

(c) Except for an airplane that has ice protection provisions that meet Appendix C of this part of those for transport category airplane type certification, no pilot may fly an airplane into known or forecast severe icing conditions.

(d) If current weather reports and briefing information relied upon by the pilot in command indicate that the forecast icing condition that would otherwise prohibit the flight will not be encountered during the flight because of changed weather conditions since the forecast, the restrictions in paragraphs (b) and (c) of this section based on forecast conditions do not apply.

§ 125.223 Airborne weather radar equipment requirements.

(a) No person may operate an airplane governed by this part in passenger-carrying operations unless approved airborne weather radar equipment is installed in the airplane.

(b) No person may begin a flight under IFR or night VFR conditions when current weather reports indicate that thunderstorms, or other potentially hazardous weather conditions that can be detected with airborne weather radar equipment, may reasonably be expected along the route to be flown, unless the airborne weather radar equipment required by paragraph (a) of this section is in satisfactory operating condition.

(c) If the airborne weather radar equipment becomes inoperative en route, the airplane must be operated under the instructions and procedures specified for that event in the manual required by § 125.71.

(d) This section does not apply to airplanes used solely within the State of Hawaii, within the State of Alaska, within that part of Canada west of longitude 130 degrees W. between latitude 70 degrees N, and latitude 53 degrees N, or during any training, test, or ferry flight.

(e) Without regard to any other provision of this part, an alternate electrical power supply is not required for airborn weather radar equipment.

§ 125.225 Flight recorders.

(a) Except as provided in paragraph (d) of this section, after October 11, 1991, no person may operate a large airplane type certificated before October 1, 1969, for operations above 25,000 feet altitude, nor a multiengine, turbine powered airplane type certificated before October 1, 1969, unless it equipped with one or more approved flight recorders that utilize a digital method of recording and storing data and a method of readily retrieving that data from the storage medium. The following information must be able to be determined within the ranges, accuracies, resolution, and recording intervals specified in Appendix D of this part:

(1) Time;
(2) Altitude;
(3) Airspeed;
(4) Vertical acceleration;
(5) Heading;
(6) Time of each radio transmission to or from air traffic control;
(7) Pitch attitude;
(8) Roll attitude;
(9) Longitudinal acceleration;
(10) Control column or pitch control surface position; and
(11) Thrust of each engine.

(b) Except as provided in paragraph (d) of this section, after October 11, 1991, no person may operate a large airplane type certificated after September 30, 1969, for operations above 25,000 feet altitude, nor a multiengine, turbine powered airplane type certificated after September 30, 1969, unless it is equipped with one or more approved flight recorders that utilize a digital method of recording and storing data and a method of readily retrieving that data from the storage medium. The following information must be able to be determined with the ranges, accuracies, resolutions, a dn recording intervals specified in Appendix D of this part:

(1) Time;
(2) Altitude;
(3) Airspeed;
(4) Vertical acceleration;
(5) Heading;
(6) Time of each radio transmission to or from air traffic control;
(7) Pitch attitude;
(8) Roll attitude;
(9) Longitudinal acceleration;
(10) Pitch trim position;
(11) control column or pitch control surface position;
(12) Control wheel or lateral control surface position;
(13) Rudder pedal or yaw control surface position;
(14) Thrust of each engine;
(15) Position of each trust reverser;
(16) Trailing edge flap or cockpit flap control position; and
(17) Leading edge flap or cockpit flap control position.

(c) After October 11, 1991, no person may operate a large airplane equipped with a digital bus and ARINC 717 digital flight data acquisition unit (DFDAU) or equivalent unless it is equipped with one or more approved flight recorders that utilize a digital method of recording and storing data and a method of readily retrieving that data from the storage medium. Any parameters specified in Appendix D of this part that are available on the digital data bus must be recorded within the ranges, accuracies, resolutions, and sampling intervals specified.

(d) No person may operate under this part an airplane that is manufactured after October 11, 1991, unless it is equipped with one or more approved flight recorders that utilize a digital method of recording and storing data and a method of readily retrieving that data from the storage medium. The parameters specified in Appendix D of this part must be recorded within the ranges, accuracies, resolutions and sampling intervals specified. For the purpose of this section "manufactured" means the point in time at which the airplane inspection acceptance records reflect that the airplane is complete and meets the FAA-approved type design data.

(e) Whenever a flight recorder required by this section is installed, it must be operated continuously from the instant the airplane begins the takeoff roll until it has completed the landing roll at an airport.

(f) Except as provided in paragraph (g) of this section, and except for recorded data erased as authorized in this paragraph, each certificate holder shall keep the recorded data prescribed in paragraph (a), (b), (c), or (d) of this section, as applicable, until the airplane has been operated for at least 25 hours of the operating time specified in §125.227(a) of this chapter. A total of 1 hour of recorded data may be erased for the purpose of testing the flight recorder or the flight recorder system. Any erasure made in accordance with this paragraph must be of the oldest recorded data accumulated at the time of testing. Except as provided in paragraph (g) of this section, no record need be kept more than 60 days.

(g) In the event of an accident or occurrence that requires immediate notification of the National Transportation Safety Board under 49 CFR Part 830 and that results in termination of the flight, the certificate holder shall remove the recording media from the airplane and keep the recorded data required by paragraph (a), (b), (c), or (d) of this section, as applicable, for at least 60 days or for a longer period upon the request of the Board or the Administrator.

(h) Each flight recorder required by this

section must be installed in accordance with the requirements of §125.1459 of this chapter in effect on August 31, 1977. The correlation required by §125.1459(c) of this chapter need be established only on one airplane of any group of airplanes.

(1) That are of the same type;

(2) On which the flight recorder models and their installations are the same; and

(3) On which there are no differences in the type design with respect to the installation of the first pilot's instruments associated with the flight recorder. The most recent instrument calibration, including the recording medium from which this calibration is derived, and the recorder correlation must be retained by the certificate holder.

(i) Each flight recorder required by this section that records the data specified in paragraphs (a), (b), (c), or (d) of this section must have an approved device to assist in locating that recorder under water.

§125.227 Cockpit voice recorders

(a) No certificate holder may operate a large turbine engine powered airplane or a large pressurized airplane with four reciprocating engines unless an approved cockpit voice recorder is installed in that airplane and is operated continuously from the start of the use of the checklist (before starting engines for the purpose of flight) to completion of the final checklist at the termination of the flight.

(b) Each certificate holder shall establish a schedule for completion, before the prescribed dates, of the cockpit voice recorder installations required by paragraph (a) of this section. In addition, the certificate holder shall identify any airplane specified in paragraph (a) of this section he intends to discontinue using before the prescribed dates.

(c) The cockpit voice recorder required by this section must also meet the following standards:

(1) The requirements of Part 25 of this chapter in effect after October 11, 1991.

(2) After September 1, 1980, each recorder container must—

(i) Be either bright orange or bright yellow;

(ii) Have reflective tape affixed to the external surface to facilitate its location under water; and

(iii) Have an approved underwater locating device on or adjacent to the container which is secured in such a manner that it is not likely to be separated during crash impact, unless the cockpit voice recorder and the flight recorder, required by § 122.225 of this chapter, are installed adjacent to each other in such a manner that they are not likely to be separated during crash impact.

(d) In complying with this section, an approved cockpit voice recorder having an erasure feature may be used so that, at any time during the operation of the recorder, information recorded more than 30 minutes earlier may be erased or otherwise obliterated.

(e) For those aircraft equipped to record the uninterrupted audio signals received by a boom or a mask microphone the flight crewmembers are required to use the boom microphone below 18,000 feet mean sea level. No person may operate a large turbine engine powered airplane or a large pressurized airplane with four reciprocating engines manufactured after October 11, 1991, or on which a cockpit voice recorder has been installed after October 11, 1991, unless it is equipped to record the uninterrupted audio signal received by a boom or mask microphone in accordance with § 25.1457 (c)(5) of this chapter.

(f) In the event of an accident or occurence requiring immediate notification of the National Transportation Safety Board under 49 CFR Part 830 of its regulations, which results in the termination of the flight, the certificate holder shall keep the recorded information for at least 60 days or, if requested by the Administrator or the Board, for a longer period. Information obtained from the record is used to assist in determining the cause of accidents or occurences in connection with investigations under 49 CFR Part 830. The Administrator does not use the record in any civil penalty or certificate action.

Subpart G — Maintenance

§ 125.241 Applicability.

This subpart prescribes rules, in addition to those prescribed in other parts of this chapter, for the maintenance of airplanes, airframes, aircraft engines, propellers, appliances, each item of survival and emergency equipment, and their component parts operated under this part.

§ 125.243 Certificate holder's responsibilities.

(a) With regard to airplanes, including airframes, aircraft engines, propellers, appliances, and survival and emergency equipment, operated by a certificate holder, that certificate holder is primarily responsible for—

(1) Airworthiness;

(2) The performance of maintenance, preventative maintenance, and alteration in accordance with applicable regulations and the certificate holder's manual;

(3) The scheduling and performance of inspections required by this part; and

(4) Ensuring that maintenance personnel make entries in the airplane maintenance log and maintenance records which meet the requirements of Part 43 of this chapter and the certificate holder's manual, and which indicate that the airplane has been approved for return to service after maintenance, preventative maintenace or alteration has been performed.

§ 125.245 Organization required to perform maintenance, preventive maintenance, and alteration.

The certificate holder must ensure that each person with whom it arranges for the performance of maintenance, preventive maintenance, alteration, or required inspection times identified in the certificate holder's manual in accordance with

§ 125.249(a)(3)(ii) must have an organization adequate to perform that work.

§ 125.247 Inspection programs and maintenance.

(a) No person may operate an airplane subject to this part unless

(1) The replacement times for life-limited parts specified in the aircraft type certificate data sheets, or other documents approved by the Administrator, are complied with;

(2) Defects disclosed between inspections, or as a result of inspection, have been corrected in accordance with Part 43 of this chapter; and

(3) The airplane, including airframe, aircraft engines, propellers, appliances, and survival and emergency equipment, and their component parts, is inspected in accordance with an inspection program approved by the Administrator.

(b) The inspection program specified in paragraph (a)(3) of this section must include at least the following:

(1) Instructions, procedures, and standards for the conduct of inspections for the particular make and model of airplane, including necessary tests and checks. The instructions and procedures must set forth in detail the parts and areas of the airframe, aircraft engines, propellers, appliances, and survival and emergency equipment required to be inspected.

(2) A schedule for the performance of inspections that must be performed under the program, expressed in terms of the time in service, calendar time, number of system operations, or any combination of these.

(c) No person may be used to perform the inspections required by this part unless that person is authorized to perform maintenance under Part 43 of this chapter.

(d) No person may operate an airplane subject to this part unless—

(1) The installed engines have been maintained in accordance with the overhaul periods recommended by the manufacturer or a program approved by the Administrator; and

(2) The engine overhaul periods are specified in the inspection programs required by § 125.247(a)(3).

(e) Inspection programs which may be approved for use under this part include, but are not limited to—

(1) A continuous inspection program which is a part of a current continuous airworthiness program approved for use by a certificate holder under Part 121 or Part 135 of this chapter;

(2) Inspection programs currently recommended by the manufacturer of the airplane, aircraft engines, propellers, appliances, or survival and emergency equipment; or

(3) An inspection program developed by a certificate holder under this part.

[Doc. No. 19779, 45 FR 67235, Oct. 9, 1980, as amended by Amdt. 125-2, 46 FR 24409, Apr. 30, 1981]

§ 125.249 Maintenance manual requirements.

(a) Each certificate holder's manual required by § 125.71 of this part shall contain, in addition to the items required by § 125.73 of this part, at least the following:

(1) A description of the certificate holders maintenance organization, when the certificate holder has such an organization.

(2) A list of those persons with whom the certificate holder has arranged for performance of inspections under this part. The list shall include the persons' names and addresses.

(3) The inspection programs required by § 125.247 of this part to be followed in the performance of inspections under this part including—

(i) The method of performing routine and nonroutine inspections (other than required inspections);

(ii) The designation of the items that must be inspected (required inspections), including at least those which if improperly accomplished could result in a failure, malfunction, or defect endangering the safe operation of the airplane;

(iii) The method of performing required inspections;

(iv) Procedures for the inspection of work performed under previously required inspection findings ("buy-back procedures");

(v) Procedures, standards, and limits necessary for required inspections and acceptance or rejection of the items required to be inspected;

(vi) Instructions to prevent any person who performs any item of work from performing any required inspection of that work; and

(vii) Procedures to ensure that work interruptions do not adversely affect required inspections and to ensure required inspections are properly completed before the airplane is released to service.

(b) In addition, each certificate holder's manual shall contain a suitable system which may include a coded system that provides for the retention of the following:

(1) A description (or reference to data acceptable to the Administrator) of the work performed.

(2) The name of the person performing the work and the person's certificate type and number.

(3) The name of the person approving the work and the person's certificate type and number.

§ 125.251 Required inspection personnel.

(a) No person may use any person to perform required inspections unless the person performing the inspection is appropriately certificated, properly trained, qualified, and authorized to do so.

(b) No person may perform a required inspection if that person performed the item of work required to be inspected.

Subpart H—Airman and Crewmember Requirements

§ 125.261 Airman: Limitations on use of services.

(a) No certificate holder may use any person as an airman nor may any person serve as an airman unless that person—

(1) Holds an appropriate current airman certificate issued by the FAA;

(2) Has any required appropriate current airman and medical certificates in that person's possession while engaged in operations under this part; and

(3) Is otherwise qualified for the operation for which that person is to be used.

(b) Each airman covered by paragraph (a) of this section shall present the certificates for inspection upon the request of the Administrator.

§ 125.263 Composition of flightcrew.

(a) No certificate holder may operate an airplane with less than the minimum flightcrew specified in the type certificate and the Airplane Flight Manual approved for that type airplane and required by this part for the kind of operation being conducted.

(b) In any case in which this part requires the performance of two or more functions for which an airman certificate is necessary, that requirement is not satisfied by the performance of multiple functions at the same time by one airman.

(c) On each flight requiring a flight engineer, at least one flight crewmember, other than the flight engineer, must be qualified to provide emergency performance of the flight engineer's functions for the safe completion of the flight if the flight engineer becomes ill or is otherwise incapacitated. A pilot need not hold a flight engineer's certificate to perform the flight engineer's functions in such a situation.

§ 125.265 Flight engineer requirements.

(a) No person may operate an airplane for which a flight engineer is required by the type certification requirements without a flight crewmember holding a current flight engineer certificate.

(b) No person may serve as a required flight engineer on an airplane unless, within the preceding 6 calendar months, that person has had at least 50 hours of flight time as a flight engineer on that type airplane, or the Administrator has checked that person on that type airplane and determined that person is familiar and competent with all essential current information and operating procedures.

§ 125.267 Flight navigator and long-range navigation equipment.

(a) No certificate holder may operate an airplane outside the 48 conterminous States and the District of Columbia when its position cannot be reliably fixed for a period of more than 1 hour, without—

(1) A flight crewmember who holds a current flight navigator certificate; or

(2) Two independent, properly functioning, and approved long-range means of navigation which enable a reliable determination to be made of the position of the airplane by each pilot seated at that person's duty station.

(b) Operations where a flight navigator or long-range navigation equipment, or both, are required are specified in the operations specifications of the operator.

§ 125.269 **Flight attendants.**

(a) Each certificate holder shall provide at least the following flight attendants on each passenger-carrying airplane used:

(1) For airplanes having more than 19 but less than 51 passengers—one flight attendant.

(2) For airplanes having more than 50 but less than 101 passengers—two flight attendants.

(3) For airplanes having more than 100 passengers—two flight attendants plus one additional flight attendant for each unit (or part of a unit) of 50 passengers above 100 passengers.

(b) The number of flight attendants approved under paragraphs (a) and (b) of this section are set forth in the certificate holder's operations specifications.

(c) During takeoff and landing, flight attendants required by this section shall be located as near as practicable to required floor level exits and shall be uniformly distributed throughout the airplane to provide the most effective egress of passengers in event of an emergency evacuation.

§ 125.271 **Emergency and emergency evacuation duties.**

(a) Each certificate holder shall, for each type and model of airplane, assign to each category of required crewmember, as appropriate, the necessary functions to be performed in an emergency or a situation requiring emergency evacuation. The certificate holder shall show those functions are realistic, can be practically accomplished, and will meet any reasonably anticipated emergency, including the possible incapacitation of individual crewmembers or their inability to reach the passenger cabin because of shifting cargo in combination cargo-passenger airplanes.

(b) The certificate holder shall describe in its manual the functions of each category of required crewmembers under paragraph (a) of this section.

Subpart I—Flight Crewmember Requirements

§ 125.281 **Pilot–in–command qualifications.**

No certificate holder may use any person, nor may any person serve, as pilot in command of an airplane unless that person—

(a) Holds at least a commercial pilot certificate, an appropriate category, class, and type rating, and an instrument rating; and

(b) Has had at least 1,200 hours of flight time as a pilot, including 500 hours of cross-country flight time, 100 hours of night flight time, including at least 10 night takeoffs and landings, and 75 hours of actual or simulated instrument flight time, at least 50 hours of which were actual flight.

§ 125.283 **Second–in–command qualifications.**

No certificate holder may use any person, nor may any person serve, as second in command of an airplane unless that person—

(a) Holds at least a commercial pilot certificate with appropriate category and class ratings, and an instrument rating; and

(b) For flight under IFR, meets the recent instrument experience requirements prescribed for a pilot in command in Part 61 of this chapter.

§ 125.285 **Pilot qualifications: Recent experience.**

(a) No certificate holder may use any person, nor may any person serve, as a required pilot flight crewmember unless within the preceding 90 days that person has made at least three takeoffs and landings in the type airplane in which that person is to serve.

The takeoffs and landings required by this paragraph may be performed in a visual simulator approved under § 125.297 to include takeoff and landing maneuvers. However, any person who fails to qualify for a 90-consecutive-day period following the date of that person's last qualification under this paragraph must reestablish recency of experience as provided in paragraph (b) of this section.

(b) A required pilot flight crewmember who has not met the requirements of paragraph (a) of this section may reestablish recency of experience by making at least three takeoffs and landings under the supervision of an authorized check airman, in accordance with the following:

(1) At least one takeoff must be made with a simulated failure of the most critical powerplant.

(2) At least one landing must be made from an ILS approach to the lowest ILS minimums authorized for the certificate holder.

(3) At least one landing must be made to a complete stop.

(c) A required pilot flight crewmember who performs the maneuvers prescribed in paragraph (b) of this section in a visual simulator must—

(1) Have previously logged 100 hours of flight time in the same type airplane in which the pilot is to serve; and

(2) Be observed on the first two landings made in operations under this part by an authorized check airman who acts as pilot in command and occupies a pilot seat. The landings must be made in weather minimums that are not less than those contained in the certificate holder's operations specifications for Category I operations and must be made within 45 days following completion of simulator testing.

(d) An authorized check airman who observes the takeoffs and landings prescribed in paragraphs (b) and (c)(3) of this section shall certify that the person being observed is proficient and qualified to perform flight duty in operations under this part, and may require any additional maneuvers that are determined necessary to make this certifying statement.

§ 125.287 Initial and recurrent pilot testing requirements.

(a) No certificate holder may use any person, nor may any person serve as a pilot, unless, since the beginning of the 12th calendar month before that service, that person has passed a written or oral test, given by the Administrator or an authorized check airman on that person's knowledge in the following areas—

(1) The appropriate provisions of Parts 61, 91, and 125 of this chapter and the operations specifications and the manual of the certificate holder;

(2) For each type of airplane to be flown by the pilot, the airplane powerplant, major components and systems, major appliances, performance and operating limitations, standard and emergency operating procedures, and the contents of the approved Airplane Flight Manual or approved equivalent, as applicable;

(3) For each type of airplane to be flown by the pilot, the method of determining compliance with weight and balance limitations for takeoff, landing, and en route operations;

(4) Navigation and use of air navigation aids appropriate to the operation of pilot authorization, including, when applicable, instrument approach facilities and procedures;

(5) Air traffic control procedures, including IFR procedures when applicable;

(6) Meteorology in general, including the principles of frontal systems, icing, fog, thunderstorms, and windshear, and, if appropriate for the operation of the certificate holder, high altitude weather;

(7) Procedures for avoiding operations in thunderstorms and hail, and for operating in turbulent air or in icing conditions; and

(8) New equipment, procedures, or techniques, as appropriate.

(b) No certificate holder may use any person, nor may any person serve, as a pilot in any airplane unless, since the beginning of the 12th calendar month before that service, that person has passed a competency check given by the Administrator or an authorized check airman in that type of airplane to determine that person's competence in practical skills and techniques in that airplane or type of airplane. The extent of the competency check shall be determined by the Administrator or authorized check airman conducting the competency check. The competency check may include any of the maneuvers and procedures currently required for the original issuance of the particular pilot certificate required for the operations authorized and appropriate to the category, class, and type of airplane involved. For the purposes of this paragraph, type, as to an airplane, means any one of a group of airplanes determined by the Administrator to have a similar means of propulsion, the same manufacturer, and no significantly different handling or flight characteristics.

(c) The instrument proficiency check required by §125.291 may be substituted for the competency check required by this section for the type of airplane used in the check.

(d) For the purposes of this part, competent performance of a procedure or maneuver by a person to be used as a pilot requires that the pilot be the obvious master of the airplane with the successful outcome of the maneuver never in doubt.

(e) The Administrator or authorized check airman certifies the competency of each pilot who passes the knowledge or flight check in the certificate holder's pilot records.

(f) Portions of a required competency check may be given in an airplane simulator or other appropriate training device, if approved by the Administrator.

§125.289 Initial and recurrent flight attendant crewmember testing requirements.

No certificate holder may use any person, nor may any person serve, as a flight attendant crewmember, unless, since the beginning of the 12th calendar month before that service, the certificate holder has determined by appropriate initial and recurrent testing that the person is knowledgeable and competent in the following areas as appropriate to assigned duties and responsibilities:

(a) Authority of the pilot in command;

(b) Passenger handling, including procedures to be followed in handling deranged persons or other persons whose conduct might jeopardize safety;

(c) Crewmember assignments, functions, and responsibilities during ditching and evacuation of persons who may need the assistance of another person to move expeditiously to an exit in an emergency;

(d) Briefing of passengers;

(e) Location and operation of portable fire extinguishers and other items of emergency equipment;

(f) Proper use of cabin equipment and controls;

(g) Location and operation of passenger oxygen equipment;

(h) Location and operation of all normal and emergency exits, including evacuation chutes and escape ropes; and

(i) Seating of persons who may need assistance of another person to move rapidly to an exit in an emergency as prescribed by the certificate holder's operations manual.

§125.291 Pilot in command: Instrument proficiency check requirements.

(a) No certificate holder may use any person, nor may any person serve, as a pilot in command of an airplane under IFR unless, since the beginning of the sixth calendar month before that service, that person has passed an instrument proficiency check and the Administrator or an authorized check airman has so certified in a letter of competency.

(b) No pilot may use any type of precision instrument approach procedure under IFR unless, since the beginning of the sixth calendar month before that use, the pilot has satisfactorily demonstrated that type of approach procedure and has been issued a letter of competency under paragraph (g) of this section. No pilot may use any type of nonprecision approach procedure under IFR unless, since the beginning of the sixth calendar month before that use, the pilot has satisfactorily demonstrated either that type of approach procedure or any other two different types of nonprecision approach procedures and has been issued a letter of competency under paragraph (g) of this section. The instrument approach procedure or procedures must include at least one straight-in approach, one circling approach, and one missed approach. Each type of approach procedure demonstrated must be conducted to published minimums for that procedure.

(c) The instrument proficiency check required by paragraph (a) of this section consists of an oral or written equipment test and a flight check under simulated or actual IFR conditions. The equipment test includes questions on emergency procedures, engine operation, fuel and lubrication systems, power settings, stall speeds, best engine-out speed, propeller and supercharge operations, and hydraulic, mechanical, and electrical systems, as appropriate. The flight check includes navigation by instruments, recovery from simulated emergencies, and standard instrument approaches involving navigational facilities which that pilot is to be authorized to use.

(1) For a pilot in command of an airplane, the instrument proficiency check must include the procedures and maneuvers for a commercial pilot certificate with an instrument rating and, if required, for the appropriate type rating.

(2) The instrument proficiency check must be given by an authorized check airman or by the Administrator.

(d) If the pilot in command is assigned to pilot only one type of airplane, that pilot must take the instrument proficiency check required by paragraph (a) of this section in that type of airplane.

(e) If the pilot in command is assigned to pilot more than one type of airplane, that pilot must take the instrument proficiency check required by paragraph (a) of this section in each type of airplane to which that pilot is assigned, in rotation, but not more than one flight check during each period described in paragraph (a) of this section.

(f) Portions of a required flight check may be given in an airplane simulator or other appropriate training device, if approved by the Administrator.

(g) The Administrator or authorized check airman issues a letter of competency to each pilot who passes the instrument proficiency check. The letter of competency contains a list of the types of instrument approach procedures and facilities authorized.

§ 125.293 Crewmember: Tests and checks, grace provisions, accepted standards.

(a) If a crewmember who is required to take a test or a flight check under this part completes the test or flight check in the calendar month before or after the calendar month in which it is required, that crewmember is considered to have completed the test or check in the calendar month in which it is required.

(b) If a pilot being checked under this subpart fails any of the required maneuvers, the person giving the check may give additional training to the pilot during the course of the check. In addition to repeating the maneuvers failed, the person giving the check may require the pilot being checked to repeat any other maneuvers that are necessary to determine the pilot's proficiency. If the pilot being checked is unable to demonstrate satisfactory performance to the person conducting the check, the certificate holder may not use the pilot, nor may the pilot serve, in the capacity for which the pilot is being checked in operations under this part until the pilot has satisfactorily completed the check.

§ 125.295 Check airman authorization: Application and issue.

Each certificate holder desiring FAA approval of a check airman shall submit a request in writing to the FAA Flight Standards district office charged with the overall inspection of the certificate holder. The Administrator may issue a letter of authority to each check airman if that airman passes the appropriate oral and flight test. The letter of authority lists the tests and checks in this part that the check airman is qualified to give, andιuhe category, class and type airplane, where appropriate, for which the check airman is qualified.

§ 125.297 Approval of airplane simulators and other training devices.

(a) Airplane simulators and other training devices approved by the Administrator may be used in checks required in this subpart.

(b) Each airplane simulator and other training device that is used in checks required under this subpart must meet the following requirements:

(1) It must be specifically approved for—

(i) The certificate holder;

(ii) The type airplane and, if applicable, the particular variation within type for which the check is being conducted; and

(iii) The particular maneuver, procedure, or crewmember function involved.

(2) It must maintain the performance, functional, and other characteristics that are required for approval.

(3) It must be modified to conform with any modification to the airplane being simulated that changes the performance, functional, or other characteristics required for approval.

Subpart J—Flight Operations

§ 125.311 Flight crewmembers at controls.

(a) Except as provided in paragraph (b) of this section, each required flight crewmember on flight deck duty must remain at the assigned duty station with seat belt fastened while the airplane is taking off or landing and while it is en route.

(b) A required flight crewmember may leave the assigned duty station—

(1) If the crewmember's absence is necessary for the performance of duties in connection with the operation of the airplane;

(2) If the crewmember's absence is in connection with physiological needs; or

(3) If the crewmember is taking a rest period and relief is provided—

(i) In the case of the assigned pilot in command, by a pilot qualified to act as pilot in command.

(ii) In the case of the assigned second in command, by a pilot qualified to act as second in command of that airplane during en route operations. However, the relief pilot need not meet the recent experience requirements of § 125.285.

§ 125.313 Manipulation of controls when carrying passengers.

No pilot in command may allow any person to manipulate the controls of an airplane while carrying passengers during flight, nor may any person manipulate the controls while carrying passengers during flight, unless that person is a qualified pilot of the certificate holder operating that airplane.

§ 125.315 Admission to flight deck.

(a) No person may admit any person to the flight deck of an airplane unless the person being admitted is—

(1) A crewmember;

(2) An FAA inspector or an authorized representative of the National Transportation Safety Board who is performing official duties; or

(3) Any person who has the permission of the pilot in command.

(b) No person may admit any person to the flight deck unless there is a seat available for the use of that person in the passenger compartment, except—

(1) An FAA inspector or an authorized representative of the Administrator or National Transportation Safety Board who is checking or observing flight operations; or

(2) A certificated airman employed by the certificate holder whose duties require an airman certificate.

§ 125.317 Inspector's credentials: Admission to pilots' compartment: Forward observer's seat.

(a) Whenever, in performing the duties of conducting an inspection, an FAA inspector presents an Aviation Safety Inspector credential, FAA Form 110A, to the pilot in command of an airplane operated by the certificate holder, the inspector must be given free and uninterrupted access to the pilot compartment of that airplane. However, this paragraph does not limit the emergency authority of the pilot in command to exclude any person from the pilot compartment in the interest of safety.

(b) A forward observer's seat on the flight deck, or forward passenger seat with headset or speaker, must be provided for use by the Administrator while conducting en route inspections. The suitability of the location of the seat and the headset or speaker for use in conducting en route inspections is determined by the Administrator.

§ 125.319 Emergencies.

(a) In an emergency situation that requires immediate decision and action, the pilot in command may take any action considered necessary under the circumstances. In such a case, the pilot in command may deviate from prescribed operations, procedures and methods, weather minimums, and this chapter, to the extent required in the interests of safety.

(b) In an emergency situation arising during flight that requires immediate decision and action by appropriate management personnel in the case of operations conducted with a flight following service and which is known to them, those personnel shall advise the pilot in command of the emergency, shall ascertain the decision of the pilot in command, and shall have the decision recorded. If they cannot communicate with the pilot, they shall declare an emergency and take any action that they consider necessary under the circumstances.

(c) Whenever emergency authority is exercised, the pilot in command or the appropriate management personnel shall keep the appropriate ground radio station fully informed of the progress of the flight. The person declaring the emergency shall send a written report of any deviation, through the operator's director of operations, to the Administrator within 10 days, exclusive of Saturdays, Sundays, and Federal holidays, after the flight is completed or, in the case of operations outside the United States, upon return to the home base.

§ 125.321 Reporting potentially hazardous meteorological conditions and irregularities of ground and navigation facilities.

Whenever the pilot in command encounters a meteorological condition or an irregularity in a ground or navigational facility in flight, the knowledge of which the pilot in command considers essential to the safety of other flights, the pilot in command shall notify an appropriate ground station as soon as practicable.

§ 125.323 Reporting mechanical irregularities.

The pilot in command shall ensure that all mechanical irregularities occurring during flight are entered in the maintenance log of the airplane at the next place of landing. Before each flight, the pilot in command shall ascertain the status of each irregularity entered in the log at the end of the preceding flight.

§ 125.325 Instrument approach procedures and IFR landing minimums.

No person may make an instrument approach at an airport except in accordance with IFR weather minimums and unless the type of instrument approach procedure to be used is listed in the certificate holder's operations specifications.

§ 125.327 Briefing of passengers before flight.

(a) Before each takeoff, each pilot in command of an airplane carrying passengers shall ensure that all passengers have been orally briefed on—

(1) Smoking;

(2) Use of seat belts;

(3) The placement of seat backs in an upright position before takeoff and landing;

(4) Location and means for opening the passenger entry door and emergency exits;

(5) Location of survival equipment;

(6) If the flight involves extended overwater operation, ditching procedures and the use of required flotation equipment;

(7) If the flight involves operations above 12,000 feet MSL, the normal and emergency use of oxygen; and

(8) Location and operation of fire extinguishers.

(b) Before each takeoff, the pilot in command shall ensure that each person who may need the assistance of another person to move expeditiously to an exit if an emergency occurs and that person's attendant, if any, has received a briefing as to the procedures to be followed if an evacuation occurs.

This paragraph does not apply to a person who has been given a briefing before a previous leg of a flight in the same airplane.

(c) The oral briefing required by paragraph (a) of this section shall be given by the pilot in command or a member of the crew. It shall be supplemented by printed cards for the use of each passenger containing—

(1) A diagram and method of operating the emergency exits; and

(2) Other instructions necessary for the use of emergency equipment on board the airplane.

Each card used under this paragraph must be carried in the airplane in locations convenient for the use of each passenger and must contain information that is appropriate to the airplane on which it is to be used.

(d) The certificate holder shall describe in its manual the procedure to be followed in the briefing required by paragraph (a) of this section.

(e) If the airplane does not proceed directly over water after takeoff, no part of the briefing required by paragraph (a)(6) of this section has to be given before takeoff but the briefing required by paragraph (a)(6) must be given before reaching the overwater part of the flight.

§125.329 Minimum altitudes for use of autopilot.

(a) Except as provided in paragraphs (b), (c), and (d) of this section, no person may use an autopilot at an altitude above the terrain which is less than 500 feet or less than twice the maximum altitude loss specified in the approved Airplane Flight Manual or equivalent for a malfunction of the autopilot, whichever is higher.

(b) When using an instrument approach facility other than ILS, no person may use an autopilot at an altitude above the terrain that is less than 50 feet below the approved minimum descent altitude for that procedure, or less than twice the maximum loss specified in the approved Airplane Flight Manual or equivalent for a malfunction of the autopilot under approach conditions, whichever is higher.

(c) For ILS approaches when reported weather conditions are less than the basic weather conditions in §91.105 of this chapter, no person may use an autopilot with an approach coupler at an altitude above the terrain that is less than 50 feet above the terrain, or the maximum altitude loss specified in the approved Airplane Flight Manual or equivalent for the malfunction of the autopilot with approach coupler, whichever is higher.

(d) Without regard to paragraph (a), (b), or (c) of this section, the Administrator may issue operations specifications to allow the use, to touchdown, of an approved flight control guidance system with automatic capability, if—

(1) The system does not contain any altitude loss (above zero) specified in the approved Airplane Flight Manual or equivalent for malfunction of the autopilot with approach coupler; and

(2) The Administrator finds that the use of the system to touchdown will not otherwise adversely affect the safety standards of this section.

§125.331 Carriage of persons without compliance with the passenger-carrying provisions of this part.

The following persons may be carried aboard an airplane without complying with the passenger-carrying requirements of this part:

(a) A crewmember.

(b) A person necessary for the safe handling of animals on the airplane.

(c) A person necessary for the safe handling of hazardous materials (as defined in Subchapter C of Title 49 CFR).

(d) A person performing duty as a security or honor guard accompanying a shipment made by or under the authority of the U.S. Government.

(e) A military courier or a military route supervisor carried by a military cargo contract operator if that carriage is specifically authorized by the appropriate military service.

(f) An authorized representative of the Administrator conducting an en route inspection.

(g) A person authorized by the Administrator.

Subpart K—Flight Release Rules

§ 125.351   Flight release authority.

(a) No person may start a flight without authority from the person authorized by the certificate holder to exercise operational control over the flight.

(b) No person may start a flight unless the pilot in command or the person authorized by the cetificate holder to exercise operational control over the flight has executed a flight release setting forth the conditions under which the flight will be conducted. The pilot in command may sign the flight release only when both the pilot in command and the person authorized to exercise operational control believe the flight can be made safely, unless the pilot in command is authorized by the certificate holder to exercise operational control and execute the flight release without the approval of any other person.

(c) No person may continue a flight from an intermediate airport without a new flight release if the airplane has been on the ground more than 6 hours.

§ 125.353   Facilities and services.

During a flight, the pilot in command shall obtain any additional available information of meteorological conditions and irregularities of facilities and services that may affect the safety of the flight.

§ 125.355   Airplane equipment.

No person may release an airplane unless it is airworthy and is equipped as prescribed.

§ 125.357   Communication and navigation facilities.

No person may release an airplane over any route or route segment unless communication and navigation facilities equal to those required by § 125.51 are in satisfactory operating condition.

§ 125.359   Flight release under VFR.

No person may release an airplane for VFR operation unless the ceiling and visibility en route, as indicated by available weather reports or forecasts, or any combination thereof, are and will remain at or above applicable VFR minimums until the airplane arrives at the airport or airports specified in the flight release.

§ 125.361   Flight release under IFR or over-the-top.

Except as provided in § 125.363, no person may release an airplane for operations under IFR or over-the-top unless appropriate weather reports or forecasts, or any combination thereof, indicate that the weather conditions will be at or above the authorized minimums at the estimated time of arrival at the airport or airports to which released.

§ 125.363   Flight release over water.

(a) No person may release an airplane for a flight that involves extended overwater operation unless appropriate weather reports or forecasts, or any combination thereof, indicate that the weather conditions will be at or above the authorized minimums at the estimated time of arrival at any airport to which released or to any required alternate airport.

(b) Each certificate holder shall conduct extended overwater operations under IFR unless it shows that operating under IFR is not necessary for safety.

(c) Each certificate holder shall conduct other overwater operations under IFR if the Administrator determines that operation under IFR is necessary for safety.

(d) Each authorization to conduct extended overwater operations under VFR and each requirement to conduct other overwater operations under IFR will be specified in the operations specifications.

§ 125.365   Alternate airport for departure.

(a) If the weather conditions at the airport of takeoff are below the landing minimums in the certificate holder's operations specifications for that airport, no person may release an airplane from that airport unless the flight release specifies an alternate airport located within the following distances from the airport of takeoff:

(1) *Airplanes having two engines.* Not more than 1 hour from the departure airport at normal cruising speed in still air with one engine inoperative.

(2) *Airplanes having three or more engines.* Not more than 2 hours from the departure airport at normal cruising speed in still air with one engine inoperative.

(b) For the purposes of paragraph (a) of this section, the alternate airport weather conditions must meet the requirements of the certificate holder's operations specifications.

(c) No person may release an airplane from an airport unless that person lists each required alternate airport in the flight release.

§125.367 Alternate airport for destination: IFR or over-the-top.

(a) Except as provided in paragraph (b) of this section, each person releasing an airplane for operation under IFR or over-the-top shall list at least one alternate airport for each destination airport in the flight release.

(b) An alternate airport need not be designated for IFR or over-the-top operations where the airplane carries enough fuel to meet the requirements of §§125.375 and 125.377 for flights outside the 48 conterminous States and the District of Columbia over routes without an available alternate airport for a particular airport of destination.

(c) For the purposes of paragraph (a) of this section, the weather requirements at the alternate airport must meet the requirements of the operator's operations specifications.

(d) No person may release a flight unless that person lists each required alternate airport in the flight release.

§125.369 Alternate airport weather minimums.

No person may list an airport as an alternate airport in the flight release unless the appropriate weather reports or forecasts, or any combination thereof, indicate that the weather conditions will be at or above the alternate weather minimums specified in the certificate holder's operations specifications for that airport when the flight arrives.

§125.371 Continuing flight in unsafe conditions.

(a) No pilot in command may allow a flight to continue toward any airport to which it has been released if, in the opinion of the pilot in command, the flight cannot be completed safely, unless, in the opinion of the pilot in command, there is no safer procedure. In that event, continuation toward that airport is an emergency situation.

§125.373 Original flight release or amendment of flight release.

(a) A certificate holder may specify any airport authorized for the type of airplane as a destination for the purpose of original release.

(b) No person may allow a flight to continue to an airport to which it has been released unless the weather conditions at an alternate airport that was specified in the flight release are forecast to be at or above the alternate minimums specified in the operations specifications for that airport at the time the airplane would arrive at the alternate airport. However, the flight release may be amended en route to include any alternate airport that is within the fuel range of the airplane as specified in §125.375 or §125.377.

(c) No person may change an original destination or alternate airport that is specified in the original flight release to another airport while the airplane is en route unless the other airport is authorized for that type of airplane.

(d) Each person who amends a flight release en route shall record that amendment.

§125.375 Fuel supply: Nonturbine and turbopropeller-powered airplanes.

(a) Except as provided in paragraph (b) of this section, no person may release for flight or take off a nonturbine or turbopropeller-powered airplane unless, considering the wind and other weather conditions expected, it has enough fuel—

(1) To fly to and land at the airport to which it is released;

(2) Thereafter, to fly to and land at the most distant alternate airport specified in the flight release; and

(3) Thereafter, to fly for 45 minutes at normal crusing fuel consumption.

(b) If the airplane is released for any flight other than from one point in the conterminous United States to another point in the conterminous United States, it must carry enough fuel to meet the requirements of paragraphs (a) (1) and (2) of this section and thereafter fly for 30 minutes plus 15 percent of the total time required to fly at normal cruising fuel consumption to the airports specified in paragraphs (a) (1) and (2) of this section, or fly for 90 minutes at normal cruising fuel consumption, whichever is less.

(c) No person may release a nonturbine or turbopropeller-powered airplane to an airport for which an alternate is not specified under § 125.367(b) unless it has enough fuel, considering wind and other weather conditions expected, to fly to that airport and thereafter to fly for 3 hours at normal cruising fuel consumption.

§ 125.377 Fuel supply: Turbine-engine-powered airplanes other than turbopropeller.

(a) Except as provided in paragraph (b) of this section, no person may release for flight or takeoff a turbine-powered airplane (other than a turbopropeller-powered airplane) unless, considering the wind and other weather conditions expected, it has enough fuel—

(1) To fly to and land at the airport to which it is released;

(2) Thereafter, to fly to and land at the most distant alternate airport specified in the flight release; and

(3) Thereafter, to fly for 45 minutes at normal cruising fuel consumption.

(b) For any operation outside the 48 conterminous United States and the District of Columbia, unless authorized by the Administrator in the operations specifications, no person may release for flight or take off a turbine-engine powered airplane (other than a turbopropeller-powered airplane) unless, considering wind and other weather conditions expected, it has enough fuel—

(1) To fly and land at the airport to which it is released;

(2) After that, to fly for a period of 10 percent of the total time required to fly from the airport of departure and land at the airport to which it was released;

(3) After that, to fly to and land at the most distant alternate airport specified in the flight release, if an alternate is required; and

(4) After that, to fly for 30 minutes at holding speed at 1,500 feet above the alternate airport (or the destination airport if no alternate is required) under standard temperature conditions.

(c) No person may release a turbine-engine-powered airplane (other than a turbopropeller airplane) to an airport for which an alternate is not specified under § 125.367(b) unless it has enough fuel, considering wind and other weather conditions expected, to fly to that airport and thereafter to fly for at least 2 hours at normal cruising fuel consumption.

(d) The Administrator may amend the operations specifications of a certificate holder to require more fuel than any of the minimums stated in paragraph (a) or (b) of this section if the Administrator finds that additional fuel is necessary on a particular route in the interest of safety.

§ 125.379 Landing weather minimums: IFR.

(a) If the pilot in command of an airplane has not served 100 hours as pilot in command in the type of airplane being operated, the MDA or DH and visibility landing minimums in the certificate holder's operations specification are increased by 100 feet and one-half mile (or the RVR equivalent). The MDA or DH and visibility minimums need not be increased above those applicable to the airport when used as an alternate airport, but in no event may the landing minimums be less than a 300-foot ceiling and 1 mile of visibility.

(b) The 100 hours of pilot-in-command experience required by paragraph (a) may be reduced (not to exceed 50 percent) by substituting one landing in operations under this part in the type of airplane for 1 required hour of pilot-in-command experience if the pilot has at least 100 hours as pilot in command of another type airplane in operations under this part.

(c) Category II minimums, when authorized in the certificate holder's operations specifications, do not apply until the pilot in command subject to paragraph (a) of this section meets the requirements of that paragraph in the type of airplane the pilot is operating.

§ 125.381 Takeoff and landing weather minimums: IFR.

(a) Regardless of any clearance from ATC, if the reported weather conditions are less than that specified in the certificate holder's operations specifications, no pilot may—

(1) Take off an airplane under IFR; or

(2) Except as provided in paragraph (c) of this section, land an airplane under IFR.

(b) Except as provided in paragraph (c) of this section, no pilot may execute an instrument approach procedure if the latest reported visibility is less than the landing minimums specified in the certificate holder's operations specifications.

(c) If a pilot initiates an instrument approach procedure when the latest weather report indicates that the specified visibility minimums exist, and a later weather report indicating below minimums conditions is received after the airplane—

(1) Is on an ILS final approach and has passed the outer marker,

(2) Is on final approach segment using a nonprecision approach procedure, or

(3) Is on PAR final approach and has been turned over to the final approach controller, the approach may be continued and a landing may be made if the pilot in command finds, upon reaching the authorized MAP or DH, that actual weather conditions are at least equal to the minimums prescribed in the operations specifications.

[Doc. No. 19779, 45 FR 67235, Oct. 9, 1980, as amended by Amdt. 125–2, 46 FR 24409, Apr. 30, 1981]

§ 125.383 Load manifest.

(a) Each certificate holder is responsible for the preparation and accuracy of a load manifest in duplicate containing information concerning the loading of the airplane. The manifest must be prepared before each takeoff and must include—

(1) The number of passengers;

(2) The total weight of the loaded airplane;

(3) The maximum allowable takeoff and landing weights for that flight;

(4) The center of gravity limits;

(5) The center of gravity of the loaded airplane, except that the actual center of gravity need not be computed if the airplane is loaded according to a loading schedule or other approved method that ensures that the center of gravity of the loaded airplane is within approved limits. In those cases, an entry shall be made on the manifest indicating that the center of gravity is within limits according to a loading schedule or other approved method:

(6) The registration number of the airplane;

(7) The origin and destination ; and

(8) Names of passengers.

(b) The pilot in command of an airplane for which a load manifest must be prepared shall carry a copy of the completed load manifest in the airplane to its destination. The certificate holder shall keep copies of completed load manifests for at least 30 days at its principal operations base, or at another location used by it and approved by the Administrator.

Subpart L—Records and Reports

§ 125.401   Crewmember record.

(a) Each certificate holder shall—

(1) Maintain current records of each crewmember that show whether or not that crewmember complies with this chapter (e.g., proficiency checks, airplane qualifications, any required physical examinations, and flight time records); and

(2) Record each action taken concerning the release from employment or physical or professional disqualification of any flight crewmember and keep the record for at least 6 months thereafter.

(b) Each certificate holder shall maintain the records required by paragraph (a) of this section at its principal operations base, or at another location used by it and approved by the Administrator.

(c) Computer record systems approved by the Administrator may be used in complying with the requirements of paragraph (a) of this section.

§ 125.403 Flight release form.

(a) The flight release may be in any form but must contain at least the following information concerning each flight:

(1) Company or organization name.

(2) Make, model, and registration number of the airplane being used.

(3) Date of flight.

(4) Name and duty assignment of each crewmember.

(5) Departure airport, destination airports, alternate airports, and route.

(6) Minimum fuel supply (in gallons or pounds).

(7) A statement of the type of operation (e.g., IFR, VFR).

(b) The airplane flight release must contain, or have attached to it, weather reports, available weather forecasts, or a combination thereof.

§ 125.405 Disposition of load manifest, flight release, and flight plans.

(a) The pilot in command of an airplane shall carry in the airplane to its destination the original or a signed copy of the—

(1) Load manifest required by § 125.383;

(2) Flight release;

(3) Airworthiness release; and

(4) Flight plan, including route.

(b) If a flight originates at the principal operations base of the certificate holder, it shall retain at that base a signed copy of each document listed in paragraph (a) of this section.

(c) Except as provided in paragraph (d) of this section, if a flight originates at a place other than the principal operations base of the certificate holder, the pilot in command (or another person not aboard the airplane who is authorized by the operator) shall, before or immediately after departure of the flight, mail signed copies of the documents listed in paragraph (a) of this section to the principal operations base.

(d) If a flight originates at a place other than the principal operations base of the certificate holder and there is at that place a person to manage the flight departure for the operator who does not depart on the airplane, signed copies of the documents listed in paragraph (a) of this section may be retained at that place for not more than 30 days before being sent to the principal operations base of the certificate holder. However, the documents for a particular flight need not be further retained at that place or be sent to the principal operations base, if the originals or other copies of them have been previously returned to the principal operations base.

(e) The certificate holder shall:

(1) Identify in its operations manual the person having custody of the copies of documents retained in accordance with paragraph (d) of this section; and

(2) Retain at its principal operations base either the original or a copy of the records required by this section for at least 30 days.

§ 125.407 Maintenance log: Airplanes.

(a) Each person who takes corrective action or defers action concerning a reported or observed failure or malfunction of an airframe, aircraft engine, propeller, or appliance shall record the action taken in the airplane maintenance log in accordance with Part 43 of this chapter.

(b) Each certificate holder shall establish a procedure for keeping copies of the airplane maintenance log required by this section in the airplane for access by appropriate personnel and shall include that procedure in the manual required by § 125.249.

§ 125.409 Reports of defects or unairworthy conditions.

(a) Each certificate holder shall report the occurrence or detection of each failure, malfunction, or defect, in a form and manner prescribed by the Administrator.

(b) The report must be made within 72 hours to the FAA Flight Standards district office in whose area the certificate holder has its principal operations base. The procedures to be used in complying with this section must be made a part of the manual procedures required by § 125.73(f).

§ 125.411 Airworthiness release or maintenance record entry.

(a) No certificate holder may operate an airplane after maintenance, preventive maintenance, or alteration is performed on the airplane unless the person performing that maintenance, preventive maintenance, or alteration prepares or causes to be prepared—

(1) An airworthiness release; or

(2) An entry in the aircraft maintenance records in accordance with the certificate holder's manual.

(b) The airworthiness release or maintenance record entry required by paragraph (a) of this section must—

(1) Be prepared in accordance with the procedures set forth in the certificate holder's manual;

(2) Include a certification that—

(i) The work was performed in accordance with the requirements of the certificate holder's manual;

(ii) All items required to be inspected were inspected by an authorized person who determined that the work was satisfactorily completed;

(iii) No known condition exists that would make the airplane unairworthy; and

(iv) So far as the work performed is concerned, the airplane is in condition for safe operation; and

(3) Be signed by a person authorized in Part 43 of this chapter to perform maintenance, preventive maintenance, and alteration.

(c) When an airworthiness release form is prepared, the certificate holder must give a copy to the pilot in command and keep a record of it for at least 60 days.

(d) Instead of restating each of the conditions of the certification required by paragraph (b) of this section, the certificate holder may state in its manual that the signature of a person authorized in Part 43 of this chapter constitutes that certification.

APPENDIX A—ADDITIONAL EMERGENCY EQUIPMENT

(a) *Means for emergency evacuation.* Each passenger-carrying landplane emergency exit (other than over-the-wing) that is more that 6 feet from the ground with the airplane on the ground and the landing gear extended must have an approved means to assist the occupants in descending to the ground. The assisting means for a floor level emergency exit must meet the requirements of § 25.809(f)(1) of this chapter in effect on April 30, 1972, except that, for any airplane for which the application for the type certificate was filed after that date, it must meet the requirements under which the airplane was type certificated. An assisting means that deploys automatically must be armed during taxiing, takeoffs, and landings. However, if the Administrator finds that the design of the exit makes compliance impractical, the Administrator may grant a deviation from the requirement of automatic deployment if the assisting means automatically erects upon deployment and, with respect to required emergency exits, if an emergency evacuation demonstration is conducted in accordance with § 125.189. This paragraph does not apply to the rear window emergency exit of DC-3 airplanes operated with less than 36 occupants, including crewmembers, and less than five exits authorized for passenger use.

(b) *Interior emergency exit marking.* The following must be complied with for each passenger-carrying airplane:

(1) Each passenger emergency exit, its means of access, and means of opening must be conspicuously marked. The identity and location of each passenger emergency exit must be recognizable from a distance equal to the width of the cabin. The location of each passenger emergency exit must be indicated by a sign visible to occupants approaching along the main passenger aisle. There must be a locating sign—

(i) Above the aisle near each over-the-wing passenger emergency exit, or at another ceiling location if it is more practical because of low headroom;

(ii) Next to each floor level passenger emergency exit, except that one sign may serve two such exits if they both can be seen readily from that sign; and

(iii) On each bulkhead or divider that prevents fore and aft vision along the passenger cabin, to indicate emergency exits beyond and obscured by it, except that if this is not possible the sign may be placed at another appropriate location.

(2) Each passenger emergency exit marking and each locating sign must meet the following:

(i) For an airplane for which the application for the type certificate was filed prior to May 1, 1972, each passenger emergency exit marking and each locating sign must be manufactured to meet the requirements of § 25.812(b) of this chapter in effect on April 30, 1972. On these airplanes, no sign may continue to be used if its luminescence (brightness) decreases to below 100 microlamberts. The colors may be reversed if it increases the emergency illumination of the passenger compartment. However, the Administrator may authorize deviation from the 2-inch background requirements if the Administrator finds that special circumstances exist that make compliance impractical and that the proposed deviation provides an equivalent level of safety.

(ii) For an airplane for which the application for the type certificate was filed on or after May 1, 1972, each passenger emergency exit marking and each locating sign must be manufactured to meet the interior emergency exit marking requirements under which the airplane was type certificated. On these airplanes, no sign may continue to be used if its luminescence (brightness) decreases to below 250 microlamberts.

(c) *Lighting for interior emergency exit markings.* Each passenger-carrying airplane must have an emergency lighting system, independent of the main lighting system. However, sources of general cabin illumination may be common to both the emergency and the main lighting systems if the power supply to the emergency lighting system is independent of the power supply to the main lighting system. The emergency lighting system must—

(1) Illuminate each passenger exit marking and locating sign; and

(2) Provide enough general lighting in the passenger cabin so that the average illumination, when measured at 40-inch intervals at seat armrest height, on the centerline of the main passenger aisle, is at least 0.05 foot-candles.

(d) *Emergency light operation.* Except for lights forming part of emergency lighting subsystems provided in compliance with § 25.812(g) of this chapter (as prescribed in paragraph (h) of this section) that serve no more than one assist means, are independent of the airplane's main emergency lighting systems, and are automatically activated when the assist means is deployed, each light required by paragraphs (c) and (h) must comply with the following:

(1) Each light must be operable manually and must operate automatically from the independent lighting system—

(i) In a crash landing; or

(ii) Whenever the airplane's normal electric power to the light is interrupted.

(2) Each light must—

(i) Be operable manually from the flight-crew station and from a point in the passenger compartment that is readily accessible to a normal flight attendant seat;

(ii) Have a means to prevent inadvertent operation of the manual controls; and

(iii) When armed or turned on at either station, remain lighted or become lighted upon interruption of the airplane's normal electric power.

Each light must be armed or turned on during taxiing, takeoff, and landing. In showing compliance with this paragraph, a transverse vertical separation of the fuselage need not be considered.

(3) Each light must provide the required level of illumination for at least 10 minutes at the critical ambient conditions after emergency landing.

(e) *Emergency exit operating handles.*

(1) For a passenger-carrying airplane for which the application for the type certificate was filed prior to May 1, 1972, the location of each passenger emergency exit operating handle and instructions for opening the exit must be shown by a marking on or near the exit that is readable from a distance of 30 inches. In addition, for each Type I and Type II emergency exit with a locking mechanism released by rotary motion of the handle, the instructions for opening must be shown by—

(i) A red arrow with a shaft at least ¾ inch wide and a head twice the width of the shaft, extending along at least 70 degrees of arc at a radius approximately equal to ¾ of the handle length; and

(ii) The word "open" in red letters 1 inch high placed horizontally near the head of the arrow.

(2) For a passenger-carrying airplane for which the application for the type certificate was filed on or after May 1, 1972, the location of each passenger emergency exit operating handle and instructions for opening the exit must be shown in accordance with the requirements under which the airplane was type certificated. On these airplanes, no operating handle or operating handle cover may continue to be used if its luminescence (brightness) decreases to below 100 microlamberts.

(f) *Emergency exit access.* Access to emergency exits must be provided as follows for each passenger-carrying airplane:

(1) Each passageway between individual passenger areas, or leading to a Type I or Type II emergency exit, must be unobstructed and at least 20 inches wide.

(2) There must be enough space next to each Type I or Type II emergency exit to allow a crewmember to assist in the evacuation of passengers without reducing the unobstructed width of the passageway below that required in paragraph (f)(1) of this section. However, the Administrator may authorize deviation from this requirement for an airplane certificated under the

provisions of Part 4b of the Civil Air Regulations in effect before December 20, 1951, if the Administrator finds that special circumstances exist that provide an equivalent level of safety.

(3) There must be access from the main aisle to each Type III and Type IV exit. The access from the aisle to these exits must not be obstructed by seats, berths, or other protrusions in a manner that would reduce the effectiveness of the exit. In addition—

(i) For an airplane for which the application for the type certificate was filed prior to May 1, 1972, the access must meet the requirements of § 25.813(c) of this chapter in effect on April 30, 1972; and

(ii) For an airplane for which the application for the type certificate was filed on or after May 1, 1972, the access must meet the emergency exit access requirements under which the airplane was certificated.

(4) If it is necessary to pass through a passageway between passenger compartments to reach any required emergency exit from any seat in the passenger cabin, the passageway must not be obstructed. However, curtains may be used if they allow free entry through the passageway.

(5) No door may be installed in any partition between passenger compartments.

(6) If it is necessary to pass through a doorway separating the passenger cabin from other areas to reach any required emergency exit from any passenger seat, the door must have a means to latch it in open position, and the door must be latched open during each takeoff and landing. The latching means must be able to withstand the loads imposed upon it when the door is subjected to the ultimate interia forces, relative to the surrounding structure, listed in § 25.561(b) of this chapter.

(g) *Exterior exit markings.* Each passenger emergency exit and the means of opening that exit from the outside must be marked on the outside of the airplane. There must be a 2-inch colored band outlining each passenger emergency exit on the side of the fuselage. Each outside marking, including the band, must be readily distinguishable from the surrounding fuselage area by contrast in color. The markings must comply with the following:

(1) If the reflectance of the darker color is 15 percent or less, the reflectance of the lighter color must be at least 45 percent. "Reflectance" is the ratio of the luminous flux reflected by a body to the luminous flux it receives.

(2) If the reflectance of the darker color is greater than 15 percent, at least a 30 percent difference between its reflectance and the reflectance of the lighter color must be provided.

(3) Exits that are not in the side of the fuselage must have the external means of opening and applicable instructions marked

conspicuously in red or, if red is inconspicuous against the background color, in bright chrome yellow and, when the opening means for such an exit is located on only one side of the fuselage, a conspicuous marking to that effect must be provided on the other side.

(h) *Exterior emergency lighting and escape route.*

(1) Each passenger-carrying airplane must be equipped with exterior lighting that meets the following requirements:

(i) For an airplane for which the application for the type certificate was filed prior to May 1, 1972, the requirements of § 25.812(f) and (g) of this chapter in effect on April 30, 1972.

(ii) For an airplane for which the application for the type certificate was filed on or after May 1, 1972, the exterior emergency lighting requirements under which the airplane was type certificated.

(2) Each passenger-carrying airplane must be equipped with a slip-resistant escape route that meets the following requirements:

(i) For an airplane for which the application for the type certificate was filed prior to May 1, 1972, the requirements of § 25.803(e) of this chapter in effect on April 30, 1972.

(ii) For an airplane for which the application for the type certificate was filed on or after May 1, 1972, the slip-resistant escape route requirements under which the airplane was type certificated.

(i) *Floor level exits.* Each floor level door or exit in the side of the fuselage (other than those leading into a cargo or baggage compartment that is not accessible from the passenger cabin) that is 44 or more inches high and 20 or more inches wide, but not wider than 46 inches, each passenger ventral exit (except the ventral exits on M-404 and CV-240 airplanes) and each tail cone exit must meet the requirements of this section for floor level emergency exits. However, the Administrator may grant a deviation from this paragraph if the Administrator finds that circumstances make full compliance impractical and that an acceptable level of safety has been achieved.

(j) *Additional emergency exits.* Approved emergency exits in the passenger compartments that are in excess of the minimum number of required emergency exits must meet all of the applicable provisions of this section except paragraph (f), (1), (2), and (3) and must be readily accessible.

(k) On each large passenger-carrying turbojet-powered airplane, each ventral exit and tailcone exit must be—

(1) Designed and constructed so that it cannot be opened during flight; and

(2) Marked with a placard readable from a distance of 30 inches and installed at a con-

spicuous location near the means of opening the exit, stating that the exit has been designed and constructed so that it cannot be opened during flight.

APPENDIX B—CRITERIA FOR DEMONSTRATION OF EMERGENCY EVACUATION PROCEDURES UNDER § 125.189

(a) *Aborted takeoff demonstration.*

(1) The demonstration must be conducted either during the dark of the night or during daylight with the dark of the night simulated. If the demonstration is conducted indoors during daylight hours, it must be conducted with each window covered and each door closed to minimize the daylight effect. Illumination on the floor or ground may be used, but it must be kept low and shielded against shining into the airplane's windows or doors.

(2) The airplane must be in a normal ground attitude with landing gear extended.

(3) Stands or ramps may be used for descent from the wing to the ground. Safety equipment such as mats or inverted life rafts may be placed on the ground to protect participants. No other equipment that is not part of the airplane's emergency evacuation equipment may be used to aid the participants in reaching the ground.

(4) The airplane's normal electric power sources must be deenergized.

(5) All emergency equipment for the type of passenger-carrying operation involved must be installed in accordance with the certificate holder's manual.

(6) Each external door and exit and each internal door or curtain must be in position to simulate a normal takeoff.

(7) A representative passenger load of persons in normal health must be used. At least 30 percent must be females. At least 5 percent must be over 60 years of age with a proportionate number of females. At least 5 percent, but not more than 10 percent, must be children under 12 years of age, prorated through that age group. Three life-size dolls, not included as part of the total passenger load, must be carried by passengers to simulate live infants 2 years old or younger. Crewmembers, mechanics, and training personnel who maintain or operate the airplane in the normal course of their duties may not be used as passengers.

(8) No passenger may be assigned a specific seat except as the Administrator may require. Except as required by item (12) of this paragraph, no employee of the certificate holder may be seated next to an emergency exit.

(9) Seat belts and shoulder harnesses (as required) must be fastened.

(10) Before the start of the demonstration, approximately one-half of the total average amount of carry-on baggage, blankets, pillows, and other similar articles must be distributed at several locations in the aisles and emergency exit access ways to create minor obstructions.

(11) The seating density and arrangement of the airplane must be representative of the highest capacity passenger version of that airplane the certificate holder operates or proposes to operate.

(12) Each crewmember must be a member of a regularly scheduled line crew, must be seated in that crewmember's normally assigned seat for takeoff, and must remain in that seat until the signal for commencement of the demonstration is received.

(13) No crewmember or passenger may be given prior knowledge of the emergency exits available for the demonstration.

(14) The certificate holder may not practice, rehearse, or describe the demonstration for the participants nor may any participant have taken part in this type of demonstration within the preceding 6 months.

(15) The pretakeoff passenger briefing required by § 125.327 may be given in accordance with the certificate holder's manual. The passengers may also be warned to follow directions of crewmembers, but may not be instructed on the procedures to be followed in the demonstration.

(16) If safety equipment as allowed by item (3) of this section is provided, either all passenger and cockpit windows must be blacked out or all of the emergency exits must have safety equipment to prevent disclosure of the available emergency exits.

(17) Not more than 50 percent of the emergency exits in the sides of the fuselage of an airplane that meet all of the requirements applicable to the required emergency exits for that airplane may be used for the demonstration. Exits that are not to be used in the demonstration must have the exit handle deactivated or must be indicated by red lights, red tape or other acceptable means, placed outside the exits to indicate fire or other reason that they are unusable. The exits to be used must be representative of all of the emergency exits on the airplane and must be designated by the certificate holder, subject to approval by the Administrator. At least one floor level exit must be used.

(18) All evacuees, except those using an over-the-wing exit, must leave the airplane by a means provided as part of the airplane's equipment.

(19) The certificate holder's approved procedures and all of the emergency equipment that is normally available, including slides, ropes, lights, and megaphones, must be fully utilized during the demonstration.

(20) The evacuation time period is completed when the last occupant has evacuated the airplane and is on the ground. Evacuees using stands or ramps allowed by item

(3) above are considered to be on the ground when they are on the stand or ramp: *Provided,* That the acceptance rate of the stand or ramp is no greater than the acceptance rate of the means available on the airplane for descent from the wing during an actual crash situation.

(b) *Ditching demonstration.* The demonstration must assume that daylight hours exist outside the airplane and that all required crewmembers are available for the demonstration.

(1) If the certificate holder's manual requires the use of passengers to assist in the launching of liferafts, the needed passengers must be aboard the airplane and participate in the demonstration according to the manual.

(2) A stand must be placed at each emergency exit and wing with the top of the platform at a height simulating the water level of the airplane following a ditching.

(3) After the ditching signal has been received, each evacuee must don a life vest according to the certificate holder's manual.

(4) Each liferaft must be launched and inflated according to the certificate holder's manual and all other required emergency equipment must be placed in rafts.

(5) Each evacuee must enter a liferaft and the crewmembers assigned to each liferaft must indicate the location of emergency equipment aboard the raft and describe its use.

(6) Either the airplane, a mockup of the airplane, or a floating device simulating a passenger compartment must be used.

(i) If a mockup of the airplane is used, it must be a life-size mockup of the interior and representative of the airplane currently used by or proposed to be used by the certificate holder and must contain adequate seats for use of the evacuees. Operation of the emergency exits and the doors must closely simulate that on the airplane. Sufficient wing area must be installed outside the over-the-wing exits to demonstrate the evacuation.

(ii) If a floating device simulating a passenger compartment is used, it must be representative, to the extent possible, of the passenger compartment of the airplane used in operations. Operation of the emergency exits and the doors must closely simulate operation on that airplane. Sufficient wing area must be installed outside the over-the-wing exits to demonstrate the evacuation. The device must be equipped with the same survival equipment as is installed on the airplane, to accommodate all persons participating in the demonstration.

APPENDIX C—ICE PROTECTION

If certification with ice protection provisions is desired, compliance with the following must be shown:

(a) The recommended procedures for the use of the ice protection equipment must be set forth in the Airplane Flight Manual.

(b) An analysis must be performed to establish, on the basis of the airplane's operational needs, the adequacy of the ice protection system for the various components of the airplane. In addition, tests of the ice protection system must be conducted to demonstrate that the airplane is capable of operating safely in continuous maximum and intermittent maximum icing conditions as described in Appendix C of Part 25 of this chapter.

(c) Compliance with all or portions of this section may be accomplished by reference, where applicable because of similarity of the designs, to analyses and tests performed by the applicant for a type certificated model.

APPENDIX D—AIRPLANE FLIGHT RECORDER SPECIFICATION

Parameters	Range	Accuracy sensor input to DFDR readout	Sampling interval (per second)	Resolution [4] read out
Time (GMT or Frame Counter) (range 0 to 4095, sampled 1 per frame).	24 Hrs	±0.125% Per Hour	0.25 (1 per 4 seconds).	1 sec.
Altitude	−1,000 ft to max certificated altitude of aircraft.	±100 to ±700 ft (See Table 1, TSO–C51a).	1	5' to 35' [1]
Airspeed	50 KIAS to V_{so}, and V_{so} to 1.2 V_D	±5%, ±3%	1	1 kt
Heading	360°	±2°	1	0.5
Normal Acceleration (Vertical)	−3g to +6g	±1% of max range excluding datum error of ±5%.	8	0.01g.
Pitch Attitude	±75°	±2°	1	0.5°
Roll Attitude	±180°	±2°	1	0.5°
Radio Transmitter Keying	On-Off (Discrete)		1	
Thrust/Power on Each Engine	Full range forward	±2%	1	0.2% [2]
Trailing Edge Flap or Cockpit Control Selection.	Full range or each discrete position	±3° or as pilot's indicator	0.5	0.5% [2]
Leading Edge Flap or Cockpit Control Selection.	Full range or each discrete position	±3° or as pilot's indicator	0.5	0.5% [2]
Thrust Reverser Position	Stowed, in transit, and reverse (Discrete)		1 (per 4 seconds per engine).	
Ground Spoiler Position/Speed Brake Selection.	Full range or each discrete position	±2% unless higher accuracy uniquely required.	1	0.2% [2]
Marker Beacon Passage	Discrete		1	
Autopilot Engagement	Discrete		1	
Longitudinal Acceleration	±1g	±1.5% max range excluding datum error of ±5%.	4	0.01g.
Pilot Input and/or Surface Position-Primary Controls (Pitch, Roll, Yaw) [3]	Full range	±2° unless higher accuracy uniquely required.	1	0.2% [2]
Lateral Acceleration	±1g	±1.5% max range excluding datum error of ±5%.	4	0.01g.
Pitch Trim Position	Full range	±3% unless higher accuracy uniquely required.	1	0.3% [2]
Glideslope Deviation	±400 Microamps	±3%	1	0.3% [2]
Localizer Deviation	±400 Microamps	±3%	1	0.3% [2]
AFCS Mode and Engagement Status	Discrete		1	
Radio Altitude	−20 ft to 2,500 ft	±2 Ft or ±3% Whichever is Greater Below 500 Ft and ±5% Above 500 Ft.		1 ft + 5% [2] above 500'
Master Warning	Discrete		1	
Main Gear Squat Switch Status	Discrete		1	
Angle of Attack (if recorded directly)	As installed	As installed	2	0.3% [2]
Outside Air Temperature or Total Air Temperature.	−50°C to +90°C	±2°C	0.5	0.3°C.
Hydraulics, Each System Low Pressure	Discrete		0.5	or 0.5% [2]
Groundspeed	As Installed	Most Accurate Systems Installed (IMS Equipped Aircraft Only).	1	0.2% [2]

If additional recording capacity is available, recording of the following parameters is recommended. The parameters are listed in order of significance:

Parameters	Range	Accuracy sensor input to DFDR readout	Sampling interval (per second)	Resolution read out
Drift Angle	When available. As installed	As installed	4	
Wind Speed and Direction	When available. As installed	As installed	4	
Latitude and Longitude	When available. As installed	As installed	4	
Brake pressure/Brake pedal position	As installed	As installed	1	
Additional engine parameters:				
EPR	As installed	As installed	1 (per engine)	
N1	As installed	As installed	1 (per engine)	
N2	As installed	As installed	1 (per engine)	
EGT	As installed	As installed	1 (per engine)	
Throttle Lever Position	As installed	As installed	1 (per engine)	
Fuel Flow	As installed	As installed	1 (per engine)	
TCAS:				
TA	As installed	As installed	1	

APPENDIX D—AIRPLANE FLIGHT RECORDER SPECIFICATION—Continued

Parameters	Range	Accuracy sensor input to DFDR readout	Sampling interval (per second)	Resolution [4] read out
RA	As installed	As installed	1	
Sensitivity level (as selected by crew).	As installed	As installed	2	
GPWS (ground proximity warning system)	Discrete		1	
Landing gear or gear selector position	Discrete		0.25 (1 per 4 seconds).	
DME 1 and 2 Distance	0-200 NM	As installed	0.25	1 mi.
Nav 1 and 2 Frequency Selection	Full range	As installed	0.25	

[1] When altitude rate is recorded. Altitude rate must have sufficient resolution and sampling to permit the derivation of altitude to 5 feet.
[2] Percent of full range.
[3] For airplanes that can demonstrate the capability of deriving either the control input on control movement (one from the other) for all modes of operation and flight regimes, the "or" applies. For airplanes with non-mechanical control systems (fly-by-wire) the "and" applies. In airplanes with split surfaces, suitable combination of inputs is acceptable in lieu of recording each surface separately.
[4] This column applies to aircraft manufactured after October 11, 1991

FEDERAL AVIATION REGULATIONS

PART 135
AIR TAXI OPERATORS AND
COMMERCIAL OPERATORS

1989 EDITION

PART 135—AIR TAXI OPERATORS
AND COMMERCIAL OPERATORS

Subpart A—General

Sec.
135.1 Applicability.
135.2 Air taxi operations with large aircraft.
135.3 Rules applicable to operations subject to this part.
135.5 Certificate and operations specifications required.
135.7 Applicability of rules to unauthorized operators.
135.9 Duration of certificate.
135.10 Compliance dates for certain rules.
135.11 Application and issue of certificate and operations specifications.
135.13 Eligibility for certificate and operations specifications.
135.15 Amendment of certificate.
135.17 Amendment of operations specifications.
135.19 Emergency operations.
135.21 Manual requirements.
135.23 Manual contents.
135.25 Aircraft requirements.
135.27 Business office and operations base.
135.29 Use of business names.
135.31 Advertising.
135.33 Area limitations on operations.
135.35 Termination of operations.
135.37 Management personnel required.
135.39 Management personnel qualifications.

135.41 Carriage of narcotic drugs, marihuana, and depressant or stimulant drugs or substances.
135.43 Crewmember certificate: International operations: Application and issue.

Subpart B—Flight Operations

135.61 General.
135.63 Recordkeeping requirements.
135.65 Reporting mechanical irregularities.
135.67 Reporting potentially hazardous meteorological conditions and irregularities of communications or navigation facilities.
135.69 Restriction or suspension of operations: Continuation of flight in an emergency.
135.71 Airworthiness check.
135.73 Inspections and tests.
135.75 Inspectors credentials: Admission to pilots' compartment: Forward observer's seat.
135.77 Responsibility for operational control.
135.79 Flight locating requirements.
135.81 Informing personnel of operational information and appropriate changes.
135.83 Operating information required.
135.85 Carriage of persons without compliance with the passenger-carrying provisions of this part.

135.87 Carriage of cargo including carry-on baggage.
135.89 Pilot requirements: Use of oxygen.
135.91 Oxygen for medical use by passengers.
135.93 Autopilot: Minimum altitudes for use.
135.95 Airmen: Limitations on use of services.
135.97 Aircraft and facilities for recent flight experience.
135.99 Composition of flight crew.
135.100 Flight crewmember duties.
135.101 Second in command required in IFR conditions.
135.103 Exception to second in command requirement: IFR operations.
135.105 Exception to second in command requirement: Approval for use of autopilot system.
135.107 Flight attendant crewmember requirement.
135.109 Pilot in command or second in command: Designation required.
135.111 Second in command required in category II operations.
135.113 Passenger occupancy of pilot seat.
135.115 Manipulation of controls.
135.117 Briefing of passengers before flight.
135.119 Prohibition against carriage of weapons.
135.121 Alcoholic beverages.
135.123 Emergency and emergency evacuation duties.
135.125 Airplane security.

Subpart C—Aircraft and Equipment

135.141 Applicability.
135.143 General requirements.
135.145 Aircraft proving tests.
135.147 Dual controls required.
135.149 Equipment requirements: General.
135.151 Cockpit voice recorders.
135.153 Ground proximity warning system.
135.155 Fire extinguishers: Passenger-carrying aircraft.
135.157 Oxygen equipment requirements.
135.158 Pitot heat indication systems.
135.159 Equipment requirements: Carrying passengers under VFR at night or under VFR over-the-top conditions.
135.161 Radio and navigational equipment: Carrying passengers under VFR at night or under VFR over-the-top.
135.163 Equipment requirements: Aircraft carrying passengers under IFR.
135.165 Radio and navigational equipment: Extended overwater or IFR operations.
135.167 Emergency equipment: Extended overwater operations.
135.169 Additional airworthiness requirements.
135.170 Materials for compartment interiors.

135.171 Shoulder harness installation at flight crewmember stations.
135.173 Airborne thunderstorm detection equipment requirements.
135.175 Airborne weather radar equipment requirements.
135.177 Emergency equipment requirements for aircraft having a passenger seating configuration of more than 19 passengers.
135.179 Inoperable instruments and equipment for multiengine aircraft.
135.181 Performance requirements: Aircraft operated over-the-top or in IFR conditions.
135.183 Performance requirements: Land aircraft operated over water.
135.185 Empty weight and center of gravity: Currency requirement.

Subpart D—VFR/IFR Operating Limitations and Weather Requirements

135.201 Applicability.
135.203 VFR: Minimum altitudes.
135.205 VFR: Visibility requirements.
135.207 VFR: Helicopter surface reference requirements.
135.209 VFR: Fuel supply.
135.211 VFR: Over-the-top carrying passengers: Operating limitations.
135.213 Weather reports and forecasts.
135.215 IFR: Operating limitations.
135.217 IFR: Takeoff limitations.
135.219 IFR: Destination airport weather minimums.
135.221 IFR: Alternate airport weather minimums.
135.223 IFR: Alternate airport requirements.
135.225 IFR: Takeoff, approach and landing minimums.
135.227 Icing conditions: Operating limitations.
135.229 Airport requirements.

Subpart E—Flight Crewmember Requirements

135.241 Applicability.
135.243 Pilot in command qualifications.
135.244 Operating experience.
135.245 Second in command qualifications.
135.247 Pilot qualifications: Recent experience.

Subpart F—Flight Crewmember Flight Time Limitations and Rest Requirements

135.261 Applicability.
135.263 Flight time limitations and rest requirements: All certificate holders.
135.265 Flight time limitations and rest requirements: Scheduled operations.
135.267 Flight time limitations and rest requirements: Unscheduled one- and two-pilot crews.

135.269 Flight time limitation and rest requirements: Unscheduled three- and four-pilot crews.
135.271 Helicopter hospital emergency medical evacuation service (HEMES).

Subpart G—Crewmember Testing Requirements

135.291 Applicability.
135.293 Initial and recurrent pilot testing requirements.
135.295 Initial and recurrent flight attendant crewmember testing requirements.
135.297 Pilot in command: Instrument proficiency check requirements.
135.299 Pilot in command: Line checks: Routes and airports.
135.301 Crewmember: Tests and checks, grace provisions, training to accepted standards.
135.303 Check pilot authorization: Application and issue.

Subpart H—Training

135.321 Applicability and terms used.
135.323 Training program: General.
135.325 Training program and revision: Initial and final approval.
135.327 Training program: Curriculum.
135.329 Crewmember training requirements.
135.331 Crewmember emergency training.
135.333 Training requirements: Handling and carriage of hazardous materials.
135.335 Approval of aircraft simulators and other training devices.
135.337 Training program: Check airmen and instructor qualifications.
135.339 Check airmen and flight instructors: Initial and transition training.
135.341 Pilot and flight attendant crewmember training programs.
135.343 Crewmember initial and recurrent training requirements.
135.345 Pilots: Initial, transition, and upgrade ground training.
135.347 Pilots: Initial, transition, upgrade, and differences flight training.
135.349 Flight attendants: Initial and transition ground training.
135.351 Recurrent training.

Subpart I—Airplane Performance Operating Limitations

135.361 Applicability.
135.363 General.
135.365 Large transport category airplanes: Reciprocating engine powered: Weight limitations.
135.367 Large transport category airplanes: Reciprocating engine powered: Takeoff limitations.
135.369 Large transport category airplanes: Reciprocating engine powered: En route limitations: All engines operating.

135.371 Large transport category airplanes: Reciprocating engine powered: En route limitations: One engine inoperative.
135.373 Part 25 transport category airplanes with four or more engines: Reciprocating engine powered: En route limitations: Two engines inoperative.
135.375 Large transport category airplanes: Reciprocating engine powered: Landing limitations: Destination airports.
135.377 Large transport category airplanes: Reciprocating engine powered: Landing limitations: Alternate airports.
135.379 Large transport category airplanes: Turbine engine powered: Takeoff limitations.
135.381 Large transport category airplanes: Turbine engine powered: En route limitations: One engine inoperative.
135.383 Large transport category airplanes: Turbine engine powered: En route limitations: Two engines inoperative.
135.385 Large transport category airplanes: Turbine engine powered: Landing limitations: Destination airports.
135.387 Large transport category airplanes: Turbine engine powered: Landing limitations: Alternate airports.
135.389 Large nontransport category airplanes: Takeoff limitations.
135.391 Large nontransport category airplanes: En route limitations: One engine inoperative.
135.393 Large nontransport category airplanes: Landing limitations: Destination airports.
135.395 Large nontransport category airplanes: Landing limitations: Alternate airports.
135.397 Small transport category airplane performance operating limitations.
135.398 Commuter category airplanes performance operating limitations.
135.399 Small nontransport category airplane performance operating limitations.

Subpart J—Maintenance, Preventive Maintenance, and Alterations

135.411 Applicability.
135.413 Responsibility for airworthiness.
135.415 Mechanical reliability reports.
135.417 Mechanical interruption summary report.
135.419 Approved aircraft inspection program.
135.421 Additional maintenance requirements.
135.423 Maintenance, preventive maintenance, and alteration organization.
135.425 Maintenance, preventive maintenance, and alteration programs.
135.427 Manual requirements.
135.429 Required inspection personnel.

135.431 Continuing analysis and surveillance.
135.433 Maintenance and preventive maintenance training program.
135.435 Certificate requirements.
135.437 Authority to perform and approve maintenance, preventive maintenance, and alterations.
135.439 Maintenance recording requirements.
135.441 Transfer of maintenance records.
135.443 Airworthiness release or aircraft log entry.

APPENDIX A—ADDITIONAL AIRWORTHINESS STANDARDS FOR 10 OR MORE PASSENGER AIRPLANES

APPENDIX B — AIRPLANE FLIGHT RECORDER SPECIFICATIONS

APPENDIX C — HELICOPTER FLIGHT RECORDER SPECIFICATIONS

APPENDIX D — AIRPLANE FLIGHT RECORDER SPECIFICATIONS

APPENDIX E — HELICOPTER FLIGHT RECORDER SPECIFICATIONS

Subpart A—General

§ 135.1 Applicability.

(a) Except as provided in paragraph (b) of this section, this part prescribes rules governing—

(1) Air taxi operations conducted under the exemption authority of Part 298 of this title;

(2) The transportation of mail by aircraft conducted under a postal service contract awarded under section 5402c of Title 39, United States Code;

(3) The carriage in air commerce of persons or property for compensation or hire as a commercial operator (not an air carrier) in aircraft having a maximum seating capacity of less than 20 passengers or a maximum payload capacity of less than 6,000 pounds, or the carriage in air commerce of persons or property in common carriage operations solely between points entirely within any state of the United States in aircraft having a maximum seating capacity of 30 seats or less or a maximum payload capacity of 7,500 pounds or less; and

(4) Each person who is on board an aircraft being operated under this part.

(b) This part does not apply to—

(1) Student instruction;

(2) Nonstop sightseeing flights that begin and end at the same airport, and are conducted within a 25 statute mile radius of that airport;

(3) Ferry or training flights;

(4) Aerial work operations, including—

(i) Crop dusting, seeding, spraying, and bird chasing;

(ii) Banner towing;

(iii) Aerial photography or survey;

(iv) Fire fighting;

(v) Helicopter operations in construction or repair work (but not including transportation to and from the site of operations); and

(vi) Powerline or pipeline patrol, or similar types of patrol approved by the Administrator;

(5) Sightseeing flights conducted in hot air balloons;

(6) Nonstop flights conducted within a 25 statute mile radius of the airport of takeoff carrying persons for the purpose of intentional parachute jumps;

(7) Helicopter flights conducted within a 25 statute mile radius of the airport of takeoff, if—

(i) Not more than two passengers are carried in the helicopter in addition to the required flight crew;

(ii) Each flight is made under VFR during the day;

(iii) The helicopter used is certificated in the standard category and complies with the 100-hour inspection requirements of Part 91 of this chapter;

(iv) The operator notifies the FAA Flight Standards District Office responsible for the geographic area concerned at least 72 hours before each flight and furnishes any essential information that the office requests;

(v) The number of flights does not exceed a total of six in any calendar year;

(vi) Each flight has been approved by the Administrator; and

(vii) Cargo is not carried in or on the helicopter;

(8) Operations conducted under Part 133 or 375 of this title;

(9) Emergency mail service conducted under section 405(h) of the Federal Aviation Act of 1958; or

(10) This part does not apply to operations conducted under the provisions of § 91.59.

[Doc. No. 16097, 43 FR 46783, Oct. 10, 1978, as amended by Amdt. 135-5, 45 FR 43162, June 26, 1980; Amdt. 135-7, 45 FR 67235, Oct. 9, 1980; Amdt. 135-20, 51 FR 40709, Nov. 7, 1986]

§ 135.2 Air taxi operations with large aircraft.

(a) Except as provided in paragraph (d) of this section, no person may conduct air taxi operations in large aircraft under an individual exemption and authorization issued by the Civil Aeronautics Board or under the exemption authority of Part 298 of this title, unless that person—

(1) Complies with the certification requirements for supplemental air carriers in Part 121 of this chapter, except that the person need not obtain, and that person is not eligible for, a certificate under that part; and

(2) Conducts those operations under the rules of Part 121 of this chapter that apply to supplemental air carriers.

However, the Administrator may issue operations specifications which require an operator to comply with the rules of Part 121 of this chapter that apply to domestic or flag air carriers, as appropriate, in place of the rules required by paragraph (a)(2) of this section, if the Administrator determines compliance with those rules is necessary to provide an appropriate level of safety for the operation.

(b) The holder of an operating certificate issued under this part who is required to comply with Subpart L of Part 121 of this chapter, under paragraph (a) of this section, may perform and approve maintenance, preventive maintenance, and alterations on aircraft having a maximum passenger seating configuration, excluding any pilot seat, of 30 seats or less and a maximum payload capacity of 7,500 pounds or less as provided in that subpart. The aircraft so maintained shall be identified by registration number in the operations specifications of the certificate holder using the aircraft.

(c) Operations that are subject to paragraph (a) of this section are not subject to §§ 135.21 through 135.43 of Subpart A and Subparts B through J of this part. Seaplanes used in operations that are subject to paragraph (a) of this section are not subject to § 121.291(a) of this chapter.

(d) Operations conducted with aircraft having a maximum passenger seating configuration, excluding any pilot seat, of 30 seats or less, and a maximum payload capacity of 7,500 pounds or less shall be conducted under the rules of this part. However, a certificate holder who is conducting operations on December 1, 1978, in aircraft described in this paragraph may continue to operate under paragraph (a) of this section.

(e) For the purposes of this part—

(1) "Maximum payload capacity" means:

(i) For an aircraft for which a maximum zero fuel weight is prescribed in FAA technical specifications, the maximum zero fuel weight, less empty weight, less all justifiable aircraft equipment, and less the operating load (consisting of minimum flight crew, foods and beverages and supplies and equipment related to foods and beverages, but not including disposable fuel or oil);

(ii) For all other aircraft, the maximum certificated takeoff weight of an aircraft, less the empty weight, less all justifiable aircraft equipment, and less the operating load (consisting of minimum fuel load, oil, and flight crew). The allowance for the weight of the crew, oil, and fuel is as follows:

(A) Crew—200 pounds for each crewmember required under this chapter.

(B) Oil—350 pounds.

(C) Fuel—the minimum weight of fuel required under this chapter for a flight between domestic points 174 nautical miles apart under VFR weather conditions that does not involve extended overwater operations.

(2) "Empty weight" means the weight of the airframe, engines, propellers, rotors, and fixed equipment. Empty weight excludes the weight of the crew and payload, but includes the weight of all fixed ballast, unusable fuel supply, undrainable oil, total quantity of engine coolant, and total quantity of hydraulic fluid.

(3) "Maximum zero fuel weight" means the maximum permissible weight of an aircraft with no disposable fuel or oil. The zero fuel weight figure may be found in either the aircraft type certificate data sheet or the approved Aircraft Flight Manual, or both.

(4) For the purposes of this paragraph, "justifiable aircraft equipment"

means any equipment necessary for the operation of the aircraft. It does not include equipment or ballast specifically installed, permanently or otherwise, for the purpose of altering the empty weight of an aircraft to meet the maximum payload capacity specified in paragraph (d) of this section.

§ 135.3 Rules applicable to operations subject to this part.

Each person operating an aircraft in operations under this part shall—

(a) While operating inside the United States, comply with the applicable rules of this chapter; and

(b) While operating outside the United States, comply with Annex 2, Rules of the Air, to the Convention on International Civil Aviation or the regulations of any foreign country, whichever applies, and with any rules of Parts 61 and 91 of this chapter and this part that are more restrictive than that Annex or those regulations and that can be complied with without violating that Annex or those regulations. Annex 2 is incorporated by reference in § 91.1(c) of this chapter.

§ 135.5 Certificate and operations specifications required.

No person may operate an aircraft under this part without, or in violation of, an air taxi/commercial operator (ATCO) operating certificate and appropriate operations specifications issued under this part, or, for operations with large aircraft having a maximum passenger seating configuration, excluding any pilot seat, of more than 30 seats, or a maximum payload capacity of more than 7,500 pounds, without, or in violation of, appropriate operations specifications issued under Part 121 of this chapter.

§ 135.7 Applicability of rules to unauthorized operators.

The rules in this part which apply to a person certificated under § 135.5 also apply to a person who engages in any operation governed by this part without an appropriate certificate and operations specifications required by § 135.5.

§ 135.9 Duration of certificate.

(a) An ATCO operating certificate is effective until surrendered, suspended or revoked. The holder of an ATCO operating certificate that is suspended or revoked shall return it to the Administrator.

(b) Except as provided in paragraphs (c) and (d) of this section, an ATCO operating certificate in effect on December 1, 1978, expires on February 1, 1979. The certificate holder must continue to conduct operations under Part 135 and the operations specifications in effect on November 30, 1978, until the certificate expires.

(c) If the certificate holder applies before February 1, 1979, for new operations specifications under this part, the operating certificate held continues in effect and the certificate holder must continue operations under Part 135 and operations specifications in effect on November 30, 1978, until the earliest of the following—

(1) The date on which new operations specifications are issued; or

(2) The date on which the Administrator notifies the certificate holder that the application is denied; or

(3) August 1, 1979.

If new operations specifications are issued under paragraph (c)(1) of this section, the ATCO operating certificate continues in effect until surrendered, suspended or revoked under paragraph (a) of this section.

(d) A certificate holder may obtain an extension of the expiration date in paragraph (c) of this section, but not beyond December 1, 1979, from the Director, Flight Standards Service, if before July 1, 1979, the certificate holder—

(1) Shows that due to the circumstances beyond its control it cannot comply by the expiration date; and

(2) Submits a schedule for compliance, acceptable to the Director, indicating that compliance will be achieved at the earliest practicable date.

(e) The holder of an ATCO operating certificate that expires, under paragraph (b), (c), or (d) of this section, shall return it to the Administrator.

§ 135.10 Compliance dates for certain rules.

After January 2, 1991, no certificate holder may use a person as a flight crewmember unless that person has completed the windshear ground training required by §§ 135.345(b)(6) and 135.351(b)(2) of this part.

(a) A certificate holder or pilot is allowed until June 1, 1979, to comply with the following sections:

(1) A third bank and pitch indicator (artificial horizon) (§ 135.149(c)).

(2) Shoulder harness at flight crewmember stations (§ 135.171(a)).

(3) Airline transport pilot certificate (§ 135.243(a)).

(b) A certificate holder is allowed until December 1, 1979, to comply with the following sections:

(1) Cockpit voice recorder (§ 135.151).

(2) Ground proximity warning system or other approved system (§ 135.153).

(3) Airborne thunderstorm detection equipment (§ 135.173).

(c) A certificate holder or pilot is allowed until August 1, 1981, to comply with the instrument rating requirements of § 135.243(b)(3).

(d) A certificate holder or pilot may obtain an extension of the compliance date in paragraph (a) or (b) of this section, but not beyond December 1, 1980, from the Director, of Flight Operations, if before the compliance date in paragraph (a) or (b) of this section—

(1) The certificate holder or pilot shows that due to the circumstances beyond its control they cannot comply by that date; and

(2) The certificate holder or pilot has submitted before that date a schedule for compliance, acceptable to the Director, indicating that compliance will be achieved at the earliest practicable date.

§ 135.11 Application and issue of certificate and operations specifications.

(a) An application for an ATCO operating certificate and appropriate operations specifications is made on a form and in a manner prescribed by the Administrator and filed with the FAA Flight Standards District Office that has jurisdiction over the area in which the applicant's principal business office is located.

(b) An applicant who meets the requirements of this part is entitled to—

(1) An ATCO operating certificate containing all business names under which the certificate holder may conduct operations and the address of each business office used by the certificate holder; and

(2) Separate operations specifications, issued to the certificate holder, containing:

(i) The type and area of operations authorized.

(ii) The category and class of aircraft that may be used in those operations.

(iii) Registration numbers and types of aircraft that are subject to an airworthiness maintenance program required by § 135.411(a)(2), including time limitations or standards for determining time limitations, for overhauls, inspections, and checks for airframes, aircraft engines, propellers, rotors, appliances, and emergency equipment.

(iv) Registration numbers of aircraft that are to be inspected under an approved aircraft inspection program under § 135.419.

(v) Additional maintenance items required by the Administrator under § 135.421.

(vi) Any authorized deviation from this part.

(vii) Any other items the Administrator may require or allow to meet any particular situation.

(c) No person holding operations specifications issued under this part may list on its operations specifications or on the current list of aircraft required by § 135.63(a)(3) any airplane listed on operations specifications issued under Part 125.

[Doc. No. 16097, 43 FR 467883, Oct. 10, 1978, as amended by Amdt. 135-24, 52 FR 20029, May 28, 1987]

§ 135.13 Eligibility for certificate and operations specifications.

(a) To be eligible for an ATCO operating certificate and appropriate operations specifications, a person must—

(1) Be a citizen of the United States, a partnership of which each member is a citizen of the United States, or a corporation or association created or organized under the laws of the United States or any state, territory, or possession of the United States, of which the president and two-thirds or more of the board of directors and other managing officers are citizens of the United States and in which at least 75 percent of the voting interest is owned or controlled by citizens of the United States or one of its possessions; and

(2) Show, to the satisfaction of the Administrator, that the person is able to conduct each kind of operation for which the person seeks authorization in compliance with applicable regulations; and

(3) Hold any economic authority that may be required by the Civil Aeronautics Board.

However, no person holding a commercial operator operating certificate issued under Part 121 of this chapter is eligible for an ATCO operating certificate unless the person shows to the satisfaction of the Administrator that the person's contract carriage business in large aircraft, having a maximum passenger seating configuration, excluding any pilot seat, of more than 30 seats or a maximum payload capacity of more than 7,500 pounds, will not result directly or indirectly from the person's air taxi business.

(b) The Administrator may deny any applicant a certificate under this part if the Administrator finds—

(1) That an air carrier or commercial operator operating certificate under Part 121 or an ATCO operating certificate previously issued to the applicant was revoked; or

(2) That a person who was employed in a position similar to general manager, director of operations, director of maintenance, chief pilot, or chief inspector, or who has exercised control with respect to any ATCO operating certificate holder, air carrier, or commercial operator whose operating certificate has been revoked, will be employed in any of those positions or a similar position, or will be in control of or have a substantial ownership interest in the applicant, and that the person's employment or control contributed materially to the reasons for revoking that certificate.

§ 135.15 Amendment of certificate.

(a) The Administrator may amend an ATCO operating certificate—

(1) On the Administrator's own initiative, under section 609 of the Federal Aviation Act of 1958 (49 U.S.C. 1429) and Part 13 of this chapter; or

(2) Upon application by the holder of that certificate.

(b) The certificate holder must file an application to amend an ATCO operating certificate at least 15 days before the date proposed by the applicant for the amendment to become effective, unless a shorter filing period is approved. The application must be on a form and in a manner prescribed by the Administrator and must be submitted to the FAA Flight Standards District Office charged with the overall inspection of the certificate holder.

(c) The FAA Flight Standards District Office charged with the overall inspection of the certificate holder grants an amendment to the ATCO operating certificate if it is determined that safety in air commerce and the public interest allow that amendment.

(d) Within 30 days after receiving a refusal to amend the operating certificate, the certificate holder may petition the Director, Flight Standards Service, to reconsider the request.

§ 135.17 Amendment of operations specifications.

(a) The FAA Flight Standards District Office charged with the overall inspection of the certificate holder may amend any operations specifications issued under this part if—

(1) It determines that safety in air commerce requires that amendment; or

(2) Upon application by the holder, that District Office determines that safety in air commerce allows that amendment.

(b) The certificate holder must file an application to amend operations specifications at least 15 days before the date proposed by the applicant for the amendment to become effective, unless a shorter filing period is approved. The application must be on a form and in a manner prescribed by the Administrator and be submitted to the FAA Flight Standards District

Office charged with the overall inspection of the certificate holder.

(c) Within 30 days after a notice of refusal to approve a holder's application for amendment is received, the holder may petition the Director of Airworthiness, for amendments pertaining to airworthiness or the Director of Flight Operations for amendments pertaining to flight operations to reconsider the refusal to amend.

(d) When the FAA Flight Standards District Office charged with the overall inspection of the certificate holder amends operations specifications, that District Office gives notice in writing to the holder of a proposed amendment to the operations specifications, fixing a period of not less than 7 days within which the holder may submit written information, views, and arguments concerning the proposed amendment. After consideration of all relevant matter presented, that District Office notifies the holder of any amendment adopted, or a rescission of the notice. The amendment becomes effective not less than 30 days after the holder receives notice of the adoption of the amendment, unless the holder petitions the Director of Airworthiness for amendments pertaining to airworthiness or the Director of Flight Operations for amendments pertaining to flight operations for reconsideration of the amendment. In that case, the effective date of the amendment is stayed pending a decision by the Director. If the Director finds there is an emergency requiring immediate action as to safety in air commerce that makes the provisions of this paragraph impracticable or contrary to the public interest, the Director notifies the certificate holder that the amendment is effective on the date of receipt, without previous notice.

[Doc. No 16097, 43 FR 46783, Oct. 10, 1978, as amended by Amdt. 135-6, 45 FR 47838, July 17, 1980]

§ 135.19 Emergency operations.

(a) In an emergency involving the safety of persons or property, the certificate holder may deviate from the rules of this part relating to aircraft and equipment and weather minimums to the extent required to meet that emergency.

(b) In an emergency involving the safety of persons or property, the pilot in command may deviate from the rules of this part to the extent required to meet that emergency.

(c) Each person who, under the authority of this section, deviates from a rule of this part shall, within 10 days, excluding Saturdays, Sundays, and Federal holidays, after the deviation, send to the FAA Flight Standards District Office charged with the overall inspection of the certificate holder a complete report of the aircraft operation involved, including a description of the deviation and reasons for it.

§ 135.21   Manual requirements.

(a) Each certificate holder, other than one who uses only one pilot in the certificate holder's operations, shall prepare and keep current a manual setting forth the certificate holder's procedures and policies acceptable to the Administrator. This manual must be used by the certificate holder's flight, ground, and maintenance personnel in conducting its operations. However, the Administrator may authorize a deviation from this paragraph if the Administrator finds that, because of the limited size of the operation, all or part of the manual is not necessary for guidance of flight, ground, or maintenance personnel.

(b) Each certificate holder shall maintain at least one copy of the manual at its principal operations base.

(c) The manual must not be contrary to any applicable Federal regulations, foreign regulation applicable to the certificate holder's operations in foreign countries, or the certificate holder's operating certificate or operations specifications.

(d) A copy of the manual, or appropriate portions of the manual (and changes and additions) shall be made available to maintenance and ground operations personnel by the certificate holder and furnished to—

(1) Its flight crewmembers; and

(2) Representatives of the Administrator assigned to the certificate holder.

(e) Each employee of the certificate holder to whom a manual or appropriate portions of it are furnished under paragraph (d)(1) of this section shall keep it up to date with the changes and additions furnished to them.

(f) Except as provided in paragraph (g) of this section, each certificate holder shall carry appropriate parts of the manual on each aircraft when away from the principal operations base. The appropriate parts must be available for use by ground or flight personnel.

(g) If a certificate holder conducts aircraft inspections or maintenance at specified stations where it keeps the approved inspection program manual, it is not required to carry the manual aboard the aircraft en route to those stations.

[Doc. No. 16097, 43 FR 46783, Oct. 10, 1978, as amended by Amdt. 135-18, 47 FR 33396, Aug. 2, 1982]

§ 135.23   Manual contents.

Each manual shall have the date of the last revision on each revised page. The manual must include—

(a) The name of each management person required under § 135.37(a) who is authorized to act for the certificate holder, the person's assigned area of responsibility, the person's duties, responsibilities, and authority, and the name and title of each person authorized to exercise operational control under § 135.77;

(b) Procedures for ensuring compliance with aircraft weight and balance limitations and, for multiengine aircraft, for determining compliance with § 135.185;

(c) Copies of the certificate holder's operations specifications or appropriate extracted information, including area of operations authorized, category and class of aircraft authorized, crew complements, and types of operations authorized;

(d) Procedures for complying with accident notification requirements;

(e) Procedures for ensuring that the pilot in command knows that required airworthiness inspections have been made and that the aircraft has been approved for return to service in compliance with applicable maintenance requirements;

(f) Procedures for reporting and recording mechanical irregularities that come to the attention of the pilot in command before, during, and after completion of a flight;

(g) Procedures to be followed by the pilot in command for determining that mechanical irregularities or defects reported for previous flights have been corrected or that correction has been deferred;

(h) Procedures to be followed by the pilot in command to obtain maintenance, preventive maintenance, and servicing of the aircraft at a place where previous arrangements have not been made by the operator, when the pilot is authorized to so act for the operator;

(i) Procedures under § 135.179 for the release for, or continuation of, flight if any item of equipment required for the particular type of operation becomes inoperative or unserviceable en route;

(j) Procedures for refueling aircraft, eliminating fuel contamination, protecting from fire (including electrostatic protection), and supervising and protecting passengers during refueling;

(k) Procedures to be followed by the pilot in command in the briefing under § 135.117;

(l) Flight locating procedures, when applicable;

(m) Procedures for ensuring compliance with emergency procedures, including a list of the functions assigned each category of required crewmembers in connection with an emergency and emergency evacuation duties under § 135.123;

(n) En route qualification procedures for pilots, when applicable;

(o) The approved aircraft inspection program, when applicable;

(p) Procedures and instructions to enable personnel to recognize hazardous materials, as defined in Title 49 CFR, and if these materials are to be carried, stored, or handled, procedures and instructions for—

(1) Accepting shipment of hazardous material required by Title 49 CFR, to assure proper packaging, marking, labeling, shipping documents, compat-

ibility of articles, and instructions on their loading, storage, and handling;

(2) Notification and reporting hazardous material incidents as required by Title 49 CFR; and

(3) Notification of the pilot in command when there are hazardous materials aboard, as required by Title 49 CFR;

(q) Procedures for the evacuation of persons who may need the assistance of another person to move expeditiously to an exit if an emergency occurs; and

(r) Other procedures and policy instructions regarding the certificate holder's operations, that are issued by the certificate holder.

[Doc. No. 16097, 43 FR 46783, Oct. 10, 1978, as amended by Amdt. 135–20, 51 FR 40709, Nov. 7, 1986]

§ 135.25   Aircraft requirements.

(a) Except as provided in paragraph (d) of this section, no certificate holder may operate an aircraft under this part unless that aircraft—

(1) Is registered as a civil aircraft of the United States and carries an appropriate and current airworthiness certificate issued under this chapter; and

(2) Is in an airworthy condition and meets the applicable airworthiness requirements of this chapter, including those relating to identification and equipment.

(b) Each certificate holder must have the exclusive use of at least one aircraft that meets the requirements for at least one kind of operation authorized in the certificate holder's operations specifications. In addition, for each kind of operation for which the certificate holder does not have the exclusive use of an aircraft, the certificate holder must have available for use under a written agreement (including arrangements for performing required maintenance) at least one aircraft that meets the requirements for that kind of operation. However, this paragraph does not prohibit the operator from using or authorizing the use of the aircraft for other than air taxi or commercial operations and does not require the certificate holder to have exclusive use of all aircraft that the certificate holder uses.

(c) For the purposes of paragraph (b) of this section, a person has exclusive use of an aircraft if that person has the sole possession, control, and use of it for flight, as owner, or has a written agreement (including arrangements for performing required maintenance), in effect when the aircraft is operated, giving the person that possession, control, and use for at least 6 consecutive months.

(d) A certificate holder may operate in common carriage, and for the carriage of mail, a civil aircraft which is leased or chartered to it without crew and is registered in a country which is a party to the Convention on International Civil Aviation if—

(1) The aircraft carries an appropriate airworthiness certificate issued by the country of registration and meets the registration and identification requirements of that country;

(2) The aircraft is of a type design which is approved under a U.S. type certificate and complies with all of the requirements of this chapter (14 CFR Chapter I) that would be applicable to that aircraft were it registered in the United States, including the requirements which must be met for issuance of a U.S. standard airworthiness certificate (including type design conformity, condition for safe operation, and the noise, fuel venting, and engine emission requirements of this chapter), except that a U.S. registration certificate and a U.S. standard airworthiness certificate will not be issued for the aircraft;

(3) The aircraft is operated by U.S.-certificated airmen employed by the certificate holder; and

(4) The certificate holder files a copy of the aircraft lease or charter agreement with the FAA Aircraft Registry, Department of Transportation, 6400 South MacArthur Boulevard, Oklahoma City, Oklahoma (Mailing address: P.O. Box 25504, Oklahoma City, Oklahoma 73125).

[Doc. No. 16097, 43 FR 46783, Oct. 10, 1978, as amended by Amdt. 135-8, 45 FR 68649, Oct. 16, 1980]

§ 135.27 Business office and operations base.

(a) Each certificate holder shall maintain a principal business office.

(b) Each certificate holder shall, before establishing or changing the location of any business office or operations base, except a temporary operations base, notify in writing the FAA Flight Standards District Office charged with the overall inspection of the certificate holder.

(c) No certificate holder who establishes or changes the location of any business office or operations base, except a temporary operations base, may operate an aircraft under this part unless the certificate holder complies with paragraph (b) of this section.

§ 135.29 Use of business names.

No certificate holder may operate an aircraft under this part under a business name that is not on the certificate holder's operating certificate.

§ 135.31 Advertising.

No certificate holder may advertise or otherwise offer to perform operations subject to this part that are not authorized by the certificate holder's operating certificate and operations specifications.

§ 135.33 Area limitations on operations.

(a) No person may operate an aircraft in a geographical area that is not specifically authorized by appropriate operations specifications issued under this part.

(b) No person may operate an aircraft in a foreign country unless that person is authorized to do so by that country.

§ 135.35 Termination of operations.

Within 30 days after a certificate holder terminates operations under this part, the operating certificate and operations specifications must be surrendered by the certificate holder to the FAA Flight Standards District Office charged with the overall inspection of the certificate holder.

§ 135.37 Management personnel required.

(a) Each certificate holder, other than one who uses only one pilot in the certificate holder's operations, must have enough qualified management personnel in the following or equivalent positions to ensure safety in its operations:

(1) Director of operations.

(2) Chief pilot.

(3) Director of maintenance.

(b) Upon application by the certificate holder, the Administrator may approve different positions or numbers of positions than those listed in paragraph (a) of this section for a particular operation if the certificate holder shows that it can perform its operations safely under the direction of fewer or different categories of management personnel.

(c) Each certificate holder shall—

(1) Set forth the duties, responsibilities, and authority of the personnel required by this section in the manual required by § 135.21;

(2) List in the manual required by § 135.21 the name of the person or persons assigned to those positions; and

(3) Within 10 working days, notify the FAA Flight Standards District Office charged with the overall inspection of the certificate holder of any change made in the assignment of persons to the listed positions.

[Doc. No. 16097, 43 FR 46783, Oct. 10, 1978, as amended by Amdt. 135–18, 47 FR 33396, Aug. 2, 1982]

§ 135.39 Management personnel qualifications.

(a) *Director of operations.* No person may serve as director of operations under § 135.37(a) unless that person knows the contents of the manual required by § 135.21, the operations specifications, the provisions of this part and other applicable regulations necessary for the proper performance of the person's duties and responsibilities and:

(1) The director of operations for a certificate holder conducting any operations for which the pilot in command is required to hold an airline transport pilot certificate must—

(i) Hold or have held an airline transport pilot certificate; and

(ii) Have at least 3 years of experience as pilot in command of an aircraft operated under this part, Part 121 or Part 127 of this chapter; or

(iii) Have at least 3 years of experience as director of operations with a certificate holder operating under this part, Part 121 or Part 127 of this chapter.

(2) The director of operations for a certificate holder who is not conducting any operation for which the pilot in command is required to hold an airline transport pilot certificate must—

(i) Hold or have held a commercial pilot certificate; and

(ii) Have at least 3 years of experience as a pilot in command of an aircraft operated under this part, Part 121 or Part 127 of this chapter; or

(iii) Have at least 3 years of experience as director of operations with a certificate holder operating under this part, Part 121 or Part 127 of this chapter.

(b) *Chief pilot.* No person may serve as chief pilot under § 135.37(a) unless that person knows the contents of the manual required by § 135.21, the operations specifications, the provisions of this part and other applicable regulations necessary for the proper performance of the person's duties, and:

(1) The chief pilot of a certificate holder conducting any operation for which the pilot in command is required to hold an airline transport pilot certificate must—

(i) Hold a current airline transport pilot certificate with appropriate ratings for at least one of the types of aircraft used; and

(ii) Have at least 3 years of experience as a pilot in command of an aircraft under this part, Part 121 or Part 127 of this chapter.

(2) The chief pilot of a certificate holder who is not conducting any operation for which the pilot in command is required to hold an airline transport pilot certificate must—

(i) Hold a current, commercial pilot certificate with an instrument rating. If an instrument rating is not required for the pilot in command under this part, the chief pilot must hold a current, commercial pilot certificate; and

(ii) Have at least 3 years of experience as a pilot in command of an aircraft under this part, Part 121 or Part 127 of this chapter.

(c) *Director of maintenance.* No person may serve as a director of maintenance under § 135.37(a) unless that person knows the maintenance sections of the certificate holder's manual, the operations specifications, the provisions of this part and other applicable regulations necessary for the proper performance of the person's duties, and—

(1) Holds a mechanic certificate with both airframe and powerplant ratings; and

(2) Has at least 3 years of maintenance experience as a certificated mechanic on aircraft, including, at the time of appointment as director of maintenance, the recent experience requirements of § 65.83 of this chapter in the same category and class of aircraft as used by the certificate holder, or at least 3 years of experience with a certificated airframe repair station, including 1 year in the capacity of approving aircraft for return to service.

(d) Deviation from this section may be authorized if the person has had equivalent aeronautical experience. The Chief of the Flight Standards Division in the region of the certificate holding district office may authorize a deviation for the director of operations, chief pilot, and the director of maintenance.

[Doc. No. 16097, 43 FR 46783, Oct. 10, 1978, as amended by Amdt. 135-18, 47 FR 33396, Aug. 2, 1982; Amdt. 133-20, 51 FR 40709, Nov. 7, 1986]

§ 135.41 Carriage of narcotic drugs, marihuana, and depressant or stimulant drugs or substances.

If the holder of a certificate issued under this part allows any aircraft owned or leased by that holder to be engaged in any operation that the certificate holder knows to be in violation of § 91.12(a) of this chapter, that operation is a basis for suspending or revoking the certificate.

§ 135.43 Crewmember certificate: International operations: Application and issue.

(a) This section provides for the issuance of a crewmember certificate to United States citizens who are employed by certificate holders as crewmembers on United States registered aircraft engaged in international air commerce. The purpose of the certificate is to facilitate the entry and clearance of those crewmembers into ICAO contracting states. They are issued under Annex 9, as amended, to the Convention on International Civil Aviation.

(b) An application for a crewmember certificate is made on FAA Form 8060-6, "Application for Crewmember Certificate," to the FAA Flight Standards District Office charged with the overall inspection of the certificate holder by whom the applicant is employed. The certificate is issued on FAA Form 8060-42, "Crewmember Certificate."

(c) The holder of a certificate issued under this section, or the certificate holder by whom the holder is employed, shall surrender the certificate for cancellation at the nearest FAA Flight Standards District Office or submit it for cancellation to the Airmen Certification Branch, AAC-260, P.O. Box 25082, Oklahoma City, Oklahoma 73125, at the termination of the holder's employment with that certificate holder.

Subpart B—Flight Operations

§ 135.61 General.

This subpart prescribes rules, in addition to those in Part 91 of this chapter, that apply to operations under this part.

§ 135.63 Recordkeeping requirements.

(a) Each certificate holder shall keep at its principal business office or at other places approved by the Administrator, and shall make available for inspection by the Administrator the following—

(1) The certificate holder's operating certificate;

(2) The certificate holder's operations specifications;

(3) A current list of the aircraft used or available for use in operations under this part and the operations for which each is equipped; and

(4) An individual record of each pilot used in operations under this part, including the following information:

(i) The full name of the pilot.

(ii) The pilot certificate (by type and number) and ratings that the pilot holds.

(iii) The pilot's aeronautical experience in sufficient detail to determine the pilot's qualifications to pilot aircraft in operations under this part.

(iv) The pilot's current duties and the date of the pilot's assignment to those duties.

(v) The effective date and class of the medical certificate that the pilot holds.

(vi) The date and result of each of the initial and recurrent competency tests and proficiency and route checks required by this part and the type of aircraft flown during that test or check.

(vii) The pilot's flight time in sufficient detail to determine compliance with the flight time limitations of this part.

(viii) The pilot's check pilot authorization, if any.

(ix) Any action taken concerning the pilot's release from employment for physical or professional disqualification.

(x) The date of the completion of the initial phase and each recurrent phase of the training required by this part.

(b) Each certificate holder shall keep each record required by paragraph (a)(3) of this section for at least 6 months, and each record required by paragraph (a)(4) of this section for at least 12 months, after it is made.

(c) For multiengine aircraft, each certificate holder is responsible for the preparation and accuracy of a load manifest in duplicate containing information concerning the loading of the aircraft. The manifest must be prepared before each takeoff and must include:

(1) The number of passengers;

(2) The total weight of the loaded aircraft;

(3) The maximum allowable takeoff weight for that flight;

(4) The center of gravity limits;

(5) The center of gravity of the loaded aircraft, except that the actual center of gravity need not be computed if the aircraft is loaded according to a loading schedule or other approved method that ensures that the center of gravity of the loaded aircraft is within approved limits. In those cases, an entry shall be made on the manifest indicating that the center of gravity is within limits according to a loading schedule or other approved method;

(6) The registration number of the aircraft or flight number;

(7) The origin and destination; and

(8) Identification of crew members and their crew position assignments.

(d) The pilot in command of an aircraft for which a load manifest must be prepared shall carry a copy of the completed load manifest in the aircraft to its destination. The certificate holder shall keep copies of completed load manifests for at least 30 days at its principal operations base, or at another location used by it and approved by the Administrator.

§ 135.65 Reporting mechanical irregularities.

(a) Each certificate holder shall provide an aircraft maintenance log to be carried on board each aircraft for recording or deferring mechanical irregularities and their correction.

(b) The pilot in command shall enter or have entered in the aircraft maintenance log each mechanical irregularity that comes to the pilot's attention during flight time. Before each flight, the pilot in command shall, if the pilot does not already know, determine the status of each irregularity entered in the maintenance log at the end of the preceding flight.

(c) Each person who takes corrective action or defers action concerning a reported or observed failure or malfunction of an airframe, powerplant, propeller, rotor, or applicance, shall record the action taken in the aircraft maintenance log under the applicable maintenance requirements of this chapter.

(d) Each certificate holder shall establish a procedure for keeping copies of the aircraft maintenance log required by this section in the aircraft for access by appropriate personnel and shall include that procedure in the manual required by § 135.21.

§ 135.67 Reporting potentially hazardous meteorological conditions and irregularities of communications or navigation facilities.

Whenever a pilot encounters a potentially hazardous meteorological condition or an irregularity in a ground communications or navigational facility in flight, the knowledge of which the pilot considers essential to the safety of other flights, the pilot shall notify an appropriate ground radio station as soon as practicable.

[Doc. No. 16097, 43 FR 46783, Oct. 1, 1978, as amended at 44 FR 26737, May 7, 1979]

§ 135.69 Restriction or suspension of operations: Continuation of flight in an emergency.

(a) During operations under this part, if a certificate holder or pilot in command knows of conditions, including airport and runway conditions, that are a hazard to safe operations, the certificate holder or pilot in command, as the case may be, shall restrict or suspend operations as necessary until those conditions are corrected.

(b) No pilot in command may allow a flight to continue toward any airport of intended landing under the conditions set forth in paragraph (a) of this section, unless, in the opinion of the pilot in command, the conditions that are a hazard to safe operations may reasonably be expected to be corrected by the estimated time of arrival or, unless there is no safer procedure. In the latter event, the continuation toward that airport is an emergency situation under § 135.19.

§ 135.71 Airworthiness check.

The pilot in command may not begin a flight unless the pilot determines that the airworthiness inspections required by § 91.169 of this chapter, or § 135.419, whichever is applicable, have been made.

§ 135.73 Inspections and tests.

Each certificate holder and each person employed by the certificate holder shall allow the Administrator, at any time or place, to make inspections or tests (including en route inspections) to determine the holder's compliance with the Federal Aviation Act of 1958, applicable regulations, and the certificate holder's operating certificate, and operations specifications.

§ 135.75 Inspectors credentials: admission to pilots' compartment: Forward observer's seat.

(a) Whenever, in performing the duties of conducting an inspection, an FAA inspector presents an Aviation Safety Inspector credential, FAA Form 110A, to the pilot in command of an aircraft operated by the certificate holder, the inspector must be given free and uninterrupted access to the pilot compartment of that aircraft. However, this paragraph does not limit the emergency authority of the pilot in command to exclude any person from the pilot compartment in the interest of safety.

(b) A forward observer's seat on the flight deck, or forward passenger seat with headset or speaker must be provided for use by the Administrator while conducting en route inspections. The suitability of the location of the seat and the headset or speaker for use in conducting en route inspections is determined by the Administrator.

§ 135.77 Responsibility for operational control.

Each certificate holder is responsible for operational control and shall list, in the manual required by § 135.21, the name and title of each person authorized by it to exercise operational control.

§ 135.79 Flight locating requirements.

(a) Each certificate holder must have procedures established for locating each flight, for which an FAA flight plan is not filed, that—

(1) Provide the certificate holder with at least the information required to be included in a VFR flight plan;

(2) Provide for timely notification of an FAA facility or search and rescue facility, if an aircraft is overdue or missing; and

(3) Provide the certificate holder with the location, date, and estimated time for reestablishing radio or telephone communications, if the flight

will operate in an area where communications cannot be maintained.

(b) Flight locating information shall be retained at the certificate holder's principal place of business, or at other places designated by the certificate holder in the flight locating procedures, until the completion of the flight.

(c) Each certificate holder shall furnish the representative of the Administrator assigned to it with a copy of its flight locating procedures and any changes or additions, unless those procedures are included in a manual required under this part.

§ 135.81 Informing personnel of operational information and appropriate changes.

Each certificate holder shall inform each person in its employment of the operations specifications that apply to that person's duties and responsibilities and shall make available to each pilot in the certificate holder's employ the following materials in current form:

(a) Airman's Information Manual (Alaska Supplement in Alaska and Pacific Chart Supplement in Pacific-Asia Regions) or a commercial publication that contains the same information.

(b) This part and Part 91 of this chapter.

(c) Aircraft Equipment Manuals, and Aircraft Flight Manual or equivalent.

(d) For foreign operations, the International Flight Information Manual or a commercial publication that contains the same information concerning the pertinent operational and entry requirements of the foreign country or countries involved.

§ 135.83 Operating information required.

(a) The operator of an aircraft must provide the following materials, in current and appropriate form, accessible to the pilot at the pilot station, and the pilot shall use them:

(1) A cockpit checklist.

(2) For multiengine aircraft or for aircraft with retractable landing gear, an emergency cockpit checklist containing the procedures required by paragraph (c) of this section, as appropriate.

(3) Pertinent aeronautical charts.

(4) For IFR operations, each pertinent navigational en route, terminal area, and approach and letdown chart.

(5) For multiengine aircraft, one-engine-inoperative climb performance data and if the aircraft is approved for use in IFR or over-the-top operations, that data must be sufficient to enable the pilot to determine compliance with § 135.181(a)(2).

(b) Each cockpit checklist required by paragraph (a)(1) of this section must contain the following procedures:

(1) Before starting engines;

(2) Before takeoff;

(3) Cruise;

(4) Before landing;

(5) After landing;

(6) Stopping engines.

(c) Each emergency cockpit checklist required by paragraph (a)(2) of this section must contain the following procedures, as appropriate:

(1) Emergency operation of fuel, hydraulic, electrical, and mechanical systems.

(2) Emergency operation of instruments and controls.

(3) Engine inoperative procedures.

(4) Any other emergency procedures necessary for safety.

§ 135.85 Carriage of persons without compliance with the passenger-carrying provisions of this part.

The following persons may be carried aboard an aircraft without complying with the passenger-carrying requirements of this part:

(a) A crewmember or other employee of the certificate holder.

(b) A person necessary for the safe handling of animals on the aircraft.

(c) A person necessary for the safe handling of hazardous materials (as defined in Subchapter C of Title 49 CFR).

(d) A person performing duty as a security or honor guard accompanying a shipment made by or under the authority of the U.S. Government.

(e) A military courier or a military route supervisor carried by a military cargo contract air carrier or commercial operator in operations under a military cargo contract, if that carriage is specifically authorized by the appropriate military service.

(f) An authorized representative of the Administrator conducting an en route inspection.

(g) A person, authorized by the Administrator, who is performing a duty connected with a cargo operation of the certificate holder.

§ 135.87 Carriage of cargo including carry-on baggage.

No person may carry cargo, including carry-on baggage, in or on any aircraft unless—

(a) It is carried in an approved cargo rack, bin, or compartment installed in or on the aircraft;

(b) It is secured by an approved means; or

(c) It is carried in accordance with each of the following:

(1) For cargo, it is properly secured by a safety belt or other tie-down having enough strength to eliminate the possibility of shifting under all normally anticipated flight and ground conditions, or for carry-on baggage, it is restrained so as to prevent its movement during air turbulence.

(2) It is packaged or covered to avoid possible injury to occupants.

(3) It does not impose any load on seats or on the floor structure that exceeds the load limitation for those components.

(4) It is not located in a position that obstructs the access to, or use of, any required emergency or regular exit, or the use of the aisle between the crew and the passenger compartment, or located in a position that obscures any passenger's view of the "seat belt" sign, "no smoking" sign, or any required exit sign, unless an auxiliary sign or other approved means for proper notification of the passengers is provided.

(5) It is not carried directly above seated occupants.

(6) It is stowed in compliance with this section for takeoff and landing.

(7) For cargo only operations, paragraph (c)(4) of this section does not apply if the cargo is loaded so that at least one emergency or regular exit is available to provide all occupants of the aircraft a means of unobstructed exit from the aircraft if an emergency occurs.

(d) Each passenger seat under which baggage is stowed shall be fitted with a means to prevent articles of baggage stowed under it from sliding under crash impacts severe enough to induce the ultimate inertia forces specified in the emergency landing condition regulations under which the aircraft was type certificated.

(e) When cargo is carried in cargo compartments that are designed to require the physical entry of a crewmember to extinguish any fire that may occur during flight, the cargo must be loaded so as to allow a crewmember to effectively reach all parts of the compartment with the contents of a hand fire extinguisher.

§ 135.89 Pilot requirements: Use of oxygen.

(a) *Unpressurized aircraft.* Each pilot of an unpressurized aircraft shall use oxygen continuously when flying—

(1) At altitudes above 10,000 feet through 12,000 feet MSL for that part of the flight at those altitudes that is of more than 30 minutes duration; and

(2) Above 12,000 feet MSL.

(b) *Pressurized aircraft.* (1) Whenever a pressurized aircraft is operated with the cabin pressure altitude more than 10,000 feet MSL, each pilot shall comply with paragraph (a) of this section.

(2) Whenever a pressurized aircraft is operated at altitudes above 25,000 feet through 35,000 feet MSL, unless each pilot has an approved quick-donning type oxygen mask—

(i) At least one pilot at the controls shall wear, secured and sealed, an oxygen mask that either supplies oxygen at all times or automatically supplies oxygen whenever the cabin pressure altitude exceeds 12,000 feet MSL; and

(ii) During that flight, each other pilot on flight deck duty shall have an oxygen mask, connected to an oxygen supply, located so as to allow immediate placing of the mask on the pilot's face sealed and secured for use.

(3) Whenever a pressurized aircraft is operated at altitudes above 35,000 feet MSL, at least one pilot at the con-

trols shall wear, secured and sealed, an oxygen mask required by paragraph (b)(2)(i) of this section.

(4) If one pilot leaves a pilot duty station of an aircraft when operating at altitudes above 25,000 feet MSL, the remaining pilot at the controls shall put on and use an approved oxygen mask until the other pilot returns to the pilot duty station of the aircraft.

§ 135.91 Oxygen for medical use by passengers.

(a) Except as provided in paragraphs (d) and (e) of this section, no certificate holder may allow the carriage or operation of equipment for the storage, generation or dispensing of medical oxygen unless the unit to be carried is constructed so that all valves, fittings, and gauges are protected from damage during that carriage or operation and unless the following conditions are met—

(1) The equipment must be—

(i) Of an approved type or in conformity with the manufacturing, packaging, marking, labeling, and maintenance requirements of Title 49 CFR Parts 171, 172, and 173, except § 173.24(a)(1);

(ii) When owned by the certificate holder, maintained under the certificate holder's approved maintenance program;

(iii) Free of flammable contaminants on all exterior surfaces; and

(iv) Appropriately secured.

(2) When the oxygen is stored in the form of a liquid, the equipment must have been under the certificate holder's approved maintenance program since its purchase new or since the storage container was last purged.

(3) When the oxygen is stored in the form of a compressed gas as defined in Title 49 CFR 173.300(a)—

(i) When owned by the certificate holder, it must be maintained under its approved maintenance program; and

(ii) The pressure in any oxygen cylinder must not exceed the rated cylinder pressure.

(4) The pilot in command must be advised when the equipment is on board, and when it is intended to be used.

(5) The equipment must be stowed, and each person using the equipment must be seated, so as not to restrict access to or use of any required emergency or regular exit, or of the aisle in the passenger compartment.

(b) No person may smoke and no certificate holder may allow any person to smoke within 10 feet of oxygen storage and dispensing equipment carried under paragraph (a) of this section.

(c) No certificate holder may allow any person other than a person trained in the use of medical oxygen equipment to connect or disconnect oxygen bottles or any other ancillary component while any passenger is aboard the aircraft.

(d) Paragraph (a)(1)(i) of this section does not apply when that equipment is furnished by a professional or medical emergency service for use on board an aircraft in a medical emergency when no other practical means of transportation (including any other properly equipped certificate holder) is reasonably available and the person carried under the medical emergency is accompanied by a person trained in the use of medical oxygen.

(e) Each certificate holder who, under the authority of paragraph (d) of this section, deviates from paragraph (a)(1)(i) of this section under a medical emergency shall, within 10 days, excluding Saturdays, Sundays, and Federal holidays, after the deviation, send to the FAA Flight Standards District Office charged with the overall inspection of the certificate holder a complete report of the operation involved, including a description of the deviation and the reasons for it.

§ 135.93 Autopilot: Minimum altitudes for use.

(a) Except as provided in paragraphs (b), (c), and (d) of this section, no person may use an autopilot at an altitude above the terrain which is less than 500 feet or less than twice the maximum altitude loss specified in the approved Aircraft Flight Manual or equivalent for a malfunction of the autopilot, whichever is higher.

(b) When using an instrument approach facility other than ILS, no person may use an autopilot at an altitude above the terrain that is less than 50 feet below the approved minimum descent altitude for that procedure, or less than twice the maximum loss specified in the approved Airplane Flight Manual or equivalent for a malfunction of the autopilot under approach conditions, whichever is higher.

(c) For ILS approaches, when reported weather conditions are less than the basic weather conditions in § 91.105 of this chapter, no person may use an autopilot with an approach coupler at an altitude above the terrain that is less than 50 feet above the terrain, or the maximum altitude loss specified in the approved Airplane Flight Manual or equivalent for the malfunction of the autopilot with approach coupler, whichever is higher.

(d) Without regard to paragraph (a), (b), or (c) of this section, the Administrator may issue operations specifications to allow the use, to touchdown, of an approved flight control guidance system with automatic capability, if—

(1) The system does not contain any altitude loss (above zero) specified in the approved Aircraft Flight Manual or equivalent for malfunction of the autopilot with approach coupler; and

(2) The Administrator finds that the use of the system to touchdown will not otherwise adversely affect the safety standards of this section.

(e) This section does not apply to operations conducted in rotorcraft.

§ 135.95 Airmen: Limitations on use of services.

No certificate holder may use the services of any person as an airman unless the person performing those services—

(a) Holds an appropriate and current airman certificate; and

(b) Is qualified, under this chapter, for the operation for which the person is to be used.

§ 135.97 Aircraft and facilities for recent flight experience.

Each certificate holder shall provide aircraft and facilities to enable each of its pilots to maintain and demonstrate the pilot's ability to conduct all operations for which the pilot is authorized.

§ 135.99 Composition of flight crew.

(a) No certificate holder may operate an aircraft with less than the minimum flight crew specified in the aircraft operating limitations or the Aircraft Flight Manual for that aircraft and required by this part for the kind of operation being conducted.

(b) No certificate holder may operate an aircraft without a second in command if that aircraft has a passenger seating configuration, excluding any pilot seat, of ten seats or more.

§ 135.100 Flight crewmember duties.

(a) No certificate holder shall require, nor may any flight crewmember perform, any duties during a critical phase of flight except those duties required for the safe operation of the aircraft. Duties such as company required calls made for such nonsafety related purposes as ordering galley supplies and confirming passenger connections, announcements made to passengers promoting the air carrier or pointing out sights of interest, and filling out company payroll and related records are not required for the safe operation of the aircraft.

(b) No flight crewmember may engage in, nor may any pilot in command permit, any activity during a critical phase of flight which could distract any flight crewmember from the performance of his or her duties or which could interfere in any way with the proper conduct of those duties. Activities such as eating meals, engaging in nonessential conversations within the cockpit and nonessential communications between the cabin and cockpit crews, and reading publications not related to the proper conduct of the flight are not required for the safe operation of the aircraft.

(c) For the purposes of this section, critical phases of flight includes all ground operations involving taxi, takeoff and landing, and all other flight operations conducted below 10,000 feet, except cruise flight.

NOTE: Taxi is defined as "movement of an airplane under its own power on the surface of an airport."

[Amdt. 135–11, 46 FR 5502, Jan. 19, 1981]

§135.101   Second in command required in IFR conditions.

Except as provided in §§ 135.103 and 135.105, no person may operate an aircraft carrying passengers in IFR conditions, unless there is a second in command in the aircraft.

§135.103   Exception to second in command requirement: IFR operations.

The pilot in command of an aircraft carrying passengers may conduct IFR operations without a second in command under the following conditions:

(a) A takeoff may be conducted under IFR conditions if the weather reports or forecasts, or any combination of them, indicate that the weather along the planned route of flight allows flight under VFR within 15 minutes flying time, at normal cruise speed, from the takeoff airport.

(b) En route IFR may be conducted if unforecast weather conditions below the VFR minimums of this chapter are encountered on a flight that was planned to be conducted under VFR.

(c) An IFR approach may be conducted if, upon arrival at the destination airport, unforecast weather conditions do not allow an approach to be completed under VFR.

(d) When IFR operations are conducted under this section:

(1) The aircraft must be properly equipped for IFR operations under this part.

(2) The pilot must be authorized to conduct IFR operations under this part.

(3) The flight must be conducted in accordance with an ATC IFR clearance.

IFR operations without a second in command may not be conducted under this section in an aircraft requiring a second in command under § 135.99.

§135.105   Exception to second in command requirement: Approval for use of autopilot system.

(a) Except as provided in §§ 135.99 and 135.111, unless two pilots are required by this chapter for operations under VFR, a person may operate an aircraft without a second in command, if it is equipped with an operative ap-

proved autopilot system and the use of that system is authorized by appropriate operations specifications. No certificate holder may use any person, nor may any person serve, as a pilot in command under this section of an aircraft operated by a Commuter Air Carrier (as defined in § 298.2 of this title) in passenger-carrying operations unless that person has at least 100 hours pilot in command flight time in the make and model of aircraft to be flown and has met all other applicable requirements of this part.

(b) The certificate holder may apply for an amendment of its operations specifications to authorize the use of an autopilot system in place of a second in command.

(c) The Administrator issues an amendment to the operations specifications authorizing the use of an autopilot system, in place of a second in command, if—

(1) The autopilot is capable of operating the aircraft controls to maintain flight and maneuver it about the three axes; and

(2) The certificate holder shows, to the satisfaction of the Administrator, that operations using the autopilot system can be conducted safely and in compliance with this part.

The amendment contains any conditions or limitations on the use of the autopilot system that the Administrator determines are needed in the interest of safety.

[Doc. No. 16097, 43 FR 46783, Oct. 10, 1978, as amended by Amdt. 135–3, 45 FR 7542, Feb. 4, 1980]

§135.107   Flight attendant crewmember requirement.

No certificate holder may operate an aircraft that has a passenger seating configuration, excluding any pilot seat, of more than 19 unless there is a flight attendant crewmember on board the aircraft.

§135.109   Pilot in command or second in command: Designation required.

(a) Each certificate holder shall designate a—

(1) Pilot in command for each flight; and

(2) Second in command for each flight requiring two pilots.

(b) The pilot in command, as designated by the certificate holder, shall remain the pilot in command at all times during that flight.

§ 135.111 Second in command required in Category II operations.

No person may operate an aircraft in a Category II operation unless there is a second in command of the aircraft.

§ 135.113 Passenger occupancy of pilot seat.

No certificate holder may operate an aircraft type certificated after October 15, 1971, that has a passenger seating configuration, excluding any pilot seat, of more than eight seats if any person other than the pilot in command, a second in command, a company check airman, or an authorized representative of the Administrator, the National Transportation Safety Board, or the United States Postal Service occupies a pilot seat.

§ 135.115 Manipulation of controls.

No pilot in command may allow any person to manipulate the flight controls of an aircraft during flight conducted under this part, nor may any person manipulate the controls during such flight unless that person is—

(a) A pilot employed by the certificate holder and qualified in the aircraft; or

(b) An authorized safety representative of the Administrator who has the permission of the pilot in command, is qualified in the aircraft, and is checking flight operations.

§ 135.117 Briefing of passengers before flight.

(a) Before each takeoff each pilot in command of an aircraft carrying passengers shall ensure that all passengers have been orally briefed on—

(1) *Smoking.* Each passenger shall be briefed on when, where, and under what conditions smoking is prohibited (including, but not limited to, the pertinent requirements of Part 252 of this title). This briefing shall include a statement that the Federal Aviation Regulations require passenger compliance with the lighted passenger information signs (if such signs are required) and posted placards. The briefing shall also include a statement (if the aircraft is equipped with a lavatory) that Federal law prohibits tampering with, disabling, or destroying any smoke detector installed in an aircraft lavatory.

(2) Use of seat belts;

(3) The placement of seat backs in an upright position before takeoff and landing;

(4) Location and means for opening the passenger entry door and emergency exits;

(5) Location of survival equipment;

(6) If the flight involves extended overwater operation, ditching procedures and the use of required flotation equipment;

(7) If the flight involves operations above 12,000 feet MSL, the normal and emergency use of oxygen; and

(8) Location and operation of fire extinguishers.

(b) Before each takeoff the pilot in command shall ensure that each person who may need the assistance of another person to move expeditiously to an exit if an emergency occurs and that person's attendant, if any, has received a briefing as to the procedures to be followed if an evacuation occurs. This paragraph does not apply to a person who has been given a briefing before a previous leg of a flight in the same aircraft.

(c) The oral briefing required by paragraph (a) of this section shall be given by the pilot in command or a crewmember.

(d) Notwithstanding the provisions of paragraph (c) of this section, for aircraft certificated to carry 19 passengers or less, the oral briefing required by paragraph (a) of this section shall be given by the pilot in command, a crewmember, or other qualified person designated by the certificate holder and approved by the Administrator.

(e) The oral briefing required by paragraph (a) shall be supplemented by printed cards which must be carried in the aircraft in locations convenient for the use of each passenger. The cards must—

(1) Be appropriate for the aircraft on which they are to be used;

(2) Contain a diagram of, and method of operating, the emergency exits; and

(3) Contain other instructions necessary for the use of emergency equipment on board the aircraft.

(f) The briefing required by paragraph (a) may be delivered by means of an approved recording playback device that is audible to each passenger under normal noise levels.

[Doc. No. 16097, 43 FR 46783, Oct. 10, 1978, as amended by Amdt. 135-9, 51 FR 40709, Nov. 7, 1986]

§ 135.119 Prohibition against carriage of weapons.

No person may, while on board an aircraft being operated by a certificate holder, carry on or about that person a deadly or dangerous weapon, either concealed or unconcealed. This section does not apply to—

(a) Officials or employees of a municipality or a State, or of the United States, who are authorized to carry arms; or

(b) Crewmembers and other persons authorized by the certificate holder to carry arms.

§ 135.121 Alcoholic beverages.

(a) No person may drink any alcoholic beverage aboard an aircraft unless the certificate holder operating the aircraft has served that beverage.

(b) No certificate holder may serve any alcoholic beverage to any person aboard its aircraft if that person appears to be intoxicated.

(c) No certificate holder may allow any person to board any of its aircraft if that person appears to be intoxicated.

§ 135.123 Emergency and emergency evacuation duties.

(a) Each certificate holder shall assign to each required crewmember for each type of aircraft as appropriate, the necessary functions to be performed in an emergency or in a situation requiring emergency evacuation. The certificate holder shall ensure that those functions can be practicably accomplished, and will meet any reasonably anticipated emergency including incapacitation of individual crewmembers or their inability to reach the passenger cabin because of shifting cargo in combination cargo-passenger aircraft.

(b) The certificate holder shall describe in the manual required under § 135.21 the functions of each category of required crewmembers assigned under paragraph (a) of this section.

§ 135.125 Airplane security.

Certificate holders conducting operations under this part shall comply with the applicable security requirements in Part 108 of this chapter.

§ 135.127 Passenger information.

(a) The no smoking signs required by § 135.177(a)(3) of this part must be turned on:

(1) During flight time on flight segments which are scheduled in the current North American Edition of the Official Airline Guide to be 2 hours or less in duration, except those flight segments between a point in the United States and point in another country; or

(2) On flight segments other than those described in paragraph (a)(1) of this section, for each takeoff and landing, and at any other time considered necessary by the pilot in command.

(b) No person may smoke while a no smoking sign is lighted, except that the pilot in command may authorize smoking on the flight deck (if it is physically separated from the passenger cabin) except during takeoff and landing.

(c) No person may smoke in any aircraft lavatory.

(d) After December 31, 1988, no person may operate an aircraft with a lavatory equipped with a smoke detector unless there is in that lavatory a sign or placard which reads: "Federal law provides for a penalty of up to $2,000 for tampering with the smoke detector installed in this lavatory."

(e) The provisions of paragraph (a)(1) of this section shall cease to be effective on April 24, 1990.

Subpart C—Aircraft and Equipment

§ 135.141 Applicability.

This subpart prescribes aircraft and equipment requirements for operations under this part. The requirements of this subpart are in addition to the aircraft and equipment requirements of Part 91 of this chapter. However, this part does not require the duplication of any equipment required by this chapter.

§ 135.143 General requirements.

(a) No person may operate an aircraft under this part unless that aircraft and its equipment meet the applicable regulations of this chapter.

(b) Except as provided in § 135.179, no person may operate an aircraft under the part unless the required instruments and equipment in it have been approved and are in an operable condition.

(c) ATC transponder equipment installed within the time periods indicated below must meet the performance and environmental requirements of the following TSO's:

(1) *Through January 1, 1992:* (i) Any class of TSO-C74b or any class of TSO-C74c as appropriate, provided that the equipment was manufactured before January 1, 1990; or

(ii) The appropriate class of TSO-C112 (Mode S).

(2) *After January 1, 1992:* The appropriate class of TSO-C112 (Mode S). For purposes of paragraph (c)(2) of this section, "installation" does not include—

(i) Temporary installation of TSO-C74b or TSO-C74c substitute equipment, as appropriate, during maintenance of the permanent equipment;

(ii) Reinstallation of equipment after temporary removal for maintenance; or

(iii) For fleet operations, installation of equipment in a fleet aircraft after removal of the equipment for maintenance from another aircraft in the same operator's fleet.

§ 135.145 Aircraft proving tests.

(a) No certificate holder may operate a turbojet airplane, or an aircraft for which two pilots are required by this chapter for operations under VFR, if it has not previously proved that aircraft or an aircraft of the same make and similar design in any operation under this part unless, in addition to the aircraft certification tests, at least 25 hours of proving tests acceptable to the Administrator have been flown by that certificate holder including—

(1) Five hours of night time, if night flights are to be authorized:

the Administrator.

(f) Each flight recorder required by this section must be installed in accordance with the requirements of §§ 23.1459, 25.1459, 27.1459 or 29.1459, as appropriate, of this chapter. The correlation required by paragraph (c) of §§ 23.1459, 25.1459, 27.1459, or 29.1459, as appropriate, of this chapter need be established only on one aircraft of a group of aircraft:

(1) That are of the same type;

(2) On which the flight recorder models and their installations are the same; and

(3) On which there are no differences in the type design with respect to the installation of the first pilot's instruments associated with the flight recorder. The most recent instrument calibration, including the recording medium from which this calibration is derived, and the recorder correlation must be retained by the certificate holder.

(g) Each flight recorder required by this section that records the data specified in paragraphs (a) and (b) this section must have an approved device to assist in locating that recorder under water.

§ 135.153 Ground proximity warning system.

No person may operate a turbojet airplane having a passenger seating configuration, excluding any pilot seat, of 10 seats or more, unless it is equipped with—

(a) A ground proximity warning system that meets § 37.201 of this chapter; or

(b) A system that conveys warnings of excessive closure rates with the terrain and any deviations below glide slope by visual and audible means. This system must—

(1) Be approved by the Director of Flight Operations; and

(2) Have a means of alerting the pilot when a malfunction occurs in the system.

(c) For the system required by this section,

the Airplane Flight Manual shall contain—

(1) Appropriate procedures for—

(i) The use of the equipment;

(ii) Proper flight crew action with respect to the equipment; and

(iii) Deactiviation for planned abnormal and emergency conditions; and

(2) An outline of all input sources that must be operating.

(d) No person may deactivate a system required by this section except under procedures in the Airplane Flight Manual.

(e) Whenever a system required by this section is deactivated, an entry shall be made in the airplane maintenance record that includes the date and time of deactivation.

(f) For a system required by paragraph (b) of this section, procedures acceptable to the FAA Flight Standards District Office charged with the overall inspection of the certificate holder shall be established by the certificate holder to ensure that the performance of the system can be appropriately monitored.

§ 135.155 Fire extinguishers: passenger-carrying aircraft.

No person may operate an aircraft carrying passengers unless it is equipped with hand fire extinguishers of an approved type for use in crew and passenger compartments as follows—

(a) The type and quantity of extinguishing agents must be suitable for the kinds of fires likely to occur.

(b) At least one hand fire extinguisher must be provided and conveniently located on the flight deck for use by the flight crew; and

(c) At least one hand fire extinguisher must be conveniently located in the passenger compartment of each aircraft having a passenger seating configuration, excluding any pilot seat, of at least 10 seats but less than 31 seats.

§ 135.157 Oxygen equipment requirements.

(a) *Unpressurized aircraft.* No person may operate an unpressurized

(2) Five instrument approach procedures under simulated or actual instrument weather conditions, if IFR flights are to be authorized; and

(3) Entry into a representative number of en route airports as determined by the Administrator.

(b) No certificate holder may carry passengers in an aircraft during proving tests, except those needed to make the tests and those designated by the Administrator to observe the tests. However, pilot flight training may be conducted during the proving tests.

(c) For the purposes of paragraph (a) of this section an aircraft is not considered to be of similar design if an alteration includes—

(1) The installation of powerplants other than those of a type similar to those with which it is certificated; or

(2) Alterations to the aircraft or its components that materially affect flight characteristics.

(d) The Administrator may authorize deviations from this section if the Administrator finds that special circumstances make full compliance with this section unnecessary.

§ 135.147 Dual controls required.

No person may operate an aircraft in operations requiring two pilots unless it is equipped with functioning dual controls. However, if the aircraft type certification operating limitations do not require two pilots, a throwover control wheel may be used in place two control wheels.

§ 135.149 Equipment requirements: General.

No person may operate an aircraft unless it is equipped with—

(a) A sensitive altimeter that is adjustable for barometric pressure:

(b) Heating or deicing equipment for each carburetor or, for a pressure carburetor, an alternate air source;

(c) For turbojet airplanes, in addition to two gyroscopic bank-and-pitch indicators (artificial horizons) for use at the pilot stations, a third indicator that—

(1) Is powered from a source independent of the aircraft's electrical generating system;

(2) Continues reliable operation for at least 30 minutes after total failure of the aircraft's electrical generating system;

(3) Operates independently of any other attitude indicating system;

(4) Is operative without selection after total failure of the aircraft's electrical generating system;

(5) Is located on the instrument panel in a position that will make it plainly visible to, and useable by, any pilot at the pilot's station; and

(6) Is appropriately lighted during all phases of operation;

(d) For aircraft having a passenger seating configuration, excluding any pilot seat, of more than 19, a public address system and a crewmember interphone system approved under § 21.305 of this chapter, which meet §§ 121.318 and 121.319, respectively, of this chapter; and

(e) For turbine powered aircraft, any other equipment as the Administrator may require.

§ 135.151 Cockpit voice recorders.

(a) After October 11, 1991, no person may operate a multiengine, turbine-powered airplane or rotorcraft having a passenger seating configuration of six or more and for which two pilots are required by certification or operating rules unless it is equipped with an approved cockpit voice recorder that:

(1) Is installed in compliance with § 23. 1457(a) (1) and (2), (b), (c), (d), (e), (f), and (g); § 25.1457(a) (1) and (2), (b), (c), (d), (e), (f), and (g); § 27.1457(a) (1) and (2), (b), (c), (d), (e), (f), and (g) or § 29.1457(a) (1) and 2, (b), (c), (d), (e), (f), and (g) of this chapter, as applicable; and

(2) Is operated continuously from the use of the check list before the flight to completion of the final check list at the end of the flight.

(b) After October 11, 1991, no person may operate a multiengine, turbine-powered airplane or rotorcraft having a passenger seating configuration of 20 or more seats unless it is equipped with an approved cockpit recorder that—

(1) Is installed in compliance with § 23. 1457, § 25.1457, § 27.1457 or § 29.1457 of this chapter, as applicable; and

(2) Is operated continuously from the use of the check list before the flight to completion of the final check list at the end of the flight.

(c) In the event of an accident, or occurrence requiring immediate notification of the National Transportation Safety Board which results in termination of the flight, the certificate holder shall keep the recorded information for at least 60 days or, if requested by the Administrator or the Board, for a longer period. Information obtained from the record may be used to assist in determining the cause of accidents or occurrences in connection with investigations. The Administrator does not use the record in any civil penalty or certificate action.

(d) For those aircraft equipped to record the uninterrupted audio signals received by a boom or mask microphone the flight crewmembers are required to use the boom microphone below 18,000 feet mean sea level. No person may operate a large turbine engine powered airplane manufactured after October 11, 1991, or on which a cockpit voice recorder has been installed after October 11, 1991, unless it is equipped to record the uninterrupted audio signal received by a boom or mask microphone in accordance with § 25. 1457(c)(5) of this chapter.

(e) In complying with this section, an approved cockpit voice recorder having an erasure feature may be used, so that during the operation of the recorder, information:

(1) Recorded in accordance with paragraph (a) of this section and recorded more than 15 minutes earlier; or

(2) Recorded in accordance with paragraph (b) of this section and recorded more than 30 minutes earlier; may be erased or otherwise obliterated.

§ 135.152 Flight recorders.

(a) No person may operate a multiengine turbine-powered airplane or rotorcraft having a passenger seating configuration, excluding any pilot seat, of 10 to 19 seats, that is brought onto the U.S. register after October 11, 1991, unless it is equipped with one or more approved flight recorders that utilize a digital method of recording and storing data, and a method of readily retrieving that data from the storage medium. The parameters specified in Appendix B or C, as applicable, of this part must be recorded within the range accuracy, resolution, and recording intervals as specified. The recorder shall retain no less than 8 hours of aircraft operation.

(b) After October 11, 1991, no person may operate a multiengine, turbine-powered airplane having a passenger seating configuration of 20 to 30 seats or a multiengine, turbine-powered rotorcraft having a passenger seating configuration of 20 or more seats unless it is equipped with one or more approved flight recorders that utilize a digital method of recording and storing data, and a method of readily retrieving that data from the storage medium. The parameters in Appendix D or E of this part, as applicable, that are set forth below, must be recorded within the ranges, accuracies, resolutions, and sampling intervals as specified.

(1) Except as provided in paragraph (b)(3) of this section for aircraft type certificated before October 1, 1969, the following parameters must be recorded:

(i) Time;
(i) Altitude;
(iii) Airspeed;
(iv) Vertical acceleration;
(v) Heading;
(vi) Time of each radio transmission to or from air traffic control;
(vii) Pitch attitude;
(viii) Roll attitude;
(ix) Longitudinal acceleration;
(x) Control column or pitch control surface position; and
(xi) Thrust of each engine.

(2) Except as provided in paragraph (b)(3) of this section for aircraft type certificated after September 30, 1969, the following parameters must be recorded:
(i) Time;
(ii) Altitude;
(iii) Airspeed;
(iv) Vertical acceleration;
(v) Heading;
(vi) Time of each radio transmission either to or from air traffic control;
(vii) Pitch attitude;

(viii) Roll attitude;
(ix) Longitudinal acceleration;
(x) Pitch trim position;
(xi) Control column or pitch control surface position; and
(xii) Control wheel or lateral control surface position;
(xiii) Rudder pedal or yaw control surface position;
(xiv) Thrust of each engine;
(xv) Position of each thrust reverser;
(xvi) Trailing edge flat or cockpit flap control position; and
(xvi) Leading edge flap or cockpit flap control position.

(3) For aircraft manufactured after October 11, 1991, all of the parameters listed in Appendix D or E of this part, as applicable, must be recorded.

(c) Whenever a flight recorder required by this section is installed, it must be operated continuously from the instant the airplane begins the takeoff roll or the rotorcraft begins the lift-off until the airplane has completed the landing roll or the rotorcraft has landed at its destination.

(d) Except as provided in paragraph (c) of this section, and except for recorded data erased as authorized in this paragraph, each certificate holder shall keep the recorded data prescribed in paragraph (a) of this section until the aircraft has been operating for at least 8 hours of the operating time specified in paragraph (c) of this section. In addition, each certificate holder shall keep the recorded data prescribed in paragraph (b) of this section for an airplane until the airplane has been operating for at least 25 hours, and for a rotorcraft until the rotorcraft has been operating for at least 10 hours, of the operating time specified in paragraph (c) of this section. A total of 1 hour of recorded data may be erased for the purpose of testing the flight recorder or the flight reocorder system. Any erasure made in accordance with this paragraph must be of the oldest recorded data accumulated at the time of testing. Except as provided in paragraph (c) of this section, no record need be kept more than 60 days.

(e) In the event of an accident or occurrence that requires the immediate notification of the National Transportation Safety Board under 49 CFR Part 830 of its regulations and that results in termination of the flight, the certificate holder shall remove the recording media from the aircraft and keep the recorded data required by paragraphs (a) and (b) of this section for at least 60 days or for a longer period upon request of the Board or

157

aircraft at altitudes prescribed in this section unless it is equipped with enough oxygen dispensers and oxygen to supply the pilots under § 135.89(a) and to supply, when flying—

(1) At altitudes above 10,000 feet through 15,000 feet MSL, oxygen to at least 10 percent of the occupants of the aircraft, other than the pilots, for that part of the flight at those altitudes that is of more than 30 minutes duration; and

(2) Above 15,000 feet MSL, oxygen to each occupant of the aircraft other than the pilots.

(b) *Pressurized aircraft.* No person may operate a pressurized aircraft—

(1) At altitudes above 25,000 feet MSL, unless at least a 10-minute supply of supplemental oxygen is available for each occupant of the aircraft, other than the pilots, for use when a descent is necessary due to loss of cabin pressurization; and

(2) Unless it is equipped with enough oxygen dispensers and oxygen to comply with paragraph (a) of this section whenever the cabin pressure altitude exceeds 10,000 feet MSL and, if the cabin pressurization fails, to comply with § 135.89 (a) or to provide a 2-hour supply for each pilot, whichever is greater, and to supply when flying—

(i) At altitudes above 10,000 feet through 15,000 feet MSL, oxygen to at least 10 percent of the occupants of the aircraft, other than the pilots, for that part of the flight at those altitudes that is of more than 30 minutes duration; and

(ii) Above 15,000 feet MSL, oxygen to each occupant of the aircraft, other than the pilots, for one hour unless, at all times during flight above that altitude, the aircraft can safely descend to 15,000 feet MSL within four minutes, in which case only a 30-minute supply is required.

(c) The equipment required by this section must have a means—

(1) To enable the pilots to readily determine, in flight, the amount of oxygen available in each source of supply and whether the oxygen is being delivered to the dispensing units; or

(2) In the case of individual dispensing units, to enable each user to make

those determinations with respect to that person's oxygen supply and delivery; and

(3) To allow the pilots to use undiluted oxygen at their discretion at altitudes above 25,000 feet MSL.

§ 135.158 **Pitot heat indication systems.**

(a) Except as provided in paragraph (b) of this section, after April 12, 1981, no person may operate a transport category airplane equipped with a flight instrument pitot heating system unless the airplane is also equipped with an operable pitot heat indication system that complies with § 25.1326 of this chapter in effect on April 12, 1978.

(b) A certificate holder may obtain an extension of the April 12, 1981, compliance date specified in paragraph (a) of this section, but not beyond April 12, 1983, from the Director of Flight Operations if the certificate holder—

(1) Shows that due to circumstances beyond its control it cannot comply by the specified compliance date; and

(2) Submits by the specified compliance date a schedule for compliance, acceptable to the Director, indicating that compliance will be achieved at the earliest practicable date.

[Amdt. 135–17, 46 FR 48306, Aug. 31, 1981]

§ 135.159 **Equipment requirements: Carrying passengers under VFR at night or under VFR over-the-top conditions.**

No person may operate an aircraft carrying passengers under VFR at night or under VFR over-the-top, unless it is equipped with—

(a) A gyroscopic rate-of-turn indicator except on the following aircraft:

(1) Helicopters with a third attitude instrument system usable through flight attitudes of ±80 degrees of pitch and ±120 degrees of roll and installed in accordance with § 29.1303(g) of this chapter.

(2) Helicopters with a maximum certificated takeoff weight of 6,000 pounds or less.

(b) A slip skid indicator.

(c) A gyroscopic bank-and-pitch indicator.

(d) A gyroscopic direction indicator.

(e) A generator or generators able to supply all probable combinations of continuous in-flight electrical loads for required equipment and for recharging the battery.

(f) For night flights—

(1) An anticollision light system;

(2) Instrument lights to make all instruments, switches, and gauges easily readable, the direct rays of which are shielded from the pilots' eyes; and

(3) A flashlight having at least two size "D" cells or equivalent.

(g) For the purpose of paragraph (e) of this section, a continuous in-flight electrical load includes one that draws current continuously during flight, such as radio equipment and electrically driven instruments and lights, but does not include occasional intermittent loads.

(h) Notwithstanding provisions of paragraphs (b), (c), and (d), helicopters having a maximum certificated takeoff weight of 6,000 pounds or less may be operated until January 6, 1988, under visual flight rules at night without a slip skid indicator, a gyroscopic bank-and-pitch indicator, or a gyroscopic direction indicator.

[Doc. No. 24550, Amdt. No. 135-20, 51 FR 40709, Nov. 7, 1986]

§ 135.161 Radio and navigational equipment: Carrying passengers under VFR at night or under VFR over-the-top.

(a) No person may operate an aircraft carrying passengers under VFR at night, or under VFR over-the-top, unless it has two-way radio communications equipment able, at least in flight, to transmit to, and receive from, ground facilities 25 miles away.

(b) No person may operate an aircraft carrying passengers under VFR over-the-top unless it has radio navigational equipment able to receive radio signals from the ground facilities to be used.

(c) No person may operate an airplane carrying passengers under VFR at night unless it has radio navigational equipment able to receive radio signals from the ground facilities to be used.

§ 135.163 Equipment requirements: Aircraft carrying passengers under IFR.

No person may operate an aircraft under IFR, carrying passengers, unless it has—

(a) A vertical speed indicator;

(b) A free-air temperature indicator;

(c) A heated pitot tube for each airspeed indicator;

(d) A power failure warning device or vacuum indicator to show the power available for gyroscopic instruments from each power source;

(e) An alternate source of static pressure for the altimeter and the airspeed and vertical speed indicators;

(f) For a single-engine aircraft, a generator or generators able to supply all probable combinations of continuous inflight electrical loads for required equipment and for recharging the battery;

(g) For multiengine aircraft, at least two generators each of which is on a separate engine, of which any combination of one-half of the total number are rated sufficiently to supply the electrical loads of all required instruments and equipment necessary for safe emergency operation of the aircraft except that for multiengine helicopters, the two required generators may be mounted on the main rotor drive train; and

(h) Two independent sources of energy (with means of selecting either), of which at least one is an engine-driven pump or generator, each of which is able to drive all gyroscopic instruments and installed so that failure of one instrument or source does not interfere with the energy supply to the remaining instruments or the other energy source, unless, for single-engine aircraft, the rate-of-turn indicator has a source of energy separate from the bank and pitch and direction indicators. For the purpose of this paragraph, for multiengine aircraft, each engine-driven source of energy must be on a different engine.

(i) For the purpose of paragraph (f) of this section, a continuous inflight electrical load includes one that draws current continuously during flight, such as radio equipment, electrically driven instruments, and lights, but does not include occasional intermittent loads.

§ 135.165 Radio and navigational equipment: Extended overwater or IFR operations.

(a) No person may operate a turbojet airplane having a passenger seating configuration, excluding any pilot seat, of 10 seats or more, or a multiengine airplane carrying passengers as a "Commuter Air Carrier" as defined in Part 298 of this title, under IFR or in extended overwater operations unless it has at least the following radio communication and navigational equipment appropriate to the facilities to be used which are capable of transmitting to, and receiving from, at any place on the route to be flown, at least one ground facility:

(1) Two transmitters, (2) two microphones, (3) two headsets or one headset and one speaker, (4) a marker beacon receiver, (5) two independent receivers for navigation, and (6) two independent receivers for communications.

(b) No person may operate an aircraft other than that specified in paragraph (a) of this section, under IFR or in extended overwater operations unless it has at least the following radio communication and navigational equipment appropriate to the facilities to be used and which are capable of transmitting to, and receiving from, at any place on the route, at least one ground facility:

(1) A transmitter, (2) two microphones, (3) two headsets or one headset and one speaker, (4) a marker beacon receiver, (5) two independent receivers for navigation, (6) two independent receivers for communications, and (7) for extended overwater operations only, an additional transmitter.

(c) For the purpose of paragraphs (a)(5), (a)(6), (b)(5), and (b)(6) of this section, a receiver is independent if the function of any part of it does not depend on the functioning of any part of another receiver. However, a receiver that can receive both communications and navigational signals may be used in place of a separate communications receiver and a separate navigational signal receiver.

§ 135.167 Emergency equipment: Extended overwater operations.

(a) No person may operate an aircraft in extended overwater operations unless it carries, installed in conspicuously marked locations easily accessible to the occupants if a ditching occurs, the following equipment:

(1) An approved life preserver equipped with an approved survivor locator light for each occupant of the aircraft. The life preserver must be easily accessible to each seated occupant.

(2) Enough approved liferafts of a rated capacity and buoyancy to accommodate the occupants of the aircraft.

(b) Each liferaft required by paragraph (a) of this section must be equipped with or contain at least the following:

(1) One approved survivor locator light.

(2) One approved pyrotechnic signaling device.

(3) Either—

(i) One survival kit, appropriately equipped for the route to be flown; or

(ii) One canopy (for sail, sunshade, or rain catcher);

(iii) One radar reflector;

(iv) One liferaft repair kit;

(v) One bailing bucket;

(vi) One signaling mirror;

(vii) One police whistle;

(viii) One raft knife;

(ix) One CO_2 bottle for emergency inflation;

(x) One inflation pump;

(xi) Two oars;

(xii) One 75-foot retaining line;

(xiii) One magnetic compass;

(xiv) One dye marker;

(xv) One flashlight having at least two size "D" cells or equivalent;

(xvi) A 2-day supply of emergency food rations supplying at least 1,000 calories per day for each person;

(xvii) For each two persons the raft is rated to carry, two pints of water or one sea water desalting kit;

(xviii) One fishing kit; and

(xix) One book on survival appropriate for the area in which the aircraft is operated.

(c) No person may operate an aircraft in extended overwater operations unless there is attached to one of the life rafts required by paragraph (a) of this section, a survival type emergency locator transmitter that meets the applicable requirements of TSO–C91. Batteries used in this transmitter must be replaced (or recharged, if the battery is rechargeable) when the transmitter has been in use for more than 1 cumulative hour, and also when 50 percent of their useful life (or for rechargeable batteries, 50 percent of their useful life of charge), as established by the transmitter manufacturer under TSO–C91, paragraph (g)(2) of this section has expired. The new expiration date for the replacement or recharged battery must be legibly marked on the outside of the transmitter. The battery useful life or useful life of charge requirements of this paragraph do not apply to batteries (such as water-activated batteries) that are essentially unaffected during probable storage intervals.

[Doc. No. 16097, 43 FR 46783, Oct. 10, 1978, as amended by Amdt. 135–4, 45 FR 38348, June 30, 1980; Amdt. 135–20, 51 FR 40710, Nov. 7, 1986]

§ 135.169 Additional airworthiness requirements.

(a) Except for commuter category airplanes, no person may operate a large airplane unless it meets the additional airworthiness requirements of §§ 121.213 through 121.283, 121.307, and 121.312 of this chapter.

(b) No person may operate a reciprocating-engine or turbopropeller-powered small airplane that has a passenger seating configuration, excluding pilot seats, of 10 seats or more unless it is type certificated—

(1) In the transport category;

(2) Before July 1, 1970, in the normal category and meets special conditions issued by the Administrator for airplanes intended for use in operations under this part;

(3) Before July 19, 1970, in the normal category and meets the additional airworthiness standards in Special Federal Aviation Regulation No. 23;

(4) In the normal category and meets the additional airworthiness standards in Appendix A;

(5) In the normal category and complies with section 1.(a) of Special Federal Aviation Regulation No. 41;

(6) In the normal category and complies with section 1.(b) of Special Federal Aviation Regulation No. 41; or

(7) In the commuter category.

(c) No person may operate a small airplane with a passenger seating configuration, excluding any pilot seat, of 10 seats or more, with a seating configuration greater than the maximum seating configuration used in that type airplane in operations under this part before August 19, 1977. This paragraph does not apply to—

(1) An airplane that is type certificated in the transport category; or

(2) An airplane that complies with—

(i) Appendix A of this part provided that its passenger seating configuration, excluding pilot seats, does not exceed 19 seats; or

(ii) Special Federal Aviation Regulation No. 41.

[Doc. No. 16097, 43 FR 46783, Oct. 10, 1978, as amended at 44 FR 53731, Sept. 17, 1979; Amdt. 135–21, 52 FR 1836, Jan. 15, 1987; 52 FR 34745, Sept. 14, 1987]

§ 135.170 Materials for compartment interiors.

No person may operate an airplane that conforms to an amended or supplemental type certificate issued in accordance with SFAR No. 41 for a maximum certificated takeoff weight in excess of 12,500 pounds, unless within one year after issuance of the initial airworthiness certificate under that SFAR, the airplane meets the compartment interior requirements set forth in § 25.853 (a), (b), (b–1), (b–2), and (b–3) of this chapter in effect on September 26, 1978.

[44 FR 53731, Sept. 17, 1979]

§ 135.171 Shoulder harness installation at flight crewmember stations.

(a) No person may operate a turbojet aircraft or an aircraft having a passenger seating configuration, excluding any pilot seat, of 10 seats or more unless it is equipped with an approved shoulder harness installed for each flight crewmember station.

(b) Each flight crewmember occupying a station equipped with a shoulder harness must fasten the shoulder harness during takeoff and landing, except that the shoulder harness may be unfastened if the crewmember cannot perform the required duties with the shoulder harness fastened.

§ 135.173 Airborne thunderstorm detection equipment requirements.

(a) No person may operate an aircraft that has a passenger seating configuration, excluding any pilot seat, of 10 seats or more in passenger-carrying operations, except a helicopter operating under day VFR conditions, unless the aircraft is equipped with either approved thunderstorm detection equipment or approved airborne weather radar equipment.

(b) After January 6, 1988, no person may operate a helicopter that has a passenger seating configuration, excluding any pilot seat, of 10 seats or more in passenger-carrying operations, under night VFR when current weather reports indicate that thunderstorms or other potentially hazardous weather conditions that can be detected with airborne thunderstorm detection equipment may reasonably be expected along the route to be flown, unless the helicopter is equipped with either approved thunderstorm detection equipment or approved airborne weather radar equipment.

(c) No person may begin a flight under IFR or night VFR conditions when current weather reports indicate that thunderstorms or other potentially hazardous weather conditions that can be detected with airborne thunderstorm detection equipment, required by paragraph (a) or (b) of this section, may reasonably be expected along the route to be flown, unless the airborne thunderstorm detection equipment is in satisfactory operating condition.

(d) If the airborne thunderstorm detection equipment becomes inoperative en route, the aircraft must be operated under the instructions and procedures specified for that event in the manual required by § 135.21.

(e) This section does not apply to aircraft used solely within the State of Hawaii, within the State of Alaska, within that part of Canada west of longitude 130 degrees W, between latitude 70 degrees N, and latitude 53 degrees N, or during any training, test, or ferry flight.

(f) Without regard to any other provision of this part, an alternate electrical power supply is not required for airborne thunderstorm detection equipment.

[Doc. No. 16097, 43 FR 46783, Oct. 10, 1978, as amended by Amdt. 135-20, 51 FR 40710, Nov. 7, 1986]

§ 135.175 Airborne weather radar equipment requirements.

(a) No person may operate a large, transport category aircraft in passenger-carrying operations unless approved airborne weather radar equipment is installed in the aircraft.

(b) No person may begin a flight under IFR or night VFR conditions when current weather reports indicate that thunderstorms, or other potentially hazardous weather conditions that can be detected with airborne weather radar equipment, may reasonably be expected along the route to be flown, unless the airborne weather radar equipment required by paragraph (a) of this section is in satisfactory operating condition.

(c) If the airborne weather radar equipment becomes inoperative en route, the aircraft must be operated under the instructions and procedures specified for that event in the manual required by § 135.21.

(d) This section does not apply to aircraft used solely within the State of Hawaii, within the State of Alaska, within that part of Canada west of longitude 130 degrees W, between latitude 70 degrees N, and latitude 53 degrees N, or during any training, test, or ferry flight.

(e) Without regard to any other provision of this part, an alternate electrical power supply is not required for airborne weather radar equipment.

§ 135.177 Emergency equipment requirements for aircraft having a passenger seating configuration of more than 19 passengers.

(a) No person may operate an aircraft having a passenger seating configuration, excluding any pilot seat, of more than 19 seats unless it is equipped with the following emergency equipment:

(1) One approved first aid kit for treatment of injuries likely to occur in flight or in a minor accident, which meets the following specifications and requirements:

(i) Each first aid kit must be dust and moisture proof, and contain only materials that either meet Federal Specifications GGK–319a, as revised, or as approved by the Administrator.

(ii) Required first aid kits must be readily accessible to the cabin flight attendants.

(iii) At time of takeoff, each first aid kit must contain at least the following or other contents approved by the Administrator:

Contents	Quantity
Adhesive bandage compressors, 1 in	16
Antiseptic swabs	20
Ammonia inhalants	10
Bandage compressors, 4 in	8
Triangular bandage compressors, 40 in	5
Burn compound, ⅛ oz or an equivalent of other burn remedy	6
Arm splint, noninflatable	1
Leg splint, noninflatable	1
Roller bandage, 4 in	4
Adhesive tape, 1-in standard roll	2
Bandage scissors	1

(2) A crash axe carried so as to be accessible to the crew but inaccessible to passengers during normal operations.

(3) Signs that are visible to all occupants to notify them when smoking is prohibited and when safety belts should be fastened. The signs must be constructed so that they can be turned on and off by a crewmember. Seat belt signs must be turned on for each takeoff and landing, and at other times considered necessary by the pilot in command. No smoking signs shall be turned on when required by § 135.127 of this part.

(4) For airplanes has the additional emergency equipment specified in § 121.310 of this chapter.

(b) Each item of equipment must be inspected regularly under inspection periods established in the operations specifications to ensure its condition for continued serviceability and immediate readiness to perform its intended emergency purposes.

§ 135.179 Inoperable instruments and equipment for multiengine aircraft.

(a) No person may take off a multiengine aircraft unless the following instruments and equipment are in an operable condition:

(1) Instruments and equipment that are either specifically or otherwise required by the airworthiness requirements under which the aircraft is type certificated and which are essential for safe operations under all operating conditions.

(2) Instruments and equipment required by an airworthiness directive to be in operable condition unless the airworthiness directive provides otherwise.

(b) No person may take off any multiengine aircraft with inoperable instruments or equipment installed, other than those described in paragraph (a) of this section, unless the following conditions are met:

(1) An approved Minimum Equipment List exists for the aircraft type.

(2) The aircraft has within it a letter of authorization, issued by the FAA Flight Standards District Office having certification responsibility for the certificate holder, authorizing operation of the aircraft under the Minimum Equipment List. The letter of authorization may be obtained by written request of the certificate holder. The Minimum Equipment List and the letter of authorization constitute a supplemental type certificate for the aircraft.

(3) The approved Minimum Equipment List must provide for the operation of the aircraft with the instruments and equipment in an inoperable condition.

(4) The aircraft records available to the pilot must include an entry describing the inoperable instruments and equipment.

(5) The aircraft is operated under all applicable conditions and limitations contained in the Minimum Equipment List and the letter authorizing the use of the list.

(c) Without regard to the requirements of paragraph (a)(1) of this section, an aircraft with inoperable instruments or equipment may be operated under a special flight permit under §§ 21.197 and 21.199 of this chapter.

§ 135.181 Performance requirements: Aircraft operated over-the-top or in IFR conditions.

(a) Except as provided in paragraphs (b) and (c) of this section, no person may—

(1) Operate a single-engine aircraft carrying passengers over-the-top or in IFR conditions; or

(2) Operate a multiengine aircraft carrying passengers over-the-top or in IFR conditions at a weight that will not allow it to climb, with the critical engine inoperative, at least 50 feet a minute when operating at the MEAs of the route to be flown or 5,000 feet MSL, whichever is higher.

(b) Notwithstanding the restrictions in paragraph (a)(2) of this section, multiengine helicopters carrying passengers offshore may conduct such operations in over-the-top or in IFR conditions at a weight that will allow the helicopter to climb at least 50 feet per minute with the critical engine inoperative when operating at the MEA of the route to be flown or 1,500 feet MSL, whichever is higher.

(c) Without regard to paragraph (a) of this section—

(1) If the latest weather reports or forecasts, or any combination of them, indicate that the weather along the planned route (including takeoff and landing) allows flight under VFR under the ceiling (if a ceiling exists) and that the weather is forecast to remain so until at least 1 hour after the estimated time of arrival at the destination, a person may operate an aircraft over-the-top; or

(2) If the latest weather reports or forecasts, or any combination of them, indicate that the weather along the planned route allows flight under VFR under the ceiling (if a ceiling exists) beginning at a point no more than 15 minutes flying time at normal cruise speed from the departure airport, a person may—

(i) Take off from the departure airport in IFR conditions and fly in IFR conditions to a point no more than 15 minutes flying time at normal cruise speed from that airport;

(ii) Operate an aircraft in IFR conditions if unforecast weather conditions are encountered while en route on a flight planned to be conducted under VFR; and

(iii) Make an IFR approach at the destination airport if unforecast weather conditions are encountered at the airport that do not allow an approach to be completed under VFR.

(d) Without regard to paragraph (a) of this section, a person may operate an aircraft over-the-top under conditions allowing—

(1) For multiengine aircraft, descent or continuance of the flight under VFR if its critical engine fails; or

(2) For single-engine aircraft, descent under VFR if its engine fails.

[Doc. No. 16097, 43 FR 46783, Oct. 10, 1978, as amended by Amdt. 135–20, 51 FR 40710, Nov. 7, 1986]

§ 135.183 Performance requirements: Land aircraft operated over water.

No person may operate a land aircraft carrying passengers over water unless—

(a) It is operated at an altitude that allows it to reach land in the case of engine failure;

(b) It is necessary for takeoff or landing;

(c) It is a multiengine aircraft operated at a weight that will allow it to climb, with the critical engine inoperative, at least 50 feet a minute, at an altitude of 1,000 feet above the surface; or

(d) It is a helicopter equipped with helicopter flotation devices.

§ 135.185 Empty weight and center of gravity: Currency requirement.

(a) No person may operate a multiengine aircraft unless the current empty weight and center of gravity are calculated from values established by actual weighing of the aircraft within the preceding 36 calendar months.

(b) Paragraph (a) of this section does not apply to—

(1) Aircraft issued an original airworthiness certificate within the preceding 36 calendar months; and

(2) Aircraft operated under a weight and balance system approved in the

operations specifications of the certificate holder.

Subpart D—VFR/IFR Operating Limitations and Weather Requirements

§ 135.201 Applicability.

This subpart prescribes the operating limitations for VFR/IFR flight operations and associated weather requirements for operations under this part.

§ 135.203 VFR: Minimum altitudes.

Except when necessary for takeoff and landing, no person may operate under VFR—

(a) An airplane—

(1) During the day, below 500 feet above the surface or less than 500 feet horizontally from any obstacle; or

(2) At night, at an altitude less than 1,000 feet above the highest obstacle within a horizontal distance of 5 miles from the course intended to be flown or, in designated mountainous terrain, less than 2,000 feet above the highest obstacle within a horizontal distance of 5 miles from the course intended to be flown; or

(b) A helicopter over a congested area at an altitude less than 300 feet above the surface.

§ 135.205 VFR: Visibility requirements.

(a) No person may operate an airplane under VFR in uncontrolled airspace when the ceiling is less than 1,000 feet unless flight visibility is at least 2 miles.

(b) No person may operate a helicopter under VFR in uncontrolled airspace at an altitude of 1,200 feet or less above the surface or in control zones unless the visibility is at least—

(1) During the day—½ mile; or

(2) At night—1 mile.

§ 135.207 VFR: Helicopter surface reference requirements.

No person may operate a helicopter under VFR unless that person has visual surface reference or, at night, visual surface light reference, sufficient to safely control the helicopter.

§ 135.209 VFR: Fuel supply.

(a) No person may begin a flight operation in an airplane under VFR unless, considering wind and forecast weather conditions, it has enough fuel to fly to the first point of intended landing and, assuming normal cruising fuel consumption—

(1) During the day, to fly after that for at least 30 minutes; or

(2) At night, to fly after that for at least 45 minutes.

(b) No person may begin a flight operation in a helicopter under VFR unless, considering wind and forecast weather conditions, it has enough fuel to fly to the first point of intended landing and, assuming normal cruising fuel consumption, to fly after that for at least 20 minutes.

§ 135.211 VFR: Over-the-top carrying passengers: Operating limitations.

Subject to any additional limitations in § 135.181, no person may operate an aircraft under VFR over-the-top carrying passengers, unless—

(a) Weather reports or forecasts, or any combination of them, indicate that the weather at the intended point of termination of over-the-top flight—

(1) Allows descent to beneath the ceiling under VFR and is forecast to remain so until at least 1 hour after the estimated time of arrival at that point; or

(2) Allows an IFR approach and landing with flight clear of the clouds until reaching the prescribed initial approach altitude over the final approach facility, unless the approach is made with the use of radar under § 91.116(f) of this chapter; or

(b) It is operated under conditions allowing—

(1) For multiengine aircraft, descent or continuation of the flight under VFR if its critical engine fails; or

(2) For single-engine aircraft, descent under VFR if its engine fails.

§ 135.213 Weather reports and forecasts.

(a) Whenever a person operating an aircraft under this part is required to use a weather report or forecast, that person shall use that of the U.S. National Weather Service, a source approved by the U.S. National Weather

Service, or a source approved by the Administrator. However, for operations under VFR, the pilot in command may, if such a report is not available, use weather information based on that pilot's own observations or on those of other persons competent to supply appropriate observations.

(b) For the purposes of paragraph (a) of this section, weather observations made and furnished to pilots to conduct IFR operations at an airport must be taken at the airport where those IFR operations are conducted, unless the Administrator issues operations specifications allowing the use of weather observations taken at a location not at the airport where the IFR operations are conducted. The Administrator issues such operations specifications when, after investigation by the U.S. National Weather Service and the FAA Flight Standards District Office charged with the overall inspection of the certificate holder, it is found that the standards of safety for that operation would allow the deviation from this paragraph for a particular operation for which an ATCO operating certificate has been issued.

§ 135.215　IFR: Operating limitations.

(a) Except as provided in paragraphs (b), (c) and (d) of this section, no person may operate an aircraft under IFR outside of controlled airspace or at any airport that does not have an approved standard instrument approach procedure.

(b) The Administrator may issue operations specifications to the certificate holder to allow it to operate under IFR over routes outside controlled airspace if—

(1) The certificate holder shows the Administrator that the flight crew is able to navigate, without visual reference to the ground, over an intended track without deviating more than 5 degrees or 5 miles, whichever is less, from that track; and

(2) The Administrator determines that the proposed operations can be conducted safely.

(c) A person may operate an aircraft under IFR outside of controlled airspace if the certificate holder has been approved for the operations and that operation is necessary to—

(1) Conduct an instrument approach to an airport for which there is in use a current approved standard or special instrument approach procedure; or

(2) Climb into controlled airspace during an approved missed approach procedure; or

(3) Make an IFR departure from an airport having an approved instrument approach procedure.

(d) The Administrator may issue operations specifications to the certificate holder to allow it to depart at an airport that does not have an approved standard instrument approach procedure when the Administrator determines that it is necessary to make an IFR departure from that airport and that the proposed operations can be conducted safely. The approval to operate at that airport does not include an approval to make an IFR approach to that airport.

§ 135.217　IFR: Takeoff limitations.

No person may takeoff an aircraft under IFR from an airport where weather conditions are at or above takeoff minimums but are below authorized IFR landing minimums unless there is an alternate airport within 1 hour's flying time (at normal cruising speed, in still air) of the airport of departure.

§ 135.219　IFR: Destination airport weather minimums.

No person may take off an aircraft under IFR or begin an IFR or over-the-top operation unless the latest weather reports or forecasts, or any combination of them, indicate that weather conditions at the estimated time of arrival at the next airport of intended landing will be at or above authorized IFR landing minimums.

§ 135.221　IFR: Alternate airport weather minimums.

No person may designate an alternate airport unless the weather reports or forecasts, or any combination of them, indicate that the weather conditions will be at or above authorized alternate airport landing minimums for that airport at the estimated time of arrival.

§ 135.223 IFR: Alternate airport requirements.

(a) Except as provided in paragraph (b) of this section, no person may operate an aircraft in IFR conditions unless it carries enough fuel (considering weather reports or forecasts or any combination of them) to—

(1) Complete the flight to the first airport of intended landing;

(2) Fly from that airport to the alternate airport; and

(3) Fly after that for 45 minutes at normal cruising speed or, for helicopters, fly after that for 30 minutes at normal cruising speed.

(b) Paragraph (a)(2) of this section does not apply if Part 97 of this chapter prescribes a standard instrument approach procedure for the first airport of intended landing and, for at least one hour before and after the estimated time of arrival, the appropriate weather reports or forecasts, or any combination of them, indicate that—

(1) The ceiling will be at least 1,500 feet above the lowest circling approach MDA; or

(2) If a circling instrument approach is not authorized for the airport, the ceiling will be at least 1,500 feet above the lowest published minimum or 2,000 feet above the airport elevation, whichever is higher; and

(3) Visibility for that airport is forecast to be at least three miles, or two miles more than the lowest applicable visibility minimums, whichever is the greater, for the instrument approach procedure to be used at the destination airport.

[Doc. No. 16097, 43 FR 46783, Oct. 10, 1978, as amended by Amdt. 135-20, 51 FR 40710, Nov. 7, 1986]

§ 135.225 IFR: Takeoff, approach and landing minimums.

(a) No pilot may begin an instrument approach procedure to an airport unless—

(1) That airport has a weather reporting facility operated by the U.S. National Weather Service, a source approved by U.S. National Weather Serv-

ice, or a source approved by the Administrator; and

(2) The latest weather report issued by that weather reporting facility indicates that weather conditions are at or above the authorized IFR landing minimums for that airport.

(b) No pilot may begin the final approach segment of an instrument approach procedure to an airport unless the latest weather reported by the facility described in paragraph (a)(1) of this section indicates that weather conditions are at or above the authorized IFR landing minimums for that procedure.

(c) If a pilot has begun the final approach segment of an instrument approach to an airport under paragraph (b) of this section and a later weather report indicating below minimum conditions is received after the aircraft is—

(1) On an ILS final approach and has passed the final approach fix; or

(2) On an ASR or PAR final approach and has been turned over to the final approach controller; or

(3) On a final approach using a VOR, NDB, or comparable approach procedure; and the aircraft—

(i) Has passed the appropriate facility or final approach fix; or

(ii) Where a final approach fix is not specified, has completed the procedure turn and is established inbound toward the airport on the final approach course within the distance prescribed in the procedure; the approach may be continued and a landing made if the pilot finds, upon reaching the authorized MDA or DH, that actual weather conditions are at least equal to the minimums prescribed for the procedure.

(d) The MDA or DH and visibility landing minimums prescribed in Part 97 of this chapter or in the operator's operations specifications are increased by 100 feet and ½ mile respectively, but not to exceed the ceiling and visibility minimums for that airport when used as an alternate airport, for each pilot in command of a turbine-powered airplane who has not served at least 100 hours as pilot in command in that type of airplane.

(e) Each pilot making an IFR takeoff or approach and landing at a military or foreign airport shall comply with applicable instrument approach procedures and weather minimums prescribed by the authority having jurisdiction over that airport. In addition, no pilot may, at that airport—

(1) Take off under IFR when the visibility is less than 1 mile; or

(2) Make an instrument approach when the visibility is less than ½ mile.

(f) If takeoff minimums are specified in Part 97 of this chapter for the takeoff airport, no pilot may take off an aircraft under IFR when the weather conditions reported by the facility described in paragraph (a)(1) of this section are less than the takeoff minimums specified for the takeoff airport in Part 97 or in the certificate holder's operations specifications.

(g) Except as provided in paragraph (h) of this section, if takeoff minimums are not prescribed in Part 97 of this chapter for the takeoff airport, no pilot may take off an aircraft under IFR when the weather conditions reported by the facility described in paragraph (a)(1) of this section are less than that prescribed in Part 91 of this chapter or in the certificate holder's operations specifications.

(h) At airports where straight-in instrument approach procedures are authorized, a pilot may take off an aircraft under IFR when the weather conditions reported by the facility described in paragraph (a)(1) of this section are equal to or better than the lowest straight-in landing minimums, unless otherwise restricted, if—

(1) The wind direction and velocity at the time of takeoff are such that a straight-in instrument approach can be made to the runway served by the instrument approach;

(2) The associated ground facilities upon which the landing minimums are predicated and the related airborne equipment are in normal operation; and

(3) The certificate holder has been approved for such operations.

§ 135.227 Icing conditions: Operating limitations.

(a) No pilot may take off an aircraft that has—

(1) Frost, snow, or ice adhering to any rotor blade, propeller, windshield,

or powerplant installation, or to an airspeed, altimeter, rate of climb, or flight attitude instrument system;

(2) Snow or ice adhering to the wings or stabilizing or control surfaces; or

(3) Any frost adhering to the wings, or stabilizing or control surfaces, unless that frost has been polished to make it smooth.

(b) Except for an airplane that has ice protection provisions that meet section 34 of Appendix A, or those for transport category airplane type certification, no pilot may fly—

(1) Under IFR into known or forecast light or moderate icing conditions; or

(2) Under VFR into known light or moderate icing conditions; unless the aircraft has functioning deicing or anti-icing equipment protecting each rotor blade, propeller, windshield, wing, stabilizing or control surface, and each airspeed, altimeter, rate of climb, or flight attitude instrument system.

(c) No pilot may fly a helicopter under IFR into known or forecast icing conditions or under VFR into known icing conditions unless it has been type certificated and appropriately equipped for operations in icing conditions.

(d) Except for an airplane that has ice protection provisions that meet section 34 of Appendix A, or those for transport category airplane type certification, no pilot may fly an aircraft into known or forecast severe icing conditions.

(e) If current weather reports and briefing information relied upon by the pilot in command indicate that the forecast icing condition that would otherwise prohibit the flight will not be encountered during the flight because of changed weather conditions since the forecast, the restrictions in paragraphs (b), (c), and (d) of this section based on forecast conditions do not apply.

[Doc. No. 16097, 43 FR 46783, Oct. 10, 1978, as amended by Amdt. 133-20, 51 FR 40710, Nov. 7, 1986]

§ 135.229 Airport requirements.

(a) No certificate holder may use any airport unless it is adequate for the proposed operation, considering such items as size, surface, obstructions, and lighting.

(b) No pilot of an aircraft carrying passengers at night may take off from, or land on, an airport unless—

(1) That pilot has determined the wind direction from an illuminated wind direction indicator or local ground communications or, in the case of takeoff, that pilot's personal observations; and

(2) The limits of the area to be used for landing or takeoff are clearly shown—

(i) For airplanes, by boundary or runway marker lights;

(ii) For helicopters, by boundary or runway marker lights or reflective material.

(c) For the purpose of paragraph (b) of this section, if the area to be used for takeoff or landing is marked by flare pots or lanterns, their use must be approved by the Administrator.

Subpart E—Flight Crewmember Requirements

§ 135.241 Applicability.

This subpart prescribes the flight crewmember requirements for operations under this part.

§ 135.243 Pilot in command qualifications.

(a) No certificate holder may use a person, nor may any person serve, as pilot in command in passenger-carrying operations of a turbojet airplane, of an airplane having a passenger seating configuration, excluding any pilot seat, of 10 seats or more, or a multiengine airplane being operated by the "Commuter Air Carrier" (as defined in Part 298 of this title), unless that person holds an airline transport pilot certificate with appropriate category and class ratings and, if required, an appropriate type rating for that airplane.

(b) Except as provided in paragraph (a) of this section, no certificate holder may use a person, nor may any person serve, as pilot in command of

an aircraft under VFR unless that person—

(1) Holds at least a commercial pilot certificate with appropriate category and class ratings and, if required, an appropriate type rating for that aircraft; and

(2) Has had at least 500 hours time as a pilot, including at least 100 hours of cross-country flight time, at least 25 hours of which were at night; and

(3) For an airplane, holds an instrument rating or an airline transport pilot certificate with an airplane category rating; or

(4) For helicopter operations conducted VFR over-the-top, holds a helicopter instrument rating, or an airline transport pilot certificate with a category and class rating for that aircraft, not limited to VFR.

(c) Except as provided in paragraph (a) of this section, no certificate holder may use a person, nor may any person serve, as pilot in command of an aircraft under IFR unless that person—

(1) Holds at least a commercial pilot certificate with appropriate category and class ratings and, if required, an appropriate type rating for that aircraft; and

(2) Has had at least 1,200 hours of flight time as a pilot, including 500 hours of cross country flight time, 100 hours of night flight time, and 75 hours of actual or simulated instrument time at least 50 hours of which were in actual flight; and

(3) For an airplane, holds an instrument rating or an airline transport pilot certificate with an airplane category rating; or

(4) For a helicopter, holds a helicopter instrument rating, or an airline transport pilot certificate with a category and class rating for that aircraft, not limited to VFR.

(d) Paragraph (b)(3) of this section does not apply when—

(1) The aircraft used is a single reciprocating-engine-powered airplane;

(2) The certificate holder does not conduct any operation pursuant to a published flight schedule which specifies five or more round trips a week between two or more points and places between which the round trips are performed, and does not transport

mail by air under a contract or contracts with the United States Postal Service having total amount estimated at the beginning of any semiannual reporting period (January 1–June 30; July 1–December 31) to be in excess of $20,000 over the 12 months commencing with the beginning of the reporting period;

(3) The area, as specified in the certificate holder's operations specifications, is an isolated area, as determined by the Flight Standards district office, if it is shown that—

(i) The primary means of navigation in the area is by pilotage, since radio navigational aids are largely ineffective; and

(ii) The primary means of transportation in the area is by air;

(4) Each flight is conducted under day VFR with a ceiling of not less than 1,000 feet and visibility not less than 3 statute miles;

(5) Weather reports or forecasts, or any combination of them, indicate that for the period commencing with the planned departure and ending 30 minutes after the planned arrival at the destination the flight may be conducted under VFR with a ceiling of not less than 1,000 feet and visibility of not less than 3 statute miles, except that if weather reports and forecasts are not available, the pilot in command may use that pilot's observations or those of other persons competent to supply weather observations if those observations indicate the flight may be conducted under VFR with the ceiling and visibility required in this paragraph;

(6) The distance of each flight from the certificate holder's base of operation to destination does not exceed 250 nautical miles for a pilot who holds a commercial pilot certificate with an airplane rating without an instrument rating, provided the pilot's certificate does not contain any limitation to the contrary; and

(7) The areas to be flown are approved by the certificate-holding FAA Flight Standards district office and are listed in the certificate holder's operations specifications.

[Doc. No. 16097, 43 FR 46783, Oct. 10, 1978; 43 FR 49975, Oct 26, 1978, as amended by Amdt. 135-15, 46 FR 30971, June 11, 1981]

§ 135.244 Operating experience.

(a) No certificate holder may use any person, nor may any person serve, as a pilot in command of an aircraft operated by a Commuter Air Carrier (as defined in § 298.2 of this title) in passenger-carrying operations, unless that person has completed, prior to designation as pilot in command, on that make and basic model aircraft and in that crewmember position, the following operating experience in each make and basic model of aircraft to be flown:

(1) Aircraft, single engine—10 hours.

(2) Aircraft multiengine, reciprocating engine-powered—15 hours.

(3) Aircraft multiengine, turbine engine-powered—20 hours.

(4) Airplane, turbojet-powered—25 hours.

(b) In acquiring the operating experience, each person must comply with the following:

(1) The operating experience must be acquired after satisfactory completion of the appropriate ground and flight training for the aircraft and crewmember position. Approved provisions for the operating experience must be included in the certificate holder's training program.

(2) The experience must be acquired in flight during commuter passenger-carrying operations under this part. However, in the case of an aircraft not previously used by the certificate holder in operations under this part, operating experience acquired in the aircraft during proving flights or ferry flights may be used to meet this requirement.

(3) Each person must acquire the operating experience while performing the duties of a pilot in command under the supervision of a qualified check pilot.

(4) The hours of operating experience may be reduced to not less than 50 percent of the hours required by this section by the substitution of one additional takeoff and landing for each hour of flight.

[Doc. No. 20011, 45 FR 7541, Feb. 4, 1980, as amended by Amdt. 135-9, 45 FR 80461, Dec. 14, 1980]

§ 135.245 Second in command qualifications.

(a) Except as provided in paragraph (b), no certificate holder may use any person, nor may any person serve, as second in command of an aircraft unless that person holds at least a commercial pilot certificate with appropriate category and class ratings and an instrument rating. For flight under IFR, that person must meet the recent instrument experience requirements of Part 61 of this chapter.

(b) A second in command of a helicopter operated under VFR, other than over-the-top, must have at least a commercial pilot certificate with an appropriate aircraft category and class rating.

[44 FR 26738, May 7, 1979]

§ 135.247 Pilot qualifications: Recent experience.

(a) No certificate holder may use any person, nor may any person serve, as pilot in command of an aircraft carrying passengers unless, within the preceding 90 days, that person has—

(1) Made three takeoffs and three landings as the sole manipulator of the flight controls in an aircraft of the same category and class and, if a type rating is required, of the same type in which that person is to serve; or

(2) For operation during the period beginning 1 hour after sunset and ending 1 hour before sunrise (as published in the Air Almanac), made three takeoffs and three landings during that period as the sole manipulator of the flight controls in an aircraft of the same category and class and, if a type rating is required, of the same type in which that person is to serve.

A person who complies with paragraph (a)(2) of this section need not comply with paragraph (a)(1) of this section.

(b) For the purpose of paragraph (a) of this section, if the aircraft is a tailwheel airplane, each takeoff must be made in a tailwheel airplane and each landing must be made to a full stop in a tailwheel airplane.

Subpart F—Flight Crewmember Flight Time Limitations and Rest Requirements

Source: Docket No. 23634, 50 FR 29320, July 18, 1985.

§ 135.261 Applicability.

Sections 135.263 through 135.271 prescribe flight time limitations and rest requirements for operations conducted under this part as follows:

(a) Section 135.263 applies to all operations under this subpart.

(b) Section 135.265 applies to:

(1) Scheduled passenger-carrying operations except those conducted solely within the state of Alaska. "Scheduled passenger-carrying operations" means passenger-carrying operations that are conducted in accordance with a published schedule which covers at least five round trips per week on at least one route between two or more points, includes dates or times (or both), and is openly advertised or otherwise made readily available to the general public, and

(2) Any other operation under this part, if the operator elects to comply with § 135.265 and obtains an appropriate operations specification amendment.

(c) Sections 135.267 and 135.269 apply to any operation that is not a scheduled passenger-carrying operation and to any operation conducted solely within the State of Alaska, unless the operator elects to comply with § 135.265 as authorized under paragraph (b)(2) of this section.

(d) Section 135.271 contains special daily flight time limits for operations conducted under the helicopter emergency medical evacuation service (HEMES).

§ 135.263 Flight time limitations and rest requirements: All certificate holders.

(a) A certificate holder may assign a flight crewmember and a flight crewmember may accept an assignment for flight time only when the applicable requirements of §§ 135.263 through 135.271 are met.

(b) No certificate holder may assign any flight crewmember to any duty with the certificate holder during any required rest period.

(c) Time spent in transportation, not local in character, that a certificate holder requires of a flight crewmember and provides to transport the crewmember to an airport at which he is to serve on a flight as a crewmember, or from an airport at which he was relieved from duty to return to his home station, is not considered part of a rest period.

(d) A flight crewmember is not considered to be assigned flight time in excess of flight time limitations if the flights to which he is assigned normally terminate within the limitations, but due to circumstances beyond the control of the certificate holder or flight crewmember (such as adverse weather conditions), are not at the time of departure expected to reach their destination within the planned flight time.

§135.265 Flight time limitations and rest requirements: Scheduled operations.

(a) No certificate holder may schedule any flight crewmember, and no flight crewmember may accept an assignment, for flight time in scheduled operations or in other commercial flying if that crewmember's total flight time in all commercial flying will exceed—

(1) 1,200 hours in any calendar year.

(2) 120 hours in any calendar month.

(3) 34 hours in any 7 consecutive days.

(4) 8 hours during any 24 consecutive hours for a flight crew consisting of one pilot.

(5) 8 hours between required rest periods for a flight crew consisting of two pilots qualified under this part for the operation being conducted.

(b) Except as provided in paragraph (c) of this section, no certificate holder may schedule a flight crewmember, and no flight crewmember may accept an assignment, for flight time during the 24 consecutive hours preceding the scheduled completion of any flight segment without a scheduled rest period during that 24 hours of at least the following:

(1) 9 consecutive hours of rest for less than 8 hours of scheduled flight time.

(2) 10 consecutive hours of rest for 8 or more but less than 9 hours of scheduled flight time.

(3) 11 consecutive hours of rest for 9 or more hours of scheduled flight time.

(c) A certificate holder may schedule a flight crewmember for less than the rest required in paragraph (b) of this section or may reduce a scheduled rest under the following conditions:

(1) A rest required under paragraph (b)(1) of this section may be scheduled for or reduced to a minimum of 8 hours if the flight crewmember is given a rest period of at least 10 hours that must begin no later than 24 hours after the commencement of the reduced rest period.

(2) A rest required under paragraph (b)(2) of this section may be scheduled for or reduced to a minimum of 8 hours if the flight crewmember is given a rest period of at least 11 hours that must begin no later than 24 hours after the commencement of the reduced rest period.

(3) A rest required under paragraph (b)(3) of this section may be scheduled for or reduced to a minimum of 9 hours if the flight crewmember is given a rest period of at least 12 hours that must begin no later than 24 hours after the commencement of the reduced rest period.

(d) Each certificate holder shall relieve each flight crewmember engaged in scheduled air transportation from all further duty for at least 24 consecutive hours during any 7 consecutive days.

§135.267 Flight time limitations and rest requirements: Unscheduled one- and two-pilot crews.

(a) No certificate holder may assign any flight crewmember, and no flight crewmember may accept an assignment, for flight time as a member of a one- or two-pilot crew if that crewmember's total flight time in all commercial flying will exceed—

(1) 500 hours in any calendar quarter.

(2) 800 hours in any two consecutive calendar quarters.

(3) 1,400 hours in any calendar year.

(b) Except as provided in paragraph (c) of this section, during any 24 consecutive hours the total flight time of the assigned flight when added to any other commercial flying by that flight crewmember may not exceed—

(1) 8 hours for a flight crew consisting of one pilot; or

(2) 10 hours for a flight crew consisting of two pilots qualified under this Part for the operation being conducted.

(c) A flight crewmember's flight time may exceed the flight time limits of paragraph (b) of this section if the assigned flight time occurs during a regularly assigned duty period of no more than 14 hours and—

(1) If this duty period is immediately preceded by and followed by a required rest period of at least 10 consecutive hours of rest;

(2) If flight time is assigned during this period, that total flight time when added to any other commercial flying by the flight crewmember may not exceed—

(i) 8 hours for a flight crew consisting of one pilot; or

(ii) 10 hours for a flight crew consisting of two pilots; and

(3) If the combined duty and rest periods equal 24 hours.

(d) Each assignment under paragraph (b) of this section must provide for at least 10 consecutive hours of rest during the 24-hour period that precedes the planned completion time of the assignment.

(e) When a flight crewmember has exceeded the daily flight time limitations in this section, because of circumstances beyond the control of the certificate holder or flight crewmember (such as adverse weather conditions), that flight crewmember must have a rest period before being assigned or accepting an assignment for flight time of at least—

(1) 11 consecutive hours of rest if the flight time limitation is exceeded by not more than 30 minutes;

(2) 12 consecutive hours of rest if the flight time limitation is exceeded by more than 30 minutes, but not more than 60 minutes; and

(3) 16 consecutive hours of rest if the flight time limitation is exceeded by more than 60 minutes.

(f) The certificate holder must provide each flight crewmember at least 13 rest periods of at least 24 consecutive hours each in each calendar quarter.

(g) The Director of Flight Operations may issue operations specifications authorizing a deviation from any specific requirement of this section if he finds that the deviation is justified to allow a certificate holder additional time, but in no case beyond October 1, 1987, to bring its operations into full compliance with the requirements of this section. Each application for a deviation must be submitted to the Director of Flight Operations before October 1, 1986. Each applicant for a deviation may continue to operate under the requirements of Subpart F of this part as in effect on September 30, 1985 until the Director of Flight Operations has responded to the deviation request.

§ 135.269 Flight time limitations and rest requirements: Unscheduled three- and four-pilot crews.

(a) No certificate holder may assign any flight crewmember, and no flight crewmember may accept an assignment, for flight time as a member of a three- or four-pilot crew if that crewmember's total flight time in all commercial flying will exceed—

(1) 500 hours in any calendar quarter.

(2) 800 hours in any two consecutive calendar quarters.

(3) 1,400 hours in any calendar year.

(b) No certificate holder may assign any pilot to a crew of three or four pilots, unless that assignment provides—

(1) At least 10 consecutive hours of rest immediately preceding the assignment;

(2) No more than 8 hours of flight deck duty in any 24 consecutive hours;

(3) No more than 18 duty hours for a three-pilot crew or 20 duty hours for a four-pilot crew in any 24 consecutive hours;

(4) No more than 12 hours aloft for a three-pilot crew or 16 hours aloft for a four-pilot crew during the maximum duty hours specified in paragraph (b)(3) of this section;

(5) Adequate sleeping facilities on the aircraft for the relief pilot;

(6) Upon completion of the assignment, a rest period of at least 12 hours;

(7) For a three-pilot crew, a crew which consists of at least the following:

(i) A pilot in command (PIC) who meets the applicable flight crewmember requirements of Subpart E of Part 135;

(ii) A PIC who meets the applicable flight crewmember requirements of Subpart E of Part 135, except those prescribed in §§ 135.244 and 135.247; and

(iii) A second in command (SIC) who meets the SIC qualifications of § 135.245.

(8) For a four-pilot crew, at least three pilots who meet the conditions of paragraph (b)(7) of this section, plus a fourth pilot who meets the SIC qualifications of § 135.245.

(c) When a flight crewmember has exceeded the daily flight deck duty limitation in this section by more than 60 minutes, because of circumstances beyond the control of the certificate holder or flight crewmember, that flight crewmember must have a rest period before the next duty period of at least 16 consecutive hours.

(d) A certificate holder must provide each flight crewmember at least 13 rest periods of at least 24 consecutive hours each in each calendar quarter.

§ 135.271 Helicopter hospital emergency medical evacuation service (HEMES).

(a) No certificate holder may assign any flight crewmember, and no flight crewmember may accept an assignment for flight time if that crewmember's total flight time in all commercial flight will exceed—

(1) 500 hours in any calendar quarter.

(2) 800 hours in any two consecutive calendar quarters.

(3) 1,400 hours in any calendar year.

(b) No certificate holder may assign a helicopter flight crewmember, and no flight crewmember may accept an assignment, for hospital emergency medical evacuation service helicopter operations unless that assignment provides for at least 10 consecutive hours of rest immediately preceding reporting to the hospital for availability for flight time.

(c) No flight crewmember may accrue more than 8 hours of flight time during any 24-consecutive hour period of a HEMES assignment, unless an emergency medical evacuation operation is prolonged. Each flight crewmember who exceeds the daily 8 hour flight time limitation in this paragraph must be relieved of the HEMES assignment immediately upon the completion of that emergency medical evacuation operation and must be given a rest period in compliance with paragraph (h) of this section.

(d) Each flight crewmember must receive at least 8 consecutive hours of rest during any 24 consecutive hour period of a HEMES assignment. A flight crewmember must be relieved of the HEMES assignment if he or she has not or cannot receive at least 8 consecutive hours of rest during any 24 consecutive hour period of a HEMES assignment.

(e) A HEMES assignment may not exceed 72 consecutive hours at the hospital.

(f) An adequate place of rest must be provided at, or in close proximity to, the hospital at which the HEMES assignment is being performed.

(g) No certificate holder may assign any other duties to a flight crewmember during a HEMES assignment.

(h) Each pilot must be given a rest period upon completion of the HEMES assignment and prior to being assigned any further duty with the certificate holder of—

(1) At least 12 consecutive hours for an assignment of less than 48 hours.

(2) At least 16 consecutive hours for an assignment of more than 48 hours.

(i) The certificate holder must provide each flight crewmember at least 13 rest periods of at least 24 consecutive hours each in each calendar quarter.

Subpart G—Crewmember Testing Requirements

§ 135.291 Applicability.

This subpart prescribes the tests and checks required for pilot and flight attendant crewmembers and for the approval of check pilots in operations under this part.

§ 135.293 Initial and recurrent pilot testing requirements.

(a) No certificate holder may use a pilot, nor may any person serve as a pilot, unless, since the beginning of the 12th calendar month before that service, that pilot has passed a written or oral test, given by the Administrator or an authorized check pilot, on that pilot's knowledge in the following areas—

(1) The appropriate provisions of Parts 61, 91, and 135 of this chapter and the operations specifications and the manual of the certificate holder;

(2) For each type of aircraft to be flown by the pilot, the aircraft powerplant, major components and systems, major appliances, performance and operating limitations, standard and emergency operating procedures, and the contents of the approved Aircraft Flight Manual or equivalent, as applicable;

(3) For each type of aircraft to be flown by the pilot, the method of determining compliance with weight and balance limitations for takeoff, landing and en route operations;

(4) Navigation and use of air navigation aids appropriate to the operation or pilot authorization, including, when applicable, instrument approach facilities and procedures;

(5) Air traffic control procedures, including IFR procedures when applicable;

(6) Meteorology in general, including the principles of frontal systems, icing, fog, thunderstorms, and windshear, and, if appropriate for the operation of the certificate holder, high altitude weather;

(7) Procedures for—

(i) Recognizing and avoiding severe weather situations;

(ii) Escaping from severe weather situations, in case of inadvertent encounters, including low-altitude windshear (except that rotorcraft pilots are not required to be tested in escaping from low-altitude windshear); and

(iii) Operating in or near thunderstorms (including best penetrating altitudes),turbulent air (including clear air turbulence), icing, hail, and other potentially hazardous meteorological conditions; and

(8) New equipment, procedures, or techniques, as appropriate.

(b) No certificate holder may use a pilot, nor may any person serve as a pilot, in any aircraft unless, since the beginning of the 12th calendar month before that service, that pilot has passed a competency check given by the Administrator or an authorized check pilot in that class of aircraft, if single-engine airplane other than turbojet, or that type of aircraft, if helicopter, multiengine airplane, or turbojet airplane, to determine the pilot's competence in practical skills and techniques in that aircraft or class of aircraft. The extent of the competency check shall be determined by the Administrator or authorized check pilot conducting the competency check. The competency check may include any of the maneuvers and procedures currently required for the original issuance of the particular pilot certificate required for the operations authorized and appropriate to the category, class and type of aircraft involved. For the purposes of this paragraph, type, as to an airplane, means any one of a group of airplanes determined by the Administrator to have a similar means of propulsion, the same manufacturer, and no significantly different handling or flight characteristics. For the purposes of this paragraph, type, as to a helicopter, means a basic make and model.

(c) The instrument proficiency check required by § 135.297 may be substituted for the competency check required by this section for the type of aircraft used in the check.

(d) For the purpose of this part, competent performance of a procedure or maneuver by a person to be used as a pilot requires that the pilot be the obvious master of the aircraft, with the successful outcome of the maneuver never in doubt.

(e) The Administrator or authorized check pilot certifies the competency of each pilot who passes the knowledge or flight check in the certificate holder's pilot records.

(f) Portions of a required competency check may be given in an aircraft simulator or other appropriate training device, if approved by the Administrator.

§135.295 Initial and recurrent flight attendant crewmember testing requirements.

No certificate holder may use a flight attendant crewmember, nor may any person serve as a flight attendant crewmember unless, since the beginning of the 12th calendar month before that service, the certificate holder has determined by appropriate initial and recurrent testing that the person is knowledgeable and competent in the following areas as appropriate to assigned duties and responsibilities—

(a) Authority of the pilot in command;

(b) Passenger handling, including procedures to be followed in handling deranged persons or other persons whose conduct might jeopardize safety;

(c) Crewmember assignments, functions, and responsibilities during ditching and evacuation of persons who may need the assistance of another person to move expeditiously to an exit in an emergency;

(d) Briefing of passengers;

(e) Location and operation of portable fire extinguishers and other items of emergency equipment;

(f) Proper use of cabin equipment and controls;

(g) Location and operation of passenger oxygen equipment;

(h) Location and operation of all normal and emergency exits, including evacuation chutes and escape ropes; and

(i) Seating of persons who may need assistance of another person to move rapidly to an exit in an emergency as prescribed by the certificate holder's operations manual.

§135.297 Pilot in command: Instrument proficiency check requirements.

(a) No certificate holder may use a pilot, nor may any person serve, as a pilot in command of an aircraft under IFR unless, since the beginning of the 6th calendar month before that service, that pilot has passed an instrument proficiency check under this section administered by the Administrator or an authorized check pilot.

(b) No pilot may use any type of precision instrument approach procedure under IFR unless, since the beginning of the 6th calendar month before that use, the pilot satisfactorily demonstrated that type of approach procedure. No pilot may use any type of nonprecision approach procedure under IFR unless, since the beginning of the 6th calendar month before that use, the pilot has satisfactorily demonstrated either that type of approach procedure or any other two different types of nonprecision approach procedures. The instrument approach procedure or procedures must include at least one straight-in approach, one circling approach, and one missed approach. Each type of approach procedure demonstrated must be conducted to published minimums for that procedure.

(c) The instrument proficiency check required by paragraph (a) of this section consists of an oral or written equipment test and a flight check under simulated or actual IFR conditions. The equipment test includes questions on emergency procedures, engine operation, fuel and lubrication systems, power settings, stall speeds, best engine-out speed, propeller and supercharger operations, and hydraulic, mechanical, and electrical systems, as appropriate. The flight check includes navigation by instruments, recovery from simulated emergencies, and standard instrument approaches involving navigational facilities which that pilot is to be authorized to use. Each pilot taking the instrument proficiency check must show that standard of competence required by §135.293(d).

(1) The instrument proficiency check must—

(i) For a pilot in command of an airplane under §135.243(a), include the procedures and maneuvers for an airline transport pilot certificate in the particular type of airplane, if appropriate; and

(ii) For a pilot in command of an airplane or helicopter under §135.243(c), include the procedures and maneuvers for a commercial pilot certificate with an instrument rating and, if required, for the appropriate type rating.

(2) The instrument proficiency check must be given by an authorized check airman or by the Administrator.

(d) If the pilot in command is assigned to pilot only one type of aircraft, that pilot must take the instrument proficiency check required by paragraph (a) of this section in that type of aircraft.

(e) If the pilot in command is assigned to pilot more than one type of aircraft, that pilot must take the instrument proficiency check required by paragraph (a) of this section in each type of aircraft to which that pilot is assigned, in rotation, but not more than one flight check during each period described in paragraph (a) of this section.

(f) If the pilot in command is assigned to pilot both single-engine and multiengine aircraft, that pilot must initially take the instrument proficiency check required by paragraph (a) of this section in a multiengine aircraft, and each succeeding check alternately in single-engine and multiengine aircraft, but not more than one flight check during each period described in paragraph (a) of this section. Portions of a required flight check may be given in an aircraft simulator or other appropriate training device, if approved by the Administrator.

(g) If the pilot in command is authorized to use an autopilot system in place of a second in command, that pilot must show, during the required instrument proficiency check, that the pilot is able (without a second in command) both with and without using the autopilot to—

(1) Conduct instrument operations competently; and

(2) Properly conduct air-ground communications and comply with complex air traffic control instructions.

(3) Each pilot taking the autopilot check must show that, while using the autopilot, the airplane can be operated as proficiently as it would be if a second in command were present to handle air-ground communications and air traffic control instructions. The autopilot check need only be demonstrated once every 12 calendar months during the instrument proficiency check required under paragraph (a) of this section.

§ 135.299 Pilot in command: Line checks: Routes and airports.

(a) No certificate holder may use a pilot, nor may any person serve, as a pilot in command of a flight unless,

since the beginning of the 12th calendar month before that service, that pilot has passed a flight check in one of the types of aircraft which that pilot is to fly. The flight check shall—

(1) Be given by an approved check pilot or by the Administrator;

(2) Consist of at least one flight over one route segment; and

(3) Include takeoffs and landings at one or more representative airports. In addition to the requirements of this paragraph, for a pilot authorized to conduct IFR operations, at least one flight shall be flown over a civil airway, an approved off-airway route, or a portion of either of them.

(b) The pilot who conducts the check shall determine whether the pilot being checked satisfactorily performs the duties and responsibilities of a pilot in command in operations under this part, and shall so certify in the pilot training record.

(c) Each certificate holder shall establish in the manual required by § 135.21 a procedure which will ensure that each pilot who has not flown over a route and into an airport within the preceding 90 days will, before beginning the flight, become familiar with all available information required for the safe operation of that flight.

§ 135.301 Crewmember: Tests and checks, grace provisions, training to accepted standards.

(a) If a crewmember who is required to take a test or a flight check under this part, completes the test or flight check in the calendar month before or after the calendar month in which it is required, that crewmember is considered to have completed the test or check in the calendar month in which it is required.

(b) If a pilot being checked under this subpart fails any of the required maneuvers, the person giving the check may give additional training to the pilot during the course of the check. In addition to repeating the maneuvers failed, the person giving the check may require the pilot being checked to repeat any other maneuvers that are necessary to determine the pilot's proficiency. If the pilot being checked is unable to demonstrate satisfactory performance to the person conducting the check, the certificate holder may not use the pilot, nor may the pilot serve, as a flight crewmember in operations under this part until the pilot has satisfactorily completed the check.

§ 135.303 Check pilot authorization: Application and issue.

Each certificate holder desiring FAA approval of a check pilot shall submit a request in writing to the FAA Flight Standards District Office charged with the overall inspection of the certificate holder. The Administrator may issue a letter of authority to each check pilot if that pilot passes the appropriate oral and flight test. The letter of authority lists the tests and checks in this part that the check pilot is qualified to give, and the category, class and type aircraft, where appropriate, for which the check pilot is qualified.

Subpart H—Training

§ 135.321 Applicability and terms used.

(a) This subpart prescribes requirements for establishing and maintaining an approved training program for crewmembers, check airmen and instructors, and other operations personnel, and for the approval and use of aircraft simulators and other training devices in the conduct of that program.

(b) For the purposes of this subpart, the following terms and definitions apply:

(1) *Initial training.* The training required for crewmembers who have not qualified and served in the same capacity on an aircraft.

(2) *Transition training.* The training required for crewmembers who have qualified and served in the same capacity on another aircraft.

(3) *Upgrade training.* The training required for crewmembers who have qualified and served as second in command on a particular aircraft type, before they serve as pilot in command on that aircraft.

(4) *Differences training.* The training required for crewmembers who have qualified and served on a particular type aircraft, when the Adminis-

trator finds differences training is necessary before a crewmember serves in the same capacity on a particular variation of that aircraft.

(5) *Recurrent training.* The training required for crewmembers to remain adequately trained and currently proficient for each aircraft, crewmember position, and type of operation in which the crewmember serves.

(6) *In flight.* The maneuvers, procedures, or functions that must be conducted in the aircraft.

§ 135.323 Training program: General.

(a) Each certificate holder required to have a training program under § 135.341 shall:

(1) Establish, obtain the appropriate initial and final approval of, and provide a training program that meets this subpart and that ensures that each crewmember, flight instructor, check airman, and each person assigned duties for the carriage and handling of hazardous materials (as defined in 49 CFR 171.8) is adequately trained to perform their assigned duties.

(2) Provide adequate ground and flight training facilities and properly qualified ground instructors for the training required by this subpart.

(3) Provide and keep current for each aircraft type used and, if applicable, the particular variations within the aircraft type, appropriate training material, examinations, forms, instructions, and procedures for use in conducting the training and checks required by this subpart.

(4) Provide enough flight instructors, check airmen, and simulator instructors to conduct required flight training and flight checks, and simulator training courses allowed under this subpart.

(b) Whenever a crewmember who is required to take recurrent training under this subpart completes the training in the calendar month before, or the calendar month after, the month in which that training is required, the crewmember is considered to have completed it in the calendar month in which it was required.

(c) Each instructor, supervisor, or check airman who is responsible for a particular ground training subject, segment of flight training, course of training, flight check, or competence check under this part shall certify as to the proficiency and knowledge of the crewmember, flight instructor, or check airman concerned upon completion of that training or check. That certification shall be made a part of the crewmember's record. When the certification required by this paragraph is made by an entry in a computerized recordkeeping system, the certifying instructor, supervisor, or check airman, must be identified with that entry. However, the signature of the certifying instructor, supervisor, or check airman, is not required for computerized entries.

(d) Training subjects that apply to more than one aircraft or crewmember position and that have been satisfactorily completed during previous training while employed by the certificate holder for another aircraft or another crewmember position, need not be repeated during subsequent training other than recurrent training.

(e) Aircraft simulators and other training devices may be used in the certificate holder's training program if approved by the Administrator.

§ 135.325   Training program and revision: Initial and final approval.

(a) To obtain initial and final approval of a training program, or a revision to an approved training program, each certificate holder must submit to the Administrator—

(1) An outline of the proposed or revised curriculum, that provides enough information for a preliminary evaluation of the proposed training program or revision; and

(2) Additional relevant information that may be requested by the Administrator.

(b) If the proposed training program or revision complies with this subpart, the Administrator grants initial approval in writing after which the certificate holder may conduct the training under that program. The Administrator then evaluates the effectiveness of the training program and advises the certificate holder of deficiencies, if any, that must be corrected.

(c) The Administrator grants final approval of the proposed training program or revision if the certificate holder shows that the training conducted under the initial approval in paragraph (b) of this section ensures that each person who successfully completes the training is adequately trained to perform that person's assigned duties.

(d) Whenever the Administrator finds that revisions are necessary for the continued adequacy of a training program that has been granted final approval, the certificate holder shall, after notification by the Administrator, make any changes in the program that are found necessary by the Administrator. Within 30 days after the certificate holder receives the notice, it may file a petition to reconsider the notice with the Administrator. The filing of a petition to reconsider stays the notice pending a decision by the Administrator. However, if the Administrator finds that there is an emergency that requires immediate action in the interest of safety, the Administrator may, upon a statement of the reasons, require a change effective without stay.

§ 135.327   Training program: Curriculum.

(a) Each certificate holder must prepare and keep current a written training program curriculum for each type of aircraft for each crewmember required for that type aircraft. The curriculum must include ground and flight training required by this subpart.

(b) Each training program curriculum must include the following:

(1) A list of principal ground training subjects, including emergency training subjects, that are provided.

(2) A list of all the training devices, mockups, systems trainers, procedures trainers, or other training aids that the certificate holder will use.

(3) Detailed descriptions or pictorial displays of the approved normal, abnormal, and emergency maneuvers, procedures and functions that will be performed during each flight training phase or flight check, indicating those maneuvers, procedures and functions that are to be performed during the

inflight portions of flight training and flight checks.

§ 135.329 Crewmember training requirements.

(a) Each certificate holder must include in its training program the following initial and transition ground training as appropriate to the particular assignment of the crewmember:

(1) Basic indoctrination ground training for newly hired crewmembers including instruction in at least the—

(i) Duties and responsibilities of crewmembers as applicable;

(ii) Appropriate provisions of this chapter;

(iii) Contents of the certificate holder's operating certificate and operations specifications (not required for flight attendants); and

(iv) Appropriate portions of the certificate holder's operating manual.

(2) The initial and transition ground training in §§ 135.345 and 135.349, as applicable.

(3) Emergency training in § 135.331.

(b) Each training program must provide the initial and transition flight training in § 135.347, as applicable.

(c) Each training program must provide recurrent ground and flight training in § 135.351.

(d) Upgrade training in §§ 135.345 and 135.347 for a particular type aircraft may be included in the training program for crewmembers who have qualified and served as second in command on that aircraft.

(e) In addition to initial, transition, upgrade and recurrent training, each training program must provide ground and flight training, instruction, and practice necessary to ensure that each crewmember—

(1) Remains adequately trained and currently proficient for each aircraft, crewmember position, and type of operation in which the crewmember serves; and

(2) Qualifies in new equipment, facilities, procedures, and techniques, including modifications to aircraft.

§ 135.331 Crewmember emergency training.

(a) Each training program must provide emergency training under this section for each aircraft type, model, and configuration, each crewmember, and each kind of operation conducted, as appropriate for each crewmember and the certificate holder.

(b) Emergency training must provide the following:

(1) Instruction in emergency assignments and procedures, including coordination among crewmembers.

(2) Individual instruction in the location, function, and operation of emergency equipment including—

(i) Equipment used in ditching and evacuation;

(ii) First aid equipment and its proper use; and

(iii) Portable fire extinguishers, with emphasis on the type of extinguisher to be used on different classes of fires.

(3) Instruction in the handling of emergency situations including—

(i) Rapid decompression;

(ii) Fire in flight or on the surface and smoke control procedures with emphasis on electrical equipment and related circuit breakers found in cabin areas;

(iii) Ditching and evacuation;

(iv) Illness, injury, or other abnormal situations involving passengers or crewmembers; and

(v) Hijacking and other unusual situations.

(4) Review of the certificate holder's previous aircraft accidents and incidents involving actual emergency situations.

(c) Each crewmember must perform at least the following emergency drills, using the proper emergency equipment and procedures, unless the Administrator finds that, for a particular drill, the crewmember can be adequately trained by demonstration:

(1) Ditching, if applicable.

(2) Emergency evacuation.

(3) Fire extinguishing and smoke control.

(4) Operation and use of emergency exits, including deployment and use of evacuation chutes, if applicable.

(5) Use of crew and passenger oxygen.

(6) Removal of life rafts from the aircraft, inflation of the life rafts, use of life lines, and boarding of passengers and crew, if applicable.

(7) Donning and inflation of life vests and the use of other individual flotation devices, if applicable.

(d) Crewmembers who serve in operations above 25,000 feet must receive instruction in the following:

(1) Respiration.

(2) Hypoxia.

(3) Duration of consciousness without supplemental oxygen at altitude.

(4) Gas expansion.

(5) Gas bubble formation.

(6) Physical phenomena and incidents of decompression.

§ 135.333   Training requirements: Handling and carriage of hazardous materials.

(a) Except as provided in paragraph (d) of this section, no certificate holder may use any person to perform, and no person may perform, any assigned duties and responsibilities for the handling or carriage of hazardous materials (as defined in 49 CFR 171.8), unless within the preceding 12 calendar months that person has satisfactorily completed initial or recurrent training in an appropriate training program established by the certificate holder, which includes instruction regarding—

(1) The proper shipper certification, packaging, marking, labeling, and documentation for hazardous materials; and

(2) The compatibility, loading, storage, and handling characteristics of hazardous materials.

(b) Each certificate holder shall maintain a record of the satisfactory completion of the initial and recurrent training given to crewmembers and ground personnel who perform assigned duties and responsibilities for the handling and carriage of hazardous materials.

(c) Each certificate holder that elects not to accept hazardous materials shall ensure that each crewmember is adequately trained to recognize those items classified as hazardous materials.

(d) If a certificate holder operates into or out of airports at which trained employees or contract personnel are not available, it may use persons not meeting the requirements of paragraphs (a) and (b) of this section to load, offload, or otherwise handle hazardous materials if these persons are supervised by a crewmember who is qualified under paragraphs (a) and (b) of this section.

§ 135.335   Approval of aircraft simulators and other training devices.

(a) Training courses using aircraft simulators and other training devices may be included in the certificate holder's training program if approved by the Administrator.

(b) Each aircraft simulator and other training device that is used in a training course or in checks required under this subpart must meet the following requirements:

(1) It must be specifically approved for—

(i) The certificate holder; and

(ii) The particular maneuver, procedure, or crewmember function involved.

(2) It must maintain the performance, functional, and other characteristics that are required for approval.

(3) Additionally, for aircraft simulators, it must be—

(i) Approved for the type aircraft and, if applicable, the particular variation within type for which the training or check is being conducted; and

(ii) Modified to conform with any modification to the aircraft being simulated that changes the performance, functional, or other characteristics required for approval.

(c) A particular aircraft simulator or other training device may be used by more than one certificate holder.

(d) In granting initial and final approval of training programs or revisions to them, the Administrator considers the training devices, methods and procedures listed in the certificate holder's curriculum under § 135.327.

[Doc. No. 16907, 43 FR 46783, Oct. 10, 1978, as amended at 44 FR 26738, May 7, 1979]

§ 135.337   Training program: Check airmen and instructor qualifications.

(a) No certificate holder may use a person, nor may any person serve, as a flight instructor or check airman in a training program established under this subpart unless, for the particular aircraft type involved, that person—

(1) Holds the airman certificate and ratings that must be held to serve as a pilot in command in operations under this part;

(2) Has satisfactorily completed the appropriate training phases for the aircraft, including recurrent training, required to serve as a pilot in command in operations under this part;

(3) Has satisfactorily completed the appropriate proficiency or competency checks required to serve as a pilot in command in operations under this part;

(4) Has satisfactorily completed the applicable training requirements of § 135.339;

(5) Holds a Class I or Class II medical certificate required to serve as a pilot in command in operations under this part;

(6) In the case of a check airman, has been approved by the Administrator for the airman duties involved; and

(7) In the case of a check airman used in an aircraft simulator only, holds a Class III medical certificate.

(b) No certificate holder may use a person, nor may any person serve, as a simulator instructor for a course of training given in an aircraft simulator under this subpart unless that person—

(1) Holds at least a commercial pilot certificate; and

(2) Has satisfactorily completed the following as evidenced by the approval of a check airman—

(i) Appropriate initial pilot and flight instructor ground training under this subpart; and

(ii) A simulator flight training course in the type simulator in which that person instructs under this subpart.

§ 135.339 Check airmen and flight instructors: Initial and transition training.

(a) The initial and transition ground training for pilot check airmen must include the following:

(1) Pilot check airman duties, functions, and responsibilities.

(2) The applicable provisions of this chapter and certificate holder's policies and procedures.

(3) The appropriate methods, procedures, and techniques for conducting the required checks.

(4) Proper evaluation of pilot performance including the detection of—

(i) Improper and insufficient training; and

(ii) Personal characteristics that could adversely affect safety.

(5) The appropriate corrective action for unsatisfactory checks.

(6) The approved methods, procedures, and limitations for performing the required normal, abnormal, and emergency procedures in the aircraft.

(b) The initial and transition ground training for pilot flight instructors, except for the holder of a valid flight instructor certificate, must include the following:

(1) The fundamental principles of the teaching-learning process.

(2) Teaching methods and procedures.

(3) The instructor-student relationship.

(c) The initial and transition flight training for pilot check airmen and pilot flight instructors must include the following:

(1) Enough inflight training and practice in conducting flight checks from the left and right pilot seats in the required normal, abnormal, and emergency maneuvers to ensure that person's competence to conduct the pilot flight checks and flight training under this subpart.

(2) The appropriate safety measures to be taken from either pilot seat for emergency situations that are likely to develop in training.

(3) The potential results of improper or untimely safety measures during training.

The requirements of paragraphs (c)(2) and (3) of this section may be accomplished in flight or in an approved simulator.

§ 135.341 Pilot and flight attendant crewmember training programs.

(a) Each certificate holder, other than one who uses only one pilot in the certificate holder's operations, shall establish and maintain an approved pilot training program, and each certificate holder who uses a flight attendant crewmember shall establish and maintain an approved flight attendant training program, that is appropriate to the operations to which each pilot and flight attendant is to be assigned, and will ensure that they are adequately trained to meet the applicable knowledge and practical testing requirements of §§ 135.293 through 135.301. However, the Administrator may authorize a deviation from this section if the Administrator finds that, because of the limited size and scope of the operation, safety will allow a deviation from these requirements.

(b) Each certificate holder required to have a training program by paragraph (a) of this section shall include in that program ground and flight training curriculums for—

(1) Initial training;
(2) Transition training;
(3) Upgrade training;
(4) Differences training; and
(5) Recurrent training.

(c) Each certificate holder required to have a training program by paragraph (a) of this section shall provide current and appropriate study materials for use by each required pilot and flight attendant.

(d) The certificate holder shall furnish copies of the pilot and flight attendant crewmember training program, and all changes and additions, to the assigned representative of the Administrator. If the certificate holder uses training facilities of other persons, a copy of those training programs or appropriate portions used for those facilities shall also be furnished. Curricula that follow FAA published curricula may be cited by reference in the copy of the training program furnished to the representative of the Administrator and need not be furnished with the program.

§ 135.343 Crewmember initial and recurrent training requirements.

No certificate holder may use a person, nor may any person serve, as a crewmember in operations under this part unless that crewmember has completed the appropriate initial or recurrent training phase of the training program appropriate to the type of operation in which the crewmember is to

serve since the beginning of the 12th calendar month before that service. This section does not apply to a certificate holder that uses only one pilot in the certificate holder's operations.

§ 135.345 Pilots: Initial, transition, and upgrade ground training.

Initial, transition, and upgrade ground training for pilots must include instruction in at least the following, as applicable to their duties:

(a) General subjects—
(1) The certificate holder's flight locating procedures;
(2) Principles and methods for determining weight and balance, and runway limitations for takeoff and landing;
(3) Enough meteorology to ensure a practical knowledge of weather phenomena, including the principles of frontal systems, icing, fog, thunderstorms, windshear and, if appropriate, high altitude weather situations;
(4) Air traffic control systems, procedures, and phraseology;
(5) Navigation and the use of navigational aids, including instrument approach procedures;
(6) Normal and emergency communication procedures;
(7) Visual cues before and during descent below DH or MDA; and
(8) Other instructions necessary to ensure the pilot's competence.

(b) For each aircraft type—
(1) A general description;
(2) Performance characteristics;
(3) Engines and propellers;
(4) Major components;
(5) Major aircraft systems (i.e., flight controls, electrical, and hydraulic), other systems, as appropriate, principles of normal, abnormal, and emergency operations, appropriate procedures and limitations;
(6) Procedures for—
(i) Recognizing and avoiding severe weather situations;
(ii) Escaping from severe weather situations, in case of inadvertent encounters, including low-altitude windshear (except that rotorcraft pilots are not required to be trained in escaping from low altitude windshear); and
(iii) Operating in or near thunderstorms (including best penetrating altitudes),turbulent air (including clear air turbulence), icing, hail, and other potentially hazardous meteorological conditions:

(7) Operating limitations;

(8) Fuel consumption and cruise control;

(9) Flight planning;

(10) Each normal and emergency procedure; and

(11) The approved Aircraft Flight Manual, or equivalent.

§ 135.347 Pilots: Initial, transition, upgrade, and differences flight training.

(a) Initial, transition, upgrade, and differences training for pilots must include flight and practice in each of the maneuvers and procedures in the approved training program curriculum.

(b) The maneuvers and procedures required by paragraph (a) of this section must be performed in flight, except to the extent that certain maneuvers and procedures may be performed in an aircraft simulator, or an appropriate training device, as allowed by this subpart.

(c) If the certificate holder's approved training program includes a course of training using an aircraft simulator or other training device, each pilot must successfully complete—

(1) Training and practice in the simulator or training device in at least the maneuvers and procedures in this subpart that are capable of being performed in the aircraft simulator or training device; and

(2) A flight check in the aircraft or a check in the simulator or training device to the level of proficiency of a pilot in command or second in command, as applicable, in at least the maneuvers and procedures that are capable of being performed in an aircraft simulator or training device.

§ 135.349 Flight attendants: Initial and transition ground training.

Initial and transition ground training for flight attendants must include instruction in at least the following—

(a) General subjects—

(1) The authority of the pilot in command; and

(2) Passenger handling, including procedures to be followed in handling deranged persons or other persons whose conduct might jeopardize safety.

(b) For each aircraft type—

(1) A general description of the aircraft emphasizing physical characteristics that may have a bearing on ditching, evacuation, and inflight emergency procedures and on other related duties;

(2) The use of both the public address system and the means of communicating with other flight crewmembers, including emergency means in the case of attempted hijacking or other unusual situations; and

(3) Proper use of electrical galley equipment and the controls for cabin heat and ventilation.

§ 135.351 Recurrent training.

(a) Each certificate holder must ensure that each crewmember receives recurrent training and is adequately trained and currently proficient for the type aircraft and crewmember position involved.

(b) Recurrent ground training for crewmembers must include at least the following:

(1) A quiz or other review to determine the crewmember's knowledge of the aircraft and crewmember position involved.

(2) Instruction as necessary in the subjects required for initial ground training by this subpart, as appropriate, including low-altitude windshear training as prescribed in § 135.345 of this part and emergency training.

(c) Recurrent flight training for pilots must include, at least, flight training in the maneuvers or procedures in this subpart, except that satisfactory completion of the check required by § 135.293 within the preceding 12 calendar months may be substituted for recurrent flight training.

Subpart I—Airplane Performance Operating Limitations *Ignore*

§ 135.361 Applicability.

(a) This subpart prescribes airplane performance operating limitations applicable to the operation of the categories of airplanes listed in § 135.363 when operated under this part.

(b) For the purpose of this subpart, "effective length of the runway," for landing means the distance from the point at which the obstruction clearance plane associated with the approach end of the runway intersects the centerline of the runway to the far end of the runway.

(c) For the purpose of this subpart, "obstruction clearance plane" means a plane sloping upward from the runway at a slope of 1:20 to the horizontal, and tangent to or clearing all obstructions within a specified area surrounding the runway as shown in a profile view of that area. In the plan view, the centerline of the specified area coincides with the centerline of the runway, beginning at the point where the obstruction clearance plane intersects the centerline of the runway and proceeding to a point at least 1,500 feet from the beginning point. After that the centerline coincides with the takeoff path over the ground for the runway (in the case of takeoffs) or with the instrument approach counterpart (for landings), or, where the applicable one of these paths has not been established, it proceeds consistent with turns of at least 4,000-foot radius until a point is reached beyond which the obstruction clearance plane clears all obstructions. This area extends laterally 200 feet on each side of the centerline at the point where the obstruction clearance plane intersects the runway and continues at this width to the end of the runway; then it increases uniformly to 500 feet on each side of the centerline at a point 1,500 feet from the intersection of the obstruction clearance plane with the runway; after that it extends laterally 500 feet on each side of the centerline.

§ 135.363 General.

(a) Each certificate holder operating a reciprocating engine powered large transport category airplane shall comply with §§ 135.365 through 135.377.

(b) Each certificate holder operating a turbine engine powered large transport category airplane shall comply with §§ 135.379 through 135.387, except that when it operates a turbo-propeller-powered large transport category airplane certificated after August 29, 1959, but previously type certificated with the same number of reciprocating engines, it may comply with §§ 135.365 through 135.377.

(c) Each certificate holder operating a large nontransport category airplane shall comply with §§ 135.389 through 135.395 and any determination of compliance must be based only on approved performance data. For the purpose of this subpart, a large nontransport category airplane is an airplane that was type certificated before July 1, 1942.

(d) Each certificate holder operating a small transport category airplane shall comply with § 135.397.

(e) Each certificate holder operating a small nontransport category airplane shall comply with § 135.399.

(f) The performance data in the Airplane Flight Manual applies in determining compliance with §§ 135.365 through 135.387. Where conditions are different from those on which the performance data is based, compliance is determined by interpolation or by computing the effects of change in the specific variables, if the results of the interpolation or computations are substantially as accurate as the results of direct tests.

(g) No person may take off a reciprocating engine powered large transport category airplane at a weight that is more than the allowable weight for the runway being used (determined under the runway takeoff limitations of the transport category operating rules of this subpart) after taking into account the temperature operating correction factors in section 4a.749a-T or section 4b.117 of the Civil Air Regulations in effect on January 31, 1965, and in the applicable Airplane Flight Manual.

(h) The Administrator may authorize in the operations specifications deviations from this subpart if special circumstances make a literal observance of a requirement unnecessary for safety.

(i) The 10-mile width specified in §§ 135.369 through 135.373 may be reduced to 5 miles, for not more than 20 miles, when operating under VFR or where navigation facilities furnish reliable and accurate identification of high ground and obstructions located outside of 5 miles, but within 10 miles, on each side of the intended track.

(j) Each certificate holder operating a commuter category airplane shall comply with § 135.398.

[Doc. No. 16097, 43 FR 46783, Oct. 10, 1978, as amended by Amdt. 135-21, 52 FR 1836, Jan. 15, 1987]

§ 135.365 **Large transport category airplanes: Reciprocating engine powered: Weight limitations.**

(a) No person may take off a reciprocating engine powered large transport category airplane from an airport located at an elevation outside of the range for which maximum takeoff weights have been determined for that airplane.

(b) No person may take off a reciprocating engine powered large transport category airplane for an airport of intended destination that is located at an elevation outside of the range for which maximum landing weights have been determined for that airplane.

(c) No person may specify, or have specified, an alternate airport that is located at an elevation outside of the range for which maximum landing weights have been determined for the reciprocating engine powered large transport category airplane concerned.

(d) No person may take off a reciprocating engine powered large transport category airplane at a weight more than the maximum authorized takeoff weight for the elevation of the airport.

(e) No person may take off a reciprocating engine powered large transport category airplane if its weight on arrival at the airport of destination will be more than the maximum authorized landing weight for the elevation of that airport, allowing for normal consumption of fuel and oil en route.

§ 135.367 **Large transport category airplanes: Reciprocating engine powered: Takeoff limitations.**

(a) No person operating a reciprocating engine powered large transport category airplane may take off that airplane unless it is possible—

(1) To stop the airplane safely on the runway, as shown by the accelerate-stop distance data, at any time during takeoff until reaching critical-engine failure speed;

(2) If the critical engine fails at any time after the airplane reaches critical-engine failure speed V_1, to continue the takeoff and reach a height of 50 feet, as indicated by the takeoff path data, before passing over the end of the runway; and

(3) To clear all obstacles either by at least 50 feet vertically (as shown by the takeoff path data) or 200 feet horizontally within the airport boundaries and 300 feet horizontally beyond the boundaries, without banking before reaching a height of 50 feet (as shown by the takeoff path data) and after that without banking more than 15 degrees.

(b) In applying this section, corrections must be made for any runway gradient. To allow for wind effect, takeoff data based on still air may be corrected by taking into account not more than 50 percent of any reported headwind component and not less than 150 percent of any reported tailwind component.

§ 135.369 **Large transport category airplanes: Reciprocating engine powered: En route limitations: All engines operating.**

(a) No person operating a reciprocating engine powered large transport category airplane may take off that airplane at a weight, allowing for normal consumption of fuel and oil, that does not allow a rate of climb (in feet per minute), with all engines operating, of at least 6.90 Vs_0 (that is, the number of feet per minute obtained by multiplying the number of knots by 6.90) at an altitude of a least 1,000 feet above the highest ground or obstruction within ten miles of each side of the intended track.

(b) This section does not apply to large transport category airplanes certificated under Part 4a of the Civil Air Regulations.

§ 135.371 **Large transport category airplanes: Reciprocating engine powered: En route limitations: One engine inoperative.**

(a) Except as provided in paragraph (b) of this section, no person operating a reciprocating engine powered large transport category airplane may take off that airplane at a weight, allowing for normal consumption of fuel and oil, that does not allow a rate of climb (in feet per minute), with one engine inoperative, of at least (0.079−0.106/

N) Vs_o^2 (where N is the number of engines installed and Vs_o is expressed in knots) at an altitude of least 1,000 feet above the highest ground or obstruction within 10 miles of each side of the intended track. However, for the purposes of this paragraph the rate of climb for transport category airplanes certificated under Part 4a of the Civil Air Regulations is 0.026 Vs_o^2.

(b) In place of the requirements of paragraph (a) of this section, a person may, under an approved procedure, operate a reciprocating engine powered large transport category airplane at an all-engines-operating altitude that allows the airplane to continue, after an engine failure, to an alternate airport where a landing can be made under § 135.377, allowing for normal consumption of fuel and oil. After the assumed failure, the flight path must clear the ground and any obstruction within five miles on each side of the intended track by at least 2,000 feet.

(c) If an approved procedure under paragraph (b) of this section is used, the certificate holder shall comply with the following:

(1) The rate of climb (as prescribed in the Airplane Flight Manual for the appropriate weight and altitude) used in calculating the airplane's flight path shall be diminished by an amount in feet per minute, equal to $(0.079-0.106/N)$ Vs_o^2 (when N is the number of engines installed and Vs_o is expressed in knots) for airplanes certificated under Part 25 of this chapter and by 0.026 Vs_o^2 for airplanes certificated under Part 4a of the Civil Air Regulations.

(2) The all-engines-operating altitude shall be sufficient so that in the event the critical engine becomes inoperative at any point along the route, the flight will be able to proceed to a predetermined alternate airport by use of this procedure. In determining the takeoff weight, the airplane is assumed to pass over the critical obstruction following engine failure at a point no closer to the critical obstruction than the nearest approved radio navigational fix, unless the Administrator approves a procedure established on a different basis upon finding that adequate operational safeguards exist.

(3) The airplane must meet the provisions of paragraph (a) of this section at 1,000 feet above the airport used as an alternate in this procedure.

(4) The procedure must include an approved method of accounting for winds and temperatures that would otherwise adversely affect the flight path.

(5) In complying with this procedure, fuel jettisoning is allowed if the certificate holder shows that it has an adequate training program, that proper instructions are given to the flight crew, and all other precautions are taken to ensure a safe procedure.

(6) The certificate holder and the pilot in command shall jointly elect an alternate airport for which the appropriate weather reports or forecasts, or any combination of them, indicate that weather conditions will be at or above the alternate weather minimum specified in the certificate holder's operations specifications for that airport when the flight arrives.

§ 135.373 Part 25 transport category airplanes with four or more engines: Reciprocating engine powered: En route limitations: Two engines inoperative.

(a) No person may operate an airplane certificated under Part 25 and having four or more engines unless—

(1) There is no place along the intended track that is more than 90 minutes (with all engines operating at cruising power) from an airport that meets § 135.377; or

(2) It is operated at a weight allowing the airplane, with the two critical engines inoperative, to climb at 0.013 Vs_o^2 feet per minute (that is, the number of feet per minute obtained by multiplying the number of knots squared by 0.013) at an altitude of 1,000 feet above the highest ground or obstruction within 10 miles on each side of the intended track, or at an altitude of 5,000 feet, whichever is higher.

(b) For the purposes of paragraph (a)(2) of this section, it is assumed that—

(1) The two engines fail at the point that is most critical with respect to the takeoff weight;

(2) Consumption of fuel and oil is normal with all engines operating up to the point where the two engines fail with two engines operating beyond that point;

(3) Where the engines are assumed to fail at an altitude above the prescribed minimum altitude, compliance with the prescribed rate of climb at the prescribed minimum altitude need not be shown during the descent from the cruising altitude to the prescribed minimum altitude, if those requirements can be met once the prescribed minimum altitude is reached, and assuming descent to be along a net flight path and the rate of descent to be 0.013 Vs_o^2 greater than the rate in the approved performance data; and

(4) If fuel jettisoning is provided, the airplane's weight at the point where the two engines fail is considered to be not less than that which would include enough fuel to proceed to an airport meeting § 135.377 and to arrive at an altitude of at least 1,000 feet directly over that airport.

§ 135.375 Large transport category airplanes: Reciprocating engine powered: Landing limitations: Destination airports.

(a) Except as provided in paragraph (b) of this section, no person operating a reciprocating engine powered large transport category airplane may take off that airplane, unless its weight on arrival, allowing for normal consumption of fuel and oil in flight, would allow a full stop landing at the intended destination within 60 percent of the effective length of each runway described below from a point 50 feet directly above the intersection of the obstruction clearance plane and the runway. For the purposes of determining the allowable landing weight at the destination airport the following is assumed:

(1) The airplane is landed on the most favorable runway and in the most favorable direction in still air.

(2) The airplane is landed on the most suitable runway considering the probable wind velocity and direction (forecast for the expected time of arrival), the ground handling characteristics of the type of airplane, and other conditions such as landing aids and terrain, and allowing for the effect of the landing path and roll of not more than 50 percent of the headwind component or not less than 150 percent of the tailwind component.

(b) An airplane that would be prohibited from being taken off because it could not meet paragraph (a)(2) of this section may be taken off if an alternate airport is selected that meets all of this section except that the airplane can accomplish a full stop landing within 70 percent of the effective length of the runway.

§ 135.377 Large transport category airplanes: Reciprocating engine powered: Landing limitations: Alternate airports.

No person may list an airport as an alternate airport in a flight plan unless the airplane (at the weight anticipated at the time of arrival at the airport), based on the assumptions in § 135.375(a) (1) and (2), can be brought to a full stop landing within 70 percent of the effective length of the runway.

§ 135.379 Large transport category airplanes: Turbine engine powered: Takeoff limitations.

(a) No person operating a turbine engine powered large transport category airplane may take off that airplane at a weight greater than that listed in the Airplane Flight Manual for the elevation of the airport and for the ambient temperature existing at takeoff.

(b) No person operating a turbine engine powered large transport category airplane certificated after August 26, 1957, but before August 30, 1959 (SR422, 422A), may take off that airplane at a weight greater than that listed in the Airplane Flight Manual for the minumum distance required for takeoff. In the case of an airplane certificated after September 30, 1958 (SR422A, 422B), the takeoff distance may include a clearway distance but the clearway distance included may not be greater than one-half of the takeoff run.

(c) No person operating a turbine engine powered large transport category airplane certificated after August 29, 1959 (SR422B), may take off that airplane at a weight greater than that listed in the Airplane Flight Manual at which compliance with the following may be shown:

(1) The accelerate-stop distance, as defined in § 25.109 of this chapter, must not exceed the length of the runway plus the length of any stopway.

(2) The takeoff distance must not exceed the length of the runway plus the length of any clearway except that the length of any clearway included must not be greater than one-half the length of the runway.

(3) The takeoff run must not be greater than the length of the runway.

(d) No person operating a turbine engine powered large transport category airplane may take off that airplane at a weight greater than that listed in the Airplane Flight Manual—

(1) For an airplane certificated after August 26, 1957, but before October 1, 1958 (SR422), that allows a takeoff path that clears all obstacles either by at least (35+0.01 D) feet vertically (D is the distance along the intended flight path from the end of the runway in feet), or by at least 200 feet horizontally within the airport boundaries and by at least 300 feet horizontally after passing the boundaries; or

(2) For an airplane certificated after September 30, 1958 (SR422A, 422B), that allows a net takeoff flight path that clears all obstacles either by a height of at least 35 feet vertically, or by at least 200 feet horizontally within the airport boundaries and by at least 300 feet horizontally after passing the boundaries.

(e) In determining maximum weights, minimum distances and flight paths under paragraphs (a) through (d) of this section, correction must be made for the runway to be used, the elevation of the airport, the effective runway gradient, and the ambient temperature and wind component at the time of takeoff.

(f) For the purposes of this section, it is assumed that the airplane is not banked before reaching a height of 50 feet, as shown by the takeoff path or net takeoff flight path data (as appropriate) in the Airplane Flight Manual,

and after that the maximum bank is not more than 15 degrees.

(g) For the purposes of this section, the terms, "takeoff distance," "takeoff run," "net takeoff flight path," have the same meanings as set forth in the rules under which the airplane was certificated.

§ 135.381 Large transport category airplanes: Turbine engine powered: En route limitations: One engine inoperative.

(a) No person operating a turbine engine powered large transport category airplane may take off that airplane at a weight, allowing for normal consumption of fuel and oil, that is greater than that which (under the approved, one engine inoperative, en route net flight path data in the Airplane Flight Manual for that airplane) will allow compliance with paragraph (a) (1) or (2) of this section, based on the ambient temperatures expected en route.

(1) There is a positive slope at an altitude of at least 1,000 feet above all terrain and obstructions within five statute miles on each side of the intended track, and, in addition, if that airplane was certificated after August 29, 1958 (SR422B), there is a positive slope at 1,500 feet above the airport where the airplane is assumed to land after an engine fails.

(2) The net flight path allows the airplane to continue flight from the cruising altitude to an airport where a landing can be made under § 135.387 clearing all terrain and obstructions within five statute miles of the intended track by at least 2,000 feet vertically and with a positive slope at 1,000 feet above the airport where the airplane lands after an engine fails, or, if that airplane was certificated after September 30, 1958 (SR422A, 422B), with a positive slope at 1,500 feet above the airport where the airplane lands after an engine fails.

(b) For the purpose of paragraph (a)(2) of this section, it is assumed that—

(1) The engine fails at the most critical point en route;

(2) The airplane passes over the critical obstruction, after engine failure at

a point that is no closer to the obstruction than the approved radio navigation fix, unless the Administrator authorizes a different procedure based on adequate operational safeguards;

(3) An approved method is used to allow for adverse winds;

(4) Fuel jettisoning will be allowed if the certificate holder shows that the crew is properly instructed, that the training program is adequate, and that all other precautions are taken to ensure a safe procedure;

(5) The alternate airport is selected and meets the prescribed weather minimums; and

(6) The consumption of fuel and oil after engine failure is the same as the consumption that is allowed for in the approved net flight path data in the Airplane Flight Manual.

§135.383 Large transport category airplanes: Turbine engine powered: En route limitations: Two engines inoperative.

(a) Airplanes certificated after August 26, 1957, but before October 1, 1958 (SR422). No person may operate a turbine engine powered large transport category airplane along an intended route unless that person complies with either of the following:

(1) There is no place along the intended track that is more than 90 minutes (with all engines operating at cruising power) from an airport that meets § 135.387.

(2) Its weight, according to the two-engine-inoperative, en route, net flight path data in the Airplane Flight Manual, allows the airplane to fly from the point where the two engines are assumed to fail simultaneously to an airport that meets § 135.387, with a net flight path (considering the ambient temperature anticipated along the track) having a positive slope at an altitude of at least 1,000 feet above all terrain and obstructions within five statute miles on each side of the intended track, or at an altitude of 5,000 feet, whichever is higher.

For the purposes of paragraph (a)(2) of this section, it is assumed that the two engines fail at the most critical point en route, that if fuel jettisoning is provided, the airplane's weight at the point where the engines fail includes enough fuel to continue to the airport and to arrive at an altitude of at least 1,000 feet directly over the airport, and that the fuel and oil consumption after engine failure is the same as the consumption allowed for in the net flight path data in the Airplane Flight Manual.

(b) Airplanes certificated after September 30, 1958, but before August 30, 1959 (SR422A). No person may operate a turbine engine powered large transport category airplane along an intended route unless that person complies with either of the following:

(1) There is no place along the intended track that is more than 90 minutes (with all engines operating at cruising power) from an airport that meets § 135.387.

(2) Its weight, according to the two-engine-inoperative, en route, net flight path data in the Airplane Flight Manual allows the airplane to fly from the point where the two engines are assumed to fail simultaneously to an airport that meets § 135.387 with a net flight path (considering the ambient temperatures anticipated along the track) having a positive slope at an altitude of at least 1,000 feet above all terrain and obstructions within five statute miles on each side of the intended track, or at an altitude of 2,000 feet, whichever is higher.

For the purpose of paragraph (b)(2) of this section, it is assumed that the two engines fail at the most critical point en route, that the airplane's weight at the point where the engines fail includes enough fuel to continue to the airport, to arrive at an altitude of at least 1,500 feet directly over the airport, and after that to fly for 15 minutes at cruise power or thrust, or both, and that the consumption of fuel and oil after engine failure is the same as the consumption allowed for in the net flight path data in the Airplane Flight Manual.

(c) Aircraft certificated after August 29, 1959 (SR422B). No person may operate a turbine engine powered large transport category airplane along an intended route unless that person complies with either of the following:

(1) There is no place along the intended track that is more than 90 min-

utes (with all engines operating at cruising power) from an airport that meets § 135.387.

(2) Its weight, according to the two-engine-inoperative, en route, net flight path data in the Airplane Flight Manual, allows the airplane to fly from the point where the two engines are assumed to fail simultaneously to an airport that meets § 135.387, with the net flight path (considering the ambient temperatures anticipated along the track) clearing vertically by at least 2,000 feet all terrain and obstructions within five statute miles on each side of the intended track. For the purposes of this paragraph, it is assumed that—

(i) The two engines fail at the most critical point en route;

(ii) The net flight path has a positive slope at 1,500 feet above the airport where the landing is assumed to be made after the engines fail;

(iii) Fuel jettisoning will be approved if the certificate holder shows that the crew is properly instructed, that the training program is adequate, and that all other precautions are taken to ensure a safe procedure;

(iv) The airplane's weight at the point where the two engines are assumed to fail provides enough fuel to continue to the airport, to arrive at an altitude of at least 1,500 feet directly over the airport, and after that to fly for 15 minutes at cruise power or thrust, or both; and

(v) The consumption of fuel and oil after the engines fail is the same as the consumption that is allowed for in the net flight path data in the Airplane Flight Manual.

§ 135.385 Large transport category airplanes: Turbine engine powered: Landing limitations: Destination airports.

(a) No person operating a turbine engine powered large transport category airplane may take off that airplane at a weight that (allowing for normal consumption of fuel and oil in flight to the destination or alternate airport) the weight of the airplane on arrival would exceed the landing weight in the Airplane Flight Manual for the elevation of the destination or alternate airport and the ambient temperature anticipated at the time of landing.

(b) Except as provided in paragraph (c), (d), or (e) of this section, no person operating a turbine engine powered large transport category airplane may take off that airplane unless its weight on arrival, allowing for normal consumption of fuel and oil in flight (in accordance with the landing distance in the Airplane Flight Manual for the elevation of the destination airport and the wind conditions anticipated there at the time of landing), would allow a full stop landing at the intended destination airport within 60 percent of the effective length of each runway described below from a point 50 feet above the intersection of the obstruction clearance plane and the runway. For the purpose of determining the allowable landing weight at the destination airport the following is assumed:

(1) The airplane is landed on the most favorable runway and in the most favorable direction, in still air.

(2) The airplane is landed on the most suitable runway considering the probable wind velocity and direction and the ground handling characteristics of the airplane, and considering other conditions such as landing aids and terrain.

(c) A turbopropeller powered airplane that would be prohibited from being taken off because it could not meet paragraph (b)(2) of this section, may be taken off if an alternate airport is selected that meets all of this section except that the airplane can accomplish a full stop landing within 70 percent of the effective length of the runway.

(d) Unless, based on a showing of actual operating landing techniques on wet runways, a shorter landing distance (but never less than that required by paragraph (b) of this section) has been approved for a specific type and model airplane and included in the Airplane Flight Manual, no person may take off a turbojet airplane when the appropriate weather reports or forecasts, or any combination of them, indicate that the runways at the destination airport may be wet or slippery at the estimated time of arrival unless the effective runway length at the destination airport is at least 115 percent of the runway length required under paragraph (b) of this section.

(e) A turbojet airplane that would be prohibited from being taken off because it could not meet paragraph (b)(2) of this section may be taken off if an alternate airport is selected that meets all of paragraph (b) of this section.

§ 135.387 Large transport category airplanes: Turbine engine powered: Landing limitations: Alternate airports.

No person may select an airport as an alternate airport for a turbine engine powered large transport category airplane unless (based on the assumptions in § 135.385(b)) that airplane, at the weight anticipated at the time of arrival, can be brought to a full stop landing within 70 percent of the effective length of the runway for turbopropeller-powered airplanes and 60 percent of the effective length of the runway for turbojet airplanes, from a point 50 feet above the intersection of the obstruction clearance plane and the runway.

§ 135.389 Large nontransport category airplanes: Takeoff limitations.

(a) No person operating a large nontransport category airplane may take off that airplane at a weight greater than the weight that would allow the airplane to be brought to a safe stop within the effective length of the runway, from any point during the takeoff before reaching 105 percent of minimum control speed (the minimum speed at which an airplane can be safely controlled in flight after an engine becomes inoperative) or 115 percent of the power off stalling speed in the takeoff configuration, whichever is greater.

(b) For the purposes of this section—

(1) It may be assumed that takeoff power is used on all engines during the acceleration;

(2) Not more than 50 percent of the reported headwind component, or not less than 150 percent of the reported tailwind component, may be taken into account;

(3) The average runway gradient (the difference between the elevations of the endpoints of the runway divided by the total length) must be considered if it is more than one-half of one percent;

(4) It is assumed that the airplane is operating in standard atmosphere; and

(5) For takeoff, "effective length of the runway" means the distance from the end of the runway at which the takeoff is started to a point at which the obstruction clearance plane associated with the other end of the runway intersects the runway centerline.

§ 135.391 Large nontransport category airplanes: En route limitations: One engine inoperative.

(a) Except as provided in paragraph (b) of this section, no person operating a large nontransport category airplane may take off that airplane at a weight that does not allow a rate of climb of at least 50 feet a minute, with the critical engine inoperative, at an altitude of at least 1,000 feet above the highest obstruction within five miles on each side of the intended track, or 5,000 feet, whichever is higher.

(b) Without regard to paragraph (a) of this section, if the Administrator finds that safe operations are not impaired, a person may operate the airplane at an altitude that allows the airplane, in case of engine failure, to clear all obstructions within five miles on each side of the intended track by 1,000 feet. If this procedure is used, the rate of descent for the appropriate weight and altitude is assumed to be 50 feet a minute greater than the rate in the approved performance data. Before approving such a procedure, the Administrator considers the following for the route, route segment, or area concerned:

(1) The reliability of wind and weather forecasting.

(2) The location and kinds of navigation aids.

(3) The prevailing weather conditions, particularly the frequency and amount of turbulence normally encountered.

(4) Terrain features.

(5) Air traffic problems.

(6) Any other operational factors that affect the operations.

(c) For the purposes of this section, it is assumed that—

(1) The critical engine is inoperative;

(2) The propeller of the inoperative engine is in the minimum drag position;

(3) The wing flaps and landing gear are in the most favorable position;

(4) The operating engines are operating at the maximum continuous power available;

(5) The airplane is operating in standard atmosphere; and

(6) The weight of the airplane is progressively reduced by the anticipated consumption of fuel and oil.

§ 135.393 Large nontransport category airplanes: Landing limitations: Destination airports.

(a) No person operating a large nontransport category airplane may take off that airplane at a weight that—

(1) Allowing for anticipated consumption of fuel and oil, is greater than the weight that would allow a full stop landing within 60 percent of the effective length of the most suitable runway at the destination airport; and

(2) Is greater than the weight allowable if the landing is to be made on the runway—

(i) With the greatest effective length in still air; and

(ii) Required by the probable wind, taking into account not more than 50 percent of the headwind component or not less than 150 percent of the tailwind component.

(b) For the purpose of this section, it is assumed that—

(1) The airplane passes directly over the intersection of the obstruction clearance plane and the runway at a height of 50 feet in a steady gliding approach at a true indicated airspeed of at least 1.3 V_{so};

(2) The landing does not require exceptional pilot skill; and

(3) The airplane is operating in standard atmosphere.

§ 135.395 Large nontransport category airplanes: Landing limitations: Alternate airports.

No person may select an airport as an alternate airport for a large nontransport category airplane unless that airplane (at the weight anticipated at the time of arrival), based on the assumptions in § 135.393(b), can be brought to a full stop landing within 70 percent of the effective length of the runway.

§ 135.397 Small transport category airplane performance operating limitations.

(a) No person may operate a reciprocating engine powered small transport category airplane unless that person complies with the weight limitations in § 135.365, the takeoff limitations in § 135.367 (except paragraph (a)(3)), and the landing limitations in §§ 135.375 and 135.377.

(b) No person may operate a turbine engine powered small transport category airplane unless that person complies with the takeoff limitations in § 135.379 (except paragraphs (d) and (f)) and the landing limitations in §§ 135.385 and 135.387.

§ 135.398 Commuter category airplanes performance operating limitations.

(a) No person may operate a commuter category airplane unless that person complies with the takeoff weight limitations in the approved Airplane Flight Manual.

(b) No person may take off an airplane type certificated in the commuter category at a weight greater than that listed in the Airplane Flight Manual that allows a net takeoff flight path that clears all obstacles either by a height of at least 35 feet vertically, or at least 200 feet horizontally within the airport boundaries and by at least 300 feet horizontally after passing the boundaries.

(c) No person may operate a commuter category airplane unless that person complies with the landing limitations prescribed in §§ 135.385 and 135.387 of this Part. For purposes of this paragraph, §§ 135.385 and 135.387 are applicable to all commuter category airplanes notwithstanding their stated applicability to turbine-engine-powered large transport category airplanes.

(d) In determining maximum weights, minimum distances and flight paths under paragraphs (a) through

(c) of this section, correction must be made for the runway to be used, the elevation of the airport, the effective runway gradient, and ambient temperature, and wind component at the time of takeoff.

(e) For the purposes of this section, the assumption is that the airplane is not banked before reaching a height of 50 feet as shown by the net takeoff flight path data in the Airplane Flight Manual and thereafter the maximum bank is not more than 15 degrees.

[Doc. No. 23516, Amdt. 135–21, 52 FR 1836, Jan. 15, 1987]

§135.399 Small nontransport category airplane performance operating limitations.

(a) No person may operate a reciprocating engine or turbopropeller-powered small airplane that is certificated under §135.169(b)(2), (3), (4), (5), or (6) unless that person complies with the takeoff weight limitations in the approved Airplane Flight Manual or equivalent for operations under this part, and, if the airplane is certificated under §135.169(b)(4) or (5) with the landing weight limitations in the Approved Airplane Flight Manual or equivalent for operations under this part.

(b) No person may operate an airplane that is certificated under §135.169(b)(6) unless that person complies with the landing limitations prescribed in §§135.385 and 135.387 of this part. For purposes of this paragraph, §§135.385 and 135.387 are applicable to reciprocating and turbopropeller-powered small airplanes notwithstanding their stated applicability to turbine engine powered large transport category airplanes.

[44 FR 53731, Sept. 17, 1979]

Subpart J—Maintenance, Preventive Maintenance, and Alterations

§135.411 Applicability.

(a) This subpart prescribes rules in addition to those in other parts of this chapter for the maintenance, preventive maintenance, and alterations for each certificate holder as follows:

(1) Aircraft that are type certificated for a passenger seating configuration, excluding any pilot seat, of nine seats or less, shall be maintained under Parts 91 and 43 of this chapter and §§135.415, 135.417, and 135.421. An approved aircraft inspection program may be used under §135.419.

(2) Aircraft that are type certificated for a passenger seating configuration, excluding any pilot seat, of ten seats or more, shall be maintained under a maintenance program in §§135.415, 135.417, and 135.423 through 135.443.

(b) A certificate holder who is not otherwise required, may elect to maintain its aircraft under paragraph (a)(2) of this section.

§135.413 Responsibility for airworthiness.

(a) Each certificate holder is primarily responsible for the airworthiness of its aircraft, including airframes, aircraft engines, propellers, rotors, appliances, and parts, and shall have its aircraft maintained under this chapter, and shall have defects repaired between required maintenance under Part 43 of this chapter.

(b) Each certificate holder who maintains its aircraft under §135.411(a)(2) shall—

(1) Perform the maintenance, preventive maintenance, and alteration of its aircraft, including airframe, aircraft engines, propellers, rotors, appliances, emergency equipment and parts, under its manual and this chapter; or

(2) Make arrangements with another person for the performance of maintenance, preventive maintenance, or alteration. However, the certificate holder shall ensure that any maintenance, preventive maintenance, or alteration that is performed by another person is performed under the certificate holder's manual and this chapter.

§135.415 Mechanical reliability reports.

(a) Each certificate holder shall report the occurrence or detection of each failure, malfunction, or defect in an aircraft concerning—

(1) Fires during flight and whether the related fire-warning system functioned properly;

(2) Fires during flight not protected by related fire-warning system;

(3) False fire-warning during flight;

(4) An exhaust system that causes damage during flight to the engine, adjacent structure, equipment, or components;

(5) An aircraft component that causes accumulation or circulation of smoke, vapor, or toxic or noxious fumes in the crew compartment or passenger cabin during flight;

(6) Engine shutdown during flight because of flameout;

(7) Engine shutdown during flight when external damage to the engine or aircraft structure occurs;

(8) Engine shutdown during flight due to foreign object ingestion or icing;

(9) Shutdown of more than one engine during flight;

(10) A propeller feathering system or ability of the system to control overspeed during flight;

(11) A fuel or fuel-dumping system that affects fuel flow or causes hazardous leakage during flight;

(12) An unwanted landing gear extension or retraction or opening or closing of landing gear doors during flight;

(13) Brake system components that result in loss of brake actuating force when the aircraft is in motion on the ground;

(14) Aircraft structure that requires major repair;

(15) Cracks, permanent deformation, or corrosion of aircraft structures, if more than the maximum acceptable to the manufacturer or the FAA; and

(16) Aircraft components or systems that result in taking emergency actions during flight (except action to shut-down an engine).

(b) For the purpose of this section, "during flight" means the period from the moment the aircraft leaves the surface of the earth on takeoff until it touches down on landing.

(c) In addition to the reports required by paragraph (a) of this section, each certificate holder shall report any other failure, malfunction, or defect in an aircraft that occurs or is detected at any time if, in its opinion, the failure, malfunction, or defect has endangered or may endanger the safe operation of the aircraft.

(d) Each certificate holder shall send each report required by this section, in writing, covering each 24-hour period beginning at 0900 hours local time of each day and ending at 0900 hours local time on the next day to the FAA Flight Standards District Office charged with the overall inspection of the certificate holder. Each report of occurrences during a 24-hour period must be mailed or delivered to that office within the next 72 hours. However, a report that is due on Saturday or Sunday may be mailed or delivered on the following Monday and one that is due on a holiday may be mailed or delivered on the next work day. For aircraft operated in areas where mail is not collected, reports may be mailed or delivered within 72 hours after the aircraft returns to a point where the mail is collected.

(e) The certificate holder shall transmit the reports required by this section on a form and in a manner prescribed by the Administrator, and shall include as much of the following as is available:

(1) The type and identification number of the aircraft.

(2) The name of the operator.

(3) The date.

(4) The nature of the failure, malfunction, or defect.

(5) Identification of the part and system involved, including available information pertaining to type designation of the major component and time since last overhaul, if known.

(6) Apparent cause of the failure, malfunction or defect (e.g., wear, crack, design deficiency, or personnel error).

(7) Other pertinent information necessary for more complete identification, determination of seriousness, or corrective action.

(f) A certificate holder that is also the holder of a type certificate (including a supplemental type certificate), a Parts Manufacturer Approval, or a Technical Standard Order Authorization, or that is the licensee of a type certificate need not report a failure, malfunction, or defect under this section if the failure, malfunction, or defect has been reported by it under § 21.3 or § 37.17 of this chapter or under the accident reporting provisions of Part 830 of the regulations of the National Transportation Safety Board.

(g) No person may withhold a report required by this section even though all information required by this section is not available.

(h) When the certificate holder gets additional information, including information from the manufacturer or other agency, concerning a report required by this section, it shall expeditiously submit it as a supplement to the first report and reference the date and place of submission of the first report.

§ 135.417 Mechanical interruption summary report.

Each certificate holder shall mail or deliver, before the end of the 10th day of the following month, a summary report of the following occurrences in multiengine aircraft for the preceding month to the FAA Flight Standards District Office charged with the overall inspection of the certificate holder:

(a) Each interruption to a flight, unscheduled change of aircraft en route, or unscheduled stop or diversion from a route, caused by known or suspected mechanical difficulties or malfunctions that are not required to be reported under § 135.415.

(b) The number of propeller featherings in flight, listed by type of propeller and engine and aircraft on which it was installed. Propeller featherings for training, demonstration, or flight check purposes need not be reported.

§ 135.419 Approved aircraft inspection program.

(a) Whenever the Administrator finds that the aircraft inspections required or allowed under Part 91 of this chapter are not adequate to meet this part, or upon application by a certificate holder, the Administrator may amend the certificate holder's operations specifications under § 135.17, to require or allow an approved aircraft inspection program for any make and model aircraft of which the certificate holder has the exclusive use of at least one aircraft (as defined in § 135.25(b)).

(b) A certificate holder who applies for an amendment of its operations specifications to allow an approved aircraft inspection program must submit that program with its application for approval by the Administrator.

(c) Each certificate holder who is required by its operations specifications to have an approved aircraft inspection program shall submit a program for approval by the Administrator within 30 days of the amendment of its operations specifications or within any other period that the Administrator may prescribe in the operations specifications.

(d) The aircraft inspection program submitted for approval by the Administrator must contain the following:

(1) Instructions and procedures for the conduct of aircraft inspections (which must include necessary tests and checks), setting forth in detail the parts and areas of the airframe, engines, propellers, rotors, and appliances, including emergency equipment, that must be inspected.

(2) A schedule for the performance of the aircraft inspections under paragraph (d)(1) of this section expressed in terms of the time in service, calendar time, number of system operations, or any combination of these.

(3) Instructions and procedures for recording discrepancies found during inspections and correction or deferral of discrepancies including form and disposition of records.

(e) After approval, the certificate holder shall include the approved aircraft inspection program in the manual required by § 135.21.

(f) Whenever the Administrator finds that revisions to an approved aircraft inspection program are necessary for the continued adequacy of the program, the certificate holder shall, after notification by the Administrator, make any changes in the program found by the Administrator to be necessary. The certificate holder may petition the Administrator to reconsider the notice to make any changes in a program. The petition must be filed with the representatives of the Administrator assigned to it within 30 days after the certificate holder receives the notice. Except in the case of an emergency requiring immediate action in the interest of safety, the filing of the petition stays the notice pending a decision by the Administrator.

(g) Each certificate holder who has an approved aircraft inspection program shall have each aircraft that is subject to the program inspected in accordance with the program.

(h) The registration number of each aircraft that is subject to an approved aircraft inspection program must be included in the operations specifications of the certificate holder.

§ 135.421 Additional maintenance requirements.

(a) Each certificate holder who operates an aircraft type certificated for a passenger seating configuration, excluding any pilot seat, of nine seats or less, must comply with the manufacturer's recommended maintenance programs, or a program approved by the Administrator, for each aircraft engine, propeller, rotor, and each item of emergency equipment required by this chapter.

(b) For the purpose of this section, a manufacturer's maintenance program is one which is contained in the maintenance manual or maintenance instructions set forth by the manufacturer as required by this chapter for the aircraft, aircraft engine, propeller, rotor or item of emergency equipment.

§ 135.423 Maintenance, preventive maintenance, and alteration organization.

(a) Each certificate holder that performs any of its maintenance (other than required inspections), preventive maintenance, or alterations, and each person with whom it arranges for the performance of that work, must have an organization adequate to perform the work.

(b) Each certificate holder that performs any inspections required by its manual under § 135.427(b) (2) or (3), (in this subpart referred to as "required inspections"), and each person with whom it arranges for the performance of that work, must have an organization adequate to perform that work.

(c) Each person performing required inspections in addition to other maintenance, preventive maintenance, or alterations, shall organize the performance of those functions so as to separate the required inspection functions from the other maintenance,

preventive maintenance, and alteration functions. The separation shall be below the level of administrative control at which overall responsibility for the required inspection functions and other maintenance, preventive maintenance, and alteration functions is exercised.

§ 135.425 Maintenance, preventive maintenance, and alteration programs.

Each certificate holder shall have an inspection program and a program covering other maintenance, preventive maintenance, and alterations, that ensures that—

(a) Maintenance, preventive maintenance, and alterations performed by it, or by other persons, are performed under the certificate holder's manual;

(b) Competent personnel and adequate facilities and equipment are provided for the proper performance of maintenance, preventive maintenance, and alterations; and

(c) Each aircraft released to service is airworthy and has been properly maintained for operation under this part.

§ 135.427 Manual requirements.

(a) Each certificate holder shall put in its manual the chart or description of the certificate holder's organization required by § 135.423 and a list of persons with whom it has arranged for the performance of any of its required inspections, other maintenance, preventive maintenance, or alterations, including a general description of that work.

(b) Each certificate holder shall put in its manual the programs required by § 135.425 that must be followed in performing maintenance, preventive maintenance, and alterations of that certificate holder's aircraft, including airframes, aircraft engines, propellers, rotors, appliances, emergency equipment, and parts, and must include at least the following:

(1) The method of performing routine and nonroutine maintenance (other than required inspections), preventive maintenance, and alterations.

(2) A designation of the items of maintenance and alteration that must be inspected (required inspections) in-

cluding at least those that could result in a failure, malfunction, or defect endangering the safe operation of the aircraft, if not performed properly or if improper parts or materials are used.

(3) The method of performing required inspections and a designation by occupational title of personnel authorized to perform each required inspection.

(4) Procedures for the reinspection of work performed under previous required inspection findings ("buy-back procedures").

(5) Procedures, standards, and limits necessary for required inspections and acceptance or rejection of the items required to be inspected and for periodic inspection and calibration of precision tools, measuring devices, and test equipment.

(6) Procedures to ensure that all required inspections are performed.

(7) Instructions to prevent any person who performs any item of work from performing any required inspection of that work.

(8) Instructions and procedures to prevent any decision of an inspector regarding any required inspection from being countermanded by persons other than supervisory personnel of the inspection unit, or a person at the level of administrative control that has overall responsibility for the management of both the required inspection functions and the other maintenance, preventive maintenance, and alterations functions.

(9) Procedures to ensure that required inspections, other maintenance, preventive maintenance, and alterations that are not completed as a result of work interruptions are properly completed before the aircraft is released to service.

(c) Each certificate holder shall put in its manual a suitable system (which may include a coded system) that provides for the retention of the following information—

(1) A description (or reference to data acceptable to the Administrator) of the work performed;

(2) The name of the person performing the work if the work is performed by a person outside the organization of the certificate holder; and

(3) The name or other positive identification of the individual approving the work.

§135.429 **Required inspection personnel.**

(a) No person may use any person to perform required inspections unless the person performing the inspection is appropriately certificated, properly trained, qualified, and authorized to do so.

(b) No person may allow any person to perform a required inspection unless, at the time, the person performing that inspection is under the supervision and control of an inspection unit.

(c) No person may perform a required inspection if that person performed the item of work required to be inspected.

(d) In the case of rotorcraft that operate in remote areas or sites, the Administrator may approve procedures for the performance of required inspection items by a pilot when no other qualified person is available, provided—

(1) The pilot is employed by the certificate holder;

(2) It can be shown to the satisfaction of the Administrator that each pilot authorized to perform required inspections is properly trained and qualified;

(3) The required inspection is a result of a mechanical interruption and is not a part of a certificate holder's continuous airworthiness maintenance program;

(4) Each item is inspected after each flight until the item has been inspected by an appropriately certificated mechanic other than the one who originally performed the item of work; and

(5) Each item of work that is a required inspection item that is part of the flight control system shall be flight tested and reinspected before the aircraft is approved for return to service.

(e) Each certificate holder shall maintain, or shall determine that each person with whom it arranges to perform its required inspections maintains, a current listing of persons who have been trained, qualified, and authorized to conduct required inspections. The persons must be identified by name, occupational title and the inspections that they are authorized to perform. The certificate holder (or person with whom it arranges to perform its required inspections) shall give written information to each person so authorized, describing the extent of that person's responsibilities, authorities, and inspectional limitations. The list shall be made available for inspection by the Administrator upon request.

[Doc. No. 16097, 43 FR 46783, Oct. 10, 1978, as amended by Amdt. No. 135-20, 51 FR 40710, Nov. 7, 1986]

§ 135.431   Continuing analysis and surveillance.

(a) Each certificate holder shall establish and maintain a system for the continuing analysis and surveillance of the performance and effectiveness of its inspection program and the program covering other maintenance, preventive maintenance, and alterations and for the correction of any deficiency in those programs, regardless of whether those programs are carried out by the certificate holder or by another person.

(b) Whenever the Administrator finds that either or both of the programs described in paragraph (a) of this section does not contain adequate procedures and standards to meet this part, the certificate holder shall, after notification by the Administrator, make changes in those programs requested by the Administrator.

(c) A certificate holder may petition the Administrator to reconsider the notice to make a change in a program. The petition must be filed with the FAA Flight Standards District Office charged with the overall inspection of the certificate holder within 30 days after the certificate holder receives the notice. Except in the case of an emergency requiring immediate action in the interest of safety, the filing of the petition stays the notice pending a decision by the Administrator.

§ 135.433   Maintenance and preventive maintenance training program.

Each certificate holder or a person performing maintenance or preventive maintenance functions for it shall have a training program to ensure that each person (including inspection personnel) who determines the adequacy of work done is fully informed about procedures and techniques and new equipment in use and is competent to perform that person's duties.

§ 135.435   Certificate requirements.

(a) Except for maintenance, preventive maintenance, alterations, and required inspections performed by repair stations certificated under the provisions of Subpart C of Part 145 of this chapter, each person who is directly in charge of maintenance, preventive maintenance, or alterations, and each person performing required inspections must hold an appropriate airman certificate.

(b) For the purpose of this section, a person "directly in charge" is each person assigned to a position in which that person is responsible for the work of a shop or station that performs maintenance, preventive maintenance, alterations, or other functions affecting airworthiness. A person who is "directly in charge" need not physically observe and direct each worker constantly but must be available for consultation and decision on matters requiring instruction or decision from higher authority than that of the person performing the work.

§ 135.437   Authority to perform and approve maintenance, preventive maintenance, and alterations.

(a) A certificate holder may perform or make arrangements with other persons to perform maintenance, preventive maintenance, and alterations as provided in its maintenance manual. In addition, a certificate holder may perform these functions for another certificate holder as provided in the maintenance manual of the other certificate holder.

(b) A certificate holder may approve any airframe, aircraft engine, propeller, rotor, or appliance for return to service after maintenance, preventive maintenance, or alterations that are performed under paragraph (a) of this section. However, in the case of a major repair or alteration, the work must have been done in accordance with technical data approved by the Administrator.

§ 135.439 Maintenance recording requirements.

(a) Each certificate holder shall keep (using the system specified in the manual required in § 135.427) the following records for the periods specified in paragraph (b) of this section:

(1) All the records necessary to show that all requirements for the issuance of an airworthiness release under § 135.443 have been met.

(2) Records containing the following information:

(i) The total time in service of the airframe, engine, propeller, and rotor.

(ii) The current status of life-limited parts of each airframe, engine, propeller, rotor, and appliance.

(iii) The time since last overhaul of each item installed on the aircraft which are required to be overhauled on a specified time basis.

(iv) The identification of the current inspection status of the aircraft, including the time since the last inspections required by the inspection program under which the aircraft and its appliances are maintained.

(v) The current status of applicable airworthiness directives, including the date and methods of compliance, and, if the airworthiness directive involves recurring action, the time and date when the next action is required.

(vi) A list of current major alterations and repairs to each airframe, engine, propeller, rotor, and appliance.

(b) Each certificate holder shall retain the records required to be kept by this section for the following periods:

(1) Except for the records of the last complete overhaul of each airframe, engine, propeller, rotor, and appliance the records specified in paragraph (a)(1) of this section shall be retained until the work is repeated or superseded by other work or for one year after the work is performed.

(2) The records of the last complete overhaul of each airframe, engine, propeller, rotor, and appliance shall be retained until the work is superseded by work of equivalent scope and detail.

(3) The records specified in paragraph (a)(2) of this section shall be re-

tained and transferred with the aircraft at the time the aircraft is sold.

(c) The certificate holder shall make all maintenance records required to be kept by this section available for inspection by the Administrator or any representative of the National Transportation Safety Board.

[Doc. No. 16097, 43 FR 46783, Oct. 10, 1978; 43 FR 49975, Oct. 26, 1978]

§ 135.441 Transfer of maintenance records.

Each certificate holder who sells a United States registered aircraft shall transfer to the purchaser, at the time of the sale, the following records of that aircraft, in plain language form or in coded form which provides for the preservation and retrieval of information in a manner acceptable to the Administrator:

(a) The records specified in § 135.439(a)(2).

(b) The records specified in § 135.439(a)(1) which are not included in the records covered by paragraph (a) of this section, except that the purchaser may allow the seller to keep physical custody of such records. However, custody of records by the seller does not relieve the purchaser of its responsibility under § 135.439(c) to make the records available for inspection by the Administrator or any representative of the National Transportation Safety Board.

§ 135.443 Airworthiness release or aircraft maintenance log entry.

(a) No certificate holder may operate an aircraft after maintenance, preventive maintenance, or alterations are performed on the aircraft unless the certificate holder prepares, or causes the person with whom the certificate holder arranges for the performance of the maintenance, preventive maintenance, or alterations, to prepare—

(1) An airworthiness release; or

(2) An appropriate entry in the aircraft maintenance log.

(b) The airworthiness release or log entry required by paragraph (a) of this section must—

(1) Be prepared in accordance with the procedure in the certificate holder's manual;

(2) Include a certification that—

(i) The work was performed in accordance with the requirements of the certificate holder's manual;

(ii) All items required to be inspected were inspected by an authorized person who determined that the work was satisfactorily completed;

(iii) No known condition exists that would make the aircraft unairworthy;

(iv) So far as the work performed is concerned, the aircraft is in condition for safe operation; and

(3) Be signed by an authorized certificated mechanic or repairman, except that a certificated repairman may sign the release or entry only for the work for which that person is employed and for which that person is certificated.

(c) Instead of restating each of the conditions of the certification required by paragraph (b) of this section, the certificate holder may state in its manual that the signature of an authorized certificated mechanic or repairman constitutes that certification.

APPENDIX A—ADDITIONAL AIRWORTHINESS STANDARDS FOR 10 OR MORE PASSENGER AIRPLANES

Applicability

1. *Applicability.* This appendix prescribes the additional airworthiness standards required by § 135.169.

2. *References.* Unless otherwise provided, references in this appendix to specific sections of Part 23 of the Federal Aviation Regulations (FAR Part 23) are to those sections of Part 23 in effect on March 30, 1967.

Flight Requirements

3. *General.* Compliance must be shown with the applicable requirements of Subpart B of FAR Part 23, as supplemented or modified in §§ 4 through 10.

Performance

4. *General.* (a) Unless otherwise prescribed in this appendix, compliance with each applicable performance requirement in sections 4 through 7 must be shown for ambient atmospheric conditions and still air.

(b) The performance must correspond to the propulsive thrust available under the particular ambient atmospheric conditions and the particular flight condition. The available propulsive thrust must correspond to engine power or thrust, not exceeding the approved power or thrust less—

(1) Installation losses; and

(2) The power or equivalent thrust absorbed by the accessories and services appropriate to the particular ambient atmospheric conditions and the particular flight condition.

(c) Unless otherwise prescribed in this appendix, the applicant must select the takeoff, en route, and landing configurations for the airplane.

(d) The airplane configuration may vary with weight, altitude, and temperature, to the extent they are compatible with the operating procedures required by paragraph (e) of this section.

(e) Unless otherwise prescribed in this appendix, in determining the critical engine inoperative takeoff performance, the accelerate-stop distance, takeoff distance, changes in the airplane's configuration, speed, power, and thrust must be made under procedures established by the applicant for operation in service.

(f) Procedures for the execution of balked landings must be established by the applicant and included in the Airplane Flight Manual.

(g) The procedures established under paragraphs (e) and (f) of this section must—

(1) Be able to be consistently executed in service by a crew of average skill;

(2) Use methods or devices that are safe and reliable; and

(3) Include allowance for any time delays, in the execution of the procedures, that may reasonably be expected in service.

5. *Takeoff*—(a) *General.* Takeoff speeds, the accelerate-stop distance, the takeoff distance, and the one-engine-inoperative takeoff flight path data (described in paragraphs (b), (c), (d), and (f) of this section), must be determined for—

(1) Each weight, altitude, and ambient temperature within the operational limits selected by the applicant;

(2) The selected configuration for takeoff;

(3) The center of gravity in the most unfavorable position;

(4) The operating engine within approved operating limitations; and

(5) Takeoff data based on smooth, dry, hard-surface runway.

(b) *Takeoff speeds.* (1) The decision speed V_1 is the calibrated airspeed on the ground at which, as a result of engine failure or other reasons, the pilot is assumed to have made a decision to continue or discontinue the takeoff. The speed V_1 must be selected by the applicant but may not be less than—

(i) $1.10 V_{S1}$;

(ii) $1.10 V_{MC}$;

(iii) A speed that allows acceleration to V_1 and stop under paragraph (c) of this section; or

(iv) A speed at which the airplane can be rotated for takeoff and shown to be adequate to safely continue the takeoff, using normal piloting skill, when the critical engine is suddenly made inoperative.

(2) The initial climb out speed V_2, in terms of calibrated airspeed, must be selected by the applicant so as to allow the gradient of climb required in section 6(b)(2), but it must not be less than V_1 or less than $1.2 V_{S1}$.

(3) Other essential take off speeds necessary for safe operation of the airplane.

(c) *Accelerate-stop distance.* (1) The accelerate-stop distance is the sum of the distances necessary to—

(i) Accelerate the airplane from a standing start to V_1; and

(ii) Come to a full stop from the point at which V_1 is reached assuming that in the case of engine failure, failure of the critical engine is recognized by the pilot at the speed V_1.

(2) Means other than wheel brakes may be used to determine the accelerate-stop distance if that means is available with the critical engine inoperative and—

(i) Is safe and reliable;

(ii) Is used so that consistent results can be expected under normal operating conditions; and

(iii) Is such that exceptional skill is not required to control the airplane.

(d) *All engines operating takeoff distance.* The all engine operating takeoff distance is the horizontal distance required to takeoff and climb to a height of 50 feet above the takeoff surface under the procedures in FAR 23.51(a).

(e) *One-engine-inoperative takeoff.* Determine the weight for each altitude and temperature within the operational limits established for the airplane, at which the airplane has the capability, after failure of the critical engine at V_1 determined under paragraph (b) of this section, to take off and climb at not less than V_2, to a height 1,000 feet above the takeoff surface and attain the speed and configuration at which compliance is shown with the en route one-engine–inoperative gradient of climb specified in section 6(c).

(f) *One-engine-inoperative takeoff flight path data.* The one-engine-inoperative takeoff flight path data consist of takeoff flight paths extending from a standing start to a point in the takeoff at which the airplane reaches a height 1,000 feet above the takeoff surface under paragraph (e) of this section.

6. *Climb*—(a) *Landing climb: All-engines-operating.* The maximum weight must be determined with the airplane in the landing configuration, for each altitude, and ambient temperature within the operational limits established for the airplane, with the most unfavorable center of gravity, and out-of-ground effect in free air, at which the steady gradient of climb will not be less than 3.3 percent, with:

(1) The engines at the power that is available 8 seconds after initiation of movement of the power or thrust controls from the minimum flight idle to the takeoff position.

(2) A climb speed not greater than the approach speed established under section 7 and not less than the greater of $1.05 V_{MC}$ or $1.10 V_{S1}$.

(b) *Takeoff climb: one-engine-inoperative.* The maximum weight at which the airplane meets the minimum climb performance specified in paragraphs (1) and (2) of this paragraph must be determined for each altitude and ambient temperature within the operational limits established for the airplane, out of ground effect in free air, with the airplane in the takeoff configuration, with the most unfavorable center of gravity, the critical engine inoperative, the remaining engines at the maximum takeoff power or thrust, and the propeller of the inoperative engine windmilling with the propeller controls in the normal position except that, if an approved automatic feathering system is installed, the propellers may be in the feathered position:

(1) *Takeoff: landing gear extended.* The minimum steady gradient of climb must be measurably positive at the speed V_1.

(2) *Takeoff: landing gear retracted.* The minimum steady gradient of climb may not be less than 2 percent at speed V_2. For airplanes with fixed landing gear this requirement must be met with the landing gear extended.

(c) *En route climb: one-engine-inoperative.* The maximum weight must be determined for each altitude and ambient temperature within the operational limits established for the airplane, at which the steady gradient of climb is not less 1.2 percent at an altitude 1,000 feet above the takeoff surface, with the airplane in the en route configuration, the critical engine inoperative, the remaining engine at the maximum continuous power or thrust, and the most unfavorable center of gravity.

7. *Landing.* (a) The landing field length described in paragraph (b) of this section must be determined for standard atmosphere at each weight and altitude within the operational limits established by the applicant.

(b) The landing field length is equal to the landing distance determined under FAR 23.75(a) divided by a factor of 0.6 for the destination airport and 0.7 for the alternate airport. Instead of the gliding approach specified in FAR 23.75(a)(1), the landing may be preceded by a steady approach down to the 50-foot height at a gradient of descent not greater than 5.2 percent (3°) at a calibrated airspeed not less than $1.3V_{S1}$.

Trim

8—*Trim* (a) *Lateral and directional trim.* The airplane must maintain lateral and directional trim in level flight at a speed of V_H or V_{MO}/M_{MO}, whichever is lower, with landing gear and wing flaps retracted.

(b) *Longitudinal trim.* The airplane must maintain longitudinal trim during the following conditions, except that it need not maintain trim at a speed greater than V_{MO}/M_{MO}:

(1) In the approach conditons specified in FAR 23.161(c) (3) through (5), except that instead of the speeds specified in those paragraphs, trim must be maintained with a stick force of not more than 10 pounds down to a speed used in showing compliance with section 7 or $1.4V_{S1}$ whichever is lower.

(2) In level flight at any speed from V_H or V_{MO}/M_{MO}, whichever is lower, to either V_x or $1.4V_{S1}$, with the landing gear and wing flaps retracted.

Stability

9. *Static longitudinal stability.* (a) In showing compliance with FAR 23.175(b) and with paragraph (b) of this section, the airspeed must return to within ±7½ percent of the trim speed.

(b) *Cruise stability.* The stick force curve must have a stable slope for a speed range of ±50 knots from the trim speed except that the speeds need not exceed V_{FC}/M_{FC} or be less than $1.4V_{S1}$. This speed range will be considered to begin at the outer extremes of the friction band and the stick force may not exceed 50 pounds with—

(1) Landing gear retracted;

(2) Wing flaps retracted;

(3) The maximum cruising power as selected by the applicant as an operating limitation for turbine engines or 75 percent of maximum continuous power for reciprocating engines except that the power need not exceed that required at V_{MO}/M_{MO};

(4) Maximum takeoff weight; and

(5) The airplane trimmed for level flight with the power specified in paragraph (3) of this paragraph.

V_{FC}/M_{FC} may not be less than a speed midway between V_{MO}/M_{MO} and V_{DF}/M_{DF}, except that, for altitudes where Mach number is the limiting factor, M_{FC} need not exceed the Mach number at which effective speed warning occurs.

(c) *Climb stability (turbopropeller powered airplanes only).* In showing compliance with FAR 23.175(a), an applicant must, instead of the power specified in FAR 23.175(a)(4), use the maximum power or thrust selected by the applicant as an operating limitation for use during climb at the best rate of climb speed, except that the speed need not be less than $1.4V_{S1}$.

Stalls

10. *Stall warning.* If artificial stall warning is required to comply with FAR 23.207, the warning device must give clearly distinguishable indications under expected conditions of flight. The use of a visual warning device that requires the attention of the crew within the cockpit is not acceptable by itself.

Control Systems

11. *Electric trim tabs.* The airplane must meet FAR 23.677 and in addition it must be shown that the airplane is safely controllable and that a pilot can perform all the maneuvers and operations necessary to effect a safe landing following any probable electric trim tab runaway which might be reasonably expected in service allowing for appropriate time delay after pilot recognition of the runaway. This demonstration must be conducted at the critical airplane weights and center of gravity positions.

Instruments: Installation

12. *Arrangement and visibility.* Each instrument must meet FAR 23.1321 and in addition:

(a) Each flight, navigation, and powerplant instrument for use by any pilot must be plainly visible to the pilot from the pilot's station with the minimum practicable deviation from the pilot's normal position and line of vision when the pilot is looking forward along the flight path.

(b) The flight instruments required by FAR 23.1303 and by the applicable operating rules must be grouped on the instrument panel and centered as nearly as practicable about the vertical plane of each pilot's forward vision. In addition—

(1) The instrument that most effectively indicates the attitude must be in the panel in the top center position;

(2) The instrument that most effectively indicates the airspeed must be on the panel directly to the left of the instrument in the top center position;

(3) The instrument that most effectively indicates altitude must be adjacent to and directly to the right of the instrument in the top center position; and

(4) The instrument that most effectively indicates direction of flight must be adjacent to and directly below the instrument in the top center position.

13. *Airspeed indicating system.* Each airspeed indicating system must meet FAR 23.1323 and in addition:

(a) Airspeed indicating instruments must be of an approved type and must be calibrated to indicate true airspeed at sea level in the standard atmosphere with a minimum practicable instrument calibration error when the corresponding pitot and static pressures are supplied to the instruments.

(b) The airspeed indicating system must be calibrated to determine the system error, i.e., the relation between IAS and CAS, in flight and during the accelerate-takeoff ground run. The ground run calibration must be obtained between 0.8 of the minimum value of V_1 and 1.2 times the maximum value of V_1, considering the approved ranges of altitude and weight. The ground run calibration is determined assuming an engine failure at the minimum value of V_1.

(c) The airspeed error of the installation excluding the instrument calibration error, must not exceed 3 percent or 5 knots whichever is greater, throughout the speed range from V_{MO} to $1.3V_{S1}$ with flaps retracted and from $1.3V_{SO}$ to V_{FE} with flaps in the landing position.

(d) Information showing the relationship between IAS and CAS must be shown in the Airplane Flight manual.

14. *Static air vent system.* The static air vent system must meet FAR 23.1325. The altimeter system calibration must be determined and shown in the Airplane Flight Manual.

Operating Limitations and Information

15. *Maximum operating limit speed V_{MO}/M_{MO}.* Instead of establishing operating limitations based on V_{NE} and V_{NO}, the applicant must establish a maximum operating limit speed V_{MO}/M_{MO} as follows:

(a) The maximum operating limit speed must not exceed the design cruising speed V_C and must be sufficiently below V_D/M_D or V_{DF}/M_{DF} to make it highly improbable that the latter speeds will be inadvertently exceeded in flight.

(b) The speed V_{MO} must not exceed $0.8V_D/M_D$ or $0.8V_{DF}/M_{DF}$ unless flight demonstrations involving upsets as specified by the Administrator indicates a lower speed margin will not result in speeds exceeding V_D/M_D or V^{DF}. Atmospheric variations, horizontal gusts, system and equipment errors, and airframe production variations are taken into account.

16. *Minimum flight crew.* In addition to meeting FAR 23.1523, the applicant must establish the minimum number and type of qualified flight crew personnel sufficient for safe operation of the airplane considering—

(a) Each kind of operation for which the applicant desires approval;

(b) The workload on each crewmember considering the following:

(1) Flight path control.

(2) Collision avoidance.

(3) Navigation.

(4) Communications.

(5) Operation and monitoring of all essential aircraft systems.

(6) Command decisions; and

(c) The accessibility and ease of operation of necessary controls by the appropriate crewmember during all normal and emergency operations when at the crewmember flight station.

17. *Airspeed indicator.* The airspeed indicator must meet FAR 23.1545 except that, the airspeed notations and markings in terms of V_{NO} and V_{NH} must be replaced by the V_{MO}/M_{MO} notations. The airspeed indicator markings must be easily read and understood by the pilot. A placard adjacent to the airspeed indicator is an acceptable means of showing compliance with FAR 23.1545(c).

Airplane Flight Manual

18. *General.* The Airplane Flight Manual must be prepared under FARs 23.1583 and 23.1587, and in addition the operating limitations and performance information in sections 19 and 20 must be included.

19. *Operating limitations.* The Airplane Flight Manual must include the following limitations—

(a) *Airspeed limitations.* (1) The maximum operating limit speed V_{MO}/M_{MO} and a statement that this speed limit may not be deliberately exceeded in any regime of flight (climb, cruise, or descent) unless a higher speed is authorized for flight test or pilot training;

(2) If an airspeed limitation is based upon compressibility effects, a statement to this effect and informaton as to any symptoms, the probable behavior of the airplane, and the recommended recovery procedures; and

(3) The airspeed limits, shown in terms of V_{MO}/M_{MO} instead of V_{NO} and V_{NE}.

(b) *Takeoff weight limitations.* The maximum takeoff weight for each airport elevation, ambient temperature, and available takeoff runway length within the range selected by the applicant may not exceed the weight at which—

(1) The all-engine–operating takeoff distance determined under section 5(b) or the accelerate-stop distance determined under section 5(c), whichever is greater, is equal to the available runway length;

(2) The airplane complies with the one-engine-inoperative takeoff requirements specified in section 5(e); and

(3) The airplane complies with the one-engine-inoperative takeoff and en route climb requirements specified in sections 6 (b) and (c).

(c) *Landing weight limitations.* The maximum landing weight for each airport elevation (standard temperature) and available landing runway length, within the range selected by the applicant. This weight may not exceed the weight at which the landing field length determined under section 7(b) is equal to the available runway length. In showing compliance with this operating limitation, it is acceptable to assume that the landing weight at the destination will be equal to the takeoff weight reduced by the normal consumption of fuel and oil en route.

20. *Performance information.* The Airplane Flight Manual must contain the performance information determined under the performance requirements of this appendix. The information must include the following:

(a) Sufficient information so that the takeoff weight limits specified in section 19(b) can be determined for all temperatures and altitudes within the operation limitations selected by the applicant.

(b) The conditions under which the performance information was obtained, including the airspeed at the 50-foot height used to determine landing distances.

(c) The performance information (determined by extrapolation and computed for the range of weights between the maximum landing and takeoff weights) for—

(1) Climb in the landing configuration; and

(2) Landing distance.

(d) Procedure established under section 4 related to the limitations and information required by this section in the form of guidance material including any relevant limitations or information.

(e) An explanation of significant or unusual flight or ground handling characteristics of the airplane.

(f) Airspeeds, as indicated airspeeds, corresponding to those determined for takeoff under section 5(b).

21. *Maximum operating altitudes.* The maximum operating altitude to which operation is allowed, as limited by flight, structural, powerplant, functional, or equipment characteristics, must be specified in the Airplane Flight Manual.

22. *Stowage provision for airplane flight manual.* Provision must be made for stowing the Airplane Flight Manual in a suitable fixed container which is readily accessible to the pilot.

23. *Operating procedures.* Procedures for restarting turbine engines in flight (including the effects of altitude) must be set forth in the Airplane Flight Manual.

Airframe Requirements

Flight Loads

24. *Engine torque.* (a) Each turbopropeller engine mount and its supporting structure must be designed for the torque effects of:

(1) The conditions in FAR 23.361(a).

(2) The limit engine torque corresponding to takeoff power and propeller speed multiplied by a factor accounting for propeller control system malfunction, including quick feathering action, simultaneously with 1g

level flight loads. In the absence of a rational analysis, a factor of 1.6 must be used.

(b) The limit torque is obtained by multiplying the mean torque by a factor of 1.25.

25. *Turbine engine gyroscopic loads.* Each turbopropeller engine mount and its supporting structure must be designed for the gyroscopic loads that result, with the engines at maximum continuous r.p.m., under either—

(a) The conditions in FARs 23.351 and 23.423; or

(b) All possible combinations of the following:

(1) A yaw velocity of 2.5 radians per second.

(2) A pitch velocity of 1.0 radians per second.

(3) A normal load factor of 2.5.

(4) Maximum continuous thrust.

26. *Unsymmetrical loads due to engine failure.* (a) Turbopropeller powered airplanes must be designed for the unsymmetrical loads resulting from the failure of the critical engine including the following conditions in combination with a single malfunction of the propeller drag limiting system, considering the probable pilot corrective action on the flight controls:

(1) At speeds between V_{mo} and V_D, the loads resulting from power failure because of fuel flow interruption are considered to be limit loads.

(2) At speeds between V_{mo} and V_c, the loads resulting from the disconnection of the engine compressor from the turbine or from loss of the turbine blades are considered to be ultimate loads.

(3) The time history of the thrust decay and drag buildup occurring as a result of the prescribed engine failures must be substantiated by test or other data applicable to the particular engine-propeller combination.

(4) The timing and magnitude of the probable pilot corrective action must be conservatively estimated, considering the characteristics of the particular engine-propeller-airplane combination.

(b) Pilot corrective action may be assumed to be initiated at the time maximum yawing velocity is reached, but not earlier than 2 seconds after the engine failure. The magnitude of the corrective action may be based on the control forces in FAR 23.397 except that lower forces may be assumed where it is shown by analysis or test that these forces can control the yaw and roll resulting from the prescribed engine failure conditions.

Ground Loads

27. *Dual wheel landing gear units.* Each dual wheel landing gear unit and its supporting structure must be shown to comply with the following:

(a) *Pivoting.* The airplane must be assumed to pivot about one side of the main gear with the brakes on that side locked. The limit vertical load factor must be 1.0 and the coefficient of friction 0.8. This condition need apply only to the main gear and its supporting structure.

(b) *Unequal tire inflation.* A 60–40 percent distribution of the loads established under FAR 23.471 through FAR 23.483 must be applied to the dual wheels.

(c) *Flat tire.* (1) Sixty percent of the loads in FAR 23.471 through FAR 23.483 must be applied to either wheel in a unit.

(2) Sixty percent of the limit drag and side loads and 100 percent of the limit vertical load established under FARs 23.493 and 23.485 must be applied to either wheel in a unit except that the vertical load need not exceed the maximum vertical load in paragraph (c)(1) of this section.

Fatigue Evaluation

28. *Fatigue evaluation of wing and associated structure.* Unless it is shown that the structure, operating stress levels, materials and expected use are comparable from a fatigue standpoint to a similar design which has had substantial satisfactory service experience, the strength, detail design, and the fabrication of those parts of the wing, wing carrythrough, and attaching structure whose failure would be catastrophic must be evaluated under either—

(a) A fatigue strength investigation in which the structure is shown by analysis, tests, or both to be able to withstand the repeated loads of variable magnitude expected in service; or

(b) A fail-safe strength investigation in which it is shown by analysis, tests, or both that catastrophic failure of the structure is not probable after fatigue, or obvious partial failure, of a principal structural element, and that the remaining structure is able to withstand a static ultimate load factor of 75 percent of the critical limit load factor at V_c. These loads must be multiplied by a factor of 1.15 unless the dynamic effects of failure under static load are otherwise considered.

Design and Construction

29. *Flutter.* For multiengine turbopropeller powered airplanes, a dynamic evaluation must be made and must include—

(a) The significant elastic, inertia, and aerodynamic forces associated with the rotations and displacements of the plane of the propeller; and

(b) Engine-propeller-nacelle stiffness and damping variations appropriate to the particular configuration.

Landing Gear

30. *Flap operated landing gear warning device.* Airplanes having retractable landing gear and wing flaps must be equipped with a warning device that functions continuously when the wing flaps are extended to a flap position that activates the warning device to give adequate warning before landing, using normal landing procedures, if the landing gear is not fully extended and locked. There may not be a manual shut off for this warning device. The flap position sensing unit may be installed at any suitable location. The system for this device may use any part of the system (including the aural warning device) provided for other landing gear warning devices.

Personnel and Cargo Accommodations

31. *Cargo and baggage compartments.* Cargo and baggage compartments must be designed to meet FAR 23.787 (a) and (b), and in addition means must be provided to protect passengers from injury by the contents of any cargo or baggage compartment when the ultimate forward inertia force is 9g.

32. *Doors and exits.* The airplane must meet FAR 23.783 and FAR 23.807 (a)(3), (b), and (c), and in addition:

(a) There must be a means to lock and safeguard each external door and exit against opening in flight either inadvertently by persons, or as a result of mechanical failure. Each external door must be operable from both the inside and the outside.

(b) There must be means for direct visual inspection of the locking mechanism by crewmembers to determine whether external doors and exits, for which the initial opening movement is outward, are fully locked. In addition, there must be a visual means to signal to crewmembers when normally used external doors are closed and fully locked.

(c) The passenger entrance door must qualify as a floor level emergency exit. Each additional required emergency exit except floor level exits must be located over the wing or must be provided with acceptable means to assist the occupants in descending to the ground. In addition to the passenger entrance door:

(1) For a total seating capacity of 15 or less, an emergency exit as defined in FAR 23.807(b) is required on each side of the cabin.

(2) For a total seating capacity of 16 through 23, three emergency exits as defined in FAR 23.807(b) are required with one on the same side as the door and two on the side opposite the door.

(d) An evacuation demonstration must be conducted utilizing the maximum number of occupants for which certification is desired. It must be conducted under simulated night conditions utilizing only the emergency exits on the most critical side of the aircraft. The participants must be representative of average airline passengers with no previous practice or rehearsal for the demonstration. Evacuation must be completed within 90 seconds.

(e) Each emergency exit must be marked with the word "Exit" by a sign which has white letters 1 inch high on a red background 2 inches high, be self-illuminated or independently internally electrically illuminated, and have a minimum luminescence (brightness) of at least 160 microlamberts. The colors may be reversed if the passenger compartment illumination is essentially the same.

(f) Access to window type emergency exits must not be obstructed by seats or seat backs.

(g) The width of the main passenger aisle at any point between seats must equal or exceed the values in the following table:

| Total seating capacity | Minimum main passenger aisle width | |
	Less than 25 inches from floor	25 inches and more from floor
10 through 23	9 inches	15 inches.

Miscellaneous

33. *Lightning strike protection.* Parts that are electrically insulated from the basic airframe must be connected to it through lightning arrestors unless a lightning strike on the insulated part—

(a) Is improbable because of shielding by other parts; or

(b) Is not hazardous.

34. *Ice protection.* If certification with ice protection provisions is desired, compliance with the following must be shown:

(a) The recommended procedures for the use of the ice protection equipment must be set forth in the Airplane Flight Manual.

(b) An analysis must be performed to establish, on the basis of the airplane's operational needs, the adequacy of the ice protection system for the various components of the airplane. In addition, tests of the ice protection system must be conducted to demonstrate that the airplane is capable of operating safely in continuous maximum and intermittent maximum icing conditions as described in Appendix C of Part 25 of this chapter.

(c) Compliance with all or portions of this section may be accomplished by reference, where applicable because of similarity of the designs, to analysis and tests performed by the applicant for a type certificated model.

35. *Maintenance information.* The applicant must make available to the owner at the time of delivery of the airplane the information the applicant considers essential for the proper maintenance of the airplane. That information must include the following:

(a) Description of systems, including electrical, hydraulic, and fuel controls.

(b) Lubrication instructions setting forth the frequency and the lubricants and fluids which are to be used in the various systems.

(c) Pressures and electrical loads applicable to the various systems.

(d) Tolerances and adjustments necessary for proper functioning.

(e) Methods of leveling, raising, and towing.

(f) Methods of balancing control surfaces.

(g) Identification of primary and secondary structures.

(h) Frequency and extent of inspections necessary to the proper operation of the airplane.

(i) Special repair methods applicable to the airplane.

(j) Special inspection techniques, such as X-ray, ultrasonic, and magnetic particle inspection.

(k) List of special tools.

Propulsion

General

36. *Vibration characteristics.* For turbopropeller powered airplanes, the engine installation must not result in vibration characteristics of the engine exceeding those established during the type certification of the engine.

37. *In flight restarting of engine.* If the engine on turbopropeller powered airplanes cannot be restarted at the maximum cruise altitude, a determination must be made of the altitude below which restarts can be consistently accomplished. Restart information must be provided in the Airplane Flight Manual.

38. *Engines.* (a) *For turbopropeller powered airplanes.* The engine installation must comply with the following:

(1) *Engine isolation.* The powerplants must be arranged and isolated from each other to allow operation, in at least one configuration, so that the failure or malfunction of any engine, or of any system that can affect the engine, will not—

(i) Prevent the continued safe operation of the remaining engines; or

(ii) Require immediate action by any crewmember for continued safe operation.

(2) *Control of engine rotation.* There must be a means to individually stop and restart the rotation of any engine in flight except that engine rotation need not be stopped if continued rotation could not jeopardize the

safety of the airplane. Each component of the stopping and restarting system on the engine side of the firewall, and that might be exposed to fire, must be at least fire resistant. If hydraulic propeller feathering systems are used for this purpose, the feathering lines must be at least fire resistant under the operating conditions that may be expected to exist during feathering.

(3) *Engine speed and gas temperature control devices.* The powerplant systems associated with engine control devices, systems, and instrumentation must provide reasonable assurance that those engine operating limitations that adversely affect turbine rotor structural integrity will not be exceeded in service.

(b) *For reciprocating engine powered airplanes.* To provide engine isolation, the powerplants must be arranged and isolated from each other to allow operation, in at least one configuration, so that the failure or malfunction of any engine, or of any system that can affect that engine, will not—

(1) Prevent the continued safe operation of the remaining engines; or

(2) Require immediate action by any crewmember for continued safe operation.

39. *Turbopropeller reversing systems.* (a) Turbopropeller reversing systems intended for ground operation must be designed so that no single failure or malfunction of the system will result in unwanted reverse thrust under any expected operating condition. Failure of structural elements need not be considered if the probability of this kind of failure is extremely remote.

(b) Turbopropeller reversing systems intended for in flight use must be designed so that no unsafe condition will result during normal operation of the system, or from any failure (or reasonably likely combination of failures) of the reversing system, under any anticipated condition of operation of the airplane. Failure of structural elements need not be considered if the probability of this kind of failure is extremely remote.

(c) Compliance with this section may be shown by failure analysis, testing, or both for propeller systems that allow propeller blades to move from the flight low-pitch position to a position that is substantially less than that at the normal flight low-pitch stop position. The analysis may include or be supported by the analysis made to show compliance with the type certification of the propeller and associated installation components. Credit will be given for pertinent analysis and testing completed by the engine and propeller manufacturers.

40. *Turbopropeller drag-limiting systems.* Turbopropeller drag-limiting systems must be designed so that no single failure or malfunction of any of the systems during normal or emergency operation results in propeller drag in excess of that for which the airplane was designed. Failure of structural elements of the drag-limiting systems need not be considered if the probability of this kind of failure is extremely remote.

41. *Turbine engine powerplant operating characteristics.* For turbopropeller powered airplanes, the turbine engine powerplant operating characteristics must be investigated in flight to determine that no adverse characteristics (such as stall, surge, or flameout) are present to a hazardous degree, during normal and emergency operation within the range of operating limitations of the airplane and of the engine.

42. *Fuel flow.* (a) For turbopropeller powered airplanes—

(1) The fuel system must provide for continuous supply of fuel to the engines for normal operation without interruption due to depletion of fuel in any tank other than the main tank; and

(2) The fuel flow rate for turbopropeller engine fuel pump systems must not be less than 125 percent of the fuel flow required to develop the standard sea level atmospheric conditions takeoff power selected and included as an operating limitation in the Airplane Flight Manual.

(b) For reciprocating engine powered airplanes, it is acceptable for the fuel flow rate for each pump system (main and reserve supply) to be 125 percent of the takeoff fuel consumption of the engine.

Fuel System Components

43. *Fuel pumps.* For turbopropeller powered airplanes, a reliable and independent power source must be provided for each pump used with turbine engines which do not have provisions for mechanically driving the main pumps. It must be demonstrated that the pump installations provide a reliability and durability equivalent to that in FAR 23.991(a).

44. *Fuel strainer or filter.* For turbopropeller powered airplanes, the following apply:

(a) There must be a fuel strainer or filter between the tank outlet and the fuel metering device of the engine. In addition, the fuel strainer or filter must be—

(1) Between the tank outlet and the engine-driven positive displacement pump inlet, if there is an engine-driven positive displacement pump;

(2) Accessible for drainage and cleaning and, for the strainer screen, easily removable; and

(3) Mounted so that its weight is not supported by the connecting lines or by the inlet or outlet connections of the strainer or filter itself.

(b) Unless there are means in the fuel system to prevent the accumulation of ice on the filter, there must be means to automatically maintain the fuel-flow if ice-clogging of the filter occurs; and

(c) The fuel strainer or filter must be of adequate capacity (for operating limitations established to ensure proper service) and of appropriate mesh to insure proper engine operation, with the fuel contaminated to a degree (for particle size and density) that can be reasonably expected in service. The degree of fuel filtering may not be less than that established for the engine type certification.

45. *Lightning strike protection.* Protection must be provided against the ignition of flammable vapors in the fuel vent system due to lightning strikes.

Cooling

46. *Cooling test procedures for turbopropeller powered airplanes.* (a) Turbopropeller powered airplanes must be shown to comply with FAR 23.1041 during takeoff, climb, en route, and landing stages of flight that correspond to the applicable performance requirements. The cooling tests must be conducted with the airplane in the configuration, and operating under the conditions that are critical relative to cooling during each stage of flight. For the cooling tests a temperature is "stabilized" when its rate of change is less than 2° F. per minute.

(b) Temperatures must be stabilized under the conditions from which entry is made into each stage of flight being investigated unless the entry condition is not one during which component and engine fluid temperatures would stabilize, in which case, operation through the full entry condition must be conducted before entry into the stage of flight being investigated to allow temperatures to reach their natural levels at the time of entry. The takeoff cooling test must be preceded by a period during which the powerplant component and engine fluid temperatures are stabilized with the engines at ground idle.

(c) Cooling tests for each stage of flight must be continued until—

(1) The component and engine fluid temperatures stabilize;

(2) The stage of flight is completed; or

(3) An operating limitation is reached.

Induction System

47. *Air induction.* For turbopropeller powered airplanes—

(a) There must be means to prevent hazardous quantities of fuel leakage or overflow from drains, vents, or other components of flammable fluid systems from entering the engine intake systems; and

(b) The air inlet ducts must be located or protected so as to minimize the ingestion of foreign matter during takeoff, landing, and taxiing.

48. *Induction system icing protection.* For turbopropeller powered airplanes, each turbine engine must be able to operate throughout its flight power range without adverse effect on engine operation or serious loss of power or thrust, under the icing conditions specified in Appendix C of Part 25 of this chapter. In addition, there must be means to indicate to appropriate flight crewmembers the functioning of the powerplant ice protection system.

49. *Turbine engine bleed air systems.* Turbine engine bleed air systems of turbopropeller powered airplanes must be investigated to determine—

(a) That no hazard to the airplane will result if a duct rupture occurs. This condition must consider that a failure of the duct can occur anywhere between the engine port and the airplane bleed service; and

(b) That, if the bleed air system is used for direct cabin pressurization, it is not possible for hazardous contamination of the cabin air system to occur in event of lubrication system failure.

Exhaust System

50. *Exhaust system drains.* Turbopropeller engine exhaust systems having low spots or pockets must incorporate drains at those locations. These drains must discharge clear of the airplane in normal and ground attitudes to prevent the accumulation of fuel after the failure of an attempted engine start.

Powerplant Controls and Accessories

51. *Engine controls.* If throttles or power levers for turbopropeller powered airplanes are such that any position of these controls will reduce the fuel flow to the engine(s) below that necessary for satisfactory and safe idle operation of the engine while the airplane is in flight, a means must be provided to prevent inadvertent movement of the control into this position. The means provided must incorporate a positive lock or stop at this idle position and must require a separate and distinct operation by the crew to displace the control from the normal engine operating range.

52. *Reverse thrust controls.* For turbopropeller powered airplanes, the propeller reverse thrust controls must have a means to prevent their inadvertent operation. The means must have a positive lock or stop at the idle position and must require a separate and distinct operation by the crew to displace the control from the flight regime.

53. *Engine ignition systems.* Each turbopropeller airplane ignition system must be considered an essential electrical load.

54. *Powerplant accessories.* The powerplant accessories must meet FAR 23.1163, and if the continued rotation of any accessory remotely driven by the engine is hazardous when malfunctioning occurs, there must be means to prevent rotation without inter-

fering with the continued operation of the engine.

Powerplant Fire Protection

55. *Fire detector system.* For turbopropeller powered airplanes, the following apply:

(a) There must be a means that ensures prompt detection of fire in the engine compartment. An overtemperature switch in each engine cooling air exit is an acceptable method of meeting this requirement.

(b) Each fire detector must be constructed and installed to withstand the vibration, inertia, and other loads to which it may be subjected in operation.

(c) No fire detector may be affected by any oil, water, other fluids, or fumes that might be present.

(d) There must be means to allow the flight crew to check, in flight, the functioning of each fire detector electric circuit.

(e) Wiring and other components of each fire detector system in a fire zone must be at least fire resistant.

56. *Fire protection, cowling and nacelle skin.* For reciprocating engine powered airplanes, the engine cowling must be designed and constructed so that no fire originating in the engine compartment can enter either through openings or by burn through, any other region where it would create additional hazards.

57. *Flammable fluid fire protection.* If flammable fluids or vapors might be liberated by the leakage of fluid systems in areas other than engine compartments, there must be means to—

(a) Prevent the ignition of those fluids or vapors by any other equipment; or

(b) Control any fire resulting from that ignition.

Equipment

58. *Powerplant instruments.* (a) The following are required for turbopropeller airplanes:

(1) The instruments required by FAR 23.1305 (a) (1) through (4), (b) (2) and (4).

(2) A gas temperature indicator for each engine.

(3) Free air temperature indicator.

(4) A fuel flowmeter indicator for each engine.

(5) Oil pressure warning means for each engine.

(6) A torque indicator or adequate means for indicating power output for each engine.

(7) Fire warning indicator for each engine.

(8) A means to indicate when the propeller blade angle is below the low-pitch position corresponding to idle operation in flight.

(9) A means to indicate the functioning of the ice protection system for each engine.

(b) For turbopropeller powered airplanes, the turbopropeller blade position indicator must begin indicating when the blade has moved below the flight low-pitch position.

(c) The following instruments are required for reciprocating engine powered airplanes:

(1) The instruments required by FAR 23.1305.

(2) A cylinder head temperature indicator for each engine.

(3) A manifold pressure indicator for each engine.

Systems and Equipments

General

59. *Function and installation.* The systems and equipment of the airplane must meet FAR 23.1301, and the following:

(a) Each item of additional installed equipment must—

(1) Be of a kind and design appropriate to its intended function;

(2) Be labeled as to its identification, function, or operating limitations, or any applicable combination of these factors, unless misuse or inadvertent actuation cannot create a hazard;

(3) Be installed according to limitations specified for that equipment; and

(4) Function properly when installed.

(b) Systems and installations must be designed to safeguard against hazards to the aircraft in the event of their malfunction or failure.

(c) Where an installation, the functioning of which is necessary in showing compliance with the applicable requirements, requires a power supply, that installation must be considered an essential load on the power supply, and the power sources and the distribution system must be capable of supplying the following power loads in probable operation combinations and for probable durations:

(1) All essential loads after failure of any prime mover, power converter, or energy storage device.

(2) All essential loads after failure of any one engine on two-engine airplanes.

(3) In determining the probable operating combinations and durations of essential loads for the power failure conditions described in paragraphs (1) and (2) of this paragraph, it is permissible to assume that the power loads are reduced in accordance with a monitoring procedure which is consistent with safety in the types of operations authorized.

60. *Ventilation.* The ventilation system of the airplane must meet FAR 23.831, and in addition, for pressurized aircraft, the ventilating air in flight crew and passenger compartments must be free of harmful or hazardous concentrations of gases and vapors in normal operation and in the event of reasonably probable failures or malfunctioning of the ventilating, heating, pressurization,

or other systems, and equipment. If accumulation of hazardous quantities of smoke in the cockpit area is reasonably probable, smoke evacuation must be readily accomplished.

Electrical Systems and Equipment

61. *General.* The electrical systems and equipment of the airplane must meet FAR 23.1351, and the following:

(a) *Electrical system capacity.* The required generating capacity, and number and kinds of power sources must—

(1) Be determined by an electrical load analysis; and

(2) Meet FAR 23.1301.

(b) *Generating system.* The generating system includes electrical power sources, main power busses, transmission cables, and associated control, regulation and protective devices. It must be designed so that—

(1) The system voltage and frequency (as applicable) at the terminals of all essential load equipment can be maintained within the limits for which the equipment is designed, during any probable operating conditions;

(2) System transients due to switching, fault clearing, or other causes do not make essential loads inoperative, and do not cause a smoke or fire hazard;

(3) There are means, accessible in flight to appropriate crewmembers, for the individual and collective disconnection of the electrical power sources from the system; and

(4) There are means to indicate to appropriate crewmembers the generating system quantities essential for the safe operation of the system, including the voltage and current supplied by each generator.

62. *Electrical equipment and installation.* Electrical equipment, controls, and wiring must be installed so that operation of any one unit or system of units will not adversely affect the simultaneous operation of any other electrical unit or system essential to the safe operation.

63. *Distribution system.* (a) For the purpose of complying with this section, the distribution system includes the distribution busses, their associated feeders, and each control and protective device.

(b) Each system must be designed so that essential load circuits can be supplied in the event of reasonably probable faults or open circuits, including faults in heavy current carrying cables.

(c) If two independent sources of electrical power for particular equipment or systems are required under this appendix, their electrical energy supply must be ensured by means such as duplicate electrical equipment, throwover switching, or multichannel or loop circuits separately routed.

64. *Circuit protective devices.* The circuit protective devices for the electrical circuits of the airplane must meet FAR 23.1357, and in addition circuits for loads which are essential to safe operation must have individual and exclusive circuit protection.

Appendix B—Airplane Flight Recorder Specifications

Parameters	Range	Installed system [1] minimum accuracy (to recovered data)	Sampling interval (per second)	Resolution [4] read out
Relative time (from recorded on prior to takeoff).	8 hr minimum	±0.125% per hour	1	1 sec.
Indicated airspeed	V$_{so}$ to V$_D$ (KIAS)	±5% or ±10 kts., whichever is greater. Resolution 2 kts. below 175 KIAS.	1	1% [3]
Altitude	−1,000 ft. to max cert. alt. of A/C	±100 to ±700 ft. (see Table 1, TSO C51-a).	1	25 to 150
Magnetic heading	360°	±5°	1	1°
Vertical acceleration	−3g to +6g	±0.2g in addition to ±0.3g maximum datum.	4 (or 1 per second where peaks, ref. to 1g are recorded).	0.03g.
Longitudinal acceleration	±1.0g	±1.5% max. range excluding datum error of ±5%.	2	0.01g.
Pitch attitude	100% of usable	±2°	1	0.8°
Roll attitude	±60° or 100% of usable range, whichever is greater.	±2°	1	0.8°
Stabilizer trim position	Full range	±3% unless higher uniquely required	1	1% [3]
Or				
Pitch control position	Full range	±3% unless higher uniquely required	1	1% [3]
Engine Power, Each Engine				
Fan or N$_i$ speed or EPR or cockpit indications used for aircraft certification.	Maximum range	±5%	1	1% [3]
Or				
Prop. speed and torque (sample once/sec as close together as practicable).			1 (prop speed), 1 (torque).	
Altitude rate [2] (need depends on altitude resolution).	±8,000 fpm	±10%. Resolution 250 fpm below 12,000 ft. indicated.	1	250 fpm Below 12,000.
Angle of attack [2] (need depends on altitude resolution).	−20° to 40° or of usable range	±2°	1	0.8% [3]
Radio transmitter keying (discrete)	On/off		1	
TE flaps (discrete or analog)	Each discrete position (U, D, T/O, AAP)		1	
Or				
	Analog 0–100% range	±3°	1	1% [3]
LE flaps (discrete or analog)	Each discrete position (U, D, T/O, AAP)		1	
Or				
	Analog 0–100% range	±3°	1	1% [3]
Thrust reverser, each engine (Discrete)	Stowed or full reverse		1	
Spoiler/speedbrake (discrete)	Stowed or out		1	
Autopilot engaged (discrete)	Engaged or disengaged		1	

[1] When data sources are aircraft instruments (except altimeters) of acceptable quality to fly the aircraft the recording system excluding these sensors (but including all other characteristics of the recording system) shall contribute no more than half of the values in this column.

[2] If data from the altitude encoding altimeter (100 ft. resolution) is used, then either one of these parameters should also be recorded. If however, altitude is recorded at a minimum resolution of 25 feet, then these two parameters can be omitted.

[3] Per cent of full range.

[4] This column applies to aircraft manufacturing after October 11, 1991

APPENDIX C—HELICOPTER FLIGHT RECORDER SPECIFICATIONS

Parameters	Range	Installed system [1] minimum accuracy (to recovered data)	Sampling interval (per second)	Resolution [3] read out
Relative time (from recorded on prior to takeoff).	8 hr minimum	±0.125% per hour	1	1 sec.
Indicated airspeed	V_{min} to V_{D} (KIAS) (minimum airspeed signal attainable with installed pilot-static system)	±5% or ±10 kts., whichever is greater	1	1 kt.
Altitude	−1,000 ft to 20,000 ft pressure altitude	±100 to ±700 ft. (see Table 1, TSO C51-a).	1	25 to 150 ft.
Magnetic heading	360°	±5°	1	1°
Vertical acceleration	−3g to +6g	±0.2g in addition to ±0.3g maximum datum.	4 (or 1 per second where peaks, ref. to 1g are recorded).	0.05g.
Longitudinal acceleration	±1.0g	±1.5% max. range excluding datum error of ±5%.	2	0.03g.
Pitch attitude	100% of usable range	±2°	1	0.8°
Roll attitude	±60° or 100% of usable range, whichever is greater.	±2°	1	0.8°
Altitude rate	±8,000 fpm	±10% Resolution 250 fpm below 12,000 ft indicated	1	250 fpm below 12,000.
Engine Power, Each Engine				
Main rotor speed	Maximum range	±5%	1	1% [2]
Free or power turbine	Maximum range	±5%	1	1% [2]
Engine torque	Maximum range	±5%	1	1% [2]
Flight Control—Hydraulic Pressure				
Primary (discrete)	High/low		1	
Secondary—if applicable (discrete)	High/low		1	
Radio transmitter keying (discrete)	On/off		1	
Autopilot engaged (discrete)	Engaged or disengaged		1	
SAS status—engaged (discrete)	Engaged/disengaged		1	
SAS fault status (discrete)	Fault/OK		1	
Flight Controls				
Collective	Full range	±3%	2	1% [2]
Pedal position	Full range	±3%	2	1% [2]
Lat. cyclic	Full range	±3%	2	1% [2]
Long. cyclic	Full range	±3%	2	1% [2]
Controllable stabilator position	Full range	±3%	2	1% [2]

[1] When data sources are aircraft instruments (except altimeters) of acceptable quality to fly the aircraft the recording system excluding these sensors (but including all other characteristics of the recording system) shall contribute no more than half of the values in this column.

[2] Per cent of full range.

[3] This column applies to aircraft manufactured after October 11, 1991

APPENDIX D—AIRPLANE FLIGHT RECORDER SPECIFICATION

Parameters	Range	Accuracy sensor input to DFDR readout	Sampling interval (per second)	resolution [4] read out
Time (GMT or Frame Counter) (range 0 to 4095, sampled 1 per frame).	24 Hrs	±0.125% Per Hour	0.25 (1 per 4 seconds).	1 sec.
Altitude	−1,000 ft to max certificated altitude of aircraft.	±100 to ±700 ft (See Table 1, TSO–C51a).	1	5' to 35' [1]
Airspeed	50 KIAS to V_{so} and V_{so} to 1.2 V_D	±5%, ±3%	1	1kt.
Heading	360°	±2°	1	0.5°
Normal Acceleration (Vertical)	−3g to +6g	±1% of max range excluding datum error of ±5%.	8	0.01g
Pitch Attitude	±75°	±2°	1	0.5°
Roll Attitude	±180°	±2°	1	0.5°
Radio Transmitter Keying	On-Off (Discrete)		1	
Thrust/Power on Each Engine	Full range forward	±2%	1 (per engine)	0 2% [2]
Trailing Edge Flap or Cockpit Control Selection.	Full range or each discrete position	±3° or as pilot's indicator	0.5	0.5% [3]
Leading Edge Flap on or Cockpit Control Selection.	Full range or each discrete position	±3° or as pilot's indicator	0.5	0.5% [3]
Thrust Reverser Position	Stowed, in transit, and reverse discrete		1 (per 4 seconds per engine).	
Ground Spoiler Position/Speed Brake Selection.	Full range or each discrete position	±2% unless higher accuracy uniquely required.	1	0 22 [2]
Marker Beacon Passage	Discrete		1	
Autopilot Engagement	Discrete		1	
Longitudinal Acceleration	±1g	±1.5% max range excluding datum error of ±5%.	4	0.01g
Pilot Input And/or Surface Position-Primary Controls (Pitch, Roll, Yaw) [3].	Full range	±2° unless higher accuracy uniquely required.	1	0 2% [3]
Lateral Acceleration	±1g	±1.5% max range excluding datum error of ±5%.	4	0.01g
Pitch Trim Position	Full range	±3% unless higher accuracy uniquely required.	1	0.3% [3]
Glideslope Deviation	±400 Microamps	±3%	1	0 3% [2]
Localizer Deviation	±400 Microamps	±3%	1	0 3% [2]
AFCS Mode And Engagement Status	Discrete		1	
Radio Altitude	−20 ft to 2,500 ft	±2 Ft or ±3% whichever is greater below 500 ft and ±5% above 500 ft.	1	1 ft + 5% [2] above 500'
Master Warning	Discrete		1	
Main Gear Squat Switch Status	Discrete		1	
Angle of Attack (if recorded directly)	As installed	As installed	2	0 3% [3]
Outside Air Temperature or Total Air Temperature.	−50°C to +90°c	±2°c	0.5	0.3 c
Hydraulics, Each System Low Pressure	Discrete		0.5	or 0 5% [2]
Groundspeed	As installed	Most accurate systems installed (IMS equipped aircraft only).	1	0 2% [3]

If additional recording capacity is available, recording of the following parameters is recommended. The parameters are listed in order of significance:

Parameters	Range	Accuracy sensor input to DFDR readout	Sampling interval (per second)	resolution read out
Drift Angle	When available. As installed	As installed	4	
Wind Speed and Direction	When available. As installed	As installed	4	
Latitude and Longitude	When available. As installed	As installed	4	
Brake pressure/Brake pedal position	As installed	As installed	1	
Additional engine parameters:				
EPR	As installed	As installed	1 (per engine)	
N1	As installed	As installed	1 (per engine)	
N2	As installed	As installed	1 (per engine)	
EGT	As installed	As installed	1 (per engine)	
Throttle Lever Position	As installed	As installed	1 (per engine)	
Fuel Flow	As installed	As installed	1 (per engine)	
TCAS:				
TA	As installed	As installed	1	
RA	As installed	As installed	1	
Sensitivity level (as selected by crew).	As installed	As installed	2	
GPWS (ground proximity warning system)	Discrete		1	
Landing gear or gear selector position	Discrete		0.25 (1 per 4 seconds)	
DME 1 and 2 Distance	0-200 NM;	As installed	0.25	1mi
Nav 1 and 2 Frequency Selection	Full range	As installed	0.25	

[1] When altitude rate is recorded. Altitude rate must have sufficient resolution and sampling to permit the derivation of altitude to 5 feet.

[2] Per cent of full range.

[3] For airplanes that can demonstrate the capability of deriving either the control input on control movement (one from the other) for all modes of operation and flight regimes, the "or" applies. For airplanes with non-mechanical control systems (fly-by-wire) the "and" applies. In airplanes with split surfaces, suitable combination of inputs is acceptable in lieu of recording each surface separately.

[4] This column applies to aircraft manufactured after October 11, 1991

APPENDIX E—HELICOPTER FLIGHT RECORDER SPECIFICATIONS

Parameters	Range	Accuracy sensor input to DFDR readout	Sampling interval (per second)	Resolution [2] read out
Time (GMT)	24 Hrs	± 0.125% Per Hour	0.25 (1 per 4 seconds)	1 sec
Altitude	−1,000 ft to max certificated altitude of aircraft.	±100 to ±700 ft (See Table 1, TSO-C51a).	1	5' to 30'
Airspeed	As the installed measuring system	±3%	1	1 kt.
Heading	360°	±2°	1	0.5°
Normal Acceleration (Vertical)	−3g to +6g	±1% of max range excluding datum error of ±5%.	8	0.01g
Pitch Attitude	±75°	±2°	2	0.5°
Roll Attitude	±180°	±2°	2	0.5°
Radio Transmitter Keying	On-Off (Discrete)		1	0.25 sec.
Power in Each Engine: Free Power Turbine Speed *and* Engine Torque.	0-130% (power Turbine Speed) Full range (Torque).	±2%	1 speed 1 torque (per engine).	0.2% [1] to 0.4% [1]
Main Rotor Speed	0-130%	±2%	2	0.3% [1]
Altitude Rate	±6,000 ft/min	As installed	2	0.2% [1]
Pilot Input—Primary Controls (Collective, Longitudinal Cyclic, Lateral Cyclic, Pedal).	Full range	±3%	2	0.5% [1]
Flight Control Hydraulic Pressure Low	Discrete, each circuit		1	
Flight Control Hydraulic Pressure Selector Switch Position, 1st and 2nd stage.	Discrete		1	
AFCS Mode and Engagement Status	Discrete (5 bits necessary)		1	
Stability Augmentation System Engage	Discrete		1	
SAS Fault Status	Discrete			
Main Gearbox Temperature Low	As installed		0.25	
Main Gearbox Temperature High	As installed	As installed	0.25	0.5% [1]
Controllable Stabilator Position	Full Range	As installed	0.5	0.5% [1]
Longitudinal Acceleration	±1g	±3%	2	0.4% [1]
		±1.5% max range excluding datum error of ±5%.	4	0.01g.
Lateral Acceleration	±1g	±1.5% max range excluding datum of ±5%.	4	0.01g.
Master Warning	Discrete		1	
Nav 1 and 2 Frequency Selection	Full range	As installed	0.25	
Outside Air Temperature	−50°C to +90°C	±2°c	0.5	0.3°c

[1] Per cent of full range.
[2] This column applies to aircraft manufactured after October 11, 1991.

FEDERAL AVIATION REGULATIONS

PART 145
REPAIR STATIONS

1989 EDITION

PART 145—REPAIR STATIONS

Subpart A—General

Sec.
145.1   Applicability.
145.2   Performance of maintenance, preventive maintenance, alterations and required inspections for an air carrier or commercial operator under the continuous airworthiness requirements of Parts 121 and 127, and for airplanes under the inspection program required by Part 125.
145.3   Certificate required.
145.11   Application and issue.
145.13   Certification of foreign repair stations: Special requirements.
145.15   Change or renewal of certificates.
145.17   Duration of certificates.
145.19   Display of certificate.
145.21   Change of location or facilities.
145.23   Inspection.
145.25   Advertising.

Subpart B—Domestic Repair Stations

145.31   Ratings.
145.33   Limited ratings.
145.35   Housing and facility requirements.
145.37   Special housing and facility requirements.
145.39   Personnel requirements.
145.41   Recommendation of persons for certification as repairmen.
145.43   Records of supervisory and inspection personnel.
145.45   Inspection systems.

145.47 Equipment and materials: Ratings other than limited ratings.
145.49 Equipment and materials: Limited rating.
145.51 Privileges of certificates.
145.53 Limitations of certificates.
145.55 Maintenance of personnel, facilities equipment, and materials.
145.57 Performance standards.
145.59 Inspection of work performed.
145.61 Performance records and reports.
145.63 Reports of defects or unairworthy conditions.

Subpart C—Foreign Repair Stations

145.71 General requirements.
145.73 Scope of work authorized.
145.75 Personnel.
145.77 General operating rules.
145.79 Records and reports.

Subpart D—Limited Ratings for Manufacturers

145.101 Application and issue.
145.103 Privileges of certificates.
145.105 Performance standards.
APPENDIX A

Subpart A—General

§ 145.1 Applicability.

(a) This part prescribes the requirements for issuing repair station certificates and associated ratings to facilities for the maintenance and alteration of airframes, powerplants, propellers, or appliances, and prescribes the general operating rules for the holders of those certificates and ratings.

(b) A certificated repair station located in the United States is called a "domestic repair station". A repair station located outside of the United States is called a "foreign repair station".

(c) A manufacturer of aircraft, aircraft engines, propellers, appliances, or parts thereof, may be issued a Repair Station Certificate with a limited rating under Subpart D of this part. Sections 145.11 through 145.79 do not apply to applicants for, or holders of, certificates issued under Subpart D of this part. Any facility where the holder of a certificate issued under Subpart D of this part exercises his privileges under that certificate may be referred to as a "manufacturer's maintenance facility."

[Doc. No. 1157, 27 FR 6662, July 13, 1962, as amended by Amdt. 145-4, 31 FR 5249, Apr. 1, 1966]

§ 145.2 Performance of maintenance, preventive maintenance, alterations and required inspections for an air carrier or commercial operator under the continuous airworthiness requirements of Parts 121 and 127, and for airplanes under the inspection program required by Part 125.

(a) Each repair station that performs any maintenance, preventive maintenance, alterations, or required inspections for an air carrier or commercial operator having a continuous airworthiness program under Part 121 or Part 127 of this chapter shall comply with Subpart L of Part 121 (except §§ 121.363, 121.369, 121.373, and 121.379) or Subpart I of Part 127 (except §§ 127.131, 127.134, 127.136, and 127.140) of this chapter, as applicable. In addition, such repair station shall perform that work in accordance with the air carrier's or commercial operator's manual.

(b) Each repair station that performs inspections on airplanes governed by Part 125 of this chapter shall do that work in accordance with the inspection program approved for the operator of the airplane.

[Amdt. 145-7, 31 FR 10614, Aug. 9, 1966, as amended by Amdt. 145-17, 45 FR 67235, Oct. 9, 1980]

§ 145.3 Certificate required.

No person may operate as a certificated repair station without, or in violation of, a repair station certificate. In addition, an applicant for a certificate may not advertise as a certificated repair station until the certificate has been issued to him.

§ 145.11 Application and issue.

(a) An application for a repair station certificate and rating, or for an additional rating, is made on a form and in a manner prescribed by the Administrator, and submitted with duplicate copies of—

(1) [Reserved]

(2) Its inspection procedures manual;

(3) A list of the maintenance functions to be performed for it, under contract, buy another agency under § 145.49 or Appendix A; and

(4) In the case of an applicant for a propeller rating (class 2) or any accessory rating (class 1, 2, or 3), a list, by type or make, as applicable, of the propeller or accessory for which he seeks approval.

(b) An applicant who meets the requirements of this part is entitled to a repair station certificate with appropriate ratings prescribing such operations specifications and limitations as are necessary in the interests of safety.

[Doc. No. 1157, 27 FR 6662, July 13, 1962, as amended by Amdt. 145-5, 31 FR 8585, June 21, 1966]

§ 145.13 Certification of foreign repair stations: Special requirements.

Before applying under § 145.11, an applicant for a foreign repair station certificate must notify the FAA office having jurisdiction over the area in which the applicant is located of his intention to so apply and send that office a statement of his reasons for wanting a repair station at his place of business. In addition to the information required by § 145.11, the applicant must furnish two copies of a suitably bound brochure, including a physical description of his facilities (with photographs), a description of his inspection system, and organizational chart, the names and titles of managing and supervisory personnel, and a list of services obtained under contract, if any, with the names of the contractors and the types of services they perform. In addition, the applicant must furnish evidence that the fee prescribed by Appendix A of Part 187 of this chapter has been paid.

[Doc. No. 1157, 27 FR 6662, July 13, 1962, as amended by Amdt. 145-20, 47 FR 35694, Aug. 16, 1982]

§ 145.15   Change or renewal of certificates.

(a) Each of the following requires the certificate holder to apply for a change in a repair station certificate, on a form and in the manner prescribed by the Administrator:

(1) A change in the location or housing and facilities of the station.

(2) A request to revise or amend a rating.

(b) If the holder of a repair station certificate sells or transfers its assets, the new owner must apply for an amended certificate, in the manner prescribed in § 145.11 and, if applicable, § 145.13.

(c) A person requesting renewal of a foreign repair station certificate shall, within 30 days before his current certificate expires, send the request to the FAA office having jurisdiction over the station. If he does not make the request within that period, he must follow the procedure prescribed in § 145.13 for applying for a new certificate, but without copies of the brochure.

[Doc. No. 1157, 27 FR 6662, July 13, 1962, as amended by Amdt. 145-8, 32 FR 15670, Nov. 14, 1967]

§ 145.17   Duration of certificates.

(a) A domestic repair station certificate or rating is effective until it is surrendered, suspended, or revoked.

(b) A foreign repair station certificate or rating expires at the end of 12 months after the date on which it was issued, unless it is sooner surrendered, suspended, or revoked. However, if the station continues to comply with § 145.71 and applies for renewal before expiration of such certificate or rating, its certificate or rating may be renewed for 24 months.

(c) The holder of a certificate that expires or is surrendered, suspended, or revoked, shall return it to the Administrator.

[Doc. No. 1157, 27 FR 6662, July 13, 1962, as amended by Amdt. 145-16, 43 FR 22643, May 25, 1978]

§ 145.19   Display of certificate.

Each holder of a repair station certificate shall display the certificate and ratings at a place in the repair station that is normally accessible to the public and is not obscured. The certificate must be available for inspection by the Administrator.

§ 145.21   Change of location or facilities.

(a) The holder of a repair station certificate may not make any change in its location or in its housing and facilities that are required by § 145.35, unless the change is approved in writing in advance.

(b) The Administrator may prescribe the conditions under which a repair station may operate while it is changing its location or housing facilities.

§ 145.23   Inspection.

Each certificated repair station shall allow the Administrator to inspect it, at any time, to determine its compliance with this part. The inspections cover the adequacy of the repair stations inspection system, records, and its general ability to comply with this part. After such an inspection is made, the repair station is notified, in writing, of any defects found during the inspection.

[Amdt. 145-5, 31 FR 8585, June 21, 1966]

§ 145.25   Advertising.

(a) Whenever the advertising of a certificated repair station indicates that it is certificated, it must clearly state its certificate number.

(b) Paragraph (a) of this section applies to advertising in—

(1) Business letterheads;

(2) Billheads and statements;

(3) Customer estimates and inspection forms;

(4) Hangar or shop signs;

(5) Magazines, periodicals, or trade journals; or

(6) Any form of promotional media.

Subpart B—Domestic Repair Stations

§ 145.31   Ratings.

The following ratings are issued under this subpart:

(a) *Airframe ratings.* (1) Class 1: Composite construction of small aircraft.

(2) Class 2: Composite construction of large aircraft.

(3) Class 3: All-metal construction of small aircraft.

(4) Class 4: All-metal construction of large aircraft.

(b) *Powerplant ratings.* (1) Class 1: Reciprocating engines of 400 horsepower or less.

(2) Class 2: Reciprocating engines of more than 400 horsepower.

(3) Class 3: Turbine engines.

(c) *Propeller ratings.* (1) Class 1: All fixed pitch and ground adjustable propellers of wood, metal, or composite construction.

(2) Class 2: All other propellers, by make.

(d) *Radio ratings.* (1) Class 1: Communication equipment: Any radio transmitting equipment or receiving equipment, or both, used in aircraft to send or receive communications in flight, regardless of carrier frequency or type of modulation used; including auxiliary and related aircraft interphone systems, amplifier systems, electrical or electronic inter-crew signaling devices, and similar equipment; but not including equipment used for navigation of the aircraft or as an aid to navigation, equipment for measuring altitude or terrain clearance, other measuring equipment operated on radio or radar principles, or mechanical, electrical, gyroscopic, or electronic instruments that are a part of communications radio equipment.

(2) Class 2: Navigational equipment: Any radio system used in aircraft for en route or approach navigation, except equipment operated on radar or pulsed radio frequency principles, but not including equipment for measuring altitude or terrain clearance or other distance equipment operated on radar or pulsed radio frequency principles.

(3) Class 3: Radar equipment: Any aircraft electronic system operated on radar or pulsed radio frequency principles.

(e) *Instrument ratings.* (1) Class 1: Mechanical: Any diaphragm, bourdon tube, aneroid, optical, or mechanically driven centrifugal instrument that is used on aircraft or to operate aircraft, including tach- ometers, airspeed indicators, pressure gauges drift sights, magnetic compasses, altimeters, or similar mechanical instruments.

(2) Class 2: Electrical: Any self-synchronous and electrical indicating instruments and systems, including remote indicating instruments, cylinder head temperature gauges, or similar electrical instruments.

(3) Class 3: Gyroscopic: Any instrument or system using gyroscopic principles and motivated by air pressure or electrical energy, including automatic pilot control units, turn and bank indicators, directional gyros, and their parts, and flux gate and gyrosyn compasses.

(4) Class 4: Electronic: Any instruments whose operation depends on electron tubes, transistors, or similar devices including capacitance type quantity gauges, system amplifiers, and engine analyzers.

(f) *Accessory ratings.* (1) Class 1: Mechanical accessories that depend on friction, hydraulics, mechanical linkage, or pneumatic pressure for operation, including aircraft wheel brakes, mechanically driven pumps, carburetors, aircraft wheel assemblies, shock absorber struts and hydraulic servo units.

(2) Class 2: Electrical accessories that depend on electrical energy for their operation, and generators, including starters, voltage regulators, electric motors, electrically driven fuel pumps magnetos, or similar electrical accessories.

(3) Class 3: electronic accessories that depend on the use of an electron tube transistor, or similar device, including supercharger, temperature, air conditioning controls, or similar electronic controls.

§ 145.33   Limited ratings.

(a) Whenever the Administrator finds it appropriate, he may issue a limited rating to a domestic repair sta-

assemblies or other operations that might be critical to the aircraft, the repair station shall provide at least one supervisor for each 10 apprentices or students, unless the apprentices or students are integrated into groups of experienced workers.

(d) Each person who is directly in charge of the maintenance functions of a repair station must be appropriately certificated as a mechanic or repairman under Part 65 of this chapter and must have had at least 18 months of practical experience in the procedures, practices, inspection methods, materials, tools, machine tools, and equipment generally used in the work for which the station is rated. Experience as an apprentice or student mechanic may not be counted in computing the 18 months of experience. In addition, at least one of the persons so in charge of maintenance functions for a station with an airframe rating must have had experience in the methods and procedures prescribed by the Administrator for returning aircraft to service after 100-hour, annual, and progressive inspections.

(e) Each limited repair station shall have employees with detailed knowledge of the particular maintenance function or technique for which it is rated, based on attending a factory school or long experience with the product or technique involved.

§ 145.41 Recommendation of persons for certification as repairmen.

(a) When a person applies for a domestic repair station certificate and rating(s) or additional rating(s) that require a repairman, that person must—

(1) Recommend at least one person for certification as a repairman;

(2) Certify to the Administrator that the person recommended meets the requirements of § 65.101 of this chapter; and

(3) Certify that the person recommended is able to perform and supervise the assigned work.

(b) Each person recommended per paragraph (a)(1) of this section must be at or above the level of shop foreman or department head or be responsible for supervising the work performed by the repair station. A quali-

fied person so recommended may be certificated as a repairman.

(Secs. 313, 314, and 601 through 610, of the Federal Aviation Act of 1958, as amended (49 U.S.C. 1354, 1355, 1421 through 1430); sec. 6(c), Dept. of Transportation Act (49 U.S.C. 1655(c)))

[Doc. No. 21269, 47 FR 33390, Aug. 2, 1982]

§ 145.43 Records of supervisory and inspection personnel.

(a) Each applicant for a domestic repair station certificate and rating, or for an additional rating, must have, and each certificated domestic repair station shall maintain, a roster of—

(1) Its supervisory personnel, including the names of the officials of the station that are responsible for its management and the names of its technical supervisors, such as foreman and crew chiefs; and

(2) Its inspection personnel, including the names of the chief inspector and those inspectors who make final airworthiness determinations before releasing an article to service.

(b) The station shall also provide a summary of the employment of each person whose name is on the roster. The summary must contain enough information as to each person on the roster to show compliance with the experience requirements of this subpart, including—

(1) His present title (e.g., chief inspector, metal shop foreman, etc.);

(2) His total years of experience in the type of work he is doing;

(3) His past employment record, with names of places and term of employment by month, and year;

(4) The scope of his present employment (e.g., airframe overhaul, airframe final assembly, engine inspection, department, etc.); and

(5) The type and number of the mechanic or repairman certificate that he holds, and the ratings on that certificate.

(c) The station shall change the roster, as necessary, to reflect—

(1) Terminating the employment of any person whose name is on the roster;

(2) Assigning any person to duties that require his name to be carried on the roster; or

standard good practices for properly protecting stored materials.

(e) The applicant must store and protect parts being assembled or disassembled, or awaiting assembly or disassembly, to eliminate the possibility of damage to them.

(f) The applicant must provide suitable ventilation for his shop, assembly, and storage areas so that the physical efficiency of his workers is not impaired.

(g) The applicant must provide adequate lighting for all work being done so that the quality of the work is not impaired.

(h) The applicant must control the température of the shop and assembly area so that the quality of the work is not impaired. Whenever special maintenance operations are being performed, such as fabric work or painting, the temperature and humidity control must be adequate to insure the airworthiness of the article being maintained.

§ 145.37 Special housing and facility requirements.

(a) In addition to the housing and facility requirements in § 145.35, an applicant for a domestic repair station certificate and rating, or for an additional rating, for airframes, powerplants, propellers, instruments, accessories, or radios must meet the requirements of paragraphs (b) to (f) of this section.

(b) An applicant for an airframe rating must provide suitable permanent housing for at least one of the heaviest aircraft within the weight class of the rating he seeks. If the location of the station is such that climatic conditions allow work to be done outside, permanent work docks may be used if they meet the requirements of § 145.35(a).

(c) An applicant for either a powerplant or accessory rating must provide suitable trays, racks, or stands for segregating complete engine or accessory assemblies from each other during assembly and disassembly. He must provide covers to protect parts awaiting assembly or during assembly to prevent dust or other foreign objects from entering into or falling on those parts.

(d) An applicant for a propeller rating must provide suitable stands, racks, or other fixtures for the proper storage of propellers after being worked on.

(e) An applicant for a radio rating must provide suitable storage facilities to assure the protection of parts and units that might deteriorate from dampness or moisture.

(f) An applicant for an instrument rating must provide a reasonably dust free shop if the shop allocated to final assembly is not air conditioned. Shop and assembly areas must be kept clean at all times to reduce the possibility of dust or other foreign objects getting into instrument assemblies.

§ 145.39 Personnel requirements.

(a) An applicant for a domestic repair station certificate and rating, or for an additional rating, must provide adequate personnel who can perform, supervise, and inspect the work for which the station is to be rated. The officials of the station must carefully consider the justifications and abilities of their employees and shall determine the abilities of its uncertificated employees performing maintenance operations on the basis of practical tests or employment records. The repair station is primarily responsible for the satisfactory work of its employees.

(b) The number of repair station employees may vary according to the type and volume of its work. However, the applicant must have enough properly qualified employees to keep up with the volume of work in process, and may not reduce the number of its employees below that necessary to efficiently produce airworthy work.

(c) Each repair station shall determine the abilities of its supervisors and shall provide enough of them for all phases of its activities. However, the Administrator may determine the ability of any supervisor by inspecting his employment and experience records or by a personal test. Each supervisor must have direct supervision over working groups but need not have over-all supervision at management level. Whenever apprentices or students are used in working groups on

tion that maintains or alters only a particular type of airframe, powerplant, propeller, radio, instrument, or accessory, or parts thereof, or performs only specialized maintenance requiring equipment and skills not ordinarily found in regular repair stations. Such a rating may be limited to a specific model aircraft, engine, or constituent part, or to any number of parts made by a particular manufacturer.

(b) Limited ratings are issued for—

(1) Airframes of a particular make and model;

(2) Engines of a particular make and model;

(3) Propellers of a particular make and model;

(4) Instruments of a particular make and model;

(5) Radio equipment of a particular make and model;

(6) Accessories of a particular make and model;

(7) Landing gear components;

(8) Floats, by make;

(9) Nondestructive inspection, testing, and processing;

(10) Emergency equipment;

(11) Rotor blades, by make and model;

(12) Aircraft fabric work; and

(13) Any other purpose for which the Administrator finds the applicant's request is appropriate.

(c) For a limited rating for specialized services, the operations specifications of the station shall contain the specification used in performing that specialized service. The specification may either be a civil or military one that is currently used by industry and approved by the Administrator or one developed by the applicant and approved by the Administrator.

§ 145.35 Housing and facility requirements.

(a) An applicant for a domestic repair station certificate and rating, or for an additional rating, must comply with paragraphs (b) to (h) of this section and provide suitable—

(1) Housing for its necessary equipment and material;

(2) Space for the work for which it seeks a rating;

(3) Facilities for properly storing, segregating, and protecting materials, parts, and supplies; and

(4) Facilities for properly protecting parts and subassemblies during disassembly, cleaning, inspection, repair, alteration, and assembly;

so that work being done is protected from weather elements, dust, and heat; workers are protected so that the work will not be impaired by their physical efficiency; and maintenance operations have efficient and proper facilities.

(b) The applicant must provide suitable shop space where machine tools and equipment are kept and where the largest amount of bench work is done. The shop space need not be partitioned but machines and equipment must be segregated whenever—

(1) Machine or woodwork is done so near an assembly area that chips or material might inadvertently fall into assembled or partially assembled work;

(2) Unpartitioned parts cleaning units are near other operations;

(3) Fabric work is done in an area where there are oils and greases;

(4) Painting or spraying is done in an area so arranged that paint or paint dust can fall on assembled or partially assembled work;

(5) Paint spraying, cleaning, or machining operations are done so near testing operations that the precision of test equipment might be affected; and

(6) In any other case the Administrator determines it is necessary.

(c) The applicant must provide suitable assembly space in an enclosed structure where the largest amount of assembly work is done. The assembly space must be large enough for the largest item to be worked on under the rating he seeks and must meet the requirements of paragraph (a) of this section.

(d) The applicant must provide suitable storage facilities used exclusively for storing standard parts, spare parts, and raw materials, and separated from shop and working space. He must organize the storage facilities so that only acceptable parts and supplies will be issued for any job, and must follow

(3) Any appreciable change in the duties and scope of assignment of any person whose name is on the roster.

(d) The station shall keep the roster and employment summaries required by this section, subject to inspection by the Administrator upon his request.

(e) A domestic repair station may not use the services of a person directly in charge of maintenance or alteration unless it keeps current records on him as required by this section.

[Doc. No. 1157, 27 FR 6662, June 13, 1962, as amended by Amdt. 145-5, 31 FR 8585, June 21, 1966; Amdt. 145-15, 41 FR 47230, Oct. 28, 1976]

§ 145.45   Inspection systems.

(a) An applicant for a repair station certificate, and rating or for an additional rating, must have an inspection system that will produce satisfactory quality control and conform to paragraphs (b) to (f) of this section.

(b) The applicant's inspection personnel must be thoroughly familiar with all inspection methods, techniques, and equipment used in their specialty to determine the quality or airworthiness of an article being maintained or altered. In addition, they must—

(1) Maintain proficiency in using various inspection aids intended for that purpose;

(2) Have available and understand current specifications involving inspection tolerances, limitations, and procedures established by the manufacturer of the product being inspected and with other forms of inspection information such as FAA airworthiness directives and bulletins; and

(3) In cases where magnetic, fluorescent, or other forms of mechanical inspection devices are to be used, be skilled in operating that equipment and be able to properly interpret defects indicated by it.

(c) The applicant must provide a satisfactory method of inspecting incoming material to insure that, before it is placed in stock for use in an aircraft or part thereof, it is in a good state of preservation and is free from apparent defects or malfunctions.

(d) The applicant must provide a system of preliminary inspection of all articles he maintains to determine the state of preservation or defects. He shall enter the results of each inspection on an appropriate form supplied by it and keep the form with the article until it is released to service.

(e) The applicant must provide a system so that before working on any airframe, powerplant, or part thereof that has been involved in an accident, it will be inspected thoroughly for hidden damage, including the areas next to the obviously damaged parts. He shall enter the results of this inspection on the inspection form required by paragraph (d) of this section.

(f) At the time he applies for a repair station certificate, the applicant must provide a manual containing inspection procedures, and thereafter maintain it in current condition at all times. The manual must explain the internal inspection system of the repair station in a manner easily understood by any employee of the station. It must state in detail the inspection requirements in paragraphs (a) to (e) of this section, and the repair station's inspection system including the continuity of inspection responsibility, samples of inspection forms, and the method of executing them. The manual must refer whenever necessary to the manufacturer's inspection standards for the maintenance of the particular article. The repair station must give a copy of the manual to each of its supervisory and inspection personnel and make it available to its other personnel. The repair station is responsible for seeing that all supervisory and inspection personnel thoroughly understand the manual.

[Doc. No. 1157, 27 FR 6662, June 13, 1962, as amended by Amdt. 145-15, 41 FR 47230, Oct. 28, 1976]

§ 145.47   Equipment and materials: Ratings other than limited ratings.

(a) An applicant for a domestic repair station certificate and rating, or for an additional rating, must have the equipment and materials necessary to efficiently perform the functions appropriate to the ratings he seeks. An applicant for an airframe, propeller, powerplant, radio, instrument, or accessory rating must be equipped to perform the functions listed in Appendix A to this part that are appropriate for the rating he seeks.

(b) The equipment and materials required by this part must be of such type that the work for which they are being used can be done competently and efficiently. The station shall ensure that all inspection and test equipment is tested at regular intervals to ensure correct calibration to a standard derived from the National Bureau of Standards or to a standard provided by the equipment manufacturer. In the case of foreign equipment, the standard of the country of manufacture may be used if approved by the Administrator. The equipment and materials required for the various ratings must be located on the premises, and under the full control of the station, unless they are used for a function that the repair station is authorized to obtain by contract. If it obtains them by contract, the repair station shall determine the airworthiness of the article involved, unless the contractor is an appropriately rated repair station.

(c) The applicant shall choose suitable tools and equipment for the functions named in Appendix A to this part, as appropriate to each of his ratings, using those the manufacturer of the article involved recommends for maintaining or altering that article, or their equivalent.

(Secs. 313, 314, and 601 through 610, of the Federal Aviation Act of 1958, as amended (49 U.S.C. 1354, 1355, 1421 through 1430); sec. 6(c), Dept. of Transportation Act (49 U.S.C. 1655(c)))

[Doc. No. 1157, 27 FR 6662, July 13, 1962, as amended by Amdt. 145–19, 47 FR 33391, Aug. 2, 1982]

§ 145.49 Equipment and materials: Limited rating.

(a) An applicant for a limited rating (other than specialized services) under § 145.33, must have the equipment and materials to perform any job function appropriate to the rating and class specified in § 145.47 for the rating he seeks. However, he need not be equipped for a function that does not apply to the particular make or model article for which he seeks a rating, if he shows that it is not necessary under the recommendations of the manufacturer of the article.

(b) An applicant for a rating for specialized services or techniques under § 145.33 must—

(1) For magnetic and penetrant inspection, have the equipment and materials for wet and dry magnetic inspection techniques, residual and continuous methods, and portable equipment for the inspection of welds both on and off the aircraft;

(2) For emergency equipment maintenance, have the equipment and materials to perform inspections, repairs, and tests of all kinds of inflated equipment, the re-packing, re-marking, re-sealing, and re-stocking of life rafts, and the weighing, refilling, and testing of carbon dioxide fire extinguishers and oxygen containers;

(3) For rotor blade maintenance, have the equipment, materials, and technical data recommended by the manufacturer; and

(4) For aircraft fabric work, have the equipment and materials to apply protective coatings to structures, machine stitch fabric panels, perform covering, sewing, and rib stitching operations, apply dope and paint using temperature and humidity control equipment, install patches, grommets, tapes, hooks, and similar equipment, and refinish entire aircraft and aircraft parts.

§ 145.51 Privileges of certificates.

A certificated domestic repair station may—

(a) Maintain or alter any airframe, powerplant, propeller, instrument, radio, or accessory, or part thereof, for which it is rated;

(b) Approve for return to service any article for which it is rated after it has been maintained or altered;

(c) In the case of a station with an airframe rating, perform 100-hour, annual or progressive inspections, and return the aircraft to service; and

(d) Maintain or alter any article for which it is rated at a place other than the repair station, if—

(1) The function would be performed in the same manner as when per-

formed at the repair station and in accordance with §§ 145.57 to 145.61;

(2) All necessary personnel, equipment, material, and technical data is available at the place where the work is to be done; and

(3) The inspection procedures manual of the station sets forth approved procedures governing work to be performed at a place other than the repair station.

However, a certificated repair station may not approve for return to service any aircraft, airframe, aircraft engine, propeller, or appliance after major repair or major alteration unless the work was done in accordance with technical data approved by the Administrator.

[Doc. No. 1157, 27 FR 6662, July 13, 1962, as amended by Amdt. 145-2, 29 FR 5451, Apr. 23, 1964]

§ 145.53   Limitations of certificates.

A certificated domestic repair station may not maintain or alter any airframe, powerplant, propeller, instrument, radio, or accessory for which it is not rated, and may not maintain or alter any article for which it is rated if it requires special technical data, equipment, or facilities that are not available to it.

§ 145.55   Maintenance of personnel, facilities, equipment, and materials.

Each certificated domestic repair station shall provide personnel, facilities equipment, and materials at least equal in quality and quantity to the standards currently required for the issue of the certificate and rating that it holds.

§ 145.57   Performance standards.

(a) Except as provided in § 145.2, each certificated domestic repair station shall perform its maintenance and alteration operations in accordance with the standards in Part 43 of this chapter. It shall maintain, in current condition, all manufacturers' service manuals, instructions, and service bulletins that relate to the articles that it maintains or alters.

(b) In addition, each certificated domestic repair station with a radio rating shall comply with those sections of Part 43 of this chapter that apply to electric systems, and shall use materials that conform to approved specifications for equipment appropriate to its rating. It shall use test apparatus, shop equipment, performance standards, test methods, alterations, and calibrations that conform to the manufacturers' specifications or instructions, approved specification, and, if not otherwise specified, to accept good practices of the aircraft radio industry.

[Doc. No. 1157, 27 FR 6662, July 13, 1962, as amended by Amdt. 145-5, 31 FR 8585, June 21, 1966; Amdt. 145-7, 31 FR 10614, Aug. 9, 1966]

§ 145.59   Inspection of work performed.

(a) Each certificated domestic repair station shall, before approving an airframe, powerplant, propeller, instrument, radio, or accessory for return to service after maintaining or altering it, have that article inspected by a qualified inspector. After performing a maintenance or alteration operation, the station shall certify on the maintenance or alteration record of the article that it is airworthy with respect to the work performed.

(b) For the purposes of paragraph (a) of this section, the qualified inspector must be a person employed by the station, who has shown by experience as a journeyman that he understands the inspection methods, techniques, and equipment used in determining the air-worthiness of the article concerned. He must also be proficient in using various types of mechanical and visual inspection aids appropriate for the article being inspected.

[Doc. No. 1157, 27 FR 6662, July 13, 1962, as amended by Amdt. 145-16, 43 FR 22643, May 25, 1978]

§ 145.61   Performance records and reports.

Each certificated domestic repair station shall maintain adequate records of all work that it does, naming the certificated mechanic or repairman who performed or supervised the work, and the inspector of that work. The station shall keep each record for at least two years after the work it applies to is done.

§ 145.63 Reports of defects or unairworthy conditions.

(a) Each certificated domestic repair station shall report to the Administrator within 72 hours after it discovers any serious defect in, or other recurring unairworthy condition of, an aircraft, powerplant, or propeller, or any component of any of them. The report shall be made on a form and in a manner prescribed by the Administrator, describing the defect or malfunction completely without withholding any pertinent information.

(b) In any case where the filing of a report under paragraph (a) of this section might prejudice the repair station, it shall refer the matter to the Administrator for a determination as to whether it must be reported. If the defect or malfunction could result in an imminent hazard to flight, the repair station shall use the most expeditious method it can to inform the Administrator.

(c) The holder of a domestic repair station certificate that is also the holder of a part 121, 127, or 135 certificate, a Type Certificate (including a Supplemental Type Certificate), a Parts Manufacturer Approval (PMA), or a TSO authorization, or that is the licensee of a Type Certificate, need not report a failure, malfunction, or defect under this section if the failure, malfunction, or defect has been reported by it, under § 21.3, § 37.17, § 121.703, § 127.313, or § 135.57 of this chapter.

[Doc. No. 1157, 27 FR 6662, July 13, 1962, as amended by Amdt. 145-9, 35 FR 3155, Feb. 19, 1970; Amdt. 145-13, 35 FR 18189, Nov. 28, 1970]

Subpart C—Foreign Repair Stations

§ 145.71 General requirements.

A repair station certificate with appropriate ratings may be issued for a foreign repair station, if the Administrator finds that the station is necessary for maintaining or altering United States registered aircraft outside of the United States. A foreign repair station must meet the requirements for a domestic repair station certificate, except those in §§ 145.39 through 145.43.

[Doc. No. 1157, 27 FR 6662, July 13, 1962, as amended by Amdt. 145-15, 41 FR 47230, Oct. 28, 1976]

§ 145.73 Scope of work authorized.

(a) A certificated foreign repair station may, with respect to United States registered aircraft, work only on aircraft that are used in operations conducted wholly or partly outside of the United States. The Administrator may prescribe operating specifications and limitations that he determines are necessary to comply with the airworthiness requirements of this chapter.

(b) A certificated foreign repair station may perform only the specific services and functions within the ratings and classes that are stated in its operating limitations.

§ 145.75 Personnel.

(a) Each applicant for a foreign repair station certificate and rating, or for an additional rating, must provide enough personnel who are able to perform, supervise, and inspect the work for which he seeks a rating, with regard being given to its volume of work.

(b) The supervisors and inspectors of each certificated foreign repair station must understand the regulations in this chapter, FAA airworthiness directives, and the maintenance and service instructions of the manufacturers of the articles to be worked on. However, they do not need airman certificates issued under this chapter and, along with the persons performing the work of the station, are not considered to be airmen within the meaning of section 101(7) of the Federal Aviation Act of 1958 (49 U.S.C. 1301) with respect to work performed in connection with their employment by the foreign repair station.

(c) In cases where the persons engaged in supervision or final inspection are not certificated under this chapter or by the country in which the station is located, their qualifications are determined by the Administrator, based on their ability to meet the requirements of paragraph (a) of this section as shown by oral or practical test or any other method the Administrator elects.

(d) No person may be responsible for the supervision or final inspection of work on an aircraft of United States registry at a foreign repair station unless he can read, write, and understand English.

§ 145.77 General operating rules.

Each certificated foreign repair station shall comply with the operating rules prescribed in Subpart B of this part, except for §§ 145.61 and 145.63, and has the privileges of a domestic repair station as provided in § 145.51.

§ 145.79 Records and reports.

(a) Each certificated foreign repair station shall maintain such records, and make such reports, with respect to United States registered aircraft, as the Administrator finds necessary, including those prescribed in paragraphs (b) and (c) of this section.

(b) Each certificated foreign repair station shall keep a record of the maintenance and alteration it performs on United States registered aircraft, in enough detail to show the make, model, identification number, and serial number of the aircraft involved, and a description of the work. In a case of major repairs or major alterations, or both, it shall report on a form and in a manner prescribed by the Administrator, giving the original copy to the aircraft owner and sending a copy to the Administrator through the FAA office having jurisdiction over the station. However, if a major repair or alteration is made on a United States scheduled flag air carrier aircraft, the report may be made in the log or other record provided by the carrier for that purpose. Upon request, the station shall make all of its maintenance and alteration records available to the Administrator.

(c) Each certificated foreign repair station shall, within 72 hours after it discovers any serious defect in, or other recurring unairworthy condition of, any aircraft, powerplant, propeller, or any component of any of them, that it works on under this part, report that defect or unairworthy condition to the Administrator.

(d) The holder of a foreign repair station certificate that is also the holder of a Type Certificate (including a Supplemental Type Certificate), a Parts Manufacturer Approval (PMA), or a TSO authorization or that is the licensee of a Type Certificate need not report a failure, malfunction, or defect under this section if the failure, malfunction, or defect has been reported by it, under § 21.3 of this chapter or § 37.17 of this chapter.

[Doc. No. 1157, 27 FR 6662, July 13, 1962, as amended by Amdt. 145-9, 35 FR 3155, Feb. 19, 1970; Amdt. 145-13, 35 FR 18189, Nov. 28, 1970]

Subpart D—Limited Ratings for Manufacturers

AUTHORITY: Secs. 313(a), 601, 602, 605, and 607, 72 Stat. 752; 49 U.S.C. 1354(a), 1421, 1422, 1425, and 1427.

SOURCE: Docket No. 1221, 31 FR 5249, Apr. 1, 1966, unless otherwise noted.

§ 145.101 Application and issue.

(a) Upon application in a form and manner prescribed by the Administrator, a repair station certificate with a limited rating for a manufacturer may be issued without further showing to—

(1) The holder or licensee of a Type Certificate who has an approved production inspection system;

(2) The holder of a Production Certificate;

(3) Any person who meets the requirements of § 21.303 of this chapter, and has the prescribed Fabrication Inspection System; and

(4) The holder of a Technical Standard Order (TSO) authorization.

(b) Limited ratings are issued under paragraph (a) of this section for—

(1) Aircraft manufactured by the holder of the rating under a Type Certificate or a Production Certificate;

(2) Aircraft engines manufactured by the holder of the rating under a Type Certificate or a Production Certificate;

(3) Propellers manufactured by the holder of the rating under a Type Certificate or a Production Certificate;

(4) Appliances manufactured by the holder of the rating (i) under a Type Certificate, (ii) under a Production Certificate, (iii) under a TSO authorization, or (iv) in accordance with § 21.303 of this chapter; and

(5) Parts manufactured by the holder of the rating under a TSO authorization or in accordance with § 21.303 of this chapter.

§ 145.103 Privileges of certificates.

(a) The holder of a repair station certificate issued under this subpart may maintain and approve for return to service any article for which it is rated, and perform preventive maintenance on that article, if certificated mechanics or repairmen are employed directly in charge of the maintenance and preventive maintenance.

(b) The privileges granted under this section apply to any location or facility unless the certificate limits the holder to specific locations or facilities.

§ 145.105 Performance standards.

Except as provided in § 145.2, each holder of a certificate issued under this subpart shall perform its maintenance and preventive maintenance operations in accordance with Part 43 of this chapter.

[Amdt. 145-7, 31 FR 10614, Aug. 9, 1966]

Appendix A

NOTE: When an asterisk (*) is shown after any job function listed in this appendix it indicates that the applicant need not have the equipment and material on his premises for performing this job function provided he contracts that particular type work to an outside agency having such equipment and material.

(a) An applicant for a Class 1, 2, 3, or 4 airframe rating must provide equipment and material necessary for efficiently performing the following job functions:

(1) Steel structural components:
Repair or replace steel tubes and fittings using the proper welding techniques when appropriate.
Anticorrosion treatment of the interior and exterior of steel parts,
Metal plating or anodizing*,
Simple machine operations such as making bushings, bolts, etc.,
Complex machine operations involving the use of planers, shapers, milling machines, etc.*,
Fabricate steel fittings,
Abrasive air blasting and chemical cleaning operations*,
Heat treatment*,
Magnetic inspection*,
Repair or rebuilt metal tanks*.

(2) Wood structure:
Splice wood spars,
Repair ribs and spars (wood),
Fabricate wood spars*,
Repair or replace metal ribs,
Interior alignment of wings,
Repair or replace plywood skin,
Treatment against wood decay.
(3) Alloy skin and structural components:
Repair and replace metal skin, using power tools and equipment,
Repair and replace alloy members and components such as tubes, channels, cowlings, fittings, attach angles, etc.,
Alignment of components using jigs or fixtures as in the case of joining fuselage sections or other similar operations,
Make up wooden forming blocks or dies,
Fluorescent inspection of alloy components*,
Fabricate alloy members and components such as tubes, channels, cowlings, fittings, attach angles, etc.*
(4) Fabric covering:
Repairs to fabric surfaces,
Recovering and refinishing of components and entire aircraft*.
(5) Control systems:
Renewing control cables, using swaging and splicing techniques,
Rigging complete control system,
Renewing or repairing all control system hinge point components such as pins, bushings, etc.,
Install control system units and components.
(6) Landing gear systems:
Renew or repair all landing gear hinge point components and attachments such as bolts, bushings, fittings, etc.,
Overhaul and repair elastic shock absorber units,
Overhaul and repair hydraulic-pneumatic shock absorber units*,
Overhaul and repair brake system components*,
Conduct retraction cycle tests,
Overhaul and repair electrical circuits,
Overhaul and repair hydraulic system components*,
Repair or fabricate hydraulic lines.
(7) Electric wiring systems:
Diagnose malfunctions,
Repair or replace wiring,
Installation of electrical equipment,
Bench check electrical components (this check is not to be confused with the more complex functional test after overhaul).
(8) Assembly operations:
Assembly of airframe component parts such as landing gear, wings, controls, etc.,
Rigging and alignment of airframe components, including the complete aircraft and control system,
Installation of powerplants,

Installation of instruments and accessories,

Assembly and fitting of cowling, fairings, etc.,

Repair and assembly of plastic components such as windshields, windows, etc.,

Jack or hoist complete aircraft.

Conduct aircraft weight and balance operations (this function will be conducted in draft-free area)*,

Balance control surfaces.

(b) An applicant for any class of powerplant rating must provide equipment and material necessary for efficiently performing the following job functions appropriate to the class of rating applied for:

(1) Classes 1 and 2. (i) Maintain and alter powerplants, including replacement of parts:

Chemical and mechanical cleaning,

Disassembly operations,

Replacement of valve guides and seats*,

Replacement of bushings, bearings, pins, inserts, etc.,

Plating operations (copper, silver, cadmium, etc.)*,

Heating operations (involving the use of recommended techniques requiring controlled heating facilities),

Chilling or shrinking operations,

Removal and replacement of studs,

Inscribing or affixing identification information,

Painting of powerplants and components,

Anticorrosion treatment for parts,

Replacement and repair of powerplant alloy sheet metal and steel components such as baffles, fittings, etc.*

(ii) Inspect all parts, using appropriate inspection aids:

Magnetic, fluorescent and other acceptable inspection aids*,

Precise determination of clearances and tolerances of all parts,

Inspection for alignment of connecting rods, crankshafts, impeller shafts, etc.,

Balancing of parts, including crankshafts, impellers, etc.*,

Inspection of valve springs.

(iii) Accomplish routine machine work:

Precision grinding, honing and lapping operations (includes crankshaft, cylinder barrels, etc.)*,

Precision drilling, tapping, boring, milling and cutting operations*,

Reaming of inserts, bushings, bearings and other similar components,

Refacing of valves.

(iv) Perform assembly operations:

Valve and ignition timing operations,

Fabricate and test ignition harnesses,

Fabricate and test rigid and flexible fluid lines,

Prepare engines for long- or short-term storage,

Functional check powerplant accessories (this check is not to be confused with the more complex performance test of overhaul)*,

Hoist engines by mechanical means,

Install engines in aircraft*,

Align and adjust engine controls*,

Installation of engines in aircraft and alignment and adjustment of engine controls, when completed, must be inspected by either an appropriately rated certificated mechanic or certificated repairman. Persons supervising or inspecting these functions must thoroughly understand the pertinent installation details involved.

(v) Test overhauled powerplants in compliance with manufacturers' recommendations: The test equipment will be the same as recommended by the manufacturers of the particular engines undergoing test or equivalent equipment that will accomplish the same purpose. The testing function may be performed by the repair station itself, or may be contracted to an outside agency. In either case the repair station will be responsible for the final acceptance of the tested engine.

(2) Class 3. Functional and equipment requirements for turbine engines will be governed entirely by the recommendations of the manufacturer, including techniques, inspection methods, and test.

(c) An applicant for any class of propeller rating must provide equipment and material necessary for efficiently performing the following job functions appropriate to the class of rating applied for:

(1) Class 1. (i) Maintain and alter propellers, including installation and replacement of parts:

Replace blade tipping,

Refinish wood propellers,

Make wood inlays,

Refinish plastic blades,

Straighten bent blades within repairable tolerances,

Modify blade diameter and profile,

Polish and buff,

Painting operations,

Remove from and reinstall on powerplants.

(ii) Inspect components, using appropriate inspection aids:

Inspect propellers for conformity with manufacturer's drawings and specifications,

Inspect hubs and blades for failures and defects, using magnetic or fluorescent inspection devices*,

Inspect hubs and blades for failures and defects, using all visual aids, including the etching of parts,

Inspect hubs for wear of splines or keyways or any other defect.

(iii) Repair or replace components: (Not applicable to this class).

(iv) Balance propellers:

Test for proper track on aircraft,

Test for horizontal and vertical unbalance (this test will be accomplished with the use of precision equipment).

(v) Test propeller pitch-changing mechanisms: (Not applicable to this class).

(2) Class 2. (i) Maintain and alter propellers, including installation and the replacement of parts:

All functions listed under paragraph (c)(1)(i) of this appendix when applicable to the make and model propeller for which a rating is sought,

Properly lubricate moving parts,

Assemble complete propeller and subassemblies, using special tools when required.

(ii) Inspect components, using appropriate inspection aids: All functions listed under paragraph (c)(1)(ii) of this appendix when applicable to the make and model propeller for which a rating is sought.

(iii) Repair or replace component parts:

Replace blades, hubs, or any of their components,

Repair or replace anti-icing devices,

Remove nicks or scratches from metal blades,

Repair or replace electrical propeller components.

(iv) Balance propellers: All functions listed under paragraph (c)(1)(iv) of this appendix when applicable to the make and model propeller for which a rating is sought.

(v) Test propeller pitch-changing mechanism:

Test hydraulically, propellers and components,

Test electrically operated propellers and components,

Test of constant speed devices*.

(d) An applicant for a radio rating must provide equipment and materials as follows:

(1) For a Class 1 (Communications) radio rating, the equipment and materials necessary for efficiently performing the job functions listed in paragraph (4) and the following job functions:

The testing and repair of headsets, speakers, and microphones.

The measuring of radio transmitter power output.

(2) For a Class 2 (Navigation) radio rating, the equipment and materials necessary for efficiently performing the job functions listed in paragraph (4) and the following job functions:

The testing and repair of headsets.

The testing of speakers.

The repair of speakers.*

The measuring of loop antenna sensitivity by appropriate methods.

The determination and compensation for quadrantal error in aircraft direction finder radio equipment.

The calibration of any radio navigational equipment, enroute and approach aids, or similar equipment, appropriate to this rating to approved performance standards.

(3) For Class 3 (Radar) radio rating, the equipment and materials necessary for efficiently performing the job functions listed in paragraph (4) and the following job functions:

The measuring of radio transmitter power output.

The metal plating of transmission lines, wave guides, and similar equipment in accordance with appropriate specifications.*

The pressurization of appropriate radar equipment with dry air, nitrogen, or other specified gases.

(4) For all classes of radio ratings, the equipment and materials necessary for efficiently performing the following job functions:

Perform physical inspection of radio systems and components by visual and mechanical methods.

Perform electrical inspection of radio systems and components by means of appropriate electrical and/or electronic test instruments.

Check aircraft wiring, antennas, connectors, relays, and other associated radio components to detect installation faults.

Check engine ignition systems and aircraft accessories to determine sources of electrical interference.

Check aircraft power supplies for adequacy and proper functioning.

Test radio instruments.*

Overhaul, test, and check dynamotors, inverters, and other radio electrical apparatus.*

Paint and refinish equipment containers.*

Accomplish appropriate methods of marking calibrations, or other information on radio control panels and other components, as required.*

Make and reproduce drawings, wiring diagrams, and other similar material required to record alterations and/or modifications to radio (photographs may be used in lieu of drawings when they will serve as an equivalent or better means of recording).*

Fabricate tuning shaft assemblies, brackets, cable assemblies, and other similar components used in radios or aircraft radio installations.*

Align tuned circuits (RF and IF).

Install and repair aircraft antennas.

Install complete radio systems in aircraft and prepare weight and balance reports* (That phase of radio installation requiring alterations to the aircraft structure must be performed, supervised, and inspected by qualified personnel).

Measure modulation values, noise, and distortion in radios.

Measure audio and radio frequencies to appropriate tolerances and perform calibration necessary for the proper operation of radios.

Measure radio component values (inductance, capacitance, resistance, etc.).

Measure radiofrequency transmission line attenuation.

Determine wave forms and phase in radios when applicable.

Determine proper aircraft radio antenna, lead-in and transmission line characteristics and locations for type of radio equipment to which connected.

Determine operational condition of radio equipment installed in aircraft by using appropriate portable test apparatus.

Determine proper location for radio antennas on aircraft.

Test all types of electronic tubes, transistors, or similar devices in equipment appropriate to the rating.

(e) An applicant for any class of instrument rating must provide equipment and material necessary for efficiently performing the following job functions, in accordance with pertinent specifications and manufacturers' recommendations, appropriate to the class of rating applied for:

(1) Class 1. (i) Diagnose instrument malfunctions: Diagnose malfunctioning of the following instruments:

Rate of climb indicators,
Altimeters,
Air speed indicators,
Vacuum indicators,
Oil pressure gauges,
Fuel pressure gauges,
Hydraulic pressure gauges,
Deicing pressure gauges,
Pitot-static tube,
Direct indicating compasses,
Accelerometer,
Direct indicating tachometers,
Direct reading fuel quantity gauges,
Optical (sextants, drift sights, etc.)*.

(ii) Maintain and alter instruments, including installation and replacement of parts:

Perform these functions on instruments listed under paragraph (e)(1)(i) of this appendix.

The function of installation includes fabrication of instrument panels and other installation structural components. The repair station should be equipped to perform this function. However, it may be contracted to a competent outside agency equipped to perform the function.

(iii) Inspect, test and calibrate instruments: Perform these functions on instruments listed under paragraph (e)(1)(i) of this appendix, on and off the aircraft, when appropriate.

(2) Class 2. (i) Diagnose instrument malfunctions: Diagnose malfunctioning of the following instruments:

Tachometers,
Synchroscope,

Electric temperature indicators,
Electric resistance type indicators,
Moving magnet type indicators,
Resistance type fuel indicators,
Warning units (oil-fuel),
Selsyn systems and indicators,
Self-synchronous systems and indicators,
Remote indicating compasses,
Fuel quantity indicators,
Oil quantity indicators,
Radio indicators,
Ammeters,
Voltmeters.

(ii) Maintain and alter instruments, including installation and the replacement of parts:

Perform these functions on instruments listed under paragraph (e)(2)(i) of this appendix.

The function of installation includes fabrication of instrument panels and other installation structural components. The repair station should be equipped to perform this function. However, it may be contracted to a competent outside agency equipped to perform the function.

(iii) Inspect, test and calibrate instruments: Perform these functions on instruments listed under paragraph (e)(2)(i) of this appendix, on and off the aircraft, when appropriate.

(3) Class 3. (i) Diagnose instrument malfunctions: Diagnose malfunctioning of the following instruments:

Turn and bank indicators,
Directional gyros,
Horizon gyros,
Auto pilot control units and components*,
Remote reading direction indicators*.

(ii) Maintain and alter instruments, including installation and replacement of parts:

Perform these functions on instruments listed under paragraph (e)(3)(i) of this appendix.

The function of installation includes fabrication of instrument panels and other installation structural components. The repair station should be equipped to perform this function. However, it may be contracted to a competent outside agency equipped to perform the function.

(iii) Inspect, test and calibrate instruments: Perform these functions on instruments listed under paragraph (e)(3)(i) of this appendix, on and off the aircraft, when appropriate.

(4) Class 4. (i) Diagnose instrument malfunctions: Diagnose malfunctioning of the following instruments:

Capacitance type quantity gauge,
Other electronic instruments,
Engine analyzers.

(ii) Maintain and alter instruments, including installation and replacement of parts:

Perform these functions on instruments listed under paragraph (e)(4)(i) of this appendix.

The function of installation includes fabrication of instrument panels and other installation structural components. The repair station should be equipped to perform this function. However, it may be contracted to a competent outside agency equipped to perform the function.

(iii) Inspect, test and calibrate instruments: Perform these functions on instruments listed under paragraph (e)(4)(i) of this appendix, on and off the aircraft, when appropriate.

(f) An applicant for a Class 1, 2, or 3 accessory rating must provide equipment and material necessary for efficiently performing the following job functions, in accordance with pertinent specifications and the manufacturers' recommendations:

(1) Diagnose accessory malfunctions.

(2) Maintain and alter accessories, including installation and the replacement of the parts.

(3) Inspect, test, and, where necessary, calibrate accessories.

(Secs. 313, 314, and 601 through 610, of the Federal Aviation Act of 1958, as amended (49 U.S.C. 1354, 1355, 1421 through 1430); sec. 6(c), Dept. of Transportation Act (49 U.S.C. 1655(c)))

[Doc. No. 1157, 27 FR 11693, Nov. 28, 1962, as amended by Amdt. 145–14, 35 FR 19349, Dec. 22, 1970; Amdt. 145–19, 47 FR 33391, Aug. 2, 1982]

AC 20- 109

DATE 1/8/79

ADVISORY CIRCULAR

DEPARTMENT OF TRANSPORTATION
Federal Aviation Administration
Washington, D.C.

Subject: SERVICE DIFFICULTY PROGRAM (GENERAL AVIATION)

1. PURPOSE. This advisory circular (AC) describes the Service Difficulty
Program as it applies to general aviation activities and provides instructions
for completion of the Malfunction or Defect Report (M or D), FAA Form 8010-4.
It solicits your participation in the Service Difficulty Program and your
cooperation in improving the quality of M or D Reports.

2. CANCELLATION. AC 20-23D, Interchange of Service Experience Mechanical
Difficulties, dated 2/12/71, is canceled.

3. FORMS. FAA Form 8010-4 (OMB: 04-R0003) Malfunction or Defect Report.
National Stock Number (NSN) 0052-00-039-1003. Unit of issue (U/I) book (25
forms per book) available from FAA General Aviation, Air Carrier, and Flight
Standards District Offices.

4. DISCUSSION. The Service Difficulty Program is an information system
designed to provide assistance to aircraft owners, operators, maintenance
organizations, manufacturers, and FAA in identifying aircraft problems
encountered during service. The program provides for the collection,
organization, analysis, and dissemination of aircraft service information so
as to improve service reliability of aeronautical products. The primary
sources of this information are the aircraft maintenance facilities, owners,
and operators. General aviation aircraft service difficulty information is
normally submitted to FAA by use of M or D Reports, FAA Form 8010-4.
Information will, however, be accepted in any usable form except when use of
FAA Form 8010-4 is required by regulation.

  a. Input. General aviation reports (M or D) are received by
local General Aviation or Flight Standards District Offices (GADO/FSDO),
reviewed for immediate impact items, and then forwarded to the Safety Data
Branch, AFS-580, Flight Standards National Field Office, Oklahoma City, for
processing. The information contained on the M or D card is stored in a
computerized data bank for retrieval and analysis. Items potentially

Initiated by: AFS- 830

1989   [AC 20-109]   ASA-517 hazardous to flight are telephoned directly to the Safety Data Branch by FAA District Office inspectors. These items are immediately referred to the type certificate holding region, Flight Standards Division, for expeditious handling.

(1) Submission of service difficulty information by the aviation public is voluntary, although certificated repair stations and air taxi/commercial operators are required by FAR's 145 and 135 to submit certain specific information.

(2) Additional service difficulty information is collected by FAA inspectors in the performance of routine aircraft and maintenance facility surveillance, accident and incident investigations, during the operation of rental aircraft, and during the conduct of pilot certification flights.

(3) Service difficulty data is retained in the computer data bank for a period of five years providing a base for the detection of trends and failure rates.

b. Output. Analysis of service difficulty information is done primarily by the Safety Data Branch. When trends are detected, they are made available to pertinent FAA field personnel for their investigation.

5. THE SAFETY DATA BRANCH. The Safety Data Branch is also an information center which responds to individual requests from the aviation community concerning service difficulties.

a. Products. The Safety Data Branch issues the Flight Standards Service Difficulty Reports (General Aviation (RIS: FS 8070-2)) daily which contains significant M or D Reports and those service difficulties reported by telephone. Highly significant items are highlighted by a black border. Items are sometimes highlighted by a black border slashed by white. This indicates a highly significant item derived from other than M or D Reports. Flight Standards Service Difficulty Reports are distributed internally to FAA Flight Standards Offices.

b. AC 43-16, General Aviation Airworthiness Alerts, contains information that is of assistance to maintenance and inspection personnel in the performance of their duties. These items are developed from M or D Reports which have been submitted. The publication is distributed free of charge to certificated repair stations, mechanics holding an inspection authorization, air taxi operators, and aviation maintenance technician schools.

c. Automatic Data Processing (ADP) Printouts. Other products available are ADP printouts, through interrogation of the computer data bank. There are 26 special "sorts" of service difficulty data which can be presented in any one of 21 formats.

   d. For details regarding service difficulty computerized data, contact
the Federal Aviation Administration, Flight Standards National Field Office,
Maintenance Analysis Center, P.O. Box 25082, Oklahoma City, Oklahoma 73125;
or phone 405-686-4171.

6. IMPORTANCE OF REPORTING. The Federal Aviation Administration requests the
cooperation of all aircraft owners, operators, mechanics, pilots, and others
in reporting service difficulties experienced with airframe, powerplants,
propellers, and appliances/components.

   a. M or D Reports provide FAA and industry with a very essential
service record of mechanical difficulties encountered in aircraft
operations. Such reports contribute to the correction of conditions or
situations which otherwise will continue to prove costly and/or cause a
serious accident or incident.

   b. Reportable Service Difficulties. Whenever a system, component or
part of an aircraft, powerplant, propeller, or appliance functions badly or
fails to operate in the normal or usual manner, it has malfunctioned and it
should be reported. Further, if a system, component, or part has a flaw or
imperfection which impairs its function or which may impair its future
function, it is defective and should be reported. While at first sight it
would appear this will generate numerous insignificant reports, the Service
Difficulty Program is designed to detect trends and any report can be very
constructive in evaluating design or maintenance reliability.

   c. When preparing a report, please furnish as much information as
possible. Attachments, such as photographs, sketches, and parts forwarded
under separate cover, should bear identifying information.

   d. Public cooperation in submitting service information is greatly
appreciated by the FAA and others who have an interest in safety. The
quantity of reports received precludes individual acknowledgement of each
report. M or D Reports (FAA Form 8010-4) are free and available at all FAA
General Aviation, Air Carrier, and Flight Standards District Offices.

7. INSTRUCTIONS FOR COMPLETION OF MALFUNCTION OR DEFECT REPORT, FAA
FORM 8010-4.

   ITEM 1. REGISTRATION NUMBER: Enter the complete aircraft registration
            number. Example: N-7523Q.

1. REGISTRATION NO.	DEPARTMENT OF TRANSPORTATION
N- **7523Q**	FEDERAL AVIATION ADMINISTRATION **MALFUNCTION OR DEFECT REPORT**

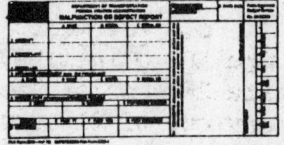

ITEM 2. <u>AIRCRAFT</u>: (Note: Always supply aircraft data if available.)

      A. <u>MAKE</u>: Enter the aircraft manufacturer's name. Any
      meaningful abbreviation will be acceptable. Example:
      Beech, Rckwl.

      B. <u>MODEL</u>: Enter aircraft model as identified on the aircraft
      data plate. Example: 180, 183, PA23-200.

      C. <u>SERIAL NUMBER</u>: Enter the serial number assigned by the
      manufacturer.

	A. MAKE	B. MODEL	C. SERIAL NO.
2. AIRCRAFT	*Cessna*	*172 B*	*1722036*

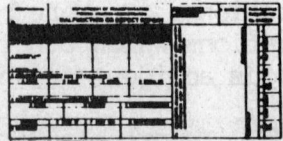

ITEM 3. <u>POWERPLANT</u>:

      A. <u>MAKE</u>: Enter engine manufacturer's name. Any meaningful
      abbreviation will be acceptable. Example: Lyc., Cont.,
      P&W.

      B. <u>MODEL</u>: Enter engine model as identified on the engine data
      plate. Example: IO540, O470R.

      C. <u>SERIAL NUMBER</u>: Enter serial number assigned by the engine
      manufacturer.

	A. MAKE	B. MODEL	C. SERIAL NO.
3. POWERPLANT	*Cont.*	*O 470R*	*L63279*

           NOTE: Propeller information, if available,
           should be included when engine failure is
           structural in nature.

ITEM 4. <u>PROPELLER</u>: (Complete only if pertinent to the problem being
      reported.)

           NOTE: Engine information, if available, should
           be completed on propeller reports for correlation
           with engine and propeller history.

A.   <u>MAKE</u>: Enter the manufacturer's name. Any meaningful abbreviation will be acceptable. Example: Hartzl, Hamstd.

B.   <u>MODEL</u>: Enter propeller model as identified in FAA type certificate data sheet/propeller specifications. Example: DHCC2Y, M74CC.

C.   <u>SERIAL NUMBER</u>: Enter serial number assigned by the propeller manufacturer.

	A. MAKE	B. MODEL	C. SERIAL NO.
4. PROPELLER	HARTZEL	HCC3Y	HC2YL2

ITEM 5.   <u>APPLIANCE/COMPONENT</u>: (Assembly that includes part)

A.   <u>NAME</u>: Enter the name of the appliance/component. The appliance/component is the assembly which includes the part. Example: When the part is a burnt wire, the component should be the system using the wire, such as VHF communication system. When the part is a bearing, the appliance should be the unit using the bearing, such as alternator, generator, starter, etc. When the part is a stringer, the component name should be fuselage, wing, or stabilizer, etc.

> NOTE: Appliance/component information should not be a repeat of major equipment identified above.

B.   <u>MAKE</u>: Enter the name of the appliance/component manufacturer. Example: Bendix, Prestolite, etc. If aircraft, engine, or propeller manufacturer is the component manufacturer, leave blank.

C.   <u>MODEL</u>: Enter the manufacturer's identification of the appliance/component. Example: AVQ75, RNA26C, S4LN20. If same as aircraft engine, or propeller, leave blank.

D.   <u>SERIAL NUMBER</u>: Enter serial number assigned by manufacturer.

5. APPLIANCE/COMPONENT (assy. that includes part)			
A. NAME	B. MAKE	C. MODEL	D. SERIAL NO.
Alternator	Prestolite	ALY6408	B625

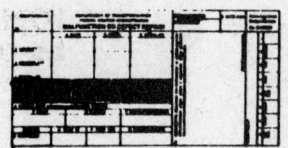

ITEM 6. SPECIFIC PART:

    A. NAME: Enter the manufacturer's name of the specific part causing the problem. Example: Bearing, stringer, hinge.

    B. NUMBER: Enter the manufacturer's part number. Example: 503445, 35K493V.

    C. PART/DEFECT LOCATION: Enter location of discrepant part or the defect. Example: right gear box, left outboard, right inboard.

    D. FAA USE: Self-explanatory.

    E. PART TT: (Part Total Time): Enter the service time of the part in whole hours. (If Part TT is unknown, use aircraft, engine, propeller, or appliance/component total time, whichever is applicable.) Example: 04278, 00032, 83568.

    F. PART TSO: (Part Time Since Overhaul): Enter the service time of the part since it was last overhauled, in whole hours. (If part TSO is unknown, use an aircraft, engine, propeller, or appliance/component time since last overhaul, whichever is applicable.) Example: 00427, 03393.

    G. PART CONDITION: Enter the word(s) which best describe the part condition. Example: cracked, broken, corroded, chafed, worn.

6. SPECIFIC PART *(of component)* CAUSING TROUBLE		
A. NAME	B. NUMBER	C. PART/DEFECT LOCATION
Bearing	35K493V	Slip ring end
FAA USE	E. PART TT	F. PART TSO	G. PART CONDITION
D. ATA CODE	02756	00351	disintegrated

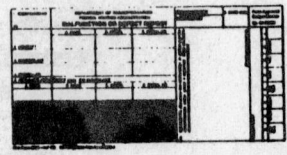

ITEM 7A.   COMMENTS: Describe the malfunction or defect and the circum-
           stances under which it occurred. State probable cause and
           recommendations to prevent recurrence. Continue on reverse
           side if needed. Powerplant TT and TSO should be shown in this
           block when it is a secondary item.

> **7A. COMMENTS** (Describe the malfunction or defect and
> the circumstances under which it occurred. State
> probable cause and recommendations to prevent
> recurrence.)
>
> *Inspection revealed Slip*
> *Ring end bearing failed*
> *due to lack of lubrication.*
> *Cause of lack unknown.*
> *Eng. TT 03872*
> *Eng. TSO 00250*
>
> Continue on reverse

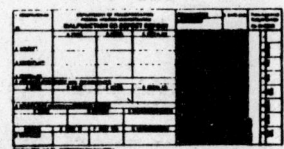

ITEM 8.   DATE SUB: Enter the date of submission, day, month, year.
          Example: 11/12/77, 2/5/78.

FAA USE ONLY	8. DATE SUB.	Form Appr. Budget Bureau No. 04-R000

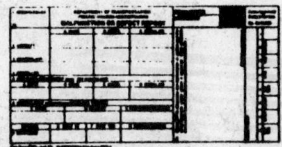

SUBMITTED BY: Enter the name (and certificate number if appropriate) of
                person submitting the report. This is not mandatory. The
                report will be entered in the system even if unsigned.

                FAA district office inspectors reviewing this report
                should show district office symbol in this area.

                Check the appropriate block to identify the organization/
                person initiating the report.

SUBMITTED BY *M. Signature*							
B.	C.	D.	E.	F.	G.	H.	I.
REP. STA.	OPER.	MECH. X	AIR TAXI	MFG.	FAA	OTHER	

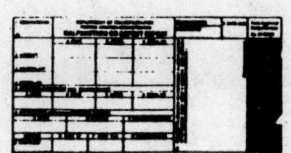

J. A. Ferrarese
J. A. FERRARESE
Acting Director, Flight Standards Service, AFS-1

**U.S. Department
of Transportation**

**Federal Aviation
Administration**

Advisory
Circular

Subject:	APPLICATION FOR U.S. AIRWORTHINESS CERTIFICATE, FAA FORM 8130-6 (OMB 2120-0018)	**Date:** 3/26/87 **AC No:** 21-12A **Initiated by:** AWS-200 **Change:**

---

1. <u>PURPOSE</u>. This advisory circular (AC) provides instructions on the preparation and submittal of Federal Aviation Administration (FAA) Form 8130-6 (issue 6-86 and subsequent) Application for Airworthiness Certificate. This application shall be completed not only to obtain an airworthiness certificate but also for any amendment or modification to a current airworthiness certificate.

2. <u>CANCELLATION</u>. AC 21-12, Application for U.S. Airworthiness Certificate, dated January 17, 1973, is cancelled.

* 3. <u>INFORMATION</u>. FAA Form 8130-6 bearing issue date (6-86) or subsequent should be used. This form is furnished by the FAA free of charge and is available at all FAA Flight Standards (FSDO) or Manufacturing Inspection District Offices (MIDO) (see Appendix 2).

4. <u>INSTRUCTIONS FOR COMPLETING FAA FORM 8130-6, APPLICATION FOR AIRWORTHINESS CERTIFICATE</u>. The applicant, or his agent, should complete Sections I through IV, or II and VI, or II and VII, as applicable for the type of airworthiness certificate being requested. The following instructions and explanations apply to the corresponding items on the form.

    a. <u>Section I. Aircraft Description</u>.

        NOTE: Do not complete this section when application is being made for a Special Flight Permit.

        (1) <u>Registration Mark</u>. Enter the U.S. nationality designator (letter "N") followed by the registration marks as shown on the aircraft registration certificate. (Reference Federal Aviation Regulations (FAR) Part 45, Subpart C.)

        (2) <u>Aircraft Builder's Name (Make)</u>. Enter the name of the manufacturer or builder as it appears on the aircraft identification (ID) plate. (Reference FAR Section 45.13(a)(1).)

            (a) For amateur-built aircraft, the aircraft make is the name of the builder. When two or more persons are involved, enter only the name of the individual that is listed first on the aircraft's ID plate.

*   (b) For aircraft built from spare and surplus parts, the aircraft builder's name would be that of the person who assembled the aircraft and not the name of the manufacturer who builds the same model of aircraft under a production approval.

---

*   (c) For surplus military aircraft (not assembled from spare and surplus parts), the builder's name will be as listed on the type certificate data sheet (TCDS).

*   (3) _Aircraft Model Designation_. Enter the model designation as shown on the aircraft ID plate. (Trade names should not be used.) (Reference FAR Section 45.13 (a)(2).)

          (a) For military aircraft being processed for civil registry, enter the civil model unless the type certificate (TC) is issued under FAR Section 21.27. In this case, the military model designation becomes the civil model designation.

          (b) For aircraft built from spare and surplus parts, the model designation should be that civil model which is shown on the TCDS to which the applicant shows conformity.

          (c) For military aircraft type certificated in the restricted category under the provisions of FAR Section 21.25(a)(2), only the military designation will be entered.

          (d) For amateur-built aircraft, the model may be any arbitrary designation as selected by the builder. If the aircraft was purchased as a kit, the model assigned by the kit supplier should be used.

*   (4) _Year of Manufacture_. Enter the year of manufacture if shown on the aircraft ID plate or as reflected in the aircraft logbook.

          (a) For aircraft eligible for standard airworthiness certificates, the year of manufacture is the date (entered by the manufacturer) the inspection records reflect that the aircraft is complete and meets the FAA-approved type design data.

          (b) For aircraft, other than the above, the year of manufacture is the date of the statement in the records, entered by the assembler/builder, establishing that the aircraft is airworthy and eligible for the certificate requested.

          (5) _Serial Number_. Enter the serial number as shown on the aircraft ID plate per FAR Section 45.13(a)(3).

          (a) For surplus military aircraft, enter the manufacturer's civil serial number. If no civil serial number exists, enter the military number.

          (b) For aircraft built from spare and surplus parts, enter the serial number assigned by the builder, providing it could not be confused with those assigned by an original manufacturer who builds the same type of aircraft under a production approval. It is suggested that a letter prefix or suffix, such as the builder's name or initials, be used with the number to provide a positive identification.

          (c) For amateur-built aircraft, the serial number may be any arbitrary number assigned by the builder.

(6) <u>Engine Builder's Name (Make)</u>. The engine make is the name of the manufacturer as it appears on the engine ID plate. (Reference FAR Section 45.13 (a)(1).) Abbreviations may be used, e.g., "P&W," "G.E.," "CMC," etc. When no engines are installed, as in the case of a glider or balloon, enter "N/A."

(7) <u>Engine Model Designation</u>. When engine(s) installed, enter the complete designation as shown on the engine ID plate; e.g., "R2800-99W," "TVO-435-AIA," "IO-470-R," etc. (Reference FAR Section 45.13(a)(2)).

(8) <u>Number of Engines</u>. When applicable, enter the quantity of engines installed on the aircraft.

(9) <u>Propeller Builder's Name (Make)</u>. Enter the name of the manufacturer as shown on the propeller identification data. Enter "N/A" if propellers are not installed. (Reference FAR Section 45.13(a)(1).)

(10) <u>Propeller Model Designation</u>. When applicable, enter the model designation as shown on the propeller identification data (Reference FAR Section 45.13(a)(2).)

(11) <u>Aircraft is Import</u>. This block should be checked only if the aircraft was manufactured in a foreign country and is being certified under the provisions of FAR Section 21.183(c).

b. <u>Section II. Certification Requested</u>. All entries in this section are generally self-explanatory. The following paragraphs reference applicable regulations and other material (including examples) to assist in the completion of the application form for each certification that may be requested.

(1) <u>Standard Airworthiness Certificate</u>.

(a) FAR Part 21, Section 21.183.

(b) AC 20-65, U.S. Airworthiness Certificates and Authorizations for Operation of Domestic and Foreign Aircraft.

(c) Appendix 1, pages 1, 2, 3, and 14 of this AC.

(2) <u>Special Airworthiness Certificate</u>.

(a) <u>Limited Airworthiness Certificate</u>.

<u>1</u> FAR Part 21, Section 21.189.

<u>2</u> AC 20-65, U.S. Airworthiness Certificates and Authorizations for Operation of Domestic and Foreign Aircraft.

<u>3</u> Appendix 1, page 4 of this AC.

(b) <u>Provisional Airworthiness Certificate</u>.

<u>1</u> FAR Part 21, Section 21.221 for a Class I certificate and Section 21.223 for a Class II certificate.

<u>2</u> Appendix 1, Page 5 of this AC.

(c) <u>Restricted Airworthiness Certificate</u>.

<u>1</u> FAR Part 21, Sections 21.25 and 21.185.

<u>2</u> AC 20-65, U.S. Airworthiness Certificates and Authorizations for Operation of Domestic and Foreign Aircraft.

<u>3</u> Appendix 1, page 6 of this AC.

(d) <u>Experimental Certificate</u>.

<u>1</u> FAR Part 21, Sections 21.191, 21.193, and 21.195.

<u>2</u> AC Nos. 20-27C, Certification and Operation of Amateur-Built Aircraft, and 20-65, U.S. Airworthiness Certificates and Authorizations for Operation of Domestic and Foreign Aircraft.

<u>3</u> Appendix 1, pages 7, 8, and 9 of this AC.

(e) <u>Special Flight Permit</u>.

<u>1</u> FAR Part 21, Sections 21.197 and 21.199.

<u>2</u> AC Nos. 20-65, U.S. Airworthiness Certificates and Authorization for Operation of Domestic and Foreign Aircraft, and 21-4B, Special Flight Permits for Operation of Overweight Aircraft.

<u>3</u> Appendix 1, pages 10, 11, and 12 of this AC.

(3) <u>Multiple Airworthiness Certificate, i.e., Standard/Restricted or Restricted/Limited</u>.

(a) FAR Part 21, Section 21.187.

(b) AC 20-65, U.S. Airworthiness Certificates and Authorization for Operation of Domestic and Foreign Aircraft.

(c) Appendix 1, page 13 of this AC.

c. <u>Section III. Owner's Certification</u>. Do not complete this section when application is being made for a Special Flight Permit.

(1) Registered Owner. Enter this information exactly as it is shown on the aircraft registration certificate. FAR Part 47 prescribes the requirements for registering aircraft under Section 501 of the Federal Aviation Act of 1958.

(2) If Dealer, Check Here. This block should be checked ONLY if the aircraft is registered under a dealer's aircraft registration certificate. (Reference FAR Part 47, Subpart C.)

*   (3) Aircraft Certification Basis (Aircraft Specification or Type Certificate Data Sheet and/or Aircraft Listing Block). This item should be completed when application is being made for a standard, provisional, limited, restricted, or multiple airworthiness certificate.   *

(a) When application is being made for a multiple airworthiness certificate, the certification basis for each certificate being requested should be entered.

(b) If the type certificate data sheet or specification for a new aircraft or model has been approved but not yet published, the date of approval, the TC or specification number, and the word "preliminary" should be entered.

(c) This item is not applicable when application is being made for an experimental certificate. "N/A" should be entered.

*   (4) Airworthiness Directives. This block should be checked to indicate compliance with all applicable Airworthiness Directives (AD). List the number of the last AD supplement available in the biweekly series, as of the date of the application, regardless of whether or not that AD supplement applies to the aircraft. (Reference FAR Part 39 and FAR Section 21.99.)   *

*   NOTE: Each AD contains an applicability statement specifying the
               product to which it applies. Some aircraft owners and
               operators mistakenly assume that AD's are not applicable to
               aircraft certificated in certain categories such as experi-
               mental or restricted. AD's, unless specifically limited
               apply to the make and model set forth in the applicability
               statement regardless of category. The type certificate and
               airworthiness certification categories are used to identify
               the product affected. (Reference AC 39-7A, Airworthiness
               Directives for General Aviation Aircraft, paragraph 9).   *

(5) Supplemental Type Certificate. This block should be checked only when one or more Supplemental Type Certificates (STC) have been incorporated. The identification number of each STC installed should be shown. If more space is required, an attachment may be used. This block is applicable to all certification categories. (Reference FAR Part 21, Subpart E.)

(6) Aircraft Operation and Maintenance Records.

(a) <u>Records in Compliance with FAR Section 91.173</u>. This block is applicable to all aircraft covered by this section and should be checked to indicate that the recordkeeping requirements of FAR Section 91.173 have been met. FAR Section 91.173 requires information which would be applicable to all aircraft; for example, FAR Section 91.173(a)(2)(ii) requires a record of the current status of life-limited parts of each airframe, engine, propeller, rotor, and appliance, while compliance with FAR Section 91.173(a)(2)(i) would require that production flight test time be entered in the aircraft's maintenance records.

(b) <u>Total Airframe Hours</u>. This block is applicable to all aircraft covered by this section. The total time in service of the aircraft, including production flight test time, should be entered.

(c) <u>Experimental Only</u>. When application is being made for the renewal of an experimental certificate, the hours flown since the previous experimental certificate was issued or renewed should be entered. If the application is for an original issuance of an experimental certificate, zero hours should be entered.

*   (7) <u>Certification</u>. If signature is of the owner's agent, a notarized letter from the registered owner authorizing the agent to act on his behalf in this matter is required.

d. <u>Section IV. Inspection Agency Verification</u>. This section should be appropriately completed only if application is being made for a standard airworthiness certificate for an aircraft being certificated under FAR Section 21.183(d). This section should be left blank for all other certification actions.

e. <u>Section V. FAA Representative Certification</u>. This section will be completed by the FAA representative that inspects the aircraft and issues the certificate.

f. <u>Section VI. Production Flight Testing</u>. This section should be completed ONLY BY A MANUFACTURER applying for a special flight permit for the purpose of flight testing production aircraft. (Reference FAR Section 21.197(a)(3).)

g. <u>Section VII. Special Flight Permit Purposes Other Than Production Flight Test</u>.

(1) <u>Item A. Description of Aircraft</u>. The entries in this section should be the same as the corresponding data recorded on the aircraft's registration certificate and, as applicable, on the aircraft's identification plate.

(2) <u>Item B. Description of Flight</u>. Self-explanatory except that:

(a) The "via" block should contain the name of an airport or city at some intermediate point in the flight to provide a general description of the route flown. For example, a flight from Kansas City, Missouri, to Dallas, Texas, may be via Wichita, Kansas, and Oklahoma City, Oklahoma. (Reference FAR Section 21.199(a)(2).)

(b) The "duration" entry should reflect the overall duration of the special flight permit and need not be the same as the planned duration of the actual flight. Factors such as fueling stops, weather conditions, overnight stops, or any other reasonable condition should be given consideration when establishing the duration. (Reference FAR Section 21.199(a)(2).)

(3) Item D. The Aircraft Does Not Meet the Applicable Airworthiness Requirements As Follows. This entry should contain in detail the ways, if any, in which the aircraft does not comply with the applicable airworthiness requirements. (Reference FAR Section 21.199(a)(4).)

(4) Item E. The Following Restrictions are Considered Necessary for Safe Operation. This entry should contain in detail the restrictions the applicant considers necessary for safe operation of the aircraft; for example, reduced airspeed or weight, turbulence avoidance, crew limitations or qualifications, and the like. (Reference FAR Section 21.199(a)(5).)

h. Section VIII. Airworthiness Documentation. This section will be completed by the FAA representative who inspects the aircraft and issues the airworthiness certificate.

5. INSTRUCTIONS FOR SUBMITTING THE COMPLETED FAA FORM 8130-6, APPLICATION FOR AIRWORTHINESS CERTIFICATE. When the applicant has completed the applicable sections and signed the FAA Form 8130-6, it should be submitted, together with any other material that may be required by the regulations for the airworthiness certification being requested, to the appropriate FAA Flight Standards District Office, Manufacturing Inspection District Office, Designated Manufacturing Inspection Representative (DMIR) or Designated Airworthiness Representative (DAR) as appropriate. When the address of the district office that will process the application is not known, it may be obtained from the FAA regional office serving the area wherein the applicant is located. Appendix 2 of this circular contains the addresses of the FAA regional offices and the geographical area governed by each.

6. HOW TO ORDER THE REFERENCED PUBLICATIONS.

a. Federal Aviation Regulations. Order from the Superintendent of Documents, U.S. Government Printing Office, Washington, D.C. 20402.

b. Advisory Circulars. Requests for the following FREE Advisory Circulars should be submitted to: Department of Transportation, Distribution Unit, M-494.3, Washington, D.C. 20590.

(1) AC No. 20-27C, Certification and Operation of Amateur-Built Aircraft.

(2) AC No. 20-65, U.S. Airworthiness Certificates and Authorizations for Operation of Domestic and Foreign Aircraft.

(3) AC No. 21-4B, Special Flight Permits for Operation of Overweight Aircraft.

7. <u>REQUEST FOR INFORMATION</u>. For additional information, interested parties should contact those offices listed in Appendix 2 of this AC.

William Sullivan

Deputy Director of Airworthiness
Office of Airworthiness

FAA FORM 8130-6 – APPLICATION FOR A STANDARD AIRWORTHINESS CERTIFICATE – NO PREVIOUS U.S. AIRWORTHINESS CERTIFICATE ISSUED

Form Approved
O.M.B. No. 2120-0018

APPLICATION FOR AIRWORTHINESS CERTIFICATE

U.S. Department of Transportation
Federal Aviation Administration

INSTRUCTIONS — Print or type. Do not write in shaded areas, these are for FAA use only. Submit original only to an authorized FAA Representative. If additional space is required, use an attachment. For special flight permits complete Sections II and VI or VII as applicable.

I. AIRCRAFT DESCRIPTION

1. REGISTRATION MARK	2. AIRCRAFT BUILDER'S NAME (Make)	3. AIRCRAFT MODEL DESIGNATION	4. YR. MFR	FAA CODING
N12345	Boeing	737-247	1985	

5. AIRCRAFT SERIAL NO.	6. ENGINE BUILDER'S NAME (Make)	7. ENGINE MODEL DESIGNATION	
19714	P&W	JT8D-9	

8. NUMBER OF ENGINES	9. PROPELLER BUILDER'S NAME (Make)	10. PROPELLER MODEL DESIGNATION	11. AIRCRAFT IS (Check if applicable)
Two	N/A	N/A	IMPORT

II. CERTIFICATION REQUESTED

APPLICATION IS HEREBY MADE FOR: (Check applicable items)

A 1 [X] STANDARD AIRWORTHINESS CERTIFICATE (Indicate category) — NORMAL | UTILITY | ACROBATIC [X] | TRANSPORT | GLIDER | BALLOON

B   SPECIAL AIRWORTHINESS CERTIFICATE (Check appropriate items)

- 2 LIMITED
- 3 PROVISIONAL (Indicate class)
  - 1 CLASS I
  - 2 CLASS II
- 4 RESTRICTED (Indicate operation(s) to be conducted)
  - 1 AGRICULTURE AND PEST CONTROL 2 AERIAL SURVEYING 3 AERIAL ADVERTISING
  - 4 FOREST (Wildlife conservation) 5 PATROLLING 6 WEATHER CONTROL
  - 7 CARRIAGE OF CARGO 8 OTHER (Specify)
- 5 EXPERIMENTAL (Indicate operation(s) to be conducted)
  - 1 RESEARCH AND DEVELOPMENT 2 AMATEUR BUILT 9 EXHIBITION
  - 2 RACING 5 CREW TRAINING MKT. SURVEY
  - 3 TO SHOW COMPLIANCE WITH FAR
- 8 SPECIAL FLIGHT PERMIT (Indicate operation to be conducted, then complete Section VI or VII as applicable on reverse side)
  - 1 FERRY FLIGHT FOR REPAIRS, ALTERATIONS, MAINTENANCE OR STORAGE
  - 2 EVACUATE FROM AREA OF IMPENDING DANGER
  - 3 OPERATION IN EXCESS OF MAXIMUM CERTIFICATED TAKE-OFF WEIGHT
  - 4 DELIVERY OR EXPORT 6 PRODUCTION FLIGHT TESTING
  - 5 CUSTOMER DEMONSTRATION FLIGHTS

C 6 MULTIPLE AIRWORTHINESS CERTIFICATE (Check ABOVE "Restricted Operation" and/or "Limited," as applicable.)

III. OWNER'S CERTIFICATION

A. REGISTERED OWNER (As shown on certificate of aircraft registration)   IF DEALER, CHECK HERE → [X]

NAME	ADDRESS
The Boeing Company	P.O. Box 3707, Seattle, Washington 98124

B. AIRCRAFT CERTIFICATION BASIS (Check applicable blocks and complete items as indicated)

[X] AIRCRAFT SPECIFICATION OR TYPE CERTIFICATE DATA SHEET (Give No. and Revision No.) **A16WE Rev. 10**

[X] AIRWORTHINESS DIRECTIVES (Check if all applicable AD's complied with and give latest AD No.) **86-03-04**

AIRCRAFT LISTING (Give page number(s)) **N/A**

SUPPLEMENTAL TYPE CERTIFICATE (List number of each STC incorporated) **N/A**

C. AIRCRAFT OPERATION AND MAINTENANCE RECORDS

[X] CHECK IF RECORDS IN COMPLIANCE WITH FAR 91.173	TOTAL AIRFRAME HOURS 17.8	EXPERIMENTAL ONLY (Enter hours flown since last certificate issued or renewed) N/A

D. CERTIFICATION — I hereby certify that I am the registered owner (or his agent) of the aircraft described above, that the aircraft is registered with the Federal Aviation Administration in accordance with Section 501 of the Federal Aviation Act of 1958, and applicable Federal Aviation Regulations, and that the aircraft has been inspected and is airworthy and eligible for the airworthiness certificate requested.

DATE OF APPLICATION	NAME AND TITLE (Print or type)	SIGNATURE
3/29/XX	John R. Doe, Airworthiness Manager	John R. Doe

IV. INSPECTION AGENCY VERIFICATION

A. THE AIRCRAFT DESCRIBED ABOVE HAS BEEN INSPECTED AND FOUND AIRWORTHY BY: (Complete this section only if FAR 21.183(d) applies)

A FAR PART 121 OR 127 CERTIFICATE HOLDER (Give Certificate No.)	B CERTIFICATED MECHANIC (Give Certificate No.)	C CERTIFICATED REPAIR STATION (Give Certificate No.)
D AIRCRAFT MANUFACTURER (Give name of firm)		

DATE	TITLE	SIGNATURE

V. FAA REPRESENTATIVE CERTIFICATION

(Check ALL applicable blocks in Items A and B)

A. I find that the aircraft described in Section I or VII meets requirements for:

THE CERTIFICATE REQUESTED
AMENDMENT OR MODIFICATION OF CURRENT AIRWORTHINESS CERTIFICATE

B. Inspection for a special flight permit under Section VII was conducted by:

FAA INSPECTOR	FAA DESIGNEE
CERTIFICATE HOLDER UNDER: FAR 65	FAR 121, 127 or 135	FAR 145

DATE	DISTRICT OFFICE	DESIGNEE'S SIGNATURE AND NO.	FAA INSPECTOR'S SIGNATURE

FAA Form 8130-6 (6-86) SUPERSEDES PREVIOUS EDITION

FAA FORM 8130-6 – APPLICATION FOR A STANDARD
AIRWORTHINESS CERTIFICATE – IMPORT GLIDER

Form Approved
O.M.B. No. 2120-0018

APPLICATION FOR AIRWORTHINESS CERTIFICATE

U.S. Department of Transportation
Federal Aviation Administration

INSTRUCTIONS — Print or type. Do not write in shaded areas; these are for FAA use only. Submit original only to an authorized FAA Representative. If additional space is required, use an attachment. For special flight permits complete Sections II and VI or VII as applicable.

I. AIRCRAFT DESCRIPTION

1. REGISTRATION MARK	2. AIRCRAFT BUILDER'S NAME (Make)	3. AIRCRAFT MODEL DESIGNATION	4. YR MFR	FAA CODING
N53B	Schleicher	AS-K13	1984	

5. AIRCRAFT SERIAL NO.	6. ENGINE BUILDER'S NAME (Make)	7. ENGINE MODEL DESIGNATION	
101	N/A	N/A	

8. NUMBER OF ENGINES	9. PROPELLER BUILDER'S NAME (Make)	10. PROPELLER MODEL DESIGNATION	11. AIRCRAFT IS (Check if applicable)
N/A	N/A	N/A	X IMPORT

II. CERTIFICATION REQUESTED

APPLICATION IS HEREBY MADE FOR: (Check applicable items)

A 1 X STANDARD AIRWORTHINESS CERTIFICATE (Indicate category) | NORMAL | UTILITY | ACROBATIC | TRANSPORT | X GLIDER | BALLOON

B SPECIAL AIRWORTHINESS CERTIFICATE (Check appropriate items)

2 LIMITED

3 PROVISIONAL (Indicate class)
1 CLASS I
2 CLASS II

4 RESTRICTED (Indicate operation(s) to be conducted)
1 AGRICULTURE AND PEST CONTROL | 3 AERIAL SURVEYING | 5 AERIAL ADVERTISING
4 FOREST (Wildlife conservation) | 6 PATROLLING | 6 WEATHER CONTROL
7 CARRIAGE OF CARGO | 9 OTHER (Specify)

4 EXPERIMENTAL (Indicate operation(s) to be conducted)
1 RESEARCH AND DEVELOPMENT | 2 AMATEUR BUILT | 7 EXHIBITION
2 RACING | 5 CREW TRAINING | MKT. SURVEY
3 TO SHOW COMPLIANCE WITH FAR

SPECIAL FLIGHT PERMIT (Indicate operation to be conducted, then complete Section VI or VII as applicable on reverse side)
2 FERRY FLIGHT FOR REPAIRS, ALTERATIONS, MAINTENANCE OR STORAGE
3 EVACUATE FROM AREA OF IMPENDING DANGER
5 OPERATION IN EXCESS OF MAXIMUM CERTIFICATED TAKE-OFF WEIGHT
4 OR EXPORT | 7 PRODUCTION FLIGHT TESTING
6 CUSTOMER DEMONSTRATION FLIGHTS

C 6 MULTIPLE AIRWORTHINESS CERTIFICATE (Check ABOVE "Restricted Operation" and "Standard" or "Limited," as applicable)

III. OWNER'S CERTIFICATION

A. REGISTERED OWNER (As shown on certificate of aircraft registration)   IF DEALER, CHECK HERE ►

NAME	ADDRESS
Elmer E. Jones	601 E. 6th St. San Diego, California 95472

B. AIRCRAFT CERTIFICATION BASIS (Check applicable blocks and complete items as indicated)

	AIRCRAFT SPECIFICATION OR TYPE CERTIFICATE DATA SHEET (Give No. and Revision No.)		AIRWORTHINESS DIRECTIVES (Check if all applicable AD's complied with and give latest AD No.)
X	G15EU	X	86-06-04

	AIRCRAFT LISTING (Give page number(s))	SUPPLEMENTAL TYPE CERTIFICATE (List number of each STC incorporated)
	N/A	N/A

C. AIRCRAFT OPERATION AND MAINTENANCE RECORDS

	CHECK IF RECORDS IN COMPLIANCE WITH FAR 91.173	TOTAL AIRFRAME HOURS		EXPERIMENTAL ONLY (Enter hours flown since last certificate issued or renewed)
X		1.0		N/A

D. CERTIFICATION — I hereby certify that I am the registered owner (or his agent) of the aircraft described above; that the aircraft is registered with the Federal Aviation Administration in accordance with Section 501 of the Federal Aviation Act of 1958, and applicable Federal Aviation Regulations, and that the aircraft has been inspected and is airworthy and eligible for the airworthiness certificate requested.

DATE OF APPLICATION	NAME AND TITLE (Print or type)	SIGNATURE
6/13/XX	Elmer E. Jones, Owner	Elmer E. Jones

IV. INSPECTION AGENCY VERIFICATION

A. THE AIRCRAFT DESCRIBED ABOVE HAS BEEN INSPECTED AND FOUND AIRWORTHY BY: (Complete this section only if FAR 21.183(d) applies)

FAR PART 121 OR 127 CERTIFICATE HOLDER (Give Certificate No.)	CERTIFICATED MECHANIC (Give Certificate No.)	CERTIFICATED REPAIR STATION (Give Certificate No.)

AIRCRAFT MANUFACTURER (Give name of firm)

DATE	TITLE	SIGNATURE

V. FAA REPRESENTATIVE CERTIFICATION

(Check ALL applicable blocks in Items A and B)   THE CERTIFICATE REQUESTED

A. I find that the aircraft described in Section I or VII meets requirements for: AMENDMENT OR MODIFICATION OF CURRENT AIRWORTHINESS CERTIFICATE

B. Inspection for a special flight permit under Section VII was conducted by:

FAA INSPECTOR | FAA DESIGNEE

CERTIFICATE HOLDER UNDER: | FAR 65 | FAR 121, 127 or 135 | FAR 145

DATE	DISTRICT OFFICE	DESIGNEE'S SIGNATURE AND NO.	FAA INSPECTOR'S SIGNATURE

FAA Form 8130-6 (6-88) SUPERSEDES PREVIOUS EDITION

FAA FORM 8130-6 – APPLICATION FOR A STANDARD AIRWORTHINESS CERTIFICATE – AIRCRAFT BUILT FROM SPARE AND SURPLUS PARTS – NO PREVIOUS U.S. AIRWORTHINESS CERTIFICATE ISSUED

Form Approved
O.M.B. No. 2120-0018

APPLICATION FOR AIRWORTHINESS CERTIFICATE

U.S. Department of Transportation
Federal Aviation Administration

INSTRUCTIONS — Print or type. Do not write in shaded areas; these are for FAA use only. Submit original only to an authorized FAA Representative. If additional space is required, use an attachment. For special flight permits complete Sections II and VI or VII as applicable.

I. AIRCRAFT DESCRIPTION

1. REGISTRATION MARK	2. AIRCRAFT BUILDER'S NAME (Make)	3. AIRCRAFT MODEL DESIGNATION	4. YR MFR	FAA CODING
N6934M	Smith	C-172M	1980	

5. AIRCRAFT SERIAL NO	6. ENGINE BUILDER'S NAME (Make)	7. ENGINE MODEL DESIGNATION	
Smith 001	Lycoming	0-320-B	

8. NUMBER OF ENGINES	9. PROPELLER BUILDER'S NAME (Make)	10. PROPELLER MODEL DESIGNATION	11. AIRCRAFT IS (Check if applicable)
One	McCauley	1C160/CTM	IMPORT

II. CERTIFICATION REQUESTED

APPLICATION IS HEREBY MADE FOR: (Check applicable items)

A 1 X STANDARD AIRWORTHINESS CERTIFICATE (Indicate category) X NORMAL | UTILITY | ACROBATIC | TRANSPORT | GLIDER | BALLOON

B SPECIAL AIRWORTHINESS CERTIFICATE (Check appropriate items)

- 2 LIMITED
- 3 PROVISIONAL (Indicate class)
  - 1 CLASS I
  - 2 CLASS II
- RESTRICTED (Indicate operation(s) to be conducted)
  - 1 AGRICULTURE AND PEST CONTROL
  - 7 FOREST (Wildlife conservation)
  - 7 CARRIAGE OF CARGO
  - 2 AERIAL SURVEYING
  - 5 PATROLLING
  - 6 OTHER (Specify)
  - 3 AERIAL ADVERTISING
  - 6 WEATHER CONTROL
- 4 EXPERIMENTAL (Indicate operation(s) to be conducted)
  - 1 RESEARCH AND DEVELOPMENT
  - 5 RACING
  - 6 TO SHOW COMPLIANCE WITH FAR
  - 2 AMATEUR BUILT
  - 3 CREW TRAINING
  - 9 EXHIBITION
  - MKT. SURVEY
- SPECIAL FLIGHT PERMIT (Indicate operation to be conducted, then complete Section VI or VII as applicable on reverse side)
  - 1 FERRY FLIGHT FOR REPAIRS, ALTERATIONS, MAINTENANCE OR STORAGE
  - 2 EVACUATE FROM AREA OF IMPENDING DANGER
  - 3 OPERATION IN EXCESS OF MAXIMUM CERTIFICATED TAKE-OFF WEIGHT
  - 4 DELIVERING OR EXPORT
  - 5 PRODUCTION FLIGHT TESTING
  - 6 CUSTOMER DEMONSTRATION FLIGHTS

C 6 MULTIPLE AIRWORTHINESS CERTIFICATE (Check ABOVE "Restricted Operation" and "Standard" or "Limited," as applicable.)

III. OWNER'S CERTIFICATION

A. REGISTERED OWNER (As shown on certificate of aircraft registration)		IF DEALER, CHECK HERE ►
NAME John R. Smith	ADDRESS 6224 Arbor Way Springfield, Tenn. 70653	

B. AIRCRAFT CERTIFICATION BASIS (Check applicable blocks and complete items as indicated)

X	AIRCRAFT SPECIFICATION OR TYPE CERTIFICATE DATA SHEET (Give No. and Revision No.) H-1, Rev. 36	X	AIRWORTHINESS DIRECTIVES (Check if all applicable AD's complied with and give latest AD No.) 86-06-04
	AIRCRAFT LISTING (Give page number(s)) N/A		SUPPLEMENTAL TYPE CERTIFICATE (List number of each STC incorporated) N/A

C. AIRCRAFT OPERATION AND MAINTENANCE RECORDS

X	CHECK IF RECORDS IN COMPLIANCE WITH FAR 91.173	TOTAL AIRFRAME HOURS 6.5		EXPERIMENTAL ONLY (Enter hours flown since last certificate issued or renewed) N/A

D. CERTIFICATION — I hereby certify that I am the registered owner (or his agent) of the aircraft described above, that the aircraft is registered with the Federal Aviation Administration in accordance with Section 501 of the Federal Aviation Act of 1958, and applicable Federal Aviation Regulations, and that the aircraft has been inspected and is airworthy and eligible for the airworthiness certificate requested.

DATE OF APPLICATION	NAME AND TITLE (Print or type)	SIGNATURE
4/23/XX	John R. Smith, Owner	*John R. Smith*

IV. INSPECTION AGENCY VERIFICATION

A. THE AIRCRAFT DESCRIBED ABOVE HAS BEEN INSPECTED AND FOUND AIRWORTHY BY: (Complete this section only if FAR 21.183(d) applies)

8	FAR PART 121 OR 127 CERTIFICATE HOLDER (Give Certificate No.)	8	CERTIFICATED MECHANIC (Give Certificate No.)	8 X	CERTIFICATED REPAIR STATION (Give Certificate No.) 4326
8	AIRCRAFT MANUFACTURER (Give name of firm)				

DATE	TITLE	SIGNATURE
4/18/XX	Chief Inspector	*Robert Corcoran*

V. FAA REPRESENTATIVE CERTIFICATION

(Check ALL applicable blocks in items A and B)

A. I find that the aircraft described in Section I or VII meets requirements for:

B. Inspection for a special flight permit under Section VII was conducted by:

	THE CERTIFICATE REQUESTED		
4	AMENDMENT OR MODIFICATION OF CURRENT AIRWORTHINESS CERTIFICATE		
	FAA INSPECTOR	FAA DESIGNEE	
	CERTIFICATE HOLDER UNDER:	FAR 65	FAR 121, 127 or 135	FAR 145

DATE	DISTRICT OFFICE	DESIGNEE'S SIGNATURE AND NO.	FAA INSPECTOR'S SIGNATURE

FAA Form 8130-6 (6-86) SUPERSEDES PREVIOUS EDITION

FAA FORM 8130-6 — APPLICATION FOR A SPECIAL
AIRWORTHINESS CERTIFICATE — LIMITED

Form Approved
O.M.B. No. 2120-0018

APPLICATION FOR AIRWORTHINESS CERTIFICATE

U.S. Department of Transportation
Federal Aviation Administration

INSTRUCTIONS — Print or type. Do not write in shaded areas; these are for FAA use only. Submit original only to an authorized FAA Representative. If additional space is required, use an attachment. For special flight permits complete Sections II and VI or VII as applicable.

I. AIRCRAFT DESCRIPTION

1. REGISTRATION MARK	2. AIRCRAFT BUILDER'S NAME (Make)	3. AIRCRAFT MODEL DESIGNATION	4. YR MFR	FAA CODING
N1256	Martin	B-26C	1943	

5. AIRCRAFT SERIAL NO.	6. ENGINE BUILDER'S NAME (Make)	7. ENGINE MODEL DESIGNATION
2256	P&W	R-2800-83AM8

8. NUMBER OF ENGINES	9. PROPELLER BUILDER'S NAME (Make)	10. PROPELLER MODEL DESIGNATION	11. AIRCRAFT IS (Check if applicable)
Two	Hamilton Standard	42E60-7/6895-8	IMPORT

II. CERTIFICATION REQUESTED

APPLICATION IS HEREBY MADE FOR: (Check applicable items)

A 1 STANDARD AIRWORTHINESS CERTIFICATE (Indicate category) NORMAL UTILITY ACROBATIC TRANSPORT GLIDER BALLOON

B X SPECIAL AIRWORTHINESS CERTIFICATE (Check appropriate items)

2 X LIMITED

5 PROVISIONAL (Indicate class) — 1 CLASS I — 2 CLASS II

3 RESTRICTED (Indicate operation(s) to be conducted)
  1 AGRICULTURE AND PEST CONTROL 2 AERIAL SURVEYING 3 AERIAL ADVERTISING
  4 FOREST (Wildlife conservation) 5 PATROLLING 6 WEATHER CONTROL
  7 CARRIAGE OF CARGO 8 OTHER (Specify)

4 EXPERIMENTAL (Indicate operation(s) to be conducted)
  1 RESEARCH AND DEVELOPMENT 2 AMATEUR BUILT 3 EXHIBITION
  2 RACING CREW TRAINING MKT. SURVEY
  3 TO SHOW COMPLIANCE WITH FAR
  4 FLIGHT FOR REPAIRS, ALTERATIONS, MAINTENANCE OR STORAGE

8 SPECIAL FLIGHT PERMIT (Indicate operation to be conducted, then complete Section VI or VII as applicable on reverse side)
  1 EVACUATE FROM AREA OF IMPENDING DANGER
  2 OPERATION IN EXCESS OF MAXIMUM CERTIFICATED TAKE-OFF WEIGHT
  4 DELIVERING OR EXPORT 5 PRODUCTION FLIGHT TESTING
  CUSTOMER DEMONSTRATION FLIGHTS

C 6 MULTIPLE AIRWORTHINESS CERTIFICATE (Check ABOVE "Restricted Operation" and "Standard" or "Limited" as applicable.)

SAMPLE

III. OWNER'S CERTIFICATION

A. REGISTERED OWNER (As shown on certificate of aircraft registration)

NAME	ADDRESS
Gas Transmission Company	1256 West 48th Street Dallas, Texas 64072

IF DEALER, CHECK HERE ▶

B. AIRCRAFT CERTIFICATION BASIS (Check applicable blocks and complete items as indicated)

AIRCRAFT SPECIFICATION OR TYPE CERTIFICATE DATA SHEET (Give No. and Revision No.)	AIRWORTHINESS DIRECTIVES (Check if all applicable AD's complied with and give latest AD No.)
X AL-33, Rev.1	X 86-01-02

AIRCRAFT LISTING (Give page number(s))	SUPPLEMENTAL TYPE CERTIFICATE (List number of each STC incorporated)
N/A	N/A

C. AIRCRAFT OPERATION AND MAINTENANCE RECORDS

CHECK IF RECORDS IN COMPLIANCE WITH FAR 91.173	TOTAL AIRFRAME HOURS	EXPERIMENTAL ONLY (Enter hours flown since last certificate issued or renewed)
X	12,632	N/A

D. CERTIFICATION — I hereby certify that I am the registered owner (or his agent) of the aircraft described above; that the aircraft is registered with the Federal Aviation Administration in accordance with Section 501 of the Federal Aviation Act of 1958, and applicable Federal Aviation Regulations, and that the aircraft has been inspected and is airworthy and eligible for the airworthiness certificate requested.

DATE OF APPLICATION	NAME AND TITLE (Print or type)	SIGNATURE
1/12/XX	George Brown, President	George Brown

IV. INSPECTION AGENCY VERIFICATION

A. THE AIRCRAFT DESCRIBED ABOVE HAS BEEN INSPECTED AND FOUND AIRWORTHY BY: (Complete this section only if FAR 21.183(d) applies)

1 FAR PART 121 OR 127 CERTIFICATE HOLDER (Give Certificate No.)	3 CERTIFICATED MECHANIC (Give Certificate No.)	5 CERTIFICATED REPAIR STATION (Give Certificate No.)
2 AIRCRAFT MANUFACTURER (Give name of firm)		

DATE	TITLE	SIGNATURE

V. FAA REPRESENTATIVE CERTIFICATION

(Check ALL applicable blocks in Items A and B)

A. I find that the aircraft described in Section I or VII meets requirements for:

4 THE CERTIFICATE REQUESTED
AMENDMENT OR MODIFICATION OF CURRENT AIRWORTHINESS CERTIFICATE

B. Inspection for a special flight permit under Section VII was conducted by:
  FAA INSPECTOR   FAA DESIGNEE
  CERTIFICATE HOLDER UNDER: FAR 65 FAR 121, 127 or 135 FAR 145

DATE	DISTRICT OFFICE	DESIGNEE'S SIGNATURE AND NO.	FAA INSPECTOR'S SIGNATURE

FAA Form 8130-6 (6-88) SUPERSEDES PREVIOUS EDITION

FAA FORM 8130-6 - APPLICATION FOR A SPECIAL
AIRWORTHINESS CERTIFICATE - PROVISIONAL

Form Approved
O.M.B. No. 2120-0018

APPLICATION FOR AIRWORTHINESS CERTIFICATE	INSTRUCTIONS — Print or type. Do not write in shaded areas; these are for FAA use only. Submit original only to an authorized FAA Representative. If additional space is required, use an attachment. For special flight permits complete Sections II and VI or VII as applicable.

U.S. Department of Transportation
Federal Aviation Administration

I. AIRCRAFT DESCRIPTION

1. REGISTRATION MARK	2. AIRCRAFT BUILDER'S NAME (Make)	3. AIRCRAFT MODEL DESIGNATION	4. YR. MFR	FAA CODING
N502A	Lockheed-Georgia Co.	382	1960	
5. AIRCRAFT SERIAL NO.	6. ENGINE BUILDER'S NAME (Make)	7. ENGINE MODEL DESIGNATION		
4100	Allison	501-D22A		
8. NUMBER OF ENGINES	9. PROPELLER BUILDER'S NAME (Make)	10. PROPELLER MODEL DESIGNATION	11. AIRCRAFT IS (Check if applicable)	
Four	Hamilton Standard	54H60-91/54H60-117	IMPORT	

II. CERTIFICATION REQUESTED

APPLICATION IS HEREBY MADE FOR: (Check applicable items)

A	1	STANDARD AIRWORTHINESS CERTIFICATE (Indicate category)		NORMAL	UTILITY	ACROBATIC	TRANSPORT	GLIDER	BALLOON

B	X	SPECIAL AIRWORTHINESS CERTIFICATE (Check appropriate items)

	2	LIMITED						
	3 X	PROVISIONAL (Indicate class)	1 X	CLASS I				
			2	CLASS II				
	4	RESTRICTED (Indicate operation(s) to be conducted)	3	AGRICULTURE AND PEST CONTROL	3	AERIAL SURVEYING	5	AERIAL ADVERTISING
			5	FOREST (Wildlife conservation)	5	PATROLLING	6	WEATHER CONTROL
			7	CARRIAGE OF CARGO	9	OTHER (Specify)		
	5	EXPERIMENTAL (Indicate operation(s) to be conducted)	1	RESEARCH AND DEVELOPMENT	2	AMATEUR BUILT	3	EXHIBITION
			4	RACING	5	CREW TRAINING	6	MKT. SURVEY
			7	TO SHOW COMPLIANCE WITH FAR				
	6	SPECIAL FLIGHT PERMIT (Indicate operation to be conducted, then complete Section VI or VII as applicable on reverse side)	1	FERRY FLIGHT FOR REPAIRS, ALTERATIONS, MAINTENANCE OR STORAGE				
			2	EVACUATE FROM AREA OF IMPENDING DANGER				
			3	OPERATION IN EXCESS OF MAXIMUM CERTIFICATED TAKE-OFF WEIGHT				
			4	DELIVERY OR EXPORT	5	PRODUCTION FLIGHT TESTING		
			6	CUSTOMER DEMONSTRATION FLIGHTS				

C	0	MULTIPLE AIRWORTHINESS CERTIFICATE (Check ABOVE "Restricted Operation" and "Standard" or "Limited," as applicable.)

III. OWNER'S CERTIFICATION

A. REGISTERED OWNER (As shown on certificate of aircraft registration)

NAME	ADDRESS	IF DEALER, CHECK HERE
Lockheed-Georgia Co.	Marietta, Georgia 30060	

B. AIRCRAFT CERTIFICATION BASIS (Check applicable blocks and complete items as indicated)

X	AIRCRAFT SPECIFICATION OR TYPE CERTIFICATE DATA SHEET (Give No. and Revision No.)	AIRWORTHINESS DIRECTIVES (Check if all applicable AD's complied with and give latest AD No.)
	A1SO	86-01-01
	AIRCRAFT LISTING (Give page number(s))	SUPPLEMENTAL TYPE CERTIFICATE (List number of each STC incorporated)
	N/A	N/A

C. AIRCRAFT OPERATION AND MAINTENANCE RECORDS

X	CHECK IF RECORDS IN COMPLIANCE WITH FAR 91.173	TOTAL AIRFRAME HOURS		EXPERIMENTAL ONLY (Enter hours flown since last certificate issued or renewed)
		10.2	0	N/A

D. CERTIFICATION — I hereby certify that I am the registered owner (or his agent) of the aircraft described above; that the aircraft is registered with the Federal Aviation Administration in accordance with Section 501 of the Federal Aviation Act of 1958, and applicable Federal Aviation Regulations, and that the aircraft has been inspected and is airworthy and eligible for the airworthiness certificate requested.

DATE OF APPLICATION	NAME AND TITLE (Print or type)	SIGNATURE
2/16/XX	James A. Jones Vice-President Engineering	J. A. Jones

IV. INSPECTION AGENCY VERIFICATION

A. THE AIRCRAFT DESCRIBED ABOVE HAS BEEN INSPECTED AND FOUND AIRWORTHY BY: (Complete this section only if FAR 21.183(d) applies)

0	FAR PART 121 OR 127 CERTIFICATE HOLDER (Give Certificate No.)	0	CERTIFICATED MECHANIC (Give Certificate No.)	0	CERTIFICATED REPAIR STATION (Give Certificate No.)
0	AIRCRAFT MANUFACTURER (Give name of firm)				

DATE	TITLE	SIGNATURE

V. FAA REPRESENTATIVE CERTIFICATION

(Check ALL applicable blocks in Items A and B)

A. I find that the aircraft described in Section I or VII meets requirements for:		THE CERTIFICATE REQUESTED
	4	AMENDMENT OR MODIFICATION OF CURRENT AIRWORTHINESS CERTIFICATE

B. Inspection for a special flight permit under Section VII was conducted by:	FAA INSPECTOR	FAA DESIGNEE			
	CERTIFICATE HOLDER UNDER:	FAR 65	FAR 121, 127 or 135	FAR 145	

DATE	DISTRICT OFFICE	DESIGNEE'S SIGNATURE AND NO.	FAA INSPECTOR'S SIGNATURE
		0	0

FAA Form 8130-6 (6-86) SUPERSEDES PREVIOUS EDITION

FAA FORM 8130-6 – APPLICATION FOR A SPECIAL
AIRWORTHINESS CERTIFICATE – RESTRICTED

Form Approved
O.M.B. No. 2120-0018

APPLICATION FOR AIRWORTHINESS CERTIFICATE

U.S. Department
of Transportation
Federal Aviation
Administration

INSTRUCTIONS — Print or type. Do not write in shaded areas, these are for FAA use only. Submit original only to an authorized FAA Representative. If additional space is required, use an attachment. For special flight permits complete Sections II and VI or VII as applicable.

I. AIRCRAFT DESCRIPTION

1. REGISTRATION MARK	2. AIRCRAFT BUILDER'S NAME (Make)	3. AIRCRAFT MODEL DESIGNATION	4. YR. MFR	FAA CODING
N7777	No. American Rockwell	S2R	1950	

5. AIRCRAFT SERIAL NO	6. ENGINE BUILDER'S NAME (Make)	7. ENGINE MODEL DESIGNATION	
1916R	P&W	R1340AN1(S3H1)	

8. NUMBER OF ENGINES	9. PROPELLER BUILDER'S NAME (Make)	10. PROPELLER MODEL DESIGNATION	11. AIRCRAFT IS (Check if applicable)
One	Hamilton Standard	12D40-305/EAC/AG 100-2	IMPORT

II. CERTIFICATION REQUESTED

APPLICATION IS HEREBY MADE FOR: (Check applicable items)

A	1	STANDARD AIRWORTHINESS CERTIFICATE (Indicate category)	NORMAL	UTILITY	ACROBATIC	TRANSPORT	GLIDER	BALLOON

B	X	SPECIAL AIRWORTHINESS CERTIFICATE (Check appropriate items)

	2	LIMITED			
		PROVISIONAL (Indicate class)	1	CLASS I	
			2	CLASS II	
	3	RESTRICTED (Indicate operation(s) to be conducted) X	1 X	AGRICULTURE AND PEST CONTROL	2	AERIAL SURVEYING	3	AERIAL ADVERTISING
			4	FOREST (Wildlife conservation)	5	PATROLLING		WEATHER CONTROL
			7	CARRIAGE OF CARGO	6	OTHER (Specify)		
	4	EXPERIMENTAL (Indicate operation(s) to be conducted)	1	RESEARCH AND DEVELOPMENT	2	AMATEUR BUILT	3	EXHIBITION
				RACING	6	CREW TRAINING		MKT SURVEY
				TO SHOW COMPLIANCE WITH FAR				
	5	SPECIAL FLIGHT PERMIT (Indicate operation to be conducted, then complete Section VI or VII as applicable on reverse side)		FERRY FLIGHT FOR REPAIRS, ALTERATIONS, MAINTENANCE OR STORAGE				
			2	EVACUATE FROM AREA OF IMPENDING DANGER				
			3	OPERATION IN EXCESS OF MAXIMUM CERTIFICATED TAKE-OFF WEIGHT				
			4	DELIVERY OR EXPORT	5	PRODUCTION FLIGHT TESTING		
				CUSTOMER DEMONSTRATION FLIGHTS				

C	6	MULTIPLE AIRWORTHINESS CERTIFICATE (Check ABOVE "Restricted Operation" and "Standard" or "Limited," as applicable.)

III. OWNER'S CERTIFICATION

A. REGISTERED OWNER (As shown on certificate of aircraft registration)		IF DEALER, CHECK HERE →
NAME: John J. Jones, R.B. Jones DBA Crop Dusters, Inc.	ADDRESS: Rt. 5 Greep_, Mississippi 39070	

B. AIRCRAFT CERTIFICATION BASIS (Check applicable blocks and complete items as indicated)

X	AIRCRAFT SPECIFICATION OR TYPE CERTIFICATE DATA SHEET (Give No. and Revision No.) A4SW Rev. 5	X	AIRWORTHINESS DIRECTIVES (Check if all applicable AD's complied with and give latest AD No.) 86-03-02
	AIRCRAFT LISTING (Give page number(s)) N/A		SUPPLEMENTAL TYPE CERTIFICATE (List number of each STC incorporated) N/A

C. AIRCRAFT OPERATION AND MAINTENANCE RECORDS

X	CHECK IF RECORDS IN COMPLIANCE WITH FAR 91.173	TOTAL AIRFRAME HOURS 210	9	EXPERIMENTAL ONLY (Enter hours flown since last certificate issued or renewed) N/A

D. CERTIFICATION — I hereby certify that I am the registered owner (or his agent) of the aircraft described above; that the aircraft is registered with the Federal Aviation Administration in accordance with Section 501 of the Federal Aviation Act of 1958, and applicable Federal Aviation Regulations, and that the aircraft has been inspected and is airworthy and eligible for the airworthiness certificate requested.

DATE OF APPLICATION	NAME AND TITLE (Print or type)	SIGNATURE
7/17/XX	John J. Jones, Co-Owner	John Jones

IV. INSPECTION AGENCY VERIFICATION

A. THE AIRCRAFT DESCRIBED ABOVE HAS BEEN INSPECTED AND FOUND AIRWORTHY BY: (Complete this section only if FAR 21.183(d) applies)

	FAR PART 121 OR 127 CERTIFICATE HOLDER (Give Certificate No.)		CERTIFICATED MECHANIC (Give Certificate No.)		CERTIFICATED REPAIR STATION (Give Certificate No.)
	AIRCRAFT MANUFACTURER (Give name of firm)				

DATE	TITLE		SIGNATURE

V. FAA REPRESENTATIVE CERTIFICATION

(Check ALL applicable blocks in items A and B)

A. I find that the aircraft described in Section I or VII meets requirements for:

B. Inspection for a special flight permit under Section VII was conducted by:

	THE CERTIFICATE REQUESTED
	AMENDMENT OR MODIFICATION OF CURRENT AIRWORTHINESS CERTIFICATE
FAA INSPECTOR	FAA DESIGNEE
CERTIFICATE HOLDER UNDER:	FAR 65	FAR 121, 127 or 135	FAR 145

DATE	DISTRICT OFFICE	DESIGNEE'S SIGNATURE AND NO.	FAA INSPECTOR'S SIGNATURE

FAA Form 8130-6 (6-86) SUPERSEDES PREVIOUS EDITION

FAA FORM 8130-6 – APPLICATION FOR A SPECIAL AIRWORTHINESS CERTIFICATE – EXPERIMENTAL AMATEUR – BUILT

Form Approved
O.M.B. No. 2120-0018

APPLICATION FOR AIRWORTHINESS CERTIFICATE

U.S. Department of Transportation
Federal Aviation Administration

INSTRUCTIONS — Print or type. Do not write in shaded areas, these are for FAA use only. Submit original only to an authorized FAA Representative. If additional space is required, use an attachment. For special flight permits complete Sections II and VI or VII as applicable.

I. AIRCRAFT DESCRIPTION

1. REGISTRATION MARK	2. AIRCRAFT BUILDER'S NAME (Make)	3. AIRCRAFT MODEL DESIGNATION	4. YR. MFR.	FAA CODING
N1234	Pratt	B-3	1986	
5. AIRCRAFT SERIAL NO.	6. ENGINE BUILDER'S NAME (Make)	7. ENGINE MODEL DESIGNATION		
001	CMC	A-65		
8. NUMBER OF ENGINES	9. PROPELLER BUILDER'S NAME (Make)	10. PROPELLER MODEL DESIGNATION	11. AIRCRAFT IS (Check if applicable)
One	Sensenich	N76AM-2-50	IMPORT

II. CERTIFICATION REQUESTED

APPLICATION IS HEREBY MADE FOR: (Check applicable items)

| A | 1 | STANDARD AIRWORTHINESS CERTIFICATE (Indicate category) | NORMAL | UTILITY | ACROBATIC | TRANSPORT | GLIDER | BALLOON |

| B | X | SPECIAL AIRWORTHINESS CERTIFICATE (Check appropriate items) |

	2	LIMITED		
	3	PROVISIONAL (Indicate class)	1	CLASS I
			2	CLASS II
	4	RESTRICTED (Indicate operation(s) to be conducted)	1	AGRICULTURE AND PEST CONTROL	2	AERIAL SURVEYING	3	AERIAL ADVERTISING
			4	FOREST (Wildlife conservation)	5	PATROLLING	6	WEATHER CONTROL
			7	CARRIAGE OF CARGO	8	OTHER (Specify)
	5 X	EXPERIMENTAL (Indicate operation(s) to be conducted)	1	RESEARCH AND DEVELOPMENT	2 X	AMATEUR BUILT	3	EXHIBITION
			4	RACING	5	CREW TRAINING	6	MKT. SURVEY
			7	TO SHOW COMPLIANCE WITH FAR
	6	SPECIAL FLIGHT PERMIT (Indicate operation to be conducted, then complete Section VI or VII as applicable on reverse side)	1	FERRY FLIGHT FOR REPAIRS, ALTERATIONS, MAINTENANCE OR STORAGE
			2	EVACUATE FROM AREA OF IMPENDING DANGER
			3	OPERATION IN EXCESS OF MAXIMUM CERTIFICATED TAKE-OFF WEIGHT
			4	DELIVERY OR EXPORT	5	PRODUCTION FLIGHT TESTING
			6	CUSTOMER DEMONSTRATION FLIGHTS

| C | 6 | MULTIPLE AIRWORTHINESS CERTIFICATE (Check ABOVE "Restricted Operation" and "Standard" or "Limited," as applicable.) |

III. OWNER'S CERTIFICATION

A. REGISTERED OWNER (As shown on certificate of aircraft registration)   IF DEALER, CHECK HERE ➔

NAME: Howard D. Pratt
John J. Smith Co-owners
ADDRESS: 2020 West St.
St. Louis, Missouri 41346

B. AIRCRAFT CERTIFICATION BASIS (Check applicable blocks and complete items as indicated)

AIRCRAFT SPECIFICATION OR TYPE CERTIFICATE DATA SHEET (Give No. and Revision No.)	AIRWORTHINESS DIRECTIVES (Check if all applicable AD's complied with and give latest AD No.)
N/A	X 86-19-01
AIRCRAFT LISTING (Give page number(s))	SUPPLEMENTAL TYPE CERTIFICATE (List number of each STC incorporated)
N/A	N/A

C. AIRCRAFT OPERATION AND MAINTENANCE RECORDS

CHECK IF RECORDS IN COMPLIANCE WITH FAR 91.173	TOTAL AIRFRAME HOURS	EXPERIMENTAL ONLY (Enter hours flown since last certificate issued or renewed)
X	0.0	0.0

D. CERTIFICATION — I hereby certify that I am the registered owner (or his agent) of the aircraft described above, that the aircraft is registered with the Federal Aviation Administration in accordance with Section 501 of the Federal Aviation Act of 1958, and applicable Federal Aviation Regulations, and that the aircraft has been inspected and is airworthy and eligible for the airworthiness certificate requested.

DATE OF APPLICATION	NAME AND TITLE (Print or type)	SIGNATURE
2/16/XX	Howard D. Pratt, Co-owner	Howard D. Pratt

IV. INSPECTION AGENCY VERIFICATION

A. THE AIRCRAFT DESCRIBED ABOVE HAS BEEN INSPECTED AND FOUND AIRWORTHY BY: (Complete this section only if FAR 21.183(d) applies)

| | FAR PART 121 OR 127 CERTIFICATE HOLDER (Give Certificate No.) | | CERTIFICATED MECHANIC (Give Certificate No.) | | CERTIFICATED REPAIR STATION (Give Certificate No.) |

| | AIRCRAFT MANUFACTURER (Give name of firm) |

| DATE | TITLE | SIGNATURE |

V. FAA REPRESENTATIVE CERTIFICATION

(Check ALL applicable blocks in items A and B)

THE CERTIFICATE REQUESTED

A. I find that the aircraft described in Section I or VII meets requirements for: ☐ AMENDMENT OR MODIFICATION OF CURRENT AIRWORTHINESS CERTIFICATE

B. Inspection for a special flight permit under Section VII was conducted by:

| | FAA INSPECTOR | FAA DESIGNEE |
| | CERTIFICATE HOLDER UNDER: | FAR 65 | FAR 121, 127 or 135 | FAR 145 |

| DATE | DISTRICT OFFICE | DESIGNEE'S SIGNATURE AND NO. | FAA INSPECTOR'S SIGNATURE |

FAA Form 8130-6 (8-88) SUPERSEDES PREVIOUS EDITION

FAA FORM 8130-6 – APPLICATION FOR A SPECIAL
AIRWORTHINESS CERTIFICATE – EXPERIMENTAL
NO PREVIOUS EXPERIMENTAL
CERTIFICATE OF AIRWORTHINESS ISSUED

Form Approved
O.M.B. No. 2120-0018

APPLICATION FOR AIRWORTHINESS CERTIFICATE

U.S. Department of Transportation
Federal Aviation Administration

INSTRUCTIONS — Print or type. Do not write in shaded areas; these are for FAA use only. Submit original only to an authorized FAA Representative. If additional space is required, use an attachment. For special flight permits complete Sections II and VI or VII as applicable.

I. AIRCRAFT DESCRIPTION

1. REGISTRATION MARK	2. AIRCRAFT BUILDER'S NAME (Make)	3. AIRCRAFT MODEL DESIGNATION	4. YR. MFR	FAA CODING
N5216	Boeing	727-228	1968	

5. AIRCRAFT SERIAL NO.	6. ENGINE BUILDER'S NAME (Make)	7. ENGINE MODEL DESIGNATION	
20540	P&W	JT8D-7	

8. NUMBER OF ENGINES	9. PROPELLER BUILDER'S NAME (Make)	10. PROPELLER MODEL DESIGNATION	11. AIRCRAFT IS (Check if applicable)
Three	N/A	N/A	IMPORT

II. CERTIFICATION REQUESTED

APPLICATION IS HEREBY MADE FOR: (Check applicable items)

A 1 STANDARD AIRWORTHINESS CERTIFICATE (Indicate category) — NORMAL | UTILITY | ACROBATIC | TRANSPORT | GLIDER | BALLOON

B [X] SPECIAL AIRWORTHINESS CERTIFICATE (Check appropriate items)

2 LIMITED

3 PROVISIONAL (Indicate class) — 1 CLASS I | 2 CLASS II

4 RESTRICTED (Indicate operation(s) to be conducted) —
- 1 AGRICULTURE AND PEST CONTROL | 3 AERIAL SURVEYING | 5 AERIAL ADVERTISING
- 6 FOREST (Wildlife conservation) | 4 PATROLLING | 6 WEATHER CONTROL
- 7 CARRIAGE OF CARGO | 9 OTHER (Specify)

4 [X] EXPERIMENTAL (Indicate operation(s) to be conducted) —
- 1 RESEARCH AND DEVELOPMENT | 2 AMATEUR BUILT | 9 EXHIBITION
- 4 RACING | 5 CREW TRAINING | MKT. SURVEY
- [X] TO SHOW COMPLIANCE WITH FAR **Part 25**
- FERRY FLIGHT FOR REPAIRS, ALTERATIONS, MAINTENANCE OR STORAGE

5 SPECIAL FLIGHT PERMIT (Indicate operation to be conducted, then complete Section VI or VII as applicable on reverse side) —
- EVACUATE FROM AREA OF IMPENDING DANGER
- OPERATION IN EXCESS OF MAXIMUM CERTIFICATED TAKE-OFF WEIGHT
- DELIVERY OR EXPORT | 5 PRODUCTION FLIGHT TESTING
- CUSTOMER DEMONSTRATION FLIGHTS

C 6 MULTIPLE AIRWORTHINESS CERTIFICATE (Check ABOVE "Restricted Operation" and "Standard" or "Limited," as applicable.)

III. OWNER'S CERTIFICATION

A. REGISTERED OWNER (As shown on certificate of aircraft registration)

IF DEALER, CHECK HERE → [X]

NAME	ADDRESS
The Boeing Company	P.O. Box 3707, Seattle, Washington 98124

B. AIRCRAFT CERTIFICATION BASIS (Check applicable blocks and complete items as indicated)

AIRCRAFT SPECIFICATION OR TYPE CERTIFICATE DATA SHEET (Give No. and Revision No.)	AIRWORTHINESS DIRECTIVES (Check if all applicable AD's complied with and give latest AD No.)
N/A	86-02-02

AIRCRAFT LISTING (Give page number(s))	SUPPLEMENTAL TYPE CERTIFICATE (List number of each STC incorporated)
N/A	N/A

C. AIRCRAFT OPERATION AND MAINTENANCE RECORDS

CHECK IF RECORDS IN COMPLIANCE WITH FAR 91.173	TOTAL AIRFRAME HOURS	EXPERIMENTAL ONLY (Enter hours flown since last certificate issued or renewed)
X	5.51	0.0

D. CERTIFICATION — I hereby certify that I am the registered owner (or his agent) of the aircraft described above, that the aircraft is registered with the Federal Aviation Administration in accordance with Section 501 of the Federal Aviation Act of 1958, and applicable Federal Aviation Regulations, and that the aircraft has been inspected and is airworthy and eligible for the airworthiness certificate requested.

DATE OF APPLICATION	NAME AND TITLE (Print or type)	SIGNATURE
1/27/XX	R.B. Smith, Airworthiness Cert. Mgr.	R.B. Smith

IV. INSPECTION AGENCY VERIFICATION

A. THE AIRCRAFT DESCRIBED ABOVE HAS BEEN INSPECTED AND FOUND AIRWORTHY BY: (Complete this section only if FAR 21.183(d) applies)

FAR PART 121 OR 127 CERTIFICATE HOLDER (Give Certificate No.)	CERTIFICATED MECHANIC (Give Certificate No.)	CERTIFICATED REPAIR STATION (Give Certificate No.)

AIRCRAFT MANUFACTURER (Give name of firm)

DATE	TITLE	SIGNATURE

V. FAA REPRESENTATIVE CERTIFICATION

A. I find that the aircraft described in Section I or VII meets requirements for:
- THE CERTIFICATE REQUESTED
- AMENDMENT OR MODIFICATION OF CURRENT AIRWORTHINESS CERTIFICATE

B. Inspection for a special flight permit under Section VII was conducted by:

	FAA INSPECTOR	FAA DESIGNEE			
	CERTIFICATE HOLDER UNDER	FAR 65	FAR 121, 127 or 135	FAR 145	

DATE	DISTRICT OFFICE	DESIGNEE'S SIGNATURE AND NO.	FAA INSPECTOR'S SIGNATURE

FAA Form 8130-6 (6-85) SUPERSEDES PREVIOUS EDITION

SAMPLE

FAA FORM 8130-6 APPLICATION FOR A SPECIAL AIRWORTHINESS CERTIFICATE – EXPERIMENTAL PREVIOUS U.S. CERTIFICATE OF AIRWORTHINESS ISSUED

Form Approved
O.M.B. No. 2120-0018

U.S. Department of Transportation — Federal Aviation Administration

APPLICATION FOR AIRWORTHINESS CERTIFICATE

INSTRUCTIONS — Print or type. Do not write in shaded areas; these are for FAA use only. Submit original only to an authorized FAA Representative. If additional space is required, use an attachment. For special flight permits complete Sections II and VI or VII as applicable.

I. AIRCRAFT DESCRIPTION

1. REGISTRATION MARK	2. AIRCRAFT BUILDER'S NAME (Make)	3. AIRCRAFT MODEL DESIGNATION	4. YR. MFR.	FAA CODING
N502CB	Cessna	500	1980	
5. AIRCRAFT SERIAL NO.	6. ENGINE BUILDER'S NAME (Make)	7. ENGINE MODEL DESIGNATION		
500-0001	UACL	JT15D-1		
8. NUMBER OF ENGINES	9. PROPELLER BUILDER'S NAME (Make)	10. PROPELLER MODEL DESIGNATION	11. AIRCRAFT IS (Check if applicable)	
Two	N/A	N/A	IMPORT	

II. CERTIFICATION REQUESTED

APPLICATION IS HEREBY MADE FOR: (Check applicable items) –

| A 1 | STANDARD AIRWORTHINESS CERTIFICATE (Indicate category) | NORMAL | UTILITY | ACROBATIC | TRANSPORT | GLIDER | BALLOON |

B [X] SPECIAL AIRWORTHINESS CERTIFICATE (Check appropriate items)

	2	LIMITED					
3		PROVISIONAL (Indicate class)	1	CLASS I			
			2	CLASS II			
4		RESTRICTED (Indicate operation(s) to be conducted)	3	AGRICULTURE AND PEST CONTROL	5	AERIAL SURVEYING	7	AERIAL ADVERTISING
			4	FOREST (Wildlife conservation)	6	PATROLLING	8	WEATHER CONTROL
			7	CARRIAGE OF CARGO	9	OTHER (Specify)	
4 [X]		EXPERIMENTAL (Indicate operation(s) to be conducted)	1	RESEARCH AND DEVELOPMENT	7	AMATEUR BUILT	9	EXHIBITION
			2	RACING	8 [X]	CREW TRAINING	[X]	MKT. SURVEY
			3	TO SHOW COMPLIANCE WITH FAR			
8		SPECIAL FLIGHT PERMIT (Indicate operation to be conducted, then complete Section VI or VII as applicable on reverse side)	1	FERRY FLIGHT FOR REPAIRS, ALTERATIONS, MAINTENANCE OR STORAGE		
			2	EVACUATE FROM AREA OF IMPENDING DANGER		
			3	OPERATION IN EXCESS OF MAXIMUM CERTIFICATED TAKE-OFF WEIGHT		
			4	DELIVERY OR EXPORT		PRODUCTION FLIGHT TESTING
			5	CUSTOMER DEMONSTRATION FLIGHTS		

| C 6 | MULTIPLE AIRWORTHINESS CERTIFICATE (Check ABOVE "Restricted Operation" and "Standard" or "Limited," as applicable.) |

III. OWNER'S CERTIFICATION

A. REGISTERED OWNER (As shown on certificate of aircraft registration)

IF DEALER, CHECK HERE → [X]

NAME	ADDRESS
Cessna Aircraft Co.	West K-42 Highway, P.O. Box 1977 Wichita, Kansas 67201

B. AIRCRAFT CERTIFICATION BASIS (Check applicable blocks and complete items as indicated)

AIRCRAFT SPECIFICATION OR TYPE CERTIFICATE DATA SHEET (Give No. and Revision No.)	AIRWORTHINESS DIRECTIVES (Check if all applicable AD's complied with and give latest AD No.)
N/A	86-01-02
AIRCRAFT LISTING (Give page number(s))	SUPPLEMENTAL TYPE CERTIFICATE (List number of each STC incorporated)
N/A	N/A

C. AIRCRAFT OPERATION AND MAINTENANCE RECORDS

CHECK IF RECORDS IN COMPLIANCE WITH FAR 91.173	TOTAL AIRFRAME HOURS	EXPERIMENTAL ONLY (Enter hours flown since last certificate issued or renewed)
X	52.0	22.0

D. CERTIFICATION — I hereby certify that I am the registered owner (or his agent) of the aircraft described above; that the aircraft is registered with the Federal Aviation Administration in accordance with Section 501 of the Federal Aviation Act of 1958, and applicable Federal Aviation Regulations; and that the aircraft has been inspected and is airworthy and eligible for the airworthiness certificate requested.

DATE OF APPLICATION	NAME AND TITLE (Print or type)	SIGNATURE
2/18/XX	A.D. Smith, Quality Control Mgr.	A. D. Smith

IV. INSPECTION AGENCY VERIFICATION

A. THE AIRCRAFT DESCRIBED ABOVE HAS BEEN INSPECTED AND FOUND AIRWORTHY BY: (Complete this section only if FAR 21.183(d) applies)

1	FAR PART 121 OR 127 CERTIFICATE HOLDER (Give Certificate No.)	3	CERTIFICATED MECHANIC (Give Certificate No.)	4	CERTIFICATED REPAIR STATION (Give Certificate No.)
2	AIRCRAFT MANUFACTURER (Give name of firm)				

DATE	TITLE	SIGNATURE

V. FAA REPRESENTATIVE CERTIFICATION

(Check ALL applicable blocks in items A and B)

A. I find that the aircraft described in Section I or VII meets requirements for:

	THE CERTIFICATE REQUESTED
	AMENDMENT OR MODIFICATION OF CURRENT AIRWORTHINESS CERTIFICATE

B. Inspection for a special flight permit under Section VII was conducted by:

FAA INSPECTOR	FAA DESIGNEE
CERTIFICATE HOLDER UNDER:	FAR 65	FAR 121, 127 or 135	FAR 145

DATE	DISTRICT OFFICE	DESIGNEE'S SIGNATURE AND NO.	FAA INSPECTOR'S SIGNATURE

FAA Form 8130-6 (6-26) SUPERSEDES PREVIOUS EDITION

SAMPLE

FAA FORM 8130-6 – APPLICATION FOR A SPECIAL
AIRWORTHINESS CERTIFICATE – SPECIAL FLIGHT
PERMIT FOR FERRY FLIGHT

(Front Side)

APPLICATION IS HEREBY MADE FOR: (Check applicable items)											
A	**1**	STANDARD AIRWORTHINESS CERTIFICATE (Indicate category)	NORMAL	UTILITY	ACROBATIC	TRANSPORT	GLIDER	BALLOON			
B	**X**	SPECIAL AIRWORTHINESS CERTIFICATE (Check appropriate items)									
		2	LIMITED								
		3	PROVISIONAL (Indicate class)	**1**	CLASS I						
				2	CLASS II						
		4	RESTRICTED (Indicate operation(s) to be conducted)	**1**	AGRICULTURE AND PEST CONTROL	**2**	AERIAL SURVEYING	**3**	AERIAL ADVERTISING		
				4	FOREST (Wildlife conservation)	**5**	PATROLLING	**6**	WEATHER CONTROL		
				7	CARRIAGE OF CARGO	**8**	OTHER (Specify)				
		5	EXPERIMENTAL (Indicate operation(s) to be conducted)	**1**	RESEARCH AND DEVELOPMENT	**2**	AMATEUR BUILT	**3**	EXHIBITION		
					RACING	**5**	CREW TRAINING		MKT SURVEY		
				10	TO SHOW COMPLIANCE WITH FAR						
		6	SPECIAL FLIGHT PERMIT (Indicate operation to be conducted, then complete Section VI or VII as applicable on reverse side)	**1**	FERRY FLIGHT FOR REPAIRS, ALTERATIONS, MAINTENANCE OR STORAGE						
				2	EVACUATE FROM AREA OF IMPENDING DANGER						
		X		**3**	OPERATION IN EXCESS OF MAXIMUM CERTIFICATED TAKE-OFF WEIGHT						
				4	DELIVERING OR EXPORT	**5**	PRODUCTION FLIGHT TESTING				
				6	CUSTOMER DEMONSTRATION FLIGHTS						
C	**9**	MULTIPLE AIRWORTHINESS CERTIFICATE (Check ABOVE "Restricted Operation" and "Standard" or "Limited" as applicable)									

(Reverse Side)

A. DESCRIPTION OF AIRCRAFT

REGISTERED OWNER	ADDRESS
Weldon H. Jackson	P.O. Box 983 Maui, Hawaii 96782
BUILDER (Make)	MODEL
Piper	PA 23-250
SERIAL NUMBER	REGISTRATION MARK
27-647	N4588P

B. DESCRIPTION OF FLIGHT — CUSTOMER DEMONSTRATION FLIGHTS ☐ (Check if applicable)

FROM	TO
El Paso, Texas	Maui, Hawaii
VIA	
San Jose, California	

DEPARTURE DATE	DURATION
3/11/XX	30 days

C. CREW REQUIRED TO OPERATE THE AIRCRAFT AND ITS EQUIPMENT.

X	PILOT	X	CO-PILOT		NAVIGATOR		OTHER (Specify)

D. THE AIRCRAFT DOES NOT MEET THE APPLICABLE AIRWORTHINESS REQUIREMENTS AS FOLLOWS

Temporary Ferry Fuel System installed in accordance with FAA Form 337, "Major Repair and Alteration" dated 3/9/XX
Gross weight not to exceed 110% of certificated maximum weight.

E. THE FOLLOWING RESTRICTIONS ARE CONSIDERED NECESSARY FOR SAFE OPERATION (Use attachment if necessary)

1. When the aircraft is in an overweight condition, the design cruise speed, V_c should not exceed 162 mph.

2. The fuel quantity should not exceed 140 gallons in the forward tank and 35 gallons in the aft tank.

3. The sequence of use of the ferry fuel tanks shall be as shown by a temporary placard installed in full view of the pilot.

F. CERTIFICATION — I hereby certify that I am the registered owner (or his agent) of the aircraft described above; that the aircraft is registered with the Federal Aviation Administration in accordance with Section 501 of the Federal Aviation Act of 1958, and applicable Federal Aviation Regulations, and that the aircraft has been inspected and is airworthy for the flight described.

DATE	NAME AND TITLE (Print or type)	SIGNATURE
3/10/XX	Don Brown, Agent	*Don Brown*

VI. SPECIAL FLIGHT FERRY FLIGHT PURPOSE OTHER THAN PRODUCTION FLIGHT TEST

II. CERTIFICATION REQUESTED

FAA FORM 8130-6 – APPLICATION FOR A SPECIAL AIRWORTHINESS CERTIFICATE – SPECIAL FLIGHT PERMIT FOR FERRY FLIGHT

(Front Side)

SAMPLE

I. CERTIFICATION REQUESTED	A	1	STANDARD AIRWORTHINESS CERTIFICATE (indicate category)		NORMAL	UTILITY	ACROBATIC	TRANSPORT	GLIDER	BALLOON	
	B	X	SPECIAL AIRWORTHINESS CERTIFICATE (Check appropriate items)								
		2	LIMITED								
		3	PROVISIONAL (Indicate class)	1	CLASS I						
				2	CLASS II						
		4	RESTRICTED (Indicate operation(s) to be conducted)	1	AGRICULTURE AND PEST CONTROL	2		AERIAL SURVEYING	3		AERIAL ADVERTISING
				4	FOREST (Wildlife conservation)	5		PATROLLING	6		WEATHER CONTROL
				7	CARRIAGE OF CARGO	8		OTHER (Specify)			
		5	EXPERIMENTAL (Indicate operation(s) to be conducted)	1	RESEARCH AND DEVELOPMENT	2		AMATEUR BUILT	3		EXHIBITION
				4		5		CREW TRAINING			MKT. SURVEY
				2	TO SHOW COMPLIANCE WITH FAR						
		8	SPECIAL FLIGHT PERMIT (Indicate operation to be conducted, then complete Section VI or VII as applicable on reverse side)	1	FERRY FLIGHT FOR REPAIRS, ALTERATIONS, MAINTENANCE OR STORAGE				X		
				2	EVACUATE FROM AREA OF IMPENDING DANGER						
				3	OPERATION IN EXCESS OF MAXIMUM CERTIFICATED TAKE-OFF WEIGHT						
				4	DELIVERING OR EXPORT			6		PRODUCTION FLIGHT TESTING	
				5	CUSTOMER DEMONSTRATION FLIGHTS						
	C	6	MULTIPLE AIRWORTHINESS CERTIFICATE (Check ABOVE "Restricted Operation" and "Standard" or "Limited" as applicable)								

(Reverse Side)

SAMPLE

A. DESCRIPTION OF AIRCRAFT

REGISTERED OWNER	ADDRESS
Robert F. Turner	4623 Mountainview Drive Waterloo, Iowa 50701
BUILDER (Make)	**MODEL**
Bellanca	14-19-2
SERIAL NUMBER	**REGISTRATION MARK**
4099	N 254B

B. DESCRIPTION OF FLIGHT   CUSTOMER DEMONSTRATION FLIGHTS ☐ (Check if applicable)

FROM	TO
Waterloo, Iowa	Des Moines, Iowa
VIA	**DEPARTURE DATE** **DURATION**
Direct	1/12/XX 1/23/XX

C. CREW REQUIRED TO OPERATE THE AIRCRAFT AND ITS EQUIPMENT

X PILOT	CO-PILOT	NAVIGATOR	OTHER (Specify)

D. THE AIRCRAFT DOES NOT MEET THE APPLICABLE AIRWORTHINESS REQUIREMENTS AS FOLLOWS:

Aircraft damaged in landing accident. Temporary repairs have been made for one flight to a repair shop at Des Moines - Dodge Airport, where permanent repairs will be made.

E. THE FOLLOWING RESTRICTIONS ARE CONSIDERED NECESSARY FOR SAFE OPERATION (Use attachment if necessary)

Airspeed should not exceed 115 m.p.h.
Landing gear should not be retracted.
No passengers or cargo should be carried.

F. CERTIFICATION – I hereby certify that I am the registered owner (or his agent) of the aircraft described above; that the aircraft is registered with the Federal Aviation Administration in accordance with Section 501 of the Federal Aviation Act of 1958, and applicable Federal Aviation Regulations, and that the aircraft has been inspected and is airworthy for the flight described.

DATE	NAME AND TITLE (Print or type)	SIGNATURE
1/06/XX	Robert F. Turner, Owner	R.F. Turner

(left margin) VII. SPECIAL FLIGHT PERMIT PERFORMED OTHER THAN PRODUCTION FLIGHT TEST

FAA FORM 8130-6 - APPLICATION FOR A
SPECIAL AIRWORTHINESS CERTIFICATE
SPECIAL FLIGHT PERMIT FOR PRODUCTION
FLIGHT TESTING

(Front Side)

(Reverse Side)

FAA-FORM 8130-6-APPLICATION FOR A MULTIPLE AIRWORTHINESS CERTIFICATE

Form Approved
O.M.B. No. 2120-0018

APPLICATION FOR AIRWORTHINESS CERTIFICATE

U.S. Department of Transportation
Federal Aviation Administration

INSTRUCTIONS — Print or type. Do not write in shaded areas; these are for FAA use only. Submit original only to an authorized FAA Representative. If additional space is required, use an attachment. For special flight permits complete Sections II and VI or VII as applicable.

I. AIRCRAFT DESCRIPTION

1. REGISTRATION MARK	2. AIRCRAFT BUILDER'S NAME (Make)	3. AIRCRAFT MODEL DESIGNATION	4. YR. MFR.	FAA CODING
N54321	Piper	PA18A-150	1951	
5. AIRCRAFT SERIAL NO.	6. ENGINE BUILDER'S NAME (Make)	7. ENGINE MODEL DESIGNATION		
18-3792	Lycoming	O-320		
8. NUMBER OF ENGINES	9. PROPELLER BUILDER'S NAME (Make)	10. PROPELLER MODEL DESIGNATION	11. AIRCRAFT IS (Check if applicable)	
One	Sensenich	M74DM	IMPORT	

II. CERTIFICATION REQUESTED

APPLICATION IS HEREBY MADE FOR: (Check applicable items)

| A | 1 | X | STANDARD AIRWORTHINESS CERTIFICATE (Indicate category) | X | NORMAL | X | UTILITY | | ACROBATIC | | TRANSPORT | | GLIDER | | BALLOON |

B — X — SPECIAL AIRWORTHINESS CERTIFICATE (Check appropriate items)

- 2 LIMITED
- 3 PROVISIONAL (Indicate class)
- X RESTRICTED (Indicate operation(s) to be conducted)
- EXPERIMENTAL (Indicate operation(s) to be conducted)
- SPECIAL FLIGHT PERMIT (Indicate operation to be conducted, then complete Section VI or VII as applicable on reverse side)

1	CLASS I
2	CLASS II
X	3	AGRICULTURE AND PEST CONTROL	4	AERIAL SURVEYING	5	AERIAL ADVERTISING
5	FOREST (Wildlife conservation)	6	PATROLLING	6	WEATHER CONTROL
7	CARRIAGE OF CARGO	8	OTHER (Specify)
9	RESEARCH AND DEVELOPMENT	2	AMATEUR BUILT	9	EXHIBITION
1	RACING	3	CREW TRAINING	MKT. SURVEY
4	TO SHOW COMPLIANCE WITH FAR
5	FERRY FLIGHT FOR REPAIRS, ALTERATIONS, MAINTENANCE OR STORAGE
6	EVACUATE FROM AREA OF IMPENDING DANGER
7	OPERATION IN EXCESS OF MAXIMUM CERTIFICATED TAKE-OFF WEIGHT
8	DELIVERY OR EXPORT	9	PRODUCTION FLIGHT TESTING
CUSTOMER DEMONSTRATION FLIGHTS

| C | 9 | X | MULTIPLE AIRWORTHINESS CERTIFICATE (Check ABOVE "Restricted Operation" and "Standard" or "Limited," as applicable.) | IF DEALER, CHECK HERE ➤ |

III. OWNER'S CERTIFICATION

A. REGISTERED OWNER (As shown on certificate of aircraft registration)

NAME	ADDRESS
North Central Airplane Corp.	Rt. 1 Box 502 Cutbank, Minn. 43692

B. AIRCRAFT CERTIFICATION BASIS (Check applicable blocks and complete items as indicated)

| X | AIRCRAFT SPECIFICATION OR TYPE CERTIFICATE DATA SHEET (Give No. and Revision No.) 1A2 Rev. 33, AR-7 Rev. 9 | X | AIRWORTHINESS DIRECTIVES (Check if all applicable AD's complied with and give latest AD No.) 86-3-06 |
| AIRCRAFT LISTING (Give page number(s)) N/A | SUPPLEMENTAL TYPE CERTIFICATE (List number of each STC incorporated) N/A |

C. AIRCRAFT OPERATION AND MAINTENANCE RECORDS

| X | CHECK IF RECORDS IN COMPLIANCE WITH FAR 91.173 | TOTAL AIRFRAME HOURS 1205 | 9 | EXPERIMENTAL ONLY (Enter hours flown since last certificate issued or renewed) N/A |

D. CERTIFICATION — I hereby certify that I am the registered owner (or his agent) of the aircraft described above; that the aircraft is registered with the Federal Aviation Administration in accordance with Section 501 of the Federal Aviation Act of 1958, and applicable Federal Aviation Regulations; and that the aircraft has been inspected and is airworthy and eligible for the airworthiness certificate requested.

DATE OF APPLICATION	NAME AND TITLE (Print or type)	SIGNATURE
3/10/XX	John Jones, President	John Jones

IV. INSPECTION AGENCY VERIFICATION

A. THE AIRCRAFT DESCRIBED ABOVE HAS BEEN INSPECTED AND FOUND AIRWORTHY BY: (Complete this section only if FAR 21.183(d) applies)

| B | FAR PART 121 OR 127 CERTIFICATE HOLDER (Give Certificate No.) | B | CERTIFICATED MECHANIC (Give Certificate No.) | B | CERTIFICATED REPAIR STATION (Give Certificate No.) |
| 9 | AIRCRAFT MANUFACTURER (Give name of firm) | | | | |

| DATE | TITLE | SIGNATURE |

V. FAA REPRESENTATIVE CERTIFICATION

(Check ALL applicable blocks in Items A and B)

A. I find that the aircraft described in Section I or VII meets requirements for:

B. Inspection for a special flight permit under Section VII was conducted by:

| THE CERTIFICATE REQUESTED |
4	AMENDMENT OR MODIFICATION OF CURRENT AIRWORTHINESS CERTIFICATE
FAA INSPECTOR	FAA DESIGNEE
CERTIFICATE HOLDER UNDER:	FAR 65	FAR 121, 127 or 135	FAR 145

| DATE | DISTRICT OFFICE | DESIGNEE'S SIGNATURE AND NO. | FAA INSPECTOR'S SIGNATURE |

FAA Form 8130-6 (9-88) SUPERSEDES PREVIOUS EDITION

FAA FORM 8130-6 – APPLICATION FOR AN
AIRWOTHINESS CERTIFICATE FOR
SURPLUS MILITARY AIRCRAFT

Form Approved
O.M.B. No. 2120-0018

APPLICATION FOR AIRWORTHINESS CERTIFICATE

U.S. Department of Transportation
Federal Aviation Administration

INSTRUCTIONS — Print or type. Do not write in shaded areas; these are for FAA use only. Submit original only to an authorized FAA Representative. If additional space is required, use an attachment. For special flight permits complete Sections II and VI or VII as applicable.

I. AIRCRAFT DESCRIPTION

1. REGISTRATION MARK	2. AIRCRAFT BUILDER'S NAME (Make)	3. AIRCRAFT MODEL DESIGNATION	4. YR. MFR	FAA CODING
N61365	Cessna	310A	1959	

5. AIRCRAFT SERIAL NO.	6. ENGINE BUILDER'S NAME (Make)	7. ENGINE MODEL DESIGNATION	
38001	Continental	0-470-M	

8. NUMBER OF ENGINES	9. PROPELLER BUILDER'S NAME (Make)	10. PROPELLER MODEL DESIGNATION	11. AIRCRAFT IS (Check if applicable)
Two	Hartzell	HC82XF-2	IMPORT

II. CERTIFICATION REQUESTED

APPLICATION IS HEREBY MADE FOR: (Check applicable items)

A | 9 | X | STANDARD AIRWORTHINESS CERTIFICATE (Indicate category) | NORMAL | UTILITY | ACROBATIC | TRANSPORT | GLIDER | BALLOON

B | | | SPECIAL AIRWORTHINESS CERTIFICATE (Check appropriate items)

- 9 LIMITED
- 0 PROVISIONAL (Indicate class) — CLASS I
- RESTRICTED (Indicate operation(s) to be conducted) — AGRICULTURE AND PEST CONTROL; FOREST (Wild. conservation); CARRYING OF CARGO; AERIAL SURVEYING; PATROLLING; OTHER (Specify); AERIAL ADVERTISING; WEATHER CONTROL
- EXPERIMENTAL (Indicate operation(s) to be conducted) — RESEARCH & DEVELOPMENT; RACING; TO SHOW COMPLIANCE WITH FAR; AMATEUR BUILT; CREW TRAINING; EXHIBITION; MKT. SURVEY
- SPECIAL FLIGHT PERMIT (Indicate operation to be conducted, then complete Section VI or VII as applicable on reverse side) — FERRY FLIGHT FOR REPAIRS, ALTERATIONS, MAINTENANCE OR STORAGE; EVACUATE FROM AREA OF IMPENDING DANGER; OPERATION IN EXCESS OF MAXIMUM CERTIFICATED TAKE-OFF WEIGHT; DELIVERING OR EXPORT; CUSTOMER DEMONSTRATION FLIGHTS; PRODUCTION FLIGHT TESTING

C | 0 | MULTIPLE AIRWORTHINESS CERTIFICATE (Check ABOVE "Restricted Operation" and "Standard" or "Limited" as applicable)

III. OWNER'S CERTIFICATION

A. REGISTERED OWNER (As shown on certificate of aircraft registration)

NAME	ADDRESS
Howard D. Pratt	1320 West St. St. Louis, Missouri 41366

B. AIRCRAFT CERTIFICATION BASIS (Check applicable blocks and complete items as indicated)

	AIRCRAFT SPECIFICATION OR TYPE CERTIFICATE DATA SHEET (Give No. and Revision No.)		AIRWORTHINESS DIRECTIVES (Check if all applicable AD's complied with and give latest AD No.)
X	3A10 Rev. 51	X	85-01-01
	AIRCRAFT LISTING (Give page number(s))		SUPPLEMENTAL TYPE CERTIFICATE (List number of each STC incorporated)
	N/A		N/A

C. AIRCRAFT OPERATION AND MAINTENANCE RECORDS

	CHECK IF RECORDS IN COMPLIANCE WITH FAR 91.173	TOTAL AIRFRAME HOURS		EXPERIMENTAL ONLY (Enter hours flown since last certificate issued or renewed)
X		9,000	9	N/A

D. CERTIFICATION — I hereby certify that I am the registered owner (or his agent) of the aircraft described above; that the aircraft is registered with the Federal Aviation Administration in accordance with Section 501 of the Federal Aviation Act of 1958, and applicable Federal Aviation Regulations, and that the aircraft has been inspected and is airworthy and eligible for the airworthiness certificate requested.

DATE OF APPLICATION	NAME AND TITLE (Print or type)	SIGNATURE
10/28/XX	Howard D. Pratt, Owner	Howard D. Pratt

IV. INSPECTION AGENCY VERIFICATION

A. THE AIRCRAFT DESCRIBED ABOVE HAS BEEN INSPECTED AND FOUND AIRWORTHY BY: (Complete this section only if FAR 21.183(d) applies)

	FAR PART 121 OR 127 CERTIFICATE HOLDER (Give Certificate No.)	9	CERTIFICATED MECHANIC (Give Certificate No.)	9	CERTIFICATED REPAIR STATION (Give Certificate No.)
9				X	4326
	AIRCRAFT MANUFACTURER (Give name of firm)				

DATE	TITLE	SIGNATURE
10/27/XX	Chief Inspector	Robert Corcoran

V. FAA REPRESENTATIVE CERTIFICATION

(Check ALL applicable blocks in items A and B)

A. I find that the aircraft described in Section I or VII meets requirements for:

B. Inspection for a special flight permit under Section VII was conducted by:

THE CERTIFICATE REQUESTED
AMENDMENT OR MODIFICATION OF CURRENT AIRWORTHINESS CERTIFICATE

FAA INSPECTOR	FAA DESIGNEE		
CERTIFICATE HOLDER UNDER:	FAR 65	FAR 121, 127 or 135	FAR 145

DATE	DISTRICT OFFICE	DESIGNEE'S SIGNATURE AND NO.	FAA INSPECTOR'S SIGNATURE

FAA Form 8130-6 (6-80) SUPERSEDES PREVIOUS EDITION

FAA Regional Office to Contact When the Address of the Appropriate
FAA Flight Standards or Manufacturing Inspection District Office Is Not Known.

Location of Applicant	Address of FAA Regional Office
Alaska, Aleutian Islands	Director, FAA 701 'C' Street, Box 14 Anchorage, Alaska 99513
Iowa, Kansas, Missouri, Nebraska	Director, FAA 601 E. 12th Street Kansas City, Missouri 64106
New York, Delaware, District of Columbia, Pennsylvania Maryland, New Jersey, West Virginia Virginia, Canada	Director, FAA JFK International Airport Jamaica, New York 11430
Europe, Africa, Middle East, Iceland, Azores	Assistant Administrator, FAA 15 Rue de la Loi B-1040 Brussels, Belgium Attn: AEU-100
Illinois, Indiana, Michigan, Minnesota, Ohio, Wisconsin, North Dakota, South Dakota	Director, FAA 2300 E. Devon Avenue Des Plaines, Illinois 60018
Connecticut, Maine, Massachusetts, New Hampshire, Rhode Island, Vermont	Director, FAA 12 New England Executive Park Burlington, Massachusetts 1803
Washington, Oregon, Idaho, Montana, Wyoming, Utah, Colorado	Director, FAA 17900 Pacific Highway South C-68966 Seattle, Washington 98168
Hawaii, Pacific Ocean area west of continental U.S. and east of Bangladesh and India including all free nations south and east of China	Manager, Flight Standards District Office 13 Honololu International Airport Air Service Corporation Building 218 Lagoon Drive, Room 215 Honolulu, Hawaii 96819
Alabama, Florida, Georgia, Kentucky, Mississippi, North Carolina, South Carolina, Tennessee, Caribbean Area, Central America, Puerto Rico, Canal Zone, Virgin Island, Swan Island	Director, FAA P.O. Box 20636 Atlanta, Georgia 30320
Arkansas, Louisiana, New Mexico, Oklahoma, Texas, Mexico	Director, FAA P.O. Box 1689 Fort Worth, Texas 76101
Arizona, California, Nevada, Wake Island, Samoa, Guam	Director, FAA P.O. Box 92007 Worldway Postal Center Los Angeles, California 0009

U.S. Department
of Transportation

**Federal Aviation
Administration**

800 Independence Ave., S.W.
Washington, D.C. 20591

**U.S. Department
of Transportation**

**Federal Aviation
Administration**

Advisory
Circular

Subject: AIRWORTHINESS DIRECTIVES	Date: 4/8/87	AC No: 39-7B
	Initiated by: AFS-340	Change:

1. PURPOSE. This advisory circular (AC) provides guidance and information to owners and operators of aircraft concerning their responsibility for complying with airworthiness directives (AD's) and recording AD compliance in the appropriate maintenance records.

2. CANCELLATION. AC 39-7A, Airworthiness Directives for General Aviation Aircraft, dated September 17, 1982, is canceled.

3. RELATED FEDERAL AVIATION REGULATIONS (FAR). FAR Part 39; FAR Part 43, Sections 43.9 and 43.11; FAR Part 91, Sections 91.163, 91.165, and 91.173.

4. BACKGROUND. Title VI of the Federal Aviation Act of 1958, as amended by Section 6 of the Department of Transportation Act, defines the Federal Aviation Administration (FAA) role regarding the promotion of safety of flight for civil aircraft. One safety function charged to the FAA is to require correction of unsafe conditions discovered in any product (aircraft, aircraft engine, propeller, or appliance) after type certification or other approval, when that condition is likely to exist or develop in other products of the same type design. AD's are used by the FAA to notify aircraft owners and operators of unsafe conditions and to require their correction. AD's prescribe the conditions and limitations, including inspections, repair, or alteration under which the product may continue to be operated. AD's are FAR codified in FAR Part 39 and issued in accordance with the public rulemaking procedures of the Administrative Procedure Act, Title 5, U.S.C. Section 553.

5. AD CATEGORIES. Since AD's are FAR, they are published in the Federal Register as amendments to FAR Part 39. Depending on the urgency, AD's are issued as follows:

   a. Normally a notice of proposed rulemaking (NPRM) for an AD is issued and published in the Federal Register when an unsafe condition is believed to exist in a product. Interested persons are invited to comment on the NPRM by submitting such written data, views, or arguments as they may desire. The comment period is usually 30 days. Proposals contained in the notice may be changed or withdrawn in light of comments received. When the final rule resulting from the NPRM is adopted, it is published in the Federal Register, printed, and distributed by first class mail to the registered owners of the products affected.

b. Emergency AD's. AD's of an urgent nature are adopted without prior notice (NPRM) under emergency procedures as immediate adopted rules. The AD's normally become effective in less than 30 days after publication in the Federal Register and are distributed by telegram or first class mail to the registered owners of the product affected.

6. AD'S WHICH APPLY TO OTHER THAN AIRCRAFT. AD's may be issued which apply to engines, propellers, or appliances installed on multiple makes or models of aircraft. When the product can be identified as being installed on a specific make or model aircraft, AD distribution is made to the registered owners of those aircraft. However, there are times when a determination cannot be made, and direct distribution to the registered owner is impossible. For this reason, aircraft owners and operators are urged to subscribe to the Summary of Airworthiness Directives which contains all previously published AD's and a biweekly supplemental service. The Summary of Airworthiness Directives is sold and distributed for the Superintendent of Documents by the FAA in Oklahoma City. AC 39-6L, Announcement of Availability--Summary of Airworthiness Directives, provides ordering information and subscription prices on these publications. AC 39-6L may be obtained, without cost, from the U.S. Department of Transportation, Utilization and Storage Section, M-443.2, Washington, D.C. 20590.

7. APPLICABILITY OF AD'S. Each AD contains an applicability statement specifying the product (aircraft, aircraft engine, propeller, or appliance) to which it applies. Some aircraft owners and operators mistakenly assume that AD's are not applicable to aircraft with experimental or restricted airworthiness certificates. Unless specifically limited, AD's apply to the make and model set forth in the applicability statement regardless of the kind of airworthiness certificate issued for the aircraft. Type certificate and airworthiness certification information are used to identify the product affected. When there is no reference to serial numbers, all serial numbers are affected. Limitations may be placed on applicability by specifying the serial number or number series to which the AD is applicable. The following are examples of AD applicability statements:

a. "Applies to Robin RA-15-150 airplanes." This statement makes the AD applicable to all airplanes of the model listed, regardless of type of airworthiness certificate issued to the aircraft and includes standard, restricted, limited, or experimental airworthiness certificates.

b. "Applies to Robin RA-15-150 airplanes except those certificated in the restricted category." This statement, or one similarly worded, incorporates all airplanes of the model listed, except those in the restricted category and is applicable to experimental aircraft.

c. "Applies to Robin RA-15-150 airplanes certificated in all categories excluding experimental aircraft." This statement incorporates all airplanes including restricted category of the model listed except those issued experimental certificates.

8. <u>AD COMPLIANCE</u>. AD's are regulations issued under FAR Part 39. Therefore, no person may operate a product to which an AD applies, except in accordance with the provisions of the AD. It should be understood that to "operate" not only means piloting the aircraft, but also causing or authorizing the product to be used. Compliance with emergency AD's can be a problem for operators of leased aircraft. The FAA has no means available for making notification to other than registered owners. Therefore, it is important that owners of leased aircraft make the AD information available to the operators leasing their aircraft as expeditiously as possible. Unless this is done, the lessee may not be aware of the AD and safety may be jeopardized.

9. <u>COMPLIANCE TIME OR DATE</u>.

   a. <u>The belief that AD compliance</u> is only required at the time of a required inspection, e.g., at 100 hours of annual inspection is <u>not</u> correct. The required compliance time is specified in each AD, and no person may operate the affected product after expiration of that stated compliance time without an exemption or a special flight authorization when the AD specifically permits such operation.

   b. <u>Compliance requirements specified in AD's</u> are established for safety reasons and may be stated in numerous ways. Some AD's are of such a serious nature they require compliance before further flight. In some instances the AD authorizes flight, provided a ferry permit is obtained, but without such authorization in the AD, further flight is prohibited. Other AD's express compliance time in terms of a specific number of hours of operation, for example, "compliance required within the next 50-hours time in service after the effective date of this AD." Compliance times may also be expressed in operational terms such as, "within the next 10 landings after the effective date of this AD." For turbine engines, compliance times are often expressed in terms of cycles. A cycle normally consists of an engine start, takeoff operation, landing, and engine shutdown. When a direct relationship between airworthiness and calendar time is identified, compliance time may be expressed as a calendar date. Another aspect of compliance times to be emphasized is that not all AD's have a one-time compliance. Repetitive inspections at specified intervals after initial compliance may be required. Repetitive inspection is used in lieu of a fix because of costs or until a fix is developed.

10. <u>ADJUSTMENTS IN COMPLIANCE REQUIREMENTS</u>. In some instances, a compliance time other than that specified in the AD would be advantageous to the owner/operator. In recognition of this need, and when equivalent safety can be shown, flexibility is provided by a statement in the AD allowing adjustment of the specified interval. When adjustment authority is provided in an AD, owners or operators desiring to make an adjustment are required to submit data substantiating their proposed adjustment to their FAA district office for consideration. The person authorized to approve adjustments in compliance requirements is normally identified in the AD.

11. <u>EQUIVALENT MEANS OF COMPLIANCE</u>. Most AD's indicate the acceptability of an equivalent means of compliance. It cannot be assumed that only one specific repair, modification, or inspection method is acceptable to correct an unsafe

condition; therefore, development of alternatives is not precluded. An equivalent means of compliance must be substantiated and "FAA approved." Normally the person authorized to approve an alternate method of compliance is indicated by title and address on the AD.

12. <u>RESPONSIBILITY FOR AD COMPLIANCE AND RECORDATION</u>. Responsibility for AD compliance always lies with the registered owner or operator of the aircraft.

    a. <u>This responsibility</u> may be met by ensuring that certificated and appropriately rated maintenance persons accomplish the maintenance required by the AD and properly record it in the maintenance records. This must be accomplished within the compliance time specified in the AD or the aircraft may not be operated.

    b. <u>Maintenance persons</u> may also have direct responsibility for AD compliance, aside from the times when AD compliance is the specific work contracted for by the owner/operator. When a 100-hour, annual, or progressive inspection, or an inspection required under FAR Parts 125 or 135 is accomplished, FAR Section 43.15(a) requires the person performing the inspection to perform it so that <u>all</u> applicable airworthiness requirements are met, which includes compliance with AD's.

    c. <u>Maintenance persons</u> should note that even though an inspection of the complete aircraft is not made, if the inspection conducted is a Progressive Inspection, an inspection required by FAR Part 125 determination of AD compliance for those portions of the aircraft inspected is required.

    d. <u>For aircraft inspected</u> in accordance with a continuous inspection program under FAR Part 91, Section 91.169(f), inspection persons are required to comply with AD's only when the portions of the inspection program provided to them require compliance. The program may require a determination of AD compliance for the entire aircraft by a general statement, or compliance with AD's applicable only to portions of the aircraft being inspected, or it may not require compliance at all. This does not mean AD compliance is not required at the compliance time or date specified in the AD. It only means that the owner or operator has elected to handle AD compliance apart from the inspection program. The owner or operator remains fully <u>responsible</u> for AD compliance.

    e. <u>The person accomplishing the AD</u> is required by FAR Part 43, Section 43.9, to record AD compliance. The entry must include those items specified in FAR Section 43.9(a)(1) through (a)(4). The owner is required, by FAR Part 91, Section 91.165, to ensure that maintenance personnel make appropriate entries and, by FAR Section 91.173, to maintain those records. It should be noted that there is a difference between the records required to be kept under FAR Section 91.173 and those FAR Section 43.9 requires maintenance personnel to make. Owners and operators may add this required information themselves or request maintenance personnel to include it in the entry they make. In either case, the owner/operator is responsible for keeping proper records.

    f. <u>Certain AD's permit pilots to perform</u> checks of some items under <u>specific conditions</u>. The AD's normally include recording requirements which are the same as those specified in FAR Section 43.9. However, if the AD does not include recording requirements for the pilot, FAR Parts 43 and 91,

Section 91.173(a)(1) and (a)(2), require the owner/operator to make and keep certain minimum records for specific times. The person who accomplished the work, who returned the aircraft to service, and the status of AD compliance are among these required records.

13. SOME AD'S REQUIRE REPETITIVE OR PERIODIC INSPECTION. In order to provide for flexibility in administering such AD's, an AD may provide for adjustment of the inspection interval to coincide with inspections required by FAR Part 91, or other regulations. The conditions under which this may be done and approval requirements are stated in the AD. If the AD does not contain such provisions, adjustments are not permitted. However, amendment, modification, or adjustment of the terms of the AD may be requested by contacting the office which issued the AD or by the petition procedures provided in FAR Part 11.

14. SUMMARY. The registered owner or operator of the aircraft is responsible for compliance with AD's applicable to airframes, powerplants, propellers, appliances, and parts and components thereof for all aircraft they operate. Maintenance personnel are also responsible for AD compliance when they accomplish an inspection required by FAR Part 91.

William T. Brennan
Acting Director of Flight Standards

**U.S. Department
of Transportation**

**Federal Aviation
Administration**

Advisory
Circular

Subject: MAINTENANCE RECORDS	Date: 1/9/84 Initiated by: AWS-340	AC No: 43-9B Change:

1. PURPOSE. This advisory circular (AC) discusses maintenance record requirements under Federal Aviation Regulations (FAR) Part 43, Sections 43.9, 43.11,
Part 91, Section 91.173, and the related responsibilities of owners, operators,
and persons performing maintenance, preventive maintenance, and alterations.

2. CANCELLATION. AC 43-9A, Maintenance Records: General Aviation Aircraft,
dated September 9, 1977, is cancelled.

3. RELATED FAR'S. FAR Parts 1, 43, 91, and 145.

4. BACKGROUND. The maintenance record requirements of Parts 43 and 91 have
remained essentially the same for several years. Certain areas, however,
continue to be misunderstood and changes to both Parts have recently been made.
Those misunderstood areas and the recent changes necessitate this reiteration of
Federal Aviation Administration (FAA) policy and an explanation of the changes.

5. DISCUSSION. Proper management of an aircraft operation begins with, and
depends upon, a good maintenance record system. Properly executed and retained
records provide owners, operators, and maintenance persons information essential
in: controlling scheduled and unscheduled maintenance; evaluating the quality of
maintenance sources; evaluating the economics and procedures of maintenance
programs; troubleshooting; and eliminating the need for reinspection and/or
rework to establish airworthiness. Only that information required to be a part
of the maintenance record should be included and retained. Voluminous and
irrelevant entries reduce the value of records in meeting their purposes.

6. MAINTENANCE RECORD REQUIREMENTS.

   a. Responsibilities. Aircraft maintenance recordkeeping is a responsibility shared by the owner/operator and maintenance persons, with the ultimate
responsibility assigned to the owner/operator by FAR Part 91, Section 91.165.
Sections 91.165 and 91.173 set forth the requirements for owners and operators,
while FAR Part 43, Sections 43.9 and 43.11 contain the requirements for
maintenance persons. In general, the requirements for owners/operators and
maintenance persons are the same; however, some small differences exist. These
differences are discussed in this AC under the rule in which they exist.

b. <u>Maintenance Record Entries Required.</u> Section 91.165 requires each owner
or operator to ensure that maintenance persons make appropriate entries in the
maintenance records to indicate the aircraft has been approved for return to
service. Thus, the prime responsibility for maintenance records lies with the
owner or operator. Section 43.9(a) requires persons performing maintenance,
preventive maintenance, rebuilding, or alteration to make entries in the
maintenance record of the equipment worked on. Maintenance persons, therefore,
share the responsibility for maintenance records.

c. <u>Maintenance Records are to be Retained.</u> Section 91.173(a) sets forth
the minimum content requirements and retention requirements for maintenance
records. Maintenance records may be kept in any format which provides record
continuity, includes required contents, lends itself to the addition of new
entries, provides for signature entry, and is not confusing. Section 91.173(b)
requires records of maintenance, alteration, and required or approved inspections to be retained until the work is repeated, superseded by other work, or
for 1 year. It also requires the records, specified in Section 91.173(a)(2), to
be retained and transferred with the aircraft at the time of sale.

> NOTE: Section 91.173(a) contains an exception regarding work accomplished
> in accordance with Section 91.171. This <u>does not</u> exclude the making of
> entries for this work, but applies to the <u>retention</u> period of the records
> for work done in accordance with this section. The exclusion is necessary
> since the retention period of 1 year is inconsistent with the 24-month
> interval of test and inspection specified in Section 91.171. Entries for
> work done per this section are to be retained for 24 months or until the
> work is repeated or superseded.

d. <u>Section 91.173(a)(1).</u> This section requires a record of maintenance,
for each aircraft (including the airframe) and each engine, propeller, rotor,
and appliance of an aircraft. This <u>does not</u> require separate or individual
records for each of these items. It <u>does</u> require the information specified in
Sections 91.173(a)(1) through 91.173(a)(2)(vi) to be kept for each item as
appropriate. As a practical matter, many owners and operators find it advantageous to keep separate or individual records since it facilitates transfer
of the record with the item when ownership changes. Section 91.173(a)(1) has
no counterpart in Section 43.9 or Section 43.11.

e. <u>Section 91.173(a)(1)(i).</u> This section requires the maintenance record
entry to include "a description of the work performed." The description should
be in sufficient detail to permit a person unfamiliar with the work to understand what was done, and the methods and procedures used in doing it. When the
work is extensive, this results in a voluminous record and involves considerable
time. To provide for this contingency, the rule permits reference to technical
data acceptable to the Administrator in lieu of making the detailed entry.
Manufacturer's manuals, service letters, bulletins, work orders, FAA advisory
circulars, Major Repair and Alteration Forms (FAA Form 337), and others, which
accurately describe what was done, or how it was done, may be referenced.
Except for the documents mentioned, which are in common usage, referenced
documents are to be made a part of the maintenance records and retained in
accordance with Section 91.173(b). Certificated repair stations frequently
work on components shipped to them when, as a consequence, the maintenance

records are unavailable. To provide for this situation, repair stations should supply owners and operators with copies of work orders written for the work, in lieu of maintenance record entries. The work order copy must include the information required by Section 91.173(a)(1) through Section 91.173(a)(1)(iii), be made a part of the maintenance record, and retained per Section 91.173(b). This procedure is not the same as that for maintenance releases discussed in paragraph 17 of this AC, and it may not be used when maintenance records are available. Section 91.173(a)(1)(i) is identical to it's counterpart, Section 43.9(a)(1), which imposes the same requirements on maintenance persons.

f. Section 91.173(a)(1)(ii) is identical to Section 43.9(a)(2) and requires entries to contain the date the work accomplished was completed. This is normally the date upon which the work is approved for return to service. However, when work is accomplished by one person and approved for return to service by another, the dates may differ. Two signatures may also appear under this circumstance; however, a single entry in accordance with Section 43.9(a)(3) is acceptable.

g. Section 91.173(a)(1)(iii) differs slightly from Section 43.9(a)(4) in that it requires the entry to indicate only the signature and certificate number of the person approving the work for return to service, and does not require the type of certificate being exercised to be indicated as does Section 43.9(a)(4). This is a new requirement of Section 43.9(a)(4), which assists owners and operators in meeting their responsibilities. Maintenance persons may indicate the type of certificate exercised by using A, P, A&P, IA, or RS for mechanic with airframe rating, with powerplant rating, with both ratings, with inspection authorization, or repair station, respectively.

h. Section 91.173(a)(2) requires six items to be made a part of the maintenance record and maintained as such. Section 43.9 does not require maintenance persons to enter these items. Section 43.11 requires some of them to be part of entries made for inspections, but they are all the responsibility of the owner or operator. The six items are discussed as follows:

(1) Section 91.173(a)(2)(i) requires a record of total time in service to be kept for the airframe, each engine, and each propeller. FAR Part 1, Section 1.1, Definitions, defines "time in service," with respect to maintenance time records, as that time from the moment an aircraft leaves the surface of the earth until it touches it at the next point of landing. Section 43.9 does not require this to be part of the entries for maintenance, preventive maintenance, rebuilding, or alterations. However, Section 43.11 requires maintenance persons to make it a part of the entries for inspections made under Parts 91, 125, and Sections 135.411(a)(1) and 135.419. It is good practice to include time in service in all entries.

(i) Some circumstances impact the owner's or operator's ability to comply with Section 91.173(a)(2)(i). For example: in the case of rebuilt engines, the owner or operator would not have a way of knowing the "total time in service," since Section 91.175 permits the maintenance record to be discontinued and the engine time to be started at "zero." In this case, the maintenance record and "time in service," subsequent to the rebuild, comprise a satisfactory record.

(ii) <u>Many components, presently in service</u>, were put into service prior to the requirements to keep maintenance records on them. Propellers are probably foremost in this group. In these instances, practicable procedures for compliance with the record requirements must be used. For example: "total time in service" may be derived using the procedures described in paragraph 13, Lost or Destroyed Records, of this AC; or if records prior to the regulatory requirements are just not available from any source, "time in service" may be kept since last complete overhaul. Neither of these procedures is acceptable when life-limited-parts status is involved or when AD compliance is a factor. Only the actual record since new may be used in these instances.

(iii) <u>Sometimes engines are assembled from modules</u> (turbojet and some turbopropeller engines) and a true "total time in service" for the total engine is not kept. If owners and operators wish to take advantage of this modular design, then "total time in service" and a maintenance record for each module is to be maintained. The maintenance records specified in Section 91.173(a)(2) are to be kept with the module.

(2) <u>Section 91.173(a)(2)(ii)</u> requires the current status of life-limited parts to be part of the maintenance record. If "total time in service" of the aircraft, engine, propeller, etc., is entered in the record when a life-limited part is installed and the "time in service" of the life-limited part is included, the normal record of time in service automatically meets this requirement.

(3) <u>Section 91.173(a)(2)(iii)</u> requires the maintenance record to indicate the time since last overhaul of all items installed on the aircraft which are required to be overhauled on a specified time basis. The explanation in paragraph 6h(2) of this AC also applies to this requirement.

(4) <u>Section 91.173(a)(2)(iv)</u> deals with the current inspection status and requires it to be reflected in the maintenance record. Again, the explanation in paragraph 6h(2) is appropriate even though Section 43.11(a)(2) requires maintenance persons to determine "time in service" of the item being inspected and to include it as part of the inspection entry.

(5) <u>Section 91.173(a)(2)(v)</u> requires the current status of applicable airworthiness directives (AD) to be a part of the maintenance record. The record is to include, at minimum, the method used to comply with the AD, the AD number, and revision date; and if the AD has requirements for recurring action, the time in service and the date when that action is required. When AD's are accomplished, maintenance persons are required to include the items specified in Section 43.9(a)(2),(3), and (4) in addition to those required by Section 91.173(a)(2)(v). An example of a maintenance record format for AD compliance is contained in Appendix 1 of this AC.

(6) <u>Section 91.173(a)(2)(vi)</u>. In the past, the owner or operator has been permitted to maintain a list of current major alterations to the airframe, engine(s), propeller(s), rotor(s), or appliances. This procedure did not produce a record of value to the owner/operator or to maintenance persons in determining the continued airworthiness of the alteration since such a record was not sufficient detail. This section of the rule has now been <u>changed</u>. It now prescribes that copies of the FAA Form 337, issued for the alteration, be made a part of the maintenance record.

7. PREVENTIVE MAINTENANCE.

    a. Preventive maintenance is defined in Part 1, Section 1.1. Part 43,
Appendix A, paragraph (c) lists those items which a pilot may accomplish under
Section 43.3(g). Section 43.7 authorizes appropriately rated repair stations
and mechanics, and persons holding at least a private pilot certificate to
approve an aircraft for return to service after they have performed preventive
maintenance. All of these persons must record preventive maintenance
accomplished in accordance with the requirements of Section 43.9. Advisory
Circular (AC)43-12, Preventive Maintenance, (as revised) contains further
information on this subject.

    b. The type of certificate exercised when maintenance or preventive
maintenance is accomplished must be indicated in the maintenance record. Pilots
may use PP, CP, or ATP to indicate private, commercial, or airline transport
pilot certificate, respectively in approving preventive maintenance for return
to service. Pilots are not authorized by Section 43.3(g) to perform preventive
maintenance on aircraft when they are operated under Parts 121, 127, 129, or
135. Pilots may only approve for return to service preventive maintenance which
they themselves have accomplished.

8. REBUILT ENGINE MAINTENANCE RECORDS.

    a. Section 91.175 provides that "zero time" may be granted to an engine
that has been rebuilt by a manufacturer or an agency approved by the
manufacturer. When this is done, the owner/operator may use a new maintenance
record without regard to previous operating history.

    b. The manufacturer or an agency approved by the manufacturer that rebuilds
and grants zero time to an engine is required by Section 91.175 to provide a
signed statement containing: (1) the date the engine was rebuilt; (2) each
change made as required by an AD; and (3) each change made in compliance with
service bulletins, when the service bulletin specifically requests an entry to
be made.

    c. Section 43.2(b) prohibits the use of the term "rebuilt" in describing
work accomplished in required maintenance records or forms unless the component
worked on has had specific work functions accomplished. These functions are
listed in Section 43.2(b) and, except for testing requirements, are the same as
those set forth in Section 91.175. When terms such as "remanufactured,"
"reconditioned," or other terms coined by various aviation enterprises are used
in maintenance records, owners and operators cannot assume that the functions
outlined in Section 43.2(b) have been done.

9. RECORDING TACHOMETERS.

    a. Time-in-service recording devices. These devices sense such things as:
electrical power on, oil pressure, wheels on the ground, etc., and from these
conditions provide an indication of time in service. With the exception of
those which sense aircraft liftoff and touchdown, the indications are
approximate.

b. Some owners and operators mistakenly believe these devices may be used in lieu of keeping time in service in the maintenance record. While they are of great assistance in arriving at time in service, such instruments, alone, do not meet the requirements of Section 91.173. For example, when the device fails and requires change, it is necessary to enter time in service and the instrument reading at the change. Otherwise, record continuity is lost.

10. MAINTENANCE RECORDS FOR AD COMPLIANCE. This subject is covered in AC 39-7, Airworthiness Directives for General Aviation Aircraft, as revised. A separate record may be kept for the airframe and each engine, propeller, rotor, and appliance, but is not required. This would facilitate record searches when inspection is needed, and when an engine, propeller, rotor, or appliance is removed, the record may be transferred with it. Such records may also be used as a schedule for recurring inspections. The format, shown in Appendix 1, is a suggested one, and adherence is not mandatory. Owners should be aware that they may be responsible for noncompliance with AD's when their aircraft are leased to foreign operators. They should, therefore, ensure that AD's are passed on to all their foreign lessees, and leases should be drafted to deal with this subject.

11. MAINTENANCE RECORDS FOR REQUIRED INSPECTIONS.

a. Section 43.11 contains the requirements for inspection entries. While these requirements are imposed on maintenance persons, owners and operators should become familiar with them in order to meet their responsibilities under Section 91.165.

b. The maintenance record requirements of Section 43.11 apply to the 100-hour, annual, and progressive inspections under Part 91; continuous inspection programs under Parts 91 and 125; Approved Airplane Inspection Programs under Part 135; and the 100-hour and annual inspections under Section 135.411(a)(1).

c. Misunderstandings persist regarding entry requirements for inspections under Section 91.169(e) (formerly Section 91.217). These requirements were formerly found in Section 43.9(a) and this contributed to misunderstanding. Appropriately rated mechanics without an inspection authorization (IA) are authorized to conduct these inspections and make the required entries. Particular attention should be given to Section 43.11(a)(7) in that it now requires a more specific statement than that previously required under Section 43.9. The entry, in addition to other items, must identify the inspection program used; identify the portion or segment of the inspection program accomplished; and contain a statement that the inspection was performed in accordance with the instructions and procedures for that program.

d. Questions continue regarding multiple entries for 100-hour/annual inspections. As discussed in paragraph 6d of this AC, neither Part 43 nor Part 91 requires separate records to be kept. Section 43.11, however, requires persons approving or disapproving equipment for return to service, after any required inspection, to make an entry in the record of that equipment. Therefore, when an owner maintains a single record, the entry of the 100-hour or annual inspection is made in that record. If the owner maintains separate records for the airframe, powerplants, and propellers, the entry for the 100-hour or annual inspection is entered in each.

12. DISCREPANCY LISTS.

a. Prior to October 15, 1982, issuance of discrepancy lists (or lists of
defects) to owners or operators was appropriate only in connection with annual
inspections under Part 91; inspections under Section 135.411(a)(1) of Part 135;
continuous inspection programs under Part 125; and inspections under
Section 91.217 of Part 91. Now, Section 43.11 requires that a discrepancy list
be prepared by a person performing any inspection required by Parts 91, 125, or
Section 135.411(a)(1) of Part 135.

b. When a discrepancy list is provided to an owner or operator, it says in
effect, "except for these discrepancies, the item inspected is airworthy." It
is imperative, therefore, that inspections be complete and that all discrepancies appear in the list. When circumstances dictate that an inspection be
terminated before it is completed, the maintenance record should clearly
indicate that the inspection was discontinued. The entry should meet all the
other requirements of Section 43.11.

c. It is no longer a requirement that copies of discrepancy lists be
forwarded to the local FAA District Office.

d. Discrepancy lists (or lists of defects) are part of the maintenance
record and the owner/operator is responsible to maintain that record in
accordance with Section 91.173(b)(3).   The entry made by maintenance persons in
the maintenance record should reference the discrepancy list when a list is
issued.

13. LOST OR DESTROYED RECORDS. Occasionally, the records for an aircraft are
lost or destroyed. This can create a considerable problem in reconstructing the
aircraft records. First, it is necessary to reestablish the total time in
service of the airframe. This can be done by: reference to other records which
reflect the time in service; research of records maintained by repair
facilities; and reference to records maintained by individual mechanics, etc.
When these things have been done and the record is still incomplete, the
owner/operator may make a notarized statement in the new record describing the
loss and establishing the time in service based on the research and the best
estimate of time in service.

a. The current status of applicable AD's may present a more formidable
problem. This may require a detailed inspection by maintenance personnel to
establish that the applicable AD's have been complied with. It can readily be
seen that this could entail considerable time, expense and, in some instances,
might require recompliance with the AD.

b. Other items required by Section 91.173(a)(2), such as the current
status of life-limited parts, time since last overhaul, current inspection
status, and current list of major alterations, may present difficult problems.
Some items may be easier to reestablish than others, but all are problems.
Losing maintenance records can be troublesome, costly, and time consuming.
Safekeeping of the records is an integral part of a good record system.

14. COMPUTERIZED RECORDS. There is a growing trend toward computerized maintenance records. Many of these systems are offered to owners/operators on a commercial basis. While these are excellent scheduling systems, alone, they normally do not meet the requirements of Sections 43.9 or 91.173. The owner/ operator who uses such a system is required to ensure that it provides the information required by Section 91.173, including signatures. If not, modification to make them complete is the owners/operators responsibility and the responsibility may not be delegated.

15. PUBLIC AIRCRAFT. Prospective purchasers of aircraft, that have been used as public aircraft, should be aware that public aircraft are not subject to the certification and maintenance requirements in the FAR's and may not have records which meet the requirements of Section 91.173. Considerable research may be involved in establishing the required records when these aircraft are purchased and brought into civil aviation. The aircraft may not be certificated or used without such records.

16. LIFE-LIMITED PARTS.

    a. Present day aircraft and powerplants commonly have life-limited parts installed. These life limits may be referred to as retirement times, service life limitations, parts retirement limitations, retirement life limits, life limitations, or other such terminology and may be expressed in hours, cycles of operation, or calendar time. They are set forth in type certificate data sheets, AD's, and operator's operations specifications, FAA-approved maintenance programs, the limitations section of FAA-approved airplane or rotorcraft flight manuals, and manuals required by operating rules.

    b. Section 91.173(a)(2)(ii) requires the owner or operator of an aircraft with such parts installed to have records containing the current status of these parts. Many owners/operators have found it advantageous to have a separate record for such parts showing the name of the part, part number, serial number, date of installation, total time in service, date removed, and signature and certificate number of the person installing or removing the part. A separate record, as described, facilitates transferring the record with the part in the event the part is removed and later reinstalled or installed on another aircraft or engine. If a separate record is not kept, the aircraft record must contain sufficient information to clearly establish the status of the life-limited parts installed.

17. MAINTENANCE RELEASE.

    a. In addition to those requirements discussed previously in this AC, Section 43.9 requires that major repairs and alterations be recorded as indicated in Appendix B of Part 43, (i.e., on FAA Form 337). An exception is provided in paragraph (b) of that appendix which allows repair stations certificated under Part 145 to use a maintenance release in lieu of the form for major repairs (and only major repairs).

    b. The maintenance release must contain the information specified in paragraph (b)(3) of Appendix B of Part 43, be made a part of the aircraft

maintenance record, and retained by the owner/operator as specified in
Section 91.173. The maintenance release is usually a special document (normally
a tag) and is attached to the product when it is approved for return to service.
The maintenance release may, however, be on a copy of the work order written for
the product. When this is done (it may be used only for major repairs) the
entry on the work order must meet paragraph (b)(3) of the appendix.

c. Some repair stations use what they call a maintenance release for other than
major repairs. This is sometimes a tag and sometimes information on a work
order. When this is done, all of the requirements of Section 43.9 must be met
(those of (b)(3) of the appendix are not applicable) and the document is to be
made and retained as part of the maintenance records under Section 91.173. This
was discussed in paragraph 6e of this AC.

18. FAA FORM 337.

a. Major repairs and alterations are to be recorded on FAA Form 337, Major
Repair and Alteration, as stated in paragraph 17. This form is executed by the
person making the repair or alteration. Provisions are made on the form for a
person other than that person performing the work to approve the repair or
alteration for return to service.

b. These forms are now required to be made part of the maintenance record
of the product repaired or altered and retained in accordance with
Section 91.173.

c. Detailed instructions for use of this form are contained in AC 43.9-1D,
Instructions for Completion of FAA Form 337, Major Repair and Alteration.

d. Some manufacturers have initiated a policy of indicating, on their
service letters and bulletins, and other documents dealing with changes to their
aircraft, whether or not the changes constitute major repairs or alterations.
They also indicate when, in their opinion, a Form 337 lies with the person
accomplishing the repairs or alterations and cannot be delegated. When there is
a question, it is advisable to contact the local office of the FAA for guidance.

19. TESTS AND INSPECTIONS FOR ALTIMETER SYSTEMS, ALTITUDE REPORTING EQUIPMENT,
AND ATC TRANSPONDERS. The recordation requirements for these tests and
inspections are the same as for other maintenance. There are essentially three
tests and inspections, (the altimeter system, the transponder system, and the
data correspondence test) each of which may be subdivided relative to who may
perform specific portions of the test. The basic authorization for performing
these tests and inspections, found in Section 43.3, are supplemented by
Sections 91.171 and 91.172. When multiple persons are involved in the
performance of tests and inspections, care must be exercised to insure proper
authorization under these three sections and compliance with Sections 43.9 and
43.9(a)(3) in particular.

20. <u>BEFORE YOU BUY</u>. This is the proper time to take a close look at the maintenance records of any used aircraft you expect to purchase. A well-kept set of maintenance records, which properly identifies all previously performed maintenance, alterations, and AD compliances, is generally a good indicator of the aircraft condition. This is not always the case, but in any event, before you buy, require the owner to produce the maintenance records for your examination, and require correction of any discrepancies found on the aircraft or in the records. Many prospective owners have found it advantageous to have a reliable unbiased maintenance person examine the maintenance records, as well as the aircraft, before negotiations have progressed too far. If the aircraft is purchased, take the time to review and learn the system of the previous owner to ensure compliance and continuity when you modify or continue that system.

M. C. Beard
Director of Airworthiness

APPENDIX 1.   AIRWORTHINESS DIRECTIVE COMPLIANCE RECORD
(SUGGESTED FORMAT)

AIRWORTHINESS DIRECTIVE COMPLIANCE RECORD

*Aircraft, Engine, Propeller, Rotor, or Appliance: Make _____ Model _____ Ser.No. _____ N _____

AD Number and Amendment Number	Date Received	Subject	Compliance Due Date Hours/Other	Method of Compliance	Date of Compliance	Airframe Total Time In Service at Compliance	Component Total Time In Service at Compliance	One-Time	Recurring	Next Comp. Due Date Hours/Other	Authorized Signature, Certificate Type and Number	Remarks

*Suggest providing a page for each category.

**U.S. Department
of Transportation**

**Federal Aviation
Administration**

800 Independence Ave., S.W.
Washington, D.C. 20591

**U.S. Department
of Transportation**

**Federal Aviation
Administration**

Advisory
Circular

Subject: INSTRUCTIONS FOR COMPLETION OF FAA FORM 337 (OMB NO. 2120-0020), MAJOR REPAIR AND ALTERATION (AIRFRAME, POWERPLANT, PROPELLER, OR APPLIANCE)	**Date:** 5/21/87 **Initiated by:** AFS-340	**AC No:** 43.9-1E **Change:**

1. <u>PURPOSE</u>. This advisory circular (AC) provides instructions for completing Federal Aviation Administration (FAA) Form 337, Major Repair and Alteration (Airframe, Powerplant, Propeller, or Appliance).

2. <u>CANCELLATION</u>. AC 43.9-1D, Instructions for Completion of FAA Form 337 (OMB 04-R0060), Major Repair and Alteration (Airframe, Powerplant, Propeller, or Appliance), dated 9/5/79, is canceled.

3. <u>RELATED FEDERAL AVIATION REGULATIONS (FAR) SECTIONS</u>. FAR Part 43, Sections 43.5, 43.7, 43.9, and Appendix B.

4. <u>INFORMATION</u>. FAA Form 337 is furnished free of charge and is available at all FAA Air Carrier (ACDO), General Aviation (GADO), Manufacturing Inspection (MIDO), and Flight Standards (FSDO) district offices, and at all International Field Offices (IFO). The form serves two main purposes; one is to provide aircraft owners and operators with a record of major repairs or alterations indicating details and approval, and the other is to provide the FAA with a copy of the form for inclusion in the aircraft records at the FAA Aircraft Registration Branch, Oklahoma City, Oklahoma.

5. <u>INSTRUCTIONS FOR COMPLETING FAA FORM 337</u>. The person who performs or supervises a major repair or major alteration should prepare FAA Form 337. The form is executed at least in duplicate and is used to record major repairs and major alterations made to an aircraft, an airframe, powerplant, propeller, appliance, or spare part. The following instructions apply to corresponding items 1 through 8 of the form as illustrated in Appendix 1.

    a. <u>Item 1 - Aircraft</u>. Information to complete the "Make," "Model," and "Serial Number" blocks will be found on the aircraft manufacturer's identification plate. The "Nationality and Registration Mark" is the same as shown on AC Form 8050-3, Certificate of Aircraft Registration.

    b. <u>Item 2 - Owner</u>. Enter the aircraft owner's complete name and address as shown on AC Form 8050-3.

Note: When a major repair or alteration is made to a spare part or appliance, items 1 and 2 will be left blank, and the original and duplicate copy of the form will remain with the part until such time as it is installed on an aircraft. The person installing the part will then enter the required information in blocks 1 and 2, give the original of the form to the aircraft owner/operator, and forward the duplicate copy to the local FAA district office within 48 hours after the work is inspected.

c. Item 3 - For FAA Use Only. Approval may be indicated in Item 3 when the FAA determines that data to be used in performing a major alteration or a major repair complies with accepted industry practices and all applicable FAR. Approval is indicated in one of the following methods. (See paragraph 6b for further details.)

(1) Approval by examination of data only - one aircraft only: "The data identified herein complies with the applicable airworthiness requirements and is approved for the above described aircraft, subject to conformity inspection by a person authorized in FAR Part 43, Section 43.7."

(2) Approval by physical inspection, demonstration, testing, etc., of the data and aircraft - one aircraft only: "The alteration (or repair) identified herein complies with the applicable airworthiness requirements and is approved for the above described aircraft, subject to conformity inspection by a person authorized in FAR Part 43, Section 43.7."

(3) Approval by examination of data only - duplication on identical aircraft. "The alteration identified herein complies with the applicable airworthiness requirements and is approved for duplication on identical aircraft make, model, and altered configuration by the original modifier."

d. 4 - Unit Identification. The information blocks under item 4 are used to identify the airframe, powerplant, propeller, or appliance repaired or altered. It is only necessary to complete the blocks for the unit repaired or altered.

e. Item 5 - Type. Enter a checkmark in the appropriate column to indicate if the unit was repaired or altered.

f. Item 6 - Conformity Statement.

(1) "A" - Agency's Name and Address. Enter name of the mechanic, repair station, or manufacturer accomplishing the repair or alteration. Mechanics should enter their name and permanent mailing address. Manufacturers and repair stations should enter the name and address under which they do business.

(2) "B" - Kind of Agency. Check the appropriate box to indicate the type of person or organization who performed the work.

(3) "C" - Certificate Number. Mechanics should enter their mechanic certificate number in this block, e.g., 1305888. Repair stations should enter their air agency certificate number and the rating or ratings under which the work was performed, e.g., 1234, Airframe Class 3. Manufacturers should enter their type production or Supplemental Type Certificate (STC) number. Manufacturers of Technical Standard Orders (TSO) appliances altering these appliances should enter the TSO number of the appliance altered.

(4) "D" - Compliance Statement: This space is used to certify that the repair or alteration was made in accordance with the FAR. When work was performed or supervised by certificated mechanics not employed by a manufacturer or repair station, they should enter the date the repair or alteration was completed and sign their full name. Repair stations are permitted to authorize persons in their employ to date and sign this conformity statement.

g. Item 7 - Approval for Return to Service. FAR Part 43 establishes the conditions under which major repairs or alterations to airframes, powerplants, propellers, and/or appliances may be approved for return to service. This portion of the form is used to indicate approval or rejection of the repair or alteration of the unit involved and to identify the person or agency making the airworthiness inspection. Check the "approved" or "rejected" box to indicate the finding. Additionally, check the appropriate box to indicate who made the finding. Use the box labeled "other" to indicate a finding by a person other than those listed. Enter the date the finding was made. The authorized person who made the finding should sign the form and enter the appropriate certificate or designation number.

h. Item 8 - Description of Work Accomplished. A clear, concise, and legible statement describing the work accomplished should be entered in item 8 on the reverse side of FAA Form 337. It is important that the location of the repair or alteration, relative to the aircraft or component, be described. The approved data used as the basis for approving the major repair or alteration for return to service should be identified and described in this area.

(1) For example, if a repair was made to a buckled spar, the description entered in this part might begin by stating, "Removed wing from aircraft and removed skin from outer 6 feet. Repaired buckled spar 49 inches from tip in accordance with . . . ." and continue with a description of the repair. The description should refer to applicable FAR sections and to the FAA-approved data used to substantiate the airworthiness of the repair or alteration. If the repair or alteration is subject to

being covered by skin or other structure, a statement should be made certifying that a precover inspection was made and that covered areas were found satisfactory.

(2) Data used as a basis for approving major repairs or alterations for return to service must be FAA-approved prior to its use for that purpose and includes: FAR (e.g., airworthiness directives), AC's (e.g., AC 43.13-1A under certain circumstances), TSO's parts manufacturing approval (PMA), FAA-approved manufacturer's instructions, kits and service handbooks, type certificate data sheets, and aircraft specifications. Other forms of approved data would be those approved by a designated engineering representative (DER), a manufacturer holding a delegation option authorization (DOA), STC's, and, with certain limitations, previous FAA field approvals. Supporting data such as stress analyses, test reports, sketches, or photographs should be submitted with the FAA Form 337. These supporting data will be returned to the applicant by the local FAA district office since only FAA Form 337 is retained as a part of the aircraft records at Oklahoma City.

(3) If additional space is needed to describe the repair or alteration, attach sheets bearing the aircraft nationality and registration mark and the date work was completed.

(4) Showing weight and balance computations under this item is not required; however, it may be done. In all cases where weight and balance of the aircraft are affected, the changes should be entered in the aircraft weight and balance records with the date, signature, and reference to the work performed on the FAA Form 337 that required the changes.

6. ADMINISTRATIVE PROCESSING. At least an original and one duplicate copy of the FAA Form 337 will be executed. FAA district office processing of the forms and their supporting data will depend upon whether previously approved or non-previously approved data was used as follows:

a. Previously Approved Data. The forms will be completed as instructed in this AC ensuring that item 7, "Approval for Return to Service," has been properly executed. Give the original of the form to the aircraft owner or operator, and send the duplicate copy to the local FAA district office within 48 hours after the work is inspected.

b. Non-previously Approved Data. The forms will be completed as instructed in this AC, leaving item 7, "Approval for Return to Service," blank. Both copies of the form, with supporting data, will be sent to the local FAA district office. When the FAA determines that the major repair or alteration data complies with applicable regulations and is in conformity with accepted industry practices, data approval will be recorded by entering an appropriate statement in item 3, "For FAA Use Only." Both forms and supporting data will be returned to the applicant who will complete item 7, "Approval for Return to Service." The applicant will give the original of the form, with its supporting data, to the aircraft owner or operator and return the duplicate copy to the local FAA district office who will, in turn, forward it to the FAA Aircraft Registration Branch, Oklahoma City, Oklahoma, for inclusion in the aircraft records.

c. Signatures on FAA Form 337 have limited purposes:

(1) A signature in item 3, "For FAA Use Only," indicates approval of the data described in that section for use in accomplishing the work described under item 8 on the reverse of FAA Form 337.

(2) A signature in item 6, "Conformity Statement," is a certification by the person performing the work that it was accomplished in accordance with applicable FAR and FAA-approved data. The certification is only applicable to that work described under item 8 on the reverse of FAA Form 337.

Note: Neither of these signatures (subparagraph c(1) and c(2)) indicate FAA approval of the work described under item 8 for return to service.

(3) A signature in item 7, "Approval for Return to Service," does not signify FAA approval unless the box to the left of "FAA Flight Standards Inspector" or "FAA Designee" is checked. The other persons listed in item 7, are authorized to "approve for return to service" if the repair or alteration is accomplished using FAA-approved data, is performed in accordance with applicable FAR, and found to conform.

d. FAA Form 337 is not authorized for use on other than U.S.-registered aircraft. If a foreign civil air authority requests the form, as a record of work performed, it may be provided. The form should be executed in accordance with the FAR and this AC. The foreign authority should be notified on the form that it is not an official record and that it will not be recorded by the FAA Aircraft Registration Branch, Oklahoma City, Oklahoma.

e. FAR Part 43, Appendix B, Paragraph (b) authorizes FAA certificated repair stations to use a work order, in lieu of FAA Form 337, for only major repairs. Such work orders should contain all the information provided on the form and in no less detail; that is, the data used as a basis of approval should be identified, a certification that the work was accomplished using that data and in accordance with the FAR, a description of the work performed (as required in item 8 of the FAA Form 337), and approval for return to service must be indicated by an authorized person. Signature, kind of certificate, and certificate number must also appear in the record (reference FAR Section 43.9).

William T. Brennan
Acting Director of Flight Standards

APPENDIX 1. FAA FORM 337 (FRONT), MAJOR REPAIR AND
ALTERATION (AIRFRAME, POWERPLANT, PROPELLER,
OR APPLIANCE)

MAJOR REPAIR AND ALTERATION (Airframe, Powerplant, Propeller, or Appliance) US Department of Transportation Federal Aviation Administration		Form Approved OMB No. 2120-0020 **For FAA Use Only** Office Identification

INSTRUCTIONS: Print or type all entries. See FAR 43.9, FAR 43 Appendix B, and AC 43.9-1 (or subsequent revision thereof) for instructions and disposition of this form. This report is required by law (49 U.S.C. 1421). Failure to report can result in a civil penalty not to exceed $1,000 for each such violation (Section 901 Federal Aviation Act of 1958).

1. Aircraft

Make: Cessna Model: 182
Serial No.: 15-10521 Nationality and Registration Mark: N-3763

2. Owner

Name (As shown on registration certificate): William Taylor
Address (As shown on registration certificate): 36 Main Street, Cambria, Pennsylvania 15946

3. For FAA Use Only

The data identified herein complies with the applicable airworthiness requirements and is approved for the above described aircraft, subject to conformity inspection by a person authorized by FAR Part 43.
AEA-GADO-19   April 5, 1986   Ralph Burlingame
District Office   Date   Signature of FAA Inspector

4. Unit Identification

Unit	Make	Model	Serial No.	Repair	Alteration
AIRFRAME	(As described in Item 1 above)			X	
POWERPLANT					
PROPELLER					
APPLIANCE	Type / Manufacturer				

6. Conformity Statement

A. Agency's Name and Address: George Morris, High Street, Johnstown, Pennsylvania 15236
B. Kind of Agency: X U.S. Certificated Mechanic
C. Certificate No.: 1305888

D. I certify that the repair and/or alteration made to the unit(s) identified in item 4 above and described on the reverse or attachments hereto have been made in accordance with the requirements of Part 43 of the U.S. Federal Aviation Regulations and that the information furnished herein is true and correct to the best of my knowledge.

Date: March 19, 1987   Signature of Authorized Individual: George Morris

7. Approval for Return To Service

Pursuant to the authority given persons specified below, the unit identified in item 4 was inspected in the manner prescribed by the Administrator of the Federal Aviation Administration and is ☑ APPROVED ☐ REJECTED

BY: X Manufacturer
Date of Approval or Rejection: April 9, 1987
Certificate or Designation No.: 237412
Signature of Authorized Individual: Donald Pauley

FAA Form 337 (4-87)

FAA FORM 337 (BACK), MAJOR REPAIR AND ALTERATION
(AIRFRAME, POWERPLANT, PROPELLER, OR APPLIANCE)

NOTICE

Weight and balance or operating limitation changes shall be entered in the appropriate aircraft record. An alteration must be compatible with all previous alterations to assure continued conformity with the applicable airworthiness requirements.

---

8. Description of Work Accomplished
(If more space is required, attach additional sheets. Identify with aircraft nationality and registration mark and date work completed.)

1. Removed right wing from aircraft and removed skin from outer 6 feet. Repaired buckled spar 49 inches from tip in accordance with attached photographs and figure 1 of drawing dated March 6, 1987.

   DATE: March 15, 1987, inspected splice in Item 1 and found it to be in accordance with data indicated. Splice is okay to cover. Inspected internal and external wing assembly for hidden damage and condition.

   Donald Pauley

   Donald Pauley, A&P 237412 IA

2. Primed interior wing structure and replaced skin P/Ns 63-0085, 63-0086, and 63-00878 with same material, 2024-T3, .025 inches thick. Rivet size and spacing all the same as original and using procedures in Chapter 2, Section 3, of AC 43.13-1A, dated 1972.

3. Replaced stringers as required and installed 6 splices as per attached drawing and photographs.

4. Installed wing, rigged aileron, and operationally checked in accordance with manufacturer's maintenance manual.

5. No change in weight or balance.

                                   END

☐ Additional Sheets Are Attached

PREFACE

This pamphlet has been prepared by the Office of Flight Standards to answer questions most frequently asked about Federal Aviation Administration (FAA) certification of aviation mechanics.

If you still have some unanswered questions after reading through this pamphlet, you should discuss them with the personnel at any of the FAA offices shown in Appendix 1. They will be pleased to advise and assist you in obtaining your aviation mechanic certificate.

Comments regarding this publication should be directed to:

U.S. Department of Transportation
Federal Aviation Administration
Office of Flight Standards
Aircraft Maintenance Division, AFS-300
800 Independence Avenue, SW.
Washington, DC 20591

This Advisory Circular supersedes AC 65-11A, dated October 1971.

William T. Brennan
William T. Brennan
Acting Director of Flight Standards

Revised April 1987

CONTENTS

	Page
Certificate ratings and requirements......................	1
Medical certificate	1
Correspondence course	1
Experience requirements	2
Military experience	3
Documentary evidence	4
Foreign national documentation............................	5
Written tests	6
Retesting after failure	7
Reference materials	8
Federal Aviation Administration offices for persons outside the United States.......................	9

Appendix 1

Federal Aviation Administration District Offices...........	1-6

Appendix 2

Reference and Study Materials	1

QUESTIONS AND ANSWERS

1. Q. What aviation mechanic certificates and ratings are
        issued by FAA?

    A. FAA issues a single mechanic certificate with an Airframe
        (A) rating, or a Powerplant (P) rating, or both (A&P)
        ratings to qualified applicants.

2. Q. What are the requirements for a mechanic certificate (license)?

    A. The requirements are prescribed by Federal Aviation Regulations,
        Part 65, Certification: Airmen Other Than Flight Crewmembers.

        An applicant must be--

        1. At least 18 years old;

        2. Able to read, write, speak, and understand the English
        language (with certain exceptions permitted);

        3. Able to meet the experience, knowledge, and skill
        requirements for at least one rating; and

        4. Able to pass all the prescribed tests within a 24-month
        period.

3. Q. Are there any general educational prerequisites for obtaining
        the mechanic certificate?

    A. No; however, some employers may require a minimum of a high
        school education.

4. Q. Do I need a medical certificate for a mechanic certificate?

    A. No.

5. Q. If I have a physical defect, will it disqualify me from getting
        a mechanic certificate?

    A. No; however, some employers may have established physical
        requirements for employment as an aviation mechanic in their
        organization.

6. Q. I wish to prepare for the FAA mechanic tests by taking
        correspondence courses during my spare time. Which courses do
        you recommend?

    A. The FAA does not recognize any correspondence courses in
        lieu of practical experience or graduation from an FAA-
        approved aviation maintenance technician school.

7. Q. What is the difference between an FAA certificate and a license?

   A. No difference. The FAA mechanic certificate is frequently referred to as a license.

8. Q. Must I have an FAA mechanic certificate to get a job as an airline mechanic?

   A. No. Possession of an FAA mechanic certificate for employment by an air carrier is not a requirement of the Federal Aviation Regulations. It is often used by the air carriers as one of several hiring requirements.

9. Q. Can I work as an aviation mechanic without being certificated?

   A. Yes, providing you work under the supervision of a certificated person and do not release aircraft to service.

10. Q. Must I hold a mechanic certificate to work in a certificated repair station?

    A   No.

11. Q. Can I obtain the necessary experience and skill to qualify for a mechanic certificate and rating(s) without attending an FAA certificated aviation maintenance technician (mechanic) school?

    A. Yes. You can obtain the necessary experience and skill by obtaining employment with any facility engaged in the construction, maintenance, and/or alteration of aircraft, powerplants, and/or appliances.

12. Q. Will my experience as a noncertificated mechanic or repairman in a repair station be qualifying experience toward a mechanic certificate?

    A. Yes, providing the experience was on airframes, powerplants, or both.

13. Q   Does the FAA issue any specialist ratings for certificated mechanics, i.e., ground equipment specialist, welder, electronics specialist?

    A. No.

14. Q. I have 10 years of experience as an Armed Forces jet
       aircraft mechanic. Why do I have to demonstrate
       knowledge and skill in such areas as woodwork, welding,
       dope and fabric, weight and balance, etc., for a civil
       mechanic certificate?

    A. Mechanic certificate privileges allow mechanics to
       perform maintenance in a large number of areas. The
       holder of a mechanic certificate is relatively
       unrestricted as to working on any particular type of
       aircraft or to specialized maintenance functions.
       Therefore, the FAA must ensure that an applicant is
       competent to perform in the broad work areas in which he
       is privileged to function.

15. Q. I was an instrument specialist in the Armed Forces. If I
       get a mechanic certificate, will I be permitted to be in
       charge of maintenance of instruments in a certificated
       repair station?

    A. No, you must also have a repairman certificate (the same
       applies to propellers).

16. Q. Where can I get information about aviation mechanic jobs?

    A. Members of the Armed Forces should check with their
       service personnel office or Project Transition Officer
       for leads on job opportunities in civil aviation. Others
       may wish to write to the personnel department of any of
       the airlines and request information about job
       opportunities at their overhaul bases. Another source of
       information is the local U.S. Employment Service Office.

17. Q. I worked 10 hours a day, 6 days a week, for a total of
       3,120 hours as an A&P mechanic apprentice during the past
       year. Since this time is equal to the number of hours
       accumulated by working 40 hours a week for 18 months,
       does this comparable mechanic experience time qualify me
       to take the mechanic written tests?

    A. No. Federal Aviation Regulations, Part 65,
       Certification: Airmen Other Than Flight Crewmembers, does
       not provide for anything less than 18 months of practical
       experience for issuance of a mechanic certificate with a
       single rating, and 30 months of practical experience
       concurrently performing the duties appropriate to both
       the airframe and powerplant ratings for a certificate
       with both A&P ratings.

18. Q. How much aviation mechanic experience do I need to
        qualify for the mechanic certificate?

    A. A minimum of 18 months of appropriate experience for each
        rating or 30 months of concurrent experience for both
        ratings.

19. Q. Must I be a graduate of an FAA certificated aviation
        maintenance technician (mechanic) school to qualify to
        take the FAA mechanic written test?

    A. No, however, graduation from the appropriate course of a
        certificated aviation maintenance technician (mechanic)
        school is one way to meet the experience requirement.

20. Q. I am a U.S. citizen, living in the United States. I have
        more than 3 years of experience as an aviation
        mechanic, how do I get a mechanic certificate (license)?

    A. Visit any of the FAA Flight Standards District Offices
        listed in Appendix 1 and present your documentary
        evidence of experience to an FAA airworthiness inspector
        for his evaluation. If the FAA inspector approves your
        documentary evidence of experience, you will be permitted
        to take the FAA mechanic written test.

21. Q. What documents must be presented to an FAA inspector for
        evaluation prior to taking the written test?

    A. Applicants (U.S. citizens) for the written test should
        present documentary evidence from former or current
        employers indicating length and type of experience.
        Applicants who were aviation mechanics in the Armed
        Forces should present their Form DD-214, Certificate of
        Release or Discharge From Active Duty, which list their
        Military Occupational Speciality (MOS) codes, schools
        attended and length of service. In addition, those
        applicants should present documents that certify training
        received, length of time served in each MOS code and
        personal evaluation records. Those applicants who are in
        the Armed Forces should present documents certifying
        training received, personnel evaluation records, and a
        letter from either their Executive Officer or
        Classification Officer indicating length of military
        service, their MOS codes, and length of service in those
        codes.

Applicants (U.S. citizens or foreign nationals) who are graduates of an FAA-certificated aviation maintenance technician (mechanic) school should present their graduation certificate. In addition to the required documents, an applicant should be prepared to present appropriate personal identification to the FAA inspector.

22. Q. **What must a foreign national show to the FAA in order to take the airframe and powerplant mechanic examinations?**

A. A foreign applicant who graduated from an FAA-approved aviation maintenance technician (mechanic) school must present an appropriate graduation certificate or certificate of completion.

1. If located in the United States, a foreign applicant (without a certificate of graduation or completion) must show the following to an FAA airworthiness inspector:

A. The ability to read, write, speak, and understand the English language.
B. Positive identification (i.e., passport).
C. A signed and detailed original statement from their employer substantiating the specific types of maintenance performed and duration of each.
D. A detailed statement obtained from the foreign airworthiness authority of the country in which the experience was gained or from an advisor of the International Civil Aviation Organization that will validate the applicant's experience.
E. All documents presented to the inspector or advisor must be signed, dated originals, and traceable to the initiator.

2. If located outside the United States, a foreign applicant (without a certificate of graduation or completion) must show the following at the time of the application:

A. Proof that he worked on U.S.-registered aircraft or for a U.S. air carrier.
B. Positive identification.
C. A signed and detailed statement from their employer substantiating the specific type of maintenance performed and duration of each.
D. A detailed statement obtained from a foreign airworthiness authority of the country in which the experience was gained or from an advisor of the International Civil Aviation Organization that will validate the applicant's experience.

E.   All documents presented to the inspector or advisor must be signed, dated originals, and traceable to the initiator.

NOTE: Applicants are not required to read, write, speak, and understand the English language if employed outside the United States by a U.S. carrier; however, mechanic certificates issued to foreign applicants who are not fluent in the English language shall be endorsed "Valid Only Outside The United States."

23. Q.   If I meet the experience requirements for the mechanic certificate, can I take the required tests while still in the Armed Forces?

    A.   Yes.

24. Q.   Can I take the mechanic written, oral, and practical tests if I am in the Armed Forces and stationed overseas?

    A.   In some instances, yes. You should contact the FAA office responsible for the general area in which you are located and request information about the feasibility of taking the tests while stationed overseas. (See question 41 for further information.)

25. Q.   How do I obtain an FAA Form 8060-7, Airman's Authorization for Written Test?

    A.   When your experience has been evaluated and approved by an FAA district office inspector, you may take the written test immediately. If that is inconvenient, request the FAA inspector to issue FAA Form 8060-7 so that you may take the written test at a later time or a different place.

26. Q.   What are the written test questions like?

    A.   Written test questions are of the objective, multiple-choice type. Questions can be answered by marking the appropriate space on a special answer sheet furnished by the FAA. Sample questions will be found in the current issue of Advisory Circular 65-2, Airframe and Powerplant Mechanics Certification Guide. (For price and availability see answer to question 37.)

27. Q.   What materials should I bring with me to take the test?

    A.   The person conducting the written test will furnish all the necessary materials for taking the written test.

Textbooks or notes of any kind are forbidden in the
examination room.

28. Q. **What document(s) must be presented prior to taking the
        mechanic oral and practical tests?**

    A. An applicant for the oral and practical tests must
        present a valid AC Form 8080-2, Airman Written Test
        Report(s), indicating that all parts of the written test
        have been passed. In addition, applicants for the oral
        and practical test may present documentation of practical
        experience obtained through previous employment, or
        training schools, or in the military services. Such
        documentation may be used by an FAA inspector or
        Designated Mechanic Examiner when determining the oral
        and practical projects to be assigned during the test.

29. Q. **If an applicant fails any part of the written or oral and
        practical test(s), how soon may he/she apply for a
        retest?**

    A. An applicant who fails any part of the written or oral
        and practical test(s) may apply for retesting 30 days
        after the date he/she failed the test. Or, before the
        30 days have expired, an applicant may present a
        statement signed by an appropriately certificated
        mechanic or an appropriately certificated repairman
        indicating that the applicant has received additional
        instruction in each of the subjects failed, and the
        airman now considers that the applicant is ready for
        retesting.

30. Q. **Who administers the mechanic oral and practical tests?**

    A. Oral and practical tests are administered by FAA
        inspectors or by Designated Mechanic Examiners.

31. Q. **Where can I get a list of the Designated Mechanic
        Examiners in a particular section of the country?**

    A. A Designated Mechanic Examiners list may be obtained from
        the appropriate FAA district office listed in Appendix 1
        and in the current issue of Advisory Circular 183-32,
        FAA Designated Maintenance Technician Examiner
        Directory.

32. Q. **How much time is permitted for completion of the airframe
        written test? For the powerplant written test?**

    A. Applicants are given 5 hours to complete each test.

33. Q. Is there a fee for taking the written test?

A. If the test is given at an FAA district office there is no fee, however, if the written test is given by a Designated Written Test Examiner there is a fee to take the test.

34. Q. Is there a fee for taking the mechanic oral and practical tests?

A. If an FAA inspector administers the tests, there is no charge; however, the testing facility, tools, materials, and supplies must be furnished or arranged for by the applicant. If a Designated Mechanic Examiner administers the tests, he/she may charge a fee; however, he/she will furnish the testing facility, and can usually arrange to furnish the tools, materials, and necessary supplies.

35. Q. Can I take the mechanic written test at night or during the weekend?

A. Yes. Arrangements for taking written tests at night or on weekends can be made with some Designated Written Test Examiners. Check with the nearest FAA district office to the location where you want to take the test for the name of the Designated Written Test Examiner.

36. Q. What document must be presented prior to retaking a written test that was previously failed?

A. A valid AC Form 8080-2, Airman Written Test Report, for the preceding test.

37. Q. Where can I obtain more detailed information about the requirements, application procedures, and the tests for a mechanic certificate?

A. The current issue of Advisory Circular 65-2 contains detailed information about the certificate requirements, application procedures, and the mechanic written, oral, and practical tests. It is available from the Superintendent of Documents, U.S. Government Printing Office, Washington, D.C. 20402, for $5.00. When ordering, give the GPO catalog number for AC 65-2, which is SN-050-007-00331-5.

38. Q. Are there any other reference materials?

A. Yes, there are many good commercial textbooks available

on loan from public libraries or may be purchased
directly from the publishers. The Superintendent of
Documents, U.S. Government Printing Office, Washington,
D.C. 20402, will provide free of charge, on request,
Guide to Federal Aviation Administration Publications
(FAA-APA-PG-9), which provides titles of aviation
publications available from GPO and the cost of each.
See Appendix 2 for further information.

39. Q. **Is there a charge for issuing the certificate?**

A. No.

40. Q. **For how long a period is the mechanic certificate valid?**

A. The mechanic certificate is valid until surrendered,
suspended, or revoked.

41. Q. **To whom should I write requesting an appointment to take
an FAA test outside the United States?**

A. If an applicant resides in Mexico, contact:

Federal Aviation Administration
Southwest Region
P.O. Box 1689
Fort Worth, TX 76101

If an applicant resides in Japan or the Far East,
contact:

Federal Aviation Administration
Flight Standards District Office No. 13
218 Lagoon Drive
Room 215
Honolulu, HI 96819

If an applicant resides in Central or South America,
contact:

Federal Aviation Administration
International Field Office
P. O. Box 592815
Miami International Airport
Miami, FL 33159

If an applicant resides in Africa (except Northern Africa) contact:

Federal Aviation Administration
American Embassy
B. P. 49
Dakar Senegal

If an applicant resides in Europe, Northern Africa, or the Middle East, contact:

Federal Aviation Administration
International Field Office No. 51
c/o American Consulate General
Siesmayer Strasse 21
Frankfurt/Main Germany.

If an applicant resides in Canada, contact:

The nearest local FAA district office (see Appendix 1).

APPENDIX 1. FAA DISTRICT OFFICES

FAA General Aviation District Offices (GADOs) and Flight Standards District Offices (FSDOs) are listed by state. You should contact the district office closest to your residence. If you reach the wrong office, you will be told which office to contact.

ALABAMA

FSDO 67B
Municipal Airport
FSS/WB Building
6500 43rd Avenue North
Birmingham, AL 35206
Phone: (205) 254-1557

ALASKA

FSDO 61
3788 University Avenue
Fairbanks, AK 99701
Phone: (907) 452-1276

FSDO 62
A.I.R. Center Building
9610 Shell Simmons Drive
Juneau, AK 99803
Phone: (907) 789-0231

FSDO 63
6601 South Airpark Place
Suite 216
Anchorage, AK 99502
Phone: (907) 243-1902

ARIZONA

FSDO 7
Scottsdale Municipal Airport
15041 North Airport Drive
Scottsdale, AZ 85260
Phone: (602) 241-2561

ARKANSAS

FSDO 65
Adams Field
FAA Building, Room 201
Little Rock, AR 72202
Phone: (501) 378-5565

CALIFORNIA

FSDO 1
Van Nuys Airport
Suite 316
7120 Hayvenhurst Avenue
Van Nuys, CA 91406
Phone: (818) 904-6291

FSDO 2
San Jose Municipal Airport
1387 Airport Boulevard
San Jose, CA 95110
Phone: (408) 291-7681

FSDO 4
Fresno Air Terminal
Suite 110
4955 East Anderson
Fresno, CA 93727
Phone: (209) 487-5306

FSDO 5
Long Beach Airport
2815 East Spring Street
Long Beach, CA 90806
Phone: (213) 426-7134

FSDO 8
Riverside Municipal Airport
6961 Flight Road
Riverside, CA 92504
Phone: (714) 351-6701

FSDO 9
Montgomery Field Airport
Suite 110
8665 Gibbs Drive
San Diego, CA 92123
Phone: (619) 293-5281

FSDO 10
5885 West Imperial Highway
Los Angeles, CA 90045
Phone: (213) 215-2150

FSDO 12
Sacramento Executive Airport
6107 Freeport Boulevard
Sacramento, CA 95822
Phone: (916) 551-1721

FSDO 14
Oakland International Airport
Earhart Road, Building L-105
P.O. Box 2397, Airport Station
Oakland, CA 94614
Phone: (415) 273-7155

COLORADO

FSDO 60 (General Aviation)
Jefferson County Airport
FAA Building 1
Broomfield, CO 80020
Phone: (303) 466-7326

FSDO 60
10455 East 25th Avenue
Suite 202
Aurora, CO 80010
Phone: (303) 340-5400

APPENDIX 1.   FAA DISTRICT OFFICES (CONTINUED)

CONNECTICUT

FSDO 63
Barnes Municipal Airport
Administration Building, First Floor
Westfield, MA 01085
Phone: (413) 568-3121

DELAWARE

FSDO 63
Scott Plaza No. 2
Fourth Floor
Philadelphia, PA 19113
Phone: (215) 596-0673

DISTRICT OF COLUMBIA

FSDO 62
Dulles International Airport
600 West Service Road
Chantilly, VA 20041
Phone: (202) 557-5360

FLORIDA

FSDO 64
St Petersburg-Clearwater Airport
Terminal Building, West Wing
Clearwater, FL 33520
Phone: (813) 531-1434

FSDO 65
Miami International Airport
Perimeter Road and N.W. 20th Street
FAA Building 3050
P.O. Box 592015
Miami, FL 33159
Phone: (305) 526-2607

FSDO 64J
Craig Municipal Airport
FAA Building
855 St John's Bluff Road
Jacksonville, FL 32211
Phone: (904) 641-7311

GEORGIA

FSDO 67
3420 Norman Berry Drive
Suite 430
College Park, GA 30354
Phone: (404) 763-7265

HAWAII

FSDO 13
Honolulu International Airport
Air Service Corporation Building
Room 215
218 Lagoon Drive
Honolulu, HI 96819
Phone: (808) 836-0615

IDAHO

FSDO 67A
Boise Airport
3975 Rickenbacker Street
Boise, ID 83705
Phone: (208) 334-1238

ILLINOIS

GADO 3
DuPage County Airport
P.O. Box H
West Chicago, IL 60185
Phone: (312) 377-4516

GADO 19
Capitol Airport
No. 3 North Airport Drive
North Quadrant
Springfield, IL 62708
Phone: (217) 492-4238

INDIANA

GADO 10
Indianapolis International Airport
6801 Pierson Drive
Indianapolis, IN 46241
Phone: (317) 247-2491

GADO 18
Michiana Regional Airport
1843 Commerce Drive
South Bend, IN 46628
Phone: (219) 236-8480

IOWA

FSDO 61
3021 Army Post Road
Des Moines, IA 50321
Phone: (515) 285-9895

APPENDIX 1.   FAA DISTRICT OFFICES (CONTINUED)

KANSAS

FSDO 64
Mid Continent Airport
Flight Standards Building
Wichita, KS   67209
Phone: (316) 926–4462

KENTUCKY

FSDO 63L
Bowman Field
FAA Building
Louisville, KY   40205
Phone: (502) 582–6116

LOUISIANA

FSDO 62
Ryan Airport
9191 Plank Road
Baton Rouge, LA   70811
Phone: (504) 356–5701

MAINE

FSDO 65
Portland International Jetport
General Aviation Terminal
Portland, ME   04102
Phone: (207) 774–4484

MARYLAND

GADO 21
Baltimore–Washington
International Airport
North Administration Building
Elm Road
Baltimore, MD   21240
Phone: (301) 859–5780

MASSACHUSETTS

FSDO 61
Civil Air Terminal Building
Second Floor
Hanscome Field
Bedford, MA   01730
Phone: (617) 273–7231

FSDO 63
Barnes Municipal Airport
Administration Building
Westfield, MA   01085
Phone: (413) 568–3121

MICHIGAN

GADO 8
Kent County International Airport
5500 44th Street, S.E.
Grand Rapids, MI   49508
Phone: (616) 456–2427

FSDO 63
Willow Run Airport
8800 Beck Road
Belleville, MI   48111
Phone: (313) 485–2550

MINNESOTA

GADO 14
Minneapolis–St. Paul International Airport
Room 201
6201 34th Avenue South
Minneapolis, MN   55450
Phone: (612) 725–3341

MISSISSIPPI

FSDO 63J
Jackson Municipal Airport
FAA Building
P.O. Box 6273, Pearl Branch
Jackson, MS   39208
Phone: (601) 960–4633

MISSOURI

FSDO 62
FAA Building
9275 Genaire Drive
Berkeley, MO   63134
Phone: (314) 425–7102

FSDO 63
Kansas City International Airport
525 Mexico City Avenue
Kansas City, MO   64153
Phone: (816) 243–3800

MONTANA

FSDO 65
Helena Airport
FAA Building, Room 3
Helena, MT   59601
Phone: (406) 449–5270

FSDO 65A
Billings Logan International Airport
Administration Building, Room 216
Billings, MT   59101
Phone: (406) 245–6179

APPENDIX 1. FAA DISTRICT OFFICES (CONTINUED)

NEBRASKA

FSDO 65
Lincoln Municipal Airport
General Aviation Building
Lincoln, NE 68524
Phone: (402) 471-5485

NEVADA

FSDO 6
241 East Reno Avenue
Suite 200
Las Vegas, NV 89119
Phone: (702) 388-6482

FSDO 11
601 South Rock Boulevard
Suite 102
Reno, NV 89502
Phone: (702) 784-5321

NEW HAMPSHIRE

FSDO 65
Portland International Jetport
General Aviation Terminal
Portland, ME 04102
Phone: (207) 774-4484

NEW JERSEY

FSDO 61
Teterboro Airport
150 Riser Road
Teterboro, NJ 07608
Phone: (201) 288-1745

NEW MEXICO

FSDO 61
2402 Kirtland Drive, S.E.
Albuquerque, NM 87106
Phone: (505) 247-0156

NEW YORK

GADO 1
Albany County Airport
CFR & M Building
Albany, NY 12211
Phone: (518) 869-8482

GADO 11
Republic Airport
Administration Building
Farmingdale, NY 11735
Phone: (516) 694-5530

GADO 17
Rochester Monroe County Airport
1295 Scottsville Road
Rochester, NY 14624
Phone: (716) 263-5880

NORTH CAROLINA

FSDO 66
Smith Reynolds Airport
Terminal Building
Second Floor
Winston Salem, NC 27105
Phone: (919) 761-3147

GADO 66C
Douglas Municipal Airport
FAA Building
5318 Morris Field Drive
Charlotte, NC 28208
Phone: (704) 392-3214

FSDO 66R
Raleigh-Durham Terminal B
Route 1, Box 486A
Morrisville, NC 27560
Phone: (919) 755-4240

NORTH DAKOTA

FSDO 64
Hector Airport
Administration Building, Room 216
P.O. Box 5496
Fargo, ND 58105
Phone: (701) 232-8949

OHIO

FSDO 65
4242 Airport Road
Lunken Airport Executive Building
Cincinnati, OH 45226
Phone: (513) 684-2183

FSDO 65
Cleveland Hopkins International Airport
Federal Facilities Office Building
Cleveland, OH 44135
Phone: (216) 267-0220

FSDO 65
Port Columbus International Airport
Lane Aviation Building, Room 234
4393 East 17 Avenue
Columbus, OH 43219
Phone: (614) 469-7476

APPENDIX 1. FAA DISTRICT OFFICES (CONTINUED)

OKLAHOMA

FSDO 67
Wiley Post Airport
FAA Building, Room 111
Bethany, OK   73008
Phone: (405) 789-5220

OREGON

FSDO 64
Portland–Hillsboro Airport
3355 N.E. Cornell Road
Hillsboro, OR   97124
Phone: (503) 221-2104

FSDO 64A
Mahlon–Sweet Airport
90606 Greenhill Road
Eugene, OR   97402
Phone: (503) 688-9721

PENNSYLVANIA

GADO 3
Allentown–Bethlehem Easton Airport
RAS Aviation Center Building
Allentown, PA   18103
Phone: (215) 264-2888

GADO 10
Capitol City Airport
Administration Building
Room 201
New Cumberland, PA   17070
Phone: (717) 782-4528

GADO 14
Allegheny County Airport
Administration Building
Room 213
West Mifflin, PA   15122
Phone: (412) 462-5507

FSDO 63
Scott Plaza No. 2
Fourth Floor
Philadelphia, PA   19113
Phone: (215) 596-0673

PUERTO RICO

FSDO 61
Puerto Rico International Airport
Room 203A
San Juan, PR   00913
Phone: (809) 791-5050

RHODE ISLAND

FSDO 63
Barnes Municipal Airport
Administration Building
Westfield, MA   01085
Phone: (413) 568-3121

SOUTH CAROLINA

FSDO 67C
Columbia Metropolitan Airport
2819 Aviation Way
West Columbia, SC   29169
Phone: (803) 765-5931

SOUTH DAKOTA

FSDO 66
Rapid City Regional Airport
Rural Route 2, Box 4750
Rapid City, SD   57701
Phone: (605) 343-2403

TENNESSEE

FSDO 63
International Airport
General Aviation Building, Room 137
2488 Winchester Road
Memphis, TN   38116
Phone: (901) 521-3820

FSDO 63N
Nashville Metropolitan Airport
Room 101
322 Knapp Boulevard
Nashville, TN   37217
Phone: (615) 251-5661

APPENDIX 1. FAA DISTRICT OFFICES (CONTINUED)

TEXAS

FSDO 63
Love Field Airport
8032 Aviation Place
Dallas, TX   75235
Phone: (214) 357-0142

FSDO 64
Hobby Airport
Room 152
8800 Paul B. Koonce Drive
Houston, TX   77061
Phone: (713) 643-6504

FSDO 66
International Airport
Route 3, Box 51
Lubbock, TX   79401
Phone: (806) 762-0335

FSDO 68
International Airport
Room 201
1115 Paul Wilkins Road
San Antonio, TX   78216
Phone: (512) 824-9535

FSDO 68SA
Miller International Airport
Terminal Building
2600 South Main Street
McAllen, TX   78503
Phone: (512) 682-4812

UTAH

FSDO 67
116 North 2400 West
Salt Lake City, UT   84116
Phone: (801) 524-4247

VERMONT

FSDO 65
Portland International Jetport
General Aviation Terminal
Portland, ME   04102
Phone: (207) 774-4484

VIRGINIA

GADO 16
Byrd International Airport
Terminal Building, Second Floor
Sandston, VA   23150
Phone: (804) 222-7494

VIRGIN ISLANDS

FSDO 61
Puerto Rico International Airport
Room 203A
San Juan, PR   00913
Phone: (809) 791-5050

WASHINGTON

FSDO 61
7300 Perimeter Road South
Seattle, WA   98108
Phone: (206) 431-2742

FSDO 61A
5620 East Rutter Avenue
Spokane, WA   99206
Phone: (509) 456-4618

WEST VIRGINIA

GADO 22
Kanawha Airport
301 Eagle Mountain Road
Charleston, WV   25311
Phone: (304) 343-4689

WISCONSIN

FSDO 61
General Mitchell Field
FAA/WB Building
5300 South Howell Avenue
Milwaukee, WI   53207
Phone: (414) 747-5531

WYOMING

FSDO 60A
Natrona County International Airport
FAA/WB Building
Casper, WY   82601
Phone: (307) 234-8959

APPENDIX 2. REFERENCE AND STUDY MATERIALS

The following publications are excellent reference and study materials for preparation to take the written and oral tests for mechanic certification.

Advisory Circulars	Titles
43.13-1A	Acceptable Methods, Techniques and Practices--Aircraft Inspection and Repair
43.13-2A	Acceptable Methods, Techniques, and Practices--Aircraft Alterations
65-2D	Airframe and Powerplant Mechanics Certification Guide
65-9A	Airframe and Powerplant Mechanics-- General Handbook
65-11A	Airframe and Powerplant Mechanics Certification Information
65-12A	Airframe and Powerplant Mechanics Powerplant Handbook
65.15A	Airframe and Powerplant Mechanics Airframe Handbook
FAA-T-8080-10A	Aviation Mechanic--General Question Book
FAA-T-8080-11A	Aviation Mechanic Powerplant Question Book
FAA-T-8080-12A	Aviation Mechanic Airframe Question Book

Note: The prices and stock numbers of the publications are subject to change. Refer to the Guide to Federal Aviation Administration Publications (FAA-APA-PG-9) for the current price, stock number, and the office where the publication can be obtained. A free copy of the Guide can be ordered from: U.S. Department of Transportation, M-443.2, Washington, D.C. 20590.